MAJOR POETS OF THE EARLIER SEVENTEENTH CENTURY

MAJOR POETS OF THE EARLIER SEVENTEENTH CENTURY

Donne · Herbert · Vaughan
Crashaw · Jonson · Herrick
Marvell

EDITED BY

BARBARA K. LEWALSKI
ANDREW J. SABOL

The Odyssey Press
A DIVISION OF THE BOBBS-MERRILL COMPANY, INC.
INDIANAPOLIS · NEW YORK

Copyright © 1973 by The Bobbs-Merrill Company, Inc.
PRINTED IN THE UNITED STATES OF AMERICA
Library of Congress Catalog Number: 70: 7893792
ISBN 0-672-63184-9 (pbk)
ISBN 0-672-53184-4
Third Printing

Contents

SEVENTEENTH CENTURY LYRIC
POTERY   xix

ABBREVIATIONS   xxxii

SOME USEFUL STUDIES OF SEVENTEENTH CENTURY
POETRY AND ITS BACKGROUNDS   xxxiii

John Donne

INTRODUCTION   3

SELECTED BIBLIOGRAPHY   16

From POEMS   21

SONGS AND SONETS   21

The good-morrow 21/ Song (Goe, and catche a falling starre) 22/ Womans constancy 23/ The undertaking 23/ The Sunne Rising 24/ The Indifferent 25/ Loves Usury 26/ The Canonization 27/ The triple Foole 28/ Lovers infinitenesse 29/ Song (Sweetest love, I do not goe) 30/ The Legacie 31/ A Feaver 32/ Aire and Angels 33/ Breake of day 34/ The Anniversarie 35/ A Valediction: of my name, in the window 36/ Twicknam garden 38/ A Valediction: of the booke 39/ Communitie 41/ Loves growth 42/ Loves exchange 43/ Confined Love 44/ The Dreame 45/ A Valediction: of weeping 46/ Loves Alchymie 47/ The Flea 48/ The Curse 49/ The Message 50/ A nocturnall upon S. Lucies day 51/ Witchcraft by a picture 52/ The Baite 53/ The Apparition 54/ The broken heart 55/ A Valediction: forbidding mourning 56/ The Extasie 57/ Loves Deitie 60/ Loves diet 61/ The Will 62/ The Funerall 63/ The Blossome 64/ The Primrose 66/ The Relique 67/ The Dampe 68/ The Dissolution 69/ A Jeat Ring sent 69/ Negative love 70/ The Prohibition 70/ The Expiration 71/ The Computation 72/ The Paradox 72/ Farewell to love 73/ A Lecture upon the Shadow 74/ Sonnet. The Token 75/ Self Love 75

ELEGIES, SATIRES, VERSE LETTERS 77

Elegie II. The Anagram 77/ Elegie V. His Picture 79/ Elegie IX. The Autumnall 79/ Elegie XI. The Bracelet 81/ Elegie XVI. On his Mistris 84/ Elegie XVIII. Loves Progresse 86/ Elegie XIX. To his Mistris going to Bed 89/ Satyre I 91/ Satyre III 94/ To the Countesse of Bedford 97/ To Sir Edward Herbert. At Julyers 99

THE ANNIVERSARY POEMS 101

A Funerall Elegie 101/ An Anatomy of the World: The First Anniversary 105/ The Second Anniversarie 119

DIVINE POEMS 135

To the Lady Magdalen Herbert 135

HOLY SONNETS (La Corona) 136

La Corona 136/ Annunciation 137/ Nativitie 137/ Temple 138/ Crucifying 138/ Resurrection 139/ Ascention 139

A LITANIE 140

HOLY SONNETS (1633) 150

To E. of D. with six holy Sonnets 150/ 1. As due by many titles . . . 151/ 2. Oh my blacke Soule! . . . 151/ 3. This is my playes last scene . . . 152/ 4. At the round earths imagin'd corners . . . 152/ 5. If poysonous minerals . . . 153/ 6. Death be not proud . . . 153/ 7. Spit in my face you Jewes 154/ 8. Why are wee by all creatures . . . 154/ 9. What if this present . . . 155/ 10. Batter my heart . . . 155/ 11. Wilt thou love God . . . 156/ 12. Father, part of his double interest 156

HOLY SONNETS (1635) 157

13. Thou hast made me . . . 157/ 14. O might those sighes and teares . . . 158/ 15. I am a little world . . . 158/ 16. If faithfull soules . . . 159

HOLY SONNETS (Westmoreland MS) 159

17. Since she whome I lovd . . . 159/ 18. Show me deare Christ . . . 160/ 19. Oh, to vex me . . . 161

OCCASIONAL POEMS AND HYMNS 162

The Crosse 162/ Upon the Annunciation and Passion falling upon one day. 1608 164/ Goodfriday, 1613. Riding Westward 165/ A Hymne to Christ, at the Authors last going into Germany 167/ A Hymne to God the Father 168/ Hymne to God my God, in my sicknesse 169

George Herbert

INTRODUCTION *173*

SELECTED BIBLIOGRAPHY *183*

THE TEMPLE *185*

The Dedication *185*

THE CHURCH-PORCH *185*

Perirrhanterium *185*/ Superliminare *204*

THE CHURCH *205*

The Altar *205*/ The Sacrifice *206*/ The Thankes-giving *215*/ The Reprisall *217*/ The Agony *217*/ The Sinner *218*/ Good Friday *219*/ Redemption *220*/ Sepulcher *220*/ Easter *221*/ Easter wings *223*/ H. Baptisme [I] *223*/ H. Baptisme [II] *224*/ Nature *224*/ Sinne [I] *225*/ Affliction [I] *226*/ Repentance *228*/ Faith *229*/ Prayer [I] *231*/ The H. Communion *231*/ Antiphon [I] *233*/ Love [I] *233*/ Love [II] *234*/ The Temper [I] *234*/ The Temper [II] *235*/ Jordan [I] *236*/ Imployment [I] *237*/ The H. Scriptures [I] *238*/ The H. Scriptures [II] *238*/ Whitsunday *239*/ Grace *240*/ Praise [I] *241*/ Affliction [II] *241*/ Mattens *242*/ Sinne [II] *243*/ Even-song *243*/ Church-monuments *244*/ Church-Musique *245*/ Anagram *246*/ Church-lock and key *246*/ The Church-floore *246*/ The Windowes *247*/ Trinity-Sunday *248*/ Content *248*/ The Quiddity *250*/ Humility *250*/ Frailty *251*/ Constancy *252*/ Affliction [III] *254*/ The Starre *254*/ Sunday *255*/ Avarice *257*/ To all Angels and Saints *258*/ Imployment [II] *259*/ Deniall *260*/ Christmas *261*/ Ungratefulnes *262*/ Sighes and Grones *263*/ The World *265*/ Coloss: 3.3. Our life is hid with Christ in God *265*/ Vanity [I] *266*/ Lent *267*/ Vertue *269*/ The Pearle *269*/ Affliction [IV] *271*/ Man *272*/ Antiphon [II] *274*/ Unkindnes *275*/ Life *276*/ Submission *276*/ Justice [I] *277*/ Charmes and Knots *277*/ Affliction [V] *278*/ Mortification *279*/ Decay *280*/ Misery *281*/ Jordan [II] *284*/ Prayer [II] *284*/ Obedience *285*/ Conscience *287*/ Sion *288*/ Home *289*/ The British Church *291*/ The Quipp *292*/ Vanity [II] *293*/ The Dawning *294*/ Jesu *295*/ Busines *295*/ Dialogue *297*/ Dulnes *298*/ Love-joy *299*/ Providence *299*/ Hope *305*/ Sinnes round *305*/ Time *306*/ Gratefulnes *307*/ Peace *308*/ Confession *310*/ Giddines *311*/ The Bunch of Grapes *312*/ Love-unknowne *313*/ Mans medly *315*/ The Storme *317*/ Paradise *317*/ The Method *318*/ Divinity *319*/ 4 Ephes: 30. Greive not the holy spirit, &c. *321*/

viii · Contents

The family 322/ The Size 323/ Artillery 325/ Churchrents or schismes 326/ Justice [II] 327/ The Pilgrimage 328/ The holdfast 329/ Complaining 330/ The Discharge 330/ Praise [II] 332/ An Offering 333/Longing 335/ The Bagge 338/ The Jewes 339/ The Collar 340/ The Glimpse 341/ Assurance 342/ The Call 344/ Clasping of hands 344/ Praise [III] 345/ Josephs coat 346/ The Pulley 347/ The Preisthood 348/ The Search 349/ Greife 352/ The Crosse 352/ The Flowre 354/ Dotage 355/ The Sonne 356/ A true Hymne 357/ The Answere 357/ A Dialogue Antheme 358/ The Water-course 358/ Selfe-condemnation 359/ Bitter-sweet 360/ The Glance 360/ The 23d Psalme 361/ Mary Magdalene 362/ Aaron 363/ The Odour. 2 Cor: 2.15 364/ The foile 365/ The Fore-runners 365/ The Rose 366/ Discipline 368/ The Invitation 369/ The Banquet 370/ The Posy 372/ A parody 373/ The Elixir 374/ A Wreath 375/ Death 375/ Doomes day 376/ Judgement 377/ Heaven 378/ Love [III] 379

THE CHURCH MILITANT   380
L'Envoy 389

Henry Vaughan

INTRODUCTION   393
SELECTED BIBLIOGRAPHY   405

SILEX SCINTILLANS

Part I   407

Authoris (de se) Emblema 407/ Dedication: To . . . Jesus Christ . . . And the . . . Virgin Mary 409/ Vain Wits and eyes 411/ Regeneration 412/ Death [I] 416/ Resurrection and Immortality 418/ Day of Judgement [I] 421/ Religion 422/ The Search 425/ Isaacs Marriage 428/ The Brittish Church 430/ The Lampe 431/ Mans fall, and Recovery 432/ The Showre 434/ Distraction 434/ The Pursuite 435/ Mount of Olives [I] 436/ The Incarnation, and Passion 437/ The Call 438/ Thou that know'st for whom I mourne 439/ Vanity of Spirit 441/ The Retreate 442/ Come, come, what doe I here? 444/ Midnight 445/ Content 446/ Joy of my life! 447/ The Storm 448/ The Morning-watch 449/ The Evening-watch 451/ Silence, and stealth of dayes! 451/ Church-Service 452/ Buriall 453/ Chearfulness 455/ Sure, there's a tye of Bodyes! 456/ Peace 457/ The Passion 458/ And do they so? 460/ The Relapse 461/ The Resolve 462/ The Match 463/ Rules and

Lessons *465*/ Corruption *470*/ H. Scriptures *471*/ Unprofitablenes *472*/ Christs Nativity *472*/ The Check *474*/ Disorder and frailty *476*/ Idle Verse *478*/ Son-dayes *479*/ Repentance *480*/ The Burial Of an Infant *483*/ Faith *483*/ The Dawning *485*/ Admission *486*/ Praise *487*/ Dressing *489*/ Easter-day *491*/ Easter Hymn *491*/ The Holy Communion *492*/ Psalm 121 *494*/ Affliction *494*/ The Tempest *496*/ Retirement *498*/ Love, and Discipline *500*/ The Pilgrimage *501*/ The Law, and the Gospel *502*/ The World *504*/ The Mutinie *506*/ The Constellation *508*/ The Shepheards *510*/ Misery *512*/ The Sap *515*/ Mount of Olives [II] *517*/ Man *518*/ I walkt the other day (to spend my hour) *519*/ Begging [I] *522*

Part II   *523*

Ascension-day *523*/ Ascension-Hymn *525*/ They are all gone into the world of light! *527*/ White Sunday *528*/ The Proffer *531*/ Cock-crowing *533*/ The Starre *535*/ The Palm-tree *536*/ Joy *537*/ The Favour *538*/ The Garland *539*/ Love-sick *540*/ Trinity-Sunday *541*/ Psalme 104 *541*/ The Bird *544*/ The Timber *546*/ The Jews *548*/ Begging [II] *550*/ Palm-Sunday *551*/ Jesus weeping [I] *553*/ The Daughter of Herodias *554*/ Jesus weeping [II] *555*/ Providence *557*/ The Knot *558*/ The Ornament *559*/ St. Mary Magdalen *560*/ The Rain-bow *562*/ The Seed growing secretly *564*/ As time one day by me did pass *566*/ Fair and yong light! *567*/ The Stone *569*/ The dwelling-place *571*/ The Men of War *572*/ The Ass *574*/The hidden Treasure *576*/ Childe-hood *577*/ The Night *579*/ Abels blood *581*/ Righteousness *582*/ Anguish *585*/ Tears *585*/ Jacobs Pillow, and Pillar *586*/ The Agreement *588*/ The day of Judgement [II] *591*/ Psalm 65 *592*/ The Throne *594*/ Death [II] *594*/ The Feast *595*/ The Obsequies *598*/ The Water-fall *599*/ Quickness *601*/ The Wreath *602*/ The Queer *602*/ The Book *603*/ To the Holy Bible *604*/ L'Envoy *605*

Richard Crashaw

INTRODUCTION   611
SELECTED BIBLIOGRAPHY   622
From STEPS TO THE TEMPLE   623
DIVINE EPIGRAMS   623
On the water of our Lords Baptisme *623*/ To the Infant Martyrs *623*/ Matthew 8 *624*/ I am the Doore *624*/ Matthew. 27 *624*/ Upon our Saviours

Tombe wherein never man was laid 625/ Luke 11 625/ Upon the Infant Martyrs 625/ Easter day 626/ On Mr. G. Herberts booke intituled the Temple of Sacred Poems, sent to a Gentlewoman 626

From THE DELIGHTS OF THE MUSES   628
Musicks Duell 628/ Wishes 633/ On Marriage 637

CARMEN DEO NOSTRO   639
Non Vi 640/ To the Noblest and best of Ladyes, the Countesse of Denbigh 640/ To the Name Above Every Name, the Name of Jesus 643/ In the Holy Nativity of Our Lord God 650/ New Year's Day 654/ In the Glorious Epiphanie of Our Lord God 656/ To the Queen's Majesty 664

THE OFFICE OF THE HOLY CROSSE: THE HOWRES   665
For the Hour of Matines 665/ For the Hour of Prime 667/ The Third 668/ The Sixt 669/ The Ninth 671/ Evensong 672/ Compline 673/ The Recommendation 675

Upon the H. Sepulcher 675/ Vexilla Regis, The Hymn of the Holy Crosse 676/ To Our B. Lord 678/ Charitas Nimia 678/ Sancta Maria Dolorum 681/ Upon the Bleeding Crucifix 685/ Upon the Crowne of Thorns 687/ Upon the Body of Our Bl. Lord, Naked and Bloody 687/ The Hymn of Sainte Thomas in Adoration of the Blessed Sacrament 688/ Lauda Sion Salvatorem 690/ Dies Irae Dies Illa 694/ The Himn O Gloriosa Domina 697/ In the Glorious Assumption of Our Blessed Lady 699/ Sainte Mary Magdalene (or The Weeper) 701/ A Hymn to the Name and Honor of the Admirable Sainte Teresa 709/ An Apologie 715/ The Flaming Heart 717/ A Song 720/ Prayer 721/ To the Same Party Councel Concerning Her Choise 724

ALEXIAS   727
The First Elegie 727/ The Seconde Elegie 728/ The Third Elegie 729

Description of a Religious House and Condition of Life 731/ An Epitaph Upon a Young Married Couple 733/ Death's Lecture at the Funeral of a Young Gentleman 734/ Temperance 735/ Hope 737/ M. Crashaws Answer for Hope 738

Ben Jonson

INTRODUCTION · 743

SELECTED BIBLIOGRAPHY 756

From EPIGRAMMES 761

I. To the Reader 762/ II. To my Booke 762/ III. To my Booke-seller 763/ IV. To King James 763/ IX. To all, to whom I write 764/ XIV. To William Camden 764/ XV. On Court-worme 765/ XVII. To the learned Critick 765/ XVIII. To my meere English Censurer 765/ XXI. On reformed Gam'ster 766/ XXII. On my first Daughter 766/ XXIII. To John Donne 766/ XXV. On Sir Voluptuous Beast 767/ XXVI. On the same Beast 767/ XXXIV. Of Death 767/ XXXVI. To the Ghost of Martial 767/ XXXVII. On Chev'rill the Lawyer 768/ XL. On Margaret Ratcliffe 768/ XLII. On Giles and Jone 769/ XLV. On my first Sonne 769/ XLIX. To Play-wright 770/ LV. To Francis Beaumont 770/ LIX. On Spies 770/ LX. To William Lord Mounteagle 771/ LXII. To Fine Lady Would-bee 771/ LXXV. On Lippe, the Teacher 772/ LXXVI. On Lucy Countesse of Bedford 772/ LXXXIV. To Lucy Countesse of Bedford 772/ LXXXVIII. On English Mounsieur 773/ LXXXIX. To Edward Allen 773/ XCII. The new Crie 774/ XCIV. To Lucy, Countesse of Bedford, with M^r. Donnes Satyres 775/ XCVI. To John Donne 776/ CI. Inviting a friend to supper 776/ CV. To Mary Lady Wroth 778/ CVII. To Captayne Hungry 779/ CVIII. To true Souldiers 780/ CXII. To a weake Gamster in Poetry 780/ CXIX. To Sir Raph Shelton 781/ CXX. Epitaph on S. P. a child of Q. El. Chappel 781/ CXXIV. Epitaph on Elizabeth, L. H. 782/ CXXX. To Alphonso Ferrabosco, on his Booke 783/ CXXXII. To Mr. Josuah Sylvester 784/ CXXXIII. On the famous Voyage 784

THE FORREST 790

I. Why I write not of Love 790/ II. To Penshurst 790/ III. To Sir Robert Wroth 793/ IV. To the World 796/ Song (V. To Celia [I]) 798/ VI. To the same 799/ Song (VII. That Women are but Mens shaddowes) 800/ VIII. To Sicknesse 800/ Song (IX. To Celia [II]) 802/ X. Praeludium 802/ XI. Epode 803/ Epistle (XII. To Elizabeth Countesse of Rutland) 807/ Epistle (XIII. To Katherine, Lady Aubigny) 810/ Ode (XIV. To Sir William Sydney, on his Birth-day) 813/ XV. To Heaven 815

From UNDER-WOOD 816

[I] POEMS OF DEVOTION 816
[1] *The Sinners Sacrifice: To the Holy Trinitie* 816; [2] *A Hymne to God the Father* 818; [3] *A Hymne On the Nativitie of my Saviour* 819

[II] A CELEBRATION OF CHARIS IN TEN LYRICK
  PEECES 820
1. *His Excuse for loving* 820; 2. *How he saw her* 820; 3. *What hee suffered* 821; 4. *Her Triumph* 822; 5. *His discourse with Cupid* 823; 6. *Clayming a second kisse by Desert* 825; 7. *Begging another, on colour of mending the former* 826; 8. *Urging her of a promise* 826; 9. *Her man described by her owne Dictamen* 827; 10. *Another Ladyes exception present at the hearing* 829
[III] *The Musicall strife* 829/ [IV] *A Song* 830/ [VIII] *The Houre-glasse* 831/ [IX] *My Picture left in Scotland* 831/ [X] *Against Jealousie* 832/ [XI] *The Dreame* 832/ [XIX] *An Elegie* 833/ [XXIII] *An Ode. To himselfe* 834/ [XXVII] *An Ode* 835/ [XXVIII] *A Sonnet: To the noble Lady, the Lady Mary Worth* 836/ [XXIX] *A Fit of Rime against Rime* 837/ [XXXVI] *A Song* 838/ [XXXVIII] *An Elegie ('Tis true, I'm broke!...)* 839/ [XXXIX] *An Elegie (To make the Doubt cleare that no Woman's true)* 843/ [XL] *An Elegie (That Love's a bitter sweet,...)* 845/ [XLI] *An Elegie (Since you must goe,...)* 846/ [XLII] *An Elegie (Let me be what I am,...)* 847/ [XLIII] *An Execration upon Vulcan* 849/ [XLVII] *An Epistle answering to one that asked to be Sealed of the Tribe of Ben* 856/ [LII] *A Poëme sent me by Sir William Burlase* 858/ *My Answer* 859/ [LVII] *To Master John Burges* 860/ [LXII] *An Epigram to K. Charles* 861/ [LXVI] *An Epigram to the Queene, then lying in* 861/ [LXVII] *An Ode, or Song, by all the Muses* 862/ [LXX] *To the immortall memorie, and friendship of that noble paire, Sir Lucius Cary, and Sir H. Morison* 864/ [LXXIX] *(New yeares, expect new gifts: Sister, your Harpe)* 868/ *A New-yeares-Gift sung to King Charles* 869

[LXXXIV] EUPHEME; OR, THE FAIRE FAME 871
1. *The Dedication of her Cradle* 872; 2. *The Song of her Descent* 873; 3. *The Picture of the Body* 874; 4. *The Mind* 875; 8. *To Kenelme, John, George* 877; 9. *Elegie on my Muse* 878

MISCELLANY 885
To the memory of my beloved, The Author Mr. William Shakespeare 885

Contents · xiii

The Songs in CYNTHIAS REVELLS 888
[Echo's] Song 888/ [Prosaites'] Song 888/ [Hedon's] Song 889/ [Amorphus'] Song 890/ The Hymne: [Hesperus sings invoking Cynthia] 890/ Palinode: [Amorphus, Phantaste, and Chorus] 891/ Song: [Mercury and Crites] 892

The Songs in POETASTER 893
Song: [1. Crispinus] 893/ [2. Hermogenes] 893/ [Horace's Ode] 894/ [Crispinus'] Song 894/ Song: (Wake, our mirth begins to die) 894/ Song: [Hermogenes and Crispinus] 895/ Song (Blush, folly, blush: here's none that feares) 895

From BARTHOLOMEW FAYRE 896
[Nightingale's Song] 896

From A PRIVATE ENTERTAINMENT AT HIGH-GATE 898
Song (See, see, ô see, who here is come a Maying!) 898

Song from THE KINGS ENTERTAINMENT AT WELBECK 899
A Dialogue Betweene the Passions, Doubt and Love 899

Songs from OBERON, THE FAERY PRINCE 900
(Buz, quoth the blue Flie) 900/ [Satyrs'] Song 901/ Silenus 902/ Song (Melt earth to sea, sea flow to ayre) 902/ The Song, by two Faies 903/ Song (The solemne rites are well begunne) 903/ Song (Nay, nay,/ You must not stay) 904/ Song (Nor yet, nor yet, O you in this night blest) 904/ Song (Gentle knights) 905/ Phosphorus 905/ Song (O yet, how early, and before her time) 905

Songs from LOVE FREED FROM IGNORANCE AND
FOLLY 906
Song (A crowne, a crowne for Loves bright head) 906/ A Dialogue (What gentle formes are these that move) 907/ Song (O what a fault, nay, what a sinne) 907/ Song (How neere to good is what is faire!) 908/ Song (What just excuse had aged Time) 908/ Song (Now, now. Gentle Love is free, and Beautie blest) 908

An Expostulacion with Inigo Jones 909/ To Inigo Marquess Would be A Corollary 912/ To a Freind an Epigram of him 913

Robert Herrick

INTRODUCTION 917
SELECTED BIBLIOGRAPHY 926
From HESPERIDES: OR, THE WORKS BOTH HUMANE & DIVINE OF ROBERT HERRICK ESQ. 929
To the Most Illustrious and Most Hopefull Prince, Charles, Prince of Wales 930/ The Argument of his Book 931/ To his Muse 931/ To his Booke 932/ When he would have his verses read 933/ Upon Julias Recovery 933/ The Parliament of Roses to Julia 934/ The Frozen Heart 934/ A Song to the Maskers 934/ To his Mistresses 935/ The Wounded Heart 935/ Soft Musick 936/ The Difference Betwixt Kings and Subjects 936/ His Answer to a Question 936/ Upon Julia's Fall 937/ No Spouse but a Sister 937/ The Pomander Bracelet 938/ The shooe tying 938/ The Carkanet 938/ Upon the losse of his Mistresses 938/ The Dream 939/ The Vine 939/ Love's play at Push-pin 940/ The Parcæ, or, Three dainty Destinies 940/ To Robin Red-brest 941/ Discontents in Devon 941/ His request to Julia 942/ Money gets the masterie 942/ The Scar-fire 942/ Upon Julia's Voice 942/ Againe 943/ The succession of the foure sweet months 943/ No Shipwrack of Vertue 943/ Upon his Sister-in-Law, Mistresse Elizab: Herrick 944/ Of Love 944/ To the King 944/ To the King and Queene, upon their unhappy distances 945/ To the reverend shade of his religious Father 945/ Delight in Disorder 946/ To Dean-Bourn, a rude River in Devon 947/ His Cavalier 947/ The Bag of the Bee 947/ A Country life: To his Brother, M. Tho: Herrick 948/ To the Painter, to draw him a Picture 952/ A Lyrick to Mirth 953/ Against Love 953/ Upon Julia's Riband 954/ The frozen Zone: or, Julia disdainfull 954/ Leanders Obsequies 955/ The Teare sent to her from Stanes 955/ His fare-well to Sack 956/ The Eye 958/ The Curse: A Song 958/ Upon the Bishop of Lincolne's Imprisonment 959/ To Electra 960/ Corinna's going a Maying 960/ To his dying Brother, Master William Herrick 962/ How Lillies came white 963/ Impossibilities to his friend 963/ To the Virgins, to make much of Time 964/ To his Friend, on the untuneable Times 964/ A Pastorall upon the birth of Prince Charles 965/ To Musique, to becalme his Fever 966/ Upon a Gentle-woman with a sweet Voice 967/ Upon Julia's breasts 968/ To the Rose 968/

To the High and Noble Prince, George, Duke, Marquesse, and Earle of Buckingham 969/ *To the King* 969/ *To the Queene* 969/ *The Poets good wishes for the most hopefull and handsome Prince, the Duke of Yorke* 970/ *To Anthea, who may command him any thing* 971/ *A Nuptiall Song, or Epithalamie, on Sir Clipseby Crew and his Lady* 972/ *Upon Shark* 976/ *Oberons Feast* 977/ *To Virgins* 978/ *To Daffadills* 979/ *Mattens, or morning Prayer* 980/ *Evensong* 980/ *The Kisse* 980/ *To the right honourable, Philip, Earle of Pembroke, and Montgomerie* 981/ *To the most learned, wise, and Arch-Antiquary, M. John Selden* 982/ *A Panegerick to Sir Lewis Pemberton* 982/ *Upon M. Ben. Johnson* 986/ *Another* 987/ *To his Nephew, to be prosperous in his art of Painting* 987/ *Clothes do but cheat and cousen us* 988/ *To Dianeme* 988/ *The mad Maids song* 988/ *A Pastorall sung to the King: Montano, Silvio, and Mirtillo, Shepheards* 989/ *Upon the Nipples of Julia's Breast* 991/ *Oberons Palace* 991/ *The parting Verse, or charge to his supposed Wife when he travelled* 995/ *To Julia* 997/ *His Winding-sheet* 997/ *To Phillis to love, and live with him* 999/ *Upon Mistresse Susanna Southwell her cheeks* 1001/ *Upon her Eyes* 1001/ *Upon her feet* 1001/ *An Ode to Sir Clipsebie Crew* 1001/ *The Apparition of his Mistresse calling him to Elizium* 1003/ *His Prayer to Ben. Johnson* 1005/ *The Night-piece, to Julia* 1005/ *A Kisse* 1006/ *Glorie* 1006/ *Poets* 1006/ *No despight to the dead* 1006/ *Connubii Flores, or the well-wishes at Weddings* 1007/ *The Hag* 1009/ *To M. Denham, on his Prospective Poem* 1010/ *His returne to London* 1011/ *Charon and Phylomel* 1011/ *To Doctor Alablaster* 1012/ *Upon Julia's Clothes* 1013/ *The Amber Bead* 1013/ *The Transfiguration* 1013/ *To the King, Upon his taking of Leicester* 1014/ *To M. Henry Lawes, the excellent Composer of his Lyricks* 1014/ *Upon Love* 1015/ *Ceremonies for Candlemasse Eve* 1015/ *Upon M. William Lawes, the rare Musitian* 1016/ *Upon Ben. Johnson* 1017/ *An Ode for him* 1017/ *To the King, Upon his welcome to Hampton-Court* 1018/ *A Bachanalian Verse* 1018/ *Upon Love* 1019/ *His teares to Thamasis* 1019/ *Twelfe night, or King and Queene* 1020/ *Charmes* 1021/ *Another* [I] 1022/ *Another* [II] 1022/ *To his Girles who would have him sportfull* 1022/ *Truth and falsehood* 1022/ *His last request to Julia* 1023/ *On Himselfe* 1023/ *To his Booke (Goe thou forth my booke, though late)* 1023/ *The end of his worke* 1023/ *To Crowne it* 1024/ *On Himselfe* 1024/ *The pillar of Fame* 1024

From HIS NOBLE NUMBERS: OR, HIS PIOUS
PIECES   1025
His Confession 1026/ His Prayer for Absolution 1026/ To finde God 1026/ What God is 1027/ Upon God 1027/ Mercy and Love 1027/ Gods Anger without Affection 1027/ God not to be comprehended 1028/ To God: an Anthem, sung in the Chappell at White-hall, before the King 1028/ Upon Time 1028/ His Letanie, to the Holy Spirit 1029/ A Thanksgiving to God, for his House 1031/ To God [I] 1032/ Neutrality loathsome 1033/ Eternitie 1033/ To his Saviour, a Child; a Present, by a child 1033/ The Parasceve, or Preparation 1034/ To God [II] 1034/ To his sweet Saviour 1035/ His Creed 1035/ The Dirge of Jephthahs Daughter: sung by the Virgins 1036/ To God, on his sicknesse 1038/ An Ode, or Psalme, to God 1038/ A Christmas Caroll, sung to the King in the Presence at White-Hall 1039/ The New-yeeres Gift, or Circumcisions Song, sung to the King in the Presence at White-Hall 1040/ The Star-Song: A Caroll to the King; sung at White-Hall 1042/ To God [III] 1043/ Good men afflicted most 1043/ To God [IV] 1044/ The white Island 1044/ Prayer 1045/ Predestination 1045/ Another 1046/ To keep a true Lent 1046/ Good Friday: Rex Tragicus 1047/ (This Crosse-Tree here) 1049/ His coming to the Sepulcher 1050

Andrew Marvell

INTRODUCTION   1053
SELECTED BIBLIOGRAPHY   1069
MISCELLANEOUS POEMS   1073
A Dialogue between the Resolved Soul, and Created Pleasure 1073/ On a Drop of Dew 1077/ The Coronet 1078/ Eyes and Tears 1079/ Bermudas 1082/ Clorinda and Damon 1083/ A Dialogue between the Soul and Body 1084/ The Nymph complaining for the death of her Faun 1085/ Young Love 1089/ To his Coy Mistress 1090/ The unfortunate Lover 1092/ The Gallery 1094/ The Fair Singer 1096/ Mourning 1097/ Daphnis and Chloe 1099/ The Definition of Love 1103/ The Picture of little T.C. in a Prospect of Flowers 1105/ Tom May's Death 1106/ The Match 1109/ The Mower against Gardens 1111/ Damon the Mower 1112/ The Mower to the Glo-Worms 1115/ The Mower's Song 1116/ Ametas and Thestylis making Hay-Ropes 1117/ Musicks Empire 1118/ The Garden 1119/ Fleckno, an

English Priest at Rome 1121/ *To his worthy Friend Doctor Witty upon his Translation of the Popular Errors* 1126/ *On Mr. Milton's Paradise lost* 1127/ *Senec. Traged. ex Thyeste Chor.* 2 1129/ *An Epitaph upon —* 1129/ *Upon the Hill and Grove at Bill-borow* 1130/ *Upon Appleton House, to my Lord Fairfax* 1133/ *On the Victory obtained by Blake over the Spaniards, in the Bay of Sanctacruze, in the Island of Teneriff* 1160/ *A Dialogue between Thyrsis and Dorinda* 1165/ *The Character of Holland* 1167/ *An Horatian Ode upon Cromwel's Return from Ireland* 1171/ *The First Anniversary of the Government under O.C.* 1174/ *Two Songs at the Marriage of the Lord Fauconberg and the Lady Mary Cromwell* 1185/ *A Poem upon the Death of O.C.* 1190/ *To his Noble Friend Mr. Richard Lovelace* 1199/ *Upon the Death of the Lord Hastings* 1200/ *An Elegy upon the Death of my Lord Francis Villiers* 1202

Appendix: Music Settings

INTRODUCTION 1209

1. Send home my long strayde eies. Giovanni Coprario 1213/ *2. Goe and catch a fallinge star.* Anon. 1215/ *3. Deerest love, I doe not goe.* Anon. 1217/ *4. So, so, leave off.* Anon. 1218/ *5. Wilt thou forgive the sinne.* John Hilton 1220/ *6. Lord, when the sense of thie sweet grace.* Anon. 1222/ *7. Bright Spark.* John Jenkins 1224/ *8. See, O see, who is heere come a Maying.* Martin Peerson 1231/ *9. O the Joyes that soone should wast.* Nathaniel Giles 1241/ *10. Yf I freely may discover.* Anon. 1244/ *11. What softer sounds are these salute the Eare.* William Lawes 1246/ *12. Heare me, O God.* Alphonso Ferrabosco II 1249/ *13. White though you be.* Nicholas Lanier 1252/ *14. Goe, goe, perjur'd man.* Robert Ramsey 1253/ *15. When as Leander (yong) was Drown'd.* Henry Lawes 1255/ *16. Gather your rose buds while you may.* William Lawes 1257/ *17. Let us sleepe this night away.* William Webb 1258/ *18. When death shall snatch us.* William Lawes 1259

Notes

John Donne 1269/ George Herbert 1279/ Henry Vaughan 1286/ Richard Crashaw 1288/ Ben Jonson 1292/ Robert Herrick 1297/ Andrew Marvell 1297

INDEX TO TITLES AND FIRST LINES *1301*

Illustrations

Title page of the first edition of Donne's *Poems* (1633)	*19*
The Lothian Portrait of John Donne (probably Dutch)	*20*
Title page of the first edition of Herbert's *The Temple* (1633)	*186*
Title page of the first edition of Vaughan's *Silex Scintillans* (1650)	*406*
Title page of the first edition of Crashaw's *Carmen Deo Nostro* (1652)	*638*
Emblem, probably by Crashaw, devised to accompany "To . . . the Countesse of Denbigh"	*639*
Emblem, probably by Crashaw, devised to accompany "The Weeper"	*701*
Title page of the first folio of Jonson's *Workes* (1616)	*759*
Title page of the first edition of Herrick's *Hesperides* (1648)	*928*
Title page of the first edition of Marvell's *Miscellaneous Poems* (1681)	*1071*
Portrait of Andrew Marvell from *Miscellaneous Poems*	*1072*
Self-Portrait of Nicholas Lanier; now in the Oxford School of Music	*1208*

Seventeenth Century Lyric Poetry

For the past two generations, those seventeenth century poets known as the metaphysicals have enjoyed a tremendous popularity, albeit for some of the wrong reasons. Recent scholarship indicates that these poets were not quite what their first enthusiastic rediscoverers thought them to be—that is, the prototypes of disoriented, doubt-ridden, self-probing modern man, and the forerunners of the style and attitudes of the modern poets. But the revisionism only enhances the intrinsic interest of these poets, for it calls attention to their great richness and variety, and demonstrates that they cannot be easily contained within the traditional definitions and classifications.

The usual classification divides the poetry of the earlier seventeenth century into metaphysical and classical kinds, with the latter-day imitators of Spenser comprising a less important third variety. Traditionally, John Donne has been regarded as the originator of the metaphysical school, which includes George Herbert, Henry Vaughan, Andrew Marvell, and (perhaps) Richard Crashaw; Ben Jonson has been designated head of the classical school, which includes his several self-styled "Sons," notably Robert Herrick, Thomas Carew, Richard Lovelace, and Sir John Suckling. As Douglas Bush has observed, the dichotomy is "sound enough to be useful, and false enough to be troublesome." The utility inheres in the fact that these critical labels have been fixed by more than three centuries' use, and that most readers do obtain a markedly different poetic experience from reading these two groups of poets. The troublesomeness is evidenced by the difficulties attending all efforts, early and late, to define the special nature and quality of metaphysical poetry.

Although early usage of the term *metaphysical* to identify a school of poetry was not common, it was influential enough to establish the label, and with it the misleading expectation that this poetry would be directly concerned with philosophical questions or would present a metaphysical system after the manner of Lucretius or Dante. However, as first used, the label had no such precise denotation but rather suggested something abstract, unnecessarily difficult, or riddled with scholastic terms and arguments. Drummond of Hawthornden, a contemporary of Donne, called upon this meaning of the term when he denounced those rebellious poets "who consulted upon her [poetry's] reformation, and endeavored to abstract her to metaphysical ideas and scholastic quiddities, denuding her of her own habits and ornaments with which she hath amused the world some thousand years." (The "ornaments" Drummond alludes to are presumably classical mythology, nature imagery, and lyricism.) Dryden used the term in a similar sense when he complained that Donne "affects the metaphysics, not only in his satires, but in his amorous verses, where nature only should reign, and perplexes the minds of the fair sex with nice speculations of philosophy, when he should engage their hearts, and entertain them with the softnesses of love." Samuel Johnson also defined metaphysical poetry in terms of the possession and display of abstruse, recondite learning—"to show their learning was their whole endeavor"—but in addition he distinguished two other characteristics which have entered into most subsequent discussions of metaphysical poetry. The first is metrical harshness: "the modulation was so imperfect that they were only found to be verses by counting the syllables." The second is a special variety of wit which Johnson brilliantly defined as a "kind of *discordia concors*; a combination of dissimilar images or discovery of occult resemblances in things apparently unlike.... The most heterogeneous ideas are yoked by violence together; nature and art are ransacked for illustrations, comparisons, and allusions."

Modern criticism, taking as its point of departure a series of essays written by T. S. Eliot in the 1920's, also asserted metaphysical poetry's divergence from earlier poetic practice, but regarded this originality as cause for adulation rather than blame, and endeavored to define its nature with greater precision. Although he subsequently altered his opinion, Eliot led many readers to find the essence of metaphysical poetry in its perfect fusion of thought and feeling, its achievement of a "direct sensuous apprehension of thought, or a re-creation of thought into feeling"—a fusion he found notably absent in English poetry after the mid-seventeenth century. Such a fusion is exemplified in Donne's "The Extasie"—at once an emotion-filled, psychological probing of the love experience and an intricate, logical argument proving the necessity for the union of physical and spiritual love. Some others who shared in the revival of metaphysical poetry in the 1920's and 1930's, such as C. M. Coffin and Basil Willey, endeavored to justify the label by pointing to genuine philosophical concerns in Donne's verse—concerns centering upon the nature of love and the nature of the universe, seen especially in terms of the conflict between the old scholastic world view and the new science. More recently, other philosophical issues or modes of perception have been proposed as fundamental to metaphysical poetry. Frank Warnke finds this poetry distinguished by an overriding concern with the metaphysical problem of the one and the many. Robert Ellrodt, in a very extensive and brilliant study of metaphysical style and sensibility, finds the distinctive metaphysical note in the poets' profound sense of the dichotomies, the paradoxes, in the nature of God, Man, and the Universe. And Earl Miner has emphasized the metaphysical poets' concern with private worlds and private experience, opposed to and often in conflict with the public world.

Most modern criticism, however, has sought to define metaphysical poetry in terms of one or more distinguishing features of poetic style or manner. Some emphasize the point that metaphysical poetry replaces the customary Elizabethan poetic imagery drawn from nature and the classics with imagery drawn from obscure, recondite areas of learning such as theology, scholastic philosophy, alchemy, medicine, cosmology, physics. For example, the opening lines of Donne's "Good Friday, 1613. Riding Westward" explore the speaker's religious devotion through the image of the movement of the spheres: "Let mans Soule be a Spheare, and then, in this,/The intelligence that moves, devotion is." Others note especially the dissonance, the disruption of lyric quality created by Donne's harsh, unmelodic speech rhythms, his complex, tortured syntax, and his use of homely, indecorous, colloquial words and phrases—words such as "wean'd," "suck'd," "snorted" from the opening lines of "The good-morrow." Still other readers point out as the predominant element of metaphysical verse its logical argumentative structure: the argument sometimes proceeds by syllogistic logic such as that which the speaker in Donne's "The Flea" uses to further his seduction proposals; sometimes by logical expansion and development of the implications of a central metaphor such as the proposition in Donne's "The Canonization" that "lovers are saints"; and sometimes by other methods of dialectical analysis.

Another critical approach locates the essence of metaphysical poetry in the multiplicity and complexity of attitudes and perspectives in a single poem, controlled through paradox, irony, and ambiguity. Thus in Donne's "The Funerall" an unrequited lover begs to have a wreath of his lady's hair buried with him, and characterizes the wreath successively as his "outward Soule" which will preserve him from corruption, as a manacle with which the lady has imprisoned him, as a religious relic of himself as martyr of love, as a foolish relic which may mislead others to idolatrous worship, and finally, simply as hair—a part of the lady whose burial will enable him to get a bit of his own back: "So, 'tis some bravery,/That since you would have none of mee, I bury some of you." Again, various critics focus on the dramatic qualities of this poetry as its most distinctive feature: the strong characterization of poetic speaker and addressee; the distinct sense of a particular setting; the presentation of experience in the present tense, acted out in the poem rather than merely recounted—all set in motion by brisk, arresting, opening lines such as, "Busie old foole, unruly Sunne," or "For Godsake hold your tongue, and let me love."

However, most readers, following Dr. Johnson's lead, have defined metaphysical poetry chiefly in terms of its wit—wit understood not merely as humor but as the play of imagination, of intellect, of perception, manifested in the sudden juxtaposition of ideas, words, and images not usually associated with each other. The vehicles of this wit are pun, oxymoron, paradox, irony, and especially the conceit—a surprising or shocking metaphor usually defined (after Johnson) as a yoking together of images from highly disparate ranges of experience. Discussions of metaphysical conceits usually distinguish two kinds: one, the condensed or telescoped image, such as that startling association of beauty and death, of life symbol and skeleton in the single line from Donne's "The Relique," "A bracelet of bright haire about the bone"; the other, the extended or expanded conceit which is developed through an entire poem or throughout several stanzas, such as, in the last three stanzas of Donne's "A Valediction: forbidding mourning," the classic comparison of the souls of the parting lovers with the two feet of a geometer's compass:

> If they [our souls] be two, they are two so
>   As stiffe twin compasses are two,
> Thy soule the fixt foot, makes no show
>   To move, but doth, if the'other doe.
>
> And though it in the center sit,
>   Yet when the other far doth rome,
> It leanes, and hearkens after it,
>   And growes erect, as that comes home.
>
> Such wilt thou be to mee, who must
>   Like th'other foot, obliquely runne.
> Thy firmnes drawes my circle just,
>   And makes me end, where I begunne.

This passage also exemplifies other commonly noted qualities of the metaphysical conceit—its organic rather than ornamental function in embodying and developing the thought of the poem, and the linking of its two terms at a single, narrow point of contact which must be apprehended intellectually rather than sensuously: thus the lovers are like compasses only in the sense that despite their separation they are joined firmly together above the plane of daily life, as the arms of the compass are joined above the plane of the map or drawing board.

Confusing though this variety of suggested approaches to and definitions of metaphysical poetry is, the confusion has been compounded by the growing suspicion among scholars and critics that the definitions have been based upon an inadequate sampling of the so-called metaphysical poetry—upon a limited portion of Donne's verse (the *Songs and Sonets*, the Holy Sonnets, a few elegies and hymns) and upon a relatively small and perhaps atypical assortment of apparently Donne-like poems from the other poets. The suspicion has also developed that the customary description of the classical poets in terms nearly opposite to those used of the metaphysicals—slight subject matter, smoothness of surface, urbanity, lyric grace, use of classical allusion and myth—may rest upon a much too superficial survey of their poetry. Accordingly, the rigorous, scholarly reexamination of seventeenth century poetry which has been in progress for over two decades has endeavored on the one hand to break through the metaphysical and classical categories in favor of broader, more imaginative approaches, and on the other hand to focus attention upon particular poems, genres, and poets.

Many recent studies of Donne and of the metaphysical school suggest that this poetry is not so much an innovation as a continuation of various traditions. Rosemond Tuve, in her seminal study *Elizabethan and Metaphysical Imagery*, inaugurated this reexamination by challenging the received view that metaphysical poetry constituted a rebellion against sensuous and ornamental Elizabethan poetry, arguing on the contrary that both Elizabethan and metaphysical poetry derive from the same poetic; that both use figures logically rather than sensuously; that both are concerned to argue abstract, general propositions rather than to depict personal, individual experience; and that both choose imagery and poetic figures according to a decorum based upon considerations of the poem's purpose and genre. Grounding her argument upon an examination of contemporary rhetorical and poetic treatises, Miss Tuve considers metaphysical poetry as an integral part of, rather than a reaction against, Elizabethan poetry, and she accounts for the quantitative increase in the use of logical structure and intellectual imagery in metaphysical poetry by such factors as the influence of Peter Ramus' new, anti-Aristotelian system of logic and rhetoric, which subordinated all other arts and sciences to logic and considered poetic images as one kind of argument.

Louis Martz has suggested another classification, subsuming the so-called metaphysical poems (along with many others) into a "meditative" poetic tradition, whose distinguishing features derive from the widespread religious practice of meditating upon religious mysteries, the life of Christ, the state of one's soul, and similar subjects. The methods for such meditation were described in detail in numerous Jesuit, Franciscan, and even Puritan handbooks of the sixteenth and seventeenth centuries. The common features of metaphysical poetry are seen by Martz to derive from common habits of meditation rather than from the influence of Donne; indeed the first exponent of the "meditative" style was the Elizabethan Jesuit poet Robert Southwell. Martz argues moreover that the usual three-part formula for meditation recommended in the handbooks is reflected in whole or in part in the structure of many seventeenth-century religious poems, and with some adaptation in that of many secular poems as well. In this view the so-called preludes to the meditation, involving a "composition of place," or vivid re-creation of some scene before the mind's eye, contribute to the dramatic element in this poetry and especially to the striking openings; the subsequent point-by-point intellectual analysis of the doctrine or mystery finds its counterpart in the logical, orderly consideration of various aspects of the poetic subject; the concluding colloquy or outpouring of the heart to God is paralleled in the personal, emotion-filled address with which many of these poems end. In addition, the fact that the meditation deliberately endeavored to fuse the three faculties of memory, intellect, and will may explain that peculiar fusion of thought and feeling which Eliot and others defined as the special feature of metaphysical poetry.

Another recent emphasis tends to break down the dichotomy between the schools of Jonson and Donne by emphasizing the very considerable area of common ground shared by the two poets. Jonson wrote three encomiastic epigrams on Donne and termed him the "first poet in the World in some things"; Donne, who honored no other contemporary writer in verse, wrote Latin verses praising Jonson's *Volpone.* Many of the "Sons of Ben" and many of the followers of Donne seem, in fact, to have learned from both masters. Also, as George Williamson points out, contemporary references identify both poets as practitioners of the "strong-lined" style, a style whose brevity, wittiness, asperity, and occasional obscurity offered a challenge to both the sensuous, decorative Petrarchan poetic style and to the ornate Ciceronian prose style. This strong-lined ideal lay behind Thomas Carew's eulogy of Donne for his "masculine expression" and his "great fancy...too stout/For their soft melting praises," and behind Owen Feltham's praise of

> solid Jonson... from whose full strong quill
> Each line did like a diamond drop distil,
> Though hard, yet clear.

Refining the "strong-lined" classification, Wesley Trimpi links Jonson and Donne yet more closely as poets who consciously adapted the classical plain style (hitherto reserved for epistolary verse, satire, epigram, and comedy) to the love lyric and to other poetic genres in an effort to achieve in these kinds also the particular qualities which both classical and Elizabethan treatises ascribed to the plain style: the accurate description of real experience, the true presentation of one's own personality, and the careful examination of philosophic truth and moral principles, all carried forth with strength, brevity, succinctness, and pregnancy of meaning. Trimpi also illuminates Jonson's divergence from, and expressed annoyance with, Donne's manner — "Done for not keeping of accent deserved hanging"; "Done himself for not being understood would perish," — by showing Jonson's preference for the Attic, Tacitean variety of the plain style over the more obscure, pointed, Senecan style characteristic of Donne.

Still another approach has attempted to relate English seventeenth century poetry to certain aspects and characteristics of contemporary European poetry, usually as manifestations of a literary baroque style analogous to the baroque in art. However, the efforts to define the literary equivalents of such artistic baroque features as the fusion of the spiritual and the sensual, the concern with illusion, the tendency to exceed the limits of the medium, and the use of extravagant ornamentation, formal imbalance, broken lines, recessed perspectives have not yet attained sufficient precision to be more than suggestive. More impressive are the comparative studies of a common metaphysical tradition linking poets in England, Italy, Spain, and elsewhere on the continent. Frank Warnke, identifying this metaphysical style as one of several seventeenth century baroque styles, defines as its common features ingenious metaphor, consistent intellectuality, radically all-inclusive diction, colloquial tone, and a shared vision—the disposition to view any particular experience in terms of total reality and accordingly to be immersed in the problems of deceptive appearances, contradictions, and multiplicity. J. A. Mazzeo identifies the conceit as the feature common to the European metaphysical movement, and finds from certain European treatises that the conceit may be regarded not merely as a witty, strained, surprising metaphor but as the means whereby the poet seeks to discover and display the analogies which God has contrived in a universe in which all realms of being—vegetable, animal, human, angelic, political states, the geocosm, the universe, God himself—are linked together through countless analogies, correspondences, and symbolic associations.

Of equal importance in the reevaluation of seventeenth century poetry has been the intensive study of particular genres and of individual authors. The fact that Elegies XXXVIII–XLI in Jonson's *Under-wood* are still controverted as to authorship between Jonson and Donne, and that XXXIX in *Under-wood* also appears as Donne's "Elegy XV" (the "Expostulation") in the 1633 volume of Donne's *Poems*, calls attention to the degree to which genre dictated style for poets of all schools in this genre-conscious age. The point is further emphasized by the vast distance between the classical decorum of Marvell's "Horatian Ode upon Cromwel's Return from Ireland" and the metaphysical wit of the same poet's emblematic lyric "On a Drop of Dew." Also, the sharp focus on the individual poet and the entire range of his production, which has been the method of several recent books, has had the happy effect of diverting attention away from broad generalizations about common features of style and toward the unique poetic experience which each of these poets can offer.

The present collection is devised to encourage intensive reading in each of the seven major lyric poets of the period, and also to provide a ready opportunity to compare them. The selections from the various poets are generous and representative; in every case except that of Herrick (whose *Hesperides* is too vast for such treatment), the poets are represented by their most significant complete book of poetry as well as by other selections. This treatment provides the reader with the opportunity — most important with Herbert's *The Temple* and Vaughan's *Silex Scintillans* but valuable also with Donne's *Songs and Sonets*, Jonson's *The Forrest*, and Crashaw's *Carmen Deo Nostro* — to encounter these poems as the poets intended, not as separate, discrete lyrics, but in volumes having substantial tonal unity, an overall structure, and certain pervasive themes.

Also, in order to show that several of the songs and lyrics in this volume were originally intended to be complemented by music, we have included a selection of contemporaneous settings by Jacobean and Caroline composers, among whom the most illustrious are Alphonso Ferrabosco II, John Coprario, Nicholas Lanier, John Wilson, and the Lawes brothers, Henry and William. All these musicians held posts, at various times in their careers, as instrumentalists, vocalists, or composers in the King's Musick, the distinguished royal organization whose function was to provide music for king and court, and the extent of their collaboration with the poets of the period was more than simply fortuitous. Jonson recognized in his "lov'd Alphonso" a composer of genius, Herrick found William Lawes a "sweet Orpheus" among a company numbering the "rare" Lanier and the "curious" Wilson, and Milton acknowledged Henry Lawes as the "Priest of *Phoebus*' choir." And as poets thought musically, so musicians thought poetically, or were encouraged to do so. Jacobean songwriters, nurtured on Thomas Morley's *Plaine and Easie Introduction to Practicall Musicke*, had been admonished to look well to the ditty and to provide a musical counterpart which might duly embellish it. Henry Lawes, anxious "to shape *Notes* to the *Words* and *Sense*," also insisted upon "right tuning the words," and John Wilson urged his fellow composers to choose good lines to which they might fashion "Notes as meet." The fruits of the collaboration of such composers with dozens of poets of the century is amply displayed in the several musical publications of John and Henry Playford; the books and their contents have been exhaustively catalogued by Cyrus Day and E. B. Murrie in their invaluable *English Song-Books: 1651–1702* (London, 1940).

In commenting upon the complementary relationship between lyric and tune, C. Day Lewis quite properly reminds us that lyrical poetry has never quite lost touch with its origin in music, and that "just as song lyrics are incomplete without music, so there are many tunes which are incomplete without words." Most poets of the seventeenth century recognized that, for the successful integration of text and tune, the shape, length, and development of a lyric depended upon the song form to be utilized by the composer. They readily grasped that pieces as dissimilar as madrigals, ballad tunes, and catches each demanded something highly individual in a ditty. They understood that concerted song forms such as the hymn, the anthem, the ballet, and the glee lent a certain impersonality to the rendition of the text. By contrast, they knew that the solo ayre, the prominent sophisticated solo song of the period, as well as the monody and the dialogue song, afforded an inescapable emphasis upon personal and often highly dramatic expression in performance. In providing a lyric for a simple ayre, for example, most poets subconsciously sensed that trimeter or tetrameter verses were far simpler to set than a series of pentameter lines, that rhyme could effectively accentuate musical cadences as well as poetic ones, that overflow lines needed to be manipulated with great care, that a refrain could contribute immeasurably in establishing the essential tone of a song, that complex or extended images frequently proved unintelligible in performance, and that abrupt changes in mood or thought in a lyric could seldom find a suitable counterpart in music. For the student wishing to explore further relationships between text and tune, an excellent guide is Wilfrid Mellers' *Harmonious Meeting*, a study centering its attention largely upon the English poetry and music of the seventeenth century, and aiming "to show that the interpenetration of words and music is not the same as a simple addition of one to the other...but...a third entity, greater and subtler than either of the contributory elements."

Yet such emphasis on the practical aspects of music as composition and performance should not obscure the century's preoccupation with *musica theorica*, or speculative music. Recent studies of John Hollander and Gretchen Finney explore a dominant concern from classical times through the seventeenth century for viewing music in relation to the theory of a universal harmony. Among the related ideas which these studies rehearse are many that reverberate in literary works from Spenser and Shakespeare to Milton and Dryden—such topics as the conception of the world as musical in all its diversified creation, the notion that music is an emblem of the everlasting harmony in heaven, the idea that music not only teaches, but gives pleasure and moves the emotions, the belief that it serves the ideal of Platonic love as a natural vehicle to attract the soul to all harmony, and the view that music can transmit celestial spirit and influence. Familiarity with such topics of *musica theorica* is ultimately essential to the appreciation of much seventeenth-century poetry, for how else can one understand the notion of *harmonia mundi* which is operative in a poem like Vaughan's "Morning-watch," the musical theory of the passions as it appears in Crashaw's "Musicks Duell," or what has been termed the "blasphemous reversal" of the idea of the music of the spheres in Dryden's "Ode for St. Cecilia's Day"?

The copy text for the works of each poet is the best early edition or manuscript, corrected by independent collation with the other most important textual sources. As we have not, for this collection, endeavored to examine all of the minor textual sources, we have been greatly indebted to the standard editions of the poets for the full record of the textual variants. With certain exceptions, all deviations from the copy text and some suggestive substantive variants are recorded in the textual notes. The exceptions, silently corrected, are obvious typesetters' errors, normalization of orthography (*i/j, s/ſ, u/v*), expansion of & and other abbreviations, and changes of *of* to *off* when that is the meaning. The critical annotations do not presume to interpret the poem, but endeavor to supply what the modern reader may need for an informed reading; for many biblical and other allusions it has seemed useful to give not only the reference but also the quotation itself, so that the reader may see at once how the material is utilized in the poem. Unless otherwise noted, all biblical quotations are from the authorized (King James) version (1611).

The editors acknowledge with thanks the courteous help accorded them by the staffs of the various libraries in which they have worked, both at home and abroad, principally the John D. Rockefeller, Jr., Library at Brown University, the Houghton Library at Harvard, the New York Public Library, the Henry E. Huntington Library and Art Gallery in San Marino, California, The British Museum, Dr. Williams' Library in London, the Bodleian Library, Library of Christ Church, St. Michael's College in Tenbury, the National Library of Scotland in Edinburgh, and the Bibliothèque Nationale. Title pages in facsimile of early editions of the poets (virtually all in the British Museum) and items transcribed from manuscript sources, including music, are reproduced with the kind permission of the authorities of the institutions possessing them; the specific indebtedness to each institution is noted in the essay introducing the selection of each of the seven poets and the music transcribed in the appendix. The Lothian Portrait of Donne is reproduced by the gracious permission of the Marquess of Lothian. Although the editors have undertaken the preparation of this volume jointly, establishing editorial procedures together and each freely advising and criticizing the contribution of the other both in text and introductory essays, the work has been so divided that B.K.L. has edited, annotated, and introduced the selections of Donne (Divine Poems and the *Anniversaries*); Herbert; Vaughan; and Crashaw; and A.J.S. has done likewise for the selections of Donne (*Songs and Sonets* and Elegies); Jonson; Herrick; and Marvell. The opening comprehensive essay is by the former, and the closing edition of texts with contemporaneous music settings is by the latter. Mrs. Toni Beckwith proved an invaluable assistant in the proofreading process.

LIST OF ABBREVIATIONS

AV	The Bible, Authorized (King James) Version (1611)
BCP	Book of Common Prayer
ELH	English Literary History
Geneva	The Bible, Geneva Version (1560)
JEGP	Journal of English and Germanic Philology
MLQ	Modern Language Quarterly
MP	Modern Philology
OED	(Oxford) New English Dictionary
Pat. Graec.	Patrologia Graeca: Patrologiae cursus completus... series Graeca, ed. J.-P. Migne. 161 vols. Paris, 1857–66.
Pat. Lat.	Patrologia Latina: Patrologiae cursus completus... series Latina, ed. J.-P. Migne. 221 vols. Paris, 1844–64.
PMLA	Publications of the Modern Language Association
PQ	Philological Quarterly
RES	Review of English Studies
SEL	Studies in English Literature
SP	Studies in Philology
UTQ	University of Toronto Quarterly

Abbreviations referring to manuscripts and editions of particular poets are noted in the final paragraph of each introductory essay.

SOME USEFUL STUDIES OF SEVENTEENTH CENTURY POETRY AND ITS BACKGROUNDS

Allen, Don Cameron. *Image and Meaning: Metaphoric Traditions in Renaissance Poetry.* Rev. ed. Baltimore, 1968.

Alvarez, Alfred. *The School of Donne.* London, 1961.

Bennett, Joan. *Five Metaphysical Poets.* Cambridge, England, 1964.

Brooks, Cleanth. *Modern Poetry and the Tradition.* Chapel Hill, N.C., 1939.

Bush, Douglas. *English Literature in the Earlier Seventeenth Century: 1600–1660.* Rev. ed. Oxford, 1962.

Colie, Rosalie. *Paradoxia Epidemica: The Renaissance Tradition of Paradox.* Princeton, N.J., 1966.

Duncan, Joseph E. *The Revival of Metaphysical Poetry: The History of a Style.* Minneapolis, Minn., 1959.

Eliot, T. S. "The Metaphysical Poets," "Andrew Marvell," in *Selected Essays.* New York and London, 1950.

Ellrodt, Robert. *L'inspiration personnelle et l'esprit du temps chez les poètes métaphysiques anglais.* 3 vols. Paris, 1960.

Finney, Gretchen L. *Musical Backgrounds for English Literature: 1580–1650.* New Brunswick, N.J., 1962.

Fisch, Harold. *Jerusalem and Albion: The Hebraic Factor in Seventeenth-Century Literature.* New York and London, 1964.

Freeman, Rosemary. *English Emblem Books.* London, 1948.

Grierson, H. J. C. "Introduction" to *Metaphysical Lyrics and Poems of the Seventeenth Century, Donne to Butler.* Oxford, 1921.

Halewood, William. *The Poetry of Grace.* New Haven, Conn., and London, 1970.

Hardison, O. B. *The Enduring Monument; A Study of the Idea of Praise in Renaissance Literary Theory and Practice.* Chapel Hill, N.C., 1962.

Hollander, John. *The Untuning of the Sky: Ideas of Music in English Poetry: 1500–1700.* Princeton, N.J., 1961.

Johnson, Samuel. "Life of Cowley," in *The Lives of the English Poets.* Dublin, 1779–81.

Keast, W. R., ed. *Seventeenth-Century English Poetry: Modern Essays in Criticism.* New York and London, 1962.

Leavis, F. R. *Revaluation: Tradition and Development in English Poetry.* London, 1936.

Leishman, J. B. *The Monarch of Wit: An Analytical and Comparative Study of the Poetry of John Donne.* 7th ed. London, 1965.

Lewis, C. Day. *The Lyric Impulse*. Cambridge, Mass., 1965.
Lovejoy, A. O. *The Great Chain of Being: A Study of the History of an Idea*. Cambridge, Mass., 1933.
Mahood, M. M. *Poetry and Humanism*. New Haven, Conn., and London, 1950.
Martz, Louis L. *The Paradise Within: Studies in Vaughan, Traherne, and Milton*. New Haven, Conn., 1964.
––––––. *The Poetry of Meditation: A Study in English Religious Literature of the Seventeenth Century*. Rev. ed. New Haven, Conn., 1962.
––––––. *The Wit of Love: Donne, Carew, Crashaw, Marvell*. Notre Dame, Indiana, and London, 1969.
Mazzeo, J. A., ed. *Reason and the Imagination: Studies in the History of Ideas: 1600 – 1800*. New York, 1962.
––––––. *Renaissance and Seventeenth-Century Studies*. New York, 1964.
Mellers, Wilfrid. *Harmonious Meeting: A Study of the Relationship between English Music, Poetry, and Theatre, c. 1600 – 1900*. London, 1965.
Miles, Josephine. *Renaissance, Eighteenth-Century, and Modern Language in English Poetry: A Tabular View*. Berkeley, Calif., 1960.
Miner, Earl. *The Metaphysical Mode from Donne to Cowley*. Princeton, N.J., 1969.
––––––. *The Cavalier Mode from Jonson to Cotton*. Princeton, N.J., 1971.
Mulder, John R. *The Temple of the Mind: Education and Literary Taste in Seventeenth-Century England*. New York, 1969.
Nicolson, Marjorie. *The Breaking of the Circle: Studies in the Effect of the "New Science" upon Seventeenth-Century Poetry*. Rev. ed. New York, 1960.
Peterson, Douglas L. *The English Lyric from Wyatt to Donne: A History of the Plain and Eloquent Styles*. Princeton, N.J., 1967.
Røstvig, Maren-Sofie. *The Happy Man: Studies in the Metamorphosis of a Classical Ideal*. 2 vols. Oslo and Oxford, 1954–58.
Smith, Hallett. *Elizabethan Poetry: A Study in Conventions, Meaning, and Expression*. Cambridge, Mass., 1952.
Stewart, Stanley. *The Enclosed Garden: The Tradition and the Image in Seventeenth-Century Poetry*. Madison, Wis., 1966.
Sypher, Wylie. *Four Stages of Renaissance Style: Transformations in Art and Literature, 1400 – 1700*. Garden City, 1955.
Tuve, Rosemond. *Elizabethan and Metaphysical Imagery: Renaissance Poetic and Twentieth Century Critics*. Chicago, 1947.
Wallerstein, Ruth. *Studies in Seventeenth-Century Poetic*. Madison, Wis., 1950.

Walton, Geoffrey. *Metaphysical to Augustan: Studies in Tone and Sensibility in the Seventeenth Century.* London, 1955.

Warnke, Frank J. *European Metaphysical Poetry.* New Haven, Conn., 1961.

White, Helen C. *The Metaphysical Poets: A Study in Religious Experience.* New York, 1936.

Willey, Basil. *The Seventeenth-Century Background: Studies in the Thought of the Age in Relation to Poetry and Religion.* New York, 1934.

Williamson, George. *The Donne Tradition: A Study in English Poetry from Donne to the Death of Cowley.* Cambridge, Mass., 1930.

———. *The Proper Wit of Poetry.* London, 1961.

———. *The Senecan Amble: A Study in Prose Form from Bacon to Collier.* Chicago, 1951.

———. *Seventeenth Century Contexts.* Rev. ed. Chicago, 1969.

———. *Six Metaphysical Poets: A Reader's Guide.* New York, 1967.

John Donne

Whether or not the so-called "metaphysical" qualities are characteristic of a distinct school or style of poetry, they are all to be found in Donne: wit, conveyed through puns, paradoxes, oxymorons, and especially conceits; logical, argumentative structure; dramatization of speaker and action; complexity of tone controlled through irony and ambiguity; learned and also colloquial imagery and diction; strained, tortuous syntax; speech-like and often unmelodic verse. Donne's poetry also exhibits a variety of attitudes, viewpoints, and feelings which are startlingly diverse and even apparently unreconcilable on the two great subjects with which he was most concerned, love and religion.

Izaak Walton, Donne's first biographer and near-contemporary, established the precedent for explaining this diversity in biographical terms. Donne was born in 1571 or 1572 into the devout Roman Catholic family of a prosperous London ironmonger. His early life was eventful and was marked by conflicting pressures. After a private education conducted in part by a Jesuit uncle, Donne studied at Oxford but did not take a degree because of religious disability. During the 1590's he became a brilliant law student at Lincoln's Inn, traveled on the Continent, and took part in Essex' expeditions in Cadiz and the Azores. During these years also he studied the religious issue carefully and at some point left the Roman Catholic for the Anglican Church (a move which opened the possibility of public employment to him); and he embarked upon a promising career as secretary to Sir Thomas Egerton, Lord Keeper of the Great Seal. Sir Richard Baker described the young Donne as "not dissolute, but very neat, a great visiter of ladies, a great frequenter of Plays, a great writer of conceited Verses." To this early period belong the witty prose *Paradoxes and Problems*, the five verse satires, and also, according to common supposition, those elegies and love poems which are risqué, amoral, frankly lustful, or gaily or bitterly cynical.

Donne's secret love marriage in 1601 to Egerton's niece, Ann More, was a major turning point in his life; when the marriage was discovered he was dismissed from his position, imprisoned briefly, cut off from hope of further public employment, and reduced to a life of financial insecurity and dependence upon patronage to support his impoverished and rapidly increasing family. In the period 1601-1615, Donne wrote numerous verse letters and tributes to friends and patrons (including the two *Anniversaries*); controversial and polemical prose works such as *Biathanatos*, a paradoxical defense of suicide; *Pseudo-Martyr* and *Ignatius his Conclave*, two satires on the Roman Catholics; and also the somewhat formalistic religious poems, the *La Corona* sonnets and *A Litanie*. In addition, the biographical critics assume that Donne's serious, tender, joyful celebrations of true love, as well as the notable renunciations of the world for love, have Ann More as subject and belong to this period of his courtship and his hardship-filled marriage. In 1615, after long hesitation, Donne was ordained in the Church of England and entered upon a distinguished career as court preacher, reader in divinity at Lincoln's Inn, and Dean of St. Paul's. His known literary production from this year until his death in 1631 includes well over one hundred and fifty sermons, the impressive book of meditations, *Devotions upon Emergent Occasions* (written during his serious illness of 1623), and a few hymns. Many critics have also ascribed, with Walton, the very personal, moving, and passionate *Holy Sonnets* to the post-ordination years, when his religious life deepened and became more intense.

But the evidence hardly sustains this idealized portrait of Donne as a latter-day St. Augustine. Most of Donne's poems were handed about in manuscript during his lifetime and, with the exception of the *First* and *Second Anniversaries* and a few occasional poems, were not collected and published until 1633, two years after his death. For the elegies and for most of the pieces in *Songs and Sonets*, the time and circumstances of composition are just not known, and so there can be no certainty about the ladies to whom the love poetry may have been addressed or the sequence in which it was written. Moreover, Walton's neat biographical classification of the religious poems is seriously challenged by Helen Gardner's evidence that the *Holy Sonnets* were written at about the same period as the more formal religious poems and some of the verse letters which utilize extravagant theological language for witty compliment.

However, we can approach the astonishing range of attitudes in Donne's poetry from more likely perspectives than that of biography. One frame of reference for any discussion of Donne must be his constant use of the dramatic monologue form, with strongly characterized speaker, addressee, and scene; this form itself ought to forestall the reading of the poems as simply lyric expressions of the author's sentiments and experiences. As Robert Ellrodt points out, the dramatic character of Donne's verse is intensified by his characteristic use of the present tense: we seem to see the speaker developing his attitudes and working out his arguments as we experience the poem. Another frame of reference is that of genre and tradition. How fruitful this approach may be has recently been shown by Helen Gardner's and Louis Martz's demonstrations that the marked differences between Donne's *La Corona* sonnets and his *Holy Sonnets* do not derive from an important change in his religious experience (as the revised dating makes clear) but from the utilization of different devotional traditions. These perspectives strongly suggest that, while Donne indeed sounded his unique note in and placed his personal stamp upon almost everything he wrote, and while all of this poetry must of course represent something in his imaginative experience, it cannot be approached as a record of actual experiences or even of "real" beliefs and attitudes. The question of sincerity—that bugbear of the literal-minded—does not properly arise in this case, for this is poetry ordered to display the variety of human experience rather than to define a unified perspective upon it. Yet the range of Donne's poetic and imaginative sensibility is revealed in the way he perceives and treats these human experiences of love and religious devotion.

The impact of genre and tradition upon Donne is especially evident when he writes in such classical genres as satire and elegy. Elizabethan verse satirists such as John Marston, Joseph Hall, and Ben Jonson produced a spate of satire in print and on the stage in the 1590's; though they consciously imitated Roman satire, their poems have, typically, a looser structure and much more realistic detail, as well as harsh, rugged metrical effects which the Elizabethans mistakenly assumed to be common in classical satire. Donne also exhibits these characteristics, and he addresses the usual Elizabethan satirical topics: corrupt courts, foppish courtiers, bad poets, foolish religious sectaries. "Satyre I," perhaps based upon Horace's Ninth of his First Book, reveals Donne's resemblance to contemporary analogues but also his heightened dramatic quality: the scenes of the speaker's walk with the foolish companion who ultimately deserts him are sharply drawn, and the speaker's language brilliantly characterizes both himself and his companion. "Satyre III," much the most interesting of the group, evidently reflects something of Donne's own religious uncertainties. It is really a hybrid form: the first part is a serious satire both of those who ignore or scorn religion and of various type characters who represent faulty sectarian religious attitudes, while the second part is a moral essay urging (without satiric or comic overtones) the search for true religion through honest doubting investigation.

That Donne's love elegies owe much to generic convention is underscored by the fact that "The Expostulation" (Donne's Elegy XV) has for four centuries been variously ascribed to both Donne and Jonson. Also, J. B. Leishman has demonstrated the influence of Ovid's *Amores* on the subject matter, the situations, the tone, and even the expressions of many of Donne's elegies—especially I, IV, VII, XII, XIX, and XX. Ovid's forty-nine love elegies are characterized by impudence, insolence, witty depravity, an amoral tone, a cynical emphasis on sex as the sole end of the man–woman relationship, and scorn of the husband or entrenched lover—and much of this can be found in Donne's poems. Yet there are important differences. Donne's speaker is more vigorous, arrogant, and certain of his mistresses' devotion, and he shows no trace of the insecurity and passionate jealousy that often plague the Ovidian lover. Also, Donne typically dramatizes and condenses what Ovid describes in leisurely and methodical fashion. Donne's Elegy XIX ("To his Mistris going to Bed") is evidently based upon *Amores* I.v, in which Ovid describes Corinna's coming to his bedside one hot noon; he undresses her slowly, cataloguing her physical beauties in detail, and then exclaims merely, "The rest, who does not know?" Donne, however, translates Ovid's past-tense narrative into the dramatic present; he heightens the erotic wit by describing the removal of each item of clothing with a series of "off with," "unpin," and "unlace" clauses, while never mentioning what the clothing covers; and he interrupts the progress of the bedroom scene to draw metaphysical analogies between undressing the lady and geographical discovery, or even the Christian-Platonic idea of the revelation of Truth hidden under external coverings or shadows.

The Italianate tradition of the paradox stands behind certain other elegies such as II, XVIII, and to some extent IX ("The Autumnall"). This last poem opens in a vein of exalted lyric praise of the older lady's beauty (the subject is Magdalen Herbert) but soon departs from this to develop in terms of sheer wit the paradoxical argument that age, for all its wrinkles like graves or trenches, is yet more attractive, more lovable, than youth. There are also highly dramatic elegies such as V ("His Picture"), XI, and XVI ("On his Mistris"). The last of these, a sophisticated lover's dissuasion of his naïve mistress, who wants to accompany him on a journey in page's disguise, is a masterpiece of witty complexity of tone; the lover combines tenderness, amusement, condescension, and a tolerant comprehension of his mistress' frailty in his descriptions of her inevitable yielding to various temptations if she should go with him, and of the foolish dreams of mishap to him which she will have if she stays home.

Donne's panegyric verse—epithalamia, epicedes and obsequies, verse letters to various patrons and patronesses, the *First* and *Second Anniversaries*—owe much to classical and Renaissance theory and practice of epideictic rhetoric and of hyperbolic compliment. Donne has several verse letters—to Henry Goodyere, Henry Wotton, Roland Woodward, and others—which are in the Jonsonian mode of judicious compliment, moral analysis, and good advice, but his more usual tone, especially to patronesses, is one of exaggerated hyperbolic praise. Hyperbole is an accepted characteristic of the panegyric genres: the person to be honored is commonly made a paragon and a compendium of all virtue, the ideal representative of his particular role in life, a sainted soul, and, in the case of a royal personage, an image and reflection of divinity. What is striking about Donne is not the hyperbole itself, but the pervasive use of theological imagery and allusion as the vehicle for praise. In the letter to Lucy Bedford beginning "Reason is our Soules left hand, Faith her right," Donne appears to take seriously the conventional trope, "the Lady is divine," and so in the course of the argument seems to conflate Lady Bedford with God himself: she is to be reached and known and loved by precisely the same means as God is. Yet this is not really the proposition: Lucy Bedford is subsequently identified as God's "Factor"—his agent or deputy—and her role is to attract our love to that divinity in herself which is in some sense the manifestation or embodiment of the Divine. This is witty compliment to be sure, but it is something more. Here, as often in his panegyric, Donne takes the occasion of praising an individual as a means to explore religious and moral truth. As Robert Ellrodt points out, he takes the person praised as the incarnation (for the purposes at hand) of All—all natural and supernatural reality.

This approach receives its most extreme development in the *Anniversaries*, written to honor Mistress Elizabeth Drury, the daughter of one of Donne's patrons who died before her fifteenth birthday and whom Donne never met. Many readers have responded to the astonishing hyperbole of the poem—in no way dictated by personal grief—as did Ben Jonson when he gruffly complained that the *First Anniversary* was "profane and full of blasphemies," and that "if it had been written of ye Virgin Marie it had been something." On such grounds, Marjorie Nicolson assumes that young Elizabeth Drury is not the subject of the poems—that they are in fact about Queen Elizabeth, who had often been eulogized as Astraea or as the Virgin Mother of her people (a Protestant substitute for the Virgin). Martz takes the poems as meditations on the effects of original sin and the promise of redemption; he finds Elizabeth Drury to be a mere occasion for such meditation and the eulogies of her to be, often, excrescences in the poems' structure. Somewhat arbitrarily, Frank Manley links Elizabeth Drury with traditional personifications of Wisdom as a woman.

Martz's observation that the poems as a whole closely resemble traditional modes of meditation, alternating passages of contempt for the world with praises of goodness, provides an important key to the poems. So does Donne's comment that he had no personal knowledge of Elizabeth Drury but rather "took such a person as might be capable of all that I could say"; she is thus "capable" not because she is a mere occasion for a poem but because, in the medieval and Elizabethan universe of analogies and correspondencies, any particular may participate in and reflect the universal. Thus the youthful innocence of the girl may reflect the lost Eden; her early death may represent the mortality and corruption of the young world occasioned by the Fall (which is the source of all subsequent mortality); her virtue may make her a figure of Astraea (Justice) whose departure from the world ended the Golden Age; and her own presumed redemption from sin by God's grace may allow her to become (as Beatrice was for Dante) an image of Heavenly Grace or even of the *Logos*, which alone can redeem corrupted man. The first poem is an *Anatomy*, a dissection and schematic analysis of the world under wrath, bereft of primal innocence, as represented by the young girl's death; the second is a *Progres*—subtitled a Contemplation—in which the speaker, by meditating on the girl as a redeemed soul, as a full participant in the Divine life of Christ (and so as a type of Christ), girds up his own soul to make its progress toward her soul, which now has ended its progress time in this world and has become a microcosm of heavenly bliss.

Donne's love poems, collected under the title *Songs and Sonets*, are presented here in their entirety, and the collection as a whole has some claim to thematic and stylistic unity and cohesiveness in that all the poems employ the dramatic mode to some degree, and together they present a vast range of attitudes and responses to the love experience—even including one, "Breake of day," in which the speaker is a woman. The 1635 editor of Donne's poems recognized the relation of the collection to contemporary sonnet sequences when he arranged the poems to begin with the awakening to love and to conclude with a farewell to love. And Donald Guss has recently demonstrated that the style and language common to the entire collection is that of the extravagant Italian Petrarchism of the fifteenth and sixteenth centuries–characterized by affected sentiment and wit, hyperbole, complication, high-flown conceits, the habit of treating tropes as literal fact and deducing conclusions from them, and the habit of utilizing esoteric Neoplatonic doctrine in arguments of love—though he indicates that Donne gives this conventional Petrarchist idiom a flexibility, a new significance, and a unique depth of human understanding.

The title, taken from *Tottel's Miscellany*, signifies the character of the volume although, formally, it is misleading. The few "songs" written to existent airs such as "The Baite," "Sweetest love, I do not goe," "Goe, and catche a falling starre," are only slightly more lyrical than the other poems, and are also untypical of Elizabethan song in their complex arguments and tight logical structures. The only formal sonnet in the collection is "The Token," an eighteen-line variant on the Shakespearean form, but the poems resemble sonnets in their compression, tight logic, and witty turns. Helen Gardner has recently called attention to a close relation between the complexity of stanzaic and metrical form and the complexity of theme and argument in these poems, though there is little solid evidence for Miss Gardner's conclusions regarding Donne's chronological development from simple to complex, in terms of both form and argument.

Although there is much dispute as to whether Donne's love poems imply a coherent philosophy of love, there can be no question that they display the richness, variety, and many-sidedness of the love experience. The collection runs the gamut of tones and attitudes on love: there are witty, gay seduction poems, such as "The Flea"; lighthearted Ovidian praises of promiscuity and amorality, such as "The Indifferent"; playful or cynical commentaries on man's or woman's inconstancy, such as "Loves Usury" and "Womans constancy"; bitter and mordant denunciations of love as a cheat and an illusion, such as "Loves Alchymie"; quasi-Petrarchan poems in which the speaker's love for a proud, unrelenting mistress is given a wryly satiric twist, such as "The Blossome" and "The Funerall"; witty but serious arguments for the glory and grandeur of a true love perfectly blending physical and spiritual elements, such as "The good-morrow," "The Canonization," and "The Extasie."

Most readers find the core of Donne's philosophy of love in the last group of poems, though there is considerable dispute as to the basis of that philosophy and little evidence to support the common assumption that these poems were written last. Grierson declares that they present a "philosophy of... love that unites contented hearts,... a justification of love as a natural passion... in which body and soul alike have their part, and of which there is no reason to repent." Helen Gardner and Donald Guss trace the debt of these poems to such Neoplatonists as Leone Ebreo for the ideal of love as spiritual and sexual union, for the concept of a microcosm composed of a pair of lovers who are complete in themselves and desire nothing but each other, and for the argument that since physical love is compatible with spiritual love, lovers united in soul should complete their union in the body. Miss Gardner asserts, however, that these "greatest poems" have finally no model and no rival, and that though Donne utilizes Neoplatonic arguments, he ignores the Neoplatonic philosophical goal of rising by stages to a wholly spiritual love.

As Douglas L. Peterson and Robert Ellrodt indicate, Donne's essential metaphysic, in the love poems as elsewhere, seems to derive from the Aristotelian idea of form realizing itself in matter and from the Christian concept of the spirit incarnate in the body. The poems argue that since the soul cannot exist in the world without the body, love must mix physical and spiritual elements; they also declare that love can be active, sensual, temporal, and at the same time contemplative and otherworldly, since the love in question is perfect in substance and subject to change only in its accidents. These attitudes provide the terms for the resolution of the witty but serious philosophy of love developed in "The Extasie," and they also explain how the lovers can at once declare absence to be no substantial threat to them in "A Valediction: forbidding mourning," yet be saddened by this diminution of their full union. In such poems as "The Sunne Rising," the lovers find in their experience an analogue of the Incarnation: the entire universe of material and spiritual values is contained, incarnated, in the little room, the lovers' bed, the lovers themselves. In "The Canonization," human love is seen as a reflection of *caritas*, and the lovers, by meeting in regard to human love precisely the demands saints meet in responding to Divine love, are worthy to be declared, analogously, saints. And in "A nocturnall upon S. Lucies day" the lover, contemplating the death of his beloved, describes an experience, as Peterson points out, of "spiritual death and sorrow analogous to that suffered throughout eternity by the damned who are denied the Beatific vision."

Donne's religious poetry, no less than his love poetry, has a freshness and immediacy that sets it apart from its predecessors and provides a model for followers and imitators, although, as with the love poetry, one can easily overstate the case for originality. The poetry bears some resemblance to English medieval lyrics which point up the paradoxes of the Christian faith, to the poetry of the English sixteenth-century Jesuit Robert Southwell, and to continental religious poets such as the French Jean de Sponde and the Spanish mystic St. John of the Cross. It also has its roots in specific devotional traditions which, as Helen Gardner shows, go far to explain the striking differences among Donne's various religious poems of similar date. Certain of Donne's poems are modeled on public liturgical forms: these include the emblematic interlinked sonnet sequence *La Corona* (1607), which imitates the Rosary devotion and which forms a chaplet or crown, with each sonnet discussing a principal event in the lives of Christ and the Virgin. Another is the long, witty poem *A Litanie* (1608?) which adapts the structure and petitions of the Litany of the Saints to private and Protestant needs, and which manifests throughout a conscious anti-asceticism, an affirmation of the Anglican *via media*, and a studied justification of the stability and ease to be found in the approved church in contrast to the Roman Catholic seekers of martyrdom. Still other poems are witty occasional pieces about various elements of liturgy: "The Crosse," "Upon the Annunciation and Passion falling upon one day."

Another group of Donne's religious poems strikes a very different note, intensely personal and often anguished; as Martz and Gardner have shown, the subject matter and structure of these poems owes much to the Ignatian formula for personal meditation on Christ's Passion and the state of one's soul. "Goodfriday, 1613. Riding Westward," displays the speaker's effort, through meditation, to place himself in appropriate relation to Christ's Passion. *Holy Sonnets* 1–16 (*c.* 1609–14) probably constitute, as Helen Gardner argues, three meditative sequences: the first group of six dealing with the Last Things, the second group of six with the love of God, and the remaining four with the general topic of sin and repentance. The "Hymne to Christ" (1619) finds in the personal circumstance of a sea journey an occasion for meditating upon evidences of God's love and protection in the sea of life; and the "Hymne to God my God, in my sicknesse" (1623 or 1631) is a deathbed meditation in which the speaker "tunes the instrument," his own soul, preparing it to become part of the heavenly harmony. Most of these poems reflect in some degree the three-part Ignatian structure of prelude, intellectual analysis, and colloquy, and especially the first stage, which involves the recreation of a scene or object before the eye of the imagination: "At the round earths imagin'd corners, blow/Your trumpets, Angells, and arise, arise/From death, you numberlesse infinities/Of soules . . ."

The religious sensibility evident in these poems is compacted of emotional tension, a strong sense of the speaker's personal unworthiness, and real agony over the question of personal salvation. The imagery and tone are often violent: God must do everything to save the speaker, who is utterly helpless. Sonnet 14 argues the speaker's need to be forcibly, violently taken by God, as a military conqueror wins back a town or as a lover ravishes a conquered lady. "Goodfriday, 1613" resolves the speaker's dilemma by showing that he can be restored to a proper relation to Christ's Passion only by receiving "corrections"—presenting his back for flogging, having his rusts burnt off. Yet the constant wit of the poems tempers this violent emotion and shows the poet in full intellectual control of his feeling. Despite Donne's ecclesiastical role, the church as such is not central to the religious experience rendered in the poems, which constantly present doctrine, mysteries, scripture, the church—the entire spectrum of religion—as manifested and embodied in the individual.

The imagery through which Donne explores the relation of the soul to God is often sexual, as the imagery through which he explores the love of man and woman is often religious—a further indication of his disposition to fuse soul and body in close, though paradoxical, union. The traditional allegories of the Song of Solomon and the writings of the mystics offer precedent for the use of sexual imagery to describe religious experience. But Donne characteristically extends and heightens such conventional paradoxes as the Bridegroom-Bride analogy, making Christ in Sonnet 14 not merely the Bridegroom but the rapist of the soul, and the True Church in Sonnet 18 not merely the Spouse of Christ but in some sense a harlot, since she "is most trew, and pleasing to thee, then/When she'is embrac'd and open to most men."

Wit is central not only to Donne's light, playful verse, but also to his most tender and serious love poems and to his religious poetry. The "Hymne to God the Father" is a profoundly serious plea for God's salvation written at a time of critical illness, but this does not prevent Donne from including several witty puns on his own name. It is evident that Donne sees no antithesis in wit and solemnity: he seems rather to expect that God himself, having contrived a universe filled with witty analogies (microcosms reflecting macrocosms), would take especial delight in a poet's witty devotions. But more than this, a remarkable feature of Donne's wit is that it goes beyond the mere display of analogies to present universal realities and religious mysteries as embodied and epitomized in the speaker's particular experiences of love and religious devotion, and in the particular individuals addressed and praised. This is, as Ellrodt recognizes, an incarnational perspective: at the heart of Donne's surprising and daring and witty effects is an imagination that constantly conflates and incarnates the great universals into the particulars of human experience.

Unless another date is indicated, the copy text for most of the poems is the first edition (1633). Poems missing from that edition and the general arrangement of the poems are supplied from the 1635 edition. A few of the *Songs and Sonets* and elegies are derived from those subsequent editions in which they first appeared, and the last three *Holy Sonnets* (unpublished in any early edition) are taken from the Westmoreland (W.) manuscript, in the Berg Collection of the New York Public Library. The texts of the *First* and *Second Anniversaries* are taken from the first editions (1611 and 1612 respectively). Copy texts have been compared with the texts of later editions (1639, 1649, 1650, 1654, 1669), and of several manuscripts, among them the Dowden (D.), Bodleian MS. Eng. Poet. e 99; British Museum Additional MS. 18647 (A18); the Norton MS. (N.), Harvard College Library MS. Eng. 966.3; the Dobell (Dob.), Harvard College Library MS. Eng. 966.4; the O'Flaherty (O'F.), Harvard College Library MS. Eng. 966.5; the Carnaby (Cy.), Harvard College Library MS. Eng. 966.1. It is not possible to discuss manuscripts here; reference should be made to the standard editions for full discussion of the stemma of the manuscripts and their claims to authority. *MSS* signifies agreement of all or most manuscripts in a particular reading. Reference is also made to a rare errata sheet for the *Anniversaries*, evidently prepared by Donne and appearing in a few 1612 copies.

We gratefully acknowledge our large debt to the standard editions, H. J. C. Grierson's (Gr.) pioneering two-volume edition of Donne's *Poems*; Helen C. Gardner's (Gd.) edition of *The Divine Poems* and *The Elegies and the Songs and Sonnets*; W. Milgate's edition of *The Satires, Epigrams and Verse Letters*; Frank Manley's (Man.) edition of *The Anniversaries*; and Evelyn M. Simpson and George R. Potter's ten-volume edition of *The Sermons of John Donne*. John T. Shawcross's *The Complete Poetry of John Donne*, the most recent edition of the poems, incorporates the latest textual discoveries.

SELECTED BIBLIOGRAPHY

EDITIONS

Gardner, Helen C., ed. *John Donne: The Divine Poems.* Oxford, 1952.

———, ed. *John Donne: The Elegies and the Songs and Sonnets.* Oxford, 1965.

Grierson, H. J. C., ed. *The Poems of John Donne.* 2 vols. Oxford, 1912.

Manley, Frank, ed. *John Donne: The Anniversaries.* Baltimore, 1963.

Milgate, W., ed. *John Donne: The Satires, Epigrams and Verse Letters.* Oxford, 1967.

Shawcross, John, ed. *The Complete Poetry of John Donne.* Garden City, N.Y., 1967.

Simpson, Evelyn M., and George R. Potter, eds. *The Sermons of John Donne.* 10 vols. Berkeley, Calif., 1953–1962.

BIOGRAPHY AND CRITICISM

Andreasen, N. J. C. *John Donne: Conservative Revolutionary.* Princeton, N.J., 1967.

——— "Theme and Structure in Donne's *Satyres*," *SEL*, III (1963), 59–75.

Bald, R. C. *John Donne: A Life.* Oxford, 1970.

Combs, Homer C., and Z. R. Sullens. *A Concordance to the English Poems of John Donne.* Chicago, 1940.

Gardner, Helen. "The Argument about 'The Ecstasy'," *Elizabethan and Jacobean Studies.* Oxford, 1959, pp. 279–306.

——— *John Donne: A Collection of Critical Essays.* Englewood Cliffs, N.J., 1962.

Gosse, Edmund. *The Life and Letters of John Donne.* 2 vols. New York, 1899.

Guss, Donald L. *John Donne, Petrarchist.* Detroit, Mich., 1966.

Hunt, Clay. *Donne's Poetry: Essays in Literary Analysis.* New Haven, Conn., 1954.

Kermode, Frank, ed. *Discussions of John Donne.* Boston, 1962.

Legouis, Pierre. *Donne the Craftsman: An Essay upon the Structure of the "Songs and Sonnets."* Paris, 1928.

Leishman, J. B. *The Monarch of Wit.* London, 1951.

Louthan, Doniphan. *The Poetry of John Donne: A Study in Explication.* New York, 1951.

McCanles, Michael. "Distinguish in Order to Unite: Donne's 'The Extasie'," *SEL*, VI (1966), 59–75.

Schleiner, Winfried. *The Imagery of John Donne's Sermons*. Providence, R.I., 1970.
Simpson, Evelyn M. *A Study of the Prose Works of John Donne*. Oxford, 1948; first published 1924.
Spencer, Theodore, ed. *A Garland for John Donne, 1631 - 1931*. Oxford, 1931.
Stein, Arnold. *John Donne's Lyrics: The Eloquence of Action*. Minneapolis, Minn., 1962.
Unger, Leonard. *Donne's Poetry and Modern Criticism*. Chicago, 1950.
Walton, Izaak. *The Lives of Dr. John Donne, Sir Henry Wotton, Mr. Richard Hooker, Mr. George Herbert*. London, 1675; often reprinted.
Webber, Joan. *Contrary Music: The Prose Style of John Donne*. Madison, Wis., 1964.
Williamson, George. "The Design of Donne's 'Anniversaries'," *MP*, LX (1963), 183-191.
Wilson, G. R., Jr. "The Interplay of Perception and Reflection: Mirror Imagery in Donne's Poetry," *SEL*, IX (1969), 107-21.

POEMS,

By J. D.

WITH

ELEGIES

ON THE AUTHORS DEATH.

LONDON.
Printed by *M. F.* for IOHN MARRIOT,
and are to be sold at his shop in St *Dunstans*
Church-yard in *Fleet-street.* 1633.

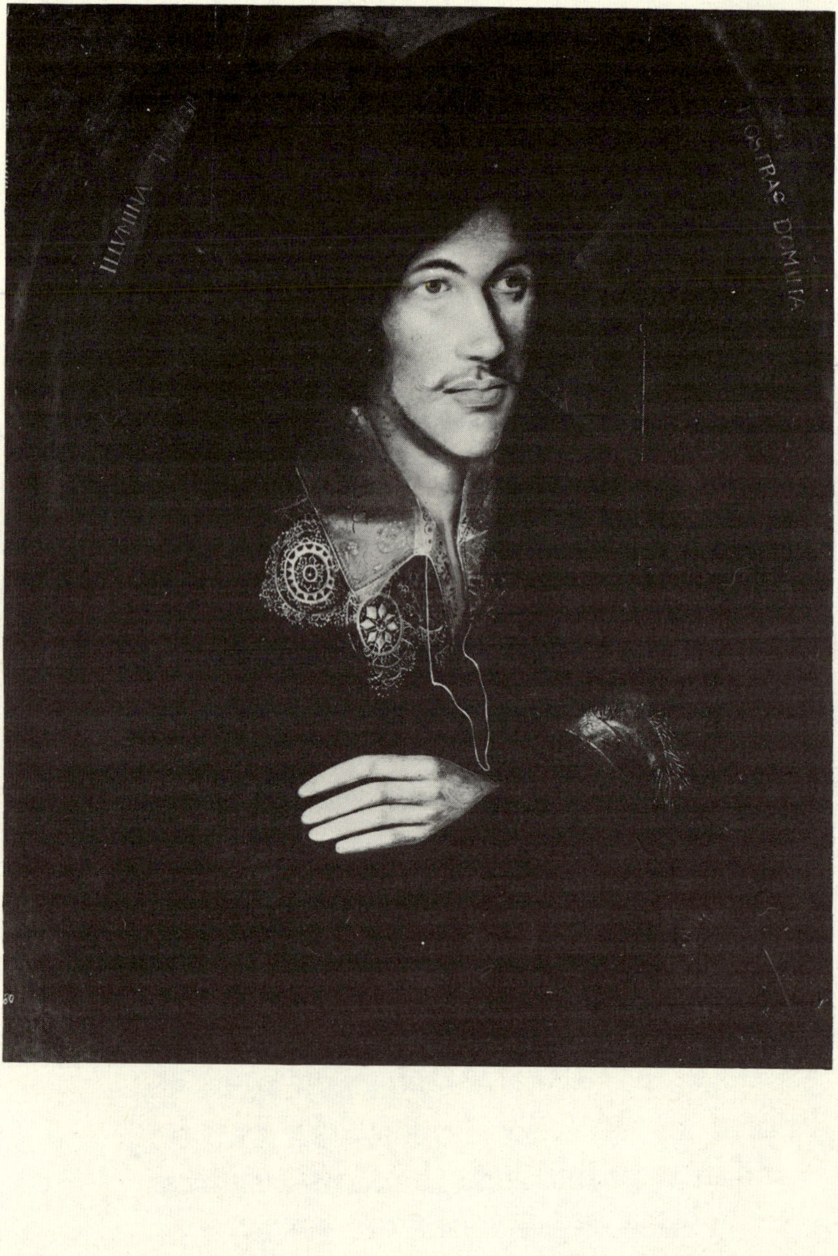

From Poems

SONGS AND SONETS

The good-morrow

I wonder by my troth, what thou, and I
Did, till we lov'd? were we not wean'd till then?
But suck'd on countrey pleasures, childishly?
Or snorted we in the seaven sleepers den?
'Twas so; But this, all pleasures fancies bee. 5
If ever any beauty I did see,
Which I desir'd, and got, 'twas but a dreame of thee.

And now good morrow to our waking soules,
Which watch not one another out of feare;
For love, all love of other sights controules, 10
And makes one little roome, an every where.
Let sea-discoverers to new worlds have gone,
Let Maps to other, worlds on worlds have showne,
Let us possesse one world, each hath one, and is one.

My face in thine eye, thine in mine appeares, 15
And true plaine hearts doe in the faces rest,
Where can we finde two better hemispheares
Without sharpe North, without declining West?

The good-morrow. 4 *seaven sleepers den*: the cave in which, according to legend, seven Christian youths of Ephesus, persecuted by the Roman Emperor Decius (*c.* 250), were walled up and spent 187 years, miraculously preserved in a deep sleep.

What ever dyes, was not mixt equally;
If our two loves be one, or, thou and I   20
Love so alike, that none doe slacken, none can die.

Song

Goe, and catche a falling starre,
   Get with child a mandrake roote,
Tell me, where all past yeares are,
   Or who cleft the Divels foot,
Teach me to heare Mermaides singing,   5
Or to keep off envies stinging,
      And finde
      What winde
Serves to'advance an honest minde.

If thou beest borne to strange sights,   10
   Things invisible to see,
Ride ten thousand daies and nights,
   Till age snow white haires on thee,
Thou, when thou retorn'st, wilt tell mee
All strange wonders that befell thee,   15
      And sweare
      No where
Lives a woman true, and faire.

If thou findst one, let mee know,
   Such a Pilgrimage were sweet,   20
Yet doe not, I would not goe,
   Though at next doore wee might meet,
Though shee were true, when you met her,
And last, till you write your letter,

   Song (Goe, and catche a falling starre). The first verse only appears in an anonymous setting for lute and voice in an early seventeenth-century manuscript (Brit. Mus. Egerton MS. 2013, f. 58v).
   2 *mandrake*: an herb with a large forked root, supposed to possess many human attributes. It was believed to cry out when uprooted. Often considered an aphrodisiac, its fruit was thought when eaten by women to promote conception.

                    Yet shee   25
                    Will bee
            False, ere I come, to two, or three.

                    Womans constancy

            Now thou hast lov'd me one whole day,
            Tomorrow when thou leav'st, what wilt thou say?
            Wilt thou then Antedate some new made vow?
                    Or say that now
            We are not just those persons, which we were?   5
            Or, that oathes made in reverentiall feare
            Of Love, and his wrath, any may forsweare?
            Or, as true deaths, true maryages untie,
            So lovers contracts, images of those,
            Binde but till sleep, deaths image, them unloose? 10
                    Or, your owne end to Justifie,
            For having purpos'd change, and falsehood; you
            Can have no way but falsehood to be true?
            Vaine lunatique, against these scapes I could
                    Dispute, and conquer, if I would,   15
                    Which I abstaine to doe,
            For by tomorrow, I may thinke so too.

                    The undertaking

                I have done one braver thing
                    Then all the *Worthies* did,
                And yet a braver thence doth spring,
                    Which is, to keepe that hid.

                It were but madnes now t'impart   5
                    The skill of specular stone,

The undertaking. 6 *specular stone*: *OED*: "a transparent or semi-transparent substance formerly used as glass or for ornamental purposes...."

When he which can have learn'd the art
    To cut it, can finde none.

So, if I now should utter this,
    Others (because no more
Such stuffe to worke upon, there is,)
    Would love but as before.

But he who lovelinesse within
    Hath found, all outward loathes,
For he who colour loves, and skinne,
    Loves but their oldest clothes.

If, as I have, you also doe
    Vertue'attir'd in woman see,
And dare love that, and say so too,
    And forget the Hee and Shee;

And if this love, though placed so,
    From prophane men you hide,
Which will no faith on this bestow,
    Or, if they doe, deride:

Then you have done a braver thing
    Then all the *Worthies* did,
And a braver thence will spring
    Which is, to keepe that hid.

The Sunne Rising

    Busie old foole, unruly Sunne,
        Why dost thou thus,
Through windowes, and through curtaines call on us?
Must to thy motions lovers seasons run?
    Sawcy pedantique wretch, goe chide
        Late schoole boyes, and sowre prentices,
   Goe tell Court-huntsmen, that the King will ride,
    Call countrey ants to harvest offices;
Love, all alike, no season knowes, nor clyme,
Nor houres, dayes, moneths, which are the rags of time.

      Thy beames, so reverend, and strong
      Why shouldst thou thinke?
I could eclipse and cloud them with a winke,
But that I would not lose her sight so long:
      If her eyes have not blinded thine,   *15*
      Looke, and to morrow late, tell mee,
  Whether both the'India's of spice and Myne
  Be where thou leftst them, or lie here with mee.
Aske for those Kings whom thou saw'st yesterday,
And thou shalt heare, All here in one bed lay.   *20*

      She'is all States, and all Princes, I,
      Nothing else is.
Princes doe but play us; compar'd to this,
All honor's mimique; All wealth alchimie.
      Thou sunne art halfe as happy'as wee,   *25*
      In that the world's contracted thus.
  Thine age askes ease, and since thy duties bee
  To warme the world, that's done in warming us.
Shine here to us, and thou art every where;
This bed thy center is, these walls, thy spheare.   *30*

The Indifferent

I can love both faire and browne,
Her whom abundance melts, and her whom want betraies,
Her who loves lonenesse best, and her who maskes and plaies,
Her whom the country form'd, and whom the town,
Her who beleeves, and her who tries,   *5*
Her who still weepes with spungie eyes,
And her who is dry corke, and never cries;
I can love her, and her, and you and you,
I can love any, so she be not true.

Will no other vice content you?   *10*
Wil it not serve your turn to do, as did your mothers?
Or have you all old vices spent, and now would finde out others?
Or doth a feare, that men are true, torment you?

Oh we are not, be not you so,
Let mee, and doe you, twenty know.   15
Rob mee, but binde me not, and let me goe.
Must I, who came to travaile thorow you,
Grow your fixt subject, because you are true?

Venus heard me sigh this song,
And by Loves sweetest Part, Variety, she swore,   20
She heard not this till now; and that it should be so no more.
She went, examin'd, and return'd ere long,
And said, alas, Some two or three
Poore Heretiques in love there bee,
Which thinke to stablish dangerous constancie.   25
But I have told them, since you will be true,
You shall be true to them, who'are false to you.

Loves Usury

For every houre that thou wilt spare mee now,
        I will allow,
Usurious God of Love, twenty to thee,
When with my browne, my gray haires equall bee;
Till then, Love, let my body raigne, and let   5
Mee travell, sojourne, snatch, plot, have, forget,
Resume my last yeares relict: thinke that yet
        We'had never met.

Let mee thinke any rivalls letter mine,
        And at next nine   10
Keepe midnights promise; mistake by the way
The maid, and tell the Lady'of that delay;
Onely let mee love none, no, not the sport:
From country grasse, to comfitures of Court,
Or cities quelque choses, let report   15
        My minde transport.

This bargaine's good; if when I'am old, I bee
        Inflam'd by thee,

If thine owne honour, or my shame, or paine,
Thou covet, most at that age thou shalt gaine.
Doe thy will then, then subject and degree,
And fruit of love, Love I submit to thee,
Spare mee till then, I'll beare it, though she bee
    One that loves mee.

The Canonization

For Godsake hold your tongue, and let me love,
    Or chide my palsie, or my gout,
My five gray haires, or ruin'd fortune flout,
    With wealth your state, your minde with Arts improve,
        Take you a course, get you a place,
        Observe his honour, or his grace,
Or the Kings reall, or his stamped face
    Contemplate, what you will, approve,
        So you will let me love.

Alas, alas, who's injur'd by my love?
    What merchants ships have my sighs drown'd?
Who saies my teares have overflow'd his ground?
    When did my colds a forward spring remove?
        When did the heats which my veines fill
        Adde one more to the plaguie Bill?
Soldiers finde warres, and Lawyers finde out still
    Litigious men, which quarrels move,
        Though she and I do love.

Call us what you will, wee'are made such by love;
    Call her one, mee another flye,
We'are Tapers too, and at our owne cost die,
    And wee in us finde the'Eagle and the Dove,
        The Phoenix ridle hath more wit

The Canonization. 7 *reall*: This is a play on *real* and *royal* in the many and varied meanings of those words.
    15 *plaguie Bill*: Bills of mortality recorded the numbers in each parish dead from the plague. See *Shakespeare Survey* 16, pp. 125 ff.

      By us, we two being one, are it.
So, to one neutrall thing both sexes fit.
      Wee dye and rise the same, and prove
      Mysterious by this love.

Wee can dye by it, if not live by love,
    And if unfit for tombes and hearse
Our legend bee, it will be fit for verse;
      And if no peece of Chronicle wee prove,
        We'll build in sonnets pretty roomes;
        As well a well wrought urne becomes
The greatest ashes, as halfe-acre tombes,
      And by these hymnes, all shall approve
      Us *Canoniz'd* for Love:

And thus invoke us: You whom reverend love
    Made one anothers hermitage;
You, to whom love was peace, that now is rage,
      Who did the whole worlds soule contract, and drove
        Into the glasses of your eyes
        So made such mirrors, and such spies,
That they did all to you epitomize,
      Countries, Townes, Courts: Beg from above
      A patterne of your love.

The triple Foole

    I am two fooles, I know,
      For loving, and for saying so
        In whining Poëtry;
But where's that wiseman, that would not be I,
      If she would not deny?
Then as th'earths inward narrow crooked lanes
Do purge sea waters fretfull salt away,
    I thought, if I could draw my paines,
Through Rimes vexation, I should them allay,
Griefe brought to numbers cannot be so fierce,
For, he tames it, that fetters it in verse.

  But when I have done so,
   Some man, his art and voice to show,
    Doth Set and sing my paine,
  And, by delighting many, frees againe   *15*
    Griefe, which verse did restraine.
  To Love and Griefe tribute of Verse belongs,
  But not of such as pleases when 'tis read;
    Both are increased by such songs,
  For both their triumphs so are published;   *20*
  And I, which was two fooles, do so grow three;
  Who are a little wise, the best fooles bee.

Lovers infinitenesse

If yet I have not all thy love,
Deare, I shall never have it all;
I cannot breath one other sigh, to move,
Nor can intreat one other teare to fall,
And all my treasure, which should purchase thee,   *5*
Sighs, teares and oathes, and letters I have spent,
Yet no more can be due to mee,
Then at the bargaine made was ment.
If then thy gift of love were partiall,
That some to mee, some should to others fall,   *10*
 Deare, I shall never have Thee All.

Or if then thou gavest mee all,
All was but All, which thou hadst then,
But if in thy heart, since, there be or shall,
New love created bee, by other men,   *15*
Which have their stocks intire, and can in teares,
In sighs, in oathes, and letters outbid mee,
This new love may beget new feares,
For, this love was not vowed by thee,
And yet it was, thy gift being generall,   *20*
The ground, thy heart is mine; what ever shall
 Grow there, deare, I should have it all.

Yet I would not have all yet,
Hee that hath all can have no more,
And since my love doth every day admit 25
New growth, thou shouldst have new rewards in store;
Thou canst not every day give me thy heart;
If thou canst give it, then thou never gavest it:
Loves riddles are, that though thy heart depart,
It stayes at home, and thou with losing savest it: 30
But wee will have a way more liberall,
Then changing hearts, to joyne them, so wee shall
   Be one, and one anothers All.

Song

Sweetest love, I do not goe,
  For wearinesse of thee,
Nor in hope the world can show
  A fitter Love for mee;
    But since that I 5
Must dye at last, 'tis best,
To use my selfe in jest
    Thus by fain'd deaths to dye;

Yesternight the Sunne went hence,
  And yet is here to day, 10
He hath no desire nor sense,
  Nor halfe so short a way:
    Then feare not mee,
But beleeve that I shall make
Speedier journeyes, since I take 15
    More wings and spurres then hee.

O how feeble is mans power,
  That if good fortune fall,
Cannot adde another houre,
  Nor a lost houre recall; 20

Song (Sweetest love, I do not goe). Anonymous settings of the early seventeenth century survive in Tenbury MS. 1018 and in Brit. Mus. Add. MS. 10037.

  But come bad chance,
 And wee joyne to'it our strength,
 And wee teach it art and length,
  It selfe o'r us to'advance.

 When thou sigh'st, thou sigh'st not winde,   *25*
  But sigh'st my soule away,
 When thou weep'st, unkindly kinde,
  My lifes blood doth decay.
   It cannot bee
 That thou lov'st mee, as thou say'st,   *30*
 If in thine my life thou waste,
  Thou are the best of mee.

 Let not thy divining heart
  Forethinke me any ill,
 Destiny may take thy part,   *35*
  And may thy feares fulfill;
   But thinke that wee
 Are but turn'd aside to sleepe;
 They who one another keepe
  Alive, ne'r parted bee.   *40*

The Legacie

When I dyed last, and, Deare, I dye
As often as from thee I goe,
Though it be but an houre agoe,
And Lovers houres be full eternity,
I can remember yet, that I   *5*
Something did say, and something did bestow;
Though I be dead, which sent mee, I should be
Mine owne executor and Legacie.

I heard mee say, Tell her anon,
That my selfe, that's you, not I,   *10*
Did kill me,'and when I felt mee dye,
I bid mee send my heart, when I was gone,
But I alas could there finde none.

When I had ripp'd me,'and search'd where hearts did lye,
It kill'd mee'againe, that I who still was true, 15
In life, in my last Will should cozen you.

Yet I found something like a heart,
But colours it, and corners had,
It was not good, it was not bad,
It was intire to none, and few had part. 20
As good as could be made by art
It seem'd, and therefore for our losses sad,
I meant to send this heart in stead of mine,
But oh, no man could hold it, for 'twas thine.

A Feaver

Oh doe not die, for I shall hate
   All women so, when thou art gone,
That thee I shall not celebrate,
   When I remember, thou wast one.

But yet thou canst not die, I know; 5
   To leave this world behinde, is death,
But when thou from this world wilt goe,
   The whole world vapors with thy breath.

Or if, when thou, the worlds soule, goest,
   It stay, 'tis but thy carkasse then, 10
The fairest woman, but thy ghost,
   But corrupt wormes, the worthyest men.

O wrangling schooles, that search what fire
   Shall burne this world, had none the wit
Unto this knowledge to aspire, 15
   That this her feaver might be it?

A Feaver. 13 *wrangling schools*: Learned controversy on the consuming of the world by fire is reflected also in Donne's prose. Cf. LXXX, Sermons (63), 1640: "Art thou able to dispute out this *Fire*, and to prove that there can be no reall, no material fire in Hell, after the dissolution of all materiall things created?"

    And yet she cannot wast by this,
        Nor long beare this torturing wrong,
    For much corruption needfull is
        To fuell such a feaver long.

    These burning fits but meteors bee,
        Whose matter in thee is soone spent.
    Thy beauty,'and all parts, which are thee,
        Are unchangeable firmament.

    Yet 'twas of my minde, seising thee,
        Though it in thee cannot persever.
    For I had rather owner bee
        Of thee one houre, then all else ever.

Aire and Angels

Twice or thrice had I loved thee,
Before I knew thy face or name;
So in a voice, so in a shapelesse flame,
Angells affect us oft, and worship'd bee,
    Still when, to where thou wert, I came
Some lovely glorious nothing I did see,
    But since, my soule, whose child love is,
Takes limmes of flesh, and else could nothing doe,
    More subtile then the parent is,
Love must not be, but take a body too,
    And therefore what thou wert, and who
        I bid Love aske, and now
That it assume thy body, I allow,
And fixe it selfe in thy lip, eye, and brow.

Whilst thus to ballast love, I thought,
And so more steddily to have gone,
With wares which would sinke admiration,
I saw, I had loves pinnace overfraught.
    Ev'ry thy haire for love to worke upon
Is much too much, some fitter must be sought;

> For, nor in nothing, nor in things
> Extreme, and scatt'ring bright, can love inhere;
> Then as an Angell, face, and wings
> Of aire, not pure as it, yet pure doth weare,
> So thy love may be my loves spheare; 25
> Just such disparitie
> As is twixt Aire and Angells puritie,
> 'Twixt womens love, and mens will ever bee.

Breake of day

'Tis true, 'tis day; what though it be?
O wilt thou therefore rise from me?
Why should we rise, because 'tis light?
Did we lie downe, because 'twas night?
Love which in spight of darknesse brought us hether, 5
Should in despight of light keepe us together.

Light hath no tongue, but is all eye;
If it could speake as well as spie,
This were the worst, that it could say,
That being well, I faine would stay, 10
And that I lov'd my heart and honor so,
That I would not from him, that had them, goe.

Must businesse thee from hence remove?
Oh, that's the worst disease of love,
The poore, the foule, the false, love can 15
Admit, but not the busied man.
He which hath businesse, and makes love, doth doe
Such wrong, as when a maryed man doth wooe.

Aire and Angels. 23 *Then as an Angell...*: Scholastic angelology, derived from Neoplatonic doctrine (which the seventeenth century inherited), reflected Plotinus' view that angels could assume a body of air or of fire, but more generally of the former.

Breake of day. The only poem in the collection addressed by a woman to her lover, this lyric belongs to the class of the *aubade*, or lover's morning song. William Corkine's setting, with a few variants in the text, first appeared in 1612, in *Second Book of Ayres*.

The Anniversarie

   All Kings, and all their favorites,
     All glory'of honors, beauties, wits,
The Sun it selfe, which makes times, as they passe,
Is elder by a yeare, now, then it was
When thou and I first one another saw: 5
All other things, to their destruction draw,
    Only our love hath no decay;
This, no to morrow hath, nor yesterday,
Running it never runs from us away,
But truly keepes his first, last, everlasting day.   10

   Two graves must hide thine and my coarse,
     If one might, death were no divorce:
Alas, as well as other Princes, wee,
(Who Prince enough in one another bee,)
Must leave at last in death, these eyes, and eares,   15
Oft fed with true oathes, and with sweet salt teares;
    But soules where nothing dwells but love,
(All other thoughts being inmates) then shall prove
This, or a love increased there above,
When bodies to their graves, soules from their graves remove.   20

   And then wee shall be throughly blest,
     But wee no more, then all the rest.
Here upon earth, we'are Kings, and none but wee
Can be such Kings, nor of such subjects bee;
Who is so safe as wee? where none can doe   25
Treason to us, except one of us two.
    True and false feares let us refraine,
Let us love nobly,'and live, and adde againe
Yeares and yeares unto yeares, till we attaine
To write threescore; this is the second of our raigne.   30

A Valediction: of my name, in the window

I
My name engrav'd herein
Doth contribute my firmnesse to this glasse,
  Which, ever since that charme, hath beene
  As hard, as that which grav'd it, was.
Thine eye will give it price enough, to mock
  The diamonds of either rock.

II
'Tis much that Glasse should bee
As all confessing, and through-shine as I,
  'Tis more, that it shewes thee to thee,
  And cleare reflects thee to thine eye.
But all such rules, loves magique can undoe;
  Here you see mee, and I am you.

III
As no one point, nor dash,
Which are but accessaries to this name,
  The showers and tempests can outwash,
  So shall all times finde mee the same;
You this intirenesse better may fulfill,
  Who have the patterne with you still.

IV
Or if too hard and deepe
This learning be, for a scratch'd name to teach,
  It, as a given deaths head keepe,
  Lovers mortalitie to preach,
Or thinke this ragged bony name to bee
  My ruinous Anatomie.

A Valediction: of my name, in the window. A valediction was a special kind of lyric (there are four thus named in *Songs and Sonets*), which is distinguished as the poetic statement of a lover's leave-taking.

V

  Then, as all my soules bee,
Emparadis'd in you, (in whom alone
 I understand, and grow and see,)
 The rafters of my body, bone
Being still with you, the Muscle, Sinew,'and Veine,
  Which tile this house, will come againe.

VI

  Till my returne, repaire
And recompact my scatter'd body so.
 As all the vertuous powers which are
 Fix'd in the starres, are said to flow
Into such characters, as graved bee
  When these starres have supremacie:

VII

  So since this name was cut
When love and griefe their exaltation had,
 No doore 'gainst this names influence shut,
 As much more loving, as more sad,
'Twill make thee; and thou shouldst, till I returne,
  Since I die daily, daily mourne.

VIII

  When thy'inconsiderate hand
Flings ope this casement, with my trembling name,
 To looke on one, whose wit or land,
 New battry to thy heart may frame,
Then thinke this name alive, and that thou thus
  In it offendst my Genius.

IX

  And when thy melted maid,
Corrupted by thy Lover's gold, and page,
 His letter at thy pillow' hath laid,
 Disputed it, and tam'd thy rage,

---

25 The traditional scholastic distinctions between the rational, vegetative (or animal), and sensitive souls may be traced to Aristotle.

And thou begin'st to thaw towards him, for this,
May my name step in, and hide his.

X

And if this treason goe 55
To'an overt act, and that thou write againe;
In superscribing, this name flow
Into thy fancy, from the pane.
So, in forgetting thou remembrest right,
And unaware to mee shalt write. 60

XI

But glasse, and lines must bee,
No meanes our firme substantiall love to keepe;
Neere death inflicts this lethargie,
And this I murmure in my sleepe;
Impute this idle talke, to that I goe, 65
For dying men talke often so.

Twicknam garden

Blasted with sighs, and surrounded with teares,
 Hither I come to seeke the spring,
 And at mine eyes, and at mine eares,
Receive such balmes, as else cure every thing:
 But O, selfe traytor, I do bring 5
The spider love, which transubstantiates all,
 And can convert Manna to gall,
And that this place may thoroughly be thought
 True Paradise, I have the serpent brought.

Twicknam garden. Lucy, Countess of Bedford, to whom both Jonson and Donne addressed several poems and epistles, lived at Twickenham from 1608 to 1617.
 1 *surrounded*: used in its root sense, *super + undare* (to rise in waves, to overflow).

'Twere wholsomer for mee, that winter did   10
    Benight the glory of this place,
    And that a grave frost did forbid
These trees to laugh and mocke mee to my face;
    But that I may not this disgrace
Indure, nor yet leave loving, Love let mee   15
    Some senslesse peece of this place bee;
Make me a mandrake, so I may grow here,
    Or a stone fountaine weeping out my yeare.

Hither with christall vyals, lovers come,
    And take my teares, which are loves wine,   20
    And try your mistresse Teares at home,
For all are false, that tast not just like mine;
    Alas, hearts do not in eyes shine,
Nor can you more judge womans thoughts by teares,
    Then by her shadow, what she weares,   25
O perverse sexe, where none is true but shee,
    Who's therefore true, because her truth kills mee.

A Valediction: of the booke

I'll tell thee now (deare Love) what thou shalt doe
    To anger destiny, as she doth us,
    How I shall stay, though she Esloygne me thus
And how posterity shall know it too;
        How thine may out-endure   5
        Sybills glory, and obscure
        Her who from Pindar could allure,
    And her, through whose helpe *Lucan* is not lame,
    And her, whose booke (they say) *Homer* did finde, and name.

A Valediction: of the booke.   3 *Esloygne*: variant of *eloign* (to remove afar off, to withdraw).

7 *Her who from Pindar*: Corinna, a rival poetess.

8 *And her, through whose helpe Lucan is not lame*: Lucan's wife, who assisted in correcting his *Pharsalia*.

9 *And her, whose book ... Homer did finde*: Gr. notes that this refers to Phantasia of Memphis, whose work Homer got from a sacred scribe named Pharis.

Study our manuscripts, those Myriades 10
    Of letters, which have past twixt thee and mee,
    Thence write our Annals, and in them will bee
To all whom loves subliming fire invades,
    Rule and example found;
    There, the faith of any ground 15
    No schismatique will dare to wound,
    That sees, how Love this grace to us affords,
To make, to keep, to use, to be these his Records:

This Booke, as long-liv'd as the elements,
    Or as the worlds forme, this all-graved tome 20
    In cypher writ, or new made Idiome;
Wee for loves clergie only'are instruments;
    When this booke is made thus,
    Should againe the ravenous
    Vandals and Goths inundate us, 25
    Learning were safe; in this our Universe
Schooles might learne Sciences, Spheares Musick, Angels Verse.

Here Loves Divines, (since all Divinity
    Is love or wonder) may finde all they seeke,
    Whether abstract spirituall love they like, 30
Their Soules exhal'd with what they do not see,
    Or loth so to amuze
    Faiths infirmitie, they chuse
    Something which they may see and use;
    For, though minde be the heaven, where love doth sit, 35
Beauty'a convenient type may be to figure it.

Here more then in their bookes may Lawyers finde,
    Both by what titles Mistresses are ours,
    And how prerogative these states devours,
Transferr'd from Love himselfe, to womankinde. 40
    Who though from heart, and eyes,
    They exact great subsidies,
    Forsake him who on them relies
    And for the cause, honour, or conscience give,
Chimeraes, vaine as they, or their prerogative. 45

Here Statesmen, (or of them, they which can reade,)
    May of their occupation finde the grounds;
    Love and their art alike it deadly wounds,
If to consider what 'tis, one proceed,
      In both they doe excell   50
      Who the present governe well,
      Whose weaknesse none doth, or dares tell;
    In this thy booke, such will their nothing see,
As in the Bible some can finde out Alchimy.

Thus vent thy thoughts; abroad I'll studie thee,   55
    As he removes farre off, that great heights takes;
    How great love is, presence best tryall makes,
But absence tryes how long this love will bee;
      To take a latitude
      Sun, or starres, are fitliest view'd   60
      At their brightest, but to conclude
    Of longitudes, what other way have wee,
But to marke when, and where the darke eclipses bee?

Communitie

    Good wee must love, and must hate ill,
    For ill is ill, and good good still,
      But there are things indifferent,
    Which wee may neither hate, nor love,
    But one, and then another prove,   5
      As wee shall find our fancy bent.

    If then at first wise Nature had
    Made women either good or bad,
      Then some wee might hate, and some chuse,
    But since shee did them so create,   10
    That we may neither love, nor hate,
      Onely this rests, All, all may use.

    If they were good it would be seene,
    Good is as visible as greene,
      And to all eyes it selfe betrayes: 15

If they were bad, they could not last,
Bad doth it selfe, and others wast,
   So, they deserve nor blame, nor praise.

But they are ours as fruits are ours,
He that but tasts, he that devours,   20
   And he that leaves all, doth as well:
Chang'd loves are but chang'd sorts of meat,
And when he hath the kernell eate,
   Who doth not fling away the shell?

Loves growth

I scarce beleeve my love to be so pure
   As I had thought it was,
   Because it doth endure
Vicissitude, and season, as the grasse;
Me thinkes I lyed all winter, when I swore,   5
My love was infinite, if spring make'it more.
But if this medicine, love, which cures all sorrow
With more, not only bee no quintessence,
But mixt of all stuffes, paining soule, or sense,
And of the Sunne his working vigour borrow,   10
Love's not so pure, and abstract, as they use
To say, which have no Mistresse but their Muse,
But as all else, being elemented too,
Love sometimes would contemplate, sometimes do.

And yet no greater, but more eminent,   15
   Love by the spring is growne;
   As, in the firmament,
Starres by the Sunne are not inlarg'd, but showne,
Gentle love deeds, as blossomes on a bough,
From loves awaken'd root do bud out now.   20
If, as in water stir'd more circles bee
Produc'd by one, love such additions take,
Those like so many spheares, but one heaven make,

For, they are all concentrique unto thee,
And though each spring doe adde to love new heate,   25
As princes doe in times of action get
New taxes, and remit them not in peace,
No winter shall abate the springs encrease.

Loves exchange

Love, any devill else but you,
Would for a given Soule give something too.
At Court your fellows every day,
Give th'art of Riming, Huntsmanship, or play,
For them which were their owne before;   5
Onely'I have nothing which gave more,
But am, alas, by being lowly, lower.

I aske no dispensation now
To falsifie a teare, or sigh, or vow,
I do not sue from thee to draw   10
A *non obstante* on natures law,
These are prerogatives, they inhere
In thee and thine; none should forsweare
Except that hee *Loves* minion were.

Give mee thy weaknesse, make mee blinde,   15
Both wayes, as thou and thine, in eies and minde;
Love, let me never know that this
Is love, or, that love childish is.
Let me not know that others know
That she knowes my paines, least that so   20
A tender shame make me mine owne new woe.

Loves exchange. 11 *non obstante*: a license to do a thing, or a dispensation from the legal penalty for a thing done, notwithstanding any statute to the contrary.

If thou give nothing, yet thou'art just,
Because I would not thy first motions trust;
Small townes which stand stiffe, till great shot
Enforce them, by warres law *condition* not. 25
Such in loves warfare is my case,
I may not article for grace,
Having put Love at last to shew this face.

This face, by which he could command
And change th'Idolatrie of any land, 30
This face, which wheresoe'r it comes,
Can call vow'd men from cloisters, dead from tombes,
And melt both Poles at once, and store
Deserts with cities, and make more
Mynes in the earth, then Quarries were before. 35

For this, Love is enrag'd with mee,
Yet kills not; if I must example bee
To future Rebells; If th'unborne
Must learne, by my being cut up, and torne:
Kill, and dissect me, Love; for this 40
Torture against thine owne end is,
Rack't carcasses make ill Anatomies.

Confined Love

Some man unworthy to be possessor
Of old or new love, himselfe being false or weake,
  Thought his paine and shame would be lesser,
If on womankind he might his anger wreake,
    And thence a law did grow, 5
    One might but one man know;
    But are other creatures so?

Are Sunne, Moone, or Starres by law forbidden,
To smile where they list, or lend away their light?

    Are birds divorc'd, or are they chidden
If they leave their mate, or lie abroad a night?
        Beasts doe no joyntures lose
        Though they new lovers choose,
        But we are made worse then those.

    Who e'r rigg'd faire ship to lie in harbors,
And not to seeke new lands, or not to deale withall?
        Or built faire houses, set trees, and arbors,
Only to lock up, or else to let them fall?
        Good is not good, unlesse
        A thousand it possesse,
        But doth wast with greedinesse.

The Dreame

Deare love, for nothing lesse then thee
Would I have broke this happy dreame,
        It was a theame
For reason, much too strong for phantasie,
Therefore thou wakd'st me wisely; yet
My Dreame thou brok'st not, but continued'st it,
Thou art so truth, that thoughts of thee suffice,
To make dreames truths; and fables histories;
Enter these armes, for since thou thoughtst it best,
Not to dreame all my dreame, let's act the rest.

As lightning, or a Tapers light,
Thine eyes, and not thy noise wak'd mee;
        Yet I thought thee
(For thou lovest truth) an Angell, at first sight,
But when I saw thou sawest my heart,
And knew'st my thoughts, beyond an Angels art,
When thou knew'st what I dreamt, when thou knew'st when
Excesse of joy would wake me, and cam'st then,
I must confesse, it could not chuse but bee
Prophane, to thinke thee any thing but thee.

>   Comming and staying show'd thee, thee,
> But rising makes me doubt, that now,
>   Thou art not thou.
> That love is weake, where feare's as strong as hee;
> 'Tis not all spirit, pure, and brave, 25
> If mixture it of *Feare, Shame, Honor* have;
> Perchance as torches which must ready bee,
> Men light and put out, so thou deal'st with mee,
> Thou cam'st to kindle, goest to come; Then I
> Will dreame that hope againe, but else would die. 30

A Valediction: of weeping

>   Let me powre forth
> My teares before thy face, whil'st I stay here,
> For thy face coines them, and thy stampe they beare,
> And by this Mintage they are something worth,
>   For thus they bee 5
>   Pregnant of thee;
> Fruits of much griefe they are, emblemes of more,
> When a teare falls, that thou falst which it bore,
> So thou and I are nothing then, when on a divers shore.
>
>   On a round ball 10
> A workeman that hath copies by, can lay
> An Europe, Afrique, and an Asia,
> And quickly make that, which was nothing, *All*,
>   So doth each teare,
>   Which thee doth weare, 15
> A globe, yea world by that impression grow,
> Till thy teares mixt with mine doe overflow
> This world, by waters sent from thee, my heaven dissolved so.
>
>   O more then Moone,
> Draw not up seas to drowne me in thy spheare, 20
> Weepe me not dead, in thine armes, but forbeare
> To teach the sea, what it may doe too soone.

> Let not the winde
> Example finde,
> To doe me more harme, then it purposeth; 25
> Since thou and I sigh one anothers breath,
> Who e'r sighes most, is cruellest, and hasts the others death.

Loves Alchymie

Some that have deeper digg'd loves Myne then I,
Say, where his centrique happinesse doth lie:
> I have lov'd, and got, and told,
But should I love, get, tell, till I were old,
I should not finde that hidden mysterie; 5
> Oh, 'tis imposture all:
And as no chymique yet th'Elixar got,
> But glorifies his pregnant pot,
> If by the way to him befall
Some odoriferous thing, or medicinall, 10
So, lovers dreame a rich and long delight,
But get a winter-seeming summers night.

Our ease, our thrift, our honor, and our day,
Shall we, for this vaine Bubles shadow pay?
> Ends love in this, that my man, 15
Can be as happy'as I can; If he can
Endure the short scorne of a Bridegroomes play?
> That loving wretch that sweares,
> 'Tis not the bodies marry, but the mindes,
> Which he in her Angelique findes, 20
> Would sweare as justly, that he heares,
In that dayes rude hoarse minstralsey, the spheares.
> Hope not for minde in women; at their best,
> Sweetnesse, and wit they'are, but, *Mummy*, possest.

Loves Alchymie. 7 *th'Elixar*: the *elixir vitae*, the elixir of life, a substance thought by alchemists to be capable of transmuting base metals into gold; also, a potion for prolonging life indefinitely.
24 *Mummy*: part of a mummy; formerly used as a drug. Sometimes it was regarded as an exudation from mummies; it has been described by one authority as "a certain odorate and pleasant liquor of the spissitude of honey."

The Flea

Marke but this flea, and marke in this,
How little that which thou deny'st me is;
It suck'd me first, and now sucks thee,
And in this flea, our two bloods mingled bee;
Thou know'st that this cannot be said   5
A sinne, nor shame, nor losse of maidenhead,
   Yet this enjoyes before it wooe,
     And pamper'd swells with one blood made of two,
   And this, alas, is more then wee would doe.

Oh stay, three lives in one flea spare,   10
Where wee almost, yea more then maryed are.
This flea is you and I, and this
Our mariage bed, and mariage temple is;
Though parents grudge, and you, w'are met,
And cloysterd in these living walls of Jet.   15
   Though use make you apt to kill mee,
     Let not to that, selfe murder added bee,
   And sacrilege, three sinnes in killing three.

Cruell and sodaine, hast thou since
Purpled thy naile, in blood of innocence?   20
Wherein could this flea guilty bee,
Except in that drop which it suckt from thee?
Yet thou triumph'st, and saist that thou
Find'st not thy selfe, nor mee the weaker now;
   'Tis true, then learne how false, feares bee; 25
     Just so much honor, when thou yeeld'st to mee,
   Will wast, as this flea's death tooke life from thee.

The Curse

Who ever guesses, thinks, or dreames he knowes
Who is my mistris, wither by this curse;
    His only,'and only'his purse
    May some dull heart to love dispose,
And shee yeeld then to all that are his foes;   5
  May he be scorn'd by one, whom all else scorne,
  Forsweare to others, what to her he'hath sworne,
  With feare of missing, shame of getting torne.

Madnesse his sorrow, gout his cramp, may hee
Make, by but thinking, who hath made him such: 10
    And may he feele no touch
    Of conscience, but of fame, and bee
Anguish'd, not that 'twas sinne, but that 'twas shee:
  In early and long scarcenesse may he rot,
  For land which had been his, if he had not   15
  Himselfe incestuously an heire begot:

May he dreame Treason, and beleeve, that hee
Meant to performe it, and confesse, and die,
    And no record tell why:
    His sonnes, which none of his may bee,   20
Inherite nothing but his infamie:
  Or may he so long Parasites have fed,
  That he would faine be theirs, whom he hath bred,
  And at the last be circumcis'd for bread:

The venom of all stepdames, gamsters gall,   25
What Tyrans, and their subjects interwish,
    What Plants, Mynes, Beasts, Foule, Fish,
    Can contribute, all ill which all
Prophets, or Poets spake; And all which shall
  Be'annex'd in schedules unto this by mee,   30
  Fall on that man; For if it be a shee
  Nature before hand hath out-cursed mee.

The Message

Send home my long strayd eyes to mee,
Which (Oh) too long have dwelt on thee,
Yet since there they have learn'd such ill,
    Such forc'd fashions,
      And false passions,   5
        That they be
        Made by thee
Fit for no good sight, keep them still.

Send home my harmlesse heart againe,
Which no unworthy thought could staine,   10
Which if it be taught by thine
    To make jestings
      Of protestings,
        And crosse both
        Word and oath,   15
Keepe it, for then 'tis none of mine.

Yet send me back my heart and eyes,
That I may know, and see thy lyes,
And may laugh and joy, when thou
    Art in anguish   20
    And dost languish
      For some one
      That will none,
Or prove as false as thou art now.

The Message. A contemporary setting (one verse only) by Giovanni Coprario (1575–1626) survives in Tenbury MS. 1019.

A nocturnall upon S. Lucies day,

Being the shortest day

'Tis the yeares midnight, and it is the dayes,
Lucies, who scarce seaven houres herself unmaskes,
   The Sunne is spent, and now his flasks
   Send forth light squibs, no constant rayes;
     The worlds whole sap is sunke: 5
The generall balme th'hydroptique earth hath drunk,
Whither as to the beds-feet life is shrunke,
Dead and enterr'd; yet all these seeme to laugh,
Compar'd with mee, who am their Epitaph.

Study me then, you who shall lovers bee   10
At the next world, that is, at the next Spring:
   For I am every dead thing,
   In whom love wrought new Alchimie.
     For his art did expresse
A quintessence even from nothingnesse,   15
From dull privations, and leane emptinesse
He ruin'd mee, and I am re-begot
Of absence, darknesse, death; things which are not.

All others, from all things, draw all that's good,
Life, soule, forme, spirit, whence they beeing have;   20
   I, by loves limbecke, am the grave
   Of all, that's nothing. Oft a flood
     Have wee two wept, and so
Drownd the whole world, us two; oft did we grow
To be two Chaosses, when we did show   25

   A nocturnall upon S. Lucies day. St. Lucy's day was 13 December (Old Style), though the shortest day of the year, the winter solstice, was actually 12 December (St. Lucy's eve). In New Style the winter solstice is, of course, 22 December.
   21 *limbecke:* variant of alembic, an apparatus much used by alchemists to distill liquids.

Care to ought else; and often absences
Withdrew our soules, and made us carcasses.

But I am by her death, (which word wrongs her)
Of the first nothing, the Elixer grown;
   Were I a man, that I were one,   *30*
    I needs must know; I should preferre,
       If I were any beast,
Some ends, some means; Yea plants, yea stones detest,
And love; all, all some properties invest.
If I an ordinary nothing were,   *35*
As shadow,'a light, and body must be here.

But I am None; nor will my Sunne renew.
You lovers, for whose sake, the lesser Sunne
   At this time to the Goat is runne
    To fetch new lust, and give it you,   *40*
      Enjoy your summer all;
Since shee enjoyes her long nights festivall,
Let mee prepare towards her, and let mee call
This houre her Vigill, and her eve, since this
Both the yeares, and the dayes deep midnight is.   *45*

Witchcraft by a picture

I fixe mine eye on thine, and there
   Pitty my picture burning in thine eye:
My picture drown'd in a transparent teare,
   When I looke lower I espie.
     Hadst thou the wicked skill   *5*
By pictures made and mard, to kill,
How many wayes mightst thou performe thy will?

But now I'have drunke thy sweet salt teares,
   And though thou poure more I'll depart;

My picture vanish'd, vanish feares,
    That I can be endamag'd by that art;
      Though thou retaine of mee
One picture more, yet that will bee,
Being in thine owne heart, from all malice free.

The Baite

Come live with mee, and bee my love,
And wee will some new pleasures prove
Of golden sands, and christall brookes,
With silken lines, and silver hookes.

There will the river whispering runne
Warm'd by thy eyes, more then the Sunne.
And there the'inamor'd fish will stay,
Begging themselves they may betray.

When thou wilt swimme in that live bath,
Each fish, which every channell hath,
Will amorously to thee swimme,
Gladder to catch thee, then thou him.

If thou, to be so seene, beest loath,
By Sunne, or Moone, thou darknest both,
And if my selfe have leave to see,
I need not their light, having thee.

Let others freeze with angling reeds,
And cut their legges, with shells and weeds,
Or treacherously poore fish beset,
With strangling snare, or windowie net:

    The Baite. Variations on the pastoral sentiment implicit here appear in similar poems, in identical meter, by Marlowe, Raleigh, and Herrick. The later poems are obvious commentaries on their predecessors.

Let coarse bold hands, from slimy nest
The bedded fish in banks out-wrest,
Or curious traitors, sleavesilke flies
Bewitch poore fishes wandring eyes.

For thee, thou needst no such deceit, 25
For thou thy selfe art thine owne bait;
That fish, that is not catch'd thereby,
Alas, is wiser farre then I.

The Apparition

When by thy scorne, O murdresse, I am dead,
        And that thou thinkst thee free
From all solicitation from mee,
Then shall my ghost come to thy bed,
And thee, fain'd vestall, in worse armes shall see; 5
Then thy sicke taper will begin to winke,
And he, whose thou art then, being tyr'd before,
Will, if thou stirre, or pinch to wake him, thinke
        Thou call'st for more,
And in false sleepe will from thee shrinke, 10
And then poore Aspen wretch, neglected thou
Bath'd in a cold quicksilver sweat wilt lye
        A veryer ghost then I;
What I will say, I will not tell thee now,
Lest that preserve thee; and since my love is spent, 15
I'had rather thou shouldst painfully repent,
Then by my threatnings rest still innocent.

The broken heart

He is starke mad, who ever sayes,
   That he hath beene in love an houre,
Yet not that love so soone decayes,
   But that it can tenne in lesse space devour;
Who will beleeve mee, if I sweare
That I have had the plague a yeare?
   Who would not laugh at mee, if I should say,
   I saw a flaske of *powder burne a day?*

Ah, what a trifle is a heart,
   If once into loves hands it come?
All other griefes allow a part
   To other griefes, and aske themselves but some;
They come to us, but us Love draws,
Hee swallows us, and never chawes:
   By him, as by chain'd shot, whole rankes doe dye,
   He is the tyran Pike, our hearts the Frye.

If 'twere not so, what did become
   Of my heart, when I first saw thee?
I brought a heart into the roome,
   But from the roome, I carried none with mee;
If it had gone to thee, I know
Mine would have taught thine heart to show
   More pitty unto mee; but Love, alas,
   At one first blow did shiver it as glasse.

Yet nothing can to nothing fall,
   Nor any place be empty quite,
Therefore I thinke my breast hath all
   Those peeces still, though they be not unite;
And now as broken glasses show
A hundred lesser faces, so
   My ragges of heart can like, wish, and adore,
   But after one such love, can love no more.

A Valediction: forbidding mourning

As virtuous men passe mildly'away,
  And whisper to their soules, to goe,
Whilst some of their sad friends doe say,
  The breath goes now, and some say, no:

So let us melt, and make no noise,
  No teare-floods, nor sigh-tempests move,
'Twere prophanation of our joyes
  To tell the layetie our love.

Moving of th'earth brings harmes and feares,
  Men reckon what it did and meant,
But trepidation of the spheares,
  Though greater farre, is innocent.

Dull sublunary lovers love
  (Whose soule is sense) cannot admit
Absence, because it doth remove
  Those things which elemented it.

But we by'a love, so much refin'd,
  That our selves know not what it is,
Inter-assured of the mind,
  Care lesse, eyes, lips, and hands to misse.

Our two soules therefore, which are one,
  Though I must goe, endure not yet
A breach, but an expansion,
  Like gold to ayery thinnesse beate.

A Valediction: forbidding mourning. This poem was quoted by Izaak Walton, in his *Life of Donne*, in connection with the vision Donne had of his wife when he visited France in 1611. See Gd. Introd., p. xxix, for a case for rejecting Walton's story.

If they be two, they are two so 25
    As stiffe twin compasses are two,
Thy soule the fixt foot, makes no show
    To move, but doth, if the'other doe.

And though it in the center sit,
    Yet when the other far doth rome, 30
It leanes, and hearkens after it,
    And growes erect, as that comes home.

Such wilt thou be to mee, who must
    Like th'other foot, obliquely runne.
Thy firmnes drawes my circle just, 35
    And makes me end, where I begunne.

The Extasie

Where, like a pillow on a bed,
    A Pregnant banke swel'd up, to rest
The violets reclining head,
    Sat we two, one anothers best;

Our hands were firmely cimented 5
    With a fast balme, which thence did spring,
Our eye-beames twisted, and did thred
    Our eyes, upon one double string.

So to'entergraft our hands, as yet
    Was all the meanes to make us one, 10
And pictures in our eyes to get
    Was all our propagation.

The Extasie. "In Neo-Platonic philosophy this was the state of mind in which the soul, escaping from the body, attained to the vision of God, the One, the Absolute." (Gr.) See in *Seventeenth Century Contexts* (1960), George Williamson's discussion of the convention of the lovers' communion in similar poems by Sidney, Greville, Lord Herbert, and Wither. See also Gd. App. D.

>   As 'twixt two equal Armies, Fate
>   Suspends uncertaine victorie,
>   Our soules, (which to advance their state,   15
>   Were gone out,) hung 'twixt her, and mee.
>
>   And whil'st our soules negotiate there,
>   Wee like sepulchrall statues lay;
>   All day, the same our postures were,
>   And wee said nothing, all the day.   20
>
>   If any, so by love refin'd,
>   That he soules language understood,
>   And by good love were growen all minde,
>   Within convenient distance stood,
>
>   He (though he knew not which soule spake,   25
>   Because both meant, both spake the same)
>   Might thence a new concoction take,
>   And part farre purer then he came.
>
>   This Extasie doth unperplex
>   (We said) and tell us what we love,   30
>   Wee see by this, it was not sexe,
>   Wee see, we saw not what did move:
>
>   But as all severall soules containe
>   Mixture of things, they know not what,
>   Love, these mixt soules, doth mixe againe,   35
>   And makes both one, each this and that.
>
>   A single violet transplant,
>   The strength, the colour, and the size,
>   (All which before was poore, and scant,)
>   Redoubles still, and multiplies.   40
>
>   When love, with one another so
>   Interinanimates two soules,
>   That abler soule, which thence doth flow,
>   Defects of lonelinesse controules.

Wee then, who are this new soule, know,
    Of what we are compos'd, and made,
For, th'Atomies of which we grow,
    Are soules, whom no change can invade.

But O alas, so long, so farre
    Our bodies why doe wee forbeare?
They'are ours, though they'are not wee, Wee are
    The'intelligences, they the spheare.

We owe them thankes, because they thus,
    Did us, to us, at first convay,
Yeelded their forces, sense, to us,
    Nor are drosse to us, but allay.

On man heavens influence workes not so,
    But that it first imprints the ayre,
Soe soule into the soule may flow,
    Though it to body first repaire.

As our blood labours to beget
    Spirits, as like soules as it can,
Because such fingers need to knit
    That subtile knot, which makes us man:

So must pure lovers soules descend
    T'affections, and to faculties,
Which sense may reach and apprehend,
    Else a great Prince in prison lies.

To'our bodies turne wee then, that so
    Weake men on love reveal'd may looke;
Loves mysteries in soules doe grow,
    But yet the body is his booke.

And if some lover, such as wee,
    Have heard this dialogue of one,
Let him still marke us, he shall see
    Small change, when we'are to bodies gone.

Loves Deitie

I long to talke with some old lovers ghost,
   Who dyed before the god of Love was borne:
I cannot thinke that hee, who then lov'd most,
   Sunke so low, as to love one which did scorne.
But since this god produc'd a destinie,
And that vice-nature, custome, lets it be;
   I must love her, that loves not mee.

Sure, they which made him god, meant not so much:
   Nor he, in his young godhead practis'd it.
But when an even flame two hearts did touch,
   His office was indulgently to fit
Actives to passives. Correspondencie
Only his subject was; It cannot bee
   Love, till I love her, that loves mee.

But every moderne god will now extend
   His vast prerogative, as far as Jove.
To rage, to lust, to write to, to commend,
   All is the purlewe of the God of Love.
Oh were wee wak'ned by this Tyrannie
To'ungod this child againe, it could not bee
   I should love her, who loves not mee.

Rebell and Atheist too, why murmure I,
   As though I felt the worst that love could doe?
Love may make me leave loving, or might trie
   A deeper plague, to make her love mee too,
Which since she loves before, I'am loth to see;
Falshood is worse then hate; and that must bee,
   If shee whom I love, should love mee.

Loves diet

To what a combersome unwieldinesse
And burdenous corpulence my love had growne,
   But that I did, to make it lesse,
   And keepe it in proportion,
Give it a diet, made it feed upon 5
That which love worst endures, *discretion*.

Above one sigh a day I'allow'd him not,
Of which my fortune, and my faults had part;
   And if sometimes by stealth he got
   A she sigh from my mistresse heart, 10
And thought to feast on that, I let him see
'Twas neither very sound, nor meant to mee.

If he wroung from mee'a teare, I brin'd it so
With scorne or shame, that him it nourish'd not;
   If he suck'd hers, I let him know 15
   'Twas not a teare, which hee had got,
His drinke was counterfeit, as was his meat;
For, eyes which rowle towards all, weepe not, but sweat.

What ever he would dictate, I writ that,
But burnt my letters; When she writ to me, 20
   And that that favour made him fat,
   I said, if any title bee
Convey'd by this, Ah, what doth it availe,
To be the fortieth name in an entaile?

Thus I reclaim'd my buzard love, to flye 25
At what, and when, and how, and where I chuse;
   Now negligent of sport I lye,
   And now as other Fawkners use,
I spring a mistresse, sweare, write, sigh and weepe:
And the game kill'd, or lost, goe talke, and sleepe. 30

The Will

Before I sigh my last gaspe, let me breath,
Great love, some Legacies; Here I bequeath
Mine eyes to *Argus*, if mine eyes can see,
If they be blinde, then Love, I give them thee;
My tongue to Fame; to'Embassadours mine eares;   5
    To women or the sea, my teares;
  Thou, Love, hast taught mee heretofore
By making mee serve her who'had twenty more,
That I should give to none, but such, as had too much before.

My constancie I to the planets give;   10
My truth to them, who at the Court doe live;
Mine ingenuity and opennesse,
To Jesuites; to Buffones my pensivenesse;
My silence to'any, who abroad hath beene;
    My mony to a Capuchin.   15
  Thou Love taught'st me, by'appointing mee
To love there, where no love receiv'd can be,
Onely to give to such as have an incapacitie.

My faith I give to Roman Catholiques;
All my good works unto the Schismaticks   20
Of Amsterdam; my best civility
And Courtship, to an Universitie;
My modesty I give to souldiers bare;
    My patience let gamesters share.
  Thou Love taught'st mee, by making mee   25
Love her that holds my love disparity,
Onely to give to those that count my gifts indignity.

The Will. 20–21 *The Schismaticks of Amsterdam:* the extreme Puritans, like Ben Jonson's Ananias and Tribulation Wholesome.

>   I give my reputation to those
>   Which were my friends; Mine industrie to foes;
>   To Schoolemen I bequeath my doubtfulnesse;   30
>   My sicknesse to Physitians, or excesse;
>   To Nature, all that I in Ryme have writ;
>   And to my company my wit;
>   Thou Love, by making mee adore
>   Her, who begot this love in mee before,   35
> Taughtst me to make, as though I gave, when I did but restore.
>
>   To him for whom the passing bell next tolls,
>   I give my physick bookes; my writen rowles
>   Of Morall counsels, I to Bedlam give;
>   My brazen medals, unto them which live   40
>   In want of bread; To them which passe among
>   All forrainers, mine English tongue.
>   Thou, Love, by making mee love one
>   Who thinkes her friendship a fit portion
> For yonger lovers, dost my gifts thus disproportion.   45
>
>   Therefore I'll give no more; But I'll undoe
>   The world by dying; because love dies too.
>   Then all your beauties will bee no more worth
>   Then gold in Mines, where none doth draw it forth.
>   And all your graces no more use shall have   50
>   Then a Sun dyall in a grave.
>   Thou Love taughtst mee, by making mee
>   Love her, who doth neglect both mee and thee,
> To'invent, and practise this one way, to'annihilate all three.

The Funerall

> Who ever comes to shroud me, do not harme
>   Nor question much
> That subtile wreath of haire, which crowns my arme;
> The mystery, the signe you must not touch,

For 'tis my outward Soule, 5
Viceroy to that, which then to heaven being gone,
    Will leave this to controule,
And keepe these limbes, her Provinces, from dissolution.

For if the sinewie thread my braine lets fall
    Through every part, 10
Can tye those parts, and make mee one of all;
These haires which upward grew, and strength and art
    Have from a better braine,
Can better do'it; Except she meant that I
    By this should know my pain, 15
As prisoners then are manacled, when they'are condemn'd to die.

What ere shee meant by'it, bury it with me,
    For since I am
Loves martyr, it might breed idolatrie,
If into others hands these Reliques came; 20
    As'twas humility
To'afford to it all that a Soule can doe,
    So, 'tis some bravery,
That since you would have none of mee, I bury some of you.

The Blossome

Little think'st thou, poore flower,
    Whom I have watch'd six or seaven dayes,
And seene thy birth, and seene what every houre
Gave to thy growth, thee to this height to raise,
And now dost laugh and triumph on this bough, 5
    Little think'st thou
That it will freeze anon, and that I shall
To morrow finde thee falne, or not at all.

Little think'st thou poore heart
    That labourest yet to nestle thee, 10
And think'st by hovering here to get a part

In a forbidden or forbidding tree,
And hop'st her stiffenesse by long siege to bow:
    Little think'st thou,
That thou to morrow, ere that Sunne doth wake,   *15*
Must with this Sunne, and mee a journey take.

  But thou which lov'st to bee
    Subtile to plague thy selfe, wilt say,
Alas, if you must goe, what's that to mee?
Here lyes my businesse, and here I will stay: *20*
You goe to friends, whose love and meanes present
    Various content
To your eyes, eares, and tongue, and every part.
If then your body goe, what need you'a heart?

  Well then, stay here; but know,   *25*
    When thou hast stayd and done thy most;
A naked thinking heart, that makes no show,
Is to a woman, but a kinde of Ghost;
How shall shee know my heart; or having none,
    Know thee for one?   *30*
Practise may make her know some other part,
But take my word, shee doth now know a Heart.

  Meet mee at London, then,
    Twenty dayes hence, and thou shalt see
Mee fresher, and more fat, by being with men,   *35*
Then if I had staid still with her and thee.
For Gods sake, if you can, be you so too:
    I would give you
There, to another friend, whom wee shall finde
As glad to have my body, as my minde.   *40*

The Primrose,
being at Montgomery Castle,
upon the hill, on which it is situate

    Upon this Primrose hill,
      Where, if Heav'n would distill
A shoure of raine, each severall drop might goe
To his owne primrose, and grow Manna so;
And where their forme, and their infinitie
      Make a terrestriall Galaxie,
      As the small starres doe in the skie:
I walke to finde a true Love; and I see
That 'tis not a mere woman, that is shee,
But must, or more, or lesse then woman bee.

    Yet know I not, which flower
      I wish; a sixe, or foure;
For should my true-Love lesse then woman bee,
She were scarce any thing; and then, should she
Be more then woman, shee would get above
      All thought of sexe, and thinke to move
      My heart to study'her, not to love;
Both these were monsters; Since there must reside
Falshood in woman, I could more abide,
She were by art, then Nature falsify'd.

    Live Primrose then, and thrive
      With thy true number five;
And women, whom this flower doth represent,
With this mysterious number be content;

The Primrose, being at Montgomery Castle.... The reference to Montgomery Castle, first appearing in the 1635 edition of the *Poems*, probably indicates that the poem was addressed to Mrs. Herbert, mother of George and of Lord Herbert of Cherbury. Gr. notes that the perfect primrose had five petals, though flowers with more or fewer might be found.

    Ten is the farthest number; if halfe ten 25
        Belonge unto each woman, then
        Each woman may take halfe us men,
Or if this will not serve their turne, Since all
Numbers are odde, or even, and they fall
First into this five, women may take us all. 30

The Relique

    When my grave is broke up againe
    Some second ghest to entertaine,
    (For graves have learn'd that woman-head
    To be to more then one a Bed)
        And he that digs it, spies 5
A bracelet of bright haire about the bone,
        Will he not let'us alone,
And thinke that there a loving couple lies,
Who hop'd that this device might be a way
To make their soules, at the last busie day, 10
Meet at this grave, and make a little stay?

    If this fall in a time, or land,
    Where mis-devotion doth command,
    Then, he that digges us up, will bring
    Us, to the Bishop, and the King, 15
        To make us Reliques; then
Thou shalt be'a Mary Magdalen, and I
        A something else thereby;
All women shall adore us, and some men;
And since at such time, miracles are sought, 20
I would have that age by this paper taught
What miracles wee harmelesse lovers wrought.

    First, we lov'd well and faithfully,
    Yet knew not what wee lov'd, nor why,
    Difference of sex no more wee knew, 25
    Then our Guardian Angells doe;

                Comming and going, wee
Perchance might kisse, but not between those meales.
                Our hands ne'r toucht the seales
Which nature, injur'd by late law, sets free.   30
These miracles wee did; but now alas,
All measure, and all language, I should passe,
Should I tell what a miracle shee was.

The Dampe

When I am dead, and Doctors know not why,
            And my friends curiositie
Will have me cut up to survay each part,
When they shall finde your Picture in my heart,
            You thinke a sodaine dampe of love   5
            Will through all their senses move,
And worke on them as mee, and so preferre
Your murder, to the name of Massacre.

Poore victories; But if you dare be brave,
            And pleasure in your conquest have,   10
First kill th'enormous Gyant, your *Disdaine*,
And let th'enchantresse *Honor*, next be slaine,
            And like a Goth and Vandall rize,
            Deface Records, and Histories
Of your owne arts and triumphs over men,   15
And without such advantage kill me then.

For I could muster up as well as you
            My Gyants, and my Witches too,
Which are vast *Constancy*, and *Secretnesse*,
But these I neyther looke for, nor professe.   20
            Kill mee as Woman, let mee die
            As a meere man; doe you but try
Your passive valor, and you shall finde than,
In that you'have odds enough of any man.

The Dissolution

    Shee'is dead; And all which die
      To their first Elements resolve;
And wee were mutuall Elements to us,
        And made of one another.
    My body then doth hers involve, 5
And those things whereof I consist, hereby
In me abundant grow, and burdenous,
        And nourish not, but smother.
    My fire of Passion, sighes of ayre,
Water of teares, and earthly sad despaire, 10
        Which my materialls bee,
But ne'r worne out by loves securitie,
Shee, to my losse, doth by her death repaire,
    And I might live long wretched so
But that my fire doth with my fuell grow. 15
        Now as those Active Kings
    Whose foraine conquest treasure brings,
Receive more, and spend more, and soonest breake:
This (which I am amaz'd that I can speake)
        This death, hath with my store 20
          My use encreas'd.
And so my soule more earnestly releas'd,
Will outstrip hers; As bullets flowen before
A latter bullet may o'rtake, the pouder being more.

A Jeat Ring sent

    Thou art not so black, as my heart,
  Nor halfe so brittle, as her heart, thou art;
What would'st thou say? shall both our properties
                         by thee bee spoke,
  Nothing more endlesse, nothing sooner broke?

Marriage rings are not of this stuffe;
Oh, why should ought lesse precious, or lesse tough
Figure our loves? Except in thy name thou have bid it say
I'am cheap, and nought but fashion, fling me'away.

Yet stay with mee since thou art come,
Circle this fingers top, which did'st her thombe.
Be justly proud, and gladly safe, that thou dost dwell with me,
She that, Oh, broke her faith, would soon breake thee.

Negative love

I never stoop'd so low, as they
Which on an eye, cheeke, lip, can prey,
   Seldome to them, which soare no higher
   Then vertue or the minde to'admire,
For sense, and understanding may
   Know, what gives fuell to their fire:
My love, though silly, is more brave,
For may I misse, when ere I crave,
If I know yet, what I would have.

If that be simply perfectest
Which can by no way be exprest
   But *Negatives*, my love is so.
   To All, which all love, I say no.
If any who deciphers best,
   What we know not, ourselves, can know,
Let him teach mee that nothing; This
As yet my ease, and comfort is,
Though I speed not, I cannot misse.

The Prohibition

Take heed of loving mee,
At least remember, I forbade it thee;
Not that I shall repaire my'unthrifty wast
Of Breath and Blood, upon thy sighes, and teares,

By being to thee then what to me thou wast,   *5*
But, so great Joy, our life at once outweares,
Then, least thy love, by my death, frustrate bee,
If thou love mee, take heed of loving mee.

    Take heed of hating mee,
Or too much triumph in the Victorie.   *10*
Not that I shall be mine owne officer,
And hate with hate againe retaliate;
But thou wilt lose the stile of conquerour,
If I, thy conquest, perish by thy hate.
Then, least my being nothing lessen thee,   *15*
If thou hate mee, take heed of hating mee.

    Yet, love and hate mee too,
So, these extreames shall ne'r their office doe;
Love mee, that I may die the gentler way;
Hate mee, because thy love'is too great for mee;   *20*
Or let these two, themselves, not me decay;
So shall I live thy Stage, not triumph bee;
Lest thou thy love and hate and mee undoe
To let mee live, Oh love and hate mee too.

The Expiration

So, so, breake off this last lamenting kisse,
    Which sucks two soules, and vapors Both away:
Turne thou ghost that way, and let mee turne this,
    And let our selves benight our happiest day;
Wee aske none leave to love; nor will we owe   *5*
    Any, so cheape a death, as saying, Goe;

Goe; and if that word have not quite kil'd thee,
    Ease mee with death, by bidding mee goe too.
Oh, if it have, let my word worke on mee,
    And a just office on a murderer doe.   *10*
Except it be too late, to kill me so,
    Being double dead, going, and bidding, goe.

The Computation

For the first twenty yeares, since yesterday,
    I scarce beleev'd, thou could'st be gone away,
For forty more, I fed on favours past,
    And forty'on hopes, that thou would'st, they might last.
Teares drown'd one hundred, and sighes blew out two,
    A thousand, I did neither thinke, nor doe,
    Or not divide, all being one thought of you;
    Or in a thousand more, forgot that too.
Yet call not this long life; But thinke that I
Am, by being dead, Immortall; Can ghosts die?

The Paradox

No Lover saith, I love, nor any other
    Can judge a perfect Lover;
Hee thinkes that else none can or will agree,
    That any loves but hee:
I cannot say I lov'd, for who can say
    Hee was kill'd yesterday?
Love with excesse of heat, more yong then old,
    Death kills with too much cold;
Wee dye but once, and who lov'd last did die,
    Hee that saith twice, doth lye:
For though hee seeme to move, and stirre a while,
    It doth the sense beguile.
Such life is like the light which bideth yet
    When the lifes light is set,
Or like the heat, which fire in solid matter
    Leaves behinde, two houres after.
Once I lov'd and dyed; and am now become
    Mine Epitaph and Tombe.
Here dead men speake their last, and so do I;
    Love-slaine, loe, here I lye.

Farewell to love

      Whilst yet to prove
I thought there was some Deitie in love,
    So did I reverence, and gave
Worship, as Atheists at their dying houre
Call, what they cannot name, an unknowne power,
    As ignorantly did I crave:
      Thus when
Things not yet knowne are coveted by men,
    Our desires give them fashion, and so
As they waxe lesser, fall, as they sise, grow.

      But, from late faire
His highnesse sitting in a golden Chaire,
    Is not lesse cared for after three dayes
By children, then the thing which lovers so
Blindly admire, and with such worship wooe;
    Being had, enjoying it decayes:
      And thence,
What before pleas'd them all, takes but one sense,
    And that so lamely, as it leaves behinde
A kinde of sorrowing dulnesse to the minde.

      Ah, cannot wee,
As well as Cocks and Lyons jocund be,
    After such pleasures, unlesse wise
Nature decreed (since each such Act, they say,
Diminisheth the length of life a day)
    This, as shee would man should despise
      The sport,
Because that other curse of being short,
    And only for a minute made to be,
Eagers desire to raise posterity.

      Since so, my minde
Shall not desire what no man else can finde;
    I'll no more dote and runne

　　　　To pursue things which had indammag'd me.
　　　　And when I come where moving beauties be,　　35
　　　　　　As men doe when the summers Sunne
　　　　　　　　Growes great,
　　　　Though I admire their greatnesse, shun their heat;
　　　　　　Each place can afford shadowes. If all faile,
　　　　'Tis but applying worme-seed to the Taile.　　40

A Lecture upon the Shadow

Stand still, and I will read to thee
A Lecture, Love, in loves philosophy.
　　　　These three houres that we have spent,
　　　　Walking here, two shadowes went
Along with us, which we ourselves produc'd;　　5
But, now the Sunne is just above our head,
　　　　We doe those shadowes tread;
　　　　And to brave clearnesse all things are reduc'd.
　　　So whilst our infant loves did grow,
　　　Disguises did, and shadowes, flow,　　10
　　　From us, and our cares; but, now 'tis not so.

That love hath not attain'd the high'st degree,
Which is still diligent lest others see.

Except our loves at this noone stay,
We shall new shadowes make the other way.　　15
　　　　As the first were made to blinde
　　　　Others; these which come behinde
Will worke upon our selves, and blind our eyes.
If our loves faint, and westwardly decline;
　　　　To me thou, falsly, thine,　　20
　　　　And I to thee mine actions shall disguise.
　　　The morning shadowes weare away,
　　　But these grow longer all the day,
　　　But oh, loves day is short, if love decay.

Love is a growing, or full constant light;　　25
And his first minute, after noone, is night.

Sonnet. The Token

Send me some Token that my hope may live,
   Or that my easelesse thoughts may sleep and rest;
Send me some honey to make sweet my hive,
   That in my passion I may hope the best.
I beg nor ribbond wrought with thine owne hands,   5
   To knit our loves in the fantastick straine
Of new-toucht youth; nor Ring to shew the stands
   Of our affection, that as that's round and plaine,
So should our loves meet in simplicity.
   No, nor the Coralls which thy wrist infold,   10
Lac'd up together with congruity,
   To shew our thoughts should rest in the same hold.
No, nor thy picture, though most gracious,
   And most desir'd, because best like the best;
Nor witty Lines, which are most copious,   15
   Within the Writings which thou hast addrest.
     Send me nor this, nor that, t'increase my store,
     But swear thou thinkst I love thee, and no more.

[Self Love]

He that cannot chuse but love,
   And strives against it still,
Never shall my fancy move,
   For he loves 'gaynst his will;

Nor he which is all his own,   5
   And can all pleasure chuse,
When I am caught he can be gone,
   And when he list refuse.

Nor he that loves none but faire,
   For such by all are sought;   10
Nor he that can for foul ones care,
   For his Judgement then is nought:

Nor he that hath wit, for he
  Will make me his jest or slave;
Nor a fool for when others, ...
  He'can neither want nor crave;   15

Nor he that still his Mistresse payes,
  For she is thrall'd therefore:
Nor he that payes not, for he sayes
  Within shee's worth no more.   20

    Is there then no kinde of men
      Whom I may freely prove?
    I will vent that humour then
      In mine own selfe love.

ELEGIES, SATIRES, VERSE LETTERS

Elegie II. The Anagram

Marry, and love thy *Flavia*, for, shee
Hath all things, whereby others beautious bee,
For, though her eyes be small, her mouth is great,
Though they be Ivory, yet her teeth be jeat,
Though they be dimme, yet she is light enough,　　　5
And though her harsh haire fall, her skinne is rough;
What though her cheeks be yellow, her haire's red,
Give her thine, and she hath a maydenhead.
These things are beauties elements, where these
Meet in one, that one must, as perfect, please.　　　10
If red and white and each good quality
Be in thy wench, ne'r aske where it doth lye.
In buying things perfum'd, we aske; if there
Be muske and amber in it, but not where.
Though all her parts be not in th'usuall place,　　　15
She'hath yet an Anagram of a good face.
If we might put the letters but one way,
In the leane dearth of words, what could wee say?
When by the Gamut some Musitions make
A perfect song, others will undertake,　　　20
By the same Gamut chang'd, to equall it.
Things simply good, can never be unfit;
She's faire as any, if all be like her,
And if none bee, then she is singular.

All love is wonder; if wee justly doe 25
Account her wonderfull, why not lovely too?
Love built on beauty, soone as beauty, dies,
Chuse this face, chang'd by no deformities;
Women are all like Angels; the faire be
Like those which fell to worse; but such as shee, 30
Like to good Angels, nothing can impaire:
'Tis lesse griefe to be foule, then to'have beene faire.
For one nights revels, silke and gold we chuse,
But, in long journeyes, cloth, and leather use.
Beauty is barren oft; best husbands say 35
There is best land, where there is foulest way.
Oh what a soveraigne Plaister will shee bee
If thy past sinnes have taught thee jealousie!
Here needs no spies, nor eunuches; her commit
Safe to thy foes; yea, to a Marmosit. 40
When Belgiaes citties, the round countries drowne,
That durty foulenesse guards, and armes the towne:
So doth her face guard her; and so, for thee,
Which, forc'd by businesse, absent oft must bee,
Shee, whose face, like clouds, turnes the day to night, 45
Who, mightier then the sea, makes Moores seem white,
Who, though seaven yeares, she in the Stews had laid,
A Nunnery durst receive, and thinke a maid,
And though in childbeds labour she did lie,
Midwifes would sweare, 'twere but a tympanie, 50
Whom, if shee'accuse her selfe, I credit lesse
Then witches, which impossibles confesse,
Whom Dildoes, bedstaves, and her velvett glasse
Would be as loth to touch, as Joseph was,
One like none, and lik'd of none, fittest were, 55
For, things in fashion every man will weare.

Elegie V. His Picture

Here take my Picture; though I bid farewell,
Thine, in my heart, where my soule dwels, shall dwell.
'Tis like me now, but I dead, 'twill be more
When wee are shadowes both, then 'twas before.
When weather-beaten I come backe; my hand   5
Perhaps with rude oares torne, or Sun beams tann'd,
My face and brest of hairecloth, and my head
With cares rash sodaine stormes, being o'rspread,
My body'a sack of bones, broken within,
And powders blew staines scatter'd on my skinne;   10
If rivall fooles taxe thee to'have lov'd a man,
So foule, and course, as, Oh, I may seeme than,
This shall say what I was: and thou shalt say,
Doe his hurts reach mee? doth my worth decay?
Or doe they reach his judging minde, that hee   15
Should now love lesse, what hee did love to see?
That which in him was faire and delicate,
Was but the milke, which in loves childish state
Did nurse it: who now is growne strong enough
To feed on that, which to'disus'd tasts seemes tough.   20

Elegie IX. The Autumnall

No *Spring*, nor *Summer* Beauty hath such grace,
    As I have seen in one *Autumnall* face;
Yong *Beauties* force our love, and that's a *Rape*,
    This doth but *counsaile*, yet you cannot scape.
If 'twere a *shame* to love, here 'twere no *shame*,   5
    Affection here takes *Reverences* name.
Were her first yeares the *Golden Age*; That's true,
    But now shee's *gold* oft tried, and ever new.
That was her torrid and inflaming time,
    This is her tolerable *Tropique clyme*.   10

Faire eyes, who askes more heate then comes from hence,
  He in a fever wishes pestilence.
Call not these wrinkles, *graves*; If *graves* they were,
  They were *Loves graves*; for else he is no where.
Yet lies not Love *dead* here, but here doth sit   15
  Vow'd to this trench, like an *Anachorit*.
And here, till hers, which must be his *death*, come,
  He doth not digge a *Grave*, but build a *Tombe*.
Here dwells he, though he sojourne ev'ry where,
  In *Progresse*, yet his standing house is here.   20
Here, where still *Evening* is; not *noone*, nor *night*;
  Where no *voluptuousnesse*, yet all *delight*.
In all her words, unto all hearers fit,
  You may at *Revels*, you at *counsaile*, sit.
This is loves timber, youth his under-wood;   25
  There he, as wine in *June*, enrages blood,
Which then comes seasonabliest, when our tast
  And appetite to other things, is past.
Xerxes strange *Lydian* love, the *Platane* tree,
  Was lov'd for age, none being so large as shee,   30
Or else because, being yong, nature did blesse
  Her youth with ages glory, *Barrennesse*.
If we love things long sought, *Age* is a thing
  Which we are fifty yeares in compassing.
If transitory things, which soone decay,   35
  Age must be lovelyest at the latest day.
But name not *Winter-faces*, whose skin's slacke;
  Lanke, as an unthrifts purse; but a soules sacke;
Whose *Eyes* seeke light within, for all here's shade;
  Whose *mouthes* are holes, rather worne out, then made;   40
Whose every tooth to'a severall place is gone,
  To vexe their soules at *Resurrection*;
Name not these living *Deaths-heads* unto mee,
  For these, not *Ancient*, but *Antique* be.

Elegie IX. 29–32 *Platane tree*: The Persian king Xerxes decked out a plane tree in Lydia with gold ornaments in order to enhance its beauty. In *N.&Q.* (1960) Mrs. K. D. Duncan-Jones finds in the works of William Browne and John Evelyn associations of barrenness with the plane tree.

> I hate extreames; yet I had rather stay 45
>   With *Tombs*, then *Cradles*, to weare out a day.
> Since such loves natural lation is, may still
>   My love descend, and journey downe the hill,
> Not panting after growing beauties, so,
>   I shall ebbe out with them, who home-ward goe. 50

Elegie XI. The Bracelet

Upon the losse of his Mistresses Chaine, for which he made satisfaction

> Not that in colour it was like thy haire,
> For Armelets of that thou maist let me weare:
> Nor that thy hand it oft embrac'd and kist,
> For so it had that good, which oft I mist:
> Nor for that silly old moralitie, 5
> That as these linkes are ty'd, our love should bee:
> Mourne I that I thy seavenfold chaine have lost:
> Nor for the luck sake; but the bitter cost.
> O, shall twelve righteous Angels, which as yet
> No leaven of vile soder did admit; 10
> Nor yet by any fault have straid or gone
> From the first state of their Creation;
> Angels, which heaven commanded to provide
> All things to me, and be my faithfull guide;
> To gaine new friends, t'appease great enemies; 15
> To comfort my soule, when I lie or rise.
> Shall these twelve innocents, by thy severe
> Sentence (dread judge) my sins great burden beare?

Elegie XI. 9 *Angels*: An elaborate series of quibbles on Angel, both in the theological and commercial senses, provides a means of establishing analogies between the spiritual and the temporal throughout this elegy. An angel was an English gold coin.

Shall they be damn'd, and in the furnace throwne,
And punisht for offences not their owne? 20
They save not me, they doe not ease my paines,
When in that hell they'are burnt and ty'd in chains:
Were they but Crownes of France, I cared not,
For, most of them their naturall Countreys rott
I think possesseth, they come here to us, 25
So leane, so pale, so lame, so ruinous.
And howsoe'r French Kings most Christian be,
Their Crownes are circumcis'd most Jewishly;
Or were they Spanish Stamps, still travelling,
That are become as Catholique as their King, 30
Those unlickt beare-whelps, unfil'd pistolets
That (more than Canon shot) availes or lets;
Which negligently left unrounded, looke
Like many angled figures, in the booke
Of some great Conjurer which would enforce 35
Nature, as these doe justice, from her course.
Which, as the soule quickens head, feet and heart,
As streames like veines, run through th'earth's every part,
Visit all Countries and have slily made
Gorgeous *France*, ruin'd: ragged and decay'd 40
Scotland, which knew no State, proud in one day:
And mangled seventeen-headed *Belgia*:
Or were it such gold as that wherewithall
Almighty *Chymiques* from each minerall,
Having by subtle fire a soule out-pull'd; 45
Are dirtely and desperately gull'd:
I would not spit to quench the fire they'are in,
For, they are guilty of much hainous Sin.
But, shall my harmlesse angels perish? Shall
I lose my guard, my ease, my food, my all? 50

24 *rott*: venereal disease, which often led to the loss of hair (cf. l. 28).

29 *Stamps*: the designs (or heads) stamped on coins, and hence the coins themselves.

32 *lets*: hinders, impedes.

42 *Belgia*: Late sixteenth-century accounts of religious warfare often refer to the seventeen provinces of the Netherlands and Belgium, which were at war with Spain. If decapitated, they would in hydra fashion sprout new heads.

Much hope which they should nourish will be dead.
Much of my able youth, and lustyhead
Will vanish, if thou love let them alone,
For thou wilt love me lesse when they are gone.
Oh be content that some lowd squeaking Cryer   55
Well-pleas'd with one leane thred-bare groat, for hire,
May like a devill roare through every street;
And gall the finders conscience if they meet.
Or let mee creepe to some dread Conjurer,
That with phantastique scheames fulfills much paper;   60
Which hath divided heaven in tenements,
And with whores, theeves, and murderers stuft his rents
So full, that though hee passe them all in sinne,
He leaves himselfe no room to enter in.
   And if, when all his art and time is spent,   65
Hee say 'twill ne'r be found; yet be content;
Receive from him that doome ungrudgingly,
Because he is the mouth of destiny.
   Thou say'st (alas) the gold doth still remaine,
Though it be chang'd, and put into a chaine,   70
So in the first falne angels, resteth still
Wisdome and knowledge; but, 'tis turn'd to ill:
As these should doe good works; and should provide
Necessities; but now must nurse thy pride,
And they are still bad angels; Mine are none;   75
For, forme gives being: and their forme is gone:
Pitty these Angels yet; their dignities
Passe Vertues, Powers, and Principalities.
   But, thou art resolute; Thy will be done;
Yet with such anguish, as her onely sonne   80
The Mother in the hungry grave doth lay,
Unto the fire these Martyrs I betray.
Good soules, (for you give life to every thing)
Good Angels, (for good messages you bring)
Destin'd you might have beene to such a one,   85
As would have lov'd and worship'd you alone:
One which would suffer hunger, nakednesse,
Yea death, ere he would make your number lesse.

But, I am guilty of your sad decay;
May your few fellowes longer with me stay.   90
    But ô thou wretched finder whom I hate
So much that I'almost pitty thy estate:
Gold being the heaviest metal amongst all,
May my most heavy curse upon thee fall:
Here fetter'd, manacled, and hang'd in chains,   95
First mayst thou bee; then chaind to hellish paines;
Or be with forraine gold brib'd to betray
Thy Country,' and faile both of that and thy pay.
May the next thing thou stoop'st to reach, containe
Poyson, whose nimble fume rot thy moist braine;   100
Or libels, or some interdicted thing,
Which negligently kept, thy ruine bring.
Lust-bred diseases rot thee;'and dwell with thee
Itching desire, and no abilitie.
May all the hurt which ever Gold hath wrought;   105
All mischiefes which all devils ever thought;
Want after plenty; poore and gouty age;
The plagues of travellers; love; and marriage
Afflict thee, and at thy lives last moment,
May thy swolne sinnes themselves to thee present.   110
    But, I forgive; repent thee, honest man:
Gold is Restorative, restore it then:
But if with it thou beest loath to'depart,
Because 'tis cordiall, would 'twere at thy heart.

Elegie XVI. On his Mistris

By our first strange and fatall interview,
By all desires which thereof did ensue,
By our long starving hopes, by that remorse
Which my words masculine perswasive force
Begot in thee, and by the memory   5
Of hurts, which spies and rivals threatned me,
I calmely beg. But by thy fathers wrath,

By all paines, which want and divorcement hath,
I conjure thee, and all the oathes which I
And thou have sworne to seale joynt constancy,   10
Here I unsweare, and overswear them thus,
Thou shalt not love by wayes so dangerous.
Temper, ô faire Love, loves impetuous rage,
Be my true Mistris still, not my faign'd Page;
I'll goe, and, by thy kinde leave, leave behinde   15
Thee, onely worthy to nurse in my minde,
Thirst to come backe; ô if thou die before,
From other landes my soule t'ward thee shall soare,
Thy (else Almighty) beautie cannot move
Rage from the Seas, nor thy love teach them love,   20
Nor tame wilde Boreas harshnesse; Thou hast reade
How roughly he in peeces shivered
Faire Orithea, whom he swore he lov'd.
Fall ill or good, 'tis madnesse to have prov'd
Dangers unurg'd; Feed on this flattery,   25
That absent Lovers one in th'other be.
Dissemble nothing, not a boy, nor change
Thy bodies habite, nor mindes; bee not strange
To thy selfe onely. All will spie in thy face
A blushing womanly discovering grace;   30
Richly cloath'd Apes, are call'd Apes, and as soone
Ecclips'd as bright we call the Moone the Moone.
Men of France, changeable Camelions,
Spittles of diseases, shops of fashions,
Loves fuellers, and the rightest company   35
Of Players, which upon the worlds stage be,

Elegie XVI. 21 *Boreas*: In Golding's translation of Ovid's *Metamorphoses* Boreas as North Wind raised a great gale (VI, 862 ff.), and enclosing himself "in smokie cloudes," caught Orithya "straught for feare,/And like a lover, verie soft and easly did her beare." Quoting a passage from Burton's *Anatomy of Melancholy* (part 3, sect. 3, memb. 1, subs. 1), Miss Gardner suggests that Donne may have confused two stories. In the latter a jealous Boreas breaks the neck of "a faire maide" transformed into a pine tree.

34 *Spittles*: lazar houses, or hospitals, where venereal diseases could be treated.

Will quickly know thee, and no lesse, alas!
Th'indifferent Italian, as we passe
His warme land, well content to think thee Page,
Will hunt thee with such lust, and hideous rage,   *40*
As *Lots* faire guests were vext. But none of these
Nor spungy hydroptique Dutch shall thee displease,
If thou stay here. O stay here, for, for thee
England is onely a worthy Gallerie,
To walke in expectation, till from thence   *45*
Our greate King call thee to his presence.
When I am gone, dreame me some happinesse,
Nor let thy lookes our long hid love confesse,
Nor praise, nor dispraise me, nor blesse nor curse
Openly loves force, nor in bed fright thy Nurse   *50*
With midnight startings, crying out, oh, oh
Nurse, ô my love is slaine, I saw him goe
O'r the white Alpes alone; I saw him I,
Assail'd, fight, taken, stabb'd, bleed, fall, and die.
Augure me better chance, except dread *Jove*   *55*
Thinke it enough for me to'have had thy love.

Elegie XVIII. Loves Progresse

Who ever loves, if he do not propose
The right true end of love, he's one that goes
To sea for nothing but to make him sick:
Love is a bear-whelp born, if we o're lick
Our love, and force it new strange shapes to take,   *5*
We erre, and of a lump a monster make.
Were not a Calf a monster that were grown
Face'd like a man, though better then his own?
Perfection is in unitie: preferr
One woman first, and then one thing in her.   *10*
I when I value gold, may think upon
The ductilness, the application,
The wholesomness, the ingenuitie,

---

41 *Lots faire guests*: The story of Lot and his guests beset by Sodomites is recounted in Gen. 19.

From rust, from soil, from fire ever free:
But if I love it, 'tis because 'tis made   15
By our new nature (Use) the soul of trade.
   All these in women we might think upon
(If women had them) and yet love but one.
Can men more injure women then to say
They love them for that, by which they're not they?   20
Makes virtue woman? must I cool my bloud
Till I both be, and find one wise and good?
May barren Angels love so. But if we
Make love to woman; virtue is not she:
As beauty's not nor wealth: He that strayes thus   25
From her to hers, is more adulterous,
Then if he took her maid. Search every sphear
And firmament, our *Cupid* is not there:
He's an infernal god and under ground,
With *Pluto* dwells, where gold and fire abound;   30
Men to such Gods, their sacrificing Coles
Did not in Altars lay, but pits and holes:
Although we see Celestial bodies move
Above the earth, the earth we Till and love:
So we her ayres contemplate, words and heart,   35
And virtues; but we love the Centrique part.
   Nor is the soul more worthy, or more fit
For love, then this, as infinit as it.
But in attaining this desired place
How much they erre; that set out at the face!   40
The hair a Forest is of Ambushes,
Of springes, snares, fetters and manacles:
The brow becalms us when 'tis smooth and plain,
And when 'tis wrinckled, shipwracks us again.
Smooth, 'tis a Paradice, where we would have   45
Immortal stay, but wrinckled 'tis a grave.
The Nose (like to the first Meridian) runs
Not 'twixt an East and West, but 'twixt two suns;

Elegie XVIII. 47 *first Meridian*: in cosmography the prime meridian is one from the intersection of which with the equator longitude is counted, both east and west. Donne here assumes that the first Meridian passes through the Canary Islands.

It leaves a Cheek, a rosie Hemisphere
On either side, and then directs us where 50
Upon the Islands fortunate we fall,
Not faint *Canaries*, but *Ambrosiall*.
Her swelling lips to which when we are come,
We anchor there, and think our selves at home,
For they seem all: there Syrens songs, and there 55
Wise Delphick Oracles do fill the ear;
There in a Creek where chosen pearls do swell
The Rhemora her cleaving tongue doth dwell.
These, and (the glorious Promontory) her Chin
Ore past, and the strayt of *Hellespont* between 60
The *Sestos* and *Abydos* of her breasts,
(Not of two Lovers, but two loves the neasts)
Succeeds a boundless sea, but that thine eye
Some Island moles may scatter'd there descry;
And Sailing towards her *India*, in that way 65
Shall at her fair Atlantick Naval stay;
Though thence the Current be thy Pilot made,
Yet ere thou be where thou wouldst be embay'd,
Thou shalt upon another Forest set,
Where many Shipwrack, and no further get. 70
When thou art there, consider what this chace
Mispent by thy beginning at the face.

  Rather set out below; practice my Art;
Some Symetry the foot hath with that part
Which thou dost seek, and is thy Map for that 75
Lovely enough to stop, but not stay at:
Least subject to disguise and change it is;
Men say the Devil never can change his.
It is the Emblem that hath figured
Firmness; 'tis the first part that comes to bed. 80
Civilitie we see refin'd: the kiss
Which at the face began, transplanted is,
Since to the hand, since to the'imperial knee,
Now at the Papal foot delights to be:

---

61 *Sestos and Abydos*: the towns on the opposing shores of the Hellespont in which respectively, in Europe and Asia Minor, Hero and Leander lived.
78 *change his*: *his* refers to the devil's cleft foot.

If Kings think that the nearer way, and do
Rise from the foot, Lovers may do so too.
For as free Spheres move faster far then can
Birds, whom the air resists, so may that man
Which goes this empty and Ætherial way,
Then if at beauties elements he stay.
Rich Nature hath in women wisely made
Two purses, and their mouths aversely laid:
They then, which to the lower tribute owe,
That way which that Exchequer looks, must go:
He which doth not, his error is as great,
As who by glister gives the Stomack meat.

Elegie XIX. To his Mistris going to Bed

Come, Madam, come, all rest my powers defie,
Until I labour, I in labour lie.
The foe oft-times having the foe in sight,
Is tir'd with standing though he never fight.
Off with that girdle, like heavens Zone glittering,
But a far fairer world incompassing.
Unpin that spangled breastplate which you wear,
That th'eyes of busie fooles may be stopt there.
Unlace your self, for that harmonious chyme,
Tells me from you, that now is your bed time.
Off with that happy busk, which I envie,
That still can be, and still can stand so nigh.
Your gown going off, such beautious state reveals,
As when through flowry meads th'hills shadow steales.
Off with that wyerie Coronet and shew
The haiery Diadem which' on your head doth grow:
Now off with those shooes, and then safely tread
In this loves hallow'd temple, this soft bed.

---

96 *glister*: colloquial variant of clyster, or enema.
Elegie XIX. The source is Ovid, *Amores*, I.v.

In such white robes, heaven's Angels us'd to be
Receiv'd by men: thou Angel bringst with thee   20
A heaven like Mahomets Paradice; and though
Ill spirits walk in white, we easly know,
By this these Angels from an evil sprite,
Those set our hairs, but these our flesh upright.
    License my roaving hands, and let them go,   25
Behind, before, above, between, below;
O my America! my new-found-land!
My Kingdom, safeliest when with one man man'd!
My Myne of precious stones: My Emperie,
How blest am I in thus discovering thee!   30
To enter in these bonds, is to be free;
Then where my hand is set, my seal shall be:
    Full nakedness! All joyes are due to thee,
As souls unbodied, bodies uncloth'd must be,
To taste whole joyes. Jems which you women use   35
Are like Atlanta's balls cast in mens views,
That when a fools eye lighteth on a Jem,
His earthly soul may covett theirs, not them:
Like pictures or like books gay coverings made,
For lay-men are all women thus arrayed.   40
Themselves are mystick books, which only we
(Whom their imputed grace will dignifie)
Must see reveal'd. Then since that I may know,
As liberally, as to a Midwife shew
Thy self: cast all, yea, this white lynnen hence;   45
There is no pennance due to innocence:
    To teach thee I am naked first; why than
What needst thou have more covering then a man?

Satyre I

Away thou fondling motley humorist,
Leave mee, and in this standing woodden chest,
Consorted with these few bookes, let me lye
In prison, and here be coffin'd, when I dye;
Here are Gods conduits, grave Divines; and here   5
Natures Secretary, the Philosopher:
And jolly Statesmen, which teach how to tie
The sinewes of a cities mistique bodie;
Here gathering Chroniclers, and by them stand
Giddie fantastique Poëts of each land.   10
Shall I leave all this constant company,
And follow headlong, wild uncertaine thee?
First sweare by thy best love, here, in earnest
(If thou which lov'st all, canst love any best)
Thou wilt not leave mee in the middle street,   15
Though some more spruce companion thou dost meet,
Not though a Captaine do come in thy way
Bright parcell gilt, with forty dead mens pay,
Not though a briske perfum'd piert Courtier
Deigne with a nod, thy courtesie to answer.   20
Nor come a velvet Justice with a long
Great traine of blew coats, twelve, or fourteen strong,
Wilt thou grin or fawne on him, or prepare
A speech to Court his beautious sonne and heire?
For better or worse take mee, or leave mee: 25
To take, and leave mee is adultery.
Oh monstrous, superstitious puritan,
Of refin'd manners, yet ceremoniall man,
That when thou meet'st one, with enquiring eyes
Dost search, and like a needy broker prize   30

Satyre I. The idea of a walk in the street with a gauche and undiscriminating companion is suggested by Horace (*Sat.* I. ix).

2 *chest*: each of the small chambers of the Benchers at Lincoln's Inn, where Donne was resident from 1592 to 1595, may have appeared to the poet as a chest standing on its end. Cf. Marvell's *Fleckno*, ll. 9–140.

22 *blew coats*: servants in livery.

The silke, and gold he weares, and to that rate
So high or low, dost raise thy formall hat:
That wilt consort none, untill thou have knowne
What lands hee hath in hope, or of his owne,
As though all thy companions should make thee   35
Jointures, and marry thy deare company.
Why should'st thou that dost not onely approve,
But in ranke itchie lust, desire, and love
The nakednesse and barrennesse to enjoy,
Of thy plumpe muddy whore, or prostitute boy   40
Hate vertue, though shee be naked, and bare:
At birth, and death, our bodies naked are;
And till our Soules be unapparrelled
Of bodies, they from blisse are banished.
Mans first blest state was naked, when by sinne   45
Hee lost that, yet hee' was cloath'd but in beasts skin,
And in this course attire, which I now weare,
With God, and with the Muses I conferre.

But since thou like a contrite penitent,
Charitably warn'd of thy sinnes, dost repent   50
These vanities, and giddinesses, loe
I shut my chamber doore, and come, lets goe.
But sooner may a cheape whore, who hath beene
Worne by as many severall men in sinne,
As are black feathers, or musk-colour hose,   55
Name her childs right true father, 'mongst all those:
Sooner may one guesse, who shall beare away
The infant of London, Heire to'an India,
And sooner may a gulling weather-Spie
By drawing forth heavens Scheme tell certainly   60
What fashion'd hats, or ruffes, or suits next yeare
Our subtile-witted antique youths will weare;
Then thou, when thou depart'st from mee, canst show
Whither, why, when, or with whom thou wouldst go.
But how shall I be pardon'd my offence   65
That thus have sinn'd against my conscience?
Now we are in the street; He first of all

58 *infant of London*: a young lady, possibly an heiress, likened to a Spanish or Portuguese infanta, as a princess royal or the daughter of a peer.

Improvidently proud, creepes to the wall,
And so imprison'd, and hem'd in by mee
Sells for a little state high libertie, 70
Yet though he cannot skip forth now to greet
Every fine silken painted foole we meet,
He them to him with amorous smiles allures,
And grins, smacks, shrugs, and such an itch endures,
As prentises, or schoole-boyes which doe know 75
Of some gay sport abroad, yet dare not goe.
And as fidlers stop lowest, at highest sound,
So to the most brave, stoops hee nigh'st the ground.
But to a grave man, he doth move no more
Then the wise politique horse would heretofore, 80
Or thou ô Elephant, or Ape will doe,
When any names the King of Spaine to you.
Now leaps he upright, Joggs me,'and cryes, Do'you see
Yonder well favour'd youth? Which? Oh, 'tis hee
That dances so divinely; Oh, said I, 85
Stand still, must you dance here for company?
Hee droopt, wee went, till one (which did excell
Th'Indians, in drinking his Tobacco well)
Met us: they talk'd; I whispered, let us goe,
'T may be you smell him not, truely I doe; 90
He heares not mee, but, on the other side
A many-colour'd Peacock having spide,
Leaves him and mee; I for my lost sheep stay;
He followes, overtakes, goes on the way,
Saying, him whom I last left, s'all repute 95
For his device, in hansoming a sute,
To judge of lace, pinke, panes, print, cut, and plight,
Of all the Court, to have the best conceit;
Our dull Comedians want him, let him goe;
But Oh, God strengthen thee, why stoop'st thou so? 100
Why, he hath travail'd. Long? No, but to me
Which understand none, he doth seeme to be

---

80 *horse*: the horse trainer Bank's gelding "Morocco" had arithmetical proficiency of a simple sort which astonished side-show spectators in London in the early 1590's. Performing elephants often are mentioned in the works of contemporary writers, though no context hints at the name of the King of Spain.

Perfect French, and Italian; I reply'd,
So is the Poxe; He answer'd not, but spy'd
More men of sort, of parts, and qualities;   105
At last his Love he in a windowe spies,
And like light dew exhal'd, he flings from mee
Violently ravish'd to his lechery.
Many were there, he could command no more;
Hee quarrell'd, fought, bled; and turn'd out of dore   110
    Directly came to mee hanging the head,
    And constantly a while must keepe his bed.

Satyre III

Kinde pitty chokes my spleene; brave scorn forbids
Those teares to issue which swell my eye-lids,
I must not laugh, nor weepe sinnes, and be wise,
Can railing then cure these worne maladies?
Is not our Mistresse faire Religion,   5
As worthy of all our Soules devotion,
As vertue was in the first blinded age?
Are not heavens joyes as valiant to asswage
Lusts, as earths honour was to them? Alas,
As wee do them in meanes, shall they surpasse   10
Us in the end, and shall thy fathers spirit
Meete blinde Philosophers in heaven, whose merit
Of strict life may be imputed faith, and heare
Thee, whom hee taught so easie wayes and neare
To follow, damn'd? O if thou dar'st, feare this.   15
This feare great courage, and high valour is.
Dar'st thou ayd mutinous Dutch, and dar'st thou lay
Thee in ships woodden Sepulchers, a prey
To leaders rage, to stormes, to shot, to dearth?
Dar'st thou dive seas, and dungeons of the earth?   20
Hast thou couragious fire to thaw the ice
Of frozen North discoveries? and thrise
Colder then Salamanders, like divine
Children in th'oven, fires of Spaine, and the line,

Whose countries limbecks to our bodies bee,   *25*
Canst thou for gaine beare? and must every hee
Which cryes not, Goddesse, to thy Mistresse, draw,
Or eate thy poysonous words? courage of straw!
O desperate coward, wilt thou seeme bold, and
To thy foes and his (who made thee to stand   *30*
Sentinell in his worlds garrison) thus yeeld,
And for forbidden warres, leave th'appointed field?
Know thy foe: the foule Devill, whom thou
Strivest to please, for hate, not love, would allow
Thee faine, his whole Realme to be quit; and as   *35*
The worlds all parts wither away and passe,
So the worlds selfe, thy other lov'd foe, is
In her decrepit wayne, and thou loving this,
Dost love a withered and worne strumpet; last,
Flesh (it selfes death) and joyes which flesh can taste,   *40*
Thou lovest; and thy faire goodly soule, which doth
Give this flesh power to taste joy, thou dost loath.
Seeke true religion. O where? Mirreus
Thinking her unhous'd here, and fled from us,
Seekes her at Rome, there, because hee doth know   *45*
That shee was there a thousand yeares agoe;
He loves her ragges so, as wee here obey
The statecloth where the Prince sate yesterday.
Crants to such brave Loves will not be inthrall'd,
But loves her onely, who at Geneva is call'd   *50*
Religion, plaine, simple, sullen, yong,
Contemptuous, yet unhansome. As among
Lecherous humors, there is one that judges
No wenches wholsome, but course country drudges.
Graius stayes still at home here, and because   *55*
Some Preachers, vile ambitious bauds, and lawes
Still new like fashions, bid him thinke that shee
Which dwels with us, is onely perfect, hee
Imbraceth her, whom his Godfathers will

Satyre III (1633). 33–42 The traditional enemies of the soul: the devil, the world, and the flesh.
    35 *quit*: to have free run of his entire realm.

Tender to him, being tender, as Wards still 60
Take such wives as their Guardians offer, or
Pay valewes. Carelesse Phrygius doth abhorre
All, because all cannot be good, as one
Knowing some women whores, dares marry none.
Graccus loves all as one, and thinkes that so 65
As women do in divers countries goe
In divers habits, yet are still one kinde,
So doth, so is Religion; and this blind-
nesse too much light breeds; but unmoved thou
Of force must one, and forc'd but one allow; 70
And the right; aske thy father which is shee,
Let him aske his; though truth and falshood bee
Neare twins, yet truth a little elder is;
Be busie to seeke her, beleeve mee this,
Hee's not of none, nor worst, that seekes the best. 75
To adore, or scorne an image, or protest,
May all be bad; doubt wisely, in strange way
To stand inquiring right, is not to stray;
To sleepe, or runne wrong, is: on a huge hill,
Cragg'd, and steep, Truth stands, and hee that will 80
Reach her, about must, and about must goe;
And what the hills suddennes resists, winne so;
Yet strive so, that before age, deaths twilight,
Thy Soule rest, for none can worke in that night.
To will, implyes delay, therefore now doe: 85
Hard deeds, the bodies paines; hard knowledge too
The mindes indeavours reach, and mysteries
Are like the Sunne, dazling, yet plaine to all eyes;
Keepe the truth which thou hast found; men do not stand
In so ill case, that God hath with his hand 90
Sign'd Kings blanck-charters to kill whom they hate,
Nor are they Vicars, but hangmen to Fate.
Foole and wretch, wilt thou let thy Soule be tyed
To mans lawes, by which she shall not be tryed

62 *valewes*: fine paid by a ward who refused a marriage arranged by his guardian.
86–87 Hard deeds are attained by the body's pains, and knowledge also is reached by the mind's endeavors; mysteries, though dazzling as the sun, are just as visible.

At the last day? Will it then boot thee 95
To say a Philip, or a Gregory,
A Harry, or a Martin taught thee this?
Is not this excuse for mere contraries,
Equally strong? cannot both sides say so?
That thou mayest rightly obey power, her bounds know; 100
Those past, her nature, and name is chang'd; to be
Then humble to her is idolatrie;
As streames are, Power is; those blest flowers that dwell
At the rough streames calme head, thrive and do well,
But having left their roots, and themselves given 105
To the streames tyrannous rage, alas are driven
Through mills, and rockes, and woods, and at last, almost
Consum'd in going, in the sea are lost:
So perish Soules, which more chuse mens unjust
Power from God claym'd, then God himselfe to trust. 110

To the Countesse of Bedford

MADAME,
Reason is our Soules left hand, Faith her right,
By these wee reach divinity, that's you;
Their loves, who have the blessings of your light,
Grew from their reason, mine from faire faith grew.

But as, although a squint lefthandednesse 5
Be'ungracious, yet we cannot want that hand,
So would I, not to'encrease, but to expresse
My faith, as I beleeve, so understand.

96–97 The lines oppose Catholic and Protestant kings (Philip II of Spain and Henry VIII) and Catholic and Protestant religious leaders (Gregory—probably Pope Gregory XIII who was active in the Council of Trent, aided Philip II, and endeavored to form a coalition against the Protestants—and Martin Luther). All of these were involved in religious coercion.

To the Countesse of Bedford. Jonson sent a copy of Donne's *Satires* to this famous patroness of poets together with an epigram introducing Donne to her. Married to the Earl in 1594, she became a luminary at James's court, often appearing in masques of the period.

Therefore I study you first in your Saints,
Those friends, whom your election glorifies,   10
Then in your deeds, accesses, and restraints,
And what you reade, and what your selfe devize.

But soone, the reasons why you'are lov'd by all
Grow infinite, and so passe reasons reach:
Then backe againe to'implicite faith I fall,   15
And rest on what the Catholique voice doth teach:

That you are good, and not one Heretique
Denies it; if he did, yet you are so.
For, rockes, which high top'd and deep rooted sticke,
Waves wash, not undermine, nor overthrow.   20

In every thing there naturally growes
A *Balsamum* to keepe it fresh, and new,
If 'twere not injur'd by extrinsique blowes;
Your birth and beauty are this Balme in you.

But, you of learning and religion,   25
And vertue,'and such ingredients, have made
A methridate, whose operation
Keepes off, or cures what can be done or said.

Yet, this is not your physicke, but your food,
A dyet fit for you; for you are here   30
The first good Angell, since the worlds frame stood,
That ever did in womans shape appeare.

Since you are then Gods masterpeece, and so
His Factor for our loves; do as you doe,
Make your returne home gracious; and bestow   35
This life on that; so make one life of two.
    For so God helpe mee,'I would not misse you there
    For all the good which you can do me here.

22 *Balsamum*: the healing fluid (balsam, or balm) which Paracelsus found in every living body and which acted as a preservative and protection from poison.
27 *methridate*: mithridate.

To Sir Edward Herbert. At Julyers

Man is a lumpe, where all beasts kneaded bee,
    Wisdome makes him an Arke where all agree;
The foole, in whom these beasts do live at jarre,
    Is sport to others, and a Theater,
Nor scapes hee so, but is himselfe their prey;   5
    All which was man in him, is eate away,
And now his beasts on one another feed,
    Yet couple'in anger, and new monsters breed;
How happy'is hee, which hath due place assign'd
    To'his beasts, and disaforested his minde!   10
Empail'd himselfe to keepe them out, not in;
    Can sow, and dares trust corne, where they have bin;
Can use his horse, goate, wolfe, and every beast,
    And is not Asse himselfe to all the rest.
Else, man not onely is the heard of swine,   15
    But he's those devills too, which did incline
Them to a headlong rage, and made them worse:
    For man can adde weight to heavens heaviest curse.
As Soules (they say) by our first touch, take in
    The poysonous tincture of Originall sinne,   20
So, to the punishments which God doth fling,
    Our apprehension contributes the sting.
To us, as to his chickins, he doth cast
    Hemlocke, and wee as men, his hemlocke taste.
We do infuse to what he meant for meat,   25
    Corrosivenesse, or intense cold or heat.
For, God no such specifique poyson hath
    As kills we know not how; his fiercest wrath
Hath no antipathy, but may be good
    At lest for physicke, if not for our food.   30
Thus man, that might be'his pleasure, is his rod,
    And is his devill, that might be his God.
Since then our businesse is, to rectifie
    Nature, to what she was, wee'are led awry
By them, who man to us in little show;   35
    Greater then due, no forme we can bestow

On him; for Man into himselfe can draw
   All, All his faith can swallow,'or reason chaw.
All that is fill'd, and all that which doth fill,
   All the round world, to man is but a pill,   40
In all it workes not, but it is in all
   Poysonous, or purgative, or cordiall,
For, knowledge kindles Calentures in some,
   And is to others icy *Opium*.
As brave as true, is that profession than   45
   Which you doe use to make; that you know man.
This makes it credible, you have dwelt upon
   All worthy bookes; and now are such an one.
Actions are authors, and of those in you
   Your friends finde every day a mart of new.   50

THE ANNIVERSARY POEMS

A Funerall Elegie

Tis lost, to trust a Tombe with such a ghest,
   Or to confine her in a Marble chest.
Alas, what's Marble, Jeat, or Porphiry,
   Priz'd with the Chrysolite of eyther eye,
Or with those Pearles, and Rubies which shee was?   5
   Joyne the two Indies in one Tombe, 'tis glas;
And so is all to her materials,
   Though every inch were ten escurials.
Yet shee's demolish'd: Can we keepe her then
   In workes of hands, or of the wits of men?   10
Can these memorials, ragges of paper, give
   Life to that name, by which name they must live?
Sickly, alas, short-liv'd, aborted bee
   Those Carkas verses, whose soule is not shee.
And can shee, who no longer would be shee,   15
   Being such a Tabernacle, stoope to bee

   The Anniversary Poems were written to commemorate the death, in December 1610, of fifteen-year-old Elizabeth Drury, daughter of Sir Robert Drury, a patron of Donne. Probably *A Funerall Elegie* was written first, although it is placed after *The First Anniversary* in both the 1611 and 1612 editions. A funeral elegy is composed for the funeral occasion; an anniversary poem commemorates a death at some annual recurrence of the date.
   A Funerall Elegie.   8 *ten escurials*: the recently erected Escorial was the residence and mausoleum of the Spanish kings.
   16 *Tabernacle*: see Donne, *Sermons* II, 221, "The *Tabernacle* it selfe was but a *mobilis domus*, and *Ecclesia portatilis*, a house without a foundation; a running, a progresse house."

In paper wrap't; Or, when she would not lie
   In such a house, dwell in an Elegie?
But 'tis no matter; we may well allow
   Verse to live so long as the world will now.   20
For her death wounded it. The world containes
   Princes for armes, and Counsailors for braines,
Lawyers for tongues, Divines for hearts, and more,
   The Rich for stomachs, and for backes the Pore;
The Officers for hands, Merchants for feet   25
   By which remote and distant Countries meet.
But those fine spirits, which doe tune and set
   This Organ, are those peeces which beget
Wonder and love; And these were shee; and shee
   Being spent, the world must needes decrepit bee.   30
For since death will proceed to triumph still,
   He can finde nothing, after her, to kill,
Except the world it selfe, so great as shee.
   Thus brave and confident may Nature bee,
Death cannot give her such another blow,   35
   Because shee cannot such another show.
But must we say shee's dead? May't not be said
   That as a sundred Clocke is peece-meale laid,
Not to be lost, but by the makers hand
   Repolish'd, without error then to stand,   40
Or as the Affrique Niger streame enwombs
   It selfe into the earth, and after comes,
(Having first made a naturall bridge, to passe
   For many leagues,) farre greater then it was,
May't not be said, that her grave shall restore   45
   Her, greater, purer, firmer, then before?
Heaven may say this, and joy in't; but can wee
   Who live, and lacke her, here this vantage see?

   28 *peeces:* musical compositions, virtuous persons.
  41–44 The Niger was often associated, as here, with the upper part of the Nile.

What is't to us, alas, if there have beene
    An Angell made a Throne, or Cherubin?
We lose by't: And as aged men are glad
    Being tastlesse growne, to joy in joyes they had,
So now the sicke starv'd world must feed upone
    This joy, that we had her, who now is gone.
Rejoyce then nature, and this world, that you
    Fearing the last fires hastning to subdue
Your force and vigor, ere it were neere gone,
    Wisely bestow'd, and layd it all on one.
One, whose cleare body was so pure, and thin,
    Because it neede disguise no thought within.
T'was but a through-light scarfe, her minde t'enroule,
    Or exhalation breath'd out from her soule.
One, whom all men who durst no more, admir'd;
    And whom, who ere had worth enough, desir'd;
As when a Temple's built, Saints emulate
    To which of them, it shall be consecrate.
But as when Heav'n lookes on us with new eyes,
    Those new starres ev'ry Artist exercise,
What place they should assigne to them they doubt,
    Argue, and agree not, till those starres go out:
So the world studied whose this peece should be,
    Till she can be no bodies else, nor shee:
But like a Lampe of Balsamum, desir'd
    Rather t'adorne, then last, shee soone expir'd;
Cloath'd in her Virgin white integrity;
    For mariage, though it doe not staine, doth dye.
To scape th'infirmities which waite upone
    Woman, shee went away, before sh'was one.
And the worlds busie noyse to overcome,
    Tooke so much death, as serv'd for *opium*.

49–51 We lose if an Angel, a member of the lowest of the nine orders of spirits whose special duty is to minister to man, is made a Throne (seventh order) or a Cherub (eighth order), both of which ranks are designated for the contemplation of God.

68 *Artist:* astronomer, usually a quack.

73–74 *Balsamum* would give a sweet odor, though oil would burn longer.

For though shee could not, nor could chuse to die,
   Shee'ath yeelded to too long an Extasie.
He which not knowing her sad History,
   Should come to reade the booke of destiny,
How faire and chast, humble and high shee'ad beene,   85
   Much promis'd, much perform'd, at not fifteene,
And measuring future things, by things before,
   Should turne the leafe to reade, and read no more,
Would thinke that eyther destiny mistooke,
   Or that some leafes were torne out of the booke.   90
But 'tis not so: Fate did but usher her
   To yeares of Reasons use, and then infer
Her destiny to her selfe; which liberty
   She tooke but for thus much, thus much to die.
Her modesty not suffering her to bee   95
   Fellow-Commissioner with destinee,
Shee did no more but die; if after her
   Any shall live, which dare true good prefer,
Every such person is her delegate,
   T'accomplish that which should have beene her fate.   100
They shall make up that booke, and shall have thankes
   Of fate and her, for filling up their blanks.
For future vertuous deeds are Legacies,
   Which from the gift of her example rise.
And 'tis in heav'n part of spirituall mirth,   105
   To see how well the good play her, on earth.

---

   92 *infer:* entrust, confer.
  106 *play her:* on a stage, which the world is, the role of the good is to imitate her.

AN ANATOMY OF THE WORLD

*Wherein, by occasion of
the untimely death of Mistris
Elizabeth Drury
the frailty and the decay
of this whole world
is represented.*

The First Anniversary

When that rich soule which to her Heaven is gone,   *The entrie into the worke.*
Whom all they celebrate, who know they have one,
(For who is sure he hath a soule, unlesse
It see, and Judge, and follow worthinesse,
And by Deedes praise it? He who doth not this,   5
May lodge an In-mate soule, but tis not his.)
When that Queene ended here her progresse time,
And, as t'her standing house, to heaven did clymbe,
Where, loth to make the Saints attend her long,
Shee's now a part both of the Quire, and Song,   10
This world, in that great earth-quake languished;
For in a common Bath of teares it bled,
Which drew the strongest vitall spirits out:

An Anatomy of the World [*The First Anniversary*]. (1611 and, with "The Second Anniversarie," 1612). An anatomy is the surgical dissection of a corpse (often performed on executed criminals), and also a schematic analysis or argument.
   6 *In-mate*: a transient lodger.
   7 *progresse*: a royal journey.
   8 *standing house*: a permanent residence or palace.
   13 *vitall spirits*: substances in the blood supposed to provide links between body and soul.

But succour'd then with a perplexed doubt,
Whether the world did loose or gaine in this, 15
(Because since now no other way there is
But goodnes, to see her, whom all would see,
All must endevour to be good as shee,)
This great consumption to a fever turn'd,
And so the world had fits; it joy'd, it mournd. 20
And, as men thinke, that Agues physicke are,
And th'Ague being spent, give over care,
So thou, sicke world, mistak'st thy selfe to bee
Well, when alas, thou'rt in a Letargee.
Her death did wound, and tame thee than, and than 25
Thou mightst have better spar'd the Sunne, or Man;
That wound was deepe, but'tis more misery,
That thou hast lost thy sense and memory.
T'was heavy then to heare thy voyce of mone,
But this is worse, that thou art speechlesse growne. 30
Thou hast forgot thy name, thou hadst; thou wast
Nothing but she, and her thou hast o'repast.
For as a child kept from the Font, untill
A Prince, expected long, come to fulfill
The Ceremonies, thou unnam'd hadst laid, 35
Had not her comming, thee her Palace made:
Her name defin'd thee, gave thee forme and frame,
And thou forgetst to celebrate thy name.
Some moneths she hath beene dead (but being dead,
Measures of times are all determined) 40
But long shee'ath beene away, long, long, yet none
Offers to tell us who it is that's gone.
But as in states doubtfull of future heyres,
When sickenes without remedy, empayres
The present Prince, they're loth it should be said, 45
The Prince doth languish, or the Prince is dead:
So mankind feeling now a generall thaw,
A strong example gone equall to law,
The Cyment which did faithfully compact
And glue all vertues, now resolv'd, and slack'd, 50

24 *Letargee*: lethargy.
40 *determined*: finished.

Thought it some blasphemy to say sh'was dead;
Or that our weakenes was discovered
In that confession; therefore spoke no more
Then tongues, the soule being gone, the losse deplore.
But though it be too late to succour thee, 55
Sicke world, yea dead, yea putrified, since shee
Thy'ntrinsique Balme, and thy preservative,
Can never be renew'd, thou never live,
I (since no man can make thee live) will trie,
What we may gaine by thy Anatomy. 60
Her death hath taught us dearely, that thou art
Corrupt and mortall in thy purest part.
Let no man say, the world it selfe being dead,
'Tis labour lost to have discovered
The worlds infirmities, since there is none 65
Alive to study this dissectione;
For there's a kind of world remaining still, *What life*
Though shee which did inanimate and fill *the world hath still.*
The world, be gone, yet in this last long night,
Her Ghost doth walke; that is, a glimmering light, 70
A faint weake love of vertue and of good
Reflects from her, on them which understood
Her worth; And though she have shut in all day,
The twi-light of her memory doth stay;
Which, from the carcasse of the old world, free, 75
Creates a new world; and new creatures be
Produc'd: The matter and the stuffe of this,
Her vertue, and the forme our practise is.
And though to be thus Elemented, arme
These Creatures, from hom-borne intrinsique harme, 80
(For all assum'd unto this Dignitee,
So many weedlesse Paradises bee,
Which of themselves produce no venemous sinne,
Except some forraine Serpent bring it in)
Yet, because outward stormes the strongest breake, 85

---

57 Man. cites Donne, *Sermons* V, 347-48: "Physitians say, that man hath in his Constitution... a naturall vertue, which they call *Balsamum suum*, his owne Balsamum, by which, any wound which a man could receive in his body, would cure it selfe...."

And strength it selfe by confidence growes weake,
This new world may be safer, being told
The dangers and diseases of the old: *The sicknesses of the world.*
For with due temper men do then forgoe,
Or covet things, when they their true worth know.   90
There is no health; Physitians say that we *Impossibility of health.*
At best, enjoy but a neutralitee.
And can there be worse sickenesse, then to know
That we are never well, nor can be so?
We are borne ruinous: poore mothers crie,   95
That children come not right, nor orderly,
Except they headlong come, and fall upon
An ominous precipitation.
How witty's ruine? how importunate
Upon mankinde? It labour'd to frustrate   100
Even Gods purpose; and made woman, sent
For mans reliefe, cause of his languishment.
They were to good ends, and they are so still,
But accessory, and principall in ill.
For that first mariage was our funerall: 105
One woman at one blow, then kill'd us all,
And singly, one by one, they kill us now.
We doe delightfully our selves allow
To that consumption; and profusely blinde,
We kill our selves to propagate our kinde.   110
And yet we doe not that; we are not men:
There is not now that mankinde, which was then
When as the Sunne, and man, did seeme to strive,
(Joynt tenants of the world) who should survive. *Shortnesse of life.*
When Stag, and Raven, and the long-liv'd tree,   115
Compar'd with man, dy'de in minoritee.
When, if a slow pac'd starre had stolne away
From the observers marking, he might stay
Two or three hundred yeares to see't againe,

95 *ruinous*: falling into ruin.
104 Women are only helpers in good, but they are leaders in evil.
107, 110 *kill*: incorporates the sexual meaning of "die," and echoes the popular belief that coitus shortens life.
115 All of these outlive modern man, though they cannot approach the longevity of the Patriarchs.

And then make up his observation plaine;   *120*
When, as the age was long, the sise was great:
Mans grouth confess'd, and recompenc'd the meat:
So spacious and large, that every soule
Did a faire Kingdome, and large Realme controule:
And when the very stature thus erect,   *125*
Did that soule a good way towards Heaven direct.
Where is this mankind now? who lives to age,
Fit to be made *Methusalem* his page?
Alas, we scarse live long enough to trie
Whether a new made clocke runne right, or lie.   *130*
Old Grandsires talke of yesterday with sorrow,
And for our children we reserve to morrow.
So short is life, that every peasant strives,
In a torne house, or field, to have three lives.
And as in lasting, so in length is man   *Smalnesse*   *135*
Contracted to an inch, who was a span.   *of stature.*
For had a man at first, in Forrests stray'd,
Or shipwrack'd in the Sea, one would have laid
A wager that an Elephant, or Whale
That met him, would not hastily assaile   *140*
A thing so equall to him: now alas,
The Fayries, and the Pigmies well may passe
As credible; mankind decayes so soone,
We're scarse our Fathers shadowes cast at noone.
Onely death addes t'our length: nor are we growne   *145*
In stature to be men, till we are none.
But this were light, did our lesse volume hold
All the old Text; or had we chang'd to gold
Their silver; or dispos'd into lesse glas,
Spirits of vertue, which then scattred was.   *150*
But'tis not so: w'are not retir'd, but dampt;
And as our bodies, so our mindes are cramp't:
'Tis shrinking, not close-weaving, that hath thus,

134 *torne*: perhaps a pun on *rented*.
145 *onely... length*: i.e., by stretching us out.
148–49 Adam and Eve lived in the Golden Age, the Patriarchs in the Silver.
149 *lesse glas*: by distillation.
151 *dampt*: extinguished.

In minde and body both bedwarfed us.
We seeme ambitious, Gods whole worke t'undoe; 155
Of nothing he made us, and we strive too,
To bring our selves to nothing backe; and we
Do what we can, to do't so soone as hee.
With new diseases on our selves we warre,
And with new phisicke, a worse Engin farre. 160
Thus man, this worlds Vice-Emperor, in whom
All faculties, all graces are at home;
And if in other Creatures they appeare,
They're but mans ministers, and Legats there,
To worke on their rebellions, and reduce 165
Them to Civility, and to mans use.
This man, whom God did wooe, and loth t'attend
Till man came up, did downe to man descend,
This man, so great, that all that is, is his,
Oh what a trifle, and poore thing he is! 170
If man were anything, he's nothing now:
Helpe, or at least some time to wast, allow
T'his other wants, yet when he did depart
With her whom we lament, he lost his hart.
She, of whom th'Aunciencts seem'd to prophesie, 175
When they call'd vertues by the name of shee,
She in whom vertue was so much refin'd,
That for Allay unto so pure a minde
Shee tooke the weaker Sex, she that could drive
The poysonous tincture, and the stayne of Eve, 180
Out of her thoughts, and deeds; and purifie
All, by a true religious Alchimy;
Shee, shee is dead; shee's dead: when thou knowest this,
Thou knowest how poore a trifling thing man is.
And learn'st thus much by our Anatomee, 185
The heart being perish'd, no part can be free.
And that except thou feed (not banquet) on

---

160 *new phisicke*: Gr. identifies this with the new mineral drugs of the Paracelsians.

172–74 Though you help or palliate man's other wants, it will be useless since he lost his heart when he parted with her.

187 *banquet*: here, a light dessert of sweetmeats, fruit, and wine (*OED*).

The supernaturall food, Religion,
Thy better Grouth growes withered, and scant;
Be more then man, or thou'rt lesse then an Ant.   190
Then, as mankinde, so is the worlds whole frame
Quite out of joynt, almost created lame:
For, before God had made up all the rest,
Corruption entred, and deprav'd the best:
It seis'd the Angels, and then first of all   195
The world did in her Cradle take a fall,
And turn'd her braines, and tooke a generall maime
Wronging each joynt of th'universall frame.
The noblest part, man, felt it first; and than
Both beasts and plants, curst in the curse of man.   *Decay of*   200
So did the world from the first houre decay,   *nature in*
                                                     other parts.
That evening was beginning of the day,
And now the Springs and Sommers which we see,
Like sonnes of women after fifty bee.
And new Philosophy cals all in doubt,   205
The Element of fire is quite put out;
The Sunne is lost, and th'earth, and no mans wit
Can well direct him, where to looke for it.
And freely men confesse, that this world's spent,
When in the Planets, and the Firmament   210
They seeke so many new; they see that this
Is crumbled out againe to his Atomis.
'Tis all in pieces, all cohaerence gone;
All just supply, and all Relation:
Prince, Subject, Father, Sonne, are things forgot,   215
For every man alone thinkes he hath got
To be a Phoenix, and that there can bee
None of that kinde, of which he is, but hee.
This is the worlds condition now, and now
She that should all parts to reunion bow,   220
She that had all Magnetique force alone,

197 *braines*: in reference to the angels as pure intellect.
202 See Gen. 1:5, "And the evening and the morning were the first day." Donne interprets the *evening* as the darkness of sin.
205 The new science discredited the concentric arrangement of the spheres, eliminated the region of fire, and identified new stars and planetary systems in the heavens.

To draw, and fasten sundred parts in one;
She whom wise nature had invented then
When she observ'd that every sort of men
Did in their voyage in this worlds Sea stray, 225
And needed a new compasse for their way;
Shee that was best, and first originall
Of all faire copies; and the generall
Steward to Fate; shee whose rich eyes, and brest,
Guilt the West Indies, and perfum'd the East; 230
Whose having breath'd in this world, did bestow
Spice on those Isles, and bad them still smell so,
And that rich Indie which doth gold interre,
Is but as single money, coyn'd from her:
She to whom this world must it selfe refer, 235
As Suburbs, or the Microcosme of her,
Shee, shee is dead; shee's dead: when thou knowst this,
Thou knowst how lame a cripple this world is.
And learnst thus much by our Anatomy,
That this worlds generall sickenesse doth not lie 240
In any humour, or one certaine part;
But, as thou sawest it rotten at the hart,
Thou seest a Hectique fever hath got hold
Of the whole substance, not to be contrould.
And that thou hast but one way, not t'admit 245
The worlds infection, to be none of it.
For the worlds subtilst immaterial parts
Feele this consuming wound, and ages darts.
For the worlds beauty is decayd, or gone,
Beauty, that's colour, and proportion. *Disformity* 250
We thinke the heavens enjoy their Sphericall *of parts*
Their round proportion embracing all.
But yet their various and perplexed course,
Observ'd in divers ages doth enforce
Men to finde out so many Eccentrique parts, 255
Such divers downe-right lines, such overthwarts,
As disproportion that pure forme. It teares
The Firmament in eight and fortie sheeres,

---

234 *single money*: small change.

255 *Eccentrique*: the eccentric circles added in the Ptolemaic theory to account for evident discrepancies in planetary movement.

And in those constellations there arise
New starres, and old do vanish from our eyes: 260
As though heav'n suffred earth-quakes, peace or war,
When new Townes rise, and olde demolish'd are.
They have empayld within a Zodiake
The free-borne Sunne, and keepe twelve signes awake
To watch his steps; the Goat and Crabbe controule, 265
And fright him backe, who els to eyther Pole,
(Did not these Tropiques fetter him) might runne:
For his course is not round; nor can the Sunne
Perfit a Circle, or maintaine his way
One inche direct; but where he rose to day 270
He comes no more, but with a cousening line,
Steales by that point, and so is Serpentine:
And seeming weary with his reeling thus,
He meanes to sleepe, being now falne nearer us.
So, of the stares which boast that they do runne 275
In Circle still, none ends where he begunne.
All their proportion's lame, it sinks, it swels.
For of Meridians, and Parallels,
Man hath weav'd out a net, and this net throwne
Upon the Heavens, and now they are his owne. 280
Loth to goe up the hill, or labor thus
To goe to heaven, we make heaven come to us.
We spur, we raine the stars, and in their race
They're diversly content t'obey our pace.
But keepes the earth her round proportion still? 285
Doth not a Tenarif, or higher Hill
Rise so high like a Rocke, that one might thinke
The floating Moone would shipwracke there, and sink?
Seas are so deepe, that Whales being strooke to day,
Perchance to morrow, scarse at middle way 290

257–62 Forty-eight constellations of stars in the Ptolemaic system, here likened to so many *shires* dividing the heavens, in which *new Townes* [stars] rise and fall; the discovery of new stars shattered the image of the heavens as stable and immutable.

267 *Tropiques:* of Cancer and Capricorn.

285 ff.: The roundness and solidity of the earth were cited by Renaissance cosmographers as evidence of its perfect circular form, but this concept was challenged by the vast oceans, the deep regions of Hell, the high mountains.

286 *Tenarif:* volcanic mountain on the largest of the Canary Islands.

Of their wish'd journeys end, the bottom, dye.
And men, to sound depths, so much line untie,
As one might justly thinke, that there would rise
At end thereof, one of th'Antipodies:
If under all, a Vault infernall be, 295
(Which sure is spacious, except that we
Invent another torment, that there must
Millions into a strait hote roome be thrust)
Then solidnes, and roundnes have no place.
Are these but warts, and pock-holes in the face 300
Of th'earth? Thinke so. But yet confesse, in this
The worlds proportion disfigured is,
That those two legges whereon it doth relie, *Disorder in*
Reward and punishment are bent awrie. *the world.*
And, Oh, it can no more be questioned, 305
That beauties best, proportion, is dead,
Since even griefe it selfe, which now alone
Is left us, is without proportion.
Shee by whose lines proportion should bee
Examin'd, measure of all Symmetree, 310
Whom had that Ancient seen, who thought soules made
Of Harmony, he would at next have said
That Harmony was shee, and thence infer,
That soules were but Resultances from her,
And did from her into our bodies go, 315
As to our eyes, the formes from objects flow:
Shee, who if those great Doctors truely said
That th'Arke to mans proportions was made,
Had beene a type for that, as that might be
A type of her in this, that contrary 320
Both Elements, and Passions liv'd at peace
In her, who caus'd all Civill warre to cease.
Shee, after whom, what forme soe're we see,

311 *Ancient:* probably Pythagoras, who described the soul in terms of musical harmony.

312 *at next:* a common Old English construction.

314 *Resultances:* something which issues, proceeds, or emanates from another thing (*OED*).

317 *those great Doctors:* perhaps Ambrose and Augustine, especially the latter, who identified the Ark as a type of Church.

Is discord, and rude incongruitee,
Shee, shee is dead, shee's dead; when thou knowst this, 325
Thou knowst how ugly a monster this world is:
And learnst thus much by our Anatomee,
That here is nothing to enamor thee:
And that, not onely faults in inward parts,
Corruptions in our braines, or in our harts, 330
Poysoning the fountaines, whence our actions spring,
Endanger us: but that if every thing
Be not done fitly'nd in proportion,
To satisfie wise, and good lookers on,
(Since most men be such as most thinke they bee) 335
They're lothsome too, by this Deformitee.
For good, and well, must in our actions meete:
Wicked is not much worse then indiscreet.
But beauties other second Element,
Colour, and lustre now, is as neere spent. 340
And had the world his just proportion,
Were it a ring still, yet the stone is gone.
As a compassionate Turcoyse which doth tell
By looking pale, the wearer is not well,
As gold fals sicke being stung with Mercury, 345
All the worlds parts of such complexion bee.
When nature was most busie, the first weeke,
Swadling the new-borne earth, God seemd to like,
That she should sport herselfe sometimes, and play,
To mingle, and vary colours every day. 350
And then, as though she could not make inow,
Himselfe his various Rainbow did allow.
Sight is the noblest sense of any one,
Yet sight hath onely color to feed on,
And color is decayd: summers robe growes 355
Duskie, and like an oft dyed garment showes.

332–38 The fitness and decorum of man's external actions almost always reflect his inner self; therefore the opinion most widely held about a man is usually right.
343–44 A commonly accepted property of this gem.
345 *stung:* given an alloy.

>   Our blushing redde, which us'd in cheekes to spred,
>   Is inward sunke, and onely our soules are redde.
>   Perchance the world might have recovered,
>   If she whom we lament had not beene dead: 360
>   But shee, in whom all white, and redde, and blue
>   (Beauties ingredients) voluntary grew,
>   As in an unvext Paradise; from whom
>   Did all things verdure, and their lustre come,
>   Whose composition was miraculous,   365
>   Being all color, all Diaphanous,
>   (For Ayre, and Fire but thicke grosse bodies were,
>   And liveliest stones but drowsie, and pale to her,)
>   Shee, shee is dead; shee's dead: when thou knowst this,
>   Thou knowst how wan a Ghost this our world is: 370
>   And learnst thus much by our Anatomee,
>   That it should more affright, then pleasure thee.
>   And that, since all faire color then did sinke,
>   Tis now but wicked vanity to thinke,
>   To color vitious deeds with good pretence,   375
>   Or with bought colors to illude mens sense.
>   Nor in ought more this worlds decay appeares,   *Weaknesse*
>   Then that her influence the heav'n forbeares,   *in the want of*
>   Or that the Elements doe not feele this,   *correspondence*
>   *of heaven and*
>   The father, or the mother barren is.   *earth.*   380
>   The clouds conceive not raine, or doe not powre
>   In the due birth-time, downe the balmy showre.
>   Th'Ayre doth not motherly sit on the earth,
>   To hatch her seasons, and give all things birth.
>   Spring-times were common cradles, but are toombes   385
>   And false-conceptions fill the generall wombs.
>   Th'Ayre showes such Meteors, as none can see,
>   Not onely what they meane, but what they bee.

357–58 *blushing redde:* see Donne, *Sermons* X, 197: "Another name of man is *Adam,* and *Adam* is no more but *earth,* and *red earth,* and the word is often used for *blushing.*"
   361–63 Man. notes that the colors of her complexion and eyes were the recognized symbols of the theological virtues (faith, love, hope) and hence make of her an *unvext Paradise.*
   380 *the father:* sky; *the mother:* earth.

Earth such new wormes, as would have troubled much,
Th'Egyptian Mages to have made more such. 390
What Artist now dares boast that he can bring
Heaven hither, or constellate any thing,·
So as the influence of those starres may bee
Imprisond in an Herbe, or Charme, or Tree,
And doe by touch, all which those starres could do? 395
The art is lost, and correspondence too.
For heaven gives little, and the earth takes lesse,
And man least knowes their trade, and purposes.
If this commerce twixt heaven and earth were not
Embarr'd, and all this trafique quite forgot, 400
Shee, for whose losse we have lamented thus,
Would worke more fully'and pow'rfully on us.
Since herbes, and roots by dying, lose not all,
But they, yea Ashes too, are medicinall,
Death could not quench her vertue so, but that 405
It would be (if not follow'd) wondred at:
And all the world would be one dying Swan,
To sing her funerall prayse, and vanish than.
But as some Serpents poison hurteth not,
Except it be from the live Serpent shot, 410
So doth her vertue need her here, to fit
That unto us; she working more then it.
But she, in whom, to such maturity,
Vertue was growne, past growth, that it must die,
She from whose influence all Impressions came, 415
But, by Receivers impotencies, lame,
Who, though she could not transubstantiate
All states to gold, yet guilded every state,
So that some Princes have some temperance;
Some Counsaylors some purpose to advance 420
The common profite; and some people have
Some stay, no more then Kings should give, to crave;
Some women have some taciturnity,
Some Nunneries, some graines of chastity.

389-90 *new wormes:* snakes of a new species discovered in America and Africa. See Exod. 7: 10-12, where at Pharaoh's command the Egyptian wise men cast down their rods, which became serpents.

She that did thus much, and much more could doe, 425
But that our age was Iron, and rusty too,
Shee, shee is dead; shee's dead: when thou knowst this,
Thou knowest how drie a Cinder this world is.
And learnst thus much by our Anatomy,
That 'tis in vaine to dew, or mollifie 430
It with thy Teares, or Sweat, or Bloud: no thing
Is worth our travaile, griefe, or perishing,
But those rich joyes, which did possesse her hart,
Of which shee's now partaker, and a part.
But as in cutting up a man that's dead, *Conclusion* 435
The body will not last out to have read
On every part, and therefore men direct
Their speech to parts, that are of most effect;
So the worlds carcasse would not last, if I
Were punctuall in this Anatomy. 440
Nor smels it well to hearers, if one tell
Them their disease, who faine would think they're wel.
Here therefore be the end: And, blessed maid,
Of whom is meant what ever hath beene said,
Or shall be spoken well by any tongue, 445
Whose name refines course lines, and makes prose song,
Accept this tribute, and his first yeares rent,
Who till his darke short tapers end be spent,
As oft as thy feast sees this widowed earth,
Will yearely celebrate thy second birth, 450
That is, thy death. For though the soule of man
Be got when man is made, 'tis borne but than
When man doth die. Our body's as the wombe,
And as a mid-wife death directs it home.
And you her creatures, whom she workes upon 455
And have your last, and best concoction
From her example, and her vertue, if you
In reverence to her, doe thinke it due,
That no one should her prayses thus reherse,
As matter fit for Chronicle, not verse, 460

430 *mollifie:* moisten.
440 *punctuall:* minute, detailed, working point by point.
456 *concoction:* refinement or purification of gold or gems.

Vouchsafe to call to minde, that God did make
A last, and lastingst peece, a song. He spake
To *Moses*, to deliver unto all,
That song: because he knew they would let fall,
The Law, the Prophets, and the History,   *465*
But keepe the song still in their memory.
Such an opinion (in due measure) made
Me this great Office boldly to invade.
Nor could incomprehensiblenesse deterre
Me, from thus trying to emprison her.   *470*
Which when I saw that a strict grave could do,
I saw not why verse might not doe so too.
Verse hath a middle nature: heaven keepes soules,
The grave keeps bodies, verse the fame enroules.

The Second Anniversarie.
Of The Progres of the Soule

Wherein: by occasion of the religious death of Mistris Elizabeth Drury *the incommodities of the soule in this life and her exaltation in the next, are contemplated.*

Nothing could make mee sooner to confesse   *The entrance*
That this world had an everlastingnesse,
Then to consider, that a yeare is runne,
Since both this lower worlds, and the Sunnes Sunne,
The Lustre, and the vigor of this All,   *5*
Did set; t'were Blasphemy, to say, did fall.
But as a ship which hath strooke saile, doth runne,

461–66 See Deut. 31–33; Moses' song (Ch. 32), composed before entry into the Promised Land, was commonly glossed as an epitome of the Law.

By force of that force which before, it wonne,
Or as sometimes in a beheaded man,
Though at those two Red seas, which freely ran,   *10*
One from the Trunke, another from the Head,
His soule be saild, to her eternall bed,
His eies will twinckle, and his tongue will roll,
As though he beckned, and cal'd backe his Soul,
He graspes his hands, and he puls up his feet,   *15*
And seemes to reach, and to step forth to meet
His soule; when all these motions which we saw,
Are but as Ice, which crackles at a thaw:
Or as a Lute, which in moist weather, rings
Her knell alone, by cracking of her strings.   *20*
So strugles this dead world, now shee is gone;
For there is motion in corruption.
As some Daies are, at the Creation nam'd,
Before the sunne, the which fram'd Daies, was fram'd,
So after this sunnes set, some show appeares,   *25*
And orderly vicisitude of yeares.
Yet a new Deluge, and of Lethe flood,
Hath drown'us all, All have forgot all good,
Forgetting her, the maine Reserve of all,
Yet in this Deluge, grosse and generall,   *30*
Thou seest mee strive for life; my life shalbe,
To bee hereafter prais'd, for praysing thee,
Immortal Mayd, who though thou wouldst refuse
The name of Mother, be unto my Muse,
A Father since her chast Ambition is,   *35*
Yearely to bring forth such a child as this.
These Hymes may worke on future wits, and so
May great Grand-children of thy praises grow.
And so, though not Revive, embalme, and spice
The world, which else would putrify with vice.   *40*
For thus, Man may extend thy progeny,
Untill man doe but vanish, and not die.

The Second Anniversarie (1612). 23–24 The Genesis account of the creation of the Sun and Moon on the fourth day gave rise to much speculation as to how the previous three days could have been distinguished as such.

34–38 Be a Father to my Muse's progeny (these hymns), which in their turn help create further progeny.

42 Refers to those yet alive at the Last Judgment.

These Hymns thy issue, may encrease so long,
As till Gods great Venite change the song.
Thirst for that time, O my insatiate soule, *A just disestimation of this world* 45
And serve thy thirst, with Gods safe-sealing Bowle.
Bee thirsty still, and drinke still till thou goe;
'Tis th'onely Health; to be Hydropique so.
Forget this rotten world; And unto thee,
Let thine owne times as an old story be, 50
Be not concern'd: study not why, nor whan;
Do not so much, as not beleeve a man.
For though to erre, be worst, to try truths forth,
Is far more busines, then this world is worth.
The World is but a Carkas; thou art fed 55
By it, but as a worme, that carcas bred;
And why shouldst thou, poore worme, consider more,
When this world will grow better then before,
Then those thy fellow-wormes doe thinke upone
That carkasses last resurrectione. 60
Forget this world, and scarse thinke of it so,
As of old cloaths, cast off a yeare agoe.
To be thus stupid is Alacrity;
Men thus lethargique have best Memory.
Looke upward; that's towards her, whose happy state 65
We now lament not, but congratulate.
Shee, to whom all this world was but a stage,
Where all sat harkning how her youthfull age
Should be emploid, because in all shee did,
Some Figure of the Golden times, was hid. 70
Who could not lacke, what ere this world could give,
Because shee was the forme, that made it live;
Nor could complaine, that this world was unfit,
To be staid in, then when shee was in it;
Shee that first tried indifferent desires 75
By vertue, and vertue by religious fires,
Shee to whose person Paradise adhear'd,

46 *safe-sealing Bowle:* the Eucharist, alluding to the seals in the foreheads of the just at the Last Judgment. (Rev. 7:3–4).
48 *Hydropique:* an insatiate thirst, as in dropsy.
53 *to try truths forth:* to test thoroughly.
72 *forme:* the soul, that gave the world life.
75 *tried:* refined, purified by fire, as metals.

As Courts to Princes; shee whose eies enspheard
Star-light inough, t'have made the South controll,
(Had shee beene there) the Star-full Northern Pole, 80
Shee, shee is gone; sheé is gone; when thou knowest this,
What fragmentary rubbidge this world is
Thou knowest, and that it is not worth a thought;
He honors it too much that thinks it nought.
Thinke then, My soule, that death is but a Groome, *Contemplation* 85
Which brings a Taper to the outward roome, *of our state in our death-bed.*
Whence thou spiest first a little glimmering light,
And after brings it nearer to thy sight:
For such approches doth Heaven make in death.
Thinke thy selfe laboring now with broken breath, 90
And thinke those broken and soft Notes to bee
Division, and thy happiest Harmonee.
Thinke thee laid on thy death bed, loose and slacke;
And thinke that but unbinding of a packe,
To take one precious thing, thy soule, from thence. 95
Thinke thy selfe parch'd with fevers violence,
Anger thine Ague more, by calling it
Thy Physicke; chide the slacknesse of the fit.
Thinke that thou hearst thy knell, and thinke no more,
But that, as Bels cal'd thee to Church before, 100
So this, to the Triumphant Church, cals thee.
Thinke Satans Sergeants round about thee bee,
And thinke that but for Legacies they thrust;
Give one thy Pride, to'another give thy Lust:
Give them those sinnes which they gave thee before, 105
And trust th'immaculate blood to wash thy score.
Thinke thy frinds weeping round, and thinke that thay
Weepe but because they goe not yet thy way.
Thinke that they close thine eyes, and thinke in this,
That they confesse much in the world, amisse, 110
Who dare not trust a dead mans eye with that,
Which they from God, and Angels cover not.
Thinke that they shroud thee up, and thinke from thence

---

80 The Northern Pole was thought to have more stars above it than the Southern.

92 *Division:* a rapid musical passage of many short notes, thought of as divisions of long notes (*OED*).

102 *Satans Sergeants:* Bailiffs, come to arrest the soul for debt.

They reinvest thee in white innocence.
Thinke that thy body rots, and (if so lowe, 115
Thy soule exalted so, thy thoughts can goe,)
Thinke the a Prince, who of themselves create
Wormes which insensibly devoure their state.
Thinke that they bury thee, and thinke that rite
Laies thee to sleepe but a saint Lucies night. 120
Thinke these things cheerefully: and if thou bee
Drowsie or slacke, remember then that shee,
Shee whose Complexion was so even made,
That which of her Ingredients should invade
The other three, no Feare, no Art could guesse: 125
So far were all remov'd from more or lesse.
But as in Mithridate, or just perfumes,
Where all good things being met, no one presumes
To governe, or to triumph on the rest,
Onely because all were, no part was best. 130
And as, though all doe know, that quantities
Are made of lines, and lines from Points arise,
None can these lines or quantities unjoynt,
And say this is a line, or this a point,
So though the Elements and Humors were 135
In her, one could not say, this governes there.
Whose even constitution might have wonne
Any disease to venter on the Sunne,
Rather then her: and make a spirit feare
That he to disuniting subject were. 140
To whose proportions if we would compare
Cubes, th'are unstable; Circles, Angulare;
Shee who was such a Chaine, as Fate emploies
To bring mankind, all Fortunes it enjoies,
So fast, so even wrought, as one would thinke, 145
No Accident, could threaten any linke,

120 *saint Lucies night:* the longest night of the year (13 December, O.S.).
123–30 Her complexion manifested a balance of humors so perfect as to seem to exempt her from the inevitable mortality resulting from the contradictions of the elements within man.
127 *Mithridate:* an antidote for poison.
137–40 The celestial matter of the sun and other planets, and the simple substance of spirits, were not subject to dissolution.
143–46 The so-called *aurea catena Homeri* (*Iliad* VIII, 19), by which all things are thought to be preserved (Man.).

Shee, shee embrac'd a sicknesse, gave it meat,
The purest Blood, and Breath, that ere it eat.
And hath taught us that though a good man hath
Title to Heaven, and plead it by his Faith,   150
And though he may pretend a conquest, since
Heaven was content to suffer violence,
Yea though he plead a long possession too,
(For they'are in Heaven on Earth, who Heavens workes do,)
Though he had right, and power, and Place before,   155
Yet Death must usher, and unlocke the doore.
Thinke further on thy selfe, my soule, and thinke;   *Incommodities*
How thou at first wast made but in a sinke;   *of the Soule*
                                                     in the Body.
Thinke that it argued some infermitee,
That those two soules, which then thou foundst in mee,   160
Thou fedst upon, And drewst into thee, both
My second soule of sence, and first of growth.
Thinke but how poore thou wast, how obnoxious,
Whom a small lump of flesh could poison thus.
This curded milke, this poore unlittered whelpe   165
My body, could, beyond escape, or helpe,
Infect thee with originall sinne, and thou
Couldst neither then refuse, nor leave it now.
Thinke that no stubborne sullen Anchorit,
Which fixt to'a Pillar, or a Grave doth sit   170
Bedded and Bath'd in all his Ordures, dwels
So fowly as our soules, in their firstbuilt Cels.
Thinke in how poore a prison thou didst lie
After, enabled but to sucke, and crie.
Thinke, when t'was growne to most, t'was a poore Inne,   175
A Province Pack'd up in two yards of skinne.
And that usurped, or threatned with the rage
Of sicknesses, or their true mother, Age.

151–52 See Matt. 11:12, "And from the days of John the Baptist until now the kingdom of heaven suffereth violence, and the violent take it by force." In commenting on this text (*Sermons* II, 220) Donne identified the violent as "zealous and spiritually valiant."

158 *sinke:* sewer, i.e., womb.

159–62 The common doctrine of man's triple soul—of growth (vegetable), of sense (animal), of reason and understanding (rational).

163 *obnoxious:* exposed.

165 *This curded milke:* see Job 10:10, "Hast thou not poured me out as milk, and curdled me like cheese."

But thinke that Death hath now enfranchis'd thee,   *Her liberty*
Thou hast thy'expansion now and libertee;   *by death.*   *180*
Thinke that a rusty Peece, discharg'd, is flowen
In peeces, and the bullet is his owne,
And freely flies: This to thy soule allow,
Thinke thy shell broke, thinke thy Soule hatch'd but now.
And thinke this slow-pac'd soule, which late did cleave,   *185*
To'a body, and went but by the bodies leave,
Twenty, perchance, or thirty mile a day,
Dispatches in a minute all the way,
Twixt Heaven, and Earth: shee staies not in the Ayre,
To looke what Meteors there themselves prepare;   *190*
She carries no desire to know, nor sense,
Whether th'Ayrs middle Region be intense,
For th'Element of fire, shee doth not know,
Whether shee past by such a place or no;
Shee baits not at the Moone, nor cares to trie,   *195*
Whether in that new world, men live, and die.
Venus retards her not, to'enquire, how shee
Can, (being one Star) Hesper, and Vesper bee;
Hee that charm'd Argus eies, sweet Mercury,
Workes not on her, who now is growen all Ey;   *200*
Who, if shee meete the body of the Sunne,
Goes through, not staying till his course be runne;
Who finds in Mars his Campe, no corps of Guard;
Nor is by Jove, nor by his father bard;
But ere shee can consider how shee went,   *205*
At once is at, and through the Firmament.
And as these stars were but so many beades
Strung on one string, speed undistinguish'd leades
Her through those spheares, as through the beades, a string,
Whose quicke succession makes it still one thing: *210*
As doth the Pith, which, least our Bodies slacke,
Strings fast the little bones of necke, and backe;
So by the soule doth death string Heaven and Earth,

189–206 The released soul is unconcerned to resolve the astronomers' quibbles, though the journey itself apparently follows Tycho Brahe's astronomy, placing Venus before Mercury (Man., citing I. A. Shapiro).

199–200 Mercury charmed Argus' hundred eyes to sleep by music and storytelling (Ovid, *Metamorphoses*, I, 622–73); the soul is now all eye, since sense perception is no longer tied to sense organs.

For when our soule enjoyes this her third birth,
(Creation gave her one, a second, grace,) 215
Heaven is as neare, and present to her face,
As colours are, and objects, in a roome
Where darknesse was before, when Tapers come.
This must, my soule, thy long-short Progresse bee;
To'advance these thoughts, remember then, that shee 220
Shee, whose faire body no such prison was,
But that a soule might well be pleas'd to passe
An Age in her; shee whose rich beauty lent
Mintage to others beauties, for they went
But for so much, as they were like to her; 225
Shee, in whose body (if wee dare prefer
This low world, to so high a mark, as shee,)
The Westerne treasure, Esterne spiceree,
Europe, and Afrique, and the unknowen rest
Were easily found, or what in them was best; 230
And when w'have made this large Discoveree,
Of all in her some one part there will bee
Twenty such parts, whose plenty and riches is
Inough to make twenty such worlds as this;
Shee, whom had they knowne, who did first betroth 235
The Tutelar Angels, and assigned one, both
To Nations, Cities, and to Companies,
To Functions, Offices, and Dignities,
And to each severall man, to him, and him,
They would have given her one for every limme; 240
Shee, of whose soule, if we may say, t'was Gold,
Her body was th'Electrum, and did hold
Many degrees of that; (we understood
Her by her sight, her pure and eloquent blood
Spoke in her cheekes, and so distinckly wrought, 245
That one might almost say, her bodie thought,)
Shee, shee, thus richly, and largely hous'd, is gone:

214 *third birth*: the birth, through death, into Heaven.
226 *prefer*: advance.
236 *Tutelar Angels*: guardian angels for individuals and special groups.
242 *Electrum*: Gr. cites Paracelsus' explanation of Electrum as a middle substance between ore and metal; it is on the way to perfection.

And chides us slow-pac'd snailes, who crawle upon
Our prisons prison, earth, nor thinke us well
Longer, then whil'st we beare our brittle shell.   250
But t'were but little to have chang'd our roome, *Her ignorance*
If, as we were in this our living Tombe   *in this life and*
Oppress'd with ignorance, we still were so,   *knowledge in the next*
Poor soule in this thy flesh what do'st thou know.
Thou know'st thy selfe so little, as thou know'st not,   255
How thou did'st die, nor how thou wast begot.
Thou neither knowst, how thou at first camest in,
Nor how thou took'st the poyson of mans sin.
Nor dost thou, (though thou knowst, that thou art so)
By what way thou art made immortall, know.   260
Thou art to narrow, wretch, to comprehend
Even thy selfe: yea though thou wouldst but bend
To know thy body. Have not all soules thought
For many ages, that our body'is wrought
Of Ayre, and Fire, and other Elements?   265
And now they thinke of new ingredients.
And one soule thinkes one, and another way
Another thinkes, and 'tis an even lay.
Knowst thou but how the stone doth enter in
The bladders Cave, and never breake the skin?   270
Knowst thou how blood, which to the hart doth flow,
Doth from one ventricle to th'other go?
And for the putrid stuffe, which thou dost spit,
Knowst thou how thy lungs have attracted it?
There are no passages so that there is   275
(For ought thou knowst) piercing of substances.
And of those many opinions which men raise
Of Nailes and Haires, dost thou know which to praise?
What hope have we to know our selves, when wee
Know not the least things, which for our use bee?   280
We see in Authors, too stiffe to recant,
A hundred controversies of an Ant.
And yet one watches, starves, freeses, and sweats,

266 *new ingredients*: salt, sulphur, and mercury, according to the Paracelsians (Man.).

To know but Catechismes and Alphabets
Of unconcerning things, matters of fact; 285
How others on our stage their parts did Act;
What Caesar did, yea, and what Cicero said.
Why grasse is greene, or why our blood is red,
Are mysteries which none have reach'd unto.
In this low forme, poore soule what wilt thou doe? 290
When wilt thou shake off this Pedantery,
Of being taught by sense, and Fantasy?
Thou look'st through spectacles; small things seeme great,
Below; But up unto the watchtowre get,
And see all things despoyld of fallacies: 295
Thou shalt not peepe through lattices of eies,
Nor heare through Laberinths of eares, nor learne
By circuit, or collections to discerne.
In Heaven thou straight know'st all, concerning it,
And what concerns it not, shall straight forget. 300
There thou (but in no other schoole) maist bee
Perchance, as learned, and as full, as shee,
Shee who all Libraries had throughly red
At home, in her owne thoughts, And practised
So much good as would make as many more: 305
Shee whose example they must all implore,
Who would or doe, or thinke well, and confesse
That aye the vertuous Actions they expresse,
Are but a new, and worse edition,
Of her some one thought, or one action: 310
Shee, who in th'Art of knowing Heaven, was growen
Here upon Earth, to such perfection,
That shee hath, ever since to Heaven shee came,
(In a far fairer print,) but read the same:
Shee, shee, not satisfied with all this waite, 315
(For so much knowledge, as would over-fraite
Another, did but Ballast her) is gone,
As well t'enjoy, as get perfectione.
And cals us after her, in that shee tooke,

292 *by sense, and Fantasy*: see Aquinas, *Sum. Theol.* I, Q.84, a.7, who explains that Spirits apprehend universals directly, but that man in the mortal condition can only abstract them from the sense images presented to Reason through the fantasy.

(Taking herselfe) our best, and worthiest booke. 320
Returne not, my soule, from this extasee, *Of our company*
And meditation of what thou shalt bee, *in this life and*
To earthly thoughts, till it to thee appeare, *in the next.*
With whom thy conversation must be there.
With whom wilt thou Converse? what station 325
Canst thou choose out, free from infection,
That wil nor give thee theirs, nor drinke in thine?
Shalt thou not finde a spungy slack Divine
Drinke and sucke in th'Instructions of Great men,
And for the word of God, vent them agen? 330
Are there not some Courts, (And then, no things bee
So like as Courts) which, in this let us see,
That wits and tongues of Libellars are weake,
Because they doe more ill, then these can speake?
The poyson'is gone through all, poysons affect 335
Chiefly the cheefest parts, but some effect
In Nailes, and Haires, yea excrements, will show;
So will the poyson of sinne, in the most low.
Up up, my drowsie soule, where thy new eare
Shall in the Angels songs no discord heare; 340
Where thou shalt see the blessed Mother-maid
Joy in not being that, which men have said.
Where shee'is exalted more for being good,
Then for her interest, of motherhood.
Up to those Patriarckes, which did longer sit 345
Expecting Christ, then they'have enjoy'd him yet.
Up to those Prophets, which now gladly see
Their Prophecies growen to be Historee.
Up to th'Apostles, who did bravely runne,
All the Sunnes course, with more light then the Sunne. 350
Up to those Martyrs, who did calmely bleed
Oyle to th'Apostles lamps, dew to their seed.
Up to those Virgins, who thought that almost
They made joyntenants with the Holy Ghost,

339–58 Man. notes that the order of the hierarchy loosely corresponds to the major headings in the Litany of the Saints.
341–42 Mary rejoices in not being free of Original Sin, for then she would have had no need for and no part in Christ's Redemption.
351–52 Cf. the proverb, "The blood of martyrs is the seed of the Church."

If they to any should his Temple give. 355
Up, up, for in that squadron there doth live
Shee, who hath carried thether, new degrees
(As to their number) to their dignitees.
Shee, who beeing to herselfe a state, enjoyd
All royalties which any state emploid, 360
For shee made wars, and triumph'd, reson still
Did not overthrow, but rectifie her will:
And shee made peace, for no peace is like this,
That beauty and chastity together kisse:
Shee did high justice; for shee crucified 365
Every first motion of rebellious pride:
And shee gave pardons, and was liberall,
For, onely herselfe except, shee pardon all:
Shee coynd, in this, that her impressions gave
To all our actions all the worth they have: 370
Shee gave protections; the thoughts of her brest
Satans rude Officers could nere arrest.
As these prerogatives being met in one,
Made her a soveraigne state, religion
Made her a Church; and these two made her all. 375
Shee who was all this All, and could not fall
To worse, by company; (for shee was still
More Antidote, then all the world was ill,)
Shee, shee doth leave it, and by Death, survive
All this, in Heaven; whither who doth not strive 380
The more, because shee'is there, he doth not know
That accidentall joyes in Heaven doe grow.
But pause, My soule, and study ere thou fall *Of essentiall joy*
On accidentall joyes, th'essentiall. *in this life and*
in the next.
Still before Accessories doe abide 385
A triall, must the principall be tride.
And what essentiall joy canst thou expect
Here upon earth? what permanent effect
Of transitory causes? Dost thou love
Beauty? (And Beauty worthyest is to move) 390

360 *royalties*: royal prerogatives, enumerated in the subsequent lines.
382 *accidentall joyes*: joys in addition to the essential joy, the beatific vision.

Poore couse'ned cose'nor, that she, and that thou,
Which did begin to love, are neither now.
You are both fluid, chang'd since yesterday;
Next day repaires, (but ill) last daies decay.
Nor are, (Although the river keep the name)   395
Yesterdaies waters, and to daies the same.
So flowes her face, and thine eies, neither now
That saint, nor Pilgrime, which your loving vow
Concernd, remaines; but whil'st you thinke you bee
Constant, you'are howrely in inconstancee.   400
Honour may have pretence unto our love,
Because that God did live so long above
Without this Honour, and then lov'd it so,
That he at last made Creatures to bestow
Honor on him; not that he needed it,   405
But that, to his hands, man might grow more fit.
But since all honors from inferiors flow,
(For they doe give it; Princes doe but show
Whom they would have so honord) and that this
On such opinions, and capacities   410
Is built, as rise, and fall, to more and lesse,
Alas, tis but a casuall happinesse.
Hath ever any man to'himselfe assigned
This or that happinesse, to'arrest his minde,
But that another man, which takes a worse,   415
Thinke him a foole for having tane that course?
They who did labour Babels tower t'erect,
Might have considerd, that for that effect,
All this whole solid Earth could not allow
Nor furnish forth Materials enow;   420
And that this Center, to raise such a place
Was far to little, to have beene the Base;
No more affoords this world, foundatione
To erect true joye, were all the meanes in one.
But as the Heathen made them severall gods,   425
Of all Gods Benefits, and all his Rods,

391–400 *couse'ned cose'nor*: poor lover *(Pilgrime)* who deludes himself and also deludes his beloved (saint) by his vows of constancy.

(For as the Wine, and Corne, and Onions are
Gods unto them, so Agues bee, and war)
And as by changing that whole precious Gold
To such small copper coynes, they lost the old, 430
And lost their onely God, who ever must
Be sought alone, and not in such a thrust,
So much mankind true happinesse mistakes;
No Joye enjoyes that man, that many makes.
Then, soule, to thy first pitch worke up againe; 435
Know that all lines which circles doe containe,
For once that they the center touch, do touch
Twice the circumference; and be thou such.
Double on Heaven, thy thoughts on Earth emploid;
All will not serve; Onely who have enjoyd 440
The sight of God, in fulnesse, can thinke it;
For it is both the object, and the wit.
This is essentiall joye, where neither hee
Can suffer Diminution, nor wee;
Tis such a full, and such a filling good; 445
Had th'Angels once look'd on him, they had stood.
To fill the place of one of them, or more,
Shee whom we celebrate, is gone before.
Shee, who had Here so much essentiall joye,
As no chance could distract, much lesse destroy; 450
Who with Gods presence was acquainted so,
(Hearing, and speaking to him) as to know
His face, in any naturall Stone, or Tree,
Better then when in Images they bee:
Who kept, by diligent devotion, 455
Gods Image, in such reparation,
Within her heart, that what decay was growen,
Was her first Parents fault, and not her own:
Who being solicited to any Act,
Still heard God pleading his safe precontract; 460

439–42 Even thy thoughts doubled, or all thy thoughts, will not suffice to apprehend God, who, being the means of knowing (wit) as well as the object of knowledge, must reveal himself.

446–50 See Aquinas, *Sum. Theol.* I, Q.63, a.6, who for the reason alluded to here decides that the evil angels must have fallen almost instantaneously after their creation.

Who by a faithfull confidence, was here
Betrothed to God, and now is married there,
Whose twilights were more cleare, then our mid day,
Who dreamt devoutlier, then most use to pray;
Who being heare fild with grace, yet strove to bee, 465
Both where more grace, and more capacitee
At once is given: shee to Heaven is gone,
Who made this world in some proportion
A heaven, and here, became unto us all,
Joye, (as our joyes admit) essentiall. 470
But could this low world joyes essentiall touch, *Of accidentall*
Heavens accidentall joyes would passe them much. *joyes in both places.*
How poore and lame, must then our casuall bee?
If thy Prince will his subjects to call thee
My Lord, and this doe swell thee, thou are than, 475
By being a greater, growen to be lesse Man.
When no Physician of Redresse can speake,
A joyfull casuall violence may breake
A dangerous Apostem in thy brest;
And whilst thou joyest in this, the dangerous rest, 480
The bag may rise up, and so strangle thee.
What eie was casuall, may ever bee.
What should the Nature change? Or make the same
Certaine, which was but casuall, when it came?
All casuall joye doth loud and plainly say, 485
Onely by comming, that it can away.
Onely in Heaven joies strength is never spent;
And accidentall things are permanent.
Joy of a soules arrivall neere decaies;
For that soule ever joyes, and ever staies. 490
Joy that their last great Consummation
Approches in the resurrection;
When earthly bodies more celestiall
Shalbe, then Angels were, for they could fall;
This kind of joy doth every day admit 495
Degrees of grouth, but none of loosing it.

---

479 *Apostem*: impostume, a swelling formed by a gathering of the humors.
482 *eie*: aye, ever, always.

In this fresh joy, tis no small part, that shee,
Shee, in whose goodnesse, he that names degree,
Doth injure her; (Tis losse to be cald best,
There where the stuffe is not such as the rest) 500
Shee, who left such a body, as even shee
Onely in Heaven could learne, how it can bee
Made better; for shee rather was two soules,
Or like to full, on both sides written Rols,
Where eies might read upon the outward skin, 505
As strong Records for God, as mindes within,
Shee, who by making full perfection grow,
Peeces a Circle, and still keepes it so,
Long'd for, and longing for'it, to heaven is gone,
Where shee receives, and gives addition. 510
Here in a place, where mis-devotion frames   *Conclusion*
A thousand praiers to saints, whose very names
The ancient Church knew not, Heaven knowes not yet,
And where, what lawes of poetry admit,
Lawes of religion, have at least the same, 515
Immortall Maid, I might invoque thy name.
Could any Saint provoke that appetite,
Thou here shouldst make mee a french convertite.
But thou wouldst not; nor wouldst thou be content,
To take this, for my second yeeres true Rent, 520
Did this Coine beare any other stampe, then his,
That gave thee power to doe, me, to say this.
Since his will is, that to posteritee,
Thou shouldest for life, and death, a patterne bee,
And that the world should notice have of this, 525
The purpose, and th'Autority is his;
Thou art the Proclamation; and I ame
The Trumpet, at whose voice the people came.

507–508 Paradoxically she adds to the circle, the traditional symbol of perfection, and yet keeps it a circle.
511–15 Donne was in Catholic France with Sir Robert Drury from November, 1611 to April, 1612; the laws of Catholicism admit invocations to the saints as the laws of poetry do to the Muses.

DIVINE POEMS

To the Lady Magdalen Herbert, of St. Mary Magdalen

Her of your name, whose fair inheritance
Bethina was, and jointure *Magdalo*:
An active faith so highly did advance,
That she once knew, more than the Church did know,
The *Resurrection*; so much good there is   5
Deliver'd of her, that some Fathers be
Loth to believe one Woman could do this;
But, think these *Magdalens* were two or three.
Increase their number, *Lady*, and their fame:
To their *Devotion*, add your *Innocence*;   10
Take so much of th'example, as of the name;
The latter half, and in some recompence
That they did harbour *Christ* himself, a Guest,
Harbour these *Hymns*, to his dear name addrest.

To the Lady.... This poem appears only in Walton, *The Life of Mr. George Herbert* (1670), pp. 25–26, following a letter dated 11 July 1607 which mentions the enclosure of some "Holy Hymns and Sonnets." These are now generally supposed to be the *La Corona* set.

2 *Magdalo*: Mary's portion of the family estate.

8 The woman who was a sinner (Luke 7:36–50), Mary of Bethany—the sister of Martha and Lazarus (John 11)—and Mary Magdalen the demoniac (Luke 8:2, Mark 16) were sometimes, though not always, assumed to be the same.

HOLY SONNETS

La Corona

I

Deigne at my hands this crown of prayer and praise,
Weav'd in my low devout melancholie,
Thou which of good, hast, yea art treasury,
All changing unchang'd Antient of dayes,
But doe not, with a vile crowne of fraile bayes, 5
Reward my muses white sincerity,
But what thy thorny crowne gain'd, that give mee,
A crowne of Glory, which doth flower alwayes;
The ends crowne our workes, but thou crown'st our ends,
For, at our end begins our endlesse rest, 10
The first last end, now zealously possest,
With a strong sober thirst, my soule attends.
'Tis time that heart and voice be lifted high,
Salvation to all that will is nigh.

La Corona. The seven poems are untitled in most manuscripts, but they have separate titles in 1633. The theme derives from Isa. 28:1,5, "Woe to the crown of pride.... Whose glorious beauty is as a fading flower.... In that day shall the Lord of hosts be for a crown of glory, and for a diadem of beauty, unto the residue of his people"; the poetic crown is composed of interwoven sonnets celebrating certain mysteries of faith in the tradition of the Rosary. Gd. calls attention to the several echoes of the Advent Offices from the Roman Breviary in the first poem.

Annunciation

2

Salvation to all that will is nigh,
That All, which alwayes is All every where,
Which cannot sinne, and yet all sinnes must beare,
Which cannot die, yet cannot chuse but die,
Loe, faithfull Virgin, yeelds himselfe to lye   5
In prison, in thy wombe; and though he there
Can take no sinne, nor thou give, yet he'will weare
Taken from thence, flesh, which deaths force may trie.
Ere by the spheares time was created, thou
Wast in his minde, who is thy Sonne, and Brother,   10
Whom thou conceiv'st, conceiv'd; yea thou art now
Thy Makers maker, and thy Fathers mother,
Thou'hast light in darke; and shutst in little roome,
Immensity cloysterd in thy deare wombe.

Nativitie

3

Immensitie cloysterd in thy deare wombe,
Now leaves his welbelov'd imprisonment,
There he hath made himselfe to his intent
Weake enough, now into our world to come;
But Oh, for thee, for him, hath th'Inne no roome?   5
Yet lay him in this stall, and from the Orient,
Starres, and wisemen will travell to prevent
Th'effect of *Herods* jealous generall doome.
Seest thou, my Soule, with thy faiths eyes, how he
Which fils all place, yet none holds him, doth lye? 10
Was not his pity towards thee wondrous high,
That would have need to be pittied by thee?
Kisse him, and with him into Egypt goe,
With his kinde mother, who partakes thy woe.

Annunciation. The striking paradoxes are medieval commonplaces.

Temple

4

With his kinde mother who partakes thy woe,
Joseph turne backe; see where your child doth sit,
Blowing, yea blowing out those sparks of wit,
Which himselfe on those Doctors did bestow;
The Word but lately could not speake, and loe   5
It sodenly speakes wonders, whence comes it,
That all which was, and all which should be writ,
A shallow seeming child, should deeply know?
His Godhead was not soule to his manhood,
Nor had time mellowed him to this ripenesse,   10
But as for one which hath a long taske, 'tis good,
With the Sunne to beginne his businesse,
He in his ages morning thus began
By miracles exceeding power of man.

Crucifying

5

By miracles exceeding power of man,
Hee faith in some, envie in some begat,
For, what weake spirits admire, ambitious, hate;
In both affections many to him ran,
But Oh! the worst are most, they will and can,   5
Alas, and do, unto the immaculate,
Whose creature Fate is, now prescribe a Fate,
Measuring selfe-lifes infinity to'a span,
Nay to an inch. Loe, where condemned hee
Beares his owne crosse, with paine, yet by and by   10
When it beares him, he must beare more and die;
Now thou art lifted up, draw mee to thee,

Temple. 9 The line alludes to and denies the ancient heresy that Christ's divine nature took, in him, the place of a human soul.

Crucifying. 12 See John 12:32, "I, if I be lifted up ... will draw all men unto me."

And at thy death giving such liberall dole,
Moyst, with one drop of thy blood, my dry soule.

Resurrection

6

Moyst with one drop of thy blood, my dry soule
Shall (though she now be in extreme degree
Too stony hard, and yet too fleshly,) bee
Freed by that drop, from being starv'd, hard, or foule,
And life, by this death abled, shall controule 5
Death, whom thy death slue; nor shall to mee
Feare of first or last death, bring miserie,
If in thy little booke my name thou enroule,
Flesh in that long sleep is not putrified,
But made that there, of which, and for which 'twas; 10
Nor can by other meanes be glorified.
May then sinnes sleep, and deaths soone from me passe,
That wak't from both, I againe risen may
Salute the last, and everlasting day.

Ascension

7

Salute the last and everlasting day,
Joy at the uprising of this Sunne, and Sonne,
Yee whose just teares, or tribulation
Have purely washt, or burnt your drossie clay;
Behold the Highest, parting hence away, 5
Lightens the darke clouds, which hee treads upon,

Resurrection. 7 *last death:* See Rev. 2:11. The first death is physical death; the second is damnation of the soul for eternity.

8 *little booke*: Donne appears to conflate the Book of Life in which the names of the elect are enrolled (Rev. 13:8, 20:12), which is not described as "little," with the "little book" of Rev. 10:2, usually glossed as the prophetic history of the Christian Church.

9–10 Flesh in death does not remain in putrefaction, but returns to earth *of which* it was made, and at length attains the glorified state *for which* it was made.

Nor doth hee by ascending, show alone,
But first hee, and hee first enters the way.
O strong Ramme, which hast batter'd heaven for mee,
Mild lambe, which with thy blood, hast mark'd the path; *10*
Bright torch, which shin'st, that I the way may see,
Oh, with thy owne blood quench thy owne just wrath,
And if thy holy Spirit, my Muse did raise,
Deigne at my hands this crowne of prayer and praise.

A LITANIE

I. THE FATHER

Father of Heaven, and him, by whom
It, and us for it, and all else, for us
Thou madest, and govern'st ever, come
And re-create mee, now growne ruinous:

Ascention. 7–8 Christ is the first man to ascend, and he also leads the triumphal procession of his redeemed to heaven. See Col. 2:15, "And having spoiled principalities and powers, he made a show of them openly, triumphing over them in it."

A Litanie. See Donne's undated letter to his friend Henry Goodyere: "Since my imprisonment in my bed, I have made a meditation in verse, which I call a Litany; the word you know imports no other then supplication, but all Churches have one forme of supplication, by that name. Amongst ancient annals (I mean some 800 years) I have met two Letanies in Latin verse, which gave me not the reason of my meditations, for in good faith I thought not upon them then, but they give me a defence, if any man, to a Lay man, and a private, impute it as a fault, to take divine and publique names, to his own little thoughts. The first of these was made by *Ratpertus* a Monk of *Suevia*; and the other by S. *Notker*.... That by which it [my litany] will deserve best acceptation, is, that neither the Roman Church need call it defective, because it abhors not the particular mention of the blessed Triumphers in heaven; nor the Reformed can discreetly accuse it, of attributing more then a rectified devotion ought to doe." (Letters, pp. 28–30). However, the litanies to which Donne refers (Migne, *Pat. Lat.* lxxxvii, col. 39 & 42) are public, not private, prayers. Donne keeps the general structure of a litany, with invocations, deprecations, supplications, but his Protestant circumlocutions to avoid direct prayer to the saints wrenches the structure of a litany as a formal prayer which repeats unvarying responses such as, *Ora pro nobis.*

    My heart is by dejection, clay,   *5*
    And by selfe-murder, red.
From this red earth, O Father, purge away
All vicious tinctures, that new fashioned
I may rise up from death, before I'am dead.

II. THE SONNE

   O Sonne of God, who seeing two things,   *10*
Sinne, and death crept in, which were never made,
   By bearing one, tryed'st with what stings
The other could thine heritage invade;
    O be thou nail'd unto my heart,
    And crucified againe,   *15*
Part not from it, though it from thee would part,
But let it be by applying so thy paine,
Drown'd in thy blood, and in thy passion slaine.

III. THE HOLY GHOST

   O Holy Ghost, whose temple I
Am, but of mudde walls, and condensed dust,   *20*
   And being sacrilegiously
Halfe wasted with youths fires, of pride and lust,
    Must with new stormes be weatherbeat;
    Double in my heart thy flame,
Which let devout sad teares intend; and let   *25*
(Though this glasse lanthorne, flesh, do suffer maime)
Fire, Sacrifice, Priest, Altar be the same.

IV. THE TRINITY

   O Blessed glorious Trinity,
Bones to Philosophy, but milke to faith,
   Which, as wise serpents, diversly   *30*
Most slipperinesse, yet most entanglings hath,

 5–6 The humor of melancholy corresponds to earth, *clay*; the clay is *red* by the self-murder of sin and also by nature, in that "Adam" (man), means "red earth."
 25 *intend:* intensify.
 26–27 The body is a *glasse lanthorne*, the *Fire* is the flame incited by the Spirit (1. 24), the *Altar* is the heart, the *Priest*, the soul.

        As you distinguish'd undistinct
        By power, love, knowledge bee,
  Give mee a such selfe different instinct,
  Of these let all mee elemented bee,   35
  Of power, to love, to know, you unnumbred three.

V. THE VIRGIN MARY

  For that faire blessed Mother-maid,
Whose flesh redeem'd us; That she-Cherubin,
  Which unlock'd Paradise, and made
One claime for innocence, and disseiz'd sinne,   40
        Whose wombe was a strange heav'n, for there
        God cloath'd himselfe, and grew,
Our zealous thankes wee poure. As her deeds were
Our helpes, so are her prayers; nor can she sue
In vaine, who hath such titles unto you.   45

VI. THE ANGELS

  And since this life our nonage is,
And wee in Wardship to thine Angels be,
  Native in heavens faire Palaces
Where we shall be but denizen'd by thee,
        As th'earth conceiving by the Sunne,   50
        Yeelds faire diversitie,
Yet never knowes which course that light doth run,
So let mee study, that mine actions bee
Worthy their sight, though blinde in how they see.

VII. THE PATRIARCHES

  And let thy Patriarches Desire   55
(Those great Grandfathers of thy Church, which saw

---

    33 *power, love, knowledge:* Donne's sequence alters the usual tradition stemming from Augustine's *De Trinitate*, ascribing Power to the Father, Wisdom to the Son, Love to the Spirit.
    38–39 The Virgin unlocked the gates of paradise which the Cherubim guarded against man (Gen. 3:24).
    40 *disseiz'd:* dispossessed. The Virgin's one claim to innocence is that she dispossessed sin; she makes no further claim of freedom from Original Sin (Gd.).
    55 See Heb. 11:16, "they desire a better country, that is, an heavenly."

    More in the cloud, then wee in fire,
Whom Nature clear'd more, then us grace and law,
      And now in Heaven still pray, that wee
        May use our new helpes right,)   60
Be satisfied, and fructifie in mee;
Let not my minde be blinder by more light
Nor Faith by Reason added, lose her sight.

VIII. THE PROPHETS

    Thy Eagle-sighted Prophets too,
Which were thy Churches Organs, and did sound   65
    That harmony, which made of two
One law, and did unite, but not confound;
      Those heavenly Poëts which did see
        Thy will, and it expresse
In rythmique feet, in common pray for mee,   70
That I by them excuse not my excesse
In seeking secrets, or Poëtiquenesse.

IX. THE APOSTLES

    And thy illustrious Zodiacke
Of twelve Apostles, which ingirt this All,
    From whom whosoever do not take   75
Their light, to darke deep pits, throw downe, and fall,
      As through their prayers, thou'hast let mee know
        That their bookes are divine;
May they pray still, and be heard, that I goe
Th'old broad way in applying; O decline   80
Mee, when my comment would make thy word mine.

57–58 The pillars of cloud and of fire which guided the Israelites out of Egypt symbolize the Law of Nature and the brighter light of Revelation (Law and Gospel); the Patriarchs saw more by the first than we by the second.
  66 The Prophets foretold Christ, who harmonized Old and New Testaments.
  70 Jerome was an originator of the tradition that many parts of the Bible were verses in classical metrical feet.
  76 They throw down others and fall themselves.

X. THE MARTYRS

And since thou so desirously
Did'st long to die, that long before thou could'st,
   And long since thou no more couldst dye,
Thou in thy scatter'd mystique body wouldst   85
      In Abel dye, and ever since
      In thine, let their blood come
To begge for us, a discreet patience
Of death, or of worse life: for Oh, to some
Not to be Martyrs, is a martyrdome.   90

XI. THE CONFESSORS

Therefore with thee triumpheth there
A Virgin Squadron of white Confessors,
   Whose bloods betroth'd, not marryed were;
Tender'd, not taken by those Ravishers:
      They know, and pray, that wee may know,   95
      In every Christian
Hourly tempestuous persecutions grow,
Tentations martyr us alive; A man
Is to himselfe a Dioclesian.

XII. THE VIRGINS

   Thy cold white snowie Nunnery,   100
Which, as thy mother, their high Abbesse, sent
   Their bodies backe againe to thee,
As thou hadst lent them, cleane and innocent,
      Though they have not obtain'd of thee,
      That, or thy Church, or I,   105
Should keep, as they, our first integrity;
Devorce thou sinne in us, or bid it die,
And call chast widowhead Virginitie.

---

86 His violent death caused Abel to be taken as a type of Christ and as the first martyr.

92 Donne links the Confessors and the Virgins, noting that the liturgical color white is used on the feast days of both.

XIII. THE DOCTORS

Thy sacred Academe above
Of Doctors, whose paines have unclasp'd, and taught   110
  Both bookes of life to us (for love
To know thy Scriptures tells us, we are wrought
    In thy other booke) pray for us there
    That what they have misdone
Or mis-said, wee to that may not adhere,   115
Their zeale may be our sinne. Lord let us runne
Meane waies, and call them stars, but not the Sunne.

XIV

And whil'st this universall Quire,
That Church in triumph, this in warfare here,
  Warm'd with one all-partaking fire   120
Of love, that none be lost, which cost thee deare,
    Prayes ceaslesly,'and thou hearken too,
    (Since to be gratious
Our taske is treble, to pray, beare, and doe)
Heare this prayer Lord, O Lord deliver us   125
From trusting in those prayers, though powr'd out thus.

XV

From being anxious, or secure,
Dead clods of sadnesse, or light squibs of mirth,
  From thinking, that great courts immure
All, or no happinesse, or that this earth   130
    Is only for our prison fram'd,
    Or that thou are covetous
To them whom thou lovest, or that they are maim'd
From reaching this worlds sweet, who seek thee thus,
With all their might, Good Lord deliver us.   135

---

111 Gd. cites Donne, *Essays in Divinity*, p. 5, "God hath two Books of life; that in the *Revelation*... which is an eternall Register of his Elect; and the *Bible* .... Our orderly love to the understanding this Book of life, testifies to us that our names are in the other."

118–26 Donne substitutes for the customary concluding petition to all the Saints a prayer which the Saints on earth and in heaven might say jointly.

XVI

    From needing danger, to bee good,
From owing thee yesterdaies teares to day,
    From trusting so much to thy blood,
That in that hope, wee wound our soule away,
        From bribing thee with Almes, to excuse   *140*
        Some sinne more burdenous,
From light affecting, in religion, newes,
From thinking us all soule, neglecting thus
Our mutuall duties, Lord deliver us.

XVII

    From tempting Satan to tempt us,   *145*
By our connivence, or slack companie,
    From measuring ill by vitious,
Neglecting to choake sins spawne, Vanitie,
        From indiscreet humilitie,
        Which might be scandalous,   *150*
And cast reproach on Christianitie,
From being spies, or to spies pervious,
From thirst, or scorne of fame, deliver us.

XVIII

    Deliver us for thy descent
Into the Virgin, whose wombe was a place   *155*
    Of midle kind; and thou being sent
To'ungratious us, staid'st at her full of grace,
        And through thy poore birth, where first thou
        Glorifiedst Povertie,
And yet soone after riches didst allow,   *160*
By accepting Kings gifts in the Epiphanie,
Deliver, and make us, to both waies free.

XIX

    And through that bitter agonie,
Which still is the agonie of pious wits,
    Disputing what distorted thee,   *165*
And interrupted evennesse, with fits,

    And through thy free confession
    Though thereby they were then
Made blind, so that thou might'st from them have gone,
Good Lord deliver us, and teach us when   *170*
Wee may not, and we may blinde unjust men.

XX

    Through thy submitting all, to blowes
Thy face, thy clothes to spoile, thy fame to scorne,
    All waies, which rage, or Justice knowes,
And by which thou could'st shew, that thou wast born,   *175*
        And through thy gallant humblenesse
        Which thou in death did'st shew,
Dying before thy soule they could expresse,
Deliver us from death, by dying so,
To this world, ere this world doe bid us goe.   *180*

XXI

    When senses, which thy souldiers are,
Wee arme against thee, and they fight for sinne,
    When want, sent but to tame, doth warre
And worke despaire a breach to enter in,
        When plenty, Gods image, and seale   *185*
        Makes us Idolatrous,
And love it, not him, whom it should reveale,
When wee are mov'd to seeme religious
Only to vent wit, Lord deliver us.

XXII

    In Churches, when the'infirmitie   *190*
Of him that speakes, diminishes the Word,
    When Magistrates doe mis-apply
To us, as we judge, lay or ghostly sword,

    167–71 Gd. notes that Donne alludes to the contemporary equivocation controversy in the story of Christ's "blinding" by truth the soldiers who came to capture him (John 18).
    174–75 By submitting [yourself to] all the ways of violence and legal action you [Christ] showed that you were truly man.

When plague, which is thine Angell, raignes,
   Or wars, thy Champions, swaie,
When Heresie, thy second deluge, gaines;
In th'houre of death, the'Eve of last judgement day,
Deliver us from the sinister way.

XXIII

   Heare us, O heare us Lord; to thee
A sinner is more musique, when he prayes,
   Then spheares, or Angels praises bee,
In Panegyrique Allelujaes,
      Heare us, for till thou heare us, Lord
      We know not what to say.
Thine eare to'our sighes, teares, thoughts gives voice and word.
O Thou who Satan heard'st in Jobs sicke day,
Heare thy selfe now, for thou in us dost pray.

XXIV

   That wee may change to evennesse
This intermitting aguish Pietie,
   That snatching cramps of wickednesse
And Apoplexies of fast sin, may die;
      That musique of thy promises,
      Not threats in Thunder may
Awaken us to our just offices;
What in thy booke, thou dost, or creatures say,
That we may heare, Lord heare us, when wee pray.

XXV

   That our eares sicknesse wee may cure,
And rectifie those Labyrinths aright,
   That wee by harkning, not procure
Our praise, nor others dispraise so invite,
      That wee get not a slipperinesse
      And senslesly decline,
From hearing bold wits jeast at Kings excesse,
To'admit the like of majestie divine,
That we may locke our eares, Lord open thine.

206 The day Job was afflicted in the body, Job 2: 4–7.

XXVI

That living law, the Magistrate,
Which to give us, and make us physicke, doth
    Our vices often aggravate,
That Preachers taxing sinne, before her growth,
      That Satan, and invenom'd men
        Which well, if we starve, dine,
When they doe most accuse us, may see then
Us to amendment heare them; thee decline;
That we may open our eares, Lord lock thine.

XXVII

That learning, thine Ambassador,
From thine allegeance wee never tempt,
    That beauty, paradises flower
For physicke made, from poyson be exempt,
      That wit, borne apt, high good to doe,
        By dwelling lazily
On Natures nothing, be not nothing too,
That our affections kill us not, nor dye,
Heare us, weake ecchoes, O thou eare, and cry.

XXVIII

Sonne of God heare us, and since thou
By taking our blood, owest it us againe,
    Gaine to thy selfe, or us allow;
And let not both us and thy selfe be slaine;
      O lambe of God, which took'st our sinne
        Which could not stick to thee,
O let it not returne to us againe,
But Patient and Physition being free,
As sinne is nothing, let it no where be.

226–34 Let all who denounce our sins — the magistrate, the preachers, Satan — see that we listen to them for our amendment but that you, God, refuse to hear their denunciations of us.

239–41 Man's wit is *apt* for the contemplation of God, but if it rests upon Nature (unsubstantial because merely derived from God) it will become worthless.

252 *nothing*: evil is defined as the privation of good, and thus of being.

HOLY SONNETS
[1633]

To E. of D. with six holy Sonnets.

See Sir, how as the Suns hot Masculine flame
   Begets strange creatures on Niles durty slime,
   In me, your fatherly yet lusty Ryme
(For, these songs are their fruits) have wrought the same;
But though the ingendring force from whence they came   5
   Bee strong enough, and nature doe admit
   Seaven to be borne at once, I send as yet
But six, they say, the seaventh hath still some maime;
   I choose your judgement, which the same degree
   Doth with her sister, your invention, hold,   10
As fire these drossie Rymes to purifie,
   Or as Elixar, to change them to gold;
You are that Alchimist which alwaies had
Wit, whose one spark could make good things of bad.

To E. of D.... The Earl of Dorset succeeded to the title in 1609, the evident date of composition of the six "holy sonnets" sent to him. Gd. argues convincingly that these were the first six of the twelve Holy Sonnets appearing in this order in 1633 and in several Group I manuscripts. This set of six meditations on the Last Things would ideally need a seventh, on the joys of Heaven, for completeness, but would yet constitute an acceptable offering.

2-7 Pliny describes the Sun's generation of creatures from the mud of the Nile, and the occurrence, in Egypt, of prodigious births of seven or more.

Holy Sonnets. 1-12 from 1633; 13-16 from 1635; 17-19 from Westmoreland.

DIVINE MEDITATIONS

1

As due by many titles I resigne
My selfe to thee, O God, first I was made
By thee, and for thee, and when I was decay'd
Thy blood bought that, the which before was thine,
I am thy sonne, made with thy selfe to shine,   5
Thy servant, whose paines thou hast still repaid,
Thy sheepe, thine Image, and till I betray'd
My selfe, a temple of thy Spirit divine;
Why doth the devill then usurpe in mee?
Why doth he steale nay ravish that's thy right?   10
Except thou rise and for thine owne worke fight,
Oh I shall soone despaire, when I doe see
That thou lov'st mankind well, yet wilt'not chuse me.
And Satan hates mee, yet is loth to lose mee. [II]

2

Oh my blacke Soule! now thou art summoned
By sicknesse, deaths herald, and champion;
Thou art like a pilgrim, which abroad hath done
Treason, and durst not turne to whence hee is fled,
Or like a thiefe, which till deaths doome be read,   5
Wisheth himselfe delivered from prison;
But damn'd and hal'd to execution,
Wisheth that still he might be imprisoned;

Roman numerals at the end of each poem indicate the conventional arrangement (Grierson's), based on the 1635 edition, in which the sonnets here numbered 13–16 were interspersed among the original twelve. In several manuscripts, these sixteen poems bear the title *Divine Meditations*. Gd. argues that the first six form a sequence on the Last Things; the second six (probably written a little later but certainly before 1614) a sequence on the love of God; the four added in the 1635 edition form a group on sin and penitence. The three from W. are unrelated, nonmeditative poems.

1. 5 See Matt. 13:43, "Then shall the righteous shine forth as the sun in the kingdom of their Father."

Yet grace, if thou repent, thou canst not lacke;
But who shall give thee that grace to beginne?   10
Oh make thy selfe with holy mourning blacke,
And red with blushing, as thou art with sinne;
Or wash thee in Christs blood, which hath this might
That being red, it dyes red soules to white. [IV]

3

This is my playes last scene, here heavens appoint
My pilgrimages last mile; and my race
Idly, yet quickly runne, hath this last pace,
My spans last inch, my minutes last point,
And gluttonous death, will instantly unjoynt   5
My body, and soule, and I shall sleepe a space,
But my'ever-waking part shall see that face,
Whose feare already shakes my every joynt:
Then, as my soule, to'heaven her first seate, takes flight,
And earth borne body, in the earth shall dwell,   10
So, fall my sinnes, that all may have their right,
To where they'are bred, and would presse me, to hell.
Impute me righteous, thus purg'd of evill,
For thus I leave the world, the flesh, the devill. [VI]

4

At the round earths imagin'd corners, blow
Your trumpets, Angells, and arise, arise
From death, you numberlesse infinities
Of soules, and to your scattred bodies goe,
All whom the flood did, and fire shall o'erthrow,   5
All whom warre, dearth, age, agues, tyrannies,

---

3. 13 The soul which bears the imputed guilt of Adam can only be saved by being imputed righteous through Christ's merits.

4. 1 See Rev. 7:1, "I saw four angels standing on the four corners of the earth."

2–4 Donne suggests here the death or sleep of the soul until the Last Judgment, though in the *Anniversaries* and in the Sermons he supposes the soul's immediate transmission to heaven.

6. *dearth*: despite manuscript authority for *death*, *dearth* (famine) seems the better reading in this list of specific causes of death—which appears as a general term in ll. 3, 8.

Despaire, law, chance, hath slaine, and you whose eyes,
Shall behold God, and never tast deaths woe.
But let them sleepe, Lord, and mee mourne a space,
For, if above all these, my sinnes abound, 10
'Tis late to aske abundance of thy grace,
When wee are there; here on this lowly ground,
Teach mee how to repent; for that's as good
As if thou'hadst seal'd my pardon, with thy blood. [VII]

5

If poysonous mineralls, and if that tree,
Whose fruit threw death on else immortall us,
If lecherous goats, if serpents envious
Cannot be damn'd; Alas; why should I bee?
Why should intent or reason, borne in mee, 5
Make sinnes, else equall, in mee, more heinous?
And mercy being easie, and glorious
To God, in his sterne wrath, why threatens hee?
But who am I, that dare dispute with thee?
O God, Oh! of thine onely worthy blood, 10
And my teares, make a heavenly Lethean flood,
And drowne in it my sinnes blacke memorie;
That thou remember them, some claime as debt,
I thinke it mercy, if thou wilt forget. [IX]

6

Death be not proud, though some have called thee
Mighty and dreadfull, for, thou art not soe,
For, those, whom thou think'st, thou dost overthrow,
Die not, poore death, nor yet canst thou kill mee;
From rest and sleepe, which but thy pictures bee, 5
Much pleasure, then from thee, much more must flow,

13-14 *Repentance* is the sign, the evidence of election and pardon.
5. 14 See Jer. 31:34.

And soonest our best men with thee doe goe,
Rest of their bones, and soules deliverie.
Thou art slave to Fate, chance, kings, and desperate men,
And dost with poyson, warre, and sicknesse dwell.　　　　10
And poppie, or charmes can make us sleepe as well,
And better then thy stroake; why swell'st thou then?
One short sleepe past, we wake eternally,
And death shall be no more, Death thou shalt die. [X]

7

Spit in my face you Jewes, and pierce my side,
Buffet, and scoffe, scourge, and crucifie mee,
For I have sinn'd, and sinn'd, and onely hee,
Who could do no iniquitie, hath dyed:
But by my death can not be satisfied　　　　5
My sinnes, which passe the Jewes impiety:
They kill'd once an inglorious man, but I
Crucifie him daily, being now glorified.
Oh let mee then, his strange love still admire:
Kings pardon, but he bore our punishment.　　　　10
And *Jacob* came cloth'd in vile harsh attire
But to supplant, and with gainfull intent:
God cloth'd himselfe in vile mans flesh, that so
Hee might be weake enough to suffer woe. [XI]

8

Why are wee by all creatures waited on?
Why doe the prodigall elements supply
Life and food to mee, being more pure then I,
Simple, and further from corruption?
Why brook'st thou, ignorant horse, subjection?　　　　5
Why dost thou bull, and bore so seelily

---

7. 8 See Heb. 6:6, "They crucify to themselves the Son of God afresh, and put him to an open shame."

11–12 Jacob disguised himself with animal hair to obtain the blessing which the blind Isaac had designated for the hairy Esau, Gen. 27:36.

8. 4 The elements, being unmixed, are less subject to corruption than man, but not wholly incorruptible, as Spirits (Gd.).

Dissemble weaknesse, and by'one mans stroke die,
Whose whole kinde, you might swallow and feed upon?
Weaker I am, woe is mee, and worse then you,
You have not sinn'd, nor need be timorous.   10
But wonder at a greater wonder, for to us
Created nature doth these things subdue,
But their Creator, whom sin, nor nature tyed,
For us, his Creatures, and his foes, hath dyed. [XII]

9

What if this present were the worlds last night?
Marke in my heart, O Soule, where thou dost dwell,
The picture of Christ crucified, and tell
Whether that countenance can thee affright,
Teares in his eyes quench the amasing light,   5
Blood fills his frownes, which from his pierc'd head fell,
And can that tongue adjudge thee unto hell,
Which pray'd forgivenesse for his foes fierce spight?
No, no; but as in my idolatrie
I said to all my profane mistresses,   10
Beauty, of pitty, foulnesse onely is
A signe of rigour: so I say to thee,
To wicked spirits are horrid shapes assign'd,
This beauteous forme assures a pitious minde. [XIII]

10

Batter my heart, three person'd God; for, you
As yet but knocke, breathe, shine, and seeke to mend;
That I may rise, and stand, o'erthrow mee,'and bend
Your force, to breake, blowe, burn and make me new.
I, like an usurpt towne, to'another due,   5
Labour to'admit you, but Oh, to no end,
Reason your viceroy in mee, mee should defend,
But is captiv'd, and proves weake or untrue,

---

9. 14 Christ's beautiful form is a Platonic guarantee of a noble and generous mind.
10. This address to the Trinity turns upon several series of three — trinities of actions and of petitions.

Yet dearely' I love you,' and would be loved faine,
But am betroth'd unto your enemie,   10
Divorce mee,'untie, or breake that knot againe,
Take mee to you, imprison mee, for I
Except you'enthrall mee, never shall be free,
Nor ever chast, except you ravish mee. [XIV]

11

Wilt thou love God, as he thee! then digest,
My Soule, this wholsome meditation,
How God the Spirit, by Angels waited on
In heaven, doth make his Temple in thy brest,
The Father having begot a Sonne most blest,   5
And still begetting, (for he ne'r begonne)
Hath deign'd to chuse thee by adoption,
Coheire to'his glory,'and Sabbaths endlesse rest;
And as a robb'd man, which by search doth finde
His stolne stuffe sold, must lose or buy'it againe: 10
The Sonne of glory came downe, and was slaine,
Us whom he'had made, and Satan stolne, to unbinde.
'Twas much, that man was made like God before,
But, that God should be made like man, much more. [XV]

12

Father, part of his double interest
Unto thy kingdome, thy Sonne gives to mee,
His joynture in the knottie Trinitie,
Hee keepes, and gives to me his deaths conquest.
This Lambe, whose death, with life the world hath blest,   5
Was from the worlds beginning slaine, and he

---

11. 4 See I Cor. 6:19, "Know ye not that your body is the temple of the Holy Ghost."
  6 This action is without end, as without beginning.
  7–8 See Rom. 8:15–17, "ye have received the Spirit of adoption.... we are the children of God... heirs of God, and joint-heirs ["co-heires," *Rheims*] with Christ...."
12. 1 *double interest:* two-fold claim.
  3 *joynture:* holding of an estate by two or more people in joint tenancy.
  6 Rev. 13:8, "the Lamb slain from the foundation of the world" ["from the beginning," *Rheims, Geneva*].

Hath made two Wills, which with the Legacie
Of his and thy kingdome, doe thy Sonnes invest,
Yet such are those laws, that men argue yet
Whether a man those statutes can fulfill;   10
None doth, but all-healing grace and Spirit,
Revive againe what law and letter kill.
Thy lawes abridgement, and thy last command
Is all but love; Oh let that last Will stand! [XVI]

[1635]

13

Thou hast made me, And shall thy worke decay?
Repaire me now, for now mine end doth haste,
I runne to death, and death meets me as fast,
And all my pleasures are like yesterday,
I dare not move my dimme eyes any way,   5
Despaire behind, and death before doth cast
Such terrour, and my feebled flesh doth waste
By sinne in it, which it t'wards hell doth weigh;
Onely thou art above, and when towards thee
By thy leave I can looke, I rise againe;   10
But our old subtle foe so tempteth me,
That not one houre my selfe I can sustaine,
Thy grace may wing me to prevent his art
And thou like Adamant draw mine iron heart. [I]

---

7 *two Wills*: the Old and New Testaments.

11–12 See John 1:17, "For the law was given by Moses, but grace and truth came by Jesus Christ."

13 *thy last command*: See John 13:34, "A new commandment I give unto you, That ye love one another."

Holy Sonnets (1635). We do not follow Gd. in reversing the positions of the second and third sonnets of this group (*15* and *16*). As a sequence on sin and repentance, these poems present in the 1635 order of appearance (interspersed among the other sonnets) a progression from tears and grief (*13*, *14*, most of *15*) to an affirmation of "fiery zeale" (*15*, ll. 10–14), to a concern with false and true varieties of both tears and zeal (*16*, ll. 9–12).

13. 13 *prevent:* frustrate.

14

O might those sighes and teares returne againe
Into my breast and eyes, which I have spent,
That I might in this holy discontent
Mourne with some fruit, as I have mourn'd in vaine;
In mine Idolatry what showres of raine   5
Mine eyes did waste? what griefs my heart did rent?
That sufferance was my sinne I now repent,
'Cause I did suffer I must suffer paine.
Th'hydroptique drunkard, and night-scouting thiefe,
The itchy Lecher, and selfe tickling proud   10
Have the remembrance of past joyes, for reliefe
Of comming ills. To (poore) me is allow'd
No ease; for, long, yet vehement griefe hath beene
Th'effect and cause, the punishment and sinne. [III]

15

I am a little world made cunningly
Of Elements, and an Angelike spright,
But black sinne hath betraid to endlesse night
My worlds both parts, and (oh) both parts must die.
You which beyond that heaven which was most high   5
Have found new sphears, and of new lands can write,
Powre new seas in mine eyes, that so I might
Drowne my world with my weeping earnestly,
Or wash it if it must be drown'd no more:
But oh it must be burnt, alas the fire   10

---

14. 7 Gr. and Gd. adopt the reading of some manuscripts, "That sufferance was my sinne, now I repent," which contrasts the tears of the speaker's lovesick days with those of his true repentance; we retain the 1635 reading which suggests that he mourns specifically for the sin of false suffering for love, a meaning that seems reinforced by ll. 8, 13-14.

9 *hydroptique:* the insatiable thirst of the dropsical.

15. 6 *new sphears:* a reference either to the newly discovered immensity of the universe or to the efforts of the Ptolemaic astronomers to save the appearances by adding new spheres and new motions; *new lands:* a reference either to the new lands of the moon seen through Galileo's telescope, or to the various new lands terrestrial explorers found.

9 See the promise to Noah of no more floods (Gen. 9:9-17), which supported the belief in the final destruction of the world by fire.

Of lust and envie have burnt it heretofore,
And made it fouler; Let their flames retire,
And burne me ô Lord, with a fiery zeale
Of thee and thy house, which doth in eating heale. [V]

16

If faithfull soules be alike glorifi'd
As Angels, then my fathers soule doth see,
And adds this even to full felicitie,
That valiantly I hels wide mouth o'rstride:
But if our mindes to these soules be descry'd   5
By circumstances, and by signes that be
Apparent in us, not immediately,
How shall my mindes white truth by them be try'd?
They see idolatrous lovers weepe and mourne,
And vile blasphemous Conjurers to call   10
On Jesus name, and Pharisaicall
Dissemblers feigne devotion. Then turne
O pensive soule, to God, for he knowes best
Thy true griefe, for he put it in my breast. [VIII]

[WESTMORELAND MS]

17

Since she whome I lovd, hath payd her last debt
To Nature, and to hers, and my good is dead,

---

13 *fiery zeale:* See Ps. 69:9, "the zeal of thine house hath eaten me up."

16. If blest souls know by immediate intuition as angels do, then my father knows of my repentance; if however they still must reason from sense impressions, then he will be misled by the similarity between my grief and zeal and other varieties of these emotions.

Westmoreland MS. These sonnets were probably written after Donne's ordination, when he was not eager to be known as a poet, and thus they had limited circulation.

17. 1 *she whome I lovd:* Donne's wife died 15 August 1617, at age thirty-three, shortly after the birth of her twelfth child.

2 *and to hers, and my good is dead:* The meaning is ambiguous. She is now dead to all good, her own and the speaker's, but also, her death is in some sense a good to herself (being in Heaven) and to him (being severed from earthly loves).

And her Soule early into heaven ravished,
Wholy in heavenly things my mind is sett.
Here the admyring her my mind did whett   5
To seeke thee God; so streames do shew the head,
But though I have found thee, and thou my thirst hast fed,
A holy thirsty dropsy melts mee yett.
But why should I begg more Love, when as thou
Dost woe my soule for hers; offring all thine: 10
And dost not only feare least I allow
My Love to Saints and Angels, things divine,
But in thy tender jealosy dost doubt
Least the World, fleshe, yea Devill putt thee out. [XVII]

18

Show me deare Christ, thy spouse, so bright and cleare.
What, is it she, which on the other shore
Goes richly painted? or which rob'd and tore
Laments and mournes in Germany and here?
Sleepes she a thousand, then peepes up one yeare?   5
Is she selfe truth and errs? now new, now outwore?
Doth she, 'and did she, and shall she evermore
On one, on seaven, or on no hill appeare?
Dwells she with us, or like adventuring knights
First travaile we to seeke and then make Love?   10
Betray kind husband thy spouse to our sights,
And let myne amorous soule court thy mild Dove,

---

10 *woe:* Gr. and Gd. alter to "wooe," but the manuscript's spelling points up a probable pun: God now woos his soul instead of hers (*for hers*) offering all his own love; but he also *woes* (causes woe to) the soul by taking her in death.

18. 1 See Rev. 19:7–8, "The marriage of the Lamb is come, and his wife hath made herself ready. And to her was granted that she should be arrayed in fine linen, clean and white" ["pure fine linnen and shining," *Geneva*].

2–4 Gd. notes that Rome is a figure of the Whore of Babylon, and Protestantism a figure of the mourning daughter of Zion, the desolate Jerusalem of Lamentations, neither of them the promised Bride. The following lines measure the foolish counterclaims of the churches against that archetypal image of the Bride.

8 The *one hill* is Mount Moriah where Solomon built the Temple, the *seaven* alludes to the Roman Church, *no hill* is the Genevan Church.

12 *thy mild Dove:* See Song of Sol. 5:2, "Open to me, my sister, my love, my dove, my undefiled."

Who is most trew, and pleasing to thee, then
When she 'is embrac'd and open to most men. [XVIII]

19

Oh, to vex me, contraryes meete in one:
Inconstancy unnaturally hath begott
A constant habit; that when I would not
I change in vowes, and in devotione.
As humorous is my contritione 5
As my prophane love, and as soone forgott:
As ridlingly distemperd, cold and hott,
As praying, as mute; as infinite, as none.
I durst not view heaven yesterday; and to day
In prayers, and flattering speaches I court God: 10
To morrow I quake with true feare of his rod.
So my devout fitts come and go away
Like a fantastique Ague: save that here
Those are my best dayes, when I shake with feare. [XIX]

OCCASIONAL POEMS AND HYMNS

The Crosse

Since Christ embrac'd the Crosse it selfe, dare I
His image, th'image of his Crosse deny?
Would I have profit by the sacrifice,
And dare the chosen Altar to despise?
It bore all other sinnes, but is it fit   5
That it should beare the sinne of scorning it?
Who from the picture would avert his eye,
How would he flye his paines, who there did dye?
From mee, no Pulpit, nor misgrounded law,
Nor scandall taken, shall this Crosse withdraw,   10
It shall not, for it cannot; for, the losse
Of this Crosse, were to mee another Crosse.
Better were worse, for, no affliction,
No Crosse is so extreme, as to have none.
Who can blot out the Crosse, which th'instrument   15
Of God, dew'd on mee in the Sacrament?
Who can deny mee power, and liberty
To stretch mine armes, and mine owne Crosse to be?
Swimme, and at every stroake, thou art thy Crosse,
The Mast and yard make one, where seas do tosse.   20
Looke downe, thou spiest out Crosses in small things;
Looke up, thou seest birds rais'd on crossed wings;
All the Globes frame, and spheares, is nothing else
But the Meridians crossing Parallels.

The Crosse. The theme relates to the medieval practice of finding reflections of theological symbols (the Trinity, the Cross) everywhere, and also to the contemporary Puritan aversion to the cross as a papist emblem.

Materiall Crosses then, good physicke bee,   25
And yet spirituall have chiefe dignity.
 These for extracted chimique medicine serve,
And cure much better, and as well preserve;
Then are you your own physicke, or need none,
When Still'd, or purg'd by tribulation.   30
For when that Crosse ungrudg'd, unto you stickes,
Then are you to your selfe, a Crucifixe.
As perchance, Carvers do not faces make,
But that away, which hid them there, do take.
Let Crosses, soe, take what hid Christ in thee,   35
And be his image, or not his, but hee.
But, as oft Alchimists doe coyners prove,
So may a selfe-dispising, get selfe-love.
And then as worst surfets, of best meates bee,
Soe is pride, issued from humility,   40
For, 'tis no child, but monster; therefore Crosse
Your joy in crosses, else, 'tis double losse,
And crosse thy senses, else, both they, and thou
Must perish soone, and to destruction bowe.
For if the'eye seeke good objects, and will take   45
No crosse from bad, wee cannot scape a snake.
So with harsh, hard, sowre, stinking, crosse the rest,
Make them indifferent; call nothing best.
But most the eye needs crossing, that can rome,
And move; To th'others th'objects must come home.   50
And crosse thy heart: for that in man alone
Points downewards, and hath palpitation.
Crosse those dejections, when it downeward tends,
And when it to forbidden heights pretends.
And as the braine through bony walls doth vent   55
By sutures, which a Crosses forme present,
So when thy braine workes, ere thou utter it,

33-34 refers to the idea that the form is *in* the material, so that the sculptor merely reveals it by chipping away the extraneous matter.
52 Gr. cites Donne, *Essays in Divinity*, pp. 59-60, "O Man... only thy heart of all others, points downwards, and onely trembles."
55-58 As the brain "vents" through sutures which trace the form of a cross upon the skull, let the product of the brain (wit) be crossed or corrected.

Crosse and correct concupiscence of witt.
Be covetous of Crosses, let none fall.
Crosse no man else, but crosse thy selfe in all. 60
Then doth the Crosse of Christ worke fruitfully
Within our hearts, when wee love harmlesly
That Crosses pictures much, and with more care
That Crosses children, which our Crosses are.

Upon the Annunciation and Passion falling upon one day. 1608

Tamely fraile body'abstaine to day; to day
My soule eates twice, Christ hither and away.
She sees him man, so like God made in this,
That of them both a circle embleme is,
Whose first and last concurre; this doubtfull day 5
Of feast or fast, Christ came, and went away;
Shee sees him nothing twice at once, who'is all;
Shee sees a Cedar plant it selfe, and fall,
Her Maker put to making, and the head
Of life, at once, not yet alive, yet dead; 10
She sees at once the virgin mother stay
Reclus'd at home, Publique at Golgotha.
Sad and rejoyc'd shee's seen at once, and seen
At almost fiftie, and at scarce fifteene.
At once a Sonne is promis'd her, and gone, 15
Gabriell gives Christ to her, He her to John;
Not fully a mother, Shee's in Orbitie,
At once receiver and the legacie;
All this, and all betweene, this day hath showne,
Th'Abridgement of Christs story, which makes one 20
(As in plaine Maps, the furthest West is East)

Upon the Annunciation and Passion. Manuscripts date poem 25 March 1608.
4 Christ's human life, ending on the same day it began, forms a circle, traditionally a symbol of God.
8 *Cedar:* type of the Godhead (Gd.).
17 *Orbitie:* "bereavement, especially of children" (*OED*).

Of the 'Angels *Ave*,' and *Consummatum est*.
How well the Church, Gods Court of faculties
Deales, in some times, and seldome joyning these;
As by the selfe-fix'd Pole wee never doe   25
Direct our course, but the next starre thereto,
Which showes where the'other is, and which we say
(Because it strayes not farre) doth never stray;
So God by his Church, neerest to him, wee know,
And stand firme, if wee by her motion goe;   30
His Spirit, as his fiery Pillar doth
Leade, and his Church, as cloud; to one end both:
This Church, by letting these daies joyne, hath shown
Death and conception in mankinde is one.
Or'twas in him the same humility,   35
That he would be a man, and leave to be:
Or as creation he hath made, as God,
With the last judgement, but one period,
His imitating Spouse would joyne in one
Manhoods extremes: He shall come, he is gone: 40
Or as though one blood drop, which thence did fall,
Accepted, would have serv'd, he yet shed all;
So though the least of his paines, deeds, or words,
Would busie a life, she all this day affords;
This treasure then, in grosse, my Soule uplay,   45
And in my life retaile it every day.

Goodfriday, 1613.

Riding Westward

Let mans Soule be a Spheare, and then, in this,
The intelligence that moves, devotion is,
And as the other Spheares, by being growne
Subject to forraigne motions, lose their owne,

31–32 The pillars of fire and of cloud which guided the Israelites out of Egypt (Exod. 13:21) symbolize God's Spirit and the Church respectively guiding mankind.

Goodfriday, 1613. Riding Westward. 1–10 The *naturall forme* of the sphere is the *intelligence* (or Angel) which moves the sphere on its natural course from

And being by others hurried every day, 5
Scarce in a yeare their naturall forme obey:
Pleasure or businesse, so, our Soules admit
For their first mover, and are whirld by it.
Hence is't, that I am carryed towards the West
This day, when my Soules forme bends toward the East. 10
There I should see a Sunne, by rising set,
And by that setting endlesse day beget;
But that Christ on this Crosse, did rise and fall,
Sinne had eternally benighted all.
Yet dare I'almost be glad, I do not see 15
That spectacle of too much weight for mee.
Who sees Gods face, that is selfe life, must dye;
What a death were it then to see God dye?
It made his owne Lieutenant Nature shrinke,
It made his footstoole crack, and the Sunne winke. 20
Could I behold those hands which span the Poles,
And tune all spheares at once peirc'd with those holes?
Could I behold that endlesse height which is
Zenith to us, and our Antipodes,
Humbled below us? or that blood which is 25
The seat of all our Soules, if not of his,
Made durt of dust, or that flesh which was worne
By God, for his apparell, rag'd, and torne?
If on these things I durst not looke, durst I
Upon his miserable mother cast mine eye, 30
Who was Gods partner here, and furnish'd thus
Halfe of that Sacrifice, which ransom'd us?

West to East, but the sphere was also subject to a contrary motion from the *primum mobile*; the natural form of man's soul is *devotion* (which on Good Friday should carry it to the East where Christ was crucified), but it accepts for its primum mobile *Pleasure or businesse*, which hurls it in a contrary direction.

17 See Exod. 33:20, "Thou canst not see my face: for there shall no man see me, and live."

20 *his footstoole:* See Isa. 66:1, "the earth is my footstool."

22 *tune all spheares:* God sets the motion of the spheres so that each will sound its characteristic note in the Platonic harmony of the spheres; some manuscripts read *turne all spheares*, emphasizing God's role as First Mover, a concept also included in *tune*.

26-27 Christ's blood, being made, like man, of the dust of the earth (Gen. 2:7), is further degraded by the crucifixion.

Though these things, as I ride, be from mine eye,
They'are present yet unto my memory,
For that looks towards them; and thou look'st towards mee, 35
O Saviour, as thou hang'st upon the tree;
I turne my backe to thee, but to receive
Corrections, till thy mercies bid thee leave.
O thinke mee worth thine anger, punish mee,
Burne off my rusts, and my deformity, 40
Restore thine Image, so much, by thy grace,
That thou may'st know mee, and I'll turne my face.

A Hymne to Christ, at the Authors last going into Germany

In what torne ship soever I embarke,
That ship shall be my embleme of thy Arke;
What sea soever swallow mee, that flood
Shall be to mee an embleme of thy blood;
Though thou with clouds of anger do disguise 5
Thy face; yet through that maske I know those eyes,
   Which, though they turne away sometimes,
      They never will despise.

I sacrifice this Iland unto thee,
And all whom I lov'd there, and who lov'd mee; 10
When I have put our seas twixt them and mee,
Put thou thy sea betwixt my sinnes and thee.
As the trees sap doth seeke the root below

A Hymne to Christ. Donne went to Germany in May, 1619, accompanying a diplomatic mission, and returned in January, 1620. See Donne's *Sermon of Valediction at my Going into Germany*, at Lincolns-Inn (18 April 1619): "and Christ Jesus remember us all in his Kingdom, to which, *though we must sail through a sea, yet it is the sea of his blood,* where no soul suffers shipwrack; though we must be blown with strange winds, with sighs and groans for our sins, yet it is the Spirit of God that blows all this wind, and shall blow away all contrary winds of diffidence or distrust in God's mercy."

In winter, in my winter now I goe,
   Where none but thee, th'Eternall root
     Of true Love I may know.

Nor thou nor thy religion dost controule,
The amorousnesse of an harmonious Soule,
But thou wouldst have that love thy selfe: As thou
Art jealous, Lord, so I am jealous now,
Thou lov'st not, till from loving more, thou free
My soule: Who ever gives, takes libertie:
   O, if thou car'st not whom I love
     Alas, thou lov'st not mee.

Seale then this bill of my Divorce to All,
On whom those fainter beames of love did fall;
Marry those loves, which in youth scattered bee
On Fame, Wit, Hopes (false mistresses) to thee.
Churches are best for Prayer, that have least light:
To see God only, I goe out of sight:
   And to scape stormy dayes, I chuse
     An Everlasting night.

A Hymne to God the Father

I

Wilt thou forgive that sinne where I begunne,
   Which was my sin, though it were done before?
Wilt thou forgive that sinne; through which I runne,
   And do run still: though still I do deplore?
     When thou hast done, thou hast not done,
       For, I have more.

A Hymne to God the Father. Walton dates it during Donne's grave illness of 1623.

II

Wilt thou forgive that sinne which I have wonne
   Others to sinne? and, made my sinne their doore?
Wilt thou forgive that sinne which I did shunne
   A yeare, or two: but wallowed in, a score?
     When thou hast done, thou hast not done,
        For I have more.

III

I have a sinne of feare, that when I have spunne
   My last thred, I shall perish on the shore;
But sweare by thy selfe, that at my death thy sonne
   Shall shine as he shines now, and heretofore;
     And, having done that, Thou haste done,
        I feare no more.

Hymne to God my God, in my sicknesse

Since I am comming to that Holy roome,
   Where, with thy Quire of Saints for evermore,
I shall be made thy Musique; As I come
   I tune the Instrument here at the dore,
   And what I must doe then, thinke now before.

Whilst my Physitians by their love are growne
   Cosmographers, and I their Mapp, who lie

Hymne to God my God, in my sicknesse (1635). Walton dates the poem 23 March 1630/31, eight days before Donne's death; another contemporary, Sir Julius Caesar, dates it December 1623, on the occasion of a very severe illness. Gr. cites Donne's Sermon on Ps. 6:8–10: "In a flat Map, there goes no more, to make West East, though they be distant in an extremity, but to paste that flat Map upon a round body, and then West and East are all one. In a flat soule, in a dejected conscience, in a troubled spirit, there goes no more to the making of that trouble, peace, then to apply that trouble to the body of the Merits, to the body of the Gospel of Christ Jesus.... The name of Christ is *Oriens*, The East."

Flat on this bed, that by them may be showne
   That this is my South-west discoverie
   Per fretum febris, by these streights to die,   *10*

I joy, that in these straits, I see my West;
   For, though theire currants yeeld returne to none,
What shall my West hurt me? As West and East
   In all flatt Maps (and I am one) are one,
   So death doth touch the Resurrection.   *15*

Is the Pacifique Sea my home? Or are
   The Easterne riches? Is *Jerusalem*?
Anyan, and *Magellan*, and *Gibraltare*,
   All streights, and none but streights, are wayes to them,
   Whether where *Japhet* dwelt, or *Cham*, or *Sem*.   *20*

We thinke that *Paradise* and *Calvarie*,
   Christs Crosse, and *Adams* tree, stood in one place;
Looke Lord, and finde both *Adams* met in me;
   As the first *Adams* sweat surrounds my face,
   May the last *Adams* blood my soule embrace.   *25*

So, in his purple wrapp'd receive mee Lord,
   By these his thornes give me his other Crowne;
And as to others soules I preach'd thy word,
   Be this my Text, my Sermon to mine owne,
   Therfore that he may raise the Lord throws down.   *30*

9–10 The *Physitians*, turned geographers, chart the speaker's symptoms and make a *South-west discoverie*, the south being the hot quarter, and the west that of the sun's setting (death); he is to die by the "heat" and "strait" (*fretum*) of fever.

16–17 These goals of the explorer — the Peaceful Sea, the Eastern Riches, the City of Peace (Jerusalem) — are also common speculative locations for the earthly paradise, the type of Heaven and hence the goal of the dying man.

18–20 *Anyan*: shown in contemporary maps as dividing America from Eastern Asia, a *streight* leading to the East. *Japhet, Cham* (Ham) and *Sem* (Shem): Noah's sons, among whom he divided the world, giving them, respectively, Europe, Africa, and Asia. *Streights* (narrow passageways, difficulties) are the way to all these continents.

21–22 A medieval commonplace held that Paradise and Calvary were in the same region, though not in the identical place.

24–25 For Christ as second Adam, see Rom. 5:12–21.

George Herbert

The religious verse of George Herbert (1593-1633) owes something to the example of John Donne, and is itself a most important influence upon the verse of Henry Vaughan and Richard Crashaw. Since Herbert's mother, the witty and gracious Magdalen Herbert, was also Donne's dear friend and patroness, she provided the two poets with some opportunities for personal contact. Though Herbert's life was less turbulent than Donne's, in certain ways their careers were parallel: both spent several agitated years trying to determine their proper profession or "calling," both served as ministers in the Church of England, and the major poetry of both received posthumous publication in the same year, 1633. However, unlike Donne, Herbert destroyed his secular verse in English (some occasional poems in Latin survive), so that his poetic reputation rests wholly upon his large and impressive book of religious verse, *The Temple*.

Born of an eminent Anglican family, Herbert was given an excellent formal education at Westminster School and Trinity College, Cambridge, where he proceeded B.A. and M.A. In 1616 he entered upon a major fellowship at Trinity, which involved tutoring, giving some university lectures, and studying divinity with a view to taking orders. But in 1620 he sought and obtained the position of Public Orator (the official spokesman and correspondent for the University), thereby taking the first steps toward a career at court, and he further prepared for such a role by being elected Member of Parliament from Montgomery in 1624. However, the changes in personnel and government policy attending upon the death of King James I in 1625 dashed his hopes of court preferment and cast Herbert into great uncertainties. He did not finally resolve upon an ecclesiastical life until 1630, when he accepted the offer of a living at the small, tranquil country parish at Bemerton in Wiltshire, thereby cutting himself off categorically from the sphere of worldly power and acclaim. Herbert preached to and served a few cottagers, whereas Donne addressed monarchs and statesmen, and none of Herbert's sermons survive. His small book on the duties of his new life, *A Priest to the Temple, or, The Country Parson*, testifies to the earnestness and joy, but also to the aristocratic uneasiness, with which he embraced his role. In chronic bad health, Herbert spent only three years at Bemerton —performing pastoral duties, writing and revising his poems, and listening to and playing music—before his untimely death in 1633. He bequeathed the manuscript of the *The Temple* to his friend Nicholas Ferrar, head of the Anglican quasi-monastic community at Little Gidding, with instructions to publish it if he thought it would "turn to the advantage of any dejected poor soul," and otherwise to burn it.

The poems of *The Church*, the collection of lyrics which comprises the major part of *The Temple*, do not have the emotional range and force of Donne's religious poems, but they nevertheless reveal a complex and profound religious sensibility. Those readers who see Herbert as the "sweet singer of Bemerton," the poet of a simple, untroubled, naive devotion to God, find apparent support in such limpid lyrics as the second part of "Easter" ("I gott mee flowrs to straw thy way"), or "Life" ("I made a posy, while the day ranne by"); yet such poems also have the tightness of construction, the exactness of diction, and the perfect control of tone that attend upon the highest artistry. The opposite approach to Herbert, as a Donne *manqué*, is founded upon poems such as "The Collar," that witty, colloquial, and audacious declaration of rebellion against the service of God which nevertheless ends (to the dismay of some readers) with the speaker's sudden, apparently weakminded submission. But the poem is not in the Donnean manner. The past tense makes clear from the start that the speaker is telling of an earlier folly, now resolved. And the Lord's call, "*Child!*," which the speaker thinks he hears, offers the precise resolution of his difficulty, for it reminds him of Paul's assurance (Gal. 4:3–7) that he is not in bondage as a slave to God, but enjoys the status of child and son, heir to the promises and the Kingdom.

It is important, then, to approach Herbert on his own terms. The primary religious concern explored in *The Church* is not (as with Donne) the question of salvation: Herbert's speaker assumes that the grace which Christ's sacrifice won has in fact been applied to him under the New Covenant. Rather, his chief concern is the maintenance and development of a personal, intimate relationship with Christ, a relationship grounded in social love. Louis Martz traces this attitude and the tone it creates to the Salesian tradition of meditation, in which the meditator sought to imitate the discourse of friend with friend. The very considerable tension and anxiety in *The Church* spring from the speaker's distress over his inability to achieve stability, ease, and steady progress in his relationship with God, over his lack of "fruition" in God's service, and over the vacillations in his own nature, purpose, and temperament. In this sense Herbert's description of the work is apt: "a picture of the many spiritual Conflicts that have past betwixt God and my Soul."

But yet Herbert's speaker does not present himself as a naked soul alone before his God, but as man in the Church, relating himself to God and Christ through liturgy, architecture and art, and the entire historical experience of the people of God. Nor does the speaker present his religious experience as idiosyncratic or unique: rather, he is a species of Christian Everyman, finding in himself a restatement of the common conflicts and experiences of the Christian life. In attempting a mimesis of this, Herbert assumes a public stance and an objectivity quite foreign to Donne.

The speaker of *The Church* is also concerned with developing and expressing a poetic theory that will explain and justify his poetic manner. One facet of this poetics is worked out in relation to Petrarchan sonneteering conventions and notably Sidney's *Astrophel and Stella*, with Christ substituted for the worthy and aloof lady, and the speaker taking the role of the distressed but aspiring lover. *The Church* as a whole rings changes upon these transmutations, and some poems point them up explicitly. "Dulnes" proclaims that Christ's bloody death makes him deserve, better than any lady, the traditional praise of being pure red and white in beauty, and that, as True or Essential Beauty, Christ especially deserves the tribute of "window-songs" (serenades) which lovers customarily address to lesser beauties. Like a Petrarchan lover, the speaker begs only a small favor: that his wits be cleared so that he may look toward Christ (since not even angels are fit to love him). In "A parody" the poet takes a secular love song (widely attributed to Donne but almost certainly by the Earl of Pembroke) and transmutes the first portion of it into a plaint to Christ. Christ is depicted as the unpredictable beloved apparently withdrawing favors and thus making the speaker suffer, but the speaker soon comes to realize that, ironically, his sin is the cause of all the vacillations, that Christ is always Love, and that unlike the cruel Petrarchan lady, "while I greive,/Thou com'st and dost releive."

The Jordan poems place Herbert among the many contemporary English and continental poets who sought to baptize the muse and enlist her in the service of God. The river Jordan is implicitly opposed to Helicon; it is the river the Israelites crossed over to enter into the Promised Land, and the river in which Christ was baptized as an earnest of the Christian's salvation. "Jordan [I]" complains that fictional subjects and conventional ornaments such as pastoral tags, allegories, and "riddling" language have wrongfully usurped the entire domain of poetry, and asserts the speaker's intention to reclaim part of this domain—to treat true (religious) subjects and to treat them "plainely." "Jordan [II]" examines more precisely the kind of plainness which the true subject requires. The speaker's initial impulse has been to use the customary poetic arts, "Curling with metaphors a plaine intention,/Decking the sence, as if it were to sell," but he discovers that this is a kind of pride, and that this weaving of the self into the sense diminishes his subject. His great insight, akin to Sidney's "Look in thy heart and write," is tendered by a "friend's" whisper: "There is in Love a sweetnes ready penn'd:/Coppy out onely that, and save expence." The implication is that the truths of nature and religion are in themselves witty and sweet because they are made so by God's love, and that, accordingly, the poet will find his appropriate manner when he treats them in terms of the imagery and symbolism which God himself used in his two books of Scripture and Nature. In the poignant "Fore-runners" the poet contemplates the signs of his old age, and with them the loss of his "sparkling notions" and "lovely enchanting Language." This is not a renunciation of his baptized metaphors: he is sorry to believe them gone back to a "sty" to serve some unworthy love. But it is a confrontation of the inevitable transiency of artistic power, and a willing acquiescence in its loss so long as the essential phrase, *"Thou art still my God,"* remains with him.

Joseph Summers has observed that "Herbert was the most consistent and interesting experimenter in the English lyric between Sidney and Yeats." His amazing variety of stanzaic forms and rhythmic patterns has some precedent in Sidney's translation of the Psalms, and is made possible by "counterpoint," a stanzaic organization in which the rhyming lines of a given stanza are of different lengths while the lines of identical length do not rhyme. *The Church* also contains a large variety of lyric kinds. The longest poem, "The Sacrifice," is a variation on a liturgical sequence, the *Improperia* or *Reproaches* of Good Friday, but a variation which greatly extends and heightens the paradoxes and ironies of the original. There are several short allegories, often modulating to parable or exemplum, such as "Humility," "The Pilgrimage," "Peace." There are fifteen sonnets, all of them using the Shakespearean form or a slight modification of it, and among them are such notable poems as "Prayer [I]," "Redemption," and the first two poems entitled "Love." Also, there are several poems identifiable by their lyrical quality and rhythmic design as hymns or songs of praise, and many of these have since been provided with musical settings. A few of these "Songs" are introduced by frame poems in very different meters: "The H. Communion," "Easter," "Christmas," and "An Offering."

Then there are many "hieroglyphic" poems, related to the emblem tradition in that they call up a visual image of something in nature or Scripture or the Church which God has invested with symbolic meaning, and also analyze that meaning poetically. However, Herbert's hieroglyphs, among which Joseph Summers distinguishes three varieties, are of quite another order of subtlety and complexity than emblem poems. One variety takes a hieroglyph from nature or religion as the content or subject of the poem. "The Church-floore," which proposes a moral meaning for every element of the church floor, resembles an explanatory poem beneath an emblem picture except for the fact that the final couplet radically extends the metaphorical dimension by identifying the floor as the human heart. "The Bunch of Grapes" takes as its starting point the popular iconographical representation of Joshua's spies carrying the grapes from the Promised Land, but instead of analyzing the liturgical or moral or typological meaning of the biblical story, the poem calls implicitly upon all these meanings in a meditation upon the absence of joy in life. A second category consists of shaped poems which present a visual hieroglyph, such as "Easter wings." This poem is much more than an exercise in ingenious typography, for not only the visual image of the wings but also the cadences of the poem show the fall and diminishing of the soul under sin and its soaring and expansion with God's grace. More complex still is the third category, in which the structure and tone of the poem present a visual or auditory hieroglyph. Examples are "Paradise," in which the paring of the rhymes displays the way in which suffering prunes souls; "Deniall," in which the chaos of the speaker's spiritual state is rendered through the disorder of the verse, which is at length restored to rhyme; and "Church-monuments," in which the dissolution of the interred bodies and of the monuments themselves is imitated by the progressive loosening of stanzaic and sentence structure in the poem.

The basic characteristic of Herbert's style is its apparent ease and simplicity, linked to a highly conscious artistry and an astonishing intellectual and emotional range. The diction is simple but the meaning of the poems is not, because Herbert all unobtrusively loads every rift with ore. Herbert's many conceits, like Donne's, often employ the technical vocabularies of law, business, science, or military practice, but Mary Ellen Rickey shows that when this occurs, the language usually has a general frame of reference as well, so that one is not forced (as with Donne) to work out all of the technical complexities of the figure in order to grasp its meaning. The conceits are often based upon traditional religious comparisons: some are brief, like the brilliant series of comparisons which comprise "Prayer

[I]," and others provide the subject of an entire poem, like the conceit of the minister as a stained glass window in "The Windowes." Perhaps Herbert's most characteristic conceits occur in the titles, which often project a metaphorical dimension upon entire poems that make no other explicit textual references to the objects named in the titles: for example, "The Collar," "Josephs coat," "The Pulley."

The poems use many other devices to extend and deepen and qualify meaning. In "The Sonne," Herbert praises the English language highly for its receptivity to puns, and he often uses puns in his titles. "The Collar," for example, refers primarily to the Christian's yoke, which seems to the speaker to be a slave's collar; but it also alludes to the collar of the clergyman, to the choler, or fit of rage, which has overtaken the speaker, and even to the Caller (the Lord) to whose call the speaker responds at length. And very often, as Miss Rickey points out, puns are used to knot together two or more strands of imagery in a poem, as the term "planted" in "Affliction [V]" links the imagery of growth and vegetation to that of firmness and stability. The poems also abound in paradoxes which have their roots in traditional Christian writing, but Herbert puts special pressure on these Christian paradoxes to give them added force. His characteristic irony is understatement, as in the surprising brevity of the final line of "Redemption," or the pervasive irony of "The Sacrifice," displaying man's tragic blindness to the magnitude and implications of the Divine sacrifice.

Another feature of Herbert's poetry is the recurrence of certain images, the significance of which is extended and deepened by such repetition. Important clusters of this kind are the stone as the Old Testament altar, as the rock Moses clave, as the human heart; music as the image of God's order, and man as God's music; Christ as the vine, as the grapes pressed in the winepress of the Passion, as the wine/blood of the Communion. These images have their sources in the Bible and, as Rosemond Tuve has shown, they depend for their force upon meanings that have accrued to them through centuries of typological interpretation, in which Old Testament type is recapitulated and fulfilled in the New Testament antitype, that is, in Christ and in the lives of Christians. "The Bunch of Grapes" shows that Herbert understood typological allusion to be God's own symbolism, inherent in the nature of things: "For as the Jews of old by *Gods* command/Travaild, and saw no towne:/So now each *Christian* hath his journey spand./Their story pennes and setts us downe." Moreover, several classical allusions function in context as imperfect figures of the Christian order. The first poem in *The Church*, "The Altar," introduces the typological perspective and Herbert's remarkable way of using it. The poem has the shape, as F. E. Hutchinson points out, of a classical altar, but its theme develops in terms of the Old Testament altar of uncut stones, untouched by any tool, which the Israelites were told to erect after crossing Jordan into the Promised Land. The poem presents the transmutation of these imperfect types: the stone altar is now the stony human heart which only God's power can cut; and the sacrifice which must be offered upon it is Christ's death, which alone can sanctify this altar.

Moreover, since *The Temple* is a conceptual and architectonic entity, several important aspects of meaning and art in Herbert's poetry can only be apprehended by seeing the volume whole. Further study of the work's overall structure is needed, but some patterns are clear. *The Temple* is an inclusive architectural metaphor, which calls up associations with the Old Testament temple (by means of the epigraph from Psalm 29:9, "In his Temple doth every man speak of his honor"), and with pagan temples (by means of the reference to the Greek sprinkling instrument, the *Perirrhanterium*, and to the *procul este profani* of Roman ritual alluded to in the verse on the *superliminare*, or portal). But both of these temples are now subsumed in the New Testament temple of the human heart: "Know ye not that ye are the temples of God, and that the Spirit of God dwelleth in you?" (I Cor. 3:16). In *The Church-Porch*, where the classical associations of *The Temple* are most in evidence, the speaker delivers to a general audience, in tones of reason and common sense, his rather dry, didactic prescriptions regarding the externals of a Christian life and the behavior befitting a Christian profession; despite the different subject matter, this poem has some affinities with classical ethical discourse.

The second element of *The Temple*, *The Church*, explores the inner dimension, the essence of the Christian experience: the relationship between Christ and the soul. In these poems (except for "The Sacrifice," which is spoken by Christ), the tone of the speaker modulates from the angry, colloquial language of "The Collar" and "Conscience" to the highly formal praise of "Antiphon [I]" and "Antiphon [II]," to the musing meditation of "Church-monuments." The audience is variously Christ, or the speaker's own soul, or his fellow Christians within the Church. The man–God relationship is explored in part by accretion of meanings: as various subjects and motifs — the Christian virtues, the actions of God toward man, man's praise of God, the work of the priest and the poet, meditations on aspects of Scripture and nature — recur again and again throughout *The Church*, they gain in depth and resonance. The man–God relationship is also seen to develop, though not by clearly defined stages. The collection begins with a series of poems which treats the basis of the relationship, Christ's sacrifice for man and man's acceptance of it. Many of the poems of the first half are concerned with such subjects as sacraments, rituals, feast days, church architecture and furniture, the events of Christ's life and their theological meaning, as if such visible matters are especially significant in the early stages of the Christian life. The poems of the second part give little attention to such topics, but instead explore ever more deeply the distresses and joys attendant upon man's relationship with God, show Christ responding more often to the speaker's addresses, and, as if all things were now sanctified to the mature Christian speaker, introduce new subjects for meditation from the natural world. The collection concludes with a group of poems on the Last Things, culminating with "Love [III]," in which Love/Christ as host welcomes the Soul as honored guest into the intimate social relationship of the Heavenly Banquet.

The Church Militant, though it may have been written earlier, forms an organic part of the unity of *The Temple*. In contrast to the interior, mystical progress of the elect soul, this poem presents the cyclic movement of the Church as a corporate society throughout history. The speaker, ostensibly addressing God, is chiefly engaged in straightforward historical exposition. The historical panorama is emphatically not a progress: the Church flees ever westward as Sin dogs its heels, destroying or taking over the communities it has established. But such a pessimistic view of the Church's role in history is perfectly traditional: after the Fall the people of God can look forward only to individual salvation, not to the victory of the Church over the world. Augustine's *City of God* shows that city in perpetual conflict with the City of Man throughout time, and Michael in *Paradise Lost* represents to Adam the woeful panorama of human history, in counterpoint to the Paradise within which the elect may attain. The corporate body can look forward only to the Final Judgment, which will display the Lord's conquests. It is in anticipation of that Judgment that the speaker of "The Church Militant" apostrophizes God even as he observes the plight of the Church in history: "How deare to mee, *O God*, thy Counsels are!/Who may with thee compare!"

The copy text is Bodleian MS. Tanner 307 (hereafter B.), probably a fair copy, made for the printer by someone at Little Gidding, of the book which Herbert sent to Farrar. Since Herbert's holograph does not survive, this manuscript is closer than any other version to the author's text, and so has highest authority. The careful and intelligent first edition of 1633 corrects several slips in language and grammar in the manuscript, but it often alters words without necessity, and it regularizes spelling, punctuation, and grammar throughout. F. E. Hutchinson adopts B.'s text for the words, and 1633's for the other elements, but the arguments for the superiority of B.'s text seem to us to hold for every aspect of it: the manuscript is more likely than the regularized edition to observe Herbert's conventions and intentions in such matters as italics, capitalizations, spellings. More important, in several poems, B.'s punctuation gives a different and, we think, better sense than 1633's heavier pointing: some examples among many are "Affliction [II]" (ll. 13-15) and "Sinne [I]" (ll. 10-12). In the present text, in addition to the normalizations noted in the general introduction, *least* is changed to *lest* silently when that is the meaning; capital letters after periods are silently supplied where needed; and lower case *c* and *r* are arbitrarily used in many doubtful cases arising from the B. scribe's almost constant employment of the same symbol for both upper and lower case forms of these two letters. Otherwise, all departures from B. are noted. Alternate readings from 1633 are given wherever there is doubt about meaning, and an earlier and incomplete manuscript, Jones B 62 in Dr. Williams' Library, London (W.), has been used as a check on some readings. F. E. Hutchinson's (H.) standard edition of Herbert's *Works* has been of inestimable value, and the editions by George Herbert Palmer and Alexander Grosart are cited on occasion as (P.) and (G.).

SELECTED BIBLIOGRAPHY

EDITIONS

Grosart, Alexander, ed. *Complete Works in Verse and Prose of George Herbert.* 3 vols. London, 1874.

Hutchinson, F. E., ed. *The Works of George Herbert.* 2nd ed. Oxford, 1945.

McCloskey, Mark, and Murphy, Paul R., eds. *The Latin Poetry of George Herbert.* Athens, Ohio, 1965.

Palmer, George Herbert, ed. *The English Works of George Herbert.* 3 vols. Boston, 1905.

BIOGRAPHY AND CRITICISM

Asals, Heather. "The Voice of George Herbert's 'The Church,'" *ELH*, XXXVI (1969), 511–28.

Bottrall, Margaret. *George Herbert.* London, 1954.

Bowers, Fredson. "Herbert's Sequential Imagery: 'The Temper,'" *MP*, LIX (1962), 202–13.

Bradner, Leicester. "New Poems by George Herbert: *The Cambridge Latin Gratulatory Anthology of 1613,*" *Renaissance News*, XV (1962), 208–11.

Chute, Marchette. *Two Gentle Men: The Lives of George Herbert and Robert Herrick.* New York, 1959.

Colie, Rosalie. "Logos in *The Temple*: George Herbert and the Shape of Content," *Journal of the Warburg and Courtauld Institutes*, XXVI (1963), 327–42.

Eliot, T. S. *George Herbert.* "Writers and Their Work," no. 152. London, 1962.

Endicott, Annabel M. "The Structure of George Herbert's *Temple*: A Reconsideration," *UTQ*, XXIV (1965), 226–37.

Hayes, Albert McHarg. "Counterpoint in Herbert," *SP*, XXXV (1938), 43–60.

Ostriker, Alicia. "Song and Speech in the Metrics of George Herbert," *PMLA*, LXXX (1965), 62–68.

Rickey, Mary Ellen. *Utmost Art: Complexity in the Verse of George Herbert.* Lexington, Ky., 1966.

Stein, Arnold. *George Herbert's Lyrics.* Baltimore, 1968.

Stewart, Stanley. "Time and *The Temple*," *SEL*, VI (1966), 97–110.

Summers, Joseph. *George Herbert: His Religion and Art.* London, 1954.

Tuve, Rosemond. *A Reading of George Herbert.* Chicago, 1952.

———. "George Herbert and *Caritas*," *Journal of the Warburg and Courtauld Institute*, XXII (1959), 303–31.

———. "Sacred 'Parody' of Love Poetry, and Herbert," *Studies in the Renaissance*, VIII (1961), 249–90.

Walker, John D. "The Architectonics of George Herbert's *The Temple*," *ELH*, XXIX (1962), 289–305.

Walton, Izaac. "The Life of Mr. George Herbert," *The Lives of Dr. John Donne, Sir Henry Wotton, Mr. Richard Hooker, Mr. George Herbert.* London, 1675. Often reprinted.

THE TEMPLE

The Dedication

Lord, *my* first *Fruits* present themselves to thee;
Yet not mine neither, for from thee they *Came*,
And must returne. Accept of them, and mee,
And make us strive, who shall sing best thy Name.
    *T*urne their eies hither, who shall make a gaine,   *5*
    Theirs, who shall hurt themselves, or mee, refraine.

THE CHURCH-PORCH

Perirrhanterium

1

Thou, whose sweet youth, and early hopes inhance
Thy rate, and price, and marke thee for a treasure;
Harken unto a verser, who may chance
Rhime thee to good, and make a bait of pleasure.
    A verse may find him, who a sermon flies,   *5*
    And turne delight into a Sacrifice.

2

Beware of Lust: It doth pollute, and foule
Whom *God* in Baptisme washt with his owne Blood.

Perirrhanterium. Greek. The instrument which sprinkles Holy Water. This sprinkling on the Church porch is a necessary purification before entering the Church.

THE
TEMPLE.

SACRED POEMS
AND
PRIVATE EJA-
CULATIONS.

By Mr. GEORGE HERBERT.

PSAL. 29.
In his Temple doth every man speak of his honour.

CAMBRIDGE:
Printed by *Thom. Buck,*
and *Roger Daniel,* printers
to the Universitie.
1633.

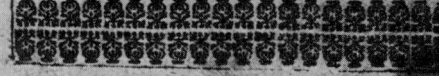

It blotts thy lesson written in thy Soule,
The holy Lines cannot be understood.   10
    How dare those eies upon a Bible looke,
    Much lesse towards *God,* whose Lust is all their booke.

3

Abstaine wholly, or wedd. Thy Bounteous *Lord*
Allows thee Choyse of paths: Take no by-waies,
But gladly welcome, what he doth afford;   15
Not grudging, that thy lust hath bounds, and staies.
    Continence hath his joy: weigh both, and so
    If rottennes have more, let *Heaven* goe.

4

If *God* had layed all common, certainely
Man would have beene th'incloser: but since now   20
God hath impal'd us, on the contrary
Man breakes the fence, and every ground will plough.
    O, what were Man, might he himselfe misplace!
    Sure to be crosse he would shift feet and face.

5

Drinke not the third glasse, which thou canst not tame,   25
When once it is within thee; but before
Mayst rule it, as thou list, and powre the shame,
Which it would powre on thee, upon the floore.
    It is most just to throw that on the ground,
    Which would throw mee there, if I keepe the round.   30

6

He, that is drunken, may his Mother kill,
Bigge with his Sister: he hath lost the raynes,
Is outlawed by himselfe: all kind of ill
Did with his liquour slide into his veines.
    The Drunkard forfets man, and doth devest   35
    All worldly right, save what he hath by beast.

---

30 *keepe the round*: refill each time the bottle is passed.

7

Shall I, to please anothers wine-sprung mind
Loose all mine owne? *God* hath given mee a measure
Short of his canne, and body: must I find
A paine in that, wherein he finds a pleasure?   *40*
    Stay at the third glasse; if thou loose thy hold,
    Then thou art modest, and the wine grows bold.

8

If reason move not Gallants, quitt the roome.
All in a shipwrack shift their severall way.
Let not a common ruine thee intombe,   *45*
Be not a beast in courtesy, but stay,
    Stay at the third cup, or forgoe the place.
    Wine above all things doth *God's* stampe deface.

9

Yet, if thou sinne in wine, or wantonnes,
Boast not thereof, nor make thy shame thy glory.   *50*
Fraylty getts pardon by submissivenes,
But he, that boasts, shuts that out of his story.
    He makes flat warre with *God,* and doth defy
    With his poore Clod of earth the spacious sky.

10

Take not his Name, who made thy mouth, in vaine.   *55*
It getts thee Nothing, and hath no excuse.
Lust and wine plead a pleasure; avarice gaine:
But the cheap swearer through his open sluce
    Lets his soule runne for nought, as little fearing:
    Were I an *Epicure*, I could bate swearing.   *60*

11

When thou doest tell anothers jest, therein
Omitt the oathes, which true witt cannot need.

39 *his canne*: the other man's wine cup.
50 Philip. 3:19, "whose God is their belly, and whose glory is in their shame."
53–54 Cf. Isa. 45:9.
60 *bate*: cease.

Pick out of tales the mirth, but not the sinne:
He pares his apple, that will cleanely feed.
   Play not away the vertue of that Name,
    Which is thy best stake, when greifes make thee tame.

12

The cheapest sins most dearely punisht are;
Because to shun them also is so cheape:
For wee have witt to marke them, and to spare.
O crumble not away thy soules faire heape.
   If thou wilt dy, the gates of hell are broad:
    Pride, and full sinnes have made the way a road.

13

Lye not; but let thy heart be true to *God*,
Thy Mouth to it, thy actions to them both.
Cowards tell lies, and those that feare the rod.
The stormy working soule spitts lies, and froth.
   Dare to be true. Nothing can need a ly.
    A fault, which needs it most, grows two thereby.

14

Fly Idlenes; which yet thou canst not fly
By dressing, mistressing, and complement.
If those take up thy day, the Sunne will cry
Against thee: For his light was onely lent.
   God gave thy soule brave wings; put not those feathers
    Into a bed, to sleepe out all ill weathers.

15

Art thou a Magistrate? then be severe.
If studious, Coppy faire, what time hath blurr'd;
Redeeme truth from his jawes. If Souldier,
Chase brave imployments with a Naked sword
   Throughout the world. Foole not; for all may have,
    If they dare try, a glorious life, or grave.

---

66 *stake*: that which is wagered in a game.
  80 *mistressing*: courting. The line comes from Donne, "To Mr. Tilman after he had taken orders" (l. 30).

16

O England, full of sinne, but most of sloth,
Spitt out thy flegme, and fill thy brest with glory.
Thy *Gentry* bleats, as if thy Native cloth
Transfus'd a sheepishness into thy story.
   Not that they all are so; but that the most
   Are gone to grasse, and in the pasture lost.

17

This losse springs cheifly from our education.
Some till their ground, but let weeds choke their son;
Some mark a Partridge, never their childs fashion;
Some ship them over, and the thing is done.
   Study this Art; make it thy great designe:
   And if *Gods* Image move thee not, let thine.

18

Some great estates provide, but doe not breed
A Mastring mind: so both are lost thereby.
Or els they breed them tender, make them need
All, that they leave. This is flatt poverty.
   For he, that needs five thousand pound to live,
   Is full as poore, as he, than needs but five.

19

The way to make thy Sonne rich is to fill
His mind with rest, before his trunke with riches:
For wealth without contentment climbs a hill
To feele those tempests, which fly over ditches.
   But if thy Sonne can make ten pound his measure
   Then all thou addest may be call'd his treasure.

20

When thou doest purpose ought within thy power,
Be sure to doe it, though it be but small.

---

92 *flegme*: the humor whose excess causes sloth.
98 Cf. Herbert, *Priest to the Temple,* chap. xxxii.
100 *ship them over*: send them on the grand tour, or to the colonies.

Constancy knitts the bones, and makes us sowre,
When wanton pleasures becken us to thrall.
   Who breakes his owne bond, forfetteth himselfe:
   What Nature made a ship, he makes a shelfe.

21

Doe all things like a man, not sneakingly.
Thinke the King sees thee still; for his *King* does.
Simpring is but a lay-hypocrisy.
Give it a corner, and the clue undoes.
   Who feares to doe ill, setts himselfe to task.
   Who feares to doe well, sure should weare a mask.

22

Looke to thy mouth; diseases enter there.
Thou hast two skonses, if thy stomack call;
Carve, or discourse; doe not a Famine feare.
Who carves, is kind to two; who talkes, to all.
   Looke on meat, thinke it durt, then eat a bitt,
   And say withall Earth to Earth I committ.

23

Slight those, who say amidst their sickly healths,
Thou liv'st by rule. What doth not so, but Man?
Houses are built by rule, and Commonwealths.
Entice the trusty Sunne, if that you can,
   From his Ecliptick line; Becken the sky.
   Who lives by rule then, keepes good Company.

24

Who keepes no guard upon himselfe, is slack,
And rots to nothing at the next great thaw.

---

117 *sowre*: sullen, austere.
120 *shelfe*: ledge, reef. Nature made him a ship but he made himself a reef to wreck that ship.
124 *clue*: ball of thread.
128 *skonses*: forts, i.e., protections.
132 Line from the burial service.
133 *sickly healths*: pledges of health in drinking from those "sick" physically and morally from drinking.

Man is a Shop of rules, a well-trust pack,
Whose every parcell underwrites a Law.
   Loose not thy selfe, nor give thy humours way:
   God gave them to thee under Lock and key.

25

By all meanes use sometimes to be alone.   *145*
Salute thy selfe; see what thy Soule doth weare.
Dare to looke in thy Chest, for 'tis thine owne;
And tumble up and downe what thou find'st there.
   Who cannot rest, till hee good-fellows find,
   He breakes up house, turnes out of doores his mind.   *150*

26

Be thrifty, but not covetous: Therefore give
Thy need, thine honour, and thy freind his due.
Never was Scraper brave Man. Gett to live;
Then live, and use it: els, it is not true,
   That thou hast gotten. Surely use alone   *155*
   Makes mony not a contemptible stone.

27

Never exceed thy Income. Youth may make
Even with the yeare; but Age, if it will hitt,
Shootes a Bow short, and lessens still his stake,
As the day lessens, and his life with it.   *160*
   Thy children, kindred, freinds upon thee call;
   Before thy journey fairely part with all.

28

Yet in thy thriving still misdoubt some evill,
Lest gaining gaine on thee, and make thee dimme
To all things els. Wealth is the Conjurers Devill;   *165*
Whom when he thinkes he hath, the Devill hath him.
   Gold thou mayst safely touch; but if it stick
   Unto thy hands, it woundeth to the quick.

  141–42 *trust*: trussed. Every part of man subscribes to some law.
  157–60 Youth may spend the year's income, but age must save for the declining years.

29

What skills it, if a bag of stones, or gold
About thy Neck doe drowne thee? raise thy head; *170*
Take starres for mony; starres not to be told
By any Art, yet to bee purchased.
   None is so wastfull as the scraping dame.
   She looseth three for one, her soule, rest, fame.

30

By no meanes runne in debt. Take thine own measure. *175*
Who cannot live on twenty pound a yeare,
Cannot on fourty: hee's a man of pleasure,
A kind of thing, that's for its selfe too deare.
   The curious unthrift makes his cloth too wide,
   And spares himselfe, but would his Taylor chide. *180*

31

Spend not on hopes. They, that by pleading cloths
Doe Fortunes seeke, when worth and service fayle,
Would have their tale beleeved for their oaths
And are like empty vessels under saile.
   Old Courtiers know this: Therefore sett out so, *185*
   As all the day thou mayest hold out to goe.

32

In Cloathes cheape handsomnes doth beare the Bell.
Wisedome's a trimmer thing, then shop ere gave.
Say not then, this with that lace will doe well,
But, this with my discretion will be brave. *190*
   Much Curiousnes is a perpetuall wooing,
   Nothing with Labour, folly long a-doing.

33

Play not for gaine, but sport. Who playes for more,
Then he can loose with pleasure, stakes his heart;

169–72 Luke 12:33, "provide yourselves bags which wax not old, a treasure in the heavens that faileth not."
180 The prodigal has too much cloth cut for his apparel, then blames the tailor for the expense (P.).

> Perhaps his wives too, and whom she hath bore:
> Servants, and *Churches* also play their part.
> > Onely a Herauld, who that way doth passe,
> > Finds his Crackt Name at length in the *Church*-glasse.

34

> If yet thou love game at so deare a rate,
> Learne this, that hath Old Gamesters dearly cost.
> Dost loose? rise up. Dost winne? Rise in that state.
> Who strive to sitt out loosing hands, are lost.
> > Game is a civil gunpouder, in peace
> > Blowing up houses with their whole encrease.

35

> In Conversation boldnes now beares sway.
> But know, that nothing can so foolish bee,
> As empty Boldnes: therefore first assay,
> To stuffe thy mind with solid Bravery;
> > Then March on Gallant. Get substantiall worth:
> > Boldnes guilds finely, and will sett it forth.

36

> Be sweet to all. Is thy complexion sowre?
> Then keepe such company; make them thy allay.
> Gett a sharp wife, a servant that will lowre.
> A Stumbler stumbles least in rugged way.
> > Commande thy selfe in cheif. He life's warre knows,
> > Whom all his passions follow, as he goes.

37

> Catch not at quarrels. He, that dares not speake
> Plainly, and home, is Coward of the two.
> Thinke not thy fame at ev'ry twitch will breake.

---

198 His name will quickly be forgotten, and even the *Herauld*, the state official responsible for reporting upon arms, genealogies, etc., will have difficulty finding it in some old church window (H.).
211 *complexion sowre*: melancholic temperament.
212 *allay*: alloy.
217–18 The coward is he who only hints an affront, not you who refuse to take it up (G.).

By great deeds show, that thou canst little doe,
    And doe them not: that shall thy wisedome bee,
    And change thy Temperance into bravery.

38

If that thy Fame with ev'ry toy be pos'd,
'Tis a thinne webbe, which poysonous fancies make.
But the great *Souldiers* honour was compos'd
Of thicker stuffe, which would endure a shake.
    Wisedome picks freinds; civility plays the rest.
    A toy shun'd cleanly passeth with the best.

39

Laugh not too much; the Witty Man laughs least:
For witt is news only to Ignorance.
Lesse at thine owne things laugh; lest in the jest
Thy Person share, and the conceit advance.
    Make not thy sport, abuses: for the fly,
    That feeds on dung, is coloured thereby.

40

Pick out of mirth, like stones out of thy ground,
Profanenes, Filthines, Abusivenes.
These are the scumme, with which course witts abound;
The fine may spare these well, yet not goe lesse.
    All things are bigge with jest: nothing that's plaine,
    But may be witty, if thou hast the vaine.

41

Witt's an unruly Engine, wildly striking
Sometimes a freind, sometimes the Engineer.
Hast thou the knack? Pamper it not with liking;
But if thou want it, buy it not too deare.
    Many, affecting witt beyond their power,
    Have gott to be a deare foole for an houre.

   223–26 Source is Bacon, *Speech Against Duels* (1614), pp. 20–21, where the soldier is identified as Gonzalo Hernandez de Cordova (1453–1515), called the Great Captain (H.).
   228 The best men will not blame your overlooking such trifles.

42

A sad wise Valour is the brave Complexion
That leads the van, and swallows up the citties.
The Gigler is a milkmaid, whom Infection,
Or a fir'd Beacon frighteth from his ditties. *250*
   Then he's the sport: the mirth then in him rests,
   And the sad man is cock of all his Jests.

43

Towards Great Persons use respective Boldnes:
That Temper gives them theirs, and yet doth take
Nothing from thine. In service care, or coldnes *255*
Doth ratably thy Fortunes marre, or make.
   Feed no Man in his Sinnes: for Adulation
   Doth make thee Parcell-devill in Damnation.

44

Envy not Greatnes: For thou mak'st thereby
Thy self the worse, and so the distance greater. *260*
Be not thine owne worme: yet such Jelousy,
As hurts not others, but may make thee better,
   Is a good spurre. Correct thy passions spite,
   Then may the beasts draw thee to happy light.

45

When Basenes is exalted, doe not bate *265*
The place its honour for the Persons sake.
The shrine is that, which thou dost venerate,
And not the beast, that beares it on his back.
   I care not, though the cloth of state should bee
   Not of rich Arras, but meane tapestry. *270*

---

252 *sad*: grave, serious.
253 *respective*: respectful.
258 *Parcell-devill*: part-devil, sharer in the devil's role.
  264 *beasts*: the passions, duly controlled by reason, are good horses to carry you to your goal.
  268 In a fable of Aesop, an ass that carried an image assumed that the reverence of the bystanders was paid to himself (H.).

46

Thy Freind put in thy bosome: weare his eies
Still in thy heart, that he may see what's there.
If cause require, thou art his sacrifice;
Thy drops of blood must pay downe all his feare.
    But Love is lost, the way of freindship's gone,
    Though David had his Jonathan, *Christ* his John.

47

Yet bee not *Surety*, if thou be a Father.
Love is a personal debt: I cannot give
My Childrens right, nor ought he take it; rather
Both freinds should dy, then hinder them to live.
    Fathers first enter bonds to Natures ends,
    And are her Sureties, ere they are a freinds.

48

If thou bee single, all thy goods, and ground
Submitt to Love: but yet not more then all.
Give one estate, as one life: None is bound
To worke for two, who brought himself to thrall.
    God made mee one Man; Love makes mee no more,
    Till labour come, and make my weaknes score.

49

In thy discourse, if thou desire to please:
All such is courteous, usefull, new, or witty.
Usefulnes comes by labour, witt by ease;
Courtesy grows in Court, News in the Citty.
    Gett a good stock of these, then draw the card,
    That suites him best, of whom thy speech is heard.

50

Entice all neatly to what they know best:
For so thou dost thy self, and him a pleasure.
(But a proud ignorance will loose his rest,

---

297 *rest*: In the card game of Primero, the stakes to be won by declaring one's hand at the proper time (*OED*).

Rather then shew his cards.) Steale from his treasure
   What to ask further: Doubts well rays'd doe lock
   The Speaker to thee, and preserve thy stock.   *300*

51

If thou be Master-gunner, spend not all,
That thou canst speake, at once; but husband it,
And give men turnes of speach: Doe not forestall
By Lavishnes thine owne, and others witt,
   As if thou mad'st thy will. A civill guest   *305*
   Will no more talk all, then eat all the feast.

52

Be calme in Arguing: For feircnes makes
Errour a fault, and truth a discourtesy.
Why should I feele another Man's mistakes,
More then his sicknesses or poverty?   *310*
   In Love I should: but Anger is not love
   Nor wisdome neither: Therefore gently move.

53

Calmnes is great advantage. He, that lets
Another chafe, may warme him at his fire,
Mark all his wanderings, and enjoy his frets;   *315*
As cunning Fencers suffer heat to tire.
   Truth dwells not in the clouds: the Bow that's there
   Doth often ayme at, never hitt the spheere.

54

Mark what another sayes: For many are
Full of themselves, and answere their owne Notion.   *320*
Take all into thee; then with equall care
Ballance each dramme of reason, like a potion.
   If truth be with thy freind, be with them both.
   Share in the conquest, and confesse a troth.

317 *Bow*: rainbow.

55

Be usefull where thou livest, that they may
Both want, and wish thy pleasing presence still.
Kindnes, good parts, great places are the way
To compasse this. Find out Mens wants, and will,
   And meet them there. All worldly joyes goe lesse
   To the one joy of doeing kindnesses.

56

Pitch thy behaviour low, thy projects high;
So shalt thou humble, and magnanimous bee.
Sink not in spirit. Who aymeth at the sky,
Shoots higher much then he, that meanes a tree.
   A graine of glory mixt with humblenes
   Cures both a Feaver, and Lethargicknes.

57

Let thy mind still be bent, still plotting where,
And when, and how, the busines may be done.
Slacknes breeds wormes; but the sure Traveller,
Though he alight sometimes, still goeth on.
   Active, and stirring spirits live alone.
   Write on the others, here lyes such-a-one.

58

Slite not the smallest losse, whether it bee
In Love, or honour: Take account of all.
Shine like the *Sunne* in every corner: See
Whether thy stock of creditt swell, or fall.
   Who say I care not, those I give for lost;
   And to instruct them, will not quitt the cost.

59

Scorne no Mans Love, though of a meane degree:
Love is a present for a Mighty King.
Much lesse make any one thy enemy.

---

339 Want of exercise was thought to breed worms.

60

All forraine wisedome doth amount to this, 355
To take all, that is given: whether wealth,
Or Love, or Language; Nothing comes amisse;
A good digestion turneth all to health.
    And then as farre, as faire behaviour may,
    Strike off all scores; None are so cleere as they. 360

61

Keepe all thy Native good, and Naturalize
All forraine of that Name; but scorne their ill:
Embrace their Activenes, not vanities.
Who follows all things, forfetteth his will.
    If thou observest strangers in each fitt, 365
    In time they'l runne thee out of all thy witt.

62

Affect in things about thee cleanlines,
That all may gladly boord thee, as a flowre.
Slovens take up their stock of Noysomnes
Before hand, and anticipate their last houre. 370
    Let thy minds sweetnes have his operation
    Upon thy Body, Cloths, and habitation.

63

In Almes regard thy meanes, and others merrit.
Thinke Heaven a better bargaine, then to give
Onely thy single market-mony for it. 375
Joine hands with *God* to make a man to live.
    Give to all something, to a good poore Man,
    Till thou Change Names, and be where he began.

---

368 *boord*: (Fr. *aborder*), approach.
371–72 Cf. *Priest to the Temple*, Ch. iii.
375 *market-mony*: lowest price.

64

Man is *Gods* Image; but a poore Man is
Christs Stampe to boote: both Images regard.   *380*
God reckons for him, counts the favour his:
Write, so much given to *God;* thou shalt be heard.
   Let thy almes goe before, and keep heavens gate
   Open for thee, or both may come too late.

65

Restore to *God* his due in Tith, and Time: *385*
A Tith purloin'd cankers the whole estate.
Sundayes observe: Thinke, when the Bells doe chime,
'Tis Angels Musique; therefore come not late.
   God then deales blessings: If a King did so,
   Who would not hast, nay give, to see the show?   *390*

66

Twice on the day his due is understood;
For all the weeke thy foode so oft he gave thee.
Thy cheere is mended; bate not of the food,
Because 'tis better, and perhaps may save thee.
   Thwart not the Mighty *God:* O bee not Crosse.   *395*
   Fast when thou wilt, but then 'tis gaine, not losse.

67

Though private prayer be a brave designe,
Yet publique hath more promises, more love.
And love's a waight to hearts, to eyes a signe.
Wee all are but Cold Suitors; let us move   *400*
   Where it is warmest: Leave thy six, and seaven;
   Pray with the most: for where most pray, is heaven.

---

383 Cf. Acts 10:4
386 Cf. Mal. 3:8–10.
391 Give God his due twice on Sunday (Morning and Evening Prayer).
396 Fast on other days, not from these Sunday services.
401 *six, and seaven*: little companies at family prayer (or conventicles).

68

When once thy foot enters the *Church,* be bare.
God is more there, then thou: for thou art there
Onely by his permission. Then beware,
And make thy selfe all reverence, and feare.
   Kneeling nere spoild silk stocking: quitt thy state;
   All equall are within the *Churche's* gate.

69

Resort to Sermons, but to Prayers most:
Praying's the end of preaching. O be drest,
Stay not for th'other pin: why thou hast lost
A joy for it worth worlds. Thus hell doth jest
   Away thy blessings, and extreemely flout thee,
   Thy Cloths being fast, but thy soule loose about thee.

70

In time of service seale up both thine eies,
And send them to thine heart; that spying sinne,
They may weepe out the staines by them did rise:
Those dores being shut, all by the eare comes in.
   Who marks in *Church*-time others symmetry,
   Makes all their beauty his deformity.

71

Let vaine, or busy thoughts have there no part.
Bring not thy plough, thy plots, thy pleasures thither.
Christ purg'd his temple; so must thou thy heart.
All worldly thoughts are but theeves mett together
   To couzin thee. Looke to thy Actions well:
   For *Churches* are either our heaven, or hell.

72

Judge not the *Preacher;* for he is thy Judge;
If thou mislike him, thou conceiv'st him not.

---

403 *bare*: bareheaded.

God calleth Preaching folly. Doe not grudge
To picke out treasures from an earthen pott.   *430*
   The worst speake something good; if all want sence,
   God takes a text, and preacheth Patience.

73

He, that gets Patience, and the blessing which
Preachers conclude with, hath not lost his paines.
He, that by being at *Church,* escapes the ditch,   *435*
Which he might fall in by companions, gaines.
   He, that loves *Gods* abode, and to combine
   With Saints on earth, shall one day with them shine.

74

Jest not at *Preachers* Language, or expression:
How know'st thou, but thy sinnes made him miscarry?   *440*
Then turne thy faults, and his into confession:
God sent him whatsoere he be; O tarry,
   And love him for his master. His condition,
   Though it be ill, makes him no ill Physition.

75

None shall in Hell such bitter pangs endure,   *445*
As those, who mock at *Gods* way of salvation.
Whom oile, and Balsoms kill, what salve can cure?
They drinke with greedines a full damnation.
   The Jews refused Thunder, and wee, folly.
   Though *God* doe hedge us in, yet who is holy?   *450*

76

Summe up at night, what thou hast done by day;
And in the morning, what thou hast to doe.
Dresse, and undresse thy soule: Mark the decay,
And growth of it. If with thy watch, that too
   Be downe, then winde up both. Since wee shall be *455*
   Most surely judg'd, make thy accounts agree.

---

  429 I Cor. 1:21, "it pleased God by the foolishness of preaching to save them that believe."
  430 II Cor. 4:7, "we have this treasure in earthen vessels."
  449 God announced the law to the Jews in Sinai amid thunder and lightning (Exod. 19:16).

77

    In breif, acquitt thee bravely; play the Man.
    Looke not on pleasures as they come, but goe.
    Deferre not the least vertue. Life's poore span
    Make not an ell by trifling in thy woe.   460
        If thou doe ill; the joy fades, not the paines:
        If well; the paine doth fade, the joy remaines.

Superliminare

    Thou, whom the former precepts have
    Sprinkled and taught, how to behave
    Thy selfe in *Church*; approach, and tast
    The *Churche's* mysticall repast.

    Avoyd, Profanenes; come not heere,   5
    Nothing, but holy, pure, and cleere,
    Or that, which groneth to be so,
    May at his perill further goe.

    461–62 H. calls attention to the long literary history of Herbert's concluding epigram, from Cato the Censor to Queen Mary I.
    Superliminare. The lintel or crossbar of the (church) doorway; a place for an inscription. Cf. Rev. 21:27.

THE CHURCH

The Altar

    A broken Altar, Lord, thy servant reares
    Made of a heart, and cimented with teares.
      Whose parts are, as thy hand did frame;
      No workemans toole hath touch'd the same.
          A heart alone   5
          Is such a stone,
          As nothing but
          Thy power doth cut,
          Wherefore each part
          Of my hard heart   10
          Meets in this frame,
          To praise thy Name.
    That, if I chance to hold my peace,
    These stones to praise thee may not cease.
    O lett thy blessed sacrifice be mine,   15
    And sanctify this Altar to be thine.

The Altar. 1–2 Ps. 51–17, "The sacrifices of God are a broken spirit: a broken and a contrite heart, O God, thou wilt not despise."

4 In Deut. 27:2–6 the Israelites are told by Moses: "... on the day when ye shall pass over Jordan ... thou shalt set thee up great stones, and plaster them with plaster.... And there shalt thou build an altar unto the Lord thy God, an altar of stones: thou shalt not lift up any iron tool upon them. Thou shalt build the altar of the Lord thy God of whole stones." Jordan is a type of Regeneration, specifically of Baptism in the New Dispensation (see the "sprinkling" of the preceding poem).

6 Cf. Zech. 7:12, "Yea, they made their hearts as an adamant stone, lest they should hear the law."

13–14 Cf. Luke 19:40, "if these should hold their peace, the stones would immediately cry out."

The Sacrifice

Oh All ye, who passe by, whose eies and mind
To worldly things are sharp, but to mee blind,
To mee, who tooke eies, that I might you finde.
            Was ever greif like mine?

The Princes of my People make a head
Against their Maker: they doe wish mee dead,
Who cannot wish, except I give them bread:
            Was ever greife like mine?

Without mee each one, who doth now mee brave,
Had to this day bin an Egyptian slave.
They use that power against mee, which I gave.
            Was ever greife like mine?

Mine owne Apostle, who the bag did beare,
Though he had all I had, did not forbeare
To sell mee also, and to put mee there.
            Was ever greif like mine?

For thirty pence he did my death devize,
Who at three hundred did the ointment prize,
Not halfe so sweet as my sweet sacrifice.
            Was ever greif like mine?

Therefore my Soule melts, and my hearts deare treasure
Drops blood (the onely beads) my words to measure.
O let this Cup passe, if it be thy pleasure.
            Was ever greif like mine?

The Sacrifice. Cf. Lam. 1:12, "Is it nothing to you, all ye that pass by? behold, and see if there be any sorrow like unto my sorrow, which is done unto me, wherewith the Lord hath afflicted me in the day of his fierce anger." Also Matt. 27:39, "And they that passed by reviled him, wagging their heads." R. Tuve, in *A Reading of George Herbert* (pp. 19–111), demonstrates that the poem's striking paradoxes and ironies, and liturgical and iconographical commonplaces, appear in the Holy Week Liturgy (specifically the *Improperia* of Good Friday) and in the medieval poetic genre of the *Complaints of Christ*, both of which present passages from Lamentations as if spoken by Christ in his Passion.

These drops being temperd with a sinners teares
A Balsome are for both the Hemispheres;
Curing all wounds, but mine, all, but my feares.
            Was ever greif like mine?

Yet my disciples sleepe, I cannot gaine
One houre of watching, but their drowsy braine
Comforts not mee, and doth my doctrine staine.
            Was ever greif like mine?

Arise, Arise, they come. Looke how they runne!
Alas what hast they make to be undone!
How with their lanterns doe they seeke the sunne!
            Was ever greif like mine?

With clubs and staves they seeke mee, as a theife,
Who am the way and Truth, the true releife,
Most true to those, who are my greatest greife.
            Was ever greif like mine?

Judas, dost thou betray mee with a kisse?
Canst thou find hell about my lips? and misse
Of life, just at the gates of life and blisse?
            Was ever greif like mine?

See they lay hold on mee, not with the hands
Of Fayth, but fury: Yet at their Commande
I suffer binding, who have loos'd their bands.
            Was ever greif like mine?

All my Disciples fly. Feare puts a barre
Betwixt my Freinds and mee; They leave the starre,
That brought the wise men of the East from farre.
            Was ever greif like mine?

38 Cf. John 14:6.
47 Ezek. 34:27, Ps. 116:16.

Then from one Ruler to another bound
They lead mee, urging, that it was not sound,
What I taught. Comments would the text confound.   55
        Was ever greif like mine?

The Preist and Rulers all false witnes seeke
'Gainst him, who seekes not life, but is the meeke
And ready Paschal Lamb of this great weeke.
        Was ever greif like mine?   60

Then they accuse me of great Blasphemie,
That I did thrust into the Diety,
Who never thought that any Robbery.
        Was ever greif like mine?

Some sayd, that I the Temple to the floore   65
In three dayes raz'd, and raysed, as before.
Why he, that built the world, can doe much more.
        Was ever greif like mine?

Then they condemne mee all with that same breath,
Which I doe give them dayly, unto death: 70
Thus Adam my first breathing rendereth.
        Was ever greif like mine?

They bind, and lead mee unto *Herod:* He
Sends mee to *Pilate*. This makes them agree;
But yet their freindship is my Enmitie.   75
        Was ever greif like mine?

Herod and all his Bands doe sett mee light,
Who teach all hands to warre, fingers to fight,
And onely am the *Lord* of *Hosts* and might.
        Was ever greif like mine?   80

57 *The Preist*: Caiaphas, the High Priest, Matt. 26:57–66.
63 Cf. Philip. 2:6, "Who, being in the form of God, thought it not robbery to be equal with God."
65–66 Cf. John 2:19.
79 Cf. Isa. 6:5.

Herod in Judgement sits, while I doe stand,
Examins mee with a censorious hand:
I him obey, who all things els command:
    Was ever greif like mine?

The *Jews* accuse mee with dispitefulnes,   *85*
And vying malice with my Gentlenes,
Pick quarrels with their onely happines.
    Was ever greif like mine?

I answere nothing, but with patience prove,
If stony hearts will melt with gentle Love.   *90*
But who does hawke at Eagles with a Dove?
    Was ever greif like mine?

My Silence rather doth augment their cry:
My Dove doth back into my bosome fly:
Because the raging waters still are high.   *95*
    Was ever greif like mine?

Harke how they cry alowd still, Crucify.
It is not fitt he live a day, they cry,
Who cannot live lesse, then æternally.
    Was ever greif like mine?   *100*

Pilate a stranger holdeth off; but they
Mine owne deare people, cry, Away, Away.
With Noyses confused frighting the day.
    Was ever greif like mine?

Yet still they shout, and cry, and stop their eares,   *105*
Putting my life among their sins and feares,
And therefore wish my Blood on them and theirs.
    Was ever greif like mine?

94–95 Cf. Gen. 8:9. Christ's *Dove* (his Love) like Noah's dove, cannot alight in the storm of their rage.
107 Cf. Matt. 27:25.

See how spite cankers things. These words, aright
Used, and wished, are the whole worlds light.   *110*
But hony is their gall: Brightnes their Night.
              Was ever greif like mine?

They choose a Murderer, and all agree
In him to doe themselves a curtesie:
For it was their owne cause, who killed mee.   *115*
              Was ever greif like mine?

And a seditious Murderer he was.
But I the Prince of peace, peace, that doth passe
All understanding, more then heaven doth glasse.
              Was ever greif like mine?   *120*

Why Cæsar is their onely King, not I.
He Clave the stony Rock, when they were dry.
But surely not their hearts, as I well try.
              Was ever greif like mine?

Ah! how they scourge me! yet my tendernes   *125*
Doubles each lash: and yet their bitternes
Winds up my greif to a mysteriousnes.
              Was ever greif like mine?

They buffett him, and box him as they list,
Who grasps the earth and heaven with his fist,   *130*
And never yet, whom he would punish, mist.
              Was ever greif like mine?

---

115 Themselves murderers (of Christ) they chose to release the murderer Barabbas instead of Christ. Cf. Mark 15:7–15.

118 Cf. Philip. 4:7.

119 Cf. I Cor. 13:12, "For now we see through a glass, darkly; but then face to face."

122 Ps. 78:16, 17, 21 (BCP), referring to God giving the Israelites water in the desert from the "stony Rock" struck by Moses' rod (Num. 20:8). The ascription of this action to Caesar is ironic but points to a typological truth: Caesar's soldier clave the side of Christ, "that spiritual Rock" (I Cor. 10:4) from which water (grace) pours forth.

130 Cf. Ps. 95:4, Prov. 30:4.

Behold they spitt on mee in scornefull wise,
Who by my spittle gave the blindman eyes,
Leaving his blindnes to my Enemies.   *135*
        Was ever greif like mine?

My face they cover, though it be devine.
As *Moses* face was vailed so is mine,
Lest on their double-darke soules either shine.
        Was ever greif like mine?   *140*

Servants and Abjects flout mee; they are witty.
Now prophesy, who strikes thee, is their ditty.
So they in mee deny themselves all pitty.
        Was ever greif like mine?

And now I am delivered unto death,   *145*
Which each one calls for so with utmost breath,
That he before mee well nigh suffereth.
        Was ever greif like mine?

Weep not, deare Freinds, since I for both have wept
When all my teares were blood, the while you slept: *150*
Your teares for your owne fortunes should be kept.
        Was ever greif like mine?

The souldiers lead mee to the common Hall,
There they deride mee, they abuse mee all;
Yet for twelve heavenly legions I could call.   *155*
        Was ever greif like mine?

Then with a scarlet robe they mee array;
Which shows my blood to be the onely way,
And cordiall left to repaire mans decay.
        Was ever greif like mine?   *160*

   138–39 Cf. Exod. 34:33.
   139 Lest either the Law or the Gospel shine on them.
   146–47 They shout so violently for my death that they nearly spend their own last breaths in doing so.
   155 Cf. Matt. 26:53.

> Then on my head a crowne of thornes I weare:
> For these are all the grapes *Sion* doth beare,
> Though I my vine planted and watered there.
> > Was ever greif like mine?
>
> So sits the earths great curse in *Adams* fall   165
> Upon my head; So I remove it all
> From th' earth unto my brows, and beare the thrall.
> > Was ever greif like mine?
>
> Then with the read they gave to mee before
> They strike my head, the rock from whence all store   170
> Of heavenly blessings issue evermore.
> > Was ever greif like mine?
>
> They bow their knees to mee, and cry, *Haile King*.
> What ever scoffes and scornfulnes can bring,
> I am the floore, the sinke, where they it fling.   175
> > Was ever greif like mine?
>
> Yet since mans Scepters are as Fraile, as Reeds,
> And thorny all their crownes, bloody their weeds,
> I who am truth turne into truth their deeds.
> > Was ever greif like mine?   180
>
> The souldiers also spitt upon that face,
> Which Angels did desire to have the grace,
> And Prophets once to see but found no place.
> > Was ever greif like mine?

161–63 Cf. Isa. 5:1–7 for imagery of the vineyard and of the house of Israel planted by God, which brought forth thorns instead of grapes.

165–66 Adam's Fall brought thorns to the earth (Gen. 3:18) and Christ's crown of thorns represents his bearing of that curse.

170 See note to l. 122.

179 Their burlesque of Christ's regal claims offers a true image of the frailty of earthly monarchy.

181–82 Cf. I Pet. 1:12.

183 Cf. Luke 10:24.

Thus trimmed, forth they bring mee to the rout, *185*
Who *Crucify him,* cry with one strong shout.
God holds his peace at Man, and Man cryes out.
        Was ever greif like mine?

They lead mee in once more, and putting then
Mine owne Cloths on, they lead mee out agen. *190*
Whom Devills fly, thus is he tost of men.
        Was ever greif like mine?

And now weary of sport, glad to ingrosse
All spite in one, counting my life their losse,
They carry mee to my most bitter crosse. *195*
        Was ever greif like mine?

My crosse I beare my selfe, untill I faint.
Then *Simon* beares it for mee by constraint,
The decreed *Burden* of each mortall *Saint.*
        Was ever greif like mine? *200*

Oh all ye, who passe by, Behold and See
Man stole the fruit, but I must climbe the tree,
The tree of life to all, but onely mee.
        Was ever greif like mine?

Lo here I hang, charg'd with a world of sinne, *205*
The greater world o' th' two: For that came in
By words, but this by sorrow I must winne.
        Was ever greif like mine?

Such sorrow as, if sinfull man could feele,
Or feele his part, he would not cease to kneele, *210*
Till all were melted, though he were all steele.
        Was ever greif like mine?

---

193 *ingrosse*: to heap up, concentrate.
199 Cf. Matt. 16:24.
202 *fruit*: Cf. Gen. 3:3-6; Tuve (pp. 86-87) calls attention to the typological tradition presenting Christ as the fruit on the tree of the Cross.
206-207 *that ... words*: the actual world was created by Divine fiat.

But, *Oh* my *God*, my *God*, why leav'st thou mee,
The Sonne, in whom thou dost delight to bee?
My *God*, My *God*—
          Never was greif like mine.

Shame teares my Soule, my Body many a wound,
Sharp Nailes peirce this, but sharper that confound,
Reproches, which are free, while I am bound.
          Was ever greif like mine?

Now heale thy self Physitian, now come downe.
Alas, I did so, when I left my crowne,
And fathers smile for you, to feele his frowne.
          Was ever greif like mine?

In healing, not my self, there doth consist
All that salvation, which ye now resist.
Your safety in my sicknes doth subsist.
          Was ever greif like mine?

Betwixt two theeves I spend my utmost breath,
As he that for some robbery suffereth.
Alas, what have I stolne from you? Death.
          Was ever greif like mine?

A King my title is, prefix'd on high,
Yet by my subjects am condemn'd to dy,
A servile death in servile company.
          Was ever greif like mine?

They give mee Vineger, mingled with gall,
But more with malice: yet, when they did call,
With *Manna*, Angels food, I fed them all.
          Was ever greif like mine?

215 Cf. Matt. 27:46. Line left unfinished.
221 Cf. Luke 4:23, Matt. 27:40, 42.
233 Cf. Matt. 27:37.
239 Ps. 78:25, "Man did eat angels' food: he sent them meat to the full." The line points to the typological relation between the manna which fed the Israelites in the desert, the multiplied loaves and fishes with which Christ fed the multitudes, and the Eucharistic bread.

They part my garments, and by lott dispose
My coat, the type of Love, which once cur'd those,
Who sought for help, never malicious foes.
              Was ever greif like mine?

Nay after death their spite shall further goe
For they will peirce my side, I full well know.
That as sin came: so sacraments might flow.
              Was ever greif like mine?

But now I dy: now all is finished.
My *woe*, mans *weale*. And now I bow my head.
Onely let others say, when I am dead,
              Never was greif like mine.

The Thankes-giving

Oh King of greif (a title strange, yet true
    To thee, of all Kings, onely due)
Oh King of wounds, how shall I greive for thee,
    Who in all greif preventest mee?
Shall I weepe blood? Why thou has wept such store
    That all thy body was one dore.
Shall I be scourged, flouted, boxed, sold?
    'Tis but to tell the tale is told.
My *God,* my *God,* why dost thou part from mee,
    Was such a greif, as cannot be.
Shall I then sing, skipping thy dolefull story,
    And side with thy triumphant glory?
Shall thy strokes be my stroking? Thornes, my flowre?
    Thy Rod, my Posy? Crosse, my Bowre?
But how then shall I imitate thee, and
    Coppy thy faire, though bloody hand?

242–43 Cf. Matt. 14:36. The sick were cured who touched the hem of his garment.

247 As Eve, the instrument of sin, was taken from Adam's side by God, so the pierced side of Christ flowed blood and water (John 19:34) signifying the Church and its sacraments.

The Thankes-giving. 4 *preventest*: goes before.

Surely I will revenge mee on thy Love,
   And try, who shall victorious prove.
If thou dost give mee wealth, I will restore
   All back unto thee by the poore.   *20*
If thou dost give mee honour, men shall see,
   The honour doth belong to thee.
I will not marry, or if she be mine,
   She and her Children shalbe thine.
My Bosome Freind, if he blaspheme thy Name,   *25*
   I will teare thence his Love and fame.
One half of mee being gone, the rest I give
   Unto some Chappell, dy or live.
As for thy Passion — but of that anone,
   When with the other I have done.   *30*
For thy predestination Ile contrive,
   That three yeares hence if I survive,
Ile build a spittle, or mend common wayes,
   But mend mine owne without delayes.
Then I will use the workes of thy creation,   *35*
   As if I us'd them, but for fashion.
The world and I will quarrel; and the yeare
   Shall not perceive, that I am here.
My Music shall find thee, and ev'ry string
   Shall have his attribute to sing.   *40*
That all together may accord in thee,
   And prove one *God*, one Harmonie.
If thou shalt give mee witt, it shall appeare,
   If thou hast given it me, 'tis here.
Nay I will read thy booke, and never move   *45*
   Till I have found therein thy Love.
Thy art of Love, which Ile turne back on thee,
   O my deare *Saviour* Victorie!
Then for thy passion — I will do for that —
   Alas, my *God,* I know not what.   *50*

---

31 He will match God's predestinating him to salvation through Christ, by predestinating himself to good works.
44 *here*: in this book of poems.

The Reprisall

    I have considerd it, and find,
There is no dealing with thy mighty passion.
For though I dy for thee, I am behind;
    My sinnes deserve the Condemnation.
    Oh make mee Innocent, that I 5
May give a disentangled state and free:
And yet thy wounds still my attempts defy,
    For by thy death I dy for thee.
    Ah was it not enough that thou
By thy eternall Glory didst outgoe mee? 10
Couldst thou not greifs sad conquests mee allow,
    But in all Victories overthrow mee?
    Yet by confession will I come
Into thy Conquest: though I can doe nought
Against thee, In thee I will overcome 15
    The Man, who once against thee fought.

The Agony

    Philosophers have measur'd mountaines,
Fadom'd the depths of seas, of states, and Kings,
Walk'd with a staff to heaven, and traced fountaines:
    But there are two vast, spacious things,
The which to measure it doth more behove: 5
Yet few there are, that sound them, Sinne, and Love.

The Reprisall. Title in W., "The Second Thanks-giving."
The Agony. H. points out that the principal metaphor derives from Isa. 63:1–3, used in the Holy Week liturgy: "Who is this that cometh from Edom... Wherefore art thou red in thine apparel, and thy garments like him that treadeth in the winefat? I have trodden the winepress alone." The typological symbolism identifies the bunch of grapes brought back by the spies out of the Promised Land (Num. 13:23) with Christ in his Passion, giving forth the saving wine of his blood (our salvation, and the Eucharistic sacrament).

>   Who would know sinne, let him repaire
> Unto Mount Olivet, there shall he see
> A man so wrung with paines, that all his haire,
> >   His skin, his garments bloody bee.   10
> Sinne is that Presse and Vice, which forceth paine
> To hunt his cruell food through ev'ry vaine.
>
> >   Who knowes not Love, let him assay
> And tast that Juice, which on the Crosse a Pike
> Did sett againe a-broach; then let him say,   15
> >   If ever he did tast the like.
> Love is that liquor sweet and most divine,
> Which my *God* feels as blood, but I, as wine.

The Sinner

> *Lord,* how I am all Ague, when I seeke,
> >   What I have treasur'd in my memory!
> Since if my soule make even with the weeke,
> Each seventh note by right is due to thee.
> I find there quarries of pil'd vanities,   5
> >   But shreds of holines, that dare not venture
> >   To shew their face, since crosse to thy decrees.
> There the circumference earth is, Heaven the center.
> In so much dregs the quintessence is small.
> >   The spirit and good extract of my heart   10
> >   Comes to about the many hundred part.
> Yet *Lord* restore thine Image, heare my call:
> >   And though my hard heart scarce to thee can grone,
> >   Remember, that thou once didst write in stone.

The Sinner. 14 Cf. Exod. 31:18. The commandments written upon tables of stone are opposed to the new covenant of grace written upon the "fleshy tables" of the heart (II Cor. 3:3) which, ironically, has also become stony.

Good Friday

    Oh my *Cheif Good*,
How shall I measure out thy blood?
How shall I count, what thee befell,
    And each greife tell?

    Shall I thy woes 5
Number according to thy foes?
Or since one starre showd thy first breath,
    Shall all thy death?

    Or shall each leaf,
Which fals in Autumne, score a greif? 10
Or cannot leaves, but fruit be signe
    Of the true vine?

    Then let each houre,
Of my whole life one greif devoure;
That thy distresse through all may runne, 15
    And be my Sunne.

    Or rather let
My severall sinnes their sorrows gett,
That as each Beast his cure doth know,
    Each sin may so. 20

Since blood is fittest, *Lord*, to write
Thy sorrows in, and bloody fight,
My heart hath store, write there, where in
One box doth ly both Inke and sinne.

That when sinne spies so many foes, 25
Thy whips, thy Nailes, thy wounds, thy woes
All come to lodge there, sinne may say,
No roome for mee, and fly away.

Sinne being gone, oh fill the place,
And keepe possession with thy grace,   30
Lest sinne take courage, and returne,
And all the writings blot or burne.

Redemption

Having bin Tenant long to a Rich *Lord,*
  Not thriving, I resolved to be bold,
  And make a suit unto him to afford
A new small-rented Lease, and cancell th'old.
In Heaven at his mannour I him sought,   5
  They told me there, that he was lately gone
  About some Land, which he had dearly bought
Long since on Earth, to take possession.
I strait return'd, and knowing his great birth,
  Sought him accordingly in great Resorts,   10
  In Citties, Theaters, Gardens, Parks, and Courts;
At length I heard a ragged noise and mirth
  Of theeves and murderers. There I him espyd,
  Who strait, *Your suit is granted,* sayd, and died.

Sepulcher

Oh Blessed body, whither art thou throwne.
No lodgeing for thee, but a cold hard stone.
So many harts on earth, and yet not one
                Receive thee?

Sure there is Roome within our hearts good store: 5
For they can lodge transgressions by the score.
Thousands of toyes dwell there; yet out of dore
                They leave thee.

Redemption. 4 *new small-rented Lease*: the new covenant of grace which cancels out the harsher, more demanding covenant of the Law.

But that, which shows them large, shows them unfitt.
What ever sinne did this pure Rock committ,   10
Which holds thee now? Who hath endited it
                of murder?

Where our hard hearts have tooke up stones to braine thee,
And missing this, most falsly did arraine thee,
Only these stones in quiet entertaine thee,   15
                and order.

And as of old the Law by heavenly art
Was writt in stone: So thou, which also art
The Letter of the word, find'st no fitt heart
                to hold thee.   20

Yet doe wee still persist, as we began,
And so should perish, but that nothing can,
Though it be cold, hard, foule, from Loving man
                withold thee.

Easter

    Rise heart; thy *Lord* is Risen. Sing his praise
              Without delayes,
    Who takes thee by the hand, that thou likewise
             With him mayst rise:
    That, as his death Calcined thee to dust,   5
    His life may make thee gold, and much more Just.

    Awake, my Lute, and struggle for thy part
             With all thy art.
    The *Crosse* taught all Wood to resound his Name,
              Who bore the same.   10
    His stretched *sinews* taught all strings, what key
    Is best to celebrate this most high Day.

Sepulcher. 13 John 10:31: "Then the Jews took up stones again to stone him."

>   Consort both *Heart* and *Lute:* and twist a song
>   Pleasant and long:
>   Or since all Musick is but three parts vyed   *15*
>   And multiplied
>   Oh let thy Blessed *Spirit* beare a part,
>   And make up our defects with his sweet art.
>
>
>   I gott mee flowrs to straw thy way,
>   I gott mee boughs off many a tree: *20*
>   But thou wast up by break of day,
>   And brought'st thy sweets along with thee.
>
>   The *Sunne* arising in the *East*
>   Though he give light, and th' *East* perfume;
>   If they should offer to contest   *25*
>   With thy arising, they presume.
>
>   Can there be any day but this,
>   Though many sunnes to shine endeavour?
>   Wee count three hundred, but wee misse:
>   There is but one, and that one ever.   *30*

Easter. 13 *twist*: weave, as in polyphonic music.
  15 *vyed*: to increase in number by addition or repetition (*OED*). The heart and lute require the Spirit, which *helpeth our infirmities* to make the third tone with them and thus form a chord (H.).

Easter wings

    Lord, who createdst Man in wealth and store,
        Though foolishly he lost the same,
            Decaying more and more,
                Till he became
                    Most poore.   5
                    With thee
                O let me rise,
            As Larks, harmoniously
        And sing this day thy Victories.
    Then shall the fall further the flight in mee.   10

    My tender Age in sorrow did beginne:
        And still with sicknesses and shame
            Thou didst so punish sinne,
                That I became
                    Most thinne.   15
                    With thee
                Let mee combine,
            And feele this day thy victorie;
        For if I impe my wing on thine,
    Affliction shall advance the flight in mee.   20

H. Baptisme [I]

As he, that sees a dark and shady grove,
    Stays not but lookes beyond it on the sky:
So when I veiw my sins, mine eyes remove
More backward still, and to that water fly
Which is above the Heavens, whose spring and vent   5
    Is in my *Deare Redeemers* peirced side.
    O blessed streames, either ye doe prevent
And stop our sinnes from growing thick and wide,
Or els give teares to drown them, as they grow.

Easter wings. 19 *impe*: in falconry, to engraft feathers in a damaged wing so as to restore or improve the powers of flight (*OED*).

  In you Redemption measures all my time,   *10*
   And spreeds the plaister equall to the crime.
You taught the *Booke of Life* my Name, that so
   Whatever future sinnes should mee miscall,
  Your first acquaintance might discredit all.

H. Baptisme [II]

    Since *Lord* to thee
   A narrow way and little gate
Is all the passage, on my infancie
   Thou didst lay hold, and antedate
    My faith in mee.   *5*

    O let me still
   Write thee great *God,* and me a child:
Let mee be soft and supple to thy will,
   Small to my selfe, to others mild,
    Behither ill.   *10*

    Although by stealth
   My flesh gett on, yet let her sister
My soule bid nothing, but preserve her wealth.
   The growth of flesh is but a blister,
    Childhood is health.   *15*

Nature

  Full of Rebellion, I would die,
   Or fight, or travell, or deny,
  That thou hast ought to doe with mee.
     O tame my heart;
    It is thy highest art   *5*
  To captivate strong holds to thee.

H. Baptisme [II]. 10 *Behither*: on this side of, short of (*OED*).
Nature. 6 Cf. II Cor. 10:4.

If thou shalt let this Venome lurke,
And in suggestions fume and worke,
My soule will turne to bubbles strait,
     And thence by kind
  Vanish into a wind,
Making thy workmanship, deceit.

O smooth my rugged heart, and there
Ingrave thy reverend Law and feare;
Or make a new one, since the old
     Is saplesse growne,
  And a much fitter stone
To hide my dust, then thee to hold.

Sinne [I]

Lord, with what care hast thou begirt us round?
 Parents first season us: then schoolemasters
Deliver us to Laws: They send us bound
To rules of reason, holy messengers,
Pulpits and Sundayes, sorrow dogging sinne,
 Afflictions sorted, anguish of all sizes,
 Fine nets and strategemes to catch us in,
Bibles layd open, millions of surprizes,
Blessings before hand, tyes of gratefulnes,
 The sound of glory ringing in our eares
 Without, our shame, within our consciences,
Angels and Grace, Eternal hopes and feares.
 Yet all these fences and their whole array
 One cunning bosome-sinne blows quite away.

13–18 Ezek. 36:26, "A new heart also will I give you.... I will take away the stony heart out of your flesh, and I will give you an heart of flesh."

Affliction [I]

When first thou didst entice to thee my heart,
        I thought the service brave.
So many Joyes I writ downe for my part,
        Besides what I might have
Out of my stock of natural delites,
Augmented with thy gracious benefites.

I looked on thy furniture so fine,
        And made it fine to mee.
Thy glorious household-stuff did mee intwine,
        And 'tice mee unto thee.
Such starres I counted mine: both Heaven and earth
Payd mee my wages in a world of mirth.

What pleasures could I want, whose King I served?
        Where joyes my fellows were:
Thus argued into hopes, my thoughts reserved
        No place for greif or feare.
Therefore my suddaine soule caught at the place,
And made her youth and fiercenes seeke thy face.

At first thou gav'st mee milk and sweetnesses,
        I had my wish and way.
My dayes were straw'd with flowres and happines,
        There was no month but May.
But with my yeares sorrow did twist and grow,
And made a party unawares for woe.

My flesh began unto my soule in paine,
        Sicknesses cleave my bones.
Consuming Agues dwell in every vaine,
        And tune my breath to grones.
Sorrow was all my soule, I scarce beleived,
Till greife did tell mee roundly, that I lived.

Affliction [I]. 25 My flesh began to complain to my soul of sickness.

When I gott health, thou took'st away my life
                    And more; for my freinds dy:
My mirth and edge was lost; a blunted knife
                    Was of more use, then I.
Thus thinne and leane without a fence or freind *35*
I was blowne through with every storme and wind.

Whereas my birth and spirit rather tooke
                    The way that takes the towne
Thou didst betray mee to a lingring booke
                    And wrap mee in a gowne. *40*
I was Intangled in the world of strife,
Before I had the powre to change my life.

Yet for I threatned oft the seege to raise,
                    Not simpring all mine age,
Thou often didst with Academick praise *45*
                    Melt and dissolve my rage.
I tooke thy sweetned pill, till I came where
I could not goe away, nor persevere.

Yet lest perchance I should too happy bee
                    In my unhappines, *50*
Turning my purge to food, thou throwest mee
                    Into more sicknesses.
Thus doth thy Power crosse-bias mee, not making
Thine owne guift good, yet mee from my waies taking.

Now I am heere, what thou wilt doe with mee, *55*
                    None of my bookes will show.
I read, and sigh, and wish I were a tree;
                    For sure then I should grow
To fruit or shade: at least some bird would trust
Her household to mee, and I should be just. *60*

32 H. identifies the friends as Ludovick Stuart, second Duke of Lennox and Richmond (d. 16 February 1623/4); James, second Marquis of Hamilton (d. 2 March 1624/5); King James I (d. 27 March 1625) — with whom, according to Walton, all Herbert's court aspirations died; Francis Bacon (d. 9 April 1626); Lancelot Andrewes (d. 26 September 1626); Herbert's mother (d. June 1627).

53 *crosse-bias*: metaphor from the game of Bowls, meaning "give me an inclination other than my own."

Yet though thou troublest mee, I must be meeke:
               In weaknes must be stout.
Well, I will change the service, and goe seeke
               Some other Master out.
Ah my Deare *God,* though I am cleane forgott,   65
Let mee not love thee, if I love thee not.

Repentance

Lord I confesse my sinne is great,
   Great is my sinne. O gently treat
With thy quick flowre, thy momentarie bloome,
        Whose life still pressing
        Is one undressing,
   A steedy aiming at a tombe.   5

Mans age is two houres worke, or three,
   Each day doth round about us see.
Thus are wee to delights; but wee are all
        To sorrows, old,   10
        If life be told,
   From what life feeleth, *Adams* fall.

O let thy height of mercy then
   Compassionate short breathed men.
Cut mee not off for my most foule transgression,   15
        I doe confesse
        My foolishnesse,
   My *God* accept of my confession.

Sweeten at length this bitter boule;
   Which thou hast powrd into my soule: 20
Thy wormewood turne to health, winds to faire weather.
        For if thou stay,
        I, and this day,
   As wee did rise, wee dy together.

Repentance. 3 *quick*: "living," and also "rapidly perishing."
22 *stay*: stay away.

> When thou for sinne rebukest man,   *25*
>   Forth with he waxeth woe and wan.
> Bitternes fills our bowells: all our hearts
>   Pine, and decay,
>   And drope away,
>   And carry with them th' other parts.   *30*
>
> But thou wilt sinne and greif destroy,
>   That so the broken bones may joy,
> And tune together in a well sett song,
>   Full of his praises,
>   Who dead men raises: *35*
>   Fractures well cur'd make us more strong.

Faith

> *Lord*, how couldst thou so much appease
> Thy wrath for sinne as, when Mans sight was dimme
> And could see little, to regard his ease,
>   And bring by Faith all things to him.
>
>   Hungry I was, and had no meat: *5*
> I did conceit a most delicious feast,
> I had it strait, and did as truly eat,
>   As ever did a welcome guest.
>
>   There is a rare outlandish root,
> Which when I could not gett I thought it heere: *10*
> That apprehension cur'd so well my foot,
>   That I can walke to heaven well neere.

25–26 Ps. 39:12, "When thou with rebukes dost chasten man for sinne, thou makest his beauty to consume away" (BCP).

32 Ps. 51:8, "that the bones which thou hast broken may rejoice."

Faith. 9–12 His walk to heaven is hampered by the serpent (Gen. 3:15) who has bruised his heel (as regenerate Christian he is both the first and the second Adam), but Christ provides an antidote against this serpent (H.).

    I owed thousands and much more.
I did beleive, that I did nothing owe,
And liv'd accordingly, my Creditor
    Beleeves so too, and lets mee goe.

    Fayth makes mee any thing, or all
That I beleive is in the sacred Story:
And where sin placeth mee in Adams Fall,
    Fayth setts mee higher in his glory.

    If I goe Lower in the booke,
What can be lower, then the common manger?
Faith puts mee there with him, who sweetly tooke
    Our flesh and frailty, Death and danger.

    If Blisse had lien in Art or strength,
None but the wise, or strong had gained it:
Where now by fayth all armes are of a length,
    One size doth all conditions fitt.

    A peasant may beleive, as much
As a great Cleark, and reach the highest stature.
Thus dost thou make proud knowledge bend and crouch,
    While grace fills up uneven Nature.

    When Creatures had no real light
Inherent in them, thou didst make the sunne,
Impute a lustre, and allow them bright
    And in this show, what *Christ* hath done.

    That, which before was darkned cleane
With bushy groves, pricking the lookers eie,
Vanishd away, when Fayth did change the scene,
    And then appear'd a glorious sky.

---

20 The glory of the Second Adam, Rom. 5:12–21.
37 *cleane*: wholly, quite.

What though my Body runne to dust?
Faith cleaves unto it, counting every graine
With an exact, and most particular trust,
    Reserving all for flesh againe.

Prayer [I]

Prayer the *Churches* banquet, Angels age,
  Gods breath in Man returning to his birth,
  The soule in paraphrase, heart in pilgrimage,
The Christian plummet sounding heaven and earth,
Engine against th'Almighty, sinners Towre,   5
  Reversed thunder, *Christ*-side-peircing speare,
  The six-dayes world transposing in an houre,
A kind of tune, which all things heare and feare,
Softnes, and peace, and joy, and love, and blisse,
  Exalted Manna, Gladnes of the best,   10
  Heaven in ordinary, Man well drest,
The milkyway, the bird of Paradise,
  Church-bels beyond the starres heard, the soules blood,
  The Land of spices, something understood.

The H. Communion

Not in rich furniture, or fine array,
    Nor in a wedge of gold,
    Thou, who for mee wast sold,
  To mee dost now thy self convey:
For so thou shouldst without mee still have binne,   5
    Leaving within mee sinne.

Prayer [I]. 1 *Angels age*: belonging to the timeless existence of the angels.
2 The breath God breathed in man (Gen. 2:7) returning to God.
7 *transposing*: transmuting, transforming.
11 *ordinary*: prayer is the common life of heaven.
The H. Communion. 2 Josh. 7:21, "When I saw among the spoils a goodly Babylonish garment, and two hundred shekels of silver, and a wedge of gold of fifty shekels weight, then I coveted them, and took them." The contrast is between the lavish Roman Catholic rites and the simple Anglican communion.

But by the way of Nourishment and strength
    Thou creep'st into my brest,
    Making thy way my rest,
   And thy small quantities my length,   10
Which spred their forces into every part,
    Meeting sins force and art.

Yet can these not gett over to my soule
    Leaping the wall, that parts
    Our souls and fleshy hearts,   15
   But as th'outworks, they may controule
My rebell-flesh, and carrying thy Name
    Affright both sinne and shame.

Onely thy grace, which with these elements comes,
    Knoweth the ready way,   20
    And hath the privy key,
   Opening the soules most subtle roomes,
While those to spirits refin'd, at doore attend,
    Dispatches from their freind.

Give mee my captive soule, or take   25
  My body also thither.
Another lift, like this, will make
  Them both to be together.

Before that sinne turn'd flesh to stone,
    And all our lumpe to leaven,   30
A fervent sigh might well have blowne
    Our innocent earth to heaven.

For sure when *Adam* did not know
    To sin, or sin to smother,
He might to heaven from Paradise goe,   35
    As from one roome t'another.

13–24 The eucharistic elements form only an external bulwark against sin and shame at the door of the soul, but grace has the key to the soul's inmost recesses (H.).

34 Or sin (know how) to smother (us).

Thou hast restor'd us to this ease
   By this thy heavenly blood
Which I can goe to when I please,
   And leave th'earth to their food. 40

Antiphon [I]

Cho. Let all the world in ev'ry corner sing,
        My *God* and King.
   Vers. The Heavens are not too high,
        His praise may thither fly.
        The Earth is not too Low, 5
        His praises there may grow.
Cho. Let all the world in ev'ry corner sing,
        My *God* and King.
   Vers. The *Church* with psalmes must shout,
        No dore can keepe them out. 10
        But above all the heart
        Must beare the longest part.
Cho. Let all the world in ev'ry corner sing,
        My *God* and King.

Love

I

Immortal *Love,* Author of this great frame,
   Sprung from that Beauty, which can never fade,
   How hath Man parceld out thy glorious Name,
And thrown it on that dust, which thou hast made,
While mortal Love doth all the title gaine. 5
   Which siding with invention, they together
   Beare all the sway, possessing heart and Braine,
(Thy workemanship), and give thee share in neither.
Witt fancies beauty, beauty raiseth witt.
   The World is theirs, they two play out the game, 10
   Thou standing by; and though thy glorious Name

Wrought our deliverance from th'infernal pitt,
    Who sings thy praise? onely a skarf or glove
    Doth warme our hands, and make them write of love.

II

Immortal Heat, o Let thy greater flame
    Attract the lesser to it: Let those fires,
    Which shall consume the world, first make it tame,
And kindle in our hearts such true desires,
As may consume our lusts, and make thee way: 5
    Then shall our hearts pant thee: then shall our braine
    All her invention on thine Altar lay;
And there in hymnes send back thy fire againe:
Our eies shall see thee, which before saw dust,
    Dust blowne by witt, till that they both were blind.   10
Thou shalt recover all thy goods in kind,
Who wert disseized by usurping lust.
    All knees shall bow to thee, all witts shall rise,
    And praise him, who did make and mend our eies.

The Temper [I]

    How should I praise thee, *Lord?* how should my rimes
        Gladly ingrave thy love in steele?
        If what my soule doth feele sometimes,
        My soule might ever feele.

    Although there were some forty heavens, or more,   5
        Sometimes I peere above them all,
        Sometimes I hardly reach a score,
        Sometimes to Hell I fall.

    O rack mee not to such a vast extent,
        Those distances belong to thee: 10

Love [II]. 6 *pant thee*: pant for thee. Cf. Ps. 42:1.
12 *disseized*: dispossessed, usually wrongfully or by force (*OED*).

> The world's too little for thy Tent,
> > A grave too bigg for mee.
>
> Wilt thou meet Armes with man, that thou dost stretch
> > A crumme of dust from heaven to hell?
> > Will great *God* measure with a wretch?   15
> > > Shall he thy stature spell?
>
> O Let mee, when thy roofe my soule hath hid,
> > O let mee roost and nestle there.
> > Then of a sinner thou art rid,
> > > And I of hope and feare.   20
>
> Yet take thy way, for sure thy way is best,
> > Stretch or contract mee, thy poore debter.
> > This is but tuning of my brest
> > > To make the Musick better.
>
> Whither I fly with Angels, fall with dust,   25
> > Thy hands made both, and I am there:
> > Thy powre and love, my love and trust
> > > Make one place ev'ry-where.

The Temper [II]

> It cannot be. Where is that mighty joy,
> > Which just now tooke up all my heart?
> > *Lord,* if thou must needs use thy dart,
> Save that; and mee, or sin for both destroy.
>
> The grosser world stands to thy word and art;   5
> > But thy diviner world of grace
> > Thou suddenly dost raise and race,
> And ev'ry day a new Creator art.

The Temper [I]. 15 In a duel, nobles will meet none but their equals.
The Temper [II]. 7 *race*: raze.

O fix thy chaire of Grace, that all my powres
    May also fix their reverence.   10
    For when thou dost depart from hence
They grow unruly, and sitt in thy bowres.

Scatter, or bind them all to bend to thee:
    Though elements change, and heaven move,
    Let not thy higher court remove,   15
But keep a standing Majesty in mee.

Jordan [I]

Who sayes that fictions onely and false haire
Become a verse? Is there in truth, no beauty?
Is all good structure in a winding staire?
May no lines passe except they doe their duty,
    Not to a true but painted Chaire?   5

Is it no verse except inchanted groves
And suddaine Arbours shaddow course-spunne lines?
Must purling streames refresh a lovers loves?
Must all be vaild, while he, that reads, divines,
    Catching the sense at two removes?   10

Shepards are honest people, let them sing:
Riddle who list for mee, and pull for prime:
I envy no mans Nightingale or spring
Nor let them punish mee with losse of rime
    Who plainely say, My *God,* My *King.*   15

Jordan [I]. The Israelites crossed the river Jordan (a type of baptism) before entering the Promised Land, Canaan (a type of Salvation). Herbert here announces the baptism of his verse to the service of God (Tuve). In his first *Eclogue* Petrarch also used Jordan as the symbol for Christian poetry.
  12 *pull for prime*: to draw for a winning hand in the card game of Primero (*OED*).

Imployment [I]

If as a flowre doth sprid and dy,
  Thou would'st extend mee to some good,
Before I were by frosts extremity
        Nipt in the bud.

The sweetnes and the praise were thine,
  But the extension and the roome,
Which in thy garland I should fill, were mine
        At thy great doome.

For as thou dost impart thy grace,
  The greater shall our glory bee.
The measure of our joyes is in this place,
        The stuffe with thee.

Let mee not languish then, and spend
  A life, as barren to thy praise,
As is the dust, to which that life doth tend,
        But with delayes.

All things are busy, onely I
  Neither bring hony with the Bees,
Nor flowres to make that, nor the husbandry
        To water these.

I am no link of thy great chaine,
  But all my company is a weed:
Lord place mee in thy consort: give one straine
        To my poore reed.

Imployment [I]. 11–12 In this life, our God-inspired activity is the *measure* of the room we occupy in God's garland (l. 6), but the *stuffe*, the substance of our joys, is with God.
    23 *consort*: many musicians playing on several instruments (*OED*).

The H. Scriptures

I

Oh Booke! infinite sweetnes! Let my heart
    Suck ev'ry letter, and a hony gaine;
    Precious for any greif in any part
To cleere the brest, to mollify all paine.
Thou art all health, health thriving till it make   5
    A full æternity. Thou art a masse
    Of strange delights, where we may wish and take.
Ladies looke here: this is the thankefull glasse,
That mends the lookers eies. This is the well
    That washes what it shows. Who can indeere   10
    Thy prayse too much! Thou art heavens Lidger here,
Working against the states of Death and Hell.
    Thou art joys handsell: heaven lyes flat in thee
    Subject to ev'ry mounters bended knee.

II

Oh that I knew how all thy lights combine,
    And the configurations of their glory;
    Seeing not onely how each verse doth shine,
But all the constellations of the story.
This verse marks that, and both doe make a motion   5
    Unto a third, that ten leaves off doth ly.
    Then as dispersed herbs do watch a potion,
These three make up some *Christians* destiny.
Such are thy secrets, which my life makes good,
    And comments on thee: for in ev'ry thing   10
    Thy words doe find mee out, and parallels bring,
And in another make mee understood.
    Starres are poore bookes, and oftentimes doe misse:
    This booke of starres lights to eternal blisse.

    The H. Scriptures I. 2 *hony gaine*: Ps. 119:103, "How sweet are thy words unto my taste! yea, sweeter than honey to my mouth!"
    11 *Lidger*: one appointed to lie or reside at a foreign court, a resident ambassador (H.).
    13 *handsell*: a first installment.
    The H. Scriptures II. 7 *watch*: verses of scripture *mark* or relate to one another so that by combination they may guide men's lives, as herbs *watch* each other in a beneficial potion. Cf. *Priest to the Temple*, Ch. iv.

Whitsunday

Listen sweet Dove unto my song,
  And spred thy golden wings in mee,
  Hatching my tender heart so long,
Till it gett wing, and fly away with thee.

  Where is that fire, which once descended
  On thy Apostles? thou didst then
  Keepe open house, richly attended,
Feasting all Commers by twelve chosen men.

  Such glorious guifts thou didst bestow,
  That th'earth did like a heaven appeare,
  The starres were comming downe to know
If they might mend their wages, and serve heere.

  The Sun, which once did shine alone,
  Hung downe his head, and wish'd for night,
  When he beheld twelve sunnes for one
Going about the world, and giving light.

  But since those pipes of gold, which brought
  That cordial water to our ground,
  Were cutt and martyred by the fault
Of those, who did themselves through their side wound,

  Thou shut'st the dore, and keep'st within,
  Scarce a good joy creeps through the chinke.
  And if the braves of conquering sinne
Did not excite thee, wee should wholy sinke.

  Lord though wee change, thou are the same,
  The same sweet *God* of Love and light:
  Restore this day for thy great Name
Unto his ancient and miraculous right.

Whitsunday. 17 *pipes of gold*: the apostles as channels conveying to others the graces they received on the first Pentecost; cf. Zech. 4:12.
  23 *braves*: defiant threats.

Grace

My stock lyes dead, and no encrease
Doth my dull husbandry improve:
O let thy graces without cease
        Drop from above.

If still the Sunne should hide his face,
Thy house would but a dungeon prove;
Thy workes Nights captives: O let grace
        Drop from above.

The dew doth ev'ry morning fall,
And shall the dew outstrip thy dove?
The dew, for which grasse cannot call
        Drop from above.

Death is still working like a Moule,
And digs my grave at each remove:
Let grace worke too, and on my soule
        Drop from above.

Sinne is still hammering my heart
Unto a hardnes, void of love:
Let supling grace to crosse his art
        Drop from above.

O Come: for thou dost know the way:
Or if to mee thou wilt not move,
Remove mee, where I need not say,
        Drop from above.

Grace. 1–4 Cf. Job 14:7–9.
1 *stock*: trunk of a tree.

Praise [I]

To write a verse or two is all the praise,
        That I can raise:
  Mend my estate in any waies,
        Thou shalt have more.

I goe to *Church;* helpe me to wings, and I   5
        Will thither fly;
  Or if I mount unto the sky
        I will doe more.

Man is all weaknes; there is no such thing
        As Prince or King,   10
  His arme is short: yet with a sling
        He may doe more.

An herbe destild, and drunk, may dwell next dore
        On the same flore
  To a brave soule: Exalt the poore,   15
        They can doe more.

O Raise mee then. Poore Bees, that work all day
        Sting my delay,
  Who have a worke as well as they,
        And much, much more.   20

Affliction [II]

        Kill mee not ev'ry day
Thou *Lord of Life*; since thy one Death for mee
    Is more, then all my Deaths can bee,
        Though I in broken pay
Dy over each houre of *Methusalems* stay.   5

Praise [I]. 11 *with a sling*: the means by which David slew Goliath, I Sam. 17 : 50. 13–16 The effects of a potion ascend to the brain and so dwell next to the soul, but the poor, if God exalt them, rise higher still and dwell next to God (H.).
Affliction [II]. 4 *broken pay*: installments.

      If all Mens teares were let
Into one common sewer, sea and brine
    What were they all compar'd to thine?
      Wherein if they were sett,
They would discolor thy most bloody sweat.   10

      Thou art my greif alone,
Thou *Lord* conceale it not: and as thou art
    All my delight; so all my smart
      Thy crosse tooke up in one,
By way of imprest, all my future mone.   15

Mattens

     I cannot ope mine eies,
    But thou art ready there to catch
     My morning-soule and sacrifice.
Then wee must needs for that day make a match.

     My *God* what is a heart,   5
    Silver, or gold, or precious stone.
     Or starre, or rainebow, or a part
Of all these things, or all of them in one?

     My *God* what is a heart,
    That thou shouldst it so ey, and woe,   10
     Powring upon it all thy art,
As if that thou had'st nothing els to doe?

     Indeed Mans whole estate
    Amounts (and richly) to serve thee:
     He did not heaven and earth create,   15
Yet studies them, not him by whom they bee.

10 *discolor*: take the color out of.
15 *imprest*: payment in advance, especially of soldiers and sailors.
Mattens. 4 *make a match*: come to agreement.

> Teach mee thy love to know,
> That this new light, which now I see,
> May both the work and workman show,
> Then by a sunne-beame I will climb to thee.   20

Sinne [II]

> O that I could a sinne once see.
> We paint the Divel foule, yet he
> Hath some good in him all agree.
> Sinne is flat opposite to th'Almighty, seeing
> It wants the good of vertue, and of beeing.   5
>
> But *God* more care of us hath had:
> If apparitions make us sadd,
> By sight of sinne we should grow madd.
> Yet as in sleepe we see foule death and live:
> So Divels are our sinnes in perspective.   10

Even-song

> Blest be the *God* of Love,
> Who gave mee eies, and light, and powre this day,
> Both to be busy, and to play.
> But much more blest be *God* above,
> Who gave mee sight alone,   5

Sinne [II]. Augustine (*Confes.* VII. xi–xv. 17–22), Aquinas (*Sum. Theol.* II, Q.48), and other theologians maintain that evil is not a substance but a privation, defect, or corruption of good; thus it has no real being and cannot be seen. We can only look upon good things corrupted, e.g., devils.

10 *perspective*: a picture or figure constructed to produce a special effect, e.g., appearing distorted or confused except when viewed from one point of view (*OED*). Devils accordingly provide a point of view or perspective from which **alone** we can see sin.

Which to himselfe he did deny:
For when he sees my waies, I dy:
But I have gott his sonne, and he hath none.

What have I brought thee home
For this thy Love? have I discharg'd the debt,   10
Which this dayes favor did begett?
I ranne, but all I brought, was fome.
Thy diet, care, and cost
Doe end in bubles, balls of winde;
Of wind to thee, whom I have crost,   15
But balls of wildfire to my troubled mind.

Yet still thou goest on,
And now with darknes closest weary eyes,
Saying to Man it doth suffice:
Henceforth repose: your work is done.   20
Thus in thy ebony boxe
Thou dost inclose us, till the day
Put our amendment in our way,
And give new wheels to our disordered clocks.

I muse, which shows more love,   25
The day or Night; that is the gale, this th'harbour.
That is the walk, and this the arbour.
Or that the garden, this the grove.
My *God,* thou art all Love.
Not one poore minute scapes thy brest,   30
But brings a favour from above;
And in this love more then in bed I rest.

Church-*monuments*

While that my soule repaires to her devotion,
Here I intombe my flesh, that it betimes
May take acquaintance of this heape of dust,

Even-song. 8 *sonne*: Son of God, and sun as source of light.

To which the blast of Deaths incessant motion,
Fed with the exhalation of our crimes,   5
Drives all at last. Therefore I gladly trust
My body to this schoole, that it may learne
To spell his elements, and find his birth
Written in dusty heraldry and lines.
Which dissolution sure doth best discerne   10
Comparing dust with dust, and earth with earth.
These laugh at Jet, and Marble put for signes,
To sever the good fellowship of dust,
And spoile the meeting. What shall point out them
When they shall bow, and kneele, and fall downe flat,   15
To kisse those heapes, which now they have in trust?
Deare Flesh, while I doe pray, learne here thy stemme
And true descent: that when thou shalt grow fatt,
And wanton in thy cravings, thou maist know,
That flesh is but the glasse, which holds the dust,   20
That measures all our time; which also shall
Be crumbled into dust. Mark here below
How tame these ashes are, how free from lust,
That thou maist fitt thy self against thy fall.

Church-*Musique*

Sweetest of sweets I thanke you. When displeasure
    Did through my body wound my mind;
You tooke mee thence, and in your house of pleasure
    A dainty lodging mee assign'd.

Now I in you without a body move,   5
    Rising and falling with your wings:
Wee both together sweetly live and love,
    Yet say sometimes, *God* help poore Kings.

Church-monuments. 12 *These*: dust and earth.
  14 *them*: the jet and marble monuments which will soon be dust themselves.
  Church-Musique. 8 Tuve cites Ps. 149:8–9, wherein the singing church is enjoined to praise God and to execute vengeance on the heathen, "To bind their kings with chains, and their nobles with fetters of iron . . . this honour have all his saints."

Comfort, I'le dy. For if you post from mee,
        Sure I shall doe so, and much more: *10*
But if I travaile in your company,
        You know the way to heavens dore.

Mary } *Anagram*
Army

How well her Name an Army doth present,
In whom the *Lord of hosts* did pitch his tent.

Church-*lock and key*

I know it is my sinne, which locks thine eares,
        And binds thy hands
Out-crying my requests, drowning my teares,
Or els the chilnes of my faint demands.

But as cold hands are angry with the fire,   *5*
        And mend it still:
So I doe lay the want of my desire,
Not on my sinnes, or coldnes, but thy will.

Yet heare, oh *God,* onely for his bloods sake
        Which pleads for mee: *10*
For though sinnes plead too, yet like stones they make
His bloods sweet current much more lowd to bee.

The Church-*floore*

Mark you the floore? that square and speckel'd stone,
        Which lookes so firme and strong,
                Is *Patience.*

Church-lock and key. 11–12 Stones make a brook run more noisily.

And th'other black and grave, wherewith each one
    Is checker'd all along, 5
        Humility.
The gentle rising, which on either hand,
    Leads to the Quire above,
        Is *Confidence.*
But the sweet cement, which in one sure band 10
    Ties the whole frame, is *Love*
        And *Charity.*

    Hither sometimes Sinne steales and staines
        The Marbles neat, and curious vaines:
But all is cleansed, when the Marble weeps. 15
    Sometimes death, puffing at the doore,
        Blows all the dust about the floore;
But while he thinkes to spoile the roome, he sweeps.
    Blest be the *Architect,* whose art
        Could build so strong in a weake heart. 20

The Windowes

Lord how can Man preach thy eternal word?
    He is a brittle crazy glasse:
Yet in thy *Temple* thou dost him afford
        This glorious and transcendent place,
        To be a window through thy grace. 5

But when thou dost anneale in glasse thy story,
    Making thy life to shine within
The holy Preachers; then the light and glory
        More reverend grows, and more doth win:
        Which els shows watrish bleake, and thin. 10

The Church-floore. 14 *neat*: delicate.

Doctrine and life, colours and light, in one
    When they combine and mingle, bring
A strong regard and awe: but speech alone
    Doth vanish like a flaring thing,
    And in the eare, not conscience ring.   *15*

Trinity-*Sunday*

Lord who hast form'd mee out of mudd,
    And hast redeem'd mee through thy blood,
    And sanctified mee to doe good,

Purge all my sins done heretofore;
    For I confesse my heavy score,   *5*
    And I will strive to sinne no more.

Enrich my heart, mouth, hands in mee
    With faith, with hope, with charitie;
    That I may runne, rise, rest with thee.

Content

Peace muttring thoughts, and doe not grudge to keep
    Within the walls of your owne brest:
Who cannot on his owne bed sweetly sleep,
    Can on anothers hardly rest.

Gad not abroad at ev'ry quest and call   *5*
    Of an untrained hope, or passion:
To court each place, or fortune, that doth fall,
    Is wantonnes in contemplation.

Marke, how the fire in flints doth quiet ly,
    Content and warme to it self alone: *10*
But when it would appeare to others eye,
    Without a knock it never shone.

Give mee the plyant mind, whose gentle measure
    Complyes, and suits with all estates:
Which can let loose to a crowne; and yet with pleasure   *15*
    Take up within a cloisters gates.

This soule doth span the world, and hang content
    From either pole unto the center;
Where in each roome of the well furnisht tent
    He lyes warme, and without adventure.   *20*

The brags of life are but a nine daies wonder,
    And after Death the fumes, that spring
From private bodies, make as bigge a thunder,
    As those, which rise from a huge King.

Onely thy *Chronicle* is lost, and yet   *25*
    Better by worms be all once spent,
Then to have hellish moths still gnaw and frett
    Thy Name in bookes, which may not rent.

When all thy deeds, whose brunt thou felst alone,
    Are chawd by others pens and tongue,   *30*
And as their witt is, their digestion,
    Thy nourisht fame is weak or strong.

Then cease, discoursing soule, till thine owne ground
    Doe not thy selfe or freinds importune:
He, that by seeking hath himselfe once found,   *35*
    Hath ever found a happy fortune.

Content. 15 *let loose to*: aim at, as an arrow at a target.
15–16 Charles V abdicated his throne for a cloister.
22–24 The corpulent body of William the Conqueror was said to give off an intolerable odor at his burial (H.).
25 The private man differs from a man of eminence only in having no chronicle; cf. Donne, "The Canonization," l. 31, "And if no peece of Chronicle we prove."

The Quiddity

My *God,* a Verse is not a Crowne,
No point of honour, or gay suit,
No hawke, or banquet, or renowne,
Nor a good sword, nor yet a Lute.

It cannot vault, or dance, or play,   5
It never was in France or Spaine,
Nor can it entertaine the day
With my great stable or Demaine.

It is no office, Art, or News,
Nor the exchange, or Busy Hall,   10
But it is that, which while I use
I am with thee, and most take all.

Humility

I saw the Vertues sitting hand in hand
In severall ranks upon an azure throne,
Where all the Beasts and Foule by their commande
Presented tokens of submission.
    Humility, who sat the lowest there   5
            To execute their call,
When by the Beasts the presents tendred were,
            Gave them about to all.

The Angry Lyon did present his paw,
Which by consent was given to *Mansuetude.*   10

The Quiddity. Scholastic term for the nature or the essence of a thing.
   12 *most take all*: Verse, as a mode of communication with God, and also as a link with the Divine creativity, excels all other goods and activities.
   Humility. 3 *Beasts*: men's natural passions. Cf. "The Church-Porch," ll. 263–64.
   10 *Mansuetude*: gentleness.

The fearefull hare her ears, which by their law
Humility did reach to *Fortitude*.
The jealous Turkey brought his corall chaine;
    That went to *Temperance*.
On *Justice* was bestowed the Foxes braine   15
    Kill'd in the way by chance.

At length the Crow bringing the Peacocks plume,
(For he would not) as they beheld the grace
Of that brave guift, each one began to fume
And challenge it, as proper to his place,   20
Till they fell out: which when the Beasts espied
    They lept upon the throne,
And if the Fox had liv'd to rule their side,
    They had depos'd each one.

Humility, who held the plume, at this   25
Did weepe so fast, that the teares trickling downe
Spoil'd all the traine: then saying, here it is
For which yee wrangle, made them turne their frowne
Against the Beasts: so jointly bandying,
    They drive them soone away: 30
And then amerc'd them double guifts to bring
    At the next Session-day.

Frailty

Lord in my silence, how doe I despise,
    What upon trust
Is styled honor, riches, or faire eyes,
    But is faire dust!

---

13 *corall chaine*: the turkey's red wattle symbolizes fleshliness or amorous jealousy (H.).
25 By their rule, the plume is due to Humility, but she alone is willing to relinquish it.
29 *bandying*: to band together, league (*OED*).

I surname them guilded clay,
    Deare earth, fine grasse or hay,
In all I think, my foot doth ever tred
    Upon their head.

But when I view abroade both regiments,
    The worlds, and thine,
Thine clad with simplenes and sad events,
    The other fine,
    Full of glory, and gay weeds,
    Brave language, braver deeds.
That, which was dust before, doth quickly rise,
    And prick mine eies.

O brooke not this, lest if what even now
    My foot did tred,
Affront those joyes, wherewith thou didst endow,
    And long since wed
    My poore soule, even sick of Love:
    It may a Babel prove
Commodious to conquer heaven and thee
    Planted in mee.

Constancy

    Who is the honest Man?
He, that doth still and strongly good pursue,
To *God,* his *Neighbour,* and *himselfe* most true:
    Whom neither force, nor fawning can
Unpinne, or wrench from giving all their due.

Frailty. 6 *Deare*: costly.
  16 *prick*: make to smart.
  Constancy. An example of the "Character" genre, a description of a particular human trait in the manner of Theophrastus.

   Whose Honesty is not
So loose or easy, that a ruffling wind
Can blow away, or glittering looke it blind:
   Who rides his sure and even trott,
While the *world* now rides by, now lags behind.   10

   Who when great trials come,
Nor seeks, nor shunnes them, but doth calmly stay,
Till he the thing and the example waigh:
   All being brought into a summe,
What place or person calls for, he doth pay.   15

   Whom none can work, or wooe
To use in any thing a trick or sleyt;
For above all things he abhorres deceits:
   His words and works and fashion too
All of a piece, and all are cleare and strait.   20

   Who never melts or thawes
At close Tentations: when the day is done
His goodnes setts not, but in dark can runne:
   The Sunne to others writeth Laws;
And is their vertue; vertue is his Sunne.   25

   Who, when he is to treat
With sick folks, women, those whom passions sway,
Allows for that, and keeps his constant way:
   Whom others faults doe not defeat,
But though men faile him, yet his part doth play.   30

   Whom nothing can procure
When the wide world runnes Bias from his will
To wryth his limbes and share, not mend the ill.
   This is the Mark-man safe and sure
Who still is right and prays to be so still.   35

---

33 The bowler writhes his shoulders after throwing the ball in a futile effort to twist it to the right course (H.).

Affliction [III]

My heart did heave, and there came forth, *O God!*
By that I knew, that thou wast in the greife
To guide and governe it to my releife,
    Making a scepter of the rod:
        Hadst thou not had thy part,   *5*
Sure the unruly sigh had broke my heart.

But since thy breath gave mee both life and shape,
Thou know'st my tallies; and when there's assign'd
So much breath to a sigh, what's then behind?
    Or if some yeares with it escape,   *10*
    The sigh then onely is
A gale to bring mee sooner to my blisse.

Thy life on earth was greif, and thou art still
Constant unto it, making it to bee
A point of honour now to greive in mee,   *15*
    And in thy members suffer ill.
        They who lament one Crosse,
Thou dying dayly, praise thee to thy losse.

The Starre

Bright sparke shott from a brighter place,
    Where beames surround my *Saviours* face,
        Canst thou be any where
        So well as there?

Yet, if thou wilt from thence depart,   *5*
    Take a bad lodging in my heart,
        For thou canst make a debter,
        And make it better.

Affliction [III]. 9–10 A sigh was thought to shorten man's life. Cf. Donne, "A Valediction: of weeping," ll. 26–27.
  17–18 *dying dayly*: Christ dies daily in his members; cf. I Cor. 15:31.

    First with thy fireworke burne to dust
        Folly, and worse then folly, lust:
            Then with thy light refine,
                And make it shine.

So disengag'd from sinne and siknes,
    Touch it with thy Celestial quicknes,
        That it may hang, and move
           After thy Love.

Then with our *Trinity* of light,
    Motion and heat, let's take our flight
        Unto the place, where thou
           Before didst bow.

Gett mee a standing there, and place
    Among the beames, which crowne the face
        Of him, who dyed to part
           Sinne and my hart:

That so among the rest I may
    Glitter, and curle, and wind, as they:
        That winding is their fashion
           Of Adoration.

Sure thou wilt joy, by gaining mee
    To fly home like a laden Bee
        Unto that hive of beames
           And garland-streames.

Sunday

    Oh Day most calme, most bright,
The fruit of this, the next worlds bud:
Th' indorsement of supreme delight,
Writ by a Freind, and with his blood.
    The couch of time: Cares balme and bay.

>   The weeke were dark, but for thy light.
>   Thy Torch doth show the way.
>
>   The other daies and thou
>   Make up one man; whose face thou art,
>   Knocking at heaven with thy brow.
>   The workydaies are the back-part,
>   The burden of the weeke lyes there,
>   Making the whole to stoop and bow,
>   Till thy release appeare.
>
>   Man had strait forward gone
>   To endles death: but thou dost pull
>   And turne us round to looke on one,
>   Whom, if wee were not very dull,
>   Wee could not chuse, but Looke on still:
>   Since there is no place so alone,
>   The which he doth not fill.
>
>   *Sundaies* the pillars are,
>   On which heavens palace arched lyes:
>   The other daies fill up the spare
>   And hollow roome with vanities.
>   They are the fruitfull beds and borders
>   In *Gods* rich garden: that is bare,
>   Which parts their ranks and orders.
>
>   The *Sundayes* of mans life,
>   Thredded together on times string,
>   Make bracelets to adorne the wife
>   Of the eternal glorious *King*.
>   On *Sunday* Heavens gate stands ope;
>   Blessings are plentifull and rife,
>   More plentifull then hope.
>
>   This day my *Saviour* rose,
>   And did inclose this light for his:
>   That, as each beast his manger knows,

Sunday. 7 Cf. Ps. 119:105.

Man might not of his fodder misse.
Christ hath tooke in this peice of ground, 40
And made a garden there for those,
    Who want Eerbs for their wound.

    The Rest of our Creation
Our great *Redeemer* did remove
With the same shake, which at his passion 45
Did th'earth and all things with it move.
As *Sampson* bore the dores away,
Christs hands, though nail'd, wrought our salvation,
    And did un-hinge that day.

    The brightnes of that day 50
Wee sullied by our foule offence:
Wherefore that robe we cast away
Having a new, at his expence,
Whose drops of blood payed the full price,
That was requir'd to make us gay, 55
    And fitt for Paradise.

    Thou art a day of mirth:
And where the weekedaies traile on ground,
Thy flight is higher, as thy birth.
O let mee take thee at the bound, 60
Leaping with thee from seven to seven,
Till that wee both, being tost from earth,
    Fly hand in hand to heaven.

Avarice

Mony, thou Bane of blisse, and sourse of woe,
    Whence com'st thou, that thou art so fresh and fine?
    I know thy Parentage is base and low:
Man found thee poore and durty in a mine.
    Surely thou didst so little contribute 5

---

47 *Sampson bore the dores away*: Judges 16:3, a common typological symbol of Christ's resurrection from the tomb.
52–53 Cf. Rev. 7:14.

>   To this great Kingdome, which thou now hast gott,
>   That he was faine, when thou wert destitute
>   To digge thee out of thy darke cave and grott:
>   Then forcing thee by fire he made thee bright,
>   Nay thou hast gott the face of man: for wee   10
>   Have with our stamp and seale transferr'd our right,
>   Thou art the man, and man but drosse to thee.
>   Man Calleth thee his wealth, who made thee rich,
>   And while he digs out thee, falls in the ditch.

To all Angels and Saints

>   Oh glorious spirits, who after all your bands
>   See the smooth face of *God* without a frowne,
>   Or strict commands:
>   Where every one is King, and hath his Crowne,
>   If not upon his head, yet in his hands.   5
>
>   Not out of envy or maliciousnes
>   Doe I forbeare to crave your special ayd:
>   I would addresse
>   My vows to thee most gladly, *Blessed Mayd*
>   And *Mother* of my *God,* in my distresse.   10
>
>   Thou art the holy mine, whence came the gold,
>   The great restorative for all decay
>   In young and old:
>   Thou art the cabinet where the Jewell lay,
>   Cheifly to thee would I my soule unfold.   15
>
>   But now, alas, I dare not: for our King,
>   Whom wee doe all joyntly adore and praise,
>   Bids no such thing:

Avarice. 10 *the face of man*: the king's head on the coin.
To all Angels and Saints. 1 *bands*: the bonds or fetters of sin which the saints once knew but now are released from.
4–5 Cf. Rev. 4:4–10.
12 Gold was believed to have medicinal powers.

And where his pleasure no injunction layes,
   'Tis your owne case, ye never move a wing.

All worship is prerogative and a flowre
Of his rich Crowne, from whom lyes no appeale
          At the last howre.
Therefore we dare not from his garland steale
To make a posy for inferiour power.

Although then others Court you, if ye know,
What's done on earth, we shall not fare the worse,
          Who doe not so:
Since we are ever ready to disburse,
If any one our *Masters* hand can show.

Imployment [II]

   He, that is weary, let him sitt.
          My soule would stirre
   And trade in curtesies and witt,
          Quitting the furre
   To cold complexions needing it.

   Man is no starre, but a quick coale
          Of mortall fire,
   Who blows it not, nor doth controule
          A faint desire,
   Lets his owne ashes choke his soule.

   When th'elements did for place contest
          With him, whose will
   Ordain'd the highest to be best:
          The earth satt still,
   And by the others is opprest.

---

  19 *injunction*: a command, not a prohibition.
  21 *prerogative*: power reserved to the monarch—here, God.
  Imployment [II]. 5 *complexions*: constitutions.
   11 Of the four elements, earth, water, air, fire, which were thought to compose all things, fire was the highest and earth the lowest and least active.

        Life is a busines, not good cheere,
            Ever in warres.
        The Sunne still shineth there or here:
            Whereas the starres
        Watch an advantage to appeare.   20

        Oh that I were an Orenge tree,
            That busy plant,
        Then should I ever laden bee,
            And never want
        Some fruit for him, that dressed mee.   25

        But wee are still too young or old;
            The Man is gone,
        Before we doe our wares unfold.
            So wee freeze on,
        Untill the Grave increase our Cold.   30

Deniall

        When my Devotions could not peirce
            Thy silent eares;
        Then was my heart broken, as was my verse:
            My brest was full of feares
                And disorder.   5

        My bent thoughts, like a brittle bow,
            Did fly asunder.
        Each tooke his way, some would to pleasures goe,
            Some to the warres and thunder
                Of Alarmes.   10

---

  22 *busy* because the orange tree bears fruit and blossoms at the same time.
  26 *too young or old*: our excuses for inaction.
  Deniall. 3 The disharmony between the soul and God is suggested by the unrhymed final line of every stanza except the last.

As good goe any where, they say,
        As to benumme
Both knees and heart, in crying night and day,
        Come, Come, my *God,* O Come,
                But no hearing.   *15*

Oh that thou shouldst give dust a tongue
        To cry to thee,
And then not heare it crying: all day long
        My heart was in my knee,
                But no hearing.   *20*

Therefore my soule lay out of sight,
        Untun'd, unstrung:
My feeble spirit, unable to looke right,
        Like a nipt blossome, hung
                Discontented.   *25*

O cheere, and tune my hartles brest,
        Deferre no time.
That so thy favours granting my request,
        They and my mind may chime,
                And mend my rime.   *30*

Christmas

All after pleasures as I ridd one day,
    My horse and I, both tir'd, Body and Mind,
    With full cry of affections, quite astray,
I tooke up in the next Inn I could find.
There when I came, whom found I, but my deare,   *5*
    My dearest *Lord,* expecting till the greif
    Of pleasures brought mee to him, ready there
To be all passengers most sweet releif.
Oh *Thou*, whose glorious, yet contracted light,
    Wrapt in Nights mantle, stole into a manger,   *10*
    Since my darke soule and brutish is thy right,

> To man of all beasts be not thou a stranger:
>> Furnish and deck my soule, that thou mayst have
>> A better Lodging, then a Rack, or Grave.

> The Shepeards sing; and shall I silent bee?   15
>> My *God,* no hymne for thee?
> My soule's a shepheard too; a flock it feeds
>> Of thoughts and words and deeds.
> The Pasture is thy word: the streames, thy grace
>> Enriching all the place.   20
> Shepheard and flock shall sing, and all my powres
>> Out-sing the day-light houres.
> Then wee will chide the Sunne for letting Night
>> Take up his place and right,
> Wee sing one Common *Lord:* wherefore he shold   25
>> Himselfe the candle hold.
> I will goe searching, till I find a Sunne
>> Shall stay, till wee have done:
> A willing Shiner, that shall shine as gladly,
>> As frostnipt Sunnes looke sadly.   30
> Then wee will sing, and shine all our owne day,
>> And one another pay.
> His beames shall cheare my brest: and both so twine
> Till even his beames sing, and my Musick shine.

Ungratefulnes

> *Lord* with what bounty and rare Clemency
>> Hast thou redeem'd us from the grave!
>> If thou hadst let us runne,
>> Gladly had man ador'd the sunne,
>> And thought his *God* most brave: 5
> Where now wee shall be better *Gods,* then hee.

Christmas. 12–14 *Rack:* place for hay or straw. Christ, placed in a rack at birth, is no stranger to beasts.
  Ungratefulnes. 4–6 Matt. 13:43, "Then shall the righteous shine forth as the sun in the kingdom of their Father."

Thou hast but two rare Cabinets, full of treasure,
    The *Trinity,* and *Incarnation:*
        Thou hast unlock'd them both,
     And made them Jewells to betroth   10
        The work of thy Creation
Unto thy selfe in everlasting pleasure.

The statelier Cabinet is the *Trinity*
    Whose sparkling light accesse denies:
        Therefore thou dost not show   15
     This fully to us, till death blow
        The dust into our eyes:
For by that powder thou wilt make us see.

But all thy sweets are packd up in the other;
    Thy mercies thither flock and flow.   20
        That as the first affrights,
     This may allure us with delights;
        Because this Bone wee know;
For wee have all of us just such another.

But Man is close, reserv'd, and dark to thee: 25
    When thou demandest but a hart,
        He cavils instantlie.
    In his poore Cabinet of bone
        Sinnes have their boxe apart,
Defrauding thee, who gavest two for one.   30

Sighes and Grones

                O doe not use mee
After my sinnes; looke not on my desert,

   16–18 H. notes that the common treatment for a horse or dog with bad eyes was to blow dust into the eyes.
   23 *Bone*: cabinet of bone (see l. 28).
   30 *two for one*: God gave us two cabinets (ll. 7–14) and asks only one heart (l. 26) in return.
   Sighes and Grones. 1–2 Ps. 103:10, "He hath not dealt with us after our sins."

But on thy glory: then thou wilt reforme
And not refuse mee: for thou onely art
The mighty *God*, but I a silly worme
                O doe not bruise mee.

                O doe not urge mee!
For what account can thy ill steward make.
I have abus'd thy stock, destroy'd thy woods,
Suck'd all thy Magazins: my head did ake,
Till it found out how to consume thy goods.
                O do not scourge mee.

                O doe not blind mee!
I have deserv'd that an *Egyptian* night
Should thicken all my powers: because my lust
Hath still sow'd figleaves to exclude thy light:
But I am frailty, and already dust.
                O doe not grind mee.

                O doe not fill mee!
With the turn'd vial of thy bitter wrath:
For thou hast other vessels full of blood,
A part whereof my *Saviour* emptied hath
Even unto death: since he dy'd for my good,
                O doe not kill mee.

                But O repreive mee.
For thou hast life and death at thy commande:
Thou art both *Judge* and *Saviour: Feast* and *Rod*,
Cordial and *Corrosive:* put not thy hand
Into the bitter box, but O my *God*,
                My *God*, releive mee.

10 *Magazins*: storehouses.
14 *an Egyptian night*: see Exod. 10:22.
16 *figleaves*: Gen. 3:7.

The World

Love built a stately house, where Fortune came,
And spinning fancies, she was heard to say,
That her fine cobwebs did support the frame,
Whereas they were supported by the same:
But Wisedome quickly swept them all away.　　　　5

Then Pleasure came, who liking not the fashion,
Began to make Balcones, Terrases,
Till she had weakned all by Alteration:
But Reverend Laws and many a proclamation
Reformed all at length with menaces.　　　　10

Then enter'd *Sinne*, and with that Sycomore,
Whose leaves first shelterd man from drought and dew,
Working and winding slyly evermore,
The inward walls and sommers cleft and tore.
But Grace shor'd these, and cut that, as it grew.　　　　15

Then *Sinne* combin'd with Death in a firme band
To raze the building to the very floore:
Which they effected, none could them withstand;
But Love and *Grace* tooke Glory by the hand,
And built a braver Palace then before.　　　　20

Coloss: 3.3.

Our life is hid with Christ in God

My words and thoughts doe both express this notion,
That *Life* hath with the sunne a double motion.

The World. 11 *Sycomore*: considered by a mistaken etymology to be a species of fig tree, whose leaves clothed Adam and Eve after the Fall.
14 *sommers*: girders, beams.
15 *these*: the walls; *that*: the sycamore.

The first *is* strait and our diurnal freind,
The other *hid,* and doth obliquely bend.
One life is wrapt *in* flesh, and tends to earth: 5
The other winds towards *Him,* whose happy birth
Taught mee to live here so, *That* still one eye
Should ayme and shoot at that, which *Is* on high:
Quitting with dayly labour all *my* pleasure
To gaine at harvest an eternall *Treasure.* 10

Vanity [I]

    The fleet Astronomer can bore,
And thred the spheres with his quick-peircing mind:
He veiws their stations, walks from dore to dore,
    Surveys, as if he had design'd
To make a purchase there: hee sees their dances, 5
    And knoweth long before,
Both their full ey'd aspects, and secret glances.

    The nimble Diver with his side
Cuts through the working waves, that he may fetch
His dearely-earned pearle, which *God* did hide 10
    On purpose from the ventrous wretch:
That he might save his life, and also hers,
    Who with excessive pride
Her owne destruction, and his danger weares.

    The subtle Chymick can devest 15
And strip the creature naked, till he find
The callow principles within their nest:
    There he imparts to them his mind,

Vanity [I]. 7 *aspects*: the relative positions of the heavenly bodies as they appear to and influence bodies on earth.
  15–21 The Chemist, seeing the principles in their essence, is as it were ad-

Admitted to their Bedchamber, before
                They appeare trimme and drest 20
To ordinary Suitors at the dore.

       What hath not Man sought out and found
But his deare God, who yet his glorious law
Embosomes in us, mellowing the ground
                With showres and frosts, with love and awe: 25
So that wee need not say, where's this commande.
                Poore Man, thou searchest round
To find out Death, but missest life at hand.

Lent

Welcome deare Feast of Lent: who loves not thee,
He loves not *Temperance* or *Authoritie*,
                But is compos'd of Passion.
The Scriptures bid us fast, the *Church* sayes now;
Give to thy *Mother,* what thou would'st allow 5
                To ev'ry Corporation.

The humble soule compos'd of Love and feare
Begins at home, and layes the burden there,
                When doctrines disagree.
He says in things, which use hath justly gott, 10
I am a Scandle to the *Church,* and not
                The *Church* is so to mee.

True *Christians* should be glad of an occasion
To use their *temperance*, seeking no evasion,
                When good is seasonable. 15
Unlesse *Authority*, which should encrease
The obligation in us, make it lesse,
                And powre it selfe disable.

---

mitted to their bedchamber, while others only see them hidden and obscure, at the door.

>   Besides the cleannes of sweet abstinence,
>   Quick thoughts and motions at a small expence, 20
>   A face not fearing light:
>   Whereas in fulnes there are sluttish fumes,
>   Sowre exhalations, and dishonest rhumes,
>   Revenging the delight.
>
>   Then those same pendant profits, which the spring 25
>   And *Easter* intimate, inlarge the thing,
>   And goodnes of the deed:
>   Neither ought other mens abuse of Lent
>   Spoile the good use, lest by that argument
>   Wee forfett all our Creed. 30
>
>   It's true we cannot reach *Christs* forti'th day,
>   Yet to goe part of that religious way
>   Is better then to rest:
>   Wee cannot reach our *Saviours* purity,
>   Yet are wee bid, Be holy, even as he. 35
>   In both let's doe our best.
>
>   Who goeth in that way, which *Christ* hath gone,
>   Is much more sure to meete with him, then one
>   That travaileth by-waies:
>   Perhaps my *God*, though he be farre before, 40
>   May turne, and take mee by the hand, and more
>   May strengthen my decayes.
>
>   Yet *Lord*, instruct us to improve our *Fast*
>   By starving sinne and taking such repast,
>   As may our faults controule: 45
>   That ev'ry Man may revell at his dore,
>   Not in his Parlar, banquetting the *Poore*,
>   And among those his soule.

Lent. 25 *pendant profits*: profits hanging like fruits to be gathered in due season. 35 See Matt. 5:48.
46 *revell at his dore*: cf. Isa. 58:6–7, "Is not this the fast that I have chosen? ... Is it not to deal thy bread to the hungry, and that thou bring the poor that are cast out to thy house?"

Vertue

Sweet Day so coole, so calme, so bright,
The Bridal of the Earth and Sky:
The Dew shall weepe thy fall to night
        For thou must dy.

Sweet Rose, whose hue angry and brave   5
Bids the rash Gazer wipe his eie:
Thy root is ever in his grave,
        And thou must dy.

Sweet Spring full of sweet dayes and roses,
A Box, where sweets compacted ly;   10
My Musique showes ye have your closes,
        And all must dy.

Onely a sweet and vertuous soule,
Like season'd timber, never gives:
But though the whole world turne to coale,   15
        Then cheifly lives.

The Pearle

Math 13.45

I know the waies of Learning; both the head
And pipes, that feed the presse, and make it runne:
What reason hath from Nature borrowed,
Or of it selfe, like a good huswife, spunne

   Vertue. 11 *closes*: cadences.
    15 *coale*: in the final conflagration; see II Pet. 3:10.
   The Pearle. Cf. Matt. 13:45–46, "Again, the kingdom of heaven is like unto a merchant man, seeking goodly pearls: Who, when he had found one pearl of great price, went and sold all that he had, and bought it."

In Laws and Policie. What the starres conspire, 5
What willing Nature speakes, what forc'd by fire.
Both the old discoveries, and the new found seas,
The stock and surplus, cause and history:
All these stand open, or I have the keyes.
             Yet I love thee. 10

I know the wayes of Honour, what maintaines
The quick returnes of curtesie and witt:
In vyes of favours, whether party gaines,
When Glory swells the heart, and moldeth it
To all expressions both of hand and eie, 15
Which on the world a true-love-knot may tie
And beare the bundle, wheresoere it goes:
How many drammes of spirit there must bee
To sell my life unto my freinds or foes.
             Yet I love thee. 20

I know the waies of Pleasure, the sweet straines,
The Lullings and the rellishes of itt:
The propositions of hott blood and braines:
What Mirth and Musique meane: what love and witt
Have done these twenty hundred yeares and more: 25
I know the projects of unbundled store.
My stuff is flesh, not brasse; my senses live,
And grumble oft; that they have more in mee
Then he, that curbs them, being but one to five.
             Yet I love thee. 30

I know all these, and have them in my hand.
Therefore not sealed, but with open eyes
I fly to thee, and fully understand,
Both the maine sale, and the commodities:
And at what rate and price I have thy love 35
With all the circumstances, that may move.

---

32 *sealed*: term for sewing up a hawk's eyes.

Yet through these labarinths, not my groveling witt,
But thy silk twist, let downe from heaven to mee,
Did both conduct, and teach mee, how by it
          To climbe to *Thee*.   40

Affliction [IV]

Broken in peices, all asunder,
        Lord hunt mee not,
        A thing forgott,
Once a poore Creature, now a wonder,
        A wonder tortur'd in the space   5
        Betwixt this world and that of grace.

My thoughts are all a case of knives,
        Wounding my heart
        With scatter'd smart,
As watring pots give flowres their lives.   10
        Nothing their fury can controule,
        While they doe wound and pink my soule.

All my attendants are at strife,
        Quitting their place
        Unto my face: 15
Nothing performes the task of life.
        The Elements are let loose to fight,
        And while I live try out their right.

Oh helpe my *God!* let not their plott
        Kill them and mee,   20
        And also thee,

---

   38 *silk twist*: cord composed of silken fibers, alluding to that by which Ariadne led Theseus out of the Labyrinth.
   Affliction [IV]. 4 Ps. 71:7, "I am as a wonder unto many; but thou art my strong refuge."
   12 *pink*: a fencing term.
   13 *attendants*: all his mental and physical faculties.

Who art my life. Dissolve the knot,
    As the Sunne scatters by his light
    All the rebellions of the night.

Then shall those powres, which work for greif,   25
    Enter thy pay,
    And day by day
Labour thy praise, and my releif,
    With care and courage building mee,
    Till I reach heaven, and much more, *Thee*.   30

Man

My God, I heard this day,
That none doth build a stately habitation,
    But he that meanes to dwell therein.
    What house more stately hath there bin
Or can be, then is Man? to whose creation   5
    All things are in decay.

    For Man is ev'ry thing,
And more: He is a Tree, yet beares no fruit;
    A Beast, yet is, or should be more:
    Reason and speach wee onely bring.   10
Parrats may thank us, if they are not mute,
    They goe upon the score.

    Man is all symmetry.
Full of proportions, one limme to another,
    And all to all the world besides: 15
    Each part may call the furthest, brother:
For head with Foot hath private amitie,
    And both with moones and tides.

Man. 18 Moon and tides were thought to influence human affairs and affect parts of the anatomy.

        Nothing hath gott so farre,
But Man hath caught and kept it, as his prey.   20
        His eyes dismount the highest starre.
        He is in little all the sphere.
Herbs gladly cure our Flesh; because that they
        Find their acquaintance there.

        For us the winds doe blow,   25
The earth doth rest, heaven move, and fountaines flow.
        Nothing wee see, but meanes our good,
        As our delight, or as our treasure.
The whole is, either our cubbord of food,
        Or cabinet of pleasure.   30

        The starres have us to bed,
Night draws the curtaine, which the sunne withdraws,
        Musick and Light attend our head.
        All things unto our flesh are kind
In their descent and being: to our mind   35
        In their Ascent and Cause.

        Each thing is full of duty:
Waters united are our navigation,
        Distinguished our habitation:
        Below our drink, above our meat;   40
Both are our cleanelines; hath one such beauty?
        Then how are all things neat!

        More servants wait on man,
Then hee'le take notice of: in ev'ry path
        He treds downe that, which doth befreind him,   45
        When sicknes makes him pale and wan.
Oh mighty Love! Man is one world, and hath
        Another to attend him.

   38–39 When the waters were distinguished from the land (Gen. 1:9–10), the latter became man's habitation.
    40 *above our meat*: the rain from above is needed to produce our food.
    41–42 If one element is so full of good uses, what excellence is in the whole?
    43–44 Cf. Donne, "Holy Sonnet 8," "Why are wee by all creatures waited on?"

                    Since then, my *God,* thou hast
            So brave a Palace built, o dwell in it,   50
                That it may dwell with thee at last.
              Till then afford us so much witt:
            That, as the World serve us, wee may serve thee,
                    And both thy servants bee.

Antiphon [II]

Chor.   Praysed be the *God* of Love,
  Men.   Here below.
  Angels. And here above.
Cho: Who hath dealt his mercies so,
  Ang: To his freind,   5
  Men.   And to his foe.
Cho: That both Grace and glorie tend
  Ang: Us of old
  Men.   And us in th'end.
Cho: The great *Shepheard* of the fold   10
  Ang: Us did make
  Men.   For us was sold.
Cho: He our foes in peices brake,
  Ang: Him wee touch,
  Men.   And him wee take.   15
Cho: Wherefore since that he is such,
  Ang: Wee adore,
  Men.   And wee do crouch.
Cho: *Lord* thy prayses should bee more.
  Men.   Wee have none,   20
  Ang: And wee no store.
Cho: Praysed be the *God* alone
         Who hath made of two folds one.

Unkindnes

Lord make mee coy and tender to offend:
In freindship first I think, if that agree,
   Which I intend
  Unto my freinds intent and end.
I would not use a freind, as I use thee.   5

If any touch my freind, or his good name,
It is my honour and my Love to free
   His blasted fame
  From the least spott or thought of blame.
I could not use a freind, as I use Thee.   10

My freind may spitt upon my curious floore;
Would he have gold, I lend it instantlie.
   But let the poore,
  And thou within them starve at doore:
I cannot use a freind, as I use Thee.   15

When that my freind pretendeth to a place,
I quitt my interest, and leave it free.
   But when thy grace
  Sues for my heart, I thee displace,
Nor would I use a freind, as I use Thee.   20

Yet can a freind what thou hast done fulfill?
O write in brasse, *My God* upon a *Tree*
   His Blood did spill
  Onely to purchase my good-will.
Yet use I not my foes, as I use thee.   25

Unkindnes. 1 *coy*: reserved (*OED*).
16 *pretendeth to*: seeks, is a candidate for.

Life

I made a posy, while the day ranne by:
Heere will I smell my remnant out, and ty
    My Life within this band.
But Time did becken to the flowres, and they
By Noone most cunningly did steale away,   5
    And witherd in my hand.

My hand was next to them, and then my heart:
I tooke without more thinking in good part
    Times gentle admonition:
Who did so sweetly deaths sad tast convey,   10
Making my mind to smell my fatall day;
    Yet sugring the suspicion.

Farewell deare Flowres, sweetly your time ye spent,
Fitt, while ye liv'd, for smell or ornament,
    And after Death for cures: 15
I follow strait without complaints or greif,
Since if my sent be good, I Care not, If
    It be as short, as yours.

Submission

But that thou art my Wisedome, Lord,
    And both mine eies are thine:
My mind would be extreamely stir'd
    For missing my designe.

Were it not better to bestow   5
    Some place and powre on mee?
Then should thy praises with mee grow,
    And share in my degree.

But when I thus dispute and greive,
    I doe resume my sight;
And pilfring what I once did give
    Disseize thee of thy right.

How know I, if thou should'st mee raise,
    That I should then raise thee?
Perhaps great places and thy praise
    Doe not so well agree.

Wherefore unto my guift I stand;
    I will no more advize:
Onely doe thou lend mee a hand,
    Since thou hast both mine eies.

Justice [I]

    I cannot skill of these thy waies.
Lord, thou didst make mee, yet thou woundest mee.
Lord, thou dost wound mee, yet thou dost releive mee.
Lord, thou releivest, yet I dy by thee.
Lord, thou dost kill mee, yet thou dost repreive mee.
    But when I marke my life and praise,
        Thy *Justice* mee most fittly paies.
For I doe praise thee, yet I praise thee not:
My praiers meane thee, yet my praiers stray:
I would doe well, yet sinne the hand hath gott:
My soule doth love thee, yet it loves delay.
    I cannot skill of these my waies.

Charmes and Knots

Who read a Chapter, when they rise,
Shall ne're be troubled with ill eies.

Charmes and Knots. The didactic aphoristic style imitates that of the Book of Proverbs and Herbert's own *Outlandish Proverbs*.

A *Poore* mans Rod, when thou dost ride,
Is both a weapon, and a guide.

Who shuts his hand, hath lost his gold:
Who opens it, hath it twice told.

Who goes to bed, and does not pray,
Maketh two Nights to ev'ry Day.

Who by aspersions throw a stone
At th'head of others, hitt their owne.

Who lookes on ground with humble eyes,
Finds himselfe there, and seeks to rise.

When th'haire is sweet through pride or lust,
The powder doth forget the dust.

Take one from ten, and what remaines?
Ten still, if Sermons goe for gaines.

In shallow waters heaven doth show;
But who drinks on, to Hell may goe.

Affliction [V]

My *God*, I red this day,
That planted Paradise was not so firme,
As was and is thy floting *Arke,* whose stay
And anchor thou art onely, to Confirme,
    And strengthen it in ev'ry age,
    When waves doe rise, and tempests rage.

At first we liv'd in pleasure,
Thine owne delights thou didst to us impart:

Affliction [V]. 3 The Ark is a type of the Church.

When wee grew wanton, thou didst use displeasure
To make us thine: yet that wee might not part,   10
    As wee at first did boord with thee,
      Now thou wouldst tast our miserie.

    There is but Joy and greif,
If either will convert us, wee are thine:
Some Angels us'd the first; if our releif   15
Take up the second, then thy double line
    And severall baits in either kind
      Furnish thy table to thy mind.

    Affliction then is ours,
Wee are the Trees, whom shaking fastens more: 20
While Blustring winds destroy the wanton bowres,
And ruffle all their curious knots and store.
    My *God* so temper joy and woe,
      That thy bright beames may tame thy bow.

Mortification

    How soone doth Man decay!
When cloths are taken from a chest of sweets
    To swaddle Infants, whose yong breath
      Scarce knows the way:
    Those clouts are little winding sheets,   5
Which do consigne and send them unto Death.

    When Boyes goe first to bed,
They step into their voluntarie graves,
    Sleepe binds them fast: onely their breath
      Makes them not dead.   10
    Successive Nights like rowling waves
Convey them quickly, who are bound for death.

---

24 *bow*: the rainbow associated with the Flood story, but also the bow as an instrument of punishment.
Mortification. 5 *clouts*: swaddling clothes.

> When Youth is frank and free,
> And calls for Musique, while his veines doe swell,
> > All day exchanging mirth and breath 15
> > In companie:
> That Musick summons to the Knell,
> Which shall befreind him at the houre of death.
>
> > When Man grows stayd and wise,
> Getting a house and home, where he may move 20
> > Within the circle of his breath,
> > Schooling his eies;
> That dumbe inclosure maketh love
> Unto the coffin, that attends his death.
>
> > When age grows low and weake, 25
> Marking his grave, and thawing ev'ry yeere,
> > Till all doe melt, and drowne his breath,
> > When he would speake:
> A chaire or litter shows the Beere,
> Which shall convey him to the house of death. 30
>
> > Man, ere he is aware,
> Hath put together a solemnity,
> > And drest his herse, while he has breath
> > As yet to spare:
> Yet *Lord,* instruct us so to dy, 35
> That all these dyings may be life in death.

Decay

> Sweet were the daies, when thou didst lodge with *Lot,*
> Struggle with *Jacob,* sitt with *Gideon,*
> Advize with *Abraham,* when thy powre could not
> Encounter *Moses* strong complaints and mone.
> > Thy words were then, *Let mee alone.* 5

33 *herse*: bier, not funeral carriage.
 Decay. 1–3 Gen. 19:3, 32:24, 18:33; Judges 6:11.
 3–5 Moses was so familiar with God that he continued to plead for his people after God bade, "Let me alone," Exod. 32:9–14.

One might have sought, and found thee presently
At some faire Oke, or Bush, or Cave, or Well:
Is my *God* this way? No, they would reply:
He is to *Sinai* gone, as wee heard tell.
      List, ye may heare great Aarons Bell.   10

But now thou dost thy self immure and close
In some one corner of a feeble heart:
Where yet both *Sinne* and *Satan*, thy old foes,
Doe pinch and straiten thee, and use much art
      To gaine thy thirds and little part.   15

I see the world grows old, when as the heat
Of thy great love once spred, as in an urne,
Doth closet up it self, and still retreat,
Cold Sinne still forcing it, till it returne,
      And Calling *Justice,* all things burne.   20

Misery

    Lord, let the Angels praise thy Name.
Man is a foolish thing, a foolish thing,
    Folly and Sinne play all his game.
His house still burnes, and yet he still doth sing,
      Man is but grasse,   5
      He knows it, fill the glasse.

    How canst thou brooke his foolishnes?
Why heele not loose a Cup of Drinke for thee.
    Bid him but temper his excesse;
Not he: he knows, where he can better bee,   10
      As he will sweare,
      Then to serve thee in feare.

---

  10 Exod. 28:33-35.
    15 *thirds*: legal term referring to the widow's legacy, the third part of the deceased husband's real property.
    Misery. 5 Isa. 40:6, "All flesh is grass."

> What strange pollutions doth he wed,
> And make his owne? as if none knew, but he.
> No man shall beat into his head, 15
> That thou within his curtaines drawne canst see.
> They are of cloth,
> Where never yet came moth.
>
> The best of Men, turne but thy hand
> For one poore minute, stumble at a pinne: 20
> They would not have their Actions scand,
> Nor any Sorrow tell them, that they sinne,
> Though it be small,
> And measure not their fall.
>
> They quarrell thee, and would give over 25
> The bargaine made to serve thee: but thy love
> Holds them unto it, and doth cover
> Their follies with the wing of thy mild dove,
> Not suffering those,
> Who would, to bee thy foes. 30
>
> My *God,* Man cannot praise thy name.
> Thou art All brightnes, perfect purity,
> The Sunne holds downe his head for shame,
> Dead with Ecclipses, when we speak of thee.
> How shall infection 35
> Presume on thy perfection?
>
> As Durty hands foule all they touch,
> And those things most, which are most pure and fine:
> So our Clay-hearts, even when wee crouch
> To sing thy praises, make them lesse divine: 40
> Yet either this,
> Or none, thy portion is.
>
> Man cannot serve thee: let him goe,
> And serve the swine: there, there is his delight:
> He doth not like this vertue, no: 45

---

16 Cf. Ps. 139:2, "Thou art... about my bed: and spiest out all my wayes" (BCP).

Give him his durt to wallow in, all night
    These preachers make
      His head to shute and Ake.

    Oh foolish man, where are thine eies?
How hast thou lost them in a croud of cares?   50
    Thou pul'st the rug, and wilt not rise,
No, not to purchase the whole pack of starres.
      There let them shine,
    Thou must goe sleepe, or dine.

    The Bird, that sees a dainty bowre   55
Made in the tree, where she was wont to sitt,
    Wonders and sings, but not his powre,
Who made the arbour: this exceeds her witt.
      But man doth know
    The spring, whence all things flow: 60

    And yet as though he knew it not,
His knowledge winks, and lets his humours raigne,
    They make his life a constant blot,
And all the blood of *God* to runne in vaine.
      Ah wretch, what verse   65
    Can thy strange waies reherse?

    Indeed at first Man was a treasure,
A Box of jewels, shop of Rarities,
    A Ring, whose posy was, My pleasure.
He was a Garden in a Paradise.   70
      Glorie and Grace
    Did crowne his heart and face.

    But Sinne hath fool'd him. Now he is
A lumpe of flesh, without a foot or wing
    To raise him to a glimpse of blisse: 75
A sick tost vessell, dashing on each thing,
      Nay his owne shelf.
    My *God* I meane my self.

77 *shelf*: a sandbank or submerged ledge of rock.

Jordan [II]

When first my lines of heavenly joyes made mention,
Such was their lustre, they did so excell,
That I sought out quaint words, and trimme invention,
My thoughts began to burnish, sprout, and swell,
Curling with metaphors a plaine intention, 5
Decking the sence, as if it were to sell.

Thousands of notions in my braine did runne,
Offring their service, if I were not sped:
I often blotted what I had begunne.
This was not quick enough, and that was dead. 10
Nothing could seeme too rich to clothe the sunne,
Much lesse those joyes, which trample on his head.

As flames doe worke and wind, when they ascend:
So did I weave my self into the sense.
But while I bustled, I might heare a freind 15
Whisper, how wide is all this long pretence;
There is in Love a sweetnes ready penn'd:
Coppy out onely that, and save expence.

Prayer [II]

Of what an easy quick accesse,
My blessed *Lord,* art thou? how suddenly
    May our requests thine eare invade?
To shew that state dislikes not easines,
    If I but lift mine eies, my suit is made: 5
Thou canst no more not heare, then thou canst dy.

Jordan [II]. See note on "Jordan [I]."
3 *invention*: a technical rhetorical term for the finding of subject matter.
4 *burnish*: spread, grow in vigor.
10 *quick*: having life, lively.
16–18 Cf. the conclusion of the first sonnet in Sidney's *Astrophel and Stella*: "Foole said my *Muse* to mee, looke in thy heart and write."

       Of what supreme almighty powre
Is thy great Arme, which spans the East and west,
       And tacks the Centre to the sphere.
By it doe all things live their measurd houre: 10
We cannot ask the thing, which is not there,
Blaming the shallownes of our request.

       Of what unmeasurable Love
Art thou possest, who, when thou couldst not dy,
       Wert faine to take our flesh and curse,   15
And for our sakes in person sinne reprove,
That by destroying that, which tyed thy purse,
Thou mightst make way for liberality.

       Since then these three wait on thy *Throne,*
Ease, Power, and *Love;* I value prayer so,   20
       That were I to leave all but one,
Wealth, fame, endowments, vertues, all shold goe.
I and deare prayer would together dwell,
And quickly gaine for each inch lost, an ell.

Obedience

       My *God,* if writings may
     Convey a Lordship any waies
Whither the buyer and the seller please;
       Let it not thee displease,
If this poore paper doe as much, as they.   5

       On it my heart doth bleed
     As many lines, as there doth need
To passe it self, and all it hath to thee.

Prayer [II]. 9 *sphere*: the crystalline sphere, the outward limit of space.
   15 *curse*: Cf. Gal. 3:13, "Christ hath redeemed us from the curse of the law, being made a curse for us: for it is written, Cursed is every one that hangeth on a tree."
   24 *ell*: a measure of length – 45 inches.
   Obedience. 8 *passe*: to convey legally.

   To which I doe agree,
And here present it, as my special Deed.   *10*

   If that hereafter pleasure
  Cavill, and claime her part and measure,
As if this passed with a reservation,
   Or some such words in fashion:
I here exclude the wrangler from thy treasure.   *15*

   Oh let thy sacred will
  All thy delight in mee fulfill.
Let mee not think an action mine owne way,
   But as thy love shall sway,
Resigning up the rudder to thy skill.   *20*

   Lord what is man to thee,
  That thou shouldst mind a rotten tree?
Yet since thou canst not chuse, but see my actions,
   So great are thy perfections
Thou mayst as well my actions guide, as see.   *25*

   Besides thy death and blood
  Showd a strange love to all our good,
Thy sorrows were in earnest: no faint proffer,
   Or superficial offer
Of what wee might not take, or be withstood.   *30*

   Wherefore I all forgoe,
  To one word onely I say, no:
Where in the Deed there was an intimation
   Of a guift or donation,
Lord, let it now by way of purchase goe.   *35*

   He, that will passe his land,
  As I have mine, may sett his hand
And heart unto this deed, when he hath red,

---

13 *reservation*: clause reserving rights in property conveyed to another.

      And make the purchase spred
  To both our goods, if he to it will stand.   *40*

      How happy were my part,
  If some kind man would thrust his heart
Into these lines? till in heavens court of rolls
      They were by winged soules
Enterd for both; farre above their desert.   *45*

Conscience

    Peace Pratler, doe not lowre.
Not a faire looke, but thou dost call it foule.
Not a sweet dish, but thou dost call it sowre.
    Musik to thee doth howle.
      By listning to thy chatting feares   *5*
      I have both lost mine eyes and eares.

    Pratler, no more, I say;
My thoughts must work, but like a noiseles sphere;
Harmonious peace must rock them all the day:
      No roome for pratlers there.   *10*
    If thou persistest, I will tell thee,
    That I have Physick to expell thee.

    And the receit shall bee
My *Saviours* blood: when ever at his boord
I doe but tast it, strait it clenseth mee,   *15*
    And leaves thee not a word,
  No, not a tooth or naile to scratch,
  And at my actions carpe, or catch.

    Yet if thou talkest still,
Besides my Physique, know there's some for thee: *20*

  42–43 Vaughan answers this plea directly in *The Match* (ll. 7–8): "Here I joyn hands, and thrust my stubborn heart/Into thy *Deed.*"
  43 *court of rolls*: Registry of legal documents.

Some wood and nailes to make a staff or Bill
　　For those, that trouble mee:
　　　The bloody Crosse of my deare *Lord*
　　　Is both my Physique and my sword.

Sion

Lord, with what glory wast thou serv'd of old,
When *Solomons Temple* stood and flourished,
　　Where most things were of purest gold,
　　The wood was all embellished
　　With flowres and carvings, mysticall and rare,　　　　5
All show'd the builders, crav'd the seeers care.

Yet all this glory, all this pompe and state
Did not affect thee much, was not thy aime,
　　Something there was, that sow'd debate:
　　Wherefore thou quit'st thy ancient claime.　　　　10
And now thy Architecture meets with sinne;
For all thy frame and fabrick is within.

There thou art struglling with a peevish heart,
Which sometimes crosseth thee, thou sometimes it:
　　The fight is hard on either part.　　　　15
　　Great *God* doth fight, he doth submitt.
All *Solomons* sea of Brasse and world of stone
Is not so deare to thee, as one good grone.

And truely brasse and stones are heavy things,
Tombes for the dead, not Temples fitt for thee;　　　　20

　　Conscience. 21-22 Cf. Ps. 23:4-5, "Thy rod and thy staff comfort me. Thou shalt prepare a table before me against them that trouble me" (BCP).
　　21 *Bill*: halberd, spear.
　　Sion. Cf. Acts 7:47-48, "But Solomon built him an house. Howbeit the most High dwelleth not in temples made with hands," and I Cor. 3:16, "Know ye not that ye are the temple of God, and that the Spirit of God dwelleth in you?"
　　17 I Kings 6:7, 7:23.

    But grones are quick, and full of wings,
        And all their motions upward bee;
And ever as they mount like larks, they sing,
    The note is sad, yet musique for a *King*.

Home

Come *Lord,* my head doth burne, my heart is sick,
    While thou dost ever, ever stay:
Thy long deferrings wound mee to the quick,
    My spirit gaspeth night and day.
        O shew thy selfe to mee,
        Or take mee up to thee.

How canst thou stay considering the pace
    The blood did make, which thou didst wast?
When I behold it trickling downe thy face,
    I never saw thing make such hast.
        O shew thy selfe to mee,
        Or take mee up to thee.

When Man was lost, thy pitty lookt about
    To see what helpe in th'earth or sky:
But there was none: at least no help without:
    The help did in thy bosome ly.
        O show thy selfe to mee,
        Or take mee up to thee.

There lay thy *Sonne*, and must he leave that nest,
    That hive of sweetnes, to remove
Thraldome from those, who would not at a feast,
    Leave one poor apple for thy love.
        O show thy selfe to mee,
        Or take mee up to thee.

He did, he came, O my *Redeemer* deare,
    After all this canst thou be strange?

So many yeares baptiz'd, and not appeare?
  As if thy Love could faile or change.
   O show thy selfe to mee,
   Or take mee up to thee.   30

Yet if thou stayest still, why must I stay?
  My *God,* what is this world to mee?
This world of woe? hence all ye clouds, away,
  Away; I must gett up and see.
   O shew thy selfe to mee,   35
   Or take mee up to thee.

What is this weary world; this meat and drink
  That chaines us by the teeth so fast?
What is this womankind, which I can wink
  Into a blacknes and distast?   40
   O show thy selfe to mee,
   Or take mee up to thee.

With one small sigh thou gav'st me th'other day
  I blasted all the Joyes about mee:
And scouling on them, as they pin'd away,   45
  Now come againe, sayd I, and flout mee.
   O show thy selfe to mee,
   Or take me up to thee.

Nothing but drought and dearth, but bush and brake,
  Which way so-e're I looke, I see.   50
Some may dreame merrily, but when they wake,
  They dresse themselves, and come to thee.
   O show thy selfe to mee,
   Or take mee up to thee.

Wee talk of harvests, there are no such things, 55
  But when wee leave our corne and hay:
There is no fruitfull yeare, but that, which brings

Home. 31 *stayest . . . stay*: stay away, delay coming.

The last and lov'd, though dreadfull day.
    O show thy selfe to mee,
    Or take mee up to thee.   60

Oh loose this frame, this knot of man unty,
    That my free soule may use her wing,
Which now is pinion'd with mortality,
    As an intangled, hamperd thing.
        Oh show thy selfe to mee,   65
        Or take mee up to thee.

What have I left, that I should stay and grone,
    The most of mee to heaven is fled:
My thoughts and joyes are all pack'd up and gone,
    And for their old acquaintance plead.   70
        O show thy selfe to mee,
        Or take mee up to thee.

Come dearest *Lord*, passe not this holy season,
    My flesh and bones and joynts doe pray:
And even my verse, when by the rime and reason   75
    The word is, *Stay,* sayes ever, *Come.*
        O show thy selfe to mee,
        Or take mee up to thee.

The British Church

I joy, Deare *Mother,* when I veiw
Thy perfect lineaments and hue.
        Both sweet and bright.
Beauty in thee takes up the place,
And dates her letters from thy face,   5
        When she doth write.

75–76 The rhyme demands *Stay* (to rhyme with *pray*) but I cry, *Come.*
  The British Church. 5 Many persons dated their letters according to the old holy days, still retained in the Church calendar.

      A fine aspect in fitt array,
      Neither too meane, nor yet too gay,
          Shows who is best.
      Outlandish lookes may not compare: 10
      For all they either painted are
          Or els undrest.

      She on the Hills, which wantonlie
      Allureth all in hope to bee
          By her preferd,   15
      Hath kiss'd so long her painted shrines,
      That even her face by kissing shines
          For her reward.

      She in the Valley is so shy
      Of dressing, that her haire doth ly   20
          About her eares:
      While she avoyds her neighbours pride,
      She wholy goes on th'other side,
          And nothing weares.

      But Dearest *Mother,* what those misse,   25
      The meane, thy praise and glory is,
          And long may bee.
      Blessed be *God,* whose Love it was
      To double-mote thee with his grace,
          And none but thee.   30

The Quipp

      The merry world did on a day
      With his traine-bands, and mates agree

---

   13 *She on the Hills*: the Roman Church.
   19 *She in the Valley*: Genevan Calvinism; cf. Donne, "Satyre III," ll. 43–62.
   29 *double-mote*: the British Church is protected (moated) against both ostentatious pride and nudity.
   The Quipp. 2 *traine-bands*: the citizen soldiers of London; here, all society.

To meet together, where I lay,
And all in sport to geere at mee.

First beauty crept into a rose, 5
Which when I pluckd not, Sir, said shee,
Tell mee, I pray, whose hands are those?
But thou shalt answeare, *Lord,* for mee.

Then Mony came, and chinking still,
What tune is this, poore man, said he: 10
I heard in *Musick* you had skill.
But thou shalt answere, *Lord,* for mee.

Then came brave Glorie puffing by
In silks, that whistled, who but he:
Hee scarce allow'd me halfe an ey. 15
But thou shalt answere, *Lord,* for mee.

Then came Quick witt and conversation,
And he would needs a confort bee,
And to be short make an Oration.
But thou shalt answere, *Lord,* for mee. 20

Yet when the houre of thy designe
To answere these fine things shall come,
Speake not at large, say, I am thine.
And then they have their answere home.

Vanity [II]

Poore silly Soule, whose hope and head lyes low,
Whose flatt delights on earth doe creep and grow,
To whom the starres shine not so faire, as eies,
Nor solid work, as false embroderies,
Heark and beware, lest what you now doe measure, 5
And write for sweet, prove a most sowre displeasure.

---

19 Perhaps an allusion to Herbert's role as Public Orator at Cambridge.

  O heare betimes, lest thy relenting
    May come to late.
  To purchase heaven for repenting
    Is no hard rate.   10
  If soules be made of earthly mold,
    Let them love gold.
    If borne on high,
  Let them unto their kindred fly:
  For they can never be at rest,   15
  Till they regaine their auncient nest.
Then Silly Soule take heed; for earthly joy
Is but a bubble, and makes thee a boy.

The Dawning

Awake, sad heart, whom sorrow ever drownes,
  Take up thine eyes, which feed on earth,
Unfold thy forehead gathered into frownes,
  Thy *Saviour* comes, and with him mirth.
    Awake, Awake,   5
And with a thankfull heart his comforts take.
  But thou dost still lament, and pine, and cry,
  And feele his death, but not his victory.

Arise sad heart. If thou doe not witstand,
  Christs resurrection thine may bee.   10
Doe not by hanging downe breake from the hand,
  Which as it riseth, raiseth thee.
    Arise, Arise.
And with his burial-linnen dry thine eyes.
  Christ left his grave-cloths, that we might, when greif   15
  Draws teares, or blood, not want an handkercheif.

The Dawning. The Easter Dawn.

Jesu

Jesu is in my heart, his sacred name
Is deeply carved there. But th'other weeke
A great Affliction broke the little frame,
Even all to peeces, which I went to seeke.
And first I found the corner, where was *I*,
After, where *ES,* and next where *U* was graved.
When I had gott these parcels, instantly
I satt mee downe to spell them, and perceived
That to my broken heart, he was, *I ease you,*
         And to my whole is *Jesu.*

Busines

      Canst be idle? canst thou play?
      Foolish Soule, who sinn'd to day?

Rivers runne, and springs each one
Know their home, and gett them gone.
Hast thou teares, or hast thou none?

If poore soule, thou hast no teares,
Would thou hadst no faults or feares.
Who hath these, those ill forbeares.

Winds still work: it is their plott,
Be the season cold, or hott.
Hast thou sighes, or hast thou not?

If thou hast no sighs or grones,
Would thou hadst no flesh and bones.
Lesser paines scape greater ones.

      But, if yet thou idle bee,
      Foolish soule, who dyed for thee?

> Who did leave his *Fathers throne*
> To assume thy flesh and bone,
> Had he life or had he none?
>
> If he had not liv'd for thee, 20
> Thou hadst dyed most wretchedlie,
> And two deaths had bin thy fee.
>
> He so farre thy good did plott,
> That his owne selfe he forgott.
> Did he dy, or did he not? 25
>
> If he had not dyed for thee,
> Thou hadst liv'd in miserie.
> Two lives worse then tenne deaths bee.
>
>> And hath any spare of breath
>> Twixt his sinnes, and *Saviours* death? 30
>
> He, that looseth gold, though drosse,
> Tells to all he meets, his crosse:
> He, that sinnes, hath he no losse?
>
> He, that finds a silver-vaine,
> Thinks on it, and thinks againe. 35
> Brings thy *Saviours* death no gaine?
>
>> Who in heart not ever kneels,
>> Neither sinne, nor *Saviour* feels.

    Busines. 22 *two deaths*: natural death and eternal death (Rev. 20:6, 14; 21:8).
    28 *Two lives*: one in misery here and one in misery hereafter.
    29–30 *spare*: that which can be given away, dispensed with (*OED*). Now has anyone a spare breath (for anything else) which is not taken up with mourning for his sins and Christ's death.

Dialogue

Sweetest *Saviour,* if my soule
    Were but worth the having,
Quickly should I then controule
    Any thought of waving.
But when all my care and paines 5
Cannot give the Name of gaines
To thy wretch so full of staines,
What delight or hope remaines?

What *Child* is the ballance thine,
    Thine the poise and measure? 10
If I say thou shalt be mine,
    Finger not my treasure.
What the gaines in having thee
Doe amount to, onely hee,
Who for Man was sold, can see; 15
That transferr'd th'accounts to mee.

But as I can see no merrit,
    Leading to this favour:
So the way to fitt mee for it
    Is beyond my savour. 20
As the reason then is thine:
So the way is none of mine.
I disclaime the whole designe,
Sinne disclaimes and I resigne.

That is all, if that I could 25
    Gett without repining,
And my Clay, my creature would
    Follow my resigning.

Dialogue. 4 *waving*: waiving (declining) the offer, and also wavering.
20 *savour*: perception, understanding (Fr. *savoir, OED*).

> That as I did freely part
> With my glory and desert,
> Left all joyes to feele all smart—
> Ah! no more: thou breakst my heart.

Dulnes

> Why doe I languish thus drooping and dull,
> As if I were all earth.
> Oh give me quicknes, that I may with mirth
> Prayse thee brim-full.
>
> The wanton lover in a curious straine
> Can praise his fairest faire;
> And with quaint metaphors her curled haire
> Curle o're againe.
>
> Thou art my Lovelines, my life, my light,
> Beauty alone to mee.
> Thy bloody death and undeserv'd, makes thee
> Pure red and white.
>
> When all perfections as but one appeere,
> That those thy forme doth show,
> The very dust, where thou dost tred and goe,
> Makes beauties heere.
>
> Where are my lines then? my approaches? veiws?
> Where are my window-songs?
> Lovers are still pretending, and even wrongs
> Sharpen their muse.

Dulnes. 12 *red and white*: the usual poetic adjectives describing the beloved's beauty.
18 *window-songs*: serenades.
19 *pretending*: seeking for favor, wooing.

But I am lost in flesh, whose sugred lyes
        Still mock mee, and grow bold,
Sure thou didst put a mind there, if I could
        Find where it lies.

Lord cleere thy guift, that with a constant witt   25
        I may but looke towards thee.
Looke onely: For to love thee, who can bee,
        What Angel fitt?

Love-joy

As on a window late I cast mine eye,
I saw a Vine drop graps with *J*, and *C*
Anneal'd on every bunch. One standing by
Ask'd, what it meant; I, who am never loth
To spend my judgement, said, it seem'd to mee   5
To be the body and the letters both
Of *Joy* and *Charity*. Sir you have not mist
The Man replied; It figures *Jesus Christ*.

Providence

O sacred Providence, who from end to end
Strongly and sweetly movest, shall I write,
And not of thee, through whom my fingers bend
To hold my quill? shall they not doe thee right?

Of all the creatures both in sea and Land   5
Onely to man thou hast made knowne thy waies,
And put the penne alone into his hand,
And made him secretary of thy praise.

---

25 *cleere*: discharge thy debt or promise.
Love-joy. See note to "The Agony." Cf. John 15:1, for Christ as the True Vine.
Providence. Many echoes of Psalm 104, titled in AV "A meditation upon the mighty power, and wonderfull providence of God" (H.).

Beasts faine would sing; Birds ditty to their notes;
Trees would be tuning on their native Lute   10
To thy renowne: but all their hands and throtes
Are brought to man, while they are lame and mute.

Man is the worlds high-preist: he doth present
The sacrifice for all; while they below
Unto the service mutter an assent   15
Such as springs use, that fall, and winds, that blow.

He, that to praise and laud thee doth refraine,
Doth not refraine unto himself alone,
But robs a thousand, who would praise thee faine,
And doth committ a worlde of sinne in one.   20

The Beasts say, *Eat mee*, but if beasts must teach,
The tongue is yours to eat, but mine to praise:
The trees say, *Pull mee*, but the hand you stretch,
Is mine to write, as it is yours to raise.

Wherefore, most *Sacred Spirit*, I here present   25
For mee and all my Fellows praise to thee:
And just it is, that I should pay the rent,
Because the benefitt accrues to mee.

Wee all aknowledge both thy powre and Love
To be exact, transcendent, and divine,   30
Who dost so strongly and so sweetly move,
While all things have their will, yet none but thine.

For either thy commande or thy permission
Lay hands on all: they are thy right and left.
The first puts on with speed and expedition,   35
The other curbs sins stealing pace and theft.

---

13 At the publication of Bacon's *Instauratio Magna* Herbert addressed him in a Latin poem as "Mundique et animarum Sacerdos unicus" (P.).

Nothing escapes them both; all must appeare,
And be dispos'd, and dress'd, and tun'd by thee,
Who sweetly temperest all: if wee could heare
Thy skill and art, what Musique would it be?

Thou art in small things great, not small in any.
Thy eeven praise can neither rise, nor fall.
Thou art in all things one, in each thing many:
For thou art infinite in one and all.

Tempests are Calme to thee, they know thy hand,
And hold it fast, as children doe their fathers,
Which cry and follow. Thou hast made poore sand
Check the proud sea, even when it swells and gathers.

Thy Cubbord serves the world. The meat is sett,
Where all may reach: no beast but knows his feed.
Birds teach us hawking; fishes have their net;
The great prey on the lesse: they on some weed.

Nothing ingendred doth prevent his meat.
Flyes have their table spred, ere they appeere.
Some creatures have in winter what to eat,
Other doe sleepe, and envy not their cheere.

How finely dost thou times and seasons spins,
And make a twist checkerd with Night and day:
Which as it lengthens winds, and winds us in,
As Bowles goe on, but turning all the way.

Each creature hath a wisedome for his good.
The Pigeons feed their tender ofspring, crying,
When they are callow; but withdraw their food
When they are fledg, that need may teach them flying.

39 *temperest*: adjust the pitch, bring into harmony.
47–48 Cf. Jer. 5:22, Job 38:11.
51 *fishes . . . net*: their wide mouths.
53 *prevent*: anticipate.
56 *cheere*: the winter fare of others.

Bees work for man, and yet they never bruse 65
Their Masters flowre, but leave it, having done,
As faire, as ever, and as fitt to use:
So both the flowre doth stay, and hony runne.

Sheep eat the grasse, and dung the ground for more.
Trees after bearing drop their leaves for soile. 70
Springs vent their streames, and by expence gett store.
Clouds coole by heat and baths by cooling boile.

Who hath the vertue to expresse the rare
And curious vertues both of herbs and stones?
Is their an herbe for that? O that thy care 75
Would show a root, that gives expressions.

And if an herbe hath powre, what have the starres?
A Rose, besides his beauty, is a cure.
Doubtles our plagues and plenty, peace and warres
Are there much surer, then our art is sure. 80

Thou has hidd mettalls, man may take them thence.
But at his perill: when he digs the place,
He makes a grave; as if the thing had sense,
And threatned man, that he should fill the space.

Even poysons praise thee. Should a thing be lost, 85
Should creatures want for want of heed their due?
Since where are poysons, antidotes are most:
The help stands close, and keeps the feare in veiw.

The Sea, which seemes to stop the traveller,
Is by a ship the speedier passage made. 90
The winds, who thinke they rule the marriner,
Are rul'd by him, and taught to serve his trade.

---

74 *vertues*: healing properties.
76 *expressions*: that which is squeezed out (expressed), that which is formulated.
80 The power of the stars over men's lives is much surer than our art of interpreting them.

And as thy house is full, so I adore
Thy curious art in marshalling thy goods.
The hils with health abound; the vales with store.   *95*
The South with Marble, North with furres and woods.

Hard things are glorious: easy things good cheap.
The Common all men have; that which is rare
Men therefore seeke to have, and care to keep.
The healthy frosts with summer-fruits compare.   *100*

Light without wind is Glasse. Warme without weight
Is wooll and furre. Coole without closenes, shade.
Speed without paines, a Horse, tall without height
A servile Hawke: low without losse a spade.

All countries have enough to serve their need: *105*
If they seek fine things, thou dost make them runne
For their offence; and then dost turne their speed
To be commerce and trade from Sunne to Sunne.

Nothing weares cloths, but Man; nothing doth need
But he, to weare them. Nothing useth fire,   *110*
But Man alone, to show his heavenly breed:
And onely he hath fuell in desire.

When th'earth was dry, thou mad'st a sea of wett:
When that lay gatherd, thou didst broch the mountaines.
When yet some places could no moisture gett,   *115*
The winds grew gardners, and the clouds good fountaines.

Raine, doe not hurt my flowres; but gently spend
Your hony drops: presse not to smell them heere.
When they are ripe, their odour will ascend,
And at your lodging with their thanks appeere.   *120*

103–104 *tall*: far from the ground; *low*: near the ground (P.).
116 *grew*: grew into.

How harsh are thornes to peares! and yet they make
A better hedge and need lesse reparation.
How smoth are silks compared with a stake,
Or with a stone! yet make no good foundation.

Sometimes thou dost divide thy guifts to man,   *125*
Sometimes unite. The Indian nutt alone
Is Clothing, Meat and Trencher, Drink and can,
Boat, cable, saile and needle, all in one.

Most herbs, that grow in brookes are hott and dry.
Cold fruits, warme kernels help against the wind.   *130*
The Lemons juice and rind cure mutually.
The whey of milk doth loose, the milk doth bind.

Thy Creatures leape not, but expresse a feast,
Where all the guests sitt close, and nothing wants.
Frogs marry Fish and flesh; Bats, Bird and Beast;   *135*
Sponges, Non-sense and sense; Mines, th'earth and plants.

To show thou art not bound, as if thy lot
Were worse then ours, sometimes thou shiftest hands.
Most things move th'underchaw, the crocodile not.
Most things sleepe lying, th'Elephant Leane or stand.   *140*

But who hath praise enough? nay who hath any?
None can expresse thy workes, but he that knows them.
And none can know thy workes, which are so many
And so complete, but onely he, that owes them.

All things, that are, though they have several waies,   *145*
Yet in their being joine with one advise

---

126 *Indian nutt*: coconut.
130 H. takes *Cold fruits* to be the object of *help*.
135 *marry*: form a link between.
136 Coal and diamonds (found in mines) once were plants.
144 *owes*: owns.

To honour thee, and so I give thee praise
In all my other hymnes, but in this twice.

Each thing, that is, although in use and name
It goe for one, hath many waies in store   150
To honour thee, and so each hymne thy fame
Extolleth many waies, yet this one more.

Hope

I gave to Hope a watch of mine: but hee
    An Anchor gave to mee.
Then an old prayer-booke I did present:
    And he an Optick sent.
With that I gave a viall, full of teares: 5
    But he a few greene eares.
Ah Loyterer, Ile no more, no more Ile bring,
    I did expect a ring.

Sinnes round

Sorry I am my *God*, sorry I am,
That my offences course it in a ring.
My thoughts are working like a busy flame,
Untill their cockatrice they hatch and bring:
And when they once have perfected their drawts,   5
My words take fire from my inflamed thoughts.

---

148 *twice*: Here the poet offers praise in his own person and as high priest of all creation (ll. 13–14, 25–26).
    Hope. The *watch* suggests that the time for the fulfillment of hope is nearly due; the *Anchor* declares the need to hold on for some time yet. The *old prayer-booke* suggests prayers long used; the *Optick* glass suggests that fulfillment is as yet far off. *Teares*, the speaker's penitence, win in return only a *few greene eares* (requiring more time and tears to ripen them) (H.).
    8 *ring*: the speaker expects the symbolic token of the Soul's marriage to her heavenly Bridegroom, but it is withheld.
    Sinnes round. 4 *cockatrice*: a fabulous creature hatched by a serpent from a cock's egg. Cf. Isa. 59:5, "[The wicked] hatch cockatrice' eggs…he that eateth of their eggs dieth."

My words take fire from my inflamed thoughts,
Which spitt it forth like the Sicilian Hill.
They vent the wares and passe them with their fauts,
And by their breathing ventilate the ill.   10
But words suffice not, where are lewd intentions:
My hands doe joyne to finish the inventions.

My hands doe joyne to finish the inventions,
And so my sins ascend three stories high,
As Babel grew, before there were dissensions.   15
Yet ill deeds loyter not: for they supply
New thoughts of sinning. Wherefore to my shame,
Sorry I am, my *God*, sorry I am.

Time

Meeting with Time, slack thing, sayd I,
Thy Sith is dull, whet it for shame.
No marveil Sir, he did reply,
If it at length deserve some blame:
    But where one man would have mee grind it,   5
    Twenty for one too sharp doe find it.

Perhaps some such of old did passe,
Who above all things lov'd this life;
To whom thy sith a hatchet was,
Which now is but a pruning knife.   10
    Christs Comming hath made man thy detter,
    Since by thy cutting he grows better.

---

  8 *Sicilian Hill*: Mount Etna.
  9 *vent*: discharge, with overtones of *vend*, sell wares.
  10 *ventilate*: To increase the flame by blowing or fanning. Cockatrices were thought to kill by their breath.

And in his blessing thou art blest:
For where thou onely wert before
An executioner at best;
Thou art a gardner now, and more,
   An usher to convey our soules
   Beyond the utmost starres and poles.

And this is that makes life so long,
While it detaines us from our *God*.
Even pleasures here encrease the wrong,
And length of dayes lengthen the rod.
   Who wants the place, where *God* doth dwell,
   Partakes already half of hell.

Of what strange length must that needs bee,
Which even Eternity excludes.
Thus farre Time heard mee patientlie,
Then chafing sayd: This man deludes.
   What doe I heere before his dore,
   He doth not crave lesse time, but more.

Gratefulnes

   Thou, that hast given so much to mee,
   Give one thing more, a gratefull heart.
   See how thy begger works on thee
        By art.

   He makes thy guifts occasion more,
   And sayes, if he in this be crost,
   All thou hast given heretofore
        Is lost.

   But thou didst reckon, when at first
   Thy word our hearts and hands did crave,
   What it would come to at the worst
        To save.

>   Perpetual knockings at thy dore,
>   Teares sullying thy transparent roomes,
>   Gift upon guift, much would have more,   *15*
>   And comes.
>
>   This notwithstanding, thou wentst on,
>   And didst allow us all our noise:
>   Nay thou hast made a sigh and grone
>   Thy joyes.   *20*
>
>   Not that thou hast not still above
>   Much better tunes, then grones can make;
>   But that these country-aires thy Love
>   Did take.
>
>   Wherefore I cry, and cry againe;   *25*
>   And in no quiet canst thou bee,
>   Till I a thankfull heart obtaine
>   Of thee.
>
>   Not thankefull, when it pleaseth mee,
>   As if thy Blessings had spare dayes,   *30*
>   But such a heart, whose pulse may bee
>   Thy praise.

Peace

>   Sweet Peace, where dost thou dwell, I humbly crave,
>   Let mee once know.
>   I sought thee in a secret cave,
>   And ask'd if Peace were there.
>   A hollow wind did seeme to answere, No   *5*
>   Goe seeke els-where.

Gratefulnes. 24 *take*: captivate, fetch.

I did; and going did a Rainebow note:
        Surely, thought I,
    This is the lace of Peaces coat:
        I will search out the matter.   10
But while I lookd, the clouds immediately
        Did breake and scatter.

Then went I to a garden, and did spy
        A gallant flowre,
    The Crowne Imperiall; sure, sayd I,   15
    Peace at the root must dwell.
But when I dig'd, I saw a worme devoure,
        What showd so well.

At length I mett a reverend good old man,
        Whom when for Peace   20
    I did demand, he thus began.
    There was a Prince of old
At Salem dwelt, who liv'd with good increase
        Of flock and fold.

He sweetly liv'd; yet sweetnes did not save   25
        His life from foes:
    But after death out of his grave
    There sprang twelve stalks of wheat,
Which many wondring at, gott some of those
        To plant and sett.   30

It prosperd strangely, and did soone disperse
        Through all the earth:
    For they, that tast it, doe reherse,
    That vertue lyes therein,
A secret vertue, bringing peace and mirth   35
        By flight of sin.

Peace: 19 *reverend good old man*: God the Father, or possibly Melchizedek.
22–24 *Salem*: Melchizedek, "King of Salem, which is, King of peace" (Heb. 7:2) brought bread and wine to Abraham (Gen. 14:18); he is a type of Christ.
28 *twelve stalks*: the twelve apostles through whom the bread of life is given.

  Take of this graine, which in my garden grows,
    And grows for you;
   Make bread of it: and that repose
    And peace, which ev'ry where   *40*
  With so much earnestnes you doe pursue,
    Is onely there.

Confession

   O what a cunning guest
 Is this same greif! within my heart I made
   Closets, and in them many a chest,
   And, like a Master in my trade,
 In those chests, boxes; in each box, a till: *5*
 Yet greif knows all, and enters, when he will.

   No scrue, no peircer can
 Into a peece of timber work and wind,
   As *Gods* afflictions into man,
   When he a torture hath design'd.   *10*
 They are too suttle for the suttlest hearts
 And fall like rhumes, upon the tendrest parts.

   Wee are the earth: and they,
 Like moules within us, heave, and cast about:
   And till they foot, and clutch their prey,   *15*
   They never coole, much lesse give out.
 No smith can make such locks, but they have keyes.
 Closets are halls to them, and hearts, high-wayes.

   Onely an open brest
 Doth shutt them out, so that they cannot enter;   *20*
   Or if they enter, cannot rest,
   But quickly seeke some new adventure.

 Confession. 19–20 *open brest*: confession, by opening the breast, paradoxically shuts out grief.

Smooth open hearts no fastning have, but fiction
Doth give a hold and handle to affliction.

   Wherefore my faults and sins,   25
Lord, I acknowledge: take thy plagues away.
  For since confession pardon wins,
   I challenge here the brightest day,
The cleerest Diamond, let them doe their best,
They shall be thick and cloudy to my brest.   30

Giddines

Oh what a thing is man! how farre from powre,
   From setled peace and rest!
He is some twenty several men at least
   Each several houre.

One while he counts of heaven as of his treasure: 5
   But then a thought creeps in,
And calls him coward, who for feare of sinne
   Will loose a pleasure.

Now he will fight it out, and to the warres;
   Now eat his bread in peace,   10
And snudge in quiet; Now he scornes encrease,
   Now all day spares.

He builds a house, which quickly downe must goe,
   As if a whirle-wind blew
And crush'd the building; and it's partly true, 15
   His mind is so.

O what a sight were man, if his attires
   Did alter with his mind,

---

30 *to*: compared to.
Giddines. 11 *snudge*: remain snug and quiet (*OED*).

And, like a Dolphins skin, his cloths combin'd
    With his desires!   20

Surely if each one saw anothers hart,
    There would be no commerce,
No sale or bargaine passe: all would disperse,
    And live a-part.

Lord, mend or rather make us: One creation   25
    Will not suffice our turne.
Except thou make us dayly, we shall spurne
    Our owne salvation.

The Bunch of Grapes

Joy, I did locke thee up. But some bad man
    Hath lett thee out againe,
And now, mee thinkes, I am, where I began
    Seven yeares agoe: one vogue and vaine,
    One aire of thoughts usurps my braine.   5
I did towards Canaan draw, but now I am
Brought back to the Red sea, the sea of shame.

For as the Jews of old by *Gods* command
    Travaild, and saw no towne:
So now each *Christian* hath his journeys spand.   10
    Their story pennes and setts us downe.
    A single deed is small renowne.
Gods workes are wide, and lett in future times,
His antient *Justice* overflows our crimes.

19 *Dolphin*: not the porpoise-like mammal but the dorado, a mackerel-like fish whose metallic colors change rapidly when it is removed from water (H.).

The Bunch of Grapes. The story of the Israelites crossing the Red Sea, wandering in the Wilderness, and attaining the Promised Land, typifies the Christian's salvation: if we do not find the Israelites' cluster of grapes, earnest of the Promised Land, we have instead Christ's Blood, the true wine.

4 *vogue*: general course or tendency (*OED*).

10 *spand*: measured, limited.

Then have wee too our guardian fires and clouds;   *15*
    Our Scripture dew drops fast.
Wee have our sands and serpents, tents and shrouds;
    Alas our murmurings come not last.
    But where's the Cluster? where's the tast
Of mine inheritance? Lord if I must borrow   *20*
Let mee, as well take up their joy, as sorrow.

But can he want the Grape, who hath the wine?
    I have their fruit and more.
Blessed be *God,* who prosperd Noahs vine,
    And made it bring forth grapes good store.   *25*
    But much more him I must adore,
Who of the Laws sowre juice sweet wine did make,
Even *God* himselfe being pressed for my sake.

Love-unknowne

Deare Freind sitt downe. The tale is long and sad.
And in my faintings I presume your Love
Will more comply, then helpe. A Lord I had,
And have, of whom some grounds, which may improve,
I hold for two lives, and both lives in mee.   *5*
To him I brought a dish of fruit one day,
And in the middle plac'd my hart. But hee,
        I sigh to say,
Look'd on a servant, who did know his eye
Better then you know mee, or (which is one)   *10*

---

15 Cf. Exod. 13:21.

16 *Our Scripture dew*: cf. Num. 11:9, "And when the dew fell upon the camp in the night, the manna fell upon it."

17 *shrowds*: shelters, especially temporary.

24–28 *Noahs vine*, fruitful under the law as an emblem of God's blessing (Gen. 9), but leading to sin and curse, is contrasted with Christ "the true Vine" (John 15:1), pressed in the wine-press of the Passion (Isa. 63:3) to become the wine of the Covenant of Grace.

Love-unknowne. 4–5 As a vassal, I hold from the Lord *some grounds* (my soul and body) to improve for this life and the next.

Then I my selfe. The servant instantly
Quitting the fruit, seized on my hart alone,
And threw it in a font, wherein did fall
A streame of blood, which issued from the side
Of a great Rock: I well remember all,   *15*
And have good cause. There it was dipt, and dyed,
And wash'd, and wrung. The very wringing yet
Enforceth teares. *Your hart was foule I feare.*
Indeed 'tis true. I did, and doe committ
Many a fault more, then my lease will beare;   *20*
Yet still ask'd pardon, and was not denied.
But you shall heare. After my heart was well,
And cleane, and faire, as I one Even-tide,
                      I sigh to tell
Walk'd by my selfe abroad, I saw a large   *25*
And spacious fornace, flaming, and thereon
A boyling caldron round about whose verge
Was in great letters sett *Affliction.*
The greatnes showd the owner. So I went
To fetch a sacrifice out of my fold,   *30*
Thinking with that, which I did thus present
To warme his Love, which I did feare grew cold.
But as my heart did tender it, the man,
Who was to take it from mee, slipt his hand,
And threw my heart into the scalding pan,   *35*
My heart, that brought it, doe you understand,
The offerers heart. *Your heart was hard I feare.*
Indeed it's true. I found a callous matter
Began to spred and to expatiate there.
But with a richer drug, then scalding water,   *40*
I bathd it often, even with holy blood,
Which at a bord, while many drunke bare wine,
A freind did steale into my cup for good,
Even taken inwardly, and most divine

---

15 The *Rock* struck by Moses (Exod. 17:6) is explained in I Cor. 10:4 as a type of Christ, "[Our fathers] drank of that spiritual Rock that followed them: and that Rock was Christ." Cf. "The Sacrifice," l. 170.

To supple hardnesses. But at the length 45
Out of the caldron getting, soone I fled
Unto my house, where to repaire the strength
Which I had lost, I hasted to my bed.
But when I thought to sleepe out all these faults,
                        I sigh to speake, 50
I found that some had stuff'd the bed with thoughts,
I would say, thornes. Deare, could my heart not breake,
When with my pleasures, even my rest was gone?
Full well I understood, who had beene there:
For I had given the key to none, but one. 55
It must be hee. *Your heart was dull, I feare.*
Indeed a slack and sleepy state of minde
Did oft possesse mee, so that when I pray'd
Though my lips went, my heart did stay behind.
But all my scores were by another payd, 60
Who tooke the debt upon him. Truely, Freind,
For ought I heare, your Master shows to you
More favour, then you wott of. Marke the end.
The font did onely, what was old, renew:
The caldron suppled, what was growne too hard: 65
The thornes did quicken, what was growne too dull:
All did but strive to mend, what you had marr'd.
Wherefore be cheer'd, and prayse him to the full
Each day, each houre, each moment of the weake,
Who faine would have you be, New, tender, quick. 70

Mans medly

        Harke, how the Birds doe sing,
              And woods doe ring.
All Creatures have their joy: and Man hath his.
        Yet if wee rightly measure,
              Mans joy and pleasure 5
Rather hereafter, then in present, is.

>   To this life things of sense
>   Make their pretence.
> In th' other Angels have a right by birth.
>   Man tyes them both alone,   10
>   And makes them one,
> With th'one hand touching heaven, with th'other earth.
>
>   In soule he mounts and flyes;
>   In flesh he dyes.
> He weares a stuff, whose thred is course and round,   15
>   But trimm'd with curious lace,
>   And should take place
> After the trimming, not the stuff and ground.
>
>   Not, that he may not heere
>   Tast of the cheere;   20
> But as birds drink, and strait lift up their head:
>   So he must sipp and thinke
>   Of better drinke,
> He may attaine to, after he is dead.
>
>   But as his joyes are double;   25
>   So is his trouble.
> He hath two winters, other things, but one.
>   Both frosts and thoughts doe nip,
>   And bite his lip;
> And he of all things feares two deaths alone. 30
>
>   Yet even the greatest griefs
>   May be releifes,
> Could he but take them right, and in their waies.
>   Happy is he, whose heart
>   Hath found the art   35
> To turne his double paines to double praise.

Mans medly. 10 *tyes*: Man alone has both the joys of earth (beasts) and heaven (angels).

15–18 Man's fit *place* should be determined not by the coarse stuff of his animal nature but by the fine lace of his higher faculties.

27 *two winters*: physical and spiritual.

30 *two deaths*: natural and eternal.

The Storme

If as the winds and waters here below
              Doe fly and flow,
My sighs and teares as busy were above;
              Sure they would move,
And much affect thee, as tempestuous times 5
Amuse poore Mortals, and object their crimes.

Starres have their stormes even in a high degree,
              As well as wee.
A throbbing conscience spurred by remorse
              Hath a strange force: 10
It quits the earth, and mounting more and more
Dares to assault thee, and beseige thy dore.

There it stands knocking to thy musicks wrong,
              And drownes the song.
Glory and *honour* are sett by, till it 15
              An answere gett.
Poets have wrong'd poore stormes: such daies are best;
They purge the aire without, within the brest.

Paradise

I blesse thee, *Lord*, because I *Growe*
Among thy trees, which in a *Rowe*
To thee both fruit and order *Owe*.

What open force, or hidden *Charme*
Can blast my fruit, or bring me *Harme*, 5
While the inclosure is thine *Arme*.

The Storme. 6 *Amuse*: bemuse, bewilder; *object*: accuse.
7 *Starres* . . .: Though seemingly serene, stars have meteor showers also.

Inclose mee still for feare I *Start*.
Bee to mee rather sharpe and *Tart*;
Then Lett mee want thy hand and *Art*.

When thou dost greater judgements *Spare*,　　　10
And with thy knife but prune and *Pare*,
Even fruitfull trees more fruitfull *Are*.

Such sharpnes shows the sweetest *Frend*.
Such cuttings rather heale, then *Rend*.
And such beginnings touch their *End*.　　　15

The Method

Poore hart lament:
For since thy *God* refuseth still,
There is some rubbe, some discontent,
　　　Which cooles his will.

Thy Father could　　　5
Quickly effect, what thou dost move;
For he is *Powre*; and sure he would;
　　　For he is *Love*.

Goe search this thing,
Tumble thy brest, and turne thy booke.　　　10
If thou hadst lost a glove or ring,
　　　Wouldst thou not looke?

What do I see
Written above there? Yesterday
I did behave mee careleslie,　　　15
　　　When I did pray.

The Method. 3 *rubbe*: impediment.
10 *turne thy booke*: examine the register of your life.

>   And should *Gods* eare
> To such indifferents chained bee,
> Who doe not theire owne motions heare?
>   Is *God* lesse free?

>   But stay! what's there?
> Late when I would have something done,
> I had a motion to forbeare,
>   Yet I went on.

>   And should Gods eare,
> Which needs not man, bee ty'd to those
> Who heare not him, but quickly heare
>   His utter foes?

>   Then once more pray.
> Down with thy knees, up with thy voice.
> Seeke pardon first, and *God* will say,
>   Glad heart rejoyce.

Divinity

> As Men, for feare the starres should sleepe and nod,
>   And trippe at night, have spheres supply'd,
> As if a starre were duller, then a clod,
>   Which knows his way without a guide:
>
> Just so the other heaven they also serve,
>   Divinities transcendent sky:
> Which with the edge of witt they cutt and carve;
>   Reason triumphes, and fayth lies by.

Divinity. 2 *spheres*: the several concentric, hollow globes imagined by the Ptolemaic astronomers as revolving about the earth and carrying with them the heavenly bodies.
    8 *lies by*: is unused.

> Could not that Wisdome, which first brochd the wine,
>   Have thickend it with definitions?   *10*
> And jagg'd his seameles coat, had that bin fine,
>   With curious questions and divisions?
>
> But all the doctrine, which he taught and gave,
>   Was Cleere, as heaven, from whence it came;
> At least those beames of truth, which onely save,   *15*
>   Surpasse in brightnes any flame.
>
> *Love GOD, and Love your Neighbour, watch and pray.*
>   *Doe as ye would be done unto.*
> Oh darke instructions; even as dark, as day!
>   Who can these *Gordian* knots undoe?   *20*
>
> But he doth bid us take his blood for wine.
>   Bid what he please, yet I am sure;
> To take and tast what he doth there designe,
>   Is all that saves, and not obscure.
>
> Then burne thy Epicycles, foolish man,   *25*
>   Breake all thy spheares, and save thy head.
> Faith needs no staffe of flesh, but stoutly can
>   To heaven alone both goe, and lead.

---

9 *brochd*: opened the cask for the wine to run out (P.).

11 *jagg'd*: slashed or pinked by way of ornament (H.).

25 *Epicycles*: in Ptolemaic astronomy, each of the seven planets was supposed to revolve in an epicycle or smaller circle, the center of which moved along a greater circle (*OED*)—an elaborate hypothesis to account for discrepancies in the Ptolemaic scheme.

4 Ephes: 30.

Greive not the holy spirit, &c.

And art thou greived, sweet and sacred Dove,
  When I am sowre,
  And crosse thy Love?
Greived for mee? The *God* of strength and powre
  Greiv'd for a worme, which when I tread,   *5*
  I passe away, and leave it dead.

Then weepe mine Eies, the *God* of Love doth greive.
  Weepe foolish hart,
  And weeping live.
For death is dry as dust. Yet if ye part,   *10*
  End as the night, whose sable hue
  Your sins expresse; melt into dew.

When sawcy mirth shall knock, or call at dore,
  Cry out, gett hence,
  Or cry no more.   *15*
Almighty *God* doth greive, he puts on sense.
  I sinne not to my greife alone,
  But to my *Gods* too, he doth grone.

Oh take thy Lute, and tune it to a straine,
  Which may with thee   *20*
  All day complaine.
There can no discord but in ceasing bee.
  Marbles can weepe, and surely strings
  More bowels have, then such hard things.

---

 4 Ephes: 30. Ephes. 4:30, "And grieve not the holy Spirit of God, whereby ye are sealed unto the day of redemption."
 10 *part*: die.
 23–24 Lute-strings are made of cat-gut; the bowels were taken as the seat of the tender emotions of pity and compassion.

> *Lord,* I adjudge my self to teares and greife, 25
> 	Even endles teares
> 	Without releife.
> If a *Cleare* spring for mee no time forbeares
> 	But runnes, although I be not dry;
> 	I am no crystall, what shall I? 30
>
> Yet if I waile not still, since still to waile
> 	Nature denies;
> 	And flesh would faile,
> If my deserts were masters of mine eies,
> 	*Lord,* pardon, for thy *Sonne* makes good 35
> 	My want of teares with store of blood.

The family

What doth this noise of thoughts within my hart
	As if they had a part?
What doe these loud complaints and puling feares
	As if there were no rule or eares?

But, Lord, the house and family are thine, 5
	Though some of them repine.
Turne out these wranglers, which defile thy seat:
	For where thou dwellest all is neat.

First Peace and Silence all disputes controule,
	Then Order plaies the soule; 10
And giving all things their sett formes and houres,
	Makes of wild woods sweet walks and bowres.

Humble Obedience neere the dore doth stand,
	Expecting a commande.
Then whom in waiting nothing seemes more slow, 15
	Nothing more quick when she doth goe.

28–32 A clear stream runs ceaselessly whether I need it or not; I am not crystal pure and hence have need of endless tears, but Nature denies them to me.
The family. 10 *plaies*: as on an instrument, to tune it.

Joyes oft are there, and greifes as oft as joyes;
        But Greifes without a noise.
Yet speake they lowder, then distemperd feares.
        What is so shrill, as silent teares?   20

This is thy house, with these it doth abound.
        And where these are not found,
Perhaps thou com'st sometimes, and for a day
        But not to make a constant stay.

The Size

        Content thee, greedy hart.
Modest and moderate Joyes to those, that have
Title to more hereafter, when they part,
        Are passing brave.
   Let th' upper springs into the low   5
   Descend and fall, and thou dost flow.

        What though some have a fraught
Of cloves and nutmegs and in cinamon saile;
If thou hast wherewithall to spice a draught,
        When greifs prevaile,   10
   And for the future time art heire
   To th' Ile of spices, is't not faire?

        To be in both worlds full
Is more then *God* was, who was hungry here.
Wouldst thou his laws of fasting disannull?   15
        Exact good cheere?
   Lay out thy joy, yet hope to save it?
   Wouldst thou both eat thy cake and have it?

        Great Joyes are all at once,
But little doe reserve themselves for more: 20

The Size. the state or status.
7 *fraught*: freight.

> Those have their hopes; these what they have, renounce,
>   And live on score.
> Those are at home; these journey still,
> And meet the rest on Sions hill.
>
>   Thy Saviour sentenc'd joy,   25
> And in the flesh condemn'd it as unfitt,
> At least in lumpe: for such doth oft destroy,
>   Whereas a bitt
> Doth tice us on to hopes of more,
> And for the present health restore.   30
>
>   A Christians state and case
> Is not a corpulent, but a thinne and spare,
> Yet active strength, whose long and bony face
>   Content and Care
> Doe seeme to equally divide,   35
> Like a pretender not a bride.
>
>   Wherefore sitt downe good hart
> Graspe not at much for feare thou losest all.
> If Comforts fell according to desert,
>   They would great frosts and snows destroy: 40
> For wee should count, since the last joy.
>
>   Then close again the seame,
> Which thou hast opened. Doe not spred thy robe
> In hope of great things. Call to mind thy dreame,
>   An earthly Globe,   45
> On whose meridian was engraven
> *These seas are teares, and heaven the haven.*

---

22 *on score*: on credit.
36 *pretender*: suitor, wooer.
39–41 If joys depended on our having earned them, they would be more infrequent and memorable than snowstorms and we should reckon time by them (H.).
46 *meridian*: a graduated ring... of brass in which an artificial globe is suspended (*OED*).

Artillery

As I one evening sat before my cell,
Mee thoughts, a starre did shoot into my lap:
I rose, and shook my cloths, as knowing well,
That from small fires comes oft no small mishap.
    When suddenly I heard one say,
    Doe as thou usest, disobey,
    Expell good motions from thy brest,
Which have the face of fire but end in rest.

I, who had heard of Musique in the spheres,
But not of speech in starres, beganne to muse:
But turning to my God, whose ministers
The starres and all things are, if I refuse,
    Dread Lord, sayd I, so oft my good,
    Then I refuse not even with blood
    To wash away my stubborne thought:
For I will doe or suffer, what I ought.

But I have also starres and shooters too
Borne, where thy servants both artilleries use.
My teares and prayers night and day doe woe,
And worke up to thee, yet thou dost refuse.
    Not, but I am, I must say still,
    Much more oblig'd to doe thy will,
    Then thou to grant mine, but because
Thy promise now hath even sett thee thy laws.

Then wee are shooters both, and thou dost daine
To enter combate with us, and contest
With thine owne Clay. But I would parley faine.
Shunne not my arrows; and behold my brest.

Artillery. 11–12 *ministers*: Cf. Ps. 104:4, "Who maketh his angels spirits; his ministers a flaming fire."
  17 *shooters*: shooting stars.

> Yet if thou shunnest, I am thine.
> I must be so, if I am mine: 30
> There is no articling with thee:
> I am but finite yet thine infinitelye.

Churchrents or schismes

> Brave Rose, alas where art thou? in the chair
> Where thou didst lately so triumph and shine
> A worme doth sitt, whose many feet and haire
> Are the more foule, the more thou wert divine.
> This, this hath done it. This did bite the root 5
> And bottome of the leaves, which when the wind
> Did once perceive it, blew thee under-foot,
> Where rude unhallowed steps doe crush and grind
>   Their beauteous glories. Onely shreds of thee,
>   And those all bitten, in thy chaire I see. 10
>
> Why doth my *Mother* blush? Is shee the rose,
> And shows it so? Indeed *Christs* precious blood
> Gave you a colour once, which when your foes
> Thought to lett out, the bleeding did you good,
> And made you looke much fresher then before. 15
> But when debates and fretting Jealousies
> Did worme and worke within you more and more,
> Your Colour vaded, and calamities
>   Turned your ruddy into pale and bleake;
>   Your health and beauty both began to breake. 20
>
> Then did your severall parts unloose and start.
> Which when your Neighbours saw, like a North-wind
> They rushed in, and cast them in the durt
> Where Pagans tred. O Mother deare and kind,

Churchrents or schismes. The Church is figured as the Rose of Sharon (Song of Sol. 2:1) in her chair of authority.
  18 *vaded*: variant of faded.
  22 *North-wind*: perhaps Scotch Presbyterianism.

Where shall I gett mee eyes enough to weepe,   *25*
As many eies as starres: since it is night,
And much of *Asia* and *Europe* fast asleepe
And even all *Africk*. Would at least I might
    With these two poore ones lick up all the dew,
    Which falls by night, and powre it out for you.   *30*

Justice [II]

O dreadfull Justice, what a fright and terrour
    Wast thou of old,
    When sin and errour
  Did show and shape thy lookes to mee,
  And through their glasse discolour thee!   *5*
He, that did but looke up, was proud and bold.

The dishes of thy ballance seemed to gape,
    Like two great pitts;
    The beame and scape
  Did like some torturing engine show,   *10*
  Thy hand above did burne and glow,
Danting the stoutest harts, the proudest witts.

But now that *Christs* pure vaile presents the sight,
    I see no feares.
    Thy hand is white,   *15*
  Thy scales like buckets, which attend
  And interchangeably descend,
Lifting to heaven from this well of teares.

For where before thou still didst call on mee,
    Now I still touch,   *20*

Justice [II]. Old Testament Justice, grounded on the Law, has lost its terrors under the New Covenant of Grace established by Christ.
   9 *scape*: the upright shaft of the balance.
   13 The veil hung before the book of the Law was opaque, "of blue, and purple, and crimson" (II Chron. 3:14), but Christ's *pure vaile* (his flesh, Heb. 10:20) is transparent (H.).

                    And harpe on thee.
              Gods promises have made thee mine,
           Why should I justice now decline?
Against mee there is none but for mee much.

The Pilgrimage

I travaild on seeing the hill, where lay
           My expectation.
    A long it was and weary way.
    The gloomy cave of desperation
I left on th' one, and on the other side   5
           The rock of pride.

And so I came to Fancies middow strowd
           With many a flowre.
    Faine would I here have made abode,
    But I was quickend by my houre.   10
So to cares copps I came, and there gott through
           With much adoe.

That led me to the wild of Passion, which
           Some call the would,
    A wasted place, but sometimes rich.   15
    Here I was robd of all my gold
Save one good Angell, which a freind had tide
           Close to my side.

At length I gott unto the gladsome hill,
           Where lay my hope,   20
    Where lay my hart, and climing still,
    When I had gain'd the brow and top,

    The Pilgrimage. 10 *my houre*: sense of the swift passage of life.
    11 *copps*: copse.
    13–14 The hilly tracts of Lincolnshire are called the wold; possibly a pun is intended: wold/would.
    17 *Angell*: a pun on the gold coin with the device of St. Michael.

A lake of brackish waters on the ground
              Was all I found.

With that abash'd and struck with many a sting   25
              Of swarming feares,
   I fell, and cryed, Alas my King,
     Can both the way and end be teares?
Yet taking heart I rose, and then perceiv'd,
              I was deceiv'd.   30

My Hill was further: So I flung away,
              Yet heard a cry
   Just as I went, none goes that way
     And lives. If that be all, sayd I,
After so foule a journey death is faire,   35
              And but a chaire.

The holdfast

I threatned to observe the strict decree
    Of my Deare God with all my powre and might.
  But I was told by one, it could not bee;
Yet I might trust in God to bee my light.
Then will I trust, sayd I, in him alone.   5
    Nay even to trust in him was also his.
  Wee must confesse, that nothing is our owne.
Then I confesse, that he my Succour is.
But to have nought is ours, not to confesse
    That wee have nought. I stood amaz'd at this,   10
  Much troubled, till I heard a freind expresse,
That all things were more ours by being his.
    What Adam had, and forfetted for all,
  Christ keepeth now, who cannot faile or fall.

---

   36 *chaire*: a sedan chair, a comfortable mode of travel.
  The holdfast. Title from Ps. 73:27, "But it is good for me to hold me fast by God" (BCP). The basis of the argument is Philip. 2:13, "For it is God which worketh in you both to will and to do of his good pleasure."

Complaining

      Doe not beguile my heart;
         Because thou art
My Powre and wisedome. Put mee not to shame:
         Because I am
  Thy Clay, that weeps, thy dust, that calls.   5

      Thou art the *Lord* of *Glory*,
         The deed and story
Are both thy due: but I a silly fly,
         That live or dy
According as the weather falls.   10

      Art thou all Justice, Lord?
         Shows not thy word
More Attributes? Am I all throat or eye
         To weepe or cry?
Have I no parts but those of greife?   15

      Let not thy wrathfull powre
         Afflict my houre,
My inch of life: or lett thy gratious powre
         Contract my houre,
That I may climbe and find releife.   20

The Discharge

  Busy inquiring heart, what wouldst thou know?
         Why dost thou pry,
And turne, and leere, and with a licorous eye
         Looke high and low,
And in thy lookings stretch and grow.   5

The Discharge. A document conveying release from an obligation; the business-legal terminology is continued in *counts, depart, right, fee.*
  3 *licorous*: desirous, lecherous.

Hast thou not made thy counts? and summ'd up all?
        Did not thy hart
Give up the whole, and with the whole depart?
        Let what will fall.
    That, which is past, who can recall?

Thy life is *Gods*, thy time to come is gone,
        And is his right.
He is thy night at Noone: he is at night
        Thy Noone alone.
    The crop is his, for he hath sowne.

And well it was for thee, when this befell,
        That *God* did make
Thy busines his, and in thy life pertake:
        For thou canst tell,
    If it be his once, all is well.

Onely the present is thy part and fee,
        And happy thou,
If though thou didst not beat thy future brow,
        Thou couldst well see,
    What present things requir'd of thee.

They ask enough: why shouldst thou further goe?
        Raise not the mudde
Of future depths, but drink the cleere and good.
        Digge not for woe
    In times to come, for it will grow.

Man and the present fitt: if he provide,
        He breakes the square.
This houre is mine: if for the next I care
        I grow too wide,
    And doe encroach upon deaths side.

---

8 *with the whole depart*: dispense with all.
21 *fee*: allotted portion.

For Death each houre environs and surrounds.
        He, that would know
And Care for future Chances, cannot goe
        Unto those grounds,
    But through a *Church*yard, which them bounds.   *40*

Things present shrink and dy; but they, that spend
        Their thoughts and sence
On future greife, doe not remove it thence,
        But it extend,
        And draw the bottome out an end.   *45*

God chaines the Dog till night. Wilt loose the chaine,
        And wake thy sorrow?
Wilt thou forestall it, and now greive to morrow
        And then againe
        Greive over freshly all thy paine?   *50*

Either greife will not come: or if it must,
        Doe not forecast.
And while it commeth, it is almost past.
        Away distrust:
        My *God* hath promis'd. He is just.   *55*

Praise [II]

King of Glory, King of Peace,
    I will love thee.
And that love may never cease,
    I will move thee.

Thou hast granted my request,   *5*
    Thou hast heard mee.

---

40 The future holds death and must be reached through death.

45 *bottome*: bottom of a skein of thread; *an end*: continuously. By anticipating, men draw out the bottom and unravel the whole spool.

48–50 Will you grieve for tomorrow's ills today, and then grieve for them over again tomorrow (H.)?

Thou didst note my working brest,
  Thou hast spard mee.

Wherefore with my utmost art
  I will sing thee,
And the creame of all my heart
  I will bring thee.

Though my sinnes against me cryed
  Thou didst cleare mee,
And alone, when they replyed
  Thou didst heare mee.

Seaven whole daies, not one in seaven
  I will praise thee.
In my heart, though not in heaven
  I can raise thee.

Thou grew'st soft and moist with teares,
  Thou relentedst.
And when Justice call'd for feares,
  Thou dissentedst.

Small it is in this poore sort
  To enrowle thee.
Even eternity is too short
  To extoll thee.

An Offering

Come! bring thy gift. If blessings were as slow,
As mens returnes, what would become of fooles?
What hast thou there? a Hart? but is it pure?
Search well and see, for hearts have many holes.
Yet one pure heart is nothing to bestow,
In *Christ* two Natures mett to be thy cure.

Praise [II]. 15 *they*: my sins.
26 *enrowle*: record in a place of honor.

O that within us hearts had propagation,
Since many guifts do challenge many harts.
Yet one if good may title to a number,
And single things grow fruitfull by deserts. *10*
In publick judgements one may be a nation,
And fence a plague, whiles others sleepe and slumber.

But all I feare is lest thy heart displease
As neither good, nor one: so oft divisions
Thy lusts have made, and not thy Lusts alone, *15*
Thy passions also have their sett partitions.
These parcell out thy heart. Recover these,
And thou mayst offer many guifts in one.

There is a balsome, or indeed a blood,
Dropping from heaven, which doth both clense and close *20*
All sorts of wounds, of such strange force it is.
Seeke out this All heale, and seeke no repose,
Untill thou find and use it to thy good:
Then bring thy guift, and lett thy hymne be this.

      Since my sadnes *25*
      Into gladnes
Lord, thou dost convert,
      O accept
      What thou hast kept,
As thy due desert. *30*

      Had I many,
      Had I any
(For this heart is none)
      All were thine
      And none of mine. *35*
Surely thine alone.

An Offering. 11–12 *one*: a king or other representative may plead for a nation and thus ward off calamity, as David and Moses did.
22 *All heale*: a general balsam for all wounds.

        Yet thy favour
        May give savour
To this poore oblation:
        And it raise   40
        To be thy praise
And bee my salvation

Longing

      With sick and famisht eyes,
With doubling knees and weary bones,
         To thee my cryes,
         To thee my grones,
To thee my sighs, my teares ascend: 5
              No end?

      My throate, my soule is hoarse,
My heart is withered like a ground,
         Which thou dost curse.
         My thoughts turne round   10
And make mee giddy, Lord, I fall,
              Yet call.

      From thee all pitty flows.
Mothers are kind, because thou art,
         And dost dispose   15
         To them a part.
Their Infants, them; and they suck thee
             More free.

      Bowells of pitty, heare!
Lord of my soule, love of my mind,   20
         Bow downe thine eare,
         Let not the wind
Scatter my words, and in the same
             Thy Name.

Longing. 9 God cursed the ground after the Fall, Gen. 3:17.

Looke on my sorrows round. 25
Marke well my fornace. O what flames,
 What heats abound!
 What greifes, what shames!
Consider, Lord, Lord, bow thine eare
 And heare. 30

Lord Jesu thou didst bow
Thy dying head upon the tree:
 O be not now
 More dead to mee.
Lord heare! Shall hee that made the eare, 35
 Not heare?

Behold thy dust doth stirre,
It moves, it creeps, it aimes at thee:
 Wilt thou deferre
 To succour mee, 40
Thy pile of dust, wherein each crumme
 Sayes, Come.

To thee helpe appertaines.
Hast thou left all things to their course,
 And layd the raines 45
 Upon the horse?
Is all lockd? hath a sinners plea
 No key?

Indeed the world's thy booke,
Where all things have their leafe assign'd: 50
 Yet a meeke Looke
 Hath interlin'd.
Thy bord is full, yet humble guests
 Find nests.

35–36 Cf. Ps. 94:9, "He that planted the eare, shall he not heare? or he that made the eye, shall he not see?" (BCP).
52 *interlin'd*: came between the lines and qualified them.

Thou tarriest, while I dy,
And fall to nothing: thou dost raigne,
        And rule on high,
        While I remaine
In bitter greife: yet am I stil'd
        Thy child.

Lord didst thou leave thy throne
Not to releive? How can it bee,
        That thou art growne
        Thus hard to mee?
Were sinne alive, good cause there were
        To beare.

But now both sinne is dead,
And all thy promises live and bide.
        That wants his head,
        These speake and chide.
And in thy bosome poure my teares,
        As theirs.

Lord Jesu, heare my heart,
Which hath been broken now so long,
        That every part
        Hath got a tongue:
Thy beggers grow, ridd them away
        To day.

My Love, my sweetnes, heare.
By these thy feet, at which my heart
        Lyes all the yeare,
        Pluck out thy dart,
And heale my troubled brest which cryes,
        Which dyes.

The Bagge

Away despaire! my Gracious Lord doth heare.
    Though windes and waves assault my keele,
    He doth preserve it: he doth steere,
    Even when the boat seemes most to reele.
    Stormes are the triumph of his art,   5
Well may he close his eies, but not his heart.

Hast thou not heard, that my Lord Jesus died?
    Then let mee tell thee a strange story.
    The *God* of powre, as he did ride
    In his Majestick robes of glory,   10
    Resolv'd to light; and so one day
He did descend, undressing all the way.

The starres his tire of light and rings obtain'd.
    The Cloud his bow, the Fire his speare,
    The sky his azure mantle gain'd.   15
    And when they askd, what he would weare,
    He smil'd and sayd, as he did goe,
He had new cloths a making here below.

When he was come, as travailers are wont,
    He did repaire unto an Inne.   20
    Both then and after many a brunt
    He did endure to cancell sinne.
    And having given the rest before,
Here he gave up his life to pay our score.

The Bagge. 4–6 *close his eies*: as on the boat in the storm on the Sea of Galilee (Matt. 8:24).
  11 *light*: alight, and also lighten his store of glories.
  13 *tire*: headpiece.
  14 *Fire*: lightning.

But as he was returning there came one 25
    That ranne upon him with a speare.
    He, who came hither all alone,
    Bringing nor man, nor armes, nor feare,
    Receivd the blow upon his side,
And straite he turnd, and to his brethren cry'd, 30

If ye have any thing to send or write,
    I have no bagge, but here is room:
    Unto my *Fathers* hands and sight
    Beleive mee, it shall safely come.
    That I shall mind, what you impart, 35
Looke you may put it very neere my heart.

Or if hereafter any of my freinds
    Will use mee in this kind, the dore
    Shall still be open; what he sends
    I will present, and somewhat more 40
    Not to his hurt. Sighs will convey
Any thing to mee. Harke, Despaire away.

The Jewes

    Poore Nation, whose sweet sappe and juice
Our cyens have purloin'd, and left you dry:
Whose streames wee gott by the Apostles sluce,
    And use in baptisme, while ye pine and dy.
Who by not keeping once, became a debter, 5
    And now by keeping loose the letter.

The Jewes. 5–6 Cf. Gal. 5:3. The Jewish nation, by not keeping the law of works (given to Adam), became a debtor to the whole of the Mosaic Law. Now by trying to keep that law (an impossible task) instead of accepting Christ's deliverance from it (Rom. 7:6) it stands to lose both letter and spirit.

  Oh that my prayers! mine, alas!
  Oh that some *Angell* might a trumpet sound;
  At which the *Church* falling upon her face
  Should cry so loud, untill the trumpe were drownd;   *10*
  And by that cry of her Deare Lord obtaine,
   That your sweet sappe might come againe.

The Collar

  I struck the board, and cryd, No more.
   I will abroad.
  What? shall I ever sigh and pine?
My lines and life are free: free as the road,
 Loose as the wind, as large as store.   *5*
   Shall I be still in suit?
  Have I no harvest but a thorne
  To lett mee blood and not restore,
What I have lost with cordiall fruit?
    Sure there was wine   *10*
  Before my sighs did dry it. There was corne
   Before my teares did drowne it.
  Is the yeare onely lost to mee?
   Have I no bayes to crowne it?
No flowres, no garlands gay? all blasted?   *15*
   All wasted?
  Not so my heart: but there is fruit,
   And thou hast hands.
  Recover all thy sigh-blowne age
On double pleasures. Leave thy cold dispute   *20*

 8–10 The Conversion of the Jews was one of the signs expected to precede the Last Judgement.
 11 *that cry*: "Father, forgive them . . . ." (Luke 23:34).
 12 Cf. Job 14:7, "For there is hope of a tree, if it be cut down, that it will sprout again."
 The Collar. 5 *store*: abundance.
 6 *in suit*: a petitioner.

Of what is fitt, and not. Forsake thy cage,
          Thy rope of sands,
Which petty thoughts have made, and made to thee
    Good cable to enforce and draw,
          And be thy law,   25
While thou didst wink and wouldst not see.
          Away, take Heed,
          I will abroad.
Call in thy deaths head there: ty up thy feares.
          He, that forbeares   30
    To suit and serve his need,
          Deserves his load.
But as I rav'd and grew more feirce and wild
          At every word,
Me thoughts I heard one calling, *Child!*   35
    And I reply'd, *My Lord.*

The Glimpse

          Whither away delight?
Thou camst but now, wilt thou so soone depart,
          And give me up to Night?
For many weekes of lingring paine and smart
But one halfe houre of comfort to my heart?   5

          Mee thinkes delight should have
More skill in Musique, and keepe better time.
          Wert thou a wind or wave,
They quickly goe, and come with lesser crime!
Flowres look about, and dy not in their prime.   10

          Thy short abode and stay
Feeds not, but addes to the desire of meat.
          Lime beg'd of old, they say,

---

24 *Good cable*: cable rope.
29 *deaths head*: the skull upon which the speaker customarily meditates.
The Glimpse. 13 *Lime*: quicklime, whose heat is increased by water.

  A neighbour spring to coole his inward heat,
  Which by the springs accesse grew much more great. *15*

   In hope of thee my heart
  Pickt here and there a crumme; and would not dy,
   But constant to his part
  When as my feares foretold this, did reply,
  A slender thred a gentle guest will ty. *20*

   Yet if the hart, that wept
  Must let thee goe, returne when it doth knock.
   Although thy heape be kept
  For future times, the droppings of the stock
  May oft break forth, and never breake the lock. *25*

   If I have more to spinne
  The wheele shall goe, so that thy stay be short.
   Thou knowst how greif and sinne
  Disturbe the worke. O make mee not their sport,
  Who by thy comming may be made a Court. *30*

Assurance

   O spitefull bitter thought,
  Bitterly spitefull thought! Could'st thou invent
  So high a torture? Is such poyson bought?
  Doubtlesse but in the way of punishment.
   When witt contrives to meete with thee, *5*
   No such rank poyson can there bee.

   Thou sayd'st but even now,
  That all was not so faire, as I conceived
  Betwixt my *God* and mee; that I allow
  And coine large hopes, but that I was deceived; *10*

---

27 *stay*: staying away.
30 *Court*: gay, festive, and regal.

Either the league was broke, or neere it,
And that I had great cause to feare it.

And what to this? what more
Could poyson, if it had a tongue, expresse?
What is thy aime? wouldst thou unlock the dore
To cold dispaires, and gnawing pensivenes?
  Wouldst thou raise Devills? I see, I know,
  I writt thy purpose long agoe.

  But I will to my Father,
Who heard thee say it. O most gracious Lord,
If all the hope and comfort, that I gather
Were from my selfe, I had not halfe a word,
  Not half a letter to oppose
  What is objected by my foes.

  But thou art my desert.
And in this league, which now my foes invade,
Thou art not onely to performe thy part,
But also mine; as when the league was made,
  Thou didst at once thy selfe endite,
  And hold my hand, while I did write.

  Wherefore if thou canst faile,
Then can thy truth and I. But while rocks stand,
And rivers stirre, thou canst not shrink or quaile;
Yea when both Rocks, and all things shall disband,
  Then shalt thou be my rock and Towre,
  And make their ruine praise thy powre.

  Now foolish thought goe on,
Spinne out thy thred, and make thereof a coat
To hide thy shame: for thou hast cast a bone
Which bounds on thee and will not downe thy throat:
  What for it selfe Love once began
  Now Love and truth will end in Man.

Assurance. 24 *foes*: bitter thoughts.
39–40 *bone/Which bounds*: bone of contention which returns.

The Call

Come my *Way*, my *Truth*, my *Life*:
Such a *Way*, as gives us breath:
Such a *Truth* as ends all strife:
Such a *Life* as killeth Death.

Come my *Light*, my *Feast*, my *Strength*. 5
Such a *Light* as shows a *Feast*:
Such a *Feast* as mends in *Length*:
Such a *Strength* as makes his *Guest*.

Come my *Joy*, my *Love*, my *Hart*.
Such a *Joy* as none can move: 10
Such a *Love* as none can part:
Such a *Hart* as *Joyes* in *Love*.

Clasping of hands

Lord, thou art mine, and I am thine,
If mine I am: and thine much more,
Then I, or ought, or can be mine.
Yet to be thine doth mee restore;
So that againe I now am mine, 5
And with advantage mine the more
Since this being mine brings with it thine,
And thou with mee dost thee restore.
　　If I without thee would be mine,
　　I neither should be mine, nor thine. 10

The Call. 2 Most journeyings put us out of breath but this *Way* gives us the *breath* of life.
　6–8 The divine *Light* sets off the Eucharistic *Feast*, which unlike most feasts, improves as it progresses and also cures its *Guest*.

Lord, I am thine and thou art mine.
So mine thou art, that something more
I may presume thee mine, then thine.
For thou didst suffer to restore
Not thee, but mee, and to be mine: 15
And with advantage mine the more,
Since thou in death wast none of thine,
Yet then as mine didst mee restore.
      O be mine still, still make me thine,
      Or rather make no Thine and Mine. 20

Praise [III]

    Lord I will meane and speake thy praise,
        Thy praise alone.
My busy hart shall spinne it all my daies.
        And when it stops for want of store,
Then will I wring it with a sigh or grone, 5
        That thou mayst yet have more.

    When thou dost favour any action,
        It runnes, it flies.
All things concurre to give it a perfection.
        That, which had but two legs before, 10
When thou dost blesse, hath twelve: one wheele doth rise
        To twenty then, or more.

    But when thou dost on busines blow,
        It hangs, it clogs.
Not all the teemes of Albion in a row 15
        Can hale or draw it out of dore.
Legs are but stumps, and Pharaohs wheeles but logs,
        And strugling hinders more.

Praise [III]. 15 *Albion*: Britain.
   17 Cf. Exod. 14:25, "[The Lord] took off their chariot wheels, that they drave them heavily."

> Thousands of things do thee imploy
> > In ruling all 20
> This spacious globe. Angels must have their joy,
> > Divels their rod, the sea his shore,
> The winds, their stint, and yet when I did call,
> > Thou heardst my call and more.
>
> I have not lost one single teare: 25
> > But when mine eies
> Did weepe to heaven, they found a bottle there,
> > (As we have boxes for the poore)
> Ready to take them in: yet of a size
> > That would containe much more. 30
>
> But after thou hadst slipt a drop
> > From thy right ey,
> (Which there did hang like streamers neere the top
> > Of some faire Church to show the sore
> And bloody battell, which thou once didst try) 35
> > The glasse was full and more.
>
> Wherefore I sing: yet since my heart,
> > Though press'd runs thin:
> O that I might some other hearts convert,
> > And so take up at use good store: 40
> That to thy chest there might be comming in
> > Both all my praise and More.

Josephs *coat*

> Wounded I sing, tormented I endite,
> > Throwne downe I fall into a bed and rest:

---

23 *stint*: limit.
27 Cf. Ps. 56:8, "Thou tellest my wanderings: put thou my tears into thy bottle."
33 *streamers*: old battle flags hung up in a church (H.).
Josephs coat. Like Joseph's coat of many colors (Gen. 37) life is variegated by joy and pain, and by the different forms of pain. Typologically, Joseph's coat

Sorrow hath chang'd its note: such is his will,
Who changeth all things, as him pleaseth best.
    For well he knows, if but one greif and smart *5*
Among my many had his full carreere,
Sure it would carry with it even my heart,
And both would runne untill they found a beere,
    To fetch the body, both being due to greif.
But he hath spoil'd the race: and given to anguish *10*
One of Joyes coats, ticing it with releif
To linger in mee, and together languish.
    I live to shew his powre, who once did bring
    My joyes to weepe; and now my greifs to sing.

The Pulley

    When *God* at first made man,
Having a glasse of blessings standing by;
Let us (sayd he) powre on him all we can:
Let the worlds riches, which dispersed ly,
    Contract into a span. *5*

    So strength first made a way,
Then Beauty flow'd, then Wisedome, Honour, Pleasure:
When almost all was out, *God* made a stay,
Perceiving that alone of all his treasure,
    Rest in the bottome lay. *10*

    For if I should (sayd he)
Bestow this Jewell also on my creature,
He would adore my guifts in stead of mee,
And rest in Nature, not the God of Nature.
    So both should loosers bee. *15*

---

is the humanity of Christ of which he was denuded at the Crucifixion (Tuve). Thus God, by giving to anguish *One of Joyes coats* (the flesh of Christ) and uniting it with us (*To linger in mee*) has afforded *releif* to our griefs.
    9 *both*: *my heart* and *the body* are both *due to greif* because of sin.
    The Pulley. Cf. the story of Pandora, who opened a box containing all the blessings of the gods, all of which slipped away and were lost except Hope.

>   Yet let him keepe the rest,
> But keepe them with repining restlesnes:
> Let him be rich and weary; that at least
> If Goodnes lead him not, yet wearines
>   May tosse him to my Brest.   20

The Preisthood

> Blest Order, which in powre dost so excell,
> That with th'one hand thou liftest to the sky,
> And with the other throwest downe to Hell
> In thy just censures; Faine would I draw nigh,
> Faine put thee on, exchanging my Lay-sword   5
>   For that of th'holy Word.
>
> But thou art fire, sacred and hallowed fire,
> And I but earth and Clay: Should I presume
> To weare thy habit, the severe attire
> My slender compositions might consume.   10
> I am both foule and brittle: much unfitt
>   To deale in Holy Writt.
>
> Yet have I often seene by cunning hand
> And force of fire what curious things are made
> Of wretched earth. Where once I scorn'd to stand, 15
> That earth is fitted by the fire and trade
> Of skilfull Artists for the boards of those
>   Who make the bravest shows.
>
> But since those great ones, be they ne're so great,
> Come from the Earth, from whence those vessles come, 20
> So that at once both feeder, dish, and meat

---

17 Cf. Augustine, *Confes.* I.i, "Thou hast made us for Thyself, and our heart is restless until it finds rest in Thee."

The Preisthood. 2–3 Cf. Matt. 16:19.

16 *That earth*: potter's clay; cf. Isa. 64:8, Jer. 18:6.

Have one beginning and one final somme,
I doe not greatly wonder at the sight,
        If earth in earth delight.

But th'holy men of *God* such vessels are,   25
As serve him up, who all the world commands:
When *God* vouchsafeth to become our fare,
Their hands convey him, who conveys their hands.
O what pure things! most pure must those things be,
        Who bring my *God* to mee!   30

Wherefore I dare not, I, put forth my hand
To hold the Arke, although it seeme to shake
Through th'old sins, and new doctrines of our Land.
Onely since *God* doth often vessels make
Of lowly matter for high uses meet,   35
        I throw mee at his feet.

There will I ly, untill my *Maker* seeke
For some meane stuffe, whereon to show his skill:
Then is my time. The distance of the meeke
Doth flatter Powre. Lest good come short of ill   40
In praising Might, the poore doe by submission
        What pride by Opposition.

The Search

    Whither, ô, whither art thou fled
        My *Lord,* My *Love?*
    My searches are my dayly bred,
        Yet never prove.

31–32 Cf. II Sam. 6:6, Uzzah rashly touched the Ark when it was shaking.
41–42 The proud flatter great ones by trying to rival their splendor; the poor flatter better by submission.

My knees peirce th'earth, mine eyes the sky, 5
    And yet the sphere
And center both to mee deny,
    That thou art there.

Yet can I marke how herbs below
    Grow greene and gay, 10
As if to meet thee they did know,
    While I decay.

Yet can I marke how starres above
    Simper and shine,
As having keyes unto thy Love, 15
    While poore I pine.

I sent a sigh to seeke thee out
    Deepe drawne, in paine,
Wingd like an arrow: but my scout
    Returnes in vaine. 20

I tun'd another (having store)
    Into a Grone;
Because the search was dumbe before:
    But all was one.

Lord dost thou some new fabrick mould, 25
    Which favour winnes,
And keeps thee present, leaving th'old
    Unto their sinnes?

Where is my God? what hidden place
    Conceales thee still? 30
What covert dare eclipse thy face?
    Is it thy will?

The Search. 14 *Simper*: twinkle.

O Let not that of any thing;
        Let rather brasse,
Or steele, or mountaines be thy ring,   35
        And I will passe.

Thy will such an entrenching is,
        As passeth thought:
To it, all strength, all subtleties
        Are things of nought.   40

Thy will such a strange distance is,
        As that to it
East and West touch, the poles doe kisse,
        And parallels meet.

Since then my greife must be as large,   45
        As is thy space,
Thy distance from mee; see my charge,
        Lord, see my case.

O take these barres, these lengths away,
        Turne and restore mee: 50
Bee not *Almighty,* let mee say,
        Against, but for mee.

When thou dost turne, and wilt be neere,
        What edge so keene,
What point so peircing can appeere   55
        To come betweene.

For as thy absence doth excell
        All distance knowne;
So doth thy neerenes beare the bell,
        Making two one.   60

---

33 *that of any thing*: of all things, let it not be thy will.
35 *ring*: fence.
42 *to it*: compared to it.
47 *charge*: burden, load of trouble.
59 *beare the bell*: take precedence.

Greife

O who will give me teares? Come all ye springs
Dwell in my head and eyes. Come clowds and raine.
My greif hath need of all the watry things,
That Nature hath produc'd. Let ev'ry vaine
Suck up a river to supply mine eies, 5
My weary weeping eies, too dry for mee,
Unlesse they get new conduits, new supplies
To beare them out, and with my state agree.
What are two shallow foords, two little spoutes
Of a lesse world, the greater is but small, 10
A narrow cupboard for my greifs and doubts,
Which want provision in the midst of all.
Verses ye are too fine a thing, too wise
For my rough sorrows: Cease, be dumbe and mute,
Give up your feet and running to mine eies, 15
And keepe your measures for some Lovers Lute,
Whose greife allows him Musick and a rime:
For mine excludes both measure, tune, and time.
                      Alas my *God*.

The Crosse

    What is this strange and uncouth thing?
To make mee sigh, and seeke, and faint, and dy
Untill I had some place, where I might sing,
    And serve thee: and not onely I,
But all my wealth and family might combine 5
To sett thy honour up, as our designe.

Greife. 1–2 Cf. Jer. 9:1.
  10 *a lesse world*: man, the microcosm; yet even the great world is small.
  15 *your feet*: with a pun upon the metrical feet.

      And then when after much delay,
Much wrastling, many a combate, this deere end,
So much desir'd, is given, to take away
      My powre to serve thee; to unbend
All my abilities, my designes confound,
And lay my threatnings bleeding on the ground.

      One Ague dwelleth in my bones,
Another in my soule (the memory
What I would doe for thee, if once my grones
      Could be allow'd for harmony):
I am in all a weake disabled thing,
Save in the sight thereof, where strength doth sting.

      Besides things sort not to my will,
Even when my will doth study thy renowne:
Thou turnest th' edge of all things on mee still,
      Taking mee up to throw mee down:
So that even when my hopes seeme to be sped,
I am to greif alive, to them as dead.

      To have my aime, and yet to bee
Further from it, then when I bent my bow;
To make my hopes my torture, and the fee
      Of all my woes another woe,
Is in the midst of delicates to need,
And even in Paradise to be a weed.

      Ah my *Deare Father,* ease my smart:
These contrarieties crush mee: these crosse Actions
Doe wind a rope about, and cutt my hart:
      And yet since these thy contradictions
Are properly a *Crosse* felt by thy Sonne
With but foure words, My words, *Thy will be done.*

The Crosse. 18 *sight thereof*: sight of the cross.
23 *sped*: brought to successful issue.
36 Christ's words on the Cross I adopt as mine.

The Flowre

How fresh, ô *Lord,* how sweet and cleane
Are thy returns! even as the flowres in spring,
    To which, besides their owne demeane,
The late-past frosts tributs of pleasure bring.
        Greife melts away   5
        Like snow in May,
As if there were no such cold thing.

Who would have thought my shriveld hart
Could have recoverd greenenesse? It was gone
    Quite under ground: as Flowres depart   10
To see their mother-root, when they have blowne;
        Where they together
        All the hard weather,
Dead to the world, keepe house unknowne.

These are thy wonders, *Lord of Powre,*   15
Killing, and quickning, bringing downe to hell,
    And up to heaven in an houre:
Making a chiming of a passing bell.
        Wee say amisse,
        This or that is,   20
Thy word is all, if wee could spell.

    O that I once past changing were
Fast in thy Paradise, where no Flowre can wither,
    Many a spring I shoot up faire,
Offring at Heaven, growing and groning thither.   25

    The Flowre. 3 *demeane*: bearing, demeanor, and also a variant of *demesne,* estate.
    18 Replacing the single-toned bell for the dead are the pleasant, varied tones of chiming bells.
    20 *is*: is unto itself, unchangeable.
    25 *Offring at*: aiming at.

        Nor doth my Flowre
        Want a spring-showre,
My sins and I joining together.

   But while I grow in a strait line
Still upwards bent, as if heaven were mine owne,
    Thy anger comes, and I decline:
What frost to that? what Pole is not the zone
        Where all things burne,
        When thou dost turne
   And the least frowne of thine is showne.

   And now in Age I bud againe,
After so many deaths I live and write,
   I once more smell the dew and raine,
And relish versing: O my onely Light,
        It cannot bee
        That I am hee
On whom thy tempests fell all night.

   These are thy wonders, *Lord of Love*,
To make us see wee are but flowres, that glide.
   Which when wee once can find and prove,
Thou hast a Garden for us, where to bide.
        Who would be more
        Swelling through store
Forfeit their Paradise by their Pride.

Dotage

False glozing Pleasures, casks of happines,
Foolish Night-fires, womens and childrens wishes,
Chases in Arras, guilded Emptinesse,

32–35 Arctic frost is nearer to the heat of the torrid zone than to the cold caused by your frown.
44 *glide*: slip away gentle.
Dotage. 1 *casks*: caskets.
2 *Night-fires: ignis fatuus*, will-o'-the-wisp.

Shaddows well mounted, Dreames in a careere,
Embroiderd Lyes, Nothing betweene two dishes, 5
   These are the pleasures heere.

True earnest sorrows, rooted miseries,
Anguish in graine, vexations ripe and blowne,
Sure-footed greifs, solid calamities,
Plaine demonstrations evident and cleere, 10
Fetching their proofs even from the very bone,
   These are the sorrows heere.

But, ô the folly of distracted men,
Who greifs in earnest, joyes in jest pursue;
Preferring, like brute beasts, a lothsome den 15
Before a court, even that above so cleere,
Where are no sorrows, but delights more true,
   Then miseries are here.

The Sonne

Let forraine Nations of their Language boast,
What fine variety each tongue affords;
I like our Language, as our Men and Coast,
Who cannot dresse it well, want witt, not words.
How neatly doe wee give one onely Name 5
To Parents issue and the *sunnes* bright starre?
A sonne is light and fruit: a fruitfull flame
Chasing the Fathers dimnesse, carried farre
From the first Man in th' East, to fresh and new
Westerne discoveries of Posterity. 10
So in one word our Lords humility
Wee turne upon him in a sense most true:
  For what *Christ* once in humblenes began,
  Wee him in glory call, The *Sonne* of *Man*.

---

 4 *in a careere*: in full development and power.
 5 H. identifies this as a Spanish proverb: when the upper or covering dish is removed, nothing is found in the lower one.
 8 *in graine*: ingrained.

A true Hymne

    My joy, my life, my crowne!
  My hart was meaning all the day,
      Somewhat it faine would say:
And still it runneth muttering up and downe
With onely this, My joy, My life, My crowne.   5

    Yet slight not these few words:
    If truly sayd, they may take part
      Among the best in art.
The finenes, which a hymne or Psalme affords,
Is, when the soule unto the lines accords.   10

    He, who craves all the mind,
  And all the soule, and strength, and time,
      If the words onely ryme,
Justly complaines, that somewhat is behind
To make his verse, or write a hymne in kind.   15

    Whereas if th'heart be moved,
  Although the verse be somewhat scant,
      God doth supply the want.
As when th'heart sayes (sighing to be approved)
O, could I love! and stops: *God* writeth, *Loved*.   20

The Answere

My comforts droppe, and melt away like snow:
I shake my head, and all the thoughts and ends,
Which my feirce youth did bandy, fall and flow
Like leaves about mee: or like sommer freinds
Flyes of estates and sunne-shine. But to all,   5
Who think mee eager, hott, and undertaking,

The Answere. 4–5 *sommer freinds*: these swarm about like flies as long as one possesses estates and wealth.

358 · *Earlier Seventeenth Century*

  But in my prosecutions slack and small,
  As a young exhalation, newly waking,
  Scorns his first bed of durt, and meanes the sky:
  But cooling by the way, grows pursy and slow,   10
  And setling to a cloud, doth live and dy
  In that darke state of teares; to all, that so
   Show mee and sett mee, I have one reply,
  Which they that know the rest, know more then I.

A Dialogue Antheme

Christian. Death.

Chr. Alas, poore Death, where is thy glory?
   Where is thy famous force, thy ancient sting?
Dea. Alas poore Mortall, void of story,
   Goe spell and read, how I have kill'd thy King.
Chr. Poore Death! and who was hurt thereby?   5
   Thy curse being layd on him, makes thee accurst.
Dea. Let Loosers talk: yet thou shalt dy,
   These Armes shall crush thee.   Chr. Spare not, doe thy worst.
   I shall be one day better then before:
   Thou so much worse, that thou shalt be no more.   10

The Water-course

  Thou who dost dwell and linger heere below,
  Since the condition of this world is fraile,
  Where of all plants afflictions soonest grow,
  If troubles overtake thee, doe not waile:
   For who can looke for lesse, that loveth $\begin{cases} \text{Life} \\ \text{Strife.} \end{cases}$ 5

  8 *exhalation*: vapor rising from damp ground.
  10 *pursy*: puffy, swollen.
  A Dialogue Antheme. Cf. Donne, "Death be not Proud."
  1–2 Cf. I Cor. 15:55, "O death, where is thy sting? O grave, where is thy victory?"

But rather turne the pipe, and waters course
To serve thy sins, and furnish thee with store
Of soveraine teares, springing from true remorse.
That so in purenes thou mayst him adore,

Who gives to Man, as he sees fitt $\begin{cases} \text{Salvation} \\ \text{Damnation.} \end{cases}$ 10

Selfe-condemnation

Thou who condemnest Jewish hate
For choosing Barrabas a murderer
    Before the *Lord* of glory,
  Looke back upon thine owne state,
Call home thine eye (that busy wanderer)   5
    That choise may be thy story.

  He, that doth love, and love amisse
This Worlds delights before true *Christian* joy,
    Hath made a *Jewish* choice:
  The world an ancient Murderer is;   10
Thousands of soules it hath and doth destroy
    With her inchanting voice.

  He, that hath made a sorry wedding
Betweene his soule and gold, and hath preferd
    False gaine before the true,   15
  Hath done what he condemnes in reading:
For he hath sold for mony his deare *Lord*,
    And is a *Judas-Jew*.

  Thus wee prevent that last great day,
And judge our selves. That light, which sin and passion   20
    Did before dimme and choke,
  When once those snuffs are taken away,
Shines bright and cleere, even unto condemnation,
    Without excuse or cloke.

Selfe-condemnation. Cf. Luke 23:18–19.

Bitter-sweet

Ah my deere angry *Lord*,
Since thou dost love, yet strike,
Cast downe, yet help afford,
Sure I will doe the like.

I will complaine, yet praise: 5
I will bewaile, approove:
And all my sowre-sweet daies
I will lament, and love.

The Glance

When first thy sweet and gracious eye
Vouchsaf'd even in the midst of youth and Night
To looke upon mee, who before did ly
    Weltring in sin;
I felt a sugred strange delight 5
Passing all cordials made by any art
Bedew, embalme, and overunne my hart,
    And take it in.

Since that time many a bitter storme
My soule hath felt, even able to destroy, 10
Had the malicious and ill-meaning harme
    His swing and sway:
But still thy sweet originall joy
Sprung from thine eye, did worke within my Soule,
And surging greifs, when they grew bold, controule, 15
    And gott the day.

If thy first glance so powrefull bee,
A mirth but open'd and seal'd up againe;
What wonders shall wee feele, when wee shall see
    Thy full-ey'd Love? 20

When thou shalt looke us out of Paine,
And one aspect of thine spend in delight
More then a Thousand Sunnes disburse in light,
In Heaven above.

The 23^d Psalme

The God of Love my Shepheard is,
    And he, that doth mee feed;
While he is mine, and I am his,
    What can I want or need.

He leads mee to the tender grasse,   5
    Where I both feed and rest,
Then to the streames that gently passe,
    In both I have the best.

Or if I stray, he doth convert,
    And bring my mind in frame: 10
And all this not for my desert,
    But for his holy Name.

Yea in Deaths shady black abode
    Well may I walk, not feare:
For thou art with mee; and thy rod   15
    To guide, thy staff to beare.

Nay thou dost make mee sitt and dine,
    Even in mine enemies sight:
My head with oile, my cuppe with wine
    Runnes over day and Night.   20

Surely thy sweet and wondrous Love
    Shall measure all my daies,
And as it never shall remove
    So neither shall thy praise.

The 23^d Psalme. H. notes Herbert's debt both to the AV and to Coverdale's version in BCP.
  10 *in frame*: in a suitable order.
  24 *thy praise*: my praise of thee.

Mary Magdalene

When Blessed *Mary* wip'd her *Saviours* feet,
(Whose precepts she had trampled on before)
And wore them for a jewell on her head,
   Shewing his steps should be the street,
   Wherein she thenceforth evermore 5
With pensive humblenes would live and tred,

She being stain'd her self, why did she strive
To make him cleane, who could not be defil'd?
Why kept she not her teares for her owne fauts,
   And not his feet? Though wee could dive 10
   In teares, like seas, our sins are pil'd
Deeper then they, in words, and workes, and thoughts.

Deare Soule, she knew, who did vouchsafe and daine
To beare her filth: and that her sins did dash
Even God himselfe. Wherefore she was not loth, 15
   As she had brought wherewith to staine,
   So to bring in wherewith to wash
And yet in washing one, she washed both.

Aaron

Holines on the Head,
Light and perfections on the Brest,
Harmonious bells below, raising the Dead,
To lead them unto life and rest.
     Thus are true Aarons drest.   5

Profanenes in my Head,
Defects and darkenes in my brest,
A noise of Passions ringing mee for Dead
Unto a place, where is no rest,
     Poore Preist thus am I drest.   10

Onely another Head
I have, another hart and brest,
Another Musique, making live not dead,
Without whom I could have no rest,
     In him I am well drest.   15

Christ is my onely *Head*,
My alone onely hart and *Brest*,
My onely Musick, striking mee even *Dead*,
That to the old man I may *Rest*,
     And be in him new *Drest*.   20

So Holy in my *Head*,
Perfect and light in my deare *Brest*,
My Doctrine tun'd by *Christ*, (who is not *Dead*
But lives in mee, while I doe *Rest*)
     Come people; *Aaron's Drest*.   25

Aaron. Cf. Exodus 28 for description of Aaron's priestly garments: a mitre with gold plate engraved "Holiness to the Lord," a breastplate or pouch containing the Urim and the Thummim ("Urim signifieth light, and Thumim, perfection," Geneva margin), and a robe with pomegranates and golden bells alternately at the hem. The Old Testament priesthood is a type of the New, and Aaron is a type of Christ's priestly role.
19 *old man*: Cf. Col. 3:9.

The Odour. 2 *Cor: 2.15*

How sweetly doth *My Master* sound! *My Master*.
    As Amber-greese leaves a rich sent
        Unto the Taster:
    So doe these words a sweet content,
An Orientall fragrancy, *My Master*.   5

With these all day I doe perfume my mind,
    My mind ever thrust into them both,
        That I might find
    What cordials make this curious broth,
This broth of smels, that feeds and fats my mind.   10

My Master, shall I speake? O that to thee
    My servant were a little so,
        As flesh may bee!
    That these two words might creepe and grow
To some degree of spicines to thee.   15

Then should the Pomander, which was before
    A speaking sweet, mend by reflection,
        And tell me more:
    For pardon of my imperfection
Would warme and worke it sweeter then before.   20

For when *My Master,* which alone is sweet,
    And even in my unworthines pleasing,
        Shall call and meet
    My servant, as thee not displeasing,
That call is but the breathing of the sweet.   25

This breathing would with gaines by sweetning mee
    (As sweet things traffick when they meet)

The Odour. 2 *Amber-greese*: ambergris, a secretion of the sperm whale, used in perfume and cookery.
16 *Pomander*: a scent ball which gives out an odor when warmed or squeezed.

Returne to thee.
And so this new commerce and sweet
Should all my life imploy and busy mee. 30

The foile

If wee Could see below
The sphere of vertue, and each shining grace
    As plainly, as that above doth show,
This were the better sky, the brighter place.

    God hath made starres the foile 5
To sett off vertues: Greifs to sett off sinning:
    Yet in this wretched world wee toile,
As if greif were not foule, nor vertue winning.

The Fore-runners

The Harbingers are come. See, see their mark,
White is their colour, and behold my head.
But must they have my Braine? must they dispark
Those sparkling notions, which therein were bred?
    Must Dulnesse turne mee to a Clod? 5
Yet have they left mee, *Thou art still my God.*

Good men ye bee, to leave me my best roome,
Even all my heart, and what is lodged there:
I passe not, I, what of the rest become,
So *Thou art still my God* be out of feare. 10
    He will be pleased with that ditty,
And if I please him, I write fine and witty.

The Fore-runners. Those sent in advance of a royal progress to procure lodgings by chalking doors. Death's harbingers thus mark the poet's head with white hair (l. 2).

3 *dispark*: turn out of a park.
6 Cf. Ps. 31:14.

Farewell sweet Phrases, Lovely Metaphores.
But will ye leave mee thus? When ye before
Of stews and Brothels onely knew the Dores, 15
Then did I wash you with my teares: and more
      Brought you to *Church* well drest and clad;
My *God* must have my best, even all I had.

Lovely enchanting Language: sugar-cane,
Honey of roses, whither wilt thou fly? 20
Hath some fond Lover tic'd thee to thy bane?
And wilt thou leave the *Church* and love a sty?
      Fy, thou wilt soile thy broiderd Coate,
And hurt thy selfe and him, that sings the note.

Let foolish Lovers, if they will love dong, 25
With canvas not with Arras cloth their shame:
Let folly speake in her own native tong.
True Beauty dwells on high. Ours is a flame,
      But borrow'd thence, to light us thither:
Beauty and beauteous words should goe together. 30

Yet, if you goe, I passe not; take your way.
For *Thou art still my God* is all that yee
Perhaps with more embellishment can say.
Goe Birds of spring: Let winter have his fee:
      Let a bleake palenes chalke the dore, 35
So all within be livelier then before.

The Rose

    Presse me not to take more pleasure
      In this world of sugred lies,
    And to use a larger measure
      Then my strict, yet welcome size.

The Rose. 12 Cf. *Obedience,* l. 8.

First there is no pleasure heere: 5
    Colour'd greifs indeed there are,
Blushing woes, that looke as cleere,
    As if they could beauty spare.

Or if such deceits there bee,
    Such delights I meant to say: 10
There are no such things to mee,
    Who have pass'd my right away.

But I will not much oppose
    Unto what you now advize:
Onely take this gentle rose, 15
    And therein my answere lyes.

What is fairer, then a rose?
    What is sweeter? yet it purgeth.
Purgings enmity disclose,
    Enmity forbearance urgeth. 20

If then all, that worldlings prize,
    Be contracted to a rose;
Sweetly there indeed it lies,
    But it biteth in the close.

So this flowre doth judge and sentence 25
    Worldly joyes to be a scourge:
For they all produce repentance,
    And repentance is a purge.

But I health not Physick chuse.
    Onely though I you oppose, 30
Say, that fairely I refuse,
    For my Answere is a *Rose*.

---

18 *purgeth*: Roses were believed to have purgative qualities.

Discipline

Throw away thy rod,
Throw away thy wrath:
        O my God,
Take the gentle path.

For my hearts desire
Unto thine is bent:
        I aspire
To a full consent.

Not a word or looke
I affect to owne,
        But by booke
And thy booke alone.

Though I faile, I weepe:
Though I halt in pace,
        Yet I creepe
To the Throne of grace.

Then let wrath remove;
Love will doe the deed
        For with Love
Stony hearts will bleed.

Love is swift of foot,
Love's a man of warre,
        And can shoot,
And can hitt from farre.

Who can scape his bow?
That, which wrought on thee,

Discipline. 22 Cf. Exod. 15:3, "The Lord is a man of war: the Lord is his name." There may also be an allusion to Cupid with his bow.

    Brought thee low,
  Needs must worke on mee.

Throw away thy rod;
Though man frailties hath,   *30*
    Thou art God:
Throw away thy wrath.

The Invitation

Come ye hither All, whose tast
    Is your wast,
Save your cost, and mend your fare.
God is heere prepar'd and drest,
    And the feast,   *5*
God, in whom all dainties are.

Come ye hither All, whom wine
    Doth define,
Naming you not to your good:
Weepe what ye have drunk amisse,   *10*
    And drink this,
Which before ye drinke is blood.

Come ye hither All, whom paine
    Doth arraigne,
Bringing all your sinnes to sight: *15*
Tast and feare not: *God* is heere
    In this cheere,
And on sinne doth cast the fright.

 The Invitation. 3 H. cites Isa. 55:1-2, "Ho, every one that thirsteth, come ye to the waters, and he that hath no money; come ye, buy, and eat; yea, come, buy wine and milk without money and without price. Wherefore do ye spend money for that which is not bread? and your labour for that which satisfieth not?"
 5 *the feast*: the Eucharist.

Come ye hither All, whom joy
               Doth destroy,   20
While ye graze without your bounds:
Heere is joy, that drowneth quite
               Your delyte,
As a flood the lower grounds.

Come ye hither All, whose Love   25
               Is your Dove,
And exalts you to the sky:
Here is Love, which having breath
               Even in death,
After Death can never dy.   30

Lord I have Invited all,
               And I shall
Still invite, still call to Thee:
For it seemes but Just and right
               In my sight,   35
Where is All, there All should bee.

The Banquet

Welcome sweet and sacred Cheere,
               Welcome Deere,
With mee, in mee live and dwell:
For thy neatnes passeth sight,
               Thy delight   5
Passeth tongue to tast, or tell.

O what sweetenes from the Bowle
               Fills my soule,
Such as is, and makes Divine:
Is some starre (fled from the sphere)   10
               Melted there,
As we sugre melt in Wine?

The Banquet. 4 *neatnes*: refined and decorous beauty.

Or hath sweetnes in the Bread
        Made a Head,
To subdue the smell of Sinne,   15
Flowres, and gummes, and powders giving
        All their living,
Lest the Enemy should winne?

Doubtles, neither Starre, nor Flowre
        Hath the powre   20
Such a sweetnes to impart:
Onely God, who gives perfumes,
        Flesh assumes,
And with it perfumes my heart.

But as Pomanders and wood   25
        Still are good,
Yet being brus'd are better sented:
God to show how farre his love
        Could improve,
Heere, as broken, is presented.   30

When I had forgott my birth,
        And on earth
In delights of earth was drown'd,
God tooke blood, and needs would bee
        Spilt with mee,   35
And so found mee on the ground.

Having rais'd mee to looke up,
        In a cup
Sweetly he doth meet my tast.
But I still being low and short,   40
        Farre from court,
Wine becomes a wing at last.

---

14 *Made a Head*: opposed.

>   For with it alone I fly
>   To the sky:
>   Where I wipe mine eies, and see,   45
>   What I seeke, for what I sue,
>   Him I veiw,
>   Who hath done so much for mee.
>
>   Let the wonder of his pitty
>   Be my ditty,   50
>   And take up my lines and life:
>   Hearken under paine of death,
>   Hands and breath;
>   Strive in this and love the Strife.

The Posy

>   Let witts contest,
>   And with their words and posies windows fill:
>   Lesse then the least
>   Of all thy mercies, is my posy still.
>
>   This on my ring,   5
>   This by my Picture, in my booke I write,
>   Whether I sing,
>   Or say, or dictate, this is my delyte.
>
>   Invention rest,
>   Comparisons goe play, witt use thy will; 10
>   Lesse then the least
>   Of all *Gods* mercies, is my *Posy* still.

The Posy: A motto. Herbert's motto, ll. 11–12, is alluded to in "The Printers to the Reader," and in Walton's *Lives*. Cf. Gen. 32:10, "I am not worthy of the least of all the mercies, and of all the truth, which thou hast shewed unto thy servant."

A parody

Soules joy, when thou art gone,
    And I alone,
    Which cannot bee,
Because thou dost abide with mee,
    And I depend on thee,   5

    Yet when thou dost suppresse
        The cheerefulnes
        Of thy abode,
And in my powres not stirre abroad,
    But leave mee to my load.   10

    O what a dampe and shade
        Doth mee invade!
        No stormy night
Can so afflict or so affright,
    As thy eclipsed light.   15

    Ah Lord, doe not withdraw,
        Lest want of aw
        Make sin appeare;
And when thou dost but shine lesse cleare,
    Say, that thou art not heere.   20

    And then, what life I have,
        While sin doth rave,
        And falsly boast,

A parody. The original is attributed to the Earl of Pembroke in Lansdowne MS. 777, where it appears, and the attribution is accepted by Grierson, though the poem also appears in every early edition of Donne's poems except that of 1633. Herbert's parody turns the opening lines from a secular to a religious use: "Soules joy, now I am gone,/And you alone,/(Which cannot be,/Since I must leave my selfe with thee,/And carry thee with me)/Yet when unto our eyes/Absense denyes/Each others sight,/And makes to us a constant night,/When others change to light."

>   That I may seeke, but thou art lost,
>   Thou and alone thou know'st.   25
>
>   O what a deadly Cold
>   Doth mee infold!
>   I half beleeve,
>   That sin sayes true, but while I greive,
>   Thou com'st and dost releive.   30

The Elixir

>   Teach mee, my *God* and *King*,
>   In all things thee to see,
>   And what I doe in any thing
>   To doe it, as for thee.
>
>   Not rudely, as a Beast,   5
>   To runne into an action:
>   But still to make thee prepossest,
>   And give it his perfection.
>
>   A man, that lookes on glasse,
>   On it may stay his eye;   10
>   Or if he pleaseth, through it passe,
>   And then the heaven espy.
>
>   All may of thee partake:
>   Nothing can be so meane,
>   Which with his Tincture (for thy sake)   15
>   Will not grow bright and cleane.

The Elixir. The elixir is identified with the philosopher's stone (l. 21), which can turn base metals to gold.
  7 *prepossest*: having a prior claim.
  15 *Tincture*: in alchemy, "a supposed spiritual or immaterial substance whose character or quality may be infused into material things" (*OED*); *for thy sake* is the tincture which can purify any action.

A servant with this clause
Makes drudgery divine:
Who sweeps a roome, as for thy laws
Makes that and th' action fine.   20

This is the famous stone
That turneth all to gold:
For that, which God doth touch and owne
Cannot for lesse be told.

A Wreath

A wreathed Garland of deserved praise,
Of praise deserved unto thee I give,
I give to thee, who knowest all my waies,
My crooked winding waies, wherein I live,
Wherein I dy, not live: for life is strait,   5
Straight as a line, and ever tends to thee,
To thee, who art more farre above deceit,
Then deceit seemes above simplicitie.
Give mee simplicitie, that I may live,
So live and like, that I may know thy waies,   10
Know them and practize them, then shall I give
For this poore wreath, give thee a crowne of praise.

Death

Death thou wast once an uncouth hideous thing,
Nothing but bones,
The sad effect of sadder grones,
Thy mouth was open but thou couldst not sing.

---

23 *touch*: testing with a touchstone to determine the fineness of gold: what God has attested as gold cannot be valued at a lesser rate.

> For wee considerd thee as at some six,　　　　　5
> 　　　　Or ten yeares hence,
> 　　After the losse of life and sence,
> Flesh being turn'd to dust, and bones to sticks.
>
> Wee look'd on this side of thee, shooting short,
> 　　　　Where wee did find　　　　10
> 　　The shels of fledg soules left behind,
> Dry dust, which sheds no teares, but may extort.
>
> But since our Saviours Death did put some blood
> 　　　　Into thy face;
> 　　Thou art growne faire and full of grace,　　　　15
> Much in request, much sought for as a good.
>
> For wee doe now behold thee gay and glad,
> 　　　　As at doomes day:
> 　　When soules shall weare their new array
> And all thy bones with beauty shall be clad.　　　　20
>
> Therefore wee can goe dy, as sleepe: and trust
> 　　　　Half, that wee have,
> 　　Unto an honest faithfull grave:
> Making our Pillows either Downe, or Dust.

Doomes day

> 　　　　Come away,
> 　　Make no delay.
> Summon all the dust to Rise,
> Till it stirre, and rubbe the eies.
> While this member jogs the other,　　　　5
> Each one whispering, Live you Brother?
>
> 　　　　Come away,
> 　　Make this the day.
> Dust, alas, no musick feels,

But thy trumpet: then it kneels,   10
As peculiar notes and straines
Cure Tarantulaes raging paines.

      Come away.
    O make no stay.
Let the graves make their confession,   15
Lest at length they plead possession:
Fleshes stubbornes may have
Red that lesson to the grave.

      Come away,
    Thy flock doth stray.   20
Some to winds their body lend,
And in them may drowne a freind:
Some in Noisome vapours grow
To a Plague and publique woe.

      Come away,   25
    Helpe our decay.
Man is out of order hurld,
Parceld out to all the world.
Lord thy broken Consort raise,
And the Musick shall be Praise.   30

Judgement

Almighty Judge, how shall poore wretches brooke
      Thy dreadfull looke,
Able a heart of Iron to appall,
      When thou shalt call
For ev'ry mans peculiar Booke!   5

Doomes day. 12 Tarantism, a hysterical malady, was supposed to be caused by the bite of the tarantula and cured by music and wild dancing (H.).
21–24 Some bodies may be scattered by winds which cause shipwreck; others may be wafted about on other winds, causing plagues.

What others meane to doe, I know not well,
   Yet I heare tell,
That some will turne thee to some leaves therein
   So voyd of sin,
  That they in merrit shall excell.   *10*

But I resolve, when thou shalt call for mine,
   That to decline,
And thrust a Testament into thy hand·
   Let that be scand.
  There thou shalt find, my faults are thine.   *15*

Heaven

O who will show mee those delights on high?
   Eccho.   I.
Thou Eccho, thou art mortall, all men know.
   Eccho.   No.
Wert thou not borne among the trees and leaves? *5*
   Eccho.   Leaves.
And are there any leaves, that still abide?
   Eccho.   Bide.
What leaves are they? impart the matter wholly.
   Eccho.   Holy. *10*
Are holy leaves the Eccho then of blisse?
   Eccho.   Yes.
Then tell mee, what is that supreme delight?
   Eccho.   Light.
Light to the mind. What shall the will enjoy? *15*
   Eccho.   Joy.
But are their cares and busines with the pleasure?
   Eccho.   Leasure.
Light, Joy, and leasure, but shall they persever?
   Eccho.   Ever. *20*

Love [III]

Love bad mee welcome. Yet my soule drew back
        Guilty of dust and sin.
But quick-ey'd Love observing mee grow slack
        From my first entrance in,
Drew neerer to mee, sweetly questioning,   5
        If I lack'd any thing.

A guest, I answer'd, worthy to be heere:
        Love said, you shalbe he.
I the unkind, ungratefull! Ah my Deere
        I cannot looke on thee.   10
Love tooke my hand, and smiling did reply,
        Who made the eyes but I?

Truth *Lord,* but I have marrd them: Let my shame
        Goe, where it doth deserve.
And know you not sayes Love, who bore the blame?   15
        My Deere, then I will serve.
You must sitt downe sayes Love, and tast my meat:
        So I did sitt and eat.

FINIS

Glory be to *God* on high
And on earth peace
Good will towards men.

THE CHURCH MILITANT

Almighty *Lord,* who from thy glorious throne
Seest and rulest all things, even as one:
The smallest Ant or Atome knows thy powre,
Knowne also to each minute of an houre.
Much more doe Common-weales acknowledge thee, 5
And wrap their policies in thy decree,
Complying with thy Counsailes, doing nought,
Which doth not meet with an eternall thought.
But above all thy *Church and Spouse* doth prove
Not the decrees of Powre, but bands of Love. 10
Early didst thou arise to plant this vine,
Which might the more indeere it to be thine.
Spices come from the East, so did thy spouse,
Trimme as the Light, sweet as the laden boughs
Of *Noahs* shady vine, chast as the Dove, 15
Prepar'd and fitted to receive thy Love.
The Course was westward, that the Sunne might light
As well our understanding, as our sight.
Where th' *Arke* did rest, there *Abraham* began
To bring the other *Arke* from *Canaan.* 20
Moses pursu'd this: but *King Solomon*
Finish'd and fix'd the old Religion.

The Church Militant. The poem is set off from *The Church* in both manuscripts and in the 1633 edition. It surveys the westward progress of the Christian Church throughout history, with Sin following closely on its heels.
12 *indeere*: bind by obligations of gratitude (*OED*).
19-22 The wanderings of Noah's ark and Moses' ark (both types of the Christian Church) are related: the place where Noah's ark rested (Ararat, Gen. 8:4) is perhaps identified with Ur (Gen. 11:31) which Abraham left to go to Canaan. Abraham and his descendants wandered from Canaan into the Philistine land and Egypt (Gen. 12:10) with that *other Arke* (the holy symbols of their religion, later identified with the Ark of the Covenant). Moses sought to return this Ark to Canaan (Exod. 37:1) but the Ark was later carried back to the Philistine land (I Sam. 5:1) until at length it was given a resting place in Solomon's Temple (II Chron. 3:1).

When it grew loose, the Jews did hope in vaine
By nailing *Christ* to fasten it againe.
But to the *Gentiles* he bore *Crosse* and all, 25
Rending with earth-quakes the Partition-wall:
Onely whereas the *Arke* in glory shone,
Now with the *Crosse*, as with a staffe, alone
Religion, like a Pilgrime, west-ward bent;
Knocking at all dores, ever, as she went. 30
Yet as the Sunne, though forward be his flight,
Listens behind him, and allowes some light,
Till all depart: So went the *Church* her way,
Letting, while one foot stept, the other stay
Among the Easterne Nations for a time, 35
Till both removed to the Westerne Clime.
To *Egypt* first she came, where they did prove
Wonders of anger once, but now of Love.
The Tenne Commandements there did flourish more,
Then the Ten bitter plagues had done before. 40
Holy *Macarius* and great *Anthony*
Made *Pharaoh, Moses,* changing th' history.
Goshen was darkenes, *Egypt* full of Lights,
Nilus for Monsters brought forth *Israelites*.
Such Powre hath mighty *Baptisme* to produce 45
For things misshapen things of highest use.
How deare to mee, *ô God,* thy Counsels are!
            Who may with thee compare!
Religion thence fled into *Greece,* where Arts
Gave her the highest place in all mens harts. 50
Learning was pos'd; *Philosophy* was sett:
Sophisters taken in a *Fishers* nett.
Plato and *Aristotle* were at a losse,

---

41 *Macarius* and *Anthony*: hermits in Upper Egypt in the fourth century A.D.
42–46 Whereas Egypt before suffered the plague of darkness (Exod. 10:21–23, 8:22) and the Children of Israel in the land of Goshen had light, this is now reversed. Now the Nile does not bring forth frogs, as when Moses sent that plague upon it, but brings forth Christians (baptized in its waters).
47–48 Refrain from Ps. 139:17 and 89:6 (BCP).
51 *pos'd ... sett*: both terms mean nonplussed, puzzled.

And wheel'd about againe to spell *Christ Crosse.*
Prayers chas'd syllogismes into their denne, 55
And *Ergo* was transform'd into *Amen.*
Though Greece tooke horse as soone, as Egypt did,
And Rome as both, yet Egypt faster rid,
And spent her period and prefixed time
Before the other. *Greece* being past her prime, 60
Religion went to *Rome,* subduing those,
Who, that they might subdue, made all their foes.
The Warrior his deere skarres no more resounds,
But seemes to yeeld *Christ* hath the greater wounds,
Wounds willingly endur'd to worke his blisse, 65
Who by an Ambush lost his *Paradise.*
The great Heart stoopes, and taketh from the dust
A sad repentance, not the spoiles of lust:
Quitting his speare lest it should peirce againe
Him in his members, who for him was slaine. 70
The *Shepheards hooke* grew to a *scepter* here,
Giving New Names and Numbers to the yeare.
But th' *Empire* dwelt in *Greece* to comfort them,
Who were cut short in *Alexanders* stemme.
In both of these Prowesse and Arts did tame, 75
And tune mens hearts against the *Gospell* came.
Which using, and not fearing, skill in th' one,
Or strength in th' other, did erect her throne.
Many a rent and strugling th' Empire knew,
(As dying things are wont) untill it flew 80
At length to *Germany,* still westward bending,
And there the *Churches* festival attending.
That as before Empire and Arts made way;
(For no lesse harbingers would serve then they)

---

54 *Christ Crosse*: a name for the alphabet, because a cross was usually prefixed to hornbooks. Philosophers thus must learn their lessons from the beginning.
67 *great Heart*: Constantine (?), who embraced Christianity.
72 The substitution of Christian holy days for pagan festivals.
73–74 The glory of the Alexandrian empire was restored when Constantine moved the capital of the Roman Empire to Byzantium.
76 *against*: before.
81–89 Spain and Germany were key powers in the Holy Roman Empire, which succeeded the Roman Empire as protector of the Church.

So they might still, and point us out the place 85
Where first the *Church* should raise her downecast face.
Strength levels grounds, art makes a garden there,
Then showres Religion, and makes all to beare.
Spaine in the *Empire* shar'd with *Germany*,
But *England* in the higher victory. 90
Giving the *Church* a *Crowne* to keepe her state,
And not goe lesse then she had done of late.
Constantines Brittish line meant this of old,
And did this mystery wrappe up and fold
Within a sheet of paper, which was rent 95
From times great *Chronicle*, and hither sent.
Thus both the *Church* and *Sunne* together ranne
Unto the farthest old Meridian.
How deare to mee, *O God,* thy Counsels are!
           Who may with thee compare! 100
Much about one and the same time and place
Both where and when the *Church* began her race,
Sinne did sett out of *Easterne Babilon,*
And travaild west-ward also journeying on,
He chidd the *Church* away, where ere he came, 105
Breaking her peace, and tainting her good name.
At first he gott to *Egypt,* and did sow
Gardens of *Gods,* which ev'ry yeere did grow,
Fresh and fine Deities. They were at great cost
Who for a *God,* cleerely a sallet lost. 110
Ah, what a thing is Man devoid of grace,
Adoring garlick with an humble face,
Begging his food of that, which he may eat,
Starving the while, he worshippeth his meat.
Who makes a root his *God,* how low is he 115
If *God* and Man be sever'd infinitelie!

90–94 Constantine's mother, Helena, was reputed to be of British birth, and Constantine's protection of the Church is here presented as a type of Britain's later role in the Reformation, giving the church a *Crowne*, i.e., setting up a national church with the King as protector.

98 *Meridian*: the highest altitude of the sun, thus the point just before its decline.

112 *Adoring garlick*: cf. Juvenal, *Sat.* xv. 9–11, Num. 11:15.

What wretchednes can give him any roome,
Whose house is foule, while he adores his broome?
None will beleive this now, though mony bee
In us the same transplanted foolerie.   *120*
Thus *Sin* in *Egypt* sneaked for a while,
His highest was an Oxe or Crocodile,
And such poore game. Thence he to *Greece* doth passe,
And being craftier much then Goodnes was,
He left behind him Garrisons of sinnes   *125*
To make good that, which ev'ry day he wins.
Heere *Sinne* tooke hart, and for a Garden-bed
Rich Shrines and Oracles he purchased:
He grew a gallant, and would needs foretell,
As well what should befall, as what befell.   *130*
Nay he became a Poet, and would serve
His pills of sublimate in that conserve.
The World came with hands and purses full
To this great Lottery, and all would pull:
But all was glorious cheating, brave deceit,   *135*
Where some poore truths were shuffled for a bait
To credit him, and to descredit those,
Who after him should braver truths disclose.
From *Greece* he went to *Rome,* and as before
He was a *God,* now he's an *Emperour.*   *140*
Nero and others lodg'd him bravely there,
Put him in trust to rule the Roman sphere.
Glory was his cheif instrument of old,
Pleasure succeeded strait, when that grew cold.
Which soone was blowne to such a mighty flame,   *145*
That though our *Saviour* did destroy the game,
Disparking Oracles, and all their treasure,

---

118 *adores his broome*: worshipers of vegetable gods neglect to use what would keep their houses clean, brooms made of twigs of the broom plant.

127 *for*: instead of.

131 The Greek oracles were often given in verse.

132 *sublimate*: mercuric chloride, whose poison in the medicinal *conserve* was concealed by the sugar coating.

137–38 *descredit those*: P. sees a reference to the Sibylline Oracles, who were thought to have prophesied Christ among the Pagans.

147 *Disparking*: expelling.

Setting affliction to encounter pleasure;
Yet did a Rogue with hope of carnall joy
Cheat the most subtle Nations. Who so coy,   *150*
So trimme, as *Greece* and *Egypt*? yet their harts
Are given over, for their curious arts
To such Mahometan stupidities,
As the Old Heathen would deeme prodigies.
How deare to mee, *O God,* thy Counsels are!   *155*
        Who may with thee compare!
Onely the West and *Rome* doe keepe them free
From this contagious infidelitie.
And this is all the Rock, whereof they boast,
As *Rome* will one day find unto her cost.   *160*
Sinne being not able to extirpate quite
The *Churches* here, bravely resolv'd one night
To be a *Church-Man* too, and weare a Mitre,
The Old debauched Ruffian would turne writer.
I saw him in his study, where he sate   *165*
Busy in Controversies sprung of late:
A Gowne and Penne became him wondrous well,
His grave aspect had more of heaven then hell:
Onely there was a handsome picture by,
To which he lent a corner of his eye.   *170*
As *Sinne* in Greece a Prophet was before,
And in Old Rome a mighty Emperour:
So now being Preist he plainely did professe
To make a jest of *Christs* three offices.
The rather since his scatter'd juglings were   *175*
United now in one both time and sphere.
From Egypt he tooke petty Deities,
From Greece oracular Infallibilities,
And from old Rome the liberty of pleasure

---

149 *Rogue*: Mohammed, who promised carnal pleasures in heaven.

159 *Rock*: Rome's claim to rest on the rock of Peter's (papal) headship and infallibility means only that she has been preserved from Mohammedan infidelity.

169–70 The often licentious Renaissance popes were great patrons of the arts.

174 *Christs three offices*: Prophet, King, Priest; Sin's caricature of all three, and her location of all these imitations at Rome, is described in the lines following.

By free dispensings of the *Churches* treasure.   *180*
Then in memoriall of his ancient throne
He did surname his palace *Babilon.*
Yet that he might the better gaine all nations,
And make that Name good by their transmigrations,
From all these places, but at divers times,   *185*
He took fine vizards to conceale his crimes.
From Egypt Anchorisme and retirednes,
Learning from Greece, from old Rome statelines,
And blending these he carried all mens eyes,
While truth sate by counting his Victories: *190*
Whereby he grew a-pace, and scorn'd to use
Such force, as once did captivate the Jews,
But did bewitch, and finely work each Nation
Into a voluntary Trans-migration.
All post to *Rome: Princes* submitt their necks,   *195*
Either to his publick foot, or private tricks.
It did not fitt his gravity to stirre,
Nor his long journey, nor his gout and furre.
Therefore he sent out able ministers,
States-men within, without dores Cloisterers.   *200*
Who without speare, or sword, or other drumme,
Then what was in their tongue, did overcome.
And having conquerd did so strangely rule,
That the whole world did seeme but the Popes mule.
As new and old *Rome* did one *Empire* twist;   *205*
So both together are one Antichrist,
Yet with two faces, as their *Janus* was,
Being in this their old crackt looking-glasse.
How deare to mee, *O God,* thy Counsels are!
            Who may with thee compare!   *210*
Thus *Sin* triumphs in Westerne *Babilon,*
Yet not as *Sin*; but as *Religion.*
Of his two thrones he made the latter best,
And to defray his journey from the East.

182 *Babilon*: the recurring biblical image for the city of iniquity, Rev. 17:5.
192 *captivate*: make captive, as Old Babylon once did the Jews.
204 *the Popes mule*: allusion to the kiss ceremonially bestowed upon *his publick foot* (l. 196), and also to his riding upon the world as on a dumb beast.

Old and new Babilon are to Hell and Night, 215
As is the Moone and Sunne to Heaven and Light.
When th' one did sett, the other did take place,
Confronting equally the Law and Grace.
They are Hells Landmarkes, Satans double crest,
They are *Sinnes* Nipples, feeding th' East and West. 220
But as in Vice the Coppy still exceedes
The Patterne, but not so in vertuous deeds:
So though *Sin* made his latter seat the better,
The latter *Church* is to the first a debter.
The second Temple could not reach the first, 225
And the late Reformation never durst
Compare with Ancient times and purer yeares;
But in the *Jews* and us deserveth teares.
Nay it shall ev'ry yeare decrease and fade,
Till such a Darkenes doe the world invade 230
At *Christs* last Comming, as his first did find.
Yet must there such proportions be assign'd
To these diminishings, as is betweene
The spacious *World* and *Jury* to be seene.
Religion stands on tiptoe in our Land, 235
Ready to passe to the *American* strand:
When hight of malice, and prodigious Lusts,
Impudent sinning, witch crafts, and distrusts
(The markes of future bane) shall fill our cup
Unto the brimme, and make our measure up, 240
When Sein shall swallow Tiber, and the Thames
By letting in them both pollutes her streames;
When Italy of us shall have her will,
And all her Calender of sins fulfill,
Whereby one may fortell, what sins next yeare 245
Shall both in *France* and *England* domineere,
Then shall *Religion* to *America* flee:

219 *double crest*: addition of the arms of another family to one's own.
225-28 The late Reformation fell as far short of the primitive Church as the Second Temple did of the first (Ezra 3:12), and alike deserves tears.
232-34 The Church will have shrunk by the time of Christ's Second Coming in proportion to its present growth from its first small beginnings in Jewry.
235-36 Walton notes that these two lines occasioned some difficulty in getting the book licensed.

They have their times of *Gospell,* even as wee.
My *God* thou dost prepare for them a way
By carrying first their Gold from them away.   250
For Gold and Grace did never yet agree:
Religion alwaies sides with povertie.
Wee thinke wee robb them, but wee think amisse.
Wee are more poore, and they more rich by this.
Thou wilt revenge their quarrel, making grace   255
To pay our debts, and leave her ancient place
To goe to them, while that, which now their Nation
But lends to us, shall be our desolation.
Yet as the *Church* shall thither westward fly;
So *Sin* shall trace and dog her instantly,   260
They have their Period also and sett times,
Both for their Vertuous Actions, and their crimes.
And where of old the *Empire* and the Arts
Ushered the *Gospell* ever in Mens harts,
Spaine hath done one, when Arts performe the other, 265
The *Church* shall come, and *Sin* the *Church* shall smother.
That when they have accomplished their round
And mett in th' East their first and ancient sound,
Judgement may meet them both and search the round.
Thus doe both lights as well in *Church,* as *sunne,* 270
Light one another, and together runne.
Thus also *Sin* and *Darknes* follow still
The *Church* and *Sunne* with all their powre and skill.
But as the *Sunne* still goes both *West* and *East;*
So also did the *Church* by going *West*   275
Still *Eastward* goe; because it drew more neere
To time and place, where *Judgement* shall appeere.
How deare to mee, ô *God,* thy Counsels are!
       Who may with thee compare!

---

265 *Spaine hath done one*: Spain used the power of Empire to bring the Gospel to South America.
268 *sound*: haven.

L'Envoy

King of Glory, King of Peace,
With the one make warre to cease,
With the other blesse thy sheep,
Thee to love, in thee to sleep.
Let not Sin devoure thy Fold   5
Bragging, that thy blood is cold,
That thy death is also dead,
While his Conquests dayly spread,
That thy Flesh hath lost his food,
And thy *Crosse* is common wood;   10
Choake him, let him say no more,
But reserve his breath in store,
Till thy Conquests and his fall
Make his sighs to use it all,
And then bargaine with the wind   15
To discharge what is behind.

Blessed be *God* alone,
Thrice Blessed Three in One.

L'Envoy. Both manuscripts continue the page heading, *The Church Militant,* above this poem, suggesting that the *Envoy* is to that poem specifically, rather than to the entire collection.

2 Cf. Ps. 46:9, "He maketh wars to cease unto the end of the earth."

Henry Vaughan

According to Vaughan's own testimony, George Herbert's example was largely responsible for making him a religious man and a religious poet. In his book of meditations, *Mount of Olives* (1652), Vaughan quotes or commends several of Herbert's poems. In the preface added in 1655 to his book of religious poems, *Silex Scintillans*, Vaughan praises Herbert as "the first, that with any effectual success attempted a *diversion* of this foul and overflowing *stream*" of unworthy secular poetry, and he identified himself as one of the many "pious *Converts*" gained by Herbert's "holy *life* and *verse*." Moreover, Vaughan's poem "The Match" responds directly to Herbert's invitation in his poem "Obedience" for "some kinde man" to join with him in the gift of the self to God. The Herbert influence is manifest in echoes and quotations throughout *Silex Scintillans*: borrowed titles, quoted first lines, closely imitated lines and passages, imitations of stanzaic forms. But Vaughan transformed these numerous borrowings, integrating them into his own poetic vision; as Joan Bennett declared, "Herbert may have made Vaughan a poet, but he did not make him in his own image."

The circumstances of Vaughan's long life (1621–1695) reveal some of the important factors affecting his poetry. Born to a Welsh family of modest means but considerable antiquity, Vaughan related himself explicitly to the Welsh tradition by adopting the title "The Silurist," thereby identifying himself with a portion of Southeast Wales supposed to have been inhabited by an ancient British tribe called the Silures. Through his twin brother Thomas, a hermetic philosopher and an author of some note, Vaughan encountered, at least casually, some of the tenets and literature of Hermeticism. Though official records are unavailable, Henry apparently attended Jesus College, Oxford, and afterwards studied at the Inns of Court, but in 1642 the commencement of the Civil War forced his return to Wales. Some of his poems intimate that he bore arms for the King; at any rate, they leave no doubt whatsoever of his intense dislike of the Puritan faction.

Unlike Herbert, Vaughan wrote and published some secular verse in the manner of the Sons of Ben: *Poems* (1646), *Olor Iscanus (The Swan of Usk)*, written about 1647 though not published until 1651, and *Thalia Rediviva* (1678), a collection of early lyrics, most of them written before 1650. Although E. L. Marilla argues the poetic quality of these secular poems, most readers find the two parts of *Silex Scintillans* (1650, 1655) to be vastly superior. And although Frank Kermode quite effectively refutes the simplistic equation of Vaughan's life and art, yet his purely artistic explanation of Vaughan's development is hardly adequate to the facts. Vaughan testifies in several places that he underwent a conversion experience sometime in the late 1640's — probably triggered by the death of his younger brother William in 1648. This experience evidently stimulated a flowering of major creative achievement in the 1650's by giving Vaughan new materials, new subjects, and a new depth of emotional involvement. He wrote little after 1655, and in his later years turned to the study and practice of medicine.

In addition to Herbert and the Scripture, Vaughan's Welsh heritage must be counted as a major influence upon his poetry. As he was fully bilingual, he readily carried over into English poetry such Welsh language habits as the ascription of gender even to nouns which are not personified, the use of *s/z* rhymes, the frequent use of assonance and consonance rhymes, constant alliteration, and the multiplication of comparisons and similes (Welsh *dyfalu*). The Welsh heritage may also account in part for Vaughan's sensitivity to nature, to the scenes of the Usk countryside — though, as E. C. Pettet notes, this aspect of Vaughan has been overemphasized. Vaughan is no premature Romantic: he does not treat nature for its own sake or in sensuously rich terms, but as a book giving lessons and as a means of contemplating God in his creatures.

Easily the most vexed issue in Vaughan criticism concerns the supposed influence of Hermeticism upon the poems. Elizabeth Holmes finds Hermeticism everywhere in Vaughan, while Ross Garner argues that Vaughan's ideas are fundamentally antipathetic to Hermetic mysticism, which is often dualistic and regards matter as evil. Garner is doubtless right to insist that the controlling perspective in Vaughan's poetry is Christian, but he also notes that eclectic assimilation of many aspects of Hermetic thought was far from uncommon among Renaissance Christians. Vaughan would seem to belong in such company. Some of Vaughan's arresting vocabulary derives its special imagistic force from the Hermetic writings—such terms as *beam, balm, balsam, essence, glance, grain, seed, hatch, influence, ray, magnetism, sympathy, tie*. Beyond this, Vaughan sometimes expresses Hermetic ideas, though usually to reinforce Christian concepts. The Neoplatonic concept of the pre-existence of the soul appears in "The Retreate," though chiefly as a metaphor for the childlike innocence the speaker longs for and hopes he may attain again by the time of his death. Such a poem as "And do they so?" is firmly based upon the biblical text (Rom. 8:19) describing the "expectation of the creature" groaning for the coming of the Lord, yet the heightened sense of the mystery and wonder of God's creation, of the sentience and quickness of all things, evidently owes something to the Hermetic idea of God's constant infusions in nature. Also, Vaughan uses the Hermetic concept of magnetic attraction between a heavenly planet and the earthly body which carries its "seed," as an analogue of God's relation to man: in "Cock-crowing," for example, the solar seed which controls the cock is an analogue of God's "seed" in man, through which he dwells in and acts upon man. Vaughan's Hermeticism is not negligible, but its function is chiefly to reinforce his Christian vision.

Another important influence, as Louis Martz shows, is the meditative tradition—not the Ignatian form with its three-part logical structure and its focus upon the Passion, but rather the Augustinian tradition of meditation upon the creatures. An influential guide to such meditation was Robert Bellarmine's *The Ascent of the Mind to God by a Ladder of Things Created* (trans. T. B. Dent [1616]), which encouraged meditation upon the "three books" of Nature, Scripture, and the Soul, noting that Scripture provides the interpretative key to the other two. Martz argues also that the Augustinian emphasis on memory, on the intuitive groping back toward a vision of Eden by means of loosely structured associations and ramifications of ideas, may explain the loose, digressive structure of many Vaughan poems. Such a poem as "I walkt the other day (to spend my hour)" is designed as a formal meditation upon a flower whose "death," wintry sojourn beneath the ground, and springtime rebirth is emblematic of man's death and restoration. In this poem, exceptionally, the customary three-part meditative structure is strictly followed: the setting of the scene, the analysis of points, the colloquy. More typical is the looser organization of such meditations on the creatures as "The Tempest," "The Starre," "The Timber."

Like Herbert, Vaughan was an Anglican, but the religious sensibility manifested in his poetry is very different. Whereas Herbert had found in Christ a man, a friend, a person to meet in a relationship, Vaughan looked to Christ primarily as a mediator, as the only means of knowing God and restoring man to union with him. Vaughan finds vestiges of the Divine everywhere, but he does not encounter a person and he is little concerned with such matters as the Passion or the Eucharist. The Incarnation is important to him, but chiefly as a witness to the immanence of the Divine in nature, as is evident in "The Incarnation, and Passion" and "The Night." Similarly, though Vaughan was greatly distressed by the Puritan threat to the British Church, his religious life was not centered in the Church to anything like the degree that Herbert's was: Martz declares perceptively that with Vaughan "it is as though the earthly church had vanished and men were left to walk alone with God."

Vaughan displays a keen awareness of the Fall and an Augustinian or even Calvinist sense of the resulting total depravity of man. Many of the poems show the speaker attempting to come to terms with the harsh fact of predestination, of the unfathomable will of God controlling man's spiritual condition. The conclusion of "Regeneration" makes clear that the Wind of the Spirit blows "Where I please," and the conclusion of "The World" indicates that the "ring" of betrothal to Christ is given only to the chosen Bride (the Church or the elect soul). A corollary to this consciousness of the Fall is the speaker's sense of the progressive decay of religion in the world since the early ages, and since early childhood in the life of the individual: he mourns lost innocence and often experiences a sense of spiritual exile, estrangement, and severance from God. At times, despite his orthodox Christian belief that evil inheres in the corrupt will rather than in matter, the speaker's distress is formulated in Neoplatonic terms: earth is a prison, matter is a clog to the spirit, and flesh is a veil or cloud obscuring the light of God.

Yet Vaughan's speaker also waxes eloquent about the Book of the Creatures as *Vestigia Dei*: he rejoices in the creatures' constancy to God's ways in comparison to the vacillations of man, and he is often exhilarated at the thought of God's nearness, his immanence in Nature. Robert Ellrodt denies to Vaughan's poetry the basis in paradox that informs the poetry of Donne, Herbert, and Crashaw, yet it would seem that this tension-filled double perspective on nature and the creatures is indeed paradoxical. Garner suggests that the paradox is implicitly resolved through a view of God as at once immanent and transcendent: Vaughan's speaker seeks to pass through the vestiges of God in nature to the higher plane of union with the transcendent God and, accordingly, sometimes praises nature and sometimes turns away from it. Yet Vaughan cannot properly be termed a mystic if one uses that term with any precision; his poems display the speaker's longing for union with the Divine but do not claim to have achieved it. Even such ecstatic poems as "The Morning-watch" and "The Night" celebrate only the merest intimations of that union which the speaker expects only in death and at the end of time.

Vaughan does not address himself at length to poetic theory, but in the 1655 preface to *Silex Scintillans* he places himself in the company of those seeking to convert the Muse to Christian themes and to the service of God. He denounces vain wits, idle words, translations into English of "the most lascivious compositions of *France* and *Italy*," love poetry which wallows in "*impure thoughts* and *scurrilous conceits*," and irreverent would-be religious poets who "dash *Scriptures*, and the *sacred Relatives* of *God* with their impious conceits." He proposes the usual remedy —a "wise exchange of *vain* and *vitious subjects*, for *divine Themes* and *Celestial praise*." Moreover, he cites Herbert as the model for this endeavor because he fitted himself for the highest poetry by making his life a true poem: "he that desires to excel in this kind of *Hagiography*, or holy writing, must strive (by all means) for *perfection* and *true holyness*... and then he will be able to write (with *Hierotheus* and holy *Herbert*) A *true Hymn*." Similarly, in "Idle Verse" (from *Silex*, Part I), the speaker denounces love poetry as the "idle talk of feav'rish souls/Sick with a scarf, or glove," and announces that he has renounced this concern of his "warmer days" for a new "Winter" severity of purpose. Vaughan's symbol for religious contemplation and true poetry is the Mount of Olives, which he uses as title for his book of meditations and for two poems on poetry in *Silex*, Part I. In the first poem the speaker laments the folly of those poets who neglect the Mount of Olives to praise the Cotswolds or Cooper's Hill; in the second he affirms that he has now found "true beauty" in God and so has undertaken a new poetic program, "sick with love I strive thy name to sing,/Thy glorious name!" "The Proffer," from *Silex*, Part II, echoes Herbert's "Jordan [I]" in declaring the poet's resolve not to debase his verse by turning back to the old poetic manner or taking up the new political fashions:

> I skill not your fine tinsel, and false hair,
> > Your Sorcery
> And smooth seducements: I'le not stuff my story
> > With your Commonwealth and glory.

Vaughan's poetic language and imagery is distinctively his own. The wit, conceits, puns, and verbal ambiguities characteristic of Herbert and Donne are not much in evidence. One finds a few domestic, homely images—of candles, rooms, streets, dressing, clothes, medicine—but most of these have biblical sources and overtones. Of first importance to Vaughan's poetic style are certain distinctive images and image clusters originating in the Bible, which carry over symbolic meaning from that source, and derive special symbolic force from their constant recurrence throughout *Silex Scintillans*. One such cluster—the familiar Light–Darkness dichotomy—explores spiritual illumination and mortal opaqueness through such images as dawn, beam, star, ray, candle, shining, brightness, cloud, veil, mist. Another cluster develops the vitality, the sentience of nature through images of green, white, "quick," flowers, roses, buds, leaves, lilies. Yet another associates images of moisture as symbols of God's grace: blood, water, spirit, dew, showers, manna. The emblem introducing *Silex* calls attention to two other dominant images which were also important for Herbert: the stony heart and the fire of God acting upon it. Something of the special intensity and the symbolic force conveyed by such image clusters is evident in the following verses from "They are all gone into the world of light!" in which the speaker contemplates the glories of the departed ones.

> I see them walking in an Air of glory,
> Whose light doth trample on my days:
> My days, which are at best but dull and hoary,
> Meer glimering and decays.
>
> . . . .
>
> If a star were confin'd into a Tomb
> Her captive flames must needs burn there;
> But when the hand that lockt her up, gives room,
> She'l shine through all the sphaere.

Vaughan's language is suffused with biblical allusions, quotations, and near-quotations which operate in several ways to extend symbolic meaning. Sometimes it is a matter of overtone: the landscapes of Vaughan's poems are often suggestive of Eden, and the biblical verses which serve as epigraphs to many of the poems set up contexts which deepen the primary meanings. Sometimes the biblical allusions function emblematically: in "Regeneration," for example, the speaker seems to encounter the biblical places and properties physically, in a fashion not unlike that of Bunyan's Pilgrim. This emblematic manner is in part allegorical, in that the events of the journey are fictions created to represent stages on the way to regeneration. But it is also symbolic, since the biblical metaphors (through the meanings which have accrued to them in centuries of exegesis and application) are felt to convey universal Christian experience, and the speaker's particular spiritual experience is shown to participate in that paradigm.

Finally, though typology is not all-pervasive in *Silex* as it is in *The Temple*, the biblical allusions often present the speaker's experience as a typological recapitulation of biblical events. "White Sunday" states explicitly that the Old Testament stories refer typologically to the modern Christian: "thy method with thy own,/Thy own dear people pens our times,/Our stories are in theirs set down/And penalties spread to our Crimes." "Mans fall, and Recovery" asserts the same point but emphasizes the Christian's advantage over the Old Testament Jews by reason of his identification with the antitype of all the types, Christ: "This [Christ's sacrifice] makes me span/My fathers journeys, and in one faire step/O're all their pilgrimage, and labours leap,/For God (made man,)/Reduc'd th'Extent of works of faith; so made/Of their *Red Sea*, a *Spring*; I wash, they wade." This typological perspective locates the speaker in the biblical story, and his experience is interpreted especially through imagery from the Song of Solomon, the Psalms, and Revelation. In "The Law, and the Gospel" the speaker sees himself recapitulating the Israelites' and the early Christians' experience with God's revelation and begs, "O plant in me thy *Gospel*, and thy *Law*." And in "The Brittish Church" he sees Christ's Passion recurring in the contemporary Puritan persecutions of the Church.

Critics often observe that Vaughan's poems do not have the tight structure and strict logical development characteristic of Donne and Herbert, but this is not necessarily a fault. Vaughan's gift is not for intellectual analysis of spiritual states, or for theological speculation in verse; rather, he often seeks to render an emotional state through an outpouring of images and associations, and uses a form appropriate to this purpose. Another stock complaint is that Vaughan's poems fail to sustain the quality of their arresting opening lines. The poem most often cited in evidence of such failure of poetic power is "The World," but this evidence develops from a misreading. The breathtaking beginning—"I saw Eternity the other night/Like a great *Ring* of pure and endless light,/All calm, as it was bright"—does not introduce a poem on the joys of heaven or the mystical experience; rather, as the title and remainder of the poem indicate, the subject is the world and the worldlings who cannot apprehend the glorious "ring" of eternity which is prepared only for the Elect Bride.

Though Vaughan is greatly indebted to Herbert in regard to versification, he does not approach Herbert's achievement of musical effects or his experimentation with varieties of stanzaic patterns and verse forms. Vaughan typically varied line lengths and stanza lengths in a single poem, as did Herbert, and he took over a few of Herbert's forms: the song introduced by a frame poem in different meter ("The Search," "Easter Hymn," "Palm-Sunday"—modeled upon Herbert's "Easter"); the hieroglyph ("The Wreath"); the list of proverbs and precepts ("Rules and Lessons," modeled upon "The Church-Porch"); the dialogue poem ("Death," "Resurrection and Immortality," "The Evening-watch"). Vaughan can manage unusual melodic textures at times, as in "They are all gone into the world of light!" In "The Water-fall" he experiments successfully with long sweeping rhythmic cadences created by enjambment and mid-line caesuras, which play against a framework of regular metrical lines and stanzas. Typically, however, Vaughan writes a long, loose, free-flowing poetic line and poetic stanza.

Like *The Temple*, *Silex Scintillans* is a unified whole; as Pettet declares, it is "a poetic work, not a collection of miscellaneous lyrics." Pettet notes that at least six poems in Part I have counterparts in Part II, that there are at least six sequences of closely interrelated poems in the two parts, and that the work presents a spiritual progress from the poems of Part I, which are dominated by the consciousness of the Fall, to those of Part II, in which the focus is rather on the life hereafter. But the case for unity is stronger still. The whole collection is set forth as the speaker's spiritual odyssey, his sojourn in the wilderness. Several poems ("The Seed growing secretly," "Begging" [II], "Providence") identify him typologically with Ishmael, the "weeping lad" who was saved in the wilderness when God heard his cries and led his mother to a fountain to "fill his bottle." Other poems continue the Pilgrimage motif: "Regeneration," "The Search," "Mans fall, and Recovery," "Vanity of Spirit," "The Pilgrimage," "The Ass," "Righteousness."

The dominant theme and tone of Part I are set by the first poem, "Regeneration." Its subject is not mystical aspiration, as is sometimes supposed, but the speaker's conversion experience. First he realizes his condition as "A Ward, and still in bonds" to sin and the Law; then he turns away from the false spring of worldly pleasures; at length he is forced to recognize that by his own efforts he cannot achieve salvation; then he experiences God's calling and restoring his soul to something like an Edenic state; and finally he recognizes that God's Spirit "bloweth where it listeth," setting apart the elect from the reprobate souls. This conversion experience ends with the speaker's urgent prayer to be numbered among the elect: "Lord, then said I, *On me one breath,/And let me dye before my death!*" "Regeneration" is followed immediately by a sequence of poems on the Last Things—"Death," "Resurrection and Immortality," "Day of Judgement"—but they are treated here in prospect, in terms of the speaker's need to prepare himself for these events.

Part I contains several poems on religious festivals and sacraments; some others which treat events in the Old Testament or the life of Christ as types of Christian experience; a few which trace man's decline from primitive or childhood purity; and many which describe spiritual and emotional states, especially those of spiritual unrest, distress over sin and the results of the Fall, frustration with the mortal condition. This tone is sounded especially in such poems as "The Search," "Unprofitablenes," "Distraction," "The Storm," "The Relapse," and "Misery"— poems which have no counterparts in Part II. There are also eight elegies in which the speaker's grief and keen sense of loss heighten for him the sharp contrast between the burdens of the earthly condition and the saints' bliss. A poem such as "Vanity of Spirit" is typical of Part I, treating as it does the speaker's longing for spiritual knowledge, his effort to understand who "circled in/Corruption with this glorious Ring," his discovery in nature of some vestiges of the divine, his discovery in himself of the image of God defaced and dismembered, and his final over-powering consciousness of mortal darkness:

> Since in these veyls my Ecclips'd Eye
> May not approach thee, (for at night
> Who can have commerce with the light?)
> I'le disapparell, and to buy
> But one half glaunce, most gladly dye.

Part I ends with the poem "Begging," whose burden is a prayer to God to "Perfect what thou hast begun."

The dominant theme and tone of Part II are also set by the opening poem. "Ascension-day" takes Christ's Ascension as a type of the speaker's progress to a higher plateau of assurance, joy, serenity, and spiritual longing: "I soar and rise/Up to the skies,/Leaving the world their day." The focus is now upon the life hereafter, and the discontents of the world count for much less in relation to the joyful expectation of the coming release into glory. The speaker's concern is now not so much with lost Edenic or primitive innocence, as with the expectation of the eschatological transformation of all things. "Ascension-day" treats Christ's Resurrection and forty-day sojourn among men as a restoration of Eden, and it concludes with the traditional typological linking of the Ascension to Judgment Day. "Ascension-Hymn," which follows, emphasizes the same motifs, stressing the Lord's promise to "Make clay ascend more quick then light." The third poem, "They are all gone into the world of light!" is in some ways the counterpart of "The World," but now the vision of the life in glory offers an ever present hope of true liberty to the soul still caught in the mists of the earthly state. Part II contains poems on the same subjects as Part I, but there are fewer on religious feasts and ceremonies and many more on objects in nature as emblems of spiritual experience: it is as if the speaker can now find the evidences of his relation to God everywhere.

Perhaps the most complex poem in Part II, and one which is typical of its special quality, is "The Night." The speaker finds in the story of Nicodemus a way to come to terms with the veils and darkness of the mortal condition, for he apprehends that Nicodemus encountered Christ's divinity at night through the veil of his flesh. Nicodemus did, in fact, at night "have commerce with the light." This recognition of the meaning of the

Incarnation, and this example of finding God in the darkness of the world help the speaker throw off the agony and distress that often accompany his longing for transcendence, for utter purity, for full, mystical union. The longing, however, remains intense: "O for that night! where I in him/Might live invisible and dim." Part II ends with a sequence of poems on the last things and on heavenly joy — "The day of Judgement," "The Throne," "Death," "The Feast," "Quickness," "The Wreath," "The Queer" — but now the Last Things are seen as imminent and the speaker seems to experience an earnest of heavenly joy on earth. Two poems on the Bible conclude the sequence, and in them the speaker assumes the posture of one near death bidding farewell to the book which has been his guide through life. The concluding poem of Part II, "L'Envoy," projects the eschatological vision of the perfection of all things, as the speaker pleads with "the new worlds new, quickning Sun" for this transformation:

> Arise, arise!
> And like old cloaths fold up these skies,
> This long worn veyl: then shine and spread
> Thy own bright self over each head,
> And through thy creatures pierce and pass
> Till all becomes thy cloudless glass,
> Transparent as the purest day.

Nevertheless, the speaker affirms his patience, his willingness to wait and serve "Till all be ready, that the train/May fully fit thy glorious reign."

Copy text for *Silex Scintillans* is the British Museum copy of the 1655 edition. In this edition the unsold sheets from 1650 (the first edition, containing Part I only) were bound together with the new material of Part II, except for two signatures (B2 and B3), which were newly set. The asterisk (*) in the text calls attention to Vaughan's marginal notes. For matters of text and interpretation I am especially indebted to L. C. Martin's standard edition of Vaughan's *Works*, cited as (M.) and to F. E. Hutchinson's biography of Vaughan, cited as (H.). The editions of French Fogle and E. K. Chambers are cited as (F.) and (Ch.).

SELECTED BIBLIOGRAPHY

EDITIONS

Chambers, E. K., ed. *The Poems of Henry Vaughan, Silurist*, intro. by H. C. Beeching. London, 1896.

Fogle, French, ed. *The Complete Poetry of Henry Vaughan*. New York, 1964.

Marilla, E. L., ed. *The Secular Poems of Henry Vaughan*. Cambridge, Mass., 1958.

Martin, L. C., ed. *The Works of Henry Vaughan*, 2nd ed. Oxford, 1957.

BIOGRAPHY AND CRITICISM

Durr, R. A. *On the Mystical Poetry of Henry Vaughan*. Cambridge, Mass., 1962.

Garner, Ross. *Henry Vaughan: Experience and the Tradition*. Chicago, 1959.

———. *The Unprofitable Servant in Henry Vaughan*. Lincoln, Neb., 1963.

Grant, P. "Hermetic Philosophy and the Nature of Man in Vaughan's *Silex Scintillans*," *JEGP*, LXVIII (1968), 406–22.

Holmes, Elizabeth. *Henry Vaughan and the Hermetic Philosophy*. Oxford, 1932.

Hutchinson, F. E. *Henry Vaughan: A Life and Interpretation*. Oxford, 1947.

Kermode, Frank. "The Private Imagery of Henry Vaughan," *RES*, I (1950), 206–25.

Mahood, M. M. *Poetry and Humanism*. London, 1950.

Marilla, E. L. "The Secular and Religious Poetry of Henry Vaughan," *MLQ*, IX (1948), 394–411.

Martz, Louis L. *The Paradise Within: Studies in Vaughan, Traherne, and Milton*. New Haven, Conn., 1964.

Pettet, E. C. *Of Paradise and Light: A Study of Vaughan's Silex Scintillans*. Cambridge, Eng., 1960.

Rickey, Mary Ellen. "Vaughan, *The Temple*, and Poetic Form," *SP*, LIX (1962), 162–70.

Spitz, Leona. "Process and Stasis: Aspects of Nature in Vaughan and Marvell," *HLQ*, XXXII (1969), 135–47.

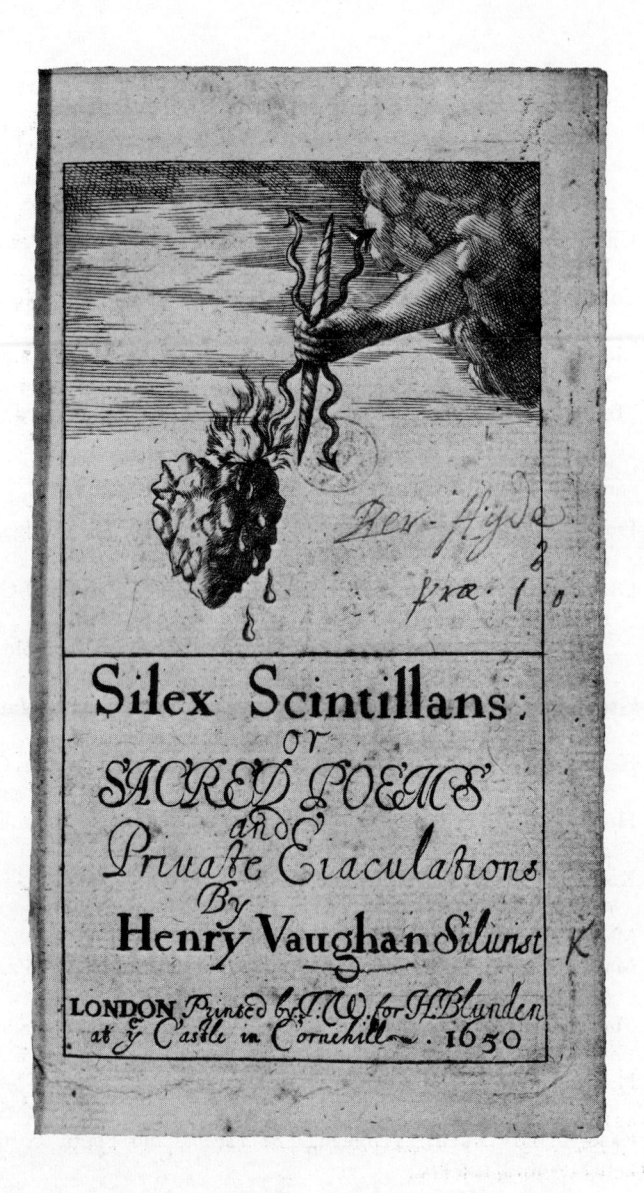

Silex Scintillans:
or
SACRED POEMS
and
Private Ejaculations
By
Henry Vaughan Silurist

LONDON Printed by T.W. for H. Blunden at ý Castle in Cornehill. 1650

SILEX SCINTILLANS:
or
Sacred Poems
and
Private Ejaculations

[PART I]

Authoris (de se) Emblema

Tentâsti, fateor, sine vulnere sœpius, & me
  Consultum voluit VOX, *sine voce, frequens;*
Ambivit placido divinior aura meatu,
  Et frustrà sancto murmure præmonuit.

   Silex Scintillans: The Flashing Flint. The subtitle acknowledges Vaughan's debt to Herbert, who used the same subtitle for *The Temple*. The 1655 edition has as motto on the title page, Job 35:10-11: "Where is God my Maker, who giveth Songs in the night? Who teacheth us more then the beasts of the earth, and maketh us wiser then the fowls of heaven?"
   Authoris (de se) Emblema. Emblem and verse appear in 1650 only; Ross Garner's translation follows:

>   Oft hast Thou wooed me, and hast made no wound;
>   And counseled me, but I have heard no sound.
>   Divinest breaths have gently sought my gain,
>   Have forewarned me with holy sighs, in vain.

Surdus eram, mutusque Silex: *Tu, (quanta tuorum* 5
  Cura tibi est!) aliâ das renovare viâ,
Permutas Curam: Jamque irritatus Amorem
  Posse negas, & vim, Vi, superare paras,
Accedis propior, molemque, & Saxea *rumpis*
  Pectora, fitque Caro, *quod fuit ante* Lapis. 10
En lacerum! Coelosque tuos ardentia tandem
  Fragmenta, & liquidas ex Adamante *genas.*
Sic olim undantes Petras, Scopulosque *vomentes*
  Curâsti, O populi providus usque tui!
Quam miranda tibi manus est! Moriendo, *revixi;* 15
  Et fractas *jam sum* ditior *inter* opes.

A flint was I, both deaf and dumb; but Thou 5
(How great Thy cure!) giv'st new ways to renew,
Changest Thy cure. Now angered, Thou dost spite
Love's skill, prepar'st to conquer might with might.
Thou draw'st near, and break'st this frame of bone,
This rocklike heart; 'tis flesh that once was stone. 10
These cuts! O Skies, these flaming shreds are Thine,
And liquid knees that once were ad'mantine.
Thus once Thou didst make water gush from stone,
Thou! ever provident of those, Thine own.
  Thy wondrous hand! I live again in dying, 15
  And rich am I, now, amid ruins lying.

13 Exod. 17:1–6 tells of Moses striking the rock, causing water to flow forth for the Israelites.

[*Dedication*]

To my most merciful, my most loving,
and dearly loved Redeemer, the ever blessed,
the onely Holy and Just one.
JESUS CHRIST,
The Son of the living GOD,
And the sacred Virgin Mary

I

My God! thou that didst dye for me,
These thy deaths fruits I offer thee;
Death that to me was life and light,
But dark and deep pangs to thy sight.
Some drops of thy all-quickning blood   5
Fell on my heart; those made it bud
And put forth thus, though Lord, before
The ground was curst, and void of store.
Indeed I had some here to hire
Which long resisted thy desire,   10
That ston'd thy servants, and did move
To have thee murthred for thy love;

To my most merciful.... Only the first poem appears in 1650, titled "The dedication." In 1655 the three dedicatory poems are preceded by a prose preface in which Vaughan denounces witty and lascivious poetry and proposes the treatment of "divine Themes and Celestial praise."

[*Dedication*] *l*. 9–12 See Matt. 21:33–41, the parable of the wicked husband — men who slew their Lord's servants (the prophets) and then His own Son (Christ).

But Lord, I have expell'd them, and so bent,
Beg, thou wouldst take thy Tenants Rent.

II

Dear Lord, 'tis finished! and now he
That copyed it, presents it thee.
'Twas thine first, and to thee returns,
From thee it shin'd, though here it burns;
If the Sun rise on rocks, is't right,   5
To call it their inherent light?
No, nor can I say, this is mine,
For, dearest Jesus, 'tis all thine.
As thy cloaths, (when thou with cloaths wert clad)
Both light from thee, and virtue had,   10
And now (as then within this place)
Thou to poor rags dost still give grace.
This is the earnest thy love sheds,
The *Candle* shining on some heads,
Till at thy charges they shall be,   15
Cloath'd all with immortality.

My dear Redeemer, the worlds light,
And life too, and my hearts delight!
For all thy mercies and thy truth
Shew'd to me in my sinful youth,
For my sad failings and my wilde   5
Murmurings at thee, when most milde:
For all my secret faults, and each
Frequent relapse and wilful Breach,
For all designs meant against thee,
And ev'ry publish'd vanity   10

[*Dedication*] *ll*. 1–4 Cf. Herbert, "Dedication" to *The Temple*.
  9–10 See the description of Christ's transfiguration, especially Mark 9:3, "And his raiment became shining, exceeding white as snow."
  14 Job 29:3, "When his candle shined upon my head, and when by his light I walked through darkness."

Which thou divinely hast forgiven,
While thy blood wash'd me white as heaven:
I nothing have to give to thee,
But this thy own gift, given to me;
Refuse it not! for now thy *Token*   15
Can tell thee where a heart is broken.

Revel. cap. 1. ver. 5,6,7.

Unto him that loved us, and washed us from our sins in his own blood. And hath made us Kings and Priests unto God and his Father; to him be glory and dominion, for ever and ever. Amen.

Behold, he cometh with clouds, and every eye shall see him, and they also which pierced him; and all kinreds of the earth shall wail because of him: even so. Amen.

[*Vain Wits and eyes*]

Vain Wits and eyes
Leave, and be wise:
Abuse not, shun not holy fire,
But with true tears wash off your mire.
Tears and these flames will soon grow kinde,   5
And mix an eye-salve for the blinde.
Tears cleanse and supple without fail,
And fire will purge your callous veyl.
Then comes the light! which when you spy,
And see your nakedness thereby,   10
Praise him, who dealt his gifts so free
In tears to you, in fire to me.

[*Vain Wits and eyes*]. In 1655 only. Vaughan perhaps intended this as a substitute for the emblem and verse of the 1650 edition.

Regeneration

A Ward, and still in bonds, one day
    I stole abroad,
It was high-spring, and all the way
    Primros'd, and hung with shade;
        Yet, was it frost within,   5
        And surly winds
Blasted my infant buds, and sinne
    Like Clouds ecclips'd my mind.

Regeneration. The thematic introduction to Part I of *Silex Scintillans*, presenting an allegory of a conversion experience culminating in the hope of election into the company of the saints. Cf. Herbert, "The Pilgrimage." M. notes some striking similarities to the opening of Thomas Vaughan's *Lumen de Lumine* (in *Works*, ed. A. E. Waite, London, 1919, pp. 243-44):

"It was about the dawning or daybreak when, tired with a tedious solitude and those pensive thoughts which attend it, after much loss and more labour, I suddenly fell asleep. Here then the day was no sooner born but strangled. I was reduced to a night of a more deep tincture than that which I had formerly spent. My fancy placed me in a region of inexpressible obscurity, and—as I thought—more than natural.... Being thus troubled to no purpose, and wearied with long endeavours, I resolved to rest myself, and seeing I could find nothing I expected if anything could find me.

"I had not long continued in this humour but I could hear the whispers of a soft wind that travelled towards me... so that I concluded myself to be in some wood or wilderness. With this gentle breath came a most heavenly, odourous air."

1 *Ward*: Rom. 8:14-15, "For as many as are led by the Spirit of God, they are the sons of God. For ye have not received the spirit of bondage again to fear; but ye have received the Spirit of adoption, whereby we cry, Abba, Father."
4 *Primros'd*: Cf. Thomas Vaughan, *Lumen*, p. 246, "Her [Thalia's] walk was green... and pearled all the way with daisies and primrose." Primrose suggests at once the springtime of youth and joy, and the "primrose path" that leads to destruction.

2

Storm'd thus; I straight perceiv'd my spring
        Meere stage, and show, 10
My walke a monstrous, mountain'd thing
        Rough-cast with Rocks, and snow;
        And as a Pilgrims Eye
            Far from reliefe,
Measures the melancholy skye 15
        Then drops, and rains for griefe,

3

So sigh'd I upwards still, at last
        'Twixt steps, and falls
I reach'd the pinacle, where plac'd
        I found a paire of scales, 20
        I tooke them up and layd
            In th'one late paines,
The other smoake, and pleasures weigh'd
        But prov'd the heavier graines;

4

With that, some cryed, *Away*; straight I 25
        Obey'd, and led
Full East, a faire, fresh field could spy
        Some call'd it, *Jacobs Bed*;
        A Virgin-soile, which no
            Rude feet ere trod, 30
Where (since he stept there,) only go
        Prophets, and friends of God.

20–24 *scales*: the speaker's repentance and grief, and the pains of his laborious ascent, do not outweigh the sinful *smoke* and *pleasures* of his life.
    28 *Jacobs Bed*: the field where Jacob slept and saw in a vision a ladder stretching from Heaven with angels ascending and descending (Gen. 28:11–12).

5

Here, I repos'd; but scarse well set,
    A grove descryed
Of stately height, whose branches met   35
    And mixt on every side;
    I entred, and once in
        (Amaz'd to see't,)
Found all was chang'd, and a new spring
    Did all my senses greet;   40

6

The unthrift Sunne shot vitall gold
    A thousand peeces,
And heaven its azure did unfold
    Checqur'd with snowie fleeces,
    The aire was all in spice   45
    And every bush
A garland wore; Thus fed my Eyes
    But all the Eare lay hush.

7

Only a little Fountain lent
    Some use for Eares,   50
And on the dumbe shades language spent
    The Musick of her teares;
    I drew here neere, and found
    The Cisterne full
Of divers stones, some bright, and round   55
    Others ill-shap'd, and dull.

---

45 *spice*: cf. Vaughan's epigraph. The echo is from the Song of Solomon, traditionally allegorizing the love of Christ for the Church or for the Soul.
49 *Fountain*: Christ, the Fountain of Life.
49–54 Song of Sol. 4:15, "A fountain of gardens, a well of living waters." Cf. John 4:10–14, Jer. 2:13.
55–58 *stones*: see 1 Pet. 2:5, "Ye also, as lively stones, are built up a spiritual house, an holy priesthood."

8

The first (pray marke,) as quick as light
        Danc'd through the floud,
But, th'last more heavy then the night
        Nail'd to the Center stood;
    I wonder'd much, but tyr'd
        At last with thought,
My restless Eye that still desir'd,
        As strange an object brought;

9

It was a banke of flowers, where I descried
        (Though 'twas mid-day,)
Some fast asleepe, others broad-eyed
        And taking in the Ray,
    Here musing long, I heard
        A rushing wind
Which still increas'd, but whence it stirr'd
        No where I could not find;

10

I turn'd me round, and to each shade
        Dispatch'd an Eye,
To see, if any leafe had made
        Least motion, or Reply,
    But while I listning sought
        My mind to ease
By knowing, where 'twas, or where not,
        It whisper'd; *Where I please.*

---

70 *wind*: the Spirit.
80 *Where I please*: John 3:8, "The wind bloweth where it listeth, and thou hearest the sound thereof, but canst not tell whence it cometh, and whither it goeth: so is every one that is born of the Spirit."

> Lord, then said I, *On me one breath,*
> *And let me dye before my death!*
>
> Cant. Cap. 5. ver. 17.
>
> Arise O North, and come thou South-wind, and blow upon my garden, that the spices thereof may flow out.

Death [I]

A Dialogue

Soule. 'Tis a sad Land, that in one day
    Hath dull'd thee thus, when death shall freeze
    Thy bloud to Ice, and thou must stay
    Tenant for Yeares, and Centuries,
    How wilt thou brook't?——   5

Body. I cannot tell,——
    But if all sence wings not with thee,
    And something still be left the dead,
    I'le wish my Curtaines off to free
    Me from so darke, and sad a bed;   10

    A neast of nights, a gloomie sphere,
    Where shadowes thicken, and the Cloud
    Sits on the Suns brow all the yeare,
    And nothing moves without a shrowd;

Soule. 'Tis so: But as thou sawest that night   15
    Wee travell'd in, our first attempts
    Were dull, and blind, but Custome straight
    Our feares, and falls brought to contempt;

---

82 *dye*: that is, to sin and to the world.
Cant. Cap. 5. ver. 17 : should read, "Cap. 4. ver. 16" (Geneva version).

Then, when the gastly *twelve* was past
We breath'd still for a blushing *East*,   20
And bad the lazie Sunne make hast,
And on sure hopes, though long, did feast;

But when we saw the Clouds to crack
And in those Cranies light appear'd,
We thought the day then was not slack,   25
And pleas'd our selves with what wee feard;

Just so it is in death. But thou
Shalt in thy mothers bosome sleepe
Whilst I each minute grone to know
How neere Redemption creepes.   30

Then shall wee meet to mixe again, and met,
'Tis last good-night, our Sunne shall never set.

Job. Cap: 10, ver. 21. 22.

Before I goe whence I shall not returne, even to the land of darknesse, and the shadow of death;
A Land of darknesse, as darkenesse it selfe, and of the shadow of death, without any order, and where the light is as darknesse.

Resurrection and Immortality

Heb. cap. 10. ve: 20

By that new, and living way, which he hath prepared for us, through the veile, which is his flesh.

Body

1

Oft have I seen, when that renewing breath
    That binds, and loosens death
Inspir'd a quickning power through the dead
    Creatures a bed,
      Some drowsie silk-worme creepe   5
      From that long sleepe
And in weake, infant hummings chime, and knell
    About her silent Cell
Untill at last full with the vitall Ray
    She wing'd away,   10
    And proud with life, and sence,
      Heav'ns rich Expence,
Esteem'd (vaine things!) of two whole Elements
    As meane, and span-extents.
Shall I then thinke such providence will be   15
    Lesse friend to me?
Or that he can endure to be unjust
    Who keeps his Covenant even with our Dust?

Resurrection and Immortality. Cf. *Hermetica*, Libellus xii, 15b, 16, ed. and trans. Walter Scott, Vol. I (Oxford, 1924), pp. 233–35: "Now this whole Kosmos... is one mass of life.... There is not, and has never been, and never will be in the Kosmos anything that is dead.... Dissolution is not death; it is only the separation of things which were combined; and they undergo dissolution not to perish, but to be made new." M. cites other relevant passages.

12–14 The butterfly (now airborne and enjoying "Heav'ns rich Expence") esteems the lower, bounded elements of earth and water as mean.

Soule

2

Poore, querulous handfull! was't for this
      I taught thee all that is?
Unbowel'd nature, shew'd thee her recruits,
        And Change of suits
     And how of death we make
        A meere mistake,
For no thing can to *Nothing* fall, but still
      Incorporates by skill,
And then returns, and from the wombe of things
        Such treasure brings
    As *Phenix*-like renew'th
        Both life, and youth;
For a preserving spirit doth still passe
      Untainted through this Masse,
Which doth resolve, produce, and ripen all
        That to it fall;
     Nor are those births which we
        Thus suffering see
Destroy'd at all; But when times restles wave
      Their substance doth deprave
And the more noble *Essence* finds his house
        Sickly, and loose,
    He, ever young, doth wing
        Unto that spring,
And *source* of spirits, where he takes his lot
     Till time no more shall rot
His passive Cottage; which (though laid aside,)
        Like some spruce Bride,
Shall one day rise, and cloath'd with shining light
        All pure, and bright
   Re-marry to the soule, for 'tis most plaine
   Thou only fal'st to be refin'd againe.

---

21 *recruits*: means of obtaining fresh supply (*OED*).

3

Then I that here saw darkly in a glasse
  But mists, and shadows passe,
And, by their owne weake *Shine,* did search the springs
  And Course of things
    Shall with Inlightned Rayes 55
    Peirce all their wayes;
And as thou saw'st, I in a thought could goe
  To heav'n, or Earth below
To reade some *Starre,* or *Min'rall,* and in State
  There often sate, 60
    So shalt thou then with me
    (Both wing'd, and free,)
Rove in that mighty, and eternall light
  Where no rude shade, or night
Shall dare approach us; we shall there no more 65
  Watch stars, or pore
Through melancholly clouds, and say
  Would it were Day!
One everlasting *Saboth* there shall runne
Without *Succession,* and without a *Sunne.* 70

Dan: Cap: 12 . ver: 13 .

But goe thou thy way untill the end be, for thou shalt rest, and stand up in thy lot, at the end of the dayes.

51 I Cor. 13:12, "For now we see through a glass, darkly; but then face to face."
57–60 Cf. *Hermetica,* Libellus xi (ii) 18, 20b, in Scott, I, 221, "Bid your soul travel to any land you choose, and sooner than you can bid it go, it will be there.... Bid it fly up to heaven, and it will have no need of wings."
68 Deut. 28:67, "at even thou shalt say, Would God it were morning!" The motto and epigraph are derived from the Geneva version of the Bible.

Day of Judgement [I]

When through the North a fire shall rush
           And rowle into the East,
And like a firie torrent brush
           And sweepe up *South*, and *West*,

When all shall streame, and lighten round   5
           And with surprizing flames
Both stars, and Elements confound
           And quite blot out their names,

When thou shalt spend thy sacred store
           Of thunders in that heate   10
And low as ere they lay before
           Thy six-dayes-buildings beate,

When like a scrowle the heavens shal passe
           And vanish cleane away,
And nought must stand of that vast space   15
           Which held up night, and day,

When one lowd blast shall rend the deepe,
           And from the wombe of earth
Summon up all that are asleepe
           Unto a second birth,   20

When thou shalt make the Clouds thy seate,
           And in the open aire
The Quick, and dead, both small and great
           Must to thy barre repaire;

O then it wilbe all too late   25
           To say, *What shall I doe?*

Day of Judgement [I]. 11–12 *Thy six-dayes-buildings*: all the six days' creations. 13 *scrowle*: Rev. 6:14, "And the heaven departed as a scroll when it is rolled together; and every mountain and island were moved out of their places."

Repentance there is out of date
        And so is *mercy* too;

Prepare, prepare me then, O God!
        And let me now begin 30
To feele my loving fathers *Rod*
        Killing the man of sinne!

Give me, O give me Crosses here,
        Still more afflictions lend,
That pill, though bitter, is most deare 35
        That brings health in the end;

Lord, God! I beg nor friends, nor wealth
        But pray against them both;
Three things I'de have, my soules chief health!
        And one of these seme loath, 40

A living *FAITH*, a *HEART* of flesh,
        The *WORLD* an Enemie,
This last will keepe the first two fresh,
        And bring me, where I'de be.

        1 Pet. 4. 7.

Now the end of all things is at hand, be you therefore sober, and watching in prayer.

Religion

    My God, when I walke in those groves,
    And leaves thy spirit doth still fan,
    I see in each shade that there growes
    An Angell talking with a man.

---

    40 *loath*: hateful, loathsome (*OED*).
    41 See Ezek. 11:19, "And I will take the stony heart out of their flesh, and will give them an heart of flesh." Epigraph is derived from the Geneva version.
    Religion. Cf. Herbert, *Decay.*

Under a *Juniper*, some house, 5
Or the coole *Mirtles* canopie,
Others beneath an *Oakes* greene boughs,
Or at some *fountaines* bubling Eye;

Here *Jacob* dreames, and wrestles; there
Elias by a Raven is fed, 10
Another time by th' Angell, where
He brings him water with his bread;

In *Abr'hams* Tent the winged guests
(O how familiar then was heaven!)
Eate, drinke, discourse, sit downe, and rest 15
Untill the Coole, and shady *Even*;

Nay thou thy selfe, my God, in *fire*,
Whirle-winds, and *Clouds*, and the *soft voice*
Speak'st there so much, that I admire
We have no Conf'rence in these daies; 20

Is the truce broke? or 'cause we have
A mediatour now with thee,
Doest thou therefore old Treaties wave
And by appeales from him decree?

Or is't so, as some green heads say 25
That now all miracles must cease?
Though thou hast promis'd they should stay
The tokens of the Church, and peace;

5-8 An angel awoke Elijah under a *Juniper* (I Kings 19:5), spoke to Zechariah from under a *Myrtle* (Zech. 1:11), spoke to Gideon under an *Oak* (Judg. 6:11), and to Hagar by a *fountain* (Gen. 16:7).
 9 See Gen. 28:11-22, 32:24-32.
 10-12 *Elias*: Elijah. See I Kings 17:3-7.
 13-16 *Abr'hams Tent*: see Gen. 18:1-8.
 17-18 God spoke to Moses in the Burning Bush (Exod. 3:2), to Job out of a whirlwind (Job 38:1), to Moses out of a cloud (Exod. 24:16), and to Elijah in "a still small voice" (I Kings 19:12).

No, no; Religion is a Spring
That from some secret, golden Mine   30
Derives her birth, and thence doth bring
Cordials in every drop, and Wine;

But in her long, and hidden Course
Passing through the Earths darke veines,
Growes still from better unto worse,   35
And both her taste, and colour staines,

Then drilling on, learnes to encrease
False *Ecchoes*, and Confused sounds,
And unawares doth often seize
On veines of *Sulphur* under ground;   40

So poison'd, breaks forth in some Clime,
And at first sight doth many please,
But drunk, is puddle, or meere slime
And 'stead of Phisick, a disease;

Just such a tainted sink we have   45
Like that *Samaritans* dead *Well*,
Nor must we for the Kernell crave
Because most voices like the *shell*.

Heale then these waters, Lord; or bring thy flock,
Since these are troubled, to the springing rock,   50
Looke downe great Master of the feast; O shine,
And turn once more our *Water* into *Wine!*

Cant. cap. 4. ver. 12.

My sister, my spouse is as a garden Inclosed, as a Spring shut up, and a fountain sealed up.

46 *Samaritans dead Well*: see John 4:6-15, in which Christ contrasts the waters of Jacob's well to the living waters which he will bring.
49-52 Moses sweetening the waters at Marah (Exod. 15:23-25) and striking water from the Rock (Exod. 17:6) are types of Christ changing water into wine at the marriage feast at Cana (John 2:1-11), itself a type of the Eucharist and of the Heavenly Feast of Christ and his saints.
Epigraph is derived from the Geneva version.

The Search

'Tis now cleare day: I see a Rose
Bud in the bright East, and disclose
The Pilgrim-Sunne; all night have I
Spent in a roving Extasie
To find my Saviour; I have been   5
As far as *Bethlem*, and have seen
His Inne, and Cradle; Being there
I met the *Wise-men*, askt them where
He might be found, or what starre can
Now point him out, grown up a Man?   10
To *Egypt* hence I fled, ran o're
All her parcht bosome to *Nile's* shore
Her yearly nurse; came back, enquir'd
Amongst the *Doctors*, and desir'd
To see the *Temple*, but was shown   15
A little dust, and for the Town
A heap of ashes, where some sed
A small bright sparkle was a bed,
Which would one day (beneath the pole,)
Awake, and then refine the whole.   20
 Tyr'd here, I come to *Sychar*; thence
To *Jacobs wel*, bequeathed since
Unto his sonnes, (where often they
In those calme, golden Evenings lay
Watring their flocks, and having spent   25
Those white dayes, drove home to the Tent
Their *well-fleec'd* traine;) And here (O fate!)
I sit, where once my Saviour sate;

The Search. 15-20 The destruction of the Temple and of Jerusalem is predicted by Christ (Luke 21:20-28) and that destruction typifies the refining fire at the end of the world. See Mal. 3:1-2, "the Lord, whom ye seek, shall suddenly come to his temple, even the messenger of the covenant, whom ye delight in.... But who may abide the day of his coming? and who shall stand when he appeareth? for he is like a refiner's fire."
 21-30 *Jacobs wel*: Jacob watered his flocks at the well (Gen. 29:2-3) and Christ, the living water, endeavored at the same well to instruct Jacob's children (John 4:6-15).

The angry Spring in bubbles swell'd
Which broke in sighes still, as they fill'd, 30
And whisper'd, *Jesus had been there*
But *Jacobs children would not heare.*
Loath hence to part, at last I rise
But with the fountain in my Eyes,
And here a fresh search is decreed 35
He must be found, where he did bleed;
I walke the garden, and there see
Idea's of his Agonie,
And moving anguishments that set
His blest face in a bloudy sweat; 40
I climb'd the Hill, perus'd the Crosse
Hung with my gaine, and his great losse,
Never did tree beare fruit like this,
Balsam of Soules, the bodyes blisse;
But, O his grave! where I saw lent 45
(For he had none,) a Monument,
An undefil'd, and new-heaw'd one,
But there was not the *Corner-stone*;
Sure (then said I,) my Quest is vaine,
Hee'le not be found, where he was slaine, 50
So mild a Lamb can never be
'Midst so much bloud, and Crueltie;
I'le to the Wilderness, and can
Find beasts more mercifull then man,
He liv'd there safe, 'twas his retreat 55
From the fierce *Jew*, and *Herods* heat,
And forty dayes withstood the fell,
And high temptations of hell;
With Seraphins there talked he
His fathers flaming ministrie, 60

44 *Balsam*: technical Hermetic term meaning a preservative to maintain a healthy balance in the body (Pettet).

45-48 Joseph of Arimathea gave Christ a tomb of hewn stone (Luke 23:53), but Christ, the *Corner-stone* (Matt. 21:42) has now arisen.

55-64 Christ's temptation in the desert (Matt. 4:1-11) prepared it as a place of refuge for his Bride, the Church. See Rev. 12:6.

He heav'nd their *walks*, and with his eyes
Made those wild shades a Paradise,
Thus was the desert sanctified
To be the refuge of his bride;
I'le thither then; see, It is day,
The Sun's broke through to guide my way.
  But as I urg'd thus, and writ down
What pleasures should my Journey crown,
What silent paths, what shades, and Cells,
Faire, virgin-flowers, and hallow'd *Wells*
I should rove in, and rest my head
Where my deare Lord did often tread,
Sugring all dangers with successe,
Me thought I heard one singing thus;

1

Leave, leave, thy gadding thoughts;
Who Pores
and spies
Still out of Doores
descries
Within them nought.

2

The skinne, and shell of things
Though faire,
are not
Thy wish, nor pray'r
but got
By meer Despair
of wings.

---

70 *Wells*: the neighborhood of a fountain or well (M.).
74 Cf. Herbert, "The Collar," l. 35.

                    3
            To rack old Elements,
                or Dust
                and say   90
            Sure here he must
                needs stay
            Is not the way,
                nor just.

    Search well another world; who studies this,   95
    Travels in Clouds, seeks *Manna*, where none is.

            Acts Cap. 17 . ver. 27, 28.

That they should seek the Lord, if happily they might feel after him, and finde him, though he be not far off from every one of us, for in him we live, and move, and have our being.

Isaacs *Marriage*

            Gen. cap. 24 . ver. 63.

And Isaac went out to pray in the field at the Even-tide, and he lift up his eyes, and saw, and behold, the Camels were coming.

    Praying! and to be married? It was rare,
    But now 'tis monstrous; and that pious care
    Though of our selves, is so much out of date,
    That to renew't were to degenerate.
    But thou a Chosen sacrifice wert given,   5
    And offer'd up so early unto heaven
    Thy flames could not be out; Religion was
    Ray'd into thee, like beams into a glasse,

Isaacs Marriage. See Gen. 24.
  5–6 See Gen. 22:1–13, the episode in which God commands Abraham to sacrifice his only son, Isaac.

Where, as thou grewst, it multipli'd and shin'd
The sacred Constellation of thy mind.　　　　　　　　　*10*
But being for a bride, prayer was such
A decryed course, sure it prevail'd not much.
Had'st ne'r an oath, nor Complement? thou wert
An odde dull sutor; Hadst thou but the art
Of these our dayes, thou couldst have coyn'd thee twenty　*15*
New sev'ral oathes, and Complements (too) plenty;
O sad, and wilde excesse! and happy those
White dayes, that durst no impious mirth expose!
When Conscience by lew'd use had not lost sense,
Nor bold-fac'd custome banish'd Innocence;　　　　　　　*20*
Thou hadst no pompous train, nor *Antick* crowd
Of young, gay swearers, with their needlesse, lowd
Retinue; All was here smooth as thy bride
And calm like her, or that mild Evening-tide;
Yet, hadst thou nobler guests: Angels did wind　　　　　*25*
And rove about thee, guardians of thy minde,
These fetch'd thee home thy bride, and all the way
Advis'd thy servant what to do, and say;
These taught him at the *well*, and thither brought
The Chast, and lovely object of thy thought;　　　　　　*30*
But here was ne'r a Complement, not one
Spruce, supple cringe, or study'd look put on,
All was plain, modest truth: Nor did she come
In *rowles* and *Curles*, mincing and stately dumb,
But in a Virgins native blush and fears　　　　　　　　　*35*
Fresh as those roses, which the day-spring wears.
O sweet, divine simplicity! O grace
Beyond a Curled lock, or painted face!
A *Pitcher* too she had, nor thought it much
To carry that, which some would scorn to touch;　　　　　*40*
With which in mild, chast language she did wooe
To draw him drink, and for his Camels too.
　And now thou knewest her coming, It was time
To get thee wings on, and devoutly climbe
Unto thy God, for Marriage of all states　　　　　　　　*45*
Makes most unhappy, or most fortunates;
This brought thee forth, where now thou didst undress

    Thy soul, and with new pinions refresh
Her wearied wings, which so restor'd did flye
Above the stars, a track unknown, and high,   50
And in her piercing flight perfum'd the ayer
Scatt'ring the *Myrrhe*, and incense of thy pray'r.
So from **Lahai-roi's* Well some spicie cloud
Woo'd by the Sun swels up to be his shrowd,
And from her moist wombe weeps a fragrant showre,   55
Which, scatter'd in a thousand pearls, each flowre
And herb partakes, where having stood awhile
And something coold the parch'd, and thirstie Isle,
The thankful Earth unlocks her self, and blends,
A thousand odours, which (all mixt,) she sends
Up in one cloud, and so returns the skies   60
That dew they lent, a breathing sacrifice.

    Thus soar'd thy soul, who (though young,) didst inherit
Together with his bloud, thy fathers spirit,
Whose active zeal, and tried faith were to thee   65
Familiar ever since thy Infancie.
Others were tym'd, and train'd up to't but thou
Diddst thy swift yeers in piety out-grow,
Age made them rev'rend, and a snowie head,
But thou wert so, e're time his snow could shed;   70
Then, who would truly limne thee out, must paint
First, a *young Patriarch*, then a *marri'd Saint*.

**A wel in the South Country where Jacob dwelt, between Cadesh, & Bered; Heb. the well of him that liveth, and seeth me.*

The Brittish Church

    Ah! he is fled!
And while these here their *mists*, and *shadows* hatch,
    My glorious head
Doth on those hills of Mirrhe, and Incense watch.
    Haste, hast my dear,   5
    The Souldiers here

The Brittish Church. 4 Song of Sol. 4:6, "Until the day break, and the shadows flee away, I will get me to the mountain of myrrh, and to the hill of frankincense." See note to l. 45, "Regeneration."

> Cast in their lots again,
>> That seamlesse coat
>> The Jews touch'd not,
> These dare divide, and stain. 10

2

>> O get thee wings!
> Or if as yet (until these clouds depart,
>> And the day springs,)
> Thou think'st it good to tarry where thou art,
>> Write in thy bookes 15
>> My ravish'd looks
> Slain flock, and pillag'd fleeces,
>> And hast thee so
>> As a young Roe
>> Upon the mounts of spices. 20

O Rosa Campi! O lilium Convallium! quomodò nunc facta es pabulum Aprorum!

The Lampe

'Tis dead night round about: Horrour doth creepe
And move on with the shades; stars nod, and sleepe,
And through the dark aire spin a firie thread
Such as doth gild the lazie glow-worms bed.
   Yet, burn'st thou here, a full day; while I spend 5
My rest in Cares, and to the dark world lend
These flames, as thou dost thine to me; I watch
That houre, which must thy life, and mine dispatch;

---

  8 *seamlesse coat*: see John 19:23–24; "White Sunday," l. 14.
  18–20 Song of Sol. 8:14, "Make haste, my beloved, and be thou like to a roe or to a young hart upon the mountains of spices."
  O Rosa . . .: "O Rose of the fields! O lily of the valley! How art thou now made food for the wild boars!"—a fusion of Song of Sol. 2:1 (Geneva version) and Ps. 80:13. See also Ezek. 29:5, 34:5, 39:4.

But still thou doest out-goe me, I can see
Met in thy flames, all acts of piety;   10
Thy light, is *Charity*; Thy heat, is *Zeale*;
And thy aspiring, active fires reveale
Devotion still on wing; Then, thou dost weepe
Still as thou burn'st, and the warme droppings creepe
To measure out thy length, as if thou'dst know   15
What stock, and how much time were left thee now;
Nor dost thou spend one teare in vain, for still
As thou dissolv'st to them, and they distill,
They're stor'd up in the socket, where they lye,
When all is spent, thy last, and sure supply,   20
And such is true repentance, ev'ry breath
Wee spend in sighes, is treasure after death;
Only, one point escapes thee; That thy Oile
Is still out with thy flame, and so both faile;
But whensoe're I'm out, both shalbe in,   25
And where thou mad'st an end, there I'le begin.

Mark Cap. 13. ver. 35.

Watch you therefore, for you know not when the master of the house commeth, at Even, or at mid-night, or at the Cock-crowing, or in the morning.

Mans fall, and Recovery

Farewell you Everlasting hills! I'm Cast
Here under Clouds, where stormes, and tempests blast
    This sully'd flowre
Rob'd of your Calme, nor can I ever make
Transplanted thus, one leafe of his t'awake,   5
    But ev'ry houre

Mans fall, and Recovery. See Rom. 5–7 for the poem's theological basis and some aspects of its language.
1 *Everlasting hills*: see Gen. 49:26.

He sleepes, and droops, and in this drowsie state
Leaves me a slave to passions, and my fate;
        Besides I've lost
A traine of lights, which in those Sun-shine dayes   *10*
Were my sure guides, and only with me stayes
        (Unto my cost,)
One sullen beame, whose charge is to dispense
More punishment, than knowledge to my sense;
        Two thousand yeares   *15*
I sojourn'd thus; at last *Jeshuruns* king
Those famous tables did from *Sinai* bring;
        These swell'd my feares,
Guilts, trespasses, and all this Inward Awe,
For sinne tooke strength, and vigour from the Law.   *20*
        Yet have I found
A plenteous way, (thanks to that holy one!)
To cancell all that e're was writ in stone,
        His saving wound
Wept bloud, that broke this Adamant, and gave   *25*
To sinners Confidence, life to the grave;
        This makes me span
My fathers journeys, and in one faire step
O're all their pilgrimage, and labours leap,
        For God (made man,)   *30*
Reduc'd th' Extent of works of faith; so made
Of their *Red Sea*, a *Spring*; I wash, they wade.

                Rom. Cap. 18. ver. 19.

As by the offence of one, the fault came on all men to condemnation; So by the Righteousness of one, the benefit abounded towards all men to the Justification of life.

  13 *One sullen beame*: the Law of Nature.
  16 *Jeshuruns king*: Israel's king, Moses. See Deut. 33:5.
    32 The Israelites *wading* in the Red Sea under the Law were the type of Christians *washed* in the Baptismal *Spring* whereby Christ frees them from sin and the Law.
  Rom. Cap.18. ver.19: should read, "Rom. Cap. 5. ver. 18." The quotation most closely resembles the version in the Geneva Bible.

The Showre

'Twas so, I saw thy birth: That drowsie Lake
From her faint bosome breath'd thee, the disease
Of her sick waters, and Infectious Ease.
      But, now at Even
        Too grosse for heaven, 5
Thou fall'st in teares, and weep'st for thy mistake.

2

Ah! it is so with me; oft have I prest
Heaven with a lazie breath, but fruitles this
Peirc'd not; Love only can with quick accesse
      Unlock the way, 10
        When all else stray
The smoke, and Exhalations of the brest.

3

Yet, if as thou doest melt, and with thy traine
Of drops make soft the Earth, my eyes could weep
O're my hard heart, that's bound up, and asleep, 15
      Perhaps at last
        (Some such showres past,)
My God would give a Sun-shine after raine.

Distraction

O knit me, that am crumbled dust! the heape
      Is all dispers'd, and cheape;
    Give for a handfull, but a thought
        And it is bought;

The Showre. 1–6 Cf. Herbert, "The Answer," ll. 8–12.

                    Hadst thou   5
Made me a starre, a pearle, or a rain-bow,
          The beames I then had shot
          My light had lessend not,
                    But now
I find my selfe the lesse, the more I grow;   10
               The world
Is full of voices; Man is call'd, and hurl'd
          By each, he answers all,
          Knows ev'ry note, and call,
                    Hence, still   15
Fresh dotage tempts, or old usurps his will.
Yet, hadst thou clipt my wings, when Coffin'd in
          This quicken'd masse of sinne,
          And saved that light, which freely thou
                    Didst then bestow,   20
                    I feare
I should have spurn'd, and said thou didst forbeare;
          Or that thy store was lesse,
          But now since thou didst blesse
                    So much,   25
I grieve, my God! that thou hast made me such.
               I grieve?
O, yes! thou know'st I doe; Come, and releive
          And tame, and keepe downe with thy light
          Dust that would rise, and dimme my sight,   30
          Lest left alone too long
               Amidst the noise, and throng,
                    Oppressed I
Striving to save the whole, by parcells dye.

The Pursuite

          Lord! what a busie, restles thing
               Hast thou made man?

The Pursuite. Cf. Vaughan, "Man," and Herbert, "The Pulley" and "Giddines."

Each day, and houre he is on wing,
    Rests not a span;
Then having lost the Sunne, and light 5
    By clouds surpriz'd
He keepes a Commerce in the night
    With aire disguis'd;
Hadst thou given to this active dust
    A state untir'd, 10
The lost Sonne had not left the huske
    Nor home desir'd;
That was thy secret, and it is
    Thy mercy too,
For when all failes to bring to blisse, 15
    Then, this must doe.
Ah! Lord! and what a Purchase will that be
To take us sick, that sound would not take thee?

Mount of Olives [I]

Sweete, sacred hill! on whose fair brow
My Saviour sate, shall I allow
    Language to love
And Idolize some shade, or grove,
Neglecting thee? such ill-plac'd wit, 5
Conceit, or call it what you please
    Is the braines fit,
    And meere disease;

2

Cotswold, and Coopers both have met
With learned swaines, and Eccho yet 10

11–12 See the parable of the Prodigal Son, Luke 15:11–32.
  Mount of Olives [I]. 9–10 *Cotswold, and Coopers*: Cotswold Hills were famous for annual races and sports, celebrated by Ben Jonson and various other poets in *Annalia Dubrensia. Upon the yeerely celebration of Mr Robert Dovers Olimpick Games upon Cotswold-Hills* (1636); Sir John Denham's *Cooper's Hill* was first published in 1642 (Ch.).

  Their pipes, and wit;
But thou sleep'st in a deepe neglect
Untouch'd by any; And what need
The sheep bleat thee a silly Lay
    That heard'st both reed   *15*
    And sheepward play?

3

Yet, if Poets mind thee well
They shall find thou art their hill,
    And fountaine too,
Their Lord with thee had most to doe;   *20*
He wept once, walkt whole nights on thee,
And from thence (his suff'rings ended,)
    Unto glorie
    Was attended;

4

Being there, this spacious ball   *25*
Is but his narrow footstoole all,
    And what we thinke
Unsearchable, now with one winke
He doth comprise; But in this aire
When he did stay to beare our Ill   *30*
    And sinne, this Hill
    Was then his Chaire.

The Incarnation, and Passion

Lord! when thou didst thy selfe undresse
Laying by thy robes of glory,
To make us more, thou wouldst be lesse,
And becam'st a wofull story.

---

16 *sheepward*: shepherd, i.e., Christ.
The Incarnation, and Passion. Cf. Herbert, "The Bagge," ll. 9–12.

To put on Clouds instead of light, 5
And cloath the morning-starre with dust,
Was a translation of such height
As, but in thee, was ne'r exprest;

Brave wormes, and Earth! that thus could have
A God Enclos'd within your Cell, 10
Your maker pent up in a grave,
Life lockt in death, heav'n in a shell;

Ah, my deare Lord! what couldst thou spye
In this impure, rebellious clay,
That made thee thus resolve to dye 15
For those that kill thee every day?

O what strange wonders could thee move
To slight thy precious bloud, and breath!
Sure it was *Love*, my Lord; for *Love*
Is only stronger far than death. 20

The Call

Come my heart! come my head!
In sighes, and teares!
'Tis now, since you have laine thus dead
Some twenty years;
Awake, awake, 5
Some pitty take
Upon your selves——
Who never wake to grone, nor weepe,
Shall be sentenc'd for their sleepe.

2

Doe but see your sad estate, 10
How many sands
Have left us, while we careles sate

With folded hands;
What stock of nights,
Of dayes, and yeares   *15*
In silent flights
Stole by our eares,
How ill have we our selves bestow'd
Whose suns are all set in a Cloud?

3

Yet, come, and let's peruse them all;   *20*
And as we passe,
What sins on every minute fall
Score on the glasse;
Then weigh, and rate
Their heavy State   *25*
Untill
The glasse with teares you fill;
That done, we shalbe safe, and good,
Those beasts were cleane, that chew'd the Cud.

[Thou that know'st for whom I mourne]

Thou that know'st for whom I mourne,
And why these teares appeare,
That keep'st account, till he returne
Of all his dust left here;
As easily thou mightst prevent   *5*
As now produce these teares,

The Call. 29 See Lev. 11:1-3.
    Thou that know'st.... 1 assumed to refer to Vaughan's younger brother William who died in 1648.

And adde unto that day he went
    A faire supply of yeares.
But 'twas my sinne that forc'd thy hand
    To cull this *Prim-rose* out,
That by thy early choice forewarn'd
    My soule might looke about.
O what a vanity is man!
    How like the Eyes quick winke
His Cottage failes; whose narrow span
    Begins even at the brink!
Nine months thy hands are fashioning us,
    And many yeares (alas!)
E're we can lisp, or ought discusse
    Concerning thee, must passe;
Yet have I knowne thy slightest things
    A *feather*, or a *shell*,
A *stick*, or *Rod* which some Chance brings
    The best of us excell,
Yea, I have knowne these shreds out last
    A faire-compacted frame
And for one *Twenty* we have past
    Almost outlive our name.
Thus hast thou plac'd in mans outside
    Death to the Common Eye,
That heaven within him might abide,
    And close eternitie;
Hence, youth, and folly (mans first shame,)
    Are put unto the slaughter,
And serious thoughts begin to tame
    The wise-mans-madnes *Laughter;*
Dull, wretched wormes! that would not keepe
    Within our first faire bed,
But out of *Paradise* must creepe
    For ev'ry foote to tread;
Yet, had our Pilgrimage bin free,
    And smooth without a thorne,

---

36 Eccles. 2:2: "I said of laughter, It is mad."

Pleasures had soil'd Eternitie,
    And *tares* had choakt the *Corne*.
Thus by the Crosse Salvation runnes,   *45*
    Affliction is a mother,
Whose painfull throws yield many sons,
    Each fairer than the other;
A silent teare can peirce thy throne,
    When lowd Joyes want a wing,   *50*
And sweeter aires streame from a grone,
    Than any arted string;
Thus, Lord, I see my gaine is great,
    My losse but little to it,
Yet something more I must intreate   *55*
    And only thou canst doe it.
O let me (like him,) know my End!
    And be as glad to find it,
And whatsoe'r thou shalt Commend,
    Still let thy Servant mind it!   *60*
Then make my soule white as his owne,
    My faith as pure, and steddy,
And deck me, Lord, with the same Crowne
    Thou hast crowned him already!

Vanity of Spirit

Quite spent with thoughts I left my Cell, and lay
Where a shrill spring tun'd to the early day.
    I beg'd here long, and gron'd to know
    Who gave the Clouds so brave a bow,
    Who bent the spheres, and circled in   *5*
    Corruption with this glorious Ring,
    What is his name, and how I might

---

44 Vaughan conflates here two parables of the sower, Matt. 13:3–23, and Matt. 13:24–30.
49–52 Cf. Herbert, "The family," ll. 17–20, and "Sion," ll. 21–24.

Descry some part of his great light.
I summon'd nature: peirc'd through all her store,
Broke up some seales, which none had touch'd before, 10
  Her wombe, her bosome, and her head.
  Where all her secrets lay a bed
  I rifled quite, and having past
  Through all the Creatures, came at last
  To search my selfe, where I did find 15
  Traces, and sounds of a strange kind.
Here of this mighty spring, I found some drills,
With Ecchoes beaten from th' eternall hills;
  Weake beames, and fires flash'd to my sight,
  Like a young East, or Moone-shine night, 20
  Which shew'd me in a nook cast by
  A peece of much antiquity,
  With Hyerogliphicks quite dismembred,
  And broken letters scarce remembred.
I tooke them up, and (much Joy'd,) went about 25
T' unite those peeces, hoping to find out
  The mystery; but this neer done,
  That little light I had was gone:
  It griev'd me much. At last, said I,
  Since in these veyls my Ecclips'd Eye 30
  May not approach thee, (for at night
  Who can have commerce with the light?)
  I'le disapparell, and to buy
  But one half glaunce, most gladly dye.

The Retreate

Happy those early dayes! when I
Shin'd in my Angell-infancy.

Vanity of Spirit. 10 Cf. Thomas Vaughan, *Coelum Terrae* (1650), p. 53 (M.).
17 *drills*: rivulets.
22 *peece*: the defaced soul.

The Retreate. See Mark 10:14–15, "Jesus...said unto them, Suffer the little children to come unto me, and forbid them not: for of such is the kingdom of God. Verily I say unto you, Whosoever shall not receive the kingdom of God as a little child, he shall not enter therein." The language of the poem also owes

Before I understood this place
Appointed for my second race,
Or taught my soul to fancy ought
But a white, Celestiall thought,
When yet I had not walkt above
A mile, or two, from my first love,
And looking back (at that short space,)
Could see a glimpse of his bright-face;
When on some *gilded Cloud*, or *flowre*
My gazing soul would dwell an houre,
And in those weaker glories spy
Some shadows of eternity;
Before I taught my tongue to wound
My Conscience with a sinfull sound,
Or had the black art to dispence
A sev'rall sinne to ev'ry sence,
But felt through all this fleshly dresse
Bright *shootes* of everlastingnesse.
   O how I long to travell back
And tread again that ancient track!
That I might once more reach that plaine,
Where first I left my glorious traine,
From whence th' Inlightned spirit sees
That shady City of Palme trees;
But (ah!) my soul with too much stay
Is drunk, and staggers in the way.
Some men a forward motion love,
But I by backward steps would move,
And when this dust falls to the urn
In that state I came return.

---

something to *Hermetica*, Libellus x, 15b, in Scott, I, 197, "Look at the soul of a child, my son, a soul that has not yet come to accept its separation from its source; for its body is still small, and has not yet grown to its full bulk. How beautiful throughout is such a soul as that!... But when the body has increased in bulk, and has drawn the soul down into its material mass, it generates oblivion; and so the soul separates itself from the Beautiful and the Good, and no longer partakes of that; and through the oblivion the soul becomes evil."

20 *shootes of everlastingnesse*: Owen Felltham (*Resolves*, I. 64 [1634], p. 197) speaks of the soul as a "shoot of everlastingnesse" (F.).

26 *City of Palme trees*: Jericho, which is shown to Moses along with other cities in the vision of the Promised Land from the top of Pisgah, Deut. 34:3.

[*Come, come, what doe I here?*]

Come, come, what doe I here?
    Since he is gone
Each day is grown a dozen year,
    And each houre, one;
    Come, come!   5
    Cut off the sum,
    By these soil'd teares!
    (Which only thou
    Know'st to be true,)
    Dayes are my feares.   10

2

Ther's not a wind can stir,
    Or beam passe by,
But strait I think (though far,)
    Thy hand is nigh;
    Come, come!   15
    Strike these lips dumb:
    This restles breath
    That soiles thy name,
    Will ne'r be tame
    Untill in death.   20

3

Perhaps some think a tombe
    No house of store,
But a dark, and seal'd up wombe,
    Which ne'r breeds more.
    Come, come!   25
    Such thoughts benum;

Come, come .... Supposed, like "Thou that know'st," to refer to the death of William Vaughan.

> But I would be
> With him I weep
> A bed, and sleep
> To wake in thee.   *30*

Midnight

> When to my Eyes
> (Whilst deep sleep others catches,)
> Thine hoast of spyes
> The starres shine in their watches,
> I doe survey   *5*
> Each busie Ray,
> And how they work, and wind,
> And wish each beame
> My soul doth streame,
> With the like ardour shin'd;   *10*
> What Emanations,
> Quick vibrations
> And bright stirs are there?
> What thin Ejections,
> Cold Affections,   *15*
> And slow motions here?

2

> Thy heav'ns (some say,)
> Are a firie-liquid light,
> Which mingling aye
> Streames, and flames thus to the sight.   *20*

Midnight. 17 *some*: the Hermeticists.
   21–32 1 John 5:6–8; "This is he that came by water and blood, even Jesus Christ.... And it is the Spirit that beareth witness, because the Spirit is truth. For there are three that bear record in heaven, the Father, the Word, and the Holy Ghost: and these three are one. And there are three that bear witness in earth, the Spirit, and the water, and the blood: and these three agree in one."
   Also, Ps. 147:18, "He sendeth out his word, and melteth them: he bloweth with his wind, and the waters flow" (BCP).

        Come then, my god!
        Shine on this bloud,
And water in one beame,
        And thou shalt see
        Kindled by thee   25
Both liquors burne, and streame.
        O what bright quicknes,
        Active brightnes,
And celestiall flowes
        Will follow after   30
        On that water,
Which thy spirit blowes!

Math. Cap. 3 . ver. XI.

  I indeed baptize you with water unto repentance, but he that commeth after me, is mightier than I, whose shooes I am not worthy to beare, he shall baptize you with the holy Ghost, and with fire.

Content

Peace, peace! I know 'twas brave,
        But this corse fleece
I shelter in, is slave
        To no such peece.
        When I am gone,   5
I shall no ward-robes leave
        To friend, or sonne
But what their own homes weave,

2

Such, though not proud, nor full,
        May make them weep,   10
And mourn to see the wooll
        Outlast the sheep;
        Poore, Pious weare!

Hadst thou bin rich, or fine
    Perhaps that teare *15*
Had mourn'd thy losse, not mine.

3

Why then these curl'd, puff'd points,
    Or a laced story?
Death sets all out of Joint
    And scornes their glory; *20*
    Some Love a *Rose*
In hand, some in the skin;
    But crosse to those,
I would have mine *within*.

[*Joy of my life!*]

Joy of my life! while left me here,
    And still my Love!
How in thy absence thou dost steere
    Me from above!
    A life well lead *5*
    This truth commends,
    With quick, or dead
    It never ends.

2

Stars are of mighty use: The night
    Is dark, and long; *10*
The Rode foul, and where one goes right,
    Six may go wrong.

    Content. 18 *laced story*: the clothes image is here related to fiction and rich ornamentation in poetry.
    [*Joy of my life!*]. 1–3 Perhaps referring to his first wife, Catherine, or to his brother William.

> One twinkling ray
> Shot o'r some cloud,
> May clear much way   *15*
> And guide a croud.

3

> Gods Saints are shining lights: who stays
> Here long must passe
> O're dark hills, swift streames, and steep ways
> As smooth as glasse;   *20*
> But these all night
> Like Candles, shed
> Their beams, and light
> Us into Bed.

4

> They are (indeed,) our Pillar-fires   *25*
> Seen as we go,
> They are that Cities shining spires
> We travell too;
> A swordlike gleame
> Kept man for sin   *30*
> First *Out*; This beame
> Will guide him *In*.

The Storm

> I see the use: and know my bloud
> Is not a Sea,

---

25 *Pillar-fires*: the Pillar of Fire (Exod. 13:21) guided the Israelites in the Wilderness.

27 *that Cities shining spires*: the heavenly Jerusalem.

29 *swordlike gleame*: Gen. 3:24, "So he drove out the man; and he placed at the east of the garden of Eden Cherubims, and a flaming sword which turned every way, to keep the way of the tree of life."

The Storm. A variation of Herbert's "The Storme," especially ll. 1–3, 17–18.

1 *use*: a moral or application (*OED*).

But a shallow, bounded floud
    Though red as he;
Yet have I flows, as strong as his,
    And boyling stremes that rave
With the same curling force, and hisse,
    As doth the mountain'd wave.

2

But when his waters billow thus,
    Dark storms, and wind
Incite them to that fierce discusse,
    Else not Inclin'd,
Thus the Enlarg'd, inraged air
    Uncalmes these to a floud,
But still the weather that's most fair
    Breeds tempests in my bloud;

3

Lord, then round me with weeping Clouds,
    And let my mind
In quick blasts sigh beneath those shrouds
    A spirit-wind,
So shall that storme purge this *Recluse*
    Which sinfull ease made foul,
And *wind*, and *water* to thy use
    Both *wash*, and *wing* my soul.

The Morning-watch

O Joyes! Infinite sweetnes! with what flowres,
And shoots of glory, my soul breakes, and buds!
    All the long houres
    Of night, and Rest

11 *discusse*: debate (*OED*).
The Morning-watch. 1 Cf. Herbert, "The H. Scriptures" (I), l. 1.

>   Through the still shrouds 5
>   Of sleep, and Clouds,
>   This Dew fell on my Breast;
>   O how it *Blouds*,
> And *Spirits* all my Earth! heark! In what Rings,
> And *Hymning Circulations* the quick world 10
>   Awakes, and sings;
>   The rising winds,
>   And falling springs,
>   Birds, beasts, all things
>   Adore him in their kinds. 15
>   Thus all is hurl'd
> In sacred *Hymnes*, and *Order*, The great *Chime*
> And *Symphony* of nature. Prayer is
>   The world in tune,
>   A spirit-voyce, 20
>   And vocall joyes
>   Whose *Eccho is* heav'ns blisse.
>   O let me climbe
> When I lye down! The Pious soul by night
> Is like a clouded starre, whose beames though sed 25
>   To shed their light
>   Under some Cloud
>   Yet are above,
>   And shine, and move
>   Beyond that mistie shrowd. 30
>   So in my Bed
> That Curtain'd grave, though sleep, like ashes, hide
> My lamp, and life, both shall in thee abide.

---

7 *Dew*: Cf. Vaughan, "The Mount of Olives," *Works*, p. 145, "O Thou! that never slumberest nor sleepest... sanctifie and supple my heart with the dew of thy divine Spirit."
10–15 Cf. Herbert, "Providence," ll. 7–12.
18–22 Cf. Herbert, "Prayer (I)," ll. 8–14.

The Evening-watch

A Dialogue

Body.   Farewell! I goe to sleep; but when
        The day-star springs, I'le wake agen.

Soul.   Goe, sleep in peace; and when thou lyest
Unnumber'd in thy dust, when all this frame
Is but one dramme, and what thou now descriest 5
        In sev'rall parts shall want a name,
Then may his peace be with thee, and each dust
Writ in his book, who ne'r betray'd mans trust!

Body.   Amen! but hark, e'r we two stray,
        How many hours do'st think 'till day? 10

Soul.   Ah! go; th'art weak, and sleepie. Heav'n
Is a plain watch, and without figures winds
All ages up; who drew this Circle even
        He fils it; Dayes, and hours are *Blinds.*
Yet, this take with thee; The last gasp of time 15
Is thy first breath, and mans *eternall Prime.*

[*Silence, and stealth of dayes!*]

    Silence, and stealth of dayes! 'tis now
        Since thou art gone,
   Twelve hundred houres, and not a brow
        But Clouds hang on.
  As he that in some Caves thick damp 5
        Lockt from the light,
   Fixeth a solitary lamp,
        To brave the night,

[Silence, and stealth of dayes!] 3 *twelve hundred houres*: the poem is set about fifty days after William Vaughan's death on or about 14 July 1648 (M.).

And walking from his Sun, when past
  That glim'ring Ray   10
Cuts through the heavy mists in haste
  Back to his day,
So o'r fled minutes I retreat
  Unto that hour
Which shew'd thee last, but did defeat   15
  Thy light, and pow'r,
I search, and rack my soul to see
  Those beams again,
But nothing but the snuff to me
  Appeareth plain;   20
That dark, and dead sleeps in its known
  And common urn,
But those fled to their Makers throne,
  There shine, and burn;
O could I track them! but souls must   25
  Track one the other,
And now the spirit, not the dust
  Must be thy brother.
Yet I have one *Pearle* by whose light
  All things I see,   30
And in the heart of Earth, and night
  Find Heaven, and thee.

Church-Service

Blest be the God of Harmony, and Love!
  The God above!
  And holy dove!
Whose Interceding, spirituall grones
  Make restless mones   5

29 *Pearle*: probably the Bible.
 Church-Service. 2–8 Rom. 8:26, "Likewise the Spirit also helpeth our infirmities:…the Spirit itself maketh intercession for us with groanings which cannot be uttered."

                For dust, and stones,
                For dust in every part,
                But a hard, stonie heart.

                        2
O how in this thy Quire of Souls I stand
                (Propt by thy hand)
                A heap of sand!
Which busie thoughts (like winds) would scatter quite
                And put to flight,
                But for thy might;
                Thy hand alone doth tame
                Those blasts, and knit my frame,

                        3
So that both stones, and dust, and all of me
                Joyntly agree
                To cry to thee,
And in this Musick by thy Martyrs bloud
                Seal'd, and made good
                Present, O God!
                The Eccho of these stones
                —— My sighes, and grones.

Buriall

O thou! the first fruits of the dead,
                And their dark bed,
When I am cast into that deep
                And senseless sleep
                The wages of my sinne,
                O then,
Thou great Preserver of all men!
                Watch o're that loose
                And empty house,
                Which I sometimes liv'd in.

2

It is (in truth!) a ruin'd peece
  Not worth thy Eyes,
And scarce a room but wind, and rain
  Beat through, and stain
    The seats, and Cells within;   *15*
      Yet thou
Led by thy Love wouldst stoop thus low,
    And in this Cott
    All filth, and spott,
  Didst with thy servant Inne.   *20*

3

And nothing can, I hourely see,
  Drive thee from me,
Thou art the same, faithfull, and just
  In life, or Dust;
    Though then (thus crumm'd) I stray   *25*
      In blasts,
Or Exhalations, and wasts
    Beyond all Eyes
    Yet thy love spies
  That Change, and knows thy Clay.   *30*

4

The world's thy boxe: how then (there tost,)
  Can I be lost?
But the delay is all; Tyme now
  Is old, and slow,
    His wings are dull, and sickly;   *35*
      Yet he
Thy servant is, and waits on thee,
  Cutt then the summe,

> Lord haste, Lord come,
> O come Lord *Jesus* quickly! 40

Rom. Cap. 8 . ver. 23 .

And not only they, but our selves also, which have the first fruits of the spirit, even wee our selves grone within our selves, waiting for the adoption, to wit, the redemption of our body.

Chearfulness

> Lord, with what courage, and delight
> I doe each thing
> When thy least breath sustaines my wing!
> I shine, and move
> Like those above, 5
> And (with much gladnesse
> Quitting sadnesse,)
> Make me faire dayes of every night.

2

> Affliction thus, meere pleasure is,
> And hap what will, 10
> If thou be in't, 'tis welcome still;
> But since thy rayes
> In Sunnie dayes
> Thou dost thus lend
> And freely spend, 15
> Ah! what shall I return for this?

Buriall. 39–40 Rev. 22:20, "He which testifieth these things saith, Surely I come quickly. Amen. Even so, come, Lord Jesus." *Quickly* puns on the meanings "speedily" and "life-giving."
Chearfulness. 9–11 Cf. Herbert, "Affliction [III]," ll. 2–4.

3

O that I were all Soul! that thou
    Wouldst make each part
Of this poor, sinfull frame pure heart!
    Then would I drown   20
    My single one,
    And to thy praise
    A Consort raise
Of *Hallelujahs* here below.

[*Sure, there's a tye of Bodyes!*]

Sure, there's a tye of Bodyes! and as they
    Dissolve (with it,) to Clay,
Love languisheth, and memory doth rust
    O'r-cast with that cold dust;
For things thus *Center'd*, without *Beames*, or *Action*   5
    Nor give, nor take *Contaction*,
And man is such a Marygold, these fled,
    That shuts, and hangs the head.

2

Absents within the Line Conspire, and *Sense*
    Things distant doth unite,   10
Herbs sleep unto the *East*, and some fowles thence
    Watch the Returns of light;
But hearts are not so kind: false, short delights
    Tell us the world is brave,
And wrap us in Imaginary flights   15
    Wide of a faithfull grave;

[*Sure, there's a tye of Bodyes!*]. 5–6 Dead bodies, lacking the *Beames* and radiations which according to the Hermetic philosophy emanate from all beings in Nature, cannot make *contact* with other beings.

9 *within the Line*: within the boundaries of life (M.). In this state, persons absent from each other are not isolated as in death, but feel bonds of sympathy uniting them.

Thus *Lazarus* was carried out of town;
    For 'tis our foes chief art
By distance all good objects first to drown,
    And then besiege the heart.   *20*
But I will be my own *Deaths-head*; and though
    The flatt'rer say, *I live*,
Because Incertainties we cannot know
    Be sure, not to believe.

Peace

My Soul, there is a Countrie
    Far beyond the stars,
Where stands a winged Centrie
    All skilfull in the wars,
There above noise, and danger   *5*
    Sweet peace sits crown'd with smiles,
And one born in a Manger
    Commands the Beauteous files,
He is thy gracious friend,
    And (O my Soul awake!)   *10*
Did in pure love descend
    To die here for thy sake,
If thou canst get but thither,
    There growes the flowre of peace,
The Rose that cannot wither,   *15*
    Thy fortresse, and thy ease;
Leave then thy foolish ranges;
    For none can thee secure,
But one, who never changes,
    Thy God, thy life, thy Cure.   *20*

17 *Lazarus'* burial *out of town* removed the unpleasant reminder of death.
21 *Deaths-head*: I will myself be the skull upon which to meditate my last end.
Peace. In manner, metrical form, and tone, this is the Vaughan poem which most closely resembles Herbert.
3-4 *Centrie*: the Archangel Michael (M.).

The Passion

      O my chief good!
      My dear, dear God!
    When thy blest bloud
Did Issue forth forc'd by the Rod,
      What pain didst thou   5
      Feel in each blow!
      How didst thou weep,
      And thy self steep
In thy own precious, saving teares!
      What cruell smart   10
      Did teare thy heart!
      How didst thou grone it
      In the spirit,
O thou, whom my soul Loves, and feares!

2

      Most blessed Vine!   15
      Whose juice so good
      I feel as Wine,
But thy faire branches felt as bloud,
      How wert thou prest
      To be my feast!   20
      In what deep anguish
      Didst thou languish,
What springs of Sweat, and bloud did drown thee!
      How in one path
      Did the full wrath   25
      Of thy great Father
      Crowd, and gather,
Doubling thy griefs, when none would own thee!

The Passion. 15–18 Cf. Herbert, "The Agony," ll. 17–18.
19–20 Cf. Herbert, "The Bunch of Grapes," ll. 27–28.

3

How did the weight
Of all our sinnes,
And death unite
To wrench, and Rack thy blessed limbes!
How pale, and bloudie
Lookt thy Body!
How bruis'd, and broke
With every stroke!
How meek, and patient was thy spirit!
How didst thou cry,
And grone on high
Father forgive,
And let them live,
I dye to make my foes inherit!

4

O blessed Lamb!
That took'st my sinne,
That took'st my shame
How shall thy dust thy praises sing!
I would I were
One hearty tear!
One constant spring!
Then would I bring
Thee two small mites, and be at strife
Which should most vie,
My heart, or eye,
Teaching my years
In smiles, and tears
To weep, to sing, thy *Death*, my *Life*.

[And do they so?]

Rom. Cap. 8 . ver. 19.

Etenim res Creatæ exerto Capite observantes expectant revelationem Filiorum Dei.

And do they so? have they a Sense
    Of ought but Influence?
Can they their heads lift, and expect,
    And grone too? why th'Elect
Can do no more: my volumes sed   5
    They were all dull, and dead,
They judg'd them senslesse, and their state
    Wholly Inanimate.
    Go, go; Seal up thy looks,
        And burn thy books.   10

2

I would I were a stone, or tree,
    Or flowre by pedigree,
Or some poor high-way herb, or Spring
    To flow, or bird to sing!
Then should I (tyed to one sure state,)   15

[*And do they so?*]. *Etenim* .... The heading is taken from Beza's version but is not quoted exactly. The poem builds upon Rom. 8:19, 21–23: "For the earnest expectation of the creature waiteth for the manifestation of the sons of God.... Because the creature itself also shall be delivered from the bondage of corruption into the glorious liberty of the children of God. For we know that the whole creation groaneth and travaileth in pain together until now. And not only they, but ourselves also, which have the firstfruits of the Spirit, even we ourselves groan within ourselves, waiting for the adoption, to wit, the redemption of our body."

The poem also invokes the Hermetic idea of the sentience of everything in Nature, caused by the Star-fire, the Divine Seed within each thing, and the shaping Divine Spirit infusing all.

2 *Influence*: the magnetic attraction and control of the stars upon beings on earth.

11–16 Cf. Herbert, "Imployment [II]," ll. 21–25.

    All day expect my date;
But I am sadly loose, and stray
    A giddy blast each way;
    O let me not thus range!
        Thou canst not change.

3

Sometimes I sit with thee, and tarry
    An hour, or so, then vary.
Thy other Creatures in this Scene
    Thee only aym, and mean;
Some rise to seek thee, and with heads
    Erect peep from their beds;
Others, whose birth is in the tomb,
    And cannot quit the womb,
      Sigh there, and grone for thee,
        Their liberty.

4

O let not me do lesse! shall they
    Watch, while I sleep, or play?
Shall I thy mercies still abuse
    With fancies, friends, or newes?
O brook it not! thy bloud is mine,
    And my soul should be thine;
O brook it not! why wilt thou stop
    After whole showres one drop?
      Sure, thou wilt joy to see
        Thy sheep with thee.

The Relapse

My God, how gracious art thou! I had slipt
    Almost to hell,
And on the verge of that dark, dreadful pit
    Did hear them yell,

But O thy love! thy rich, almighty love
    That sav'd my soul,
And checkt their furie, when I saw them move,
    And heard them howl;
O my sole Comfort, take no more these wayes,
    This hideous path,
And I wil mend my own without delayes,
    Cease thou thy wrath!
I have deserv'd a thick, Egyptian damp,
    Dark as my deeds,
Should *mist* within me, and put out that lamp
    Thy spirit feeds;
A darting Conscience full of stabs, and fears;
    No shade but *Yewgh*,
Sullen, and sad Ecclipses, Cloudie Spheres,
    These are my due.
But he that with his bloud, (a price too deere,)
    My scores did pay,
Bid me, by vertue from him, chalenge here
    The brightest day;
Sweet, downie thoughts; soft *Lilly*-shades; Calm streams;
    Joyes full, and true;
Fresh, spicie mornings; and eternal beams
    These are his due.

The Resolve

I have consider'd it; and find
    A longer stay
Is but excus'd neglect. To mind
    One path, and stray

The Relapse. 11 Cf. Herbert, "The Thankes-giving," l. 34.
9–12 Cf. Herbert, "Discipline," ll. 1–4.
13–14 Cf. Herbert, "Sighes and Grones," ll. 14–15.
18 *Yewgh*: Yew trees were traditionally associated with mourning.
25–28 The imagery owes something to the Song of Solomon.
The Resolve. ll. 11–28 printed in the 1650 edition of *Wits Recreation* (M.).
1 Cf. Herbert, "The Reprisall," l. 1.

Into another, or to none, 5
    Cannot be love;
When shal that traveller come home,
    That will not move?
If thou wouldst thither, linger not,
    Catch at the place, 10
Tell youth, and beauty they must rot,
    They'r but a *Case*;
Loose, parcell'd hearts wil freeze: The Sun
    With scatter'd locks
Scarce warms, but by contraction 15
    Can heat rocks;
Call in thy *Powers*; run, and reach
    Home with the light,
Be there, before the shadows stretch,
    And *Span* up night; 20
Follow the *Cry* no more: there is
    An ancient way
All strewed with flowres, and happiness
    And fresh as *May*;
There turn, and turn no more; Let wits 25
    Smile at fair eies,
Or lips; But who there weeping sits,
    Hath got the *Prize*.

The Match

Dear friend! whose holy, ever-living lines
    Have done much good
To many, and have checkt my blood,

---

10 Cf. Herbert, "Affliction [I]," l. 17.
12 *Case*: chance, occurrence (*OED*).
19-20 *Span up*: to extend (*OED*).
22-24 Cf. Herbert, "Affliction [I]," ll. 20-22.
The Match. A compact.
1 *friend*: Herbert. Vaughan here takes up the invitation proffered by Herbert in "Obedience," ll. 36-43.

My fierce, wild blood that still heaves, and inclines,
  But is still tam'd
   By those bright fires which thee inflam'd;
Here I joyn hands, and thrust my stubborn heart
  Into thy *Deed*,
   There from no *Duties* to be freed,
And if hereafter *youth*, or *folly* thwart
  And claim their share,
   Here I renounce the pois'nous ware.

II

Accept, dread Lord, the poor Oblation,
  It is but poore,
   Yet through thy Mercies may be more.
O thou! that canst not wish my souls damnation,
  Afford me life,
   And save me from all inward strife!
Two *Lifes* I hold from thee, my gracious Lord,
  Both cost thee deer,
   For one, I am thy Tenant here;
The other, the true life, in the next world
  And endless is,
   O let me still mind *that* in *this!*
To thee therefore my *Thoughts*, *Words*, *Actions*
  I do resign,
   Thy will in all be done, not mine.
Settle my *house*, and shut out all distractions
  That may unknit
   My heart, and thee planted in it;
Lord *Jesu!* thou didst bow thy blessed head
  Upon a tree,
   O do as much, now unto me!
O hear, and heal thy servant! Lord, strike dead
  All lusts in me,
   Who onely wish life to serve thee!
Suffer no more this dust to overflow
  And drown my eies,

10–12 Cf. Herbert, "Obedience," ll. 11–15.
19–23 Cf. Herbert, "Longing," ll. 31–36.

> But seal, or pin them to thy skies.
> And let this *grain* which here in tears I sow   40
> Though *dead*, and *sick*,
> Through thy *Increase* grow *new*, and *quick*.

Rules and Lessons

When first thy Eies unveil, give thy Soul leave
To do the like; our Bodies but forerun
The spirits duty; True hearts spread, and heave
Unto their God, as flow'rs do to the Sun.
> Give him thy first thoughts then; so shalt thou keep   5
> Him company all day, and in him sleep.

Yet, never sleep the Sun up; Prayer shou'd
Dawn with the day; There are set, awful hours
'Twixt heaven, and us; The *Manna* was not good
After Sun-rising, far-day sullies flowres.   10
> Rise to prevent the Sun; sleep doth sins glut,
> And heav'ns gate opens, when this world's is shut.

Walk with thy fellow-creatures: note the *hush*
And *whispers* amongst them. There's not a *Spring*,
Or *Leafe* but hath his *Morning-hymn*; Each *Bush*   15
And *Oak* doth know *I AM*; canst thou not sing?
> O leave thy Cares, and follies! go this way
> And thou art sure to prosper all the day.

Serve God before the world; let him not go
Until thou hast a blessing, then resigne   20
The whole unto him; and remember who

Rules and Lessons. The metrical form and didactic manner are inspired by Herbert's "The Church-Porch."
  9–10 Cf. Exod. 16:19–21.
  11 Cf. Wisd. of Sol. 16:28, "we must prevent the Sun to give thee thanks" (Apocrypha).
  19–22 See Gen. 32:24–32, and Gen. 35:14. Jacob wrestled with God before daybreak and would not cease until he had obtained a blessing, and he also poured oil upon the stone pillar at Bethel as an offering to God.

Prevail'd by *wrestling* ere the *Sun* did *shine*.
    Poure *Oyle* upon the *stones*, weep for thy sin,
    Then journey on, and have an eie to heav'n.

Mornings are *Mysteries*; the first worlds *Youth*,   25
Mans *Resurrection*, and the futures *Bud*
Shrowd in their births: The Crown of life, light, truth
Is stil'd their *starre*, the *stone*, and *hidden food*.
    Three *blessings* wait upon them, two of which
    Should move; They make us *holy, happy*, rich.   30

When the world's up, and ev'ry swarm abroad,
Keep thou thy temper, mix not with each Clay;
Dispatch necessities, life hath a load
Which must be carri'd on, and safely may.
    Yet keep those cares without thee, let the heart   35
    Be Gods alone, and choose the better part.

Through all thy *Actions*, *Counsels*, and *Discourse*,
Let *Mildness*, and *Religion* guide thee out,
If truth be thine, what needs a brutish force?
But what's not *good*, and *just* ne'r go about.   40
    Wrong not thy Conscience for a rotten stick,
    That gain is dreadful, which makes spirits sick.

To God, thy Countrie, and thy friend be true,
If *Priest*, and *People* change, keep thou thy ground.
Who sels Religion, is a *Judas Jew*,   45
And, oathes once broke, the soul cannot be sound.
    The perjurer's a devil let loose: what can
    Tie up his hands, that dares mock God, and man?

Seek not the same steps with the *Crowd*; stick thou
To thy sure trot; a Constant, humble mind   50
Is both his own Joy, and his Makers too;

---

28 Rev. 2:17, "To him that overcometh will I give to eat of the hidden manna, and will give him a white stone" (H.).
31–36 See Luke 10:38–42.
45 Cf. Herbert, "Selfe-condemnation," ll. 17–18.

Let folly dust it on, or lag behind.
> A sweet *self-privacy* in a right soul
> Out-runs the Earth, and lines the utmost pole.

To all that seek thee, bear an open heart; 55
Make not thy breast a *Labyrinth*, or *Trap*;
If tryals come, this wil make good thy part,
For honesty is safe, come what can hap;
> It is the good mans *feast*; The prince of flowres
> Which thrives in *storms*, and smels best after *showres*. 60

Seal not thy Eyes up from the poor, but give
Proportion to their *Merits*, and thy *Purse*;
Thou mai'st in Rags a mighty Prince relieve
Who, when thy sins call for't, can fence a Curse.
> Thou shalt not lose one *mite*. Though waters stray, 65
> The Bread we cast returns in fraughts one day.

Spend not an hour so, as to weep another,
For tears are not thine own; If thou giv'st words
Dash not thy *friend*, nor *Heav'n*; O smother
A vip'rous thought; some *Syllables* are *Swords*. 70
> Unbitted tongues are in their penance double,
> They shame their *owners*, and the *hearers* trouble.

Injure not modest bloud, whose *spirits* rise
In judgement against *Lewdness*; that's base wit
That voyds but *filth*, and *stench*. Hast thou no prize 75
But *sickness*, or *Infection*? stifle it.
> Who makes his jests of sins, must be at least
> If not a very *devill*, worse than a *Beast*.

Yet, fly no friend, if he be such indeed,
But meet to quench his *Longings*, and thy *Thirst*; 80
Allow your Joyes *Religion*; That done, speed

---

54 *lines*: reaches (*OED*).
63 *Prince*: Christ. See Matt. 25:34–46.
64 *fence*: ward off.

And bring the same man back, thou wert at first.
    Who so returns not, cannot pray aright
    But shuts his door, and leaves God out all night.

To highten thy *Devotions*, and keep low   85
All mutinous thoughts, what busines e'r thou hast
Observe God in his works; here *fountains* flow,
Birds sing, *Beasts* feed, *Fish* leap, and th' *Earth* stands fast;
    Above are restles *motions*, running *Lights*,
    Vast Circling *Azure*, giddy *Clouds*, days, nights.   90

When *Seasons* change, then lay before thine Eys
His wondrous *Method*; mark the various *Scenes*
In heav'n; *Hail*, *Thunder*, *Rain-bows*, *Snow*, and *Ice*,
Calmes, *Tempest*, *Light*, and *darknes* by his means;
    Thou canst not misse his Praise; Each *tree, herb, flowre*   95
    Are shadows of his *wisedome*, and his Pow'r.

To *meales* when thou doest come, give him the praise
Whose *Arm* supply'd thee; Take what may suffice,
And then be thankful; O admire his ways
Who fils the worlds unempty'd granaries!   100
    A thankles feeder is a *Theif*, his feast
    A very *Robbery*, and himself no *guest*.

High-noon thus past, thy time decays; provide
Thee other thoughts; Away with friends, and mirth;
The Sun now stoops, and hasts his beams to hide   105
Under the dark, and melancholy Earth.
    All but preludes thy End. Thou art the man
    Whose *Rise, hight*, and *Descent* is but a span.

Yet, set as he doth, and 'tis well. Have all
Thy Beams home with thee: trim thy *Lamp*, buy *Oyl*,   110
And then set forth; who is thus drest, The *Fall*
Furthers his glory, and gives death the foyl.
    Man is a *Summers day*; whose *youth*, and *fire*
    Cool to a glorious *Evening*, and Expire.

When night comes, lift thy deeds; make plain the way 115
'Twixt Heaven, and thee; block it not with delays,
But perfect all before thou sleep'st; Then say
Ther's one Sun more strung on my Bead of days.
    What's good score up for Joy; The bad wel scann'd
    Wash off with tears, and get thy *Masters* hand. 120

Thy Accounts thus made, spend in the grave one houre
Before thy time; Be not a stranger there
Where thou may'st sleep whole ages; Lifes poor flowr
Lasts not a night sometimes. Bad spirits fear
    This Conversation; But the good man lyes 125
    Intombed many days before he dyes.

Being laid, and drest for sleep, Close not thy Eys
Up with thy Curtains; Give thy soul the wing
In some good thoughts; So when the day shall rise
And thou *unrak'st* thy *fire*, those *sparks* will bring 130
    New *flames*; Besides where these lodge vain *heats* mourn
    And die; That *Bush* where God is, shall not burn.

When thy *Nap's* over, stir thy fire, unrake
In that *dead age*; one beam i'th' dark outvies
Two in the day; Then from the *Damps*, and *Ake* 135
Of night shut up thy *leaves*, be Chast; God prys
    Through thickest nights; Though then the Sun be far
    Do thou the works of *Day*, and rise a *Star*.

Briefly, *Doe as thou would'st be done unto,*
Love God, and Love thy Neighbour; Watch, and Pray. 140
These are the *Words*, and *Works* of life; This do,
And live; who doth not thus, hath lost *Heav'ns way.*
    O lose it not! look up, wilt Change those *Lights*
    For *Chains* of *Darknes*, and *Eternal Nights*?

121–26 Cf. Herbert, "Church-monuments."
132 See Exod. 3:2.
139–42 Cf. Herbert, "Divinitie," ll. 17–18.

Corruption

    Sure, It was so. Man in those early days
        Was not all stone, and Earth,
    He shin'd a little, and by those weak Rays
        Had some glimpse of his birth.
    He saw Heaven o'r his head, and knew from whence   *5*
        He came (condemned,) hither,
    And, as first Love draws strongest, so from hence
        His mind sure progress'd thither.
    Things here were strange unto him: Swet, and till,
        All was a thorn, or weed,   *10*
    Nor did those last, but (like himself,) dyed still
        As soon as they did *Seed*,
    They seem'd to quarrel with him; for that Act
        That fel him, foyl'd them all,
    He drew the Curse upon the world, and Crackt   *15*
        The whole frame with his fall.
    This made him long for *home*, as loath to stay
        With murmurers, and foes;
    He sigh'd for *Eden*, and would often say
        Ah! what bright days were those!   *20*
    Nor was Heav'n cold unto him; for each day
        The vally, or the Mountain
    Afforded visits, and still *Paradise* lay
        In some green shade, or fountain.
    Angels lay *Leiger* here; Each Bush, and Cel,   *25*
        Each Oke, and high-way knew them,
    Walk but the fields, or sit down at some *wel*,
        And he was sure to view them.
    Almighty *Love!* where art thou now? mad man
        Sits down, and freezeth on,   *30*

Corruption. 1–8 Cf. "The Retreate."
    13–16 Cf. Thomas Vaughan, *Anthroposophia Theomagica* (Waite, Works, p. 45), "The curse followed, and the impure seeds were joined with the pure, and they reign to this hour in our bodies; and not in us alone but in every other natural thing."
    21–28 Cf. "Religion," ll. 1–20.
    25 *Leiger*: resident, as a resident ambassador.

He raves, and swears to stir nor fire, nor fan,
    But bids the thread be spun.
I see, thy Curtains are Close-drawn; Thy bow
    Looks dim too in the Cloud,
Sin triumphs still, and man is sunk below 35
    The Center, and his shrowd;
All's in deep sleep, and night; Thick darknes lyes
    And hatcheth o'r thy people;
But hark! what trumpets that? what Angel cries
    Arise! Thrust in thy sickle. 40

H. Scriptures

Welcome dear book, souls Joy, and food! The feast
    Of Spirits, Heav'n extracted lyes in thee;
    Thou art lifes Charter, The Doves spotless neast
Where souls are hatch'd unto Eternitie.

In thee the hidden stone, the *Manna* lies, 5
    Thou are the great *Elixir*, rare, and Choice;
    The Key that opens to all Mysteries,
The *Word* in Characters, God in the *Voice*.

O that I had deep Cut in my hard heart
    Each line in thee! Then would I plead in groans 10
    Of my Lords penning, and by sweetest Art
Return upon himself the *Law*, and *Stones*.
    Read here, my faults are thine. This Book, and I
    Will tell thee so; *Sweet Saviour thou didst dye*!

---

  40 Rev. 14:18, "And another angel came ... and cried with a loud cry to him that had the sharp sickle, saying, Thrust in thy sharp sickle, and gather the clusters of the vine of the earth; for her grapes are fully ripe."
  H. Scriptures. 5 See Rev. 2:17, quoted at the end of "The Mutinie."
  9–12 Cf. Herbert, "The Altar," ll. 5–8.
  13 Cf. Herbert, "Judgement," l. 15.

Unprofitablenes

How rich, O Lord! how fresh thy visits are!
'Twas but Just now my bleak leaves hopeles hung
    Sullyed with dust and mud;
Each snarling blast shot through me, and did share
Their Youth, and beauty, Cold showres nipt, and wrung   5
    Their spiciness, and bloud;
But since thou didst in one sweet glance survey
Their sad decays, I flourish, and once more
    Breath all perfumes, and spice;
I smell a dew like *Myrrh*, and all the day   10
Wear in my bosome a full Sun; such store
    Hath one beame from thy Eys.
But, ah, my God! what fruit hast thou of this?
What one poor leaf did ever I yet fall
    To wait upon thy wreath?   15
Thus thou all day a thankless weed doest dress,
And when th'hast done, a stench, or fog is all
    The odour I bequeath.

CHRISTS Nativity

Awake, glad heart! get up, and Sing,
It is the Birth-day of thy King,
    Awake! awake!
    The Sun doth shake
Light from his locks, and all the way   5
Breathing Perfumes, doth spice the day.

2

Awak, awak! heark, how th'*wood* rings,
Winds whisper, and the busie *springs*

Unprofitablenes. 1 Cf. Herbert, "The Flower," ll. 1–2.
Christs Nativity. 7–12 Cf. Herbert, "Mans medly," ll. 1–2, and "Providence,"
ll. 13–16.

      A Consort make;
        Awake, awake!
Man is their high-priest, and should rise
To offer up the sacrifice.

3

I would I were some *Bird*, or Star,
Flutt'ring in woods, or lifted far
      Above this *Inne*
      And Rode of sin!
Then either Star, or *Bird*, should be
Shining, or singing still to thee.

4

I would I had in my best part
Fit Roomes for thee! or that my heart
      Were so clean as
      Thy manger was!
But I am all filth, and obscene,
Yet, if thou wilt, thou canst make clean.

5

Sweet *Jesu!* will then; Let no more
This Leper haunt, and soyl thy door,
      Cure him, Ease him
      O release him!
And let once more by mystick birth
The Lord of life be borne in Earth.

II.

How kind is heav'n to man! If here
      One sinner doth amend

---

18 Cf. Herbert, "Christmas," ll. 31–34.

Strait there is Joy, and ev'ry sphere
    In musick doth Contend;
And shall we then no voices lift?   35
    Are mercy, and salvation
Not worth our thanks? Is life a gift
    Of no more acceptation?
Shal he that did come down from thence,
    And here for us was slain,   40
Shal he be now cast off? no sense
    Of all his woes remain?
Can neither Love, nor suff'rings bind?
    Are we all stone, and Earth?
Neither his bloudy passions mind,   45
    Nor one day blesse his birth?
Alas, my God! Thy birth now here
    Must not be numbred in the year.

The Check

Peace, peace! I blush to hear thee; when thou art
    A dusty story
A speechlesse heap, and in the midst my heart
    In the same livery drest
        Lyes tame as all the rest;   5
When six years thence digg'd up, some youthfull Eie
    Seeks there for Symmetry
But finding none, shal leave thee to the wind,
    Or the next foot to Crush,
        Scatt'ring thy kind   10
    And humble dust, tell then dear flesh
        Where is thy glory?

    45–48 On 23 December 1644, a Puritan Parliament abolished the observance of Christmas and Good Friday.

2

As he that in the midst of day Expects
    The hideous night,
Sleeps not, but shaking off sloth, and neglects,   *15*
    Works with the Sun, and sets
    Paying the day its debts;
That (for Repose, and darknes bound,) he might
    Rest from the fears i'th'night;
So should we too. All things teach us to die   *20*
    And point us out the way
    While we passe by
    And mind it not; play not away
    Thy glimpse of light.

3

View thy fore-runners: Creatures giv'n to be   *25*
    Thy youths Companions,
Take their leave, and die; Birds, beasts, each tree
    All that have growth, or breath
    Have one large language, *Death*.
O then play not! but strive to him, who Can   *30*
    Make these sad shades pure Sun,
Turning their mists to beams, their damps to day,
    Whose pow'r doth so excell
    As to make Clay
    A spirit, and true glory dwell   *35*
    In dust, and stones.

4

Heark, how he doth Invite thee! with what voice
    Of Love, and sorrow
He begs, and Calls: *O that in these thy days*
    Thou knew'st but thy own good!   *40*
    Shall not the Crys of bloud,

Of Gods own bloud awake thee? He bids beware
    Of drunknes, surfeits, Care,
But thou sleep'st on; wher's now thy protestation,
    Thy Lines, thy Love? Away, 45
        Redeem the day,
    The day that gives no observation,
        Perhaps to morrow.

Disorder and frailty

When first thou didst even from the grave
And womb of darknes becken out
My brutish soul, and to thy slave
Becam'st thy self, both guide, and Scout;
    Even from that hour 5
Thou gotst my heart; And though here tost
    By winds, and bit with frost
        I pine, and shrink
        Breaking the link
'Twixt thee, and me; And oftimes creep 10
Into th' old silence, and dead sleep,
    Quitting thy way
    All the long day,
Yet, sure, my God! I love thee most.
    Alas, thy love! 15

2

I threaten heaven, and from my Cell
Of Clay, and frailty break, and bud
Touch'd by thy fire, and breath; Thy bloud
Too, is my Dew, and springing wel.
    But while I grow 20
And stretch to thee, ayming at all
    Thy stars, and spangled hall,
        Each fly doth tast,
        Poyson, and blast

My yielding leaves; sometimes a showr   25
Beats them quite off, and in an hour
    Not one poor shoot
    But the bare root
Hid under ground survives the fall.
    Alas, frail weed!   30

3

Thus like some sleeping Exhalation
(Which wak'd by heat, and beams, makes up
Unto that Comforter, the Sun,
And soars, and shines; But e'r we sup
    And walk two steps   35
Cool'd by the damps of night, descends,
  And, whence it sprung, there ends,)
    Doth my weak fire
    Pine, and retire,
And (after all my hight of flames,)   40
In sickly Expirations tames
    Leaving me dead
    On my first bed
Untill thy Sun again ascends.
    Poor, falling Star!   45

4

O, is! but give wings to my fire,
And hatch my soul, untill it fly
Up where thou art, amongst thy tire
Of Stars, above Infirmity;
    Let not perverse,   50
And foolish thoughts adde to my Bil
  Of forward sins, and Kil
    That seed, which thou
    In me didst sow,

Disorder and frailty. 31–37 Cf. Herbert, "The Answere," ll. 8–12.
46 *O, is!*: probably a form of "yes" (M.).
46–48 Cf. Herbert, "Whitsunday," ll. 1–4.

> But dresse, and water with thy grace 55
> Together with the seed, the place;
> And for his sake
> Who died to stake
> His life for mine, tune to thy will
> My heart, my verse. 60

Hosea Cap. 6. ver. 4.

O Ephraim what shall I do unto thee? O Judah how shall I intreat thee? for thy goodness is as a morning Cloud, and as the early Dew it goeth away.

Idle Verse

Go, go, queint folies, sugred sin,
  Shadow no more my door;
I will no longer Cobwebs spin,
  I'm too much on the score.

For since amidst my youth, and night, 5
  My great preserver smiles,
Wee'l make a Match, my only light,
  And Joyn against their wiles;

Blind, desp'rate *fits*, that study how
  To dresse, and trim our shame, 10
That gild rank poyson, and allow
  Vice in a fairer name;

The *Purles* of youthfull bloud, and bowles,
  Lust in the Robes of Love,
The idle talk of feav'rish souls 15
  Sick with a scarf, or glove;

Epigraph is derived from the Geneva version.
  Idle Verse. 13 *Purles*: the action or sound of purling, as a rill (*OED*); *bowles*: bowels, center of feeling.
  16 Cf. Herbert, "Love [I]," ll. 13–14.

>   Let it suffice my warmer days
>   Simper'd, and shin'd on you,
>   Twist not my Cypresse with your Bays,
>   Or Roses with my Yewgh;   20
>
>   Go, go, seek out some greener thing,
>   It snows, and freezeth here;
>   Let Nightingales attend the spring,
>   Winter is all my year.

Son-dayes

> Bright shadows of true Rest! some shoots of blisse,
>   Heaven once a week;
> The next worlds gladnes prepossest in this;
>   A day to seek;
>
> Eternity in time; the steps by which   5
> We Climb above all ages; Lamps that light
> Man through his heap of dark days; and the rich,
> And full redemption of the whole weeks flight.
>
>   2
> The Pulleys unto headlong man; times bower;
>   The narrow way;   10
> Transplanted Paradise; Gods walking houre;
>   The Cool o'th' day;
>
> The Creatures *Jubile*; Gods parle with dust;
> Heaven here; Man on those hills of Myrrh, and flowres;

---

18 Cf. Herbert, "The Search," ll. 13–14.

Son-dayes. The title carries the common Sun/Son pun. In form the poem closely resembles Herbert's "Prayer [I]," while the language and imagery owe much to Herbert's "Sunday."

9 Cf. Herbert, "The Pulley."

11–12 Gen. 3:8, "And they [Adam and Eve] heard the voice of the Lord God walking in the garden in the cool of the day."

Angels descending; the Returns of Trust; 15
A Gleam of glory, after six-days-showres.

3

The Churches love-feasts; Times Prerogative,
          And Interest
Deducted from the whole; The Combs, and hive,
          And home of rest. 20

The milky way Chalkt out with Suns; a Clue
That guides through erring hours; and in full story
A taste of Heav'n on earth; the pledge, and Cue
Of a full feast; And the Out Courts of glory.

Repentance

Lord, since thou didst in this vile Clay
    That sacred Ray
Thy spirit plant, quickning the whole
With that one grains Infused wealth,
My forward flesh creept on, and subtly stole 5
Both growth, and power, Checking the health
And heat of thine: That little gate
And narrow way, by which to thee
The Passage is, He term'd a grate
And Entrance to Captivitie; 10
Thy laws but nets, where some small birds
(And those but seldome too) were caught,
Thy Promises but empty words
Which none but Children heard, or taught.
This I believed: And though a friend 15
Came oft from far, and whisper'd, *No*;
Yet that not sorting to my end
I wholy listen'd to my foe.

Repentance. 5–9·Cf. Herbert, "H. Baptisme [II]."
9 *He*: my flesh.

Wherefore, pierc'd through with grief, my sad
Seduced soul sighs up to thee, 20
To thee who with true light art Clad
And seest all things just as they be.
Look from thy throne upon this Rowl
Of heavy sins, my high transgressions,
Which I Confesse with all my soul, 25
My God, Accept of my Confession.
      It was last day
(Touch'd with the guilt of my own way)
I sate alone, and taking up
      The bitter Cup, 30
Through all thy fair, and various store
Sought out what might outvie my score.
    The blades of grasse, thy Creatures feeding,
    The trees, their leafs; the flowres, their seeding;
    The Dust, of which I am a part, 35
    The Stones much softer than my heart,
    The drops of rain, the sighs of wind,
    The Stars to which I am stark blind,
    The Dew thy herbs drink up by night,
    The beams they warm them at i'th' light, 40
    All that have signature or life,
    I summon'd to decide this strife,
    And lest I should lack for Arrears,
    A spring ran by, I told her tears,
    But when these came unto the scale, 45
    My sins alone outweigh'd them all.
O my dear God! my life, my love!
Most blessed lamb! and mildest dove!
Forgive your penitent Offender,
And no more his sins remember, 50
Scatter these shades of death, and give
Light to my soul, that it may live;

---

41 *signature*: cf. H. Nollius, *Hermetical Physick*, trans. H. Vaughan (1656), *Works*, ed. Martin, p. 583, "*De Signatoris rerum*, that is to say, Of those impressions and Characters, which God hath communicated to, and marked (as I may say) all his Creatures with."

Cut me not off for my transgressions,
Wilful rebellions, and suppressions,
But give them in those streams a part 55
Whose spring is in my Saviours heart.
Lord, I confesse the heynous score,
And pray, I may do so no more,
Though then all sinners I exceed
O think on this; *Thy Son did bleed*; 60
O call to mind his wounds, his woes,
His Agony, and bloudy throws;
Then look on all that thou hast made,
And mark how they do fail, and fade,
The heavens themselves, though fair and bright 65
Are dark, and unclean in thy sight,
How then, with thee, Can man be holy
Who doest thine Angels charge with folly?
O what am I, that I should breed
Figs on a thorne, flowres on a weed! 70
I am the gourd of sin, and sorrow
Growing o'r night, and gone to morrow,
In all this *Round* of life and death
Nothing's more vile than is my breath,
Profanenes on my tongue doth rest, 75
Defects, and darknes in my brest,
Pollutions all my body wed,
And even my soul to thee is dead,
Only in him, on whom I feast,
Both soul, and body are well drest, 80
    His pure perfection quits all score,
      And fills the Boxes of his poor;
He is the Center of long life, and light,
I am but finite, He is Infinite.
O let thy *Justice* then in him Confine, 85
And through his merits, make thy mercy mine!

    65–66 Job 25:5, "Yea, the stars are not pure in his sight."
    68 Job 4:18, "Behold, he put no trust in his servants; and his angels he charged with folly."
    71–72 Jonah 4:10, "Thou hast had pity on the gourd, for the which thou hast not laboured, neither madest it grow; which came up in a night, and perished in a night."
    75–80 Cf. Herbert, "Aaron," ll. 6–15.

The Burial
Of an Infant

Blest Infant Bud, whose Blossome-life
Did only look about, and fal,
Wearyed out in a harmles strife
Of tears, and milk, the food of all;

Sweetly didst thou expire: Thy soul 5
Flew home unstain'd by his new kin,
For ere thou knew'st how to be foul,
Death *wean'd* thee from the world, and sin.

Softly rest all thy Virgin-Crums!
Lapt in the sweets of thy young breath, 10
Expecting till thy Saviour Comes
To *dresse* them, and *unswadle* death.

Faith

Bright, and blest beame! whose strong projection
    Equall to all,
Reacheth as well things of dejection
    As th' high, and tall;
How hath my God by raying thee 5
    Inlarg'd his spouse,
And of a private familie
    Made open house?
All may be now Co-heirs; no noise
    Of *Bond*, or *Free* 10
Can Interdict us from those Joys
    That wait on thee,

Faith. 9-10 Rom. 8:16-17, "The Spirit itself beareth witness with our spirit, that we are the children of God: And if children, then heirs; heirs of God, and joint-heirs with Christ." Also I Cor. 12:13, "For by one Spirit are we all baptized into one body, whether we be Jews or Gentiles, whether we be bond or free."

The Law, and Ceremonies made
    A glorious night,
Where Stars, and Clouds, both light, and shade   *15*
    Had equal right;
But, as in nature, when the day
    Breaks, night adjourns,
Stars shut up shop, mists pack away,
    And the Moon mourns;   *20*
So when the Sun of righteousness
    Did once appear,
That Scene was chang'd, and a new dresse
    Left for us here;
Veiles became useles, Altars fel,   *25*
    Fires smoking die;
And all that sacred pomp, and shel
    Of things did flie;
Then did he shine forth, whose sad fall,
    And bitter fights   *30*
Were figur'd in those mystical,
    And Cloudie Rites;
And as i'th' natural Sun, these three,
    Light, *motion*, *heat*,
So are now *Faith*, *Hope*, *Charity*   *35*
    Through him Compleat;
Faith spans up blisse; what sin, and death
    Put us quite from,
Lest we should run for't out of breath,
    Faith brings us home;   *40*
So that I need no more, but say
    I do believe,
And my most loving Lord straitway
    Doth answer, *Live*.

The Dawning

Ah! what time wilt thou come? when shall that crie
    The *Bridegroome's Comming!* fil the sky?
Shall it in the Evening run
When our words and works are done?
Or wil thy all-surprizing light   5
    Break at midnight?
When either sleep, or some dark pleasure
Possesseth mad man without measure;
Or shal these early, fragrant hours
    Unlock thy bowres?   10
And with their blush of light descry
Thy locks crown'd with eternitie;
Indeed, it is the only time
That with thy glory doth best chime,
All now are stirring, ev'ry field   15
    Ful hymns doth yield,
The whole Creation shakes off night,
And for thy shadow looks the light,
Stars now vanish without number,
Sleepie Planets set, and slumber,   20
The pursie Clouds disband, and scatter,
All expect some sudden matter,
Not one beam triumphs, but from far
    That morning-star;

O at what time soever thou   25
(Unknown to us,) the heavens wilt bow,
And, with thy Angels in the *Van*,
Descend to Judge poor careless man,
Grant, I may not like puddle lie
In a Corrupt securitie,   30

The Dawning. See Matt. 25:1–13, especially verses 6, 13: "And at midnight there was a cry made, Behold the bridegroom cometh; go ye out to meet him.... Watch therefore, for ye know neither the day nor the hour wherein the Son of man cometh."
  21 *pursie*: swollen, heavy (*OED*).

Where, if a traveller water crave,
He finds it dead, and in a grave;
But as this restless, vocall *Spring*
All day, and night doth run, and sing,
And though here born, yet is acquainted 35
Elsewhere, and flowing keeps untainted;
So let me all my busie age
In thy free services ingage,
And though (while here) of force I must
Have Commerce somtimes with poor dust, 40
And in my flesh, though vile, and low,
As this doth in her Channel, flow,
Yet let my Course, my aym, my Love,
And chief acquaintance be above;
So when that day, and hour shal come 45
In which thy self wil be the Sun,
Thou'lt find me drest and on my way,
Watching the Break of thy great day.

Admission

How shril are silent tears? when sin got head
    And all my Bowels turn'd
To brasse, and iron; when my stock lay dead,
    And all my powers mourn'd;
Then did these drops (for Marble sweats, 5
    And Rocks have tears,)
As rain here at our windows beats,
    Chide in thine Ears;

2

No quiet couldst thou have: nor didst thou wink,
    And let thy Begger lie, 10

Admission. 1 Cf. Herbert, "*The family,*" l. 20.
3 Cf. Herbert, "Grace," l. 1.

But e'r my eies could overflow their brink
    Didst to each drop reply;
Bowels of Love! at what low rate,
    And slight a price
Dost thou relieve us at thy gate,   15
    And stil our Cries?

3

Wee are thy Infants, and suck thee; If thou
    But hide, or turn thy face,
Because where thou art, yet, we cannot go,
    We send tears to the place,   20
These find thee out, and though our sins
    Drove thee away,
Yet with thy love that absence wins
    Us double pay.

4

O give me then a thankful heart! a heart   25
    After thy own, not mine;
So after thine, that all, and ev'ry part
    Of mine, may wait on thine;
O hear! yet not my tears alone,
    Hear now a floud,   30
A floud that drowns both tears, and grones,
    My Saviours bloud.

Praise

    King of Comforts! King of life!
        Thou hast cheer'd me,
    And when fears, and doubts were rife,
        Thou hast cleer'd me!

13–17 Cf. Herbert, "Longing," ll. 14–20.
Praise. Cf. Herbert, "Praise [II]," for the metrical form of ll. 1–32.

> Not a nook in all my Breast 5
>   But thou fill'st it,
> Not a thought, that breaks my rest,
>   But thou kill'st it;
>
> Wherefore with my utmost strength
>   I wil praise thee, 10
> And as thou giv'st line, and length,
>   I wil raise thee;
>
> Day, and night, not once a day
>   I will blesse thee,
> And my soul in new array 15
>   I will dresse thee;
>
> Not one minute in the year
>   But I'l mind thee,
> As my seal, and bracelet here
>   I wil bind thee; 20
>
> In thy word, as if in heaven
>   I wil rest me,
> And thy promise 'til made even
>   There shall feast me.
>
> Then, thy sayings all my life 25
>   They shal please me,
> And thy bloudy wounds, and strife
>   They wil ease me;
>
> With thy grones my daily breath
>   I will measure, 30
> And my life hid in thy death
>   I will treasure.
>
>   Though then thou art
>   Past thought of heart
> All perfect fulness, 35

    And canst no whit
    Accesse admit
From dust and dulness;

    Yet to thy name
    (As not the same *40*
With thy bright Essence,)
    Our foul, Clay hands
    At thy Commands
Bring praise, and Incense;

    If then, dread Lord, *45*
    When to thy board
Thy wretch comes begging,
    He hath a flowre
    Or (to his pow'r,)
Some such poor Off'ring; *50*

    When thou hast made
    Thy begger glad,
And fill'd his bosome,
    Let him (though poor,)
    Strow at thy door *55*
That one poor Blossome.

Dressing

O thou that lovest a pure, and whitend soul!
That feedst among the Lillies, 'till the day
Break, and the shadows flee; touch with one Coal
My frozen heart; and with thy secret key

Dressing. 2–3 Song of Sol. 2:16–17, "My beloved is mine, and I am his: he feedeth among the lilies. Until the day break, and the shadows flee away."
3 *touch with one Coal*: see Isaiah 6:6–7.
4–5 Cf. Herbert, "The H. Communion," ll. 21–22.

Open my desolate rooms; my gloomie Brest 5
With thy cleer fire refine, burning to dust
These dark Confusions, that within me nest,
And soyl thy Temple with a sinful rust.

Thou holy, harmless, undefil'd high-priest!
The perfect, ful oblation for all sin, 10
Whose glorious conquest nothing can resist,
But even in babes doest triumph still and win;

    Give to thy wretched one
      Thy mysticall *Communion*,
        That, absent, he may see, 15
        Live, die, and rise with thee;
Let him so follow here, that in the end
He may take thee, as thou doest him intend.

    Give him thy private seal,
      Earnest, and sign; Thy gifts so deal 20
        That these forerunners here
        May make the future cleer;
Whatever thou dost bid, let faith make good,
Bread for thy body, and Wine for thy blood.

    Give him (with pitty) love, 25
      Two flowres that grew with thee above;
        Love that shal not admit
        Anger for one short fit,
And pitty of such a divine extent
That may thy members, more than mine, resent. 30

    Give me, my God! thy grace,
      The beams, and brightnes of thy face,
        That never like a beast
        I take thy sacred feast,
Or the dread mysteries of thy blest bloud 35
Use, with like Custome, as my Kitchin food.

5–8 Cf. Herbert, "The Starre," ll. 9–12.
30 *resent*: show traces of, give forth (*OED*).

       Some sit to thee, and eat
      Thy body as their Common meat,
        O let not me do so!
     Poor dust should ly still low,   40
Then kneel my soul, and body; kneel, and bow;
If *Saints*, and *Angels* fal down, much more thou.

Easter-day

Thou, whose sad heart, and weeping head lyes low,
    Whose Cloudy brest cold damps invade,
Who never feel'st the Sun, nor smooth'st thy brow,
    But sitt'st oppressed in the shade,
          Awake, awake,   5
And in his Resurrection partake,
    Who on this day (that thou might'st rise as he,)
    Rose up, and cancell'd two deaths due to thee.

Awake, awake; and, like the Sun, disperse
    All mists that would usurp this day;   10
Where are thy Palmes, thy branches, and thy verse?
    Hosanna! heark; why doest thou stay?
          Arise, arise,
And with his healing bloud anoint thine Eys,
    Thy inward Eys; his bloud will cure thy mind,   15
    Whose spittle only could restore the blind.

Easter Hymn

    Death, and darkness get you packing,
    Nothing now to man is lacking,

  Easter-day. Greatly indebted for meter, theme, and language to Herbert's "The Dawning."
  8 *two deaths*: the death of the body, and the eternal death of the soul, Rev. 20:6, 14; 21:8.
  16 See John 9:6-7.

All your triumphs now are ended,
And what *Adam* marr'd, is mended;
Graves are beds now for the weary, 5
Death a nap, to wake more merry;
Youth now, full of pious duty,
Seeks in thee for perfect beauty,
The weak, and aged tir'd, with length
Of daies, from thee look for new strength, 10
And Infants with thy pangs Contest
As pleasant, as if with the brest;
    Then, unto him, who thus hath thrown
Even to Contempt thy kingdome down,
And by his blood did us advance 15
Unto his own Inheritance,
To him be glory, power, praise,
From this, unto the last of daies.

The Holy Communion

Welcome sweet, and sacred feast; welcome life!
    Dead I was, and deep in trouble;
But grace, and blessings came with thee so rife,
    That they have quicken'd even drie stubble;
        Thus soules their bodies animate, 5
        And thus, at first, when things were rude,
            Dark, void, and Crude
They, by thy Word, their beauty had, and date;
        All were by thee,
        And stil must be, 10
        Nothing that is, or lives,
    But hath his Quicknings, and reprieves
            As thy hand opes, or shuts;
        Healings, and Cuts,
    Darkness, and day-light, life, and death 15
Are but meer leaves turn'd by thy breath.

The Holy Communion. 1 See Herbert, "The Banquet," ll. 1-2.
  9-16 Pettet describes this passage as a "sustained hermetic account of God's continuous intervention in his creation."

                    Spirits without thee die,
                        And blackness sits
                        On the divinest wits,
                As on the Sun Ecclipses lie.
            But that great darkness at thy death
            When the veyl broke with thy last breath,
                        Did make us see
                        The way to thee;
            And now by these sure, sacred ties,
                        After thy blood
                        (Our sov'rain good,)
                        Had clear'd our eies,
                        And given us sight;
            Thou dost unto thy self betroth
                Our souls, and bodies both
                In everlasting light.

Was't not enough that thou hadst payd the price
                        And given us eies
When we had none, but thou must also take
                        Us by the hand
                        And keep us still awake,
                            When we would sleep,
                            Or from thee creep,
            Who without thee cannot stand?

            Was't not enough to lose thy breath
                And blood by an accursed death,
                    But thou must also leave
                    To us that did bereave
            Thee of them both, these seals the means
                        That should both cleanse
                        And keep us so,
                            Who wrought thy wo?
                O rose of *Sharon*! O the Lilly
                        Of the valley!

22 See Matt. 27: 45, 51.
35–39 See Matt. 26:40, 71.
49–50 See Song of Sol. 2:1.

How art thou now, thy flock to keep,
Become both *food*, and *Shepheard* to thy sheep!

Psalm 121

Up to those bright, and gladsome hils
    Whence flowes my weal, and mirth,
I look, and sigh for him, who fils
    (Unseen,) both heaven, and earth.

He is alone my help, and hope,   5
    That I shall not be moved,
His watchful Eye is ever ope,
    And guardeth his beloved;

The glorious God is my sole stay,
    He is my Sun, and shade,   10
The cold by night, the heat by day,
    Neither shall me invade.

He keeps me from the spite of foes,
    Doth all their plots controul,
And is a shield (not reckoning those,)   15
    Unto my very soul.

Whether abroad, amidst the Crowd,
    Or els within my door,
He is my Pillar, and my Cloud,
    Now, and for evermore.   20

Affliction

Peace, Peace; It is not so. Thou doest miscall
    Thy Physick; Pils that change
Thy sick Accessions into setled health,
This is the great *Elixir* that turns gall

  To wine, and sweetness; Poverty to wealth,   5
   And brings man home, when he doth range.
  Did not he, who ordain'd the day,
     Ordain night too?
  And in the greater world display
   What in the lesser he would do?   10
All flesh is Clay, thou know'st; and but that God
   Doth use his rod,
And by a fruitfull Change of frosts, and showres
   Cherish, and bind thy *pow'rs*,
Thou wouldst to weeds, and thistles quite disperse,   15
  And be more wild than is thy verse;
Sickness is wholsome, and Crosses are but curbs
  To check the mule, unruly man,
They are heavens husbandry, the famous fan
  Purging the floor which Chaff disturbs.   20
Were all the year one constant Sun-shine, wee
   Should have no flowres,
All would be drought, and leanness; not a tree
   Would make us bowres;
Beauty consists in colours; and that's best   25
  Which is not fixt, but flies, and flowes.
The settled *Red* is dull, and *whites* that rest
  Something of sickness would disclose.
   Vicissitude plaies all the game,
     Nothing that stirrs,   30
    Or hath a name,
  But waits upon this wheel,
Kingdomes too have their Physick, and for steel,
   Exchange their peace, and furrs.
   Thus doth God *Key* disorder'd man   35
    (Which none else can,)

 Affliction. 11 Vaughan conflates Isaiah 40:6, "All flesh is grass," and Gen. 2:7, "And the Lord God formed man of the dust of the ground."
 19–20 Matt. 3:12, "Whose fan is in his hand, and he will throughly purge his floor, and . . . burn up the chaff."
 29–32 Cf. Felltham, *Resolves* I. 41 (p. 133), "'Tis *vicissitude* that maintaines the *Worlde*."

Tuning his brest to rise, or fall;
And by a sacred, needfull art
Like strings, stretch ev'ry part
Making the whole most Musicall.   40

The Tempest

How is man parcell'd out? how ev'ry hour
   Shews him himself, or somthing he should see?
   This late, long heat may his Instruction be,
And tempests have more in them than a showr.

     When nature on her bosome saw   5
        Her Infants die,
     And all her flowres wither'd to straw,
        Her brests grown dry;
     She made the Earth their nurse, and tomb,
        Sigh to the sky,   10
     'Til to those sighes fetch'd from her womb
        Rain did reply,
     So in the midst of all her fears
        And faint requests
     Her Earnest sighes procur'd her tears   15
        And fill'd her brests.

O that man could do so! that he would hear
   The world read to him! all the vast expence
   In the Creation shed, and slav'd to sence
Makes up but lectures for his eie, and ear.   20

Sure, mighty love foreseeing the discent
   Of this poor Creature, by a gracious art
   Hid in these low things snares to gain his heart,
And layd surprizes in each Element.

37–40 Cf. Herbert, "The Temper [I]," ll. 21–24.
The Tempest. Contains many allusions to Herbert, especially to "Misery."
1 Cf. Herbert, "Doomes' day," ll. 27–28.
23–24 Cf. Herbert, "Sinne [I]," ll. 7–8.

All things here shew him heaven; *Waters* that fall 25
    Chide, and fly up; *Mists* of corruptest fome
    Quit their first beds and mount; trees, herbs, flowres, all
Strive upwards stil, and point him the way home.

How do they cast off grossness? only *Earth*,
    And *Man* (like *Issachar*) in lodes delight, 30
    Water's refin'd to *Motion*, Aire to *Light*,
Fire to all* three, but man hath no such mirth.   *Light, Motion, heat.

Plants in the *root* with Earth do most Comply,
    Their *Leafs* with water, and humiditie,
    The *Flowres* to air draw neer, and subtiltie, 35
And *seeds* a kinred fire have with the sky.

All have their *keyes*, and set *ascents*; but man
    Though he knows these, and hath more of his own,
    Sleeps at the ladders foot; alas! what can
These new discoveries do, except they drown? 40

Thus groveling in the shade, and darkness, he
    Sinks to a dead oblivion; and though all
    He sees, (like *Pyramids*,) shoot from this ball
And less'ning still grow up invisibly,

Yet hugs he stil his durt; The *stuffe* he wears 45
    And painted trimming takes down both his eies,
    Heaven hath less beauty than the dust he spies,
And money better musick than the *Spheres*.

Life's but a blast, he knows it; what? shal straw,
    And bul-rush-fetters temper his short hour? 50

25-40 Cf. Herbert, "Man," ll. 25-36.
30 *Issachar*: Cf. Gen. 49:14-15, "Issachar... bowed his shoulder to bear, and became a servant unto tribute."
31-32 Cf. Herbert, "The Starre," ll. 17-18.
33-36 The imagery is drawn from the Hermetic scheme of attractions and correspondencies in nature.
37 *keyes*: notes in the great scale of being.
37-53 Cf. Herbert, "Misery," ll. 5-6, 45-46, 49-50, 59-62.

> Must he nor sip, nor sing? grows ne'r a flowr
> To crown his temples? shal dreams be his law?

> O foolish man! how hast thou lost thy sight?
> How is it that the Sun to thee alone
> Is grown thick darkness, and thy bread, a stone? 55
> Hath flesh no softness now? mid-day no light?

> Lord! thou didst put a soul here; If I must
> Be broke again, for flints will give no fire
> Without a steel, O let thy power cleer
> Thy gift once more, and grind this flint to dust! 60

Retirement

> Who on yon throne of Azure sits,
> Keeping close house
> Above the morning-starre,
> Whose meaner showes,
> And outward utensils these glories are 5
> That shine and share
> Part of his mansion; He one day
> When I went quite astray
> Out of meer love
> By his mild Dove 10
> Did shew me home, and put me in the way.

2

> Let it suffice at length thy fits
> And lusts (said he,)
> Have had their wish, and way;
> Presse not to be 15

51–52 Cf. Herbert, "The Collar," ll. 13–15.
Retirement. Contains many Herbert allusions, and also imitates Herbert's tone and logical development.

Still thy own foe, and mine; for to this day
    I did delay,
And would not see, but chose to wink,
    Nay, at the very brink
      And edge of all
    When thou wouldst fall
My *love-twist* held thee up, my *unseen link*.

3

I know thee well; for I have fram'd
    And hate thee not,
    Thy spirit too is mine;
    I know thy lot,
Extent, and end, for my hands drew the line
    Assigned thine;
    If then thou would'st unto my seat,
    'Tis not th'applause, and feat
      Of dust, and clay
    Leads to that way,
But from those follies a resolv'd Retreat.

4

Now here below where yet untam'd
    Thou doest thus rove
    I have a house as well
    As there above,
In it my *Name*, and *honour* both do dwell
    And shall untill
    I make all new; there nothing gay
    In perfumes, or Array,
      Dust lies with dust
    And hath but just
The same Respect, and room, with ev'ry clay.

---

22 Cf. Herbert, "The Pearle," ll. 38–40.
40 Rev. 21:5, "And he that sat upon the throne said, Behold, I make all things new."

5

>A faithful school where thou maist see 45
> In Heraldrie
>Of stones, and speechless Earth
> Thy true descent;
>Where dead men preach, who can turn feasts, and mirth
> To funerals, and *Lent*. 50
>There dust that out of doors might fill
> Thy eies, and blind thee still,
> Is fast asleep;
> Up then, and keep
>Within those doors, (my doors) dost hear? *I will*. 55

Love, and Discipline

Since in a land not barren stil
(Because thou dost thy grace distil,)
My lott is faln, Blest be thy will!

And since these biting frosts but kil
Some tares in me which choke, or spil 5
That seed thou sow'st, Blest be thy skil!

Blest be thy Dew, and blest thy frost,
And happy I to be so crost,
And cur'd by Crosses at thy cost.

The Dew doth Cheer what is distrest, 10
The frosts ill weeds nip, and molest,
In both thou workst unto the best.

45–48 Cf. Herbert, "Church-monuments," ll. 6–9, 17–18.
55 Cf. Herbert, "The Collar," l. 36.
Love, and Discipline. The form owes something to Herbert's "Paradise," although the rhymes are not here created by deletion of letters.
5 *spil*: kill. See Matt. 13:24–30, the story of the tares and the wheat.

Thus while thy sev'ral mercies plot,
And work on me now cold, now hot,
The work goes on, and slacketh not,   15

For as thy hand the weather steers,
So thrive I best, 'twixt joyes, and tears,
And all the year have some grean Ears.

The Pilgrimage

As travellours when the twilight's come,
And in the sky the stars appear,
The past daies accidents do summe
With, *Thus wee saw there, and thus here.*

Then *Jacob*-like lodge in a place   5
(A place, and no more, is set down,)
Where till the day restore the race
They rest and dream homes of their own.

So for this night I linger here,
And full of tossings too and fro,   10
Expect stil when thou wilt appear
That I may get me up, and go.

I long, and grone, and grieve for thee,
For thee my words, my tears do gush,
O that I were but where I see!   15
Is all the note within my Bush.

As Birds rob'd of their native wood,
Although their Diet may be fine,

17–18 Cf. Herbert, "Hope," ll. 5–6.
  The Pilgrimage. 5–8 Gen. 28:11–12, 17, "And he [Jacob] lighted upon a certain place, and tarried there all night." He beheld there the ladder from Heaven with angels ascending and descending.

        Yet neither sing, nor like their food,
        But with the thought of home do pine;   *20*

        So do I mourn, and hang my head,
        And though thou dost me fullnes give,
        Yet look I for far better bread
        Because by this man cannot live.

        O feed me then! and since I may   *25*
        Have yet more days, more nights to Count,
        So strengthen me, Lord, all the way,
        That I may travel to thy Mount.

              Heb. Cap. XI. ver. 13.

And they Confessed, that they were strangers, and Pilgrims on the earth.

The Law, and the Gospel

    Lord, when thou didst on *Sinai* pitch
And shine from *Paran*, when a firie Law
Pronounc'd with thunder, and thy threats did thaw
Thy Peoples hearts, when all thy weeds were rich
        And Inaccessible for light,   *5*
            Terrour, and might,
How did poor flesh (which after thou didst weare,)
        Then faint, and fear!
Thy Chosen flock, like leafs in a high wind,
Whisper'd obedience, and their heads Inclin'd.   *10*

27–28 I Kings 19:8, "Then he [Elijah] arose, and did eat and drinke [the food supplied by the angel], and walked in the strength of that meate fourtie dayes and fourtie nights, unto Horeb the mount of God" (Geneva).
    The Law, and the Gospel. 1–10 See Exod. 19:18–25, 24:15–17, 33:18–23.
    1–3 Deut. 33:2, "The Lord came from Sinai, and rose up from Seir unto them; he shined forth from mount Paran, and he came with ten thousands of saints: from his right hand went a fiery law for them."

2

But now since we to *Sion* came,
And through thy bloud thy glory see,
With filial Confidence we touch ev'n thee;
And where the other mount all clad in flame,
    And threatning Clouds would not so much
        As 'bide the touch,
We Climb up this, and have too all the way
        Thy hand our stay,
Nay, thou tak'st ours, and (which ful Comfort brings)
Thy Dove too bears us on her sacred wings.

3

Yet since man is a very brute
And after all thy Acts of grace doth kick,
Slighting that health thou gav'st, when he was sick,
Be not displeas'd, If I, who have a sute
    To thee each houre, beg at thy door
        For this one more;
O plant in me thy *Gospel*, and thy *Law*,
        Both *Faith*, and *Awe*;
So twist them in my heart, that ever there
I may as wel as *Love*, find too thy *fear*!

4

Let me not spil, but drink thy bloud,
Not break thy fence, and by a black Excess
Force down a Just Curse, when thy hands would bless;
Let me not scatter, and despise my food,

---

11 *Sion*: the mountain on which the Temple at Jerusalem was placed, hence the type of the new dispensation of Grace, and of the Heavenly Jerusalem. See Rev. 14:1, "Lo, a Lamb stood on the mount Sion, and with him an hundred forty and four thousand, having his Father's name written in their foreheads."

>   Or nail those blessed limbs again   35
>   Which bore my pain;
>   So Shall thy mercies flow: for while I fear,
>   I know, thou'lt bear,
>   But should thy mild Injunction nothing move me,
>   I would both think, and Judge I did not love thee.   40

>   *John Cap. 14. ver. 15.*

>   *If ye love me, keep my Commandements.*

The World

>   I Saw Eternity the other night
>   Like a great *Ring* of pure and endless light,
>   All calm, as it was bright,
>   And round beneath it, Time in hours, days, years
>   Driv'n by the spheres   5
>   Like a vast shadow mov'd, In which the world
>   And all her train were hurl'd;
>   The doting Lover in his queintest strain
>   Did their Complain,
>   Neer him, his Lute, his fancy, and his flights,   10
>   Wits sour delights,
>   With gloves, and knots the silly snares of pleasure
>   Yet his dear Treasure
>   All scatter'd lay, while he his eys did pour
>   Upon a flowr.   15

>   2
>   The darksome States-man hung with weights and woe
>   Like a thick midnight-fog mov'd there so slow
>   He did nor stay, nor go;

The World. 1–7 See Plato, *Timaeus*, 37d (H.).
8 Cf. Herbert, "Dulnes," l. 5.

Condemning thoughts (like sad Ecclipses) scowl
    Upon his soul,
And Clouds of crying witnesses without
    Pursued him with one shout.
Yet dig'd the Mole, and lest his ways be found
    Workt under ground,
Where he did Clutch his prey, but one did see
    That policie,
Churches and altars fed him, Perjuries
    Were gnats and flies,
It rain'd about him bloud and tears, but he
    Drank them as free.

3

The fearfull miser on a heap of rust
Sate pining all his life there, did scarce trust
    His own hands with the dust,
Yet would not place one peece above, but lives
    In feare of theeves.
Thousands there were as frantick as himself
    And hug'd each one his pelf,
The down-right Epicure plac'd heav'n in sense
    And scornd pretence
While others slipt into a wide Excesse
    Said little lesse;
The weaker sort slight, triviall wares Inslave
    Who think them brave,
And poor, despised truth sate Counting by
    Their victory.

4

Yet some, who all this while did weep and sing,
And sing, and weep, soar'd up into the *Ring*,
    But most would use no wing.

44–45 Cf. Herbert, "The Church Militant," l. 190.

O fools (said I,) thus to prefer dark night
    Before true light, 50
To live in grots, and caves, and hate the day
    Because it shews the way,
The way which from this dead and dark abode
    Leads up to God,
A way where you might tread the Sun, and be 55
    More bright than he.
But as I did their madnes so discusse
    One whisper'd thus,
This Ring the Bride-groome did for none provide
    But for his bride. 60

John Cap. 2. ver. 16, 17.

All that is in the world, the lust of the flesh, the lust of the Eys, and the pride of life, is not of the father, but is of the world.

And the world passeth away, and the lusts thereof, but he that doth the will of God abideth for ever.

The Mutinie

Weary of this same Clay, and straw, I laid
Me down to breath, and casting in my heart

49–54 Cf. Plato, *Republic* vii, 514–517: "Behold! human beings living in an underground cave.... At first when any of them is liberated and compelled suddenly to...look toward the light, he will suffer sharp pains, the glare will distress him.... And if he is compelled to look straight at the light, will he not have a pain in his eyes which will make him turn away... And suppose once more, that he is reluctantly dragged up a steep and rugged ascent, and held fast until he is forced into the presence of the sun himself, is he not likely to be pained and irritated?" (trans. Jowett).

60 *bride*: Rev. 19:7–8, "the marriage of the Lamb is come, and his wife hath made herself ready. And to her was granted that she should be arrayed in fine linen, clean and white: for the fine linen is the righteousness of saints." The last lines of the poem imply the doctrine of predestination.

John Cap. 2...: should read I John 2:16, 17.

The Mutinie. Owes a general debt to Herbert, "The Collar."

1–14 See accounts in Exodus 1 and 5 of the Israelites laboring in Egypt in brick-making.

The after-burthens, and griefs yet to come,
    The heavy sum
So shook my brest, that (sick and sore dismai'd)　　　　5
My thoughts, like water which some stone doth start
Did quit their troubled Channel, and retire
Unto the banks, where, storming at those bounds,
They murmur'd sore; But I, who felt them boyl
    And knew their Coyl,　　　　10
Turning to him, who made poor sand to tire
And tame proud waves, If yet these barren grounds
    And thirstie brick must be (said I)
      My taske, and Destinie,

2

Let me so strive and struggle with thy foes　　　　15
(Not thine alone, but mine too,) that when all
Their Arts and force are built unto the height
    That Babel-weight
May prove thy glory, and their shame; so Close
And knit me to thee, That though in this vale　　　　20
Of sin, and death I sojourn, yet one Eie
May look to thee, To thee the finisher
And Author of my faith; so shew me home
    That all this fome
And frothie noise which up and down doth flie　　　　25
May find no lodging in mine Eie, or Eare,
    O seal them up! that these may flie
      Like other tempests by.

3

Not but I know thou hast a shorter Cut
To bring me home, than through a wildernes,　　　　30

11–12 Cf. Herbert, "Providence," ll. 47–48.

22–23 Heb. 12:1–2, "let us lay aside every weight, and the sin which doth so easily beset us, and let us run with patience the race that is set before us, Looking unto Jesus the author and finisher of our faith."

30–31 *wildernes,/A Sea...*: the way God took to lead the Israelites to the Promised Land.

> A Sea, or Sands and Serpents; Yet since thou
>   (As thy words show)
> Though in this desart I were wholy shut,
> Canst light and lead me there with such redress
> That no decay shal touch me; O be pleas'd   35
> To fix my steps, and whatsoever path
> Thy sacred and eternal wil decreed
>   For thy bruis'd reed
> O give it ful obedience, that so seiz'd
> Of all I have, I may nor move thy wrath   40
>   Nor grieve thy *Dove*, but soft and mild
>   Both live and die thy Child.

Revel. Cap. 2. ver. 17.

To him that overcometh wil I give to eate of the hidden Manna, *and I wil give him a white stone, and in the stone a new name written, which no man knoweth, saving he that receiveth it.*

The Constellation

> Fair, order'd lights (whose motion without noise
>   Resembles those true Joys
> Whose spring is on that hil where you do grow
>   And we here tast sometimes below,)
>
> With what exact obedience do you move   5
>   Now beneath, and now above,
> And in your vast progressions overlook
>   The darkest night, and closest nook!
>
> Some nights I see you in the gladsome East,
>   Some others neer the West,   10
> And when I cannot see, yet do you shine
>   And beat about your endles line.

37 See Isa. 42:3.
40 See Ephes. 4:30, and Herbert, "Grieve not the Holy Spirit," l. 1.

Silence, and light, and watchfulnes with you
    Attend and wind the Clue,
No sleep, nor sloth assailes you, but poor man   *15*
    Still either sleeps, or slips his span.

He grops beneath here, and with restless Care
    First makes, then hugs a snare,
Adores dead dust, sets heart on Corne and grass
    But seldom doth make heav'n his glass.   *20*

Musick and mirth (if there be musick here)
    Take up, and tune his year,
These things are Kin to him, and must be had,
    Who kneels, or sighs a life is mad.

Perhaps some nights hee'l watch with you, and peep   *25*
    When it were best to sleep,
Dares know Effects, and Judge them long before,
    When th'herb he treads knows much, much more.

But seeks he your *Obedience, Order, Light,*
    Your calm and wel-train'd flight,   *30*
Where, though the glory differ in each star,
    Yet is there peace still, and no war?

Since plac'd by him who calls you by your names
    And fixt there all your flames,
Without Command you never acted ought   *35*
    And then you in your Courses fought.

But here Commission'd by a black self-wil
    The sons the father kil,
The Children Chase the mother, and would heal
    The wounds they give, by crying, zeale.   *40*

The Constellation. 14 *Clue*: ball of yarn.
16 *slips his span*: neglects to take advantage of his life span (*OED*).
31 I Cor. 15:41, "for one star differeth from another star in glory."
36 Judg. 5:20, "the stars in their courses fought against Sisera."
37 ff. Allusions to the violence and disorder of the Puritan Revolution and perhaps to the execution of Charles I.

Then Cast her bloud, and tears upon thy book
    Where they for fashion look,
And like that Lamb which had the Dragons voice
    Seem mild, but are known by their noise.

Thus by our lusts disorder'd into wars
    Our guides prove wandring stars,
Which for these mists, and black days were reserv'd,
    What time we from our first love swerv'd.

Yet O for his sake who sits now by thee
    All crown'd with victory,
So guide us through this Darknes, that we may
    Be more and more in love with day;

Settle, and fix our hearts, that we may move
    In order, peace, and love,
And taught obedience by thy whole Creation,
    Become an humble, holy nation.

Give to thy spouse her perfect, and pure dress,
    Beauty and *holiness*,
And so repair these Rents, that men may see
    And say, *Where God is, all agree.*

The Shepheards

Sweet, harmles lives! (on whose holy leisure
    Waits Innocence and pleasure,)
Whose leaders to those pastures, and cleer springs,
    Were *Patriarchs*, Saints, and Kings,
How happend it that in the dead of night
    You only saw true light,

---

43 Rev. 13:11, "And I beheld another beast coming up out of the earth; and he had two horns like a lamb, and he spake as a dragon."
46 *Our guides*: perhaps the clergy.
57–58 See note to "The World," l. 60.

While *Palestine* was fast a sleep, and lay
    Without one thought of Day?
Was it because those first and blessed swains
    Were pilgrims on those plains
When they receiv'd the promise, for which now
    'Twas there first shown to you?
'Tis true, he loves that Dust whereon they go
    That serve him here below,
And therefore might for memory of those
    His love there first disclose;
But wretched *Salem* once his love, must now
    No voice, nor vision know,
Her stately Piles with all their height and pride
    Now languished and died,
And *Bethlems* humble Cotts above them stept
    While all her Seers slept;
Her Cedar, firr, hew'd stones and gold were all
    Polluted through their fall,
And those once sacred mansions were now
    Meer emptiness and show,
This made the Angel call at reeds and thatch,
    Yet where the shepheards watch,
And Gods own lodging (though he could not lack,)
    To be a common *Rack*;
No costly pride, no soft-cloath'd luxurie
    In those thin Cels could lie,
Each stirring wind and storm blew through their Cots
    Which never harbour'd plots,
Only Content, and love, and humble joys
    Lived there without all noise,
Perhaps some harmless cares for the next day
    Did in their bosomes play,
As where to lead their sheep, what silent nook,
    What springs or shades to look,
But that was all; And now with gladsome care

The Shepheards. 17 *Salem*: Jerusalem, city of the Jews and the Old Law, now repudiated.
    23–26 the Temple.
    30 *Rack*: manger.
    37–41 Cf. Milton, "On the Morning of Christ's Nativity," ll. 91–92, "Perhaps their loves, or else their sheep,/Was all that did their silly thoughts so busy keep."

        They for the town prepare,
   They leave their flock, and in a busie talk
         All towards *Bethlem* walk
To see their souls great shepheard, who was come   *45*
        To bring all straglers home,
Where now they find him out, and taught before
        That Lamb of God adore,
That Lamb whose daies great Kings and Prophets wish'd
        And long'd to see, but miss'd.   *50*
The first light they beheld was bright and gay
        And turn'd their night to day,
But to this later light they saw in him,
        Their day was dark, and dim.

Misery

   Lord, bind me up, and let me lye
   A Pris'ner to my libertie,
   If such a state at all can be
   As an Impris'ment serving thee;
   The wind, though gather'd in thy fist,   *5*
   Yet doth it blow stil where it list,
   And yet shouldst thou let go thy hold
   Those gusts might quarrel and grow bold.
     As waters here, headlong and loose
   The lower grounds stil chase, and choose,   *10*
   Where spreading all the way they seek
   And search out ev'ry hole, and Creek;
   So my spilt thoughts winding from thee
   Take the down-rode to vanitie,
   Where they all stray and strive, which shal   *15*
   Find out the first and steepest fal;
   I cheer their flow, giving supply

49–50 Cf. Luke 10:24.
Misery. 5 Prov. 30:4, "who hath gathered the wind in his fists?"
6 See John 3:8.

To what's already grown too high,
And having thus perform'd that part
Feed on those vomits of my heart. 20
I break the fence my own hands made
Then lay that trespasse in the shade,
Some fig-leafs stil I do devise
As if thou hadst nor ears, nor Eyes.
Excesse of friends, of words, and wine 25
Take up my day, while thou dost shine
All unregarded, and thy book
Hath not so much as one poor look.
If thou steal in amidst the mirth
And kindly tel me, *I am Earth*, 30
I shut thee out, and let that slip,
Such Musick spoils good fellowship.
Thus wretched I, and most unkind,
Exclude my dear God from my mind,
Exclude him thence, who of that Cel 35
Would make a Court, should he there dwel.
He goes, he yields; And troubled sore
His holy spirit grieves therefore,
The mighty God, th' eternal King
Doth grieve for Dust, and Dust doth sing. 40
But I go on, haste to Devest
My self of reason, till opprest
And buried in my surfeits I
Prove my own shame and miserie.
Next day I call and cry for thee 45
Who shouldst not then come neer to me,
But now it is thy servants pleasure
Thou must (and dost) give him his measure.
Thou dost, thou com'st, and in a showr
Of healing sweets thy self dost powr 50
Into my wounds, and now thy grace
(I know it wel,) fils all the place;

23-24 Cf. Herbert, "Sighes and Grones," ll. 15-16.
35-36 Cf. Herbert, "The Glimpse," ll. 29-30.

I sit with thee by this new light,
And for that hour th'art my delight,
No man can more the world despise
Or thy great mercies better prize.
I School my Eys, and strictly dwel
Within the Circle of my Cel,
That Calm and silence are my Joys
Which to thy peace are but meer noise.
At length I feel my head to ake,
My fingers Itch, and burn to take
Some new Imployment, I begin
To swel and fome and fret within.
   "The Age, the present times are not
   "To snudge in, and embrace a Cot,
   "Action and bloud now get the game,
   "Disdein treads on the peaceful name,
   "Who sits at home too bears a loade
   "Greater than those that gad abroad.
Thus do I make thy gifts giv'n me
The only quarrellers with thee,
I'd loose those knots thy hands did tie,
Then would go travel, fight or die.
Thousands of wild and waste Infusions
Like waves beat on my resolutions,
As flames about their fuel run
And work, and wind til all be done,
So my fierce soul bustles about
And never rests til all be out.
Thus wilded by a peevish heart
Which in thy musick bears no part
I storm at thee, calling my peace
A Lethargy, and meer disease,
Nay, those bright beams shot from thy eys
To calm me in these mutinies

57–58 Cf. Herbert, "Mortification," ll. 20–22.
65–71 Cf. Herbert, "Giddines," ll. 9–11.
66 *snudge*: to remain snug, to nestle (F.).
74 Cf. Herbert, "Nature," ll. 1–2.

I stile meer tempers, which take place
At some set times, but are thy grace.
    Such is mans life, and such is mine
The worst of men, and yet stil thine,   90
Stil thine thou know'st, and if not so
Then give me over to my foe.
Yet since as easie 'tis for thee
To make man good, as bid him be,
And with one glaunce (could he that gain,)   95
To look him out of all his pain,
O send me from thy holy hil
So much of strength, as may fulfil
All thy delight (what e'r they be)
And sacred Institutes in me;   100
Open my rockie heart, and fil
It with obedience to thy wil,
Then seal it up, that as none see,
So none may enter there but thee.
    O hear my God! hear him, whose bloud   105
Speaks more and better for my good!
O let my Crie come to thy throne!
My crie not pour'd with tears alone,
(For tears alone are often foul)
But with the bloud of all my soul,   110
With spirit-sighs, and earnest grones,
Faithful and most repenting mones,
With these I crie, and crying pine
Till thou both mend and make me thine.

The Sap

Come sapless Blossom, creep not stil on Earth
    Forgetting thy first birth;

---

96 Cf. Herbert, "The Glance," l. 21.
   The Sap. Much influenced by Herbert's "Peace," especially ll. 17–18, 22–23, 27–39.

'Tis not from dust, or if so, why dost thou
    Thus cal and thirst for dew?
It tends not thither, if it doth, why then 5
    This growth and stretch for heav'n?
Thy root sucks but diseases, worms there seat
    And claim it for their meat.
Who plac'd thee here, did something then Infuse
    Which now can tel thee news. 10
There is beyond the Stars an hil of myrrh
    From which some drops fal here,
On it the Prince of *Salem* sits, who deals
    To thee thy secret meals,
There is thy Country, and he is the way 15
    And hath withal the key.
Yet liv'd he here sometimes, and bore for thee
    A world of miserie,
For thee, who in the first mans loyns didst fal
    From that hil to this vale, 20
And had not he so done, it is most true
    Two deaths had bin thy due;
But going hence, and knowing wel what woes
    Might his friends discompose,
To shew what strange love he had to our good 25
    He gave his sacred bloud
By wil our sap, and Cordial; now in this
    Lies such a heav'n of bliss,
That, who but truly tasts it, no decay
    Can touch him any way, 30
Such secret life, and vertue in it lies
    It wil exalt and rise
And actuate such spirits as are shed
    Or ready to be dead,
And bring new too. Get then this sap, and get 35
    Good store of it, but let

---

13 *Prince of Salem*: Melchisedec, here as in Herbert's poem a type of Christ, "King of Salem, which is, King of peace" (Heb. 7:2).
  17–22 Cf. Herbert, "Busines," ll. 20–22, 26–28.
  22 *Two deaths*: See note to "Easter-day," l. 8.

    The vessel where you put it be for sure
        To all your pow'r most pure;
    There is at all times (though shut up) in you
        A powerful, rare dew,   40
    Which only grief and love extract; with this
        Be sure, and never miss,
    To wash your vessel wel: Then humbly take
        This balm for souls that ake,
    And one who drank it thus, assures that you   45
        Shal find a Joy so true,
    Such perfect Ease, and such a lively sense
        Of grace against all sins,
    That you'l Confess the Comfort such, as even
        Brings to, and comes from Heaven.   50

Mount of Olives [II]

When first I saw true beauty, and thy Joys
Active as light, and calm without all noise
Shin'd on my soul, I felt through all my powr's
Such a rich air of sweets, as Evening showrs
Fand by a gentle gale Convey and breath   5
On some parch'd bank, crown'd with a flowrie wreath;
Odors, and Myrrh, and balm in one rich floud
O'r-ran my heart, and spirited my bloud,
My thoughts did swim in Comforts, and mine eie
Confest, *The world did only paint and lie.*   10
And where before I did no safe Course steer
But wander'd under tempests all the year,
Went bleak and bare in body as in mind,
And was blow'n through by ev'ry storm and wind,
I am so warm'd now by this glance on me,   15
That, midst all storms I feel a Ray of thee;
So have I known some beauteous *Paisage* rise

Mount of Olives [II]. Much influenced by Herbert, "The Flowre" (M.).
14 Cf. Herbert, "Affliction [I]," l. 36 (H.).
17 *Paisage*: landscape.

  In suddain flowres and arbours to my Eies,
  And in the depth and dead of winter bring
  To my Cold thoughts a lively sense of spring.   20
   Thus fed by thee, who dost all beings nourish,
  My wither'd leafs again look green and flourish,
  I shine and shelter underneath thy wing
  Where sick with love I strive thy name to sing,
  Thy glorious name! which grant I may so do   25
  That these may be thy *Praise*, and my *Joy* too.

Man

  Weighing the stedfastness and state
 Of some mean things which here below reside,
 Where birds like watchful Clocks the noiseless date
  And Intercourse of times divide,
 Where Bees at night get home and hive, and flowrs 5
   Early, aswel as late,
 Rise with the Sun, and set in the same bowrs;

      2

  I would (said I) my God would give
 The staidness of these things to man! for these
 To his divine appointments ever cleave,   10
  And no new business breaks their peace;
 The birds nor sow, nor reap, yet sup and dine,
   The flowres without clothes live,
 Yet *Solomon* was never drest so fine.

 Man. 12–14 Luke 12 : 24, 27, "Consider the ravens: for they neither sow nor reap; which neither have storehouse nor barn; and God feedeth them.... Consider the lilies how they grow: they toil not, they spin not; and yet I say unto you, that Solomon in all his glory was not arrayed like one of these."

3

Man hath stil either toyes, or Care,   *15*
He hath no root, nor to one place is ty'd,
But ever restless and Irregular
    About this Earth doth run and ride,
He knows he hath a home, but scarce knows where,
        He sayes it is so far   *20*
That he hath quite forgot how to go there.

4

He knocks at all doors, strays and roams,
Nay hath not so much wit as some stones have
Which in the darkest nights point to their homes,
    By some hid sense their Maker gave;   *25*
Man is the shuttle, to whose winding quest
        And passage through these looms
God order'd motion, but ordain'd no rest.

[*I walkt the other day (to spend my hour)*]

I walkt the other day (to spend my hour,)
    Into a field
Where I sometimes had seen the soil to yield
    A gallant flowre,
But Winter now had ruffled all the bowre   *5*
    And curious store
I knew there heretofore.

15–28 Cf. Herbert, "Giddines."
28 Cf. Herbert, "The Pulley," ll. 16–20.
   [*I walkt the other day*...]. 1–4 Cf. Herbert, "Peace," ll. 13–14. The allegorical narrative method also derives from "Peace."

2

Yet I whose search lov'd not to peep and peer
    I'th' face of things
Thought with my self, there might be other springs   *10*
    Besides this here
Which, like cold friends, sees us but once a year,
    And so the flowre
      Might have some other bowre.

3

Then taking up what I could neerest spie   *15*
    I digg'd about
That place where I had seen him to grow out,
    And by and by
I saw the warm Recluse alone to lie
    Where fresh and green   *20*
      He lived of us unseen.

4

Many a question Intricate and rare
    Did I there strow,
But all I could extort was, that he now
    Did there repair   *25*
Such losses as befel him in this air
    And would e'r long
      Come forth most fair and young.

5

This past, I threw the Clothes quite o'r his head,
    And stung with fear   *30*
Of my own frailty dropt down many a tear
    Upon his bed,
Then sighing whisper'd, *Happy are the dead!*
    What peace doth now
      Rock him asleep below?   *35*

15–21 Cf. Herbert, "The Flowre," ll. 8–14.

6

And yet, how few believe such doctrine springs
    From a poor root
Which all the Winter sleeps here under foot
    And hath no wings
To raise it to the truth and light of things,   40
    But is stil trod
    By ev'ry wandring clod.

7

O thou! whose spirit did at first inflame
    And warm the dead,
And by a sacred Incubation fed   45
    With life this frame
Which once had neither being, forme, nor name,
    Grant I may so
    Thy steps track here below,

8

That in these Masques and shadows I may see   50
    Thy sacred way,
And by those hid ascents climb to that day
    Which breaks from thee
Who art in all things, though invisibly;
    Shew me thy peace,   55
    Thy mercy, love, and ease,

9

And from this Care, where dreams and sorrows raign
    Lead me above
Where Light, Joy, Leisure, and true Comforts move
    Without all pain,   60
There, hid in thee, shew me his life again
    At whose dumbe urn
    Thus all the year I mourn.

43–47 Pettet notes the Hermetic language and conception of creation.
59 Cf. Herbert, "Heaven," l. 19.
61 *his life*: probably his brother William.

Begging [I]

King of Mercy, King of Love,
In whom I live, in whom I move,
Perfect what thou hast begun,
Let no night put out this Sun;
Grant I may, my chief desire!　　　　5
Long for thee, to thee aspire,
Let my youth, my bloom of dayes
Be my Comfort, and thy praise,
That hereafter, when I look
O'r the sullyed, sinful book,　　　　10
I may find thy hand therein
Wiping out my shame, and sin.
O it is thy only Art
To reduce a stubborn heart,
And since thine is victorie,　　　　15
Strong holds should belong to thee;
Lord then take it, leave it not
Unto my dispose or lot,
But since I would not have it mine,
O my God, let it be thine!　　　　20

Jude ver. 24, 25.

Now unto him that is able to keep us from falling, and to present us faultless before the presence of his glory with exceeding joy,

To the only wise God, our Saviour, be glory, and majesty, Dominion and power, now and ever, Amen.

Begging [I]. 13–16 Cf. Herbert, "Nature," ll. 4–6.

[PART II]

Ascension-day

Lord Jesus! with what sweetness and delights,
Sure, holy hopes, high joys and quickning flights
Dost thou feed thine! O thou! the hand that lifts
To him, who gives all good and perfect gifts.
Thy glorious, bright Ascension (though remov'd   5
So many Ages from me) is so prov'd
And by thy Spirit seal'd to me, that I
Feel me a sharer in thy victory.
        I soar and rise
           Up to the skies,   10
              Leaving the world their day,
          And in my flight,
          For the true light
              Go seeking all the way;
I greet thy Sepulchre, salute thy Grave,   15
That blest inclosure, where the Angels gave
The first glad tidings of thy early light,
And resurrection from the earth and night.
I see that morning in thy* Converts tears,
Fresh as the dew, which but this dawning wears!   20
I smell her spices, and her ointment yields
As rich a scent as the new Primros'd-fields:
The Day-star smiles, and light with the deceast
Now shines in all the Chambers of the East.
What stirs, what posting intercourse and mirth   25
Of Saints and Angels glorifie the earth?

*St. Mary Magdalene

Ascension-day. This poem introduces the central themes of Part II, treating an advance to a higher stage in the spiritual life.
19-22 Mary Magdalene, who first discovered Christ's resurrection from the tomb (John 20:1-18), was often identified with Mary of Bethany who anointed Jesus' feet (John 12:3).

What sighs, what whispers, busie stops and stays;
Private and holy talk fill all the ways?
They pass as at the last great day, and run
In their white robes to seek the risen Sun; 30
I see them, hear them, mark their haste, and move
Amongst them, with them, wing'd with faith and love.
Thy forty days more secret commerce here,
After thy death and Funeral, so clear
And indisputable, shews to my sight 35
As the Sun doth, which to those days gave light.
I walk the fields of *Bethani* which shine
All now as fresh as *Eden*, and as fine.
Such was the bright world, on the first seventh day,
Before man brought forth sin, and sin decay; 40
When like a Virgin clad in *Flowers* and *green*
The pure earth sat, and the fair woods had seen
No frost, but flourish'd in that youthful vest,
With which their great Creator had them drest:
When Heav'n above them shin'd like molten glass, 45
While all the Planets did unclouded pass;
And Springs, like dissolv'd Pearls their Streams did pour
Ne'r marr'd with floods, nor anger'd with a showre.
With these fair thoughts I move in this fair place,
And the last steps of my milde Master trace; 50
I see him leading out his chosen Train,
All sad with tears, which like warm Summer rain
In silent drops steal from their holy eyes,
Fix'd lately on the Cross, now on the skies.
And now (eternal Jesus!) thou dost heave 55
Thy blessed hands to bless, these thou dost leave;
The cloud doth now receive thee, and their sight
Having lost thee, behold two men in white!

57–62 Acts 1:10–11. "And while they looked stedfastly toward heaven as he went up, behold, two men stood by them in white apparel; Which also said, Ye men of Galilee, why stand ye gazing up into heaven? this same Jesus, which is taken up from you into heaven, shall so come in like manner as ye have seen him go into heaven." The poem builds upon the typological relation between Christ's Ascension and his Second Coming.

Two and no more: *what two attest, is true,*
Was thine own answer to the stubborn Jew. 60
Come then thou faithful witness! come dear Lord
Upon the Clouds again to judge this world!

Ascension-Hymn

      Dust and clay
    Mans antient wear!
    Here you must stay,
    But I elsewhere;
Souls sojourn here, but may not rest; 5
Who will ascend, must be undrest.

    And yet some
    That know to die
    Before death come,
    Walk to the skie 10
Even in this life; but all such can
Leave behinde them the old Man.

    If a star
    Should leave the Sphaere,
    She must first mar 15
    Her flaming wear,
And after fall, for in her dress
Of glory, she cannot transgress.

    Man of old
    Within the line 20
    Of *Eden* could
    Like the Sun shine
All naked, innocent and bright,
And intimate with Heav'n, as light;

   59–60 John 8:17, "It is also written in your law, that the testimony of two men is true."
   Ascension-Hymn. 12 See Col. 3:9.

But since he 25
That brightness soil'd,
His garments be
All dark and spoil'd,
And here are left as nothing worth,
Till the Refiners fire breaks forth. 30

Then comes he!
Whose mighty light
Made his cloathes be
Like Heav'n, all bright;
The Fuller, whose pure blood did flow 35
To make stain'd man more white then snow.

Hee alone
And none else can
Bring bone to bone
And rebuild man, 40
And by his all subduing might
Make clay ascend more quick then light.

30–36 Mal. 3:2, "But who may abide the day of his coming? and who shall stand when he appeareth? for he is like a refiner's fire, and like fullers' soap." Also, Mark 9:3, of Christ's Transfiguration, "And his raiment became shining, exceeding white as snow; so as no fuller on earth can white them."
39–42 See Ezek. 37:7, Philip. 3:21.

[*They are all gone into the world of light!*]

They are all gone into the world of light!
    And I alone sit lingring here;
Their very memory is fair and bright,
    And my sad thoughts doth clear.

It glows and glitters in my cloudy brest   5
    Like stars upon some gloomy grove,
Or those faint beams in which this hill is drest,
    After the Sun's remove.

I see them walking in an Air of glory,
    Whose light doth trample on my days: 10
My days, which are at best but dull and hoary,
    Meer glimering and decays.

O holy hope! and high humility,
    High as the Heavens above!
These are your walks, and you have shew'd them me   15
    To kindle my cold love,

Dear, beauteous death! the Jewel of the Just,
    Shining no where, but in the dark;
What mysteries do lie beyond thy dust;
    Could man outlook that mark!   20

He that hath found some fledg'd birds nest, may know
    At first sight, if the bird be flown;
But what fair Well, or Grove he sings in now,
    That is to him unknown.

And yet, as Angels in some brighter dreams   25
    Call to the soul, when man doth sleep:

[*They are all gone* . . .]. 23 *Well*: the neighborhood of a well or fountain (M.).

So some strange thoughts transcend our wonted theams,
    And into glory peep.

If a star were confin'd into a Tomb
    Her captive flames must needs burn there;
But when the hand that lockt her up, gives room,
    She'l shine through all the sphaere.

O Father of eternal life, and all
    Created glories under thee!
Resume thy spirit from this world of thrall
    Into true liberty.

Either disperse these mists, which blot and fill
    My perspective (still) as they pass,
Or else remove me hence unto that hill,
    Where I shall need no glass.

White Sunday

Wellcome white day! a thousand Suns,
  Though seen at once, were black to thee;
For after their light, darkness comes,
  But thine shines to eternity.

Those flames which on the Apostles rush'd
  At this great feast, and in a tyre
Of cloven Tongues their heads all brush'd,
  And crown'd them with Prophetic fire:

Can these new lights be like to those,
  These lights of Serpents like the Dove?

---

38 *perspective*: telescope.
White Sunday. Cf. Herbert, "Whitsunday."
5–8 Acts 2:3–4, "And there appeared unto them cloven tongues like as of fire, and it sat upon each of them. And they were all filled with the Holy Ghost, and began to speak with other tongues."
6 *tyre*: head dress.

Thou hadst no *gall*, ev'n for thy foes,
And thy two wings were *Grief* and *Love*.

Though then some boast that fire each day,
And on Christs coat pin all their shreds;
Not sparing openly to say,   15
His candle shines upon their heads:

Yet while some rays of that great light
Shine here below within thy Book,
They never shall so blinde my sight
But I will know which way to look.   20

For though thou doest that great light lock,
And by this lesser commerce keep:
Yet by these glances of the flock
I can discern Wolves from the Sheep.

Not, but that I have wishes too,   25
And pray, *These last may be as first*,
Or better; but thou long ago
Hath said, *These last should be the worst*.

Besides, thy method with thy own,
Thy own dear people pens our times,   30
Our stories are in theirs set down
And penalties spread to our Crimes.

---

14 *their shreds*: The Puritan deformations of doctrine are *pinned* to Christ's coat (the Church) on the plea of the special illumination of the Spirit.

16 See Job 29:2-3, "Oh that I were as in months past.... When his candle shined upon my head, and when by his light I walked through darkness."

24 Matt. 7:15, "Beware of false prophets, which come to you in sheep's clothing, but inwardly they are ravening wolves."

26 Matt. 19:30, "But many that are first shall be last; and the last shall be first."

28 II Tim. 3:1, 13, "This know also, that in the last days perilous times shall come.... evil men and seducers shall wax worse and worse, deceiving, and being deceived."

29-32 Cf. Herbert, "The Bunch of Grapes," ll. 11, 14 (H.).

Again, if worst and worst implies
A State, that no redress admits,
Then from thy Cross unto these days 35
The *rule* without *Exception* fits.

And yet, as in nights gloomy page
One silent star may interline:
So in this last and lewdest age,
Thy antient love on some may shine. 40

For, though we hourly breath decays,
And our best *note* and highest *ease*
Is but meer changing of the *keys*,
And a *Consumption* that doth please;

Yet thou the great eternal Rock 45
Whose height above all ages shines,
Art still the same, and canst unlock
Thy waters to a soul that pines.

Since then thou art the same this day
And ever, as thou wert of old, 50
And nothing doth thy love allay
But our hearts dead and sinful cold:

As thou long since wert pleas'd to buy
Our drown'd estate, taking the Curse
Upon thy self, so to destroy 55
The knots we tyed upon thy purse,

So let thy grace now make the way
Even for thy love; for by that means
We, who are nothing but foul clay,
Shal be fine gold, which thou didst cleanse. 60

45 *Rock*: the rock struck by Moses; see Exod. 17:6, I Cor. 10:4.
55–56 Cf. Herbert, *"Prayer* [II]," ll. 17–18.
59–62 Cf. Mal. 3:2–3, "he is like a refiner's fire.... And he shall sit as a refiner and purifier of silver: and he shall purify the sons of Levi, and purge them as gold and silver."

O come! refine us with thy fire!
Refine us! we are at a loss.
Let not thy stars for *Balaams* hire
Dissolve into the common dross!

The Proffer

Be still black Parasites,
    Flutter no more;
Were it still winter, as it was before,
    You'd make no flights;
But now the dew and Sun have warm'd my bowres,   *5*
  You flie and flock to suck the flowers.

But you would honey make:
    These buds will wither,
And what you now extract, in harder weather
    Will serve to take;   *10*
Wise husband will (you say) there wants prevent,
  Who do not so, too late repent.

O poys'nous, subtile fowls!
    The flyes of hell
That buz in every ear, and blow on souls   *15*
    Until they smell
And rot, descend not here, nor think to stay,
  I've read, who 'twas, drove you away.

---

63 *thy stars*: God's modern prophets, or his modern prophecies.
63-64 Balak sought to *hire* Balaam for gold and silver (Num. 22:17-18) to curse Israel, but God prevented him and instead made him prophesy of the "*Star*" out of Jacob," i.e. David and, typologically, Christ.
    The Proffer. H. suggests (*Life*, 124-25) that Vaughan may have received offers of a position under the Commonwealth.
11 *prevent*: anticipate.
18 *I've read*: Exod. 8:31, "And the Lord did according to the word of Moses; and he removed the swarms of flies from Pharaoh, from his servants, and from his people."

    Think you these longing eyes,
        Though sick and spent,   20
    And almost famish'd, ever will consent
        To leave those skies,
    That glass of souls and spirits, where well drest
        They shine in white (like stars) and rest.

    Shall my short hour, my inch,   25
        My one poor sand,
    And crum of life, now ready to disband
        Revolt and flinch,
    And having born the burthen all the day,
        Now cast at night my Crown away?   30

    No, No; I am not he,
        Go seek elsewhere.
    I skill not your fine tinsel, and false hair,
        Your Sorcery
    And smooth seducements: I'le not stuff my story 35
        With your Commonwealth and glory.

    There are, that will sow tares
        And scatter death
    Amongst the quick, selling their souls and breath
        For any wares;   40
    But when thy Master comes, they'l finde and see
        There's a reward for them and thee.

    Then keep the antient way!
        Spit out their phlegm
    And fill thy brest with home; think on thy dream: 45
        A calm, bright day!
    A Land of flowers and spices! the word given,
        If these be fair, O what is Heaven!

37–42 See parable of the Sower, Matt. 13:24–30, 37–40.
44–45 Cf. Herbert, "The Church-Porch," l. 92.
45–48 Cf. Herbert, "The Size," ll. 44–47.

Cock-crowing

Father of lights! what Sunnie seed,
What glance of day hast thou confin'd
Into this bird? To all the breed
This busie Ray thou hast assign'd;
     Their magnetisme works all night,   5
     And dreams of Paradise and light.

Their eyes watch for the morning-hue,
Their little grain expelling night
So shines and sings, as if it knew
The path unto the house of light.   10
     It seems their candle, howe'r done,
     Was tinn'd and lighted at the sunne.

If such a tincture, such a touch,
So firm a longing can impowre
Shall thy own image think it much   15
To watch for thy appearing hour?
     If a meer blast so fill the sail,
     Shall not the breath of God prevail?

     O thou immortall light and heat!
     Whose hand so shines through all this frame,   20

Cock-crowing. Many classical and Christian sources identify the cock as a sacred bird, the symbol of Divine light. Relevant also are Hermetic descriptions of the magnetic attraction between the sun and stars and the creatures, owing to the Seed or ray of Star-fire implanted in each. Cf. Thomas Vaughan, *Anima Magica Abscondita* (Waite, p. 81), "The Soul...is guided in her operations by a spiritual metaphysical grain, a seed or glance of light, simple and without any mixture, descending from the first Father of Lights."

1 Cf. Jas. 1:17.

10 *house of light*: cf. title of Thomas Vaughan's treatise *Aula Lucis, or, The House of Light* (1652).

11-12 *tinn'd*: kindled. Cf. Thomas Vaughan, *Lumen de Lumine* (1651), "Within this fantastic circle stands a Lamp, and it typifies the Light of Nature. This is the secret Candle of God, which He hath tinned in the elements.... Every natural body is a kind of black lantern; it carries the candle within it.... The great world hath the Sun for his life and candle" (Waite, pp. 266-67).

13 *tincture*: a spiritual principle or immaterial substance, whose quality may be infused into matter (*OED*).

That by the beauty of the seat,
We plainly see, who made the same.
  Seeing thy seed abides in me,
  Dwell thou in it, and I in thee.

To sleep without thee, is to die;   25
Yea, 'tis a death partakes of hell:
For where thou dost not close the eye
It never opens, I can tell.
  In such a dark, Ægyptian border,
  The shades of death dwell and disorder. 30

If joyes, and hopes, and earnest throws,
And hearts, whose Pulse beats still for light
Are given to birds; who, but thee, knows
A love-sick souls exalted flight?
  Can souls be track'd by any eye   35
  But his, who gave them wings to flie?

Onely this Veyle which thou hast broke,
And must be broken yet in me,
This veyle, I say, is all the cloke
And cloud which shadows thee from me.   40
  This veyle thy full-ey'd love denies,
  And onely gleams and fractions spies.

O take it off! make no delay,
But brush me with thy light, that I
May shine unto a perfect day,   45
And warme me at thy glorious Eye!
  O take it off! or till it flee,
  Though with no Lilie, stay with me!

29 *Ægyptian border*: Exod. 10:22, "And Moses stretched forth his hand toward heaven; and there was a thick darkness in all the land of Egypt three days."
37–42 *Veyle*: the veil before the Ark containing the Old Testament Law, metaphorically seen as obscuring its meaning (II Cor. 3:15–16); here, the mortal condition itself.
48 *no Lilie*: Song of Sol. 6:2–3, "My beloved is gone down into his garden, to the beds of spices, to feed in the gardens, and to gather lilies. I am my beloved's, and my beloved is mine: he feedeth among the lilies." Though the speaker's soul is not such a lily, he begs the "bridegroom" to *stay*.

The Starre

What ever 'tis, whose beauty here below
Attracts thee thus and makes thee stream and flow,
      And wind and curle, and wink and smile,
         Shifting thy gate and guile:

Though thy close commerce nought at all imbarrs   5
My present search, for Eagles eye not starrs,
      And still the lesser by the best
         And highest good is blest:

Yet, seeing all things that subsist and be,
Have their Commissions from Divinitie,   10
      And teach us duty, I will see
         What man may learn from thee.

First, I am sure, the Subject so respected
Is well-disposed, for bodies once infected,
      Deprav'd or dead, can have with thee   15
         No hold, nor sympathie.

Next, there's in it a restless, pure desire
And longing for thy bright and vitall fire,
      Desire that never will be quench'd,
         Nor can be writh'd, nor wrench'd.   20

These are the Magnets which so strongly move
And work all night upon thy light and love,
      As beauteous shapes, we know not why,
         Command and guide the eye.

The Starre. Also indebted to Hermetic imagery.
  1–4 Cf. Thomas Vaughan, *Magia Adamica* (Waite, p. 128), "Look up then to heaven, and when thou seest the celestial fires move in their swift and glorious circles, think also there are below some cold natures which they overlook and about which they move incessantly, to heat and concoct them."
  3–4 Cf. Herbert, "The Starre," ll. 25–26.

Earlier Seventeenth Century

    For where desire, celestiall, pure desire   25
    Hath taken root, and grows, and doth not tire,
        There God a Commerce states, and sheds
        His Secret on their heads.

    This is the Heart he craves; and who so will
    But give it him, and grudge not; he shall feel   30
        That God is true, as herbs unseen
        Put on their youth and green.

The Palm-tree

Deare friend sit down, and bear awhile this shade
As I have yours long since; This Plant, you see
So prest and bow'd, before sin did degrade
Both you and it, had equall liberty

With other trees: but now shut from the breath   5
And air of *Eden*, like a male-content
It thrives no where. This makes these weights (like death
And sin) hang at him; for the more he's bent

The more he grows. Celestial natures still
Aspire for home; This *Solomon* of old   10
By flowers and carvings and mysterious skill
Of Wings, and Cherubims, and Palms foretold.

This is the life which hid above with Christ
In God, doth always (hidden) multiply,
And spring, and grow, a tree ne'r to be prick'd,   15
A Tree, whose fruit is immortality.

    The Palm-tree. 1 Cf. Herbert, "Love-unknown," l. 1.
    10–12 See the descriptions of the Temple, I Kings 6:29; Cf. Herbert, "Sion," ll. 1–5.
    13–16 Col. 3:3-4, "For ye are dead, and your life is hid with Christ in God. When Christ, who is our life, shall appear, then shall ye also appear with him in glory." See also Herbert, "Our life is hid with Christ in God."

Here Spirits that have run their race and fought
And won the fight, and have not fear'd the frowns
Nor lov'd the smiles of greatness, but have wrought
Their masters will, meet to receive their Crowns.   20

Here is the patience of the Saints: this Tree
Is water'd by their tears, as flowers are fed
With dew by night; but One you cannot see
Sits here and numbers all the tears they shed.

Here is their faith too, which if you will keep   25
When we two part, I will a journey make
To pluck a Garland hence, while you do sleep
And weave it for your head against you wake.

Joy

Be dumb course measures, jar no more; to me
There is no discord, but your harmony.
False, jugling sounds; a grone well drest, where care
Moves in disguise, and sighs afflict the air:
Sorrows in white; griefs tun'd; a sugerd Dosis   5
Of Wormwood, and a Deaths-head crown'd with Roses.
He weighs not your forc'd accents, who can have
A lesson plaid him by a winde or wave.
Such numbers tell their days, whose spirits be
Lull'd by those Charmers to a Lethargy.   10
   But as for thee, whose faults long since require
More eyes then stars; whose breath could it aspire
To equal winds: would prove too short: Thou hast
Another mirth, a mirth though overcast

---

21 Rev. 14:12, "Here is the patience of the saints: here are they that keep the commandments of God, and the faith of Jesus."
Joy. 5 *Dosis*: dose.
6 In Wisd. of Sol. 2:8, the wicked say, "Let us crown ourselves with rosebuds before they be withered" (F.).

With clouds and rain, yet full as calm and fine 15
As those *clear heights* which above tempests shine.
    Therefore while the various showers
    Kill and cure the tender flowers,
    While the winds refresh the year
    Now with clouds, now making clear, 20
    Be sure under pains of death
    To ply both thine eyes and breath.
        As leafs in Bowers
        Whisper their hours,
        And Hermit-wells 25
        Drop in their Cells:
    So in sighs and unseen tears
    Pass thy solitary years,
And going hence, leave written on some Tree,
Sighs make joy sure, and shaking fastens thee. 30

The Favour

O thy bright looks! thy glance of love
Shown, and but shown me from above!
Rare looks! that can dispense such joy
As without wooing wins the coy,
And makes him mourn, and pine and dye 5
Like a starv'd Eaglet, for thine eye
Some kinde herbs here, though low and far,
Watch for, and know their loving star.
O let no star compare with thee!
Nor any herb out-duty me! 10
So shall my nights and mornings be
Thy time to shine, and mine to see.

29–30 Cf. Herbert, "Affliction [V]," l. 20.
The Favour. See notes to "The Starre."

The Garland

Thou, who dost flow and flourish here below,
To whom a falling star and nine dayes glory,
Or some frail beauty makes the bravest shew,
Hark, and make use of this ensuing story.

  When first my youthful, sinfull age 5
    Grew master of my wayes,
  Appointing errour for my Page,
    And darknesse for my dayes;
  I flung away, and with full crie
    Of wild affections, rid 10
  In post for pleasures, bent to trie
    All gamesters that would bid.
  I played with fire, did counsell spurn,
    Made life my common stake;
  But never thought that fire would burn, 15
    Or that a soul could ake.
  Glorious deceptions, gilded mists,
    False joyes, phantastick flights,
  Peeces of sackcloth with silk-lists,
    These were my prime delights. 20
  I sought choice bowres, haunted the spring,
    Cull'd flowres and made me posies:
  Gave my fond humours their full wing,
    And crown'd my head with Roses.
  But at the height of this Careire 25
    I met with a dead man,
  Who noting well my vain Abear,
    Thus unto me began:
  Desist fond fool, be not undone,

The Garland. 9–11 Cf. Herbert, "Christmas," ll. 1–3.
24 See note to "Joy," l. 6.
27 *Abear*: going astray (from Lat. *aberrare*).
29–36 I Pet. 1:24–25, "For all flesh is as grass, and all the glory of man as the flower of grass. The grass withereth, and the flower thereof falleth away: But the word of the Lord endureth for ever." Cf. Isa. 40:6–8. Also I Pet. 5:4, "And when the chief Shepherd shall appear, ye shall receive a crown of glory that fadeth not away."

> What thou hast cut to day 30
> Will fade at night, and with this Sun
> Quite vanish and decay.

Flowres gather'd in this world, die here; if thou
Wouldst have a wreath that fades not, let them grow,
And grow for thee; who spares them here, shall find 35
A Garland, where comes neither rain, nor wind.

Love-sick

JESUS, my life! how shall I truly love thee?
O that thy Spirit would so strongly move me,
That thou wert pleas'd to shed thy grace so farr
As to make man all pure love, flesh a star!
A star that would ne'r set, but ever rise, 5
So rise and run, as to out-run these skies,
These narrow skies (narrow to me) that barre,
So barre me in, that I am still at warre,
At constant warre with them. O come and rend,
Or bow the heavens! Lord bow them and descend, 10
And at thy presence make these mountains flow,
These mountains of cold Ice in me! Thou art
Refining fire, O then refine my heart,
My foul, foul heart! Thou art immortall heat,
Heat motion gives; Then warm it, till it beat, 15
So beat for thee, till thou in mercy hear,
So hear that thou must open: open to
A sinfull wretch, A wretch that caus'd thy woe,
Thy woe, who caus'd his weal; so far his weal
That thou forgott'st thine own, for thou didst seal 20
Mine with thy blood, thy blood which makes thee mine,
Mine ever, ever; And me ever thine.

Love-sick. The interlinked lines imitate Herbert's "A Wreath."
13–15 See note to "Ascension-Hymn," ll. 30–36.

Trinity-Sunday

O holy, blessed, glorious three,
Eternall witnesses that be
In heaven, One God in trinitie!

As here on earth (when men with-stood,)
The Spirit, Water, and the Blood,   5
Made my Lords Incarnation good:

So let the *Anty-types* in me
Elected, bought and seal'd for free,
Be own'd, sav'd, *Sainted* by you three!

Psalme 104

Up, O my soul, and blesse the Lord. O God,
    My God, how great, how very great art thou!
Honour and majesty have their abode
        With thee, and crown thy brow.

Thou cloath'st thy self with light, as with a robe,   5
    And the high, glorious heav'ns thy mighty hand
Doth spread like curtains round about this globe
        Of Air, and Sea, and Land.

The beams of thy bright Chambers thou dost lay
    In the deep waters, which no eye can find;   10
The clouds thy chariots are, and thy path-way
        The wings of the swift wind.

In thy celestiall, gladsome messages
    Dispatch'd to holy souls, sick with desire
And love of thee, each willing Angel is   15
        Thy minister in fire.

Trinity-Sunday. Follows the form of Herbert's "Trinity-Sunday." See note to "Midnight," ll. 21–32.

Thy arm unmoveable for ever laid
    And founded the firm earth; then with the deep
As with a vail thou hidst it, thy floods plaid
    Above the mountains steep.   20

At thy rebuke they fled, at the known voice
    Of their Lords thunder they retir'd apace:
Some up the mountains past by secret ways,
    Some downwards to their place.

For thou to them a bound hast set, a bound   25
    Which (though but sand) keeps in and curbs whole seas:
There all their fury, fome and hideous sound
    Must languish and decrease.

And as thy care bounds these, so thy rich love
    Doth broach the earth, and lesser brooks lets forth,   30
Which run from hills to valleys, and improve
    Their pleasure and their worth.

These to the beasts of every field give drink;
    There the wilde asses swallow the cool spring:
And birds amongst the branches on their brink   35
    Their dwellings have and sing.

Thou from thy upper Springs above, from those
    Chambers of rain, where Heav'ns large bottles lie,
Doest water the parch'd hills, whose breaches close
    Heal'd by the showers from high.   40

Grass for the cattel, and herbs for mans use
    Thou mak'st to grow; these (blest by thee) the earth
Brings forth, with wine, oyl, bread: All which infuse
    To mans heart strength and mirth.

Psalme 104. 26 Cf. Herbert, "Providence," ll. 47–48.

Thou giv'st the trees their greenness, ev'n to those 45
    Cedars in *Lebanon*, in whose thick boughs
The birds their nests build; though the Stork doth choose
    The fir-trees for her house.

To the wilde goats the high hills serve for folds,
    The rocks give Conies a retyring place: 50
Above them the cool Moon her known course holds,
    And the Sun runs his race.

Thou makest darkness, and then comes the night;
    In whose thick shades and silence each wilde beast
Creeps forth, and pinch'd for food, with scent and sight 55
    Hunts in an eager quest.

The Lyons whelps impatient of delay
    Roar in the covert of the woods, and seek
Their meat from thee, who doest appoint the prey
    And feed'st them all the week. 60

This past, the Sun shines on the earth, and they
    Retire into their dens; Man goes abroad
Unto his work, and at the close of day
    Returns home with his load.

O Lord my God, how many and how rare 65
    Are thy great works! In wisdom hast thou made
Them all, and this the earth, and every blade
    Of grass, we tread, declare.

So doth the deep and wide sea, wherein are
    Innumerable, creeping things both small 70
And great: there ships go, and the shipmens fear
    The comely spacious Whale.

These all upon thee wait; that thou maist feed
    Them in due season: what thou giv'st, they take:
Thy bounteous open hand helps them at need, 75
    And plenteous meals they make.

When thou doest hide thy face (thy face which keeps
    All things in being) they consume and mourn:
When thou with-draw'st their breath, their vigour sleeps,
    And they to dust return.   80

Thou send'st thy spirit forth, and they revive,
    The frozen earths dead face thou dost renew.
Thus thou thy glory through the world dost drive,
    And to thy works art true.

Thine eyes behold the earth, and the whole stage   85
    Is mov'd and trembles, the hills melt and smoke
With thy least touch: lightnings and winds that rage
    At thy rebuke are broke.

Therefore as long as thou wilt give me breath
    I will in songs to thy great name imploy   90
That gift of thine, and to my day of death
    Thou shalt be all my joy.

Ile *spice* my thoughts with thee, and from thy word
    Gather true comforts; but the wicked liver
Shall be consum'd. O my soul, bless thy Lord!   95
    Yea, blesse thou him for ever!

The Bird

Hither thou com'st: the busie wind all night
Blew through thy lodging, where thy own warm wing
Thy pillow was. Many a sullen storm
(For which course man seems much the fitter born,)
    Rain'd on thy bed   5
    And harmless head.

The Bird. 4 *course*: with pun on coarse.

And now as fresh and chearful as the light
Thy little heart in early hymns doth sing
Unto that *Providence*, whose unseen arm
Curb'd them, and cloath'd thee well and warm.   10
    All things that be, praise him; and had
        Their lesson taught them, when first made.

So hills and valleys into singing break,
And though poor stones have neither speech nor tongue,
While active winds and streams both run and speak,   15
Yet stones are deep in admiration.
Thus Praise and Prayer here beneath the Sun
Make lesser mornings, when the great are done.

For each inclosed Spirit is a star
    Inlightning his own little sphaere,   20
Whose light, though fetcht and borrowed from far,
    Both mornings makes, and evenings there.

But as these Birds of light make a land glad,
Chirping their solemn Matins on each tree:
So in the shades of night some dark fowls be,   25
Whose heavy notes make all that hear them, sad.

    The Turtle then in Palm-trees mourns,
        While Owls and Satyrs howl;
    The pleasant Land to brimstone turns
        And all her streams grow foul.   30

Brightness and mirth, and love and faith, all flye,
Till the Day-spring breaks forth again from high.

13-18 Isa. 55:12, "For ye shall go out with joy, and be led forth with peace: the mountains and the hills shall break forth before you into singing, and all the trees of the field shall clap their hands."

27-32 Luke 1:78-79, "Through the tender mercy of our God; whereby the dayspring from on high hath visited us, To give light to them that sit in darkness and in the shadow of death, to guide our feet into the way of peace."

The Timber

Sure thou didst flourish once! and many Springs,
Many bright mornings, much dew, many showers
Past ore thy head: many light *Hearts* and *Wings*
Which now are dead, lodg'd in thy living bowers.

And still a new succession sings and flies; 5
Fresh Groves grow up, and their green branches shoot
Towards the old and still enduring skies,
While the low *Violet* thrives at their root.

But thou beneath the sad and heavy *Line*
Of death, dost waste all senseless, cold and dark; 10
Where not so much as dreams of light may shine,
Nor any thought of greenness, leaf or bark.

And yet (as if some deep hate and dissent,
Bred in thy growth betwixt high winds and thee,
Were still alive) thou dost great storms resent 15
Before they come, and know'st how near they be.

Else all at rest thou lyest, and the fierce breath
Of tempests can no more disturb thy ease;
But this thy strange resentment after death
Means onely those, who broke (in life) thy peace. 20

So murthered man, when lovely life is done,
And his blood freez'd, keeps in the Center still
Some secret sense, which makes the dead blood run
At his approach, that did the body kill.

And is there any murth'rer worse then sin? 25
Or any storms more foul then a lewd life?
Or what *Resentient* can work more within,
Then true remorse, when with past sins at strife?

The Timber. 27 *Resentient*: that which causes a change of feeling (*OED*).

He that hath left lifes vain joys and vain care,
And truly hates to be detain'd on earth,   *30*
Hath got an house where many mansions are,
And keeps his soul unto eternal mirth.

But though thus dead unto the world, and ceas'd
From sin, he walks a narrow, private way;
Yet grief and old wounds make him sore displeas'd,   *35*
And all his life a rainy, weeping day.

For though he should forsake the world, and live
As meer a stranger, as men long since dead;
Yet joy it self will make a right soul grieve
To think, he should be so long vainly lead.   *40*

But as shades set off light, so tears and grief
(Though of themselves but a sad blubber'd story)
By shewing the sin great, shew the relief
Far greater, and so speak my Saviors glory.

If my way lies through deserts and wilde woods;   *45*
Where all the Land with scorching heat is curst;
Better, the pools should flow with rain and floods
To fill my bottle, then I die with thirst.

Blest showers they are, and streams sent from above
Begetting *Virgins* where they use to flow;   *50*
And trees of life no other waters love,
These upper springs and none else make them grow.

---

31 John 14:2, "In my Father's house are many mansions."

48 *fill my bottle*: the speaker identifies himself with the child Ishmael (Gen. 21:9-21) whom God preserved in the wilderness by leading his mother Hagar to a well to fill her bottle.

49-56 Rev. 22:1-2, "And he shewed me a pure river of water of life, clear as crystal....and on either side of the river, was there the tree of life, which bare twelve manner of fruits, and yielded her fruit every month." Also Rev. 14:3-4, "they sung as it were a new song before the throne...the hundred and forty and four thousand, which were redeemed from the earth. These are they which were not defiled with women; for they are virgins."

But these chaste fountains flow not till we dye;
Some drops may fall before, but a clear spring
And ever running, till we leave to fling 55
Dirt in her way, will keep above the skie.

Rom. Cap. 6. ver. 7.

He that is dead, is freed from sin.

The Jews

When the fair year
Of your deliverer comes,
And that long frost which now benums
Your hearts shall thaw; when Angels here
Shall yet to man appear, 5
And familiarly confer
Beneath the Oke and Juniper:
When the bright *Dove*
Which now these many, many Springs
Hath kept above, 10
Shall with spread wings
Descend, and living waters flow
To make drie dust, and dead trees grow;

O then that I
Might live, and see the Olive bear 15
Her proper branches! which now lie
Scattered each where,
And without root and sap decay

The Jews. Cf. Herbert, "The Jews."
4–8 Cf. "Religion," ll. 5–8. Cf. Herbert, "Decay," ll. 6–8.
14–18 Rom. 11:24–26, "For if thou [the gentiles] wert cut out of the olive tree which is wild by nature, and wert grafted contrary to nature into a good olive tree: how much more shall these [Jews], which be the natural branches, be grafted into their own olive tree?... blindness in part is happened to Israel, until the fulness of the Gentiles be come in. And so all Israel shall be saved."

Cast by the husband-man away.
          And sure it is not far!
For as your fast and foul decays
Forerunning the bright morning-star,
Did sadly note his healing rayes
Would shine elsewhere, since you were blind,
And would be cross, when God was kinde:
          So by all signs
Our fulness too is now come in,
And the same Sun which here declines!
And sets, will few hours hence begin
To rise on you again, and look
Towards old *Mamre* and *Eshcols* brook.
          For surely he
Who lov'd the world so, as to give
His onely Son to make it free,
Whose spirit too doth mourn and grieve
To see man lost, will for old love
From your dark hearts this veil remove.

Faith sojourn'd first on earth in you,
You were the dear and chosen stock:
The Arm of God, glorious and true,
Was first reveal'd to be your rock.

You were the *eldest* childe, and when
Your stony hearts despised love,
The *youngest*, ev'n the Gentiles then
Were chear'd, your jealousie to move.

  22–24 See Mal. 4:2, "But unto you that fear my name shall the Sun of righteousness arise with healing in his wings."

  31 *Mamre*: Hebron, a portion of the land promised to Abraham, the Promised Land (Gen. 13:14–18); *Eshcols brook*: place in Hebron from which Joshua's spies cut the bunch of grapes as a sample of the products of the Promised Land (Num. 13:22–24), these grapes being a commonly accepted typological symbol for Christ. Cf. Herbert, "The Bunch of Grapes."

  32–35 See John 3:16.

  37 II Cor. 3:14, "But their minds were blinded: for until this day remaineth the same veil untaken away in the reading of the old testament; which veil is done away in Christ."

  41 See Deut. 32:4.

Thus, Righteous Father! doest thou deal
With Brutish men; Thy gifts go round
By turns, and timely, and so heal
The lost Son by the newly found.

Begging [II]

I, do not go! thou know'st, I'le dye!
My *Spring* and *Fall* are in thy book!
Or, if thou goest, do not deny
To lend me, though from far, one look!

My sins long since have made thee strange, 5
A very stranger unto me;
No morning-meetings since this change,
Nor evening-walks have I with thee.

Why is my God thus slow and cold,
When I am most, most sick and sad? 10
Well fare those blessed days of old
When thou didst hear the *weeping Lad!*

O do not thou do as I did,
Do not despise a Love-sick heart!
What though some clouds defiance bid 15
Thy Sun must shine in every part.

Though I have spoil'd, O spoil not thou!
Hate not thine own dear gift and token!
Poor birds sing best, and prettiest show,
When their nest is faln and broken. 20

Dear Lord! restore thy ancient peace,
Thy quikning friendship, mans bright wealth!
And if thou wilt not give me ease
From sicknesse, give my spirit health!

Begging [II]. 12 *weeping Lad*: Ishmael. See note to "Timber," l. 48.

Palm-Sunday

Come, drop your branches, strow the way
          Plants of the day!
Whom sufferings make most green and gay.

The King of grief, the man of sorrow
Weeping still, like the wet morrow,   5
Your shades and freshness comes to borrow.
Put on, put on your best array;
Let the joy'd rode make holy-day,
And flowers that into fields do stray,
Or secret groves, keep the high-way.   10

Trees, flowers and herbs; birds, beasts and stones,
That since man fell, expect with groans
To see the lamb, which all at once,
Lift up your heads and leave your moans!
          For here comes he   15
          Whose death will be
Mans life, and your full liberty.

Hark! how the children shril and high
          Hosanna cry,
Their joys provoke the distant skie,   20
Where thrones and Seraphins reply,
And their own Angels shine and sing
          In a bright ring:
          Such yong, sweet mirth
          Makes heaven and earth   25
Joyn in a joyful Symphony,

Palm-Sunday. See Matt. 21:8–16, John 12:12–15.
4 Cf. Herbert, "The Thankes-giving," l. 1.
11–17 See note to [And do they so?].

> The harmless, yong and happy Ass,
> Seen long before* this came to pass,
> Is in these joys an high partaker
> Ordain'd, and made to bear his Maker.   30
>
> Dear feast of Palms, of Flowers and Dew!
> Whose fruitful dawn sheds hopes and lights;
> Thy bright solemnities did shew,
> The third glad day through two sad nights.
>
> I'le get me up before the Sun,   35
> I'le cut me boughs off many a tree,
> And all alone full early run
> To gather flowers to wellcome thee.
>
> Then like the *Palm*, though wrong, I'le bear,
> I will be still a childe, still meek   40
> As the poor Ass, which the proud jear,
> And onely my dear *Jesus* seek.
>
> If I lose all, and must endure
> The proverb'd griefs of holy *Job*,
> I care not, so I may secure   45
> But one *green Branch* and a *white robe*.
>
> *Zechariah, chap. 9. ver. 9.

   27–30 See Zech. 9:9, and John 12:15, "Fear not, daughter of Sion: behold, thy King cometh, sitting on an ass's colt."
   35–38 Cf. Herbert, "Easter," ll. 19–22.
   46 Rev. 7:9, "After this...a great multitude...stood before the throne, and before the Lamb, clothed with white robes, and palms in their hands"; the Palm Sunday branches thus foreshadow the victory palms of the Saints.

Jesus weeping [I]

S. Luke 19. ver. 41.

Blessed, unhappy City! dearly lov'd
But still unkinde! art this day nothing mov'd!
    Art senseless still? O can'st thou sleep
    When God himself for thee doth weep!
    Stiff-necked *Jews*! your fathers breed   5
    That serv'd the calf, not *Abr'ams* seed,
    Had not the Babes *Hosanna* cryed,
    The stones had spoke, what you denyed.

Dear *Jesus* weep on! pour this latter
Soul-quickning rain, this living water   10
    On their dead hearts; but (O my fears!)
    They will drink blood, that despise tears.
    My dear, bright Lord! my Morning-star!
    Shed this live-dew on fields which far
    From hence long for it! shed it there,   15
    Where the starv'd earth groans for one tear!

This land, though with thy hearts blest extract fed,
Will nothing yield but thorns to wound thy head.

Jesus weeping [I]. Luke 19:41, "And when he was come near, he beheld the city [Jerusalem], and wept over it."

6 *calf*: the Golden Calf, made and worshiped by the Jews while Moses (*Abr'ams seed*) was receiving the Decalogue from God; see Exod. 32:1-6.

7 Matt. 21:15-16, "And when the chief priests and scribes saw...the children crying in the temple, and saying, Hosanna to the son of David; they were sore displeased....And Jesus saith unto them, Yea; have ye never read, Out of the mouth of babes and sucklings thou hast perfected praise?"

8 Luke 19:40, "I tell you that, if these should hold their peace, the stones would immediately cry out."

The Daughter of Herodias
St. Matth. chap. 14. ver. 6. &c.

Vain, sinful Art! who first did fit
Thy lewd loath'd *Motions* unto *sounds*,
And made grave *Musique* like wilde *wit*
Erre in loose airs beyond her bounds?

What fires hath he heap'd on his head?
Since to his sins (as needs it must,)
His *Art* adds still (though he be dead,)
New fresh accounts of blood and lust.

Leave then* yong Sorceress; the *Ice*
Will those coy spirits cast asleep,
Which teach thee now to please* his eyes
Who doth thy lothsome mother keep.

But thou hast pleas'd so well, he swears,
And gratifies thy sin with vows:
His shameless lust in publick wears,
And to thy soft arts strongly bows.

Skilful Inchantress and true bred!
Who out of evil can bring forth good?
Thy mothers nets in thee were spred,
She tempts to *Incest*, thou to *blood*.

*Her name was Salome; *in passing over a frozen river, the ice broke under her, and chopt off her head.*
*Herod Antipas.

The Daughter of Herodias. Salome asked for the head of John the Baptist as a reward.

Jesus weeping [II]

St. John chap. 11. ver. 35.

My dear, Almighty Lord! why dost thou weep?
Why dost thou groan and groan again,
    And with such deep,
Repeated sighs thy kinde heart pain,
Since the same sacred breath which thus   5
    Doth Mourn for us,
Can make mans dead and scatter'd bones
Unite, and raise up all that dyed, at once?

O holy groans! Groans of the Dove!
O healing tears! the tears of love!   10
    Dew of the dead! which makes dust move
And spring, how is't that you so sadly grieve,
    Who can relieve?

Should not thy sighs refrain thy store
Of tears, and not provoke to more?   15
    Since two afflictions may not raign
In one at one time, as some feign.
Those blasts, which o'r our heads here stray,
If showers then fall, will showers allay,
As those poor Pilgrims oft have tryed,   20
Who in this windy world abide.

Dear Lord! thou art all grief and love,
But which thou art most, none can prove.

Jesus weeping [II]. John 11:35, "Jesus wept." The context is Christ's raising Lazarus from the grave, John 11:11-44.

  7-8 Ezek. 37:5, 12, "Thus saith the Lord God unto these bones; Behold, I will cause breath to enter into you, and ye shall live....O my people, I will open your graves, and cause you to come up out of your graves."

  9 *Groans of the Dove*: Rom. 8:26, "the Spirit itself maketh intercession for us with groanings which cannot be uttered."

Thou griev'st, man should himself undo,
And lov'st him, though he works thy wo. 25

'Twas not that vast, almighty measure
Which is requir'd to make up life,
(Though purchas'd with thy hearts dear treasure,)
    Did breed this strife
Of grief and pity in thy brest, 30
The throne where peace and power rest:
But 'twas thy love that (without leave,)
Made thine eyes melt, and thy heart heave;
For though death cannot so undo
What thou hast done, (but though man too 35
Should help to spoil) thou canst restore
All better far then 'twas before;
Yet, thou so full of pity art
(Pity which overflows thy heart!)
That, though the Cure of all mans harm 40
Is nothing to thy glorious arm,
Yet canst not thou that free Cure do,
But thou must sorrow for him too.

    Then farewel joys! for while I live,
My business here shall be to grieve: 45
A grief that shall outshine all joys
For mirth and life, yet without noise.
A grief, whose silent dew shall breed
Lilies and Myrrhe, where the curs'd seed
Did sometimes rule. A grief so bright 50
'Twill make the Land of darkness light;
And while too many sadly roam,
Shall send me (*Swan-like*) singing home.

Psal. 73. ver. 25.

Whom have I in heaven but thee? and there is none upon earth, that I desire besides thee.

Providence

    Sacred and secret hand!
By whose assisting, swift command
The Angel shewd that holy Well,
Which freed poor *Hagar* from her fears,
And turn'd to smiles the begging tears 5
Of yong, distressed *Ishmael*.

    How in a mystick Cloud
(Which doth thy strange sure mercies shroud)
Doest thou convey man food and money
Unseen by him, till they arrive 10
Just at his mouth, that thankless hive
Which kills thy Bees, and eats thy honey!

    If I thy servant be
(Whose service makes ev'n captives free,)
A fish shall all my tribute pay, 15
The swift-wing'd Raven shall bring me meat,
And I, like Flowers shall still go neat,
As if I knew no moneth but *May*.

    I will not fear what man,
With all his plots and power can; 20
Bags that wax old may plundered be,
But none can sequester or let

Providence. 1–6 See note to "The Timber," l. 48.
   13–15 Matt. 17:24–27. When asked for tribute money, Christ commanded Peter to take up the first fish he caught, which had the tribute money in its mouth.
   16 The ravens fed Elijah in hiding, I Kings 17:6.
   18 Cf. Herbert, "Affliction [I]," l. 22.
   19–30 Matt. 6:19–20, 26, "Lay not up for yourselves treasures upon earth, where moth and rust doth corrupt, and where thieves break through and steal: But lay up for yourselves treasures in heaven.... Behold the fowls of the air: for they sow not, neither do they reap, nor gather into barns; yet your heavenly Father feedeth them."

  A state that with the Sun doth set
  And comes next morning fresh as he.

   Poor birds this doctrine sing,   25
  And herbs which on dry hills do spring
  Or in the howling wilderness
  Do know thy dewy morning-hours,
  And watch all night for mists or showers,
  Then drink and praise thy bounteousness.   30

   May he for ever dye
  Who trusts not thee! but wretchedly
  Hunts gold and wealth, and will not lend
  Thy service, nor his soul one day:
  May his Crown, like his hopes, be clay,   35
  And what he saves, may his foes spend!

   If all my portion here,
  The measure given by thee each year
  Were by my causless enemies
  Usurp'd; it never should me grieve   40
  Who know, how well thou canst relieve,
  Whose hands are open as thine eyes.

   Great King of love and truth!
  Who would'st not hate my froward youth,
  And wilt not leave me, when grown old;   45
  Gladly will I, like *Pontick* sheep,
  Unto their wormwood-diet keep
  Since thou hast made thy Arm my fold.

The Knot

  Bright Queen of Heaven! Gods Virgin Spouse!
   The glad worlds blessed maid!

46–47 Pliny, *Nat. Hist.* 27:28, notes that Pontic sheep eat wormwood (M.).

Whose beauty tyed life to thy house,
    And brought us saving ayd.

Thou art the true Loves-knot; by thee   5
    God is made our Allie,
And mans inferior Essence he
    With his did dignifie.

For Coalescent by that Band
    We are his body grown,   10
Nourished with favors from his hand
    Whom for our head we own.

And such a Knot, what arm dares loose,
    What life, what death can sever?
Which us in him, and him in us   15
    United keeps for ever.

The Ornament

The lucky world shewd me one day
Her gorgeous Mart and glittering store,
Where with proud haste the rich made way
To buy, the poor came to adore.

Serious they seem'd and bought up all   5
The latest Modes of pride and lust,
Although the first must surely fall,
And the last is most loathsome dust.

But while each gay, alluring wear
With idle hearts and busie looks   10
They viewd, (for idleness hath there
Laid up all her Archives and books.)

The Ornament. Cf. Herbert, "The Quip."

Quite through their proud and pompous file
Blushing, and in meek weeds array'd
With native looks, which knew no guile,   15
Came the sheep-keeping *Syrian* Maid.

Whom strait the shining Row all fac'd
Forc'd by her artless looks and dress,
While one cryed out, We are disgrac'd!
For she is bravest, you confess.   20

St. Mary Magdalen

Dear, beauteous Saint! more white then day,
When in his naked, pure array;
Fresher then morning-flowers which shew
As thou in tears dost, best in dew.
How art thou chang'd! how lively-fair,   5
Pleasing and innocent an air,
Not tutor'd by thy glass, but free,
Native and pure shines now in thee!
But since thy beauty doth still keep
Bloomy and fresh, why dost thou weep?   10
This dusky state of sighs and tears
Durst not look on those smiling years,
When *Magdal*-castle was thy seat,
Where all was sumptuous, rare and neat.
Why lies this *Hair* despised now   15
Which once thy care and art did show?
Who then did dress the much lov'd toy,
In *Spires*, *Globes*, angry *Curls* and coy,
Which with skill'd negligence seem'd shed
About thy curious, wilde, yong head?   20

---

16 *Maid*: Rachel; Gen. 29:9, 17, "Rachel was beautiful and well favoured."
St. Mary Magdalen. See Mark 14:3, "And being in Bethany in the house of Simon the leper... there came a woman having an alabaster box of ointment of spikenard very precious; and she brake the box, and poured it on his head."
13 See note on Donne, "To the Lady Magdalen Herbert," l. 2.

Why is this rich, this *Pistic* Nard
Spilt, and the box quite broke and marr'd?
What pretty sullenness did hast
Thy easie hands to do this waste?
Why art thou humbled thus, and low   25
As earth, thy lovely head dost bow?
Dear *Soul!* thou knew'st, flowers here on earth
At their Lords foot-stool have their birth;
Therefore thy wither'd self in haste
Beneath his blest feet thou didst cast,   30
That at the root of this green tree
Thy great decays restor'd might be.
Thy curious vanities and rare;
Odorous ointments kept with care,
And dearly bought, (when thou didst see   35
They could not cure, nor comfort thee,)
Like a wise, early Penitent
Thou sadly didst to him present,
Whose interceding, meek and calm
Blood is the worlds all-healing *Balm*.   40
This, this Divine Restorative
Call'd forth thy tears, which ran in live
And hasty drops, as if they had
(Their Lord so near) sense to be glad.
Learn, *Ladies*, here the faithful cure   45
Makes beauty lasting, fresh and pure;
Learn *Marys* art of tears, and then
Say, *You have got the day from men.*
Cheap, mighty Art! her Art of love,
Who lov'd much, and much more could move;   50

Her Art! whose memory must last
Till truth through all the world be past,
Till his abus'd, despised flame
Return to Heaven, from whence it came,
And send a fire down, that shall bring   55
Destruction on his ruddy wing.

21 *Pistic Nard*: spikenard.
50 Luke 7:47, "Her sins, which are many, are forgiven; for she loved much."

> Her Art! whose pensive, weeping eyes,
> Were once sins loose and tempting spies,
> But now are fixed stars, whose light
> Helps such dark straglers to their sight. 60
>
> Self-boasting *Pharisee*! how blinde
> A Judge wert thou, and how unkinde?
> It was impossible, that thou
> Who wert all false, should'st true grief know;
> Is't just to judge her faithful tears 65
> By that foul rheum thy false eye wears?
>
> *This Woman* (say'st thou) *is a sinner:*
> And sate there none such at thy dinner?
> Go Leper, go; wash till thy flesh
> Comes like a childes, spotless and fresh; 70
> He is still leprous, that still paints:
> Who Saint themselves, they are no *Saints*.

The Rain-bow

Still yong and fine! but what is still in view
We slight as old and soil'd, though fresh and new.
How bright wert thou, when *Shems* admiring eye
Thy burnisht, flaming *Arch* did first descry!
When *Terah, Nahor, Haran, Abram, Lot*, 5
The youthful worlds gray fathers in one knot,
Did with intentive looks watch every hour
For thy new light, and trembled at each shower!
When thou dost shine darkness looks white and fair,

61–72 *Pharisee*: Simon the Pharisee (Luke 7:39–50) complained that Jesus allowed himself to be touched by Mary, a sinner; he is identified with Simon the Leper (Mark 14:3).

70 II Kings 5:14. After Naaman the Leper bathed in Jordan "his flesh came again like unto the flesh of a little child."

The Rain-bow. 3 *Shem*: son of Noah.

5 See Gen. 11:24–27 for their generations.

Storms turn to Musick, clouds to smiles and air: 10
Rain gently spends his honey-drops, and pours
Balm on the cleft earth, milk on grass and flowers.
Bright pledge of peace and Sun-shine! the sure tye
Of thy Lords hand, the* object of his eye.
When I behold thee, though my light be dim, 15
Distant and low, I can in thine see him,
Who looks upon thee from his glorious throne
And mindes the Covenant 'twixt *All* and *One*.
O foul, deceitful men! my God doth keep
His promise still, but we break ours and sleep. 20
After the *Fall,* the first sin was in *Blood,*
And *Drunkenness* quickly did succeed the flood;
But since *Christ* dyed, (as if we did devise
To lose him too, as well as *Paradise,*)
These two grand sins we joyn and act together, 25
Though blood and drunkeness make but foul, foul weather.
Water (though both Heavens windows and the deep,
Full forty days o'r the drown'd world did weep,)
Could not reform us, and blood (in despight)
Yea Gods own blood we tread upon and slight. 30
So those bad daughters, which God sav'd from fire,
While *Sodom* yet did smoke, lay with their sire.

Then peaceful, signal bow, but in a cloud
Still lodged, where all thy unseen arrows shrowd,
I will on thee, as on a Comet look, 35
A Comet, the sad worlds ill-boding book;
Thy light as luctual and stain'd with woes
I'le judge, where penal flames sit mixt and close.
For though some think, thou shin'st but to restrain
Bold storms, and simply dost attend on rain, 40

10-11 Cf. Herbert, "Providence," ll. 117-18.
13-18 Gen. 9:16, "And the bow shall be in the cloud; and I will look upon it, that I may remember the everlasting covenant between God and every living creature of all flesh."
21-22 Cain's murder of Abel succeeded the Fall; Noah's drunkenness, the Flood.
27-28 See Gen. 7:11-12.
31-32 Lot's daughters, Gen. 19:30-38.

Yet I know well, and so our sins require,
Thou dost but Court cold rain, till *Rain* turns *Fire*.

*Gen. chap. 9. ver. 16.

The Seed growing secretly
S. Mark 4. 26.

If this worlds friends might see but once
What some poor man may often feel,
Glory, and gold, and Crowns and Thrones
They would soon quit and learn to kneel.

My dew, my dew! my early love,
My souls bright food, thy absence kills!
Hover not long, eternal Dove!
Life without thee is loose and spills.

Something I had, which long ago
Did learn to suck, and sip, and taste,
But now grown sickly, sad and slow,
Doth fret and wrangle, pine and waste.

O spred thy sacred wings and shake
One living drop! one drop life keeps!
If pious griefs Heavens joys awake,
O fill his bottle! thy childe weeps!

Slowly and sadly doth he grow,
And soon as left, shrinks back to ill;
O feed that life, which makes him blow
And spred and open to thy will!

41–42 Cf. Herbert, "Decay," ll. 16–20.
The Seed growing secretly. Mark 4:26–27, "So is the kingdom of God, as if a man should cast seed into the ground; And should sleep, and rise night and day, and the seed should spring and grow up, he knoweth not how."
16 *childe*: Ishmael. See note to "The Timber," l. 48.

For thy eternal, living wells
None stain'd or wither'd shall come near:
A fresh, immortal *green* there dwells,
And spotless *white* is all the wear.

Dear, secret *Greenness*! nurst below 25
Tempests and windes, and winter-nights,
Vex not, that but ône sees thee grow,
That *One* made all these lesser lights.

If those bright joys he singly sheds
On thee, were all met in one Crown, 30
Both Sun and Stars would hide their heads;
And Moons, though full, would get them down.

Let glory be their bait, whose mindes
Are all too high for a low Cell:
Though Hawks can prey through storms and winds, 35
The poor Bee in her hive must dwel.

Glory, the Crouds cheap tinsel still
To what most takes them, is a drudge;
And they too oft take good for ill,
And thriving vice for vertue judge. 40

What needs a Conscience calm and bright
Within it self an outward test?
Who breaks his glass to take more light,
Makes way for storms into his rest.

Then bless thy secret growth, nor catch 45
At noise, but thrive unseen and dumb;
Keep clean, bear fruit, earn life and watch,
Till the white winged Reapers come!

21-24 See note to "The Timber," ll. 49-56, and note to "Palm-Sunday," l. 46.
25-26 Cf. Herbert, "The Flowre," ll. 8-14.
48 Matt. 13:39, "the harvest is the end of the world; and the reapers are the angels."

[*As time one day by me did pass*]

As time one day by me did pass
    Through a large dusky glasse
    He held, I chanc'd to look
    And spyed his curious book
Of past days, where sad Heav'n did shed   5
A mourning light upon the dead.

Many disordered lives I saw
    And foul records which thaw
    My kinde eyes still, but in
    A fair, white page of thin   10
And ev'n, smooth lines, like the Suns rays,
Thy name was writ, and all thy days.

O bright and happy Kalendar!
    Where youth shines like a star
    All pearl'd with tears, and may   15
    Teach age, *The Holy way*;
Where through thick pangs, high agonies
Faith into life breaks, and death dies.

As some meek *night-piece* which day quails,
    To candle-light unveils: 20
    So by one beamy line
    From thy bright lamp did shine
In the same page thy humble grave
Set with green herbs, glad hopes and brave.

Here slept my thoughts dear mark! which dust   25
    Seem'd to devour, like rust;
    But dust (I did observe)
    By hiding doth preserve,

[*As time one day*...]. 2–3 I Cor. 13:12, "For now we see through a glass, darkly."

  As we for long and sure recruits,
   Candy with sugar our choice fruits.   *30*

O calm and sacred bed where lies
  In deaths dark mysteries
  A beauty far more bright
  Then the noons cloudless light;
For whose dry dust green branches bud   *35*
And robes are bleach'd in the *Lambs* blood.

Sleep happy ashes! (blessed sleep!)
  While haplesse I still weep;
  Weep that I have out-liv'd
  My life, and unreliev'd   *40*
Must (soul-lesse shadow!) so live on,
Though life be dead, and my joys gone.

[*Fair and yong light!*]

Fair and yong light! my guide to holy
Grief and soul-curing melancholy;
Whom living here I did still shun
As sullen night-ravens do the Sun,
And lead by my own foolish fire   *5*
Wandred through darkness, dens and mire.
How am I now in love with all
That I term'd then meer bonds and thrall,
And to thy name, which still I keep,
Like the surviving turtle, weep!   *10*
O bitter curs'd delights of men!
Our souls diseases first, and then
Our bodies: poysons that intreat
With fatal sweetness, till we eat;

---

29 *recruits*: supplies.
36 Rev. 7:14, "These are they which...have washed their robes, and made them white in the blood of the Lamb."
[*Fair and yong light!*]. Probably Vaughan's first wife, Catherine (H.).

How artfully do you destroy, 15
That kill with smiles and seeming joy?
If all the subtilties of vice
Stood bare before unpractic'd eyes,
And every act she doth commence
Had writ down its sad consequence, 20
Yet would not men grant, their ill fate
Lodged in those false looks, till too late.
O holy, happy, healthy heaven,
Where all is pure, where all is even,
Plain, harmless, faithful, fair and bright, 25
But what Earth breaths against thy light!
How blest had men been, had their *Sire*
Liv'd still in league with thy chaste fire,
Nor made life through her long descents,
A slave to lustful Elements! 30
I did once read in an old book
Soil'd with many a weeping look,
That the seeds of foul sorrows be
The finest things that are, to see.
So that fam'd fruit which made all dye 35
Seem'd fair unto the womans eye.
If these supplanters in the shade
Of Paradise, could make man fade,
How in this world should they deter
This world, their fellow-murtherer! 40
And why then grieve we to be sent
Home by our first fair punishment,
Without addition to our woes
And lingring wounds from weaker foes?
Since that doth quickly freedom win, 45
For he that's dead, is freed from sin.

O that I were winged and free
And quite undrest just now with thee,
Where freed souls dwel by living fountains

46 Rom. 6:7.

> On everlasting, spicy mountains! 50
> Alas! my God! take home thy sheep;
> This world but laughs at those that weep.

The Stone

Josh. chap. 24. ver. 27.

> I have it now:
> But where to act, that none shall know,
> Where I shall have no cause to fear
> An eye or ear,
> What man will show? 5
> If nights, and shades, and secret rooms,
> Silent as tombs,
> Will nor conceal nor assent to
> My dark designs, what shall I do?
> Man I can bribe, and woman will 10
> Consent to any gainful ill,
> But these dumb creatures are so true,
> No gold nor gifts can them subdue.
> *Hedges have ears*, said the old *sooth*,
> And ev'ry bush is somethings booth; 15
> This cautious fools mistake, and fear
> Nothing but man, when ambush'd there.
>
> But I (Alas!)
> Was shown one day in a strange glass
> That busie commerce kept between 20
> God and his Creatures, though unseen.

---

50 Song of Sol. 8:14, "Make haste, my beloved, and be thou like to a roe or to a young hart upon the mountains of spices," and Rev. 7:17, "For the Lamb... shall lead them unto living fountains of waters."

The Stone. Josh. 24:27, "And Joshua said unto all the people, Behold, this stone shall be a witness unto us; for it hath heard all the words of the Lord which he spake unto us: it shall be therefore a witness unto you, lest ye deny your God."

    They hear, see, speak,
And into loud discoveries break,
As loud as blood. Not that God needs
Intelligence, whose spirit feeds   25
All things with life, before whose eyes,
Hell and all hearts stark naked lyes.
But* he that judgeth as he hears,
He that accuseth none, so steers
His righteous course, that though he knows 30
All that man doth, conceals or shows,
Yet will not he by his own light
(Though both all-seeing and all right,)
Condemn men; but will try them by
A process, which ev'n mans own eye   35
Must needs acknowledge to be just.
    Hence sand and dust
Are shak'd for witnesses, and stones
Which some think dead, shall all at once
With one attesting voice detect   40
Those secret sins we least suspect.
For know, wilde men, that when you erre
Each thing turns Scribe and Register,
And in obedience to his Lord,
Doth your most private sins record.   45

    The *Law* delivered to the *Jews*,
Who promis'd much, but did refuse
Performance, will for that same deed
Against them by a *stone* proceed;
Whose substance, though 'tis hard enough, 50
Will prove their hearts more stiff and tuff.
But now, since God on himself took
What all mankinde could never brook,

 *John, chap. 5. ver. 30. 45.

28–29 John 5:30, 45, "I can of mine own self do nothing: as I hear, I judge: and my judgment is just.... Do not think that I will accuse you to the Father: there is one that accuseth you, even Moses, in whom ye trust."

If any (for he all invites)
His easie yoke rejects or slights, 55
The *Gospel* then (For 'tis his word
And not himself* shall judge the world)
Will by loose *Dust* that man arraign,
As one then dust more vile and vain.

*St. John, chap. 12. ver. 47, 48.

The dwelling-place
S. John, chap. 1. ver. 38, 39.

What happy, secret fountain,
Fair shade, or mountain,
Whose undiscover'd virgin glory
Boasts it this day, though not in story,
Was then thy dwelling? did some cloud 5
Fix'd to a Tent, descend and shrowd
My distrest Lord? or did a star
Becken'd by thee, though high and far,
In sparkling smiles haste gladly down
To lodge light, and increase her own? 10
My dear, dear God! I do not know
What lodged thee then, nor where, nor how;
But I am sure, thou dost now come
Oft to a narrow, homely room,
Where thou too hast but the least part, 15
My God, I mean *my sinful heart.*

55–56 John 12:47–48, "And if any man hear my words, and believe not, I judge him not: for I came not to judge the world, but to save the world. He that rejecteth me, and receiveth not my words, hath one that judgeth him: the word that I have spoken, the same shall judge him in the last day."

The dwelling-place. John 1:38–39, "They said unto him, Rabbi . . . where dwellest thou? He saith unto them, Come and see. They came and saw where he dwelt, and abode with him that day."

The Men of War
S. Luke, chap. 23. ver. 11.

If any have an ear
Saith holy* John, then let him hear.
He that into Captivity
Leads others, shall a Captive be.
Who with the sword doth others kill,　　　　5
A sword shall his blood likewise spill.
Here is the patience of the Saints,
And the true faith, which never faints.

Were not thy word (dear Lord!) my light,
How would I run to endless night,　　　　10
And persecuting thee and thine,
Enact for *Saints* my self and mine.
But now enlighten'd thus by thee,
I dare not think such villany;
Nor for a temporal self-end　　　　15
Successful wickedness commend.
For in this bright, instructing verse
Thy Saints are not the Conquerers;
But patient, meek, and overcome
Like thee, when set at naught and dumb.　　　　20
Armies thou hast in Heaven, which fight,
And follow thee all cloath'd in white,
But here on earth (though thou hast need)
Thou wouldst no legions, but wouldst bleed.

The Men of War. Luke 23:11, "And Herod with his men of war set him at nought, and mocked him, and arrayed him in a gorgeous robe, and sent him again to Pilate."

1-2 Rev. 13:9-10, "If any man have an ear, let him hear. He that leadeth into captivity shall go into captivity: he that killeth with the sword must be killed with the sword. Here is the patience and the faith of the saints."

12 Probably an allusion to the militant Puritan "Saints."

23-24 Cf. Matt. 26:53, "Thinkest thou that I cannot now pray to my Father, and he shall presently give me more than twelve legions of angels?"

The sword wherewith thou dost command 25
Is in thy mouth, not in thy hand,
And all thy Saints do overcome
By thy blood, and their Martyrdom.
But seeing Soldiers long ago
Did spit on thee, and smote thee too; 30
Crown'd thee with thorns, and bow'd the knee,
But in contempt, as still we see,
I'le marvel not at ought they do,
Because they us'd my Savior so;
Since of my *Lord* they had their will, 35
The servant must not take it ill.

Dear *Jesus* give me patience here,
And faith to see my Crown as near
And almost reach'd, because 'tis sure
If I hold fast and slight the *Lure*. 40
Give me humility and peace,
Contented thoughts, innoxious ease,
A sweet, revengeless, quiet minde,
And to my greatest haters kinde.
Give me, my God! a heart as milde 45
And plain, as when I was a childe;
That when *thy Throne is set*, and all
These *Conquerors* before it fall,
I may be found (preserv'd by thee)
Amongst that chosen company, 50
Who by no blood (here) overcame
But the blood of the *blessed Lamb*.

*Revel. cap. 13. ver. 10.

25–26 Rev. 19:15, "And out of his mouth goeth a sharp sword, that with it he should smite the nations"; the sword was usually interpreted as the Gospel.
51–52 Rev. 12:11, "And they overcame him [Satan] by the blood of the Lamb, and by the word of their testimony."

The Ass

St. Matt. 21.

Thou! who didst place me in this busie street
Of flesh and blood, where two ways meet:
The *One* of goodness, peace and life,
The *other* of death, sin and strife;
Where frail visibles rule the minde,
And present things finde men most kinde:
Where obscure cares the *mean* defeat,
And splendid vice destroys the *great*;
As thou didst set no law for me,
But that of perfect liberty,
Which neither tyres, nor doth corrode,
But is a *Pillow*, not a *Load*:
So give me grace ever to rest,
And build on it, because the best;
Teach both mine eyes and feet to move
Within those bounds set by thy love;
Grant I may soft and lowly be,
And minde those things I cannot see;
Tye me to faith, though above reason,
Who question power, they speak treason:
Let me thy Ass be onely wise
To carry, not search mysteries;
Who carries thee, is by thee lead,
Who argues, follows his own head.
To check bad motions, keep me still
Amongst the dead, where thriving ill
Without his brags and conquests lies,
And truth (opprest here) gets the prize.
At all times, whatsoe'r I do,
Let me not fail to question, who

The Ass. Matt. 21:1-11 tells of Christ's ride into Jerusalem on an ass. The ass was commonly taken as a symbol of patience and humility.
9-10 See Jas. 1:25.

Shares in the *act*, and puts me to't?
And if not thou, let not me do't.
Above all, make me love the poor,
Those burthens to the rich mans door,
Let me admire those, and be kinde 35
To low estates, and a low minde.
If the world offers to me ought,
That by thy book must not be sought,
Or though it should be lawful, may
Prove not expedient for thy way; 40
To shun that peril, let thy grace
Prevail with me to shun the place.
Let me be wise to please thee still,
And let men call me what they will.

   When thus thy milde, instructing hand 45
Findes thy poor *foal* at thy command,
When he from wilde is become wise,
And slights that most, which men most prize,
When all things here to thistles turn
Pricking his lips, till he doth mourn 50
And hang the head, sighing for those
Pastures of life, where the Lamb goes:
O then, just then! break or untye
These bonds, this sad captivity,
This leaden state, which men miscal 55
Being and life, but is dead thrall.
And when (O God!) the Ass is free,
In a state known to none but thee;
O let him by his *Lord* be led,
To living springs, and there be fed 60
Where light, joy, health and perfect peace
Shut out all pain and each disease;
Where death and frailty are forgotten,
And bones rejoyce, which once were broken!

   53–60 Job 39:5, 8, "Who hath sent out the wild ass free? or who hath loosed the bands of the wild ass?... The range of the mountains is his pasture, and he searcheth after every green thing."
   64 Ps. 51:8, "Make me to hear joy and gladness; that the bones which thou hast broken may rejoice."

The hidden Treasure

S. Matt. 13. 44.

What can the man do that succeeds the* King?
Even what was done before, and no new thing.
Who shews me but one grain of sincere light?
False stars and fire-drakes, the deceits of night
Set forth to fool and foil thee, do not boast; 5
Such Coal-flames shew but Kitchin-rooms at most.
And those I saw search'd through; yea those and all
That these three thousand years time did let fall
To blinde the eyes of lookers-back, and I
Now all is done, finde all is vanity. 10
Those secret searches, which afflict the wise,
Paths that are hidden from the *Vulturs* eyes
I saw at distance, and where grows that fruit
Which others onely grope for and dispute.
    The worlds lov'd wisdom (for the worlds friends think 15
There is none else) did not the dreadful brink
And precipice it leads to, bid me flie
None could with more advantage use, then I.
    Mans favorite sins, those tainting appetites
Which nature breeds, and some fine clay invites, 20
With all their soft, kinde arts and easie strains
Which strongly operate, though without pains,
Did not a greater beauty rule mine eyes,
None would more dote on, nor so soon entice.
But since these sweets are sowre, and poyson'd here 25
Where the impure seeds flourish all the year,
And private Tapers will but help to stray
Ev'n those, who *by them* would finde out the day,

The hidden Treasure. Matt. 13:44, "the kingdom of heaven is like unto treasure hid in a field; the which when a man hath found, he hideth, and for joy thereof goeth and selleth all that he hath, and buyeth that field."
  4 *fire-drakes*: fiery meteors.
  12–13 Job 28:7, "There is a path which no fowl knoweth, and which the vulture's eye hath not seen."

I'le seal my eyes up, and to thy commands
Submit my wilde heart, and restrain my hands;   30
I will do nothing, nothing know, nor see
But what thou bidst, and shew'st, and teachest me.
Look what thou gav'st; all that I do restore
But for one thing, though purchas'd once before.

*Ecclesiastes, chap. 2. 12.

Childe-hood

I cannot reach it; and my striving eye
Dazles at it, as at eternity.
    Were now that Chronicle alive,
Those white designs which children drive,
And the thoughts of each harmless hour,   5
With their content too in my pow'r,
Quickly would I make my path even,
And by meer playing go to Heaven.
    Why should men love
A Wolf, more then a Lamb or Dove?   10
Or choose hell-fire and brimstone streams
Before bright stars, and Gods own beams?
Who kisseth thorns, will hurt his face,
But flowers do both refresh and grace,
And sweetly living (*fie on men!*)   15
Are when dead, medicinal then.
If seeing much should make staid eyes,
And long experience should make wise;
Since all that age doth teach, is ill,
Why should I not love childe-hood still?   20
Why if I see a rock or shelf,
Shall I from thence cast down my self,

Childe-hood. See notes to "The Retreate."
14–16 Cf. Herbert, "Life," ll. 13–15.

> Or by complying with the world,
> From the same precipice be hurl'd?
> Those observations are but foul
> Which make me wise to lose my soul.
>
> And yet the *Practice* worldlings call
> Business and weighty action all,
> Checking the poor childe for his play,
> But gravely cast themselves away.
>
>   Dear, harmless age! the short, swift span,
> Where weeping virtue parts with man;
> Where love without lust dwells, and bends
> What way we please, without self-ends.
>
> An age of mysteries! which he
> Must live twice, that would Gods face see;
> Which *Angels* guard, and with it play,
> Angels! which foul men drive away.
>
> How do I study now, and scan
> Thee, more then ere I studyed man,
> And onely see through a long night
> Thy edges, and thy bordering light!
> O for thy Center and mid-day!
> For sure that is the *narrow way*.

---

36 *live twice*: Mark 10:15, "Whosoever shall not receive the kingdom of God as a little child, he shall not enter therein."

44 *narrow way*: Matt. 7:14, "Strait is the gate, and narrow is the way, which leadeth unto life."

The Night

John 3.2.

    Through that pure *Virgin-shrine*,
That sacred vail drawn o'r thy glorious noon,
That men might look and live as Glo-worms shine,
        And face the Moon:
    Wise *Nicodemus* saw such light   5
As made him know his God by night.

    Most blest believer he!
Who in that land of darkness and blinde eyes
Thy long expected healing wings could see,
        When thou didst rise,   10
    And what can never more be done,
Did at mid-night speak with the Sun!

    O who will tell me, where
He found thee at that dead and silent hour!
What hallow'd solitary ground did bear   15
        So rare a flower,
    Within whose sacred leafs did lie
The fulness of the Deity.

    No mercy-seat of gold,
No dead and dusty *Cherub*, nor carv'd stone,   20
But his own living works did my Lord hold
        And lodge alone;

The Night. John 3:1-2, "There was a man of the Pharisees, named Nicodemus, a ruler of the Jews: The same came to Jesus by night, and said unto him, Rabbi, we know that thou art a teacher come from God."

    2 *vail*: Heb. 10:20, "By a new and living way, which he hath consecrated for us, through the veil, that is to say, his flesh."

    3 *That man might look and live*: Exod. 33:20, "And he [God] said, Thou canst not see my face: for there shall no man see me, and live;" *Glo-worms shine* only under the moon (not the sun).

    9 See note to "The Jews," ll. 22-24.

    19-22 Exod. 25:17-18, "And thou shalt make a mercy seat of pure gold.... And thou shalt make two cherubims of gold." Cf. also Herbert, "Sion," ll. 1-5.

> Where *trees* and *herbs* did watch and peep
> And wonder, while the *Jews* did sleep.
>
> Dear night! this worlds defeat, 25
> The stop to busie fools; cares check and curb;
> The day of Spirits; my souls calm retreat
> Which none disturb!
> *Christs** progress, and his prayer time;
> The hours to which high Heaven doth chime. 30
>
> Gods silent, searching flight:
> When my Lords head is fill'd with dew, and all
> His locks are wet with the clear drops of night;
> His still, soft call;
> His knocking time; The souls dumb watch, 35
> When Spirits their fair kinred catch.
>
> Were all my loud, evil days
> Calm and unhaunted as is thy dark Tent,
> Whose peace but by some *Angels* wing or voice
> Is seldom rent; 40
> Then I in Heaven all the long year
> Would keep, and never wander here.
>
> But living where the Sun
> Doth all things wake, and where all mix and tyre
> Themselves and others, I consent and run 45
> To ev'ry myre,
> And by this worlds ill-guiding light,
> Erre more then I can do by night.

29 Mark 1:35, "And in the morning, rising up a great while before day, he went out...and...prayed." Luke 21:37, "at night he went out, and abode in the mount that is called the mount of Olives."

32–35 Song of Sol. 5:2, "I sleep, but my heart waketh: it is the voice of my beloved that knocketh, saying, Open to me, my sister, my love, my dove, my undefiled: for my head is filled with dew, and my locks with the drops of the night." Also Rev. 3:20, "Behold, I stand at the door, and knock," and I Kings 19:12 alluding to God speaking to Elijah in "a still small voice."

There is in God (some say)
A deep, but dazling darkness; As men here   50
Say it is late and dusky, because they
    See not all clear;
  O for that night! where I in him
  Might live invisible and dim.

*Mark, chap. 1. 35. Luke, chap. 21. 37.

Abels blood

Sad, purple well! whose bubling eye
Did first against a Murth'rer cry;
Whose streams still vocal, still complain
    Of bloody *Cain*,
And now at evening are as red   5
As in the morning when first shed.
    If single thou
(Though single voices are but low,)
Could'st such a shrill and long cry rear
As speaks still in thy makers ear,   10
What thunders shall those men arraign
Who cannot count those they have slain,
Who bath not in a shallow flood,
But in a deep, wide sea of blood?
A sea, whose lowd waves cannot sleep,   15
But *Deep* still calleth upon *deep*:
Whose urgent *sound* like unto that
Of many waters, beateth at

---

49 *some say*: cf. Dionysius the Areopagite, Epist. v, *Opera*, Pat. Lat. I, cols. 1073–74 (M.). Also, Thomas Vaughan, *Lumen de Lumine* (Waite, p. 269): "there is above all degree of intelligence a certain infinite, inaccessible fire or light. Dionysius calls it Divine Darkness, because it is invisible and incomprehensible."

Abels blood. Cf. Gen. 4:10, "And he [God] said, What hast thou done? the voice of thy brother's blood crieth unto me from the ground." The poem considers the modern martyrs of the Civil War, and especially the slain King Charles (ll. 33–37) in terms of the slain Abel and the crucified Christ, his antitype.

16 Ps. 42:7, "Deep calleth unto deep at the noise of thy waterspouts."
17–18 Rev. 1:15, "his voice as the sound of many waters."

>   The everlasting doors above,
>   Where souls behind the altar move,   20
>   And with one strong, incessant cry
>   Inquire *How long?* of the most high.
>   Almighty Judge!
>   At whose just laws no just men grüdge;
>   Whose blessed, sweet commands do pour   25
>   Comforts and joys, and hopes each hour
>   On those that keep them; O accept
>   Of his vow'd heart, whom thou hast kept
>   From bloody men! and grant, I may
>   That sworn memorial duly pay   30
>   To thy bright arm, which was my light
>   And leader through thick death and night!
>   I, may that flood,
>   That proudly spilt and despis'd blood,
>   Speechless and calm, as Infants sleep!   35
>   Or if it watch, forgive and weep
>   For those that spilt it! May no cries
>   From the low earth to high Heaven rise,
>   But what (like his, whose blood peace brings)
>   Shall (when they rise) *speak better things*   40
>   Then *Abels* doth! may *Abel* be
>   Still single heard, while these agree
>   With his milde blood in voice and will,
>   *Who* pray'd for those that did him kill!

Righteousness

>   Fair, solitary path! Whose blessed shades
>   The old, white Prophets planted first and drest:

19-24 Ps. 24:7, "Lift up your heads, O ye gates; and be ye lift up, ye everlasting doors." Also Rev. 6:10, "And they cried with a loud voice, saying, How long, O Lord, holy and true, dost thou not judge and avenge our blood on them that dwell on the earth?"

40-41 Heb. 12:24, "And to Jesus the mediator of the new covenant, and to the blood of sprinkling, that speaketh better things than that of Abel."

Righteousness. The poem is a tissue of biblical allusions, notably from Psalm 15 and Matthew 5-7, the Sermon on the Mount; its rhetorical form owes much to Herbert's "Constancy."

1 *path*: Ps. 23:3, "he leadeth me in the paths of righteousness."

Leaving for us (whose goodness quickly fades,)
A shelter all the way, and bowers to rest.

Who is the man that walks in thee? who loves
Heav'ns secret solitude, those fair abodes
Where turtles build, and careless sparrows move
Without to morrows evils and future loads?

Who hath the upright heart, the single eye,
The clean, pure hand, which never medled pitch?
Who sees *Invisibles*, and doth comply
With hidden treasures that make truly rich?

    He that doth seek and love
        The things above,
Whose spirit ever poor, is meek and low;
    Who simple still and wise,
        Still homewards flies,
Quick to advance, and to retreat most slow.

    Whose acts, words and pretence
        Have all one sense,
One aim and end; who walks not by his sight:
    Whose eyes are both put out,
        And goes about
Guided by faith, not by exterior light.

    Who spills no blood, nor spreds
        Thorns in the beds
Of the distrest, hasting their overthrow;

7–8 Matt. 6:26, "Behold the fowls of the air: for they sow not, neither do they reap ... yet your heavenly Father feedeth them."

9 *upright heart*: see Ps. 7:10; *single eye*: Matt. 6:22, "The light of the body is the eye: if therefore thine eye be single, thy whole body shall be full of light."

10 Ps. 24:4, "He that hath clean hands, and a pure heart." Also Ecclus. 13:1, "He that toucheth pitch shall be defiled" (*Apocrypha*).

11 *Invisibles*: Rom. 1:20, "For the invisible things of him from the creation of the world are clearly seen."

12–15 *hidden treasures*: Matt. 5:3, 5, "Blessed are the poor in spirit.... Blessed are the meek."

21–24 Heb. 11:1, "Now faith is the substance of things hoped for, the evidence of things not seen." Also II Cor. 5:7, "For we walk by faith, not by sight."

>   Making the time they had
>   Bitter and sad
>   Like *Chronic* pains, which surely kill, though slow.   *30*

>   Who knows earth nothing hath
>   Worth love or wrath,
>   But in his *hope* and *Rock* is ever glad.
>   Who seeks and follows peace,
>   When with the ease   *35*
>   And health of conscience it is to be had.

>   Who bears his cross with joy
>   And doth imploy
>   His heart and tongue in prayers for his foes;
>   Who lends, not to be paid,   *40*
>   And gives full aid
>   Without that bribe which Usurers impose.

>   Who never looks on man
>   Fearful and wan,
>   But firmly trusts in God; the great mans measure   *45*
>   Though high and haughty must
>   Be ta'en in dust,
>   But the good man is Gods peculiar treasure.

>   Who doth thus, and doth not
>   These good deeds blot   *50*
>   With bad, or with neglect; and heaps not wrath
>   By secret filth, nor feeds
>   Some snake, or weeds,
>   Cheating himself; That man walks in this path.

   33 *hope*: I Tim. 1:1, "Lord Jesus Christ, which is our hope." *Rock*: I Cor. 10:4, "for they drank of that spiritual Rock ... and that Rock was Christ."
   38–42 Matt. 5:44, "Love your enemies...pray for them which despitefully use you, and persecute you." Also Luke 6:35, "lend, hoping for nothing again."
   48 Exod. 19:5, "Now therefore, if ye will obey my voice indeed, and keep my covenant, then ye shall be a peculiar treasure unto me."

Anguish

My God and King! to thee
 I bow my knee,
I bow my troubled soul, and greet
With my foul heart thy holy feet.
Cast it, or tread it! It shall do   5
Even what thou wilt, and praise thee too.

My God, could I weep blood,
 Gladly I would;
Or if thou wilt give me that Art,
Which through the eyes pours out the hart,   10
I will exhaust it all, and make
My self all tears, a weeping lake.

O! 'tis an easie thing
 To write and sing;
But to write true, unfeigned verse   15
Is very hard! O God, disperse
These weights, and give my spirit leave
To act as well as to conceive!

O my God, hear my cry;   20
 Or let me dye! ———

Tears

O when my God, my glory brings
 His white and holy train,
Unto those clear and living *Springs*,
 Where comes no *stain!*

Anguish. 13–16 Cf. Herbert, "Praise [I]," and "A true Hymne."
Tears. See note to "The Timber," ll. 49–56, and to "The Ass."

Where all is *light*, and *flowers*, and *fruit*, 5
    And *joy*, and *rest*,
Make me amongst them ('tis my suit!)
    The last one, and the least.

And when they all are fed, and have
    Drunk of thy living stream, 10
Bid thy poor Ass (with tears I crave!)
    Drink after them.

Thy love claims highest thanks, my sin
    The lowest pitch:
But if he pays, who *loves much*, then 15
    Thou hast made beggers rich.

Jacobs Pillow, and Pillar

I see the Temple in thy Pillar rear'd,
And that dread glory, which thy children fear'd,
In milde, clear visions, without a frown,
Unto thy solitary self is shown.
'Tis number makes a Schism: throngs are rude, 5
And God himself dyed by the multitude.
This made him put on clouds, and fire and smoke,
Hence he in thunder to thy Off spring spoke;
The small, still voice, at some low Cottage knocks,
But a strong wind must break thy lofty rocks. 10

Jacobs Pillow, and Pillar. Jacob, fleeing from his brother Esau, saw a vision of a ladder with angels ascending and descending, and heard God's voice promising to protect him and his seed (Gen. 28:10–22). Then Jacob (28:18–19) "rose up early in the morning, and took the stone that he had put for his pillows, and set it up for a pillar, and poured oil upon the top of it. And he called the name of that place Beth-el."

7–8 Exod. 19:18, "And mount Sinai was altogether on a smoke, because the Lord descended upon it in fire...and the whole mount quaked greatly" when God delivered the Decalogue to Moses.

9 *small, still voice*: God spoke so to Elijah, I Kings 19:12.

The first true worship of the worlds great King
From private and selected hearts did spring,
But he most willing to save all mankinde,
Inlarg'd that light, and to the bad was kinde.
Hence Catholick or Universal came   15
A most fair notion, but a very name.
For this rich Pearl, like some more common stone,
When once made publique, is esteem'd by none.
Man slights his Maker, when familiar grown,
And sets up laws, to pull his honor down.   20
This God forsaw: And when slain by the crowd
(Under that stately and mysterious cloud
Which his death scatter'd) he foretold the place,
And form to serve him in, should be true grace
And the meek heart, not in a Mount, nor at   25
Jerusalem, with blood of beasts, and fat.
A heart is that dread place, that awful Cell,
That secret Ark, where the milde Dove doth dwell
When the proud waters rage: when Heathens rule
By Gods permission, and man turns a Mule.   30
This little *Goshen*, in the midst of night,
And Satans seat, in all her Coasts hath light,
Yea *Bethel* shall have Tithes (saith *Israels* stone)
And vows and visions, though her foes crye, None.
Thus is the solemn temple sunk agen   35
Into a Pillar, and conceal'd from men.
And glory be to his eternal Name!
Who is contented, that this holy flame
Shall lodge in such a narrow pit, till he
With his strong arm turns our captivity.   40

21–23 I Cor. 10:1–2, "all our fathers were under the cloud.... And were all baptized unto Moses in the cloud and in the sea."

25–30 I Cor. 3:16, "Know ye not that ye are the temple of God, and that the Spirit of God dwelleth in you?"

31–32 *Goshen*: When the plague of darkness was visited upon Egypt, only the Israelites who dwelt in the Land of Goshen "had light in their dwellings."

33–34 Gen. 28:22, After his dream Jacob vowed, "this stone, which I have set for a pillar, shall be God's house: and of all that thou shalt give me I will surely give the tenth unto thee." Lines 31 ff. may allude to the Anglican Church's sufferings under Puritan rule.

But blessed *Jacob*, though thy sad distress
Was just the same with ours, and nothing less,
For thou a brother, and blood-thirsty too
Didst flye,* whose children wrought thy childrens wo:
Yet thou in all thy solitude and grief,   45
On stones didst sleep and found'st but cold relief;
Thou from the Day-star a long way didst stand
And all that distance was Law and command.
But we a healing Sun by day and night,
Have our sure Guardian, and our leading light;   50
What thou didst hope for and believe, we finde
And feel a friend most ready, sure and kinde.
Thy pillow was but type and shade at best,
But we the substance have, and on him rest.

Obadiah chap. I. 11. Amos chap. I. 11:

The Agreement

I wrote it down. But one that saw
And envyed that Record, did since
Such a mist over my minde draw,
It quite forgot that purpos'd glimpse.
    I read it sadly oft, but still   5
    Simply believ'd, 'twas not my Quill;

At length, my lifes kinde Angel came,
And with his bright and busie wing
Scatt'ring that cloud, shewd me the flame
Which strait, like Morning-stars did sing,   10
    And shine, and point me to a place,
    Which all the year sees the Suns face.

The Agreement. John 6:44, "No man can come to me, except the Father which hath sent me draw him: and I will raise him up at the last day." The speaker considers the evidences of his election.
  6 *not my Quill*: not my writing, does not pertain to me.
  10 *Morning-stars*: See Job 38:7.

O beamy book! O my mid-day
Exterminating fears and night!
The mount, whose white Ascendents may
Be in conjunction with true light!
    My thoughts, when towards thee they move,
    Glitter and kindle with thy love.

Thou art the oyl and the wine-house:
Thine are the present healing leaves,
Blown from the tree of life to us
By his breath whom my dead heart heaves.
    Each page of thine hath true life in't,
    And Gods bright minde exprest in print.

Most modern books are blots on thee,
Their doctrine chaff and windy fits:
Darken'd along, as their scribes be,
With those foul storms, when they were writ;
    While the mans zeal lays out and blends
    Onely self-worship and self-ends.

Thou art the faithful, pearly rock,
The Hive of beamy, living lights,
Ever the same, whose diffus'd stock
Entire still, wears out blackest nights.
    Thy lines are rays, the true Sun sheds;
    Thy leaves are healing wings he spreads.

For until thou didst comfort me,
I had not one poor word to say:
Thick busie clouds did multiply,
And said, I was no childe of day;
    They said, my own hands did remove
    That candle given me from above.

---

13 *beamy book*: the Bible.
42 *candle*: Prov. 20:27, "The spirit of man is the candle of the Lord."

O God! I know and do confess
My sins are great and still prevail,
Most heynous sins and numberless!
But thy *Compassions* cannot fail.
    If thy sure mercies can be broken,
    Then all is true, my foes have spoken.

But while time runs, and after it
Eternity, which never ends,
Quite through them both, still infinite
Thy Covenant by *Christ* extends;
    No sins of frailty, nor of youth
    Can foil his merits, and thy truth.

And this I hourly finde, for thou
Dost still renew, and purge and heal:
Thy care and love, which joyntly flow
New Cordials, new *Cathartics* deal.
    But were I once cast off by thee
    I know (my God!) this would not be.

Wherefore with tears (tears by thee sent)
I beg, my faith may never fail!
And when in death my speech is spent,
O let that silence then prevail!
    O chase in that *cold calm* my foes,
    And hear my hearts last private throws!

So thou, who didst the work begin
(For *I till* drawn came not to thee*)
Wilt finish it, and by no sin
Will thy free mercies hindred be.
    For which, O God, I onely can
    Bless thee, and blame unthankful man.

**St. John, chap. 6. ver. 44. 65.*

The day of Judgement [II]

O day of life, of light, of love!
The onely day dealt from above!
A day so fresh, so bright, so brave
Twill shew us each forgotten grave,
And make the dead, like flowers, arise   5
Youthful and fair to see new skies.
All other days, compar'd to thee,
Are but lights weak minority,
They are but veils, and Cypers drawn
Like Clouds, before thy glorious dawn.   10
O come, arise, shine, do not stay
          Dearly lov'd day!
The fields are long since white, and I
With earnest groans for freedom cry,
My fellow-creatures too say, *Come!*   15
And stones, though speechless, are not dumb.
When shall we hear that glorious voice
          Of life and joys?
That voice, which to each secret bed
          Of my Lords dead,   20
Shall bring true day, and make dust see,
The way to immortality.
When shall those first white Pilgrims rise,
Whose holy, happy Histories
(Because they sleep so long) some men   25
Count but the blots of a vain pen?
          Dear Lord! make haste,
Sin every day commits more waste,
And thy old enemy, which knows
His time is short, more raging grows.   30
Nor moan I onely (though profuse)
Thy Creatures bondage and abuse;

The day of Judgement [II]. See note to [And do they so?].
13 John 4:35, "look on the fields; for they are white already to harvest."

> But what is highest sin and shame,
> The vile despight done to thy name;
> The forgeries, which impious wit   35
> And power force on Holy Writ,
> With all detestable designs
> That may dishonor those pure lines.
> O God! though mercy be in thee
> The greatest attribute we see,   40
> And the most needful for our sins;
> Yet, when thy mercy nothing wins
> But meer disdain, let not man say
> *Thy arm doth sleep*; but write this day
> Thy judging one: Descend, descend!   45
> Make all things new! and without end!

Psalm 65

> *Sions* true, glorious God! on thee
> Praise waits in all humility.
> All flesh shall unto thee repair,
> To thee, O thou that hearest prayer!
> But sinful words and works still spread   5
> And over-run my heart and head;
> Transgressions make me foul each day,
> O purge them, purge them all away!
>
>   Happy is he! whom thou wilt choose
> To serve thee in thy blessed house!   10
> Who in thy holy Temple dwells,
> And fill'd with joy, thy goodness tells!
> King of Salvation! by strange things
> And terrible, Thy Justice brings
> Man to his duty. Thou alone   15
> Art the worlds hope, and but thee, none.

44 Isa. 51:9, "Awake, awake, put on strength, O arm of the Lord."

Sailers that flote on flowing seas
Stand firm by thee, and have sure peace.
Thou still'st the loud waves, when most wild
And mak'st the raging people mild. 20
Thy arm did first the mountains lay
And girds their rocky heads this day.
The most remote, who know not thee,
At thy great works astonish'd be.
The *outgoings* of the *Even* and *Dawn*, 25
In *Antiphones* sing to thy Name
Thou visit'st the low earth, and then
Water'st it for the sons of men,
Thy upper river, which abounds
With fertil streams, makes rich all grounds, 30
And by thy mercies still supplied
The sower doth his bread provide.
Thou water'st every ridge of land
And settlest with thy secret hand
The furrows of it; then thy warm 35
And opening showers (restrain'd from harm)
Soften the mould, while all unseen
The blade grows up alive and green.
The year is with thy goodness crown'd,
And all thy paths drop fatness round, 40
They drop upon the wilderness,
For thou dost even the desarts bless,
And hills full of springing pride,
Wear fresh adornments on each side.
The fruitful flocks fill every Dale, 45
And purling Corn doth cloath the Vale;
They shout for joy, and joyntly sing,
Glory to the eternal King!

The Throne

Revel. chap. 20. ver. 11.

When with these eyes clos'd now by thee,
      But then restor'd,
The great and white throne I shall see
      Of my dread Lord:
And lowly kneeling (for the most   5
      Stiff then must kneel)
Shall look on him, at whose high cost
      (Unseen) such joys I feel.

What ever arguments, or skill
      Wise heads shall use,   10
Tears onely and my blushes still
      I will produce.
And should those speechless beggers fail,
      Which oft have won;
Then taught by thee, I will prevail,   15
      And say, *Thy will be done!*

Death [II]

Though since thy first sad entrance by
      Just *Abels* blood,
'Tis now six thousand years well nigh,
And still thy sov'rainty holds good:
Yet by none art thou understood.   5
We talk and name thee with much ease
      As a tryed thing,

The Throne. Rev. 20:11–12, "And I saw a great white throne, and him that sat on it, from whose face the earth and the heaven fled away.... And I saw the dead, small and great, stand before God... and the dead were judged out of those things which were written in the books, according to their works."

And every one can slight his lease
As if it ended in a Spring,
Which shades and bowers doth rent-free bring.   10

To thy dark land these heedless go:
                But there was *One*,
Who search'd it quite through to and fro,
And then returning, like the Sun
Discover'd all, that there is done.   15

And since his death, we throughly see
                All thy dark way;
Thy shades but thin and narrow be,
Which his first looks will quickly fray:
Mists make but triumphs for the day.   20

As harmless violets, which give
                Their virtues here
For salves and syrups, while they live,
Do after calmly disappear,
And neither grieve, repine, nor fear: 25

So dye his servants; and as sure
                Shall they revive.
Then let not dust your eyes obscure,
But lift them up, where still alive,
Though fled from you, their spirits hive.   30

The Feast

O come away,
Make no delay,
        Come while my heart is clean and steddy!

The Feast. The poem treats the Communion as a celebration of Christ's Passion and as a type of the heavenly "Marriage Supper of the Lamb."

While Faith and Grace
Adorn the place,
 Making dust and ashes ready.

No bliss here lent
Is permanent,
 Such triumphs poor flesh cannot merit;
Short sips and sights
Endear delights,
 Who seeks for more, he would inherit.

Come then true bread,
Quickning the dead,
 Whose eater shall not, cannot dye,
Come, antedate
On me that state
 Which brings poor dust the victory.

I, victory
Which from thine eye
 Breaks as the day doth from the east,
When the spilt dew,
Like tears doth shew
 The sad world wept to be releast.

Spring up, O wine,
And springing shine
 With some glad message from his heart,
Who did, when slain,
These means ordain
 For me to have in him a part.

Such a sure part
In his blest heart,

---

 12 *inherit*: enjoy the heavenly inheritance now.
 13 *true bread*: John 6:51, "I am the living bread which came down from heaven: if any man eat of this bread, he shall live for ever."

> The well, where living waters spring,
> That with it fed
> Poor dust though dead 35
> Shall rise again, and live and sing.
>
> O drink and bread
> Which strikes death dead,
> The food of mans immortal being!
> Under veyls here 40
> Thou art my chear,
> Present and sure without my seeing.
>
> How dost thou flye
> And search and pry
> Through all my parts, and like a quick 45
> And knowing lamp
> Hunt out each damp,
> Whose shadow makes me sad or sick?
>
> O what high joys
> The Turtles voice 50
> And songs I hear! O quickning showers
> Of my Lords blood
> You make rocks bud
> And crown dry hils with wells and flowers!
>
> For this true ease 55
> This healing peace,
> For this taste of living glory,
> My soul and all,
> Kneel down and fall
> And sing his sad victorious story. 60

33–36 Rev. 7:17, "For the Lamb which is in the midst of the throne shall feed them, and shall lead them unto living fountains of waters."

49–54 Song of Sol. 2:12, "The flowers appear on the earth; the time of the singing of birds is come, and the voice of the turtle is heard in our land."

    O thorny crown
    More soft then down!
        O painful Cross, my bed of rest!
    O spear, the key
    Opening the way!   65
        O thy worst state, my onely best!

    Oh! all thy griefs
    Are my reliefs,
        And all my sins, thy sorrows were!
    And what can I,   70
    To this reply;
        What (O God!) but a silent tear?

    Some toil and sow,
    That wealth may flow,
        And dress this earth for next years meat: 75
    But let me heed,
    Why thou didst bleed,
    And what in the next world to eat.

        Revel. chap. 19. ver. 9.

Blessed are they, which are called unto the marriage Supper of the Lamb.

The Obsequies

Since dying for me, thou didst crave no more
        Then common pay,
    Some few true tears, and those shed for
        My own ill way;
    With a cheap, plain remembrance still   5
        Of thy sad death,
    Because forgetfulness would kill
        Even lifes own breath:

61–69 Cf. Herbert, "The Thankes-giving," ll. 13–14.

I were most foolish and unkinde
        In my own sense,
Should I not ever bear in minde
If not thy mighty love, my own defense.
Therefore, those loose delights and lusts, which here
        Men call good chear,
   I will close girt and tyed
For mourning sack-cloth wear, all mortified.

   Not but that mourners too, can have
        Rich weeds and shrouds;
For some wore *White* ev'n in thy grave,
And Joy, like light, shines oft in clouds:
But thou, who didst mans whole life earn,
Doest so invite, and woo me still,
That to be merry I want skill,
        And time to learn.
Besides, those Kerchiefs sometimes shed
        To make me brave,
I cannot finde, but where thy head
Was once laid for me in thy grave.
Thy grave! To which my thoughts shal move
Like Bees in storms unto their Hive,
That from the murd'ring worlds false love
Thy death may keep my soul alive.

The Water-fall

With what deep murmurs through times silent stealth
Doth thy transparent, cool and watry wealth
        Here flowing fall,
        And chide, and call,
As if his liquid, loose Retinue staid

The Obsequies.   19 *some*: the two angels at Jesus' tomb; see John 20:12.

>   Lingring, and were of this steep place afraid,
>   The common pass
>   Where, clear as glass,
>   All must descend
>   Not to an end:
> But quickned by this deep and rocky grave,
> Rise to a longer course more bright and brave.
>
>   Dear stream! dear bank, where often I
>   Have sate, and pleas'd my pensive eye,
>   Why, since each drop of thy quick store
>   Runs thither, whence it flow'd before,
>   Should poor souls fear a shade or night,
>   Who came (sure) from a sea of light?
>   Or since those drops are all sent back
>   So sure to thee, that none doth lack,
>   Why should frail flesh doubt any more
>   That what God takes, hee'l not restore?
>
>   O useful Element and clear!
>   My sacred wash and cleanser here,
>   My first consigner unto those
>   Fountains of life, where the Lamb goes!
>   What sublime truths, and wholesome themes,
>   Lodge in thy mystical, deep streams!
>   Such as dull man can never finde
>   Unless that Spirit lead his minde,
>   Which first upon thy face did move,
>   And hatch'd all with his quickning love.
>   As this loud brooks incessant fall
>   In streaming rings restagnates all,

The Water-fall. 15 *quick*: living.

23 *useful*: in that it is the substance in which man is baptized, and also in pointing out *uses* (lessons, truths, doctrines, applications) to man.

25–26 See Rev. 7:17.

31–32 Gen. 1:2, "And the earth was without form, and void; and darkness was upon the face of the deep. And the spirit of God moved upon the face of the waters." The Vulgate reads, "Spiritus Domini incubabat aquis."

34 *restagnates*: to become or remain stagnant (*OED*).

Which reach by course the bank, and then
Are no more seen, just so pass men.
O my invisible estate,
My glorious liberty, still late!
Thou art the Channel my soul seeks,
Not this with Cataracts and Creeks.

Quickness

False life! a foil and no more, when
         Wilt thou be gone?
Thou foul deception of all men
That would not have the true come on.

Thou art a Moon-like toil; a blinde
         Self-posing state;
A dark contest of waves and winde;
A meer tempestuous debate.

Life is a fix'd, discerning light,
         A knowing Joy;
No chance, or fit: but ever bright,
And calm and full, yet doth not cloy.

'Tis such a blissful thing, that still
         Doth vivifie,
And shine and smile, and hath the skill
To please without Eternity.

Thou art a toylsom Mole, or less
         A moving mist.
But life is, what none can express,
A quickness, which my God hath kist.

---

38 Rom. 8:21, "the glorious liberty of the children of God."

The Wreath

Since I in storms us'd most to be
    And seldom yielded flowers,
How shall I get a wreath for thee
    From those rude, barren hours?

The softer dressings of the Spring,
    Or Summers later store
I will not for thy temples bring,
    Which *Thorns*, not *Roses* wore.

But a twin'd wreath of *grief* and *praise*,
Praise soil'd with tears, and tears again
Shining with joy, like dewy days,
This day I bring for all thy pain,
Thy causless pain! and sad as death;
Which sadness breeds in the most vain,
(O not in vain!) now beg thy breath;
Thy quickning breath, which gladly bears
Through saddest clouds to that glad place,
Where cloudless Quires sing without tears,
Sing thy just praise, and see thy face.

The Queer

O tell me whence that joy doth spring
    Whose diet is divine and fair,
Which wears heaven, like a bridal ring,
    And tramples on doubts and despair?

Whose Eastern traffique deals in bright
    And boundless Empyrean themes,

The Wreath. Cf. Herbert, "A Wreath."
The Queer. The index to *Silex* (1655) lists *Quere*, meaning query.
3 Cf. "The World," ll. 59–60.

Mountains of spice, Day-stars and light,
Green trees of life, and living streams?

Tell me, O tell who did thee bring
And here, without my knowledge, plac'd,   10
Till thou didst grow and get a wing,
A wing with eyes, and eyes that taste?

Sure, *holyness* the *Magnet* is,
And *Love* the *Lure*, that woos thee down;
Which makes the high transcendent bliss   15
Of knowing thee, so rarely known.

The Book

Eternal God! maker of all
That have liv'd here, since the mans fall;
The Rock of ages! in whose shade
They live unseen, when here they fade.

Thou knew'st this *papyr*, when it was   5
Meer *seed*, and after that but *grass*;
Before 'twas *drest* or *spun*, and when
Made *linen*, who did *wear* it then:
What were their lifes, their thoughts and deeds
Whither good *corn*, or fruitless *weeds*.   10

  Thou knew'st this *Tree*, when a green *shade*
Cover'd it, since a *Cover* made,
And where it flourish'd, grew and spread,
As if it never should be dead.

  Thou knew'st this harmless *beast*, when he   15
Did live and feed by thy decree
On each green thing; then slept (well fed)

7–8 See note to "Timber," ll. 49–56.

Cloath'd with this *skin*, which now lies spred
A *Covering* o're this aged book,
Which makes me wisely weep and look
On my own dust; meer dust it is,
But not so dry and clean as this.
Thou knew'st and saw'st them all and though
Now scatter'd thus, dost know them so.

    O knowing, glorious spirit! when
Thou shalt restore trees, beasts and men,
When thou shalt make all new again,
Destroying onely death and pain,
Give him amongst thy works a place,
Who in them lov'd and sought thy face!

To the Holy Bible

O Book! lifes guide! how shall we part,
And thou so long seiz'd of my heart!
Take this last kiss, and let me weep
True thanks to thee, before I sleep.

    Thou wert the first put in my hand,
When yet I could not understand,
And daily didst my yong eyes lead
To letters, till I learnt to read.
But as rash youths, when once grown strong
Flye from their Nurses to the throng,
Where they new Consorts choose, and stick
To those, till either hurt or sick:
So with that first light gain'd from thee
Ran I in chase of vanity,
Cryed dross for gold, and never thought
My first cheap Book had all I sought.
Long reign'd this vogue; and thou cast by
With meek, dumb look didst woo mine eye,
And oft left open would'st convey

A sudden and most searching ray 20
Into my soul, with whose quick touch
Refining still, I strugled much.
By this milde art of love at length
Thou overcam'st my sinful strength,
And having brought me home, didst there 25
Shew me that pearl I sought elsewhere.
Gladness, and peace, and hope, and love,
The secret favors of the Dove,
Her quickning kindness, smiles and kisses,
Exalted pleasures, crowning blisses, 30
Fruition, union, glory, life
Thou didst lead to, and still all strife.
Living, thou wert my souls sure ease,
And dying mak'st me go in peace:
Thy next *Effects* no tongue can tell; 35
Farewel O book of God! farewel!

S Luke chap. 2. ver. 14.

*Glory be to God in the highest, and on
Earth peace, good will towards men.*

L'Envoy

O the new worlds new, quickning Sun!
Ever the same, and never done!
The seers of whose sacred light
Shall all be drest in shining white,
And made conformable to his 5
Immortal shape, who wrought their bliss,
      Arise, arise!

To the Holy Bible. 26 Matt. 13:45–46, "The kingdom of heaven is like unto a merchant man, seeking goodly pearls: Who, when he had found one pearl of great price, went and sold all that he had, and bought it."

L'Envoy. 4 Rev. 7:9.

And like old cloaths fold up these skies,
This long worn veyl: then shine and spread
Thy own bright self over each head, 10
And through thy creatures pierce and pass
Till all becomes thy cloudless glass,
Transparent as the purest day
And without blemish or decay,
Fixt by thy spirit to a state 15
For evermore immaculate.
A state fit for the sight of thy
Immediate, pure and unveil'd eye,
A state agreeing with thy minde,
A state thy birth, and death design'd: 20
A state for which thy creatures all
Travel and groan, and look and call.
O seeing thou hast paid our score,
Why should the curse reign any more?
But since thy number is as yet 25
Unfinish'd, we shall gladly sit
Till all be ready, that the train
May fully fit thy glorious reign.
Onely, let not our haters brag,
Thy seamless coat is grown a rag, 30
Or that thy truth was not here known,
Because we forc'd thy judgements down.
Dry up their arms, who vex thy spouse,
And take the glory of thy house
To deck their own; then give thy saints 35
That faithful zeal, which neither faints
Nor wildly burns, but meekly still
Dares own the truth, and shew the ill.
Frustrate those cancerous, close arts
Which cause solution in all parts, 40

21–22 See note to [And do they so?].
22 Rom. 8:22, "the whole creation groaneth and travaileth in pain together until now."
30 *seamless coat*: See John 19:23; here, the Church.
40 *solution*: dissolution.

And strike them dumb, who for meer words
Wound thy beloved, more then swords.
Dear Lord, do this! and then let grace
Descend, and hallow all the place.
Incline each hard heart to do good,   45
And cement us with thy sons blood,
That like true sheep, all in one fold
We may be fed, and one minde hold.
Give watchful spirits to our guides!
For sin (like water) hourly glides   50
By each mans door, and quickly will
Turn in, if not obstructed still.
Therefore write in their hearts thy law,
And let these long, sharp judgements aw
Their very thoughts, that by their clear   55
And holy lives, mercy may here
Sit regent yet, and blessings flow
As fast, as persecutions now.
So shall we know in war and peace
Thy service to be our sole ease,   60
With prostrate souls adoring thee,
Who turn'd our sad captivity!

S. Clemens apud Basil:

Ζῆ ὁ Θεὸς, καὶ ὁ κύριος Ἰησοῦς Χριστὸς,
καὶ τὸ πνεῦμα τὸ ἅγιον.

Epigraph   Vaughan has revised his source to produce an epigraph in the imperative mood, encapsulating the spirit of the final, apocalyptic poem — "Live, O God, and the Lord Jesus Christ, and the Holy Spirit." In the original, Basil in *Liber de Spirito Sancto*, xxxix (*Opera, Pat. Graec.* xxxii. 201), quotes St. Clement as follows:

Ζη, φησὶν, ὁ Θεὸς, χαὶ ὁ Κύριος Ἰησοῦς
Χριστὸς, χαὶ τὸ πνεῦμα τὸ ἅγιον.

Richard Crashaw

The title of Crashaw's first and second collections of sacred poems, *Steps to the Temple*, is a graceful acknowledgment of Herbert's leadership in the field of sacred lyric poetry, but not a proclamation of artistic indebtedness such as Vaughan's poems everywhere manifest. In a presentation poem accompanying a copy of *The Temple*, Crashaw praises Herbert as an "Angell" and his book as embodying "Divinest love." But Crashaw's religious and poetic sensibility differs greatly from that of Herbert, Donne, or any other lyric poet of the period: only the poem "Charitas Nimia" suggests Herbert's tone and manner, and only "Loves Horoscope" at all recalls Donne's characteristic development and exploitation of a single conceit. Joseph Beaumont—if he was the friend who wrote the preface to the 1646 *Steps to the Temple*—accurately defines Crashaw's relation to Herbert in terms of their common dedication to sacred verse, terming Crashaw "Herbert's second, but equall, who hath retriv'd Poetry of late, and return'd it up to its Primitive use; Let it bound back to heaven gates, whence it came."

Crashaw's conversion to Roman Catholicism and his deep involvement in its devotional life was in some respects the natural expression of his temperament and religious affinities, though without the catalyst of the Civil War he might not have taken this step. Born in 1612, the son of a Puritan divine who was especially noted for his hatred of popery and the Jesuits, Crashaw was educated first at the Charterhouse and then at Pembroke College, Cambridge, where he commenced B.A. in 1634. Pembroke was a center of Laudian Anglicanism, as was also Peterhouse, where Crashaw was elected fellow in 1636, and these influences attached him firmly to High Church ritual,

Catholic art, and Arminian doctrine. During these years Crashaw also had some association with Ferrar's Anglican religious community, Little Gidding, which evidently supplied the subject of his poem, "Description of a Religious House and Condition of Life." By 1639 he was an Anglican priest, curate of Little St. Mary's, and college catechist, or lecturer, at Peterhouse; a contemporary wrote that his sermons "ravished more like poems," but apparently none of them has survived.

This idyllic life at Peterhouse, which Crashaw later called his "little contentfull kingdom," was violently disrupted by the Civil War. In 1643 the Puritans occupied Cambridge, and Crashaw fled in January, 1644, in a futile effort to avoid being expelled from his fellowship for religious reasons. Sometime in 1645, destitute, he took up residence in Paris, where Queen Henrietta Maria and the English court were in exile; and sometime during that year he became a Roman Catholic. Subsequently he went to Rome, where, after considerable delay, Queen Henrietta's intercession with the Pope obtained for him a position in Cardinal Palotto's retinue. In April, 1649, he was given the minor post of *beneficiatus* at the Santa Casa at Loreto, revered as the house Christ lived in while at Nazareth, and in August of that same year he died.

This is not the place for definition or discussion of the much-abused term *baroque*, but it is important to note that the chief influences on Crashaw stem from that far-flung European artistic movement, and that Crashaw is perhaps the only important English poet who can be called "baroque" with complete accuracy. In all the arts, the baroque impulse attempted to render the spiritual through and in terms of the sensuous, and the movement was reinforced by the Counter-Reformation emphasis upon the senses in ritual, in the veneration of images, and in the doctrine of transubstantiation. Favorite themes and motifs which recur again and again in baroque painting, sculpture, and literature are angels and cherubs, the infant Jesus, the crucified Savior with his wounds streaming blood, the weeping Magdalen, the ecstatic Teresa (as in Bernini's masterpiece), and various swooning mystics and agonized martyrs. The baroque style, to note only its obvious and undisputed characteristics, is exuberant, rhetorical, sensuous, grandiose, agitated, splendidly ornamented; it endeavors to dissolve lines and forms, to transcend the limits of each genre or medium.

Among the baroque literary influences upon Crashaw was the emblem, a genre uniting picture (engraving) and poetry, which spread throughout Catholic and Protestant Europe in the sixteenth and seventeenth centuries in the form of emblem books. Religious emblems usually depict human figures as allegories or personifications of states of the soul or other abstractions; a motto and a short poem interpret the picture. Often emblems translate scriptural metaphor, intended to be comprehended conceptually, into bluntly visual terms, e.g., portraying Christ knocking at a door in a palpable, fleshly heart. Crashaw included emblem engravings in his last collection of religious poems, *Carmen Deo Nostro*, and he is generally assumed to have executed two of them himself—the padlocked heart which prefaces the dedicatory poem to the Countess of Denbigh, and the Magdalen with bleeding, flaming, winged heart and weeping eyes, which prefaces "The Weeper." In some sense, then, these poems are emblem poems, interpreting the pictures. More generally, Crashaw's sensuous and sometimes grotesque metaphors owe something to the emblem method of making visual and literal the abstract and figurative. Another significant influence, as Mario Praz has demonstrated, is the Latin epigram as practiced by continental Jesuits such as Jacob Bidermann and Franciscus Remond. A terse, pointed, witty form usually concluding with a surprising turn, the Jesuit epigram developed a highly sophisticated rhetoric comprised especially of pun, paradox, and antithesis and created a common fund of witty metaphors and conceits upon which Crashaw drew, even in poems which are not formally epigrams.

But the most considerable baroque influence upon Crashaw was Gianbattista Marino (1569–1625) and the literary style known as Marinism—a style characterized by rhetorical floridity and elaborate ornament, sensuous and often cloying description, slight and slow-paced narrative, the use of sensuous metaphors for sacred themes and objects, and an abundance of antitheses, oxymorons, paradoxes, and especially conceits. The Marinist conceits produce witty surprise, but differ from the Donnean conceits, as Austin Warren notes, in that they are chiefly within the range of the palpable, comparing things to other things, one sense perception to that of another sense. Crashaw could find English precedent for many aspects of this style in the poetry of the Jesuit poet Robert Southwell and in Giles Fletcher's *Christ's Victory and Triumph*, which devotes twenty stanzas to a florid, sensuous description of Christ's eyes. But Marino is the chief influence: his romantic epic *Adone* was extremely popular throughout Europe; the English poet Drummond of Hawthornden translated some of his lyrics; and Crashaw himself translated the first part of Marino's *Strage degli Innocenti* — softening and further elaborating the imagery but also sharpening the metaphors.

The temperament and religious sensibility which Crashaw manifests in his poetry are clearly cast in the Counter-Reformation mold. His favorite subjects are the common baroque themes — the wounds and blood of the crucified Lord, the sorrows and sufferings of the Blessed Mother, the tears of the penitent Magdalen, the love-wounds and ecstasies of the mystic Teresa. Unlike Donne or Herbert, Crashaw does not offer an intellectual analysis of theological doctrine or of his own psychological responses to religious experience; rather, as Robert Ellrodt notes, he simply contemplates the Christian paradoxes and mysteries in awe and wonder. This focus upon the object adored rather than upon the self makes for a kind of objectivity— of attitude though not of effect. Crashaw's often strained wit prevents a dramatic presentation of the sacred personages as personalities. And the frequent pleas of Crashaw's poetic speaker to experience in himself and share in the events he contemplates — the wounds and pain of the crucifixion or the love-wounds of the mystics — makes Crashaw's special sensibility a prominent element in all his poems.

That special sensibility is probably the source of the difficulty for the considerable number of readers who dislike Crashaw. As Mary Ellen Rickey notes, Crashaw tends, whatever the subject, to emphasize the same sensory qualities — warmth, softness, sweetness. Any reader could readily list Crashaw's favorite rhymes, nouns, and descriptive terms: breasts and nests, wounds and swoons, darts and hearts; kisses, blood, tears; sweet, dear, delicious, milky, rosy, blushing, bleeding, warm, soft. These are all-pervasive, and they constitute a field of private symbolic reference for Crashaw. But their very frequency gives to Crashaw's verse the soft luxuriance, the lack of toughness, the suggestion of unwholesomeness which prompted Warren to declare that "Weakness is, for Crashaw, real; evil scarcely is," and Douglas Bush to observe that in Crashaw "Over-ripeness is all." Moreover, Crashaw's emphasis upon the senses sometimes renders traditional Christian paradoxes so literally that they become tasteless, or grotesque, or almost blasphemous. A notable example is "Prayer: An Ode," which applies the conventional bridegroom–bride imagery to the relation of Christ and the soul so explicitly as to suggest a bedroom scene rather than the mystical union.

But the obverse of this fault is Crashaw's great merit as a poet. Though he did not always succeed, he alone among the English religious poets attempted the poetic rendering of religious ecstasy and rapture. Whether or not he was a mystic in any strict sense, it is obvious that he craved the mystical union. His verses "To the Morning. Satisfaction for sleepe" reveal that he regarded poetry itself as a means of ecstatic vision, in which the fancy wings to heaven and brings back,

> *Enthusiasticke* flames, such as can give
> Marrow to my plumpe *Genius*, make it live
> Drest in the glorious madnesse of a Muse,
> Whose feet can walke the milky way, and chuse
> Her starry Throne; whose holy heats can warme
> The Grave, and hold up an exalted arme
> To lift me from my lazy Urne, to climbe
> Upon the stooped shoulders of old Time;
> And trace Eternity.

To counterbalance his failures Crashaw has some amazing successes in creating the experience of rapture: "Musicks Duell," which renders the ecstasy produced by music; the ode "To the Name Above Every Name," which conveys religious rapture. Crashaw's apparent formlessness, metrical irregularity, and plethora of seemingly confused images are explicable in terms of this intention, for it is by collapsing the logical categories of thought and producing a synesthetic blending of sensations, a phantasmagoria, a constant metamorphosis of one thing into another, that Crashaw suggests transcendence.

Though Crashaw's poetic production was not extensive, he worked in several kinds. His Latin epigrams, published as *Epigrammata Sacra* in 1634, are all on New Testament texts, and probably many of them were composed as academic exercises at Pembroke, when Crashaw, as a Greek scholar, had to write Latin and Greek verses on the Scripture texts for every Sunday and feast day of the year. They are among the best Latin epigrams written by an Englishman, and many of those which he transposed into English are notable for their metallic wit and their sometimes shocking metaphors: Christ's wounds are both mouths and eyes; the Holy Innocents' milk becomes lilies and their blood, roses; the infant Christ drinks milk from Mary's breast but she must soon drink blood from his.

Crashaw's secular poems, *The Delights of the Muses*, were published with the first edition of *Steps to the Temple* in 1646 and are for the most part translations or occasional elegies or compliments, usually in couplet form. "Wishes To his (supposed) Mistresse" is an elegant exception, a triumph in the Jonsonian manner of simplicity and restraint, developing a Jonsonian theme of balance and order in the affections. But the *chef-d'oeuvre* of the secular verse is "Musicks Duell," Crashaw's elaboration to three times the original length of Famianus Strada's fifty-eight-line poem on the contest between a nightingale and a lutanist. This is musical poetry, but not in the simple sense of the imitation of musical sounds by means of liquid vowels, smooth and gliding syntax, sound repetitions, and onomatopoeia—though all of these devices are present in abundance. Rather, Crashaw's concern here is to find metaphorical equivalents for the ecstatic sensations of listening to music, to convey by appropriate formal means the contest between melodic and harmonic music. In creating melody, the nightingale's whole soul is poured "Into loose exstasies" and she is placed "Above her selfe." But the lutanist wins the contest, for he can produce harmony, the analogue of the music of the spheres which orders the whole cosmos, and as he does so his soul seems to be "snatcht out at his Eares/By a strong

Extasy" and seated "In th'*Empyraeum* of pure Harmony." As the poem builds toward these climactic ecstasies and especially that of the lutanist, its meter becomes more and more irregular, pauses and stops and parenthetical expressions multiply, and sentence structure loosens—as if the normal categories of perception are disintegrating. The concomitant blending of sounds and synesthesia suggest a new mode of perception in the ecstatic experience.

In the second edition (1648) of *Steps to the Temple*, Crashaw included versions of the Office of the Holy Cross and of several famous medieval hymns—among them the *Adoro Te*, the *Lauda Sion*, the *Vexilla Regis*, the *Dies Irae*. Crashaw subtitled his version of the *Stabat Mater* "A Patheticall descant upon the devout Plainsong," and indeed the term "descant" describes all of these translations: they are florid, ornamental obbligatos which elaborate the images, add many images not warranted by the originals, and increase the adjectival count (as Sister Margaret Claydon shows) by as much as 300 percent. As Ruth Wallerstein argues, Crashaw's version of *O Gloriosa Domina* is perhaps the most successful of these translations; he evidently found the subject sympathetic and he approached it with imaginative freedom, exploiting its conceits and paradoxes but eschewing his usual lush sensuousness. The least successful by all odds is the *Dies Irae*, where Crashaw's subjectivity, adjectival ornamentation, and tender, pathetic tone utterly destroy the somber magnificence of the original.

Crashaw's most distinctive pieces are his original hymns and odes, which vary in tone and style. "The Weeper," as Mario Praz notes, is little more than a rosary of independent epigrams, most of them commonplaces. The Magdalen's tears become mere objects for witty wordplay, the Magdalen as a person is quite obscured, and the conceits are often in notoriously bad taste: her tears are cream for the Cherubs' breakfast in heaven; her eyes are "two walking baths; Two weeping motions;/ Portable, and compendious oceans." By contrast, the hymn "In the Holy Nativity" has a Murillo-like prettiness. Though it addresses the witty problem of finding for Jesus a resting-place at once warm enough and pure enough for his needs, and though it employs dialogue (or rather antiphonal exchange) among the shepherd speakers, the constant repetition of such terms as "sweet," "dear," "soft," produces a uniform, all-pervasive tone of melting sweetness.

Of quite a different order is the hymn "To the Name Above Every Name," whose structure, as Louis Martz shows, closely follows the *Scala Meditatoria* of Mauburnus. Here Crashaw's customary sensory imagery has become wholly symbolic, for it attaches to no sensible object—only to the "Name" whose glory the speaker meditates upon with increasing fervor until at length he sees and ecstatically welcomes its advent into the "dark world." "A Hymn to... Sainte Teresa" celebrates the fusion of martyrdom and mysticism in Teresa's experience, rendering it through the sensuous imagery of love and marriage, pain and death: her ecstasy is a "sweet and subtle PAIN," a "death more mysticall and high." The "Hymn" is an impressive whole, modulating in tone according to Teresa's changing spiritual states, but it does not attain the magnificence of the final lines of "The Flaming Heart," wherein the speaker conveys his own intense longing for Teresian ecstasy in a litany of witty antitheses and sharply pointed paradoxes. "In the Glorious Epiphanie" is Crashaw's only treatment of the mysticism of the *Via Negativa*, the renunciation of images in order to seek God in the Dark Night of the Soul—whose emblem here is the sun's eclipse. The poem is in some ways Crashaw's most "metaphysical" work, both in theme and style. It treats the antithesis between the sun of the universe, which was worshiped as a pagan god and taken as the emblem of worldly wisdom, and the heavenly Sun/Son whose worship supplants all other worship and whose light shows all other light to be darkness. Here, appropriately, Crashaw eschews color imagery and most other sensory imagery as well, developing the poem through the analysis and exploitation of the paradoxes and symbolic meanings conveyed through the light-darkness polarity.

Though Crashaw wrote in several forms, and though he revised his poems constantly, we can speak of his "development" only in a limited sense. His revisions were chiefly additions and elaborations, not radical changes; and he did not abandon the bad taste of "The Weeper" when he became capable of writing the concluding lines of "The Flaming Heart." One discernible line of development is the movement from the epigram (and the closed couplet) to the ode form—that is, from restricted, highly controlled forms to freer, dithyrambic, seemingly formless works. Rickey's recent study suggests, however, that this formlessness is only apparent, that in fact Crashaw's treatment of rhyme devices outlines and emphasizes the logical structures in these poems, and that in his revisions this structural use of rhyme patterns is sharpened. Also, Crashaw's later poems, translations, and revisions tend, through an increase in the use of imperatives, apostrophes, direct quotations, and the mixture of present and future tense, to emphasize the dramatic or meditative role of the speaker as he strives progressively to become one with the object he contemplates.

Another line of development is toward the symbolic use of sensory imagery; in many of Crashaw's best poems the imagery has become a ceremonial formula with both public and private symbolic significance, George W. Williams has noted some of these recurrent symbols: the imagery of feasts, creation, and overflowing rivers connotes abundance; drops of water, drops of blood, crumbs of the Eucharist suggest the great in the little; the imagery of white and red, lilies and roses, diamonds and rubies, tears and blood, and milky and rosy things connotes purity and ardor; various images of liquidity—blood, milk, tears, wine— suggest the movement and metamorphosis of all created things; nests, breasts, and rosy dawns are nascent symbols, connoting beginnings. Yet Williams' affirmation that Crashaw's images are to be read strictly on the symbolic level can be sustained only for a few works such as the hymn "To the Name Above Every Name" and the final lines of "The Flaming Heart"; in most of the poems, whatever the symbolic reference, the sensory qualities of the imagery remain too insistent and too pervasive to be wholly transcended.

Carmen Deo Nostro (1652), Crashaw's last collection of religious poetry, is presented here in its entirety, because it appears to have been planned, or at least arranged, as a whole work. The evidence for this is less clear than in the cases of Herbert and Vaughan: this volume contains many poems published in Crashaw's earlier collections, and, since it appeared posthumously, the arrangement could have been the work of Thomas Car. Yet, as L. C. Martin and Austin Warren agree, it was very probably planned by Crashaw before he left Paris for Rome. The book's ordering conception would seem to be the celebration of the liturgy and devotions of Crashaw's new Roman Catholic faith. Evidence for this is the new poem to the Countess of Denbigh urging her to join the Roman Church, which stands as a dedicatory and introductory poem to the volume; the addition of the many emblems, which in Counter-Reformation fashion fuse the arts in the service of devotion; the explicit identification here of the several medieval hymns Crashaw translated, to which he earlier gave titles obscuring his sources; and the arrangement of the poems in this volume in a definite liturgical order, in marked contrast to the haphazard arrangement of the two editions of *Steps to the Temple*.

After the introductory poem identifying Lady Denbigh as a "heav'n-intreated HEART," long irresolute, who ought now to respond to heaven by joining the Roman Church, the first large group of poems follows the course of the Church's liturgical devotion in the temporal cycle of feast days. First come the Christmastide poems on the Nativity, the Circumcision, the Epiphany. These are preceded by the hymn "To the Name Above Every Name," which alludes to the Christmastide Feast of the Holy Name of Jesus but also, by way of introduction, subsumes and generalizes the Christmas themes, and, by its petitions of anticipation and longing, suggests Advent. Next come a series of epigrams and hymns on the Passion and Crucifixion and the sorrowful mother, introduced by Crashaw's version of the liturgical prayer, The Office of the Holy Cross. Immediately following this are versions of Thomas Aquinas' two hymns on the Eucharist, the fruit of the Passion; the *Lauda Sion* was associated with the feast of Corpus Christi (the Thursday after Trinity Sunday). The section on the temporal cycle concludes with Crashaw's version of the *Dies Irae*, a meditation on the Day of Judgment used on 2 November, the feast commemorating all the dead. The next large group of poems relates to the Sanctoral cycle of feast days, beginning with two poems on the Virgin, followed by "The Weeper" celebrating the Magdalen, then the three Teresian poems and "A Song," which is set forth as Teresa's formulation of her own mystical experience or else the speaker's imaginative identification with that experience. The remaining poems depart from the liturgical focus to consider various modes of Christian life and death: two poems recommend the virginal life as the means to mystical union with Christ; the Alexis elegies look at such a choice from the uncomprehending worldly perspective of the bereaved wife of St. Alexis; the "Description of a Religious House" celebrates the "monastic" life at Little Gidding; several epitaphs propose meditation upon death as the culmination of all modes of life; and the poem "Temperance" concludes in this version with added lines on the easy death of the temperate man. The final poem is the Cowley–Crashaw debate on "Hope," presented as a dialogue in all previous versions but here as two separate poems, no doubt so that the reader may take at the conclusion of the volume the full force of Crashaw's defense of hope as a foretaste of eternity.

Copy texts of the poems printed here are the first edition (1646) of *Steps to the Temple* (for the epigrams), the first edition (1646) of *The Delights of the Muses* (for the secular poems), and the first edition (1652) of *Carmen Deo Nostro*. The copy texts are corrected for obvious errors and occasionally altered to better readings by comparison with the other printed and manuscript versions of the various poems, but no effort is made in the textual apparatus to record the significant variants among these versions. In Crashaw's case, the changes from version to version of a given poem are often so extensive as to make the versions quite different poems. For matters of text and interpretation we are especially indebted to L. C. Martin's standard edition of Crashaw's Poems (Oxford, 1957), cited as (M.).

SELECTED BIBLIOGRAPHY

EDITIONS

Martin, L. C., ed. *The Poems English Latin and Greek of Richard Crashaw.* 2nd ed. Oxford, 1957.

Williams, George W., ed., *The Complete Poetry of Richard Crashaw.* New York, 1970.

BIOGRAPHY AND CRITICISM

Adams, R. M. "Taste and Bad Taste in Metaphysical Poetry: Richard Crashaw and Dylan Thomas," *Hudson Review*, VIII (1955), 61–77.

Claydon, Sister Margaret. *Richard Crashaw's Paraphrases.* Washington, D.C., 1960.

Madsen, William G. "A Reading of 'Musicks Duell,'" in A. D. Wallace and W. O. Ross, eds., *Studies in Honor of John Wilcox.* Detroit, Mich., 1958.

Praz, Mario. "Richard Crashaw and the Baroque," *The Flaming Heart.* New York, 1958.

Raspa, Anthony, "Crashaw and the Jesuit Poetic," *UTQ*, XXXVI (1966) 37–54.

Rickey, Mary Ellen. *Rhyme and Meaning in Richard Crashaw.* Lexington, Ky., 1961.

Strier, Richard. "Crashaw's Other Voice," *SEL*, IX (1969), 133–51.

Wallerstein, Ruth. *Richard Crashaw: A Study in Style and Poetic Development*, Madison, Wis., 1935.

Warren, Austin. *Richard Crashaw: A Study in Baroque Sensibility.* Ann Arbor, Mich., 1957.

Williams, George W. *Image and Symbol in the Sacred Poetry of Richard Crashaw.* Columbia, S.C., 1963.

From STEPS TO THE TEMPLE

DIVINE EPIGRAMS

On the water of our Lords Baptisme

    Each blest drop, on each blest limme,
    Is washt it selfe, in washing him:
    Tis a Gemme while it stayes here,
    While it falls hence 'tis a Teare.

To the Infant Martyrs

Goe smiling soules, your new built Cages breake,
In Heav'n you'l learne to sing ere here to speake,
Nor let the milky fonts that bath your thirst,
          Bee your delay;
The place that calls you hence, is at the worst   5
          Milke all the way.

    Divine Epigrams. All of the epigrams included here have Latin counterparts in Crashaw's *Epigrammata Sacra* (1634), a cycle of epigrams based upon subjects drawn from the Gospels for the Sundays and feast days of the Church year.

Matthew 8

I am not worthy that thou should'st come under my roofe

Thy God was making hast into thy roofe,
    Thy humble faith and feare keepes him aloofe:
Hee'l be thy Guest, because he may not be,
    Hee'l come — into thy house? no, into thee.

I am the Doore

And now th'art set wide ope, The Speare's sad Art,
    Lo! hath unlockt thee at the very Heart:
Hee to himselfe (I feare the worst)
        And his owne hope
Hath *shut* these Doores of Heaven, that durst   5
        Thus set them *ope*.

Matthew. 27

And he answered them nothing

O Mighty *Nothing*! unto thee,
Nothing, wee owe all things that bee.
God spake once when hee all things made,
Hee sav'd all when hee *Nothing* said.
The world was made of *Nothing* then;   5
'Tis made by *Nothyng* now againe.

Matthew 8. Matthew 8:8.
I am the Doore. 3 *Hee*: the soldier who pierced Christ's side with a lance.
Matthew. 27. Matt. 27:14. The allusion is to Christ's silence when accused by the priests and elders before Pilate.

Upon our Saviours Tombe wherein never man was laid

How Life and Death in Thee
                Agree?
Thou had'st a virgin Wombe
                And Tombe.
A *Joseph* did betroth   5
                Them both.

Luke 11

Blessed be the paps which Thou hast sucked

Suppose he had been Tabled at thy Teates,
  Thy hunger feeles not what he eates:
Hee'l have his Teat e're long (a bloody one)
  The mother then must suck the Son.

Upon the Infant Martyrs

To see both blended in one flood
The Mothers Milke, the Childrens blood,
Makes me doubt if Heaven will gather,
Roses hence, or *Lillies* rather.

    Upon our Saviours Tombe.... 5 *Joseph:* according to legend Christ's tomb was provided by Joseph of Arimathea.
    Luke 11. Luke 11:27. Christ's apparent negation of the woman's praise of his mother provides the basis for a grotesque antithesis between Christ's painless feeding at Mary's breast, and her spiritual nourishment from the blood flowing from his side, the source of all mankind's salvation.

Easter day

Rise, Heire of fresh Eternity,
    From thy Virgin Tombe:
Rise mighty man of wonders! and thy world with thee,
   Thy Tombe, the universall East,
      Natures new wombe,   5
Thy Tombe, faire Immortalities perfum'd Nest.

Of all the Gloryes Make Noone gay
    This is the Morne.
This rocke buds forth the fountaine of the streames of Day.
   In joyes white Annals live this houre,   10
      When life was borne,
No cloud scoule on his radiant lids, no tempest lowre.

Life, by this light's Nativity
    All creatures have.
Death onely by this Dayes just Doome is forc't to Dye;   15
   Nor is Death forc'd; for may hee ly
      Thron'd in thy Grave;
Death will on this condition be content to Dy.

On Mr. G. Herberts *booke intituled* the Temple of Sacred Poems, *sent to a Gentlewoman*

Know you faire, on what you looke;
Divinest love lyes in this booke:
Expecting fire from your eyes,
To kindle this his sacrifice.

Easter day. Cf. George Herbert, "Easter."
15, 18 Cf. Donne, "Holy Sonnet VI" (X), l. 14.
On Mr. G. Herberts booke. . . . A testimony of Crashaw's admiration for Herbert.

When your hands unty these strings,   5
Thinke you have an Angell by th'wings.
One that gladly will bee nigh,
To wait upon each morning sigh.
To flutter in the balmy aire,
Of your well perfumed prayer.   10
These white plumes of his heele lend you,
Which every day to heaven will send you:
To take acquaintance of the spheare,
And all the smooth faced kindred there.
    And though *Herberts* name doe owe   15
    These devotions, fairest; know
    That while I lay them on the shrine
    Of your white hand, they are mine.

From THE DELIGHTS OF THE MUSES

Musicks Duell

Now Westward *Sol* had spent the richest Beames
Of Noons high Glory, when hard by the streams
Of *Tiber*, on the sceane of a greene plat,
Under protection of an Oake; there sate
A sweet Lutes-master: in whose gentle aires   5
Hee lost the Dayes heat, and his owne hot cares.
   Close in the covert of the leaves there stood
A Nightingale, come from the neighbouring wood:
(The sweet inhabitant of each glad Tree,
Their Muse, their *Syren*, harmlesse *Syren* shee)   10
There stood she listning, and did entertaine
The Musicks soft report: and mold the same
In her owne murmures, that what ever mood
His curious fingers lent, her voyce made good:
The man perceiv'd his Rivall, and her Art,   15
Dispos'd to give the light-foot Lady sport

Musicks Duell. A very free translation of a Latin poem by the Jesuit Famianus Strada (1572–1649) first published in *Prolusiones Academicae, Oratoriae, Historiae, Poeticae* (Coloniae Agrippinae, 1617), Lib. II, Prolus. VI. Poet. Acad. II, pp. 353–55. Austin Warren notes that Strada's poem had been paraphrased by several other English and continental poets, among them John Ford, William Strode, and Gianbattista Marino, and that there were many allusions in the seventeenth century to a duel between a nightingale and singers or musicians. Crashaw's poem is three times the length of Strada's, and ll. 57–156 are a development from only fifteen lines of the original.

Awakes his Lute, and 'gainst the fight to come
Informes it, in a sweet *Praeludium*
Of closer straines, and ere the warre begin,
Hee lightly skirmishes on every string
Charg'd with a flying touch: and streightway shee
Carves out her dainty voyce as readily,
Into a thousand sweet distinguish'd Tones,
And reckons up in soft divisions,
Quicke volumes of wild Notes; to let him know
By that shrill taste, shee could doe something too.
 His nimble hands instinct then taught each string
A capring cheerefullnesse; and made them sing
To their owne dance; now negligently rash
Hee throwes his Arme, and with a long drawne dash
Blends all together; then distinctly tripps
From this to that; then quicke returning skipps
And snatches this againe, and pauses there.
Shee measures every measure, every where
Meets art with art; sometimes as if in doubt
Not perfect yet, and fearing to bee out
Trayles her playne Ditty in one long-spun note,
Through the sleeke passage of her open throat:
A cleare unwrinckled song, then doth shee point it
With tender accents, and severely joynt it
By short diminutives, that being rear'd
In controverting warbles evenly shar'd,
With her sweet selfe shee wrangles. Hee amazed
That from so small a channell should be rais'd
The torrent of a voyce, whose melody
Could melt into such sweet variety
Straines higher yet; that tickled with rare art
The tatling strings (each breathing in his part)
Most kindly doe fall out; the grumbling Base
In surly groanes disdaines the Trebles Grace.
The high-perch't treble chirps at this, and chides,

18 *Praeludium*: a movement or piece forming the introduction to a musical work.
 24 *divisions*: rapid melodic passages, originally conceived as dividing successions of long notes into short ones.

Untill his finger (Moderatour) hides
And closes the sweet quarrell, rowsing all
Hoarce, shrill, at once; as when the Trumpets call
Hot Mars to th'Harvest of Deaths field, and woo 55
Mens hearts into their hands; this lesson too
Shee gives him backe; her supple Brest thrills out
Sharpe Aires, and staggers in a warbling doubt
Of dallying sweetnesse, hovers ore her skill,
And folds in wav'd notes with a trembling bill, 60
The plyant Series of her slippery song.
Then starts shee suddenly into a Throng
Of short thicke sobs, whose thundring volleyes float,
And roule themselves over her lubricke throat
In panting murmurs, still'd out of her Breast 65
That ever-bubling spring; the sugred Nest
Of her delicious soule, that there does lye
Bathing in streames of liquid Melodie;
Musicks best seed-plot, whence in ripend Aires
A Golden-headed Harvest fairely reares 70
His Honey-dropping tops, plow'd by her breath
Which there reciprocally laboureth
In that sweet soyle. It seemes a holy quire
Founded to th'Name of great *Apollo's* lyre,
Whose sylver-roofe rings with the sprightly notes 75
Of sweet-lipp'd Angell-Imps, that swill their throats
In creame of Morning *Helicon*, and then
Preferre soft Anthems to the Eares of men,
To woo them from their Beds, still murmuring
That men can sleepe while they their Mattens sing: 80
(Most divine service) whose so early lay,
Prevents the Eye-lidds of the blushing day.
There might you heare her kindle her soft voyce,
In the close murmur of a sparkling noyse,
And lay the ground-worke of her hopefull song, 85
Still keeping in the forward streame, so long
Till a sweet whirle-wind (striving to gett out)
Heaves her soft Bosome, wanders round about,
And makes a pretty Earthquake in her Breast,

77 *Helicon*: the mountain home of the Muses.

Till the fledg'd Notes at length forsake their Nest; 90
Fluttering in wanton shoales, and to the Sky
Wing'd with their owne wild Eccho's pratling fly.
Shee opes the floodgate, and lets loose a Tide
Of streaming sweetnesse, which in state doth ride
On the wav'd backe of every swelling straine, 95
Rising and falling in a pompous traine.
And while shee thus discharges a shrill peale
Of flashing Aires; shee qualifies their zeale
With the coole Epode of a graver Noat,
Thus high, thus low, as if her silver throat 100
Would reach the brasen voyce of warr's hoarce Bird;
Her little soule is ravisht: and so pour'd
Into loose extasies, that shee is plac't
Above her selfe, Musicks *Enthusiast.*

    Shame now and anger mixt a double staine 105
In the Musitians face; yet once againe
(Mistresse) I come; now reach a straine my Lute
Above her mocke, or bee for ever mute.
Or tune a song of victory to mee,
Or to thy selfe, sing thine owne Obsequie; 110
So said, his hands sprightly as fire hee flings,
And with a quavering coynesse tasts the strings.
The sweet-lip't sisters musically frighted,
Singing their feares are fearfully delighted.
Trembling as when *Appollo's* golden haires 115
Are fan'd and frizled, in the wanton ayres
Of his owne breath: which marryed to his lyre
Doth tune the *Sphaeares*, and make Heavens selfe looke higher,
From this to that, from that to this hee flyes
Feeles Musicks pulse in all her Arteryes, 120
Caught in a net which there *Appollo* spreads,
His fingers struggle with the vocall threads,
Following those little rills, hee sinkes into
A Sea of *Helicon*; his hand does goe
Those parts of sweetnesse which with *Nectar* drop, 125
Softer then that which pants in *Hebe's* cup.

---

99 *Epode*: the third section of a lyric ode, following the strophe and antistrophe.
101 *warr's hoarce Bird*: the raven.
113 *The sweet-lip't sisters*: the Muses.

The humourous strings expound his learned touch,
By various Glosses; now they seeme to grutch,
And murmur in a buzzing dinne, then gingle
In shrill tongu'd accents: striving to bee single.   130
Every smooth turne, every delicious stroake
Gives life to some new Grace; thus doth h'invoke
Sweetnesse by all her Names; thus, bravely thus
(Fraught with a fury so harmonious)
The Lutes light *Genius* now does proudly rise,   135
Heav'd on the surges of swolne Rapsodyes.
Whose flourish (Meteor-like) doth curle the aire
With flash of high-borne fancyes: here and there
Dancing in lofty measures, and anon
Creeps on the soft touch of a tender tone: 140
Whose trembling murmurs melting in wild aires
Runs to and fro, complaining his sweet cares
Because those pretious mysteryes that dwell,
In musick's ravish't soule hee dare not tell,
But whisper to the world: thus doe they vary   145
Each string his Note, as if they meant to carry
Their Masters blest soule (snatcht out at his Eares
By a strong Extasy) through all the sphaeares
Of Musicks heaven; and seat it there on high
In th'*Empyraeum* of pure Harmony.   150
At length (after so long, so loud a strife
Of all the strings, still breathing the best life
Of blest variety attending on
His fingers fairest revolution
In many a sweet rise, many as sweet a fall)   155
A full-mouth *Diapason* swallowes all.

   This done, hee lists what shee would say to this,
And shee although her Breath's late exercise
Had dealt too roughly with her tender throate,
Yet summons all her sweet powers for a Noate   160
Alas! in vaine! for while (sweet soule) shee tryes
To measure all those wild diversities

---

128 *grutch*: onomatopoeic word meaning to grumble or complain.
  156 *Diapason*: a swelling burst of harmony; the entire range of a musical instrument or voice, here, apparently, caught up in one sound.

Of chatt'ring stringes, by the small size of one
Poore simple voyce, rais'd in a Naturall Tone;
Shee failes, and failing grieves, and grieving dyes.   165
Shee dyes; and leaves her life the Victors prise,
Falling upon his Lute; ô fit to have
(That liv'd so sweetly) dead, so sweet a Grave!

Wishes

To his (supposed) Mistresse

Who ere shee bee,
That not impossible shee
That shall command my heart and mee;

Where ere shee lye,
Lock't up from mortall Eye,   5
In shady leaves of Destiny:

Till that ripe Birth
Of studied fate stand forth,
And teach her faire steps to our Earth;

Till that Divine   10
Idaea, take a shrine
Of Chrystall flesh, through which to shine:

Meet you her my wishes,
Be speake her to my blisses,
And bee yee call'd my absent kisses.   15

I wish her Beauty,
That owes not all his Duty
To gaudy Tire, or glistring shoo-ty.

Wishes.... First published in *Witts Recreations* (1641) in a much shorter version.
18 *Tire*: attire; *shoo-ty*: shoelace.

Something more than
Taffeta or Tissew can, 20
Or rampant feather, or rich fan.

More then the spoyle
Of shop, or silkewormes Toyle
Or a bought blush, or a set smile.

A face thats best 25
By its owne beauty drest,
And can alone command the rest.

A face made up
Out of no other shop,
Then what natures white hand sets ope. 30

A cheeke where Youth,
And Blood, with Pen of Truth
Write, what the Reader sweetly ru'th.

A Cheeke where growes
More then a Morning Rose: 35
Which to no Boxe his being owes.

Lipps, where all Day
A lovers kisse may play,
Yet carry nothing thence away.

Lookes that oppresse 40
Their richest Tires but dresse
And cloath their simplest Nakednesse.

Eyes, that displaces
The Neighbour Diamond, and out faces
That Sunshine by their owne sweet Graces. 45

Tresses, that weare
Jewells, but to declare
How much themselves more pretious are.

Whose native Ray,
Can tame the wanton Day 50
Of Gems, that in their bright shades play.

Each Ruby there,
Or Pearle that dare appeare,
Bee its owne blush, bee its owne Teare.

A well tam'd Heart, 55
For whose more noble smart,
Love may bee long chusing a Dart.

Eyes, that bestow
Full quivers on loves Bow;
Yet pay lesse Arrowes then they owe. 60

Smiles, that can warme
The blood, yet teach a charme,
That Chastity shall take no harme.

Blushes, that bin
The burnish of no sin, 65
Nor flames of ought too hot within.

Joyes, that confesse,
Vertue their Mistresse,
And have no other head to dresse.

Feares, fond and flight, 70
As the coy Brides, when Night
First does the longing lover right.

Teares, quickly fled,
And vaine, as those are shed
For a dying Maydenhead. 75

---

70 *flight*: fleeting.

Dayes, that need borrow,
No part of their good Morrow,
From a fore spent night of sorrow.

Dayes, that in spight
Of Darkenesse, by the Light
Of a cleere mind are Day all Night.

Nights, sweet as they,
Made short by lovers play,
Yet long by th'absence of the Day.

Life, that dares send
A challenge to his end,
And when it comes say *Welcome Friend*.

Sydnaean showers
Of sweet discourse, whose powers
Can Crowne old Winters head with flowers.

Soft silken Houers,
Open sunnes, shady Bowers,
Bove all; Nothing within that lowres.

What ere Delight
Can make Dayes forehead bright;
Or give Downe to the Wings of Night.

In her whole frame,
Have Nature all the Name,
Art and ornament the shame.

Her flattery,
Picture and Poesy,
Her counsell her owne vertue bee.

---

88 *Sydnaean showers*: a testimony of Crashaw's admiration for Sidney.

>   I wish, her store
>   Of worth may leave her poore
>   Of wishes; And I wish — No more.   105
>
>   Now if Time knowes
>   That her whose radiant Browes,
>   Weave them a Garland of my vowes;
>
>   Her whose just Bayes,
>   My future hopes can raise,   110
>   A trophie to her present praise;
>
>   Her that dares bee,
>   What these Lines wish to see:
>   I seeke no further, it is shee.
>
>   'Tis shee, and heere   115
>   Lo I uncloath and cleare,
>   My wishes cloudy Character.
>
>   May shee enjoy it,
>   Whose merit dare apply it,
>   But Modesty dares still deny it.   120
>
>   Such worth as this is,
>   Shall fixe my flying wishes,
>   And determine them to kisses.
>
>   Let her full Glory,
>   My fancyes, fly before yee,   125
>   Be ye my fictions; But her story.

On Marriage

>   I Would be married, but I'de have no Wife,
>   I would be married to a single Life.

126 *story*: history.

CARMEN DEO NOSTRO,

TE DECET HYMNVS SACRED POEMS,

COLLECTED,
CORRECTED,
AVGMENTED,
Most humbly Presented,

TO

MY LADY THE COVNTSSE OF DENBIGH

BY

Her most deuoted Seruant.

R. C.

In heaty acknowledgment of his immortall obligation to her Goodnes & Charity.

AT PARIS,

By PETER TARGA, Printer to the Arch-bishope of Paris, in S. Victors streete at the golden sunne.

M. DC. LII.

CARMEN DEO NOSTRO
Te Decet Hymnus
Sacred Poems

Non Vi

*'Tis not the work of force but skill
To find the way into man's will.
'Tis love alone can hearts unlock.
Who knowes the* WORD, *he needs not knock.*

To the Noblest and best of Ladyes, the Countesse of Denbigh

Perswading her to Resolution in Religion, and to render her selfe without further delay into the Communion of the Catholick Church.

To the Noblest.... First published in 1652 as the dedication to the *Carmen Deo Nostro*; a much different version printed separately in 1653. Susan, Countess of Denbigh, was the daughter of Sir George Villiers, the sister of the Duke of Buckingham, and patroness of Crashaw; she entered the Roman Church at Easter, 1651, two years after Crashaw's death. The prefatory emblem — a padlocked heart — is thought to be Crashaw's own drawing; Praz notes its similarity to an emblem in the Dutch collection *Af-beeldinghe van d'eerst eeuwe der Societeyt Jesu* (Antwerp, 1640), p. 140. Another familiar emblem, the heart wounded by Love's dart or arrows, supplies the imagery of ll. 45-46.

What heav'n-intreated HEART is This?
Stands trembling at the gate of blisse;
Holds fast the door, yet dares not venture
Fairly to open it, and enter.
Whose DEFINITION is a doubt   5
Twixt life and death, twixt in and out.
Say, lingring fair! why comes the birth
Of your brave soul so slowly forth?
Plead your pretences (o you strong
In weaknes!) why you choose so long   10
In labor of your selfe to ly,
Nor daring quite to live nor dy?
Ah linger not, lov'd soul! a slow
And late consent was a long no,
Who grants at last, long time tryd   15
And did his best to have deny'd.
What magick bolts, what mystick Barres
Maintain the will in these strange warres!
What fatall, yet fantastick, bands
Keep The free Heart from it's own hands!   20
So when the year takes cold, we see
Poor waters their owne prisoners be.
Fetter'd, and lockt up fast they ly
In a sad selfe-captivity.
The' astonisht nymphs their flood's strange fate deplore, 25
To see themselves their own severer shore.
Thou that alone canst thaw this cold,
And fetch the heart from it's strong Hold;
Allmighty LOVE! end this long warr,
And of a meteor make a starr.   30
O fix this fair INDEFINITE.
And'mongst thy shafts of soveraign light
Choose out that sure decisive dart
Which has the Key of this close heart,

---

26 *their own severer shore*: the water nymphs become this as the water turns to winter ice.

Knowes all the corners of't, and can controul 35
The self-shutt cabinet of an unsearcht soul.
O let it be at last, love's houre.
Raise this tall Trophee of thy Powre;
Come once the conquering way; not to confute
But kill this rebell-word, IRRESOLUTE, 40
That so, in spite of all this peevish strength
Of weaknes, she may write RESOLV'D AT LENGTH.
Unfold at length, unfold fair flowre
And use the season of love's showre,
Meet his well-meaning Wounds, wise heart! 45
And hast to drink the wholsome dart.
That healing shaft, which heavn till now
Hath in love's quiver hid for you.
O Dart of love! arrow of light!
O happy you, if it hitt right, 50
It must not fall in vain, it must
Not mark the dry regardles dust.
Fair one, it is your fate; and brings
Æternall worlds upon it's wings.
Meet it with wide-spread armes; and see 55
It's seat your soul's just center be.
Disband dull feares; give faith the day.
To save your life, kill your delay;
It is love's seege; and sure to be
Your triumph, though his victory. 60
'Tis cowardise that keeps this feild
And want of courage not to yeild.
Yeild then, ô yeild, that love may win
The Fort at last, and let life in.
Yeild quickly. Lest perhaps you prove 65
Death's prey, before the prize of love.
This Fort of your fair selfe, if't be not won,
He is repulst indeed; But you' are undone.

To the Name Above Every Name, the Name of Jesus

A Hymn

I sing the NAME which None can say
But touch't with An interiour RAY:
The Name of our New PEACE; our Good:
Our Blisse: and Supernaturall Blood:
The Name of All our Lives and Loves. 5
Hearken, And Help, ye holy Doves!
The high-born Brood of Day; you bright
Candidates of blissefull Light,
The HEIRS Elect of Love; whose Names belong
Unto The everlasting life of Song; 10
All ye wise SOULES, who in the wealthy Brest
Of This unbounded NAME build your warm Nest.
Awake, MY glory. SOUL, (if such thou be,
And That fair WORD at all referr to Thee)
    Awake and sing 15
    And be All Wing;
Bring hither thy whole SELF; and let me see
What of thy Parent HEAVN yet speakes in thee.
    O thou art Poore
    Of noble POWRES, I see, 20

To the Name.... First published in 1648 with the title "On the name of Jesus"; only slight verbal changes in 1652. Praz notes that its source is the medieval *Jubilus de nomine Domine* attributed to St. Bernard. The day which the ode celebrates is evidently the Feast of the Holy Name of Jesus; in Crashaw's time it was not yet permanently fixed in the Roman Calendar but was usually celebrated during Christmastide—on 14 or 15 January, or the second Sunday after Epiphany. In the old Sarum Use the feast was on 7 August. The poem's placement before the Christmastide poems in this collection may reflect the Sarum date, or may be simply because it anticipates the Christmastide themes and Advent longing. The imagery of ll.225ff. draws upon the *Introit* for the Feast of the Holy Name (from Philip. 2: 10–11): "In the Name of Jesus let every knee bow, of those that are in heaven, on earth, and under the earth: and let every tongue confess that the Lord Jesus Christ is in the glory of God the Father" (Missale Romanum).

6 *Doves*: the angel choirs, or the choirs of elect saints.

And full of nothing else but empty ME,
Narrow, and low, and infinitely lesse
Then this GREAT mornings mighty Busynes.
    One little WORLD or two
    (Alas) will never doe.   *25*
    We must have store.
Goe, SOUL, out of thy Self, and seek for More.
    Goe and request
Great NATURE for the KEY of her huge Chest
Of Heavns, the self involving Sett of Sphears   *30*
(Which dull mortality more Feeles then heares)
    Then rouse the nest
Of nimble ART, and traverse round
The Aiery Shop of Soul-appeasing Sound:
And beat a summons in the Same   *35*
    All-soveraign Name
To warn each severall kind
And shape of sweetnes, Be they such
    As sigh with supple wind
    Or answer Artfull Touch,   *40*
That they convene and come away
To wait at the love-crowned Doores of
    This Illustrious DAY.
Shall we dare This, my Soul? we'l doe't and bring
No Other note for't, but the Name we sing.   *45*
    Wake LUTE and HARP
    And every sweet-lipp't Thing
    That talkes with tunefull string;
Start into life, And leap with me
Into a hasty Fitt-tun'd Harmony.   *50*
    Nor must you think it much
    T'obey my bolder touch;
I have Authority in LOVE'S name to take you
And to the worke of Love this morning wake you,

---

24 *World*: 1648 reads *word*, but the alteration vastly strengthens the poem, pointing to the inadequacy of the speaker, even as microcosm, to offer fit praise.
30–31 *Sphears*: after the Fall, mankind could no longer hear the music of the spheres.

                    Wake; In the Name   55
Of HIM who never sleeps, All Things that Are,
                    Or, what's the same,
                    Are Musicall;
                    Answer my Call
                    And come along;   60
Help me to meditate mine Immortall Song.
Come, ye soft ministers of sweet sad mirth,
Bring All your houshold stuffe of Heavn on earth;
O you, my Soul's most certain Wings,
Complaining Pipes, and prattling Strings,   65
          Bring All the store
Of SWEETS you have; And murmur that you have no more.
          Come, ne'er to part,
          NATURE and ART!
          Come; and come strong,   70
To the conspiracy of our Spatious song.
          Bring All the Powres of Praise
Your Provinces of well-united WORLDS can raise;
Bring All your LUTES and HARPS of HEAVN and EARTH;
What e're cooperates to The common mirthe   75
          Vessells of vocall Joyes,
Or You, more noble Architects of Intellectuall Noise,
Cymballs of Heav'n, or Humane sphears,
Solliciters of SOULES or EARES;
          And when you'are come, with All   80
That you can bring or we can call;
          O may you fix
          For ever here, and mix
          Your selves into the long
And everlasting series of a deathlesse SONG;   85
Mix All your many WORLDS, Above,
And loose them into ONE of Love.
          Chear thee my HEART!
          For Thou too hast thy Part
          And Place in the Great Throng   90
Of This unbounded All-imbracing SONG.
          Powres of my Soul, be Proud!
          And speake lowd

> To All the dear-bought Nations This Redeeming Name,
> And in the wealth of one Rich WORD proclaim 95
> New Similes to Nature.
>   May it be no wrong
> Blest Heavns, to you, and your Superiour song,
> That we, dark Sons of Dust and Sorrow,
>   A while Dare borrow 100
> The Name of Your Delights and our Desires,
> And fitt it to so farr inferior LYRES.
> Our Murmurs have their Musick too,
> Ye mighty ORBES, as well as you,
>   Nor yeilds the noblest Nest 105
> Of warbling SERAPHIM to the eares of Love,
> A choicer Lesson then the joyfull BREST
>   Of a poor panting Turtle-Dove.
> And we, low Wormes have leave to doe
> The Same bright Busynes (ye Third HEAVENS) with you. 110
> Gentle SPIRITS, doe not complain.
>   We will have care
>   To keep it fair,
> And send it back to you again.
> Come, lovely NAME! Appeare from forth the Bright 115
>   Regions of peacefull Light
> Look from thine own Illustrious Home,
> Fair KING of NAMES, and come.
> Leave All thy native Glories in their Georgeous Nest,
> And give thy Self a while The gracious Guest 120
> Of humble Soules, that seek to find
>   The hidden Sweets
>   Which man's heart meets
> When Thou art Master of the Mind.
> Come, lovely Name; life of our hope! 125
> Lo we hold our HEARTS wide ope!
> Unlock thy Cabinet of DAY
> Dearest Sweet, and come away.
>   Lo how the thirsty Lands
> Gasp for thy Golden Showres! with longstretch't Hands 130

129 ff. The allusions review the Advent themes of waiting for Christ's coming.

>   Lo how the laboring EARTH
>   That hopes to be
>   All Heaven by THEE,
>   Leapes at thy Birth.
> The'attending WORLD, to wait thy Rise,   135
>   First turn'd to eyes;
> And then, not knowing what to doe;
> Turn'd Them to TEARES, and spent Them too.
> Come ROYALL Name; and pay the expence
> Of All this Pretious Patience.   140
>   O come away
> And kill the DEATH of This Delay.
> O see, so many WORLDS of barren yeares
> Melted and measur'd out in Seas of TEARES.
> O see, The WEARY liddes of wakefull Hope   145
> (LOVE'S Eastern windowes) All wide ope
>   With Curtains drawn,
> To catch The Day-break of Thy DAWN.
> O dawn, at last, long look't for Day!
> Take thine own wings, and come away.   150
> Lo, where Aloft it comes! It comes, Among
> The Conduct of Adoring SPIRITS, that throng
> Like diligent Bees, And swarm about it.
>   O they are wise;
> And know what SWEETES are suck't from out it.   155
>   It is the Hive,
>   By which they thrive,
> Where All their Hoard of Hony lyes.
> Lo where it comes, upon The snowy DOVE'S
> Soft Back; And brings a Bosom big with Loves.   160
> WELCOME to our dark world, Thou
>   Womb of Day!
> Unfold thy fair Conceptions; And display
> The Birth of our Bright Joyes.
>   O thou compacted   165
> Body of Blessings: spirit of Soules extracted!
> O dissipate thy spicy Powres
> (Clowd of condensed sweets) and break upon us
>   In balmy showrs;

O fill our senses, And take from us 170
All force of so Prophane a Fallacy
To think ought sweet but that which smells of Thee.
Fair, flowry Name; In none but Thee
And Thy Nectareall Fragrancy,
      Hourly there meetes 175
An universall SYNOD of All sweets;
By whom it is defined Thus
      That no Perfume
      For ever shall presume
To passe for Odoriferous, 180
But such alone whose sacred Pedigree
Can prove it Self some kin (sweet name) to Thee.
SWEET NAME, in Thy each Syllable
A Thousand Blest ARABIAS dwell;
A Thousand Hills of Frankincense; 185
Mountains of myrrh, and Beds of spices,
And ten Thousand PARADISES
The soul that tasts thee takes from thence.
How many unknown WORLDS there are
Of Comforts, which Thou hast in keeping! 190
How many Thousand Mercyes there
In Pitty's Soft lap ly a sleeping!
Happy he who has the art
      To awake them,
      And to take them 195
Home, and lodge them in his HEART.
O that it were as it was wont to be!
When thy old Freinds of Fire, All full of Thee,
Fought against Frowns with smiles; gave Glorious chase
To Persecutions; And against the Face 200
Of DEATH and feircest Dangers, durst with Brave
And sober pace march on to meet A GRAVE.
On their Bold BRESTS about the world they bore thee
And to the Teeth of Hell stood up to teach thee,
In Center of their inmost Soules they wore thee, 205
Where Rackes and Torments striv'd, in vain, to reach thee.

198 *Freinds of Fire*: the early Christian martyrs.

   Little, alas, thought They
Who tore the Fair Brests of thy Freinds,
   Their Fury but made way
For Thee; And serv'd therein Thy glorious ends.   *210*
What did Their weapons but with wider pores
Inlarge thy flaming-brested Lovers
   More freely to transpire
   That impatient Fire
The Heart that hides Thee hardly covers.   *215*
What did their Weapons but sett wide the Doores
For Thee: Fair, purple Doores, of love's devising;
The Ruby windowes which inrich't the EAST
Of Thy so oft repeated Rising.
Each wound of Theirs was Thy new Morning;   *220*
And reinthron'd thee in thy Rosy Nest,
With blush of thine own Blood thy day adorning,
It was the witt of love o'reflowd the Bounds
Of WRATH, and made thee way through All Those WOUNDS.
Wellcome dear, All-Adored Name!   *225*
   For sure there is no Knee
   That knowes not THEE.
Or if there be such sonns of shame,
   Alas what will they doe
   When stubborn Rocks shall bow   *230*
And Hills hang down their Heavn-saluting Heads
   To seek for humble Beds
Of Dust, where in the Bashfull shades of night
Next to their own low NOTHING they may ly,
And couch before the dazeling light of thy dread majesty.   *235*
They that by Love's mild Dictate now
   Will not Adore thee,
Shall Then with Just Confusion, bow
   And break before thee.

---

222 The reference to Christ's own wounds alludes to the Feast of the Circumcision, associated with the Holy Name as the time at which that Name was formally conferred.

230ff. The perspective is here extended from the First Coming to the Second, the Last Judgment.

IN THE HOLY NATIVITY OF OUR LORD GOD

A Hymn

Sung as by the Shepheards

Chorus
Come we shepheards whose blest Sight
Hath mett love's Noon in Nature's night;
  Come lift we up our loftyer Song
And wake the SUN that lyes too long.

  To all our world of well-stoln joy   5
He slept; and dream't of no such thing.
  While we found out Heavn's fairer ey
And Kis't the Cradle of our KING.
  Tell him He rises now, too late
To show us ought worth looking at.   10

Tell him we now can show Him more
Then He e're show'd to mortall Sight;
  Then he Himselfe e're saw before;
Which to be seen needes not His light.
  Tell him, Tityrus, where th'hast been,   15
Tell him, Thyrsis, what th'hast seen.

  Tityrus. Gloomy night embrac't the Place
Where The Noble Infant lay.
  The BABE look't up and shew'd his Face;

In the Holy Nativity.... First published in 1646 with title "A Hymne of the Nativity, sung by the Shepheards." 1646 is shorter, has no choric refrains, and otherwise differs considerably from 1648 and 1652, which are nearly identical.

In spite of Darknes, it was DAY.   20
 It was THY day, SWEET! and did rise
Not from the EAST, but from thine EYES.

 Chorus.   It was THY day, Sweet, etc.

 Thyrs. WINTER chidde aloud; and sent
The angry North to wage his warres.   25
 The North forgott his feirce Intent;
And left perfumes in stead of scarres.
 By those sweet eyes' persuasive powrs
Where he mean't frost, he scatter'd flowrs.

 Chorus. By those sweet eyes', etc.   30

 Both. We saw thee in thy baulmy Nest,
Young dawn of our æternall DAY!
 We saw thine eyes break from their EASTE
And chase the trembling shades away.
 We saw thee; and we blest the sight   35
We saw thee by thine own sweet light.

 Tity. Poor WORLD (said I) what wilt thou doe
To entertain this starry STRANGER?
 Is this the best thou canst bestow?
A cold, and not too cleanly, manger?   40
 Contend, ye powres of heav'n and earth.
To fitt a bed for this huge birthe.

 Cho.   Contend ye powers, etc.

 Thyr. Proud world, said I; cease your contest
And let the MIGHTY BABE alone.   45
 The Phænix builds the Phænix' nest.
LOV'S architecture is his own.
 The BABE whose birth embraves this morn,
Made his own bed e're he was born.

32 *Young dawn*: the infant Christ is this because the Nativity begins the work of our Redemption.

Cho. The BABE whose, etc. 50

Tit. I saw the curl'd drops, soft and slow,
Come hovering o're the place's head;
  Offring their whitest sheets of snow
To furnish the fair INFANT'S bed:
  Forbear, said I; be not too bold. 55
Your fleece is white But t'is too cold.

Cho. Forbear, sayd I, etc.

Thyr. I saw the obsequious SERAPHIMS
Their rosy fleece of fire bestow.
  For well they now can spare their wings 60
Since HEAVN itself lyes here below.
  Well done, said I: but are you sure
Your down so warm, will passe for pure?

Cho. Well done sayd I, etc.

Tity. No no. your KING'S not yet to seeke 65
Where to repose his ROYALL HEAD
  See see, how soon his new-bloom'd CHEEK
Twixt's mother's brests is gone to bed.
  Sweet choise, said we! no way but so
Not to ly cold, yet sleep in snow. 70

Cho. Sweet choise, said we, etc.

Both. We saw thee in thy baulmy nest,
Bright dawn of our æternall Day!
  We saw thine eyes break from thir EAST
And chase the trembling shades away. 75
  We saw thee: and we blest the sight.
We saw thee, by thine own sweet light.

Cho. We saw thee, etc.

Full Chorus

    Wellcome, all WONDERS in one sight!
Æternity shutt in a span.
    Sommer in Winter. Day in Night.
Heaven in earth, and GOD in MAN.
    Great little one! whose all-embracing birth
Lifts earth to heaven, stoopes heav'n to earth.

    WELLCOME. Though nor to gold nor silk,
To more then Cæsar's birth right is;
    Two sister-seas of Virgin-Milk,
With many a rarely-temper'd kisse
    That breathes at once both MAID and MOTHER,
Warmes in the one, cooles in the other.

    WELCOME, though not to those gay flyes
Guilded ith' Beames of earthly kings;
    Slippery soules in smiling eyes;
But to poor Shepheards, home-spun things:
    Whose Wealth's their flock; whose witt, to be
Well read in their simplicity.
    Yet when young April's husband showrs
Shall blesse the fruitfull Maja's bed
    We'l bring the First-born of her flowrs
To kisse thy FEET and crown thy HEAD.
    To thee, dread lamb! whose love must keep
The shepheards, more then they the sheep.
    To THEE, meek Majesty! soft KING
Of simple GRACES and sweet LOVES.
    Each of us his lamb will bring,
Each his pair of sylver Doves;
    Till burnt at last in fire of Thy fair eyes,
Our selves become our own best SACRIFICE.

85ff. Christ is made welcome, not to gold and silver, but to a birthright exceeding Caesar's, the Virgin's milk.

91 *flyes*: parasites, flatterers (*OED*).

New Year's Day

Rise, thou best and brightest morning!
Rosy with a double Red;
   With thine own blush thy cheeks adorning
And the dear drops this day were shed.

All the purple pride that laces 5
The crimson curtains of thy bed,
   Guilds thee not with so sweet graces
Nor setts thee in so rich a red.

Of all the fair-cheek't flowrs that fill thee
None so fair thy bosom strowes, 10
   As this modest maiden lilly
Our sins have sham'd into a rose.

Bid thy golden GOD, the Sun,
Burnisht in his best beames rise,
   Put all his red-ey'd Rubies on; 15
These Rubies shall putt out their eyes.

Let him make poor the purple east,
Search what the world's close cabinets keep,
   Rob the rich births of each bright nest
That flaming in their fair beds sleep, 20

Let him embrave his own bright tresses
With a new morning made of gemmes;
   And wear, in those his wealthy dresses,
Another Day of Diadems.

New Year's Day. First published in 1646 with the title "An Himne for the Circumcision day of Our Lord"; 1646 differs considerably and 1648 only slightly from the text of 1652. Cf. Milton, "On the Morning of Christ's Nativity," for a similar conception of the sun robbed of splendor by Christ's coming.

    When he hath done all he may   25
To make himselfe rich in his rise,
    All will be darknes to the Day
That breakes from one of these bright eyes.

    And soon this sweet truth shall appear
Dear BABE, ere many dayes be done,   30
    The morn shall come to meet thee here,
And leave her own neglected Sun.

    Here are Beautyes shall bereave him
Of all his eastern Paramours.
    His Persian Lovers all shall leave him,   35
And swear faith to thy sweeter Powres.

In the Glorious EPIPHANIE of Our Lord God

A Hymn
Sung as by the Three Kings

Bright BABE! Whose awfull beautyes make
The morn incurr a sweet mistake;
(2.) For whom the'officious heavns devise
To disinheritt the sun's rise,
(3.) Delicately to displace
The Day, and plant it fairer in thy face;   5
(1.) O thou born KING of loves,
    (2.) Of lights,
    (3.) Of joyes!
Cho. Look up, sweet BABE, look up and see   10
    For love of Thee
    Thus farr from home
    The EAST is come
To seek her self in thy sweet Eyes.
(1.) We, who strangely went astray,   15
    Lost in a bright
    Meridian night,

In the Glorious Epiphanie.... First published in 1648 with the title "A Hymne for the Epiphanie. Sung as by the three Kings"; the two versions differ only slightly. The poem turns on the antithesis between the natural sun, worshiped by various pagan cults and supposed to have a birthday at the winter solstice (22 December), and the Heavenly Sun/Son. The Epistle for Epiphany, drawn from Isa. 60:1-3 is suggestive for the imagery of the poem and for the sun comparison: "Arise, be enlightened, O Jerusalem: for thy light is come, and the glory of the Lord is risen upon thee. For behold darkness shall cover the earth, and a mist the people: but the Lord shall arise upon thee, and His glory shall be seen upon thee. And the Gentiles shall walk in thy light, and kings in the brightness of thy rising" (Missale Romanum).

(2.) A Darkenes made of too much day,
  (3.) Becken'd from farr
  By thy fair starr,
Lo at last have found our way.
Cho. TO THEE, thou DAY of night! thou east of west!
Lo we at last have found the way.
To thee, the world's great universal east.
The Generall and indifferent DAY.
(1.) All-circling point. All centring sphear.
The World's one, round, Æternall year.
(2.) Whose full and all-unwrinkled face
Nor sinks nor swells with time or place;
(3.) But every where and every while
Is One Consistent solid smile;
  (1.) Not vext and tost
  (2.) 'Twixt spring and frost,
(3.) Nor by alternate shredds of light
Sordidly shifting hands with shades and night.
Cho. O little all! in thy embrace
The world lyes warm, and likes his place.
Nor does his full Globe fail to be
Kist on Both his cheeks by Thee.
Time is too narrow for thy YEAR
Nor makes the whole WORLD thy half-sphear.
  (1.) To Thee, to Thee
  From him we flee
(2.) From HIM, whom by a more illustrious ly,
The blindness of the world did call the eye;
(3.) To HIM, who by These mortall clouds hast made
Thy self our sun, though thine own shade.
(1.) Farewell, the world's false light.
  Farewell, the white
  Ægypt! a long farewell to thee
  Bright IDOL; black IDOLATRY.
The dire face of inferior DARKNES, kis't
And courted in the pompus mask of a more specious mist.
  (2.) Farewell, farewell
  The proud and misplac't gates of hell,
  Pertch't, in the morning's way

And double-guilded as the doores of DAY.
The deep hypocrisy of DEATH and NIGHT
More desperately dark, Because more bright.
  (3.) Welcome, the world's sure Way!
  HEAVN'S wholsom ray.
  Cho. Wellcome to us; and we
  (SWEET) to our selves, in THEE.
(1.) The deathles HEIR of all thy FATHER'S day!
  (2.) Decently Born.
Embosom'd in a much more Rosy MORN,
The Blushes of thy All-unblemish't mother.
  (3.) No more that other
  Aurora shall sett ope
Her ruby casements, or hereafter hope
  From mortall eyes
To meet Religious welcomes at her rise.
Cho. We (Pretious ones!) in you have won
A gentler MORN, a juster sun.
(1.) His superficiall Beames sun-burn't our skin;
  (2.) But left within
(3.) The night and winter still of death and sin.
Cho. Thy softer yet more certaine DARTS
Spare our eyes, but peirce our HARTS.
(1.) Therfore with HIS proud persian spoiles
(2.) We court thy more concerning smiles.
  (3.) Therfore with his Disgrace
We guild the humble cheek of this chast place;
Cho. And at thy FEET powr forth his FACE.
(1.) The doating nations now no more
Shall any day but THINE adore.
(2.) Nor (much lesse) shall they leave these eyes
For cheap Ægyptian Deityes.
(3.) In whatsoe're more Sacred shape
Of Ram, He-goat, or reverend ape,
Those beauteous ravishers opprest so sore
The too-hard-tempted nations.
  (1.) Never more
By wanton heyfer shall be worn

(2.) A Garland, or a guilded horn.   95
The altar-stall'd ox, fatt OSYRIS now
      With his fair sister cow,
(3.) Shall kick the clouds no more; But lean and tame,
Cho. See his horn'd face, and dy for shame.
And MITHRA now shall be no name.   100
(1.) No longer shall the immodest lust
Of Adulterous GODLES dust
(2.) Fly in the face of heav'n; As if it were
The poor world's Fault that he is fair.
(3.) Nor with perverse loves and Religious RAPES   105
Revenge thy Bountyes in their beauteous shapes;
And punish Best Things worst; Because they stood
Guilty of being much for them too Good.
(1.) Proud sons of death! that durst compell
Heav'n it self to find them hell;   110
(2.) And by strange witt of madnes wrest
From this world's EAST the other's WEST.
(3.) All-Idolizing wormes! that thus could crowd
And urge Their sun into thy cloud;
Forcing his sometimes eclips'd face to be   115
A long deliquium to the light of thee.
Cho. Alas with how much heavyer shade
The shamefac't lamp hung down his head
      For that one eclipse he made
      Then all those he suffered!   120
(1.) For this he look't so bigg; and every morn
With a red face confes't this scorn.
Or hiding his vex't cheeks in a hir'd mist
Kept them from being so unkindly kis't.
(2.) It was for this the day did rise   125
      So oft with blubber'd eyes.
For this the evening wept; and we ne're knew
      But call'd it deaw.
      (3.) This dayly wrong

---

116 *deliquium:* fault, crime.

Silenc't the morning-sons, and damp't their song 130
Cho. Nor was't our deafnes, but our sins, that thus
Long made th'Harmonious orbes all mute to us.
      (1.) Time has a day in store
      When this so proudly poor
And self-oppressed spark, that has so long 135
By the love-sick world bin made
Not so much their sun as SHADE,
Weary of this Glorious wrong
From them and from himself shall flee
For shelter to the shadow of thy TREE; 140
Cho. Proud to have gain'd this pretious losse
And chang'd his false crown for thy CROSSE.
(2.) That dark Day's clear doom shall define
Whose is the Master FIRE, which sun should shine.
That sable judgment-seat shall by new lawes 145
Decide and settle the Great cause
      Of controverted light,
Cho. And natur's wrongs rejoyce to doe thee right.
(3.) That forfeiture of noon to night shall pay
All the idolatrous thefts done by this night of day; 150
And the Great Penitent presse his own pale lipps
With an elaborate love-eclipse
      To which the low world's lawes
      Shall lend no cause
Cho. Save those domestick which he borrowes 155
From our sins and his own sorrowes.
(1.) Three sad hour's sackcloth then shall show to us
His penance, as our fault, conspicuous.
(2.) And he more needfully and nobly prove
The nation's terror now then erst their love. 160

    130 *morning-sons:* see Job 38:7, in reference to the Creation, "When the morning stars sang together, and all the sons of God shouted for joy." The allusion is evidently to the angelic choirs (related immediately after, l. 132, to the music of the spheres), both now inaudible to man because of sin.
    151 *Great Penitent:* at the Crucifixion the Sun will do penance for his sin of being worshiped as a God by being eclipsed; not Nature's laws, but his own "domestick" or private concerns will cause this event, which is foreshadowed in the Epiphany by the Magi's adoration.

(3.) Their hated loves changd into wholsom feares,
Cho. The shutting of his eye shall open Theirs.
(1.) As by a fair-ey'd fallacy of day
Miss-ledde before they lost their way,
So shall they, by the seasonable fright 165
Of an unseasonable night,
Loosing it once again, stumble'on true LIGHT.
(2.) And as before his too-bright eye
Was Their more blind idolatry,
So his officious blindnes now shall be 170
Their black, but faithfull perspective of thee;
    (3.) His new prodigious night,
Their new and admirable light;
The supernaturall DAWN of Thy pure day.
    While wondring they 175
(The happy converts now of him
Whom they compell'd before to be their sin)
    Shall henceforth see
To kisse him only as their rod
Whom they so long courted as GOD, 180
Cho. And their best use of him they worship't be
To learn of Him at least, to worship Thee.
(1.) It was their Weaknes woo'd his beauty;
    But it shall be
Their wisdome now, as well as duty, 185
To'injoy his Blott; and as a large black letter
Use it to spell Thy beautyes better;
And make the night it self their torch to thee.
(2.) By the oblique ambush of this close night
    Couch't in that conscious shade 190
The right-ey'd Areopagite
Shall with a vigorous guesse invade
And catche thy quick reflex; and sharply see

---

191 *The right-ey'd Areopagite:* Dionysius, the pseudo-Areopagite, was said to have been converted by the eclipse at the Crucifixion. Crashaw alludes here and below to his *De Mystica Theologia (Patrologia Graeca* III, ed. J. P. Migne, Paris, 1857, cols. 997–1064) as teaching the *Via Negativa*, a systematic negation of sensuous perceptions and images (sinfully used in the old sun-worship) so as to find God in "Divine Darkness," as a "pure intelligentiall Prey."

    On this dark Ground
    To descant THEE.   *195*
(3.) O prize of the rich SPIRIT! with what feirce chase
    Of his strong soul, shall he
    Leap at thy lofty FACE,
And seize the swift Flash, in rebound
From this obsequious cloud;   *200*
    Once call'd a sun;
    Till dearly thus undone,
Cho. Till thus triumphantly tam'd (o ye two
Twinne SUNNES!) and taught now to negotiate you.
(1.) Thus shall that reverend child of light,   *205*
(2.) By being scholler first of that new night,
Come forth Great master of the mystick day;
(3.) And teach obscure MANKIND a more close way
By the frugall negative light
Of a most wise and well-abused Night   *210*
To read more legible thine originall Ray,
Cho. And make our Darknes serve THY day;
Maintaining t'wixt thy world and ours
A commerce of contrary powres,
    A mutuall trade   *215*
    'Twixt sun and SHADE,
By confederat BLACK and WHITE
Borrowing day and lending night.
(1.) Thus we, who when with all the noble powres
That (at thy cost) are call'd, not vainly, ours   *220*
    We vow to make brave way
Upwards, and presse on for the pure intelligentiall Prey;
    (2.) At lest to play
    The amorous Spyes
And peep and proffer at thy sparkling Throne;   *225*
(3.) In stead of bringing in the blissfull PRIZE
    And fastening on Thine eyes,
    Forfeit our own
    And nothing gain
But more Ambitious losse, at lest of brain;   *230*
Cho. Now by abased liddes shall learn to be
Eagles; and shutt our eyes that we may see.

The Close

Therefore to THEE and thine Auspitious ray
    (Dread sweet!) lo thus
      At lest by us,   235
The delegated EYE of DAY
Does first his Scepter, then HIMSELF in solemne tribute pay.
    Thus he undresses
      His sacred unshorn treses;
At thy adored FEET, thus, he layes down   240
    (1.) His gorgeous tire
    Of flame and fire,
(2.) His glittering ROBE, (3.) his sparkling CROWN,
(1.) His GOLD, (2.) his MIRRH, (3.) his FRANKINCENCE,
[Cho.] To which He now has no pretence.   245
For being show'd by this day's light, how farr
He is from sun enough to make THY starr,
His best ambition now, is but to be
Somthing a brighter SHADOW (sweet) of thee.
Or on heavn's azure forehead high to stand   250
Thy golden index; with a duteous Hand
Pointing us Home to our own sun
The world's and his HYPERION.

To the Queen's Majesty

MADAME.
'Mongst those long rowes of crownes that guild your race,
These Royall sages sue for decent place.
The day-break of the nations; their first ray;
When the Dark WORLD dawn'd into Christian DAY
And smil'd i'th' BABE'S bright face, the purpling Bud   5
And Rosy dawn of the right Royall blood;
Fair first-fruits of the LAMB. Sure KINGS in this;
They took a kingdom while they gave a kisse.
But the world's Homage, scarse in These well blown,
We read in you (Rare Queen) ripe and full-grown.   10
For from this day's rich seed of Diadems
Does rise a radiant croppe of Royalle stemms,
A Golden harvest of crown'd heads, that meet
And crowd for kisses from the LAMB'S white feet.
In this Illustrious throng, your lofty floud   15
Swells high, fair Confluence of all highborn Bloud!
With your bright head whole groves of scepters bend
Their wealthy tops; and for these feet contend.
So swore the LAMB'S dread sire. And so we see't.
Crownes, and the HEADS they kisse, must court these FEET. 20
Fix here, fair Majesty! May your Heart ne're misse
To reap new CROWNES and KINGDOMS from that kisse.
Nor may we misse the joy to meet in you
The aged honors of this day still new.
May the great time, in you, still greater be   25
While all the YEAR is your EPIPHANY,
While your each day's devotion duly brings
Three KINGDOMES to supply this day's three KINGS.

To the Queen's Majesty. First published in 1648 with the title, "To the Queenes Majestie upon his dedicating to her the foregoeing Hymne"; text varies only slightly from 1652. This compliment to Henrietta Maria on the occasion of the Epiphany relates her, as a sovereign, to the Three Kings.

THE OFFICE OF THE HOLY CROSSE

THE HOWRES

For the Hour of Matines

The Versicle

LORD, by thy Sweet and Saving SIGN,

The Responsory

Defend us from our foes and Thine.
V. Thou shallt open my lippes, O LORD.
R. And my mouth shall shew forth thy Prayse.
V. O GOD make speed to save me.
R. O LORD make hast to help me.   *5*
GLORY be to the FATHER,
 and to the SON,
 and to the H. GHOST.
 As it was in the beginning, is now, and ever shall be, world without end. Amen.   *10*

The Office of the Holy Crosse. First published in 1648 in a condensed version, with parts differently distributed, under various titles. The original is one of several special offices developed in imitation of the prescribed Divine Office, especially for monastic and popular devotion. It was in many Books of Hours, and also in the vernacular Sarum Primers, published in Queen Mary's reign and in constant use at Little Gidding, where Crashaw had first access to these formularies of Roman Catholic worship in England. In the Sarum Use the Hours of the Holy Cross were to be recited daily during Lent after the regular Hours of the Office. See William Maskell, *Monumenta Ritualia Ecclesiae Anglicanae* III (Oxford, 1882), x–xiv, 40, 47–61, 66–74. Crashaw's translation is very free.

THE HYMN

The wakefull Matines hast to sing,
The unknown sorrows of our king,
The FATHER'S word and wisdom, made
MAN, for man, by man's betraid;   15
The world's price sett to sale, and by the bold
Merchants of Death and sin, is bought and sold.
Of his Best Freinds (yea of himself) forsaken,
By his worst foes (because he would) beseig'd and taken.

The Antiphona

All hail, fair TREE.   20
Whose Fruit we be.
What song shall raise
Thy seemly praise.
Who broughtst to light
Life out of death, Day out of night.   25

The Versicle

Lo, we adore thee,
Dread LAMB! And bow thus low before thee;

The Responsor

'Cause, by the covenant of thy CROSSE,
Thou'hast sav'd at once the whole world's losse.

The Prayer

O Lord JESU-CHRIST, son of the living GOD! interpose, I pray thee, thine own pretious death, thy CROSSE and Passion, betwixt my soul and thy judgment, now and in the hour of my death. And vouchsafe to graunt unto me thy grace and mercy; unto all quick and dead, remission and rest; to thy church peace and concord; to us sinners life and glory everlasting. Who livest and reignest with the FATHER, in the unity of the HOLY GHOST, one GOD, world without end.   Amen.

For the Hour of Prime

The Versicle
Lord by thy sweet and saving SIGN

The Responsor
Defend us from our foes and thine.
V. Thou shalt open.
R. And my mouth.
V. O GOD make speed.
R. O LORD make hast.
  Glory be to.
  As it was in.

THE HYMN

The early PRIME blushes to say
She could not rise so soon, as they
Call'd Pilat up; to try if He
Could lend them any cruelty.
    Their hands with lashes arm'd, their toungs
      with lyes,
And loathsom spittle, blott those beauteous eyes,
The blissfull springs of joy; from whose all-chearing Ray
The fair starrs fill their wakefull fires, the sun him-
    selfe drinks Day.

The Antiphona
    Victorious SIGN
    That now dost shine,
    Transcrib'd above
Into the land of light and love;
    O let us twine
    Our rootes with thine,
    That we may rise
Upon thy wings, and reach the skyes.

The Versicle
Lo we adore thee
Dread LAMB! and fall
Thus low before thee   25

The Responsor
'Cause by the Convenant of thy CROSSE
Thou'hast sav'd at once the whole world's losse.

The Prayer
O Lord JESU-CHRIST, *etc.*   30

The Third

The Versicle
Lord, by thy sweet and saving SIGN

The Responsor
Defend us from our foes and thine.
  V. Thou shalt open.
  R. And my mouth.
  V. O GOD make speed.   5
  R. O LORD make hast.
  V. Glory be to.
  R. As it was in the.

THE HYMN

The Third hour's deafen'd with the cry
Of crucify him, crucify.   10
So goes the vote (nor ask them, Why?)
Live Barabbas! and let GOD dy.
But there is witt in wrath, and they will try
A HAIL more cruell than their crucify.
For while in sport he weares a spitefull crown,   15

The serious showres along his decent
        Face run sadly down.

The Antiphona
CHRIST when he dy'd
Deceivd the CROSSE;
And on death's side   20
Threw all the losse.
The captive world awak't, and found
The prisoners loose, the Jalyor bound.

The Versicle
Lo we adore thee
Dread LAMB, and fall   25
    thus low before thee

The Responsor
'Cause by the convenant of the CROSSE
Thou'has sav'd at once the whole world's losse.

The Prayer
O Lord JESU-CHRIST, *etc.*   30

The Sixt

The Versicle
Lord by thy sweet and saving SIGN,

The Responsor
Defend us from our foes and thine.
V. Thou shalt open.
R. And my mouth.
V. O GOD make speed.   5
R. O LORD make hast.
V. Glory be.
R. As it was in.

THE HIMN

Now is The noon of sorrow's night;
High in his patience, as their spite.
Lo the faint LAMB, with weary limb
Beares that huge tree which must bear Him.
That fatall plant, so great of fame
For fruit of sorrow and of shame,
Shall swell with both for HIM; and mix
All woes into one CRUCIFIX.
Is tortur'd Thirst, it selfe, too sweet a cup?
GALL, and more bitter mocks, shall make it up.
Are NAILES blunt pens of superficiall smart?
Contempt and scorn can send sure wounds to search
   the inmost Heart.

The Antiphona

O deare and sweet Dispute
'Twixt death's and LOVE'S farr different FRUIT!
Different as farr
As antidotes and poysons are.
By that first fatall TREE
Both life and liberty
Were sold and slain;
By this they both look up, and live again.

The Versicle

Lo we adore thee
Dread LAMB! and bow thus low before thee;

The Responsor

'Cause by the convenant of thy CROSSE
Thou'hast sav'd the world from certain losse.

The Prayer

O Lord JESU-CHRIST, *etc.*

The Ninth

The Versicle
Lord by thy sweet and saving SIGN

The Responsor
Defend us from our foes and thine.
v. Thou shalt open.
r. And my mouth.
v. O GOD make speed.
r. O LORD make hast.
  Glory be to.
  As it was in.

THE HYMN

The ninth with awfull horror hearkened to
  those groanes
Which taught attention ev'n to rocks and STONES
Hear, FATHER, hear! thy LAMB (at last) complaines.
Of some more painfull thing then all his paines.
Then bowes his all-obedient head, and dyes
His own lov's, and our sin's GREAT SACRIFICE.
The sun saw That; And would have seen no more;
The center shook. Her uselesse veil th' inglorious
  Temple tore.

The Antiphona
O strange mysterious strife
Of open DEATH and hidden LIFE!
When on the crosse my king did bleed,
LIFE seem'd to dy, DEATH dy'd indeed.

The Versicle
Lo we adore thee
Dread LAMB! and fall
  thus low before thee

The Responsor
'Cause by the convenant of thy CROSSE
Thou'hast sav'd at once the whole world's losse.   *25*

The Prayer
O Lord JESU-CHRIST, *etc.*

Evensong

The Versicle
Lord, by thy sweet and saving SIGN

The Responsor
Defend us from our foes and thine.
v. Thou shalt open.
r. And my mouth.
v. O GOD make speed.
r. O LORD make hast.
v. Glory be to.   *5*
r. As it was in the.

THE HYMN

But there were Rocks would not relent at This.
Lo, for their own hearts, they rend his.   *10*
Their deadly hate lives still; and hath
A wild reserve of wanton wrath;
Superfluous SPEAR! But there's a HEART stands by
Will look no wounds be lost, no deaths shall dy.
Gather now thy Greif's ripe FRUIT. Great mother-maid!   *15*
Then sitt thee down, and sing thine Ev'nsong in the sad
    TREE'S shade.

The Antiphona
O sad, sweet TREE!
Wofull and joyfull we

Both weep and sing in shade of thee.
When the dear NAILES did lock
And graft into thy gracious Stock
    The hope; the health,
    The worth, the wealth
Of all the ransom'd WORLD, thou hadst the power
    (In that propitious Hour)
    To poise each pretious limb,
And prove how light the World was, when it weighd with HIM.
    Wide maist thou spred
Thine Armes; And with thy bright and blisfull head
O'relook all Libanus. Thy lofty crown
The king himself is; Thou his humble THRONE.
Where yeilding and yet conquering he
Prov'd a new path of patient Victory.
When wondring death by death was slain,
And our Captivity his Captive ta'ne.

The Versicle
Lo we adore thee
Dread LAMB! and bow thus low before thee;

The Responsor
'Cause by the convenant of thy CROSSE
Thou'hast sav'd the world from certain losse.

THE PRAYER
O lord JESU-CHRIST, *etc.*

Compline

The Versicle
Lord by thy sweet and saving SIGN,

The Responsor
Defend us from our foes and thine.
V. Thou shalt open.
R. And my mouth.
V. O GOD make speed.
R. O LORD make hast.
V. Glory be.
R. As it was in.

THE HIMN

The Complin hour comes last, to call
Us to our own LIVE'S funerall.
Ah hartlesse task! yet hope takes head;
And lives in Him that here lyes dead.
Run, MARY, run! Bring hither all the BLEST
ARABIA, for thy Royall Phœnix'nest;
Pour on thy noblest sweets, Which, when they touch
This sweeter BODY, shall indeed be such.
But must thy bed, lord, be a borow'd grave
Who lend'st to all things All the LIFE they have.
O rather use this HEART, thus farr a fitter STONE,
'Cause, though a hard and cold one, yet it is thine owne.
     Amen.

The Antiphona
 O save us then
 Mercyfull KING of men!
 Since thou wouldst needs be thus
A SAVIOUR, and at such a rate, for us;
 Save us, o save us, lord.
We now will own no shorter wish, nor name a narrower word.
  Thy blood bids us be bold.
  Thy Wounds give us fair hold.
  Thy Sorrows chide our shame.
Thy Crosse, thy Nature, and thy name

Advance our claim
And cry with one accord
Save them, o save them, lord.

The Recommendation

These Houres, and that which hover's o're my END,
Into thy hands, and hart, lord I, commend.

Take Both to Thine Account, that I and mine
In that Hour, and in these, may be all thine.

That as I dedicate my devoutest BREATH 5
To make a kind of LIFE for my lord's DEATH,

So from his living, and life-giving DEATH,
My dying LIFE may draw a new, and never fleeting BREATH.

Upon the H. Sepulcher

Here where our LORD once lay'd his Head,
Now the grave lyes Buryed.

The Recommendation. First published in 1648. Prefaced in 1652 by an engraving and motto signed by J. Messager, who did several of the engravings in this volume.

Upon the H. Sepulcher. First published in 1646, with the title "Upon the Sepulchre of our Lord."

Vexilla Regis, the Hymn of the Holy Crosse

I

Look up, languishing Soul! Lo where the fair
BADG of thy faith calls back thy care,
    And biddes thee ne're forget
    Thy life is one long Debt
Of love to Him, who on this painfull TREE   5
Paid back the flesh he took for thee.

II

Lo, how the streames of life, from that full nest
Of loves, thy lord's too liberall brest,
    Flow in an amorous floud
    Of WATER wedding BLOOD.   10
With these he wash't thy stain, transfer'd thy smart,
And took it home to his own heart.

III

But though great LOVE, greedy of such sad gain
Usurp't the Portion of THY pain,
    And from the nailes and spear   15
    Turn'd the steel point of fear,
Their use is chang'd, not lost; and now they move
Not stings of wrath, but wounds of love.

IV

Tall TREE of life! thy truth makes good
What was till now ne're understood,   20

Vexilla Regis.... First published in 1648 with lines 37–42 omitted. The original is a medieval hymn attributed to Fortunatus; it was first sung in 569 A.D., and was established in Roman ritual as a sequence to be chanted during the Mass of the Presanctified on Good Friday, and as a hymn to be sung at Vespers from the Saturday before Passion Sunday to Maundy Thursday. See Sister Margaret Claydon, *Richard Crashaw's Paraphrases,* for texts of the Latin hymns and sequences Crashaw rendered, and for a study of his manner as a translator.

> Though the prophetick king
> Struck lowd his faithful string.
> It was thy wood he meant should make the THRONE
> For a more then SALOMON.

V

> Larg throne of love! Royally spred
> With purple of too Rich a red.
>   Thy crime is too much duty;
>   Thy Burthen, too much beauty;
> Glorious, or Greivous more? thus to make good
> Thy costly excellence with thy KING'S own BLOOD.

VI

> Even ballance of both worlds! our world of sin,
> And that of grace heavn way'd in HIM,
>   Us with our price thou weighed'st;
>   Our price for us thou payed'st;
> Soon as the right-hand scale rejoyc't to prove
> How much Death weigh'd more light then love.

VII

> Hail, our alone hope! let thy fair head shoot
> Aloft; and fill the nations with thy noble fruit.
>   The while our hearts and we
>   Thus graft our selves on thee;
> Grow thou and they. And be thy fair increase
> The sinner's pardon and the just man's peace.

> Live, o for ever live and reign
> The LAMB whom his own love hath slain!
> And let thy lost sheep live to'inherit
> That KINGDOM which this CROSSE did merit.
>   AMEN.

To Our B. Lord
Upon the Choise of His Sepulchur

How life and death in Thee
    Agree!
Thou hadst a virgin womb,
    And tomb.
A JOSEPH did betroth   5
    Them both.

Charitas Nimia
or
The Dear Bargain

Lord, what is man? why should he coste thee
So dear? what had his ruin lost thee?
Lord what is man? that thou hast overbought
  So much a thing of nought?

Love is too kind, I see; and can   5
Make but a simple merchant man.
'Twas for such sorry merchandise
Bold Painters have putt out his Eyes.

Alas, sweet lord, what wer't to thee
If there were no such wormes as we?   10
Heav'n ne're the lesse still heavn would be,
    Should Mankind dwell
    In the deep hell.
What have his woes to doe with thee?

Charitas Nimia . . . . First published in 1648 without stanza divisions.

  Let him goe weep　　　　　　　　　　*15*
  O're his own wounds;
  SERAPHIMS will not sleep
Nor spheares let fall their faithfull rounds.

 Still would The youthfull SPIRITS sing;
And still thy spatious Palace ring.　　　　　　*20*
Still would those beauteous ministers of light
  Burn all as bright,

 And bow their flaming heads before thee
Still thrones and Dominations would adore thee
Still would those ever-wakefull sons of fire　　*25*
  Keep warm thy prayse
  Both nights and dayes,
And teach thy lov'd name to their noble lyre.

 Let froward Dust then doe it's kind;
And give it self for sport to the proud wind.　*30*
Why should a peice of peevish clay plead shares
In the Æternity of thy old cares?
Why shouldst thou bow thy awfull Brest to see
What mine own madnesses have done with me?

 Should not the king still keepe his throne　　*35*
Because some desperate Fool's undone?
Or will the world's Illustrious eyes
Weep for every worm that dyes;

  Will the gallant sun
  E're the lesse glorious run?
Will he hang down his golden head　　　　　　*40*
Or e're the sooner seek his western bed,
  Because some foolish fly
  Growes wanton, and will dy?

 If I were lost in misery,　　　　　　　　　*45*
What was it to thy heavn and thee?

What was it to thy pretious blood
If my foul Heart call'd for a floud?

What if my faithlesse soul and I
    Would needs fall in 50
    With guilt and sin,
What did the Lamb, that he should dy?
What did the lamb, that he should need,
When the wolf sins, himself to bleed?

    If my base lust, 55
Bargain'd with Death and well-beseeming dust
    Why should the white
    Lamb's bosom write
    The purple name
    Of my sin's shame? 60

Why should his unstaind brest make good
My blushes with his own heart-blood?

O my SAVIOUR, make me see
How dearly thou hast payd for me

That lost again my LIFE may prove 65
As then in DEATH, so now in love.

Sancta Maria Dolorum

or

The Mother of Sorrows

A Patheticall descant upon
the devout Plainsong

of

STABAT MATER
DOLOROSA

I

In shade of death's sad TREE
    Stood Dolefull SHEE.
Ah SHE! now by none other
Name to be known, alas, but SORROW'S MOTHER.
    Before her eyes   5
Her's, and the whole world's joyes,
Hanging all torn she sees; and in his woes
And Paines, her Pangs and throes.
Each wound of His, from every Part,
All, more at home in her owne heart.   10

II

    What kind of marble than
    Is that cold man
    Who can look on and see,

Sancta Maria Dolorum.... First published in 1648 with the title "The Mother of Sorrowes." The 1652 subtitle identifies the source, Jacopone da Todi's (1230–1302) well-known hymn, *Stabat Mater Dolorosa*, which appeared by the fifteenth century in several European missals as the sequence for the Feast of the Seven Sorrows of the Virgin. The feast was usually celebrated on Friday of Passion Week although it was not extended to the whole church until 1727.

Not keep such noble sorrowes company?
    Sure ev'en from you 15
    (My Flints) some drops are due
To see so many unkind swords contest
    So fast for one soft Brest.
While with a faithfull, mutuall, floud
Her eyes bleed TEARES, his wounds weep BLOOD. 20

III

    O costly intercourse
    Of deaths, and worse
    Divided loves. While son and mother
Discourse alternate wounds to one another;
    Quick Deaths that grow 25
    And gather, as they come and goe:
His Nailes write swords in her, which soon her heart
    Payes back, with more then their own smart,
Her SWORDS, still growing with his pain,
Turn SPEARES, and straight come home again. 30

IV

    She sees her son, her GOD,
    Bow with a load
    Of borrowd sins; And swimme
In woes that were not made for Him.
    Ah hard command 35
    Of love! Here must she stand
Charg'd to look on, and with a stedfast ey
    See her life dy:
Leaving her only so much Breath
As serves to keep alive her death. 40

V

    O Mother turtle-dove!
    Soft sourse of love
    That these dry lidds might borrow
Somthing from thy full Seas of sorrow!

>   O in that brest 45
>   Of thine (the noblest nest
> Both of love's fires and flouds) might I recline
>   This hard, cold, Heart of mine!
> The chill lump would relent, and prove
> Soft, subject for the seige of love. 50

VI

>   O teach those wounds to bleed
>   In me; me, so to read
>   This book of loves, thus writ
> In lines of death, my life may coppy it
>   With loyall cares. 55
>   O let me, here, claim shares;
> Yeild somthing in thy sad prærogative
>   (Great Queen of greifes) and give
> Me too my teares; who, though all stone,
> Think much that thou shouldst mourn alone. 60

VII

>   Yea let my life and me
>   Fix here with thee,
>   And at the Humble foot
> Of this fair TREE take our eternall root.
>   That so we may 65
>   At least be in loves way;
> And in these chast warres while the wing'd wounds flee
>   So fast' twixt him and thee,
> My brest may catch the kisse of some kind dart,
> Though as at second hand, from either heart. 70

VIII

>   O you, your own best Darts
>   Dear, dolefull hearts!
>   Hail; and strike home and make me see
> That wounded bosomes their own weapons be.
>   Come wounds! come darts! 75
>   Nail'd hands! and peirced hearts!

  Come your whole selves, sorrow's great son and
    mother!
   Nor grudge a yonger-Brother
Of greifes his portion, who (had all their due)
One single wound should not have left for you.   *80*

IX

  Shall I, sett there
  So deep a share
  (Dear wounds) and onely now
In sorrows draw no Dividend with you?
  O be more wise   *85*
  If not more soft, mine eyes!
Flow, tardy founts! and into decent showres
  Dissolve my Dayes and Howres.
And if thou yet (faint soul!) deferr
To bleed with him, fail not to weep with her.   *90*

X

  Rich Queen, lend some releife;
  At least an almes of greif
  To'a heart who by sad right of sin
Could prove the whole sume (too sure) due to him.
  By all those stings   *95*
  Of love, sweet bitter things,
Which these torn hands transcrib'd on thy true heart
  O teach mine too the art
To study him so, till we mix
Wounds; and become one crucifix.   *100*

XI

  O let me suck the wine
  So long of this chast vine
  Till drunk of the dear wounds, I be
A lost Thing to the world, as it to me.
  O faithfull freind   *105*
  Of me and of my end!

Fold up my life in love; and lay't beneath
    My dear lord's vitall death.
Lo, heart, thy hope's whole Plea! Her pretious Breath
Powr'd out in prayrs for thee; thy lord's in death.   110

Upon the Bleeding Crucifix

A Song

I

Jesu, no more! It is full tide.
From thy head and from thy feet,
From thy hands and from thy side
All the purple Rivers meet.

II

What need thy fair head bear a part   5
In showres, as if thine eyes had none?
What need They help to drown thy heart,
That strives in torrents of it's own?

III

Thy restlesse feet now cannot goe
For us and our eternall good,   10
As they were ever wont. What though?
They swimme. Alas, in their own floud.

IV

Thy hands to give, thou canst not lift;
Yet will thy hand still giving be.
It gives but ô, it self's the gift.   15
It gives though bound; though bound 'tis free.

Upon the Bleeding Crucifix.... First published in 1646 with the title "On the bleeding wounds of our crucified Lord"; in 1648 with the title "On the bleeding body of our crucified Lord."

V

But ô thy side, thy deep-digg'd side!
That hath a double Nilus going.
Nor ever was the pharian tide
Half so fruitfull, half so flowing.   20

VI

No hair so small, but payes his river
To this red sea of thy blood
Their little channells can deliver
Somthing to the Generall floud.

VII

But while I speak, whither are run   25
All the rivers nam'd before?
I counted wrong. There is but one;
But ô that one is one all ore.

VIII

Rain-swoln rivers may rise proud,
Bent all to drown and overflow.   30
But when indeed all's overflow'd
They themselves are drowned too.

IX

This thy blood's deluge, a dire chance
Dear LORD to thee, to us is found
A deluge of Deliverance;   35
A deluge least we should be drown'd.

N'ere wast thou in a sense so sadly true,
The WELL of living WATERS, Lord, till now.

---

19 *pharian:* of or pertaining to the island of Pharos, in Egypt; here, the Nile's tide.

Upon the Crowne of Thorns
Taken Downe From the head of our Bl. Lord, all Bloody

Know'st thou This, Souldier? 'Tis a much-
    chang'd plant which yet
        Thy selfe didst sett.

O who so hard a Husbandman did ever find 5
        A soile so kind?

Is not the soile a kind one, which returnes
        Roses for Thornes?

Upon the Body of Our Bl. Lord, Naked and Bloody

They'have left thee naked, LORD, O that they had!
This garment too I would they had deny'd.

Thee with thy self they have too richly clad;
Opening the purple wardrobe in thy side.

O never could there be garment too good 5
For thee to wear, But this, of thine own Blood.

Upon the Crowne.... First published in 1646 in a longer version titled "Upon the Thornes taken downe from our Lords head bloody"; 1648 version is substantially that of 1652.

Upon the Body.... First published in 1646 with the title "On our crucified Lord Naked, and bloody"; 1648 retains the 1646 title.

The Hymn of Sainte Thomas
in Adoration of the Blessed Sacrament

ADORO TE

With all the powres my poor Heart hath
Of humble love and loyall Faith,
Thus lowe (my hidden life!) I bow to thee
Whom too much love hath bow'd more low for me.
Down down, proud sense! Discourses dy.   5
Keep close, my soul's inquiring ey!
Nor touch nor tast must look for more
But each sitt still in his own Dore.

Your ports are all superfluous here,
Save That which lets in faith, the eare.   10
Faith is my skill. Faith can beleive
As fast as love new lawes can give.
Faith is my force. Faith strength affords
To keep pace with those powrfull words.
And words more sure, more sweet, then they   15
Love could not think, truth could not say.

O let thy wretch find that releife
Thou didst afford the faithfull theife.
Plead for me, love! Alleage and show
That faith has farther, here, to goe   20
And lesse to lean on. Because than
Though hidd as GOD, wounds writt thee man,

The Hymn of Sainte Thomas.... First published in 1648 with the title "A Hymne to Our Saviour by the Faithfull Receiver of the Sacrament." This strong, austere hymn had been incorporated into the Missal in 1570 among the prayers of preparation and thanksgiving for Holy Communion, and it is placed in this volume in conjunction with St. Thomas' sequence for Corpus Christi, which immediately follows. Crashaw's version keeps the same number of stanzas as the original, but greatly expands them.

Thomas might touch; None but might see
At least the suffring side of thee;
And that too was thy self which thee did cover,　　25
But here ev'n That's hid too which hides the other.

  Sweet, consider then, that I
Though allow'd nor hand nor eye
To reach at thy lov'd Face; nor can
Tast thee GOD, or touch thee MAN　　30
Both yet beleive; And wittnesse thee
My LORD too and my GOD, as lowd as He.

  Help, Lord, my Faith, my Hope increase;
And fill my portion in thy peace.
Give love for life; nor let my dayes　　35
Grow, but in new powres to thy name and praise.

  O dear memoriall of that Death
Which lives still, and allowes us breath!
Rich, Royall food! Bountyfull BREAD!
Whose use denyes us to the dead;　　40
Whose vitall gust alone can give
The same leave both to eat and live;
Live ever Bread of loves, and be
My life, my soul, my surer selfe to mee.

  O soft self-wounding Pelican!　　45
Whose brest weepes Balm for wounded man.
Ah this way bend thy benign floud
To'a bleeding Heart that gaspes for blood.
That blood, whose least drops soveraign be
To wash my worlds of sins from me.　　50
Come love! Come LORD! and that long day
For which I languish, come away.
When this dry soul those eyes shall see,
And drink the unseal'd sourse of thee.
When Glory's sun faith's shades shall chase,　　55
And for thy veil give me thy FACE.
                    AMEN

Lauda Sion Salvatorem
The Hymn for
the Bl. Sacrament

I

Rise, Royall SION! rise and sing
Thy soul's kind shepheard, thy hart's KING:
Stretch all thy powres; call if you can
Harpes of heavn to hands of man.
This soveraign subject sitts above 5
The best ambition of thy love.

II

Lo the BREAD of LIFE, this day's
Triumphant Text, provokes thy prayse.
The living and life-giving bread,
To the great twelve distributed 10
When LIFE, himself, at point to dy
Of love, was his own LEGACY.

III

Come, love! and let us work a song
Lowd and pleasant, sweet and long;
Let lippes and Hearts lift high the noise 15
Of so just and solemn joyes,
Which on his white browes this bright day
Shall hence for ever bear away.

Lauda Sion .... First published in 1648 with the title "A Hymne on the B. Sacrament." The original, Aquinas' sequence for Corpus Christi (the Thursday after Trinity Sunday) was commissioned by Urban IV for the establishment of that feast in 1264. Severely doctrinal and objective, it seems to restrain Crashaw's inventiveness somewhat, and his version, though more ornamented and subjective, remains fairly close to the text and rather pedestrian.

IV

Lo the new LAW of a new LORD
With a new Lamb blesses the Board.
The aged Pascha pleads not yeares
But spyes love's dawn, and disappeares.
Types yeild to TRUTHES; shades shrink away;
And their NIGHT dyes into our Day.

V

But lest THAT dy too, we are bid
Ever to doe what he once did.
And by a mindfull, mystick breath
That we may live, revive his DEATH;
With a well-bles't bread and wine
Transsum'd, and taught to turn divine.

VI

The Heavn-instructed house of FAITH
Here a holy Dictate hath
That they but lend their Form and face,
Themselves with reverence leave their place,
Nature, and name, to be made good
By'a nobler Bread, more needfull BLOOD.

VII

Where nature's lawes no leave will give,
Bold FAITH takes heart, and dares beleive.
In different species, names not things
Himself to me my SAVIOUR brings,
As meat in That, as Drink in this;
But still in Both one CHRIST he is.

---

39 *names not things:* the name "flesh" is applied to the bread, and the name "blood" to the wine, but Christ is in reality wholly present in both.

VIII

The Receiving Mouth here makes
Nor wound nor breach in what he takes.
Let one, or one THOUSAND be
Here Dividers, single he
Beares home no lesse, all they no more,
Nor leave they both lesse then before.

IX

Though in it self this SOVERAIN FEAST
Be all the same to every Guest,
Yet on the same (life-meaning) Bread
The child of Death eates himself Dead.
Nor is't love's fault, but sin's dire skill
That thus from LIFE can DEATH distill.

X

When the blest signes thou broke shall see,
Hold but thy Faith intire as he
Who, howsoe're clad, cannot come
Lesse then whole CHRIST in every crumme.
In broken formes a stable FAITH
Untouch't her pretious TOTALL hath.

XI

Lo the life-food of ANGELLS then
Bow'd to the lowly mouths of men!
The children's BREAD; the Bridegroom's WINE,
Not to be cast to dogges, or swine.

XII

Lo, the full, finall, SACRIFICE
On which all figures fix't their eyes.

---

55 *blest signes ... broke:* although the signs (bread and wine) may be mere crumbs or particles, Christ is wholly present.

The ransom'd ISACK, and his ramme;
The MANNA, and the PASCHAL Lamb.

XIII

JESU MASTER, Just and true!
Our FOOD, and faithfull SHEPHARD too! 70
O by thy self vouchsafe to keep,
As with thy selfe thou feed'st thy SHEEP.

XIV

O let that love which thus makes thee
Mix with our low Mortality,
Lift our lean Soules, and sett us up 75
Convictors of thine own full cup,
Coheirs of SAINTS. That so all may
Drink the same wine; and the same WAY.
Nor chang the PASTURE, but the PLACE;
To feed of THEE in thine own FACE. 80
         AMEN.

---

67 *ransom'd Isack:* Isaac was replaced on the sacrificial altar by a ram, the Israelites ate manna in the desert, the paschal lamb was offered and eaten at Passover — all types (foreshadowings) of the Eucharist.

76 *Convictors:* co-sharers in a banquet, table-companions (*OED*).

Dies Irae Dies Illa

The Hymn of the Church,
in Meditation of the Day of Judgment

I

Hears't thou, my soul, what serious things
Both the Psalm and sybyll sings
Of a sure judge, from whose sharp Ray
The world in flames shall fly away.

II

O that fire! before whose face   5
Heavn and earth shall find no place.
O those eyes! whose angry light
Must be the day of that dread Night.

III

O that trump! whose blast shall run
An even round with the circling Sun.   10
And urge the murmuring graves to bring
Pale mankind forth to meet his king.

Dies Irae. First published in 1648 with the title "A Hymne in meditation of the day of judgement." The original is a thirteenth-century hymn, probably by the Franciscan monk Thomas of Celeno; it is used as a sequence in the Requiem Mass and also in the Mass of 2 November which commemorates all the dead. A comparison of Crashaw's first stanza with that of the original provides a measure of how Crashaw has softened this sternly magnificent hymn: "Dies irae, dies illa,/ Solvet Saeclum in favilla,/Teste David cum Sibylla.

2 Both David as a representative of the Hebrew Covenant and the Sybil as representative of the Gentiles are seen as testifying to the Day of Judgment in this wholly conventional linking of the two orders of prophecy. Several of David's psalms call for and predict Judgment, and St. Augustine, *De Civitate Dei* XVIII, quotes a passage from the Cumaean Sybil as foretelling the end of the world.

IV

Horror of nature, hell and Death!
When a deep Groan from beneath
Shall cry we come, we come and all
The caves of night answer one call.

V

O that Book! whose leaves so bright
Will sett the world in severe light.
O that Judge! whose hand, whose eye
None can indure; yet none can fly.

VI

Ah then, poor soul, what wilt thou say?
And to what Patron chuse to pray?
When starres themselves shall stagger; and
The most firm foot no more then stand.

VII

But thou giv'st leave (dread Lord) that we
Take shelter from thy self, in thee;
And with the wings of thine own dove
Fly to thy scepter of soft love.

VIII

Dear, remember in that Day
Who was the cause thou cams't this way.
Thy sheep was stray'd; And thou wouldst be
Even lost thy self in seeking me.

IX

Shall all that labour, all that cost
Of love, and ev'n that losse, be lost?
And this lov'd soul, judg'd worth no lesse
Then all that way, and werynesse?

X

Just mercy then, thy Reckning be
With my price, and not with me:
Twas pay'd at first with too much pain,
To be pay'd twice; or once, in vain. 40

XI

Mercy (my judge) mercy I cry
With blushing Cheek and bleeding ey,
The conscious colors of my sin
Are red without and pale within.

XII

O let thine own soft bowells pay 45
Thy self; And so discharge that day.
If sin can sigh, love can forgive.
O say the word, my Soul shall live.

XIII

Those mercyes which thy MARY found
Or who thy crosse confes't and crown'd, 50
Hope tells my heart, the same loves be
Still alive; and still for me.

XIV

Though both my Prayres and teares combine,
Both worthlesse are; For they are mine.
But thou thy bounteous self still be; 55
And show thou art, by saving me.

XV

O when thy last Frown shall proclaim
The flocks of goates to folds of flame,
And all thy lost sheep found shall be,
Let *come ye blessed* then call me. 60

57–60 Cf. Matt. 25:32–46.

XVI

When the dread ITE shall divide
Those Limbs of death from thy left side,
Let those life-speaking lipps command
That I inheritt thy right hand.

XVII

O hear a suppliant heart; all crush't
And crumbled into contrite dust.
My hope, my fear! my Judge, my Freind!
Take charge of me, and of my END.

The Himn
O Gloriosa Domina

Hail, most high, most humble one!
Above the world; below thy SON,
Whose blush the moon beauteously marres
And staines the timerous light of stares.
He that made all things, had not done
Till he had made Himself thy son.
The whole world's host would be thy guest
And board himself at thy rich BREST.
O boundles Hospitality!
The FEAST of all things feeds on thee.
   The first Eve, mother of our FALL,
E're she bore any one, slew all.
Of Her unkind gift might we have
The inheritance of a hasty GRAVE;

---

61 *Ite*: Latin, "go," "depart."

The Himn O Gloriosa.... First published in 1648 with the title "The Virgin-Mother." The original is a sixteen-line (or sometimes twenty-line) Latin hymn assigned to Lauds for the feasts of the Virgin in the Roman Breviary; as such it is a fit celebration of the Virgin in all her roles and an apt choice as the first of the poems dealing with the Sanctoral cycle.

3 *Whose blush...marres:* whose humble, human blush is more glorious than the celestial light of moon and stars.

Quick burye'd in the wanton TOMB 15
    Of one forbidden bitt;
Had not a Better FRUIT forbidden it.
    Had not thy healthfull womb
    The world's new eastern window bin
And given us heav'n again, in giving HIM. 20
Thine was the Rosy DAWN that sprung the Day
Which renders all the starres she stole away.
    Let then the Aged world be wise, and all
Prove nobly, here, unnaturall.
'Tis gratitude to forgett that other 25
And call the maiden Eve their mother.
    Yee redeem'd Nations farr and near,
    Applaud your happy selves in her,
    (All you to whom this love belongs)
And keep't alive with lasting songs. 30
    Let hearts and lippes speak lowd; and say
Hail, door of life: and sourse of day!
The door was shutt, the fountain seal'd;
Yet LIGHT was seen and LIFE reveald.
The DOORE was shut, yet let in day, 35
The fountain seald, yet life found way.
    Glory to thee, great virgin's son
In bosom of thy FATHER'S blisse.
    The same to thee, sweet SPIRIT be done;
As ever shall be, was, and is. 40
              AMEN

---

19 *eastern window*: giving upon the East, that is, the place where the New Sun, Christ, will rise.

21 *Rosy Dawn*: she is the new Aurora who heralded the new Day, Christ.

22 *starres*: the saints. Christ will restore, render up, all the Holy Ones who have hitherto been barred from heaven by Adam's fall.

24 *nobly, here, unnaturall*: to forget our mother (Eve) is unnatural, but in this case it is noble, and is proper gratitude to Mary.

26 *maiden Eve*: Mary, the Second Eve.

31 ff: some of the imagery of the last lines derives from the Song of Solomon.

In the Glorious Assumption
of Our Blessed Lady

THE HYMN

Hark! she is call'd, the parting houre is come.
Take thy Farewell, poor world! heavn must goe home.
A peice of heav'nly earth; Purer and brighter
Then the chast starres, whose choise lamps come to light her
While through the crystall orbes, clearer then they   5
She climbes; and makes a farre more milkey way.
She's calld. Hark, how the dear immortall dove
Sighes to his sylver mate rise up, my love!
Rise up, my fair, my spottlesse one!
The winter's past, the rain is gone.   10
The spring is come, the flowrs appear
No sweets, but thou, are wanting here.
    Come away, my love!
    Come away, my dove! cast off delay,
    The court of heav'n is come   15
    To wait upon thee home; Come come away!
    The flowrs appear.
Or quickly would, wert thou once here.
The spring is come, or if it stay,
'Tis to keep time with thy delay.   20
The rain is gone, except so much as we
Detain in needfull teares to weep the want of thee.
    The winter's past.
    Or if he make lesse hast,
His answer is, why she does so.   25
If sommer come not, how can winter goe.
    Come away, come away.

In the Glorious Assumption.... First published in 1646 in a different version (ll. 17–34 omitted) with the title "On the Assumption"; 1648 version closely resembles 1652. The hymn celebrates the Feast of the Assumption (15 August), using the imagery of the Song of Solomon (2: 10–13) — a use suggested by the traditional identification of the Bridegroom with Christ and the Bride with the pure soul.

The shrill winds chide, the waters weep thy stay;
The fountains murmur; and each loftyest tree
Bowes low'st his heavy top, to look for thee.   *30*
      Come away, my love.
      Come away, my dove, etc.
She's call'd again. And will she goe?
When heavn bidds come, who can say no?
Heavn calls her, and she must away.   *35*
Heavn will not, and she cannot stay.
GOE then; goe GLORIOUS.
      On the golden wings
Of the bright youth of heavn, that sings
Under so sweet a Burthen. Goe,   *40*
Since thy dread son will have it so.
And while thou goest, our song and we
Will, as we may, reach after thee.
HAIL, holy Queen of humble hearts!
We in thy prayse will have our parts.   *45*
      Thy pretious name shall be
      Thy self to us; and we
      With holy care will keep it by us.
      We to the last
      Will hold it fast   *50*
      And no ASSUMPTION shall deny us.
      All the sweetest showres
      Of our fairest flowres
      Will we strow upon it.
      Though our sweets cannot make   *55*
      It sweeter, they can take
      Themselves new sweetnes from it.
MARIA, men and Angels sing
MARIA, mother of our KING.
    LIVE, rosy princesse, LIVE. And may the bright   *60*
Crown of a most incomparable light
Embrace thy radiant browes. O may the best
Of everlasting joyes bath thy white brest.
LIVE, our chast love, the holy mirth
Of heavn; the humble pride of earth.   *65*
Live, crown of woemen; Queen of men.

Live mistresse of our song. And when
Our weak desires have done their best,
Sweet Angels come, and sing the rest.

Sainte Mary Magdalene

or

The Weeper

Loe where a WOUNDED HEART with Bleeding EYES conspire.
Is she a FLAMING Fountain, or a Weeping fire!

Sainte Mary Magdalene. First published in 1646 in a shorter version entitled "The Weeper," as the introductory poem in that volume. 1652 closely follows 1648 version. The poem's chief debts are to Epigram XXIX, Lib. I of Franciscus Remond's *Epigrammata et Elegiae* (Antwerp, 1606) and to several of Marino's poems about the Magdalen. The emblem is probably Crashaw's own drawing and the poem is among his most Marinist works. The basic situation is the story in Luke 7:36–50 of the sinner who anointed Christ's feet with tears and ointment and wiped them with her hair; there is allusion also (st. xxvi) to the Magdalen's legendary thirty years' penitence in the Desert. Her feast was 22 July.

The Weeper

I

Hail, sister springs!
Parents of sylver-footed rills!
Ever bubling things!
Thawing crystall! snowy hills,
Still spending, never spent! I mean
Thy fair eyes, sweet MAGDALENE!

II

Heavens thy fair eyes be;
Heavens of ever-falling starres.
'Tis seed-time still with thee
And starres thou sow'st, whose harvest dares
Promise the earth to counter shine
Whatever makes heavn's forhead fine.

III

But we'are deceived all.
Starres indeed they are too true;
For they but seem to fall,
As Heavn's other spangles doe.
It is not for our earth and us
To shine in Things so pretious.

IV

Upwards thou dost weep.
Heavn's bosome drinks the gentle stream.
Where th'milky rivers creep,
Thine floates above; and is the cream.
Waters above th'Heavns, what they be
We'are taught best by thy TEARES and thee.

19ff. See Ecclus. 35:16–17, "Do not the widows teares runne downe to the cheeke.... For from the cheeke they goe up even to heaven" (Douay).

V

Every morn from hence
A brisk Cherub somthing sippes
Whose sacred influence
Addes sweetnes to his sweetest Lippes.
Then to his musick. And his song
Tasts of this Breakfast all day long.

VI

Not in the evening's eyes
When they Red with weeping are
For the Sun that dyes,
Sitts sorrow with a face so fair,
No where but here did ever meet
Sweetnesse so sad, sadnesse so sweet.

VII

When sorrow would be seen
In her brightest majesty
(For she is a Queen)
Then is she drest by none but thee.
Then, and only then, she weares
Her proudest pearles; I mean, thy TEARES.

VIII

The deaw no more will weep
The primrose's pale cheek to deck,
The deaw no more will sleep
Nuzzel'd in the lilly's neck;
Much reather would it be thy TEAR,
And leave them Both to tremble here.

IX

There's no need at all
That the balsom-sweating bough
So coyly should let fall
His med'cinable teares; for now
Nature hath learn't to'extract a deaw
More soveraign and sweet from you.

X

  Yet let the poore drops weep 55
  (Weeping is the ease of woe)
  Softly let them creep,
  Sad that they are vanquish't so.
They, though to others no releife,
Balsom maybe, for their own greife. 60

XI

  Such the maiden gemme
  By the purpling vine put on,
  Peeps from her parent stemme
  And blushes at the bridegroomes sun.
This watry Blossom of thy eyn, 65
Ripe, will make the richer wine.

XII

  When some new bright Guest
  Takes up among the starres a room,
  And Heavn will make a feast,
  Angels with crystal violls come 70
And deaw from these full eyes of thine
Their master's Water: their own Wine.

XIII

  Golden though he be,
  Golden Tagus murmures tho;
  Were his way by thee, 75
  Content and quiet he would goe.
So much more rich would he esteem
Thy sylver, then his golden stream.

XIV

  Well does the May that lyes
  Smiling in thy cheeks, confesse 80

---

74 *Golden Tagus*: one of the principal rivers in Spain, celebrated for its golden sand (Pliny IV. 22.115; Catullus XX. 30).

  The April in thine eyes.
  Mutuall sweetnesse they expresse.
No April ere lent kinder showres,
Nor May return'd more faithfull flowres.

XV

  O cheeks! Bedds of chast loves   *85*
  By your own showres seasonably dash't
  Eyes! nests of milky doves.
  In your own wells decently washt,
O wit of love! that thus could place
Fountain and Garden in one face.   *90*

XVI

  O sweet Contest; of woes
  With loves, of teares with smiles disputing!
  O fair, and Freindly Foes,
  Each other kissing and confuting!
While rain and sunshine, Cheekes and Eyes   *95*
Close in kind contrarietyes.

XVII

  But can these fair Flouds be
  Freinds with the bosom fires that fill thee!
  Can so great flames agree
  Æternall Teares should thus distill thee!   *100*
O flouds, o fires! o suns ô showres!
Mixt and made freinds by love's sweet powres.

XVIII

  Twas his well-pointed dart
  That digg'd these wells, and drest this Vine;
  And taught the wounded HEART   *105*
  The way into these weeping Eyn.
Vain loves avant! bold hands forbear!
The lamb hath dipp't his white foot here.

XIX

    And now where're he strayes,
    Among the Galilean mountaines,   *110*
    Or more unwellcome wayes,
    He's follow'd by two faithfull fountaines;
Two walking baths; two weeping motions;
Portable, and compendious oceans.

XX

    O Thou, thy lord's fair store!   *115*
    In thy so rich and rare expenses,
    Even when he show'd most poor,
    He might provoke the wealth of Princes.
What Prince's wanton'st pride e're could
Wash with Sylver, wipe with Gold.   *120*

XXI

    Who is that King, but he
    Who calls't his Crown to be call'd thine,
    That thus can boast to be
    Waited on by a wandring mine,
A voluntary mint, that strowes   *125*
Warm sylver shoures where're he goes!

XXII

    O pretious Prodigall!
    Fair spend-thrift of thy self! thy measure
    (Mercilesse love!) is all.
    Even to the last Pearle in thy treasure.   *130*
All places, Times, and objects be
Thy teare's sweet opportunity.

XXIII

    Does the day-starre rise?
    Still thy starres doe fall and fall
    Does day close his eyes?   *135*
    Still the FOUNTAIN weeps for all.
Let night or day doe what they will,
Thou hast thy task; thou weepest still.

XXIV

    Does thy song lull the air?
    Thy falling teares keep faithfull time.   *140*
    Does thy sweet-breath'd praier
    Up in clouds of incense climb?
Still at each sigh, that is, each stop,
A bead, that is, A TEAR, does drop.

XXV

    At these thy weeping gates,   *145*
    (Watching their watry motion)
    Each winged moment waits,
    Takes his TEAR, and gets him gone.
By thine Ey's tinct enobled thus
Time layes him up; he's pretious.   *150*

XXVI

    Not, so long she lived,
    Shall thy tomb report of thee;
    But, so long she greived,
    Thus must we date thy memory.
Others by moments, months, and yeares   *155*
Measure their ages; thou, by TEARES.

XXVII

    So doe perfumes expire.
    So sigh tormented sweets, opprest
    With proud unpittying fire.
    Such Teares the suffring Rose that's vext   *160*
With ungentle flames does shed,
Sweating in a too warm bed.

XXVIII

    Say, ye bright brothers,
    The fugitive sons of those fair Eyes
    Your fruitfull mothers!   *165*
    What make you here? what hopes can 'tice
You to be born? what cause can borrow
You from Those nests of noble sorrow?

XXIX

    Whither away so fast?
    For sure the sordid earth   *170*
    Your Sweetnes cannot tast
    Nor does the dust deserve your birth.
Sweet whither hast you then? o say
Why you trip so fast away?

XXX

    We goe not to seek,   *175*
    The darlings of Auroras bed,
    The rose's modest Cheek
    Nor the violet's humble head.
Though the Feild's eyes too WEEPERS be
Because they want such TEARES as we.   *180*

XXXI

    Much lesse mean we to trace
    The Fortune of inferior gemmes,
    Preferr'd to some proud face
    Or pertch't upon fear'd Diadems.
Crown'd Heads are toyes. We goe to meet   *185*
A worthy object, our lord's FEET.

A Hymn
to the Name and Honor
of the Admirable
Sainte Teresa,

Foundresse of the Reformation of the Discalced Carmelites, both men and Women; A Woman for Angelicall heigth of speculation, for Masculine courage of performance, more then a woman. Who Yet a child, out ran maturity, and durst plott a Martyrdome

    Love, thou art Absolute sole lord
    OF LIFE and DEATH. To prove the word,
    Wee'l now appeal to none of all
    Those thy old Souldiers, Great and tall,
    Ripe Men of Martyrdom, that could reach down   5
    With strong armes, their triumphant crown;
    Such as could with lusty breath
    Speak lowd into the face of death
    Their Great LORD'S glorious name, to none

A Hymn to... Teresa. First published in 1646 in a different version with the title "In memory of the Vertuous and Learned Lady Madre de Teresa that sought an early Martyrdome." 1648 keeps 1646 title, and 1652 closely follows 1648. This poem and also "The Flaming Heart" (below) were evidently inspired by Teresa's autobiography, *La Vida de la Santa Madre Teresa de Jesus*, trans. into English in 1642 (by Toby Matthew?) as *The Flaming Hart or the Life of the Glorious S. Teresa* (Antwerp, 1642). The liturgy for her feast day (15 October) includes a hymn at Matins and Lauds opposing, like this poem, her early search for martyrdom among the barbarians and her later role as victim of Love. Her books, especially *The Way of Perfection* and *The Interior Castle*, are guides to mystical experience.

Of those whose spatious Bosomes spread a throne 10
For LOVE at larg to fill: spare blood and sweat;
And see him take a private seat,
Making his mansion in the mild
And milky soul of a soft child.
 Scarse has she learn't to lisp the name 15
Of Martyr; yet she thinks it shame
Life should so long play with that breath
Which spent can buy so brave a death.
She never undertook to know
What death with love should have to doe; 20
Nor has she e're yet understood
Why to show love, she should shed blood
Yet though she cannot tell you why,
She can LOVE, and she can DY.
 Scarse has she Blood enough to make 25
A guilty sword blush for her sake;
Yet has she 'a HEART dares hope to prove
How much lesse strong is DEATH then LOVE.
 Be love but there; let poor six yeares
Be pos'd with the maturest Feares 30
Man trembles at, you straight shall find
LOVE knowes no nonage, nor the MIND.
'Tis LOVE, not YEARES or LIMBS that can
Make the Martyr, or the man.
 LOVE touch't her HEART, and lo it beates 35
High, and burnes with such brave heates;
Such thirsts to dy, as dares drink up,
A thousand cold deaths in one cup.
Good reason. For she breathes All fire.
Her weake brest heaves with strong desire 40
Of what she may with fruitles wishes
Seek for amongst her MOTHER'S kisses.
 Since 'tis not to be had at home
She'l travail to a Martyrdom.
No home for hers confesses she 45
But where she may a Martyr be.
 Sh'el to the Moores; And trade with them,
For this unvalued Diadem.

She'l offer them her dearest Breath,
With CHRIST'S Name in't, in change for death.   50
Sh'el bargain with them; and will give
Them GOD; teach them how to live
In him: or, if they this deny,
For him she'l teach them how to DY.
So shall she leave amongst them sown   55
Her LORD'S Blood; or at least her own.
  FAREWEL then, all the world! Adieu.
TERESA is no more for you.
Farewell, all pleasures, sports, and joyes,
(Never till now esteemed toyes)   60
Farewell what ever deare may bee,
MOTHER'S armes or FATHER'S knee
Farewell house, and farewell home!
SHE'S for the Moores, and MARTYRDOM.
  SWEET, not so fast! lo thy fair Spouse   65
Whom thou seekst with so swift vowes,
Calls thee back, and bidds thee come
T'embrace a milder MARTYRDOM.
  Blest powres forbid, Thy tender life
Should bleed upon a barborous knife;   70
Or some base hand have power to race
Thy Brest's chast cabinet, and uncase
A soul kept there so sweet, ô no;
Wise heavn will never have it so.
THOU art love's victime; and must dy   75
A death more mysticall and high.
Into love's armes thou shalt let fall
A still-surviving funerall.
His is the DART must make the DEATH

---

79 *His is the Dart*: Love's arrow (an emblematic transference from Cupid's arrow) is here and in "The Flaming Heart" derived from an experience described in Teresa's autobiography (1642 translation, p. 419): "It pleased our Blessed Lord, that I should have sometimes, this following Vision. I saw an Angell very neer me, towards my left side, and he appeared to me, in a Corporeall forme.... He was not great; but rather little; yet withall, he was of very much beautie. His face was so inflamed, that he appeared to be of those most Superiour Angells, who seem to be, all in a fire; and he well might be of them, whome we

Whose stroke shall tast thy hallow'd breath; 80
A Dart thrice dip't in that rich flame
Which writes thy spouse's radiant Name
Upon the roof of Heav'n; where ay
It shines, and with a soveraign ray
Beates bright upon the burning faces 85
Of soules which in that name's sweet graces
Find everlasting smiles. So rare,
So spirituall, pure, and fair
Must be th'immortall instrument
Upon whose choice point shall be sent 90
A life so lou'd; And that there be
Fitt executioners for Thee,
The fair'st and first-born sons of fire
Blest SERAPHIM, shall leave their quire
And turn love's souldiers, upon THEE 95
To exercise their archerie.
   O how oft shalt thou complain
Of a sweet and subtle PAIN.
Of intolerable JOYES;
Of a DEATH, in which who dyes 100
Loves his death, and dyes again.
And would for ever so be slain.
And lives, and dyes; and knowes not why
To live, But that he thus may never leave to Dy.
   How kindly will thy gentle HEART 105
Kisse the sweetly-killing DART!
And close in his embraces keep
Those delicious Wounds, that weep
Balsom to heal themselves with. Thus
When These thy DEATHS, so numerous, 110

---

call Seraphins.... I saw, that he had a long Dart of gold in his hand; and at the end of the iron below, me thought, there was a little fire; and I conceaved, that he thrust it, some severall times, through my verie Hart, after such a manner, as that it passed the verie inwards, of my Bowells; and when he drew it back, me thought, it carried away, as much, as it had touched within me; and left all that, which remained, wholy inflamed with a great love of Almightye God. The paine of it, was so excessive, that it forced me to utter those groanes; and the suavitie, which that extremitie of paine gave, was also so very excessive, that there was no desiring at all, to be ridd of it; nor can the Soule then, receave anie contentment at all, in lesse, then God Almightie himself."

Shall all at last dy into one,
And melt thy Soul's sweet mansion;
Like a soft lump of incense, hasted
By too hott a fire, and wasted
Into perfuming clouds, so fast   *115*
Shalt thou exhale to Heavn at last
In a resolving SIGH, and then
O what? Ask not the Tongues of men.
Angells cannot tell, suffice,
Thyselfe shall feel thine own full joyes   *120*
And hold them fast for ever. There,
So soon as thou shalt first appear,
The MOON of maiden starrs, thy white
MISTRESSE, attended by such bright
Soules as thy shining self, shall come   *125*
And in her first rankes make thee room;
Where 'mongst her snowy family
Immortall wellcomes wait for thee.
 O what delight, when reveal'd LIFE shall stand
And teach thy lipps heav'n with his hand;   *130*
On which thou now maist to thy wishes
Heap up thy consecrated kisses.
What joyes shall seize thy soul, when she
Bending her blessed eyes on thee
(Those second Smiles of Heav'n) shall dart *135*
Her mild rayes through thy melting heart!
 Angels, thy old freinds, there shall greet thee
Glad at their own home now to meet thee.
 All thy good WORKES which went before
And waited for thee, at the door,   *140*
Shall own thee there, and all in one
Weave a constellation
Of CROWNS, with which the KING thy spouse
Shall build up thy triumphant browes.
 All thy old woes shall now smile on thee *145*
And thy paines sitt bright upon thee
All thy sorrows here shall shine,

---

135 *Those second Smiles of Heav'n*: Mary's smiles.

All thy SUFFRINGS be divine.
TEARES shall take comfort, and turn gemms
And WRONGS repent to Diademms. *150*
Ev'n thy Death shall live; and new
Dresse the soul that erst they flew.
Thy wounds shall blush to such bright scarres
As keep account of the LAMB'S warres.
   Those rare WORKES where thou shalt leave writt, *155*
Love's noble history, with witt
Taught thee by none but him, while here
They feed our soules, shall cloth THINE there.
Each heavnly word by whose hid flame
Our hard Hearts shall strike fire, the same *160*
Shall flourish on thy browes, and be
Both fire to us and flame to thee;
Whose light shall live bright in thy FACE
By glory, in our hearts by grace.
   Thou shalt look round about, and see *165*
Thousands of crown'd Soules throng to be
Themselves thy crown, sons of thy vowes
The virgin-births with which thy soveraign spouse
Made fruitfull thy fair soul. Goe now
And with them all about thee bow *170*
To Him, put on (hee'l say) put on
(My rosy love) That thy rich zone
Sparkling with the sacred flames
Of thousand soules, whose happy names
Heav'n keeps upon thy score. (Thy bright *175*
Life brought them first to kisse the light
That kindled them to starrs.) and so
Thou with the LAMB, thy lord, shalt goe;
And whereso'ere he setts his white
Stepps, walk with HIM those wayes of light *180*
Which who in death would live to see,
Must learn in life to dy like thee.

---

167 *sons of thy vowes*: the religious whose order she has founded and reformed (the order of Mount Carmel), and those her books have inspired.

An Apologie
for the Fore-going Hymne
as having been writt when the author was yet among the protestantes.

    Thus have I back again to thy bright name
(Fair floud of holy fires!) transfus'd the flame
I took from reading thee, tis to thy wrong
I know, that in my weak and worthlesse song
Thou here art sett to shine where thy full day   5
Scarse dawnes. O pardon if I dare to say
Thine own dear bookes are guilty. For from thence
I learn't to know that love is eloquence.
That hopefull maxime gave me hart to try
If, what to other tongues is tun'd so high,   10
Thy praise might not speak English too; forbid
(By all thy mysteryes that here ly hidde)
Forbid it, mighty Love! let no fond Hate
Of names and wordes, so farr præjudicate.
Souls are not SPANIARDS too, one freindly floud   15
Of BAPTISM blends them all into a blood.
CHRIST'S faith makes but one body of all soules
And love's that body's soul, no law controwlls
Our free traffique for heav'n, we may maintaine
Peace, sure, with piety, though it come from SPAIN.   20
What soul so e're, in any language, can
Speak heav'n like her's is my souls country-man.
O 'tis not spanish, but 'tis heav'n she speaks!
'Tis heav'n that lyes in ambush there, and breaks
From thence into the wondring reader's brest;   25

An Apologie.... First published in 1646 with title "An Apologie for the precedent Hymne"; in 1648 the poem follows "The Flaming Heart" and is titled "An Apologie for the precedent Hymnes on Teresa." The title may mean that the poem was written while Crashaw was in England, among the Protestants, and that it is an apologia, a justification, to his Spanish-hating countrymen for his praise of Teresa.

    Who feels his warm HEART hatch'd into a nest
    Of little EAGLES and young loves, whose high
    Flights scorn the lazy dust, and things that dy.
      There are enow whose draughts (as deep as hell)
    Drink up al SPAIN in sack. Let my soul swell   *30*
    With thee, strong wine of love! let others swimme
    In puddles; we will pledge this SERAPHIM
    Bowles full of richer blood then blush of grape
    Was every guilty of. Change we too 'our shape
    (My soul,) Some drink from men to beasts, o then   *35*
    Drink we till we prove more, not lesse, then men,
    And turn not beasts, but Angels. Let the king
    Me ever into these his cellars bring
    Where flowes such wine as we can have of none
    But HIM who trod the wine-presse all alone.   *40*
    Wine of youth, life, and the sweet Deaths of love;
    Wine of immortall mixture; which can prove
    It's Tincture from the rosy nectar; wine
    That can exalt weak EARTH; and so refine
    Our dust, that at one draught, mortality   *45*
    May drink it self up, and forget to dy.

---

    40 *Him who trod the wine-presse all alone*: see Isa. 63:3, "I have trodden the winepress alone; and of the people there was none with me," commonly applied to Christ in the Passion and by extension (as here) to the Eucharist as the sacrament of his Blood.

The Flaming Heart

Upon the Book and Picture of the seraphicall saint, Teresa, (As She Is Usually Expressed with a Seraphim Biside Her.)

Well meaning readers! you that come as freinds,
And catch the pretious name this peice pretends;
Make not too much hast to' admire
That fair-cheek't fallacy of fire.
That is a SERAPHIM, they say   5
And this the great TERESIA.
Readers, be rul'd by me; and make
Here a well-plac't and wise mistake.
You must transpose the picture quite,
And spell it wrong to read it right;   10
Read HIM for her, and her for him;
And call the SAINT the SERAPHIM.
  Painter, what didst thou understand
To put her dart into his hand!
See, even the yeares and size of him   15
Showes this the mother SERAPHIM.
This is the mistresse flame; and duteous he
Her happy fire-works, here, comes down to see.
O most poor-spirited of men!
Had thy cold Pencil kist her PEN   20

The Flaming Heart.... First published in 1648 with the title "The flaming Heart. Upon the booke and picture of Teresa. As she is usually expressed with a Seraphim beside her"; ll. 85–108 added in 1652. See note to "A Hymn to the Name...," quoting Teresa's description of her "transverberations," the basis for this poem. Crashaw uses as his point of departure a painting of this subject, a favorite baroque theme, which must have rather resembled in conception that of Bernini's famous sculpture in the Church of S. Maria della Vittoria in Rome: the swooning, passive saint whose strong face and swirling robes nevertheless suggest masculine energy, and the youthful, sweet-faced, smiling seraph with a golden dart.

Thou couldst not so unkindly err
To show us This faint shade for HER.
Why man, this speakes pure mortall frame;
And mockes with female FROST love's manly flame.
One would suspect thou meant'st to paint 25
Some weak, inferiour, woman saint.
But had thy pale-fac't purple took
Fire from the burning cheeks of that bright Booke
Thou wouldst on her have heap't up all
That could be found SERAPHICALL; 30
What e're this youth of fire weares fair,
Rosy fingers, radiant hair,
Glowing cheek, and glistering wings,
All those fair and flagrant things,
But before all, that fiery DART 35
Had fill'd the Hand of this great HEART.
 Doe then as equall right requires,
Since HIS the blushes be, and her's the fires,
Resume and rectify thy rude design;
Undresse thy Seraphim into MINE. 40
Redeem this injury of thy art;
Give HIM the vail, give her the dart.
 Give Him the vail; that he may cover
The Red cheeks of a rivall'd lover.
Asham'd that our world, now, can show 45
Nests of new Seraphims here below.
 Give her the DART for it is she
(Fair youth) shootes both thy shaft and THEE.
Say, all ye wise and well-peirc't hearts
That live and dy amidst her darts, 50
What is't your tastfull spirits doe prove
In that rare life of Her, and love?
Say and bear wittnes. Sends she not
A SERAPHIM at every shott?
What magazins of immortall ARMES there shine! 55
Heavn's great artillery in each love-spun line.

50 *her darts*: her writings.

Give then the dart to her who gives the flame;
Give him the veil, who kindly takes the shame.
    But if it be the frequent fate
Of worst faults to be fortunate;   60
If all's præscription; and proud wrong
Hearkens not to an humble song;
For all the gallantry of him,
Give me the suffring SERAPHIM.
His be the bravery of all those Bright things,   65
The glowing cheekes, the glistering wings;
The Rosy hand, the radiant DART;
Leave HER alone THE FLAMING HEART.
    Leave her that; and thou shalt leave her
Not one loose shaft but love's whole quiver.   70
For in love's feild was never found
A nobler weapon then a WOUND.
Love's passives are his activ'st part.
The wounded is the wounding heart.
O HEART! the æquall poise of lov'es both parts   75
Bigge alike with wound and darts,
Live in these conquering leaves; live all the same;
And walk through all tongues one triumphant FLAME
Live here, great HEART; and love and dy and kill;
And bleed and wound; and yeild and conquer still.   80
Let this immortall life wherere it comes
Walk in a crowd of loves and MARTYRDOMES.
Let mystick DEATHS wait on't; and wise soules be
The love-slain wittnesses of this life of thee.
O sweet incendiary! shew here thy art,   85
Upon this carcasse of a hard, cold, hart,
Let all thy scatter'd shafts of light, that play
Among the leaves of thy larg Books of day,
Combin'd against this BREST at once break in
And take away from me my self and sin,   90
This gratious Robbery shall thy bounty be;
And my best fortunes such fair spoiles of me.
O thou undanted daughter of desires!
By all thy dowr of LIGHTS and FIRES;

By all the eagle in thee, all the dove; 95
By all thy lives and deaths of love;
By thy larg draughts of intellectuall day,
And by thy thirsts of love more large then they;
By all thy brim-fill'd Bowles of feirce desire
By thy last Morning's draught of liquid fire; 100
By the full kingdome of that finall kisse
That seiz'd thy parting Soul, and seal'd thee his;
By all the heav'ns thou hast in him
(Fair sister of the SERAPHIM!)
By all of HIM we have in THEE; 105
Leave nothing of my SELF in me.
Let me so read thy life, that I
Unto all life of mine may dy.

A Song

Lord, when the sense of thy sweet grace
Sends up my soul to seek thy face.
Thy blessed eyes breed such desire,
I dy in love's delicious Fire.
   O love, I am thy SACRIFICE. 5
Be still triumphant, blessed eyes.
Still shine on me, fair suns! that I
Still may behold, though still I dy.

Second part.

Though still I dy, I live again;
Still longing so to be still slain, 10
So gainfull is such losse of breath,
I dy even in desire of death.

---

95 *eagle...dove*: see Teresa's autobiography, p. 274: "She is not yet, become so true an Eaglet, of this swift, and strong Eagle, which bred her, as that she can be able to looke earnestly upon this Sunne...but when she lookes in, upon her self, her eyes are stopped up, with clay; and so this poore Dove, is blind." Cf. Donne, "The Canonization," l. 22, "And wee in us finde the Eagle and the Dove."
  A Song. First published in 1648 with the title "A Song of Divine Love."

Still live in me this loving strife
Of living DEATH and dying LIFE.
For while thou sweetly slayest me   *15*
Dead to my selfe, I live in Thee.

Prayer

An Ode, Which Was Præfixed to a little Prayer-book givin to a young Gentle-woman

Lo here a little volume, but great Book!
A nest of new-born sweets;
Whose native fires disdaining
To ly thus folded, and complaining
Of these ignoble sheets,   *5*
Affect more comly bands
(Fair one) from thy kind hands
And confidently look
To find the rest
Of a rich binding in your BREST.   *10*
It is, in one choise handfull, heavenn; and all
Heavn's Royall host; incamp't thus small
To prove that true schooles use to tell,
Ten thousand Angels in one point can dwell.
It is love's great artillery   *15*
Which here contracts itself, and comes to ly
Close couch't in your white bosom: and from thence
As from a snowy fortresse of defence,
Against the ghostly foes to take your part,
And fortify the hold of your chast heart.   *20*
It is an armory of light
Let constant use but keep it bright,

Prayer: An Ode.... First published in 1646 with the title "On a prayer booke sent to Mrs. M. R." Manuscript version identifies the "book" as the Book of Common Prayer, which relates the poem to Crashaw's High Anglican liturgical period, but he omits the identification here. The poem is Crashaw's most considerable attempt to generalize about the mystical experience, using the traditional imagery of the Song of Solomon.

        You'l find it yeilds
To holy hands and humble hearts
        More swords and sheilds   25
Then sin hath snares, or Hell hath darts.
        Only be sure
        The hands be pure
That hold these weapons; and the eyes
Those of turtles, chast and true;   30
        Wakefull and wise;
Here is a freind shall fight for you,
Hold but this book before your heart;
Let prayer alone to play his part,
        But ô the heart   35
        That studyes this high ART
        Must be a sure house-keeper;
        And yet no sleeper.
        Dear soul, be strong.
        MERCY will come e're long   40
And bring his bosom fraught with blessings,
Flowers of never fading graces
To make immortall dressings
For worthy soules, whose wise embraces
Store up themselves for HIM, who is alone   45
The SPOUSE of Virgins and the Virgin's son.
But if the noble BRIDEGROOM, when he come,
Shall find the loytering HEART from home;
        Leaving her chast aboad
        To gadde abroad   50
Among the gay mates of the god of flyes;
To take her pleasure and to play
And keep the devill's holyday;
To dance ith'sunshine of some smiling
        But beguiling   55
Spheares of sweet and sugred Lyes,
        Some slippery Pair
        Of false, perhaps as fair,

---

51 *god of flyes*: the literal meaning of the Hebrew name, Beelzebub, often used in reference to Satan.

Flattering but forswearing eyes;
Doubtlesse some other heart
    Will gett the start
Mean while, and stepping in before
Will take possession of that sacred store
Of hidden sweets and holy joyes.
WORDS which are not heard with EARES
(Those tumultous shops of noise)
Effectuall wispers, whose still voice
The soul it selfe more feeles then heares;
Amorous languishments; luminous trances;
SIGHTS which are not seen with eyes;
Spirituall and soul-peircing glances
Whose pure and subtil lightning flyes
Home to the heart, and setts the house on fire
And melts it down in sweet desire
    Yet does not stay
To ask the windows leave to passe that way;
Delicious DEATHS; soft exalations
Of soul; dear and divine annihilations;
    A thousand unknown rites
Of joyes and rarefy'd delights;
A hundred thousand goods, glories, and graces,
    And many a mystick thing
    Which the divine embraces
Of the deare spouse of spirits with them will bring
    For which it is no shame
That dull mortality must not know a name.
    Of all this store
Of blessings and ten thousand more
    (If when he come
    He find the Heart from home)
    Doubtlesse he will unload
    Himself some other where,
    And poure abroad
    His pretious sweets
On the fair soul whom first he meets.
O fair, ô fortunate! O riche, ô dear!
O happy and thrice happy she

> Selected dove
> Who ere she be,
> Whose early love.   100
> With winged vowes
Makes hast to meet her morning spouse
And close with his immortall kisses.
Happy indeed, who never misses
To improve that pretious hour,   105
> And every day
> Seize her sweet prey
All fresh and fragrant as he rises
Dropping with a baulmy Showr
A delicious dew of spices;   110
O let the blissfull heart hold fast
Her heavnly arm-full, she shall tast
At once ten thousand paradises;
> She shall have power
> To rifle and deflour   115
The rich and roseall spring of those rare sweets
Which with a swelling bosome there she meets
> Boundles and infinite
> Bottomles treasures
Of pure inebriating pleasures.   120
Happy proof! she shal discover
> What joy, what blisse,
How many Heav'ns at once it is
To have her GOD become her LOVER.

To the Same Party
Councel Concerning Her Choise

> Dear, heavn-designed SOUL!
> Amongst the rest
Of suters that beseige your Maiden brest,

To the Same . . . . First published in 1648.

   Why may not I
   My fortune try
And venture to speak one good word
Not for my self alas, but for my dearer LORD?
You'ave seen allready, in this lower sphear
Of froth and bubbles, what to look for here.
Say, gentle soul, what can you find
   But painted shapes,
   Peacocks and Apes,
   Illustrious flyes,
Guilded dunghills, glorious LYES,
   Goodly surmises
   And deep disguises,
Oathes of water, words of wind?
TRUTH biddes me say, 'tis time you cease to trust
Your soul to any son of dust.
'Tis time you listen to a braver love,
   Which from above
   Calls you up higher
   And biddes you come
   And choose your roome
Among his own fair sonnes of fire,
   Where you among
   The golden throng
That watches at his palace doores
   May passe along
And follow those fair starres of yours;
Starrs much too fair and pure to wait upon
The false smiles of a sublunary sun.
Sweet, let me prophesy that at last t'will prove
   Your wary love
Layes up his purer and more pretious vowes,
And meanes them for a farre more worthy SPOUSE
Then this world of Lyes can give ye
'Evn for Him with whom nor cost,
Nor love, nor labour can be lost;
Him who never will deceive ye.
Let not my lord, the Mighty lover
Of soules, disdain that I discover

>   The hidden art
> Of his high stratagem to win your heart,
>   It was his heavnly art 45
>   Kindly to crosse you
>   In your mistaken love,
>   That, at the next remove
>   Thence he might tosse you
>   And strike your troubled heart 50
> Home to himself; to hide it in his brest
>   The bright ambrosiall nest,
> Of love, of life, and everlasting rest.
>   Happy Mystake!
>   That thus shall wake 55
> Your wise soul, never to be wonne
> Now with a love below the sun.
> Your first choyce failes, ô when you choose agen
> May it not be amongst the sonnes of Men.

49–51 Cf. Herbert, "The Pulley," ll. 19–20.

ALEXIAS

The Complaint of the Forsaken Wife of Sainte Alexis

The First Elegie

I late the roman youth's lov'd prayse and pride,
Whom long none could obtain, though thousands try'd,
Lo here am left (alas), For my lost mate
T'embrace my teares, and kisse an unkind FATE.
Sure in my early woes starres were at strife,   *5*
And try'd to make a WIDOW ere a WIFE.
Nor can I tell (and this new teares doth breed)
In what strange path my lord's fair footsteppes bleed.
O knew I where he wander'd, I should see
Some solace in my sorrow's certainty   *10*
I'd send my woes in words should weep for me.
(Who knowes how powrfull well-writt praires would be?)
Sending's too slow a word, my selfe would fly.
Who knowes my own heart's woes so well as I?
But how shall I steal hence? ALEXIS thou   *15*
Ah thou thy self, alas, hast taught me how.
Love too, that leads the way, would lend the wings

Alexias.... First published in 1648 among *The Delights of the Muses*; title omits the word *Sainte*. The three elegies draw upon Latin elegies 1, 5, and 2 in Franciscus Remond's *Epigrammata et Elegiae* (Antwerp, 1606), often reprinted in the seventeenth century. Crashaw's rendering is very free. Alexis, a fifth-century Roman saint, fled his father's house on the night of his marriage to a King's daughter, in order to devote himself entirely to God, although according to several formulations (as here) she was willing to live as a virgin with him. He wandered through the world as a beggar for seventeen years and lived another seventeen years as a beggar, unrecognized, in his father's house. The elegies do not celebrate the Saint, but treat the pathetic state of the uncomprehending, abandoned wife, offering hereby a striking counterpoint to the advice in the preceding poem to the Soul to seek only a heavenly lover.

To bear me harmlesse through the hardest things.
And where love lends the wing, and leads the way,
What dangers can there be dare say me nay?   20
If I be shipwrack't, Love shall teach to swimme.
If drown'd; sweet is the death indur'd for HIM,
The noted sea shall change his name with me;
I, 'mongst the blest STARRES a new name shall be.'
And sure where lovers make their watry graves   25
The weeping mariner will augment the waves.
For who so hard, but passing by that way
Will take acquaintance of my woes, and say
Here t'was the roman MAID found a hard fate
While through the world she sought her wandring mate.   30
Here perish't she, poor heart, heavns, be my vowes
As true to me, as she was to her spouse.
O live, so rare a love! live! and in thee
The too frail life of femal constancy.
Farewell; and shine, fair soul, shine there above   35
Firm in thy crown, as here fast in thy love.
There thy lost fugitive thou'hast found at last.
Be happy; and for ever hold him fast.

The Seconde Elegie

Though All the joyes I had fleed hence with Thee,
Unkind! yet are my TEARES still true to me
I'am wedded ore again since thou art gone;
Nor couldst thou, cruell, leave me quite alone.
ALEXIS' widdow now is sorrow's wife.   5
With him shall I weep out my weary life.
Wellcome, my sad sweet Mate! Now have I gott
At last a constant love that leaves me not.
Firm he, as thou art false, Nor need my cryes
Thus vex the earth and teare the beauteous skyes.   10
For him, alas, n'ere shall I need to be
Troublesom to the world, thus, as for thee.
For thee I talk to trees; with silent groves
Expostulate my woes and much-wrong'd loves.

Hills and relentlesse rockes, or if there be
Things that in hardnesse more allude to thee;
To these I talk in teares, and tell my pain;
And answer too for them in teares again.
How oft have I wept out the weary sun!
My watry hour-glasse hath old time outrunne.
O I am learned grown, Poor love and I
Have study'd over all astrology.
I'am perfect in heavn's state, with every starr
My skillfull greife is grown familiar.
Rise, fairest of those fires; whate're thou be
Whose rosy beam shall point my sun to me.
Such as the sacred light that erst did bring
The EASTERN princes to their infant king.
O rise, pure lamp! and lend thy golden ray
That weary love at last may find his way.

The Third Elegie

Rich, churlish LAND! that hid'st so long in thee,
My treasures, rich, alas, by robbing mee.
Needs must my miseryes owe that man a spite
Who e're he be was the first wandring knight.
O had he nere been at that cruell cost
NATURE'S virginity had nere been lost.
Seas had not bin rebuk't by sawcy oares
But ly'n lock't up safe in their sacred shores.
Men had not spurn'd at mountaines; nor made warrs
With rocks; nor bold hands struck the world's strong barres.
Nor lost in too larg bounds, our little Rome
Full sweetly with it selfe had dwell't at home.
My poor ALEXIS, then in peacefull life,
Had under some low roofe lov'd his plain wife.
But now, ah me, from where he has no foes
He flyes; and into willfull exile goes.

The Third Elegie. 1 *churlish Land*: in that it hid Alexis from her.
6 *Nature's virginity*: Nature would have remained untouched, unexploited, had it not been for the first wandering knight.

Cruell return. Or tell the reason why
Thy dearest parents have deserv'd to dy.
And I, what is my crime I cannot tell.
Unlesse it be a crime to'have lov'd too well. 20
If Heates of holyer love and high desire
Make bigge thy fair brest with immortall fire,
What needs my virgin lord fly thus from me,
Who only wish his virgin wife to be?
Wittnesse, chast heavns! no happyer vowes I know 25
Then to a virgin GRAVE untouch't to goe.
Love's truest Knott by venus is not ty'd;
Nor doe embraces onely make a bride.
The QUEEN of angels, (and men chast as You)
Was MAIDEN WIFE and MAIDEN MOTHER too. 30
CECILIA, Glory of her name and blood
With happy gain her maiden vowes made good.
The lusty bridegroom made approach: young man,
Take heed (said she) take heed, VALERIAN!
My bosome's guard, a SPIRIT great and strong, 35
Stands arm'd, to sheild me from all wanton wrong.
My Chastity is sacred; and my sleep
Wakefull, her dear vowes undefil'd to keep.
PALLAS beares armes, forsooth, and should there be
No fortresse built for true VIRGINITY? 40
No gaping gorgon, this. None, like the rest
Of your learn'd lyes. Here you'l find no such jest.
I'am yours, O were my GOD, my CHRIST so too,
I'd know no name of love on earth but you.
He yeilds, and straight Baptis'd, obtains the grace 45
To gaze on the fair souldier's glorious face.
Both mixt at last their blood in one rich bed
Of rosy MARTYRDOME, twice Married.
O burn our hymen bright in such high Flame.
Thy torch, terrestriall love, have here no name. 50

29 *(and men...)*: the sense of the parentheses must be, "and *of* men chaste as you."
31 *Cecilia*: one of the several legends about St. Cecilia, patroness of music, is recounted here.

How sweet the mutuall yoke of man and wife,
When holy fires maintain love's Heavnly life!
But I, (so help me heavn my hopes to see)
When thousands sought my love, lov'd none but Thee.
Still, as their vain teares my firm vowes did try,   55
ALEXIS, he alone is mine (said I)
Half true, alas, half false, proves that poor line!
ALEXIS is alone; But is not mine.

Description of a Religious House and Condition of Life
(Out of Barclay)

No roofes of gold o're riotous tables shining
Whole dayes and suns devour'd with endlesse dining;
No sailes of tyrian sylk proud pavements sweeping;
Nor ivory couches costlyer slumbers keeping;
False lights of flairing gemmes; tumultous joyes;   5
Halls full of flattering men and frisking boyes;

Description.... First published in 1648 with the title "Description of a religious house." Cf. John Barclay, *Argenis* (Leyden, 1630), p. 613:

> Non isthic aurata domus, luxuque fluentes
> Sunt epulae, spondave sopor pretiosus eburna,
> Aut in carbaseo Tyrius velamine murex.
> Non gemma vibrante nitor, non persona cantu
> Limina, non prono famulantum examina collo,
> Atque avidas quicquid trahit in certamina gentes;
> Sed nemora, & nudae rupes, neglectaque squalent
> Confraga: Sunt epulae viles, jussaeque quietis
> Hora brevis: Duro velantur corpora texto:
> Et labor in pretio, & vitam mors longa fatigat.
> At neque crudeles Dirae, vilique flagello
> Saevit cura ferox: falso non abditus ore
> Ipse sua insanus furit in praecordia livor.
> Alma quies parvisque habitat concordia tectis,
> Et semper niveo veri de pectore risus.
> Ipsa suae meminit stirpis, seseque Deisque
> Meus fruitur fœlix, & novit in astra reverti.

Warren (p. 39) observes that Crashaw in this poem was "assuredly commemorating Little Gidding."

Whate're false showes of short and slippery good
Mix the mad sons of men in mutuall blood.
But WALKES and unshorn woods; and soules, just so
Unforc't and genuine; but not shady tho.   10
Our lodgings hard and homely as our fare.
That chast and cheap, as the few clothes we weare.
Those, course and negligent, As the naturall lockes
Of these loose groves, rough as th'unpolish't rockes.
A hasty Portion of præscribed sleep;   15
Obedient slumbers? that can wake and weep,
And sing, and sigh, and work, and sleep again;
Still rowling a round sphear of still-returning pain.
Hands full of harty labours; Paines that pay
And prize themselves; doe much, that more they may,   20
And work for work, not wages; let to morrow's
New drops, wash off the sweat of this daye's sorrows.
A long and dayly-dying life, which breaths
A respiration of reviving deaths.
But neither are there those ignoble stings   25
That nip the bosome of the world's best things,
And lash Earth-laboring souls.
No cruell guard of diligent cares, that keep
Crown'd woes awake; as things too wise for sleep.
But reverent discipline, and religious fear,   30
And soft obedience, find sweet biding here;
Silence, and sacred rest; peace, and pure joyes;
Kind loves keep house, ly close, and make no noise,
And room enough for Monarchs, while none swells
Beyond the kingdomes of contentfull Cells.   35
The self-remembring SOUL sweetly recovers
Her kindred with the starrs; not basely hovers
Below; But meditates her immortall way
Home to the originall sourse of LIGHT and intellectuall Day.

An Epitaph Upon a Young Married Couple
Dead and Buryed Together

To these, whom DEATH again did wed,
This GRAVE'S their second Marriage-bed.
For though the hand of fate could force
'Twixt SOUL and BODY a Divorce,
It could not sunder man and WIFE,　　　　5
'Cause They Both lived but one life.
Peace, good Reader. Doe not weep.
Peace, The Lovers are asleep.
They, sweet Turtles, folded ly
In the last knott love could ty.　　　　10
And though they ly as they were dead,
Their Pillow stone, their sheetes of lead,
(Pillow hard, and sheetes not warm)
Love made the bed; They'l take no harm
Let them sleep: let them sleep on.　　　　15
Till this stormy night be gone,
Till the' Æternall morrow dawn;
Then the curtaines will be drawn
And they wake into a light,
Whose day shall never dy in Night.　　　　20

An Epitaph . . . . First published in a shorter version in 1646 with the title "An Epitaph upon Husband and Wife, which died, and were buried together." 1652 closely follows the 1648 version.

Death's Lecture at the Funeral of a Young Gentleman

Dear Reliques of a dislodg'd SOUL, whose lack
Makes many a mourning paper put on black!
O stay a while, ere thou draw in thy head
And wind thy self up close in thy cold bed.
Stay but a little while, untill I call   5
A summons worthy of thy funerall.
Come then, YOUTH, BEAUTY, and blood!
        All ye soft powres.
Whose sylken flatteryes swell a few fond howres
Into a false æternity. Come man;   10
Hyperbolized NOTHING! know thy span;
Take thine own measure here: down, down, and bow
Before thy self in thine idæa; thou
Huge emptynes! contract thy self; and shrinke
All thy wide circle to a Point. O sink   15
Lower and lower yet; till thy leane size
Call heavn to look on thee with narrow eyes.
Lesser and lesser yet; till thou begin
To show a face, fitt to confesse thy Kin,
Thy neigbourhood to NOTHING.   20
Proud lookes, and lofty eyliddes, here putt on
Your selves in your unfaign'd reflexion,
Here, gallant ladyes! this unpartiall glasse
(Though you be painted) showes you your true face.
These death-seal'd lippes are they dare give the ly 25
To the lowd Boasts of poor Mortality.
These curtain'd windows, this retired eye
Outstares the liddes of larg-look't tyranny.

Death's Lecture .... First published in 1646 with the title "Upon Mr. Stani-nough's Death"; 1652 closely follows the slightly altered version in 1648. James Stanenough was fellow of Queen's College, Cambridge, and was buried in the College chapel 5 March 1634/5 (M.).

This posture is the brave one: this that lyes
Thus low, stands up (me thinkes,) thus and defies   30
The world. All-daring dust and ashes! only you
Of all interpreters read Nature True.

Temperance

or

The Cheap Physitian
Upon the Translation of Lessius

Goe now; and with some daring drugg
Bait thy disease. And whilst they tugge,
Thou to maintain their pretious strife
Spend the dear treasures of thy life.
Goe, take physick. Doat upon   5
Some big-nam'd composition.
Th'Oraculous DOCTOR'S mystick bills;
Certain hard WORDS made into pills,
And what at last shalt' gain by these?
Only a costlyer disease.   10
That which makes us have no need
Of physick, that's PHYSICK indeed.
Hark hither, Reader! wilt thou see
Nature her own physitian be?
Wilt' see a man, all his own wealth,   15
His own musick, his own health;
A man whose sober soul can tell

Temperance.... First published, beginning at l. 13, with the English translation of Leonard Lessius, *Hygiasticon: Or, The right course of preserving Life and Health unto extream old Age*... (Cambridge, 1634); published in 1646 and 1648 with the title "In praise of Lessius his rule of health"; ll. 45–52 added in 1652. Leonard Leys, or Lessius (1554–1623) was a Jesuit philosopher at Douay; his *Hygiasticon* was first published in 1613, and the English translation has been somewhat questionably attributed to Nicholas Ferrar (M.).

How to wear her garments well.
Her garments, that upon her sitt
As garments should doe, close and fitt; 20
A well-cloth'd soul; that's not opprest
Nor choak't with what she should be drest.
A soul sheath'd in a christall shrine;
Through which all her bright features shine;
As when a peice of wanton lawn 25
A thinne, aeriall veil, is drawn
Or'e beauty's face; seeming to hide
More sweetly showes the blushing bride.
A soul, whose intellectuall beames
No mists doe mask, no lazy steames. 30
A happy soul, that all the way
To HEAVN rides in a summer's day.
Wouldst' see a man, whose well-warm'd blood
Bathes him in a genuine flood!
A man, whose tuned humors be 35
A seat of rarest harmony?
Wouldst see blith lookes, fresh cheekes beguil
Age? wouldst see december smile?
Wouldst' see nests of new roses grow
In a bed of reverend snow? 40
Warm thoughts, free spirits flattering
Winter's selfe into a SPRING.
In summe, wouldst see a man that can
Live to be old, and still a man?
Whose latest and most leaden houres 45
Fall with soft wings, stuck with soft flowres;
And when life's sweet fable ends,
Soul and body part like freinds;
No quarrells, murmurs, no delay;
A KISSE, a SIGH, and so away. 50
This rare one, reader, wouldst thou see?
Hark hither; and thy self be HE.

Hope

Hope whose weak beeing ruin'd is
Alike if it succeed or if it misse!
Whom ill or good does equally confound
And both the hornes of fate's dilemma wound.
       Vain shadow; that dost vanish quite   5
       Both at full noon and perfect night!
The starres have not a possibility
       Of blessing Thee.
If thinges then from their end we happy call,
'Tis hope is the most hopelesse thing of all.   10
  Hope, thou bold Taster of delight!
Who in stead of doing so, devourst it quite.
Thou bringst us an estate, yet leav'st us poor
By clogging it with legacyes before.
       The joyes which we intire should wed   15
       Come deflour'd-virgins to our bed.
Good fortunes without gain imported be
       Such mighty custom's paid to Thee,
For joy like wine kep't close, does better tast;
If it take air before his spirits wast.   20
  Hope fortun's cheating lottery
Where for one prize, an hundred blankes there be.
Fond archer, hope. Who tak'st thine aime so farr
That still or short or wide thine arrowes are
       Thinne empty cloud which th'eye deceives   25
       With shapes that our own fancy gives.
A cloud which gilt and painted now appeares
       But must drop presently in teares
When thy false beames o're reason's light prevail,

Hope. Cowley's poem was published in *The Mistresse,* 1647, with his own "Answer for Hope"; in 1646 Cowley's "Hope" and Crashaw's "Answer" were published in alternating stanzas, as a dialogue, under the title "On Hope, By way of Question and Answer, between A. COWLEY, and R. CRASHAW." 1648 also prints it as a single poem in dialogue.

By IGNES FATUI for north starres we sail. 30
   Brother of fear more gayly clad.
The merryer fool oth two, yet quite as mad.
Sire of repentance, child of fond desire
That blow'st the chymick and the lover's fire.
   Still leading them insensibly' on 35
   With the strong witchcraft of Anon.
By thee the one does changing nature through
   Her endlesse labyrinth's pursue,
And th'other chases woman; while she goes
More wayes and turnes then hunted nature knowes. 40

               M. COWLEY.

M. Crashaws Answer for Hope

Dear hope! earth's dowry, and heavn's debt!
The entity of those that are not yet.
Subtlest, but surest beeing! Thou by whom
Our nothing has a definition!
   Substantiall shade! whose sweet allay 5
   Blends both the noones of night and day.
Fates cannot find out a capacity
   Of hurting thee.
From Thee their lean dilemma, with blunt horn,
Shrinkes, as the sick moon from the wholsome morn. 10
  Rich hope! love's legacy, under lock
Of faith! still spending, and still growing stock!
Our crown-land lyes above yet each meal brings
A seemly portion for the sonnes of kings.
   Nor will the virgin joyes we wed 15
   Come lesse unbroken to our bed,
Because that from the bridall cheek of blisse
   Thou steal'st us down a distant kisse.

---

30 *Ignes Fatui*: false fires, wandering and misleading lights which might be mistaken for the reliable guide, the North Star.

Hope's chast stealth harmes no more joye's maidenhead
Then spousall rites prejudge the marriage bed.
   Fair hope! our earlyer Heav'n! by thee
Young time is taster to eternity.
Thy generous wine with age growes strong, not sowre.
Nor does it kill thy fruit, to smell thy flowre.
       Thy golden, growing, head never hangs down
       Till in the lappe of loves full noone
It falls; and dyes! o no, it melts away
    As does the dawn into the day.
As lumpes of sugar loose themselves; and twine
Their supple essence with the soul of wine.
   Fortune? alas, above the world's low warres
Hope walks; and kickes the curld heads of conspiring starres.
Her keel cutts not the waves where These winds stirr
Fortune's whole lottery is one blank to her.
       Her shafts, and shee fly farre above,
       And forrage in the fields of light and love.
Sweet hope! kind cheat! fair fallacy! by thee
   We are not WHERE nor What we be,
But WHAT and WHERE we would be. Thus art thou
Our absent PRESENCE, and our future NOW.
Faith's sister! nurse of fair desire!
Fear's antidote! a wise and well-stay'd fire!
Temper twixt chill despair, and torrid joy!
Queen Regent in yonge love's minority!
       Though the vext chymick vainly chases
       His fugitive gold through all her faces;
Though love's more feirce, more fruitlesse, fires assay
       One face more fugitive then all they;
True hope's a glorious hunter and her chase,
The GOD of nature in the feilds of grace.

VIVE JESU

Ben Jonson

It is only in recent times that the achievement of Jonson as a poet has been recognized and that literary historians have accorded his nondramatic poetry as a whole any measure of appreciation or sympathy. In Jonson's later life, an informal master–disciple relationship developed between himself and a few Cavalier poets who styled themselves "the Sons of Ben." Imitating him, this group, which included Herrick, Carew, and Waller as its most illustrious members, immersed themselves in the Roman poets and absorbed to varying degrees their pagan ideals as well as their clarity and elegance of manner. Only six months after his death in 1637, many of the "Sons," contributing with dozens of other admirers to a volume of elegies entitled *Jonsonus Virbius*, already regarded Jonson as a dramatist of note who wrote comedies of a trenchant and brittle-witted variety, and they praised him especially for his learning, his spontaneity, his wit, his good sense.

Although Dryden, at the end of the seventeenth century, spoke respectfully of Jonson the poet as "a professed Imitator of Horace," most of his critical attention, like that of his followers, was directed to the plays. Pope, comparing Jonson to Shakespeare, unerringly predicted that the world would "exalt the one at the expense of the other," and, indeed, critics in the next few decades found as much in Jonson's works to deprecate as in Shakespeare's to commend. Virtually the sole apologist of stature at the turn of the eighteenth century was Jonson's editor William Gifford. Supporting Jonson against the asperities of Malone, who had dismissed the masques as "bungling shows" and the tragedy of *Catiline* as "deservedly damned," Gifford found Jonson possessing "extraordinary requisites for the stage, joined to a stream of poetry always manly, frequently lofty, and sometimes almost sublime...."

It was not until the nineteenth century that critics turned their attention to Jonson's nondramatic poetry, but except for admiring a handful of songs, they judged it largely in negative terms. For every Gifford who lamented that the author had not left "a further selection" of the epigrams, there were many like Scott, who castigated Jonson for "coarseness of taste"; or like Swinburne, who, though he considered some of the epigrams good, found that "the worst are so bad, so foul if not so dull, so stupid if not so filthy, that the student stands aghast with astonishment"; or like John Addington Symonds, who deplored "the grossness of the poet's muse," complaining that Jonson "did not shine in purely lyric composition."

In the last three decades, in an evident effort to redress the misjudgments of the past, Jonson scholars have produced no fewer than four editions of the complete poems, several short studies centering on the nondramatic poems, and two extended monographs devoted to this poetry. A concurrent re-examination of the masques, which comprise a larger segment of Jonson's dramatic work than most suspect, and which contain several of his most exquisite songs, has led to reappraisals which have brought a new stature to their author. When the dramatic works — the sixteen plays and the more than twenty-five masques — are viewed in relation to the three collections of verse — *Epigrammes*, *The Forrest*, and *Under-Wood* — what emerges clearly is the sense that the satiric Jonson, the acerbic critic of the indignant plays, is counterbalanced by the man who "painted virtues," the spokesman for the ideal life as seen in the masques, and that the ample dimensions of the world-view of the dramatist find their most positive and succinct statement in the nondramatic poetry.

London bred, Jonson knew city life intimately, and detailed references to it abound in his various works throughout his career. Born in 1573, the posthumous son of a clergyman of Scottish ancestry (his stepfather was a master bricklayer), he was indebted to "a friend" for his education at Westminster School with the classical scholar William Camden. He took no earned degree at either Oxford or Cambridge, but he told William Drummond of Hawthornden in 1619 that "He was Master of

Arts in both the Universities by their favour not his studie." His learning in the classics was prodigious, moving an anonymous contemporary to describe him in a commendatory sonnet not only as "Tun'd to the highest key of antiant Rome," but "Retorning all her musick, with his owne."

Surviving details of his life, though few, fill out a picture of a vigorous and forthright man of integrity, uninhibited by the prudential virtues, who displayed something of the recklessness of the bohemian. He never was a solid family man, although he married Anne Lewis in 1594 and became the father of several children, none of whom, unfortunately, survived him. Argumentative and quarrelsome by nature, he was twice apprehended in his career by the authorities for writing plays considered seditious. He frequently engaged in disputes with theatrical associates, and on one occasion killed a fellow actor in a duel. He did not hesitate to embrace Catholicism in a period when to be a Catholic in England involved the greatest danger, nor did he scruple to return to the Anglican fold when honest belief dictated the change.

During his theatrical career, from the early 1590's until the early 1630's, he wrote for a variety of children's troupes and adult companies, including, in certain periods, the King's Men, and on one occasion he acted in a production with Shakespeare. Jonson viewed the dramatist as moralist and teacher, not merely as entertainer, and his chief comedies—*Volpone* (1606), *The Alchemist* (1610), and *Bartholomew Fayre* (1614)—reveal him as an incisive satirist of men who are conditioned by their "humours," or follies and affectations, and must be purged of them in order to become responsible members of the social community.

Though he wrote no plays after 1614 which are considered stageworthy today, Jonson showed throughout his career no diminution in his abilities as masque librettist. As masque writer for the Jacobean court, he became an eloquent spokesman for the ideals of royalty and aristocracy. In *Queens* (1609), for example, Jonson exalted the monarchy through Queen Anne, who appeared in the performance *in propria persona* among the greatest queens of legend and history; in *Oberon* (1611) he honored Prince Henry on his institution as Prince of Wales by identifying him as chief masquer with the fairy King and by associating him with all the marvels of the realm of faerie; and in *Augurs* (1622) he celebrated both King James and Prince Charles as irreproachable helmsmen of the British state. These are occasional dramatic pieces in the grand Renaissance style. In imaginative appeal as well as in poetic finish, they have no rivals in the masques of the age.

In an age when few writers announced critical principles, Jonson's are clearly set forth in *Timber, or Discoveries*, a collection of short essays on various aspects of the writer and his craft, first published in the second Folio of 1640-41. For Jonson, the poet, like the orator, has a public responsibility; he considers poetry the noblest of all arts, since it speaks to the understanding and not merely to the senses, and its object is profit as well as pleasure. What the poet is expected to invent shows us Jonson's high regard for his office:

> I could never thinke the study of *Wisdome* confin'd only to the Philosopher: or of *Poetry* to the *Divine*: or of *State* to the *Politicke*. But that he which can faine a *Common-wealth* (which is the *Poet*) can governe it with *Counsels,* strengthen it with *Lawes,* correct it with *Judgements,* informe it with *Religion,* and *Morals;* is all these. Wee doe not require in him meere *Elocution;* or an excellent faculty in verse; but the exact knowledge of all vertues; and their Contraries; with ability to render the one lov'd, the other hated, by his proper embattaling them.

In manner Jonson clearly aligns himself with the anti-Ciceronians, reacting against a florid style and advocating the cultivation of the *plain style*, an epistolary style well adapted to serve as the vehicle of satire, comedy, epistle, and epigram, the genres in which he was especially interested. Ease and relaxation, he insists, are profitable to all studies: "The true Artificer will not run away from nature ... or depart from life ... but speake to the capacity of his hearers." He admires one writer because he never forced language, never "went out of the high way of *speaking*; but for some great necessity," and never utilized figures "for ornament, but for ayde."

Pithy anticipations of several of Jonson's critical views appear in the informal observations recorded by Drummond when the poet visited Scotland early in 1619. Preserved in the famous *Conversations*, these have both the virtues and the limitations of an unedited report. What is abundantly clear is that Jonson had little sympathy for the poetry of the Elizabethans, and frequently was exceedingly censorious. To Drummond he reported that "Spencers stanzaes pleased him not, nor his matter," that Samuel Daniel was "no poet," that Michael Drayton's "Long Verses pleased him not," that Shakespeare, introducing in one play a shipwreck in Bohemia, where there is no sea coast, "wanted Arte," and that Sidney "did not keep a Decorum in making every one speak as well as himself." When not literary gossip at its most negligible, some of this table-talk constitutes incisive criticism, raising questions of considerable importance concerning genre, subject matter, and style.

His more immediate contemporaries elicited from him equally provocative comments. Drummond further records that Jonson "esteemeth John Done the first poet in the World in some things," but he "deserved hanging... for not keeping of accent." Indeed, Jonson went on to say that "Donne himself, for not being understood, would perish." Others he dismissed with little ceremony for reasons largely personal: Raleigh, because he "esteemed more of fame than conscience"; and Beaumont, because he "loved too much himself and his own verses." He belittled Marston, his would-be satirist, declaring that Marston wrote his chaplain father-in-law's sermons and that his father-in-law wrote Marston's comedies. Of far greater interest are Jonson's reports to Drummond on his own method of composing: "that he wrot all his [verses] first in prose, for so his master Cambden had Learned him"; "That [his] Verses stood by sense without either Colour's or accent"; and that he had presumed to tell King James that the latter's tutor Buchanan "had corrupted his eare... and learned him to sing Verses, when he should have read them." Like Donne, who, according to Jonson, had completed all his best pieces before he was twenty-five, Jonson himself had finished an important part of his poetry relatively early in his career. His *Epigrammes* were entered in the Stationers' Register in 1612.

Jonson considered the *Epigrammes*, first published in the Folio of 1616, "the ripest of my studies." Martial was his chief guide in his use of the epigram, although he was familiar with a host of Renaissance imitators from More to Donne. He admired the brevity and the informal, conversational manner associated with the genre, as well as its opportunities for wit. In talking with Drummond, he criticized Sir John Harington's pieces because "they were Narrations and not Epigrams," and Sir John Davies' because "they expressed in the end, what should have been understood." The epigram's variable length, like its diversity in subject matter and extensive tonal range, greatly appealed to him. He regarded the genre as "the bravest sort of verses," and Drummond reports that he "cursed Petrarch for redacting Verses to Sonnets, which he said were like that Tirrants bed, wher some who were too short were racked, others too long cut short."

In this collection of well over a hundred pieces, Jonson observes, describes, and judges the society of contemporary London with taste and decorum as well as with shrewdness and perception. He recognizes that epigrams in the aggregate comprise a public kind of poetry, presupposing the ideal of an ordered community of men to be viewed by a detached though morally implicated observer and assessor of experience. As epigrammatist, Jonson subjects life in its diversified activity to the keenest scrutiny. For him, all conduct must meet the bar of good sense, rational behavior, taste, and virtue. His judgments on man as a member of society are ordinarily implicit rather than overt, and the moral responses of his readers are usually gained through comparisons and contrasts or through juxtapositions of generalized and particularized accounts of men and their doings.

A vivid Jacobean society, alternately magnificent and just, then squalid and corrupt, is evoked by the epigrams as they survey the extensive range of human activity from man at his best to men at their worst. The portrait of the individual personage addressed is always positively rendered, while the description of the type figure is invariably satirical. Thus Robert Cecil, Earl of Salisbury, is justly praised for his virtuous conduct as statesman, while the aspiring politico, Captayne Hungry, is ridiculed for his adeptness in rifling the top-secret portfolios of his superiors. Lucy, Countess of Bedford, famed patroness of poets, is extolled as "the *Muses* evening, as their morning-starre," while Fine Lady Would-bee is derided for undergoing an abortion. Francis Beaumont, "That unto mee dost such religion use," merits Jonson's love while Play-wright is castigated for demanding of the poet epigrams full of "bawdrie" and "obscenity." Figures in similar pairs can be found throughout the collection, embracing all professions and occupations, from the king himself to courtiers, tilters, and *grandes dames*, to scholars, poets, and booksellers, to divines, actors, and musicians, to tapsters, tavern habitués, and bawds.

It is refreshing to find that Jonson's tonal range in this collection is broad enough to include several epigrams which are tender and gentle in manner, to counterbalance those which are curt and waspish. Such is the epitaph on the death of Salomon Pavy, the boy actor of a choir-boy troupe, who was best remembered for his excellent portrayals of old men; and such also is the epigram inviting a friend to supper, which casually extols the conjunction of good food and talk. As a further contrast, there are several pieces in a bold and Rabelaisian manner, such as "On the famous Voyage," a mock-heroic poem which memorializes the zany progress of a pair of contemporary wags through a series of rollicking escapades along the waterfront of a seamy section of London. In sharp contrast there are also the tempered and even-measured tributes to such famous Jacobean personages as Sir John Rowe, Lord Mounteagle, the Earl of Salisbury, the Countess of Bedford, tributes which make Jonson the greatest occasional poet England ever had. It is the ability to see his subjects not only for themselves but also as distinguished members of a well-ordered community which marks Jonson's special contribution to this kind of poetry.

A second collection of poems also appeared in the 1616 Folio. It was entitled *The Forrest*, after the manner of the ancients who, Jonson explains, were wont to speak of their pieces as *sylva*. Consisting of fifteen poems (for the most part epistles, odes, and songs), the collection introduces a tonal palette quite different from that of the *Epigrammes*. Here the idealizing, nonsatiric Jonson dominates; it is the painter of virtue who speaks, and on subjects not broached in the earlier collection. The Jonson of the epigrams — now trenchant, now almost grudging in his tributes — yields here to a poet warmer and more kindly disposed to his subjects, and more willing to reveal himself. We are confronted with a figure at once bluff, rugged, and scrupulously honest, hearty, witty, and fond of the good life. Time and again he preaches the simple doctrine that man can keep "true state" by virtue of his intelligence, his sense of morality, and the strength of his will. He can learn to dominate his senses, and also to reciprocate that true love which has the power to combine "the soft and sweetest mindes/In equall knots."

The majority of the poems of *The Forrest* describe a way of life which is stoic in principle but Epicurean within the limits granted by that austere code. Its exponents, ideally, are the aristocracy, best exemplified by the lord and the lady of the manor-house. "To Penshurst," one of the earliest of several seventeenth-century country-house poems, reveals Jonson's wholehearted espousal of the way of life led at such a seat as that of the Sidney family, presided over by the great lord Sir Robert (brother to Sir Philip) and his good lady. Sir Robert Wroth, sometimes resident at Durance, a similar seat, is likewise praised for his sense of manly duty and responsibility as master of his domains, as sportsman, and as soldier; his "noblest spouse," Lady Mary, daughter of Sir Robert Sidney, is honored as his graceful consort sprung from a race of heroes. In other urbane epistles Jonson extends similar gracious address to such other titled patronesses as Lady Aubigny, whom he praises for her virtue, for her conscience, and for the chaste love she bears her lord, and the Countess of Rutland, one of Jonson's several stars of "purest light" among the nobility who made him shine "rapt with rage divine." It is not surprising that in even a trifling song such as "That Women are but Mens shaddowes" (written for the Countess of Pembroke as a penance after a dispute with her lord, so Jonson told Drummond), the grounds are set forth upon which the ideal relationship between man and woman may subsist.

On occasion in this collection Jonson's subjects are subordinated to the way of life he extols. In the poem beginning "And must I sing?" Jonson whimsically questions what the ideal subject matter for poetry should be and what gods or worthies he ought to invoke to inspire his active Muse. Deciding to rely on his own intuition, he unequivocally sets forth his credo in "Epode" in a series of epigrammatically terse couplets. He boldly underscores the fundamental assumptions of man as master of his destiny even though he recognizes that his mental powers are ever subject to the depredations of the passions. He distinguishes true love from blind desire as "an essence, farre more gentle, fine, /Pure, perfect, nay divine." The poem, emphasizing man's capacity for friendship and love, serves as one of the chief repositories of Jonson's views about society as an organism reflecting at once the symmetry of the universe or macrocosm, and the capacity for harmonious composition within the world of man or microcosm.

The largest collection of Jonson's poetry was not published until after his death, in the Folio of 1640-41. Entitled *Underwoods* (or *Under-Wood*), it comprises "workes of divers nature, and matter congested." These are "lesser Poems, of later growth," Jonson explains, and are so entitled because of the relation they bear to *The Forrest*. The collection contains eighty-nine pieces, most of them substantial in length. Even though the collection is not unified by theme, the diversity of content and the maturity of manner are appealing. Here, lucid and graceful songs, ranking among Jonson's supreme achievements, alternate with pithy epigrams, and epistles cast in the conscious prosaic mold of weighty generalization contrast sharply with elegies more fervidly amorous than critics usually grant. As a group these intimate pieces display Jonson's plain style at its most flexible. Through a masterful colloquial utterance extending from vituperation and expostulation to admiring and ingratiating compliment, Jonson comes closest in these pieces to developing the dramatic monologue in a fashion inimitably his own.

Under-Wood contains several well-defined groups of poems. It opens with a tripartite hymn celebrating the Holy Trinity which displays, rather unexpectedly, the poet's contrite penitence and complete submissiveness. This is followed by a small masterpiece, "A Celebration of Charis in ten Lyrick Peeces," a semi-dramatic piece of generous length establishing through its ambivalent tone of whimsey and seriousness the ideals of aristocratic womanhood and manhood, and presenting the principals in an avowedly Platonic but actually sensual relationship. It is, on one level, a sustained paean to abstract beauty, and on another—since the poet is transformed to stone at the sight of the proud beauty, and Cupid's bow and arrows are rendered ineffectual by her eyes—a playful satire upon Petrarchan formulae. Near the end of the collection appears still another substantial piece, "Eupheme; or, The Faire Fame," Jonson's most extended endeavor in the elegiac genre. It was intended to contain ten separate poems celebrating the memory of Lady Venetia Digby, wife of the Caroline worthy Sir Kenelm Digby. In the piece entitled "Elegie on my Muse," Jonson praises Lady Digby in extravagant terms as a pious and devoted wife and mother, though his tribute is in quite a different vein from that of Donne in speaking of Mistress Drury in his *Anniversaries*. The elegy is otherwise memorable as one of the chief statements of Jonson's commitment to traditional Christian values.

Several poems in *Under-Wood* deal with the theme of the poet's dedication to "Poesie" as distinguished from "worded Balladrie." Jonson can show scorn for "chattring Pies" (XXIII), and he can reduce rhyme to a delightful absurdity as "the rack of finest wits" (XXIX). At the same time, he never tires of showing how his Muse is continually inspired by worthy subjects. In XXVIII he compliments Lady Wroth for making him not only a better lover but a better poet, and in LXXXIV he celebrates Lady Venetia Digby as his Muse. Another group, Elegies XXXVIII–XLII, reveals Jonson assuming the Donnean manner of fierce dramatic intensity in love poetry. In one elegy, addressing an offended mistress in the language of abject submission, he protests apologetically in an endless series of rhetorical questions. In others, he approaches the mischievous taunting manner of a sardonic anti-Petrarchan thoroughly immersed in Jacobean slang. Wesley Trimpi finds that in such pieces even the worn comparisons of conventional love poetry are given a passionate plainness rarely equaled in English literature. It is hardly surprising that some authorities have not hesitated to ascribe some or all of this group of elegies to Donne.

Various poems in *Under-Wood* reveal the poet's preoccupation, in his later years, with personal as well as public matters. He greets his monarch and his queen on every due occasion, from celebrating a birthday to opening a new wine cellar, and he displays an appropriate anxiety in anticipating each payment of his pension. He honors personal friends like Sir Lucius Cary and Sir Henry Morrison in eloquent odes, and he is equally prepared to denigrate personal antagonists like the scenic designer Inigo

Jones when the latter receives a royal appointment to fill an office beyond his capacities. The most impressive of the personal poems, entitled "An Execration upon Vulcan," is a magnificently sustained mock-heroic invective against the god of fire for allowing the poet's quarters in London to be completely destroyed. In the course of an amusing tongue-lashing, Jonson surveys his gutted chambers with a nice sense of epic magnification, comparing them with the three great London edifices ravaged by fire in his lifetime — St. Paul's steeple, the Globe Theater, and Whitehall — each a world in itself. "An Execration" reflects certain dominant strains of the entire collection and links together in subject matter and manner both the personal and the public poet. In it, Jonson asserts, if only inversely, his essential civility and urbanity, and he does so with penetrating wit and a racy manner.

The songs comprise another extensive body of Jonson's lyric poetry, to be found in the plays and the masques and more sparingly in *The Forrest* and *Under-Wood*. Jonson's songs have always been appreciated precisely because they display so admirably the essential requirements of the genre: simplicity, brevity, and elegance. Some poets consider that the musical quality of a song depends upon diction, rhyme, and prosody; like Swinburne, they speak of "singing power" of words alone. Others (and Jonson unmistakably belongs to this second group) think of a song rather as an assemblage of words intended to be sung to an actual tune which may heighten or complement the text. Although his knowledge of music in its technical details could hardly equal that of a poet like Campion, Jonson certainly recognized that the successful integration of text and tune required him to understand certain fundamental aspects of the song forms of his own age.

Songs usually are spoken of as the most personal kind of lyric expression. What Jonson has achieved in his songs, however, is a quality which is unexpectedly impersonal and detached, though hardly as cold or formal as some critics would maintain. The fact that his songs are most often imbedded in a dramatic context, to be sung usually by characters which are more types than individuals, underscores the universality of their sentiments. Although consideration of Jonson's dramatic use of song is beyond the scope of our anthology, it may briefly be noted here that the seven songs woven into the matrix of *Cynthias Revells* display dramatist and poet working hand in hand to crystallize dominant ideas, attitudes, and actions in the play. These songs are strikingly diversified in tone and manner. The famous "Slow, slow, fresh fount," with its flawlessly-paced prosody marking out mutability, contrasts sharply in tempo with the brisk patter song, "Come follow me, my wagges," a boisterous beggars' song which evokes the uninhibited street cries of the day. The ecstatically elegant "O, that joy so soone should waste," to be sung by the voluptuary Hedon to his mistress over the prospect of a kiss, is complemented by the palinode, or song of recantation, a parody of the chanted litany at the conclusion of the play which seeks on a secular level to purge men of all ill humors and to redeem the court of Cynthia from all insipidities. In each instance, the effectiveness of the song is dependent in no small measure upon the subtlety of humor, which is achieved variously through parody, hyperbole, or a magic jingling quality reminding us, on occasion, of the origin of song as charm. Though the tonal contribution of these songs is of considerable importance to the play, each can stand alone effectively.

As a rule most masque songs, in contrast to songs in plays, reveal a ceremoniousness, a sense of ritual, of a piece with the entertainments of which they form a not inconsiderable part. In view of the formality of most masque speeches, the way in which Jonson preserves his songs from woodenness or heaviness is remarkable, particularly when, as in *The Masque of Beauty*, he fashions them to bear the weight of his guiding ideas, in this case the creation of the world through Love. Yet their use is more normally guided by the plot movements of the myths and allegories which serve as the basis of most masques, as well as by the special structure developed in the masque of Jonson's day. Hence he uses songs to interpret complex dances which are hieroglyphs, for the chief participants of the masque, the courtly blue bloods, always express themselves in the movements of dance, never in speech or song. He frequently uses songs as charms to effect transformations, and he sees them as useful devices to solve various other plotting exigencies: the presenter's address to the State, the invitation to the revels, the signal to close the festivities, the farewell song. The fact that the songs are never cast as the personal expression of the vocalist or chorus, who are almost invariably anonymous, but rather are always directed to the masquers, describing, guiding, or praising them, emphasizes the generality of their sentiments.

Since the vocal and instrumental resources available to Jonson were extensive for his day, his lyrics are often cast in unusual forms to achieve interesting effects: he is fond of echo devices, and he likes to alternate various solo and chorus passages. His variations in stanzaic forms are diversely complex, and there is some basis, as Willa Evans has shown, for believing that he created irregular patterns to be effectively complemented by the music. In *Oberon*, the satyrs who sing "Buz, quoth the blue Flie," are given a text appropriate to a catch, while a chorus of Faies, in the solemnly moving "Melt earth to sea," celebrates James as the wonder of all tongues, ears, and eyes in a lyric which lends itself admirably to a choral setting.

The breadth and universality of Jonson's utterance in the masque lyrics strike one as notably impressive, for their deceptive simplicity tends to obscure the fact that they admirably distill the ideas more fully developed in the matrix of the blank verse in which these lyrics appear. In place of an automatic emotional response, they demand of the listener some degree of intellectual application. In them Jonson joins together two aspects of himself, the occasional poet *par excellence* and the lyricist of flawless workmanship. The result, to be seen in masque after masque, is the celebration of a society of talent and virtue, hierarchically ordered, in which the aristocracy of his day—for royalty moved in their midst as chief performers—could enact their relationship to constituted authority, survey their responsibilities as well as privileges, and ultimately not only comprehend the great gulf which could lie between actuality and ideality in the conduct of life, but also recognize that their capacity and potential for achieving noble ends were virtually limitless.

The standard critical edition of Jonson is that of C. H. Herford and Percy and Evelyn Simpson, cited in the notes as H. & S. Other complete editions of the present century are those of Bernard H. Newdigate, George Burke Johnston, and William B. Hunter, Jr. Like the selection from Jonson's poetry edited by John Hollander, these contain critical introductions and annotations of value. The photographic reproduction of the *Epigrams, The Forest, Underwoods* from the first editions prepared by Hoyt H. Hudson for the Facsimile Text Society includes substantial bibliographical notes.

The copy text for the selections from the *Epigrammes* and *The Forrest* is the Folio of 1616 (F), and for the selections from *Under-Wood*, the Folio of 1640/41 (F2). The copy text of the songs from the plays, entertainments, and masques is that folio containing the earlier version. The commendatory verses to Shakespeare reproduce the version of the 1623 Folio, and the three poems on Inigo Jones are derived from the versions in an Ellesmere manuscript in the Henry E. Huntington Library, #EL8729.

SELECTED BIBLIOGRAPHY
EDITIONS

Epigrams, The Forest, Underwoods. Reproduced from the first editions, with a bibliographic note by Hoyt H. Hudson. New York, 1936.

Gifford, William, ed. *The Works of Ben Jonson.* 9 vols. London, 1816. (Poetry, vols. 8-9.) This edition was reprinted in one volume in 1838 and partially revised by Francis Cunningham in 1871 (3 vols.) and in 1875 (11 vols.).

Herford, C. H., and Simpson, Percy and Evelyn, eds. *Ben Jonson.* 11 vols. Oxford, 1925-52. (Introduction to poetry, vol. 2; Masques, vol. 7; Poetry, vol. 8; Commentary, vol. 11.)

Hollander, John, ed. *Ben Jonson.* New York, 1961.

Hunter, William B., Jr., ed. *The Complete Poetry.* New York, 1963.

Johnston, George Burke, ed. *Poems of Ben Jonson.* Cambridge, Mass., 1954.

Newdigate, Bernard H., ed. *The Poems of Ben Jonson.* Oxford, 1936.

Orgel, Stephen, ed. *Ben Jonson: The Complete Masques.* New Haven, Conn., 1969.

Whalley, Peter, ed. *The Works of Ben Jonson.* 7 vols. London, 1756. (Poetry, vol. 6.)

BIOGRAPHY AND CRITICISM

Atkins, J. W. H. *English Literary Criticism: The Renascence.* London, 1947.
Beaurline, L. A. "The Selective Principle in Jonson's Shorter Poems," *Criticism,* VIII (1966), 64-74.
Bradbrook, F. W. "Ben Jonson's Poetry," in Boris Ford, ed., *A Guide to English Literature,* vol. 3. Harmondsworth, Middlesex, 1956.
Briggs, W. D. "Source-Material for Jonson's *Epigrams* and *Forest,*" *Class. Philol.,* XI (1916), 169-90.
———. "Source-Material for Jonson's *Underwoods* and Miscellaneous Poems," *MP,* XV (1917), 227-312.
———. "Studies in Ben Jonson, III-V," *Anglia,* XXXIX (1916), 16-44, 209-52, 310-18.
Cubeta, P. M. "Ben Jonson's Religious Lyrics," *JEGP,* LXII (1963), 96-110.
———. "'A Celebration of Charis': An Evaluation of Jonsonian Poetic Strategy," *ELH,* XXV (1958), 163-80.
———. "A Jonsonian Ideal: 'To Penshurst,'" *PQ,* XLII (1963), 14-24.
Evans, W. McC. *Ben Jonson and Elizabethan Music.* Lancaster, Pa., 1929. Reprinted with a new preface, New York, 1965.
Hudson, H. H. *The Epigram in the English Renaissance.* Princeton, N.J., 1947.
Johnston, G. B. *Ben Jonson: Poet.* New York, 1945.
Knights, L. C. "Tradition and Ben Jonson," *Scrutiny,* IV (1935), 140-57.
McEuen, Kathryn A. *Classical Influence upon the Tribe of Ben: A Study of Classical Elements in the Nondramatic Poetry of Ben Jonson and His Circle.* Cedar Rapids, Iowa, 1939.
Maclean, Hugh. "Ben Jonson's Poems: Notes on the Ordered Society," in Millar Maclure and F. W. Watts, eds., *Essays ... Presented to A. S. P. Woodhouse.* Toronto, 1964.
Parfitt, G. A. E. "Ethical Thought and Ben Jonson's Poetry," *SEL,* IX (1969), 123-34.
Putney, R. D. "'This So Subtile Sport': Some Aspects of Jonson's Epigrams," *Colorado Studies in Language and Literature,* X (1966), 37-56.
Sabol, A. J. *A Score for "Lovers Made Men."* Providence, R. I., 1963.
———. *Songs and Dances for the Stuart Masque.* Providence, R. I., 1959.

Spanos, W. V. "The Real Toad in the Jonsonian Garden: Resonance in the Nondramatic Poetry," *JEGP*, LXVIII (1969), 1–23.

Stein, Arnold. "Plain Style, Plain Criticism, Plain Dealing, and Ben Jonson," *ELH*, XXX (1963), 306–16.

Swinburne, Algernon Charles. *A Study of Ben Jonson*. London, 1889.

Symonds, J. A. *Ben Jonson*. London, 1888.

Trimpi, Wesley. *Ben Jonson's Poems: A Study of the Plain Style*. Stanford, Calif., 1962.

Walker, R. S., ed. *Ben Jonson's "Timber; or, Discoveries."* Syracuse, N.Y., 1953. (Contains the essay "Ben Jonson's Lyric Poetry.")

Walton, Geoffrey. "The Tone of Ben Jonson's Poetry," in *Metaphysical to Augustan*. London, 1955.

Wheeler, C. F. *Classical Mythology in the Plays, Masques, and Poems of Ben Jonson*. Princeton, N.J., 1938.

Whipple, T. K. *Martial and the English Epigram from Sir Thomas Wyatt to Ben Jonson*. Berkeley, Calif., 1925.

THE
WORKES
OF
Beniamin Jonson

— neque, me, vt miretur turba,
laboro:
Contentus paucis lectoribus.

Imprinted at London by Will Stansby

An°. D. 1616.

From EPIGRAMMES

TO THE GREAT
EXAMPLE OF
HONOR AND
VERTUE,
THE MOST NOBLE
WILLIAM,
EARLE OF PEMBROKE,
L. CHAMBERLAYNE, &C.

MY LORD. *While you cannot change your merit, I dare not change your title: It was that made it, and not I. Under which name, I here offer to your Lo: the ripest of my studies, my* Epigrammes; *which, though they carry danger in the sound, doe not therefore seeke your shelter: For, when I made them, I had nothing in my conscience, to expressing of which I did need a cypher. But, if I be falne into those times, wherein, for the likenesse of vice, and facts, every one thinks anothers ill deeds objected to him; and that in their ignorant and guiltie mouthes, the common voyce is (for their securitie)* Beware the Poet, *confessing, therein, so much love to their diseases, as they would rather make a partie for them, then be either rid, or told of them: I must expect, at your Lo: hand, the protection of truth, and libertie, while you are constant to your owne goodnesse. In thankes whereof, I returne*

Epigrammes. Dedication. William Herbert, Earl of Pembroke (1580–1630), was the son of Mary Sidney, Countess of Pembroke, patroness of several poets. The Shakespeare First Folio of 1623 was also dedicated to this lord and to his teacher, the Earl of Montgomery.

you the honor of leading forth so many good, and great names (as my verses mention on the better part) to their remembrance with posteritie. Amongst whom, if I have praysed, unfortunately, any one, that doth not deserve; or, if all answere not, in all numbers, the pictures I have made of them: I hope it will be forgiven me, that they are no ill pieces, though they be not like the persons. But I foresee a neerer fate to my booke, then this: that the vices therein will be own'd before the vertues (though, there, I have avoyded all particulars, as I have done names) and that some will be so readie to discredit me, as they will have the impudence to belye themselves. For, if I meant them not, it is so. Nor, can I hope otherwise. For, why should they remit any thing of their riot, their pride, their selfe-love, and other inherent graces, to consider truth or vertue; but, with the trade of the world, lend their long eares against men they love not: and hold their deare Mountebanke, *or* Jester, *in farre better condition, then all the studie, or studiers of* humanitie? *For such, I would rather know them by their visards, still, then they should publish their faces, at their perill, in my* Theater, *where* CATO, *if he liv'd, might enter without scandall.*

Your Lo: most faithfull honorer,
BEN. JONSON.

I. *To the Reader*

Pray thee take care, that tak'st my booke in hand,
  To reade it well: that is, to understand.

II. *To my Booke*

It will be look'd for, booke, when some but see
  Thy title, *Epigrammes*, and nam'd of mee,
Thou should'st be bold, licentious, full of gall,
  Wormewood, and sulphure, sharpe, and tooth'd withall;
Become a petulant thing, hurle inke, and wit,   *5*
  As mad-men stones: not caring whom they hit.

Deceive their malice, who could wish it so.
   And by thy wiser temper, let men know
Thou art not covetous of least selfe fame,
   Made from the hazard of anothers shame: 10
Much lesse with lewd, prophane, and beastly phrase,
   To catch the worlds loose laughter, or vaine gaze.
He that departs with his owne honesty
   For vulgar praise, doth it too dearely buy.

III. *To my Booke-seller*

Thou, that mak'st gaine thy end, and wisely well,
   Call'st a booke good, or bad, as it doth sell,
Use mine so, too: I give thee leave. But crave
   For the lucks sake, it thus much favour have,
To lye upon thy stall, till it be sought;   5
   Not offer'd, as it made sute to be bought;
Nor have my title-leafe on posts, or walls,
   Or in cleft-sticks, advanced to make calls
For termers, or some clarke-like serving-man,
   Who scarse can spell th'hard names: whose knight lesse can.   10
If, without these vile arts, it will not sell,
   Send it to *Bucklers-bury*, there 'twill, well.

IV. *To King James*

   How, best of Kings, do'st thou a scepter beare!
     How, best of *Poets*, do'st thou laurell weare!
   But two things, rare, the FATES had in their store,
     And gave thee both, to shew they could no more.

   III. To my Booke-seller. Written originally to the bookseller John Stepneth, in 1612 (H. & S.).
   12 *Bucklers-bury*: area in London inhabited by grocers, who could make use of wrapping paper.
   IV. To King James. 2 *Poets*: King James's verses were published in his lifetime and have been since.

For such a *Poet*, while thy dayes were greene, 5
   Thou wert, as chiefe of them are said t'have beene.
And such a Prince thou art, wee daily see,
   As chiefe of those still promise they will bee.
Whom should my *Muse* then flie to, but the best
   Of Kings for grace; of *Poets* for my test? 10

IX. *To all, to whom I write*

May none, whose scatter'd names honor my booke,
   For strict degrees of ranke, or title looke:
'Tis 'gainst the manners of an *Epigram*:
   And, I a *Poet* here, no *Herald* am.

XIV. *To William Camden*

CAMDEN, most reverend head, to whom I owe
   All that I am in arts, all that I know,
(How nothing's that?) to whom my countrey owes
   The great renowne, and name wherewith shee goes.
Then thee the age sees not that thing more grave, 5
   More high, more holy, that shee more would crave.
What name, what skill, what faith hast thou in things!
   What sight in searching the most antique springs!
What weight, and what authoritie in thy speech!
   Man scarse can make that doubt, but thou canst teach. 10
Pardon free truth, and let thy modestie,
   Which conquers all, be once over-come by thee.
Many of thine this better could, then I,
   But for their powers, accept my pietie.

XIV. To William Camden. Camden (1551–1623) was Jonson's teacher and is frequently praised by the poet. His *Britannia* (1586) was a long work in Latin celebrating Britain's illustrious past.

xv. *On Court-worme*

All men are wormes: But this no man. In silke
   'Twas brought to court first wrapt, and white as milke;
Where, afterwards, it grew a butter-flye:
   Which was a cater-piller. So't will dye.

xvii. *To the learned Critick*

May others feare, flie, and traduce thy name,
   As guiltie men doe magistrates: glad I,
That wish my poemes a legitimate fame,
   Charge them, for crowne, to thy sole censure hye.
And, but a sprigge of bayes, given by thee,   5
   Shall out-live gyrlands, stolne from the chast tree.

xviii. *To my meere English Censurer*

To thee, my way in *Epigrammes* seemes new,
   When both it is the old way, and the true.
Thou saist, that cannot be: for thou hast seene
   DAVIS, and WEEVER, and the best have beene,
And mine come nothing like. I hope so. Yet,   5
   As theirs did with thee, mine might credit get:
If thou'ldst but use thy faith, as thou didst then,
   When thou wert wont t'admire, not censure men.
Pr'y thee beleeve still, and not judge so fast,
   Thy faith is all the knowledge that thou hast.   10

XVIII. To my...Censurer. John Davies' *Epigrams* appeared in the same volume as Marlowe's *Elegies* (based on Ovid), published about 1590. John Weever's *Epigrammes* appeared in 1599.

XXI. *On reformed Gam'ster*

Lord, how is GAM'STER chang'd! his haire close cut!
    His neck fenc'd round with ruffe! his eyes halfe shut!
His clothes two fashions of, and poore! his sword
    Forbidd' his side! and nothing, but the word
Quick in his lips! who hath this wonder wrought?   5
    The late tane bastinado. So I thought.
What severall wayes men to their calling have!
    The bodies stripes, I see, the soule may save.

XXII. *On my first Daughter*

Here lyes to each her parents ruth,
MARY, the daughter of their youth:
Yet, all heavens gifts, being heavens due,
It makes the father, lesse, to rue.
At sixe moneths end, shee parted hence   5
With safetie of her innocence;
Whose soule heavens Queene, (whose name shee beares)
In comfort of her mothers teares,
Hath plac'd amongst her virgin-traine:
Where, while that sever'd doth remaine,   10
This grave partakes the fleshly birth.
Which cover lightly, gentle earth.

XXIII. *To John Donne*

DONNE, the delight of PHŒBUS, and each *Muse*,
    Who, to thy one, all other braines refuse;
    Whose every worke, of thy most earely wit,

XXI. *On reformed Gam'ster.* 1 *haire close cut*: traditional Puritan fashion.
XXII. *On my first Daughter.* Jonson was married to Anne Lewis in 1594. The death date of the six-month-old daughter of this marriage has been variously put at 1596 or 1598.

Came forth example, and remaines so, yet:
Longer a knowing, then most wits doe live.
   And which no'affection praise enough can give!
To it, thy language, letters, arts, best life,
   Which might with halfe mankind maintayne a strife.
All which I meant to praise, and, yet, I would;
   But leave, because I cannot as I should!

XXV. *On Sir Voluptuous Beast*

While BEAST instructs his faire, and innocent wife,
   In the past pleasures of his sensuall life,
Telling the motions of each petticote,
   And how his GANIMEDE mov'd, and how his goate,
And now, her (hourely) her owne cucqueane makes,
   In varied shapes, which for his lust shee takes:
What doth he else, but say, leave to be chast,
   Just wife, and, to change me, make womans hast.

XXVI. *On the same Beast*

Then his chast wife, though BEAST now know no more,
   He'adulters still: his thoughts lye with a whore.

XXXIV. *Of Death*

   He that feares death, or mournes it, in the just,
   Shewes of the resurrection little trust.

XXXVI. *To the Ghost of Martial*

MARTIAL, thou gav'st farre nobler *Epigrammes*
   To thy DOMITIAN, than I can my JAMES:
But in my royall subject I passe thee,
   Thou flattered'st thine, mine cannot flatter'd bee.

XXXVII. *On Chev'rill the Lawyer*

No cause, nor client fat, will CHEV'RILL leese,
  But as they come, on both sides he takes fees,
And pleaseth both. For while he melts his greace
  For this: that winnes, for whom he holds his peace.

XL. *On Margaret Ratcliffe*

Marble, weepe, for thou dost cover
A dead beautie under-neath thee,
Rich, as nature could bequeath thee:
Grant then, no rude hand remove her.
All the gazers on the skies   5
Read not in faire heavens storie,
Expresser truth, or truer glorie,
Then they might in her bright eyes.
Rare, as wonder, was her wit;
And like, *Nectar* ever flowing: 10
Till time, strong by her bestowing,
Conquer'd hath both life and it.
Life, whose griefe was out of fashion,
In these times. Few so have ru'de
Fate, in a brother. To conclude,   15
For wit, feature, and true passion,
Earth, thou hast not such another.

    XXXVII. *On Chev'rill the Lawyer.* 1 *Chev'rill*: soft elastic leather made of kid-skin.
    XL. *On Margaret Ratcliffe.* A daughter of Sir John Ratcliffe and a maid of honor to Queen Elizabeth; she died in 1599, grief-stricken at the news of her brother's death in Ireland.

XLII. *On Giles and Jone*

Who sayes that GILES and JONE at discord be?
    Th'observing neighbours no such mood can see.
Indeed, poore GILES repents he married ever.
    But that his JONE doth too. And GILES would never,
By his free will, be in JONES company.   5
    No more would JONE he should. GILES riseth early,
And having got him out of doores is glad.
    The like is JONE. But turning home, is sad.
And so is JONE. Oft-times, when GILES doth find
    Harsh sights at home, GILES wisheth he were blind.   10
All this doth JONE. Or that his long yearn'd life
    Were quite out-spun. The like wish hath his wife.
The children, that he keepes, GILES sweares are none
    Of his begetting. And so sweares his JONE.
In all affections shee concurreth still.   15
    If, now, with man and wife, to will, and nill
The selfe-same things, a note of concord be:
    I know no couple better can agree!

XLV. *On my first Sonne*

Farewell, thou child of my right hand, and joy;
    My sinne was too much hope of thee, lov'd boy,
Seven yeeres tho'wert lent to me, and I thee pay,
    Exacted by thy fate, on the just day.
O, could I loose all father, now. For why   5
    Will man lament the state he should envie?
To have so soone scap'd worlds, and fleshes rage,
    And, if no other miserie, yet age?
Rest in soft peace, and, ask'd, say here doth lye
    BEN. JONSON his best piece of *poetrie*.   10

XLV. *On my first Sonne*. Drummond of Hawthornden recorded 1603 as the date of the death of Jonson's first son, Benjamin.

For whose sake, hence-forth, all his vowes be such,
As what he loves may never like too much.

XLIX. *To Play-wright*

Play-wright me reades, and still my verses damnes,
   He sayes, I want the tongue of *Epigrammes*;
I have no salt: no bawdrie he doth meane.
   For wittie, in his language, is obscene.
PLAY-WRIGHT, I loath to have thy manners knowne   5
   In my chast booke: professe them in thine owne.

LV. *To Francis Beaumont*

How I doe love thee BEAUMONT, and thy *Muse*,
   That unto me dost such religion use!
How I doe feare my selfe, that am not worth
   The least indulgent thought thy pen drops forth!
At once thou mak'st me happie, and unmak'st;   5
   And giving largely to me, more thou tak'st.
What fate is mine, that so it selfe bereaves?
   What art is thine, that so thy friend deceives?
When even there, where most thou praysest mee,
   For writing better, I must envie thee.   10

LIX. *On Spies*

SPIES, you are lights in state, but of base stuffe,
Who, when you'have burnt your selves downe to the snuffe,
Stinke, and are throwne away. End faire enough.

LX. *To William Lord Mounteagle*

Loe, what my countrey should have done (have rais'd
    An obeliske, or columne to thy name,
Or, if shee would but modestly have prais'd
    Thy fact, in brasse or marble writ the same)
I, that am glad of thy great chance, here doo!   5
    And proud, my worke shall out-last common deeds,
Durst thinke it great, and worthy wonder too,
    But thine, for which I doo't, so much exceeds!
My countries parents I have many knowne;
    But saver of my countrey thee alone.   10

LXII. *To Fine Lady Would-bee*

Fine MADAME WOULD-BEE, wherefore should you feare,
    That love to make so well, a child to beare?
The world reputes you barren: but I know
    Your 'pothecarie, and his drug sayes no.
Is it the paine affrights? that's soone forgot.   5
    Or your complexions losse? you have a pot,
That can restore that. Will it hurt your feature?
    To make amends, yo'are thought a wholesome creature.
What should the cause be? Oh, you live at court:
    And there's both losse of time, and losse of sport   10
In a great belly. Write, then on thy wombe,
    Of the not borne, yet buried, here's the tombe.

LX. To William Lord Mounteagle. Having exposed the Gunpowder Plot of 1605 to blow up the Houses of Parliament, William Parker, Lord Mounteagle (1575–1622), was rewarded with a pension.

LXXV. *On Lippe, the Teacher*

I cannot thinke there's that antipathy
   'Twixt *puritanes*, and *players*, as some cry;
Though LIPPE, at PAULS, ranne from his text away,
   T'inveigh 'gainst playes: what did he then but play?

LXXVI. *On Lucy Countesse of Bedford*

This morning, timely rapt with holy fire,
   I thought to forme unto my zealous *Muse*,
What kinde of creature I could most desire,
   To honor, serve, and love; as *Poets* use.
I meant to make her faire, and free, and wise,   5
   Of greatest bloud, and yet more good then great;
I meant the day-starre should not brighter rise,
   Nor lend like influence from his lucent seat.
I meant shee should be curteous, facile, sweet,
   Hating that solemne vice of greatnesse, pride;   10
I meant each softest vertue, there should meet,
   Fit in that softer bosome to reside.
Onely a learned, and a manly soule
   I purpos'd her; that should, with even powers,
The rock, the spindle, and the sheeres controule   15
   Of destinie, and spin her owne free houres.
Such when I meant to faine, and wish'd to see,
   My *Muse* bad, *Bedford* write, and that was shee.

LXXXIV. *To Lucy Countesse of Bedford*

MADAME, I told you late how I repented,
   I ask'd a lord a buck, and he denyed me;

LXXVI. *On Lucy Countesse of Bedford*. Lucy Harrington (1581–1627) was a bluestocking and great patroness of poets who helped and inspired Jonson, Donne, and Drayton. She took part in several court masques.

And, ere I could aske you, I was prevented:
   For your most noble offer had supply'd me.
Straight went I home; and there most like a *Poet*,   5
   I fancied to my selfe, what wine, what wit
I would have spent: how every *Muse* should know it,
   And PHŒBUS-selfe should be at eating it.
O *Madame*, if your grant did thus transferre mee,
   Make it your gift. See whither that will beare mee.   10

LXXXVIII. *On English Mounsieur*

Would you beleeve, when you this MOUNSIEUR see,
   That his whole body should speake *french*, not he?
That so much skarfe of *France*, and hat, and fether,
   And shooe, and tye, and garter should come hether,
And land on one, whose face durst never bee   5
   Toward the sea, farther then halfe-way tree?
That he, untravell'd, should be *french* so much,
   As *french*-men in his companie, should seeme *dutch*?
Or had his father, when he did him get,
   The *french* disease, with which he labours yet?   10
Or hung some MOUNSIEURS picture on the wall,
   By which his damme conceiv'd him, clothes and all?
Or is it some *french* statue? No: 'T doth move,
   And stoupe, and cringe. O then, it needs must prove
The new *french*-taylors motion, monthly made,   15
   Daily to turne in PAULS, and helpe the trade.

LXXXIX. *To Edward Allen*

If *Rome* so great, and in her wisest age,
   Fear'd not to boast the glories of her stage,

LXXXIX. *To Edward Allen*. Allen (1566–1626), famous tragedian of the Admiral's Men, was rival to Burbage in Shakespeare's company. He possibly played Jeronimo in Kyd's *Spanish Tragedy*, a play which Philip Henslowe had hired Jonson to augment.

    As skilfull ROSCIUS, and grave ÆSOPE, men,
        Yet crown'd with honors, as with riches, then;
    Who had no lesse a trumpet of their name,   5
        Then CICERO, whose every breath was fame:
    How can so great example dye in mee,
        That, ALLEN, I should pause to publish thee?
    Who both their graces in thy selfe hast more
        Out-stript, then they did all that went before: 10
    And present worth in all dost so contract,
        As others speake, but onely thou dost act.
    Weare this renowne. 'Tis just, that who did give
        So many *Poets* life, by one should live.

XCII. *The new Crie*

Ere cherries ripe, and straw-berries be gone,
    Unto the cryes of *London* Ile adde one;
Ripe statesmen, ripe: They grow in every street.
    At sixe and twentie, ripe. You shall 'hem meet,
And have 'hem yeeld no favour, but of state.   5
    Ripe are their ruffes, their cuffes, their beards, their gate,
And grave as ripe, like mellow as their faces.
    They know the states of *Christendome*, not the places:
Yet have they seene the maps, and bought 'hem too,
    And understand 'hem, as most chapmen doe.   10
The councels, projects, practises they know,
    And what each prince doth for intelligence owe,
And unto whom: They are the almanacks
    For twelve yeeres yet to come, what each state lacks.
They carry in their pockets TACITUS,   15
    And the GAZETTI, or GALLO-BELGICUS:
And talke reserv'd, lock'd up, and full of feare,
    Nay, aske you, how the day goes, in your eare.
Keepe a *starre*-chamber sentence close, twelve dayes:

    XCII. *The new Crie.* 16 *Gallo-Belgicus*: refers to a register of news first published in Cologne. The date of the English translation is 1614.

  And whisper what a Proclamation sayes.   *20*
They meet in sixes, and at every mart,
  Are sure to con' the catalogue by hart;
Or, every day, some one at RIMEE'S looks,
  Or BILS, and there he buyes the names of books.
They all get *Porta*, for the sundrie wayes   *25*
  To write in cypher, and the severall keyes,
To ope' the character. They'have found the sleight
  With juyce of limons, onions, pisse, to write.
To breake up seales, and close 'hem. And they know,
  If the *States* make peace, how it will goe   *30*
With *England*. All forbidden bookes they get.
  And of the poulder-plot, they will talke yet.
At naming the *French* King, their heads they shake,
  And at the *Pope*, and *Spaine* slight faces make.
Or 'gainst the Bishops, for the Brethren, raile,   *35*
  Much like those Brethren; thinking to prevaile
With ignorance on us, as they have done
  On them: And therefore doe not onely shunne
Others more modest, but contemne us too,
  That know not so much state, wrong, as they doo.   *40*

XCIV. *To Lucy, Countesse of Bedford, with M^r. Donnes Satyres*

LUCY, you brightnesse of our spheare, who are
  Life of the *Muses* day, their morning-starre!
If workes (not th'authors) their owne grace should looke,
  Whose poemes would not wish to be your booke?

23-24 *Rimee's ... Or Bils*: James Rime (or Rymer) and John Bill were London printers and booksellers.
25 Giovanni Baptista della Porta was the authority on secret codes and cyphers.
32 The reference to the Gunpowder Plot dates the poem after 1605.
XCIV. To Lucy ... with Mr. Donnes Satyres. Cf. Epigrammes LXXVI and XXIII.

> But these, desir'd by you, the makers ends 5
>   Crowne with their owne. Rare poemes aske rare friends.
> Yet, *Satyres*, since the most of mankind bee
>   Their un-avoided subject, fewest see:
> For none ere tooke that pleasure in sinnes sense,
>   But, when they heard it tax'd, tooke more offence. 10
> They, then, that living where the matter is bred,
>   Dare for these poemes, yet, both aske, and read,
> And like them too; must needfully, though few,
>   Be of the best: and 'mongst those, best are you.
> LUCY, you brightnesse of our spheare, who are 15
>   The *Muses* evening, as their morning-starre.

XCVI. *To John Donne*

> Who shall doubt, DONNE, where I a *Poet* bee,
>   When I dare send my *Epigrammes* to thee?
> That so alone canst judge, so'alone dost make:
>   And, in thy censures, evenly, dost take
> As free simplicitie, to dis-avow, 5
>   As thou hast best authoritie, t'allow.
> Reade all I send: and, if I find but one
>   Mark'd by thy hand, and with the better stone,
> My title's seal'd. Those that for claps doe write,
>   Let pui'nees, porters, players praise delight, 10
> And, till they burst, their backs, like asses load:
>   A man should seeke great glorie, and not broad.

CI. *Inviting a friend to supper*

> To night, grave sir, both my poore house, and I
>   Doe equally desire your companie:

XCVI. To John Donne. Cf. XCIV.
1 *where*: whether.
8 *the better stone*: In ancient Rome the better (white) stone marked the happy day.
10 *pui'nees*: puisnes, or juniors.

Not that we thinke us worthy such a ghest,
  But that your worth will dignifie our feast,
With those that come; whose grace may make that seeme
  Something, which, else, could hope for no esteeme.
It is the faire acceptance, Sir, creates
  The entertaynment perfect: not the cates.
Yet shall you have, to rectifie your palate,
  An olive, capers, or some better sallade
Ushring the mutton; with a short-leg'd hen,
  If we can get her, full of egs, and then,
Limons, and wine for sauce: to these, a coney
  Is not to be despair'd of, for our money;
And, though fowle, now, be scarce, yet there are clarkes,
  The skie not falling, thinke we may have larkes.
Ile tell you of more, and lye, so you will come:
  Of partrich, pheasant, wood-cock, of which some
May yet be there; and godwit, if we can:
  Knat, raile, and ruffe too. How so ere, my man
Shall reade a piece of VIRGIL, TACITUS,
  LIVIE, or of some better booke to us,
Of which wee'll speake our minds, amidst our meate;
  And Ile professe no verses to repeate:
To this, if ought appeare, which I know not of,
  That will the pastrie, not my paper, show of.
Digestive cheese, and fruit there sure will bee;
  But that, which most doth take my *Muse*, and mee,
Is a pure cup of rich *Canary*-wine,
  Which is the *Mermaids*, now, but shall be mine:
Of which had HORACE, or ANACREON tasted,
  Their lives, as doe their lines, till now had lasted.
Tabacco, Nectar, or the *Thespian* spring,
  Are all but LUTHERS beere, to this I sing.
Of this we will sup free, but moderately,
  And we will have no *Pooly'*, or *Parrot* by;

CI. Inviting a friend to supper. 20 *Knat* [knot], *raile, and ruffe*: these wading birds were considered great delicacies for the table.

34 *Luthers beere*: Sack was considered superior to German beer.

36 Robert Pooly (or Poley), government informer, was present at Marlowe's death, which took place in an inn-yard fracas after supper on 30 May, 1593. The unidentified Parrot was very likely also an agent.

    Nor shall our cups make any guiltie men:
      But, at our parting, we will be, as when
    We innocently met. No simple word,
      That shall be utter'd at our mirthfull boord,   40
    Shall make us sad next morning: or affright
      The libertie, that wee'll enjoy to night.

CV. *To Mary Lady Wroth*

MADAME, had all antiquitie beene lost,
  All historie seal'd up, and fables crost;
That we had left us, nor by time, nor place,
  Least mention of a *Nymph*, a *Muse*, a *Grace*,
But even their names were to be made a-new,   5
  Who could not but create them all, from you?
He, that but saw you weare the wheaten hat,
  Would call you more then CERES, if not that:
And, drest in shepheards tyre, who would not say:
  You were the bright OENONE, FLORA, or *May*?   10
If dancing, all would cry th'*Idalian* Queene,
  Were leading forth the *Graces* on the greene:
And, armed to the chase, so bare her bow
  DIANA'alone, so hit, and hunted so.
There's none so dull, that for your stile would aske,   15
  That saw you put on PALLAS plumed caske:
Or, keeping your due state, that would not cry,
  There JUNO sate, and yet no Peacock by.
So are you *Natures Index*, and restore,
  I'your selfe, all treasure lost of th'age before.   20

CV. To Mary Lady Wroth. Jonson dedicated *The Alchemist* to her as "the Lady most deserving her name and blood." Daughter of Sir Robert Sidney, she married Sir Robert Wroth (1576-1614) in 1604. An epistle (No. III of *The Forrest*) is addressed to Sir Robert.

CVII. *To Captayne Hungry*

Doe what you come for, Captayne, with your newes;
    That's, sit, and eate: doe not my eares abuse.
I oft looke on false coyne, to know't from true:
    Not that I love it, more, then I will you.
Tell the grosse *Dutch* those grosser tales of yours,   *5*
    How great you were with their two Emperours;
And yet are with their Princes: Fill them full
    Of your *Moravian* horse, *Venetian* bull.
Tell them, what parts yo'have tane, whence run away,
    What States yo'have gull'd, and which yet keepes yo'in pay.   *10*
Give them your services, and embassies
    In *Ireland, Holland, Sweden,* pompous lies,
In *Hungary,* and *Poland, Turkie* too;
    What at *Ligorne, Rome, Florence* you did doe:
And, in some yeere, all these together heap'd,   *15*
    For which there must more sea, and land be leap'd,
If but to be beleev'd you have the hap,
    Then can a flea at twise skip i'the Map.
Give your yong States-men, (that first make you drunke,
    And then lye with you, closer, then a punque,   *20*
For newes) your *Ville-royes,* and *Silleries,*
    Janin's, your *Nuncio's,* and your *Tuilleries,*
Your *Arch-Dukes* Agents, and your *Beringhams,*
    That are your wordes of credit. Keepe your Names
Of *Hannow, Shieter-huissen, Popenheim,*   *25*
    Hans-spiegle, Rotteinberg, and *Boutersheim,*
For your next meale: this you are sure of. Why
    Will you part with them, here, unthriftely?
Nay, now you puffe, tuske, and draw up your chin,
    Twirle the poore chaine you run a feasting in.   *30*
Come, be not angrie, you are HUNGRY; eate;
    Doe what you come for, Captayne, There's your meate.

CVII. *To Captayne Hungry.* 21–22 *Ville-royes*...*Silleries*...*Janin's*: the Seigneur de Villeroy, the Marquis de Sillery, and Pierre Jeannin were government officials and statesmen under Henry IV of France.

CVIII. *To true Souldiers*

Strength of my Countrey, whilst I bring to view
    Such as are misse-call'd Captaynes, and wrong you;
And your high names: I doe desire, that thence
    Be nor put on you, nor you take offence.
I sweare by your true friend, my *Muse*, I love   5
    Your great profession; which I once, did prove:
And did not shame it with my actions, then,
    No more, then I dare now doe, with my pen.
He that not trusts me, having vow'd thus much,
    But's angry for the Captayne, still: is such.   10

CXII. *To a weake Gamster in Poetry*

With thy small stocke, why art thou ventring still,
    At this so subtile sport: and play'st so ill?
Think'st thou it is meere fortune, that can win?
    Or thy ranke setting? that thou dar'st put in
Thy all, at all: and what so ere I doe,   5
    Art still at that, and think'st to blow me'up too?
I cannot for the stage a *Drama* lay,
    Tragick, or *Comick*; but thou writ'st the play.
I leave thee there, and giving way, entend
    An *Epick* poeme; thou hast the same end.   10
I modestly quit that, and thinke to write,
    Next morne, an *Ode*: Thou mak'st a song ere night.
I passe to *Elegies*; Thou meet'st me there:
    To *Satyres*; and thou dost pursue me. Where,
Where shall I scape thee? in an *Epigramme*?   15
    O, (thou cry'st out) that is thy proper game.

  CVIII. To true Souldiers. This epigram was "only once spoken upon the stage," according to the Apologetical Dialogue to *Poetaster*, published in 1601.
  CXII. To a weake Gamster in Poetry. This epigram contains several references to technical terms in the card game primero, including the following: *setting* (l. 4), *blow me 'up* (l. 6), *plucke* (l. 18), *save thy rest* (l. 21), and *make thee prime* (l. 22).

Troth, if it be, I pitty thy ill lucke;
   That both for wit, and sense, so oft dost plucke,
And never art encounter'd, I confesse:
   Nor scarce dost colour for it, which is lesse.   20
Pr'y thee, yet save thy rest; give ore in time:
   There's no vexation, that can make thee prime.

CXIX. *To Sir Raph Shelton*

Not he that flies the court for want of clothes,
   At hunting railes, having no guift in othes,
Cryes out 'gainst cocking, since he cannot bet,
   Shuns prease, for two maine causes, poxe, and debt,
With me can merit more, then that good man,   5
   Whose dice not doing well, to'a pulpit ran.
No, SHELTON, give me thee, canst want all these,
   But dost it out of judgement, not disease;
Dar'st breath in any ayre; and with safe skill,
   Till thou canst finde the best, choose the least ill.   10
That to the vulgar canst thy selfe apply,
   Treading a better path, not contrary;
And, in their errors maze, thine owne way know:
   Which is to live to conscience, not to show.
He, that, but living halfe his age, dyes such;   15
   Makes, the whole longer, then 'twas given him, much.

CXX. *Epitaph on S. P. a child of Q. El. Chappel*

Weepe with me all you that read
   This little storie:

CXIX. *To Sir Raph Shelton.* Knighted in 1607, Shelton was a wag among courtiers in the early part of the century. John Harington, in *Apology for Ajax* (1596), pictured him impaneled on a mock jury, and John Chamberlain characterized him as a buffoon. Jonson accepts this view of him by making him one of the heroes of the mock-heroic epigram CXXXIII "On the famous Voyage."

CXX. *Epitaph on S. P*....Salomon Pavy acted in Jonson's *Cynthias Revells* (1600) and also in *Poetaster* (1601).

And know, for whom a teare you shed,
   Death's selfe is sorry.
'Twas a child, that so did thrive
   In grace, and feature,
As *Heaven* and *Nature* seem'd to strive
   Which own'd the creature.
Yeeres he numbred scarse thirteene
   When *Fates* turn'd cruell,
Yet three fill'd *Zodiackes* had he beene
   The stages jewell;
And did act (what now we mone)
   Old men so duely,
As, sooth, the *Parcæ* thought him one,
   He plai'd so truely.
So, by error, to his fate
   They all consented;
But viewing him since (alas, too late)
   They have repented.
And have sought (to give new birth)
   In bathes to steepe him;
But, being so much too good for earth,
   Heaven vowes to keepe him.

CXXIV. *Epitaph on Elizabeth, L. H.*

Would'st thou heare, what man can say
   In a little? Reader, stay.
Under-neath this stone doth lye
   As much beautie, as could dye:
Which in life did harbour give
   To more vertue, then doth live.

CXXIV. *Epitaph on Elizabeth, L. H.* Elizabeth, Lady Hatton, has been suggested as the subject of this epitaph (H. & S.). Intentional obscurity makes identification virtually impossible.

>   If, at all, shee had a fault,
>   Leave it buryed in this vault.
>   One name was ELIZABETH,
>   Th'other let it sleepe with death: 10
>   Fitter, where it dyed, to tell,
>   Then that it liv'd at all. Farewell.

CXXX. *To Alphonso Ferrabosco, on his Booke*

> To urge, my lov'd ALPHONSO, that bold fame,
>   Of building townes, and making wilde beasts tame,
> Which *Musick* had; or speake her knowne effects,
>   That shee removeth cares, sadnesse ejects,
> Declineth anger, perswades clemencie, 5
>   Doth sweeten mirth, and heighten pietie,
> And is t'a body, often, ill inclin'd,
>   No lesse a sov'raigne cure, then to the mind;
> T'alledge, that greatest men were not asham'd,
>   Of old, even by her practise to be fam'd; 10
> To say, indeed, shee were the soule of heaven,
>   That the eight spheare, no lesse, then planets seaven,
> Mov'd by her order, and the ninth more high,
>   Including all, were thence call'd harmonie:
> I, yet, had utter'd nothing on thy part, 15
>   When these were but the praises of the Art.
> But when I have said, the proofes of all these bee
>   Shed in thy Songs; tis true: but short of thee.

CXXX. *To Alphonso Ferrabosco*.... Ferrabosco (1575–1628), who ranks in eminence as a composer with Byrd, wrote the vocal and instrumental music to several masques of Jonson. His *Ayres*, to which this epigram was prefixed, was published in 1609.

CXXXII. *To M^r. Josuah Sylvester*

If to admire were to commend, my praise
   Might then both thee, thy worke and merit raise:
But, as it is (the Child of Ignorance,
   And utter stranger to all ayre of *France*)
How can I speake of thy great paines, but erre?   5
   Since they can only judge, that can conferre.
Behold! the reverend shade of BARTAS stands
   Before my thought, and (in thy right) commands
That to the world I publish, for him, this;
   BARTAS *doth wish thy* English *now were his.*   10
So well in that are his inventions wrought,
   As his will now be the translation thought,
Thine the *originall*; and *France* shall boast,
   No more, those mayden glories shee hath lost.

CXXXIII. *On the famous Voyage*

No more let *Greece* her bolder fables tell
   Of HERCULES, or THESEUS going to *hell*,
ORPHEUS, ULYSSES: or the *Latine Muse*,
   With tales of *Troyes* just knight, our faiths abuse:
We have a SHELTON, and a HEYDEN got,   5
   Had power to act, what they to faine had not.
All, that they boast of STYX, of ACHERON,
   COCYTUS, PHLEGETON, our have prov'd in one;
The filth, stench, noyse: save only what was there
   Subtly distinguish'd, was confused here.   10
Their wherry had no saile, too; ours had none:
   And in it, two more horride knaves, then CHARON.

CXXXII. *To M^r. Josuah Sylvester.* Sylvester (1563–1618), at one time in the service of Prince Henry (d. 1612), translated Du Bartas' *Divine Weeks*. This epigram appeared in the first edition of the translation in 1605. The influence of this French Huguenot in the early seventeenth century was vast.
CXXXIII. *On the famous Voyage.* 5 *Shelton*: cf. Epigram CXIX. Heyden has not been identified (H. & S.).
8 *in one*: the reference is to Fleet Ditch (H. & S.).

Arses were heard to croake, in stead of frogs;
   And for one CERBERUS, the whole coast was dogs.
Furies there wanted not: each scold was ten.   *15*
   And, for the cryes of *Ghosts*, women, and men,
Laden with plague-sores, and their sinnes, were neard,
   Lash'd by their consciences, to die, affeard.
Then let the former age, with this content her,
   Shee brought the *Poets* forth, but ours th'adventer.   *20*

THE VOYAGE IT SELFE

I sing the brave adventure of two wights,
And pitty 'tis, I cannot call 'hem knights:
One was; and he, for brawne, and braine, right able
To have beene stiled of King ARTHURS table.
The other was a squire, of faire degree;   *25*
But, in the action, greater man then hee:
Who gave, to take at his returne from *Hell*,
His three for one. Now, lordings, listen well.
   It was the day, what time the powerfull *Moone*
Makes the poore *Banck-side* creature wet it' shoone,   *30*
In it' owne hall; when these (in worthy scorne
Of those that put out moneyes, on returne
From *Venice, Paris*, or some in-land passage
Of sixe times to, and fro, without embassage,
Or him that backward went to *Berwicke*, or which   *35*
Did dance the famous Morrisse, unto *Norwich*)
At *Bread-streets* Mermaid, having din'd, and merry,
Propos'd to goe to *Hol'borne* in a wherry:
A harder tasque, then either his to *Bristo'*,
Or his to *Antwerpe*. Therefore, once more, list ho'.   *40*
   A *Docke* there is, that called is AVERNUS,
Of some *Bride-well*, and may, in time, concerne us
All, that are readers: but, me thinkes 'tis od,
That all this while I have forgot some *god*,
Or *goddesse* to invoke, to stuffe my verse;   *45*

35-36 *which/Did dance*: in 1599 William Kempe, comedian in Shakespeare's troupe, danced from London to Norwich in nine days.

And with both bombard-stile, and phrase, rehearse
The many perills of this *Port*, and how
Sans helpe of SYBIL, or a golden bough,
Or magick sacrifice, they past along!
ALCIDES, be thou succouring to my song.   50
Thou hast seene *hell* (some say) and know'st all nookes there,
Canst tell me best, how every *Furie* lookes there,
And art a *god*, if *Fame* thee not abuses,
Alwayes at hand, to aide the merry *Muses*.
Great *Club-fist*, though they backe, and bones be sore,   55
Still, with thy former labours; yet, once more,
Act a brave worke, call it thy last adventry:
But hold my torch, while I describe the entry
To this dire passage. Say, thou stop thy nose:
'Tis but light paines: Indeede this *Dock's* no rose.   60
   In the first jawes appear'd that ugly monster,
Ycleped *Mud*, which, when their oares did once stirre,
Belch'd forth an ayre, as hot, as at the muster
Of all your night-tubs, when the carts doe cluster,
Who shall discharge first his merd-urinous load;   65
Thorough her wombe they make their famous road,
Betweene two walls; where, on one side to scar men,
Were seene your ugly *Centaures*, yee call Car-men,
Gorgonian scolds, and *Harpyes*: on the other
Hung stench, diseases, and old filth, their mother,   70
With famine, wants, and sorrowes many a dosen,
The least of which was to the plague a cosen.
But they unfrighted passe, though many a privie
Spake to'hem louder, then the oxe in LIVIE;
And many a sinke pour'd out her rage anenst'hem;   75
But still their valour, and their vertue fenc't'hem,
And, on they went, like CASTOR brave, and POLLUX:
Ploughing the mayne. When, see (the worst of all lucks)
They met the second Prodigie, would feare a
Man, that had never heard of a *Chimæra*.   80
One said, it was bold BRIAREUS, or the beadle,
(Who hath the hundred hands when he doth meddle)
The other thought it HYDRA, or the rock
Made of the trull, that cut her fathers lock:
But, comming neere, they found it but a liter,   85

So huge, it seem'd, they could by no meanes quite her.
Backe, cry'd their brace of CHARONS: they cry'd, no,
No going backe; on still you rogues, and row.
How hight the place? a voyce was heard, COCYTUS.
Row close then slaves. Alas, they will beshite us. 90
No matter, stinkards, row. What croaking sound
Is this we heare? of frogs? No, guts wind-bound,
Over your heads: Well, row. At this a loud
Crack did report it selfe, as if a cloud
Had burst with storme, and downe fell *ab excelsis*, 95
Poore MERCURY, crying out on PARACELSUS,
And all his followers, that had so abus'd him:
And, in so shitten sort, so long had us'd him:
For (where he was the god of eloquence,
And subtiltie of mettalls) they dispense 100
His spirits, now, in pills, and eeke in potions,
Suppositories, cataplasmes, and lotions.
But many Moones there shall not wane (quoth hee)
(In the meane time, let 'hem imprison mee)
But I will speake (and know I shall be heard) 105
Touching this cause, where they will be affeard
To answere me. And sure, it was th'intent
Of the grave fart, late let in parliament,
Had it beene seconded, and not in fume
Vanish'd away: as you must all presume 110
Their MERCURY did now. By this, the stemme
Of the hulke touch'd, and, as by POLYPHEME
The slie ULYSSES stole in a sheepes-skin,
The well-greas'd wherry now had got betweene,
And bad her *fare-well sough*, unto the lurden: 115
Never did bottome more betray her burden;
The meate-boate of Beares colledge, *Paris-garden*,
Stunke not so ill; nor, when shee kist, KATE ARDEN.
Yet, one day in the yeere, for sweet 'tis voyc't,
And that is when it is the Lord *Maiors* foist. 120
    By this time had they reach'd the *Stygian* poole,
By which the *Masters* sweare, when, on the stoole
Of worship, they their nodding chinnes doe hit

117 *Paris-garden*: adjacent to the Globe Theater; the place for bearbaiting.
120 *foist*: state barge.

Against their breasts. Here, sev'rall ghosts did flit
About the shore, of farts, but late departed,   125
White, black, blew, greene, and in more formes out-started,
Then all those *Atomi* ridiculous,
Whereof old DEMOCRITE, and HILL NICHOLAS,
One said, the other swore, the world consists.
These be the cause of those thicke frequent mists   130
Arising in that place, through which, who goes,
Must trie the un-used valour of a nose:
And that ours did. For, yet, no nare was tainted,
Nor thumbe, nor finger to the stop acquainted,
But open, and un-arm'd encounter'd all: 135
Whether it languishing stucke upon the wall,
Or were precipitated downe the jakes,
And, after, swom abroad in ample flakes,
Or, that it lay, heap'd like an usurers masse,
All was to them the same, they were to passe,   140
And so they did, from STIX, to ACHERON:
The ever-boyling floud. Whose bankes upon
Your *Fleet*-lane *Furies*; and hot cookes doe dwell,
That, with still-scalding steemes, make the place *hell*.
The sinkes ran grease, and haire of meazled hogs,   145
The heads, houghs, entrailes, and the hides of dogs:
For, to say truth, what scullion is so nastie,
To put the skins, and offall in a pastie?
Cats there lay divers had beene flead, and rosted,
And, after mouldie growne, againe were tosted,   150
Then, selling not, a dish was tane to mince'hem,
But still, it seem'd, the ranknesse did convince'hem.
For, here they were throwne in with'the melted pewter,
Yet drown'd they not. They had five lives in future.
But 'mong'st these *Tiberts*, who do'you thinke there was?   155
Old BANKES the juggler, our PYTHAGORAS,
Grave tutor to the learned horse. Both which,
Being, beyond sea, burned for one witch:

---

128 *Hill Nicholas*: Nicholas Hill (d. 1610) was the disciple of Democritus in promulgating an atomic theory.
 155 *Tiberts*: cats; cf. Mercutio's epithet for Tybalt as "Prince of cats."
 156 *Bankes the juggler*: his "mathematical" horse, well known in the 1590's, could beat out with his hoof any number suggested by his master.

Their spirits transmigrated to a cat:
And, now, above the poole, a face right fat   160
With great gray eyes, are lifted up, and mew'd;
Thrise did it spit: thrise div'd. At last, it view'd
Our brave *Heroes* with a milder glare,
And, in a pittious tune, began. How dare
Your daintie nostrills (in so hot a season,   165
When every clerke eates artichokes, and peason,
Laxative lettuce, and such windie meate)
Tempt such a passage? when each privies seate
Is fill'd with buttock? And the walls doe sweate
Urine, and plaisters? when the noise doth beate   170
Upon your eares, of discords so un-sweet?
And out-cryes of the damned in the *Fleet?*
Cannot the *Plague* bill keepe you backe? nor bells
Of loud SEPULCHRES with their hourely knells,
But you will visit grisly PLUTO'S hall?   175
Behold where CERBERUS, rear'd on the wall
Of *Hol'borne* (three sergeants heads) lookes ore,
And stayes but till you come unto the dore!
Tempt not his furie, PLUTO is away:
And MADAME CAESAR, great PROSERPINA,   180
Is now from home. You lose your labours quite,
Were you JOVE'S sonnes, or had ALCIDES might.
They cry'd out PUSSE. He told them he was BANKES,
That had, so often, shew'd'hem merry prankes.
They laugh't, at his laugh-worthy fate. And past   185
The tripple head without a sop. At last,
Calling for RADAMANTHUS, that dwelt by,
A sope-boyler; and ÆACUS him nigh,
Who kept an ale-house; with my little MINOS,
An ancient pur-blinde fletcher, with a high nose;   190
They tooke'hem all to witnesse of their action:
And so went bravely backe, without protraction.
   In memorie of which most liquid deed,
The citie since hath rais'd a Pyramide.
And I could wish for their eterniz'd sakes,   195
My *Muse* had plough'd with his, that sung A-JAX.

173 *Plague bill*: list of dead periodically issued by every parish in plague time.

THE FORREST

I. *Why I write not of Love*

    Some act of *Love's* bound to reherse,
    I thought to binde him, in my verse:
    Which when he felt, Away (quoth hee)
    Can Poets hope to fetter mee?
    It is enough, they once did get   5
    MARS, and my *Mother*, in their net:
    I weare not these my wings in vaine.
    With which he fled me: and againe,
    Into my ri'mes could ne're be got
    By any arte. Then wonder not,   10
    That since, my numbers are so cold,
    When *Love* is fled, and I grow old.

II. *To Penshurst*

Thou art not, PENSHURST, built to envious show,
    Of touch, or marble; nor canst boast a row
Of polish'd pillars, or a roofe of gold:
    Thou hast no lantherne, whereof tales are told;

    The Forrest. This collection was first printed in the 1616 folio. As in *Under-Wood* and *Timber* (cf. their prefatory notes), Jonson follows the ancients in such a title as *Silvae*.
    II. To Penshurst. Penshurst was the seat of the Sidney family.
    2 *touch*: short for touchstone, often applied to black marble.
    4 *lantherne*: an erection with windowed or glazed apertures set upon a dome or a building to admit light and air.

Or stayre, or courts; but stand'st an ancient pile,   *5*
   And these grudg'd at, art reverenc'd the while.
Thou joy'st in better markes, of soyle, of ayre,
   Of wood, of water: therein thou art faire.
Thou hast thy walkes for health, as well as sport:
   Thy *Mount*, to which the *Dryads* doe resort,   *10*
Where PAN, and BACCHUS their high feasts have made,
   Beneath the broad beech, and the chest-nut shade;
That taller tree, which of a nut was set,
   At his great birth, where all the *Muses* met.
There, in the writhed barke, are cut the names   *15*
   Of many a SYLVANE, taken with his flames.
And thence, the ruddy *Satyres* oft provoke
   The lighter *Faunes*, to reach thy *Ladies oke*.
Thy copp's, too, nam'd of GAMAGE, thou hast there,
   That never failes to serve thee season'd deere,   *20*
When thou would'st feast, or exercise thy friends.
   The lower land, that to the river bends,
Thy sheepe, thy bullocks, kine, and calves doe feed:
   The middle grounds thy mares, and horses breed.
Each banke doth yeeld thee coneyes; and the topps   *25*
   Fertile of wood, ASHORE, and SYDNEY'S copp's,
To crowne thy open table, doth provide
   The purpled pheasant, with the speckled side:
The painted partrich lyes in every field,
   And, for thy messe, is willing to be kill'd.   *30*
And if the high swolne *Medway* faile thy dish,
   Thou hast thy ponds, that pay thee tribute fish,
Fat, aged carps, that runne into thy net.
   And pikes, now weary their owne kinde to eat,
As loth, the second draught, or cast to stay,   *35*
   Officiously, at first, themselves betray.
Bright eeles, that emulate them, and leape on land,
   Before the fisher, or into his hand.
Then hath thy orchard fruit, thy garden flowers,

---

14 *his*: refers to the birth of Sir Philip Sidney in 1554.
19 Barbara Gamage married Sir Robert Sidney in 1584.
26 *Ashore*: Ashour wood still exists today (H. & S.).

  Fresh as the ayre, and new as are the houres.   *40*
The earely cherry, with the later plum,
 Fig, grape, and quince, each in his time doth come:
The blushing apricot, and woolly peach
 Hang on thy walls, that every child may reach.
And though thy walls be of the countrey stone,   *45*
 They'are rear'd with no mans ruine, no mans grone,
There's none, that dwell about them, wish them downe;
 But all come in, the farmer, and the clowne:
And no one empty-handed, to salute
 Thy lord, and lady, though they have no sute.   *50*
Some bring a capon, some a rurall cake,
 Some nuts, some apples; some that thinke they make
The better cheeses, bring 'hem; or else send
 By their ripe daughters, whom they would commend
This way to husbands; and whose baskets beare   *55*
 An embleme of themselves, in plum, or peare.
But what can this (more then expresse their love)
 Adde to thy free provisions, farre above
The neede of such? whose liberall boord doth flow,
 With all, that hospitalitie doth know!   *60*
Where comes no guest, but is allow'd to eate,
 Without his feare, and of thy lords owne meate:
Where the same beere, and bread, and selfe-same wine,
 That is his Lordships, shall be also mine.
And I not faine to sit (as some, this day,   *65*
 At great mens tables) and yet dine away.
Here no man tells my cups; nor, standing by,
 A waiter, doth my gluttony envy:
But gives me what I call, and lets me eate,
 He knowes, below, he shall finde plentie of meate,   *70*
Thy tables hoord not up for the next day,
 Nor, when I take my lodging, need I pray
For fire, or lights, or livorie: all is there;
 As if thou, then, wert mine, or I raign'd here:
There's nothing I can wish, for which I stay.   *75*
  That found King JAMES, when hunting late, this way,
With his brave sonne, the Prince, they saw thy fires
 Shine bright on every harth as the desires

Of thy *Penates* had beene set on flame,
    To entertayne them; or the countrey came,   *80*
With all their zeale, to warme their welcome here.
    What (great, I will not say, but) sodayne cheare
Did'st thou, then, make 'hem! and what praise was heap'd
    On thy good lady, then! who, therein, reap'd
The just reward of her high huswifery,   *85*
    To have her linnen, plate, and all things nigh,
When shee was farre: and not a roome, but drest,
    As if it had expected such a guest!
These, PENSHURST, are thy praise, and yet not all.
    Thy lady's noble, fruitfull, chaste withall.   *90*
His children thy great lord may call his owne:
    A fortune, in this age, but rarely knowne.
They are, and have beene taught religion: Thence
    Their gentler spirits have suck'd innocence.
Each morne, and even, they are taught to pray,   *95*
    With the whole houshold, and may, every day,
Reade, in their vertuous parents noble parts,
    The mysteries of manners, armes, and arts.
Now, PENSHURST, they that will proportion thee
    With other edifices, when they see   *100*
Those proud, ambitious heaps, and nothing else,
    May say, their lords have built, but thy lord dwells.

III. *To Sir Robert Wroth*

How blest art thou, canst love the countrey, WROTH,
    Whether by choice, or fate, or both;
And, though so neere the citie, and the court,
    Art tane with neithers vice, nor sport:
That at great times, art no ambitious guest   *5*
    Of Sheriffes dinner, or Maiors feast.

---

91 *thy great lord*: Sir Robert. His brother Sir Philip was killed at the battle of Zutphen in 1586.

III. To Sir Robert Wroth. Sir Robert Wroth (d. 1614), son-in-law of Sir Robert Sidney, married Lady Mary Sidney in 1604.

Nor com'st to view the better cloth of state;
  The richer hangings, or crowne-plate;
Nor throng'st (when masquing is) to have a sight
  Of the short braverie of the night;   10
To view the jewells, stuffes, the paines, the wit
  There wasted, some not paid for yet!
But canst, at home, in thy securer rest,
  Live, with un-bought provision blest;
Free from proud porches, or their guilded roofes,   15
  'Mongst loughing heards, and solide hoofes:
Along'st the curled woods, and painted meades,
  Through which a serpent river leades
To some coole, courteous shade, which he calls his,
  And makes sleepe softer then it is!   20
Or, if thou list the night in watch to breake,
  A-bed canst heare the loud stag speake,
In spring, oft roused for thy masters sport,
  Who, for it, makes thy house his court;
Or with thy friends, the heart of all the yeere,   25
  Divid'st, upon the lesser Deere;
In autumne, at the Partrich makes a flight,
  And giv'st thy gladder guests the sight;
And, in the winter, hunt'st the flying hare,
  More for thy exercise, then fare;   30
While all, that follow, their glad eares apply
  To the full greatnesse of the cry:
Or hauking at the river, or the bush,
  Or shooting at the greedie thrush,
Thou dost with some delight the day out-weare,   35
  Although the coldest of the yeere!
The whil'st the severall seasons thou hast seene
  Of flowrie fields, of cop'ces greene,
The mowed meddowes, with the fleeced sheepe,
  And feasts, that either shearers keepe;   40
The ripened eares, yet humble in their height,
  And furrowes laden with their weight;
The apple-harvest, that doth longer last;

21–24 Like his monarch, Sir Robert was a keen sportsman.

The hogs return'd home fat from mast;
The trees cut out in log; and those boughes made 45
   A fire now, that lent a shade!
Thus PAN, and SYLVANE, having had their rites,
   COMUS puts in, for new delights;
And fills thy open hall with mirth, and cheere,
   As if in SATURNES raigne it were; 50
APOLLO'S harpe, and HERMES lyre resound,
   Nor are the *Muses* strangers found:
The rout of rurall folke come thronging in,
   (Their rudenesse then is thought no sinne)
Thy noblest spouse affords them welcome grace; 55
   And the great *Heroes*, of her race,
Sit mixt with losse of state, or reverence.
   Freedome doth with degree dispense.
The jolly wassall walkes the often round,
   And in their cups, their cares are drown'd: 60
They thinke not, then, which side the cause shall leese,
   Nor how to get the lawyer fees.
Such, and no other was that age, of old,
   Which boasts t'have had the head of gold.
And such since thou canst make thine owne content, 65
   Strive, WROTH, to live long innocent.
Let others watch in guiltie armes, and stand
   The furie of a rash command,
Goe enter breaches, meet the cannons rage,
   That they may sleepe with scarres in age. 70
And shew their feathers shot, and cullors torne,
   And brag, that they were therefore borne.
Let this man sweat, and wrangle at the barre,
   For every price, in every jarre,
And change possessions, oftner with his breath, 75
   Then either money, warre, or death:
Let him, then hardest sires, more disinherit,
   And each where boast it as his merit,
To blow up orphanes, widdowes, and their states;

55–56 *Thy noblest spouse...her race*: refers to Lady Mary Wroth. Cf. Epigrams CIII and CV.

  And thinke his power doth equall *Fates*.   80
Let that goe heape a masse of wretched wealth,
  Purchas'd by rapine, worse then stealth,
And brooding o're it sit, with broadest eyes,
  Not doing good, scarce when he dyes.
Let thousands more goe flatter vice, and winne,   85
  By being organes to great sinne,
Get place, and honor, and be glad to keepe
  The secrets, that shall breake their sleepe:
And, so they ride in purple, eate in plate,
  Though poyson, thinke it a great fate.   90
But thou, my WROTH, if I can truth apply,
  Shalt neither that, nor this envy:
Thy peace is made; and, when man's state is well,
  'Tis better, if he there can dwell.
God wisheth, none should wracke on a strange shelfe: 95
  To him, man's dearer, then t'himselfe.
And, howsoever we may thinke things sweet,
  He alwayes gives what he knowes meet;
Which who can use is happy: Such be thou.
  Thy morning's, and thy evening's vow   100
Be thankes to him, and earnest prayer, to finde
  A body sound, with sounder minde;
To doe thy countrey service, thy selfe right;
  That neither want doe thee affright,
Nor death; but when thy latest sand is spent,   105
  Thou maist thinke life, a thing but lent.

IV. *To the World*

A farewell for a Gentle-woman, vertuous and noble

  False world, good-night: since thou hast brought
   That houre upon my morne of age,
  Hence-forth I quit thee from my thought,
   My part is ended on thy stage.

Doe not once hope, that thou canst tempt
    A spirit so resolv'd to tread
Upon thy throate, and live exempt
    From all the nets that thou canst spread.
I know thy formes are studyed arts,
    Thy subtle wayes, be narrow straits;
Thy curtesie but sodaine starts,
    And what thou call'st thy gifts are baits.
I know too, though thou strut, and paint,
    Yet art thou both shrunke up, and old,
That onely fooles make thee a saint,
    And all thy good is to be sold.
I know thou whole art but a shop
    Of toyes, and trifles, traps, and snares,
To take the weake, or make them stop:
    Yet art thou falser then thy wares.
And, knowing this, should I yet stay,
    Like such as blow away their lives,
And never will redeeme a day,
    Enamor'd of their golden gyves?
Or, having scap'd, shall I returne,
    And thrust my necke into the noose,
From whence, so lately, I did burne,
    With all my powers, my selfe to loose?
What bird, or beast, is knowne so dull,
    That fled his cage, or broke his chaine,
And tasting ayre, and freedome, wull
    Render his head in there againe?
If these, who have but sense, can shun
    The engines, that have them annoy'd;
Little, for me, had reason done,
    If I could not thy ginnes avoyd.
Yes, threaten, doe. Alas I feare
    As little, as I hope from thee:
I know thou canst nor shew, nor beare
    More hatred, then thou hast to mee.
My tender, first, and simple yeeres
    Thou did'st abuse, and then betray;
Since stird'st up jealousies and feares,

                When all the causes were away.
            Then, in a soile hast planted me,   45
                Where breathe the basest of thy fooles;
            Where envious arts professed be,
                And pride, and ignorance the schooles,
            Where nothing is examin'd, weigh'd,
                But, as 'tis rumor'd, so beleev'd: 50
            Where every freedome is betray'd,
                And every goodnesse tax'd, or griev'd.

            But, what we'are borne for, we must beare:
                Our fraile condition it is such,
            That, what to all may happen here,   55
                If't chance to me, I must not grutch.
            Else, I my state should much mistake,
                To harbour a divided thought
            From all my kinde: that, for my sake,
                There should a miracle be wrought.   60
            No, I doe know, that I was borne
                To age, misfortune, sicknesse, griefe:
            But I will beare these, with that scorne,
                As shall not need thy false reliefe.
            Nor for my peace will I goe farre,   65
                As wandrers doe, that still doe rome,
            But make my strengths, such as they are,
                Here in my bosome, and at home.

Song

V. *To Celia* [I]

            Come my CELIA, let us prove,
            While we may, the sports of love;
            Time will not be ours, for ever:
            He, at length, our good will sever.
            Spend not then his guifts in vaine.   5
            Sunnes, that set, may rise againe:

V. To Celia [I]. First published as a song in *Volpone* in 1607. A setting by Ferrabosco appears in his *Ayres* (1609).

But if once we loose this light,
'Tis, with us, perpetuall night.
Why should we deferre our joyes?
Fame, and rumor are but toyes.   10
Cannot we delude the eyes
Of a few poore houshold spyes?
Or his easier ears beguile,
So removed by our wile?
'Tis no sinne, loves fruit to steale,   15
But the sweet theft to reveale:
To be taken, to be seene,
These have crimes accounted beene.

VI. *To the same*

Kisse me, sweet: The warie lover
Can your favours keepe, and cover,
When the common courting jay
All your bounties will betray.
Kisse againe: no creature comes.   5
Kisse, and score up wealthy summes
On my lips, thus hardly sundred,
While you breath. First give a hundred,
Then a thousand, then another
Hundred, then unto the tother   10
Adde a thousand, and so more:
Till you equall with the store,
All the grasse that *Rumney* yeelds,
Or the sands in *Chelsey* fields,
Or the drops in silver *Thames*,   15
Or the starres, that guild his streames,
In the silent sommer-nights,
When youths ply their stolne delights.
That the curious may not know
How to tell 'hem, as they flow,

VI. To the same. 19–22 This concluding quatrain is appended to the song in *Volpone* beginning "Come my Celia..."; cf. V above. This song, like the preceding, is in part derived from Catullus' lyric V, beginning "Vivamus, mea Lesbia."

And the envious, when they find
What their number is, be pin'd.

Song

VII. *That Women are but Mens shaddowes*

Follow a shaddow, it still flies you;
   Seeme to flye it, it will pursue:
So court a mistris, shee denyes you;
   Let her alone, shee will court you.
Say, are not women truely, then,   5
   Stil'd but the shaddowes of us men?
At morne, and even, shades are longest;
   At noone, they are or short, or none:
So men at weakest, they are strongest,
   But grant us perfect, they're not knowne.   10
Say, are not women truely, then,
   Stil'd but the shaddowes of us men?

VIII. *To Sicknesse*

Why, *Disease*, dost thou molest
Ladies? and of them the best?
Doe not men, ynow of rites
To thy altars, by their nights
Spent in surfets: and their dayes,   5
And nights too, in worser wayes?
   Take heed, *Sicknesse*, what you doe,
   I shall feare, you'll surfet too.
Live not we, as, all thy stalls,

VII. That Women are but Mens shaddowes. Jonson's composition of this piece is recorded by Drummond in his *Conversations*: "Pembrok and his Lady discoursing the Earl said the Woemen were mens shadowes, and she maintained y^m, both appealing to Johnson, he affirmed it true, for which my Lady gave a pennance to prove it in Verse, hence his Epigrame." Jonson adapted his song from a Latin lyric of Barthélemi Aneau (see *N. & Q.*, III, viii, 187).

Spittles, pest-house, hospitalls,
Scarce will take our present store?
   And this age will build no more:
'Pray thee, feed contented, then,
Sicknesse; onely on us men.
   Or if needs thy lust will tast
   Woman-kinde; devoure the wast
   Livers, round about the towne.
But, forgive me, with thy crowne
They maintayne the truest trade,
And have more diseases made.
   What should, yet, thy pallat please?
   Daintinesse, and softer ease,
   Sleeked limmes, and finest blood?
If thy leanenesse love such food,
There are those, that, for thy sake,
Doe enough; and who would take
Any paines; yea, thinke it price,
To become thy sacrifice.
That distill their husbands land
In decoctions; and are mann'd
With ten Emp'ricks, in their chamber,
Lying for the spirit of amber.
That for th'oyle of *Talke*, dare spend
More then citizens dare lend
Them, and all their officers.
That, to make all pleasure theirs,
Will by coach, and water goe,
Every stew in towne to know;
Dare entayle their loves on any,
Bald, or blinde, or nere so many:
And, for thee, at common game,
Play away, health, wealth, and fame.
These, *disease*, will thee deserve:
And will, long ere thou should'st starve
On their beds, most prostitute,
Move it, as their humblest sute,
In thy justice to molest
None but them, and leave the rest.

Song

IX. *To Celia.* [II]

Drinke to me, onely, with thine eyes,
   And I will pledge with mine;
Or leave a kisse but in the cup,
   And Ile not looke for wine.
The thirst, that from the soule doth rise,   5
   Doth aske a drinke divine:
But might I of JOVE'S *Nectar* sup,
   I would not change for thine.
I sent thee, late, a rosie wreath,
   Not so much honoring thee,   10
As giving it a hope, that there
   It could not withered bee.
But thou thereon did'st onely breath,
   And sent'st it backe to mee:
Since when it growes, and smells, I sweare,   15
   Not of it selfe, but thee.

X. [*Praeludium*]

And must I sing? what subject shall I chuse?
Or whose great name in *Poets* heaven use?
For the more countenance to my active *Muse*?

HERCULES? alas his bones are yet sore,
With his old earthly labours. T'exact more,   5
Of his dull god-head, were sinne. Ile implore

X. [*Praeludium*]. XI. *Epode*. Both poems were first printed in Robert Chester's *Love's Martyr* (1601) among the "Diverse Poetical Essaies" on the subject of *The Phoenix and Turtle*, the phoenix representing womanly perfection and the turtle male constancy. Other poets represented in this portion of the volume are Shakespeare, Chapman, and Marston.

PHŒBUS. No? tend thy cart still. Envious day
Shall not give out, that I have made thee stay,
And foundred thy hot teame, to tune my lay.

Nor will I beg of thee, *Lord of the vine*, 10
To raise my spirits with thy conjuring wine,
In the greene circle of thy Ivy twine.

PALLAS, nor thee I call on, mankinde maid,
That, at thy birth, mad'st the poore Smith affraid,
Who, with his axe, thy fathers mid-wife plaid. 15

Goe, crampe dull MARS, light VENUS, when he snorts,
Or, with thy *Tribade* trine, invent new sports,
Thou, nor thy loosenesse with my making sorts.

Let the *old boy*, your sonne, ply his old taske,
Turne the stale prologue to some painted maske, 20
His absence in my verse, is all I aske.

HERMES, the cheater, shall not mix with us,
Though he would steale his sisters PAGASUS,
And riffle him: or pawne his PETASUS.

Nor all the ladies of the *Thespian lake*, 25
(Though they were crusht into one forme) could make
A beautie of that merit, that should take

My *Muse* up by *commission*: No, I bring
My owne true fire. Now my thought takes wing,
And now an *Epode* to deepe eares I sing. 30

XI. *Epode*

Not to know vice at all, and keepe true state,
    Is vertue, and not *Fate*:

X. [*Praeludium*]. 24 *riffle*: raffle; *Petasus*: Hermes' hat.

Next, to that vertue, is to know vice well,
    And her blacke spight expell.
Which to effect (since no brest is so sure,   5
    Or safe, but shee'll procure
Some way of entrance) we must plant a guard
    Of thoughts to watch, and ward
At th'eye and eare (the ports unto the minde)
    That no strange, or unkinde   10
Object arrive there, but the heart (our spie)
    Give knowledge instantly,
To wakefull reason, our affections king:
    Who (in th'examining)
Will quickly taste the treason, and commit   15
    Close, the close cause of it.
'Tis the securest policie we have,
    To make our sense our slave.
But this true course is not embrac'd by many:
    By many? scarse by any.   20
For either our affections doe rebell,
    Or else the sentinell
(That should ring larum to the heart) doth sleepe,
    Or some great thought doth keepe
Backe the intelligence, and falsely sweares,   25
    Th'are base, and idle feares
Whereof the loyall conscience so complaines.
    Thus, by these subtle traines,
Doe severall passions invade the minde,
    And strike our reason blinde.   30
Of which usurping rancke, some have thought love
    The first; as prone to move
Most frequent tumults, horrors, and unrests,
    In our enflamed brests:
But this doth from the cloud of error grow,   35
    Which thus we over-blow.
The thing, they here call Love, is blinde Desire,
    Arm'd with bow, shafts, and fire;
Inconstant, like the sea, of whence 'tis borne,
    Rough, swelling, like a storme: 40
With whom who sailes, rides on the surge of feare,

  And boyles, as if he were
In a continuall tempest. Now, true Love
  No such effects doth prove;
That is an essence, farre more gentle, fine,   45
  Pure, perfect, nay divine;
It is a golden chaine let downe from heaven,
  Whose linkes are bright, and even.
That falls like sleepe on lovers, and combines
  The soft, and sweetest mindes   50
In equall knots: This beares no brande, nor darts,
  To murther different hearts,
But, in a calme, and god-like unitie,
  Preserves communitie.
O, who is he, that (in this peace) enjoyes   55
  Th'*Elixir* of all joyes?
A forme more fresh, then are the *Eden* bowers,
  And lasting, as her flowers:
Richer then *Time*, and as *Time's* vertue, rare.
  Sober, as saddest care: 60
A fixed thought, an eye un-taught to glance;
  Who (blest with such high chance)
Would, at suggestion of a steepe desire,
  Cast himselfe from the spire
Of all his happinesse? But soft: I heare   65
  Some vicious foole draw neare,
That cryes, we dreame, and sweares, there's no such thing,
  As this chaste love we sing.
Peace, Luxurie, thou art like one of those
  Who, being at sea, suppose,   70
Because they move, the continent doth so:
  No, vice, we let thee know
Though thy wild thoughts with sparrowes wings doe flye,
  Turtles can chastly dye;
And yet (in this t'expresse our selves more cleare)   75
  We doe not number, here,
Such spirits as are onely continent,
  Because lust's meanes are spent:
Or those, who doubt the common mouth of fame,
  And for their place, and name,   80

Cannot so safely sinne. Their chastitie
    Is meere necessitie.
Nor meane we those, whom vowes and conscience
    Have fill'd with abstinence:
Though we acknowledge, who can so abstayne,   85
    Makes a most blessed gayne.
He that for love of goodnesse hateth ill,
    Is more crowne-worthy still,
Then he, which for sinnes penaltie forbeares.
    His heart sinnes, though he feares.   90
But we propose a person like our Dove,
    Grac'd with a Phœnix love;
A beautie of that cleere, and sparkling light,
    Would make a day of night,
And turne the blackest sorrowes to bright joyes: 95
    Whose od'rous breath destroyes
All taste of bitternesse, and makes the ayre
    As sweet, as shee is fayre.
A body so harmoniously compos'd,
    As if *Nature* disclos'd   100
All her best symmetrie in that one feature!
    O, so divine a creature
Who could be false to? chiefly, when he knowes
    How onely shee bestowes
The wealthy treasure of her love on him;   105
    Making his fortunes swim
In the full floud of her admir'd perfection?
    What savage, brute affection,
Would not be fearefull to offend a dame
    Of this excelling frame?   110
Much more a noble, and right generous mind
    (To vertuous moods inclin'd)
That knowes the waight of guilt: He will refraine
    From thoughts of such a straine.
And to his sense object this sentence ever,   115
    Man may securely sinne, but safely never.

Epistle

XII. *To Elizabeth Countesse of Rutland*

MADAME,
Whil'st that, for which, all vertue now is sold,
   And almost every vice, almightie gold,
That which, to boote with hell, is thought worth heaven,
   And, for it, life, conscience, yea, soules are given,
Toyles, by grave custome, up and downe the court,   5
   To every squire, or groome, that will report
Well, or ill, onely, all the following yeere,
   Just to the waight their this dayes-presents beare;
While it makes huishers serviceable men,
   And some one apteth to be trusted, then,   10
Though never after; whiles it gaynes the voyce
   Of some grand peere, whose ayre doth make rejoyce
The foole that gave it; who will want, and weepe,
   When his proud patrons favours are asleepe;
While thus it buyes great grace, and hunts poore fame;   15
   Runs betweene man, and man; 'tweene dame, and dame;
Solders crackt friendship; makes love last a day;
   Or perhaps lesse: whil'st gold beares all this sway,
I, that have none (to send you) send you verse.
   A present which (if elder writs reherse   20
The truth of times) was once of more esteeme,
   Then this, our guilt, nor golden age can deeme,
When gold was made no weapon to cut throtes,
   Or put to flight ASTREA, when her ingots
Were yet unfound, and better plac'd in earth,   25
   Then, here, to give pride fame, and peasants birth.
But let this drosse carry what price it will

XII. Epistle To Elizabeth Countesse of Rutland. The folio of 1616 prints only through l. 93 ("wheresoere he be..."); the rest of the poem is recoverable through manuscript. After l. 93, F. reads "The rest is lost." H. & S. point out that in 1616 the concluding lines would have been tasteless in view of the Earl of Rutland's known impotence. H. & S. further indicate that this is a New Year's Day gift sent the Countess on New Year's Day, 1600, as the last eight lines show.

With noble ignorants, and let them still,
Turne, upon scorned verse, their quarter-face:
    With you, I know, my offring will find grace.
For what a sinne 'gainst your great fathers spirit,
    Were it to thinke, that you should not inherit
His love unto the *Muses*, when his skill
    Almost you have, or may have, when you will?
Wherein wise *Nature* you a dowrie gave,
    Worth an estate, treble to that you have.
Beautie, I know, is good, and bloud is more;
    Riches thought most: But, *Madame*, thinke what store
The world hath seene, which all these had in trust,
    And now lye lost in their forgotten dust.
It is the *Muse*, alone, can raise to heaven,
    And, at her strong armes end, hold up, and even,
The soules, shee loves. Those other glorious notes,
    Inscrib'd in touch or marble, or the cotes
Painted, or carv'd upon our great-mens tombs,
    Or in their windowes; doe but prove the wombs,
That bred them, graves: when they were borne, they di'd,
    That had no *Muse* to make their fame abide.
How many equall with the *Argive* Queene,
    Have beautie knowne, yet none so famous seene?
ACHILLES was not first, that valiant was,
    Or, in an armies head, that, lockt in brasse,
Gave killing strokes. There were brave men, before
    AJAX, or IDOMEN, or all the store,
That HOMER brought to *Troy*; yet none so live:
    Because they lack'd the sacred pen, could give
Like life unto 'hem. Who heav'd HERCULES
    Unto the starres? or the *Tyndarides*?
Who placed JASONS ARGO in the skie?
    Or set bright ARIADNES crowne so high?
Who made a lampe of BERENICES hayre?
    Or lifted CASSIOPEA in her chayre?
But onely *Poets*, rapt with rage divine?
    And such, or my hopes faile, shall make you shine.
You, and that other starre, that purest light,
    Of all LUCINA'S traine; LUCY the bright.

Then which, a nobler heaven it selfe knowes not.
   Who, though shee have a better verser got,
(Or *Poet*, in the court account) then I,
   And, who doth me (though I not him) envy,   *70*
Yet, for the timely favours shee hath done,
   To my lesse sanguine *Muse*, wherein she'hath wonne
My gratefull soule, the subject of her powers,
   I have already us'd some happy houres,
To her remembrance; which when time shall bring   *75*
   To curious light, to notes, I then shall sing,
Will prove old ORPHEUS act no tale to be:
   For I shall move stocks, stones, no lesse then he.
Then all, that have but done my *Muse* least grace,
   Shall thronging come, and boast the happy place   *80*
They hold in my strange *poems*, which, as yet,
   Had not their forme touch'd by an English wit.
There like a rich, and golden *pyramede*,
   Borne up by statues, shall I reare your head,
Above your under carved ornaments,   *85*
   And show, how, to the life, my soule presents
Your forme imprest there: not with tickling rimes,
   Or common places, filch'd, that take these times,
But high, and noble matter, such as flies
   From braines entranc'd, and fill'd with extasies;   *90*
Moodes, which the god-like SYDNEY oft did prove,
   And your brave friend, and mine so well did love.
Who wheresoere he be, on what deare coast,
   Now thincking on you though to England lost,
For that firme grace he holds in your regard,   *95*
   I that am gratefull for him have prepard
This hastie sacrifice wherrin I reare
   A vowe, as new and ominous as the yeare,
Before his swift and circled race be run,
   My best of wishes; may you beare a sonne.   *100*

Epistle

XIII. *To Katherine, Lady Aubigny*

'Tis growne almost a danger to speake true
   Of any good minde, now: There are so few.
The bad, by number, are so fortified,
   As what th'have lost t'expect, they dare deride.
So both the prais'd, and praisers suffer: Yet,   5
   For others ill, ought none their good forget.
I, therefore, who professe my selfe in love
   With every vertue, wheresoere it move,
And howsoever; as I am at fewd
   With sinne and vice, though with a throne endew'd;   10
And, in this name, am given out dangerous
   By arts, and practise of the vicious,
Such as suspect them selves, and thinke it fit
   For their owne cap'tall crimes, t'indite my wit;
I, that have suffer'd this; and, though forsooke   15
   Of *Fortune*, have not alter'd yet my looke,
Or so my selfe abandon'd, as because
   Men are not just, or keepe no holy lawes
Of nature, and societie, I should faint;
   Or feare to draw true lines, 'cause others paint: 20
I, *Madame*, am become your praiser. Where,
   If it may stand with your soft blush to heare,
Your selfe but told unto your selfe, and see
   In my character, what your features bee,
You will not from the paper slightly passe: 25
   No lady, but, at some time, loves her glasse.
And this shall be no false one, but as much
   Remov'd, as you from need to have it such.
Looke then, and see your selfe. I will not say
   Your beautie; for you see that every day: 30

XIII. *Epistle To Katherine, Lady Aubigny.* Her husband Esmé, Lord Aubigny (later Duke of Lennox), was celebrated by Jonson in the dedication to *Sejanus* (1605) as "no less noble by virtue than blood." Jonson lived in his house in Blackfriars for five years, from 1602 to 1607.

And so doe many more. All which can call
   It perfect, proper, pure, and naturall,
Not taken up o'th'doctors, but as well
   As I, can say, and see it doth excell.
That askes but to be censur'd by the eyes: 35
   And, in those outward formes, all fooles are wise.
Nor that your beautie wanted not a dower,
   Doe I reflect. Some alderman has power,
Or cos'ning farmer of the customes so,
   T'advance his doubtfull issue, and ore-flow   40
A Princes fortune: These are gifts of chance,
   And raise not vertue; they may vice enhance.
My mirror is more subtile, cleere, refin'd,
   And takes, and gives the beauties of the mind.
Though it reject not those of FORTUNE: such   45
   As bloud, and match. Wherein, how more then much
Are you engaged to your happy fate,
   For such a lot! that mixt you with a state
Of so great title, birth, but vertue most,
   Without which, all the rest were sounds, or lost.   50
'Tis onely that can time, and chance defeat:
   For he, that once is good, is ever great.
Wherewith, then, *Madame*, can you better pay
   This blessing of your starres, then by that way
Of vertue, which you tread? what if alone?   55
   Without companions? 'Tis safe to have none.
In single paths, dangers with ease are watch'd:
   Contagion in the prease is soonest catch'd.
This makes, that wisely you decline your life,
   Farre from the maze of custome, error, strife,   60
And keepe an even, and unalter'd gaite;
   Not looking by, or backe (like those, that waite
Times, and occasions, to start forth, and seeme)
   Which though the turning world may dis-esteeme,
Because that studies spectacles, and showes,   65
   And after varyed, as fresh objects goes,
Giddie with change, and therefore cannot see
   Right, the right way: yet must your comfort bee
Your conscience, and not wonder, if none askes

  For truthes complexion, where they all weare maskes.   *70*
Let who will follow fashions, and attyres,
 Maintayne their liedgers forth, for forraine wyres,
Melt downe their husbands land, to poure away
 On the close groome, and page, on new-yeeres day,
And almost, all dayes after, while they live;   *75*
 (They finde it both so wittie, and safe to give.)
Let'hem on poulders, oyles, and paintings, spend,
 Till that no usurer, nor his bawds dare lend
Them, or their officers: and no man know,
 Whether it be a face they weare, or no.   *80*
Let'hem waste body, and state; and after all,
 When their owne Parasites laugh at their fall,
May they have nothing left, whereof they can
 Boast, but how oft they have gone wrong to man:
And call it their brave sinne. For such there be   *85*
 That doe sinne onely for the infamie:
And never thinke, how vice doth every houre,
 Eate on her clients, and some one devoure.
You, *Madame*, yong have learn'd to shunne these shelves,
 Whereon the most of mankinde wracke themselves,   *90*
And, keeping a just course, have earely put
 Into your harbor, and all passage shut
'Gainst stormes, or pyrats, that might charge your peace;
 For which you worthy are the glad encrease
Of your blest wombe, made fruitfull from above,   *95*
 To pay your lord the pledges of chast love:
And raise a noble stemme, to give the fame,
 To CLIFTON'S bloud, that is deny'd their name.
Grow, grow, faire tree, and as thy branches shoote,
 Heare, what the *Muses* sing about thy roote,   *100*
By me, their priest (if they can ought divine)
 Before the moones have fill'd their tripple trine,
To crowne the burthen which you goe withall,
 It shall a ripe and timely issue fall,
T'expect the honors of great 'AUBIGNY: *105*
 And greater rites, yet writ in mysterie,
But which the *Fates* forbid me to reveale.
 Onely, thus much, out of a ravish'd zeale,

Unto your name; and goodnesse of your life,
    They speake; since you are truely that rare wife,   *110*
Other great wives may blush at: when they see
    What your try'd manners are, what theirs should bee.
How you love one, and him you should; how still
    You are depending on his word, and will;
Not fashion'd for the court, or strangers eyes;   *115*
    But to please him, who is the dearer prise
Unto himselfe, by being so deare to you.
    This makes, that your affections still be new,
And that your soules conspire, as they were gone
    Each into other, and had now made one.   *120*
Live that one, still; and as long yeeres doe passe,
    Madame, be bold to use this truest glasse:
Wherein, your forme, you still the same shall finde;
    Because nor it can change, nor such a minde.

Ode

XIV. *To Sir William Sydney, on his Birth-day*

Now that the harth is crown'd with smiling fire,
    And some doe drinke, and some doe dance,
        Some ring,
        Some sing,
    And all doe strive t'advance   *5*
The gladnesse higher:
    Wherefore should I
    Stand silent by,
        Who not the least,
    Both love the cause, and authors of the feast?   *10*
Give me my cup, but from the *Thespian* well,
    That I may tell to SYDNEY, what
        This day
        Doth say,

XIV. Ode To Sir William Sydney, on his Birth-day. Sir William Sidney (1590–1612) was son to Sir Robert Sidney, and nephew to Sir Philip. He was knighted in January 1611.

    And he may thinke on that 15
Which I doe tell:
        When all the noyse
          Of these forc'd joyes,
            Are fled and gone,
              And he, with his best *Genius* left alone. 20
This day sayes, then, the number of glad yeeres
    Are justly summ'd, that make you man;
          Your vow
          Must now
    Strive all right wayes it can, 25
T'out-strip your peeres:
        Since he doth lacke
          Of going backe
            Little, whose will
              Doth urge him to runne wrong, or to stand still. 30
Nor can a little of the common store,
    Of nobles vertue, shew in you;
          Your blood
          So good
    And great, must seeke for new, 35
And studie more:
        Not weary, rest
          On what's deceast.
            For they, that swell
              With dust of ancestors, in graves but dwell. 40
'Twill be exacted of your name, whose sonne,
    Whose nephew, whose grand-child you are;
          And men
          Will, then,
    Say you have follow'd farre, 45
When well begunne:
        Which must be now,
          They teach you, how.
            And he that stayes
              To live untill to morrow'hath lost two dayes. 50
So may you live in honor, as in name,
    If with this truth you be inspir'd,

> So may
> This day
> Be more, and long desir'd: 55
> And with the flame
> Of love be bright,
> As with the light
> Of bone-fires. Then
> The Birth-day shines, when logs not burne, but men. 60

xv. *To Heaven*

Good, and great GOD, can I not thinke of thee,
   But it must, straight, my melancholy bee?
Is it interpreted in me disease,
   That, laden with my sinnes, I seeke for ease?
O, be thou witnesse, that the reynes dost know, 5
   And hearts of all, if I be sad for show,
And judge me after: if I dare pretend
   To ought but grace, or ayme at other end.
As thou art all, so be thou all to mee,
   First, midst, and last, converted one, and three; 10
My faith, my hope, my love: and in this state,
   My judge, my witnesse, and my advocate.
Where have I beene this while exil'd from thee?
   And whither rap'd, now thou but stoup'st to mee?
Dwell, dwell here still: O, being every-where, 15
   How can I doubt to finde thee ever here?
I know my state, both full of shame, and scorne,
   Conceiv'd in sinne, and unto labour borne,
Standing with feare, and must with horror fall,
   And destin'd unto judgement, after all. 20
I feele my griefes too, and there scarce is ground,
   Upon my flesh t'inflict another wound.
Yet dare I not complaine, or wish for death
   With holy PAUL, lest it be thought the breath
Of discontent; or that these prayers bee 25
   For wearinesse of life, not love of thee.

From UNDER-WOOD

Consisting of Divers Poems

Martial — *Cineri, gloria sera venit.*

TO THE READER
With the same leave, the Ancients call'd that kind of body Sylva, *or* ῞Υλη, *in which there were workes of divers nature, and matter congested; as the multitude call Timber-trees, promiscuously growing, a* Wood, *or* Forrest: *so am I bold to entitle these lesser Poems, of later growth, by this of* Under-wood, *out of the Analogie they hold to the* Forrest, *in my former booke, and no otherwise.*

BEN. JOHNSON.

[I] *Poems of Devotion*

[1] *The Sinners Sacrifice*
To the Holy Trinitie

1. O holy, blessed, glorious *Trinitie*
Of persons, still one God, in *Unitie*,
The faithfull mans beleeved Mysterie,
   Helpe, helpe to lift

Under-Wood. The prefatory note shows that Jonson had begun to arrange for publication of the poems in this section, and that he regarded the collection as being analogous to *The Forrest.* It first appeared in the second folio edition, *Workes* (1640–41), a few years after his death. Variants in the poems in some

2. My selfe up to thee, harrow'd, torne, and bruis'd
By sinne, and Sathan; and my flesh misus'd,
As my heart lies in peeces, all confus'd,
        O take my gift.
3. All-gracious God, the *Sinners sacrifice*,
A broken heart thou wert not wont despise,
But 'bove the fat of rammes, or bulls, to prize
        An offring meet,
4. For thy acceptance. O, behold me right,
And take compassion on my grievous plight.
What odour can be, then a heart contrite,
        To thee more sweet?
5. *Eternall Father*, God, who did'st create
This All of nothing, gavest it forme, and fate,
And breath'st into it, life, and light, with state
        To worship thee.
6. *Eternall God the Sonne*, who not denyd'st
To take our nature; becam'st man, and dyd'st,
To pay our debts, upon thy Crosse, and cryd'st
        All's done in me.
7. *Eternall Spirit*, God from both proceeding,
Father and Sonne; the Comforter, in breeding
Pure thoughts in man: with fiery zeale them feeding
        For acts of grace.
8. Increase those acts, ô glorious *Trinitie*
Of persons, still one God in *Unitie*;
Till I attaine the long'd-for mysterie
        Of seeing your face.
9. Beholding one in three, and three in one,
A *Trinitie*, to shine in *Unitie*;
The gladdest light, darke man can thinke upon;
        O grant it me!
10. Father, and Sonne, and Holy Ghost, you three
All coeternall in your Majestie,
Distinct in persons, yet in Unitie
        One God to see.

---

copies of F2 suggest that a considerable number of corrections were made while the printing was in progress. The epigraph is from an epigram of Martial (I. xxv. 8): "Glory comes to the departed too late."

11. My Maker, Saviour, and my Sanctifier,
To heare, to meditate, sweeten my desire,
With grace, with love, with cherishing intire,
    O, then how blest;
12. Among thy Saints elected to abide,   45
And with thy Angels, placed side, by side,
But in thy presence, truly glorified
    Shall I there rest?

[2] *A Hymne to God the Father*

Heare mee, O God!
    A broken heart,
    Is my best part:
Use still thy rod,
    That I may prove   5
    Therein, thy Love.

If thou hadst not
    Beene sterne to mee,
    But left me free,
I had forgot   10
    My selfe and thee.

For, sin's so sweet,
    As minds ill bent
    Rarely repent,
Untill they meet   15
    Their punishment.

Who more can crave
    Then thou hast done:
    That gav'st a Sonne,
To free a slave?   20
    First made of nought;
    With all since bought.

Sinne, Death, and Hell,
    His glorious Name

[I.2] *A Hymne*... A contemporaneous setting by Alphonso Ferrabosco II arranged for voice and lute is included in this volume.

  Quite overcame,   25
Yet I rebell,
  And slight the same.

  But, I'le come in,
   Before my losse,
   Me farther tosse,
  As sure to win   30
   Under his Crosse.

[3] *A Hymne*

On the Nativitie of my Saviour

I sing the birth, was borne to night,
The Author both of Life, and light;
  The Angels so did sound it,
And like the ravish'd Sheep'erds said,
Who saw the light, and were afraid,   5
  Yet search'd, and true they found it.

The Sonne of God, th'Eternall King,
That did us all salvation bring,
  And freed the soule from danger;
Hee whom the whole world could not take,   10
The Word, which heaven, and earth did make;
  Was now laid in a Manger.

The Fathers wisedome will'd it so,
The Sonnes obedience knew no No,
  Both wills were in one stature;   15
And as that wisedome had decreed,
The Word was now made Flesh indeed,
  And tooke on him our Nature.

What comfort by him doe wee winne?
Who made himselfe the price of sinne,   20
  To make us heires of glory?

To see this Babe, all innocence;
A Martyr borne in our defence;
Can man forget this Storie?

[II] *A Celebration of Charis in ten Lyrick Peeces*
1. *His Excuse for loving*

Let it not your wonder move,
Lesse your laughter; that I love.
Though I now write fiftie yeares,
I have had, and have my Peeres;
Poëts, though devine are men: 5
Some have lov'd as old agen.
And it is not alwayes face,
Clothes, or Fortune gives the grace;
Or the feature, or the youth:
But the Language, and the Truth, 10
With the Ardor, and the Passion,
Gives the Lover weight, and fashion.
If you then will read the Storie,
First, prepare you to be sorie,
That you never knew till now, 15
Either whom to love, or how:
But be glad, as soone with me,
When you know, that this is she,
Of whose Beautie it was sung,
She shall make the old man young, 20
Keepe the middle age at stay,
And let nothing high decay,
Till she be the reason why,
All the world for love may die.

2. *How he saw her*

I beheld her, on a Day,
When her looke out-flourisht May:

And her dressing did out-brave
All the Pride the fields than have:
Farre I was from being stupid,   *5*
For I ran and call'd on *Cupid*;
Love if thou wilt ever see
Marke of glorie, come with me;
Where's thy Quiver? bend thy Bow:
Here's a shaft, thou art to slow!   *10*
And (withall) I did untie
Every Cloud about his eye;
But, he had not gain'd his sight
Sooner, then he lost his might,
Or his courage; for away   *15*
Strait hee ran, and durst not stay,
Letting Bow and Arrow fall,
Nor for any threat, or Call,
Could be brought once back to looke.
I foole-hardie, there up tooke   *20*
Both the Arrow he had quit,
And the Bow: which thought to hit
This my object. But she threw
Such a Lightning (as I drew)
At my face, that tooke my sight,   *25*
And my motion from me quite;
So that there, I stood a stone,
Mock'd of all: and call'd of one
(Which with griefe and wrath I heard)
Cupids Statue with a Beard,   *30*
Or else one that plaid his Ape,
In a *Hercules*-his shape.

3. *What hee suffered*

After many scornes like these,
Which the prouder Beauties please,
She content was to restore
Eyes and limbes; to hurt me more
And would on Conditions, be   *5*

Reconcil'd to Love, and me:
First, that I must kneeling yeeld
Both the Bow, and shaft I held
Unto her; which Love might take
At her hand, with oath, to make 10
Mee, the scope of his next draught
Aymed, with that selfe-same shaft.
He no sooner heard the Law,
But the Arrow home did draw
And (to gaine her by his Art) 15
Left it sticking in my heart:
Which when she beheld to bleed,
She repented of the deed,
And would faine have chang'd the fate,
But the Pittie comes too late. 20
Looser-like, now, all my wreake
Is, that I have leave to speake,
And in either Prose, or Song,
To revenge me with my Tongue,
Which how Dexterously I doe 25
Heare and make Example too.

4. *Her Triumph*

See the Chariot at hand here of Love
   Wherein my Lady rideth!
Each that drawes, is a Swan, or a Dove,
   And well the Carre Love guideth.
As she goes, all hearts doe duty 5
     Unto her beauty;
And enamour'd, doe wish, so they might
     But enjoy such a sight,
That they still were, to run by her side,
Through Swords, through Seas, whether she would ride. 10

Doe but looke on her eyes, they doe light
   All that Loves world compriseth!

[II.4] *Her Triumph*. 11–30 These lines first appeared in Jonson's *The Devil is*

Doe but looke on her Haire, it is bright
  As Loves starre when it riseth!
Doe but marke her forhead's smoother   15
  Then words that sooth her!
And from her arched browes, such a grace
  Sheds itselfe through the face,
As alone there triumphs to the life
All the Gaine, all the Good, of the Elements strife.   20

Have you seene but a bright Lillie grow,
  Before rude hands have touch'd it?
Ha' you mark'd but the fall o' the Snow
  Before the soyle hath smutch'd it?
Ha' you felt the wooll o' the Bever?   25
  Or Swans Downe ever?
Or have smelt o' the bud o' the Brier?
  Or the Nard in the fire?
Or have tasted the bag of the Bee?
O so white! O so soft! O so sweet is she!   30

5. *His discourse with* Cupid

Noblest *Charis*, you that are
Both my fortune, and my Starre!
And doe governe more my blood,
Then the various Moone the flood!
Heare, what late Discourse of you,   5
Love, and I have had; and true.
'Mongst my Muses finding me,
Where he chanc't your name to see
Set, and to this softer straine;
Sure, said he, if I have Braine,   10
This here sung, can be no other
By description, but my Mother!
So hath *Homer* prais'd her haire;

---

an Ass (Act II, sc. 6), acted in Blackfriars in 1616. A contemporary setting attributed to Robert Johnson of ll. 21–30 survives in several manuscripts of the period.

So, *Anacreon* drawne the Ayre
Of her face, and made to rise 15
Just about her sparkling eyes,
Both her Browes, bent like my Bow.
By her lookes I doe her know,
Which you call my Shafts. And see!
Such my Mothers blushes be, 20
As the Bath your verse discloses
In her cheekes, of Milke, and Roses;
Such as oft I wanton in;
And, above her even chin,
Have you plac'd the banke of kisses, 25
Where you say, men gather blisses,
Rip'ned with a breath more sweet,
Then when flowers, and West-winds meet?
Nay, her white and polishd neck,
With the Lace that doth it deck, 30
Is my Mothers! Hearts of slaine
Lovers, made into a Chaine!
And betweene each rising breast,
Lyes the Valley, cal'd my nest,
Where I sit and proyne my wings 35
After flights; and put new stings
To my shafts! Her very Name,
With my Mothers is the same.
I confesse all, I replide,
And the Glasse hangs by her side, 40
And the Girdle 'bout her waste,
All is *Venus:* save unchaste.
But alas, thou seest the least
Of her good, who is the best
Of her Sex; But could'st thou, *Love,* 45
Call to mind the formes, that strove
For the Apple, and those three
Make in one, the same were shee.
For this Beauty yet doth hide,
Something more then thou hast spi'd. 50
Outward Grace weake love beguiles:
Shee is *Venus,* when she smiles,

But shee's *Juno*, when she walkes,
And *Minerva*, when she talkes.

6. *Clayming a second kisse by Desert*

Charis, guesse, and doe not misse,
Since I drew a Morning kisse
From your lips, and suck'd an ayre
Thence, as sweet, as you are faire,
    What my Muse and I have done: 5
Whether we have lost, or wonne,
If by us, the oddes were laid,
That the Bride (allow'd a Maid)
Look'd not halfe so fresh, and faire,
With th'advantage of her haire, 10
And her Jewels, to the view
Of th'Assembly, as did you!
    Or, that did you sit, or walke,
You were more the eye, and talke
Of the Court, to day, then all 15
Else that glister'd in *White-hall*;
So, as those that had your sight,
Wisht the Bride were chang'd to night,
And did thinke, such Rites were due
To no other Grace but you! 20
    Or, if you did move to night
In the Daunces, with what spight
Of your Peeres, you were beheld,
That at every motion sweld
So to see a Lady tread, 25
As might all the Graces lead,
And was worthy (being so seene)
To be envi'd of the Queene.
Or if you would yet have stay'd,
Whether any would up-braid 30
To himselfe his losse of Time;
Or have charg'd his sight of Crime,
To have left all sight for you:

Guesse of these, which is the true;
And, if such a verse as this, 35
May not claime another kisse.

7. *Begging another, on colour of mending the former*

For *Loves*-sake, kisse me once againe,
  I long, and should not beg in vaine,
    Here's none to spie, or see;
    Why doe you doubt, or stay?
I'le taste as lightly as the Bee, 5
That doth but touch his flower, and flies away.
  Once more, and (faith) I will be gone.
  Can he that loves, aske lesse then one?
    Nay, you may erre in this,
    And all your bountie wrong: 10
This could be call'd but halfe a kisse.
What w'are but once to doe, we should doe long;
  I will but mend the last, and tell
  Where, how it would have relish'd well;
    Joyne lip to lip, and try: 15
    Each suck others breath.
And whilst our tongues perplexed lie,
Let who will thinke us dead, or wish our death.

8. *Urging her of a promise*

Charis one day in discourse
Had of Love, and of his force,
Lightly promis'd, she would tell
What a man she could love well:
And that promise set on fire 5
All that heard her, with desire.
With the rest, I long expected,
When the worke would be effected:
But we find that cold delay,

And excuse spun every day, 10
As, untill she tell her one,
We all feare, she loveth none.
Therefore, *Charis*, you must do't,
For I will so urge you to't
You shall neither eat, nor sleepe, 15
No, nor forth your window peepe,
With your emissarie eye,
To fetch in the Formes goe by:
And pronounce, which band or lace,
Better fits him, then his face; 20
Nay I will not let you sit
'Fore your Idoll Glasse a whit,
To say over every purle
There; or to reforme a curle;
Or with Secretarie *Sis* 25
To consult, if *Fucus* this
Be as good, as was the last:
All your sweet of life is past,
Make accompt unlesse you can,
(And that quickly) speake your Man. 30

9. *Her man described by her owne Dictamen*

Of your Trouble, *Ben*, to ease me,
I will tell what Man would please me.
I would have him if I could,
Noble; or of greater Blood:
Titles, I confesse, doe take me; 5
And a woman God did make me,
French to boote, at least in fashion,
And his Manners of that Nation.
   Young Il'd have him to, and faire,
Yet a man; with crisped haire 10
Cast in thousand snares, and rings
For *Loves* fingers, and his wings:
Chestnut colour, or more slack
Gold, upon a ground of black.

Venus, and *Minerva's* eyes 15
For he must looke wanton-wise.
   Eye-brows bent like *Cupids* bow,
Front, an ample field of snow;
Even nose, and cheeke (withall)
Smooth as is the Billiard Ball: 20
Chin, as woolly as the Peach,
And his lip should kissing teach,
Till he cherish'd too much beard,
And make *Love* or me afeard.
   He would have a hand as soft 25
As the Downe, and shew it oft;
Skin as smooth as any rush,
And so thin to see a blush
Rising through it e're it came;
All his blood should be a flame 30
Quickly fir'd as in beginners
In loves schoole, and yet no sinners.
   'Twere to long to speake of all,
What we harmonie doe call
In a body should be there. 35
Well he should his clothes to weare;
Yet no Taylor help to make him;
Drest, you still for man should take him;
And not thinke h'had eat a stake,
Or were set up in a Brake. 40
   Valiant he should be as fire,
Shewing danger more then ire.
Bounteous as the clouds to earth;
And as honest as his Birth.
All his actions to be such, 45
As to doe nothing too much.
Nor o're-praise, nor yet condemne;
Nor out-valew, nor contemne;
Nor doe wrongs, nor wrongs receave;
Nor tie knots, nor knots unweave; 50
And from basenesse to be free,
As he durst love Truth and me.

Such a man, with every part,
I could give my very heart;
But of one, if short he came, 55
I can rest me where I am.

10. *Another Ladyes exception present at the hearing*

For his Mind, I doe not care,
That's a Toy, that I could spare:
Let his Title be but great,
His Clothes rich, and band sit neat,
Himselfe young, and face be good, 5
All I wish is understood.
What you please, you parts may call,
'Tis one good part I'ld lie withall.

[III] *The Musicall strife;*
In a Pastorall Dialogue

SHEE

Come with our Voyces, let us warre,
   And challenge all the Spheares,
Till each of us be made a Starre,
   And all the world turne Eares.

HEE

At such a Call, what beast or fowle, 5
   Of reason emptie is!
What Tree or stone doth want a soule?
   What man but must lose his?

[III] *The Musicall strife* ... This poem was quoted by Jonson to Drummond on the occasion of the poet's visit to Scotland in 1619.

SHEE

Mixe then your Notes, that we may prove
    To stay the running floods?
To make the Mountaine Quarries move?
    And call the walking woods?

HEE

What need of mee? doe you but sing
    Sleepe, and the Grave will wake.
No tunes are sweet, nor words have sting,
    But what those lips doe make.

SHEE

They say the Angells marke each Deed,
    And exercise below,
And out of inward pleasure feed
    On what they viewing know.

HEE

O sing not you then, lest the best
    Of Angels should be driven
To fall againe; at such a feast,
    Mistaking earth for heaven.

SHEE

Nay, rather both our soules bee straynd
    To meet their high desire;
So they in state of Grace retain'd,
    May wish us of their Quire.

[IV] *A Song*

Oh doe not wanton with those eyes,
    Lest I be sick with seeing;
Nor cast them downe, but let them rise,
    Lest shame destroy their being:
O, be not angry with those fires,

  For then their threats will kill me;
 Nor looke too kind on my desires,
  For then my hopes will spill me;
 O, doe not steepe them in thy Teares,
  For so will sorrow slay me;   *10*
 Nor spread them as distract with feares,
  Mine owne enough betray me.

[VIII] *The Houre-glasse*

Doe but consider this small dust,
Here running in the Glasse,
  By Atomes mov'd;
Could you beleeve, that this,
   The body was   *5*
    Of one that lov'd?
And in his Mistress flame, playing like a flye,
 Turn'd to cinders by her eye?
Yes; and in death, as life unblest,
   To have't exprest,   *10*
Even ashes of lovers find no rest.

[IX] *My Picture left in Scotland*

I now thinke, Love is rather deafe, then blind,
 For else it could not be,
   That she,
Whom I adore so much, should so slight me,
 And cast my love behind: *5*
I'm sure my language to her, was as sweet,
  And every close did meet
  In sentence, of as subtile feet,
   As hath the youngest Hee,

 [VIII] *The Houre-glasse.* The *Conversations* record that a copy of this poem was sent to Drummond by the poet.
 [IX] *My Picture left in Scotland.* This poem is mentioned in the Drummond *Conversations*. It was written shortly before 1619.

That sits in Shadow of *Apollo's* tree.   10
Oh, but my conscious feares
    That flie my thoughts betweene,
    Tell me that she hath seene
My hundreds of gray haires,
    Told seven and fortie yeares,   15
Read so much wast, as she cannot imbrace
My mountaine belly, and my rockie face,
And all these through her eyes, have stopt her eares.

[X] *Against Jealousie*

Wretched and foolish Jealousie,
How cam'st thou thus to enter me?
    I ne're was of thy kind;
    Nor have I yet the narrow mind
        To vent that poore desire,   5
That others should not warme them at my fire:
    I wish the Sun should shine
On all mens Fruit, and flowers, as well as mine.

But under the Disguise of love
Thou sai'st, thou only cam'st to prove   10
    What my Affections were.
    Think'st thou that love is help'd by feare?
    Goe, get thee quickly forth.
Loves sicknesse, and his noted want of worth
    Seeke doubting Men to please;   15
I ne're will owe my health to a disease.

[XI] *The Dreame*

Or Scorne, or pittie on me take,
I must the true Relation make,
    I am undone to Night;
Love in a subtile Dreame disguis'd,

Hath both my heart and me surpriz'd, 5
Whom never yet he durst attempt t'awake;
Nor will he tell me for whose sake
    He did me the Delight,
    Or Spight,
But leaves me to inquire, 10
In all my wild desire
    Of sleepe againe, who was his Aid,
    And sleepe so guiltie and afraid,
As since he dares not come within my sight.

[XIX] *An Elegie*

By those bright Eyes, at whose immortall fires
    Love lights his torches to inflame desires;
By that faire Stand, your forehead, whence he bends
    His double Bow, and round his Arrowes sends;
By that tall Grove, your haire; whose globy rings 5
    He flying curles, and crispeth, with his wings;
By those pure bathes your either cheeke discloses,
    Where he doth steepe himselfe in Milke and Roses;
And lastly by your lips, the banke of kisses,
    Where men at once may plant, and gather blisses: 10
Tell me (my lov'd Friend) doe you love or no?
    So well as I may tell in verse, 'tis so?
You blush, but doe not: friends are either none,
    (Though they may number bodyes) or but one.
I'le therefore aske no more, but bid you love; 15
    And so that either may example prove
Unto the other; and live patternes, how
    Others, in time may love, as we doe now.
Slip no occasion; As time stands not still,
    I know no beautie, nor no youth that will. 20
To use the present, then, is not abuse,
    You have a Husband is the just excuse
Of all that can be done him; Such a one
    As would make shift, to make himselfe alone,

That which we can, who both in you, his Wife, 25
   His Issue, and all Circumstance of life
As in his place, because he would not varie,
   Is constant to be extraordinarie.

[XXIII] *An Ode. To himselfe*

Where do'st thou carelesse lie
   Buried in ease and sloth?
Knowledge, that sleepes, doth die;
And this Securitie,
   It is the common Moath, 5
That eats on wits, and Arts, and destroyes them both.

Are all th'*Aonian* springs
   Dri'd up? lyes *Thespia* wast?
Doth *Clarius* Harp want strings,
That not a Nymph now sings! 10
   Or droop they as disgrac't,
To see their Seats and Bowers by chattring Pies defac't?

If hence thy silence be,
   As 'tis too just a cause;
Let this thought quicken thee, 15
Minds that are great and free,
   Should not on fortune pause,
'Tis crowne enough to vertue still, her owne applause.

What though the greedie Frie
   Be taken with false Baytes 20
Of worded Balladrie,
And thinke it Poësie?
   They die with their conceits,
And only pitious scorne, upon their folly waites.

[XXIII] *An Ode. To himselfe.* The last two lines of this poem are virtually identical with the closing lines of the "Apologetical Dialogue" of *Poetaster*; this appendage was first printed in the Folio of 1616.

> Then take in hand thy Lyre,   *25*
>   Strike in thy proper straine,
> With *Japhets* lyne, aspire
> *Sols* Chariot for new fire,
>   To give the word againe:
> Who aided him, will thee, the issue of *Joves* braine.   *30*
>
> And since our Daintie age,
>   Cannot indure reproofe,
> Make not thy selfe a Page,
> To that strumpet the Stage,
>   But sing high and aloofe,   *35*
> Safe from the wolves black jaw, and the dull Asses hoofe.

[XXVII] *An Ode*

> *Hellen*, did *Homer* never see
> Thy beauties, yet could write of thee?
> Did *Sappho* on her seven-tongu'd Lute,
> So speake (as yet it is not mute)
> Of *Phaos* forme? or doth the Boy   *5*
> In whom *Anacreon* once did joy,
> Lie drawne to life, in his soft Verse,
> As he whom *Maro* did rehearse?
> Was *Lesbia* sung by learn'd *Catullus*?
> Or *Delia's* Graces, by *Tibullus*?   *10*
> Doth *Cynthia*, in *Propertius* song
> Shine more, then she the Stars among?
> Is *Horace* his each love so high
> Rap't from the Earth, as not to die?
> With bright *Lycoris*, *Gallus* choice,   *15*
> Whose fame hath an eternall voice?
> Or hath *Corynna*, by the name
> Her *Ovid* gave her, dimn'd the fame
> Of *Cæsars* Daughter, and the line
> Which all the world then styl'd devine?   *20*
> Hath *Petrarch* since his *Laura* rais'd

    Equall with her? or *Ronsart* prais'd
    His new *Cassandra*, 'bove the old,
    Which all the Fate of *Troy* foretold?
    Hath our great *Sydney*, *Stella* set,   25
    Where never Star shone brighter yet?
    Or *Constables* Ambrosiack Muse
    Made *Dian*, not his notes refuse?
    Have all these done (and yet I misse
    The Swan that so relish'd *Pancharis*)   30
    And shall not I my *Celia* bring,
    Where men may see whom I doe sing?
    Though I, in working of my song
    Come short of all this learned throng,
    Yet sure my tunes will be the best,   35
    So much my Subject drownes the rest.

[XXVIII] *A Sonnet*

To the noble Lady, the Lady Mary Worth

I that have been a lover, and could shew it,
  Though not in these, in rithmes not wholly dumbe,
  Since I exscribe your Sonnets, am become
A better lover, and much better Poët.
Nor is my Muse, or I asham'd to owe it   5
  To those true numerous Graces; whereof some,
  But charme the Senses, others over-come
Both braines and hearts; and mine now best doe know it:
For in your verse all *Cupids* Armorie,
  His flames, his shafts, his Quiver, and his Bow,   10
  His very eyes are yours to overthrow.

[XXVII] *An Ode.* 30 *Swan*: To Hugh Holland's *Pancharis*, a poem published in 1603, Jonson contributed a dedicatory poem. Holland provided commendatory verses for Jonson's *Sejanus* (1605) and also for the Shakespeare First Folio (1623).

[XXVIII] *A Sonnet To ... Lady Mary Worth.* Lady Mary Worth (Wroth) was also the addressee of Jonson's Epigrams CIII and CV.

But then his Mothers sweets you so apply,
   Her joyes, her smiles, her loves, as readers take
   For *Venus Ceston*, every line you make.

[XXIX] *A Fit of Rime against Rime*

    Rime, the rack of finest wits,
    That expresseth but by fits,
        True Conceipt,
    Spoyling Senses of their Treasure,
    Cosening Judgement with a measure,   5
        But false weight.
    Wresting words, from their true calling;
    Propping Verse, for feare of falling
        To the ground.
    Joynting Syllabes, drowning Letters,   10
    Fastning Vowells, as with fetters
        They were bound!
    Soone as lazie thou wert knowne,
    All good Poëtrie hence was flowne,
        And Art banish'd.   15
    For a thousand yeares together,
    All *Pernassus* Greene did wither,
        And wit vanish'd.
    Pegasus did flie away,
    At the Wells no Muse did stay,   20
        But bewail'd.
    So to see the Fountaine drie,
    And *Apollo's* Musique die,
        All light failed!
    Starveling rimes did fill the Stage,   25
    Not a Poët in an Age,
        Worth crowning.
    Not a worke deserving Baies,
    Nor a lyne deserving praise,
        Pallas frowning;   30
    Greeke was free from Rimes infection,

>   Happy Greeke by this protection,
>   Was not spoyled.
>   Whilst the Latin, Queene of Tongues,
>   Is not yet free from Rimes wrongs,   35
>   But rests foiled.
>   Scarce the hill againe doth flourish,
>   Scarce the world a Wit doth nourish,
>   To restore
>   *Phœbus* to his Crowne againe;   40
>   And the Muses to their braine;
>   As before.
>   Vulgar Languages that want
>   Words, and sweetnesse, and be scant
>   Of true measure,   45
>   *Tyran* Rime hath so abused,
>   That they long since have refused,
>   Other ceasure;
>   He that first invented thee,
>   May his joynts tormented bee,   50
>   Cramp'd forever;
>   Still may Syllabes jarre with time,
>   Stil may reason warre with rime,
>   Resting never.
>   May his Sense, when it would meet   55
>   The cold tumor in his feet,
>   Grow unsounder.
>   And his Title be long foole,
>   That in rearing such a Schoole,
>   Was the founder.   60

[XXXVI] *A Song*

LOVER

Come, let us here enjoy the shade,
For love, in shadow best is made.
Though Envie oft his shadow be,
None brookes the Sun-light worse then he.

MISTRES

Where love doth shine, there needs no Sunne, 5
All lights into his one doth run;
Without which all the world were darke;
Yet he himselfe is but a sparke.

ARBITER

A sparke to set whole worlds a-fire,
Who more they burne, they more desire, 10
And have their being, their waste to see;
And waste still, that they still might bee.

CHORUS

Such are his powers, whom time hath stil'd,
Now swift, now slow, now tame, now wild;
Now hot, now cold, now fierce, now mild. 15
The eldest God, yet still a Child.

[XXXVIII] *An Elegie*

'Tis true, I'm broke! Vowes, Oathes, and all I had
   Of Credit lost. And I am now run madde:
Or doe upon my selfe some desperate ill;
   This sadnesse makes no'approaches, but to kill.
It is a Darknesse hath blockt up my sense, 5
   And drives it in to eat on my offence,

[XXXVIII–XLI] Elegies. Of these four elegies, the second (XXXIX), which also appears in the 1633, 1635, and 1639 editions of John Donne's *Poems* under the title of "The Expostulation," is very likely to be attributed to Donne. Several of Jonson's critics, notably Swinburne and C. H. Herford, have, on purely stylistic grounds (for not a shred of external evidence exists), concluded that XXXVIII, XL, and XLI are also to be attributed to Donne. The editors of this book agree with Percy and Evelyn Simpson (*Ben Jonson*, XI, 66–72) and with J. B. Leishman (*The Monarch of Wit*, 7th ed., 1965, Ch. 3) in attributing the three disputed pieces to Jonson.

Or there to sterve it: helpe O you that may
   Alone lend succours, and this furie stay,
Offended Mistris, you are yet so faire,
   As light breakes from you, that affrights despaire,   10
And fills my powers with perswading joy,
   That you should be too noble to destroy.
There may some face or menace of a storme
   Looke forth, but cannot last in such forme.
If there be nothing worthy you can see   15
   Of Graces, or your mercie here in me
Spare your owne goodnesse yet; and be not great
   In will and power, only to defeat.
God, and the good, know to forgive, and save.
   The ignorant, and fooles, no pittie have.   20
I will not stand to justifie my fault,
   Or lay the excuse upon the Vintners vault;
Or in confessing of the Crime be nice,
   Or goe about to countenance the vice,
By naming in what companie 'twas in,   25
   As I would urge Authoritie for sinne.
No, I will stand arraign'd, and cast, to be
   The Subject of your Grace in pardoning me,
And (Stil'd your mercies Creature) will live more
   Your honour now, then your disgrace before.   30
Thinke it was frailtie, Mistris, thinke me man,
   Thinke that your selfe like heaven forgive me can;
Where weaknesse doth offend, and vertue grieve,
   There greatnesse takes a glorie to relieve.
Thinke that I once was yours, or may be now;   35
   Nothing is vile, that is a part of you:
Errour and folly in me may have crost
   Your just commands; yet those, not I be lost.
I am regenerate now, become the child
   Of your compassion; Parents should be mild: 40
There is no Father that for one demerit,
   Or two, or three, a Sonne will dis-inherit,
That is the last of punishments is meant;
   No man inflicts that paine, till hope be spent:
An ill-affected limbe (what e're it aile)   45

We cut not off, till all Cures else doe faile:
And then with pause; for sever'd once, that's gone,
    Would live his glory that could keepe it on:
Doe not despaire my mending; to distrust
    Before you prove a medicine, is unjust.   50
You may so place me, and in such an ayre
    As not alone the Cure, but scarre be faire.
That is, if still your Favours you apply,
    And not the bounties you ha' done, deny.
Could you demand the gifts you gave, againe!   55
    Why was't? did e're the Cloudes aske back their raine?
The Sunne his heat, and light, the ayre his dew?
    Or winds the Spirit, by which the flower so grew?
That were to wither all, and make a Grave
    Of that wise Nature would a Cradle have!   60
Her order is to cherish, and preserve,
    Consumptions nature to destroy, and sterve.
But to exact againe what once is given,
    Is natures meere obliquitie! as Heaven
Should aske the blood, and spirits he hath infus'd   65
    In man, because man hath the flesh abus'd.
O may your wisdome take example hence,
    God lightens not at mans each fraile offence,
He pardons, slips, goes by a world of ills,
    And then his thunder frights more, then it kills.   70
He cannot angrie be, but all must quake,
    It shakes even him, that all things else doth shake.
And how more faire, and lovely lookes the world
    In a calme skie, then when the heaven is horl'd
About in Cloudes, and wrapt in raging weather   75
    As all with storme, and tempest ran together.
O imitate that sweet Serenitie
    That makes us live, not that which calls to die
In darke, and sullen mornes; doe we not say
    This looketh like an Execution day?   80
And with the vulgar doth it not obtaine
    The name of Cruell weather, storme, and raine?
Be not affected with these markes too much
    Of crueltie, lest they doe make you such.

But view the mildnesse of your Makers state, 85
   As I the penitents here emulate:
He when he sees a sorrow such as this,
   Streight puts off all his Anger, and doth kisse
The contrite Soule, who hath no thought to win
   Upon the hope to have another sin 90
Forgiven him; And in that lyne stand I
   Rather then once displease you more, to die,
To suffer tortures, scorne, and Infamie,
   What Fooles, and all their Parasites can apply;
The wit of Ale, and *Genius* of the Malt 95
   Can pumpe for; or a Libell without salt
Produce; though threatning with a coale, or chalke
   On every wall, and sung where e're I walke.
I number these as being of the Chore
   Of Contumelie, and urge a good man more 100
Then sword, or fire, or what is of the race
   To carry noble danger in the face:
There is not any punishment, or paine,
   A man should flie from, as he would disdaine.
Then Mistresse here, here let your rigour end, 105
   And let your mercie make me asham'd t'offend.
I will no more abuse my vowes to you,
   Then I will studie falshood, to be true.
O, that you could but by dissection see
   How much you are the better part of me; 110
How all my Fibres by your Spirit doe move,
   And that there is no life in me, but love.
You would be then most confident, that tho
   Publike affaires command me now to goe
Out of your eyes, and be awhile away; 115
   Absence, or Distance, shall not breed decay.
Your forme shines here, here fixed in my heart.
   I may dilate my selfe, but not depart.
Others by common Stars their courses run,
   When I see you, then I doe see my Sun, 120
Till then 'tis all but darknesse, that I have;
   Rather then want your light, I wish a grave.

[XXXIX] *An Elegie*

To make the Doubt cleare that no Woman's true,
    Was it my fate to prove it full in you?
Thought I but one had breath'd the purer Ayre,
    And must she needs be false, because she's faire?
It is your beauties Marke, or of your youth,   5
    Or your perfection not to studie truth;
Or thinke you heaven is deafe? or hath no eyes?
    Or those it has, winke at your perjuries?
Are vowes so cheape with women? or the matter
    Whereof they are made, that they are writ in water;   10
And blowne away with wind? or doth their breath
    Both hot and cold at once, threat life and death?
Who could have thought so many accents sweet
    Tun'd to our words, so many sighes should meet
Blowne from our hearts, so many othes and teares   15
    Sprinkled among? All sweeter by our feares,
And the Devine Impression of stolne kisses,
    That seal'd the rest, could now prove emptie blisses?
Did you draw bonds to forfeit? Signe, to breake,
    Or must we read you quite from what you speake,   20
And find the truth out the wrong way? or must
    He first desire you false, would wish you just?
O, I prophane! though most of women be,
    The common Monster, Love shall except thee;
My dearest Love, how ever jealousie,   25
    With Circumstance might urge the contrarie.
Sooner I'le thinke the Sunne would cease to cheare
    The teeming Earth, and that forget to beare;
Sooner that Rivers would run back, or Thames
    With ribs of Ice in June would bind his streames: 30
Or Nature, by whose strength the world indures,
    Would change her course, before you alter yours:
But, O, that trecherous breast, to whom, weake you
    Did trust our counsells, and we both may rue,
Having his falshood found too late! 'twas he   35

That made me cast you Guiltie, and you me.
Whilst he, black wretch, betray'd each simple word
   We spake unto the comming of a third!
Curst may he be that so our love hath slaine,
   And wander wretched on the earth, as *Cain*,   40
Wretched as he, and not deserve least pittie;
   In plaguing him let miserie be wittie.
Let all eyes shun him, and he shun each eye,
   Till he be noysome as his infamie;
May he without remorse deny God thrice,   45
   And not be trusted more on his soules price;
And after all selfe-torment, when he dyes,
   May Wolves teare out his heart, Vultures his eyes,
Swyne eat his Bowels, and his falser Tongue,
   That utter'd all, be to some Raven flung,   50
And let his carrion corse be a longer feast
   To the Kings Dogs, then any other beast.
Now I have curst, let us our love revive;
   In me the flame was never more alive.
I could begin againe to court and praise,   55
   And in that pleasure lengthen the short dayes
Of my lifes lease; like Painters that doe take
   Delight, not in made workes, but whilst they make.
I could renew those times, when first I saw
   Love in your eyes, that gave my tongue the Law   60
To like what you lik'd, and at Masques, or Playes,
   Commend the selfe-same Actors, the same wayes;
Aske how you did? and often with intent
   Of being officious, grow impertinent;
All which were such lost pastimes, as in these   65
   Love was as subtly catch'd as a Disease.
But, being got, it is a treasure, sweet,
   Which to defend, is harder then to get;
And ought not be prophan'd on either part,
   For though 'tis got by chance, 'tis kept by art.   70.

[XL] *An Elegie*

That Love's a bitter sweet, I ne're conceive
   Till the sower Minute comes of taking leave,
And then I taste it. But as men drinke up
   In hast the bottome of a med'cin'd Cup,
And take some sirrup after; so doe I 5
   To put all relish from my memorie
Of parting, drowne it in the hope to meet
   Shortly againe: and make our absence sweet.
This makes me, Mistress, that sometime by stealth
   Under another Name, I take your health; 10
And turne the Ceremonies of those Nights
   I give, or owe my friends, into your Rites,
But ever without blazon, or least shade
   Of vowes so sacred, and in silence made,
For though Love thrive, and may grow up with cheare, 15
   And free societie, hee's borne else-where,
And must be bred, so to conceale his birth,
   As neither wine doe rack it out, or mirth.
Yet should the Lover still be ayrie and light,
   In all his Actions rarified to spright; 20
Not like a *Midas* shut up in himselfe,
   And turning all he toucheth into pelfe,
Keepe in reserv'd in his Dark-lanterne face,
   As if that ex'lent Dulnesse were Loves grace;
No Mistress no, the open merrie Man 25
   Moves like a sprightly River, and yet can
Keepe secret in his Channels what he breedes
   'Bove all your standing waters, choak'd with weedes.
They looke at best like Creame-bowles, and you soone
   Shall find their depth: they're sounded with a spoone. 30
They may say Grace, and for Loves Chaplaines passe;
   But the grave Lover ever was an Asse;
Is fix'd upon one leg, and dares not come
   Out with the other, for hee's still at home;
Like the dull wearied Crane that (come on land) 35
   Doth while he keepes his watch, betray his stand.

  Where he that knowes will like a Lapwing flie
   Farre from the Nest, and so himselfe belie
  To others as he will deserve the Trust
   Due to that one, that doth believe him just.   *40*
  And such your Servant is, who vowes to keepe
   The Jewell of your name, as close as sleepe
  Can lock the Sense up, or the heart a thought,
   And never be by time, or folly brought,
Weaknesse of braine, or any charme of Wine,   *45*
   The sinne of Boast, or other countermine
  (Made to blow up loves secrets) to discover
   That Article, may not become our lover:
  Which in assurance to your brest I tell,
   If I had writ no word, but Deare, farewell.   *50*

[XLI] *An Elegie*

  Since you must goe, and I must bid farewell,
   Heare, Mistress, your departing servant tell
  What it is like: And doe not thinke they can
   Be idle words, though of a parting Man;
  It is as if a night should shade noone-day,   *5*
   Or that the Sun was here, but forc't away;
  And we were left under that Hemisphere,
   Where we must feele it Darke for halfe a yeare.
  What fate is this to change mens dayes and houres,
   To shift their seasons, and destroy their powers!   *10*
  Alas I ha' lost my heat, my blood, my prime,
   Winter is come a Quarter e're his Time,
  My health will leave me; and when you depart,
   How shall I doe sweet Mistris for my heart?
  You would restore it? No, that's worth a feare,   *15*
   As if it were not worthy to be there:
  O, keepe it still; for it had rather be
   Your sacrifice, then here remaine with me.
  And so I spare it. Come what can become
   Of me, I'le softly tread unto my Tombe;   *20*

Or like a Ghost walke silent amongst men,
    Till I may See both it and you agen.

[XLII] *An Elegie*

Let me be what I am, as *Virgil* cold;
    As *Horace* fat; or as *Anacreon* old;
No Poets verses yet did ever move,
    Whose Readers did not thinke he was in love.
Who shall forbid me then in Rithme to bee   5
    As light, and Active as the youngest hee
That from the Muses fountaines doth indorse
    His lynes, and hourely sits the Poets horse?
Put on my Ivy Garland, let me see
    Who frownes, who jealous is, who taxeth me.   10
Fathers, and Husbands, I doe claime a right
    In all that is call'd lovely: take my sight
Sooner then my affection from the faire.
    No face, no hand, proportion, line, or Ayre
Of beautie; but the Muse hath interest in: 15
    There is not worne that lace, purle, knot or pin,
But is the Poëts matter: And he must
    When he is furious love, although not lust.
But then content, your Daughters and your Wives,
    (If they be faire and worth it) have their lives   20
Made longer by our praises. Or, if not,
    Wish, you had fowle ones, and deformed got;
Curst in their Cradles, or there chang'd by Elves,
    So to be sure you doe injoy your selves.
Yet keepe those up in sackcloth too, or lether,   25
    For Silke will draw some sneaking Songster thither.
It is a ryming Age, and Verses swarme
    At every stall; The Cittie Cap's a charme.
But I who live, and have liv'd twentie yeare
    Where I may handle Silke, as free, and neere,   30
As any Mercer; or the whale-bone man
    That quilts those bodies, I have leave to span:

Have eaten with the Beauties, and the wits,
   And braveries of Court, and felt their fits
Of love, and hate: and came so nigh to know   35
   Whether their faces were their owne, or no.
It is not likely I should now looke downe
   Upon a Velvet Petticote, or a Gowne,
Whose like I have knowne the Taylors Wife put on
   To doe her Husbands rites in, e're 'twere gone   40
Home to the Customer: his Letcherie
   Being, the best clothes still to præoccupie.
Put a Coach-mare in Tissue, must I horse
   Her presently? Or leape thy Wife of force,
When by thy sordid bountie she hath on,   45
   A Gowne of that, was the Caparison?
So I might dote upon thy Chaires and Stooles
   That are like cloath'd, must I be of those fooles
Of race accompted, that no passion have
   But when thy Wife (as thou conceiv'st) is brave?   50
Then ope thy wardrobe, thinke me that poore Groome
   That, from the Foot-man, when he was become
An Officer there, did make most solemne love,
   To ev'ry Petticote he brush'd, and Glove
He did lay up, and would adore the shooe,   55
   Or slipper was left off, and kisse it too,
Court every hanging Gowne, and after that,
   Lift up some one, and doe, I tell not what.
Thou didst tell me; and wert o're-joy'd to peepe
   In at a hole, and see these Actions creepe   60
From the poore wretch, which though he play'd in prose,
   He would have done in verse, with any of those
Wrung on the Withers, by Lord Loves despight,
   Had he had the facultie to reade, and write!
Such Songsters there are store of; witnesse he   65
   That chanc'd the lace, laid on a Smock, to see,
And straight-way spent a Sonnet; with that other
   That (in pure Madrigall) unto his Mother
Commended the French-hood, and Scarlet gowne
   The Lady Mayresse pass'd in through the Towne,   70
Unto the Spittle Sermon. O, what strange

    Varietie of Silkes were on th'Exchange!
Or in Moore-fields! this other night, sings one,
    Another answers, 'Lasse those Silkes are none,
In smiling *L'envoye*, as he would deride   75
    Any Comparison had with his Cheap-side.
And vouches both the Pageant, and the Day,
    When not the Shops, but windowes doe display
The Stuffes, the Velvets, Plushes, Fringes, Lace,
    And all the originall riots of the place: 80
Let the poore fooles enjoy their follies, love
    A Goat in Velvet; or some block could move
Under that cover; an old Mid-wives hat!
    Or a Close-stoole so cas'd; or any fat
Bawd, in a Velvet scabberd! I envy   85
    None of their pleasures! nor will aske thee, why
Thou art jealous of thy Wifes, or Daughters Case:
    More then of eithers manners, wit, or face!

[XLIII] *An Execration upon* Vulcan

And why to me this, thou lame Lord of fire,
    What had I done that might call on thine ire?
Or urge thy Greedie flame, thus to devoure
    So many my Yeares-labours in an houre?
I ne're attempted, *Vulcan*, 'gainst thy life;   5
    Nor made least line of love to thy loose Wife;
Or in remembrance of thy afront, and scorne
    With Clownes, and Tradesmen, kept thee clos'd in horne.
'Twas *Jupiter* that hurl'd thee headlong downe,
    And *Mars*, that gave thee a Lanthorne for a Crowne: 10
Was it because thou wert of old denied
    By *Jove* to have *Minerva* for thy Bride,
That since thou tak'st all envious care and paine,
    To ruine any issue of the braine?

[XLIII] *An Execration upon Vulcan*. This poem memorializes the event of a fire in Jonson's quarters which consumed his library and several manuscripts in 1623.

Had I wrote treason there, or heresie,   *15*
  Imposture, witchcraft, charmes, or blasphemie,
I had deserv'd then, thy consuming lookes,
  Perhaps, to have beene burned with my bookes.
But, on thy malice, tell me, didst thou spie
  Any, least loose, or scurrile paper, lie   *20*
Conceal'd, or kept there, that was fit to be,
  By thy owne vote, a sacrifice to thee?
Did I there wound the honours of the Crowne?
  Or taxe the Glories of the Church, and Gowne?
Itch to defame the State? or brand the Times?   *25*
  And my selfe most, in some selfe-boasting Rimes?
If none of these, then why this fire? Or find
  A cause before; or leave me one behind.
Had I compil'd from *Amadis de Gaule,*
  Th'*Esplandians, Arthur's, Palmerins,* and all   *30*
The learned Librarie of *Don Quixote*;
  And so some goodlier monster had begot,
Or spun out Riddles, and weav'd fiftie tomes
  Of *Logogriphes,* and curious *Palindromes,*
Or pomp'd for those hard trifles *Anagrams,*   *35*
  Or *Eteostichs,* or those finer flammes
Of Egges, and Halberds, Cradles, and a Herse,
  A paire of Scisars, and a Combe in verse;
Acrostichs, and *Telestichs,* on jumpe names,
  Thou then hadst had some colour for thy flames,   *40*
On such my serious follies; But, thou'lt say,
  There were some pieces of as base allay,
And as false stampe there; parcels of a Play,
  Fitter to see the fire-light, then the day;
Adulterate moneys, such as might not goe: *45*
  Thou should'st have stay'd, till publike fame said so.
Shee is the Judge, Thou Executioner,
  Or if thou needs would'st trench upon her power,
Thou mightst have yet enjoy'd thy crueltie
  With some more thrift, and more varietie: *50*

---

30 *Esplandian*: the son of Amadis. Anthony Munday's translation of *Amadis de Gaule* was published in 1618/19.

Thou mightst have had me perish, piece, by piece,
    To light Tobacco, or save roasted Geese,
Sindge Capons, or poore Pigges, dropping their eyes;
    Condemn'd me to the Ovens with the pies;
And so, have kept me dying a whole age,   55
    Not ravish'd all hence in a minutes rage.
But that's a marke, wherof thy Rites doe boast,
    To make consumption, ever where thou go'st;
Had I fore-knowne of this thy least desire
    T'have held a Triumph, or a feast of fire,   60
Especially in paper; that, that steame
    Had tickled your large Nosthrill: many a Reame
To redeeme mine, I had sent in; enough,
    Thou should'st have cry'd, and all beene proper stuffe.
The *Talmud*, and the *Alcoran* had come,   65
    With pieces of the *Legend*; The whole summe
Of errant Knight-hood, with the Dames, and Dwarfes;
    The charmed Boates, and the inchanted Wharfes,
The *Tristram's, Lanc'lots, Turpins,* and the *Peer's,*
    All the madde *Rolands,* and sweet *Oliveer's*;   70
To *Merlins* Marvailes, and his *Caballs* losse,
    With the Chimæra of the *Rosie-Crosse,*
Their Seales, their Characters, Hermetique rings,
    Their Jemme of Riches, and bright Stone, that brings
Invisibilitie, and strength, and tongues: 75
    The art of kindling the true Coale, by lungs;
With *Nicholas Pasquill's*, Meddle with your match,
    And the strong lines, that so the time doe catch;
Or Captaine *Pamphlets* horse, and foot; that sallie
    Upon th'Exchange, still out of Popes-head-Alley;   80
The weekly Corrants, with *Pauls* Seale; and all
    Th'admir'd discourses of the Prophet *Ball:*
These, had'st thou pleas'd either to dine, or sup,
    Had made a meale for *Vulcan* to lick up.
But in my Deske, what was there to accite   85
    So ravenous, and vast an appetite?

---

77 *Nicholas Pasquill's*: Nicholas Breton's five pamphlets on Pasquil appeared between 1600 and 1602.

I dare not say a body, but some parts
    There were of search, and mastry in the Arts.
All the old *Venusine*, in *Poëtrie*,
    And lighted by the *Stagerite*, could spie,   90
Was there made English: with the Grammar too,
    To teach some that, their Nurses could not doe,
The puritie of Language; and among
    The rest, my journey into *Scotland* song,
With all th'adventures; Three bookes not afraid   95
    To speake the fate of the *Sicilian* Maid
To our owne Ladyes; and in storie there
    Of our fift *Henry*, eight of his nine yeare;
Wherein was oyle, beside the succour spent,
    Which noble *Carew, Cotton, Selden* lent: 100
And twice-twelve-yeares stor'd up humanitie,
    With humble Gleanings in Divinitie;
After the Fathers, and those wiser Guides
    Whom Faction had not drawne to studie sides.
How in these ruines, *Vulcan*, thou dost lurke,   105
    All soote, and embers! odious, as thy worke!
I now begin to doubt, if ever Grace,
    Or Goddesse, could be patient of thy face.
Thou woo *Minerva*! or to wit aspire!
    'Cause thou canst halt, with us in Arts, and Fire!   110
Sonne of the Wind! for so thy mother gone
    With lust conceiv'd thee; Father thou hadst none:
When thou wert borne, and that thou look'st at best,
    She durst not kisse, but flung thee from her brest.
And so did *Jove*, who ne're meant thee his Cup: 115
    No mar'le the Clownes of *Lemnos* tooke thee up,

---

  89 *the old Venusine*: Horace.
  90 *the Stagerite*: Aristotle.
  91 *the Grammar*: Jonson had written an English grammar. See H. & S., vol. VIII.
  94 *my journey into Scotland*: this work has not survived in any other version.
  96 *Sicilian Maid*: Argenis, the subject of a Latin romance by John Barclay, translated by Jonson at the invitation of King James. It was entered in the Stationers' Register on 2 October 1623.
  100 Richard Carew (1555–1620), Sir Robert Cotton (1571–1631), and John Selden (1574–1654) were all learned friends of Jonson.

For none but Smiths would have made thee a God.
    Some Alchimist there may be yet, or odde
Squire of the Squibs, against the Pageant day,
    May to thy name a *Vulcanale* say;   120
And for it lose his eyes with Gun-powder,
    As th'other may his braines with Quicksilver.
Well-fare the Wise-men yet, on the *Banckside*,
    My friends, the Watermen! They could provide
Against thy furie, when to serve their needs,   125
    They made a *Vulcan* of a sheafe of Reedes,
Whom they durst handle in their holy-day coates,
    And safely trust to dresse, not burne their Boates.
But, O those Reeds! thy meere disdaine of them,
    Made thee beget that cruell Stratagem,   130
(Which, some are pleas'd to stile but thy madde pranck)
    Against the *Globe*, the Glory of the *Banke*.
Which, though it were the Fort of the whole Parish,
    Flanck'd with a Ditch, and forc'd out of a Marish,
I saw with two poore Chambers taken in   135
    And raz'd; e're thought could urge, this might have beene!
See the worlds Ruines! nothing but the piles
    Left! and wit since to cover it with Tiles.
The Brethren, they streight nois'd it out for Newes,
    'Twas verily some Relique of the Stewes;   140
And this a Sparkle of that fire let loose
    That was lock'd up in the *Winchestrian* Goose
Bred on the *Banck*, in time of Poperie,
    When *Venus* there maintain'd the Misterie.
But, others fell, with that conceipt by the eares,   145
    And cry'd, it was a threatning to the beares;
And that accursed ground, the *Parish-Garden*:
    Nay, sigh'd a Sister, 'twas the Nun, *Kate Arden*

119 *Squire of the Squibs*: John Squire's *The Triumphs of Peace* was the Lord Mayor's show performed on 30 October 1620.
132 The Globe, the theater of the King's Men, was burned to the ground in 1613 during a performance of *Henry VIII*. The thatch was ignited by wadding from cannon shots.
142 *Winchestrian Goose*: one afflicted with venereal disease. The stews on the Surrey side of the Thames were located in the liberties under the jurisdiction of the Bishop of Winchester.

Kindled the fire! But, then did one returne,
    No Foole would his owne harvest spoile, or burne!   *150*
If that were so, thou rather would'st advance
    The place, that was thy Wives inheritance.
O no, cry'd all. *Fortune*, for being a whore,
    Scap'd not his Justice any jot the more:
He burnt that Idoll of the *Revels* too: *155*
    Nay, let *White-Hall* with Revels have to doe,
Though but in daunces, it shall know his power;
    There was a Judgement shew'n too in an houre.
Hee is true *Vulcan* still! He did not spare
    Troy, though it were so much his *Venus* care.   *160*
Foole, wilt thou let that in example come?
    Did not she save from thence, to build a *Rome?*
And what hast thou done in these pettie spights,
    More then advanc'd the houses, and their rites?
I will not argue thee, from those of guilt,   *165*
    For they were burnt, but to be better built.
'Tis true, that in thy wish they were destroy'd,
    Which thou hast only vented, not enjoy'd.
So would'st th'have run upon the *Rolls* by stealth,
    And didst invade part of the Common-wealth,   *170*
In those Records, which were all Chronicles gone,
    Will be remembred by *Six Clerkes*, to one.
But, say all sixe, Good Men, what answer yee?
    Lyes there no Writ, out of the *Chancerie*
Against this *Vulcan?* No Injunction?   *175*
    No order? no Decree? Though we be gone
At *Common-Law:* Me thinkes in his despight
    A Court of *Equitie* should doe us right.
But to confine him to the Brew-houses,
    The Glasse-house, Dye-fats, and their Fornaces;   *180*
To live in Sea-coale, and goe forth in smoake;
    Or lest that vapour might the Citie choake,

---

156 *White-Hall*: The Banqueting House, scene of many court masques, was burned down in January, 1618.

169 *Rolls*: a chancery office—Six Clerks' Office—was consumed by fire in December, 1621.

Condemne him to the Brick-kills, or some Hill-
    foot (out in *Sussex*) to an iron Mill,
Or in small Fagots have him blaze about
    Vile Tavernes, and the Drunkards pisse him out;
Or in the *Bell*-Mans Lanthorne, like a spie,
    Burne to a snuffe, and then stinke out, and die:
I could invent a sentence, yet were worse,
    But I'le conclude all in a civill curse.
Pox on your flameship, *Vulcan*; if it be
    To all as fatall as't hath beene to me,
And to *Pauls-Steeple*; which was unto us
    'Bove all your Fire-workes, had at *Ephesus*,
Or *Alexandria*; and though a Divine
    Losse remaines yet, as unrepair'd as mine.
Would you had kept your Forge at *Ætna* still,
    And there made Swords, Bills, Glaves, and Armes your fill;
Maintain'd the trade at *Bilbo*; or else-where;
    Strooke in at *Millan* with the Cutlers there;
Or stay'd but where the Fryar, and you first met,
    Who from the Divels-Arse did Guns beget,
Or fixt in the *Low-Countrey's*, where you might
    On both sides doe your mischiefes with delight;
Blow up, and ruine, myne, and countermyne,
    Make your Petards, and Granats, all your fine
Engines of Murder, and receive the praise
    Of massacring Man-kind so many wayes.
We aske your absence here, we all love peace,
    And pray the fruites thereof, and the increase;
So doth the *King*, and most of the *Kings men*
    That have good places: therefore once agen,
Pox on thee, *Vulcan*, thy *Pandora's* pox,
    And all the Evils that flew out of her box
Light on thee: Or if those plagues will not doo,
    Thy Wives pox on thee, and *Bess Broughtons* too.

---

  192 The steeple of St. Paul's was struck by lightning in June, 1561, and set afire.
  216 *Bess Broughton*: a well-known London courtesan who died of venereal disease.

[XLVII] *An Epistle answering to one that asked to be Sealed of the Tribe of* Ben

Men that are safe, and sure, in all they doe,
   Care not what trials they are put unto;
They meet the fire, the Test, as Martyrs would;
   And though Opinion stampe them not, are gold;
I could say more of such, but that I flie   5
   To speake my selfe out too ambitiously,
And shewing so weake an Act to vulgar eyes,
   Put conscience and my right to compromise.
Let those that meerely talke, and never thinke,
   That live in the wild Anarchie of Drinke   10
Subject to quarrell only; or else such
   As make it their proficiencie, how much
They'ave glutted in, and letcher'd out that weeke,
   That never yet did friend, or friendship seeke
But for a Sealing: let these men protest.   15
   Or th'other on their borders, that will jeast
On all Soules that are absent; even the dead;
   Like flies, or wormes, which mans corrupt parts fed:
That to speake well, thinke it above all sinne,
   Of any Companie but that they are in,   20
Call every night to Supper in these fitts,
   And are received for the Covey of Witts;
That censure all the Towne, and all th'affaires,
   And know whose ignorance is more then theirs;
Let these men have their wayes, and take their times   25
   To vent their Libels, and to issue rimes.
I have no portion in them, nor their deale
   Of newes they get, to strew out the long meale,
I studie other friendships, and more one,
   Then these can ever be; or else wish none.   30
What is't to me whether the French Designe

Be, or be not, to get the *Val-telline?*
Or the States Ships sent forth belike to meet
   Some hopes of *Spaine* in their West-Indian Fleet?
Whether the Dispensation yet be sent,   35
   Or that the Match from *Spaine* was ever meant?
I wish all well, and pray high heaven conspire
   My Princes safetie, and my Kings desire,
But if for honour, we must draw the Sword,
   And force back that, which will not be restor'd,   40
I have a body, yet, that spirit drawes
   To live, or fall, a Carkasse in the cause.
So farre without inquirie what the States,
   Brunsfield, and *Mansfield* doe this yeare, my fates
Shall carry me at Call; and I'le be well,   45
   Though I doe neither heare these newes, nor tell
Of *Spaine* or *France*; or were not prick'd downe one
   Of the late Mysterie of reception,
Although my Fame, to his, not under-heares,
   That guides the Motions, and directs the beares.   50
But that's a blow, by which in time I may
   Lose all my credit with my Christmas Clay,
And animated *Porc'lane* of the Court,
   I, and for this neglect, the courser sort
Of earthen Jarres, there may molest me too: 55
   Well, with mine owne fraile Pitcher, what to doe
I have decreed; keepe it from waves, and presse;
   Lest it be justled, crack'd, made nought, or lesse:
Live to that point I will, for which I am man,
   And dwell as in my Center, as I can,   60
Still looking too, and ever loving heaven;
   With reverence using all the gifts thence given.
'Mongst which, if I have any friendships sent

[XLVII] *An Epistle...Tribe of Ben.* 32 *Val-telline*: a valley in the Alps captured by the French in 1624.

  44 *Mansfield*: Ernest, Count of Mansfield, commanded the army of Frederick, Elector Palatine, son-in-law to James I. Mansfield visited England in 1624.

  50 Scenic designer Inigo Jones and actor Edward Allen were among those sent to Southampton to arrange for the reception of the Spanish Infanta in June, 1623.

    Such as are square, wel-tagde, and permanent,
Not built with Canvasse, paper, and false lights   65
    As are the Glorious Scenes, at the great sights;
And that there be no fev'ry heats, nor colds,
    Oylie Expansions, or shrunke durtie folds,
But all so cleare, and led by reasons flame,
    As but to stumble in her sight were shame.   70
These I will honour, love, embrace, and serve:
    And free it from all question to preserve.
So short you read my Character, and theirs
    I would call mine, to which not many Staires
Are asked to climbe. First give me faith, who know   75
    My selfe a little. I will take you so,
As you have writ your selfe. Now stand, and then
    Sir, you are Sealed of the Tribe of *Ben*.

[LII] *A Poëme sent me by Sir* William Burlase
The Painter to the Poet

To paint thy Worth, if rightly I did know it,
And were but Painter halfe like thee, a Poët;
    Ben, I would show it:
But in this skill, m'unskilfull pen will tire,
Thou, and thy worth, will still be found farre higher;   5
    And I a Lier.
Then, what a Painter's here? or what an eater
Of great attempts! when as his skil's no greater,
    And he a Cheater?
Then what a Poet's here! whom, by Confession   10
Of all with me, to paint without Digression
    There's no Expression.

[LII] *A Poëme ... by Sir William Burlase.* Burlase died in 1629.

My Answer
The Poet to the Painter

Why? though I seeme of a prodigious wast,
I am not so voluminous, and vast,
But there are lines, wherewith I might b'embrac'd.

'Tis true, as my wombe swells, so my backe stoupes,
And the whole lumpe growes round, deform'd, and droupes,   5
But yet the Tun at *Heidelberg* had houpes.

You were not tied, by any Painters Law
To square my Circle, I confesse; but draw
My Superficies: that was all you saw.

Which if in compasse of no Art it came   10
To be described by a *Monogram*,
With one great blot, yo'had form'd me as I am.

But whilst you curious were to have it be
An *Archetipe*, for all the world to see,
You made it a brave piece, but not like me.   15

O, had I now your manner, maistry, might,
Your Power of handling shadow, ayre, and spright,
How I would draw, and take hold and delight.

But, you are he can paint; I can but write:
A Poet hath no more but black and white,   20
Ne knowes he flatt'ring Colours, or false light.

Yet when of friendship I would draw the face,
A letter'd mind, and large heart would place
To all posteritie; I will write *Burlase*.

[LVII] *To Master* John Burges

    Father *John Burges*,
    Necessitie urges
    My wofull crie,
    To Sir *Robert Pie:*
    And that he will venter 5
    To send my *Debentur.*
    Tell him his *Ben*
    Knew the time, when
    He lov'd the Muses;
    Though now he refuses 10
    To take Apprehension
    Of a yeares Pension,
    And more is behind:
    Put him in mind
    Christmas is neere; 15
    And neither good Cheare,
    Mirth, fooling, nor wit,
    Nor any least fit
    Of gambol, or sport
    Will come at the Court, 20
    If there be no money,
    No Plover, or Coney
    Will come to the Table,
    Or Wine to enable
    The Muse, or the Poet, 25
    The Parish will know it.
Nor any quick-warming-pan helpe him to bed,
  If the 'Chequer be emptie, so will be his Head.

[LVII] *To Master John Burges.* Burges was a clerk of the Exchequer (H. & S.).
4 Sir Robert Pie was also connected with the Exchequer.

[LXII] *An Epigram to K.* Charles *for a 100. pounds he sent me in my sicknesse*
1629

   Great CHARLES, among the holy gifts of grace
      Annexed to thy Person, and thy place,
   Tis not enough (thy pietie is such)
      To cure the call'd *Kings Evill* with thy touch;
   But thou wilt yet a Kinglier mastrie trie,   5
      To cure the *Poëts Evill*, Povertie:
   And, in these Cures, do'st so thy selfe enlarge,
      As thou dost cure our *Evill*, at thy charge.
   Nay, and in this, thou show'st to value more
      One *Poët*, then of other folke ten score.   10
   O pietie! so to weigh the poores estates!
   O bountie! so to difference the rates!
   What can the *Poët* wish his *King* may doe,
      But, that he cure the Peoples Evill too?

[LXVI] *An Epigram to the Queene, then lying in*
1630

Haile *Mary*, full of grace, it once was said,
   And by an Angell, to the blessed'st Maid
The Mother of our Lord: why may not I
   (Without prophanenesse) yet, a Poët, cry
Haile *Mary*, full of honours, to my Queene,   5
   The Mother of our Prince? When was there seene
(Except the joy that the first *Mary* brought,
   Whereby the safetie of Man-kind was wrought)
So generall a gladnesse to an Isle

> To make the hearts of a whole Nation smile,   *10*
> As in this Prince? Let it be lawfull, so
> To compare small with great, as still we owe
> Glorie to God. Then, Haile to *Mary*! spring
> Of so much safetie to the Realme, and King.

[LXVII] *An Ode, or Song, by all the Muses*

In celebration of her Majesties birth-day

1630

> 1. CLIO.   Up publike joy, remember
>   This sixteenth of *November*,
>   Some brave un-common way:
>   And though the Parish-steeple
>   Be silent, to the people   *5*
>   Ring thou it Holy-day.
> 2. MEL.   What, though the thriftie Tower
>   And Gunnes there, spare to poure
>   Their noises forth in Thunder:
>   As fearfull to awake   *10*
>   This Citie, or to shake
>   Their guarded gates asunder?
> 3. THAL.   Yet, let our Trumpets sound;
>   And cleave both ayre and ground,
>   With beating of our Drum's: *15*
>   Let every Lyre be strung,
>   Harpe, Lute, Theorbo sprung,
>   With touch of daintie thum's!
> 4. EUT.   That when the Quire is full,
>   The Harmony may pull   *20*
>   The Angels from their Spheares:

[LXVII] *An Ode* ... *1630*. Queen Henrietta Maria, consort of Charles I, was the daughter of Henry IV (*Harry*, l. 26) of France and the sister of Louis XIII (*Lewis*, l. 27).

5. TERP.	And each intelligence May wish it selfe a sense; Whilst it the Dittie heares. Behold the royall *Mary*,	25
	The Daughter of great *Harry!* And Sister to just *Lewis!* Comes in the pompe, and glorie Of all her Brothers storie,	
6. ERAT.	And of her Fathers prowesse! Shee showes so farre above	30
	The fained Queene of Love. This sea-girt Isle upon: As here no *Venus* were; But, that shee raigning here,	35
7. CALLI.	Had got the *Ceston* on! See, see our active *King*	
	Hath taken twice the Ring Upon his pointed Lance: Whilst all the ravish'd rout Doe mingle in a shout,	40
8. URA.	Hay! for the flowre of *France!* This day the Court doth measure	
	Her joy in state, and pleasure; And with a reverend feare, The Revells, and the Play, Summe up this crowned day,	45
9. POLY.	Her two and twenti'th yeare! Sweet! happy *Mary!* All	
	The People her doe call! And this the wombe divine, So fruitfull, and so faire, Hath brought the Land an Heire! And *Charles* a *Caroline!*	50

36 *Ceston*: a girdle or belt.

[LXX] *To the immortall memorie,
and friendship of that noble paire,
Sir* Lucius Cary, *and Sir* H. Morison

THE TURNE

Brave Infant of *Saguntum*, cleare
Thy comming forth in that great yeare,
When the Prodigious *Hannibal* did crowne
His rage, with razing your immortall Towne.
Thou, looking then about, 5
E're thou wert halfe got out,
Wise child, did'st hastily returne,
And mad'st thy Mothers wombe thine urne.
How summ'd a circle didst thou leave man-kind
Of deepest lore, could we the Center find! 10

THE COUNTER-TURNE

Did wiser Nature draw thee back,
From out the horrour of that sack,
Where shame, faith, honour, and regard of right
Lay trampled on; the deeds of death, and night,
Urg'd, hurried forth, and horld 15
Upon th'affrighted world:
Sword, fire, and famine, with fell fury met;
And all on utmost ruine set;
As, could they but lifes miseries fore-see,
No doubt all Infants would returne like thee? 20

[LXX] *To the immortall memorie...Sir H. Morison.* The poem celebrates the friendship of Sir Lucius Cary, second Viscount Falkland (d. 1643), a man of great learning who became Secretary of State in 1642, and Sir Henry Morison, who died (l. 45) at Carmarthon in 1629. Morison's sister married Falkland in 1630.

THE STAND

For, what is life, if measur'd by the space,
Not by the act?
Or masked man, if valu'd by his face,
Above his fact?
Here's one out-liv'd his Peeres,   25
And told forth fourescore yeares;
He vexed time, and busied the whole State;
Troubled both foes, and friends;
But ever to no ends:
What did this Stirrer, but die late?   30
How well at twentie had he falne, or stood!
For three of his foure-score, he did no good.

THE TURNE

Hee entred well, by vertuous parts,
Got up and thriv'd with honest arts:
He purchas'd friends, and fame, and honours then,   35
And had his noble name advanc'd with men:
But weary of that flight,
Hee stoop'd in all mens sight
To sordid flatteries, acts of strife,
And sunke in that dead sea of life   40
So deep, as he did then death's waters sup;
But that the Corke of Title boy'd him up.

THE COUNTER-TURNE

Alas, but *Morison* fell young:
Hee never fell, thou fall'st, my tongue.
Hee stood, a Souldier to the last right end,   45
A perfect Patriot, and a noble friend,
But most a vertuous Sonne.
All Offices were done
By him, so ample, full, and round,

In weight, in measure, number, sound,
As though his age imperfect might appeare,
His life was of Humanitie the Spheare.

THE STAND

Goe now, and tell out dayes summ'd up with feares,
And make them yeares;
Produce thy masse of miseries on the Stage,
To swell thine age;
Repeat of things a throng,
To shew thou hast beene long,
Not liv'd; for life doth her great actions spell,
By what was done and wrought
In season, and so brought
To light: her measures are, how well
Each syllab'e answer'd, and was form'd, how faire;
These make the lines of life, and that's her ayre.

THE TURNE

It is not growing like a tree
In bulke, doth make man better bee;
Or standing long an Oake, three hundred yeare,
To fall a logge, at last, dry, bald, and seare:
A Lillie of a Day,
Is fairer farre, in May,
Although it fall, and die that night;
It was the Plant, and flowre of light.
In small proportions, we just beauties see:
And in short measures, life may perfect bee.

THE COUNTER-TURNE

Call, noble *Lucius*, then for Wine,
And let thy lookes with gladnesse shine:
Accept this garland, plant it on thy head,
And thinke, nay know, thy *Morison's* not dead.
Hee leap'd the present age,

Possest with holy rage,   80
To see that bright eternall Day:
Of which we *Priests*, and *Poëts* say
Such truths, as we expect for happy men,
And there he lives with memorie; and *Ben*

THE STAND

Jonson, who sung this of him, e're he went   85
Himselfe to rest,
Or taste a part of that full joy he meant
To have exprest,
In this bright *Asterisme:*
Where it were friendships schisme,   90
(Were not his *Lucius* long with us to tarry)
To separate these twi-
Lights, the *Dioscuri;*
And keepe the one halfe from his *Harry*.
But fate doth so alternate the designe,   95
Whilst that in heav'n, this light on earth must shine.

THE TURNE

And shine as you exalted are;
Two names of friendship, but one Starre:
Of hearts the union. And those not by chance
Made, or indentur'd, or leas'd out t'advance   100
The profits for a time.
No pleasures vaine did chime,
Of rimes, or ryots, at your feasts,
Orgies of drinke, or fain'd protests:
But simple love of greatnesse, and of good;   105
That knits brave minds, and manners, more then blood.

THE COUNTER-TURNE

This made you first to know the Why
You lik'd, then after, to apply
That liking; and approach so one the tother,

Till either grew a portion of the other: 110
Each stiled by his end,
The Copie of his friend.
You liv'd to be the great surnames,
And titles, by which all made claimes
Unto the Vertue. Nothing perfect done, 115
But as a CARY, or a MORISON.

THE STAND

And such a force the faire example had,
As they that saw
The good, and durst not practise it, were glad
That such a Law 120
Was left yet to Man-kind;
Where they might read, and find
Friendship, indeed, was written, not in words:
And with the heart, not pen,
Of two so early men, 125
Whose lines her rowles were, and records.
Who, e're the first downe bloomed on the chin,
Had sow'd these fruits, and got the harvest in.

[LXXIX]

New yeares, expect *new* gifts: Sister, your Harpe,
   Lute, Lyre, Theorbo, all are call'd to day.
Your change of Notes, the *flat*, the *meane*, the *sharpe*,
   To shew the rites, and t'usher forth the way
Of the *New Yeare*, in a new silken warpe, 5
   To fit the softnesse of our *Yeares*-gift: When
   We sing the best of *Monarchs, Masters, Men;*
For, had we here said lesse, we had sung nothing then.

A New-yeares-Gift sung to King CHARLES 1635

Rector Chori.	To day old *Janus* opens the new yeare,
	And shuts the old. Haste, haste, all loyall Swaines,
	That know the times, and seasons when t'appeare,
	And offer your just service on these plaines;
	Best Kings expect first-fruits of your glad gaines. 5
	1. PAN is the great Preserver of our bounds.
	2. To him we owe all profits of our grounds.
	3. Our milke. 4. Our fells. 5. Our fleeces. 6. and first Lambs.
	7. Our teeming Ewes, 8. and lustie-mounting Rammes.
	9. See where he walkes with MIRA by his side. 10
Chor.	Sound, sound his praises loud, and with his, hers divide.
Shep.	Of PAN wee sing, the best of Hunters, PAN,
	That drives the Hart to seeke unused wayes,
	And in the chase, more then SYLVANUS can,
Chor.	Heare, ô you Groves, and, Hills, resound his praise. 15
Nym.	Of brightest MIRA, doe we raise our Song,
	Sister of PAN, and glory of the Spring:
	Who walkes on Earth as *May* still went along,
Chor.	Rivers, and Vallies, *Eccho* what wee sing.
Shep.	Of PAN wee sing, the Chief of Leaders, PAN, 20
	That leades our flocks and us, and calls both forth
	To better Pastures then great PALES can:
Chor.	Heare, O you Groves, and, Hills, resound his worth.
Nymp.	Of brightest MIRA, is our Song; the grace
	Of all that Nature, yet, to life did bring; 25
	And were shee lost, could best supply her place,

[LXXIX] *A New-yeares-Gift . . . 1635.* Jonson returned to his 1620 masque, *Pan's Anniversary,* for some material adapted here. The text of the last two stanzas (ll. 38–58) prefaced by an adaptation of ll. 1–2 were apparently the basis of a setting by Nicholas Lanier, for so the text appears in Bodleian MS. Ashmole 36–37, f. 166, where it is headed "A pastorall Song, to the King on New-yeares day: An° dmi 1633."

Chor.   Rivers, and Valleys, *Eccho* what wee sing.

  1. Where ere they tread th'enamour'd ground,
     The Fairest flowers are always found;
  2. As if the beauties of the yeare,   *30*
     Still waited on 'hem where they were.
  1. Hee is the Father of our peace;
  2. Shee, to the Crowne, hath brought encrease.
  1. Wee know no other power then his,
     PAN only our great Shep'ard is,   *35*
Chorus. Our great, our good. Where one's so drest
     In truth of colours, both are best.

Haste, haste you hither, all you gentler Swaines,
That have a Flock, or Herd, upon these plaines;
This is the great Preserver of our bounds,   *40*
To whom you owe all duties of your grounds;
Your Milkes, your Fells, your Fleeces, and first Lambes,
Your teeming Ewes, as well as mounting Rammes.
Whose praises let's report unto the Woods,
That they may take it eccho'd by the Floods.   *45*
  'Tis hee, 'tis hee, in singing hee,
  And hunting, PAN, exceedeth thee.
  Hee gives all plentie, and encrease,
  Hee is the author of our peace.

Where e're he goes upon the ground,   *50*
The better grasse, and flowers are found.
To sweeter Pastures lead hee can,
Then ever PALES could, or PAN;
Hee drives diseases from our Folds,
The theefe from spoyle, his presence holds.   *55*
PAN knowes no other power then his,
This only the great Shep'ard is.
    'Tis hee, 'tis hee, etc.

[LXXXIV] EUPHEME; OR, THE FAIRE FAME

Left to Posteritie
Of that truly-noble Lady, the Lady
VENETIA DIGBY, late Wife of Sir
KENELME DIGBY, Knight: A Gentleman
absolute in all Numbers;
Consisting of these
Ten Pieces

The Dedication of her CRADLE.
The Song of her DESCENT.
The Picture of her BODY.
Her MIND.
Her being chosen a MUSE.
Her faire OFFICES.
Her happie MATCH.
Her hopefull ISSUE.
Her ΑΠΟΘΕΩΣΙΣ, or Relation to the Saints.
Her Inscription, or CROWNE.

Vivam amare voluptas, defunctam Religio.
Stat.

[LXXXIV] *Eupheme; or, The Faire Fame.* A group of nine poems (some incomplete; some lost) celebrating the virtues of Lady Venetia Digby, who in spite of parental opposition became the wife of Jonson's friend Sir Kenelm Digby. The poems were written in her lifetime. At her death in 1633, Jonson sent them to her husband, who eventually became editor of Jonson's second folio of 1640/41. The epigraph, from Statius' *Silvae*, may thus be translated: "The Voluptuous is a lover of life; the Religious, of death."

1. *The Dedication of her CRADLE*

Faire FAME, who art ordain'd to crowne
With ever-greene, and great renowne,
Their Heads, that ENVY would hold downe
    With her, in shade

Of Death, and Darknesse; and deprive
Their names of being kept alive,
By THEE, and CONSCIENCE, both who thrive
    By the just trade

Of Goodnesse still; Vouchsafe to take
This CRADLE, and for Goodnesse sake,
A dedicated Ensigne make
    Thereof, to TIME.

That all Posteritie, as wee,
Who read what the CREPUNDIA bee,
May something by that twilight see
    'Bove rattling Rime.

For, though that Rattles, Timbrels, Toyes,
Take little Infants with their noyse,
As prop'rest gifts, to Girles, and Boyes,
    Of light expence;

Their Corrals, Whistles, and prime Coates,
Their painted Maskes, their paper Boates,
With Sayles of silke, as the first notes
    Surprize their sense:

Yet, here are no such Trifles brought,
No cobweb Call's; no Surcoates wrought
With Gold, or Claspes, which might be bought
    On every Stall.

1. *The Dedication of her Cradle.* 14 *Crepundia*: a child's toy, or rattle.
26 *Call's*: cauls, coverings of network for the head worn by women.

But, here's a Song of her DESCENT;
And Call to the high Parliament   30
Of Heaven; where SERAPHIM take tent
    Of ord'ring all.

This, utter'd by an antient BARD,
Who claimes (of reverence) to be heard,
As comming with his Harpe, prepar'd   35
    To chant her 'gree,

Is sung: as als'her getting up
By JACOBS Ladder, to the top
Of that eternall Port kept ope'
    For such as SHEE.   40

2. *The Song of her DESCENT*

I sing the just, and uncontrol'd Descent
  Of Dame VENETIA DIGBY, styl'd The Faire:
For Mind, and Body, the most excellent
  That ever Nature, or the later Ayre
Gave two such Houses as NORTHUMBERLAND,   5
  And STANLEY, to the which shee was Co-heire.
Speake it, you bold PENATES, you that stand
  At either Stemme, and know the veines of good
Run from your rootes; Tell, testifie the grand
  Meeting of Graces, that so swell'd the flood   10
Of vertues in her, as, in short, shee grew
  The wonder of her Sexe, and of your Blood.
And tell thou, ALDE-LEGH, None can tell more true
  Thy Neeces line, then thou that gav'st thy Name
Into the Kindred, whence thy *Adam* drew   15
  Meschines honour with the *Cestrian* fame
Of the first *Lupus*, to the Familie
  By *Ranulph* ─────────
[The rest of this Song is lost.]

2. *The Song of her Descent.* 1 *uncontrol'd*: undisputed.

3. *The Picture of the BODY*

Sitting, and ready to be drawne,
   What makes these Velvets, Silkes, and Lawne,
   Embroderies, Feathers, Fringes, Lace,
   Where every lim takes like a face?

Send these suspected helpes, to aide
   Some Forme defective, or decay'd;
   This beautie without falshood fayre,
   Needs nought to cloath it but the ayre.

Yet something, to the Painters view,
   Were fitly interpos'd; so new:
   Hee shall, if he can understand,
   Worke with my fancie, his owne hand.

Draw first a Cloud: all save her neck;
   And, out of that, make Day to breake;
   Till, like her face, it doe appeare,
   And Men may thinke, all light rose there.

Then let the beames of that, disperse
   The Cloud, and show the Universe;
   But at such distance, as the eye
   May rather yet adore, then spy.

The Heaven design'd, draw next a Spring,
   With all that Youth, or it can bring:
   Foure Rivers branching forth like Seas,
   And Paradise confining these.

Last, draw the circles of this Globe,
   And let there be a starry Robe
   Of Constellations 'bout her horld;
   And thou hast painted beauties world.

But, Painter, see thou doe not sell
   A Copie of this peece; nor tell 30
   Whose 'tis: but if it favour find,
   Next sitting we will draw her mind.

4. *The* MIND

Painter, yo'are come, but may be gone,
   Now I have better thought thereon,
   This worke I can performe alone;
   And give you reasons more then one.

Not, that your Art I doe refuse: 5
   But here I may no colours use.
   Beside, your hand will never hit,
   To draw a thing that cannot sit.

You could make shift to paint an Eye,
   An Eagle towring in the skye, 10
   The Sunne, a Sea, or soundlesse Pit;
   But these are like a Mind, not it.

No, to expresse Mind to sense,
   Would aske a Heavens Intelligence;
   Since nothing can report that flame, 15
   But what's of kinne to whence it came.

Sweet Mind, then speake your selfe, and say,
   As you goe on, by what brave way
   Our Sense you doe with knowledge fill,
   And yet remaine our wonder still. 20

I call you *Muse*; now make it true:
   Hence-forth may every line be you;
   That all may say, that see the frame,
   This is no Picture, but the same.

A Mind so pure, so perfect fine, 25
   As 'tis not radiant, but divine:
   And so disdaining any tryer;
   'Tis got where it can try the fire.

There, high exalted in the Spheare,
   As it another Nature were,   30
   It moveth all; and makes a flight
   As circular, as infinite.

Whose Notions when it will expresse
   In speech; it is with that excesse
   Of grace, and Musique to the eare,   35
   As what it spoke, it planted there.

The Voyce so sweet, the words so faire,
   As some soft chime had stroak'd the ayre;
   And, though the sound were parted thence,
   Still left an Eccho in the sense.   40

But, that a Mind so rapt, so high,
   So swift, so pure, should yet apply
   It selfe to us, and come so nigh
   Earths grossnesse; There's the how, and why.

Is it because it sees us dull,   45
   And stuck in clay here, it would pull
   Us forth, by some Celestiall slight
   Up to her owne sublimed hight?

Or hath she here, upon the ground,
   Some Paradise, or Palace found   50
   In all the bounds of beautie fit
   For her t'inhabit? There is it.

Thrice happy house, that hast receipt
   For this so loftie forme, so streight,
   So polisht, perfect, round, and even,   55
   As it slid moulded off from Heaven.

Not swelling like the Ocean proud,
   But stooping gently, as a Cloud,
   As smooth as Oyle pour'd forth, and calme
   As showers; and sweet as drops of Balme.   60

Smooth, soft, and sweet, in all a floud
   Where it may run to any good;
   And where it stayes, it there becomes
   A nest of odorous spice, and gummes.

> In action, winged as the wind,   65
> > In rest, like spirits left behind
> > Upon a banke, or field of flowers,
> > Begotten by that wind, and showers.
>
> In thee, faire Mansion, let it rest,
> > Yet know, with what thou art possest,   70
> > Thou entertaining in thy brest,
> > But such a Mind, mak'st God thy Guest.

A whole quaternion in the middest of this Poem is lost, containing entirely the three next pieces of it, and all of the fourth (which in the order of the whole, is the eighth) excepting the very end: which at the top of the next quaternion goeth on thus:

But, for you (growing Gentlemen) the happy branches of two so illustrious Houses as these, where from your honour'd Mother is in both lines descended; let me leave you this last Legacie of Counsell; which so soone as you arrive at yeares of mature Understanding, open you (Sir) that are the eldest, and read it to your Brethren, for it will concerne you all alike. Vowed by a faithfull Servant, and Client of your Familie, with his latest breath expiring it.

B.J.

8. *To Kenelme, John, George*

> Boast not these Titles of your Ancestors;
> > (Brave Youths) th'are their possessions, none of yours:
> > When your owne Vertues, equall'd have their Names,
> > 'Twill be but faire, to leane upon their *Fames*;
> > For they are strong Supporters: But, till then,   5
> > The greatest are but growing Gentlemen.
> > It is a wretched thing to trust to reedes;
> > Which all men doe, that urge not their owne deeds
> > Up to their Ancestors; the rivers side,
> > By which yo'are planted, shew's your fruit shall bide: 10
> > Hang all your roomes, with one large Pedigree:
> > 'Tis Vertue alone, is true Nobilitie.
> > Which Vertue from your Father, ripe, will fall;
> > Study illustrious Him, and you have all.

9. Elegie on my Muse

The truly honoured Lady, the Lady VENETIA DIGBY;
who living, gave me leave to call her so.
Being
Her ΑΠΟΘΕΩΣΙΣ, or Relation to the Saints.
Sera quidem tanto struitur medicina dolori.

'Twere time that I dy'd too, now shee is dead,
   Who was my *Muse*, and life of all I sey'd.
The Spirit that I wrote with, and conceiv'd,
   All that was good, or great in me she weav'd,
And set it forth; the rest were Cobwebs fine,   5
   Spun out in name of some of the old *Nine*!
To hang a window, or make darke the roome,
   Till swept away, th'were cancell'd with a broome!
Nothing, that could remaine, or yet can stirre
   A sorrow in me, fit to wait to her!   10
O! had I seene her laid out a faire Corse,
   By *Death*, on Earth, I should have had remorse
On *Nature*, for her: who did let her lie,
   And saw that portion of herselfe to die.
Sleepie, or stupid Nature, couldst thou part   15
   With such a *Raritie*, and not rowse *Art*
With all her aydes, to save her from the seize
   Of *Vulture death*, and those relentlesse cleies?
Thou wouldst have lost the *Phœnix*, had the kind
   Beene trusted to thee: not to 't selfe assign'd.   20
Looke on thy sloth, and give thy selfe undone,
   (For so thou art with me) now shee is gone.
My wounded mind cannot sustaine this stroke,
   It rages, runs, flies, stands, and would provoke
The world to ruine with it; in her *Fall*,   25
   I summe up mine owne breaking, and wish all.

---

9. *Elegy on my Muse.* The Latin epigraph may thus be translated: "Late indeed is the remedy compounded for such grief."

Thou hast no more blowes, *Fate*, to drive at one:
   What's left a *Poët*, when his *Muse* is gone?
Sure, I am dead, and know it not! I feele
   Nothing I doe; but, like a heavie wheele,   30
Am turned with an others powers. My Passion
   Whoorles me about, and to blaspheme in fashion!
I murmure against *God*, for having ta'en
   Her blessed Soule, hence, forth this valley vane
Of teares, and dungeon of calamitie!   35
   I envie it the Angels amitie!
The joy of Saints! the *Crowne* for which it lives,
   The glorie, and gaine of rest, which the place gives!
Dare I prophane, so irreligious bee
   To 'greet, or grieve her soft Euthanasee!   40
So sweetly taken to the Court of blisse,
   As spirits had stolne her *Spirit*, in a kisse,
From off her pillow, and deluded bed;
   And left her lovely body unthought dead!
Indeed, she is not dead! but laid to sleepe   45
   In earth, till the last *Trumpe* awake the *Sheepe*
And *Goates* together, whither they must come
   To heare their Judge, and his eternall doome;
To have that finall retribution,
   Expected with the fleshes restitution.   50
For, as there are three *Natures, Schoolemen* call
   One *corporall*, only; th'other *spirituall*,
Like single; so, there is a third, commixt,
   Of *Body* and *Spirit* together, plac'd betwixt
Those other two; which must be judg'd, or crown'd: 55
   This as it guilty is, or guiltlesse found,
Must come to take a sentence, by the sense
   Of that great Evidence, the *Conscience*!
Who will be there, against that day prepar'd,
   T'accuse, or quit all *Parties* to be heard!   60
O *Day* of joy, and suretie to the just!
   Who in that feast of *Ressurrection* trust!
That great eternall *Holy-day* of rest,
   To Body, and Soule! where *Love* is all the guest!

And the whole *Banquet* is full sight of *God!* 65
   Of joy the *Circle*, and sole *Period!*
All other gladnesse, with the thought is barr'd;
   Hope, hath her end! and *Faith* hath her reward!
This being thus: why should my tongue, or pen
   Presume to interpell that fulnesse, when 70
Nothing can more adorne it, then the seat
   That she is in, or, make it more compleat?
Better be dumbe, then superstitious!
   Who violates the God-head, is most vitious
Against the Nature he would worship. *Hee* 75
   Will honour'd be in all simplicitie!
Have all his actions wondred at, and view'd
   With silence, and amazement! not with rude,
Dull, and prophane, weake, and imperfect eyes,
   Have busie search made in his mysteries! 80
Hee knowes, what worke h'hath done, to call this *Guest*,
   Out of her noble body, to this *Feast*:
And give her place, according to her blood
   Amongst her *Peeres*, those Princes of all good!
Saints, Martyrs, Prophets, with those *Hierarchies,* 85
   Angels, Arch-angels, Principalities,
The *Dominations, Vertues,* and the *Powers,*
   The *Thrones,* the *Cherube,* and *Seraphick* bowers,
That, planted round, there sing before the *Lamb,*
   A new Song to his praise, and great *I AM:* 90
And she doth know, out of the shade of Death,
   What 'tis t'enjoy, an everlasting breath!
To have her captiv'd spirit freed from flesh,
   And on her Innocence, a garment fresh
And white, as that, put on: and in her hand 95
   With boughs of Palme, a crowned *Victrice* stand!
And will you, worthy Sonne, Sir, knowing this,
   Put black, and mourning on? and say you misse
A *Wife*, a *Friend*, a *Lady*, or a *Love*;
   Whom her *Redeemer*, honour'd hath above 100
Her fellowes, with the oyle of gladnesse, bright
   In heav'n *Empire*, and with a robe of light?
Thither, you hope to come; and there to find

That pure, that pretious, and exalted mind
You once enjoy'd: A short space severs yee,   *105*
  Compar'd unto that long eternitie,
That shall re-joyne yee. Was she, then, so deare,
  When shee departed? you will meet her there,
Much more desir'd, and dearer then before,
  By all the wealth of blessings, and the store   *110*
Accumulated on her, by the *Lord*
  Of life, and light, the Sonne of *God*, the *Word!*
There, all the happy soules, that ever were,
  Shall meet with gladnesse in one *Theatre*;
And each shall know, there, one anothers face: *115*
  By beatifick vertue of the Place.
There shall the Brother, with the Sister walke,
  And Sons, and Daughters, with their Parents talke;
But all of *God*; They still shall have to say,
  But make him *All in All*, their *Theme*, that *Day:*   *120*
That happy *Day*, that never shall see night!
  Where *Hee* will be, all Beautie to the *Sight*;
Wine, or delicious fruits, unto the *Taste;*
  A Musique in the *Eares*, will ever last;
Unto the *Sent*, a Spicerie, or Balme;   *125*
  And to the *Touch*, a Flower, like soft as Palme.
Hee will all Glory, all Perfection be,
  God, in the *Union*, and the *Trinitie!*
That holy, great, and glorious Mysterie,
  Will there revealed be in Majestie!   *130*
By light, and comfort of spirituall *Grace*;
  The vision of our *Saviour*, face, to face
In his humanitie! To heare him preach
  The price of our *Redemption*, and to teach
Through his inherent righteousnesse, in death,   *135*
  The safetie of our soules, and forfeit breath!
What fulnesse of beatitude is here?
  What love with mercy mixed doth appeare?
To style us Friends, who were, by Nature, Foes?
  Adopt us Heires, by grace, who were of those   *140*
Had lost our selves? and prodigally spent
  Our native portions, and possessed rent;

Yet have all debts forgiven us, and advance
  B'imputed right to an inheritance
In his eternall Kingdome, where we sit   145
  Equall with Angels, and Co-heires of it.
Nor dare we under blasphemy conceive
  He that shall be our supreme Judge, should leave
Himselfe so un-inform'd of his elect,
  Who knowes the hearts of all, and can dissect   150
The smallest Fibre of our flesh; he can
  Find all our Atomes from a point t'a span!
Our closest Creekes, and Corners, and can trace
  Each line, as it were graphick, in the face.
And best he knew her noble Character,   155
  For 'twas himselfe who form'd, and gave it her.
And to that forme, lent two such veines of blood
  As nature could not more increase the flood
Of title in her! All Nobilitie
  (But pride, that schisme of incivilitie)   160
She had, and it became her! she was fit
  T'have knowne no envy, but by suffring it!
She had a mind as calme, as she was faire;
  Not tost or troubled with light Lady-aire;
But, kept an even gate, as some streight tree   165
  Mov'd by the wind, so comely moved she.
And by the awfull manage of her Eye
  She swaid all bus'nesse in the Familie!
To one she said, Doe this, he did it; So
  To another, Move; he went; To a third, Go,   170
He run; and all did strive with diligence
  T'obey, and serve her sweet Commandements,
She was in one, a many parts of life;
  A tender *Mother*, a discreeter *Wife*,
A solemne *Mistresse*, and so good a *Friend*,   175
  So charitable, to religious end,
In all her petite actions, so devote,
  As her whole life was now become one note
Of Pietie, and private holinesse.
  She spent more time in teares her selfe to dresse   180

For her devotions, and those sad essayes
   Of sorrow, then all pompe of gaudy daies:
And came forth ever cheered, with the rod
   Of divine Comfort, when sh'had talk'd with *God*.
Her broken sighes did never misse whole sense:
   Nor can the bruised heart want eloquence:
For, Prayer is the Incense most perfumes
   The holy Altars, when it least presumes.
And hers were all Humilitie! they beat
   The doore of *Grace*, and found the *Mercy-Seat*.
In frequent speaking by the pious Psalmes
   Her solemne houres she spent, or giving Almes,
Or doing other deeds of Charitie,
   To cloath the naked, feed the hungry. Shee
Would sit in an Infirmery, whole dayes
   Poring, as on a Map, to find the wayes
To that eternall Rest, where now sh'hath place
   By sure Election, and predestin'd grace!
Shee saw her Saviour, by an early light;
   Incarnate in the Manger, shining bright
On all the world! Shee saw him on the Crosse
   Suffring, and dying to redeeme our losse!
Shee saw him rise, triumphing over Death
   To justifie; and quicken us in breath!
Shee saw him too, in glory to ascend
   For his designed worke the perfect end
Of raising, judging, and rewarding all
   The kind of Man, on whom his doome should fall!
All this by *Faith* she saw, and fram'd a Plea,
   In manner of a daily *Apostrophe*,
To him should be her Judge, true *God*, true *Man*,
   Jesus, the onely gotten *Christ*! who can
As being Redeemer, and Repairer too
   (Of lapsed Nature) best know what to doe,
In that great Act of judgement: which the *Father*
   Hath given wholly to the Sonne (the rather
As being the Sonne of *Man*) to shew his *Power*,
   His *Wisdome*, and his *Justice*, in that houre,

> The last of houres, and shutter up of all;
>   Where first his *Power* will appeare, by call
> Of all are dead to life! His *Wisdome* show
>   In the discerning of each conscience, so!
> And most his *Justice*, in the fitting parts,
>   And giving dues to all Mankinds deserts!
> In this sweet *Extasie*, she was rapt hence.
>   Who reades, will pardon my Intelligence,
> That thus have ventur'd these true straines upon;
>   To publish her a *Saint*. My *Muse* is gone.
>
>
>
> *In pietatis memoriam*
> *quam præstas*
> Venetiæ *tuæ illustrissim:*
> *Marit: dign:* Digbeie
> *Hanc* ΑΠΟΘΕΩΣΙΝ, *tibi, tuisque sacro.*
>
>
>
> The Tenth, being her Inscription, or CROWNE, is lost.

---

229 ff. The Latin may thus be rendered: "In memory of the piety which you maintain for your most illustrious and worthy consort, Venetia Digby, I tender to you and to your honor this apotheosis."

MISCELLANY

Including Songs from the Plays and Masques

To the memory of my beloved,
The Author
MR. WILLIAM SHAKESPEARE:
And
what he hath left us

To draw no envy (*Shakespeare*) on thy name,
   Am I thus ample to thy Booke, and Fame:
While I confesse thy writings to be such,
   As neither *Man*, nor *Muse*, can praise too much.
'Tis true, and all mens suffrage. But these wayes   5
   Were not the paths I meant unto thy praise:
For seeliest Ignorance on these may light,
   Which, when it sounds at best, but eccho's right;
Or blinde Affection, which doth ne're advance
   The truth, but gropes, and urgeth all by chance;   10
Or crafty Malice, might pretend this praise,
   And thinke to ruine, where it seem'd to raise.
These are, as some infamous Baud, or Whore,
   Should praise a Matron. What could hurt her more?

To the memory of... Mr. William Shakespeare. Text from *Mr. William Shakespeares Comedies, Histories, & Tragedies* (First Folio, 1623).

But thou art proofe against them, and indeed
    Above th'ill fortune of them, or the need.
I, therefore will begin. Soule of the Age!
    The applause! delight! the wonder of our Stage!
My *Shakespeare*, rise; I will not lodge thee by
    Chaucer, or *Spenser*, or bid *Beaumont* lye
A little further, to make thee a roome:
    Thou art a Moniment, without a tombe,
And art alive still, while thy Booke doth live,
    And we have wits to read, and praise to give.
That I not mixe thee so, my braine excuses;
    I meane with great, but disproportion'd *Muses*:
For, if I thought my Judgement were of yeeres,
    I should commit thee surely with thy peeres,
And tell, how farre thou didst our *Lily* out-shine,
    Or sporting *Kid*, or *Marlowes* mighty line.
And though thou hadst small *Latine*, and lesse *Greeke*,
    From thence to honour thee, I would not seeke
For names; but call forth thund'ring *Æschilus*,
    Euripides, and *Sophocles* to us,
Paccuvius, *Accius*, him of *Cordova* dead,
    To life againe, to heare thy Buskin tread,
And shake a Stage: Or, when thy Sockes were on,
    Leave thee alone, for the comparison
Of all, that insolent *Greece*, or haughtie *Rome*
    Sent forth, or since did from their ashes come.
Triúmph, my *Britaine*, thou hast one to showe,
    To whom all Scenes of *Europe* homage owe.
He was not of an age, but for all time!
    And all the *Muses* still were in their prime,
When like *Apollo* he came forth to warme
    Our eares, or like a *Mercury* to charme!
Nature her selfe was proud of his designes,

---

31 *small Latine...Greeke*: the phrase may be traced to A. S. Minturno's *L'arte Poetica*; see A. H. Gilbert, *Literary Criticism: Plato to Dryden* (Detroit, 1962), pp. 282ff.

35 *Paccuvius, Accius*: Latin tragic poets of the second century B.C. whose tragedies were adapted from their greater Greek counterparts. A few hundred lines only of the dramatic writing of each are extant. Horace speaks of both; *him of Cordova*: the dramatist Seneca.

And joy'd to weare the dressing of his lines!
Which were so richly spun, and woven so fit,
  As, since, she will vouchsafe no other Wit.
The merry *Greeke*, tart *Aristophanes*,
  Neat *Terence*, witty *Plautus*, now not please;
But antiquated, and deserted lye
  As they were not of Natures family.
Yet must I not give Nature all: Thy Art,
  My gentle *Shakespeare*, must enjoy a part.
For though the *Poets* matter, Nature be,
  His Art doth give the fashion. And, that he,
Who casts to write a living line, must sweat,
  (Such as thine are) and strike the second heat
Upon the *Muses* anvile: turne the same,
  (And himselfe with it) that he thinkes to frame;
Or for the lawrell, he may gaine a scorne,
  For a good *Poet's* made, as well as borne.
And such wert thou. Looke how the fathers face
  Lives in his issue, even so, the race
Of *Shakespeares* minde, and manners brightly shines
  In his well torned, and true-filed lines:
In each of which, he seemes to shake a Lance,
  As brandish't at the eyes of Ignorance.
Sweet Swan of *Avon*! what a sight it were
  To see thee in our waters yet appeare,
And make those flights upon the bankes of *Thames*,
  That so did take *Eliza*, and our *James*!
But stay, I see thee in the *Hemisphere*
  Advanc'd, and made a Constellation there!
Shine forth, thou Starre of *Poets*, and with rage,
  Or influence, chide, or cheere the drooping Stage;
Which, since thy flight from hence, hath mourn'd like night,
  And despaires day, but for thy Volumes light.

The Songs in CYNTHIAS REVELLS

[Echo's] Song

Slow, slow, fresh fount, keepe time with my salt teares;
   Yet slower, yet, ô faintly gentle springs:
List to the heavy part the musique beares,
   "Woe weepes out her division, when shee sings."
      Droupe hearbs, and flowres;   5
      Fall griefe in showres;
      "Our beauties are not ours":
          O, I could still
(Like melting snow upon some craggie hill,)
      drop, drop, drop, drop,   10
Since natures pride is, now, a wither'd daffodill.

[Prosaites'] Song

Come follow me, my wagges, and say as I say.
   There's no riches but in ragges; hey day, hey day.
   You that professe this arte, come away, come away,
And helpe to beare a part.   Hey day; hey day.
      Beare-wards, and Blackingmen.   5
      Corne-cutters, and Carmen.
      Sellers of mar-king stones.
      Gatherer's up of Marow-bones.
      Pedlers, and Puppit-players.
      Sow-gelders, and Sooth-saiers.   10

[*Prosaites'*] *Song*: Marginal gloss at ll. 25–26 in the quarto of 1600 designates the song as "Beggars rime."

Gipsies and Jaylers,
Rat-catchers, and Raylers,
Beadles, and Ballad-singers.
Fidlers, and Fadingers.
Thomalins, and Tinkers.   15
Scavengers, and Skinkers.
There goes the Hare away.
      Hey day, Hey day.
Bawds and blinde Doctors.
Paritors, and spittle Proctors.   20
Chymists, and Cuttlebungs.
Hookers, and Horne-thums.
With all cast commaunders
Turn'd Post-knights, or Pandars.
Juglers, and Jesters.   25
Borrowers of Testers.
And all the troope of trashe
That're allied to the lash,
Come, and Joyne with your Jags
Shake up your muscle-bags.   30
For Beggary beares the sway,
Then sing: cast care away,
      Hey day, hey day.

[Hedon's] Song

O, that joy so soone should waste!
  or so sweet a blisse
    as a kisse,
Might not for ever last!
So sugred, so melting, so soft, so delicious,   5

---

14 *Fadingers*: those who either dance the Irish jig-like fading, or sing its often indelicate refrain.

15 *Thomalins*: wandering beggars. Cf. Edgar of *King Lear*, who disguises himself as "Poor Tom."

20 *Proctors*: those supposedly licensed to collect alms on behalf of the occupants of a "spital-house."

24 *Post-knights*: Knights of the Post, notorious perjurors.

30 *muscle-bags*: thighs. Cf. honey-bags of bees.

  The dew that lyes on roses,
  When the morne her selfe discloses,
   is not so precious.
O, rather then I would it smother,
Were I to taste such another;   *10*
   It should bee my wishing
   That I might dye kissing.

[*Amorphus'*] *Song*

Thou more then most sweet glove,
 Unto my more sweet love,
 Suffer me to store with kisses
This emptie lodging, that now misses
  The pure rosie hand, that ware thee,   *5*
  Whiter then the kid, that bare thee.
   Thou art soft, but that was softer;
   CUPIDS selfe hath kist it ofter,
   Then e're he did his mothers doves,
   Supposing her the Queene of loves,   *10*
    That was thy Mistresse,
    Best of gloves.

The Hymne

[*Hesperus sings invoking Cynthia*]

Queene, and *Huntresse*, chaste, and faire,
Now the *Sunne* is laid to sleepe,
Seated, in thy silver chaire,
State in wonted manner keepe:
 HESPERUS intreats thy light,   *5*
 Goddesse, excellently bright.

Earth, let not thy envious shade
Dare it selfe to interpose;

CYNTHIAS shining orbe was made
Heaven to cleere, when day did close: 10
  Blesse us then with wished sight,
  Goddesse, excellently bright.

Lay thy bow of pearle apart,
And thy cristall-shining quiver;
Give unto the flying hart 15
Space to breathe, how short soever:
  Thou that mak'st a day of night,
  Goddesse, excellently bright.

Palinode

[*Amorphus, Phantaste, and Chorus*]

AMO. From *spanish* shrugs, *french* faces, smirks, irps, and all affected humours:
    CHORUS. *Good* MERCURY *defend us.*
PHA. From secret friends, sweet servants, loves, doves, and such phantastique humours. 5
    CHORUS. *Good* MERCURY *defend us.*
AMO. From stabbing of armes, flap-dragons, healths, whiffes, and all such swaggering humours.
    CHORUS. *Good* MERCURY *defend us.*
PHA. From waving of fannes, coy glaunces, glickes, cringes, and all 10
such simpring humours.
    CHORUS. *Good* MERCURY *defend us.*
AMO. From making love by atturny, courting of puppets, and paying for new acquaintance.
    CHORUS. *Good* MERCURY *defend us.* 15

  Palinode. This song is a recantation or renunciation of foolish and wanton activities engaged in by would-be lovers of either sex, unknowing victims of self-love.
  1 *irps*: origin unknown. From its context it seems to refer to some gesture or body movement.
  7 *whiffes*: inhalations of tobacco smoke.
  10 *glickes*: gleeks, ogling looks or glances.

PHA. From perfum'd dogs, munkeyes, sparrowes, dildo's, and parachito's.
  CHORUS. *Good* MERCURY *defend us.*
AMO. From wearing bracelets of haire, shooe-ties, gloves, garters, and rings with poesies.
  CHORUS. *Good* MERCURY *defend us.*
PHA. From pargetting, painting, slicking, glazing, and renewing old riveld faces.
  CHORUS. *Good* MERCURY *defend us.*
AMO. From squiring to tilt-yards, play-houses, pageants, and all such publique places.
  CHORUS. *Good* MERCURY *defend us.*
PHA. From entertayning one gallant to gull an other, and making fooles of either.
  CHORUS. *Good* MERCURY *defend us.*
AMO. From belying ladies favours, noble-mens countenance, coyning counterfet imployments, vaine-glorious taking to them other mens services, and all *selfe-loving* humours.
  CHORUS. *Good* MERCURY *defend us.*

Song

[*Mercury and Crites*]

Now each one drie his weeping eyes.
  And to the well of knowledge haste;
Where purged of your maladies,
  You may of sweeter waters taste:
    And, with refined voice, report
    The grace of *Cynthia*, and her court.

The Songs in POETASTER

Song

[1. *Crispinus*]

If I freely may discover,
What would please me in my lover:
    I would have her faire, and wittie,
    Savouring more of court, then cittie;
    A little proud, but full of pittie: 5
    Light, and humorous in her toying,
    Oft building hopes, and soone destroying,
    Long, but sweet in the enjoying,
Neither too easie, nor too hard:
All extremes I would have bard.   10

[2. *Hermogenes*]

Shee should be allow'd her passions,
So they were but us'd as fashions;
    Sometimes froward, and then frowning,
    Sometimes sickish, and then swowning,
    Every fit, with change, still crowning.   15
    Purely jealous, I would have her,
    Then onely constant when I crave her.
    'Tis a vertue should not save her.
Thus, nor her delicates would cloy me,
Neither her peevishnesse annoy me.   20

[*Horace's Ode*]

    Swell me a bowle with lustie wine,
Till I may see the plump LYAEUS swim
      Above the brim:
I drinke, as I would wright,
In flowing measure, fill'd with flame, and spright.   5

[*Crispinus'*] *Song*

Love is blinde, and a wanton;
    In the whole world, there is scant
    one such another:
    No, not his *Mother*.
He hath pluckt her *doves*, and *sparrowes*,   5
To feather his sharpe arrowes,
    And alone prevaileth,
    Whilst sicke VENUS waileth.
But if CYPRIS once recover
The wag; it shall behove her   10
    To looke better to him:
    Or shee will undoe him.

Song

Wake, our mirth begins to die:
Quicken it with tunes, and wine:
Raise your notes, you're out: fie, fie,
This drouzinesse is an ill signe.
    We banish him the queere of Gods,   5
      That droops agen:
      Then all are men,
For here's not one, but nods.

Song

[*Hermogenes and Crispinus*]

HERM. Then, in a free and lofty straine,
    Our broken tunes we thus repaire;
CRIS. And we answere them againe,
    Running division on the panting aire:
AMBO.   To celebrate this feast of *sense*,   5
    As free from scandall, as offence.
HERM.   Here is *beautie*, for the eye;
CRIS.   For the eare, sweet *melodie*;
HERM.   *Ambrosiack odours*, for the smell;
CRIS.   Delicious *nectar*, for the taste;   10
AMBO.   For the touch, a *ladies waste*;
    Which doth all the rest excell!

Song

Blush, *folly*, blush: here's none that feares
The wagging of an asses eares,
Although a woolvish case he weares.
Detraction is but basenesse varlet;
And apes are apes, though cloth'd in scarlet.   5

From BARTHOLOMEW FAYRE

[Nightingale's Song]

To the tune of Paggingtons Pound

    My masters and friends, and good people draw neere,
    And looke to your purses, for that I doe say;
    And though little money, in them you doe beare,
    It cost more to get, then to lose in a day.
        You oft have beene told,   5
        Both the young and the old;
    And bidden beware of the cutpurse so bold:
Then if you take heed not, free me from the curse,
Who both give you warning for and the cutpurse.
Youth, youth, thou hadst better bin starv'd by thy Nurse,   10
Then live to be hanged for cutting a purse.

    It hath bin upbrayded to men of my trade,
    That often times we are the cause of this crime.
    Alacke and for pitty, why should it be said?
    As if they regarded or places, or time.   15
        Examples have been
        Of some that were seen,
    In Westminster Hall, yea the pleaders between,
Then why should the Judges be free from this curse,
More then my poore selfe, for cutting the purse?   20
Youth, youth, thou hadst better bin starv'd by thy Nurse,
Then live to be hanged for cutting a purse.

    At Worc'ter 'tis knowne well, and even i' the Jayle,
    A Knight of good worship did there shew his face,
    Against the foule sinners, in zeale for to rayle,   25
    And lost (*ipso facto*) his purse in the place.

> Nay, once from the Seat
> Of Judgement so great,
> A Judge there did lose a faire pouch of velvete.
> O Lord for thy mercy, how wicked or worse, 30
> Are those that so venture their necks for a purse!
> Youth, youth, [thou hadst better bin starv'd by thy Nurse,
> Then live to be hanged for cutting a purse.]
>
> At Playes and at Sermons, and at the Sessions,
> 'Tis daily their practice such booty to make: 35
> Yea, under the Gallowes, at Executions,
> They sticke not the *Stare-abouts* purses to take.
> Nay one without grace,
> At a better place,
> At *Court*, and in *Christmas*, before the Kings face, 40
> Alacke then for pitty must I beare the curse,
> That onely belongs to the cunning cutpurse?
> Youth, youth, thou hadst better [bin starv'd by thy Nurse,
> Then live to be hanged for cutting a purse.]
>
> But O, you vile nation of cutpurses all, 45
> Relent and repent, and amend and be sound,
> And know that you ought not, by honest mens fall,
> Advance your owne fortunes, to die above ground,
> And though you goe gay,
> In silkes as you may, 50
> It is not the high way to heaven, (as they say).
> Repent then, repent you, for better, for worse:
> And kisse not the Gallowes for cutting a purse.
> Youth, youth, thou hadst better bin sterv'd by thy Nurse,
> Then live to be hanged for cutting a purse. 55

From A PRIVATE ENTERTAINMENT AT HIGH-GATE

Here, AURORA, ZEPHYRUS, *and* FLORA, *began this song in three parts*

Song

See, see, ô see, who here is come a Maying!
    The master of the Ocean;
    And his beautious ORIAN:
  Why left we off our playing?
      To gaze, to gaze,   5
On them, that gods no lesse then men amaze.
  Up *Nightingale*, and sing
    Jug, jug, jug; jug, jug, jug; jug, jug, jug;
  Raise *Larke* thy note, and wing,
  All birds their musique bring,   10
  Sweet *Robin, Linet, Thrush,*
  Record, from every bush,
    The welcome of the King
    And Queene:
Whose like were never seene,   15
  For good, for faire.
Nor can be; though fresh *May,*
  Should every day
  Invite a severall paire,
No, though shee should invite a severall paire.   20

Song from A Private Entertainment at High-gate. Part of the royal shows which began the Coronation proceedings in 1604 for James I and Queen Anne. The piece was performed at the estate of Sir William Cornwallis (d. 1611) on May-day in the morning in a setting near London from which one could view the city and the surrounding countryside.

Song from THE KINGS ENTERTAINMENT AT WELBECK

A DIALOGUE BETWEENE THE PASSIONS, DOUBT AND LOVE

DOUBT. What softer sounds are these salute the Eare
        From the large Circle of the Hemispheare,
        As if the Center of all sweets met here!
LOVE. It is the breath, and Soule of every thing,
        Put forth by Earth, by Nature, and the Spring,   5
        To speake the Welcome, Welcome of the King.

CHORUS.   The joy of plants, the spirit of flowers,
Of   The smell, and verdure of the bowers,
Affections,   The waters murmure; with the showers
Joy.   Distilling on the new-fresh howers: 10
Delight, &c. The whistling winds, and birds, that sing
            The Welcome of our great, good King.
       Welcome, O Welcome, is the generall voyce,
       Wherein all Creatures practize to rejoyce.

            The second Straine.   15
LOVE. When was old Sherewood's head more quaintly curl'd?
       Or look'd the Earth more greene upon the world?
       Or Natures Cradle more inchas'd, and purl'd?
       When did the Aire so smile, the Winds so chime?

Song from the Kings Entertainment at Welbeck. In 1633, when Charles I was en route to Edinburgh to be crowned, he was invited by the Earl of Newcastle to Welbeck in Nottinghamshire, and this entertainment graced the occasion. In 1634 the entertainment was repeated for Queen Henrietta as she visited the northern parts in progress.

	As Quiristers of Season, and the Prime!	20
Dou[bt].	If what they doe, be done in their due time.	

Chorus. Hee makes the time for whom 'tis done,
         From whom the warmth, heat, life, begun,
         Into whose fostring armes doe run
         All that have being from the Sun.   25
         Such is the fount of light, the King,
         The heart, that quickens ev'ry thing,
       And makes the Creatures language all one voyce;
       In Welcome, Welcome, Welcome, to rejoyce:
       Welcome is all our Song, is all our sound,   30
       The Treble part, the Tenor, and the Ground.

Songs from
OBERON, THE FAERY PRINCE

A Masque of Prince Henries

... the Satyres *fell sodainely
into this catch.*

    Buz, quoth the blue Flie,
      Hum, quoth the Bee:
    Buz, and hum, they crie,
      And so doe wee.
    In his eare, in his nose,   5
      Thus, doe you see?
    He eat the dormouse,
      Else it was hee.

Songs from Oberon. Performed on 1 January 1611 at Whitehall, this masque displayed Prince Henry as Oberon.

[Satyrs'] Song

Now, my cunning lady, Moone,
Can you leave the side, so soone,
   Of the boy, you keepe so hid?
Mid-wife JUNO sure will say,
This is not the proper way   5
   Of your palenesse to be rid.
But, perhaps, it is your grace
To weare sicknesse i'your face,
   That there might be wagers laid,
   Still, by fooles, you are a maid.   10

Come, your changes overthrow,
What your looke would carry so;
   Moone, confesse then, what you are.
And be wise, and free to use
Pleasures, that you now doe loose;   15
   Let us *Satyres* have a share.
Though our forms be rough, and rude
Yet our acts may be endew'd
   With more vertue: Every one
   Cannot be ENDYMION.   20

The song ended: They fell sodainely into an antique dance, full of gesture, and swift motion, and continued it, till the crowing of the cock: At which they were interrupted by SILENUS.

Silenus

>   Stay, the cheerefull *Chanticleere*   25
>   Tells you, that the time is neere:
>   See, the gates alreadie spread!
>   Every *Satyre* bow his head.

There the whole palace open'd, and the nation of Faies *were discover'd, some with instruments, some bearing lights; others singing; and within a farre 30 off in perspective, the knights masquers sitting in their severall sieges: At the further end of all,* OBERON, *in a chariot, which to a lowd triumphant musique began to move forward, drawne by two white beares, and on either side guarded by three* SYLVANES, *with one going in front.*

Song

>   Melt earth to sea, sea flow to ayre,
>   And ayre flie into fire,
>   Whilst we, in tunes, to ARTHURS chayre
>   Beare OBERONS desire;
>   Then which there nothing can be higher,   40
>   Save *JAMES*, to whom it flyes:
>   But he the wonder is of tongues, of eares, of eyes.
>   Who hath not heard, who hath not seene,
>   Who hath not sung his name?
>   The soule, that hath not, hath not beene;   45
>   But is the very same
>   With buryed sloth, and knowes not fame,
>   Which doth him best comprise:
>   For he the wonder is of tongues, of eares, of eyes.

---

31 *knights masquers*: the names of the blue bloods who danced in the masque have not been recovered.

The Song, by two Faies

1. Seeke you majestie, to strike?
    Bid the world produce his like.
2. Seeke you glorie, to amaze?
    Here, let all eyes stand at gaze.
1.}
2.} Seeke you wisedome, to inspire?   5
    Touch, then, at no others fire.
1. Seeke you knowledge, to direct?
    Trust to his, without suspect.
2. Seeke you pietie, to lead?
    In his foot-steps, only, tread.   10
CHO.} Every vertue of a king,
    And of all, in him, we sing.

Then, the lesser Faies dance forth their dance; which ended, A full song fol-lowes, by all the voyces.

Song

The solemne rites are well begunne;
    And, though but lighted by the moone,
They shew as rich, as if the sunne
    Had made this night his noone.
But may none wonder, that they are so bright,   20
The moone now borrowes from a greater light:
        Then, princely OBERON,
            Goe on,
This is not every night.

There OBERON, *and the knights dance out the first masque-dance: which was follow'd with this song.*

Song

>   Nay, nay,
>   You must not stay,
>   Nor be weary, yet;   30
>   This's no time to cast away;
>   Or, for *Faies* so to forget
>   The vertue of their feet.
>   Knottie legs, and plants of clay
>   Seeke for ease, or love delay.   35
>   But with you it still should fare
>   As, with the ayre of which you are.

After which, they danced forth their second masque-dance, and were againe excited by a song.

Song   40

>   1. Nor yet, nor yet, O you in this night blest,
>   Must you have will, or hope to rest.
>   2. If you use the smallest stay,
>   You'll be overtane by day.
>   1. And these beauties will suspect   45
>   That their formes you doe neglect,
>   If you doe not call them forth:
>   2. Or that you have no more worth
>   Then the course, and countrey *Faery*,
>   That doth haunt the harth, or dairy.   50

Then follow'd the measures, coranto's, galliards, &c. till PHOSPHORUS, *the day-starre appear'd, and call'd them away; but first they were invited home, by one of the* SYLVANES, *with this song.*

Song

    Gentle knights,   55
Know some measure of your nights.
Tell the high-grac'd OBERON,
It is time, that we were gone.
    Here be formes, so bright, and aery,
        And their motions so they vary   60
    As they will enchant the *Faery*,
        If you longer, here, should tarry.

Phosphorus

To rest, to rest; The *Herald* of the day,
Bright PHOSPHORUS commands you hence; Obay.   65
The *Moone* is pale, and spent; and winged night
Makes head-long haste, to flie the mornings sight:
Who, now, is rising from her blushing warres,
And, with her rosie hand, puts backe the starres.
Of which my selfe, the last, her harbinger,   70
But stay, to warne you, that you not defer
Your parting longer. Then, doe I give way,
As night hath done, and so must you, to day.

*After this, they danc'd their last dance, into the worke. And with a full song,
the starre vanish'd, and the whole machine clos'd.*   75

Song

O yet, how early, and before her time,
    The envious *Morning* up doth clime,
    Though shee not love her bed!

What haste the jealous *Sunne* doth make, 80
His fiery horses up to take,
  And once more shew his head!
Lest, taken with the brightnesse of this night,
The world should wish it last, and never misse his light.

Songs from LOVE FREED FROM IGNORANCE AND FOLLY

A Masque of her Majesties

Graces

THEIR SONG CROWNING CUPID.

  A crowne, a crowne, for LOVES bright head,
    Without whose happie wit
  All forme, and beautie had beene dead,
    And we had di'd with it. 5
  For what are all the graces
  Without good formes, and faces?
    Then *Love* receive the due reward
    Those *Graces* have prepard. 10
CHO. And may no hand, no tongue, no eie
    Thy merit, or their thankes envie.

Songs from Love Freed from Ignorance and Folly. Performed on 3 February, 1611, this was a court masque in which Queen Anne danced as Queen of the Orient attended by her ladies as the Daughters of the Morn.

A Dialogue betweene the CHORUS *and the* GRACES.

What gentle formes are these that move 15
    To honour *Love*?
They are the bright and golden lights
    That grace his nights.
      And shot from *Beauties* eyes,
They looke like faire AURORAS streames. 20
They are her fairer daughters beames,
    Who now doth rise.
  Then night is lost, or fled away;
For where such *Beautie* shines, is ever day.

The Masque daunce followed. 25
That done, one of the PRIESTS *alone sung.*

PRIE.   O what a fault, nay, what a sinne
    In *Fate*, or *Fortune* had it beene,
    So much beautie to have lost!
    Could the world with all her cost 30
    Have redeem'd it?   CHO. No, no, no.

      PRIE.   How so?

CHO.   It would *Nature* quite undoe,
    For losing these, you lost her too.

The Measures and Revells follow. 35
Then another of the Priests *alone.*

How neere to good is what is faire!
    Which we no sooner see,
But with the lines, and outward aire
    Our senses taken be. 40
We wish to see it still, and prove,
    What waies wee may deserve,
We court, we praise, we more then love.
    We are not griev'd to serve.

The last Masque-daunce. 45
And after it, this full Song.

What just excuse had aged *Time*,
    His wearie limbes now to have eas'd,
And sate him downe without his crime,
    While every thought was so much pleas'd! 50
But he so greedie to devoure
    His owne, and all that hee brings forth,
Is eating every piece of houre
    Some object of the rarest worth.
Yet this is rescued from his rage, 55
As not to die by time, or age.
    For beautie hath a living name,
    And will to heaven, from whence it came.

The going out.

Now, now. Gentle *Love* is free, and *Beautie* blest 60
    With the sight it so much long'd to see.
Let us the *Muses* PRIESTS, and GRACES goe to rest,
    For in them our labours happie bee.
Then, then, angry *Musique* sound, and teach our feet,
    How to move in time, and measure meet: 65
Thus should the *Muses* PRIESTS, and GRACES goe to rest,
    Bowing to the Sunne, throned in the West.

An Expostulacion with Inigo Jones

    Master Surveyor, you that first begann
From thirty pound in pipkins, to the Man
You are; from them leapt forth an Architect,
Able to talk of Euclide, and correct
Both him and Archimede; damne Architas   5
The noblest Ingenyre that ever was!
Controll Ctesibius: overbearing us
With mistooke Names out of Vitruvius!
Drawne Aristotle on us! and thence showne
How much Architectonice is your owne!   10
Whether the buylding of the Stage or Scene!
Or making of the propertyes it meane?
Vizors or Anticks? or it comprehend
Something your Surship doth not yet intend!
By all your Titles, and whole style at once   15
Of Tyre-man, Mounte-banck, and Justice Jones,
I doe salute you! Are you fitted yet?
Will any of these express your place? or witt?
Or are you soe ambitious 'bove your peers!
You would be'an Asinigo, by your Ears?   20
Why much good doo't you! Be what beast you will,
You'l be as Langley sayd, an Inigo still.
    What makes your Wretchednes to bray soe loud
In Towne and Court? Are you growne rich? and proud?
Your Trappings will not change you. Change your mynd.   25

An Expostulacion with Inigo Jones. Jonson's career-long feud with Inigo Jones, architect and scene-designer, came to a head in 1631 after the performance of *Chloridia* in Shrovetide, and this satire together with the corollary and the epigram are usually dated shortly after its performance. Details of the quarrel are clearly outlined by H. & S. in volume XI (App. XXIV). From George Chapman's vindictive "Invective against Ben Jonson," parts of which are quoted by H. & S., it would appear that Jonson had temerariously delivered the expostulation against Jones at court in the very presence of the King.

Noe velvet Sheath you weare, will alter kynde.
A wodden Dagger, is a Dagger of wood
Though gold or Ivory haftes would make it good.
What is the cause you pompe it soe? I aske,
And all men eccho you have made a Masque. 30
I chyme that too: And I have mett with those
That doe cry up the Machine, and the Showes!
The majesty of Juno in the Cloudes,
And peering forth of Iris in the Shrowdes!
Th'ascent of Lady Fame which none could spy 35
Not they that sided her, Dame Poetry,
Dame History, Dame Architecture too,
And Goody Sculpture, brought with much adoe
To hold her up. O Showes! Showes! Mighty showes!
The Eloquence of Masques! What need of Prose 40
Or Verse, or Sense t'express Immortall you?
You are the Spectacles of State! Tis true
Court Hieroglyphicks! and all Artes affoord
In the mere perspective of an Inch board!
You aske noe more then certeyne politique Eyes, 45
Eyes that can pierce into the Misteryes
Of many Coulors! read them! and reveale
Mythology there painted on slit deale!
Oh, to make Boardes to speake! There is a taske.
Painting and Carpentry are the Soule of Masque. 50
Pack with your pedling Poetry to the Stage,
This is the money-gett, Mechanick Age!
To plant the Musick where noe Eare can reach!
Attyre the Persons as noe thought can teach
Sense, what they are! which by a specious fyne 55
Terme of the Architects is calld Designe!
But in the practisd truth Destruction is
Of any Art, besyde what he calls his!
Whither? oh whither will this Tire-man growe?
His name is Σκενοποιος wee all knowe, 60
The maker of the Propertyes! in summe
The Scene! the Engyne! but he now is come
To be the Musick Master! Fabler too!

He is, or would be the mayne Dominus doe
All in'the Worke! And soe shall still for Ben: 65
Be Inigo, the Whistle, and his men!
Hee's warme on his feet now he sayes, and can
Swim without Corke! Why, thank the good Queen Anne!
I am too fat t'envy him. He too leane
To be worth Envy. Henceforth I doe meane 70
To pitty him, as smiling at his Feat
Of Lanterne-lerry, with fuliginous heat
Whirling his Whymseys, by a subtilty
Suckt from the Veynes of shop-philosophy.
What would he doe now, gi'ng his mynde that waye 75
In presentacion of some puppet play!
Should but the King his Justice-hood employ
In setting forth of such a solemne Toye!
How would he firke? lyke Adam overdooe
Up, and about? Dyve into Cellars too 80
Disguisd? and thence drag forth Enormity?
Discover Vice? Commit Absurdity?
Under the Morall? shewe he had a Pate
Moulded, or stroakt up to survey a State!
O wise Surveyor! wyser Architect! 85
But wisest Inigo! who can reflect
On the new priming of thy old Signe postes
Reviving with fresh coulors the pale Ghosts
Of thy dead Standards: or (with miracle) see
Thy twice conceyvd, thrice payd for Imagery? 90
And not fall downe before it? and confess
Allmighty Architecture? who noe less
A Goddess is, then paynted Cloth, Deal-boards,
Vermilion, Lake, or Cinnopar affoards
Expression for! with that unbounded lyne 95
Aymd at in thy omnipotent Designe!
What Poesy ere was painted on a wall
That might compare with thee? what story shall
Of all the Worthyes hope t'outlast thy one,
Soe the Materialls be of Purbeck stone! 100
Lyve long the Feasting Roome. And ere thou burne

Againe, thy Architect to ashes turne!
Whom not ten fyres, nor a Parlyament can
With all Remonstrance make an honest man.

To Inigo Marquess Would be
A Corollary

But cause thou hearst the mighty king of Spaine
Hath made his Inigo Marquess, wouldst thou fayne
Our Charles should make thee such? T'will not become
All Kings to doe the self same deeds with some!
Besydes, his Man may merit it, and be   5
A Noble honest Soule! what's this to thee?
He may have skill and judgment to designe
Cittyes and Temples! thou a Cave for Wyne,
Or Ale! He build a Pallace! Thou a Shopp
With slyding Windowes, and false Lights a top!   10
He draw a Forum, with quadriviall Streets!
Thou paint a Lane, where Thumb the Pygmy meets!
He some Colossus to bestryde the Seas,
From the famd Pillars of old Hercules!
Thy Canvas Gyant, at some Channell aymes,   15
Or Dowgate Torrent falling into Thames:
And stradling shews the Boyes Brown paper fleet,
Yearly set out there, to sayle downe the Street.
Your Workes thus differing, troth let soe your style:
Content thee to be Pancridge Earle the whyle;   20
An Earle of show: for all thy worke is Showe;
But when thou turnst a Reall Inigo;
Or canst of truth the least intrenchment pitch,
Wee'll have thee styld the Marquess of New-Ditch.

To a Freind an Epigram of him

Sir Inigo doeth fear it as I heare
(And labours to seem worthy of that feare)
That I should wryte upon him some sharp Verse,
Able to eat into his bones, and pierce
The Marrow! Wretch, I quitt thee of thy paine   5
Thou'rt too ambitious: and dost fear in vaine!
The Lybian Lion hunts noe butter-flyes,
He makes the Camell and dull Ass his prize.
If thou be soe desyrous to be read,
Seek out some hungry painter, that for bread,   10
With rotten chalk, or Cole upon a wall,
Will well designe thee, to be viewd of all
That sit upon the Common Draught; or Strand!
Thy Forehead is too narrow for my Brand.

                              BEN: JOHNSON:

Robert Herrick

Herrick called his *Hesperides* "this my rich Plantation," and it contains well over a thousand poems of varying length and kind. Even though Swinburne did not recognize in the work any underlying unity, regarding it "a diet of alternate sweetmeats and emetics," most readers have felt it to be a harmoniously related collection.

"The Argument of his Book," the introductory poem, is essentially a catalogue of the subjects Herrick intends to treat, and through the lists of doublets, both complementary and antithetical, he establishes at the outset the principle of unity in diversity which informs the entire volume. The subject matter includes nature and the seasons, festivals sacred and profane, youth and love, myths and legends, and even hell and heaven. From the subjects recorded, it is readily evident that Herrick's subject matter aims to embrace first the whole of the natural world in its rich diversity, then man and his changing activities both private and public, and finally the supernatural world in both its secular and sacred guises.

As one leafs through the collection, the contents seem arranged sometimes chronologically, sometimes thematically. Viewed in its entirety, the volume aptly displays *"Times trans-shifting."* The poems underscore the pagan preoccupation with transience, yet they often unexpectedly temper it by establishing parallels and correspondences between past and present, ideality and actuality, and contemplation and activity. In more specific contexts, the tension may be seen as subsisting between courtly sophistication and rural innocence, between Epicurean placidity and Christian commitment, or between Cavalier insouciance and Puritan rigidity. Opposing points of view, most evident in the pagan and pious pieces, do not invite the reader's alternating acceptance and rejection so much as his consideration of means of reconciliation. It is not surprising that *Hesperides*, which in its ample dimensions includes the devotional pieces under the title *His Noble Numbers*, is the only collection which Herrick gathered together and published. It is a life's work, epitomizing and integrating all that he thought and cherished. Upon the variegated pieces which make up the total design of its mosaic he exercised the art of a lapidary.

Hesperides contains dozens of epigrammatic couplets, balanced by several blank-verse pieces of generous length. There are also many songs, odes, and dialogues, among which may be found in categories of even greater particularity aubades and valedictions, epithalamia and dirges, panegyrics and satirical squibs, pastorals and anacreontics. The range exploits all the principal types of lyric utterance in which the Roman poets excelled, and in which Herrick, like his avowed master Jonson, had thoroughly immersed himself. In Herrick's verses the classical attitudes and manners serve as the basis for a delicate neo-paganism, subtly transmuted to appeal to a Caroline audience of taste and refinement. Infused with the Roman spirit, Herrick's poems may be seen as the *apologia* of a divine of some learning but little pretension who provides a celebration of a way of life which joins the natural, human, and divine spheres in a series of interrelated miniatures of flawless artistry.

For Herrick, the life of sweet content in the natural world is of inestimable importance, and his poems often emphasize the daily round of activities of a life lived close to nature. In "A Country life," a poem addressed to his brother Thomas, the traditional doctrines of the Golden Age, as adopted by the Elizabethan poets, are expressed in several well-turned phrases: the country's "sweet simplicity" provides a means to become "the sooner innocent"; it permits one "to know vertue" and "to live well"; it encourages man "to confine desires." A natural world to be enjoyed for its own beauties, the country delights both eye and ear with its damasked meadows and pebbly streams, its purling springs and well-woven bowers. From its perspective, one can look "more with wonder then with feare" as Fame tells of states, of countries, courts, and kings; and when one hears that "Vice rules the Most, or All at Court," one's devout wishes are only that "Vertue had, and mov'd her Sphere." Against such a backdrop, Spenser's Colin Clout and Pastorella had taught how the Blatant Beast might be subdued, and Shakespeare's Florizel and Perdita, in the course of their disportings, had shown their sin-sick elders how to regain a vision of the prelapsarian world. And insofar as the pastoral tradition sets a value on ideality and emphasizes a lost innocence, in these respects it provides a background for Marvell and Milton, those garden poets *par excellence* who follow Herrick. Both explore man's fall from grace in terms which at first glance seem far removed from such a convention-ridden genre as the pastoral.

Herrick's poetry of the idealized world has a freshness and spontaneity in keeping with his own imaginative vision of that world. On a few occasions, often in the more formally constructed dialogue pieces intended to be sung, a Silvio and a Montano, or an Amyntas and a Mirtillo, may display rather artificial Arcadian attitudes as they share their roundelays, extol a flower-bedecked mistress, or entreat Pan and Pallas to bring their sweet-sad passions to an end. But in general, in his desire to turn the Iron Age into gold, Herrick does not rely on imaginary Arcadias, traditional nymphs and shepherds, nor the usual classical deities to watch over them. Instead, he portrays plowmen and farm hands, recognizable types who whistle to their teams as they till the soil. Or, he provides his country-house poems with a lord and lady or with a gentleman farmer who, as they survey their domains, may see "a present God-like Power/Imprinted in each Herbe and Flower" and realize that "the best compost for the Lands/Is the wise Masters Feet, and Hands." In a poem celebrating the country life Herrick depicts just such a master in the person of Endimion Porter, actively superintending his holdings yet free enough to enjoy hunting and to engage in the wholesome activities that are significant parts of country holidays and festivals: wakes, tilting matches, Maypole dancing, morris dancing, shearing feasts, harvest homes, wassails, mummeries, and Christmas revels. In "A Panegerick to Sir Lewis Pemberton" he praises this knight's unstinting generosity, comparing him first to a Roman tribune and then to "that *Hospitable God*," Jove himself. This is the *"Princely Pemberton,"* he concludes, "who can/Teach man to keepe a God in man."

It is a commonplace to observe that Herrick seldom describes nature for its own sake, and rarely in any great detail. He may concentrate on a daffodil, but only to compare its brief life-span with man's. Although he often stresses nature's regeneration as a pattern for man's renewal, Herrick insists that the chief lesson to be derived from nature is the enjoyment of life to the full in one's prime. He distinguishes between living merrily and living well, and for him the good life is not only one lived amid nature, but one in which labor plays a proper part.

Living well is living the life of total immersion in experience, and it is through sexual experience, the distillation of intense engagement in life, that one may most directly show one's response to the world of the senses. Thus the large class of amatory poems in *Hesperides* which provocatively touch upon the sex experience. Modern criticism properly cautions that the poet here does not explore the relations between two identifiable individuals, and that biographical speculations about how a middle-aged country parson spent dull winter evenings distort rather than clarify the meaning of these poems. Julia, "dearest of thousands," the quintessence of feminine beauty and the perfection of bearing, thus stands as the idealized symbol toward which man's admiration and desires are directed, and the host of attractive ladies only glimpsed in obscurer glades of *Hesperides* serve as minor representatives, variations on a basic theme, of the richness and diversity of feminine charm and grace.

Together these ladies comprise a gallery of warmly tinted sketches of pretty mistresses endowed with effortless grace and modesty, to which is sometimes added a certain archness or sauciness in manner. Corinna, Sapho, Electra, or Dianeme—each catches something from the remote past as well as from Herrick's present as she engages in a characteristic activity—tying a shoe, working a sampler, or bedecking herself with a bracelet or a carcanet. Mute, except when singing seductively to the lute (for Herrick has as much enthusiasm for music as Shakespeare and Campion), each makes an impact through her physical charms, and these especially as displayed in bodily movement.

Her eyes, if not the liquefaction of her clothes, may intoxicate innocents like the poet. Since his mistresses are each endowed with differing personal traits—Anthea, for example, is discreet and timid; Lucia, joyous and light-hearted; and Corinna, once she rises to go a-Maying, wild-spirited and aggressive—there is every reason for the poet to respond variously to each, now with tenderness, now with frivolity, and now wantonness. Herrick never omits observing and never wearies of recording each trifle of the lady's garb, down to such elegant artifices as the wearing of flowers and perfumes. And yet, despite the roguish and self-conscious immediate delight the speaker takes in describing his beauties, one senses that in a Keatsian way forever will they be fair, and forever will the poet pay them court, always at a distance. In these miniatures, love is often treated delicately and humorously, and most frequently with that teasing uncertainty which is the product of an obliquely described dramatic situation. Not a little of the effectiveness of Herrick's love poetry is dependent upon the subtle use of implied narrative as well as upon the winsomeness and charm of the speaker, an abject admirer who impresses his tastes and responses upon all that he describes.

Frankly pagan, the attitudes Herrick expresses toward love in these poems bear only a tenuous relationship to the Petrarchan cult of the Elizabethan lyricists; they resemble more closely the views of Ovid and Horace. It is only in such formal pieces as the epithalamia that Herrick honors wedded love, and even here the emphasis falls upon the eager expectancy of the lovers as they approach the bridal bed. In particular, the Horatian ideal of love as a refined amusement, as a voluntary surrender of the spirit but never an unmastered passion, has left an imprint upon the poet. Like Horace, he poses as one wearying of a single love, preferring, at least in imagination, to surround himself with a host of mistresses. It is hardly surprising that when he does not translate Horace directly he easily echoes and transmutes the sentiments of the Latin poet's odes and epodes.

Although the chief emphasis in *Hesperides* falls upon the daily round of domestic and amatory activities in a natural setting, the poet momentarily disrupts this life, at well-spaced intervals in the collection, to reach into a less immediate time to lament the drowning of Leander, to recall the dancing of masquers at a

Twelfth Night revel at Whitehall in his youth, or to explore imaginatively the dimensions and appointments of Oberon's palace. Yet it is not all idyll and fancy: one of the dominant contrasts in the collection is between the world of public concerns in city and court and the world of private tranquillity idealized in a pastoral setting. Seen in its immediate historical context, the serious world is a Royalist world, echoes of whose civil war battles resound to Herrick's country retreat from as far as Chester and Worcester and from as close as Cornwall. Herrick attempts no justification of the Royalist cause beyond the true-blue Englishman's admiration for his monarch and the occasional praise of those worthies who support the royal cause in battle. He is no apologist for, say, Archbishop Laud, and one senses that for Herrick his virtual exile in Devonshire was to a great extent self-imposed.

This sophisticated world of affairs, as the poet knows it, is inhabited by men of talent, occasionally titled figures, but more often friends who have distinguished themselves in professional life. Those friends whom he considers deserving of a place in his book include clergymen, lawyers, doctors, scholars, and soldiers, as well as painters, musicians, and poets. In the encomiastic poems of Jonson and Donne the blue-blooded intelligentsia predominate. In those of Herrick the emphasis is upon lesser figures, but those actively engaged in their field of endeavor. He comforts the Bishop of Lincoln, imprisoned for having revealed secrets of the Privy Council, even though this prelate had dealt unkindly with the poet himself. He lauds his honored friend Master John Weare of Silverton, Counsellor-at-law, for upholding pious principles. On no less than three occasions he pays tribute to his friend Master John Wickes, who as doctor and clergyman (he had been ordained with Herrick in 1623) lived an Epicurean life in keeping with the poet's ideals. In the scholarly realm he commends Doctor William Alabaster, who in his writings on mystical theology read the history of his own age in terms of scriptural prophecy, Master John Hamar, classicist, whose Latin epigrams (one is subjoined to the poet's portrait in *Hesperides*) he considers worthy rivals of Martial's, and Master John Selden, "arch-antiquary" and "demi-God," whose vast erudition served the poet as a firm foundation for his work. He singles out Van Dyck, who had painted Charles I and his courtiers, as "the glory of the world," and he is one of the first of his age to recognize the true greatness of the Caroline masque composer William Lawes, whose untimely death at the battle of Chester he deplores. He regards Henry Lawes as "the excellent Composer of his Lyricks," and hearing in his music strains of his distinguished fellow musicians Gotière, Wilson, and Lanier, compliments him for uniting the artistry of all three.

By contrast, the poets of the contemporary scene, except for Jonson, are seldom referred to explicitly. Denham is praised for the "brave, bold, and sweet Maronian Muse of his 'Cooper's Hill,'" but for any observation on Donne or Herbert one must turn to certain of Herrick's poems which comment broadly upon well-known pieces of theirs. One, entitled "Impossibilities to his friend," shows Herrick trifling with the impossibility theme made famous by "Goe, and catch a falling star," and another, beginning "Love brought me to a silent Grove," is an obvious imitation of the manner of Herbert's dramatized personifications. Jonson, "the rare Arch-poet," brings to mind convivial meetings and stands as a reminder to Herrick that he must husband his poetic talent. But apart from lamenting the demise of the stage after Jonson's death, this Son of Ben has little else to say about Jonson as either poet or dramatist.

Herrick insisted that man's active life need not be limited to his professional endeavors or his love experiences. For him it was also to be concerned with the life of the spirit. Although it is often remarked that his sacred verse displays relatively little individuality, and that it seldom departs from the conservative norms of the Anglican tenets of faith as his generation understood them, it is rarely noted that its essential character is the inevitable product of an eager nature, impatient and unhesitant, seeking to be immersed in a religious experience which could remove all endangering doubts and subtleties. Certainly Herrick's sacred pieces do not display the intense personal commitment found in Donne, Herbert, or Crashaw, but then, theirs do not always show the admirable simplicity and directness (if not perfunctoriness) that many of his pieces possess. His is a sacred poetry of affirmation and declaration which announces unequivocally in its epigraph that "we... know when we intend to state the truth." Doctrinal matters of a predictable sort are often encapsulated in a sententious couplet or quatrain. No questioning disturbs the easy faith of the poet, and little sense of mystery is aroused by his contemplation of God's workings. It is a poetry largely devoid of ambiguity or complex meanings, and the tranquil acceptance of doctrine is seldom disrupted by paradox or irony.

Such religious ideas as Herrick states are hardly of the type that would have prompted disputes or controversy among fellow Anglicans. He concerns himself largely with the central and unchanging tenets of orthodox Christianity, enunciated if not in the Scriptures, then in the works of the early Church Fathers: that God is best known by not defining him; that he likes to bring good men to the field, and to have them skirmish there; that predestination (in an anti-Calvinist view) is not responsible for any man's Fall, though it explains his standing; that man, continually enmeshed in sin, can find salvation only in God's love and mercy; that the ransomed sinner inherits heaven not by merit but only by Christ's mercies; and that the pleasures of the "white Island," Herrick's eternity, have no contact with "sorrowes streames" of this world. Apart from almost total immersion in the Scriptures, whose images, phrases, and cadences leave their mark on virtually every poem in *His Noble Numbers*, Herrick shows a familiarity with the writings of St. Augustine, St. Ambrose, and St. Thomas, as well as with those of such contemporaries as John Gregory, whose *Notes and Observations upon Some Passages of Scripture*, published in Oxford in 1646, is the precise source from which he derived the substance of several of the epigrams included among his sacred pieces.

Although Herrick's sacred verse seldom explicates theological nuances, much of it is devoted to demonstrating through ceremonies and rites precisely how one participates in worship, or how one engages in living the Christian life. Many poems rehearse in some detail the procedures undertaken by the Christian seeking salvation: we are familiarized with the speaker's confession, which then becomes *our* confession, and so forth with his prayer for absolution, his litany, his thanksgiving to God, his preparation for the Communion, his Credo. Other poems describe in circumstantial detail the solemnities and festivals of the liturgical year. Reading those poems intended for Christmas, New Year's Day, or Epiphany, for example, becomes an act of worship, and the eager expectancy and quiet joy which they elicit make them by far the most memorable of his festive pieces. In this class of sacred verse Herrick clearly surpasses all his contemporaries. Following the necessary rubrics of performance (even where contemporary musical settings no longer survive) enables us to respond imaginatively with the mind's ear to such pieces as "What sweeter musick can we bring." Such elaborate choral pieces as these have their counterparts in the secular poems describing and celebrating holidays and folk festivals. The latter also provide a means for immersing oneself imaginatively in such experiences as going a-Maying or preparing the hock cart, and these also are infused with an infectious spontaneity.

Except for a few epigrams, the pieces of *His Noble Numbers* sustain the persona of the speaker already introduced in *Hesperides*, thus establishing a consistency in point of view and a sense of unity for the entire volume. Herrick's dealings with God are sometimes colloquially direct ("Pardon me, God, once more I Thee intreat"); sometimes personally quaint, as if he were addressing a Julia or an Anthea ("Lord, I am like to *Misletoe*"); and on occasion even skirting the erotic when, in addressing his Savior as a child, he urges his reader to try to win a kiss "From those mellifluous lips of his." He engages in colloquies with God, whose unexpressed responses may be deduced only through the persistency of the penitent's questions.

It is in the sweet simplicity and sincerity of such "pious" pieces as these that Herrick is at his most effective and vital; his more abstract pronouncements of doctrine remain merely coldly correct. Though one looks in vain in Herrick's religious verse for any passionate intellectual analysis in the manner of Donne, for anything approximating Vaughan's delight in the soul, or for any anticipation of the ecstatic self-abandonment of Traherne, there is a plain and sweet reasonableness in his manner which presumably displays something of the directness of this practical churchman in dealing with his flock. Closest to him among his contemporaries is Herbert, who likewise displays a great admiration for the ritual of formal worship.

Older criticism has usefully categorized much of seventeenth-century poetry in terms of its main classes of subject matter: nature poems, love poems, occasional poems, and sacred poems. Though among his immediate contemporaries Herrick is clearly outdistanced in devotional poetry by Donne and Herbert, and in occasional poetry by Jonson (who in this class has no peer among English poets), he nonetheless maintains a special position of preeminence as a poet of nature and of love. None of his contemporaries equals him as a poet of nature in those special terms inimitably his own which are defined in poem after poem of *Hesperides*. The final distinction may involve not so much matter as tone. And there is no poet of love in his century who sings against such an idealized natural background with such simple eloquence and unfettered joy—and with such consummate virtuosity—the glories of taking our pleasures in the very real delights of this world while we may.

The copy text for this selection of Herrick's poems is *Hesperides* with *His Noble Numbers* (London, 1648).

The following complete editions deserve special notice from among the several editions of Herrick's poetry issued during the past century: those of W. Carew Hazlitt, Alexander B. Grosart, Henry Morley, Alfred Pollard, George Saintsbury, F. W. Moorman, L. C. Martin, and J. Max Patrick. While many of these contain illuminating introductions, the two latest are of utmost importance to students of Herrick because of their extensive annotations and their inclusion of several items from manuscript sources.

SELECTED BIBLIOGRAPHY

EDITIONS

Child, Francis J., ed. *Hesperides*. 2 vols. Boston, 1854.
Grosart, Alexander B., ed. *Complete Poems*. London, 1876.
Hazlitt, W. Carew, ed. *Hesperides: The Poems, and Other Remains of Robert Herrick*. 2 vols. London, 1869.
Maitland, Thomas, ed. *The Works of Robert Herrick*. 2 vols Edinburgh, 1823.
Martin, L. C., ed. *Poetical Works*. Oxford, 1956; rev. ed., 1965.

Moorman, F. W., ed. *The Poetical Works of Robert Herrick*. Oxford, 1915.
Nott, John, ed. *Select Poems from the Hesperides*. Bristol, 1810.
Patrick, J. Max, ed. *The Complete Poetry of Robert Herrick*. Garden City, N.Y., 1963.
Pollard, Alfred W., ed. *The Hesperides and Noble Numbers*. With a preface by Algernon Charles Swinburne. 2 vols. London, 1891.
Saintsbury, George, ed. *The Poetical Works of Robert Herrick*. 2 vols. London, 1893.

BIOGRAPHY AND CRITICISM

Aiken, Pauline. *The Influence of the Latin Elegists on English Lyric Poetry, 1600–1650, with Particular Reference to the Works of Robert Herrick*. Univ. of Maine Studies, Second Series, no. 22. Orono, Me., 1932.
Chute, Marchette. *Two Gentle Men: The Lives of George Herbert and Robert Herrick*. New York, 1959.
Delattre, Floris. *Robert Herrick: Contribution à l'Etude de la Poésie Lyrique en Angleterre au Dix-septième Siècle*. Paris, 1912.
Deming, R. H. "Herrick's Funeral Poems," *SEL*, IX (1969), 153–67.
Evans, W. McC. *Henry Lawes: Musician and Friend of Poets*. New York, 1941.
McEuen, Kathryn A. *Classical Influence upon the Tribe of Ben: A Study of Classical Elements in the Nondramatic Poetry of Ben Jonson and His Circle*. Cedar Rapids, Iowa, 1939.
Moorman, F. W. *Robert Herrick: A Biographical and Critical Study*. London, 1910.
Musgrove, S. *The Universe of Robert Herrick*. Auckland, 1950.
Press, John. *Robert Herrick*. London, 1961.
Rollin, R. B. *Robert Herrick*. New York, 1966.
Starkman, M. K. "*Noble Numbers* and the Poetry of Devotion," in J. A. Mazzeo, ed., *Reason and the Imagination: Studies in the History of Ideas, 1600–1800*. New York, 1962.
Swinburne, Algernon Charles. *Studies in Prose and Poetry*. London, 1894.
Whitaker, T. R. "Herrick and the Fruits of the Garden," *ELH*, XXII (1955), 16–33.
Willey, Basil. "Robert Herrick: 1591–1674," *Church Quarterly Review*, CLVI (1955), 248–55.
Woodward, D. H. "Herrick's Oberon Poems," *JEGP*, LXIV (1965), 270–84.

HESPERIDES:
OR,
THE WORKS
BOTH
HUMANE & DIVINE
OF
ROBERT HERRICK Esq.

OVID.
Effugient avidos Carmina nostra Rogos.

LONDON,
Printed for *John Williams*, and *Francis Eglesfield*,
and are to be sold by *Tho: Hunt*, Book-seller
in *Exon*. 1648.

From HESPERIDES or, The Works both Humane & Divine of Robert Herrick Esq.

Tempora cinxisset Foliorum densior umbra:
  Debetur Genio Laurea Sylva tuo.
Tempora et Illa Tibi mollis redimisset Oliva;
  Scilicet excludis Versibus Arma tuis.
Admisces Antiqua Novis, Iucunda Severis:
  Hinc Iuvenis discat, Fœmina, Virgo, Senex
Ut solo minor es Phœbo, sic major es Unus
  Omnibus, Ingenio, Mente, Lepore, Stylo.
W. Marshall Fecit.
                              scripsit I.H.C.W.M.

Hesperides or, The Works both Humane & Divine of Robert Herrick Esq. was first published in London in 1648 by John Williams and Francis Eglesfield. This edition stands as the sole authority for the vast majority of Herrick's poems, and since its printing was supervised by the author, who provided a list of errata at the beginning of the volume, it is the source of a relatively accurate text. Of the well over fourteen hundred poems in the volume, only nine (according to J. M. Patrick, in his edition of the poems) were published before 1648, and the earliest in 1633. The dates of composition of only forty may be established with any precision, usually by the events they commemorate. A few were composed as early as 1623, the year of the poet's ordination, while virtually the whole of *His Noble Numbers or, His Pious Pieces* were written within a short period in 1647 or 1648. The 1647 date on the title page before the second division may be explained as an indication of the relatively long period it took the compositor to set up both *Hesperides* and *His Noble Numbers*. Presumably the 1647 date of the latter division had in actuality become 1648, and this new date appeared on the title page of *Hesperides*, apparently prepared last. An entry in the Stationers' Register on 29 April 1640 serves as an indication that a volume of Herrick's was then planned for publication. None is known to have survived, and the edition very likely never appeared.

[*Title page.*] Motto from Ovid's *Amores*, III, ix, 28, for whose *defugient* Herrick has substituted *effugient*: "Our songs alone shall escape destruction."

[*Frontispiece.*] The initials at the foot of the Latin verses, I.H.C.W.M., stand for John Harman, Master of Westminster College (c. 1594–1670), scholar,

To the Most Illustrious, and Most Hopefull Prince, Charles, Prince of Wales

Well may my Book come forth like Publique Day,
When such a *Light* as *You* are leads the way:
Who are my Works *Creator*, and alone
The *Flame* of it, and the *Expansion*.
And look how all those heavenly Lamps acquire   5
Light from the Sun, that *inexhausted Fire*:
So all my *Morne*, and *Evening Stars* from You
Have their *Existence*, and their *Influence* too.
Full is my Book of Glories; but all These
By You become *Immortall Substances*.   10

---

physician, poet, and friend of Herrick. Herrick addressed an epigram to him. The Latin verses have been thus translated by A. B. Grosart, in his edition of Herrick (1876):

> A denser shade of leaves thy brows should bind;
> A laurel grove is due to such a mind.
> The peaceful olive should those brows entwine,
> For arms are banished from such verse as thine.
> Old things with new thou blendest, grave with gay:
> Hence young and old, mother and maid may say,
> Phoebus except, all else thou dost outvie
> In style, and beauty, and capacity.

[*The Prefatory Poem.*] *To...Charles, Prince of Wales*. The Prince's birth on 29 May 1630 was followed, as many poets of the day noted, by the appearance of Hesperus, the evening star. This fact adds still another dimension to the title beyond those noted here: that the ancients associated the garden of Hesperus (inhabited by nymphs descended from him) with the Fortunate Isles, situated at the western end of the earth; and that Herrick thought of his poems as fruits of the western country, Devonshire, where, as vicar of Dean Prior, he composed the larger part of *Hesperides*.

The Argument of his Book

I sing of *Brooks*, of *Blossomes*, *Birds*, and *Bowers:*
Of *April*, *May*, of *June*, and *July*-Flowers.
I sing of *May-poles*, *Hock-carts*, *Wassails*, *Wakes*,
Of *Bride-grooms*, *Brides*, and of their *Bridall-cakes*.
I write of *Youth*, of *Love*, and have Accesse 5
By these, to sing of cleanly-*Wantonnesse*.
I sing of *Dewes*, of *Raines*, and piece by piece
Of *Balme*, of *Oyle*, of *Spice*, and *Amber-Greece*.
I sing of *Times trans-shifting*; and I write
How *Roses* first came *Red*, and *Lillies White*. 10
I write of *Groves*, of *Twilights*, and I sing
The Court of *Mab*, and of the *Fairie-King*.
I write of *Hell*; I sing (and ever shall)
Of *Heaven*, and hope to have it after all.

To his Muse

Whither *Mad maiden* wilt thou roame?
Farre safer 'twere to stay at home:
Where thou mayst sit, and piping please
The poore and private *Cottages*.
Since *Coats*, and *Hamlets*, best agree 5
With this thy meaner Minstralsie.
There with the Reed, thou mayst expresse.
The Shepherds Fleecie happinesse:
And with thy *Eclogues* intermixe
Some smooth, and harmlesse *Beucolicks*. 10
There on a Hillock thou mayst sing

The Argument of his Book. 3 *Hock-carts*: the cart or wagon which carried home the last load of the harvest (*OED*).

Unto a handsome Shephardling;
Or to a Girle (that keeps the Neat)
With breath more sweet then Violet.
There, there, (perhaps) such Lines as These   15
May take the simple *Villages*.
But for the Court, the Country wit
Is despicable unto it.
Stay then at home, and doe not goe
Or flie abroad to seeke for woe.   20
Contempts in Courts and Cities dwell;
No *Critick* haunts the Poore mans Cell:
Where thou mayst hear thine own Lines read
By no one tongue, there, censured.
That man's unwise will search for Ill,   25
And may prevent it, sitting still.

To his Booke

While thou didst keep thy *Candor* undefil'd,
Deerely I lov'd thee; as my first-borne child:
But when I saw thee wantonly to roame
From house to house, and never stay at home;
I brake my bonds of Love, and bad thee goe,   5
Regardlesse whether well thou sped'st, or no.
On with thy fortunes then, what e're they be;
If good I'le smile, if bad I'le sigh for Thee.

When he would have his verses read

In sober mornings, doe not thou reherse
The holy incantation of a verse;
But when that men have both well drunke, and fed,
Let my Enchantments then be sung, or read.
When Laurell spirts 'ith fire, and when the Hearth 5
Smiles to it selfe, and guilds the roofe with mirth;
When up the *Thyrse* is rais'd, and when the sound
Of sacred *Orgies* flyes, A round, A round.
When the *Rose* raignes, and locks with ointments shine,
Let rigid *Cato* read these Lines of mine. 10

Upon Julias Recovery

Droop, droop no more, or hang the head
Ye *Roses* almost withered;
Now strength, and newer Purple get,
Each here declining *Violet*.
O *Primroses*! let this day be 5
A Resurrection unto ye;
And to all flowers ally'd in blood,
Or sworn to that sweet Sister-hood:
For Health on *Julia's* cheek hath shed
Clarret, and Creame commingled. 10
And those her lips doe now appeare
As beames of *Corrall*, but more cleare.

When he would have ... read. 7 *Thyrse*: A *Javelin* twind with *Ivy* (Herrick's note).
8 *Orgies*: Songs to *Bacchus* (Herrick's note).
Upon Julias Recovery. 12 *beames*: branches.

The Parliament of Roses to Julia

I dreamt the Roses one time went
To meet and sit in Parliament:
The place for these, and for the rest
Of flowers, was thy spotlesse breast:
Over the which a State was drawne   5
Of Tiffanie, or Cob-web Lawne;
Then in that *Parly*, all those powers
Voted the Rose; the Queen of flowers.
But so, as that her self should be
The maide of Honour unto thee.   10

The Frozen Heart

I freeze, I freeze, and nothing dwels
In me but Snow, and *ysicles*.
For pitties sake give your advice,
To melt this snow, and thaw this ice;
I'le drink down Flames, but if so be   5
Nothing but love can supple me;
I'le rather keepe this frost, and snow,
Then to be thaw'd, or heated so.

A Song to the Maskers

1. Come down, and dance ye in the toyle
    Of pleasures, to a Heate;
   But if to moisture, Let the oyle
    Of Roses be your sweat.

2. Not only to your selves assume   5
    These sweets, but let them fly;
   From this, to that, and so Perfume
    E'ne all the standers by.

3. As Goddess *Isis* (when she went,
    Or glided through the street)   *10*
  Made all that touch't her with her scent,
    And whom she touch't, turne sweet.

To his Mistresses

Helpe me! helpe me! now I call
To my pretty *Witchcrafts* all:
Old I am, and cannot do
That, I was accustom'd to.
Bring your *Magicks, Spels, and Charmes,*   *5*
To enflesh my thighs, and armes:
Is there no way to beget
In my limbs their former heat?
Æson had (as *Poets* faine)
Baths that made him young againe: *10*
Find that *Medicine* (if you can)
For your drie-decrepid man:
Who would faine his strength renew,
Were it but to pleasure you.

The Wounded Heart

Come bring your *sampler*, and with Art,
  Draw in't a wounded Heart:
    And dropping here, and there:
Not that I thinke, that any Dart,
  Can make your's bleed a teare: *5*
    Or peirce it any where;
Yet doe it to this end: that I,

To his Mistresses. 9 *Æson*: Purged with brimstone, fire, and water by an enchantress, King Æson undergoes a transformation. In Golding's translation of Ovid's *Metamorphoses* (VII, ll. 340ff. and 376ff.) his "withered corse grew fulsome, faire and fresh."

May by
This secret see,
Though you can make
That *Heart* to bleed, your's ne'r will ake
For me.

Soft Musick

The mellow touch of musick most doth wound
The soule, when it doth rather sigh, then sound.

The Difference Betwixt Kings and Subjects

Twixt Kings and Subjects ther's this mighty odds,
Subjects are taught by *Men*; Kings by the *Gods*.

His Answer to a Question

Some would know
    Why I so
Long still doe tarry,
    And ask why
    Here that I
Live, and not marry?
    Thus I those
    Doe oppose;
What man would be here,
    Slave to Thrall,
    If at all
He could live free here?

Upon Julia's Fall

Julia was carelesse, and withall,
She rather took, then got a fall:
The wanton *Ambler* chanc'd to see
Part of her leggs sinceritie:
And ravish'd thus, It came to passe,   5
The Nagge (like to the *Prophets Asse*)
Began to speak, and would have been
A telling what rare sights h'ad seen:
And had told all; but did refraine,
Because his Tongue was ty'd againe.   10

No Spouse but a Sister

A bachelour I will
Live as I have liv'd still,
And never take a wife
To crucifie my life:
But this I'le tell ye too,   5
What now I meane to doe;
A Sister (in the stead
Of Wife) about I'le lead;
Which I will keep embrac'd,
And kisse, but yet be chaste.   10

Upon Julia's Fall. 6 *Prophets Asse*: Balaam's ass, struck thrice, protests his ill usage by speaking to his master. He (but not Balaam) was able to see the Angel of the Lord opposing his master's way with drawn sword. See Num. 22:30.

No Spouse but a Sister. Herrick's deceased brother's wife, Elizabeth, kept house for him at Dean Prior.

The Pomander Bracelet

To me my *Julia* lately sent
A Bracelet richly Redolent:
The Beads I kist, but most lov'd her
That did perfume the Pomander.

The shooe tying

Anthea bade me tye her shooe;
I did; and kist the Instep too:
And would have kist unto her knee,
Had not her Blush rebuked me.

The Carkanet

Instead of Orient Pearls of Jet,
I sent my Love a Karkanet:
About her spotlesse neck she knit
The lace, to honour me, or it:
Then think how wrapt was I to see   5
My Jet t'enthrall such Ivorie.

Upon the losse of his Mistresses

I have lost, and lately, these
Many dainty Mistresses:
Stately *Julia*, prime of all;
Sapho next, a principall:
Smooth *Anthea*, for a skin   5

The Carkanet. An ornamental chain, necklace, or collar, usually of gold or jeweled.

White, and Heaven-like Chrystalline:
Sweet *Electra*, and the choice
Myrha, for the Lute, and Voice.
Next, *Corinna*, for her wit,
And the graceful use of it:
With *Perilla*: All are gone;
Onely *Herrick's* left alone,
For to number sorrow by
Their departures hence, and die.

The Dream

Me thought, (last night) love in an anger came,
And brought a rod, so whipt me with the same:
Mirtle the twigs were, meerly to imply;
Love strikes, but 'tis with gentle crueltie.
Patient I was: Love pitifull grew then,
And stroak'd the stripes, and I was whole agen.
Thus like a Bee, *Love-gentle* stil doth bring
Hony to salve, where he before did sting.

The Vine

I dream'd this mortal part of mine
Was Metamorphoz'd to a Vine;
Which crawling one and every way,
Enthrall'd my dainty *Lucia*.
Me thought, her long small legs and thighs
I with my *Tendrils* did surprize;
Her Belly, Buttocks, and her Waste
By my soft *Nerv'lits* were embrac'd:

The Dream. 3 *Mirtle*: The myrtle was held sacred to Venus and is used as an emblem of love (*OED*).

About her head I writhing hung,
And with rich clusters (hid among
The leaves) her temples I behung:
So that my *Lucia* seem'd to me
Young *Bacchus* ravisht by his tree.
My curles about her neck did craule,
And armes and hands they did enthrall:
So that she could not freely stir,
(All parts there made one prisoner.)
But when I crept with leaves to hide
Those parts, which maids keep unespy'd,
Such fleeting pleasures there I took,
That with the fancie I awook;
And found (Ah me!) this flesh of mine
More like a *Stock*, then like a *Vine*.

Love's play at Push-pin

Love and my selfe (beleeve me) on a day
At childish Push-pin (for our sport) did play:
I put, he pusht, and heedless of my skin,
Love prickt my finger with a golden pin:
Since which, it festers so, that I can prove
'Twas but a trick to poyson me with love:
Little the wound was; greater was the smart;
The finger bled, but burnt was all my heart.

The Parcæ, or, Three dainty Destinies

The Armilet

Three lovely Sisters working were
(As they were closely set)

Love's play at Push-pin. 2 *Push-pin*: a child's game, in which each player pushes or fillips his pin with the object of crossing that of another player (*OED*).

Of soft and dainty Maiden-haire,
    A curious *Armelet*.
I smiling, ask'd them what they did? 5
    (Faire *Destinies* all three)
Who told me, they had drawn a thred
    Of Life, and 'twas for me.
They shew'd me then, how fine 'twas spun;
    And I reply'd thereto, 10
I care not now how soone 'tis done,
    Or cut, if cut by you.

To Robin Red-brest

Laid out for dead, let thy last kindnesse be
With leaves and mosse-work for to cover me:
And while the Wood-nimphs my cold corps inter,
Sing thou my Dirge, sweet-warbling Chorister!
For Epitaph, in Foliage, next write this, 5
  Here, here the Tomb of Robin Herrick is.

Discontents in Devon

More discontents I never had
    Since I was born, then here;
Where I have been, and still am sad,
    In this dull *Devon-shire*:
Yet justly too I must confesse; 5
    I ne'r invented such
Ennobled numbers for the Presse,
    Then where I loath'd so much.

The Parcæ.... 4 *Armelet*: Like a bracelet, it was sometimes made of "soft and dainty maiden-haire," as Herrick elsewhere describes one.

His request to Julia

Julia, if I chance to die
Ere I print my Poetry;
I most humbly thee desire
To commit it to the fire:
Better 'twere my Book were dead,　　　　5
Then to live not perfected.

Money gets the masterie

Fight thou with shafts of silver, and o'rcome,
When no force else can get the masterdome.

The Scar-fire

Water, water I desire,
Here's a house of flesh on fire:
Ope' the fountains and the springs,
And come all to Buckittings:
What ye cannot quench, pull downe;　　　　5
Spoile a house, to save a towne:
Better tis that one shu'd fall,
Then by one, to hazard all.

Upon Julia's Voice

So smooth, so sweet, so silv'ry is thy voice,
As, could they hear, the Damn'd would make no noise,
But listen to thee, (walking in thy chamber)
Melting melodious words, to Lutes of Amber.

The Scar-fire. A sudden conflagration (*OED*).
Upon Julia's Voice. 4 *of Amber*: inlaid with amber.

Againe

When I thy singing next shall heare,
Ile wish I might turne all to eare,
To drink in Notes, and Numbers; such
As blessed soules cann't heare too much:
Then melted down, there let me lye   5
Entranc'd, and lost confusedly:
And by thy Musique strucken mute,
Die, and be turn'd into a Lute.

The succession of the foure sweet months

First, *April*, she with mellow showrs
Opens the way for early flowers;
Then after her comes smiling *May*,
In a more rich and sweet aray:
Next enters *June*, and brings us more   5
Jems, then those two, that went before:
Then (lastly) *July* comes, and she
More wealth brings in, then all those three.

No Shipwrack of Vertue

To a friend

Thou sail'st with others, in this *Argus* here;
Nor wrack, or *Bulging* thou hast cause to feare:
But trust to this, my noble passenger;
Who swims with Vertue, he shall still be sure
(*Ulysses*-like) all tempests to endure;   5
And 'midst a thousand gulfs to be secure.

Againe. 3 *Numbers*: verses.

Upon his Sister-in-Law, Mistresse Elizab: Herrick

First, for Effusions due unto the dead,
My solemne Vowes have here accomplished:
Next, how I love thee, that my griefe must tell,
Wherein thou liv'st for ever. Deare farewell.

Of Love

A Sonet

How Love came in, I do not know,
Whether by th'eye, or eare, or no:
Or whether with the soule it came
(At first) infused with the same:
Whether in part 'tis here or there, 5
Or, like the soule, whole every where:
This troubles me: but I as well
As any other, this can tell;
That when from hence she does depart,
The out-let then is from the heart. 10

To the King

Upon his comming with his Army into the West

Welcome, most welcome to our Vowes and us,
Most great, and universall *Genius!*
The Drooping West, which hitherto has stood

Upon his Sister-in-Law .... She died in April, 1643.
To The King .... Charles marched into Cornwall in the summer of 1644.
2 *Genius*: guardian spirit, or angel.

As one, in long-lamented-window-hood;
Looks like a Bride now, or a bed of flowers, 5
Newly refresh't, both by the Sun, and showers.
War, which before was horrid, now appears
Lovely in you, brave Prince of Cavaliers!
A deale of courage in each bosome springs
By your accesse; (*O you the best of Kings!*) 10
Ride on with all white *Omens*; so, that where
Your Standard's up, we fix a Conquest there.

To the King and Queene, upon their unhappy distances

Woe, woe to them, who (by a ball of strife)
Doe, and have parted here a Man and Wife:
CHARLS the best Husband, while MARIA strives
 To be, and is, the very best of Wives:
Like Streams, you are divorc'd; but 'twill come, when 5
These eyes of mine shall see you mix agen.
Thus speaks the *Oke*, here; *C.* and *M.* shall meet,
Treading on *Amber*, with their silver-feet:
Nor wil't be long, ere this accomplish'd be;
The words found true, *C. M.* remember me. 10

To the reverend shade of his religious Father

That for seven *Lusters* I did never come
To doe the *Rites* to thy Religious Tombe:
That neither haire was cut, or true teares shed

---

11 *white*: propitious, favorable (*OED*).
   To the King and Queene.... In 1642 and again in 1644, Queen Henrietta Maria returned to France to seek support for the Royalist cause.
   8 *silver-feet*: both frequently danced in masque productions of the 1630's.
   To the ... Father. Nicholas Herrick died in a fall from the window of his house on 9 November 1592.

By me, o'r thee, *(as justments to the dead)*
Forgive, forgive me; since I did not know 5
Whether thy bones had here their Rest, or no.
But now 'tis known, Behold; behold, I bring
Unto thy Ghost, th'Effused Offering:
And look, what Smallage, Night-shade, Cypresse, Yew,
Unto the shades have been, or now are due, 10
Here I devote; And something more then so;
I come to pay a Debt of Birth I owe.
Thou gav'st me life, (but Mortall;) For that one
Favour, Ile make full satisfaction;
For my life mortall, Rise from out thy Herse, 15
And take a life immortall from my Verse.

Delight in Disorder

A sweet disorder in the dresse
Kindles in cloathes a wantonnesse:
A Lawne about the shoulders thrown
Into a fine distraction:
An erring Lace, which here and there 5
Enthralls the Crimson Stomacher:
A Cuffe neglectfull, and thereby
Ribbands to flow confusedly:
A winning wave (deserving Note)
In the tempestuous petticote: 10
A carelesse shooe-string, in whose tye
I see a wilde civility:
Doe more bewitch me, then when Art
Is too precise in every part.

To Dean-Bourn, *a rude River in* Devon

by which sometimes he lived

Dean-Bourn, farewell; I never look to see
Deane, or thy watry incivility.
Thy rockie bottome, that doth teare thy streams,
And makes them frantick, ev'n to all extreames;
To my content, I never sho'd behold,   5
Were thy streames silver, or the rocks all gold.
Rockie thou art; and rockie we discover
Thy men; and rockie are thy wayes all over.
O men, O manners; There, and ever knowne
To be *A Rockie Generation!*   10
A people currish; churlish as the seas;
And rude (almost) as rudest Salvages.
With whom I did, and may re-sojourne when
Rocks turn to Rivers, Rivers turn to Men.

His Cavalier

Give me that man, that dares bestride
The active Sea-horse, and with pride,
Through that huge field of waters ride:
Who, with his looks too, can appease
The ruffling winds and raging Seas,   5
In mid'st of all their outrages.
This, this a virtuous man can doe,
Saile against Rocks, and split them too;
I! and a world of Pikes passe through.

The Bag of the Bee

About the sweet bag of a Bee,
    Two *Cupids* fell at odds;

            And whose the pretty prize shu'd be,
               They vow'd to ask the Gods.

         Which *Venus* hearing; thither came,   5
            And for their boldness stript them:
         And taking thence from each his flame;
            With rods of *Mirtle* whipt them.

         Which done, to still their wanton cries,
            When quiet grown sh'ad seen them,   10
         She kist, and wip'd thir dove-like eyes;
            And gave the Bag between them.

A Country life: To his Brother, M. Tho: Herrick

Thrice, and above, blest (my soules halfe) art thou,
   In thy both Last, and Better Vow:
Could'st leave the City, for exchange, to see
   The Countries sweet simplicity:
And it to know, and practice; with intent   5
   To grow the sooner innocent:
By studying to know vertue; and to aime
   More at her nature, then her name:
The last is but the least; the first doth tell
   Wayes lesse to live, then to live well: 10
And both are knowne to thee, who now can'st live
   Led by thy conscience; to give
Justice to soone-pleas'd nature; and to show,
   Wisdome and she together goe,
And keep one Centre: This with that conspires,   15
   To teach Man to confine desires:

A Country life: To his Brother.... Three years older than the poet, Thomas left his native Leicestershire as a young man to take a position with a London mercer. He retired to a small farm in about 1610.

And know, that Riches have their proper stint,
    In the contented mind, not mint.
And can'st instruct, that those who have the itch
    Of craving more, are never rich.
These things thou know'st to'th'height, and dost prevent
    That plague; because thou art content
With that Heav'n gave thee with a warie hand,
    (More blessed in thy Brasse, then Land)
To keep cheap Nature even, and upright;
    To coole, not cocker Appetite.
Thus thou canst tearcely live to satisfie
    The belly chiefly; not the eye:
Keeping the barking stomach wisely quiet,
    Lesse with a neat, then needfull diet.
But that which most makes sweet thy country life,
    Is, the fruition of a wife:
Whom (Stars consenting with thy Fate) thou hast
    Got, not so beautifull, as chast:
By whose warme side thou dost securely sleep
    (While Love the Centinell doth keep)
With those deeds done by day, which ne'r affright
    Thy silken slumbers in the night.
Nor has the darknesse power to usher in
    Feare to those sheets, that know no sin.
But still thy wife, by chast intentions led,
    Gives thee each night a Maidenhead.
The Damaskt medowes, and the peebly streames
    Sweeten, and make soft your dreames:
The Purling springs, groves, birds, and well-weav'd Bowrs,
    With fields enameled with flowers,
Present their shapes; while fantasie discloses
    Millions of *Lillies* mixt with *Roses*.
Then dream, ye heare the Lamb by many a bleat
    Woo'd to come suck the milkie Teat:
While *Faunus* in the Vision comes to keep,
    From rav'ning wolves, the fleecie sheep.

---

27 *tearcely*: tersely.

With thousand such enchanting dreams, that meet
    To make sleep not so sound, as sweet:
Nor can these figures so thy rest endeare, 55
    As not to rise when *Chanticlere*
Warnes the last Watch; but with the Dawne dost rise
    To work, but first to sacrifice;
Making thy peace with heav'n, for some late fault,
    With Holy-meale, and spirting-salt. 60
Which done, thy painfull Thumb this sentence tells us,
    Jove for our labour all things sells us.
Nor are thy daily and devout affaires
    Attended with those desp'rate cares,
Th'industrious Merchant has; who for to find 65
    Gold, runneth to the Western Inde,
And back again, (tortur'd with fears) doth fly,
    Untaught, to suffer Poverty.
But thou at home, blest with securest ease,
    Sitt'st, and beleev'st that there be seas, 70
And watrie dangers; while thy whiter hap,
    But sees these things within thy Map.
And viewing them with a more safe survey,
    Mak'st easie Feare unto thee say,
A heart thrice wall'd with Oke, and Brasse, that man 75
    Had, first, durst plow the Ocean.
But thou at home without or tyde or gale,
    Canst in thy Map securely saile:
Seeing those painted Countries; and so guesse
    By those fine Shades, their Substances: 80
And from thy Compasse taking small advice,
    Buy'st Travell at the lowest price.
Nor are thine eares so deafe, but thou canst heare
    (Far more with wonder, then with feare)
Fame tell of States, of Countries, Courts, and Kings; 85
    And beleeve there be such things:
When of these truths, thy happyer knowledge lyes,
    More in thine eares, then in thine eyes.

---

60 *spirting-salt*: a salt that enspirits or causes to burst forth.

And when thou hear'st by that too-true-Report,
    Vice rules the Most, or All at Court: *90*
Thy pious wishes are, (though thou not there)
    Vertue had, and mov'd her Sphere.
But thou liv'st fearlesse; and thy face ne'r shewes
    Fortune when she comes, or goes.
But with thy equall thoughts, prepar'd dost stand,   *95*
    To take her by the either hand:
Nor car'st which comes the first, the foule or faire;
    A wise man ev'ry Way lies square.
And like a surly *Oke* with storms perplext;
    Growes still the stronger, strongly vext.   *100*
Be so, bold spirit; Stand Center-like, unmov'd;
    And be not onely thought, but prov'd
To be what I report thee; and inure
    Thy selfe, if want comes to endure:
And so thou dost: for thy desires are   *105*
    Confin'd to live with private *Larr*:
Not curious whether Appetite be fed,
    Or with the first, or second bread.
Who keep'st no proud mouth for delicious cates:
    Hunger makes coorse meats, delicates.   *110*
Can'st, and unurg'd, forsake that Larded fare,
    Which Art, not Nature, makes so rare;
To taste boyl'd Nettles, Colworts, Beets, and eate
    These, and sowre herbs, as dainty meat?
While soft Opinion makes thy *Genius* say,   *115*
    Content makes all Ambrosia.
Nor is it, that thou keep'st this stricter size
    So much for want, as exercise:
To numb the sence of Dearth, which sho'd sinne haste it,
    Thou might'st but onely see't, not taste it.   *120*
Yet can thy humble roofe maintaine a Quire
    Of singing Crickits by thy fire:

---

    98 *square*: referring to Aristotle's *Ethics* (Ch. X), George Puttenham, in *The Arte of English Poesie* (ed. G. Smith, *Eliz. Critical Essays*. II, 104) speaks of a constant-minded man "not easily overthrowne" as "a square man."
    115 *Genius*: the Lar, or household god, of l. 106.

And the brisk Mouse may feast her selfe with crums,
    Till that the green-ey'd Kitling comes.
Then to her Cabbin, blest she can escape   125
    The sudden danger of a Rape.
And thus thy little-well-kept-stock doth prove,
    Wealth cannot make a life, but Love.
Nor art thou so close-handed, but can'st spend
    (Counsell concurring with the end)   130
As well as spare: still conning o'r this Theame,
    To shun the first, and last extreame.
Ordaining that thy small stock find no breach,
    Or to exceed thy Tether's reach:
But to live round, and close, and wisely true   135
    To thine owne selfe; and knowne to few.
Thus let thy Rurall Sanctuary be
    Elizium to thy wife and thee;
There to disport your selves with golden measure:
    For seldome use commends the pleasure.   140
Live, and live blest; thrice happy Paire; Let Breath,
    But lost to one, be th'others death.
And as there is one Love, one Faith, one Troth,
    Be so one Death, one Grave to both.
Till when, in such assurance live, ye may   145
    Nor feare, or wish your dying day.

To the Painter, to draw him a Picture

Come, skilfull *Lupo*, now, and take
Thy *Bice*, thy *Umber*, *Pink*, and *Lake*;
And let it be thy Pensils strife,
To paint a Bridgeman to the life:
Draw him as like too, as you can,   5
An old, poore, lying, flatt'ring man:
His cheeks be-pimpled, red and blue;
His nose and lips of mulbrie hiew.
Then for an easie fansie; place

A Burling iron for his face: 10
Next, make his cheeks with breath to swell,
And for to speak, if possible:
But do not so; for feare, lest he
Sho'd by his breathing, poyson thee.

A Lyrick to Mirth

While the milder Fates consent,
Let's enjoy our merryment:
Drink, and dance, and pipe, and play;
Kisse our *Dollies* night and day:
Crown'd with clusters of the Vine;   5
Let us sit, and quaffe our wine.
Call on *Bacchus*; chaunt his praise;
Shake the *Thyrse*, and bite the *Bayes*:
Rouze *Anacreon* from the dead;
And return him drunk to bed: 10
Sing o're *Horace*; for ere long
Death will come and mar the song:
Then shall *Wilson* and *Gotiere*
Never sing, or play more here.

Against Love

When ere my heart, Love's warmth, but entertaines,
O Frost! O Snow! O Haile forbid the Banes.
One drop now deads a spark; but if the same

To the Painter.... 10 *Burling iron*: a pair of tweezers or small pincers for extracting the knots from wool (*OED*).
A Lyrick to Mirth. 8 *Thyrse*: a javelin entwined with ivy; *bite the Bayes*: to chew bay leaves; so the Latin poets accounted for inspiration.
13 *Wilson and Gotiere*: The former was a famous singer and composer of ayres who became professor of music at Oxford; the latter was a virtuoso lutanist who came from France to England in the entourage of Queen Henrietta Maria.

Once gets a force, Floods cannot quench the flame.
Rather then love, let me be ever lost; 5
Or let me 'gender with eternall frost.

Upon Julia's *Riband*

As shews the Aire, when with a Rain-bow grac'd;
So smiles that Riband 'bout my *Julia's* waste:
Or like——Nay 'tis that *Zonulet* of love,
Wherein all pleasures of the world are wove.

The frozen Zone: or, Julia *disdainfull*

Whither? Say, whither shall I fly,
To slack these flames wherein I frie?
   To the Treasures, shall I goe,
   Of the Raine, Frost, Haile, and Snow?
   Shall I search the under-ground, 5
   Where all Damps, and Mists are found?
   Shall I seek (for speedy ease)
   All the floods, and frozen seas?
   Or descend into the deep,
   Where eternall cold does keep? 10
   These may coole; but there's a Zone
   Colder yet then any one:
   That's my *Julia's* breast; where dwels
   Such destructive Ysicles;
As that the Congelation will 15
Me sooner starve, then those can kill.

Leanders *Obsequies*

When as *Leander* young was drown'd,
No heart by love receiv'd a wound;
But on a Rock himselfe sate by,
There weeping sup'rabundantly.
Sighs numberlesse he cast about,   5
And all his Tapers thus put out:
His head upon his hand he laid;
And sobbing deeply, thus he said,
Ah cruell Sea! and looking on't,
Wept as he'd drowne the Hellespont.   10
And sure his tongue had more exprest,
But that his teares forbad the rest.

The Teare sent to her from *Stanes*

1. Glide gentle streams, and beare
    Along with you my teare
        To that coy Girle;
        Who smiles, yet slayes
        Me with delayes;   5
    And strings my tears as Pearle.

2. See! see she's yonder set,
    Making a Carkanet
        Of Maiden-flowers!
        There, there present   10
        This Orient,
    And Pendant Pearle of ours.

3. Then say, I've sent one more
    Jem to enrich her store;

Leanders Obsequies. 2 *love*: Cupid.

        And that is all 15
        Which I can send,
          Or vainly spend,
    For tears no more will fall.

4. Nor will I seek supply
   Of them, the spring's once drie; 20
      But Ile devise,
      (Among the rest)
      A way that's best
   How I may save mine eyes.

5. Yet say; sho'd she condemne 25
   Me to surrender them;
      Then say; my part
      Must be to weep
      Out them, to keep
   A poore, yet loving heart. 30

6. Say too, She wo'd have this;
   She shall: Then my hope is,
      That when I'm poore,
      And nothing have
      To send, or save; 35
   I'm sure she'll ask no more.

His fare-well to Sack

Farewell thou Thing, time-past so knowne, so deare
To me, as blood to life and spirit: Neare,
Nay, thou more neare then kindred, friend, man, wife,
Male to the female, soule to body: Life
To quick action, or the warme soft side   5
Of the resigning, yet resisting Bride.
The kisse of Virgins; First-fruits of the bed;

  His fare-well to Sack. A complementary "Welcome to Sack" also appears in *Hesperides.*

Soft speech, smooth touch, the lips, the Maiden-head:
These, and a thousand sweets, co'd never be
So neare, or deare, as thou wast once to me. 10
O thou the drink of Gods, and Angels! Wine
That scatter'st Spirit and Lust; whose purest shine,
More radiant then the Summers Sun-beams shows;
Each way illustrious, brave; and like to those
Comets we see by night; whose shagg'd portents 15
Fore-tell the comming of some dire events:
Or some full flame, which with a pride aspires,
Throwing about his wild, and active fires.
'Tis thou, above Nectar, O Divinest soule!
(Eternall in thy self) that canst controule 20
That, which subverts whole nature, grief and care;
Vexation of the mind, and damn'd Despaire.
'Tis thou, alone, who with thy Mistick Fan,
Work'st more then Wisdome, Art, or Nature can,
To rouze the sacred madnesse; and awake 25
The frost-bound-blood, and spirits; and to make
Them frantick with thy raptures, flashing through
The soule, like lightning, and as active too.
'Tis not *Apollo* can, or those thrice three
Castalian Sisters, sing, if wanting thee. 30
Horace, Anacreon both had lost their fame,
Had'st thou not fill'd them with thy fire and flame.
Phœbean splendour! and thou *Thespian* spring!
Of which, sweet Swans must drink, before they sing
Their true-pac'd-Numbers, and their Holy-Layes, 35
Which makes them worthy *Cedar*, and the *Bayes*.
But why? why longer doe I gaze upon
Thee with the eye of admiration?
Since I must leave thee; and enforc'd, must say
To all thy witching beauties, Goe, Away. 40
But if thy whimpring looks doe ask me why?
Then know, that Nature bids thee goe, not I.
'Tis her erroneous self has made a braine
Uncapable of such a Soveraigne,

23 *Fan*: an instrument for winnowing grain (*OED*).

As is thy powerfull selfe. Prethee not smile; 45
Or smile more inly; lest thy looks beguile
My vowes denounc'd in zeale, which thus much show thee,
That I have sworn, but by thy looks to know thee.
Let others drink thee freely; and desire
Thee and their lips espous'd; while I admire, 50
And love thee; but not taste thee. Let my Muse
Faile of thy former helps; and onely use
Her inadult'rate strength: what's done by me
Hereafter, shall smell of the Lamp, not thee.

The Eye

   Make me a heaven; and make me there
Many a lesse and greater spheare.
Make me the straight, and oblique lines;
The Motions, Lations, and the Signes.
Make me a Chariot, and a Sun; 5
And let them through a Zodiac run:
Next, place me Zones, and Tropicks there;
With all the Seasons of the Yeare.
Make me a Sun-set; and a Night:
And then present the Mornings-light 10
Cloath'd in her Chamlets of Delight.
To these, make Clouds to poure downe raine;
With weather foule, then faire againe.
And when, wise Artist, that thou hast,
With all that can be, this heaven grac't; 15
Ah! what is then this curious skie,
But onely my *Corinna's* eye?

The Curse
A Song

   Goe perjur'd man; and if thou ere return
To see the small remainders in mine Urne:

When thou shalt laugh at my Religious dust;
And ask, Where's now the colour, forme and trust
Of Womans beauty? and with hand more rude 5
Rifle the Flowers which the Virgins strew'd:
Know, I have pray'd to Furie, that some wind
May blow my ashes up, and strike thee blind.

Upon the Bishop of Lincolne's *Imprisonment*

Never was Day so over-sick with showres,
But that it had some intermitting houres.
Never was Night so tedious, but it knew
The Last Watch out, and saw the Dawning too.
Never was Dungeon so obscurely deep, 5
Wherein or Light, or Day, did never peep.
Never did Moone so ebbe, or seas so wane,
But they left Hope-seed to fill up againe.
So you, my Lord, though you have now your stay,
Your Night, your Prison, and your Ebbe; you may 10
Spring up afresh; when all these mists are spent,
And Star-like, once more, guild our Firmament.
Let but That Mighty *Cesar* speak, and then,
All bolts, all barres, all gates shall cleave; as when
That Earth-quake shook the house, and gave the stout 15
Apostles, way (unshackled) to goe out.
This, as I wish for, so I hope to see;
Though you (my Lord) have been unkind to me:
To wound my heart, and never to apply
(When you had power) the meanest remedy: 20
Well; though my griefe by you was gall'd, the more;
Yet I bring Balme and Oile to heal your sore.

Upon the...Imprisonment. A churchman with political expectations, John Williams, Bishop of Lincoln, was twice sent to the Tower: in 1637 for subornation of perjury, and in 1641, when he was impeached with eleven other bishops by the House of Commons. The nature of his unkindness to the poet (l. 18) is unknown.

To Electra

    Ile come to thee in all those shapes
    As *Jove* did, when he made his rapes:
    Onely, Ile not appeare to thee,
    As he did once to *Semele*.
    Thunder and Lightning Ile lay by,   5
    To talk with thee familiarly.
    Which done, then quickly we'll undresse
    To one and th'others nakednesse.
    And ravisht, plunge into the bed,
    (Bodies and souls commingled)   10
    And kissing, so as none may heare,
    We'll weary all the Fables there.

Corinna's *going a Maying*

Get up, get up for shame, the Blooming Morne
Upon her wings presents the god unshorne.
        See how *Aurora* throwes her faire
        Fresh-quilted colours through the aire:
        Get up, sweet-Slug-a-bed, and see   5
        The Dew-bespangling Herbe and Tree.
Each Flower has wept, and bow'd toward the East,
Above an houre since; yet you not drest,
        Nay! not so much as out of bed?
        When all the Birds have Mattens seyd,   10
        And sung their thankfull Hymnes: 'tis sin,
        Nay, profanation to keep in,
When as a thousand Virgins on this day,
Spring, sooner then the Lark, to fetch in May.

Rise; and put on your Foliage, and be seene   15
To come forth, like the Spring-time, fresh and greene;
        And sweet as *Flora*. Take no care

>   For Jewels for your Gowne, or Haire:
>   Feare not; the leaves will strew
>   Gemms in abundance upon you:
> Besides, the childhood of the Day has kept,
> Against you come, some *Orient Pearls* unwept:
>   Come, and receive them while the light
>   Hangs on the Dew-locks of the night:
>   And *Titan* on the Eastern hill
>   Retires himselfe, or else stands still
> Till you come forth. Wash, dresse, be briefe in praying:
> Few Beads are best, when once we goe a Maying.
>
> Come, my *Corinna*, come; and comming, marke
> How each field turns a street; each street a Parke
>   Made green, and trimm'd with trees: see how
>   Devotion gives each House a Bough,
>   Or Branch: Each Porch, each doore, ere this,
>   An Arke a Tabernacle is
> Made up of white-thorn neatly enterwove;
> As if here were those cooler shades of love.
>   Can such delights be in the street,
>   And open fields, and we not see't?
>   Come, we'll abroad; and let's obay
>   The Proclamation made for May:
> And sin no more, as we have done, by staying;
> But my *Corinna*, come, let's goe a Maying.
>
> There's not a budding Boy, or Girle, this day,
> But is got up, and gone to bring in May.
>   A deale of Youth, ere this, is come
>   Back, and with *White-thorn* laden home.
>   Some have dispatcht their Cakes and Creame,
>   Before that we have left to dreame:
> And some have wept, and woo'd, and plighted Troth,
> And chose their Priest, ere we can cast off sloth:
>   Many a green-gown has been given;
>   Many a kisse, both odde and even:
>   Many a glance too has been sent
>   From out the eye, Loves Firmament:

Many a jest told of the Keyes betraying 55
This night, and Locks pickt, yet w'are not a Maying.

Come, let us goe, while we are in our prime;
And take the harmlesse follie of the time.
    We shall grow old apace, and die
    Before we know our liberty. 60
    Our life is short; and our dayes run
    As fast away as do's the Sunne:
And as a vapour, or a drop of raine
Once lost, can ne'r be found againe:
    So when or you or I are made 65
    A fable, song, or fleeting shade;
    All love, all liking, all delight
    Lies drown'd with us in endlesse night.
Then while time serves, and we are but decaying;
Come, my *Corinna*, come, let's goe a Maying. 70

To his dying Brother, Master William Herrick

Life of my life, take not so soone thy flight,
But stay the time till we have bade Good night.
Thou hast both Wind and Tide with thee; Thy way
As soone dispatcht is by the Night, as Day.
Let us not then so rudely henceforth goe 5
Till we have wept, kist, sigh't, shook hands, or so.
There's paine in parting; and a kind of hell,
When once true-lovers take their last Fare-well.
What? shall we two our endlesse leaves take here
Without a sad looke, or a solemne teare? 10
He knowes not Love, that hath not this truth proved,
Love is most loth to leave the thing beloved.
Pay we our Vowes, and goe; yet when we part,
Then, even then, I will bequeath my heart

To his dying Brother .... Dead by June, 1632.

Into thy loving hands: For Ile keep none 15
To warme my Breast, when thou my Pulse art gone.
No, here Ile last, and walk (a harmless shade)
About this Urne, wherein thy Dust is laid,
To guard it so, as nothing here shall be
Heavy, to hurt those sacred seeds of thee. 20

How Lillies came white

White though ye be; yet, Lillies, know,
From the first ye were not so:
    But Ile tell ye
    What befell ye;
Cupid and his Mother lay 5
In a Cloud; while both did play,
He with his pretty finger prest
The rubie niplet of her breast;
Out of the which, the creame of light,
    Like to a Dew, 10
    Fell downe on you,
    And made ye white.

Impossibilities to his friend

My faithful friend, if you can see
The Fruit to grow up, or the Tree:
If you can see the colour come
Into the blushing Peare, or Plum:
If you can see the water grow 5
To cakes of Ice, or flakes of Snow:
If you can see, that drop of raine
Lost in the wild sea, once againe:
If you can see, how Dreams do creep
Into the Brain by easie sleep: 10
Then there is hope that you may see
Her love me once, who now hates me.

To the Virgins, to make much of Time

1. Gather ye Rose-buds while ye may,
   Old Time is still a flying:
   And this same flower that smiles to day,
   To morrow will be dying.

2. The Glorious Lamp of Heaven, the Sun, 5
   The higher he's a getting;
   The sooner will his Race be run,
   And neerer he's to Setting.

3. That Age is best, which is the first,
   When Youth and Blood are warmer; 10
   But being spent, the worse, and worst
   Times, still succeed the former.

4. Then be not coy, but use your time;
   And while ye may, goe marry:
   For having lost but once your prime, 15
   You may for ever tarry.

To his Friend, on the untuneable Times

Play I co'd once; but (gentle friend) you see
My Harp hung up, here on the Willow tree.
Sing I co'd once; and bravely too enspire
(With luscious Numbers) my melodious Lyre.
Draw I co'd once (although not stocks or stones, 5
Amphion-like) men made of flesh and bones,
Whether I wo'd; but (ah!) I know not how,
I feele in me, this transmutation now.

To his Friend .... 2 *Willow tree*: see Ps. 137:2.

Griefe, (my deare friend) has first my Harp unstrung;
Wither'd my hand, and palsie-struck my tongue.   10

A Pastorall upon the birth of Prince Charles, Presented to the King, and Set by Mr. Nic: Laniere

The Speakers, MIRTILLO, AMINTAS, *and* AMARILLIS.

Amin.   Good day, *Mirtillo.*   *Mirt.* And to you no lesse:
And all faire Signs lead on our Shepardesse.
Amar.   With all white luck to you.   *Mirt.* But say, what news
Stirs in our Sheep-walk?   *Amin.* None, save that my Ewes,
My Weathers, Lambes, and wanton Kids are well,   5
Smooth, faire, and fat, none better I can tell:
Or that this day *Menalchas* keeps a feast
For his Sheep-shearers.   *Mir.* True, these are the least.
But dear *Amintas*, and sweet *Amarillis,*
Rest but a while here, by this bank of Lillies.   10
And lend a gentle eare to one report
The Country has.   *Amint.* From whence?   *Amar.* From whence?
   Mir. The Court.
Three dayes before the shutting in of *May*,
(With whitest Wool be ever crown'd that day!)   15
To all our joy, a sweet-fac't child was borne,
More tender then the childhood of the Morne.
Chor.   *Pan* pipe to him, and bleats of lambs and sheep,
Let Lullaby the pretty Prince asleep!
Mirt.   And that his birth sho'd be more singular,   20
At Noone of Day, was seene a silver Star,
Bright as the Wise-mens Torch, which guided them
To Gods sweet Babe, when borne at *Bethlehem*;

A Pastorall...Set by Mr. Nic: Laniere. Prince Charles was born 29 May 1630. Lanier, Master of the King's Musick under Charles I, was a masque composer and ayre writer of considerable eminence. He also set the poet's "How Lillies came white."

While Golden Angels (some have told to me)
Sung out his Birth with Heav'nly Minstralsie.   25
Amint.   O rare! But is't a trespasse if we three
Sho'd wend along his Baby-ship to see?
Mir.   Not so, not so.   *Chor.* But if it chance to prove
At most a fault, 'tis but a fault of love.
Amar.   But deare *Mirtillo*, I have heard it told,   30
Those learned men brought *Incense, Myrrhe,* and *Gold*,
From Countries far, with store of Spices, (sweet)
And laid them downe for Offrings at his feet.
Mirt.   'Tis true indeed; and each of us will bring
Unto our smiling, and our blooming King,   35
A neat, though not so great an Offering.
Amar.   A Garland for my Gift shall be
Of flowers, ne'r suckt by th'theeving Bee:
And all most sweet; yet all lesse sweet then he.
Amint.   And I will beare along with you   40
Leaves dropping downe the honyed dew,
With oaten pipes, as sweet, as new.
Mirt.   And I a Sheep-hook will bestow,
To have his little King-ship know,
As he is Prince, he's Shepherd too.   45
Chor.   Come let's away, and quickly let's be drest,
And quickly give, *The swiftest Grace is best.*
And when before him we have laid our treasures,
We'll blesse the Babe, Then back to Countrie pleasures.

To Musique, to becalme his Fever

1. Charm me asleep, and melt me so
      With thy Delicious Numbers;
    That being ravisht, hence I goe
      Away in easie slumbers.
        Ease my sick head,   5
        And make my bed,
      Thou Power that canst sever

   From me this ill:
   And quickly still:
   Though thou not kill
    My Fever.

2. Thou sweetly canst convert the same
  From a consuming fire,
Into a gentle-licking flame,
  And make it thus expire,
   Then make me weep
   My paines asleep;
And give me such reposes,
  That I, poore I,
   May think, thereby,
   I live and die
    'Mongst Roses.

3. Fall on me like a silent dew,
  Or like those Maiden showrs,
Which, by the peepe of day, doe strew
  A Baptime o're the flowers.
   Melt, melt my paines,
   With thy soft straines;
That having ease me given,
   With full delight,
   I leave this light;
   And take my flight
    For Heaven.

Upon a Gentlewoman with a sweet Voice

So long you did not sing, or touch your Lute,
We knew 'twas Flesh and Blood, that there sate mute.
But when your Playing, and your Voice came in,
'Twas no more you then, but a *Cherubin*.

Upon Julia's *breasts*

Display thy breasts, my *Julia*, there let me
Behold that circummortall purity:
Between whose glories, there my lips Ile lay,
Ravisht, in that faire *Via Lactea*.

To the Rose
Song

1. Goe happy Rose, and enterwove
    With other Flowers, bind my Love.
       Tell her too, she must not be,
       Longer flowing, longer free,
       That so oft has fetter'd me. 5

2. Say (if she's fretfull) I have bands
    Of Pearle, and Gold, to bind her hands:
       Tell her, if she struggle still,
       I have Mirtle rods, (at will)
       For to tame, though not to kill. 10

3. Take thou my blessing, thus, and goe,
    And tell her this, but doe not so,
       Lest a handsome anger flye,
       Like a Lightning, from her eye,
       And burn thee'up, as well as I. 15

Upon Julia's breasts. 2 *circummortall:* "above" the merely mortal.
4 *Via Lactea:* the Milky Way.
   To the Rose. Song. See Martial, *Epigrams* VII, 89, for the piece beginning "*I, felix rosa* . . . ," to which Herrick is indebted for his opening lines.

To the High and Noble Prince, GEORGE, Duke, Marquesse, and Earle of Buckingham

Never my Book's perfection did appeare,
Til I had got the name of VILLARS here.
Now 'tis so full, that when therein I look,
I see a Cloud of Glory fills my Book.
Here stand it stil to dignifie our Muse, 5
Your sober Hand-maid; who doth wisely chuse,
Your Name to be a *Laureat Wreathe* to Hir,
Who doth both love and feare you *Honour'd Sir.*

To the King

If when these Lyricks (CESAR) You shall heare,
And that *Apollo* shall so touch Your eare,
As for to make this, that, or any one
Number, Your owne, by free Adoption;
That Verse, of all the Verses here, shall be 5
The Heire to This *great Realme of Poetry.*

To the Queene

Goddesse of Youth, and Lady of the Spring.
(*Most fit to be the Consort to a King*)
Be pleas'd to rest you in *This Sacred Grove,*
Beset with *Mirtles*; whose each leafe drops Love.
Many a sweet-fac't *Wood-Nymph* here is seene, 5
Of which chast *Order You* are now the *Queene:*

Witnesse their *Homage*, when they come and strew
Your Walks with Flowers, and give their Crowns to you.
Your Leavie-Throne (with *Lilly*-work) possesse;
And be both *Princesse* here, and *Poetresse*. 10

The Poets good wishes for the most hopefull and handsome Prince, the Duke of Yorke

May his pretty Duke-ship grow
Like t'a Rose of *Jericho*:
Sweeter far, then ever yet
Showrs or Sun-shines co'd beget.
May the Graces, and the Howers   5
Strew his hopes, and Him with flowers:
And so dresse him up with Love,
As to be the Chick of *Jove*.
May the thrice-three-Sisters sing
Him the Soveraigne of their Spring: 10
And entitle none to be
Prince of *Hellicon*, but He.
May his soft foot, where it treads,
Gardens thence produce and Meads:
And those Meddowes full be set   15
With the Rose, and Violet.
May his ample Name be knowne
To the last succession:
And his actions high be told
Through the world, but writ in gold.   20

The Poets good wishes for... the Duke of Yorke. Prince James was born 14 October 1633.

To Anthea, *who may command him any thing*

[1.] Bid me to live, and I will live
    Thy Protestant to be:
  Or bid me love, and I will give
    A loving heart to thee.

2. A heart as soft, a heart as kind,
    A heart as sound and free,
  As in the whole world thou canst find,
    That heart Ile give to thee.

3. Bid that heart stay, and it will stay,
    To honour thy Decree:
  Or bid it languish quite away,
    And't shall doe so for thee.

4. Bid me to weep, and I will weep,
    While I have eyes to see:
  And having none, yet I will keep
    A heart to weep for thee.

5. Bid me despaire, and Ile despaire,
    Under that *Cypresse* tree:
  Or bid me die, and I will dare
    E'en Death, to die for thee.

6. Thou art my life, my love, my heart,
    The very eyes of me:
  And hast command of every part,
    To live and die for thee.

A Nuptiall Song, or Epithalamie, on Sir Clipseby Crew and his Lady

1. What's that we see from far? the spring of Day
Bloom'd from the East, or faire Injewel'd May
    Blowne out of April; or some New-
    Star fill'd with glory to our view,
        Reaching at heaven,   5
To adde a nobler Planet to the seven?
    Say, or doe we not descrie
Some Goddesse, in a cloud of Tiffanie
    To move, or rather the
    Emergent *Venus* from the Sea?   10

2. 'Tis she! 'tis she! or else some more Divine
Enlightned substance; mark how from the Shrine
    Of holy Saints she paces on,
    Treading upon *Vermilion*
        And *Amber*; Spice-   15
ing the Chafte Aire with fumes of Paradise.
    Then come on, come on, and yeeld
A savour like unto a blessed field,
    When the bedabled Morne
Washes the golden eares of corne.   20

3. See where she comes; and smell how all the street
Breathes Vine-yards and Pomgranats: O how sweet!
    As a fir'd Altar, is each stone,
    Perspiring pounded Cynamon.
        The Phenix nest,   25
Built up of odours, burneth in her breast.
    Who therein wo'd not consume
His soule to Ash-heaps in that rich perfume?

A Nuptiall Song...on Sir Clipseby Crew.... Son of Sir Ranulphe Crewe, he married June, second daughter of Sir John Pulteney, on 7 July 1627. She died in 1639, in her thirtieth year.

                    Bestroaking Fate the while
                He burnes to Embers on the Pile.   30

4.   *Himen, O Himen!* Tread the sacred ground;
Shew thy white feet, and head with Marjoram crown'd:
            Mount up thy flames, and let thy Torch
            Display the Bridegroom in the porch,
                        In his desires   35
More towring, more disparkling then thy fires:
            Shew her how his eyes do turne
And roule about, and in their motions burne
                Their balls to Cindars: haste,
                Or else to ashes he will waste.   40

5.   Glide by the banks of Virgins then, and passe
The Shewers of Roses, lucky-foure-leav'd grasse:
            The while the cloud of younglings sing,
            And drown yee with a flowrie Spring:
                        While some repeat   45
Your praise, and bless you, sprinkling you with Wheat:
            While that others doe divine;
Blest is the Bride, on whom the Sun doth shine;
                And thousands gladly wish
                You multiply, as doth a Fish.   50

6.   And beautious Bride we do confess y'are wise,
In dealing forth these bashfull jealousies:
            In Lov's name do so; and a price
            Set on your selfe, by being nice:
                        But yet take heed;   55
What now you seem, be not the same indeed,
            And turne *Apostate*: Love will
Part of the way be met; or sit stone-still.
                On then, and though you slow-
                ly go, yet, howsoever, go.   60

7.   And now y'are enter'd; see the Codled Cook
Runs from his *Torrid Zone*, to prie, and look,
            And blesse his dainty Mistresse: see,

       The Aged point out, This is she,
           Who now must sway 65
The House (Love shield her) with her Yea and Nay:
       And the smirk Butler thinks it
Sin, in's Nap'rie, not to express his wit;
           Each striving to devise
       Some gin, wherewith to catch your eyes. 70

8.   To bed, to bed, kind Turtles, now, and write
This the short'st day, and this the longest night;
       But yet too short for you: 'tis we,
       Who count this night as long as three,
           Lying alone, 75
Telling the Clock strike Ten, Eleven, Twelve, One.
       Quickly, quickly then prepare;
And let the Young-men and the Bride-maids share
           Your Garters; and their joynts
       Encircle with the Bride-grooms Points. 80

9.   By the Brides eyes, and by the teeming life
Of her green hopes, we charge ye, that no strife
       (Farther then Gentlenes tends) gets place
       Among ye, striving for her lace:
           O doe not fall 85
Foule in these noble pastimes, lest ye call
       Discord in, and so divide
The youthfull Bride-groom, and the fragrant Bride:
           Which Love fore-fend; but spoken,
       Be't to your praise, no peace was broken. 90

10.   Strip her of Spring-time, tender-whimpring-maids,
Now *Autumne's* come, when all those flowrie aids
       Of her Delayes must end; Dispose
       That *Lady-smock*, that *Pansie*, and that *Rose*
           Neatly apart; 95
But for *Prick-madam*, and for *Gentle-heart;*
       And soft-*Maidens-blush*, the Bride
Makes holy these, all others lay aside:

   Then strip her, or unto her
  Let him come, who dares undo her.

11. And to enchant yee more, see every where
About the Roofe a *Syren* in a Sphere;
   (As we think) singing to the dinne
   Of many a warbling *Cherubim*:
     O marke yee how
The soule of Nature melts in numbers: now
   See, a thousand *Cupids* flye,
To light their Tapers at the Brides bright eye.
   To Bed; or her they'l tire,
  Were she an Element of fire.

12. And to your more bewitching, see, the proud
Plumpe Bed beare up, and swelling like a cloud,
   Tempting the two too modest; can
   Yee see it brusle like a Swan,
     And you be cold
To meet it, when it woo's and seemes to fold
   The Armes to hugge it? throw, throw
Your selves into the mighty over-flow
    Of that white Pride, and Drowne
   The night, with you, in floods of Downe.

13. The bed is ready, and the maze of Love
Lookes for the treaders; every where is wove
   Wit and new misterie; read, and
   Put in practise, to understand
     And know each wile,
Each hieroglyphick of a kisse or smile;
   And do it to the full; reach
High in your own conceipt, and some way teach
    Nature and Art, one more
   Play, then they ever knew before.

14. If needs we must for Ceremonies-sake,
Blesse a *Sack-posset*; Luck go with it; take

    The Night-Charme quickly; you have spells,
    And magicks for to end, and hells,
      To passe; but such   *135*
And of such Torture as no one would grutch
    To live therein for ever: Frie
And consume, and grow again to die,
      And live, and in that case,
    Love the confusion of the place.   *140*

15. But since It must be done, dispatch, and sowe
Up in a sheet your Bride, and what if so
    It be with Rock, or walles of Brasse,
    Ye Towre her up, as *Danae* was;
      Thinke you that this,   *145*
Or hell it selfe a powerfull Bulwarke is?
    I tell yee no; but like a
Bold bolt of thunder he will make his way,
      And rend the cloud, and throw
    The sheet about, like flakes of snow.   *150*

16. All now is husht in silence; *Midwife-moone*,
With all her *Owle-ey'd* issue begs a boon
    Which you must grant; that's entrance; with
    Which extract, all we can call pith
      And quintiscence   *155*
Of Planetary bodies; so commence
    All faire *Constellations*
Looking upon yee, that Two Nations
      Springing from two such Fires,
    May blaze the vertue of their Sires.   *160*

Upon Shark
Epig.

  Shark, when he goes to any publick feast,
  Eates to ones thinking, of all there, the least.

What saves the master of the House thereby?
When if the servants search, they may descry
In his wide Codpeece, (dinner being done)   5
Two Napkins cram'd up, and a silver Spoone.

Oberons *Feast*

Shapcot! To thee the Fairy State
I with discretion, dedicate.
Because thou prizest things that are
Curious, and un-familiar.
Take first the feast; these dishes gone;   5
Wee'l see the Fairy-Court anon.

A little mushroome table spred,
After short prayers, they set on bread;
A Moon-parcht grain of purest wheat,
With some small glit'ring gritt, to eate   10
His choyce bitts with; then in a trice
They make a feast lesse great then nice.
But all this while his eye is serv'd,
We must not thinke his eare was stearv'd:
But that there was in place to stir   15
His Spleen, the chirring Grashopper;
The merry Cricket, puling Flie,
The piping Gnat for minstralcy.
And now, we must imagine first,
The Elves present to quench his thirst   20
A pure seed-Pearle of Infant dew,
Brought and besweetned in a blew
And pregnant violet; which done,
His kitling eyes begin to runne
Quite through the table, where he spies   25
The hornes of paperie Butterflies,

Oberons Feast. 1 *Shapcot*: Thomas Shapcott, lawyer, was close friend to Herrick. *Alumni Oxon.* records that he was a gentleman from Exeter, Devonshire, who matriculated at Exeter College in Oxford in 1633 at the age of sixteen.

Of which he eates, and tastes a little
Of that we call the Cuckoes spittle.
A little Fuz-ball-pudding stands
By, yet not blessed by his hands, 30
That was too coorse; but then forthwith
He ventures boldly on the pith
Of sugred Rush, and eates the sagge
And well bestrutted Bees sweet bagge:
Gladding his pallat with some store 35
Of Emits eggs; what wo'd he more?
But Beards of Mice, a Newt's stew'd thigh,
A bloated Earewig, and a Flie;
With the Red-capt worme, that's shut
Within the concave of a Nut, 40
Browne as his Tooth. A little Moth,
Late fatned in a piece of cloth:
With withered cherries; Mandrakes eares;
Moles eyes; to these, the slain-Stags teares:
The unctuous dewlaps of a Snaile; 45
The broke-heart of a Nightingale
Ore-come in musicke; with a wine,
Ne're ravisht from the flattering Vine,
But gently prest from the soft side
Of the most sweet and dainty Bride, 50
Brought in a dainty daizie, which
He fully quaffs up to bewitch
His blood to height; this done, commended
Grace by his Priest; *The feast is ended.*

To Virgins

Heare ye Virgins, and Ile teach,
What the times of old did preach.
Rosamond was in a Bower

46–47: *Nightingale*: see Crashaw's poem.
50 *Bride*: bridewort.
To Virgins. 3 *Rosamond*: mistress of Henry II.

Kept, as *Danae* in a Tower:
But yet Love (who subtile is) 5
Crept to that, and came to this.
Be ye lockt up like to these,
Or the rich *Hesperides*;
Or those Babies in your eyes,
In their Christall Nunneries; 10
Notwithstanding Love will win,
Or else force a passage in:
And as coy be, as you can,
Gifts will get ye, or the man.

To Daffadills

[1.] Faire Daffadills, we weep to see
    You haste away so soone:
As yet the early-rising Sun
    Has not attain'd his Noone.
        Stay, stay, 5
Untill the hasting day
        Has run
But to the Even-song;
And, having pray'd together, we
    Will goe with you along. 10

2. We have short time to stay, as you,
    We have as short a Spring;
As quick a growth to meet Decay,
    As you, or any thing.
        We die, 15
As your hours doe, and drie
        Away,
Like to the Summers raine;
Or as the pearles of Mornings dew
    Ne'r to be found againe. 20

---

8 *Hesperides*: The daughters of Hesperus were reputedly guarded by a dragon.

Mattens, or morning Prayer

When with the Virgin morning thou do'st rise,
Crossing thy selfe; come thus to sacrifice:
First wash thy heart in innocence, then bring
Pure hands, pure habits, pure, pure every thing.
Next to the Altar humbly kneele, and thence, 5
Give up thy soule in clouds of frankinsence.
Thy golden Censors fil'd with odours sweet,
Shall make thy actions with their ends to meet.

Evensong

Beginne with *Jove*; then is the worke halfe done;
And runnes most smoothly, when tis well begunne.
Jove's is the first and last: The Morn's his due,
The midst is thine; But *Joves* the Evening too;
As sure a *Mattins* do's to him belong, 5
So sure he layes claime to the *Evensong*.

The Kisse
A Dialogue

1. Among thy Fancies, tell me this,
   What is the thing we call a kisse?
2. I shall resolve ye, what it is.

   It is a creature born and bred
   Between the lips, (all cherrie-red,) 5
   By love and warme desires fed,
Chor. And makes more soft the Bridall Bed.

		2.	It is an active flame, that flies,	
			First, to the Babies of the eyes;	
			And charmes them there with lullabies;	10
	Chor.		And stils the Bride too, when she cries.	

      2. Then to the chin, the cheek, the eare,
         It frisks, and flyes, now here, now there,
         'Tis now farre off, and then tis nere;
Chor.   And here, and there, and every where.   15

      1. Ha's it a speaking virtue? 2. Yes;
      1. How speaks it, say? 2. Do you but this,
         Part your joyn'd lips, then speaks your kisse;
Chor.   And this loves sweetest language is.

      1. Has it a body? 2. I, and wings   20
         With thousand rare encolourings:
         And as it flyes, it gently sings,
Chor.   Love, honie yeelds; but never stings.

To the right honourable, Philip, *Earle of Pembroke, and Montgomerie*

How dull and dead are books, that cannot show
A *Prince of Pembroke*, and that *Pembroke*, you!
You, who are High born, and a Lord no lesse
Free by your fate, then Fortunes mightinesse,
Who hug our Poems (Honourd Sir) and then   5
The paper gild, and Laureat the pen.
Nor suffer you the Poets to sit cold,
But warm their wits, and turn their lines to gold.
Others there be, who righteously will swear

To the...Earle of Pembroke, and Montgomerie. Philip Herbert, nephew of Sidney and dedicatee of the Shakespeare Folio of 1623.

Those smooth-pac't Numbers, amble every where; 10
And these brave Measures go a stately trot;
Love those, like these; regard, reward them not.
But you my Lord, are One, whose hand along
Goes with your mouth, or do's outrun your tongue;
Paying before you praise; and cockring wit, 15
Give both the Gold and Garland unto it.

To the most learned, wise, and Arch-Antiquary, M. John Selden

I who have favour'd many, come to be
Grac't (now at last) or glorifi'd by thee.
Loe, I, the Lyrick Prophet, who have set
On many a head the Delphick Coronet,
Come unto thee for Laurell, having spent 5
My wreaths on those, who little gave or lent.
Give me the *Daphne*, that the world may know it,
Whom they neglected, thou hast crown'd a Poet.
A City here of *Heroes* I have made,
Upon the rock, whose firm foundation laid, 10
Shall never shrink, where making thine abode,
Live thou a *Selden*, that's a Demi-god.

A Panegerick to Sir Lewis Pemberton

Till I shall come again, let this suffice,
    I send my salt, my sacrifice
To Thee, thy Lady, younglings, and as farre
    As to thy *Genius* and thy *Larre*;

A Panegerick to Sir Lewis Pemberton. Alumni Cant. reports that he was knighted in 1607, became Sheriff of Northamptonshire in 1620, married Alice, daughter of Thomas Bowles of Hertfordshire, and died in 1640.

To the worn Threshold, Porch, Hall, Parlour, Kitchin, 5
    The fat-fed smoking Temple, which in
The wholsome savour of thy mighty Chines
    Invites to supper him who dines,
Where laden spits, warp't with large Ribbs of Beefe,
    Not represent, but give reliefe 10
To the lanke-Stranger, and the sowre Swain;
    Where both may feed, and come againe:
For no black-bearded *Vigil* from thy doore
    Beats with a button'd-staffe the poore:
But from thy warm-love-hatching gates each may 15
    Take friendly morsels, and there stay
To Sun his thin-clad members, if he likes,
    For thou no Porter keep'st who strikes.
No commer to thy Roofe his *Guest-rite* wants;
    Or staying there, is scourg'd with taunts 20
Of some rough Groom, who (yirkt with Corns) sayes, Sir
    Y'ave dipt too long i'th Vinegar;
And with our Broth and bread, and bits; Sir, friend,
    Y'ave farced well, pray make an end;
Two dayes y'ave larded here; a third, yee know, 25
    Makes guests and fish smell strong; pray go
You to some other chimney, and there take
    Essay of other giblets; make
Merry at anothers hearth; y'are here
    Welcome as thunder to our beere: 30
Manners knowes distance, and a man unrude
    Wo'd soon recoile, and not intrude
His Stomach to a second Meale. No, no,
    Thy house, well fed and taught, can show
No such crab'd vizard: Thou hast learnt thy Train, 35
    With heart and hand to entertain:
And by the Armes-full (with a Brest unhid)
    As the old Race of mankind did,
When eithers heart, and eithers hand did strive
    To be the nearer Relative: 40
Thou do'st redeeme those times; and what was lost
    Of antient honesty, may boast

>   It keeps a growth in thee; and so will runne
>   A course in thy Fames-pledge, *thy Sonne*.
> Thus, like a *Roman Tribune*, thou thy gate 45
>   Early setts ope to feast, and late:
> Keeping no *currish Waiter* to affright,
>   With blasting eye, the appetite,
> Which fain would waste upon thy Cates, but that
>   The *Trencher-creature* marketh what 50
> Best and more suppling piece he cuts, and by
>   Some private pinch tels danger's nie
> A hand too desp'rate, or a knife that bites
>   Skin deepe into the Porke, or lights
> Upon some part of Kid, as if mistooke, 55
>   When checked by the Butlers look.
> No, no, thy bread, thy wine, thy jocund Beere
>   Is not reserv'd for *Trebius* here,
> But all, who at thy table seated are,
>   Find equall freedome, equall fare; 60
> And Thou, like to that *Hospitable God*,
>   *Jove*, joy'st when guests make their abode
> To eate thy Bullocks thighs, thy Veales, thy fat
>   Weathers, and never grudged at.
> The *Phesant*, *Partridge*, *Gotwit*, *Reeve*, *Ruffe*, *Raile*, 65
>   The *Cock*, the *Curlew*, and the *quaile*;
> These, and thy choicest viands do extend
>   Their taste unto the lower end
> Of thy glad table: not a dish more known
>   To thee, then unto any one: 70
> But as thy meate, so thy *immortall wine*
>   Makes the smirk face of each to shine,
> And spring fresh *Rose-buds*, while the salt, the wit
>   Flowes from the Wine, and graces it:
> While Reverence, waiting at the bashfull board, 75
>   Honours my Lady and my Lord.
> No scurrile jest; no open Sceane is laid
>   Here, for to make the face affraid;

58 *Trebius*: a friend to the epicure Lucullus who is attacked in Juvenal's Satire V.

But temp'rate mirth dealt forth, and so discreet-
    ly that it makes the meate more sweet; *80*
And adds perfumes unto the Wine, which thou
    Do'st rather poure forth, then allow
By cruse and measure; thus devoting Wine,
    As the *Canary* Isles were thine:
But with that wisdome, and that method, as *85*
    No One that's there his guilty glasse
Drinks of distemper, or ha's cause to cry
    Repentance to his liberty.
No, thou know'st order, Ethicks, and ha's read
    All Oeconomicks, know'st to lead *90*
A House-dance neatly, and can'st truly show,
    How farre a Figure ought to go,
Forward, or backward, side-ward, and what pace
    Can give, and what retract a grace;
What Gesture, Courtship; Comliness agrees, *95*
    With those thy primitive decrees,
To give subsistance to thy house, and proofe,
    What *Genii* support thy roofe,
Goodnes and *Greatnes*; not the oaken Piles;
    For these, and marbles have their whiles *100*
To last, but not their ever: Vertues Hand
    It is, which builds, 'gainst Fate to stand.
Such is thy house, whose firme foundations trust
    Is more in thee, then in her dust,
Or depth, these last may yeeld, and yearly shrinke, *105*
    When what is strongly built, no chinke
Or yawning rupture can the same devoure,
    But fixt it stands, by her own power,
And well-laid bottome, on the iron and rock,
    Which tryes, and counter-stands the shock, *110*
And *Ramme* of time and by vexation growes
    The stronger: *Vertue dies when foes*
Are wanting to her exercise, but great
    And large she spreads by dust, and sweat.
Safe stand thy Walls, and Thee, and so both will, *115*
    Since neithers height was rais'd by th' ill
Of others; since no Stud, no Stone, no Piece,

     Was rear'd up by the Poore-mans fleece:
No Widowes Tenement was rackt to guild
     Or fret thy Seeling, or to build   *120*
A *Sweating-Closset*, to annoint the silke-
     soft-skin, or bath in *Asses milke*:
Nor *Orphans* pittance, left him, serv'd to set
     The Pillars up of *lasting Jet*,
For which their cryes might beate against thine eares, *125*
     Or in the dampe Jet read their Teares.
No *Planke* from *Hallowed* Altar, do's appeale
     To yond' *Star-chamber*, or do's seale
A curse to Thee, or Thine; but all things even
     Make for thy peace, and pace to heaven. *130*
Go on directly so, as just men may
     A thousand times, more sweare, then say,
This is that *Princely Pemberton*, who can
     Teach man to keepe a God in man:
And when wise Poets shall search out to see   *135*
     Good men, *They find them all in Thee*.

Upon M. Ben. Johnson
Epig.

After the rare Arch-Poet JOHNSON dy'd,
The Sock grew loathsome, and the Buskins pride,
Together with the Stages glory stood
Each like a poore and pitied widowhood.
The Cirque prophan'd was; and all postures rackt: *5*
For men did strut, and stride, and stare, not act.
Then temper flew from words; and men did squeake,
Looke red, and blow, and bluster, but not speake:
No Holy-Rage, or frantick-fires did stirre,

Upon M. Ben Johnson .... Jonson died in 1637.

Or flash about the spacious Theater. 10
No clap of hands, or shout, or praises-proofe
Did crack the Play-house sides, or cleave her roofe.
Artlesse the Sceane was; and that monstrous sin
Of deep and *arrant ignorance* came in;
Such ignorance as theirs was, who once hist 15
At thy unequal'd Play, the *Alchymist*:
Oh fie upon 'em! Lastly too, all witt
In utter darkenes did, and still will sit
Sleeping the lucklesse Age out, till that shee
Her Resurrection ha's again with Thee. 20

Another

Thou had'st the wreath before, now take the Tree;
That henceforth none be *Laurel crown'd but Thee.*

To his Nephew, to be prosperous in his art of Painting

On, as thou hast begunne, brave youth, and get
The Palme from *Urbin, Titian, Tintarret,*
Brugel and *Coxie,* and the workes out-doe,
Of *Holben,* and That mighty *Ruben* too.
So draw, and paint, as none may do the like, 5
No, not the glory of the World, *Vandike.*

To his Nephew .... 2 *Urbin*: Raphael, who was born in the ducal city of Urbino.
3 *Coxie*: Michael van Coxcyen, the Flemish painter, died in 1592.
6 *Vandike*: Van Dyck often painted English royalty and nobility in the Caroline period.

Clothes do but cheat and cousen us

Away with silks, away with Lawn,
Ile have no Sceans, or Curtains drawn:
Give me my Mistresse, as she is,
Drest in her nak't simplicities:
For as my Heart, ene so mine Eye
Is wone with flesh, not *Drapery*.

To Dianeme

Shew me thy feet; shew me thy legs, thy thighes;
Shew me Those *Fleshie Principalities*;
Shew me that Hill (where smiling Love doth sit)
Having a living Fountain under it.
Shew me thy waste; Then let me there withall,
By the *Assention* of thy Lawn, see All.

The mad Maids song

1. Good morrow to the Day so fair;
    Good morning Sir to you:
   Good morrow to mine own torn hair
    Bedabled with the dew.

2. Good morning to this Prim-rose too;
    Good morrow to each maid;
   That will with flowers the *Tomb* bestrew,
    Wherein my Love is laid.

3. Ah! woe is me, woe, woe is me,
    Alack and welladay!

>   For pitty, Sir, find out that Bee,
>   Which bore my Love away.
>
> 4. I'le seek him in your *Bonnet* brave;
>   Ile seek him in your eyes;
>   Nay, now I think th'ave made his grave
>   I'th' bed of strawburies.
>
> 5. Ile seek him there; I know, ere this,
>   The cold, cold Earth doth shake him;
>   But I will go, or send a kisse
>   By you, Sir, to awake him.
>
> 6. Pray hurt him not; though he be dead,
>   He knowes well who do love him,
>   And who with green-turfes reare his head,
>   And who do rudely move him.
>
> 7. He's soft and tender (Pray take heed)
>   With bands of Cow-slips bind him;
>   And bring him home, but 'tis decreed,
>   That I shall never find him.

A Pastorall sung to the King: Montano, Silvio, *and* Mirtillo, *Shepheards*

Mon. Bad are the times.   *Sil.* And wors then they are we.
Mon. Troth, bad are both; worse fruit, and ill the tree:
The feast of Shepheards fails.   *Sil.* None crowns the cup
Of *Wassaile* now, or sets the *quintell* up:
And He, who us'd to leade the Country-round,
Youthfull *Mirtillo*, Here he comes, Grief drownd.
Ambo. Lets cheer him up.   *Sil.* Behold him weeping ripe.
Mirt. Ah! *Amarillis*, farewell mirth and pipe;

A Pastorall sung to the King . . . .   4 *quintell*: quintain, an object to be tilted at.

Since thou art gone, no more I mean to play,
To these smooth Lawns, my mirthfull Roundelay.   10
Dear *Amarillis!*   *Mon.* Hark!   *Sil.* mark: *Mir.* this earth grew sweet
Where, *Amarillis*, Thou didst set thy feet.
  Ambo. Poor pittied youth!   *Mir.* And here the breth of kine
And sheep, grew more sweet, by that breth of Thine.
This flock of wooll, and this rich lock of hair,   15
This ball of *Cow-slips*, these she gave me here.
Sil. Words sweet as Love it self. *Montano*, Hark.
Mirt. This way she came, and this way too she went;
How each thing smells divinely redolent!
Like to a field of beams, when newly blown;   20
Or like a medow being lately mown.
Mon. A sweet-sad passion.——
Mirt. In dewie-mornings when she came this way,
Sweet Bents wode bow, to give my Love the day:
And when at night, she folded had her sheep,   25
Daysies wo'd shut, and closing, sigh and weep.
Besides (Ai me!) since she went hence to dwell,
The voices Daughter nea'r spake syllable.
But she is gone.   *Sil. Mirtillo*, tell us whether.
Mirt. Where she and I shall never meet together.   30
Mont. Fore-fend it *Pan*, and *Pales* do thou please
To give an end: *Mir.* To what?   *Sil.* such griefs as these.
Mirt. Never, O never! Still I may endure
The wound I suffer, never find a cure.
Mont. Love for thy sake will bring her to these hills   35
And dales again: *Mir.* No I will languish still;
And all the while my part shall be to weepe;
And with my sighs, call home my bleating sheep:
And in the Rind of every comely tree
Ile carve thy name, and in that name kisse thee: 40
Mont. Set with the Sunne, thy woes: *Sil.* The day grows old:
And time it is our full-fed flocks to fold.

  31 *Pales*: The festival of Pales, the Roman goddess of cattle and pasture, took place on 21 April.

Chor. The shades grow great; but greater growes our sorrow,
                But lets go steepe
                Our eyes in sleepe;   45
                And meet to weepe
                        To morrow.

Upon the Nipples of Julia's *Breast*

Have ye beheld (with much delight)
A red-Rose peeping through a white?
Or else a Cherrie (double grac't)
Within a Lillie? Center plac't?
Or ever mark't the pretty beam,   5
A Strawberry shewes halfe drown'd in Creame?
Or seen rich Rubies blushing through
A pure smooth Pearle, and Orient too?
So like to this, nay all the rest,
Is each neate Niplet of her brest.   10

Oberons *Palace*

After the Feast (my *Shapcot*) see,
The Fairie Court I give to thee:
Where we'le present our *Oberon* led
Halfe tipsie to the Fairie Bed,
Where *Mab* he finds; who there doth lie   5
Not without mickle majesty.
Which, done; and thence remov'd the light,
We'l wish both Them and Thee, good night.

Full as a Bee with Thyme, and Red,
As Cherry harvest, now high fed   10
For Lust and action; on he'l go,

Oberons Palace. 1 *Shapcot*: see "Oberons Feast."

To lye with *Mab*, though all say no.
Lust ha's no eares; He's sharpe as thorn;
And fretfull, carries Hay in's horne,
And lightning in his eyes; and flings   *15*
Among the Elves, (if mov'd) the stings
Of peltish wasps; we'l know his Guard
Kings though th'are hated, will be fear'd.
Wine lead him on. Thus to a Grove
(Sometimes devoted unto Love)   *20*
Tinseld with *Twilight*, He, and They
Lead by the shine of Snails; a way
Beat with their num'rous feet, which by
Many a neat perplexity,
Many a turn, and man' a crosse-   *25*
Track they redeem a bank of mosse
Spungie and swelling, and farre more
Soft then the finest Lemster Ore.
Mildly disparkling, like those fiers,
Which break from the Injeweld tyres   *30*
Of curious Brides; or like those mites
Of Candi'd dew in Moony nights.
Upon this *Convex*, all the flowers,
(Nature begets by th' Sun, and showers,)
Are to a wilde digestion brought,   *35*
As if Loves *Sampler* here was wrought:
Or *Citherea's Ceston*, which
All with temptation doth bewitch.
Sweet Aires move here; and more divine
Made by the breath of great-ey'd kine,   *40*
Who as they lowe empearl with milk
The four-leav'd grasse, or mosse-like silk.
The breath of *Munkies* met to mix
With *Musk-flies*, are th' *Aromaticks*,
Which cense this Arch; and here and there,   *45*
And farther off, and every where,
Throughout that *Brave Mosaick* yard

28 *Lemster Ore*: fine wool from Leominster.
43 *Munkies*: the monkey-flower has a gaping corolla.

Those Picks or Diamonds in the Card:
With peeps of Harts, of Club and Spade
Are here most neatly inter-laid. 50
Many a Counter, many a Die,
Half rotten, and without an eye,
Lies here abouts; and for to pave
The excellency of this Cave,
Squirrils and childrens teeth late shed, 55
Are neatly here enchequered.
With brownest *Toadstones*, and the Gum
That shines upon the blewer Plum.
The nails faln off by Whit-flawes: Art's
Wise hand enchasing here those warts, 60
Which we to others (from our selves)
Sell, and brought hither by the Elves.
The tempting Mole, stoln from the neck
Of the shie Virgin, seems to deck
The holy Entrance; where within 65
The roome is hung with the blew skin
Of shifted Snake: enfreez'd throughout
With eyes of Peacocks Trains, and Trout-
flies curious wings; and these among
Those silver-pence, that cut the tongue 70
Of the red infant, neatly hung.
The glow-wormes eyes; the shining scales
Of silv'rie fish; wheat-strawes, the snailes
Soft Candle-light; the Kitling's eyne;
Corrupted wood; serve here for shine. 75
No glaring light of bold-fac't Day,
Or other over radiant Ray
Ransacks this roome; but what weak beams
Can make reflected from these jems,
And multiply; Such is the light, 80
But ever doubtfull Day, or night.
By this quaint Taper-light he winds
His Errours up; and now he finds
His Moon-tann'd *Mab*, as somewhat sick,

---

59 *Whit-flawes*: whitlows, an inflammation of the fingers or toes.

And (Love knowes) tender as a chick. 85
Upon six plump *Dandillions*, high-
Rear'd, lyes her Elvish-majestie:
Whose woollie-bubbles seem'd to drowne
Hir *Mab-ship* in obedient Downe.
For either sheet, was spread the Caule 90
That doth the Infants face enthrall,
When it is born: (by some enstyl'd
The luckie *Omen* of the child)
And next to these two blankets ore-
Cast of the finest *Gossamore*. 95
And then a Rug of carded wooll,
Which, *Spunge-like* drinking in the dull-
Light of the Moon, seem'd to comply,
Cloud-like, the *daintie Deitie*.
Thus soft she lies: and over-head 100
A *Spinners* circle is bespread,
With Cob-web-curtains: from the roof
So neatly sunck, as that no proof
Of any tackling can declare
What gives it hanging in the Aire. 105
The Fringe about this, are those *Threds*
Broke at the Losse of *Maiden-heads*:
And all behung with these pure Pearls,
Dropt from the eyes of *ravisht Girles*
Or *writhing Brides*; when, (panting) they 110
Give unto Love the straiter way.
For Musick now; He has the cries
Of fained-lost-Virginities;
The which the *Elves* make to excite
A more unconquer'd appetite. 115
The Kings undrest; and now upon
The Gnats-watch-word the *Elves* are gone.
And now the bed, and *Mab* possest
Of this great-little-kingly-Guest.
We'll nobly think, what's to be done, 120
He'll do no doubt; *This flax is spun.*

The parting Verse, or charge to his supposed Wife when he travelled

Go hence, and with this parting kisse,
Which joyns two souls, remember this;
Though thou beest young, kind, soft, and faire,
And may'st draw thousands with a haire:
Yet let these glib temptations be 5
Furies to others, Friends to me.
Looke upon all; and though on fire
Thou set'st their hearts, let chaste desire
Steere Thee to me; and thinke (me gone)
In having all, that thou hast none. 10
Nor so immured wo'd I have
Thee live, as dead and in thy grave;
But walke abroad, yet wisely well
Stand for my comming, Sentinell.
And think (as thou do'st walke the street) 15
Me, or my shadow thou do'st meet.
I know a thousand greedy eyes
Will on thy Feature tirannize,
In my short absence; yet behold
Them like some Picture, or some Mould 20
Fashion'd like Thee; which though 'tave eares
And eyes, it neither sees or heares.
Gifts will be sent, and Letters, which
Are the expressions of that itch,
And salt, which frets thy Suters; fly 25
Both, lest thou lose thy liberty:
For that once lost, thou't fall to one,
Then prostrate to a million.
But if they wooe thee, do thou say,
(As that chaste Queen of *Ithaca* 30

The parting Verse.... Cf. Donne's valedictions and his elegy entitled "His Picture."

Did to her suitors) this web done
(Undone as oft as done) I'm wonne;
I will not urge Thee, for I know,
Though thou art young, thou canst say no,
And no again, and so deny, 35
Those thy Lust-burning *Incubi*.
Let them enstile Thee Fairest fair,
The Pearle of Princes, yet despaire
That so thou art, because thou must
Believe, Love speaks it not, but Lust; 40
And this their Flatt'rie do's commend
Thee chiefly for their pleasures end.
I am not jealous of thy Faith,
Or will be; for the Axiome saith,
He that doth suspect, do's haste 45
A gentle mind to be unchaste.
No, live thee to thy selfe, and keep
Thy thoughts as cold, as is thy sleep:
And let thy dreames be only fed
With this, that I am in thy bed. 50
And thou then turning in that Sphere,
Waking shalt find me sleeping there.
But yet if boundlesse Lust must skaile
Thy Fortress, and will needs prevaile;
And wildly force a passage in, 55
Banish consent, and 'tis no sinne
Of Thine; so *Lucrece* fell, and the
Chaste *Syracusian Cyane*.
So *Medullina* fell, yet none
Of these had imputation 60
For the least trespasse; 'cause the mind
Here was not with the act combin'd.
The body sins not, 'tis the Will
That makes the Action, good, or ill.
And if thy fall sho'd this way come, 65
Triumph in such a Martirdome.
I will not over-long enlarge
To thee, this my religious charge.

Take this compression, so by this
Means I shall know what other kisse 70
Is mixt with mine; and truly know,
Returning, if't be mine or no:
Keepe it till then; and now my Spouse,
For my wisht safety pay thy vowes,
And prayers to *Venus*; if it please 75
The *Great-blew-ruler* of the Seas;
Not many full-fac't-moons shall waine,
Lean-horn'd, before I come again
As one triumphant; when I find
In thee, all faith of Woman-kind. 80
Nor wo'd I have thee thinke, that Thou
Had'st power thy selfe to keep this vow;
But having scapt temptations shelfe,
Know vertue taught thee, not thy selfe.

To Julia

Julia when thy *Herrick* dies,
   Close thou up thy Poets eyes:
And his last breath, let it be
   Taken in by none but Thee.

His Winding-sheet

Come thou, who art the Wine, and wit
     Of all I've writ:
The Grace, the Glorie, and the best
     Piece of the rest.
Thou art of what I did intend 5
     The All, and End.

69 *compression*: embrace.
76 *Great-blew-ruler*: Neptune.

And what was made, was made to meet
            Thee, thee my sheet.
Come then, and be to my chast side
            Both Bed, and Bride.   10
We two (as Reliques left) will have
            One Rest, one Grave.
And, hugging close, we will not feare
            Lust entring here:
Where all Desires are dead, or cold   15
            As is the mould:
And all Affections are forgot,
            Or Trouble not.
Here, here the Slaves and Pris'ners be
            From Shackles free: 20
And weeping Widowes long opprest
            Doe here find rest.
The wronged Client ends his Lawes
            Here, and his Cause.
Here those long suits of Chancery lie   25
            Quiet, or die:
And all Star-chamber-Bils doe cease,
            Or hold their peace.
Here needs no Court for our Request,
            Where all are best;   30
All wise; all equall; and all just
            Alike i'th'dust.
Nor need we here to feare the frowne
            Of Court, or Crown.
Where Fortune bears no sway o're things,   35
            There all are Kings.
In this securer place we'l keep,
            As lull'd asleep;
Or for a little time we'l lye,
            As Robes laid by;   40
To be another day re-worne,
            Turn'd, but not torn:

His Winding-sheet. 29 *Court...Request*: a former court of record for the relief of persons petitioning the King (*OED*).

Or like old Testaments ingrost,
   Lockt up, not lost:
And for a while lye here conceal'd,   *45*
   To be reveal'd
Next, at that great Platonick yeere,
   And then meet here.

To Phillis *to love, and live with him*

Live, live with me, and thou shalt see
The pleasures Ile prepare for thee:
What sweets the Country can afford
Shall blesse thy Bed, and blesse thy Board.
The soft sweet Mosse shall be thy bed,   *5*
With crawling Woodbine over-spread:
By which the silver-shedding streames
Shall gently melt thee into dreames.
Thy clothing next, shall be a Gowne
Made of the Fleeces purest Downe.   *10*
The tongues of Kids shall be thy meate;
Their Milke thy drinke; and thou shalt eate
The Paste of Filberts for thy bread
With Cream of Cowslips buttered:
Thy Feasting-Tables shall be Hills   *15*
With *Daisies* spread, and *Daffadils*;
Where thou shalt sit, and *Red-brest* by,
For meat, shall give thee melody.
Ile give thee Chaines and Carkanets
Of *Primroses* and *Violets*.   *20*
A Bag and Bottle thou shalt have;
That richly wrought, and This as brave;
So that as either shall expresse

---

 43 *Testaments ingrost*: wills written in fair copies and hence in proper form.
 47 *Platonick yeere*: a cycle in which heavenly bodies were supposed to go through all their possible movements and return to their original relative positions, sometimes identified with the period of revolution of the equinoxes, about 25,800 years (*OED*).

The Wearer's no meane Shepheardesse.
At Sheering-times, and yearely Wakes, 25
When *Themilis* his pastime makes,
There thou shalt be; and be the wit,
Nay more, the Feast, and grace of it.
On Holy-dayes, when Virgins meet
To dance the Heyes with nimble feet; 30
Thou shalt come forth, and then appeare
The *Queen of Roses* for that yeere.
And having danc't ('bove all the best)
Carry the Garland from the rest.
In Wicker-baskets Maids shal bring 35
To thee, (my dearest Shepharling)
The blushing Apple, bashfull Peare,
And shame-fac't Plum, (all simp'ring there)
Walk in the Groves, and thou shalt find
The name of *Phillis* in the Rind 40
Of every straight, and smooth-skin tree;
Where kissing that, Ile twice kisse thee.
To thee a Sheep-hook I will send,
Be-pranckt with Ribbands, to this end,
This, this alluring Hook might be 45
Lesse for to catch a sheep, then me.
Thou shalt have Possets, Wassails fine,
Not made of Ale, but spiced Wine;
To make thy Maids and selfe free mirth,
All sitting neer the glitt'ring Hearth. 50
Thou sha't have Ribbands, Roses, Rings,
Gloves, Garters, Stockings, Shooes, and Strings
Of winning Colours, that shall move
Others to Lust, but me to Love.
These (nay) and more, thine own shal be, 55
If thou wilt love, and live with me.

Upon Mistresse Susanna Southwell her cheeks

Rare are thy cheeks *Susanna*, which do show
Ripe Cherries smiling, while that others blow.

Upon her Eyes

Cleere are her eyes,
Like purest Skies.
Discovering from thence
A Babie there
That turns each Sphere, 5
Like an Intelligence.

Upon her feet

Her pretty feet
Like snailes did creep
A little out, and then,
As if they started at Bo-peep,
Did soon draw in agen. 5

An Ode to Sir Clipsebie Crew

1. Here we securely live, and eate
    The Creame of meat;
  And keep eternal fires,

Upon Mistresse Susanna Southwell.... She was presumably a relative of Sir Thomas Southwell and his lady, for which pair Herrick had composed an epithalamium.
Upon her Eyes. 6 *Intelligence*: a rational being who may be incorporeal, like an angelic essence moving the spheres.

> By which we sit, and doe Divine
> > As Wine 5
> > And Rage inspires.
>
> 2. If full we charme; then call upon
> > *Anacreon*
> > To grace the frantick Thyrse:
> And having drunk, we raise a shout 10
> > Throughout
> > To praise his Verse.
>
> 3. Then cause we *Horace* to be read,
> > Which sung, or seyd,
> > A Goblet, to the brim, 15
> Of Lyrick Wine, both swell'd and crown'd,
> > A Round
> > We quaffe to him.
>
> 4. Thus, thus, we live, and spend the houres
> > In Wine and Flowers: 20
> > And make the frollick yeere,
> The Month, the Week, the instant Day
> > To stay
> > The longer here.
>
> 5. Come then, brave Knight, and see the Cell 25
> > Wherein I dwell;
> > And my Enchantments too;
> Which Love and noble freedome is;
> > And this
> > Shall fetter you. 30
>
> 6. Take Horse, and come; or be so kind,
> > To send your mind
> > (Though but in Numbers few)
> And I shall think I have the heart,
> > Or part 35
> > Of *Clipseby Crew*.

The Apparition of his Mistresse calling him to Elizium

Desunt nonnulla ——

Come then, and like two Doves with silv'rie wings,
Let our soules flie to'th' shades, where ever springs
Sit smiling in the Meads; where Balme and Oile,
Roses and Cassia crown the untill'd soyle.
Where no disease raignes, or infection comes   5
To blast the Aire, but *Amber-greece* and *Gums*.
This, that, and ev'ry Thicket doth transpire
More sweet, then *Storax* from the hallowed fire:
Where ev'ry tree a wealthy issue beares
Of fragrant Apples, blushing Plums, or Peares: 10
And all the shrubs, with sparkling spangles, shew
Like Morning-Sun-shine tinsilling the dew.
Here in green Meddowes sits eternall May,
Purfling the Margents, while perpetuall Day
So double gilds the Aire, as that no night   15
Can ever rust th'Enamel of the light.
Here, naked Younglings, handsome Striplings run
Their Goales for Virgins kisses; which when done,
Then unto Dancing forth the learned Round
Commixt they meet, with endlesse Roses crown'd.   20
And here we'l sit on Primrose-banks, and see
Love's *Chorus* led by *Cupid*; and we'l be
Two loving followers too unto the Grove,
Where Poets sing the stories of our love.
There thou shalt hear Divine *Musaus* sing   25
Of *Hero*, and *Leander*; then Ile bring

The Apparition ... calling him to Elizium. Elysium was the dwelling place of the happy souls after death, celebrated by the ancient poets. *Desunt nonnulla*: an incomplete poem (lit. "some things are lacking").
 1 *Doves with silv'rie wings*: see Ps. 68:13.
 8 *Storax*: a balsam.

Thee to the Stand, where honour'd *Homer* reades
His *Odisees*, and his high *Iliads*.
About whose Throne the crowd of Poets throng
To heare the incantation of his tongue: 30
To *Linus*, then to *Pindar*; and that done,
Ile bring thee *Herrick* to *Anacreon*,
Quaffing his full-crown'd bowles of burning Wine,
And in his Raptures speaking Lines of Thine,
Like to His subject; and as his Frantick- 35
Looks, shew him truly *Bacchanalian* like,
Besmear'd with Grapes; welcome he shall thee thither,
Where both may rage, both drink and dance together.
Then stately *Virgil*, witty *Ovid*, by
Whom faire *Corinna* sits, and doth comply 40
With Yvorie wrists, his Laureat head, and steeps
His eye in dew of kisses, while he sleeps.
Then soft *Catullus*, sharp-fang'd *Martial*,
And towring *Lucan, Horace, Juvenal*,
And Snakie *Perseus*, these, and those, whom Rage 45
(Dropt for the jarres of heaven) fill'd t'engage
All times unto their frenzies; Thou shalt there
Behold them in a spacious Theater.
Among which glories, (crown'd with sacred Bayes,
And flatt'ring Ivie) Two recite their Plaies, 50
Beumont and *Fletcher*, Swans, to whom all eares
Listen, while they (like Syrens in their Spheres)
Sing their *Evadne*; and still more for thee
There yet remaines to know, then thou can'st see
By glim'ring of a fancie: Doe but come, 55
And there Ile shew thee that capacious roome
In which thy Father *Johnson* now is plac't,
As in a Globe of Radiant fire, and grac't
To be in that Orbe crown'd (that doth include
Those Prophets of the former Magnitude) 60
And he one chiefe; But harke, I heare the Cock,
(The Bell-man of the night) proclaime the clock
Of late struck one; and now I see the prime
Of Day break from the pregnant East, 'tis time

I vanish; more I had to say; 65
But Night determines here, Away.

His Prayer to Ben. Johnson

[1.] When I a Verse shall make,
Know I have praid thee,
For old *Religions* sake,
Saint *Ben* to aide me.

2. Make the way smooth for me, 5
When I, thy *Herrick*,
Honouring thee, on my knee
Offer my *Lyrick*.

3. Candles Ile give to thee,
And a new Altar; 10
And thou Saint *Ben*, shalt be
Writ in my *Psalter*.

The Night-piece, to Julia

[1.] Her Eyes the Glow-worme lend thee,
The Shooting Starres attend thee;
And the Elves also,
Whose little eyes glow,
Like the sparks of fire, befriend thee. 5

2. No *Will-o'th'-Wispe* mis-light thee;
Nor Snake, or Slow-worme bite thee:
But on, on thy way
Not making a stay,
Since Ghost ther's none to affright thee. 10

3.   Let not the darke thee cumber;
        What though the Moon do's slumber?
            The Starres of the night
            Will lend thee their light,
    Like Tapers cleare without number.   15

4.   Then *Julia* let me wooe thee,
        Thus, thus to come unto me:
            And when I shall meet
            Thy silv'ry feet,
    My soule Ile poure into thee.   20

A Kisse

What is a Kisse? Why this, as some approve;
The sure sweet-Sement, Glue, and Lime of Love.

Glorie

I make no haste to have my Numbers read.
Seldome comes Glorie till a man be dead.

Poets

Wantons we are; and though our words be such,
Our Lives do differ from our Lines by much.

No despight to the dead

Reproach we may the living; not the dead:
'*Tis cowardice to bite the buried.*

Glorie. 2 *Seldome...dead*: the line translates Martial's *Cineri gloria sera venit* (see *Epigrams*, I 25, 8). Jonson used this motto as the epigraph for *Under-Wood*.

Connubii Flores, *or the well-wishes at Weddings*

Chorus Sacerdotum

1. From the Temple to your home
   May a thousand blessings come!
   And a sweet concurring stream
   Of all joyes, to joyn with them.

Chorus Juvenum

2.   Happy day   5
   Make no long stay
         Here
   In thy Sphere;
   But give thy place to night,
         That she,   10
         As Thee,
         May be
   Partaker of this sight.
   And since it was thy care
   To see the Younglings wed;   15
   'Tis fit that Night, the Paire,
   Sho'd see safe brought to Bed.

Chorus Senum

3. Go to your banquet then, but use delight,
   So as to rise still with an appetite.
   Love is a thing most nice; and must be fed   20
   To such a height; but never surfeited.
   What is beyond the mean is ever ill:
   'Tis best to feed Love; but not over-fill:
   Go then discreetly to the Bed of pleasure;
   And this remember, *Vertue keepes the measure.*   25

Connubii Flores . . . . The speakers are Choruses of Priests, Young Men, Old Men, Virgins, Shepherds, and Matrons.

Chorus Virginum

4. Luckie signes we have discri'd
   To encourage on the Bride;
   And to these we have espi'd,
   Not a kissing *Cupid* flyes
   Here about, but has his eyes,
   To imply your Love is wise.

Chorus Pastorum

5. Here we present a fleece
      To make a peece
         Of cloth;
   Nor Faire, must you be loth
   Your Finger to apply
      To huswiferie.
         Then, then begin
            To spin:
   And (Sweetling) marke you, what a Web will come
   Into your Chests, drawn by your painfull Thumb.

Chorus Matronarum

6. Set you to your Wheele, and wax
      Rich, by the Ductile Wool and Flax.
   Yarne is an Income; and the Huswives thread
   The Larder fils with meat; the Bin with bread.

Chorus Senum

7. Let wealth come in by comely thrift,
      And not by any sordid shift:
         'Tis haste
         Makes waste:
         Extreames have still their fault;
   The softest Fire makes the sweetest Mault.
   Who gripes too hard the dry and slip'rie sand,
   Holds none at all, or little in his hand.

Chorus Virginum

8. Goddesse of Pleasure, Youth and Peace,
    Give them the blessing of encrease: 55
    And thou *Lucina*, that do'st heare
    The vowes of those, that children beare:
    When as her Aprill houre drawes neare,
    Be thou then propitious there.

Chorus Juvenum

9. Farre hence be all speech, that may anger move: 60
Sweet words must nourish soft and gentle Love.

Chorus Omnium

10. Live in the Love of Doves, and having told
The Ravens yeares, go hence more Ripe then old.

The Hag

[1.]   The Hag is astride,
          This night for to ride;
    The Devill and shee together:
          Through thick, and through thin,
          Now out, and then in, 5
    Though ne'r so foule be the weather.

2.   A Thorn or a Burr
          She takes for a Spurre:
    With a lash of a Bramble she rides now,
          Through Brakes and through Bryars, 10
          O're Ditches, and Mires,
    She followes the Spirit that guides now.

3.   No Beast, for his food,
          Dares now range the wood;

> But husht in his laire he lies lurking: *15*
> While mischeifs, by these,
> On Land and on Seas,
> At noone of Night are a working.
>
> 4. The storme will arise,
> And trouble the skies;   *20*
> This night, and more for the wonder,
> The ghost from the Tomb
> Affrighted shall come,
> Cal'd out by the clap of the Thunder.

To M. Denham, *on his Prospective Poem*

> Or lookt I back unto the Times hence flown,
> To praise those Muses, and dislike our own?
> Or did I walk those *Pean*-Gardens through,
> To kick the Flow'rs, and scorn their odours too?
> I might (and justly) be reputed (here)   *5*
> One nicely mad, or peevishly severe.
> But by *Apollo!* as I worship wit,
> (Where I have cause to burn perfumes to it:)
> So, I confesse, 'tis somwhat to do well
> In our high art, although we can't excell,   *10*
> Like thee; or dare the Buskins to unloose
> Of thy brave, bold, and sweet *Maronian* Muse.
> But since I'm cal'd (rare *Denham*) to be gone,
> Take from thy *Herrick* this conclusion:
> 'Tis dignity in others, if they be   *15*
> Crown'd Poets; yet live Princes under thee:
> The while their wreaths and Purple Robes do shine;
> Lesse by their own jemms, then those beams of thine.

To M. Denham.... John Denham (1615–1669) wrote "Cooper's Hill" on a prospect or view near Windsor.

3 *Pean*: in heraldry, one of the furs, the ground being sable, and the spots or tufts orange.

His returne to London

From the dull confines of the drooping West,
To see the day spring from the pregnant East,
Ravisht in spirit, I come, nay more, I flie
To thee, blest place of my Nativitie!
Thus, thus with hallowed foot I touch the ground, 5
With thousand blessings by thy Fortune crown'd.
O fruitfull Genius! that bestowest here
An everlasting plenty, yeere by yeere.
O *Place!* O *People!* Manners! fram'd to please
All *Nations, Customes, Kindreds, Languages!* 10
I am a free-born *Roman*; suffer then,
That I amongst you live a Citizen.
London my home is: though by hard fate sent
Into a long and irksome banishment;
Yet since cal'd back; henceforward let me be, 15
O native countrey, repossest by thee!
For, rather then I'le to the West return,
I'le beg of thee first here to have mine Urn.
Weak I am grown, and must in short time fall;
Give thou my sacred Reliques Buriall. 20

Charon *and* Phylomel

A Dialogue Sung

Ph. *Charon!* O Gentle *Charon!* let me wooe thee,
   By tears and pitie now to come unto mee.
Ch. What voice so sweet and charming do I heare?
   Say what thou art.   *Ph.* I prithee first draw neare.

Charon and Phylomel....   Turned into a nightingale, Philomela seeks passage to Hades, following her sister Procne (see l. 16) in death. She had been violated and deprived of her tongue by Procne's husband, Tereus.

Ch. A sound I heare, but nothing yet can see,
    Speak where thou art. *Ph.* O *Charon* pittie me!
    I am a bird, and though no name I tell,
    My warbling note will say I'm *Phylomel*.
Ch. What's that to me, I waft nor fish or fowles,
    Nor Beasts (fond thing) but only humane soules.
Ph. Alas for me! *Ch.* Shame on thy witching note,
    That made me thus hoist saile, and bring my Boat:
    But Ile returne; what mischief brought thee hither?
Ph. A deale of Love, and much, much Griefe together.
Ch. What's thy request? *Ph.* That since she's now beneath
    Who fed my life, I'le follow her in death.
Ch. And is that all? I'm gone. *Ph.* By love I pray thee,
Ch. Talk not of love, all pray, but few soules pay me.
Ph. Ile give thee vows and tears. *Ch.* Can tears pay skores
    For mending sails, for patching Boat and Oares?
Ph. I'le beg a penny, or Ile sing so long,
    Till thou shalt say, I've paid thee with a song.
Ch. Why then begin, and all the while we make
    Our slothfull passage o're the Stygian Lake,
    Thou and I'le sing to make these dull Shades merry,
    Who els with tears wo'd doubtles drown my ferry.

To Doctor Alablaster

Nor art thou lesse esteem'd, that I have plac'd
(Amongst mine honour'd) Thee (almost) the last:
In great Processions many lead the way
To him, who is the triumph of the day,
As these have done to Thee, who art the one,
One onely glory of a million,
In whom the spirit of the Gods do's dwell,
Firing thy soule, by which thou dost foretell

To Doctor Alablaster. William Alabaster (1576–1640), Latin poet and divine, was a friend of Jonson, Selden, and Herrick; he was noted for his recondite studies in cabalistic divinity.

When this or that vast *Dinastie* must fall
Downe to a *Fillit* more *Imperiall*.   10
When this or that *Horne* shall be broke, and when
Others shall spring up in their place agen:
When times and seasons and all yeares must lie
Drown'd in the Sea of wild Eternitie:
When the *Black Dooms-day Bookes* (as yet unseal'd)   15
Shall by the mighty *Angell* be reveal'd:
And when the Trumpet which thou late hast found
Shall call to Judgment; tell us when the sound
Of this or that great Aprill day shall be,
And next the Gospell wee will credit thee.   20
Meane time like Earth-wormes we will craule below,
And wonder at Those Things that thou dost know.

Upon Julia's Clothes

When as in silks my *Julia* goes,
Then, then (me thinks) how sweetly flowes
That liquefaction of her clothes.
Next, when I cast mine eyes and see
That brave Vibration each way free;   5
O how that glittering taketh me!

The Amber Bead

I saw a Flie within a Beade
Of Amber cleanly buried:
The Urne was little, but the room
More rich then *Cleopatra's* Tombe.

The Transfiguration

Immortall clothing I put on,
So soone as *Julia* I am gon
To mine eternall Mansion.

Thou, thou art here, to humane sight
Cloth'd all with incorrupted light;
But yet how more admir'dly bright

Wilt thou appear, when thou art set
In thy refulgent Thronelet,
That shin'st thus in thy counterfeit?

TO THE KING,
Upon his taking of Leicester

This Day is Yours *Great CHARLES*! and in this War
Your Fate, and Ours, alike Victorious are.
In her white Stole; now Victory do's rest
Enspher'd with Palm on Your Triumphant Crest.
Fortune is now Your Captive; other Kings
Hold but her hands; You hold both hands and wings.

To M. Henry Lawes, *the excellent Composer of his Lyricks*

Touch but thy Lire (my *Harrie*) and I heare
From thee some raptures of the rare *Gotire*.
Then if thy voice commingle with the String
I heare in thee the rare *Laniere* to sing;
Or curious *Wilson*: Tell me, canst thou be
Less then *Apollo*, that usurp'st such Three?
Three, unto whom the whole world give applause;
Yet their Three praises, praise but One; that's *Lawes*.

To M. Henry Lawes .... The Caroline composers and performers mentioned here—Gotière, Lanier, and Wilson—were all friends of the distinguished Henry.

Upon Love

Love brought me to a silent Grove,
    And shew'd me there a Tree,
Where some had hang'd themselves for love,
    And gave a Twist to me.

The Halter was of silk, and gold,   5
    That he reacht forth unto me:
No otherwise, then if he would
    By dainty things undo me.

He bade me then that Neck-lace use;
    And told me too, he maketh   10
A glorious end by such a Noose,
    His Death for Love that taketh.

'Twas but a dream; but had I been
    There really alone;
My desp'rate feares, in love, had seen   15
    Mine Execution.

Ceremonies for Candlemasse Eve

Down with the Rosemary and Bayes,
    Down with the Misleto;
In stead of Holly, now up-raise
    The greener Box (for show.)

The Holly hitherto did sway;   5
    Let Box now domineere;
Untill the dancing Easter-day,
    Or Easters Eve appeare.

Then youthfull Box which now hath grace,
    Your houses to renew;   10

        Grown old, surrender must his place,
           Unto the crisped Yew.

        When Yew is out, then Birch comes in,
           And many Flowers beside;
        Both of a fresh, and fragrant kinne   15
           To honour Whitsontide.

        Green Rushes then, and sweetest Bents,
           With cooler Oken boughs;
        Come in for comely ornaments,
           To re-adorn the house.   20
Thus times do shift; each thing his turne do's hold;
New things succeed, as former things grow old.

Upon M. William Lawes, *the rare Musitian*

Sho'd I not put on Blacks, when each one here
Comes with his Cypresse, and devotes a teare?
Sho'd I not grieve (my *Lawes*) when every Lute,
Violl, and Voice, is (by thy losse) struck mute?
Thy loss brave man! whose Numbers have been hurl'd,   5
And no less prais'd, then spread throughout the world.
Some have Thee call'd *Amphion*; some of us,
Nam'd thee *Terpander*, or sweet *Orpheus*:
Some this, some that, but all in this agree,
Musique had both her birth, and death with Thee.   10

Upon M. William Lawes.... Serving with the Royalist forces, William Lawes was fatally shot at the siege of Chester in September, 1645.

Upon Ben. Johnson

Here lyes *Johnson* with the rest
Of the Poets; but the Best.
Reader, wo'dst thou more have known?
Aske his Story, not this Stone.
That will speake what this can't tell   5
Of his glory. *So farewell.*

An Ode for him

Ah *Ben*!
Say how, or when
Shall we thy Guests
Meet at those *Lyrick* Feasts,
Made at the *Sun*,   5
The *Dog*, the triple *Tunne*?
Where we such clusters had,
As made us nobly wild, not mad;
And yet each Verse of thine
Out-did the meate, out-did the frolick wine.   10

My *Ben*
Or come agen:
Or send to us,
Thy wits great over-plus;
But teach us yet   15
Wisely to husband it;
Lest we that Tallent spend:
And having once brought to an end
That precious stock; the store
Of such a wit the world sho'd have no more.   20

TO THE KING,
Upon his welcome to Hampton-Court
Set and Sung

Welcome, *Great Cesar*, welcome now you are,
As dearest Peace, after destructive Warre:
Welcome as slumbers; or as beds of ease
After our long, and peevish sicknesses.
O *Pompe of Glory!* Welcome now, and come   5
To re-possess once more your long'd-for home.
A thousand Altars smoake; a thousand thighes
Of Beeves here ready stand for Sacrifice.
Enter and prosper; while our eyes doe waite
For an *Ascendent* throughly *Auspicate*:   10
Under which signe we may the former stone
Lay of our safeties new foundation:
That done; *O Cesar*, live, and be to us,
Our *Fate*, our *Fortune*, and our *Genius*;
To whose free knees we may our temples tye   15
As to a still protecting Deitie.
That sho'd you stirre, we and our Altars too
May (*Great Augustus*) *goe along with You.*
Chor. Long live the King; and to accomplish this,
We'l from our owne, adde far more years to his.   20

A Bachanalian Verse

[1.]   Drinke up
Your Cup,
But not spill Wine;
For if you
Do,   5
'Tis an ill signe;

To the King.... Charles I, apprehended by the Parliamentary army, took up his abode at Hampton Court on 24 August 1647.

2.   That we
        Foresee,
    You are cloy'd here,
        If so, no   10
        Hoe,
    But avoid here.

Upon Love,

by way of question and answer

I bring ye love: *Quest.* What will love do?
    Ans. Like, and dislike ye:
I bring ye love: *Quest.* What will love do?
    Ans. Stroake ye to strike ye.
I bring ye love: *Quest.* What will Love do?   5
    Ans. Love will be-foole ye:
I bring ye love: *Quest.* What will love do?
    Ans. Heate ye to coole ye:
I bring ye love: *Quest.* What will love do?
    Ans. Love gifts will send ye: 10
I bring ye love: *Quest.* What will love do?
    Ans. Stock ye to spend ye:
I bring ye love: *Quest.* What will love do?
    Ans. Love will fulfill ye:
I bring ye love: *Quest.* What will love do?   15
    Ans. Kisse ye, to kill ye.

His teares to Thamasis

I send, I send here my supremest kiss
To thee my *silver-footed Thamasis.*
No more shall I reiterate thy Strand,
Whereon so many Stately Structures stand:
Nor in the summers sweeter evenings go,   5

His teares to Thamasis.   The Thames.

To bath in thee (as thousand others doe.)
No more shall I a long thy christall glide,
In Barge (with boughes and rushes beautifi'd)
With soft-smooth Virgins (for our chast disport)
To *Richmond, Kingstone,* and to *Hampton-Court:*   10
Never againe shall I with Finnie-Ore
Put from, or draw unto the faithfull shore:
And Landing here, or safely Landing there,
Make way to my *Beloved Westminster:*
Or to the *Golden-cheap-side,* where the earth   15
Of *Julia Herrick* gave to me my Birth.
May all clean *Nimphs* and curious water Dames,
With Swan-like state, flote up and down thy streams:
No drought upon thy wanton waters fall
To make them Leane, and languishing at all.   20
No ruffling winds come hither to discease
Thy pure, and *Silver-wristed Naides.*
Keep up your state ye streams; and as ye spring,
Never make sick your Banks by surfeiting.
Grow young with Tydes, and though I see ye never,   25
Receive this vow, *so fare-ye-well for ever.*

Twelfe night, or King *and* Queene

Now, now the mirth comes
With the cake full of plums,
Where Beane's the *King* of the sport here;
Beside we must know,
The Pea also   5
Must revell, as *Queene,* in the Court here.

Twelfe night, or King and Queene.   For the eve of the twelfth day of Christmas, *The Oxford Dictionary of the Christian Church* (F. L. Cross, ed.) notes: "The 'Twelfth Cake' was an ornamental cake made for the occasion, containing a bean or a coin, the drawer of which became the 'King' or 'Queen' of the festivities." Here the pea takes the place of the bean.

Begin then to chuse,
 (This night as ye use)
Who shall for the present delight here,
 Be a *King* by the lot, 10
 And who shall not
Be Twelfe-day *Queene* for the night here.

 Which knowne, let us make
 Joy-sops with the cake;
And let not a man then be seen here, 15
 Who unurg'd will not drinke
 To the base from the brink
A health to the King and the Queene here.

 Next crowne the bowle full
 With gentle lambs-wooll; 20
Adde sugar, nutmeg and ginger,
 With store of ale too;
 And thus ye must doe
To make the wassaile a swinger.

 Give then to the King 25
 And Queene wassailing;
And though with ale ye be whet here;
 Yet part ye from hence,
 As free from offence,
As when ye innocent met here. 30

Charmes

This Ile tell ye by the way,
Maidens when ye Leavens lay,
Crosse your Dow, and your dispatch,
Will be better for your Batch.

Another [I]

In the morning when ye rise
Wash your hands, and cleanse your eyes.
Next be sure ye have a care,
To disperse the water farre.
For as farre as that doth light,   5
So farre keepes the evill Spright.

Another [II]

If ye feare to be affrighted
When ye are (by chance) benighted:
In your Pocket for a trust,
Carrie nothing but a Crust:
For that holy piece of Bread,   5
Charmes the danger, and the dread.

To his Girles who would have him sportfull

Alas I can't, for tell me how
Can I be gamesome (aged now)
Besides ye see me daily grow
Here Winter-like, to Frost and Snow.
And I ere long, my Girles shall see,   5
Ye quake for cold to looke on me.

Truth and falsehood

Truth by her own simplicity is known,
Falsehood by Varnish and Vermillion.

His last request to Julia

I have been wanton, and too bold I feare,
To chafe o're much the Virgins cheek or eare:
Beg for my Pardon *Julia; He doth winne*
Grace with the Gods, who's sorry for his sinne.
That done, my *Julia*, dearest *Julia*, come, 5
And go with me to chuse my Buriall roome:
My Fates are ended; when thy *Herrick* dyes,
Claspe thou his Book, then close thou up his Eyes.

On Himselfe

Il'e write no more of Love; but now repent
Of all those times that I in it have spent.
Ile write no more of life; but wish twas ended,
And that my dust was to the earth commended.

To his Booke

Goe thou forth my booke, though late;
Yet be timely fortunate.
It may chance good-luck may send
Thee a kinsman, or a friend,
That may harbour thee, when I, 5
With my fates neglected lye.
If thou know'st not where to dwell,
See, the fier's by: *Farewell.*

The end of his worke

Part of the worke remaines; one part is past:
And here my ship rides having Anchor cast.

To Crowne it

My wearied Barke, O Let it now be Crown'd!
The Haven Reacht to which I first was bound.

On Himselfe

The worke is done: young men, and maidens set
Upon my curles the *Mirtle Coronet*,
Washt with sweet ointments; Thus at last I come
To suffer in the Muses *Martyrdome*:
But with this comfort, if my blood be shed, 5
The Muses will weare blackes, when I am dead.

The pillar of Fame

Fames pillar here, at last, we set,
Out-during *Marble, Brasse,* or *Jet*,
 Charm'd and enchanted so,
 As to withstand the blow
  Of overthrow: 5
  Nor shall the seas,
  Or OUTRAGES
  Of storms orebear
  What we up-rear
  Tho Kingdoms fal, 10
 This pillar never shall
 Decline or waste at all;
But stand for ever by his owne
Firme and well fixt foundation.

To his Book's end this last line he'd have plac't,
Jocond his Muse was; but his Life was chast.

From HIS
NOBLE NUMBERS
or,
His Pious Pieces,

Wherein (*amongst other things*)
he sings the Birth of his CHRIST:
and sighes for his Saviours suffe-
ring on the Crosse

HESIOD

Ἴδμεν ψεύδεα πολλὰ λέγειν ἐτύμοισιν ὁμοῖα
Ἴδμεν δ', εὖτ' ἐθέλωμεν, ἀληθέα μυθήσασθαι.

His Noble Numbers. [*Title page.*] The epigraph, a quotation from Hesiod's *Theogony,* ll. 21–28, may be translated thus: "We know how to tell many false things true-seeming, but we know how to speak the real truth when we will." The *Theogony* is a work which attempts to reduce to order the stories of the origin of the earth and the origin and relationships of the gods. It is one of the principal sources for our knowledge of the mythology of the early Greeks.

His Confession

Look how our foule Dayes do exceed our faire;
And as our bad, more then our good Works are:
Ev'n so those Lines, pen'd by my wanton Wit,
Treble the number of these good I've writ.
Things precious are least num'rous: Men are prone   5
To do ten Bad, for one Good Action.

His Prayer for Absolution

For Those my unbaptized Rhimes,
Writ in my wild unhallowed Times;
For every sentence, clause and word,
That's not inlaid with Thee, (my Lord)
Forgive me God, and blot each Line   5
Out of my Book, that is not Thine.
But if, 'mongst all, thou find'st here one
Worthy thy Benediction;
That One of all the rest, shall be
The Glory of my Work, and Me.   10

To finde God

Weigh me the Fire; or, canst thou find
A way to measure out the Wind;
Distinguish all those Floods that are
Mixt in that watrie Theater;
And tast thou them as saltlesse there,   5
As in their Channell first they were.
Tell me the People that do keep
Within the Kingdomes of the Deep;

To finde God. Cf. Donne's Song, "Goe, and catch a falling starre."

Or fetch me back that Cloud againe,
Beshiver'd into seeds of Raine;
Tell me the motes, dust, sands, and speares
Of Corn, when Summer shakes his eares;
Shew me that world of Starres, and whence
They noiselesse spill their Influence:
This if thou canst; then shew me Him
That rides the glorious *Cherubim*.

What God is

God is above the sphere of our esteem,
And is the best known, not defining Him.

Upon God

God is not onely said to be
An *Ens*, but *Supraentitie*.

Mercy and Love

God hath two wings, which He doth ever move,
The one is Mercy, and the next is Love:
Under the first the Sinners ever trust;
And with the last he still directs the Just.

Gods Anger without Affection

God when He's angry here with any one,
His wrath is free from perturbation;
And when we think His looks are sowre and grim,
The alteration is in us, not Him.

God not to be comprehended

'Tis hard to finde God, but to comprehend
Him, as He is, is labour without end.

To God:
an Anthem, sung in the Chappell at White-Hall, before the King

Verse.   My God, I'm wounded by my sin,
             And sore without, and sick within:
Ver. Chor. I come to Thee, in hope to find
             Salve for my body, and my mind.
Verse.   In *Gilead* though no Balme be found,   5
             To ease this smart, or cure this wound;
Ver. Chor. Yet, Lord, I know there is with Thee
             All saving health, and help for me.
Verse.   Then reach Thou forth that hand of Thine,
             That powres in oyle, as well as wine.   10
Ver. Chor. And let it work, for I'le endure
             The utmost smart, so Thou wilt cure.

Upon Time

    Time was upon
The wing, to flie away;
    And I cal'd on
Him but a while to stay;
    But he'd be gone,   5
For ought that I could say.

   He held out then,
A Writing, as he went;
   And askt me, when
False man would be content
   To pay agen,
What God and Nature lent.

   An houre-glasse,
In which were sands but few,
   As he did passe,
He shew'd, and told me too,
   Mine end near was,
And so away he flew.

His Letanie, to the Holy Spirit

1. In the houre of my distresse,
   When temptations me oppresse,
   And when I my sins confesse,
     Sweet Spirit comfort me!

2. When I lie within my bed,
   Sick in heart, and sick in head,
   And with doubts discomforted,
     Sweet Spirit comfort me!

3. When the house doth sigh and weep,
   And the world is drown'd in sleep,
   Yet mine eyes the watch do keep;
     Sweet Spirit comfort me!

4. When the artlesse Doctor sees
   No one hope, but of his Fees,
   And his skill runs on the lees;
     Sweet Spirit comfort me!

5. When his Potion and his Pill,
   His, or none, or little skill,
   Meet for nothing, but to kill;
       Sweet Spirit comfort me!

6. When the passing-bell doth tole,
   And the Furies in a shole
   Come to fright a parting soule;
       Sweet Spirit comfort me!

7. When the tapers now burne blew,
   And the comforters are few,
   And that number more then true;
       Sweet Spirit comfort me!

8. When the Priest his last hath praid,
   And I nod to what is said,
   'Cause my speech is now decaid;
       Sweet Spirit comfort me!

9. When (God knowes) I'm tost about,
   Either with despaire, or doubt;
   Yet before the glasse be out,
       Sweet Spirit comfort me!

10. When the Tempter me pursu'th
    With the sins of all my youth,
    And halfe damns me with untruth;
        Sweet Spirit comfort me!

11. When the flames and hellish cries
    Fright mine eares, and fright mine eyes,
    And all terrors me surprize;
        Sweet Spirit comfort me!

12. When the Judgment is reveal'd,
    And that open'd which was seal'd,
    When to Thee I have appeal'd;
        Sweet Spirit comfort me!

A Thanksgiving to God, for his House

Lord, Thou hast given me a cell
    Wherein to dwell;
And little house, whose humble Roof
    Is weather-proof;
Under the sparres of which I lie   5
    Both soft, and drie;
Where Thou my chamber for to ward
    Hast set a Guard
Of harmlesse thoughts, to watch and keep
    Me, while I sleep.   10
Low is my porch, as is my Fate,
    Both void of state;
And yet the threshold of my doore
    Is worn by'th poore,
Who thither come, and freely get   15
    Good words, or meat:
Like as my Parlour, so my Hall
    And Kitchin's small:
A little Butterie, and therein
    A little Byn,   20
Which keeps my little loafe of Bread
    Unchipt, unflead:
Some brittle sticks of Thorne or Briar
    Make me a fire,
Close by whose living coale I sit,   25
    And glow like it.
Lord, I confesse too, when I dine,
    The Pulse is Thine,
And all those other Bits, that bee
    There plac'd by Thee;   30
The Worts, the Purslain, and the Messe
    Of Water-cresse,
Which of Thy kindnesse Thou hast sent;
    And my content
Makes those, and my beloved Beet,   35
    To be more sweet.

'Tis thou that crown'st my glittering Hearth
      With guiltlesse mirth;
And giv'st me Wassaile Bowles to drink,
      Spic'd to the brink.   40
Lord, 'tis thy plenty-dropping hand,
      That soiles my land;
And giv'st me, for my Bushell sowne,
      Twice ten for one:
Thou mak'st my teeming Hen to lay   45
      Her egg each day:
Besides my healthfull Ewes to beare
      Me twins each yeare:
The while the conduits of my Kine
      Run Creame, (for Wine.)   50
All these, and better Thou dost send
      Me, to this end,
That I should render, for my part,
      A thankfull heart;
Which, fir'd with incense, I resigne,   55
      As wholly Thine;
But the acceptance, that must be,
      My Christ, by Thee.

To God [I]

Make, make me Thine, my gracious God,
Or with thy staffe, or with thy rod;
And be the blow too what it will,
Lord, I will kisse it, though it kill:
Beat me, bruise me, rack me, rend me,   5
Yet, in torments, I'le commend Thee:
Examine me with fire, and prove me
To the full, yet I will love Thee:
Nor shalt thou give so deep a wound,
But I as patient will be found.   10

Neutrality loathsome

God will have all, or none; serve Him, or fall
Down before *Baal*, *Bel*, or *Belial:*
Either be hot, or cold: God doth despise,
Abhorre, and spew out all Neutralities.

Eternitie

1. O Yeares! and Age! Farewell:
    Behold I go,
    Where I do know
 Infinitie to dwell.

2. And these mine eyes shall see   5
    All times, how they
    Are lost i'th' Sea
 Of vast Eternitie.

3. Where never Moone shall sway
    The Starres; but she,   10
    And Night, shall be
 Drown'd in one endlesse Day.

To his Saviour, a Child; a Present, by a child

Go prettie child, and beare this Flower
Unto thy little Saviour;
And tell Him, by that Bud now blown,
He is the *Rose of Sharon* known:
When thou hast said so, stick it there   5
Upon his Bibb, or Stomacher:
And tell Him, (for good handsell too)

      That thou hast brought a Whistle new,
      Made of a clean strait oaten reed,
      To charme his cries, (at time of need:)   10
      Tell Him, for Corall, thou hast none;
      But if thou hadst, He sho'd have one;
      But poore thou art, and knowne to be
      Even as monilesse, as He.
      Lastly, if thou canst win a kisse   15
      From those mellifluous lips of his;
      Then never take a second on,
      To spoile the first impression.

The Parasceve, or Preparation

To a Love-Feast we both invited are:
The figur'd Damask, or pure Diaper,
Over the golden Altar now is spread,
With Bread, and Wine, and Vessells furnished;
The *sacred Towell*, and the *holy Eure*   5
Are ready by, to make the Guests all pure:
Let's go (my *Alma*) yet e're we receive,
Fit, fit it is, we have our *Parasceve*.
Who to that *sweet Bread* unprepar'd doth come
Better he starv'd, then but to tast one crumme.   10

To God [II]

God is all-sufferance here; here He doth show
No Arrow nockt, onely a stringlesse Bow:
His Arrowes flie; and all his stones are hurl'd
Against the wicked, in another world.

The Parasceve, or Preparation.   The evening before the Jewish Sabbath.

To his sweet Saviour

Night hath no wings, to him that cannot sleep;
And Time seems then, not for to flie, but creep;
Slowly her chariot drives, as if that she
Had broke her wheele, or crackt her axeltree.
Just so it is with me, who list'ning, pray 5
The winds, to blow the tedious night away;
That I might see the cheerfull peeping day.
Sick is my heart; O Saviour! do Thou please
To make my bed soft in my sicknesses:
Lighten my candle, so that I beneath 10
Sleep not for ever in the vaults of death:
Let me Thy voice betimes i'th morning heare;
Call, and I'le come; say Thou, the when, and where:
Draw me, but first, and after Thee I'le run,
And make no one stop, till my race be done. 15

His Creed

I do believe, that die I must,
And be return'd from out my dust:
I do believe, that when I rise,
Christ I shall see, with these same eyes:
I do believe, that I must come, 5
With others, to the dreadfull Doome:
I do believe, the bad must goe
From thence, to everlasting woe:
I do believe, the good, and I,
Shall live with Him eternally: 10
I do believe, I shall inherit
Heaven, by Christs mercies, not my merit:
I do believe, the One in Three,
And Three in perfect Unitie:
Lastly that JESUS is a Deed 15
Of Gift from God: *And heres my Creed.*

The Dirge of Jephthahs Daughter: sung by the Virgins

1. O Thou, the wonder of all dayes!
   O Paragon, and Pearle of praise!
   O Virgin-martyr, ever blest
                 Above the rest
   Of all the Maiden-Traine! We come,   5
   And bring fresh strewings to thy Tombe.

2. Thus, thus, and thus we compasse round
   Thy harmlesse and unhaunted Ground;
   And as we sing thy Dirge, we will
                 The Daffadill,   10
   And other flowers, lay upon
   (The Altar of our love) thy Stone.

3. Thou wonder of all Maids, li'st here,
   Of Daughters all, the Deerest Deere;
   The eye of Virgins; nay, the Queen   15
                 Of this smooth Green,
   And all sweet Meades; from whence we get
   The Primrose, and the Violet.

4. Too soon, too deere did *Jephthah* buy,
   By thy sad losse, our liberty: 20
   His was the Bond and Cov'nant, yet
                 Thou paid'st the debt,
   Lamented Maid! he won the day,
   But for the conquest thou didst pay.

5. Thy Father brought with him along   25
   The Olive branch, and Victors Song:
   He slew the Ammonites, we know,
                 But to thy woe;
   And in the purchase of our Peace,
   The Cure was worse then the Disease.   30

6. For which obedient zeale of thine,
   We offer here, before thy Shrine,
   Our sighs for Storax, teares for Wine;
      And to make fine,
   And fresh thy Herse-cloth, we will, here,   35
   Foure times bestrew thee ev'ry yeere.

7. Receive, for this thy praise, our teares:
   Receive this offering of our Haires:
   Receive these Christall Vialls fil'd
      With teares, distil'd   40
   From teeming eyes; to these we bring,
   Each Maid, her silver Filleting,

8. To guild thy Tombe; besides, these Caules,
   These Laces, Ribbands, and these Faules,
   These Veiles, wherewith we use to hide   45
      The Bashfull Bride,
   When we conduct her to her Groome:
   All, all we lay upon thy Tombe.

9. No more, no more, since thou art dead,
   Shall we ere bring coy Brides to bed;   50
   No more, at yeerly Festivalls
      We Cowslip balls,
   Or chaines of Columbines shall make,
   For this, or that occasions sake.

10. No, no; our Maiden-pleasures be   55
    Wrapt in the winding-sheet, with thee:
    'Tis we are dead, though not i'th grave:
       Or, if we have
    One seed of life left, 'tis to keep
    A Lent for thee, to fast and weep.   60

11. Sleep in thy peace, thy bed of Spice;
    And make this place all Paradise:
    May Sweets grow here! and smoke from hence,
       Fat Frankincense:

           Let Balme, and Cassia send their scent   65
           From out thy Maiden-Monument.

    12.   May no Wolfe howle, or Screech-Owle stir
           A wing about thy Sepulcher!
           No boysterous winds, or stormes, come hither,
                        To starve, or wither   70
           Thy soft sweet Earth! but (like a spring)
           Love keep it ever flourishing.

    13.   May all shie Maids, at wonted hours,
           Come forth, to strew thy Tombe with flow'rs:
           May Virgins, when they come to mourn,   75
                        Male-Incense burn
           Upon thine Altar! then return,
           And leave thee sleeping in thy Urn.

To God, on his sicknesse

       What though my Harp, and Violl be
       Both hung upon the Willow-tree?
       What though my bed be now my grave,
       And for my house I darknesse have?
       What though my healthfull dayes are fled,   5
       And I lie numbred with the dead?
       Yet I have hope, by Thy great power,
       To spring; though now a wither'd flower.

An Ode, or Psalme, to God

                   Deer God,
                If thy smart Rod
             Here did not make me sorrie,
                 I sho'd not be
                   With Thine, or Thee,   5
              In Thy eternall Glorie.

> But since
> Thou didst convince
> My sinnes, by gently striking;
> Add still to those   10
> First stripes, new blowes,
> According to Thy liking.
>
> Feare me,
> Or scourging teare me;
> That thus from vices driven,   15
> I may from Hell
> Flie up, to dwell
> With Thee, and Thine in Heaven.

A *Christmas* Caroll, *sung to the King in the Presence at* White-Hall

Chor. What sweeter musick can we bring,
Then a Caroll, for to sing
The Birth of this our heavenly King?
Awake the Voice! Awake the String!
Heart, Eare, and Eye, and every thing   5
Awake! the while the active Finger
Runs division with the Singer.

From the Flourish they came to the Song.

1. Dark and dull night, flie hence away,
    And give the honour to this Day,
    That sees *December* turn'd to *May*.   10

An Ode, or Psalme, to God. 8 *convince*: vanquish.
13 *Feare me*: inspire me with fear.
  A Christmas Caroll, sung to the King.... 7 *division*: a variation on, or accompaniment to, a theme or "plain-song."
  Flourish: fanfare; *Song*: Herrick intended the carol to be sung by four solo voices and a chorus. No contemporary setting appears to have survived.

2. If we may ask the reason, say;
   The why, and wherefore all things here
   Seem like the Spring-time of the yeere?

3. Why do's the chilling Winters morne
   Smile, like a field beset with corne?   15
   Or smell, like to a Meade new-shorne,
   Thus, on the sudden?   4. Come and see
   The cause, why things thus fragrant be:
   'Tis He is borne, whose quickning Birth
   Gives life and luster, publike mirth,   20
   To Heaven, and the under-Earth.

Chor. We see Him come, and know him ours,
   Who, with His Sun-shine, and His showers,
   Turnes all the patient ground to flowers.

1. The Darling of the world is come,   25
   And fit it is, we finde a roome
   To welcome Him.   2. The nobler part
   Of all the house here, is the heart,

Chor. Which we will give Him; and bequeath
   This Hollie, and this Ivie Wreath,   30
   To do Him honour; who's our King,
   And Lord of all this Revelling.

The Musicall Part was composed by
M. Henry Lawes.

The New-yeeres Gift, or Circumcisions Song, sung to the King in the Presence at White-Hall

1. Prepare for Songs; He's come, He's come;
   And be it sin here to be dumb,
   And not with Lutes to fill the roome.

2. Cast Holy Water all about,
    And have a care no fire gos out,   5
       But 'cense the porch, and place throughout.

3. The Altars all on fier be;
    The Storax fries; and ye may see,
       How heart and hand do all agree,
To make things sweet.   *Chor.* Yet all less sweet then He.   10

4. Bring Him along, most pious Priest,
    And tell us then, when as thou seest
       His gently-gliding, Dove-like eyes,
    And hear'st His whimp'ring, and His cries;
       How canst thou this Babe circumcise?   15

5. Ye must not be more pitifull then wise;
    For, now unlesse ye see Him bleed,
       Which makes the Bapti'me; 'tis decreed,
The Birth is fruitlesse: *Chor.* Then the *work God speed.*

1. Touch gently, gently touch; and here   20
    Spring Tulips up through all the yeere;
       And from His sacred Bloud, here shed,
May Roses grow, to crown His own deare Head.

Chor.   Back, back again; each thing is done
    With zeale alike, as 'twas begun;   25
       Now singing, homeward let us carrie
    The Babe unto His Mother *Marie*;
       And when we have the Child commended
To her warm bosome, then our Rites are ended.

              Composed by M. *Henry Lawes.*

The Star-Song: A Caroll to the King; sung at White-Hall

The Flourish of Musick: then followed the Song

1. Tell us, thou cleere and heavenly Tongue,
   Where is the Babe but lately sprung?
   Lies He the Lillie-banks among?

2. Or say, if this new Birth of ours
   Sleeps, laid within some Ark of Flowers,   5
   Spangled with deaw-light; thou canst cleere
   All doubts, and manifest the where.

3. Declare to us, bright Star, if we shall seek
   Him in the Mornings blushing cheek,
   Or search the beds of Spices through,   10
   To find him out?

Star. No, this ye need not do;
   But only come, and see Him rest
   A Princely Babe in's Mothers Brest.

Chor. He's seen, He's seen, why then a Round,   15
   Let's kisse the sweet and holy ground;
   And all rejoyce, that we have found
   A King, before conception crown'd.

4. Come then, come then, and let us bring
   Unto our prettie *Twelfth-Tide King*,   20
   Each one his severall offering;

Chor. And when night comes, wee'l give Him wassailing:
   And that His treble Honours may be seen,
   Wee'l chuse Him King, and make His Mother Queen.

The Star-Song.... Intended for Epiphany.
24 *King...Queen*: see note to "Twelfe night, or King and Queene."

To God [III]

With golden Censers, and with Incense, here,
Before Thy Virgin-Altar I appeare,
To pay Thee that I owe, since what I see
In, or without; all, all belongs to Thee:
Where shall I now begin to make, for one   5
Least loane of Thine, half Restitution?
Alas! I cannot pay a jot; therefore
I'le kisse the Tally, and confesse the score.
Ten thousand Talents lent me, Thou dost write:
'Tis true, my God; *but I can't pay one mite*.   10

Good men afflicted most

God makes not good men wantons, but doth bring
Them to the field, and, there, to skirmishing;
With trialls those, with terrors these He proves,
And hazards those most, whom the most He loves:
For *Sceva*, darts; for *Cocles*, dangers; thus   5
He finds a fire for mighty *Mutius*;
Death for stout *Cato*; and besides all these,
A poyson too He has for *Socrates*;
Torments for high *Attilius*; and, with want,

Good men afflicted most. 5 *Sceva*: a centurion in Caesar's army who fought valorously at the battle of Dyrrhachium; *Cocles*: Publius Horatius Cocles, who kept the entire army of Porsenna at bay at the Sublician bridge.
6 *Mutius:* Scevola thrust his hand into a brazier of burning coals to show his indifference to death.
9 *Attilius*: A. Regulus preferred to submit himself to the most excruciating tortures at the hands of the Carthaginians, rather than urge the Roman Senate to assent to a peace as one way of securing his release from captivity.

Brings in *Fabricius* for a Combatant: *10*
But, bastard-slips, and such as He dislikes,
He never brings them once to th' push of Pikes.

To God [IV]

Lord, I am like to *Misletoe*,
Which has no root, and cannot grow,
Or prosper, but by that same tree
It clings about; so I by Thee.
What need I then to feare at all,   *5*
So long as I about Thee craule?
But if that Tree sho'd fall, and die,
Tumble shall heav'n, and down will I.

The white Island
or place of the Blest

In this world (the *Isle of Dreames*)
While we sit by sorrowes streames,
Teares and terrors are our theames
    Reciting:

But when once from hence we flie,   *5*
More and more approaching nigh
Unto young Eternitie
    Uniting:

In that *whiter Island*, where
Things are evermore sincere;   *10*

---

10 *Fabricius*: a Roman consul of unshakable integrity whose refusal of bribes offered by King Pyrrhus meant meeting the army of that King on the field.

Candor here, and lustre there
            Delighting:

There no monstrous fancies shall
Out of hell an horrour call,
To create (or cause at all)   15
            Affrighting.

There in calm and cooling sleep
We our eyes shall never steep;
But eternall watch shall keep,
            Attending   20

Pleasures, such as shall pursue
Me immortaliz'd, and you;
And fresh joyes, as never too
            Have ending.

Prayer

A Prayer, that is said alone,
Starves, having no companion.
Great things ask for, when thou dost pray,
And those great are, which ne're decay.
Pray not for silver, rust eats this;   5
Ask not for gold, which metall is:
Nor yet for houses, which are here
But earth: *such vowes nere reach Gods eare.*

Predestination

Predestination is the Cause alone
Of many standing, but of fall to none.

Another

Art thou not destin'd? then, with hast, go on
To make thy faire *Predestination*:
If thou canst change thy life, God then will please
To change, or call back, His past *Sentences*.

To keep a true Lent

1. Is this a Fast, to keep
    The Larder leane?
        And cleane
  From fat or Veales, and Sheep?

2. Is it to quit the dish
    Of Flesh, yet still
        To fill
  The platter high with Fish?

3. Is it to fast an houre,
    Or rag'd to go,
        Or show
  A down-cast look, and sowre?

4. No: 'tis a Fast, to dole
    Thy sheaf of wheat,
        And meat,
  Unto the hungry Soule.

5. It is to fast from strife,
    From old debate,

To keep a true Lent. 10 *rag'd*: ragged.

And hate;
To circumcise thy life.   20

6. To shew a heart grief-rent;
To sterve thy sin,
Not Bin;
And that's to keep thy Lent.

Good Friday: Rex Tragicus,
or *Christ going to His Crosse*

Put off Thy Robe of *Purple*, then go on
To the sad place of execution:
Thine houre is come; and the Tormentor stands
Ready, to pierce Thy tender Feet, and Hands.
Long before this, the base, the dull, the rude,   5
Th' inconstant, and unpurged Multitude
Yawne for Thy coming; some e're this time crie,
How He deferres, how loath He is to die!
Amongst this scumme, the Souldier, with his speare,
And that sowre Fellow, with his *vineger*,   10
His *spunge*, and *stick*, do ask why Thou dost stay?
So do the *Skurfe* and *Bran* too: Go Thy way,
Thy way, Thou guiltlesse man, and satisfie
By Thine approach, each their beholding eye.
Not as a thief, shalt Thou ascend the mount,   15
But like a Person of some high account:
The *Crosse* shall be Thy *Stage*; and Thou shalt there
The spacious field have for Thy *Theater*.
Thou art that *Roscius*, and that markt-out man,
That must this day act the Tragedian,   20
To wonder and affrightment: Thou art He,
Whom all the flux of Nations comes to see;
Not those poor Theeves that act their parts with Thee:
Those act without regard, when once a *King*,

And *God*, as Thou art, comes to suffering. 25
No, No, this *Scene* from Thee takes life and sense,
And soule and spirit plot, and excellence.
Why then begin, great King! ascend Thy Throne,
And thence proceed, to act Thy Passion
To such an height, to such a period rais'd, 30
As Hell, and Earth, and Heav'n may stand amaz'd.
God, and good Angells guide Thee; and so blesse
Thee in Thy severall parts of bitternesse;
That those, who see Thee nail'd unto the Tree,
May (though they scorn Thee) praise and pitie Thee. 35
And we (Thy Lovers) while we see Thee keep
The Lawes of Action, will both sigh, and weep;
And bring our Spices, to embalm Thee dead;
That done, we'l see Thee sweetly buried.

> *This Crosse-Tree here*
> *Doth* Jesus *beare,*
> *Who sweet'ned first,*
> *The Death accurs't.*

Here all things ready are, make hast, make hast away;
For, long this work wil be, and very short this Day.
Why then, go on to act: Here's wonders to be done,
Before the last least sand of Thy ninth houre be run;
Or e're dark Clouds do dull, or dead the Mid-dayes Sun.

> Act when Thou wilt,
> Bloud will be spilt;
> Pure Balm, that shall
> Bring Health to All.
> Why then, Begin
> To powre first in
> Some Drops of Wine,
> In stead of Brine,
> To search the Wound,
> So long unsound:
> And, when that's done,
> Let Oyle, next, run,
> To cure the Sore
> Sinne made before.
> And O! Deare Christ,
> E'en as Thou di'st,
> Look down, and see
> Us weepe for Thee.
> And tho (Love knows)
> Thy dreadfull Woes
> Wee cannot ease;
> Yet doe Thou please,
> Who Mercie art,
> T'accept each Heart,
> That gladly would
> Helpe, if it could.
> Meane while, let mee,
> Beneath this Tree,
> This Honour have,
> To make my grave.

His coming to the Sepulcher

Hence they have born my Lord: Behold! the Stone
Is rowl'd away; and my sweet Saviour's gone!
Tell me, white Angell; what is now become
Of Him, we lately seal'd up in this Tombe?
Is He, from hence, gone to the shades beneath,   5
To vanquish Hell, as here He conquer'd Death?
If so; I'le thither follow, without feare;
And live in Hell, if that my *Christ* stayes there.

Of all the good things whatsoe're we do,
God is the ΑΡΧΗ, and the ΤΕΛΟΣ too.

[*Untitled closing couplet.*]   2 The Greek words are *Arche* and *Telos*, the beginning and ending.

Andrew Marvell

In his poems Marvell frequently displays an acute awareness of a fundamental cleavage in man's consciousness, often opposing human activity and contemplation or contrasting engagement in and retirement from experience. While on the one hand he portrays the actual world as an alluring place in which to be and move, he simultaneously evokes an imaginative world of essences with which he longs to commune but which, because of his temporal preoccupations, he can glimpse only intermittently. Time and again he establishes a polarity between two prime absolutes such as Body and Soul, or between Created Pleasure and the Resolved Soul, and he then sets these antithetical personifications in motion to conduct animated debates during whose course individual states of being are rigorously analyzed. In such encounters he invariably maintains an impartial balance in assessing the virtues and the deficiencies of divergent approaches to experience, a procedure to which he adheres even when, turning aside from formal contention, he attempts to describe the simplest essence or explain the most trivial occurrence, for to him all experience is equivocal. Ultimately he reveals himself as a poet of unexpected profundity, to whom ambiguity and irony of expression if not inevitable are essential instruments for accentuating the paradoxical.

Marvell does not formulate a philosophy, nor does he subscribe to any established system of thought. He finds experience, it would seem, far too complex to define in categorical assertions, and man himself, by his very nature, incapable of assessing what his role in the world should be. A basic contradiction frustrates the shaping of a world view, and it centers itself on the impossibility of achieving a world of innocence within what is necessarily a world of experience. In depicting a world where man's transcendent aspirations are limited by his mortality, he often allows opposing views in a given poem or group of poems to remain in a state of unresolved tension, and the presence of such balanced irreconcilables usually gives rise to conflicting interpretations which depend upon the reader's personal views of the evidence.

The opposition may be seen, for example, between the views of the poet as maker and the poet as prophet, the one Christian and the other classical. It may concern the relative value of cultivated gardens and natural wilderness, or the ambiguous good accompanying fulfilled love or self-sufficient chastity. The reader may have to measure the degree of praise or blame to be accorded to figures as different as Cromwell, King Charles I, or General Fairfax as they immerse themselves in experience or withdraw from it, or he may have to evaluate the achievement not only of poets like Milton and Lovelace but even poetasters like Richard Flecknoe and Thomas May. The contraries recur in various poems: fate and free will, war and peace, expectation and accomplishment, eternity and transiency. Insofar as a balance is scrupulously maintained in his evaluation of each pair, Marvell may be said to be uncommitted. Yet the chief difficulty in accepting this view lies in his extraordinary elusiveness, which is often ingeniously complicated by his subtle detachment from the experiences he describes.

Though the poems often suggest an active mind playing over vast areas of philosophic thought they never mention particular thinkers nor use their special terminologies. In making use of the ordinary materials of experience, Marvell displays a paradoxical simplicity which is at first engaging and then momentarily disquieting. What on first reading is direct statement involving concrete objects—a drop of dew, a rope of hay, a fawn, a statue—gradually assumes a significance beyond the merely literal to include the emblematic—the pastoral garland of flowers juxtaposed with the Christian garland of thorns—and then embraces even the typological—the literal truth of the description of Appleton House, as Maren-Sofie Røstvig has demonstrated, embodying simultaneously the moral truth of the importance of humility, the allegorical truth of the house as but an inn in the pilgrimage of the soul, and the ultimate truth of the housemaster relationship as a reflection of the body-soul relationship. The drop of dew, Marvell tells us explicitly, mirrors "The greater Heaven in an Heaven less," and such perspectives make his lyric poems metaphysical in the primary sense of the word: they are pieces which speculate about man and his nature and his relation to reality.

Ever since the early part of this century, when Sir Herbert Grierson characterized Marvell as "the most interesting personality between Donne and Dryden, and at his very best a finer poet than either," and when T. S. Eliot fastened upon his special blend of wit and imagination as the basis for his permanent appeal, Marvell's reputation as a lyric poet has grown to such a height that there is no need to justify his importance, let alone prove his excellence. It is therefore hard to realize that although Lamb had liked his "witty delicacy," and that Tennyson had been specially taken by "the magnificent hyperbole" of "To his Coy Mistress," the prevailing tendency at the turn of the present century was still to think of Marvell chiefly as a political writer and satirist of the Commonwealth and Restoration periods.

Born at Winestead in Holderness, Yorkshire, on 31 March 1621, the son of an Anglican clergyman of liberal persuasion, Marvell was educated first at Hull Grammar School. Although he was enrolled at Trinity College, Cambridge, in a period when the intellectual life of that university was largely dominated by the views of such Platonists as Peter Sterry, Benjamin Whichcote, John Smith, and Henry More, no record survives of their impact upon him. Not much is known of his student enthusiasms beyond the report that at one time he was attracted to Catholicism, nor is much known of his activities immediately after his departure from the university in September, 1641. In the mid-1640's, while many of his contemporaries were involved in the Civil War, he was on a continental tour. He was in Rome in 1645, visiting the poet Flecknoe. On his return he served in 1650 or 1651 as tutor to Mary, daughter of Lord Fairfax, the general of the Parliamentary forces who had recently resigned his command and retired to his country seat at Nun Appleton. Two letters of 1653 attest both to Marvell's scholarly attainments and presumably to his advocacy of the Parliamentary cause. In the first, addressed to John Bradshaw, President of the Council, Milton, then Latin Secretary *extraordinarius* to the Commonwealth, recommends that Marvell be made Latin Secretary in the office of the Secretary of State; Marvell probably took up his post in September of 1657. The second letter, from Marvell to Cromwell, comments favorably on the progress of the Protector's ward, William Dutton, whom the poet had been engaged to tutor in the house of one of the fellows at Eton.

Although Marvell's later life is far more completely documented, his biographer Augustine Birrell aptly notes that "A more elusive, non-recorded character is hardly to be found. We know all about him, but very little of him." After the death of Cromwell in 1658, Marvell spent virtually the remainder of his life as Member of Parliament representing Hull, and some three hundred of his letters directed to a long line of mayors survive in that city's archives, attesting to his dedication as a civil servant. In addition to the *Miscellaneous Poems* of 1681 (Marvell died in 1678), which contains all the lyrical pieces together with a few Latin poems, some satires, and the Cromwell eulogies, there is also a collection of satires, published in 1689, entitled *Poems on Affairs of State*. Students of Marvell's prose are unanimous in singling out for emphasis *The Rehearsal Transpros'd* (published in two parts in 1672 and 1673), which is especially notable for its championing of religious tolerance.

Marvell is an anomalous figure whose poetry is so diverse in its manner and subject matter that it is difficult to categorize him easily as either a Puritan or a Cavalier poet. For some of his critics, it becomes a nice point to determine at what period in his life he turned aside from the Royalist way of life to espouse the cause of the Parliamentarians, and a nicer point to decide the extent, nature, and even sincerity of his admiration for Cromwell. Similarly, he defies obvious identification with poets exclusively metaphysical, Spenserian, or Jonsonian. Although he is able to compose an intensely personal religious lyric like "The Coronet" in the manner of Herbert, and to manipulate a conceit in a poem like "Eyes and Tears" in accents not far removed from Donne's, neither poem represents a habitual manner. And even if the marriage songs addressed to Lord Fauconberg and Lady Mary Cromwell suggest the spontaneity of the dialogues of Spenser's *Shepheardes Calender*, and the satires on Flecknoe and May recall the pungent raillery of Jonson's "Famous Voyage," none of these, again, epitomizes the essential manner of Marvell. Although certain critics like Dennis Davison view him as having passed successively through a series of phases or periods, each of which reflects a specific influence in his development, the limited confines of his poetry (virtually all his lyric poetry was written between the late 1640's and the early 1650's) hardly permit the work to represent a many-faceted career or to document a spiritual autobiography.

Certain poems or groups of poems have not infrequently been discussed in terms of genre. Marvell can evoke a pastoral world not far removed from that of the Fletchers, Browne, or Herrick, and he can people it with nymphs and shepherds who recall classical attitudes but often relate them to the preoccupations of the seventeenth century. In depicting this ideal world he can introduce innovations into traditional kinds of pastoral poems—the blazon, the elegy, the dialogue, and even the extended country-house poem—in a fresh and vital way. In the opinion of Frank Kermode, pastoral poetry in the tradition of the ancients comes to an end with Marvell, while H. R. Swardson finds that Marvell carries the natural innocence of the classical pastoral a step further into a yet more primitive state, which he chooses to describe as a presexual or nonsexual innocence that nourishes the mind and provides a kind of philosophical or religious retreat from the world. As with pastorals, Marvell is capable of making utmost use of the *données* of a relatively restricted class of poem such as the Horatian ode, and both R. H. Syfret and J. S. Coolidge have recently shown that recognition of classical antecedents of "Upon Cromwel's Return from Ireland" adds fuller dimensions to the appreciation and understanding of a poem long considered an enigma by Marvell exegetes.

Some readers emphasize the importance of viewing Marvell as apologist for various philosophical movements of the mid-seventeenth century. Muriel Bradbrook and M. G. Lloyd Thomas find that the striking parallelism between some aspects of the poems and Spinoza's thought is centered chiefly in Marvell's elevation of matter to a position equal to that of mind, which compares with the philosopher's view of the twin attitudes of thought and extension. Also significant is Marvell's treatment of the passions, which suggests Spinoza's theory that the passions cease to be passions as soon as a clear and distinct idea of them is formed. For Maren-Sofie Røstvig, the principles of Neoplatonic philosophy as set forth in the Hermetic corpus (a series of *libelli* presenting what some men in the seventeenth century regarded as a divinely inspired account of the creation of the world) are indispensable to an understanding of such key poems as "The Garden" and "Upon Appleton House." The doctrines of the Cambridge Platonists, as utilized and modified by Marvell, merit an extended treatment in H. E. Toliver's study of the poet and undergird his explication of particular poems.

Pierre Legouis, who believes that particular philosophical hobbyhorses can be ridden too hard, finds the political, historical, and biographical contexts of the poems of utmost importance. The dedication of his recently revised study of the poet to Marvell's distinguished editor and annotator H. M. Margoliouth testifies that his is the approach of the literary historian, who painstakingly collects, arranges, interprets, and relates facts and details, both significant and trivial, about the poet's life and work. His study provides a solidly documented foundation of which the critic impatient of historical background had better take due cognizance. In keeping with this approach, J. M. Wallace subjects to careful scrutiny Marvell's Loyalism and, in a detailed study, treats the poet as a member of that central group of moderate men who neither wholly espoused the causes of the Royalists or the Puritans.

Somewhat different in ultimate aim from the historians of literature are those critics concerned with Marvell's artistry. More than a generation ago Victoria Sackville-West, in an incisive though circumscribed critique of the poet, concentrated on "To his Coy Mistress" as the apogee of Marvell's art, praising it for its paradoxical compression and luxuriance: "The whole poem is as tight and hard as a knot; yet as spilling and voluptuous as a horn of plenty." Two recent writers have extended considerably the Marvellian dimensions through fresh awareness. Ann Berthoff sees the lyric poems as "unified by the master theme of the soul's response to temporality," and perceiving the nice relationship existing between matter and manner, suggests exploring Marvell's intellectual power and subtlety through the ways of his imagination, which she takes to be "conceptual in its resources and allegorical in its expression." In a comprehensive study of Marvell's art, Rosalie Colie brings to the forefront "Upon Appleton House" as a poem which the twentieth century somewhat belatedly has recognized as a very important, if not great, poem of the seventeenth century, and she persuasively demonstrates the way in which the poet's strange juxtaposition of elements from widely disparate contexts—rhetorical, iconographic, religious, scientific—contributes at once to the poem's richness, achieving an impressive unity amid almost mad multiplicity.

Even a casual survey of Marvell's complete poetic output, which is considerably smaller than that of any of his contemporaries here anthologized, indicates that it is composed of lyric and discursive pieces, the former class containing mostly nature poems and love poems, and the latter class composed of occasional poems and satires. Although the categories are not mutually exclusive, there is some profit in maintaining them in a discussion of attitudes and manner, if only to show how the originality of Marvell's thought transcends easy classification.

Marvell's nature poetry usually makes the first impact upon the reader. The conscious artificiality of the old pastoralism is often replaced in his work by a refreshing realism, and old conventions are fired with new meanings. The idealization of experience which pastoral poetry traditionally postulates—that luxurious life of a Golden Age unblemished by anything more serious than the loss of a song contest or a shepherd's crook—is sometimes maintained, but more often it is transformed into an existence in which the passions have wrought havoc. Grasshoppers and frogs, moving instinctively and abruptly, may symbolize the pastoral's thoughtless unconcern for the genuine problems of experience, but the serpent may sometimes raise its head threateningly when man introduces a disquiet, a disunity, and ultimately a discordant chaos into nature's order. Chief among Marvell's innovations is the endowment of the traditionally one-dimensional shepherds of pastoralism with unexpected depth of character. Of no less moment is the replacement of the picturesque backdrop with a nature that is sentient and vital.

In its most positive contexts, Marvell's nature is animate and responsive to man. Associated with it is the color green, which underscores the ideas of fertility and fecundity, and which often is contrasted with the pinks and reds of the disruptive passions. Never static, nature is always seen as transient and evanescent, although paradoxically it is often described as the ultimate source of man's repose and tranquillity. It is never spoken of as the repository of any divine elements; no pantheism is to be associated with it. Nor does the presentation of its flora or fauna display the precise and detailed knowledge of a naturalist; rather, natural objects are invested with human concepts. Sometimes this natural world is incarnated in geometric shapes or architectural patterns, and on occasion its fruits and flowers are endowed with souls and its trees are made to speak with a startling animation.

The poetry of Marvell reveals alternately the wild and the cultivated states of nature, constantly comparing and contrasting worlds of innocence and experience. Yet, as Joseph Summers perceptively notes, the state of natural wildness, for Marvell, is not intrinsically superior to the state of cultivated nature displayed in gardens. The virtue of either depends upon its use by the poet, for the garden may recall the paradisal state as well as the Fall. Several of his poems describe the prelapsarian state of nature in terms of freshness and vitality. The most idyllic treatment of this is in "Bermudas," in which an island paradise, seen from a distance by Puritan voyagers, is exultantly hymned as an Eden of innocence and eternal springs, free from monsters, storms, and prelates' rages. Such an idealized state is also described in "The Garden," Marvell's most famous nature poem, where nature's "Fair quiet" is associated with "repose" and "delicious Solitude," and is treated as all-sufficient for man if he meets it with all passion spent. In place of the physical allurements of love ("our Passions heat"), it can supply a wondrous life in which fruits and flowers may carry on a vital kind of courtship with man. Stanley Stewart, arguing for an allegorical interpretation of this poem in terms of the Song of Songs, finds that the context of the Canticles would adequately explain the aggressive role of the garden as it pursues, captures, and embraces the Beloved. In this view even the trees become emblems of divine love and of its productive effects. As a result, the mind achieves the contemplative state which is the goal of meditation, and is able to create new worlds; and the Soul, as in Yeats's poem, is able to clap hands and sing, preparing itself for "longer flight." By contrast many critics have noted that the Mower poems deal with man's treatment, or mistreatment, of nature. In the first of these the Mower inveighs against lecherous man for seducing the world and perverting nature, once "most plain and pure," by the construction of artificial gardens, whose soil, scientifically treated to bring forth unnatural varieties of flowers and fruits, thus prevents the vital sexual forces from operating in keeping with their natures.

Marvell's nature, however, whether plain and pure or ordered and cultivated, does not exist for itself so much as for its relation with man. In some of his dialogues, the typical interchanges between shepherds and shepherdesses blend attitudes both pagan and Christian in keeping with the mild didacticism long associated with the genre. In one, an unfrequented cave is Love's shrine for Clorinda, but it is Virtue's grave for Damon, who urges Clorinda dutifully to join the natural world in singing the praises of Pan (traditionally identified with Christ). In another, so persuasively does Thyrsis paint for Dorinda the pleasures of that paradise, Elysium, that she eagerly simulates death through a drug-induced sleep. In still another dialogue, Ametas wins his suit to Thestylis by inexorably pursuing the logic of the analogy of making hay-ropes: where both twist the same way rather than contrariwise, neither love nor hay-ropes can be made.

From such conventional figures as these, Marvell easily passes to more subtle studies, and in a deceptively simple way he is able to endow his men and women with a profundity which is often suggested by merely a few circumstantial details. He is primarily interested in the innermost natures of his young lovers, and his many love poems often reveal surprisingly modern attitudes and preoccupations. Like Donne, he rejects the artificiality of Petrarchism, replacing it with a realism full of unexpected contrarieties, at times even surpassing his eminent predecessor in tapping the subliminal and in devising a symbolic world of extraordinary brilliance to depict it. Though the women he creates may superficially recall the delicate and arch innocents of Herrick's *Hesperides*, Marvell's favorite figures are either excessively naive or calculatingly cynical.

A central irony often encountered in Marvell's love poems is the contrast between the search for a kind of perfect love, on the one hand, and the melting away of that love's satisfactions in its very attainment, on the other. Most readers, immediately struck by the vexations of the love poems, are tempted to conclude that for Marvell love in its physical realization somehow mars that marriage of true minds which alone insures the ideal relationship. The speaker of "The Definition of Love" attests to the ideality of love, and then promptly denies the possibility of its existence. In a central figure Marvell compares ideal lovers to parallel lines, which even in infinity can never meet. When a union is effected, like that between Celia and the speaker in "The Match" (who represent respectively Nature and Love), the conjunction occurs not as a result of reciprocal affection but simply as a magnetic fusion mechanically achieved at the ironic moment when each most indulgently contemplates his own beauty.

For L. W. Hyman, Marvell's view of man's happiness in the garden-state, where he "walk'd without a Mate," has as its basis the tradition found in an old Rabbinic legend that Adam was originally androgynous. Maren-Sofie Røstvig has traced this idea in even greater detail to the Hermetic corpus, where, at one early stage in the creation of the world (as described in the first *libellus*), men were thought to have been hermaphroditic, only later to be divided into sexes and enjoined by God to conceive and multiply.

Since the chief stumbling blocks to the happiness or equanimity of lovers are the passions, it is inevitable that Marvell glorifies, above all, young love, which is at its most ideal before the passions are called into play. Like Blake's Thel, the nymph in "The Picture of little T. C. in a Prospect of Flowers" will grow to fear wanton love. The Mower, smitten by Juliana, assaults the grasses with his scythe and then slashes his own ankle as a sign of his invasion of the world of passion, a symbol of his fall. In contrast, the nymph complaining of the death of her fawn rejects her lover Sylvio (his name significantly suggests either wildness or all the good to be associated with the green world of the forest) and worships instead his gift of the gentle beast. Though this act may at first symbolize modesty and innocence, it later becomes possessiveness, the fruit of a kind of inversion which she does not comprehend. In this complex poem it may be the nymph's self-deception which is ultimately responsible for the fawn's death, or it may be the wanton troopers who are to blame. In "Daphnis and Chloe," the dissembling hero is portrayed more overtly; his casual fabrication of motives to justify his departure from his lady exposes his hypocrisy. At other times it is the lady who is the false aggressor: her weeping, Marvell slyly hints in "Eyes and Tears," may have no connection whatsoever with grief; or she may appear, as in "The Gallery," in the harrowing guise of murderess and enchantress, as well as in the innocuous garb of fair and tender shepherdess.

On occasion, Marvell scores his most telling strokes through overstatement. In his most famous poem, "To his Coy Mistress" (often treated as a striking example of the *carpe diem* theme of the period), the lover may be interpreted, largely because of the extravagant imagery of the poem, as an overenthusiastic and hence ironic apologist for immediate gratification when confronted with the idea of mutability. Similarly overwrought is "The unfortunate Lover," a highly-colored poem in which Marvell insists that we recognize the falsity of the storybook picture of love as a good meriting sympathy. Here the passion-painted knight, the banneret whose appropriate heraldic colors are sable and gules, undergoes a melodramatically exhausting career which is delicately but none the less pointedly satirized as he progresses from birth ("In a *Cesarian Section*") to death ("a Lover drest/In his own Blood").

For most Marvell devotees, the occasional poems and satires are of far less moment than the lyric pieces and indeed belong to the world of history. In his relatively few occasional poems — seven are addressed to friends, and even fewer record particular events — one often senses that Marvell writes not so much out of choice as out of duty. Unlike Jonson, whose feeling for the ordered society and whose admiration for certain of its members he shares only indifferently (though he recognizes his own public responsibilities as a civil servant), Marvell seldom seems to approach this kind of poem with relish or pleasure. Whether he writes in Latin or English, it often is an occasion rather than a person which attracts him, and the nature of his response is often dependent upon the opportunities offered him to treat certain favorite themes.

A few of the occasional poems may be selected for comment from among subjects as diverse as the following: the death from smallpox of Lord Hastings, at the age of nineteen, on the eve of his marriage; the fall of Lord Villiers in a skirmish near Kingston-on-Thames during the Civil War; the return of Cromwell from Ireland; the victory of Blake over the Spaniards at Santa Cruz; the first anniversary of the government under Cromwell; the publication of Lovelace's *Lucasta* and of Milton's *Paradise Lost*. In the less memorable of these pieces Marvell gives up his favorite octosyllabics for rhymed pentameter couplets, and what becomes immediately evident is a loss of concentration, inevitability, and, particularly in the longer pieces, a center of gravity, though not one jot of wit.

Not a little interest has been generated for the Hastings poem, if only because it shows Marvell emulating certain metaphysical mannerisms through the panache of his learned allusions, recording almost flippantly that the misfortune of Hastings' early death had regrettably not permitted him to feast upon the Tree of Life as he had on that of Knowledge. More sustained is the panegyric addressed to Villiers, who is described in grandiloquent epic terms bordering on the mock heroic as a Hector struck down in battle, paradoxically dividing with his steel whole troops as he cuts his epitaph on either side to deal Death itself a death-blow. The Lovelace poem is amusing in its almost facetious treatment of the poet as love's lover, and the poem praising Milton adroitly sidesteps the usual encomiastic banalities by an initial skeptical inquiry as to whether the author of *Paradise Lost* would be able to develop that poem's serious theme with due ceremony. The piece praising Blake's victory as the work of a resolved soul exhibits the utmost of tonal control; it vividly contrasts the proud pomp of the Spanish fleet "rais'd by Tyranny, and rais'd for War" with the "resistless genious" of a peace-loving hero seen against the idyllic background of the "sweet" Canary Isles "by Nature blest."

Yet none of these occasional pieces has won even a modicum of the acclaim granted to the somberly measured "Horatian Ode" which, in spite of (or perhaps because of) conflicting interpretations, continues to attract readers and to elicit enlightened commentary. It provides a good example of the prismatic nature of some of Marvell's poems, whose individual facets light up differing points in successive readings. Thus, one reading may emphasize Cromwell's restlessness and forthrightness, and another Charles I's calmness in submitting to Fate's ministrations. On another occasion the poet's championship of the great Parliamentarian may obscure for the moment his devotion and sympathy for the beloved monarch mounting the scaffold at Whitehall, or the glorification of "adventrous War" may take precedence over the "inglorious Arts of Peace."

In his later years Marvell established himself as an incisive commentator on the world of his time, and published several verse satires on various political figures. These appeared in 1689 as *Poems on Affairs of State*. A fruitful reading of them, as both Legouis and Wallace have shown, is inevitably dependent upon a close knowledge of historical events surrounding the Restoration. They complement his lyric pieces in an extraordinary way, showing the poet who discoursed so elegantly on a drop of dew to be quite capable of immersing himself in the world.

The *Miscellaneous Poems* of 1681, however, contains three pieces of formal verse satire of more general interest: "Tom May's Death," "Fleckno, an English Priest at Rome," and "The Character of Holland." Each of these, in its own highly individual manner, shows Marvell in tune with his century in centering his satires upon literary and religious as well as political themes. Thomas May and Richard Flecknoe serve as suitable figures for satire for Marvell, just as Inigo Jones and Thomas Sheldon had served for Jonson and Elkanah Settle and Thomas Shadwell would serve for Dryden.

Marvell is aware of the need for including in his satires a moral norm against which the extravagances of his figures may be seen, yet he shrewdly makes use of narrators whose essential *personae* add no little complexity by making any such norm virtually impossible to establish. In "Tom May's Death," the literary dictator Ben Jonson appears, not without some self-consciousness, in Elysium, to chide and scold the bumbling poetaster-translator of Lucan for failing to wrest the poet laureateship from his rival Davenant. Here poet and poetaster alike seem to be victims of Marvell's derision. In "Fleckno," the youthful narrator visiting the poet-priest is endowed with such rare ingenuousness and civility that his most incisive strokes against the Jesuit are at first naive and unintentional. Confronted by the priest's witty equivocation, the narrator grows perceptibly in sophistication. In "The Character of Holland," a facetious spokesman for the Commonwealth dismisses with typical English condescension the inconsequential grotesqueries of the Dutch and the meanness of the land they inhabit. Marvell's stance here is intentionally vague. Especially pertinent in contexts such as these is T. S. Eliot's observation that Marvell's lyric poetry displays "that precise taste... which finds for him the proper degree of seriousness for every subject which he treats."

Like Dryden, who sought to elevate satire to an exalted position, Marvell attempted to slay with finesse. In his satires there is little vituperation, but there are admirable bold utterances, as well as several memorable passages of whimsey and wit. Most readers admire the straightforward march of his heroic couplets, skillfully varied by the occasional inclusion of feminine rhymes or by the adroit placement of the caesura, but most frequently by the choice of arresting epithets. May, at first a "Gazet writer" inspired by a "Tankard-bearing Muse," later becomes "Chronicler to *Spartacus*," and Flecknoe is urbanely diminished as "This *Basso Relievo* of a man." Somewhat more crudely, Holland is reduced to "This indigested vomit of the Sea" and "th'Off-scouring of the *Brittish Sand*."

Much of the effectiveness of these satires depends upon Marvell's use of such devices as the balanced antithesis and the cadenced polysyllabic, but some of their charm comes from their literary associations. The picture of Jonson taxing May as a "servil' wit, and Mercenary Pen" is introduced by lines echoing Jonson on Shakespeare, and it is precisely the kind of comment that was often leveled at Jonson in his lifetime. The Miltonic echo in "The last distemper of the sober Brain" anticipates the scriptural echo of Pope, who introduces his Arabella Fermor at that famed card game to utter, with epic magnification, "Let spades be trump!" The theological puns so insistently injected in "Fleckno" achieve a kind of immortality in Dryden's later satire "MacFlecknoe," which takes as its point of departure Marvell's piece in order to belittle Shadwell as the son of that raffish mid-century priest.

Whether Marvell expresses himself in the lyric, the satire, or the discursive political poem, certain characteristics of his manner remain constant and define a mode singularly his own. Turning aside from the recondite allusions and verbal extravagances of the full-blown metaphysical manner, he uses instead the simple word, homely figure, undecorated phrase. Spontaneity supplants self-consciousness. The term "conceit" becomes a thing of a past age. Most of the poems of Marvell are memorable for a striking beauty which is in part dependent upon their unfettered grace of phrase and their unforced rhymes, and in part upon a syntactic strength capable of supporting the irony and paradox pervading them. They often make a telling impact by imparting a vivid sense of the wondrousness of life, and they frequently do so through highly dramatic means for which the monologue and the dialogue provide only the frame. Their strongest claim, however, lies in their elusiveness: they require the reader to set his own imagination to work on the one hand to uncover a poet obscured through his own subtleties, and on the other to come to terms with his personal views of experience by attempting to resolve those which the poet has set forth as uncannily enigmatic if not profoundly complex.

The copy text of Marvell's poems is that of the *Miscellaneous Poems* of 1681, a slim folio which in the textual notes is denoted as "F." The British Museum copy (C. 59. i. 8) and one other are the only two which contain "An Horatian Ode" and "The First Anniversary," and only the former contains "A Poem upon the Death of O. C." (ll. 1–184), a poem canceled in every other surviving copy. A completed version of this poem with the concluding lines (185–324) was first printed in the collected edition of Captain Edward Thompson (Th.). Thompson possibly made use of a manuscript version of this poem recently acquired by the Bodleian (MS Eng. poet. d. 49), which also contains manuscript versions of the two Cromwell poems cited above. Omitted in the present edition from the *Miscellaneous Poems* are fourteen pieces in Latin, both verses and prose, a few of which, like "Rus" and "Hortus," are Latin renderings of pieces printed also in English. The order of the remaining English poems is not disturbed. F. contains the following English poems which had been printed before 1681:

> To his worthy Friend Doctor Witty....
> The Character of Holland (ll. 1–100)
> The First Anniversary....
> On the Victory obtained by Blake....
> On Mr. Milton's *Paradise lost*
> A Dialogue between Thyrsis and Dorinda

On occasion, variant readings have been taken from the earlier editions. Textual notes record the source of these readings, as well as some early emendations first made by Thomas Cooke in his collected edition of 1726.

Three additional poems (not in the 1681 folio) are also included:

1. "To his Noble Friend Mr. Richard Lovelace, upon his Poems," which is reprinted from Lovelace's *Lucasta* (1649), where it appears as one of several commendatory poems.

2. "Upon the Death of the Lord Hastings," which is reprinted from *Lachrymae Musarum*, collected and set forth by R. B[rome], 1649 and 1650. The copy text here is that of the edition of 1650.

3. "An Elegy upon the Death of my Lord Francis Villiers," which exists in a single exemplar in the library of Worcester College, Oxford, from which it is here reprinted. The attribution of this poem to Marvell is conjectural.

Poems on Affairs of State, which includes the satires of Marvell and of several of his contemporaries, appeared in twelve editions from 1689 to 1716. It is this vast miscellany of political poems which is currently being re-edited under the guidance of George deF. Lord for the Yale University Press. The great nineteenth-century edition of A. B. Grosart is important in that it includes letters and prose works as well as poems. The standard twentieth-century edition of the poems and letters, to which every student is obligated, is the richly annotated edition of H. M. Margoliouth (Mar.). The recent edition of the complete poetry by George deF. Lord is of some importance if only because it raises questions about the accepted canon of Marvell's poetry and because some of its readings are derived from a copy of the 1681 *Miscellaneous Poems* with extensive manuscript additions acquired by the Bodleian Library in 1946 (catalogued as Eng. poet. d. 49). Other recent editions of selections from the poetry by Dennis Davison, Hugh MacDonald (Mac.), and J. H. Summers, are distinguished by perceptive introductory essays.

SELECTED BIBLIOGRAPHY

EDITIONS

Cooke, Thomas, ed. *The Works of Andrew Marvell.* 2 vols. London, 1726.
Davison, Dennis, ed. *Selected Poetry and Prose of Andrew Marvell.* London, 1952.
Grierson, H. J. C., ed. *Metaphysical Lyrics and Poems of the Seventeenth Century: Donne to Butler.* Oxford, 1921.
Grosart, A. B., ed. *The Complete Works of Andrew Marvell.* 4 vols. London, 1872–1875.
Kermode, Frank, ed. *The Selected Poetry of Marvell.* New York, 1967.
Lord, G. deF., ed. *Complete Poetry of Andrew Marvell.* New York, 1968.
———. *Poems of Affairs of State.* Vol. I. New Haven, Conn., 1963.
MacDonald, Hugh, ed. *The Poems of Andrew Marvell.* Cambridge, Mass., 1952.
Margoliouth, H. M., ed. *The Poems and Letters of Andrew Marvell.* 2 vols. Oxford, 1927; 3rd ed. rev. Pierre Legouis and E. E. Duncan-Jones (1971).
Summers, J. H., ed. *Marvell.* New York, 1966.
Thompson, Edward. *Works of Andrew Marvell.* 3 vols. London, 1776.

BIOGRAPHY AND CRITICISM

Berthoff, Ann E. *The Resolved Soul: A Study of Marvell's Major Poems.* Princeton, N.J., 1970.
Birrell, Augustine. *Andrew Marvell.* London, 1906.
Bradbrook, M. C., and M. G. Lloyd Thomas. *Andrew Marvell.* Cambridge, England, 1940.

Colie, Rosalie L. *"My Ecchoing Song": Andrew Marvell's Poetry of Criticism.* Princeton, N.J., 1970.

Coolidge, John S. "Marvell and Horace," *MP*, LXIII (1965), 111-20.

Cullen, Patrick. *Spenser, Marvell, and Renaissance Pastoral.* Cambridge, Mass., 1970.

Eliot, T. S. "Andrew Marvell," in *Selected Essays: 1917 - 1932.* New York, 1932.

Evett, David. "'Paradice's Only Map': The *Topos* of the *Locus Amoenus* and the Structure of Marvell's *Upon Appleton House*," *PMLA*, LXXXV (1970), 504-13.

Guild, Nicholas. "Marvell's 'The Nymph Complaining for the Death of her Faun,'" *MLQ*, XXIX (1968), 385-94.

Hyman, L. W. *Andrew Marvell.* New York, 1964.

Kermode, Frank. *English Pastoral Poetry from the Beginnings to Marvell.* London, 1952.

Legouis, Pierre. *André Marvell: poète, puritain, patriote, 1621 - 78.* Paris, 1928. Rev., abridged, and trans. as *Andrew Marvell: Poet, Puritan, Patriot.* Oxford, 1965.

Leishman, J. B. *The Art of Marvell's Poetry.* London, 1966.

Lord, George deF., ed. *Andrew Marvell: A Collection of Critical Essays.* Englewood Cliffs, N.J., 1968.

Røstvig, Maren-Sofie. "Andrew Marvell's 'The Garden': A Hermetic Poem," *English Studies*, XL (1959), 65-76.

———. "'Upon Appleton House' and the Universal History of Man," *English Studies*, XLII (1961), 337-51.

Sackville-West, Victoria. *Andrew Marvell.* London, 1929.

Summers, J. H. "Marvell's 'Nature,'" *ELH*, XX (1953), 121-35.

Stewart, Stanley N. *The Enclosed Garden: The Tradition and the Image in Seventeenth-Century Poetry.* Madison, Wis., 1966.

Swardson, H. R. *Poetry and the Fountain of Light: Observations on the Conflict Between Christian and Classical Traditions in Seventeenth-Century Poetry.* Columbia, Mo., 1962.

Syfret, R. H. "Marvell's 'Horatian Ode,'" *RES*, XII (1961), 160-72.

Tayler, E. W. *Nature and Art in Renaissance Literature.* New York and London, 1964.

Toliver, H. E. *Marvell's Ironic Vision.* New Haven, Conn., 1965.

Wallace, J. M. *Destiny His Choice: The Loyalism of Andrew Marvell.* Cambridge, England, 1968.

MISCELLANEOUS
POEMS.

BY
ANDREW MARVELL, Esq;
Late Member of the Honourable House of Commons.

LONDON,
Printed for Robert Boulter, at the Turks-Head
in Cornhill. M.DC.LXXXI.

Andr. Marvell. Esq.

MISCELLANEOUS POEMS

TO THE READER

These are to Certifie every Ingenious Reader, that all these Poems, as also the other things in this Book contained, are Printed according to the exact Copies of my late dear Husband, under his own Hand-Writing, being found since his Death among his other Papers, Witness my Hand this 15th day of *October*, 1680.

Mary Marvell.

A Dialogue between the Resolved Soul, and Created Pleasure

Courage my Soul, now learn to wield
The weight of thine immortal Shield.
Close on thy Head thy Helmet bright.
Ballance thy Sword against the Fight.
See where an Army, strong as fair,   5
With silken Banners spreads the air.

To the Reader. Mary Marvell: this was Mary Palmer, alias Mrs. Andrew Marvell, the poet's London landlady, who evidently at his request took a house in Great Russell Street in 1677, to shelter two distant Yorkshire relations of the poet from the harsh bankruptcy laws of the time. Of the *Miscellaneous Poems*, Pierre Legouis says (p. 121), "This publication may have been at the time no more than a move in a cheating game played by people of whom none was too honest or at least scrupulous...." See F. S. Tupper in *PMLA*, LIII (1938), 267-92. The poet died in this house on 16 August 1678.

Now, if thou bee'st that thing Divine,
In this day's Combat let it shine:
And shew that Nature wants an Art
To conquer one resolved Heart.

Pleasure

Welcome the Creations Guest,
Lord of Earth, and Heavens Heir.
Lay aside that Warlike Crest,
And of Nature's banquet share:
Where the Souls of fruits and flow'rs
Stand prepar'd to heighten yours.

Soul

I sup above, and cannot stay
To bait so long upon the way.

Pleasure

On these downy Pillows lye,
Whose soft Plumes will thither fly:
On these Roses strow'd so plain
Lest one Leaf thy Side should strain.

Soul

My gentler Rest is on a Thought,
Conscious of doing what I ought.

Pleasure

If thou bee'st with Perfumes pleas'd,
Such as oft the Gods appeas'd,
Thou in fragrant Clouds shalt show
Like another God below.

Soul

A Soul that knowes not to presume
Is Heaven's and its own perfume.

Pleasure

Every thing does seem to vie
Which should first attract thine Eye:
But since none deserves that grace,
In this Crystal view *thy* face.

Soul

When the Creator's skill is priz'd, 35
The rest is all but Earth disguis'd.

Pleasure

Heark how Musick then prepares
For thy Stay these charming Aires;
Which the posting Winds recall,
And suspend the Rivers Fall. 40

Soul

Had I but any time to lose,
On this I would at all dispose.
Cease Tempter. None can chain a mind
Whom this sweet Chordage cannot bind.

CHORUS

Earth cannot shew so brave a Sight 45
As when a single Soul does fence
The Batteries of alluring Sense,
And Heaven views it with delight.
   Then persevere: for still new Charges sound:
   And if thou overcom'st thou shalt be crown'd. 50

Pleasure

All this fair, and soft, and sweet,
  Which scatteringly doth shine,
Shall within one Beauty meet,
  And she be only thine.

Soul

If things of Sight such Heavens be, 55
What Heavens are those we cannot see?

Pleasure

Where so e're thy Foot shall go
   The minted Gold shall lie;
Till thou purchase all below,
   And want new Worlds to buy. 60

Soul

Wer't not a price who'ld value Gold?
And that's worth nought that can be sold.

Pleasure

Wilt thou all the Glory have
   That War or Peace commend?
Half the World shall be thy Slave 65
   The other half thy Friend.

Soul

What Friends, if to my self untrue?
What Slaves, unless I captive you?

Pleasure

Thou shalt know each hidden Cause;
   And see the future Time: 70
Try what depth the Centre draws;
   And then to Heaven climb.

Soul

None thither mounts by the degree
Of Knowledge, but Humility.

CHORUS

Triumph, triumph, victorious Soul; 75
The World has not one Pleasure more:
The rest does lie beyond the Pole,
And is thine everlasting Store.

On a Drop of Dew

See how the Orient Dew,
Shed from the Bosom of the Morn
   Into the blowing Roses,
Yet careless of its Mansion new;
For the clear Region where 'twas born 5
   Round in its self incloses:
   And in its little Globes Extent,
Frames as it can its native Element.
   How it the purple flow'r does slight,
     Scarce touching where it lyes, 10
   But gazing back upon the Skies,
     Shines with a mournful Light;
       Like its own Tear,
Because so long divided from the Sphear.
   Restless it roules and unsecure, 15
     Trembling lest it grow impure:
Till the warm Sun pitty it's Pain,
And to the Skies exhale it back again.
   So the Soul, that Drop, that Ray
Of the clear Fountain of Eternal Day, 20
Could it within the humane flow'r be seen,

On a Drop of Dew. In the original edition, the English version of this poem is followed by the Latin version entitled "Rus." Similarly, "The Garden" (see below) is followed by "Hortus." Both Grierson and Margoliouth, in their notes to their editions of the poems, consider that the Latin was in each case written first.

      Remembering still its former height,
      Shuns the sweat leaves and blossoms green;
      And, recollecting its own Light,
Does, in its pure and circling thoughts, express   *25*
The greater Heaven in an Heaven less.
      In how coy a Figure wound,
      Every way it turns away:
      So the World excluding round,
      Yet receiving in the Day.   *30*
      Dark beneath, but bright above:
      Here disdaining, there in Love.
How loose and easie hence to go:
How girt and ready to ascend.
      Moving but on a point below,   *35*
It all about does upwards bend.
Such did the Manna's sacred Dew destil;
White, and intire, though congeal'd and chill.
Congeal'd on Earth: but does, dissolving, run
Into the Glories of th' Almighty Sun.   *40*

The Coronet

When for the Thorns with which I long, too long,
    With many a piercing wound,
    My Saviours head have crown'd,
I seek with Garlands to redress that Wrong:
    Through every Garden, every Mead,   *5*
I gather flow'rs (my fruits are only flow'rs)
    Dismantling all the fragrant Towers
That once adorn'd my Shepherdesses head.
And now when I have summ'd up all my store,
    Thinking (so I my self deceive)   *10*
    So rich a Chaplet thence to weave
As never yet the king of Glory wore:
    Alas I find the Serpent old

---

39 Exod. 16:21 (Mar.).

>   That, twining in his speckled breast,
>   About the flow'rs disguis'd does fold,
>   With wreaths of Fame and Interest.
> Ah, foolish Man, that would'st debase with them,
> And mortal Glory, Heavens Diadem
> But thou who only could'st the Serpent tame,
> Either his slipp'ry knots at once untie,
> And disintangle all his winding Snare:
> Or shatter too with him my curious frame:
> And let these wither, so that he may die,
> Though set with Skill and chosen out with Care.
> That they, while Thou on both their Spoils dost tread,
> May crown thy Feet, that could not crown thy Head.

Eyes and Tears

I

> How wisely Nature did decree,
> With the same Eyes to weep and see!
> That, having view'd the object vain,
> They might be ready to complain.

II

> And, since the Self-deluding Sight,
> In a false Angle takes each hight;
> These Tears which better measure all,
> Like wat'ry Lines and Plummets fall.

III

> Two Tears, which Sorrow long did weigh
> Within the Scales of either Eye,
> And then paid out in equal Poise,
> Are the true price of all my Joyes.

The Coronet. 22 *curious frame*: refers to the rich Chaplet (l. 11), used figuratively for "poem."

IV

What in the World most fair appears,
Yea even Laughter, turns to Tears:
And all the Jewels which we prize,
Melt in these Pendants of the Eyes.

V

I have through every Garden been,
Amongst the Red, the White, the Green;
And yet, from all the flow'rs I saw,
No Hony, but these Tears could draw.

VI

So the all-seeing Sun each day
Distills the World with Chymick Ray;
But finds the Essence only Showers,
Which straight in pity back he powers.

VII

Yet happy they whom Grief doth bless,
That weep the more, and see the less:
And, to preserve their Sight more true,
Bath still their Eyes in their own Dew.

VIII

So *Magdalen*, in Tears more wise
Dissolv'd those captivating Eyes,
Whose liquid Chaines could flowing meet
To fetter her Redeemers feet.

Eyes and Tears. 29–32 A Latin version of this stanza appears at the end of the poem in the 1681 edition.

IX

Not full sailes hasting loaden home,
Nor the chast Ladies pregnant Womb,
Nor *Cynthia* Teeming show's so fair, 35
As two Eyes swoln with weeping are.

X

The sparkling Glance that shoots Desire,
Drench'd in these Waves, does lose it fire.
Yea oft the Thund'rer pitty takes
And here the hissing Lightning slakes. 40

XI

The Incense was to Heaven dear,
Not as a Perfume, but a Tear.
And Stars shew lovely in the Night,
But as they seem the Tears of Light.

XII

Ope then mine Eyes your double Sluice, 45
And practise so your noblest Use.
For others too can see, or sleep;
But only humane Eyes can weep.

XIII

Now like two Clouds dissolving, drop,
And at each Tear in distance stop: 50
Now like two Fountains trickle down:
Now like two floods o'return and drown.

XIV

Thus let your Streams o'reflow your Springs,
Till Eyes and Tears be the same things:
And each the other's difference bears; 55
These weeping Eyes, those seeing Tears.

Bermudas

    Where the remote *Bermudas* ride
In th' Oceans bosome unespy'd,
From a small Boat, that row'd along,
The listning Winds receiv'd this Song.
       What should we do but sing his Praise   5
That led us through the watry Maze,
Unto an Isle so long unknown,
And yet far kinder than our own?
Where he the huge Sea-Monsters wracks,
That lift the Deep upon their Backs.   10
He lands us on a grassy Stage;
Safe from the Storms, and Prelat's rage.
He gave us this eternal Spring,
Which here enamells every thing;
And sends the Fowl's to us in care,   15
On daily Visits through the Air.
He hangs in shades the Orange bright,
Like golden Lamps in a green Night.
And does in the Pomgranates close,
Jewels more rich than *Ormus* show's.   20
He makes the Figs our mouths to meet;
And throws the Melons at our feet.
But Apples plants of such a price,
No Tree could every bear them twice.
With Cedars, chosen by his hand,   25
From *Lebanon*, he stores the Land.
And makes the hollow Seas, that roar,
Proclaime the Ambergris on shoar.
He cast (of which we rather boast)
The Gospels Pearl upon our Coast.   30
And in these Rocks for us did frame

Bermudas. John Oxenbridge, Fellow of Eton, in whose house Marvell lodged in 1653 while tutor to Cromwell's ward, William Dutton, had twice visited the Bermudas. Pierre Legouis finds that "this lyrical piece encloses in its coloured crystal the legend of Puritan emigration."
    23 *Apples*: pineapples.

A Temple, where to sound his Name.
Oh let our Voice his Praise exalt,
Till it arrive at Heavens Vault:
Which thence (perhaps) rebounding, may   35
Eccho beyond the *Mexique Bay*.
Thus sung they, in the *English* boat,
An holy and a chearful Note,
And all the way, to guide their Chime,
With falling Oars they kept the time.   40

Clorinda and Damon

C. Damon come drive thy flocks this way.
D. No: 'tis too late they went astray.
C. I have a grassy Scutcheon spy'd,
    Where *Flora* blazons all her pride.
    The Grass I aim to feast thy Sheep: 5
    The Flow'rs I for thy Temples keep.
D. Grass withers; and the Flow'rs too fade.
C. Seize the short Joyes then, ere they vade.
    Seest thou that unfrequented Cave?
D. That den? C. Loves Shrine. D. But Virtue's Grave.   10
C. In whose cool bosome we may lye
    Safe from the Sun. D. not Heaven's Eye.
C. Near this, a Fountaines liquid Bell
    Tinkles within the concave Shell.
D. Might a Soul bath there and be clean,   15
    Or slake its Drought? C. What is't you mean?
D. These once had been enticing things,
    Clorinda, Pastures, Caves, and Springs.
C. And what late change? D. The other day
    Pan met me. C. What did great *Pan* say?   20
D. Words that transcend poor Shepherds skill,
    But He ere since my Songs does fill:
    And his Name swells my slender Oate.
C. Sweet must *Pan* sound in *Damons* Note.
D. *Clorinda's* voice might make it sweet.   25
C. Who would not in *Pan's* Praises meet?

CHORUS

Of Pan *the flowry Pastures sing,*
Caves eccho, and the Fountains ring.
Sing then while he doth us inspire;
For all the World is our Pan's *Quire.* 30

A Dialogue between the Soul and Body

Soul

   O who shall, from this Dungeon, raise
A Soul inslav'd so many wayes?
With bolts of Bones, that fetter'd stands
In Feet; and manacled in Hands.
Here blinded with an Eye; and there 5
Deaf with the drumming of an Ear.
A soul hung up, as 'twere, in Chains
Of Nerves, and Arteries, and Veins.
Tortur'd, besides each other part,
In a vain Head, and double Heart. 10

Body

   O who shall me deliver whole,
From bonds of this Tyrannic Soul?
Which, stretcht upright, impales me so,
That mine own Precipice I go;
And warms and moves this needless Frame: 15
(A Fever could but do the same.)
And, wanting where its spight to try,
Has made me live to let me dye.
A Body that could never rest,
Since this ill Spirit it possest. 20

Soul

   What Magick could me thus confine
With anothers Grief to pine?

Where whatsoever it complain,
I feel, that cannot feel, the pain.
And all my Care its self employes,
That to preserve, which me destroys:
Constrain'd not only to indure
Diseases, but, whats worse, the Cure:
And ready oft the Port to gain,
Am Shipwrackt into Health again.

Body

But Physick yet could never reach
The Maladies Thou me dost teach;
Whom first the Cramp of Hope does Tear:
And then Palsie Shakes of Fear.
The Pestilence of Love does heat:
Or Hatred's hidden Ulcer eat.
Joy's chearful Madness does perplex:
Or Sorrow's other Madness vex.
Which Knowledge forces me to know;
And memory will not foregoe.
What but a Soul could have the wit
To build me up for Sin so fit?
So Architects do square and hew,
Green Trees that in the Forest grew.

The Nymph complaining for the death of her Faun

The wanton Troopers riding by
Have shot my Faun and it will dye.
Ungentle men! They cannot thrive
To kill thee. Thou neer didst alive
Them any harm: alas nor cou'd
Thy death yet do them any good.
I'me sure I never wisht them ill;
Nor do I for all this; nor will:
But, if my simple Pray'rs may yet

Prevail with Heaven to forget 10
Thy murder, I will Joyn my Tears
Rather then fail. But, O my fears!
It cannot dye so. Heavens King
Keeps register of every thing:
And nothing may we use in vain. 15
Ev'n Beasts must be with justice slain;
Else Men are made their *Deodands*.
Though they should wash their guilty hands
In this warm life blood, which doth part
From thine, and wound me to the Heart, 20
Yet could they not be clean: their Stain
Is dy'd in such a Purple Grain.
There is not such another in
The World, to offer for their Sin.

    Unconstant *Sylvio*, when yet 25
I had not found him counterfeit,
One morning (I remember well)
Ty'd in this silver Chain and Bell,
Gave it to me: nay and I know
What he said then; I'me sure I do. 30
Said He, look how your Huntsman here
Hath taught a Faun to hunt his *Dear*.
But *Sylvio* soon had me beguil'd.
This waxed tame; while he grew wild,
And quite regardless of my Smart, 35
Left me his Faun, but took his Heart.

    Thenceforth I set my self to play
My solitary time away,
With this: and very well content,
Could so mine idle Life have spent. 40
For it was full of sport; and light
Of foot, and heart; and did invite,
Me to its game: it seem'd to bless

The Nymph complaining for the death of her Faun. 17 *Deodands*: literally, things given or things forfeited. A deodand was an animal or thing which, because it had been the immediate cause of the death of a person, was given to God as an expiatory offering, that is, forfeited to the crown, to be applied to charitable uses.

Its self in me. How could I less
Than love it? O I cannot be 45
Unkind, t'a Beast that loveth me.
　　Had it liv'd long, I do not know
Whether it too might have done so
As *Sylvio* did: his Gifts might be
Perhaps as false or more than he. 50
But I am sure, for ought that I
Could in so short a time espie,
Thy Love was far more better then
The love of false and cruel men.
　　With sweetest milk, and sugar, first 55
I it at mine own fingers nurst.
And as it grew, so every day
It wax'd more white and sweet than they.
It had so sweet a Breath! And oft
I blusht to see its foot more soft, 60
And white, (shall I say then my hand?)
NAY any Ladies of the Land.
　　It is a wond'rous thing, how fleet
'Twas on those little silver feet.
With what a pretty skipping grace, 65
It oft would challenge me the Race:
And when 'thad left me far away,
'Twould stay, and run again, and stay.
For it was nimbler much than Hindes;
And trod, as on the four Winds. 70
　　I have a Garden of my own,
But so with Roses over grown,
And Lillies, that you would it guess
To be a little Wilderness.
And all the Spring time of the year 75
It onely loved to be there.
Among the beds of Lillyes, I
Have sought it oft, where it should lye;
Yet could not, till it self would rise,
Find it, although before mine Eyes. 80
For, in the flaxen Lillies shade,
It like a bank of Lillies laid.

Upon the Roses it would feed,
Until its Lips ev'n seem'd to bleed:
And then to me 'twould boldly trip, 85
And print those Roses on my Lip.
But all its chief delight was still
On Roses thus its self to fill:
And its pure virgin Limbs to fold
In whitest sheets of Lillies cold. 90
Had it liv'd long, it would have been
Lillies without, Roses within.
   O help! O help! I see it faint:
And dye as calmely as a Saint.
See how it weeps. The Tears do come 95
Sad, slowly dropping like a Gumme.
So weeps the wounded Balsome: so
The holy Frankincense doth flow.
The brotherless *Heliades*
Melt in such Amber Tears as these. 100
   I in a golden Vial will
Keep these two crystal Tears; and fill
It till it do o'reflow with mine;
Then place it in *Diana's* Shrine.
   Now my sweet Faun is vanish'd to 105
Whether the Swans and Turtles go:
In fair *Elizium* to endure,
With milk-white Lambs, and Ermins pure.
O do not run too fast: for I
Will but bespeak thy Grave, and dye. 110
   First my unhappy Statue shall
Be cut in Marble; and withal,
Let it be weeping too: but there
Th'Engraver sure his Art may spare;
For I so truly thee bemoane, 115
That I shall weep though I be Stone:
Until my Tears, still dropping, wear
My breast, themselves engraving there.

  99–100 *Heliades*: the three sisters of Phaëton, who attempted to drive the chariot of the Sun and was struck down by a thunderbolt from Zeus. The sisters were transformed into willow trees, and their tears fell in amber drops.

There at my feet shalt thou be laid,
Of purest Alabaster made: 120
For I would have thine Image be
White as I can, though not as Thee.

Young Love

I

Come little Infant, Love me now,
   While thine unsuspected years
Clear thine aged Fathers brow
   From cold Jealousie and Fears.

II

Pretty surely 'twere to see 5
   By young Love old Time beguil'd:
While our Sportings are as free
   As the Nurses with the Child.

III

Common Beauties stay fifteen;
   Such as yours should swifter move; 10
Whose fair Blossoms are too green
   Yet for Lust, but not for Love.

IV

Love as much the snowy Lamb
   Or the wanton Kid does prize,
As the lusty Bull or Ram, 15
   For his morning Sacrifice.

V

Now then love me: time may take
   Thee before thy time away:
Of this Need wee'l Virtue make,
   And learn Love before we may. 20

VI

So we win of doubtful Fate;
   And, if good she to us meant,
We that Good shall antedate,
   Or, if ill, that Ill prevent.

VII

Thus as Kingdomes, frustrating   25
   Other Titles to their Crown,
In the craddle crown their King,
   So all Forraign Claims to drown,

VIII

So, to make all Rivals vain,
   Now I crown thee with my Love: 30
Crown me with thy Love again,
   And we both shall Monarchs prove.

To his Coy Mistress

Had we but World enough, and Time,
This coyness Lady were no crime.
We would sit down, and think which way
To walk, and pass our long Loves Day.
Thou by the *Indian Ganges* side   5
Should'st Rubies find: I by the Tide
Of *Humber* would complain. I would
Love you ten years before the Flood:
And you should if you please refuse
Till the Conversion of the *Jews*.   10
My vegetable Love should grow
Vaster then Empires, and more slow.
An hundred years should go to praise
Thine Eyes, and on thy Forehead Gaze.

Two hundred to adore each Breast: 15
But thirty thousand to the rest.
An Age at least to every part,
And the last Age should show your Heart.
For Lady you deserve this State;
Nor would I love at lower rate. 20
    But at my back I alwaies hear
Times winged Charriot hurrying near:
And yonder all before us lye
Desarts of vast Eternity.
Thy Beauty shall no more be found; 25
Nor, in thy marble Vault, shall sound
My ecchoing Song: then Worms shall try
That long preserv'd Virginity:
And your quaint Honour turn to dust;
And into ashes all my Lust. 30
The Grave's a fine and private place,
But none I think do there embrace.
    Now therefore, while the youthful hew
Sits on thy skin like morning lew,
And while thy willing Soul transpires 35
At every pore with instant Fires,
Now let us sport us while we may;
And now, like am'rous birds of prey,
Rather at once our Time devour,
Than languish in his slow-chapt pow'r. 40
Let us roll all our Strength, and all
Our sweetness, up into one Ball:
And tear our Pleasures with rough strife,
Thorough the Iron gates of Life.
Thus though we cannot make our Sun 45
Stand still, yet we will make him run.

To his Coy Mistress. 34 *lew*: warmth, or heat-haze. Lord retains F.'s *glew* as a variant form of *glow*.

40 *slow-chapt*: slowly devouring.

The unfortunate Lover

I

Alas, how pleasant are their dayes
With whom the Infant Love yet playes!
Sorted by pairs, they still are seen
By Fountains cool, and Shadows green.
But soon these Flames do lose their light, 5
Like Meteors of a Summers night:
Nor can they to that Region climb,
To make impression upon Time.

II

'Twas in a Shipwrack, when the Seas
Rul'd, and the Winds did what they please, 10
That my poor Lover floting lay,
And, e're brought forth, was cast away:
Till at the last the master-Wave
Upon the Rock his Mother drave;
And there she split against the Stone, 15
In a *Cesarian Section*.

III

The Sea him lent these bitter Tears
Which at his Eyes he alwaies bears.
And from the Winds the Sighs he bore,
Which through his surging Breast do roar. 20
No Day he saw but that which breaks,
Through frighted Clouds in forked streaks.
While round the ratling Thunder hurl'd,
As at the Fun'ral of the World.

IV

While Nature to his Birth presents 25
This masque of quarreling Elements;

The unfortunate Lover. 16 *Section*: pronounced as three syllables.

A num'rous fleet of Corm'rants black,
That sail'd insulting o're the Wrack,
Receiv'd into their cruel Care,
Th' unfortunate and abject Heir: 30
Guardians most fit to entertain
The Orphan of the *Hurricane*.

V

They fed him up with Hopes and Air,
Which soon digested to Despair.
And as one Corm'rant fed him, still 35
Another on his Heart did bill.
Thus while they famish him, and feast,
He both consumed, and increast:
And languished with doubtful Breath,
Th'*Amphibium* of Life and Death. 40

VI

And now, when angry Heaven wou'd
Behold a spectacle of Blood,
Fortune and He are call'd to play
At sharp before it all the day:
And Tyrant Love his brest does ply 45
With all his wing'd Artillery.
Whilst he, betwixt the Flames and Waves,
Like *Ajax*, the mad Tempest braves.

VII

See how he nak'd and fierce does stand,
Cuffing the Thunder with one hand; 50
While with the other he does lock,
And grapple, with the stubborn Rock:
From which he with each Wave rebounds,
Torn into Flames, and ragg'd with Wounds.
And all he saies, a Lover drest 55
In his own Blood does relish best.

36 *bill*: peck (*OED*).
44 *At sharp*: with sharp weapons, as rapiers.

VIII

This is the only *Banneret*
That ever Love created yet:
Who though, by the Malignant Starrs,
Forced to live in Storms and Warrs; 60
Yet dying leaves a Perfume here,
And Musick within every Ear:
And he in Story only rules,
In a Field *Sable* a Lover *Gules*.

The Gallery

I

Clora come view my Soul, and tell
Whether I have contriv'd it well.
Now all its several lodgings lye
Compos'd into one Gallery;
And the great *Arras*-hangings, made   5
Of various Faces, by are laid;
That, for all furniture, you'l find
Only your Picture in my Mind.

II

Here Thou art painted in the Dress
Of an Inhumane Murtheress;   10
Examining upon our Hearts
Thy fertile Shop of cruel Arts:
Engines more keen than ever yet
Adorned Tyrants Cabinet;
Of which the most tormenting are   15
Black Eyes, red Lips, and curled Hair.

---

57 *Banneret*: a knight dubbed on the field of battle for bravery displayed in the presence of the king.

III

But, on the other side, th'art drawn
Like to *Aurora* in the Dawn;
When in the East she slumb'ring lyes,
And stretches out her milky Thighs;
While all the morning Quire does sing,
And *Manna* falls, and Roses spring;
And, at thy Feet, the wooing Doves
Sit perfecting their harmless Loves.

IV

Like an Enchantress here thou show'st,
Vexing thy restless Lover's Ghost;
And, by a Light obscure, dost rave
Over his Entrails, in the Cave;
Divining thence, with horrid Care,
How long thou shalt continue fair;
And (when inform'd) them throw'st away,
To be the greedy Vultur's prey.

V

But, against that, thou sit'st a float
Like *Venus* in her pearly Boat.
The *Halycons*, calming all that's nigh,
Betwixt the Air and Water fly.
Or, if some rowling Wave appears,
A Mass of Ambergris it bears.
Nor blows more Wind than what may well
Convoy the Perfume to the Smell.

VI

These Pictures and a thousand more,
Of Thee, my Gallery dost store;
In all the Forms thou can'st invent
Either to please me, or torment:
For thou alone to people me,

Art grown a num'rous Colony;
And a Collection choicer far
Then or *White-hall's*, or *Mantua's* were.

VII

But, of these Pictures and the rest,
That at the Entrance likes me best: 50
Where the same Posture, and the Look
Remains, with which I first was took.
A tender Shepherdess, whose Hair
Hangs loosely playing in the Air,
Transplanting Flow'rs from the green Hill, 55
To crown her Head, and Bosome fill.

The Fair Singer

I

To make a final conquest of all me,
Love did compose so sweet an Enemy,
In whom both Beauties to my death agree,
Joyning themselves in fatal Harmony;
That while she with her Eyes my Heart does bind, 5
She with her Voice might captivate my Mind.

II

I could have fled from One but singly fair:
My dis-intangled Soul it self might save,
Breaking the curled trammels of her hair.
But how should I avoid to be her Slave, 10
Whose subtile Art invisibly can wreath
My Fetters of the very Air I breath?

The Gallery. 48 Charles I's great collection of paintings at Whitehall was enriched by the purchase of canvases from the collection of the Gonzagas, Dukes of Mantua.

III

It had been easie fighting in some plain,
Where Victory might hang in equal choice.
But all resistance against her is vain, 15
Who has th'advantage both of Eyes and Voice.
And all my Forces needs must be undone,
She having gained both the Wind and Sun.

Mourning

I

You, that decipher out the Fate
Of humane Off-springs from the Skies,
What mean these Infants which of late
Spring from the Starrs of *Chlora's* Eyes?

II

Here Eyes confus'd, and doubled ore, 5
With Tears suspended ere they flow;
Seem bending upwards, to restore
To Heaven, whence it came, their Woe.

III

When, molding of the watry Sphears,
Slow drops unty themselves away; 10
As if she, with those precious Tears,
Would strow the ground where *Strephon* lay.

IV

Yet some affirm, pretending Art,
Her Eyes have so her Bosome drown'd,
Only to soften near her Heart 15
A place to fix another Wound.

V

And, while vain Pomp does her restrain
Within her solitary Bowr,
She courts her self in am'rous Rain;
Herself both *Danae* and the Showr. 20

VI

Nay others, bolder, hence esteem
Joy now so much her Master grown,
That whatsoever does but seem
Like Grief, is from her Windows thrown.

VII

Nor that she payes, while she survives, 25
To her dead Love this Tribute due;
But casts abroad these Donatives,
At the installing of a new.

VIII

How wide they dream! The *Indian* Slaves
That sink for Pearl through Seas profound, 30
Would find her Tears yet deeper Waves
And not of one the bottom sound.

IX

I yet my silent Judgment keep,
Disputing not what they believe:
But sure as oft as Women weep, 35
It is to be suppos'd they grieve.

Daphnis and Chloe

I

Daphnis must from Chloe part:
Now is come the dismal Hour
That must all his Hopes devour,
All his Labour, all his Art.

II

Nature, her own Sexes foe, 5
Long had taught her to be coy:
But she neither knew t'enjoy,
Nor yet let her Lover go.

III

But, with this sad News surpriz'd,
Soon she let that Niceness fall; 10
And would gladly yield to all,
So it had his stay compriz'd.

IV

Nature so her self does use
To lay by her wonted State,
Lest the World should separate; 15
Sudden Parting closer glews.

V

He, well read in all the wayes
By which men their Siege maintain,
Knew not that the Fort to gain
Better 'twas the Siege to raise. 20

VI

But he came so full possest
With the Grief of Parting thence,

That he had not so much Sence
As to see he might be blest.

VII

Till Love in her Language breath'd 25
Words she never spake before;
But then Legacies no more
To a dying Man bequeath'd.

VIII

For, Alas, the time was spent,
Now the latest minut's run 30
When poor *Daphnis* is undone,
Between Joy and Sorrow rent.

IX

At that *Why*, that *Stay my Dear*,
His disorder'd Locks he tare;
And with rouling Eyes did glare, 35
And his cruel Fate forswear.

X

As the Soul of one scarce dead,
With the shrieks of Friends aghast,
Looks distracted back in hast,
And then streight again is fled. 40

XI

So did wretched *Daphnis* look,
Frighting her he loved most.
At the last, this Lovers Ghost
Thus his Leave resolved took.

XII

Are my Hell and Heaven Joyn'd 45
More to torture him that dies?

Could departure not suffice,
But that you must then grow kind?

XIII

Ah my *Chloe* how have I
Such a wretched minute found, 50
When thy Favours should me wound
More than all thy Cruelty?

XIV

So to the condemned Wight
The delicious Cup we fill;
And allow him all he will, 55
For his last and short Delight.

XV

But I will not now begin
Such a Debt unto my Foe;
Nor to my Departure owe
What my Presence could not win. 60

XVI

Absence is too much alone:
Better 'tis to go in peace,
Than my Losses to increase
By a late Fruition.

XVII

Why should I enrich my Fate? 65
'Tis a Vanity to wear,
For my Executioner,
Jewels of so high a rate.

XVIII

Rather I away will pine
In a manly stubborness 70

XIX

Than be fatted up express
For the *Canibal* to dine.

XIX

Whilst this grief does thee disarm,
All th' Enjoyment of our Love
But the ravishment would prove 75
Of a Body dead while warm.

XX

And I parting should appear
Like the Gourmand *Hebrew* dead,
While he Quailes and *Manna* fed,
And does through the Desert err. 80

XXI

Or the Witch that midnight wakes
For the Fern, whose magick Weed
In one minute casts the Seed,
And invisible him makes.

XXII

Gentler times for Love are ment: 85
Who for parting pleasure strain
Gather Roses in the rain,
Wet themselves and spoil their Sent.

XXIII

Farewel therefore all the fruit
Which I could from Love receive: 90
Joy will not with Sorrow weave,
Nor will I this Grief pollute.

Daphnis and Chloe. 78–80 in Num. 11, the children of Israel, wandering in the desert, are smitten by the Lord with a great plague as punishment for their greed in devouring the manna and quail sent to them.

XXIV

Fate I come, as dark, as sad,
As thy Malice could desire;
Yet bring with me all the Fire 95
That Love in his Torches had.

XXV

At these words away he broke;
As who long has praying ly'n,
To his Heads-man makes the Sign,
and receives the parting stroke. 100

XXVI

But hence Virgins all beware.
Last night he with *Phlogis* slept;
This night for *Dorinda* kept;
And but rid to take the Air.

XXVII

Yet he does himself excuse; 105
Nor indeed without a Cause.
For, according to the Lawes,
Why did *Chloe* once refuse?

The Definition of Love

I

My Love is of a birth as rare
As 'tis for object strange and high:
It was begotten by despair
Upon Impossibility.

II

Magnanimous Despair alone 5
Could show me so divine a thing,

Where feeble Hope could ne'r have flown
But vainly flapt its Tinsel Wing.

III

And yet I quickly might arrive
Where my extended Soul is fixt,   *10*
But Fate does Iron wedges drive,
And alwaies crouds it self betwixt.

IV

For Fate with jealous Eye does see
Two perfect Loves; nor lets them close:
Their union would her ruine be,   *15*
And her Tyrannick pow'r depose.

V

And therefore her Decrees of Steel
Us as the distant Poles have plac'd,
(Though Loves whole World on us doth wheel)
Not by themselves to be embrac'd.   *20*

VI

Unless the giddy Heaven fall,
And Earth some new Convulsion tear;
And, us to joyn, the World should all
Be cramp'd into a *Planisphere*.

VII

As Lines so Loves *oblique* may well   *25*
Themselves in every Angle greet:
But ours so truly *Paralel*,
Though infinite can never meet.

VIII

Therefore the Love which us doth bind,
But Fate so enviously debarrs,   *30*
Is the Conjunction of the Mind,
And Opposition of the Stars.

The Picture of little T.C. in a Prospect of Flowers

I

See with what simplicity
This Nimph begins her golden daies!
In the green Grass she loves to lie,
And there with her fair Aspect tames
The Wilder flow'rs, and gives them names: 5
But only with the Roses playes;
        And them does tell
What Colour best becomes them, and what Smell.

II

Who can foretel for what high cause
This Darling of the Gods was born!   10
Yet this is She whose chaster Laws
The wanton Love shall one day fear,
And, under her command severe,
See his Bow broke and Ensigns torn.
        Happy, who can   15
Appease this virtuous Enemy of Man!

III

O then let me in time compound,
And parly with those conquering Eyes;
Ere they have try'd their force to wound,
Ere, with their glancing wheels, they drive   20
In Triumph over Hearts that strive,
And them that yield but more despise.
        Let me be laid,
Where I may see thy Glories from some Shade.

The Picture of little T. C. . . . Mar., in "Andrew Marvell: Some Biographical Points," *MLR*, XVII (1922), suggests that little T. C. was possibly Theophila Cornewall.

IV

Mean time, whilst every verdant thing 25
It self does at thy Beauty charm,
Reform the errours of the Spring;
Make that the Tulips may have share
Of sweetness, seeing they are fair;
And Roses of their thorns disarm: 30
      But most procure
That Violets may a longer Age endure.

V

But O young beauty of the Woods,
Whom Nature courts with fruits and flow'rs,
Gather the Flow'rs, but spare the Buds; 35
Lest *Flora* angry at thy crime,
To kill her Infants in their prime,
Do quickly make th' Example Yours;
      And, ere we see,
Nip in the blossome all our hopes and Thee. 40

Tom May's Death

As one put drunk into the Packet-boat,
Tom May was hurry'd hence and did not know't.
But was amaz'd on the Elysian side,
And with an Eye uncertain, gazing wide,
Could not determine in what place he was, 5
For whence in Stevens ally Trees or Grass.

Tom May's Death. Thomas May (1595–1650), best known to the court of Charles I as the translator of Lucan's *Pharsalia*, is here depicted among the shades of the ancient world waiting to succeed Ben Jonson as Poet Laureate. When Davenant won this honor after Jonson's death in 1637, May turned to support the Puritan cause and wrote a history (l. 76) of those turbulent times, praising such public figures as Cromwell and Fairfax. To L. W. Hyman, a recent critic of Marvell, this poem, written in 1650, represents "the clearest expression (as well as the last) of Marvell's Royalist beliefs...."

Nor where the Popes head, nor the Mitre lay,
Signs by which still he found and lost his way.
At last while doubtfully he all compares,
He saw near hand, as he imagin'd *Ares*.
Such did he seem for corpulence and port,
But 'twas a man much of another sort;
'Twas *Ben* that in the dusky Laurel shade
Amongst the Chorus of old Poets laid,
Sounding of ancient Heroes, such as were
The Subjects Safety, and the Rebel's Fear.
But how a double headed Vulture Eats,
Brutus and *Cassius* the Peoples cheats.
But seeing *May* he varied streight his Song,
Gently to signifie that he was wrong.
Cups more then civil of *Emathian* wine,
I sing (said he) and the *Pharsalian* Sign,
Where the Historian of the Common-wealth
In his own Bowels sheath'd the conquering health.
By this *May* to himself and them was come,
He found he was translated, and by whom.
Yet then with foot as stumbling as his tongue
Prest for his place among the Learned throng.
But *Ben*, who knew not neither foe nor friend,
Sworn Enemy to all that do pretend,
Rose more then ever he was seen severe,
Shook his gray locks, and his own Bayes did tear
At this intrusion. Then with Laurel wand,
The awful Sign of his supream command,
At whose dread Whisk *Virgil* himself does quake,
And *Horace* patiently its stroke does take,
As he crowds in he whipt him ore the pate
Like *Pembroke* at the Masque, and then did rate.

   Far from these blessed shades tread back agen
Most servil' wit, and Mercenary Pen.
Polydore, Lucan, Allan, Vandale, Goth,
Malignant Poet and Historian both.

---

38 *Pembroke*: at the first performance of Shirley's *Triumph of Peace* (3 February 1634, at Whitehall), the Lord Chamberlain, against whom May had "come athwart," broke his truncheon over the translator's shoulders.

Go seek the novice Statesmen, and obtrude
On them some Romane cast similitude,
Tell them of Liberty, the Stories fine, 45
Until you all grow Consuls in your wine.
Or thou *Dictator* of the glass bestow
On him the *Cato*, this the *Cicero*.
Transferring old *Rome* hither in your talk,
As *Bethlem's* House did to *Loretto* walk. 50
Foul Architect that hadst not Eye to see
How ill the measures of these States agree.
And who by *Romes* example *England* lay,
Those but to *Lucan* do continue *May*.
But thee nor Ignorance nor seeming good 55
Misled, but malice fixt and understood.
Because some one than thee more worthy weares
The sacred Laurel, hence are all these teares?
Must therefore all the World be set on flame,
Because a Gazet writer mist his aim? 60
And for a Tankard-bearing Muse must we
As for the Basket *Guelphs* and *Gibellines* be?
When the Sword glitters ore the Judges head,
And fear has Coward Churchmen silenced,
Then is the Poets time, 'tis then he drawes, 65
And single fights forsaken Vertues cause.
He, when the wheel of Empire, whirleth back,
And though the World's disjointed Axel crack,
Sings still of ancient Rights and better Times,
Seeks wretched good, arraigns successful Crimes. 70
But thou base man first prostituted hast
Our spotless knowledge and the studies chast.
Apostatizing from our Arts and us,
To turn the Chronicler to *Spartacus*.
Yet wast thou taken hence with equal fate, 75
Before thou couldst great *Charles* his death relate.
But what will deeper wound thy little mind,
Hast left surviving *Davenant* still behind
Who laughs to see in this thy death renew'd,
Right Romane poverty and gratitude. 80
Poor Poet thou, and grateful Senate they,

Who thy last Reckoning did so largely pay.
And with the publick gravity would come,
When thou hadst drunk thy last to lead thee home.
If that can be thy home where *Spencer* lyes 85
And reverend *Chaucer*, but their dust does rise
Against thee, and expels thee from their side,
As th'Eagles Plumes from other birds divide.
Nor here thy shade must dwell, Return, Return,
Where Sulphrey *Phlegeton* does ever burn. 90
The *Cereberus* with all his Jawes shall gnash,
Megæra thee with all her Serpents lash.
Thou rivited unto *Ixion's* wheel
Shalt break, and the perpetual Vulture feel.
'Tis just what Torments Poets ere did feign, 95
Thou first Historically shouldst sustain.
   Thus by irrevocable Sentence cast,
   May only Master of these Revels past.
   And streight he vanisht in a Cloud of pitch,
   Such as unto the Sabboth bears the Witch. 100

The Match

I

Nature had long a Treasure made
  Of all her choisest store;
Fearing, when She should be decay'd,
  To beg in vain for more.

II

Her *Orientest* Colours there, 5
  And Essences most pure,
With sweetest Perfumes hoarded were,
  All as she thought secure.

III

She seldom them unlock'd, or us'd,
  But with the nicest care; 10

For, with one grain of them diffus'd,
    She could the World repair.

IV

But likeness soon together drew
    What she did separate lay;
Of which one perfect Beauty grew,
    And that was *Celia*.

V

Love wisely had of long fore-seen
    That he must once grow old;
And therefore stor'd a Magazine,
    To save him from the cold.

VI

He kept the several Cells repleat
    With Nitre thrice refin'd;
The Naphta's and the Sulphurs heat,
    And all that burns the Mind.

VII

He fortifi'd the double Gate,
    And rarely thither came;
For, with one Spark of these, he streight
    All Nature could inflame.

VIII

Till, by vicinity so long,
    A nearer Way they sought;
And, grown magnetically strong,
    Into each other wrought.

IX

Thus all his fewel did unite
    To make one fire high:
None ever burn'd so hot, so bright:
    And *Celia* that am I.

X

So we alone the happy rest,
  Whilst all the World is poor,
And have within our Selves possest
  All Love's and Nature's store.   40

The Mower against Gardens

Luxurious Man, to bring his Vice in use,
  Did after him the World seduce:
And from the fields the Flow'rs and Plants allure,
  Where Nature was most plain and pure.
He first enclos'd within the Gardens square   5
  A dead and standing pool of Air:
And a more luscious Earth for them did knead,
  Which stupifi'd them while it fed.
The Pink grew then as double as his Mind;
  The nutriment did change the kind.   10
With strange perfumes he did the Roses taint.
  And Flow'rs themselves were taught to paint.
The Tulip, white, did for complexion seek;
  And learn'd to interline its cheek:
Its Onion root they then so high did hold,   15
  That one was for a Meadow sold.
Another World was search'd, through Oceans new,
  To find the *Marvel of Peru*.
And yet these Rarities might be allow'd,
  To Man, that sov'raign thing and proud;   20
Had he not dealt between the Bark and Tree,
  Forbidden mixtures there to see.
No Plant now knew the Stock from which it came;
  He grafts upon the Wild the Tame:
That the uncertain and adult'rate fruit   25
  Might put the Palate in dispute.
His green *Seraglio* has its Eunuchs too;

　　　　Lest any Tyrant him out-doe.
And in the Cherry he does Nature vex,
　　　To procreate without a Sex.
'Tis all enforc'd; the Fountain and the Grot;
　　　While the sweet Fields do lye forgot:
Where willing Nature does to all dispence
　　　A wild and fragrant Innocence:
And *Fauns* and *Faryes* do the Meadows till,
　　　More by their presence then their skill.
Their Statues polish'd by some ancient hand,
　　　May to adorn the Gardens stand:
But howso'ere the Figures do excel,
　　　The *Gods* themselves with us do dwell.

Damon *the Mower*

I

Heark how the Mower *Damon* Sung,
With love of *Juliana* stung!
While ev'ry thing did seem to paint
The Scene more fit for his complaint.
Like her fair Eyes the day was fair;
But scorching like his am'rous Care.
Sharp like his Sythe his Sorrow was,
And wither'd like his Hopes the Grass.

II

Oh what unusual Heats are here,
Which thus our Sun-burn'd Meadows sear!
The Grass-hopper its pipe gives ore;
And hamstring'd Frogs can dance no more.
But in the brook the green Frog wades;
And Grass-hoppers seek out the shades.
Only the Snake, that kept within,
Now glitters in its second skin.

III

This heat the Sun could never raise,
Nor Dog-star so inflame's the dayes.
It from an higher Beauty grow'th,
Which burns the Fields and Mower both: 20
Which made the Dog, and makes the Sun
Hotter then his own *Phaeton*.
Not *July* causeth these Extremes,
But *Juliana's* scorching beams.

IV

Tell me where I may pass the Fires 25
Of the hot day, or hot desires.
To what cool Cave shall I descend,
Or to what gelid Fountain bend?
Alas! I look for Ease in vain,
When Remedies themselves complain. 30
No moisture but my Tears do rest,
Nor Cold but in her Icy Breast.

V

How long wilt Thou, fair Shepheardess,
Esteem me, and my Presents less?
To Thee the harmless Snake I bring, 35
Disarmed of its teeth and sting.
To Thee *Chameleons* changing-hue,
And Oak leaves tipt with hony due.
Yet thou ungrateful hast not sought
Nor what they are, nor who them brought. 40

VI

I am the Mower *Damon*, known
Through all the Meadows I have mown.
On me the Morn her dew distills
Before her darling Daffadils.
And, if at Noon my toil me heat, 45
The Sun himself licks off my Sweat.

While, going home, the Ev'ning sweet
In cowslip-water bathes my feet.

VII

What, though the piping Shepherd stock
The plains with an unnum'red Flock, 50
This Sithe of mine discovers wide
More ground then all his Sheep do hide.
With this the golden fleece I shear
Of all these Closes ev'ry Year.
And though in Wooll more poor then they, 55
Yet am I richer far in Hay.

VIII

Nor am I so deform'd to sight,
If in my Sithe I looked right;
In which I see my Picture done,
As in a crescent Moon the Sun. 60
The deathless Fairyes take me oft
To lead them in their Danses soft:
And, when I tune my self to sing,
About me they contract their Ring.

IX

How happy might I still have mow'd, 65
Had not Love here his Thistles sow'd!
But now I all the day complain,
Joyning my Labour to my Pain;
And with my Sythe cut down the Grass,
Yet still my Grief is where it was: 70
But, when the Iron blunter grows,
Sighing I whet my Sythe and Woes.

X

While thus he threw his Elbow round,
Depopulating all the Ground,
And, with his whistling Sythe, does cut 75
Each stroke between the Earth and Root,

The edged Stele by careless chance
Did into his own Ankle glance;
And there among the Grass fell down,
By his own Sythe, the Mower mown.   *80*

XI

Alas! said He, these hurts are slight
To those that dye by Loves despight.
With Shepherds-purse, and Clowns-all-heal,
The Blood I stanch, and Wound I seal.
Only for him no Cure is found,
Whom *Julianas* Eyes do wound.   *85*
'Tis death alone that this must do:
For Death thou art a Mower too.

The Mower to the Glo-Worms

I

Ye living Lamps, by whose dear light
The Nightingale does sit so late,
And studying all the Summer-night,
Her matchless Songs does meditate;

II

Ye Country Comets, that portend   *5*
No War, nor Princes funeral,
Shining unto no higher end
Then to presage the Grasses fall;

III

Ye Glo-worms, whose officious Flame
To wandring Mowers shows the way,   *10*
That in the Night have lost their aim,
And after foolish Fires do stray;

IV

Your courteous Lights in vain you wast,
Since *Juliana* here is come,
For She my Mind hath so displac'd   15
That I shall never find my home.

The Mower's Song

I

My Mind was once the true survey
Of all these Medows fresh and gay;
And in the greenness of the Grass
Did see its Hopes as in a Glass;
When *Juliana* came, and She   5
What I do to the Grass, does to my Thoughts and Me.

II

But these, while I with Sorrow pine,
Grew more luxuriant still and fine;
That not one Blade of Grass you spy'd,
But had a Flower on either side;   10
When *Juliana* came, and She
What I do to the Grass, does to my Thoughts and Me.

III

Unthankful Medows, could you so
A fellowship so true forego,
And in your gawdy May-games meet,   15
While I lay trodden under feet?
When *Juliana* came, and She
What I do to the Grass, does to my Thoughts and Me.

IV

But what you in Compassion ought,
Shall now by my Revenge be wrought: 20
And Flow'rs, and Grass, and I and all,

Will in one common Ruine fall.
For *Juliana* comes, and She
What I do to the Grass, does to my Thoughts and Me.

V

And thus, ye Meadows, which have been 25
Companions of my thoughts more green,
Shall now the Heraldry become
With which I shall adorn my Tomb;
For *Juliana* comes, and She
What I do to the Grass, does to my Thoughts and Me. 30

Ametas *and* Thestylis *making Hay-Ropes*

I. *Ametas*

Think'st Thou that this Love can stand,
Whilst Thou still dost say me nay?
Love unpaid does soon disband:
Love binds Love as Hay binds Hay.

II. *Thestylis*

Think'st Thou that this Rope would twine 5
If we both should turn one way?
Where both parties so combine,
Neither Love will twist nor Hay.

III. *Ametas*

Thus you vain Excuses find,
Which your selve and us delay: 10
And Love tyes a Womans Mind
Looser then with Ropes of Hay.

IV. *Thestylis*

What you cannot constant hope
Must be taken as you may.

V. *Ametas*

 Then let's both lay by our Rope,   *15*
 And go kiss within the Hay.

Musicks Empire

I

First was the World as one great Cymbal made,
Where Jarring Windes to infant Nature plaid.
All Musick was a solitary sound,
To hollow Rocks and murm'ring Fountains bound.

II

Jubal first made the wilder Notes agree;   *5*
And *Jubal* tuned Musicks *Jubilee*:
He call'd the *Ecchoes* from their sullen Cell,
And built the Organs City where they dwell.

III

Each sought a consort in that lovely place;
And Virgin Trebles wed the manly Base.   *10*
From whence the Progeny of numbers new
Into harmonious Colonies withdrew.

IV

Some to the Lute, some to the Viol went,
And others chose the Cornet eloquent.
These practising the Wind, and those the Wire,   *15*
To sing Mens Triumphs, or in Heavens quire.

V

Then Musick, the Mosaique of the Air,
Did of all these a solemn noise prepare:
With which She gain'd the Empire of the Ear,
Including all between the Earth and Sphear.   *20*

VI

Victorious sounds! yet here your Homage do
Unto a gentler Conqueror then you;
Who though He flies the Musick of his praise,
Would with you Heavens Hallelujahs raise.

The Garden

How vainly men themselves amaze
To win the Palm, the Oke, or Bayes;
And their uncessant Labours see
Crown'd from some single Herb or Tree,
Whose short and narrow verged Shade   5
Does prudently their Toyles upbraid;
While all Flow'rs and all Trees do close
To weave the Garlands of repose.

II

Fair quiet, have I found thee here,
And Innocence thy Sister dear!   10
Mistaken long, I sought you then
In busie Companies of Men.
Your sacred Plants, if here below,
Only among the Plants will grow.
Society is all but rude,   15
To this delicious Solitude.

III

No white nor red was ever seen
So am'rous as this lovely green.
Fond Lovers, cruel as their Flame,
Cut in these Trees their Mistress name.   20

Musicks Empire. 22 *Conqueror*: very likely refers to Fairfax.

Little, Alas, they know, or heed,
How far these Beauties Hers exceed!
Fair Trees! where s'eer your barkes I wound,
No Name shall but your own be found.

IV

When we have run our Passions heat,
Love hither makes his best retreat.
The *Gods*, that mortal Beauty chase,
Still in a Tree did end their race.
Apollo hunted *Daphne* so,
Only that She might Laurel grow.
And *Pan* did after *Syrinx* speed,
Not as a Nymph, but for a Reed.

V

What wond'rous Life is this I lead!
Ripe Apples drop about my head;
The Luscious Clusters of the Vine
Upon my Mouth do crush their Wine;
The Nectaren, and curious Peach,
Into my hands themselves do reach;
Stumbling on Melons, as I pass,
Insnar'd with Flow'rs, I fall on Grass.

VI

Mean while the Mind, from pleasure less,
Withdraws into its happiness:
The Mind, that Ocean where each kind
Does streight its own resemblance find;
Yet it creates, transcending these,
Far other Worlds, and other Seas;
Annihilating all that's made
To a green Thought in a green Shade.

VII

Here at the Fountains sliding foot,
Or at some Fruit-trees mossy root,
Casting the Bodies Vest aside,

My Soul into the boughs does glide:
There like a Bird it sits, and sings,
Then whets, and combs its silver Wings;
And, till prepar'd for longer flight, 55
Waves in its Plumes the various Light.

VIII

Such was that happy Garden-state,
While Man there walk'd without a Mate:
After a Place so pure, and sweet,
What other Help could yet be meet! 60
But 'twas beyond a Mortal's share
To wander solitary there:
Two Paradises 'twere in one
To live in Paradise alone.

IX

How well the skilful Gardner drew 65
Of flow'rs and herbes this Dial new;
Where from above the milder Sun
Does through a fragrant Zodiack run;
And, as it works, th'industrious Bee
Computes its time as well as we. 70
How could such sweet and wholsome Hours
Be reckon'd but with herbs and flow'rs!

Fleckno, *an English Priest at* Rome

Oblig'd by frequent visits of this man,
Whom as Priest, Poet, and Musician,
I for some branch of *Melchizedeck* took,
(Though he derives himself from *my Lord Brooke*)
I sought his Lodging; which is at the Sign 5

Fleckno, an English Priest at Rome. Richard Flecknoe, also satirized by Dryden later in the century, was a poet who visited Rome in 1645–46.

Of the sad *Pelican*; Subject divine
For Poetry: There three Stair-Cases high,
Which signifies his triple property,
I found at last a Chamber, as 'twas said,
But seem'd a Coffin set on the Stairs head.   10
Not higher then Seav'n, nor larger then three feet;
Only there was nor Seeling, nor a Sheet,
Save that th'ingenious Door did as you come
Turn in, and shew to Wainscot half the Room.
Yet of his State no man could have complain'd;   15
There being no Bed where he entertain'd:
And though within one Cell so narrow pent,
He'd *Stanza's* for a whole Appartement.

   Straight without further information,
In hideous verse, he, and a dismal tone,   20
Begins to exercise; as if I were
Possest; and sure the *Devil* brought me there.
But I, who now imagin'd my self brought
To my last Tryal, in a serious thought
Calm'd the disorders of my youthful Breast,   25
And to my Martyrdom prepared Rest.
Only this frail Ambition did remain,
The last distemper of the sober Brain,
That there had been some present to assure
The future Ages how I did indure: 30
And how I, silent, turn'd my burning Ear
Towards the Verse; and when that could not hear,
Held him the other; and unchanged yet,
Ask'd still for more, and pray'd him to repeat:
Till the Tyrant, weary to persecute,   35
Left off, and try'd t'allure me with his Lute.

   Now as two Instruments, to the same key
Being tun'd by Art, if the one touched be
The other opposite as soon replies,
Mov'd by the Air and hidden Sympathies;   40
So while he with his gouty fingers craules

---

18 *Stanza's*: there is a bilingual pun on this Italian word for "room" and "strophe."

Over the Lute, his murmuring Belly calls,
Whose hungry Guts to the same streightness twin'd
In Echo to the trembling Strings repin'd.
   I, that perceiv'd now what his Musick ment,   45
Ask'd civilly if he had eat this Lent.
He answered yes; with such, and such an one.
For he has this of gen'rous, that alone
He never feeds; save only when he tryes
With gristly Tongue to dart the passing flyes.   50
I ask'd if he eat flesh. And he, that was
So hungry that though ready to say *Mass*
Would break his fast before, said he was Sick,
And th'*Ordinance* was only Politick.
Nor was I longer to invite him: Scant   55
Happy at once to make him Protestant,
And Silent. Nothing now Dinner stay'd
But till he had himself a Body made.
I mean till he were drest: for else so thin
He stands, as if he only fed had been   60
With consecrated Wafers: and the *Host*
Hath sure more flesh and blood then he can boast.
This *Basso Relievo* of a man,
Who as a Camel tall, yet easly can
The Needles Eye thread without any stich,   65
(His only impossible is to be rich)
Left his too suttle Body, growing rare,
Should leave his Soul to wander in the Air,
He therefore circumscribes himself in rimes;
And swaddled in's own papers seaven times,   70
Wears a close Jacket of poetick Buff,
With which he doth his third Dimension Stuff.
Thus armed underneath, he over all
Does make a primitive *Sotana* fall;
And above that yet casts an antick Cloak,   75
Worn at the first Counsel of *Antioch*;
Which by the *Jews* long hid, and Disesteem'd,
He heard of by Tradition, and redeem'd.
But were he not in this black habit deck't,
This half transparent Man would soon reflect   80

Each colour that he past by; and be seen,
As the *Chamelion*, yellow, blew, or green.
  He drest, and ready to disfurnish now
His Chamber, whose compactness did allow
No empty place for complementing doubt, 85
But who came last is forc'd first to go out;
I meet one on the Stairs who made me stand,
Stopping the passage, and did him demand:
I answer'd he is here *Sir*; but you see
You cannot pass to him but thorow me. 90
He thought himself affronted; and reply'd,
I whom the Pallace never has deny'd
Will make the way here; I said *Sir* you'l do
Me a great favour, for I seek to go.
He gathring fury still made sign to draw; 95
But himself there clos'd in a Scabbard saw
As narrow as his Sword's; and I, that was
Delightful, said there can no Body pass
Except by penetration hither, where
Two make a crowd, nor can three Persons here 100
Consist but in one substance. Then, to fit
Our peace, the Priest said I too had some wit:
To prov't, I said, the place doth us invite
By its own narrowness, Sir, to unite.
He ask'd me pardon; and to make me way 105
Went down, as I him follow'd to obey.
But the propitiatory Priest had straight
Oblig'd us, when below, to celebrate
Together our attonement: so increas'd
Betwixt us two the Dinner to a Feast. 110
  Let it suffice that we could eat in peace;
And that both Poems did and Quarrels cease
During the Table; though my new made Friend
Did, as he threatned, ere 'twere long intend
To be both witty and valiant: I loth, 115
Said 'twas too late, he was already both.
  But now, Alas, my first Tormentor came,
Who satisfy'd with eating, but not tame
Turns to recite; though Judges most severe

After th'Assizes dinner mild appear, 120
And on full stomach do condemn but few:
Yet he more strict my sentence doth renew;
And draws out of the black box of his Breast
Ten quire of paper in which he was drest.
Yet that which was a greater cruelty 125
Then *Nero's* Poem he calls charity:
And so the *Pelican* at his door hung
Picks out the tender bosome to its young.
   Of all his Poems there he stands ungirt
Save only two foul copies for his shirt: 130
Yet these he promises as soon as clean.
But how I loath'd to see my Neighbour glean
Those papers, which he pilled from within
Like white fleaks rising from a Leaper's skin!
More odious then those raggs which the *French* youth 135
At ordinaries after dinner show'th,
When they compare their *Chancres* and *Poulains*.
Yet he first kist them, and after takes pains
To read; and then, because he understood
Not one Word, thought and swore that they were good. 140
But all his praises could not now appease
The provok't Author, whom it did displease
To hear his Verses, by so just a curse,
That were ill made condemn'd to be read worse:
And how (impossible) he made yet more 145
Absurdityes in them then were before.
For he his untun'd voice did fall or raise
As a deaf Man upon a Viol playes,
Making the half points and the periods run
Confus'der then the atomes in the Sun. 150
Thereat the Poet swell'd, with anger full,
And roar'd out, like *Perillus* in's own *Bull*;
Sir you read false. That any one but you
Should know the contrary. Whereat, I, now
Made Mediator, in my room, said, Why? 155
To say that you read false *Sir* is no Lye.
Thereat the waxen Youth relented straight;
But saw with sad dispair that was too late.

For the disdainful Poet was retir'd
Home, his most furious Satyr to have fir'd   160
Against the Rebel; who, at this struck dead,
Wept bitterly as disinherited.
Who should commend his Mistress now? Or who
Praise him? both difficult indeed to do
With truth. I counsell'd him to go in time,   165
Ere the fierce Poets anger turn'd to rime.
   He hasted; and I, finding my self free,
As one scap't strangely from Captivity,
Have made the Chance be painted; and go now
To hang it in *Saint Peter's* for a Vow.   170

To his worthy Friend Doctor Witty upon his Translation of the Popular Errors

Sit further, and make room for thine own fame,
Where just desert enrolles thy honour'd Name
The good Interpreter. Some in this task
Take off the Cypress vail, but leave a mask,
Changing the Latine, but do more obscure   5
That sense in *English* which was bright and pure.
So of Translators they are Authors grown,
For ill Translators make the Book their own.
Others do strive with words and forced phrase
To add such lustre, and so many rayes,   10
That but to make the Vessel shining, they
Much of the precious Metal rub away.
He is Translations thief that addeth more,
As much as he that taketh from the Store
Of the first Author. Here he maketh blots   15
That mends; and added beauties are but spots.
   Cælia whose English doth more richly flow

To his worthy Friend Doctor Witty.... 17 *Cælia*: very likely Mary Fairfax, daughter of the general. Marvell, who often celebrates the general and his

Then *Tagus*, purer then dissolved snow,
And sweet as are her lips that speak it, she
Now learns the tongues of *France* and *Italy*; 20
But she is *Cælia* still: no other grace
But her own smiles commend that lovely face;
Her native beauty's not Italianated,
Nor her chast mind into the *French* translated:
Her thoughts are *English*, though her sparkling wit 25
With other Language doth them fitly fit.
   Translators learn of her: but stay I slide
Down into Error with the Vulgar tide;
Women must not teach here: the Doctor doth
Stint them to Cawdles, Almond-milk, and Broth. 30
Now I reform, and surely so will all
Whose happy Eyes on thy Translation fall.
I see the people hastning to thy Book,
Liking themselves the worse the more they look,
And so disliking, that they nothing see 35
Now worth the liking, but thy Book and thee.
And (if I Judgment have) I censure right;
For something guides my hand that I must write.
You have Translations statutes best fulfil'd.
That handling neither sully nor would guild. 40

On Mr. Milton's *Paradise lost*

When I beheld the Poet blind, yet bold,
In slender Book his vast Design unfold,
Messiah Crown'd, *Gods* Reconcil'd Decree,
Rebelling *Angels*, the Forbidden Tree,
Heav'n, Hell, Earth, Chaos, All; the Argument 5
Held me a while misdoubting his Intent,
That he would ruine (for I saw him strong)
The sacred Truths to Fable and old Song,

---

household, was presumably resident at Appleton House as early as 1650 in a tutorial capacity to this "Cælia," to whom he taught languages.

(So *Sampson* groap'd the Temples Posts in spight)
The World o'rewhelming to revenge his Sight.   10

   Yet as I read, soon growing less severe,
I lik'd his Project, the success did fear;
Through that wide Field how he his way should find
O're which lame Faith leads Understanding blind;
Lest he perplext the things he would explain,   15
And what was easie he should render vain.

   Or if a Work so infinite he spann'd,
Jealous I was that some less skilful hand
(Such as disquiet alwayes what is well,
And by ill imitating would excell)   20
Might hence presume the whole Creations day
To change in Scenes, and show it in a Play.

   Pardon me, *mighty Poet*, nor despise
My causeless, yet not impious, surmise.
But I am now convinc'd, and none will dare   25
Within thy Labours to pretend a Share.
Thou hast not miss'd one thought that could be fit,
And all that was improper dost omit:
So that no room is here for Writers left,
But to detect their Ignorance or Theft.   30

   That Majesty which through thy Work doth Reign
Draws the Devout, deterring the Profane.
And things divine thou treatst of in such state
As them preserves, and Thee inviolate.
At once delight and horrour on us seize,   35
Thou singst with so much gravity and ease;
And above humane flight dost soar aloft,
With Plume so strong, so equal, and so soft.
The *Bird* nam'd from that *Paradise* you sing
So never Flags, but alwaies keeps on Wing.   40

   Where couldst thou Words of such a compass find?
Whence furnish such a vast expense of Mind?
Just Heav'n Thee, like *Tiresias*, to requite,
Rewards with *Prophesie* thy loss of Sight.

   Well mightst thou scorn thy Readers to allure   45
With tinkling Rhime, of thy own Sense secure;
While the *Town-Bays* writes all the while and spells,

And like a Pack-Horse tires without his Bells.
Their Fancies like our bushy Points appear,
The Poets tag them; we for fashion wear. 50
I too transported by the *Mode* offend,
And while I meant to *Praise* thee, must Commend.
Thy verse created like thy *Theme* sublime,
In Number, Weight, and Measure, needs not *Rhime*.

Senec. Traged. ex Thyeste Chor. 2

Stet quicunque volet potens
Aulæ culmine lubrico &c.

Translated

Climb at *Court* for me that will
Tottering favors Pinacle;
All I seek is to lye still.
Settled in some secret Nest
In calm Leisure let me rest; 5
And far of the publick Stage
Pass away my silent Age.
Thus when without noise, unknown,
I have liv'd out all my span,
I shall dye, without a groan, 10
An old honest Country man.
Who expos'd to others Ey's,
Into his own Heart ne'r pry's,
Death to him's a Strange surprise.

An Epitaph upon ———

Enough: and leave the rest to Fame.
'Tis to commend her but to name.
Courtship, which living she declin'd,
When dead to offer were unkind.

Where never any could speak ill,   *5*
Who would officious Praises spill?
Nor can the truest Wit or Friend,
Without Detracting, her commend.
To say she liv'd a *Virgin* chast,
In this Age loose and all unlac't;   *10*
Nor was, when Vice is so allow'd,
Of *Virtue* or asham'd, or proud;
That her Soul was on *Heaven* so bent
No Minute but it came and went;
That ready her last Debt to pay   *15*
She summ'd her Life up ev'ry day;
Modest as Morn; as Mid-day bright;
Gentle as Ev'ning; cool as Night;
'Tis true: but all so weakly said;
'Twere more Significant, *She's Dead.*   *20*

Upon the Hill and Grove at Bill-borow

To the Lord Fairfax

I

See how the arched Earth does here
Rise in a perfect Hemisphere!
The stiffest Compass could not strike
A Line more circular and like;
Nor softest Pensel draw a Brow   *5*
So equal as this Hill does bow.
It seems as for a Model laid,
And that the World by it was made.

Upon the Hill and Grove at Bill-borow. Bilbrough, near the Fairfax estates at Nun Appleton, is not very distant from Hull, the city in which Marvell spent his early years and which he represented with great distinction in Parliament later in life.

II

Here learn ye Mountains more unjust,
Which to abrupter greatness thrust,
That do with your hook-shoulder'd height
The Earth deform and Heaven fright.
For whose excrescence ill design'd,
Nature must a new Center find,
Learn here those humble steps to tread,
Which to securer Glory lead.

III

See what a soft access and wide
Lyes open to its grassy side;
Nor with the rugged path deterrs
The feet of breathless Travellers.
See then how courteous it ascends,
And all the way it rises bends;
Nor for it self the height does gain,
But only strives to raise the Plain.

IV

Yet thus it all the field commands,
And in unenvy'd Greatness stands,
Discerning further then the Cliff
Of Heaven-daring *Teneriff*.
How glad the weary Seamen hast
When they salute it from the Mast!
By Night the Northern Star their way
Directs, and this no less by Day.

V

Upon its crest this Mountain grave
A Plume of aged Trees does wave.
No hostile hand durst ere invade
With impious Steel the sacred Shade.
For something alwaies did appear
Of the *great Masters* terrour there:

And Men could hear his Armour still
Ratling through all the Grove and Hill. 40

VI

Fear of the *Master*, and respect
Of the great *Nymph* did it protect;
Vera the *Nymph* that him inspir'd,
To whom he often here retir'd,
And on these Okes ingrav'd her Name; 45
Such Wounds alone these Woods became:
But ere he well the Barks could part
'Twas writ already in their Heart.

VII

For they ('tis credible) have sense,
As we, of Love and Reverence, 50
And underneath the Courser Rind
The *Genius* of the house do bind.
Hence they successes seem to know,
And in their *Lord's* advancement grow;
But in no Memory were seen 55
As under this so streight and green.

VIII

Yet now no further strive to shoot,
Contented if they fix their Root.
Nor to the winds uncertain gust,
Their prudent Heads too far intrust. 60
Onely sometimes a flutt'ring Breez
Discourses with the breathing Trees;
Which in their modest Whispers name
Those Acts that swell'd the Cheek of Fame.

---

41 *Master*: Thomas, third Baron Fairfax (1612–1671), the great general often commended by Marvell, married Anne Vere, the daughter of Sir Horace Vere, in 1637. Fairfax resigned his appointment as commander in chief of the Puritan forces in 1650 because he did not wish to lead an unprovoked attack into Scotland. He returned to Nun Appleton.

IX

Much other Groves, say they, then these 65
And other Hills him once did please.
Through Groves of Pikes he thunder'd then,
And Mountains rais'd of dying Men.
For all the *Civick Garlands* due
To him our Branches are but few. 70
Nor are our Trunks enow to bear
The *Trophees* of one fertile Year.

X

'Tis true, the Trees nor ever spoke
More certain *Oracles* in Oak.
But Peace (if you his favour prize) 75
That Courage its own Praises flies.
Therefore to your obscurer Seats
From his own Brightness he retreats:
Nor he the Hills without the Groves,
Nor Height but with Retirement loves. 80

Upon Appleton House, to my Lord Fairfax

I

Within this sober Frame expect
Work of no Forrain *Architect*;
That unto Caves the Quarries drew,
And Forrests did to Pastures hew;
Who of his great Design in pain 5
Did for a Model vault his Brain,
Whose Columnes should so high be rais'd
To arch the Brows that on them gaz'd.

II

Why should of all things Man unrul'd
Such unproportion'd dwellings build? 10

The Beasts are by their Denns exprest:
And Birds contrive an equal Nest;
The low roof'd Tortoises do dwell
In cases fit of Tortoise-shell:
No Creature loves an empty space; 15
Their Bodies measure out their Place.

III

But He, superfluously spread,
Demands more room alive then dead.
And in his hollow Palace goes
Where Winds as he themselves may lose. 20
What need of all this Marble Crust
T'impark the wanton Mote of Dust,
That thinks by Breadth the World t'unite
Though the first Builders fail'd in Height?

IV

But all things are composed here 25
Like Nature, orderly and near:
In which we the Dimensions find
Of that more sober Age and Mind,
When larger sized Men did stoop
To enter at a narrow loop; 30
As practising, in doors so strait,
To strain themselves through *Heavens Gate*.

V

And surely when the after Age
Shall hither come in *Pilgrimage*,
These sacred Places to adore, 35
By *Vere* and *Fairfax* trod before,
Men will dispute how their Extent
Within such dwarfish Confines went:
And some will smile at this, as well
As *Romulus* his Bee-like Cell. 40

VI

Humility alone designs
Those short but admirable Lines,
By which, ungirt and unconstrain'd,
Things greater are in less contain'd.
Let others vainly strive t'immure   45
The *Circle* in the *Quadrature*!
These *holy Mathematicks* can
In ev'ry Figure equal Man.

VII

Yet thus the laden House does sweat,
And scarce indures the *Master* great: 50
But where he comes the swelling Hall
Stirs, and the *Square* grows *Spherical*;
More by his *Magnitude* distrest,
Then he is by its straitness prest:
And too officiously it slights   55
That in it self which him delights.

VIII

So Honour better Lowness bears,
Then That unwonted Greatness wears.
Height with a certain Grace does bend,
But low Things clownishly ascend.   60
And yet what needs there here Excuse
Where ev'ry Thing does answer Use?
Where neatness nothing can condemn,
Nor Pride invent what to contemn?

IX

A Stately *Frontispice of Poor*   65
Adorns without the open Door:
Nor less the Rooms within commends
Daily new *Furniture of Friends*.
The House was built upon the Place
Only as for *a Mark of Grace*;   70

    And for an *Inn* to entertain
    Its *Lord* a while, but not remain.

        X

    Him *Bishops-Hill*, or *Denton* may,
    Or *Bilbrough*, better hold then they:
    But Nature here hath been so free   *75*
    As if she said leave this to me.
    Art would more neatly have defac'd
    What she had laid so sweetly wast;
    In fragrant Gardens, shaddy Woods,
    Deep Meadows, and transparent Floods.   *80*

        XI

    While with slow Eyes we these survey,
    And on each pleasant footstep stay,
    We opportunly may relate
    The Progress of this Houses Fate.
    A *Nunnery* first gave it birth.   *85*
    For *Virgin Buildings* oft brought forth.
    And all that Neighbour-Ruine shows
    The Quarries whence this dwelling rose.

        XII

    Near to this gloomy Cloysters Gates
    There dwelt the blooming Virgin *Thwates*, *90*
    Fair beyond Measure, and an Heir
    Which might Deformity make fair.

  Upon Appleton House.... 73–74 *Bishops-Hill...Bilbrough*: these are all manor houses which made up the Fairfax estates; they were located within a thirty-mile radius of Appleton House.
  90 *Virgin Thwates*: Isabel Thwaites of Denton, Askwith, and Bishops Hill married Sir William Fairfax in 1518, after a long courtship. By this union, Nun Appleton House, built on the lands of the Cistercian priory of Appleton, was secured for the Fairfax heirs, and the attempts of the Prioress, Lady Anna Langton, guardian of the Virgin Thwaites, to win her as a bride of the Church (ll. 157–58) were of no avail. At the dissolution of the priory in 1542, the house came into the possession of the Fairfax family.

And oft She spent the Summer Suns
Discoursing with the *Suttle Nunns*.
Whence in these Words one to her weav'd, 95
(As 'twere by Chance) Thoughts long conceiv'd.

XIII

'Within this holy leisure we
'Live innocently as you see.
'These walls restrain the World without,
'But hedge our Liberty about. 100
'These Bars inclose that wider Den
'Of those wild Creatures, called Men.
'The Cloyster outward shuts its Gates,
'And, from us, locks on them the Grates.

XIV

'Here we, in shining Armour white, 105
'Like *Virgin Amazons* do fight.
'And our chast *Lamps* we hourly trim,
'Lest the great *Bridegroom* find them dim.
'Our *Orient* Breaths perfumed are
'With insense of incessant Pray'r. 110
'And Holy-water of our Tears
'Most strangely our Complexion clears.

XV

'Not Tears of Grief; but such as those
'With which calm Pleasure overflows;
'Or Pity, when we look on you 115
'That live without this happy Vow.
'How should we grieve that must be seen
'Each one a *Spouse*, and each a *Queen*;
'And can in *Heaven* hence behold
'Our brighter Robes and Crowns of Gold? 120

XVI

'When we have prayed all our Beads,
'Some One the holy *Legend* reads;

'While all the rest with Needles paint
'The Face and Graces of the *Saint*.
'But what the Linnen can't receive
'They in their Lives do interweave.
'This Work the *Saints* best represents;
'That serves for *Altar's Ornaments*.

XVII

'But much it to our work would add
'If here your hand, your Face we had:
'By it we would *our Lady* touch;
'Yet thus She you resembles much.
'Some of your Features, as we sow'd,
'Through ev'ry *Shrine* should be bestow'd.
'And in one Beauty we would take
'Enough a thousand *Saints* to make.

XVIII

'And (for I dare not quench the Fire
'That me does for your good inspire)
''Twere Sacriledge a Man t'admit
'To holy things, for *Heaven* fit.
'I see the *Angels* in a Crown
'On you the Lillies show'ring down:
'And round about you Glory breaks,
'That something more then humane speaks.

XIX

'All Beauty, when at such a height,
'Is so already consecrate.
'*Fairfax* I know; and long ere this
'Have mark'd the Youth, and what he is.
'But can he such a *Rival* seem
'For whom you *Heav'n* should disesteem?
'Ah, no! and 'twould more Honour prove
'He your *Devoto* were, then *Love*.

XX

'Here live beloved, and obey'd:
'Each one your Sister, each your Maid.
'And, if our Rule seem strictly pend, 155
'The Rule it self to you shall bend.
'Our *Abbess* too, now far in Age,
'Doth your succession near presage.
'How soft the yoke on us would lye,
'Might such fair Hands as yours it tye! 160

XXI

'Your voice, the sweetest of the Quire,
'Shall draw *Heav'n* nearer, raise us higher.
'And your Example, if our Head,
'Will soon us to perfection lead.
'Those Virtues to us all so dear, 165
'Will straight grow Sanctity when here:
'And that, once sprung, increase so fast
'Till Miracles it work at last.

XXII

'Nor is our *Order* yet so nice,
'Delight to banish as a Vice. 170
'Here Pleasure Piety doth meet;
'One perfecting the other Sweet.
'So through the mortal fruit we boyl
'The Sugars uncorrupting Oyl:
'And that which perisht while we pull, 175
'Is thus preserved clear and full.

XXIII

'For such indeed are all our Arts;
'Still handling Natures finest Parts.
'Flow'rs dress the Altars; for the Clothes,
'The Sea-born Amber we compose; 180

'Balms for the griv'd we draw; and Pasts
'We mold, as Baits for curious tasts.
'What need is here of Man? unless
'These as sweet Sins we should confess.

XXIV

'Each Night among us to your side 185
'Appoint a fresh and Virgin Bride;
'Whom if *our Lord* at midnight find,
'Yet Neither should be left behind.
'Where you may lye as chast in Bed,
'As Pearls together billetted. 190
'All Night embracing Arm in Arm,
'Like Chrystal pure with Cotton warm.

XXV

'But what is this to all the store
'Of Joys you see, and may make more!
'Try but a while, if you be wise: 195
'The Tryal neither Costs, nor Tyes.
Now *Fairfax* seek her promis'd faith:
Religion that dispensed hath;
Which She hence forward does begin;
The *Nuns* smooth Tongue has suckt her in. 200

XXVI

Oft, though he knew it was in vain,
Yet would he valiantly complain.
'Is this that *Sanctity* so great,
'An Art by which you finly'r cheat?
'Hypocrite Witches, hence *avant*, 205
'Who though in prison yet inchant!
'Death only can such Theeves make fast,
'As rob though in the Dungeon cast.

XXVII

'Were there but, when this House was made,
'One Stone that a just Hand had laid, 210

'It must have fall'n upon her Head
'Who first Thee from thy Faith misled.
'And yet, how well soever ment,
'With them 'twould soon grow fraudulent:
'For like themselves they alter all, 215
'And vice infects the very Wall.

XXVIII

'But sure those Buildings last not long,
'Founded by Folly, kept by Wrong.
'I know what Fruit their Gardens yield,
'When they it think by Night conceal'd. 220
'Fly from their Vices. 'Tis thy state,
'Not Thee, that they would consecrate.
'Fly from their Ruine. How I fear
'Though guiltless lest thou perish there.

XXIX

What should he do? He would respect 225
Religion, but not Right neglect:
For first Religion taught him Right,
And dazled not but clear'd his sight.
Sometimes resolv'd his Sword he draws,
But reverenceth then the Laws: 230
For Justice still that Courage led;
First from a Judge, then Souldier bred.

XXX

Small Honour would be in the Storm.
The *Court* him grants the lawful Form;
Which licens'd either Peace or Force, 235
To hinder the unjust Divorce.
Yet still the *Nuns* his Right debar'd,
Standing upon their holy Guard.
Ill-counsell'd Women, do you know
Whom you resist, or what you do? 240

XXXI

Is not this he whose Offspring fierce
Shall fight through all the *Universe*;
And with successive Valour try
France, Poland, either *Germany*;
Till one, as long since prophecy'd, 245
His Horse through conquer'd *Britain* ride?
Yet, against Fate, his Spouse they kept;
And the great Race would intercept.

XXXII

Some to the Breach against their Foes
Their *Wooden Saints* in vain oppose. 250
Another bolder stands at push
With their old *Holy-Water Brush*.
While the disjointed *Abbess* threads
The gingling Chain-shot of her *Beads*.
But their lowd'st Cannon were their Lungs; 255
And sharpest Weapons were their Tongues.

XXXIII

But, waving these aside like Flyes,
Young *Fairfax* through the Wall does rise.
Then th'unfrequented Vault appear'd,
And superstitions vainly fear'd. 260
The *Relicks false* were set to view;
Only the Jewels there were true.
But truly bright and holy *Thwaites*
That weeping at the *Altar* waites.

XXXIIII

But the glad Youth away her bears, 265
And to the *Nuns* bequeaths her Tears:
Who guiltily their Prize bemoan,
Like Gipsies that a Child hath stoln.
Thenceforth (as when th'Inchantment ends
The Castle vanishes or rends) 270

The wasting Cloister with the rest
Was in one instant dispossest.

XXXV

At the demolishing, this Seat
To *Fairfax* fell as by Escheat.
And what both *Nuns* and *Founders* will'd   275
'Tis likely better thus fulfill'd.
For if the *Virgin* prov'd not theirs,
The *Cloyster* yet remained hers.
Though many a *Nun* there made her Vow,
'Twas no *Religious House* till now.   280

XXXVI

From that blest Bed the *Heroe* came,
Whom *France* and *Poland* yet does fame:
Who, when retired here to Peace,
His warlike Studies could not cease;
But laid these Gardens out in sport   285
In the just Figure of a Fort;
And with five Bastions it did fence,
As aiming one for ev'ry Sense.

XXXVII

When in the *East* the Morning Ray
Hangs out the Colours of the Day,   290
The Bee through these known Allies hums,
Beating the *Dian* with its *Drumms*.
Then Flow'rs their drowsie Eylids raise,
Their Silken Ensigns each displays,
And dries its Pan yet dank with Dew,   295
And fills its Flask with Odours new.

XXXVIII

These, as their *Governour* goes by,
In fragrant Vollyes they let fly;

---

281 *Heroe*: Sir Thomas Fairfax (d. 1599), son of Sir William and Lady Isabel.

    And to salute their *Governess*
    Again as great a charge they press: *300*
    None for the *Virgin Nymph*; for She
    Seems with the Flow'rs a Flow'r to be.
    And think so still! though not compare
    With Breath so sweet, or Cheek so faire.

XXXIX

    Well shot ye Firemen! Oh how sweet,   *305*
    And round your equal Fires do meet;
    Whose shrill report no Ear can tell,
    But Ecchoes to the Eye and smell.
    See how the Flow'rs, as at *Parade*,
    Under their *Colours* stand displaid: *310*
    Each *Regiment* in order grows,
    That of the Tulip Pinke and Rose.

XL

    But when the vigilant *Patroul*
    Of Stars walks round about the *Pole*,
    Their Leaves, that to the stalks are curl'd,   *315*
    Seem to their Staves the *Ensigns* furl'd.
    Then in some Flow'rs beloved Hut
    Each Bee as Sentinel is shut;
    And sleeps so too: but, if once stir'd,
    She runs you through, or askes *the Word*.   *320*

XLI

    Oh Thou, that dear and happy Isle
    The Garden of the World ere while,
    Thou *Paradise* of four Seas,
    Which *Heaven* planted us to please,
    But, to exclude the World, did guard   *325*
    With watry if not flaming Sword;
    What luckless Apple did we tast,
    To make us Mortal, and Thee Wast?

XLII

Unhappy! shall we never more
That sweet *Militia* restore, 330
When Gardens only had their Towrs,
And all the Garrisons were Flowrs,
When Roses only Arms might bear,
And Men did rosie Garlands wear?
Tulips, in several Colours barr'd, 335
Were then the *Switzers* of our *Guard*.

XLIII

The *Gardiner* had the *Souldiers* place,
And his more gentle Forts did trace.
The Nursery of all things green
Was then the only *Magazeen*. 340
The *Winter Quarters* were the Stoves,
Where he the tender Plants removes.
But War all this doth overgrow:
We Ord'nance Plant and Powder sow.

XLIV

And yet their walks one on the Sod 345
Who, had it pleased him and *God*,
Might once have made our Gardens spring
Fresh as his own and flourishing.
But he preferr'd to the *Cinque Ports*
These five imaginary Forts: 350
And, in those half-dry Trenches, spann'd
Pow'r which the Ocean might command.

XLV

For he did, with his utmost Skill,
Ambition weed, but *Conscience* till.
Conscience, that Heaven-nursed Plant, 355

---

345 *one on the Sod*: the great General Fairfax.

Which most our Earthly Gardens want.
A prickling leaf it bears, and such
As that which shrinks at ev'ry touch;
But Flowrs eternal, and divine,
That in the Crowns of Saints do shine. 360

XLVI

The sight does from these *Bastions* ply,
Th'invisible *Artilery*;
And at proud *Cawood Castle* seems
To point the *Battery* of its Beams.
As if it quarrell'd in the Seat 365
Th'Ambition of its *Prelate* great.
But ore the Meads below it plays,
Or innocently seems to gaze.

XLVII

And now to the Abbyss I pass
Of that unfathomable Grass, 370
Where Men like Grashoppers appear,
But Grashoppers are Gyants there:
They, in there squeking Laugh, contemn
Us as we walk more low then them:
And, from the Precipices tall 375
Of the green spir's, to us do call.

XLVIII

To see Men through this Meadow Dive,
We wonder how they rise alive.
As, under Water, none does know
Whether he fall through it or go. 380
But, as the Marriners that sound,
And show upon their Lead the Ground,
They bring up Flow'rs so to be seen,
And prove they've at the Bottom been.

XLIX

No Scene that turns with Engines strange 385
Does oftner then these Meadows change,
For when the Sun the Grass hath vext,
The tawny Mowers enter next;
Who seem like *Israalites* to be,
Walking on foot through a green Sea. 390
To them the Grassy Deeps divide,
And crowd a Lane to either Side.

L

With whistling Sithe, and Elbow strong,
These Massacre the Grass along:
While one, unknowing, carves the *Rail*, 395
Whose yet unfeather'd Quils her fail.
The Edge all bloody from its Breast
He draws, and does his stroke detest;
Fearing the Flesh untimely mow'd
To him a Fate as black forebode. 400

LI

But bloody *Thestylis*, that waites
To bring the mowing Camp their Cates,
Greedy as Kites has trust it up,
And forthwith means on it to sup:
When on another quick She lights, 405
And cryes, he call'd us *Israelites*;
But now, to make his saying true,
Rails rain for Quails, for Manna Dew.

LII

Unhappy Birds! what does it boot
To build below the Grasses Root; 410
When Lowness is unsafe as Hight,
And Chance o'retakes what scapeth spight?
And now your Orphan Parents Call

Sounds your untimely Funeral.
Death-Trumpets creak in such a Note, 415
And 'tis the *Sourdine* in their Throat.

LIII

Or sooner hatch or higher build:
The Mower now commands the Field;
In whose new Traverse seemeth wrought
A Camp of Battail newly fought: 420
Where, as the Meads with Hay, the Plain
Lyes quilted ore with Bodies slain:
The Women that with forks it fling,
Do represent the Pillaging.

LIV

And now the careless Victors play, 425
Dancing the Triumphs of the Hay;
Where every Mowers wholesome Heat
Smells like an *Alexanders sweat*.
Their Females fragrant as the Mead
Which they in *Fairy Circles* tread: 430
When at their Dances End they kiss,
Their new-made Hay not sweeter is.

LV

When after this 'tis pil'd in Cocks,
Like a calm Sea it shews the Rocks:
We wondring in the River near 435
How Boats among them safely steer.
Or, like the *Desert Memphis Sand*,
Short *Pyramids* of Hay do stand.
And such the *Roman Camps* do rise
In Hills for Soldiers Obsequies. 440

LVI

This *Scene* again withdrawing brings
A new and empty Face of things;
A levell'd space, as smooth and plain,
As Clothes for *Lilly* strecht to stain.

The World when first created sure 445
Was such a Table rase and pure.
Or rather such is the *Toril*
Ere the Bulls enter at Madril.

LVII

For to this naked equal Flat,
Which *Levellers* take Pattern at, 450
The Villagers in common chase
Their Cattle, which it closer rase;
And what below the Sith increast
Is pincht yet nearer by the Beast.
Such, in the painted World, appear'd 455
Davenant with th'Universal Heard.

LVIII

They seem within the polisht Grass
A Landskip drawen in Looking-Glass.
And shrunk in the huge Pasture show
As Spots, so shap'd, on Faces do. 460
Such Fleas, ere they approach the Eye,
In Multiplying Glasses lye.
They feed so wide, so slowly move,
As *Constellations* do above.

LIX

Then, to conclude these pleasant Acts, 465
Denton sets ope its *Cataracts*;
And makes the Meadow truly be
(What it but seem'd before) a Sea.
For, jealous of its *Lords* long stay,
It try's t'invite him thus away. 470
The River in it self is drown'd,
An Isl's th'astonish'd Cattle round.

---

456 *Davenant*: in his epic *Gondibert*, "an universal Herd" is mentioned (II. vi) as appearing on the sixth day of Creation.

LX

Let others tell the *Paradox*,
How Eels now bellow in the Ox;
How Horses at their Tails do kick, 475
Turn'd as they hang to Leeches quick;
How Boats can over Bridges sail;
And Fishes do the Stables scale.
How *Salmons* trespassing are found;
And Pikes are taken in the Pound. 480

LXI

But I, retiring from the Flood,
Take Sanctuary in the Wood;
And, while it lasts, my self imbark
In this yet green, yet growing Ark;
Where the first Carpenter might best 485
Fit Timber for his Keel have Prest.
And where all Creatures might have shares,
Although in Armies, not in Paires.

LXII

The double Wood of ancient Stocks
Link'd in so thick, an Union locks, 490
It like two *Pedigrees* appears,
On one hand *Fairfax*, th'other *Veres*:
Of whom though many fell in War,
Yet more to Heaven shooting are:
And, as they Natures Cradle deckt, 495
Will in green Age her Hearse expect.

LXIII

When first the Eye this Forrest sees
It seems indeed as *Wood* not *Trees*:
As if their Neighbourhood so old
To one great Trunk them all did mold. 500
There the huge Bulk takes place, as ment
To thrust up a *Fifth Element*;

And stretches still so closely wedg'd
As if the Night within were hedg'd.

LXIV

Dark all without it knits; within
It opens passable and thin;
And in as loose an order grows,
As the *Corinthean Porticoes.*
The arching Boughs unite between
The Columnes of the Temple green;
And underneath the winged Quires
Echo about their tuned Fires.

LXV

The *Nightingale* does here make choice
To sing the Tryals of her Voice.
Low Shrubs she sits in, and adorns
With Musick high the squatted Thorns.
But highest Oakes stoop down to hear,
And listning Elders prick the Ear.
The Thorn, lest it should hurt her, draws
Within the Skin its shrunken claws.

LXVI

But I have for my Musick found
A Sadder, yet more pleasing Sound:
The *Stock-doves*, whose fair necks are grac'd
With Nuptial Rings their Ensigns chast;
Yet always, for some Cause unknown,
Sad pair unto the Elms they moan.
O why should such a Couple mourn,
That in so equal Flames do burn!

LXVII

Then as I carless on the Bed
Of gelid *Straw-berryes* do tread,
And through the Hazles thick espy
The hatching *Thrastles* shining Eye,
The *Heron* from the Ashes top,
The eldest of its young lets drop,

    As if it Stork-like did pretend
    That *Tribute* to *its Lord* to send.

LXVIII

But most the *Hewel's* wonders are,
Who here has the *Holt-felsters* care.
He walks still upright from the Root,
Meas'ring the Timber with his Foot;
And all the way, to keep it clean,
Doth from the Bark the Wood-moths glean.
He, with his Beak, examines well
Which fit to stand and which to fell.

LXIX

The good he numbers up, and hacks;
As if he mark'd them with the Ax.
But where he, tinkling with his Beak,
Does find the hollow Oak to speak,
That for his building he designs,
And through the tainted Side he mines.
Who could have thought the *tallest Oak*
Should fall by such a *feeble Strok'*!

LXX

Nor would it, had the Tree not fed
A *Traitor-worm*, within it bred.
(As first our *Flesh* corrupt within
Tempts impotent and bashful *Sin*.)
And yet that *Worm* triumphs not long,
But serves to feed the *Hewels young*.
While the Oake seems to fall content,
Viewing the Treason's Punishment.

LXXI

Thus I, *easie Philosopher*,
Among the *Birds* and *Trees* confer:
And little now to make me, wants
Or of the *Fowles*, or of the *Plants*.

Give me but Wings as they, and I 565
Streight floting on the Air shall fly:
Or turn me but, and you shall see
I was but an inverted Tree.

LXXII

Already I begin to call
In their most learned Original: 570
And where I Language want, my Signs
The Bird upon the Bough divines;
And more attentive there doth sit
Then if She were with Lime-twigs knit.
No Leaf does tremble in the Wind 575
Which I returning cannot find.

LXXIII

Out of these scatter'd *Sibyls* Leaves
Strange *Prophecies* my Phancy weaves:
And in one History consumes,
Like *Mexique Paintings*, all the *Plumes*. 580
What *Rome, Greece, Palestine,* ere said
I in this light *Mosaick* read.
Thrice happy he who, not mistook,
Hath read in *Natures mystick Book.*

LXXIV

And see how Chance's better Wit 585
Could with a Mask my studies hit!
The Oak-Leaves me embroyder all,
Between which Caterpillars crawl:
And Ivy, with familiar trails,
Me licks, and clasps, and curles, and hales. 590
Under this *antick Cope* I move
Like some great *Prelate of the Grove,*

LXXV

Then, languishing with ease, I toss
On Pallets swoln of Velvet Moss;

While the Wind, cooling through the Boughs, 595
Flatters with Air my panting Brows.
Thanks for my Rest ye *Mossy Banks*,
And unto you *cool Zephyr's* Thanks,
Who, as my Hair, my Thoughts too shed,
And winnow from the Chaff my Head. 600

LXXVI

How safe, methinks, and strong, behind
These Trees have I incamp'd my Mind;
Where Beauty, aiming at the Heart,
Bends in some Tree its useless Dart;
And where the World no certain Shot 605
Can make, or me it toucheth not.
But I on it securely play,
And gaul its Horsemen all the Day.

LXXVII

Bind me ye *Woodbines* in your 'twines,
Curle me about ye gadding *Vines*, 610
And Oh so close your Circles lace,
That I may never leave this Place:
But, lest your Fetters prove too weak,
Ere I your Silken Bondage break,
Do you, *O Brambles*, chain me too, 615
And courteous *Briars* nail me through.

LXXVIII

Here in the Morning tye my Chain,
Where the two Woods have made a Lane;
While, like a *Guard* on either side,
The Trees before their *Lord* divide; 620
This, like a long and equal Thread,
Betwixt two *Labyrinths* does lead.
But, where the Floods did lately drown,
There at the Ev'ning stake me down.

LXXIX

For now the Waves are fal'n and dry'd,   625
And now the Meadows fresher dy'd;
Whose Grass, with moister colour dasht,
Seems as green Silks but newly washt.
No *Serpent* new nor *Crocodile*
Remains behind our little *Nile*;   630
Unless it self you will mistake,
Among these Meads the only Snake.

LXXX

See in what wanton harmless folds
It ev'ry where the Meadow holds;
And its yet muddy back doth lick,   635
Till as a *Chrystal Mirrour* slick;
Where all things gaze themselves, and doubt
If they be in it or without.
And for his shade which therein shines,
Narcissus like, the *Sun* too pines.   640

LXXXI

Oh what a Pleasure 'tis to hedge
My Temples here with heavy sedge;
Abandoning my lazy Side,
Stretcht as a Bank unto the Tide;
Or to suspend my sliding Foot   645
On the Osiers undermined Root,
And in its Branches tough to hang,
While at my Lines the Fishes twang!

LXXXII

But now away my Hooks, my Quills,
And Angles, idle Utensils.   650
The *young Maria* walks to night:

---

651 *Maria*: the daughter of the general (who had been Marvell's tutee in the early 1650's) married George Villiers, second Duke of Buckingham, in

Hide trifling Youth thy Pleasures slight.
'Twere shame that such judicious Eyes
Should with such Toyes a Man surprize;
She that already is the *Law* 655
Of all her *Sex*, her *Ages Aw*.

LXXXIII

See how loose Nature, in respect
To her, it self doth recollect;
And every thing so whisht and fine,
Starts forth with to its *Bonne Mine*. 660
The *Sun* himself, of *Her* aware,
Seems to descend with greater Care;
And lest *She* see him go to Bed,
In blushing Clouds conceales his Head.

LXXXIV

So when the Shadows laid asleep 665
From underneath these Banks do creep,
And on the River as it flows
With *Eben Shuts* begin to close;
The modest *Halcyon* comes in sight,
Flying betwixt the Day and Night; 670
And such an horror calm and dumb,
Admiring Nature does benum.

LXXXV

The viscous Air, wheres'ere She fly,
Follows and sucks her Azure dy;
The gellying Stream compacts below, 675
If it might fix her shadow so;
The stupid Fishes hang, as plain
As *Flies* in *Chrystal* overt'ane;
And Men the silent *Scene* assist,
Charm'd with the *Saphir-winged Mist*. 680

1657. Commentators often overlook the fact that in 1657 Lady Mary Cromwell married into the Fairfax family, into a branch only two generations removed from the main line. Her husband was Thomas, second Viscount and first Earl Fauconberg (1627–1700).

LXXXVI

Maria such, and so doth hush
The *World*, and through the *Ev'ning* rush.
No new-born *Comet* such a Train
Draws through the Skie, nor Star new-slain.
For streight those giddy Rockets fail,   685
Which from the putrid Earth exhale,
But by her *Flames*, in *Heaven* try'd,
Nature is wholly *vitrifi'd*.

LXXXVII

'Tis *She* that to these Gardens gave
That wondrous Beauty which they have;   690
She streightness on the Woods bestows;
To *Her* the Meadow sweetness owes;
Nothing could make the River be
So Chrystal-pure but only *She*;
She yet more Pure, Sweet, Streight, and Fair,   695
Then Gardens, Woods, Meads, Rivers are.

LXXXVIII

Therefore what first *She* on them spent,
They gratefully again present.
The Meadow Carpets where to tread;
The Garden Flow'rs to Crown *Her* Head;   700
And for a Glass the limpid Brook,
Where *She* may all *her* Beautyes look;
But, since *She* would not have them seen,
The Wood about *her* draws a Skreen.

LXXXIX

For *She*, to higher Beauties rais'd,   705
Disdains to be for lesser prais'd.
She counts her Beauty to converse
In all the Languages as *hers*;

Nor yet in those *her self* imployes
But for the *Wisdome*, not the *Noyse*; 710
Nor yet that *Wisdome* would affect,
But as 'tis *Heavens Dialect*.

XC

Blest Nymph! that couldst so soon prevent
Those *Trains* by Youth against thee meant;
Tears (watry Shot that pierce the Mind;) 715
And *Sighs* (Loves Cannon charg'd with Wind;)
True Praise (That breaks through all defence;)
And *feign'd complying Innocence*;
But knowing where this *Ambush* lay,
She scap'd the safe, but roughest Way. 720

XCI

This 'tis to have been from the first
In a *Domestick Heaven* nurst,
Under the *Discipline* severe
Of *Fairfax*, and the starry *Vere*;
Where not one object can come nigh 725
But pure, and spotless as the Eye;
And *Goodness* doth it self intail
On *Females*, if there want a *Male*.

XCII

Go now fond Sex that on your Face
Do all your useless Study place, 730
Nor once at Vice your Brows dare knit
Lest the smooth Forehead wrinkled sit:
Yet your own Face shall at you grin,
Thorough the Black-bag of your Skin;
When *knowledge* only could have fill'd 735
And *Virtue* all those *Furrows* till'd .

XCIII

Hence *She* with Graces more divine
Supplies beyond her *Sex* the *Line*;

And, like a *sprig of Misleto*,
On the *Fairfacian Oak* does grow;   740
Whence, for some universal good,
The *Priest* shall cut the sacred Bud;
While her *glad Parents* most rejoice,
And make their *Destiny* their *Choice*.

XCIV

Mean time ye Fields, Springs, Bushes, Flow'rs,   745
Where yet She leads her studious Hours,
(Till Fate her worthily translates,
And find a *Fairfax* for our *Thwaites*)
Employ the means you have by Her,
And in your kind your selves preferr;   750
That, as all *Virgins* She preceds,
So you all *Woods, Streams, Gardens, Meads*.

XCV

For you *Thessalian Tempe's Seat*
Shall now be scorn'd as obsolete;
Aranjuez, as less, disdain'd;   755
The *Bel-Retiro* as constrain'd;
But name not the *Idalian Grove*,
For 'twas the Seat of wanton Love;
Much less the Dead's *Elysian Fields*,
Yet nor to them your Beauty yields.   760

XCVI

'Tis not, what once it was, the *World*;
But a rude heap together hurl'd;
All negligently overthrown,
Gulfes, Deserts, Precipices, Stone.
Your lesser *World* contains the same.   765
But in more decent Order tame;

755-56 *Aranjuez...Bel-Retiro*: [Buen-Retiro] royal retreats on the Tagus, near Madrid, for Philip II. The former is about 30 miles from the city, and the latter in the present century has been surrounded by the growing city.

You Heaven's Center, Nature's Lap.
And Paradice's only Map.

XCVII

But now the *Salmon-Fishers* moist
Their *Leathern Boats* begin to hoist; 770
And, like *Antipodes* in Shoes,
Have shod their *Heads* in their *Canoos.*
How *Tortoise like*, but not so slow,
These rational *Amphibii* go?
Let's in: for the dark *Hemisphere* 775
Does now like one of them appear.

On the Victory obtained by Blake over the Spaniards, in the Bay of Sanctacruze, in the Island of Teneriff 1657

Now does *Spains* Fleet her spatious wings unfold,
Leaves the new World and hastens for the old:
But though the wind was fair, they slowly swoome
Frayted with acted Guilt, and Guilt to come:
For this rich load, of which so proud they are, 5
Was rais'd by Tyranny, and rais'd for War;
Every capatious Gallions womb was fill'd,
With what the Womb of wealthy Kingdomes yield,
The new Worlds wounded Intrails they had tore,

On the Victory obtained by Blake.... The poem memorializes the victory won in June, 1657 by the English navy under Blake, off Tenerife in the Canary Islands. Mar. points out that the poem is clearly addressed to Cromwell. Blake died before the fleet returned to England in August of the same year (and hence after the writing of this poem).

For wealth wherewith to wound the old once more. 10
Wealth which all others Avarice might cloy,
But yet in them caus'd as much fear, as Joy.
For now upon the Main, themselves they saw,
That boundless Empire, where you give the Law,
Of winds and waters rage, they fearful be, 15
But much more fearful are your Flags to see.
Day, that to those who sail upon the deep,
More wish't for, and more welcome is then sleep,
They dreaded to behold, Least the Sun's light,
With *English* Streamers, should salute their sight: 20
In thickest darkness they would choose to steer,
So that such darkness might suppress their fear;
At length theirs vanishes, and fortune smiles;
For they behold the sweet Canary Isles;
One of which doubtless is by Nature blest 25
Above both Worlds, since 'tis above the rest.
For least some Gloominess might stain her sky,
Trees there the duty of the Clouds supply;
O noble Trust which Heaven on this Isle poures,
Fertile to be, yet never need her showres. 30
A happy People, which at once do gain
The benefits without the ills of rain.
Both health and profit, Fate cannot deny;
Where still the Earth is moist, the Air still dry;
The jarring Elements no discord know, 35
Fewel and Rain together kindly grow;
And coolness there, with heat doth never fight,
This only rules by day, and that by Night.
Your worth to all these Isles, a just right brings,
The best of Lands should have the best of Kings. 40
And these want nothing Heaven can afford,
Unless it be, the having you their Lord;
But this great want, will not a long one prove,
Your Conquering Sword will soon that want remove.
For *Spain* had better, shee'l ere long confess, 45
Have broken all her Swords, then this one Peace,
Casting that League off, which she held so long,
She cast off that which only made her strong.

Forces and art, she soon will feel, are vain,
Peace, against you, was the sole strength of *Spain*. 50
By that alone those Islands she secures,
Peace made them hers, but War will make them yours;
There the indulgent Soil that rich Grape breeds,
Which of the Gods the fancied drink exceeds;
They still do yield, such is their pretious mould, 55
All that is good, and are not curst with Gold.
With fatal Gold, for still where that does grow,
Neither the Soyl, nor People quiet know.
Which troubles men to raise it when 'tis Oar,
And when 'tis raised, does trouble them much more. 60
Ah, why was thither brought that cause of War,
Kind Nature had from thence remov'd so far.
In vain doth she those Islands free from Ill,
If fortune can make guilty what she will.
But whilst I draw that Scene, where you ere long, 65
Shall conquests act, your present are unsung.

    For *Sanctacruze* the glad Fleet takes her way,
And safely there casts Anchor in the Bay.
Never so many with one joyful cry,
That place saluted, where they all must dye. 70
Deluded men! Fate with you did but sport,
You scap't the Sea, to perish in your Port.
'Twas more for *Englands* fame you should dye there,
Where you had most of strength, and least of fear.

    The Peek's proud height, the *Spaniards* all admire, 75
Yet in their brests, carry a pride much higher.
Onely to this vast hill a power is given,
At once both to Inhabit Earth and Heaven.
But this stupendious Prospect did not neer,
Make them admire, so much as they did fear. 80

    For here they met with news, which did produce,
A grief, above the cure of Grapes best juice.
They learn'd with Terrour, that nor Summers heat,
Nor Winters storms, had made your Fleet retreat.
To fight against such Foes, was vain they knew, 85
Which did the rage of Elements subdue.
Who on the Ocean that does horror give,

To all besides, triumphantly do live.
   With hast they therefore all their Gallions moar,
And flank with Cannon from the Neighbouring shore.   *90*
Forts, Lines, and Sconces all the Bay along,
They build and act all that can make them strong.
   Fond men who know not whilst such works they raise,
They only Labour to exalt your praise.
Yet they by restless toyl, became at Length,   *95*
So proud and confident of their made strength,
That they with joy their boasting General heard,
Wish then for that assault he lately fear'd.
His wish he has, for now undaunted *Blake*,
With winged speed, for *Sanctacruze* does make.   *100*
For your renown, his conquering Fleet does ride,
Ore Seas as vast as is the *Spaniards* pride.
Whose Fleet and Trenches view'd, he soon did say,
We to their Strength are more oblig'd then they.
Wer't not for that, they from their Fate would run,   *105*
And a third World seek out our Armes to shun.
Those Forts, which there, so high and strong appear,
Do not so much suppress, as shew their fear.
Of speedy Victory let no man doubt,
Our worst works past, now we have found them out.   *110*
Behold their Navy does at Anchor lye,
And they are ours, for now they cannot fly.
   This said, the whole Fleet gave it their applause,
And all assumes your courage, in your cause.
That Bay they enter, which unto them owes,   *115*
The noblest wreaths, that Victory bestows.
Bold *Stainer* Leads, this Fleets design'd by fate,
To give him Lawrel, as the Last did Plate.
   The Thund'ring Cannon now begins the Fight,
And though it be at Noon, creates a Night.   *120*
The Air was soon after the fight begun,
Far more enflam'd by it, then by the Sun.
Never so burning was that Climate known,
War turn'd the temperate, to the Torrid Zone.
   Fate these two Fleets, between both Worlds had brought.   *125*
Who fight, as if for both those Worlds they fought.

Thousands of wayes, Thousands of men there dye,
Some Ships are sunk, some blown up in the skie.
Nature never made Cedars so high aspire,
As Oakes did then, Urg'd by the active fire. 130
Which by quick powders force, so high was sent,
That it return'd to its own Element.
Torn Limbs some leagues into the Island fly,
Whilst others lower, in the Sea do lye.
Scarce souls from bodies sever'd are so far, 135
By death, as bodies there were by the War.
Th'all-seeing Sun, neer gaz'd on such a sight,
Two dreadful Navies there at Anchor Fight.
And neither have, or power, or will to fly;
There one must Conquer, or there both must dye. 140
Far different Motives yet, engag'd them thus,
Necessity did them, but Choice did us.
   A choice which did the highest worth express,
And was attended by as high success.
For your resistless genious there did Raign, 145
By which we Laurels reapt ev'n on the Mayn.
So prosperous Stars, though absent to the sence,
Bless those they shine for, by their Influence.
   Our Cannon now tears every Ship and Sconce,
And o're two Elements Triumphs at once. 150
Their Gallions sunk, their wealth the Sea does fill,
The only place where it can cause no Ill.
   Ah would those Treasures which both Indies have,
Were buryed in as large, and deep a grave,
Wars chief support with them would buried be, 155
And the Land owe her peace unto the Sea.
Ages to come, your conquering Arms will bless,
There they destroy, what had destroy'd their Peace.
And in one War the present age may boast,
The certain seeds of many Wars are lost. 160
   All the Foes Ships destroy'd, by Sea or fire,
Victorious *Blake*, does from the Bay retire,
His Seige of *Spain* he then again pursues,
And there first brings of his success the news;
The saddest news that ere to *Spain* was brought, 165

Their rich Fleet sunk, and ours with Lawrel fraught.
Whilst fame in every place, her Trumpet blowes,
And tells the World, how much to you it owes.

A Dialogue between Thyrsis *and* Dorinda

Dorinda. When Death shall part us from these Kids,
And shut up our divided Lids,
Tell me, *Thirsis*, prethee do,
Whither thou and I shall go.

Thyrsis. To the Elizium: (*Dorinda.*) oh where is't?   5

Thyrsis. A Chast Soul can never mis't.

Dorinda. I know no way but one, our home:
Is our Cell Elizium?

Thyrsis. Cast thine Eye to yonder Skie,
There the milky way doth lye;   10
'Tis a sure but rugged way,
That leads to Everlasting day.

Dorinda. There Birds may nest, but how shall I,
That have no wings and cannot fly?

Thyrsis. Do not sigh (fair Nimph) for fire   15
Hath no wings, yet doth aspire
Till it hit against the pole,
Heaven's the Center of the Soul.

Dorinda. But in Elizium how do they
Pass Eternity away?   20

A Dialogue between Thyrsis and Dorinda. A truncated version of this poem appears in British Museum Add. MS. 31432, ff. 12v-14r (William Lawes's autograph manuscript song book), where it is attributed to him. Lawes, fighting with the Royalists, died in 1645.

Thyrsis. Oh! ther's neither hope nor fear.
 Ther's no Wolf, no Fox, no Bear;
 No need of Dog to fetch our stray,
 Our Lightfoot we may give away;
 No Oatepipes needful, there thy Eares 25
 May feast with Musick of the Spheares.

Dorinda. Oh Sweet! how I my future state,
 By silent thinking, Antidate:
 I preethe let us spend out time to come
 In talking of *Elizium*. 30

Thyrsis. Then I'le go on: There sheep are full
 Of sweetest grass, and softest wooll;
 There birds sing Consort, garlands grow,
 Cool winds do whisper, springs do flow.
 There alwayes is a rising Sun, 35
 And day is ever but begun.
 Shepheards there bear equal sway,
 And every Nimph's a Queen of *May*.

Dorinda. Ah me! (*Thyrsis.*) *Dorinda*, why do'st Cry?

Dorinda. I'm sick, I'm sick, and fain would dye; 40
 Convince me now that this is true,
 By bidding, with mee, all adieu.

Thyrsis. I cannot live without thee, I;
 I'le for thee, much more with thee dye.

Dorinda. Then let us give *Corilla* charge o'th Sheep, 45
 And thou and I'le pick poppies, and them steep
 In wine, and drink on't even till we weep:
 So shall we smoothly pass away in sleep.

The Character of Holland

Holland, that scarce deserves the name of *Land*,
As but th'Off-scouring of the *Brittish Sand*;
And so much Earth as was contributed
By *English Pilots* when they heav'd the Lead;
Or what by th'Oceans slow alluvion fell,   5
Of shipwrackt Cockle and the Muscle-shell:
This indigested vomit of the Sea
Fell to the *Dutch* by just Propriety.

   Glad then, as Miners that have found the Oar,
They with mad labour fish'd the *Land* to *Shoar*;   10
And div'd as desperately for each piece
Of Earth, as if't had been of *Ambergreece*;
Collecting anxiously small Loads of Clay,
Less then what building Swallows bear away;
Or then those Pills which sordid Beetles roul,   15
Tranfusing into them their Dunghil Soul.

   How did they rivet, with Gigantick Piles,
Thorough the Center their new-catched Miles;
And to the stake a strugling Country bound,
Where barking Waves still bait the forced Ground;   20
Building their *watry Babel* far more high
To reach the *Sea*, then those to scale the *Sky*.

   Yet still his claim the Injur'd Ocean laid,
And oft at Leap-frog ore their Steeples plaid:
As if on purpose it on Land had come   25
To shew them what's their *Mare Liberum*.
A daily deluge over them does boyl;
The Earth and Water play at *Level-coyl*;
The Fish oft-times the Burger dispossest,
And sat not as a Meat but as a Guest;   30
And oft the *Tritons* and the *Sea-Nymphs* saw
Whole sholes of *Dutch* serv'd up for *Cabillau*;

The Character of Holland. 26 *Mare Liberum*: in a book of that title published in 1609, Grotius discussed freedom on European seas.
28 *Level-coyl*: lever-de-cul, a rough-and-tumble game.
32 *Cabillau*: the French *cabillaud*, fresh codfish.

Or as they over the new Level rang'd
For pickled *Herring*, pickled *Heeren* chang'd.
Nature, it seem'd, asham'd of her mistake,   35
Would throw their Land away at *Duck* and *Drake*.
    Therefore *Necessity*, that first made *Kings*,
Something like *Government* among them brings.
For as with *Pygmees* who best kills the *Crane*,
Among the *hungry* he that treasures *Grain*,   40
Among the *blind* the one-ey'd *blinkard* reigns,
So rules among the *drowned* he that *draines*.
Not who first see the *rising Sun* commands,
But who could first discern the *rising Lands*.
Who best could know to pump an Earth so leak,   45
Him they their *Lord* and *Country's Father* speak.
To make a *Bank* was a great *Plot of State*;
Invent a *Shov'l* and be a *Magistrate*.
Hence some small *Dyke-grave* unperceiv'd invades
The *Pow'r*, and grows as 'twere a *King of Spades*.   50
But for less envy some *joynt States* endures,
Who look like a *Commission of the Sewers*.
For these *Half-anders*, half wet, and half dry,
Nor bear *strict service*, nor *pure Liberty*.
    'Tis probable *Religion* after this   55
Came next in order; which they could not miss.
How could the *Dutch* but be converted, when
Th'*Apostles* were so many Fishermen?
Besides the Waters of themselves did rise,
And, as their Land, so them did re-baptize.   60
Though *Herring* for their *God* few voices mist,
And *Poor-John* to have been th' *Evangelist*.
Faith, that could never Twins conceive before,
Never so fertile, spawn'd upon this shore:
More pregnant then their *Marg'ret*, that laid down   65
For *Hans-in-Kelder* of a whole *Hans-Town*.

49 *Dyke-grave*: an officer in charge of dikes and levees.
53 *Half-anders*: as opposed to Hol-anders.
65 *Marg'ret*: a legendary Dutch countess, said to have had at a single birth as many children as there are days in the year.
66 *Hans-in-Kelder*: child in the womb.

Sure when *Religion* did it self imbark,
And from the *East* would *Westward* steer its Ark,
It struck, and splitting on this unknown ground,
Each one thence pillag'd the first piece he found: 70
Hence *Amsterdam*, *Turk-Christian-Pagan-Jew*,
Staple of Sects and Mint of Schisme grew;
That *Bank of Conscience*, where not one so strange
Opinion but finds Credit, and Exchange.
In vain for *Catholicks* our selves we bear; 75
The *universal Church* is onely there.
Nor can Civility there want for *Tillage*,
Where wisely for their *Court* they chose a *Village*.
How fit a Title clothes their *Governours*,
Themselves the *Hogs* as all their Subjects *Bores*! 80
   Let it suffice to give their Country Fame
That it had one *Civilis* call'd by Name,
Some Fifteen hundred and more years ago;
But surely never any that was so.
   See but their *Mairmaids* with their *Tails of Fish*, 85
Reeking at *Church* over the *Chafing-Dish*.
A vestal Turf enshrin'd in Earthen Ware
Fumes through the loop-holes of a wooden Square.
Each to the *Temple* with these *Altars* tend,
But still does place it at her *Western End*: 90
While the fat steam of *Female Sacrifice*
Fills the *Priests Nostrils* and puts out his *Eyes*.
   Or what a spectacle the *Skipper gross*,
A Water-Hercules Butter-Coloss,
Tunn'd up with all their sev'ral *Towns of Beer*; 95
When Stagg'ring upon some Land, *Snick and Sneer*,
They try, like Statuaries, if they can,
Cut out each others *Athos* to a Man:
And carve in their large Bodies, where they please,
The Armes of the *United Provinces*. 100
   But when such Amity at home is show'd;
What then are their confederacies abroad?
Let this one court'sie witness all the rest,
When their whole Navy they together prest,
Not Christian Captives to redeem from Bands: 105

Or intercept the Western golden Sands:
No, but all ancient Rights and Leagues must vail,
Rather then to the *English* strike their sail;
To whom their weather-beaten *Province* ows
It self, when as some greater Vessel tows 110
A Cock-boat tost with the same wind and fate;
We buoy'd so often up their *sinking State*.
 Was this *Jus Belli & Pacis*; could this be
Cause why their *Burgomaster of the Sea*
Ram'd with Gun-powder, flaming with Brand wine, 115
Should raging hold his Linstock to the Mine?
While, with feign'd *Treaties*, they invade by stealth
Our sore new circumcised *Common wealth*.
 Yet of his vain Attempt no more he sees
Then of *Case-Butter* shot and *Bullet-Cheese*. 120
And the torn Navy stagger'd with him home,
While the Sea laught it self into a foam,
'Tis true since that (as fortune kindly sports,)
A wholesome Danger drove us to our Ports.
While half their banish'd keels the Tempest tost, 125
Half bound at home in Prison to the frost:
That ours mean time at leizure might careen,
In a calm Winter, under Skies Serene.
As the obsequious Air and Waters rest,
Till the dear *Halcyon* hatch out all its nest. 130
The *Common wealth* doth by its losses grow;
And, like its own Seas, only Ebbs to flow.
Besides that very Agitation laves,
And purges out the corruptible waves.
 And now again our armed *Bucentore* 135
Doth yearly their *Sea-Nuptials* restore.
And how the *Hydra of seaven Provinces*
Is strangled by our *Infant Hercules*.
Their Tortoise wants its vainly stretched neck;
Their Navy all our Conquest or our Wreck: 140
Or, what is left, their *Carthage* overcome
Would render fain unto our better *Rome*.

---

135 *Bucentore*: the state barge of the Venetian Republic (It. *bucintoro*).

Unless our *Senate*, lest their Youth disuse,
The War, (but who would) Peace if begg'd refuse.
  For now of nothing may our *State* despair,   *145*
Darling of Heaven, and of Men the Care;
Provided that they be what they have been,
Watchful abroad, and honest still within.
For while our *Neptune* doth a *Trident* shake,
Steel'd with those piercing Heads, *Dean, Monck* and *Blake:*   *150*
And while *Jove* governs in the highest Sphere,
Vainly in *Hell* let *Pluto* domineer.

An Horatian *Ode upon* Cromwel's *Return from* Ireland

    The forward Youth that would appear
    Must now forsake his *Muses* dear,
        Nor in the Shadows sing
        His Numbers languishing.
    'Tis time to leave the Books in dust,   *5*
    And oyl th'unused Armours rust:
        Removing from the Wall
        The Corslet of the Hall.
    So restless *Cromwell* could not cease
    In the inglorious Arts of Peace,   *10*
        But through adventrous War
        Urged his active Star.
    And, like the three-fork'd Lightning, first
    Breaking the Clouds where it was nurst,
        Did through his own Side   *15*
        His fiery way divide.
    For 'tis all one to Courage high
    The Emulous or Enemy;

---

  150 *Dean, Monck and Blake*: these three generals were at sea together from 26 November 1652 until Dean's death on 3 June 1653. These facts permit us to date the poem, or at least its latter half.
  An Horatian Ode . . . . Cromwell returned from Ireland in May of 1650 to take part in the Scottish campaign.

   And with such to inclose
  Is more then to oppose.   20
Then burning through the Air he went,
And Pallaces and Temples rent:
   And *Caesars* head at last
   Did through his Laurels blast.
'Tis Madness to resist or blame   25
The force of angry Heavens flame:
   And, if we would speak true,
   Much to the Man is due.
Who, from his private Gardens, where
He liv'd reserved and austere,   30
   As if his highest plot
   To plant the Bergamot,
Could by industrious Valour climbe
To ruine the great Work of Time,
   And cast the Kingdome old   35
   Into another Mold.
Though Justice against Fate complain,
And plead the antient Rights in vain:
   But those do hold or break
   As Men are strong or weak.   40
Nature that hateth emptiness,
Allows of penetration less:
   And therefore must make room
   Where greater Spirits come.
What Field of all the Civil Wars,   45
Where his were not the deepest Scars?
   And *Hampton* shows what part
   He had of wiser Art.
Where, twining subtile fears with hope,
He wove a Net of such a scope,   50
   That *Charles* himself might chase
   To *Caresbrooks* narrow case.
That thence the *Royal Actor* born
The *Tragick Scaffold* might adorn:
   While round the armed Bands 55
   Did clap their bloody hands.
He nothing common did or mean

Upon that memorable Scene:
   But with his keener Eye
   The Axes edge did try: 60
Nor call'd the *Gods* with vulgar spight
To vindicate his helpless Right,
   But bow'd his comely Head,
   Down as upon a Bed.
This was that memorable Hour   65
Which first assur'd the forced Pow'r.
   So when they did design
   The *Capitols* first Line,
A bleeding Head where they begun,
Did fright the Architects to run;   70
   And yet in that the *State*
   Foresaw it's happy Fate.
And now the *Irish* are asham'd
To see themselves in one Year tam'd:
   So much one Man can do,   75
   That does both act and know.
They can affirm his Praises best,
And have, though overcome, confest
   How good he is, how just,
   And fit for highest Trust: 80
Nor yet grown stiffer with Command,
But still in the *Republick's* hand:
   How fit he is to sway
   That can so well obey.
He to the *Commons Feet* presents   85
A *Kingdome*, for his first years rents:
   And, what he may, forbears
   His Fame to make it theirs:
And has his Sword and Spoyls ungirt,
To lay them at the *Publick's* skirt.   90
   So when the Falcon high
   Falls heavy from the Sky,
She, having kill'd, no more does search,
But on the next green Bow to pearch;
   Where, when he first does lure,   95
   The Falckner has her sure.

What may not then our *Isle* presume
While Victory his Crest does plume!
   What may not others fear
   If thus he crown each Year!   100
A *Cæsar* he ere long to *Gaul*,
To *Italy* an *Hannibal*;
   And to all States not free
   Shall *Clymacterick* be.
The *Pict* no shelter now shall find   105
Within his party-colour'd Mind;
   But from this Valour sad
   Shrink underneath the Plad:
Happy if in the tufted brake
The *English Hunter* him mistake;   110
   Nor lay his Hounds in near
   The *Caledonian* Deer.
But thou the Wars and Fortunes Son
March indefatigably on;
   And for the last effect   115
   Still keep thy Sword erect:
Besides the force it has to fright
The Spirits of the shady Night,
   The same *Arts* that did *gain*
   A *Pow'r* must it *maintain*.   120

The First Anniversary
of the Government under O.C.

Like the vain Curlings of the Watry maze,
Which in smooth streams a sinking Weight does raise;
So Man, declining alwayes, disappears
In the weak Circles of increasing Years;
And his short Tumults of themselves Compose,   5

The First Anniversary . . . . Intended for December, 1654 (Cromwell had been named protector one year earlier), the poem first appeared in 1655, when Marvell was still tutor at Eton to William Dutton, the ward of Cromwell. In ll. 108ff. Marvell alludes to apocalyptic prophecies appearing in Dan. 7–8 and Rev. 12–20.

While flowing Time above his Head does close.
   Cromwell alone with greater Vigour runs,
(Sun-like) the Stages of succeeding Suns:
And still the Day which he doth next restore,
Is the just Wonder of the Day before.
Cromwell alone doth with new Lustre spring,
And shines the Jewel of the yearly Ring.
   'Tis he the force of scatter'd Time contracts,
And in one Year the work of Ages acts:
While heavy Monarchs make a wide Return,
Longer, and more Malignant then *Saturn*:
And though they all *Platonique* years should raign,
In the same Posture would be found again.
Their earthy Projects under ground they lay,
More slow and brittle then the *China* clay:
Well may they strive to leave them to their Son,
For one Thing never was by one King don.
Yet some more active for a Frontier Town
Took in by Proxie, beggs a false Renown;
Another triumphs at the publick Cost,
And will have Wonn, if he no more have Lost;
They fight by Others, but in Person wrong,
And only are against their Subjects strong;
Their other Wars seem but a feign'd contest,
This Common Enemy is still opprest;
If Conquerors, on them they turn their might;
If Conquered, on them they wreak their Spight:
They neither build the Temple in their dayes,
Nor Matter for succeeding Founders raise;
Not sacred Prophecies consult within,
Much less themselves to perfect them begin;
No other care they bear of things above,
But with Astrologers divine, and *Jove*,
To know how long their Planet yet Reprives
From the deserved Fate their guilty lives:
Thus (Image-like) an useless time they tell,
And with vain Scepter strike the hourly Bell;
Nor more contribute to the state of Things,
Then wooden Heads unto the Viols strings.

> While indefatigable *Cromwell* hyes, 45
> And cuts his way still nearer to the Skyes,
> Learning a Musique in the Region clear,
> To tune this lower to that higher Sphere.
>
>   So when *Amphion* did the Lute command,
> Which the God gave him, with his gentle hand, 50
> The rougher Stones, unto his Measures hew'd,
> Dans'd up in order from the Quarreys rude;
> This took a Lower, that an Higher place,
> As he the Treble alter'd, or the Base:
> No Note he struck, but a new Story lay'd, 55
> And the great Work ascended while he play'd.
>
>   The listning Structures he with Wonder ey'd.
> And still new Stopps to various Time apply'd:
> Now through the Strings a Martial rage he throws,
> And joyning streight the *Theban* Tow'r arose; 60
> Then as he strokes them with a Touch more sweet,
> The flocking Marbles in a Palace meet;
> But, for he most the graver Notes did try,
> Therefore the Temples rear'd their Columns high:
> Thus, ere he ceas'd, his sacred Lute creates 65
> Th'harmonious City of the seven Gates.
>
>   Such was that wondrous Order and Consent,
> When *Cromwell* tun'd the ruling Instrument;
> While tedious Statesmen many years did hack,
> Framing a Liberty that still went back; 70
> Whose num'rous Gorge could swallow in an hour
> That Island, which the Sea cannot devour:
> Then our *Amphion* issues out and sings,
> And once he struck, and twice, the pow'rful Strings.
>
>   The Commonwealth then first together came, 75
> And each one enter'd in the willing Frame;
> All other Matter yields, and may be rul'd;
> But who the Minds of stubborn Men can build?
> No Quarry bears a Stone so hardly wrought,
> Nor with such labour from its Center brought; 80
> None to be sunk in the Foundation bends,
> Each in the House the highest Place contends,
> And each the Hand that lays him will direct,

And some fall back upon the Architect;
Yet all compos'd by his attractive Song, 85
Into the Animated City throng.
    The Common-wealth does through their Centers all
Draw the Circumf'rence of the publique Wall;
The crossest Spirits here do take their part,
Fast'ning the Contignation which they thwart; 90
And they, whose Nature leads them to divide,
Uphold, this one, and that the other Side;
But the most Equal still sustein the Height,
And they as Pillars keep the Work upright;
While the resistance of opposed Minds, 95
The Fabrick as with Arches stronger binds,
Which on the Basis of a Senate free,
Knit by the Roofs Protecting weight agree.
    When for his Foot he thus a place had found,
He hurles e'r since the World about him round; 100
And in his sev'ral Aspects, like a Star,
Here shines in Peace, and thither shoots a War.
While by his Beams observing Princes steer,
And wisely court the Influence they fear;
O would they rather by his Pattern won, 105
Kiss the approaching, nor yet angry Son;
And in their numbred Footsteps humbly tread
The path where holy Oracles do lead;
How might they under such a Captain raise
The great Designes kept for the latter Dayes! 110
But mad with Reason, so miscall'd, of State
They know them not, and what they know not, hate.
Hence still they sing Hosanna to the Whore,
And her whom they should Massacre adore:
But Indians whom they should convert, subdue; 115
Nor teach, but traffique with, or burn the Jew.
    Unhappy Princes, ignorantly bred,
By Malice some, by Errour more misled;
If gracious Heaven to my Life give length,
Leisure to Time, and to my Weakness Strength, 120
Then shall I once with graver Accents shake
Your Regal sloth, and your long Slumbers wake:

Like the shrill Huntsman that prevents the East,
Winding his Horn to Kings that chase the Beast.
 Till then my Muse shall hollow far behind   *125*
Angelique *Cromwell* who outwings the wind;
And in dark Nights, and in cold Dayes alone
Pursues the Monster thorough every Throne:
Which shrinking to her *Roman* Den impure,
Gnashes her Goary teeth; nor there secure.   *130*
 Hence oft I think, if in some happy Hour
High Grace should meet in one with highest Pow'r,
And then a seasonable People still
Should bend to his, as he to Heavens will,
What we might hope, what wonderful Effect   *135*
From such a wish'd Conjuncture might reflect.
Sure, the mysterious Work, where none withstand,
Would forthwith finish under such a Hand:
Fore-shortned Time its useless Course would stay,
And soon precipitate the latest Day.   *140*
But a thick Cloud about that Morning lyes,
And intercepts the Beams of Mortal eyes,
That 'tis the most which we determine can,
If these the Times, then this must be the Man.
And well he therefore does, and well has guest,   *145*
Who in his Age has always forward prest:
And knowing not where Heavens choice may light,
Girds yet his Sword, and ready stands to fight;
But Men alas, as if they nothing car'd,
Look on, all unconcern'd, or unprepar'd;   *150*
And Stars still fall, and still the Dragons Tail
Swinges the Volumes of its horrid Flail.
For the great Justice that did first suspend
The World by Sin, does by the same extend.
Hence that blest Day still counterpoysed wastes,   *155*
The Ill delaying, what th'Elected hastes;
Hence landing Nature to new Seas is tost,
And good Designes still with their Authors lost.
 And thou, great *Cromwell*, for whose happy birth
A Mold was chosen out of better Earth;   *160*
Whose Saint-like Mother we did lately see

Live out an Age, long as a Pedigree;
That she might seem, could we the Fall dispute,
T'have smelt the Blossome, and not eat the Fruit;
Though none does of more lasting Parents grow,   *165*
But never any did them Honor so;
Though thou thine Heart from Evil still unstain'd,
And always hast thy Tongue from fraud refrain'd;
Thou, who so oft through Storms of thundring Lead
Hast born securely thine undaunted Head,   *170*
Thy Brest through ponyarding Conspiracies,
Drawn from the Sheath of lying Prophecies;
Thee proof beyond all other Force or Skill,
Our Sins endanger, and shall one day kill.

  How near they fail'd, and in thy sudden Fall   *175*
At once assay'd to overturn us all.
Our brutish fury strugling to be Free,
Hurry'd thy Horses while they hurry'd thee.
When thou hadst almost quit thy Mortal cares,
And soyl'd in Dust thy Crown of silver Hairs.   *180*
Let this one Sorrow interweave among
The other Glories of our yearly Song.
Like skilful Looms which through the costly threed
Of purling Ore, a shining wave do shed:
So shall the Tears we on past Grief employ,   *185*
Still as they trickle, glitter in our Joy.
So with more Modesty we may be True,
And speak as of the Dead the Praises due:
While impious Men deceiv'd with pleasure short,
On their own Hopes shall find the Fall retort.   *190*
But the poor Beasts wanting their noble Guide,
What could they more? shrunk guiltily aside.
First winged Fear transports them far away,
And leaden Sorrow then their flight did stay.
See how they each his towring Crest abate,   *195*
And the green Grass, and their known Mangers hate,
Nor through wide Nostrils snuffe the wanton air,
Nor their round Hoofs, or curled Mane's compare;
With wandring Eyes, and restless Ears they stood,
And with shrill Neighings ask'd him of the Wood.   *200*

Thou *Cromwell* falling, not a stupid Tree,
Or Rock so savage, but it mourn'd for thee:
And all about was heard a Panique groan,
As if that Natures self were overthrown.
It seem'd the Earth did from the Center tear; 205
It seem'd the Sun was faln out of the Sphere:
Justice obstructed lay, and Reason fool'd;
Courage disheartned, and Religion cool'd.
A dismal Silence through the Palace went,
And then loud Shreeks the vaulted Marbles rent. 210
Such as the dying Chorus sings by turns,
And to deaf Seas, and ruthless Tempests mourns,
When now they sink, and now the plundring Streams
Break up each Deck, and rip the Oaken seams.

But thee triumphant hence the firy Carr, 215
And firy Steeds had born out of the Warr,
From the low World, and thankless Men above,
Unto the Kingdom blest of Peace and Love:
We only mourn'd our selves, in thine Ascent,
Whom thou hadst left beneath with Mantle rent. 220

For all delight of Life thou then didst lose,
When to Command, thou didst thy self Depose;
Resigning up thy Privacy so dear,
To turn the headstrong Peoples Charioteer;
For to be *Cromwell* was a greater thing, 225
Then ought below, or yet above a King:
Therefore thou rather didst thy Self depress,
Yielding to Rule, because it made thee Less.

For, neither didst thou from the first apply
Thy sober Spirit unto things too High, 230
But in thine own Fields exercisedst long,
An healthful Mind within a Body strong;
Till at the Seventh time thou in the Skyes,
As a small Cloud, like a Mans hand didst rise;
Then did thick Mists and Winds the air deform, 235
And down at last thou pow'rdst the fertile Storm;
Which to the thirsty Land did plenty bring,
But though forewarn'd, o'r-took and wet the King.

What since he did, an higher Force him push'd

Still from behind, and it before him rush'd, 240
Though undiscern'd among the tumult blind,
Who think those high Decrees by Man design'd.
'Twas Heav'n would not that his Pow'r should cease,
But walk still middle betwixt War and Peace;
Choosing each Stone, and poysing every weight, 245
Trying the Measures of the Bredth and Height;
Here pulling down, and there erecting New,
Founding a firm State by Proportions true.

    When *Gideon* so did from the War retreat,
Yet by the Conquest of two Kings grown great, 250
He on the Peace extends a Warlike power,
And *Is'rel* silent saw him rase the Tow'r;
And how he *Succoths* Elders durst suppress,
With Thorns and Briars of the Wilderness.
No King might ever such a Force have done; 255
Yet would not he be Lord, nor yet his Son.

    Thou with the same strength, and an Heart as plain,
Didst (like thine Olive) still refuse to Reign;
Though why should others all thy Labor spoil,
And Brambles be anointed with thine Oyl, 260
Whose climbing Flame, without a timely stop,
Had quickly Levell'd every Cedar's top.
Therefore first growing to thy self a Law,
Th'ambitious Shrubs thou in just time didst aw.

    So have I seen at Sea, when whirling Winds, 265
Hurry the Bark, but more the Seamens minds,
Who with mistaken Course salute the Sand,
And threat'ning Rocks misapprehend for Land;
While baleful *Tritons* to the shipwrack guide.
And Corposants along the Tacklings slide. 270
The Passengers all wearyed out before,
Giddy, and wishing for the fatal Shore;
Some lusty Mate, who with more careful Eye
Counted the Hours, and ev'ry Star did spy,
The Helm does from the artless Steersman strain, 275
And doubles back unto the safer Main.
What though a while they grumble discontent,
Saving himself he does their loss prevent.

'Tis not a Freedome, that where All command;
Nor Tyranny, where One does them withstand: 280
But who of both the Bounders knows to lay
Him as their Father must the State obey.
 Thou, and thine House, like *Noah's* Eight did rest,
Left by the Wars Flood on the Mountains crest:
And the large Vale lay subject to thy Will, 285
Which thou but as an Husbandman wouldst Till:
And only didst for others plant the Vine
Of Liberty, not drunken with its Wine.
 That sober Liberty which men may have,
That they enjoy, but more they vainly crave: 290
And such as to their Parents Tents do press,
May shew their own, not see his Nakedness.
 Yet such a *Chammish* issue still does rage,
The Shame and Plague both of the Land and Age,
Who watch'd thy halting, and thy Fall deride, 295
Rejoycing when thy Foot had slipt aside;
That their new King might the fifth Scepter shake,
And make the World, by his Example, Quake:
Whose frantique Army should they want for Men
Might muster Heresies, so one were ten. 300
What thy Misfortune, they the Spirit call,
And their Religion only is to Fall.
Oh *Mahomet*! now couldst thou rise again,
Thy Falling-sickness should have made thee Reign,
While *Feake* and *Simpson* would in many a Tome, 305
Have writ the Comments of thy sacred Foame:
For soon thou mightst have past among their Rant
Wer't but for thine unmoved Tulipant;
As thou must needs have own'd them of thy band

---

283 *Noah's Eight*: Cromwell was the father of two sons and four daughters.

291–92 *Parents Tents*: see Gen. 9, for Ham (cf. Cham, and the adjective *Chammish* of l. 293), second son of Noah, who had seen the nakedness of his father.

297 *fifth Scepter*: a reference to the fifth monarchy of Dan. 7: 17–18.

298 *make the World...Quake*: an oblique reference to the falling sickness associated with the Quakers and Mahomet (l. 303) alike.

305 *Feake* and *Simpson*: Christopher Feake and Sydrach Simpson were imprisoned in 1654 for preaching sedition against Cromwell (Mar.).

    For prophecies fit to be *Alcorand*.   310
      Accursed Locusts, whom your King does spit
Out of the Center of th'unbottom'd Pit;
Wand'rers, Adult'rers, Lyers, *Munser's* rest,
Sorcerers, Atheists, Jesuites, Possest;
You who the Scriptures and the Laws deface   315
With the same liberty as Points and Lace;
Oh Race most hypocritically strict!
Bent to reduce us to the ancient Pict;
Well may you act the *Adam* and the *Eve*;
Ay, and the Serpent too that did deceive.   320
      But the great Captain, now the danger's ore,
Makes you for his sake Tremble one fit more;
And, to your spight, returning yet alive
Does with himself all that is good revive.
      So when first Man did through the Morning new   325
See the bright Sun his shining Race pursue,
All day he follow'd with unwearied sight,
Pleas'd with that other World of moving Light;
But thought him when he miss'd his setting beams,
Sunk in the Hills, or plung'd below the Streams.   330
While dismal blacks hung round the Universe,
And Stars (like Tapers) burn'd upon his Herse:
And Owls and Ravens with their screeching noyse
Did make the Fun'rals sadder by their Joyes.
His weeping Eyes the doleful Vigils keep,   335
Not knowing yet the Night was made for sleep:
Still to the West, where he him lost, he turn'd,
And with such accents, as Despairing, mourn'd:
Why did mine Eyes once see so bright a Ray;
Or why Day last no longer then a Day?   340
When streight the Sun behind him he descry'd,
Smiling serenely from the further side.

---

313 *Munser's rest*: the residue, or sediment, of Münster, chief city of Westphalia taken over by the Anabaptists in 1634. In *The Unfortunate Traveller*, Thomas Nashe takes his gallant through that city in late Tudor times, and treats with abhorrence the sect's strange practices in abolishing law, private property, and marriage in their zeal for the Holy City. It is possible that *Munser* may also refer obliquely to Thomas Münzer, a founder of that sect.

So while our Star that gives us Light and Heat,
Seem'd now a long and gloomy Night to threat,
Up from the other World his Flame he darts, 345
And Princes shining through their windows starts;
Who their suspected Counsellors refuse,
And credulous Ambassadors accuse.

'Is this, saith one, the Nation that we read
'Spent with both Wars, under a Captain dead? 350
'Yet rig a Navy while we dress us late;
'And ere we Dine, rase and rebuild our State.
'What Oaken Forrests, and what golden Mines!
'What Mints of Men, what Union of Designes!
'Unless their Ships, do, as their Fowle proceed 355
'Of shedding Leaves, that with their Ocean breed.
'Theirs are not Ships, but rather Arks of War,
'And beaked Promontories sail'd from far;
'Of floting Islands a new Hatched Nest;
'A Fleet of Worlds, of other Worlds in quest; 360
'An hideous shole of wood-Leviathans,
'Arm'd with three Tire of brazen Hurricans;
'That through the Center shoot their thundring side
'And sink the Earth that does at Anchor ride.
'What refuge to escape them can be found, 365
'Whose watry Leaguers all the world surround?
'Needs must we all their Tributaries be,
'Whose Navies hold the Sluces of the Sea.
'The Ocean is the Fountain of Command,
'But that once took, we Captives are on Land. 370
'And those that have the Waters for their share,
'Can quickly leave us neither Earth nor Air.
'Yet if through these our Fears could find a pass;
'Through double Oak, and lin'd with treble Brass;
'That one Man still, although but nam'd, alarms 375
'More then all Men, all Navies, and all Arms.
'Him, all the Day, Him, in late Nights I dread,
'And still his Sword seems hanging o're my head.
'The Nation had been ours, but his one Soul
'Moves the great Bulk, and animates the whole. 380
'He Secrecy with Number hath inchas'd,
'Courage with Age, Maturity with Hast:

'The Valiants Terror, Riddle of the Wise;
'And still his Fauchion all our Knots unties.
'Where did he learn those Arts that cost us dear?   385
'Where below Earth, or where above the Sphere?
'He seems a King by long Succession born,
'And yet the same to be a King does scorn.
'Abroad a King he seems, and something more,
'At Home a Subject on the equal Floor.   390
'O could I once him with our Title see,
'So should I hope yet he might Dye as wee.
'But let them write his Praise that love him best,
'It grieves me sore to have thus much confest.
   Pardon, great Prince, if thus their Fear or Spight   395
More then our Love and Duty do thee Right.
I yield, nor further will the Prize contend;
So that we both alike may miss our End:
While thou thy venerable Head dost raise
As far above their Malice as my Praise.   400
And as the *Angel* of our Commonweal,
Troubling the Waters, yearly mak'st them Heal.

Two Songs at the Marriage of the Lord Fauconberg *and the Lady* Mary Cromwell

First

Chorus. Endymion. Luna.

Chorus

Th' *Astrologers* own Eyes are set,
And even Wolves the Sheep forget;
Only *this Shepheard*, late and soon,
Upon this Hill outwakes the *Moon*.
Heark how he sings, with sad delight,   5
Thorough the clear and silent Night.

384 *Fauchion*: falchion, or sword.

Endymion

Cynthia, O Cynthia, turn thine Ear,
Nor scorn *Endymions* plaints to hear.
As we our Flocks, so you command
The fleecy Clouds with silver wand.

Cynthia

If thou a *Mortal,* rather sleep;
Or if a *Shepheard,* watch thy Sheep.

Endymion

The *Shepheard,* since he saw thine Eyes,
And *Sheep* are both thy *Sacrifice.*
Nor merits he a *Mortal's* name,
That burns with an *immortal Flame.*

Cynthia

I have enough for me to do,
Ruling the Waves that Ebb and flow.

Endymion

Since thou disdain'st not then to share
On Sublunary things thy care;
Rather restrain these double Seas,
Mine Eyes uncessant deluges.

Cynthia

My wakeful Lamp all night must move,
Securing their Repose above.

Endymion

If therefore thy resplendent Ray
Can make a Night more bright then Day;
Shine thorough this obscurer Brest,
With shades of deep Despair opprest.

Chorus

Courage, *Endymion*, boldly Woo,
Anchises was a *Shepheard* too: *30*
Yet is *her younger Sister* laid
Sporting with him in *Ida's shade*:
   And *Cynthia*, though the strongest,
Seeks but the honour to have held out longest.

Endymion

Here unto *Latmos Top* I climbe: *35*
How far below thine *Orbe* sublime?
O why, as well as Eyes to see,
Have I not Armes that reach to thee?

Cynthia

'Tis needless then that I refuse,
Would you but your own Reason use.   *40*

Endymion

Though I so high may not pretend,
It is the same so you descend.

Cynthia

These Stars would say I do them wrong,
Rivals each one for thee to strong.

Endymion

The Stars are fix'd unto their *Sphere*,   *45*
And cannot, though they would, come near.
Less Loves set of each others praise,
While *Stars* Eclypse by mixing Rayes.

Cynthia

That Cave is dark.

Endymion

    Then none can spy: 50
Or shine Thou there and 'tis the Sky.

Chorus

  Joy to *Endymion*,
For he has *Cynthia's* favour won.
  And *Jove* himself approves
With his serenest influence their Loves. 55
  For he did never love to pair
  His Progeny above the Air;
  But to be honest, valiant, wise,
Makes *Mortals* matches fit for *Deityes*.

Second Song
Hobbinol. Phillis. Tomalin.

Hobbinol

Phillis, *Tomalin*, away:
Never such a merry day.
For *the Northern Shepheards Son*
Has *Menalca's daughter* won.

Phillis

Stay till I some flow'rs ha' ty'd 5
In a Garland for the Bride.

Tomalin

If thou would'st a Garland bring,
Phillis you may wait the Spring:
They ha' chosen such an hour
When *She* is the only flow'r. 10

Phillis

Let's not then at least be seen
Without each a Sprig of Green.

Hobbinol

Fear not; at *Menalca's Hall*
There is Bayes enough for all.
He when Young as we did graze,   15
But when Old he planted Bayes.

Tomalin

Here *She* comes; but with a Look
Far more catching then my Hook.
'Twas those Eyes, I now dare swear,
Led our Lambs we knew not where.   20

Hobbinol

Not our Lambs own Fleeces are
Curl'd so lovely as her Hair:
Nor our Sheep new Wash'd can be
Half so white or sweet as *She*.

Phillis

He so looks as fit to keep   25
Somewhat else then silly *Sheep*.

Hobbinol

Come, lets in some Carol new
Pay to Love and Them their due.

All

  Joy to that *happy Pair*,
Whose Hopes united banish our Despair.   30
  What *Shepheard* could for Love pretend,
Whil'st all the *Nymphs* on *Damon's* choice attend?
  What *Shepherdess* could hope to wed
  Before *Marina's* turn were sped?
    Now lesser Beauties may take place,   35
    And meaner Virtues come in play;
        While they,

                    Looking from high,
                    Shall grace
        Our Flocks and us with a propitious Eye.   *40*
          But what is most, the gentle Swain
          No more shall need of Love complain;
          But Virtue shall be Beauties hire,
        And those be equal that have equal Fire.
                Marina yields. Who dares be coy?   *45*
        Or who despair, now *Damon* does enjoy?
                    Joy to that happy Pair,
        Whose Hopes united banish our Despair.

A Poem upon the Death of O. C.

That Providence which had so long the care
Of *Cromwell's* head, and numbred ev'ry hair,
Now in its self (the Glass where all appears)
Had seen the period of his golden Years:
And thenceforth onely did attend to trace,   *5*
What death might least so fair a Life deface.
   The People, which what most they fear esteem,
Death when more horrid so more noble deem;
And blame the last *Act*, like *Spectators* vain,
Unless the *Prince* whom they applaud be slain.   *10*
Nor Fate indeed can well refuse that right
To those that liv'd in War, to dye in Fight.
   But long his *Valour* none had left that could
Indanger him, or *Clemency* that would.
And he whom Nature all for Peace had made,   *15*
But angry Heaven unto War had sway'd,
And so less useful where he most desir'd,
For what he least affected was admir'd,
Deserved yet an End whose ev'ry part
Should speak the wondrous softness of his Heart.   *20*

A Poem upon the Death of O. C. Cromwell's death on 3 September 1658 was preceded by that of his second daughter, Elizabeth, on 6 August of the same year. She had married John Claypole in 1646, and was the mother of four children. The Francisca of l. 245 is Cromwell's youngest daughter Frances. The Richard of l. 305, made protector on the day of his father's death, resigned the title in April, 1659.

To *Love* and *Grief* the fatal Writ was sign'd;
(Those nobler weaknesses of humane Mind,
From which those Powers that issu'd the Decree,
Although immortal, found they were not free.)
That they, to whom his Breast still open lyes, 25
In gentle Passions should his Death disguise:
And leave succeeding Ages cause to mourn,
As long as Grief shall weep, or Love shall burn.
   Streight does a slow and languishing Disease
Eliza, Natures and his darling, seize. 30
Her when an infant, taken with her Charms,
He oft would flourish in his mighty Arms;
And, lest their force the tender burthen wrong,
Slacken the vigour of his Muscles strong;
Then to the Mothers brest her softly move, 35
Which while she drain'd of Milk she fill'd with Love.
But as with riper Years her Virtue grew,
And ev'ry minute adds a Lustre new;
When with meridian height her Beauty shin'd,
And thorough that sparkled her fairer Mind; 40
When She with Smiles serene and Words discreet
His hidden Soul at ev'ry turn could meet;
Then might y' ha' daily his Affection spy'd,
Doubling that knot which Destiny had ty'd.
While they by sence, not knowing, comprehend 45
How on each other both their Fates depend.
With her each day the pleasing Hours he shares,
And at her Aspect calms his growing Cares;
Or with a Grandsire's joy her Children sees
Hanging about her neck or at his knees. 50
Hold fast dear Infants, hold them both or none;
This will not stay when once the other's gone.
   A silent fire now wasts those Limbs of Wax,
And him within his tortur'd Image racks.
So the Flowr with'ring which the Garden crown'd, 55
The sad Root pines in secret under ground.
Each Groan he doubled and each Sigh he sigh'd,
Repeated over to the restless Night.
No trembling String compos'd to numbers new,

Answers the touch in Notes more sad more true. 60
She lest He grieve hides what She can her pains,
And He to lessen hers his Sorrow feigns:
Yet both perceiv'd, yet both conceal'd their Skills,
And so diminishing increast their ills:
That whether by each others grief they fell, 65
Or on their own redoubled, none can tell.

   And now *Eliza's* purple Locks were shorn,
Where She so long her *Fathers* fate had worn:
And frequent lightning to her Soul that flyes,
Devides the Air, and opens all the Skyes: 70
And now his Life, suspended by her breath,
Ran out impetuously to hasting Death.
Like polish'd Mirrours, so his steely Brest
Had ev'ry figure of her woes exprest;
And with the damp of her last Gasps obscur'd, 75
Had drawn such staines as were not to be cur'd.
Fate could not either reach with single stroke,
But the dear Image fled the Mirrour broke.

   Who now shall tell us more of mournful Swans,
Of Halycons kind, or bleeding Pelicans? 80
No downy breast did ere so gently beat,
Or fan with airy plumes so soft an heat.
For he no duty by his height excus'd,
Nor though a *Prince* to be a *Man* refus'd:
But rather then in his *Eliza's* pain 85
Not love, not grieve, would neither live nor reign:
And in himself so oft immortal try'd,
Yet in compassion of another dy'd.

   So have I seen a Vine, whose lasting Age
Of many a Winter hath surviv'd the rage. 90
Under whose shady tent Men ev'ry year
At its rich bloods expence their Sorrows chear,
If some dear branch where it extends its life
Chance to be prun'd by an untimely knife,
The Parent-Tree unto the Grief succeeds, 95
And through the Wound its vital humour bleeds;
Trickling in watry drops, whose flowing shape
Weeps that it falls ere fix'd into a Grape.

So the dry Stock, no more that spreading Vine,
Frustrates the Autumn and the hopes of Wine.
    A secret Cause does sure those Signs ordain
Fore boding Princes falls, and seldom vain.
Whether some Kinder Pow'rs, that wish us well,
What they above cannot prevent, foretell;
Or the great World do by consent presage,
As hollow Seas with future Tempests rage:
Or rather Heav'n, which us so long foresees,
Their fun'rals celebrates while it decrees.
But never yet was any humane Fate
By nature solemniz'd with so much state.
He unconcern'd the dreadful passage crost;
But oh what pangs that Death did Nature cost!
First the great *Thunder* was shot off, and sent
The Signal from the starry Battlement.
The *Winds* receive it, and its force out-do,
As practising how they could thunder too:
Out of the Binders Hand the Sheaves they tore,
And thrash'd the Harvest in the airy floore;
Or of huge Trees, whose growth with his did rise,
The deep foundations open'd to the Skyes.
Then heavy *Showres* the winged Tempests lead,
And pour the Deluge ore the *Chaos* head.
The Race of warlike *Horses* at his Tomb
Offer themselves in many an *Hecatomb*;
With pensive head towards the ground they fall,
And helpless languish at the tainted Stall.
Numbers of *Men* decrease with pains unknown,
And hasten not to see his Death their own.
Such Tortures all the Elements unfix'd,
Troubled to part where so exactly mix'd.
And as through Air his wasting Spirits flow'd,
The Universe labour'd beneath their load.
    Nature it seem'd with him would Nature vye;
He with *Eliza*, It with him would dye.
    He without noise still travell'd to his End,
As silent Suns to meet the Night descend.
The *Stars* that for him fought had only pow'r

Left to determine now his fatal Hour;
Which, since they might not hinder, yet they cast
To chuse it worthy of his *Glories* past.   140
   No part of time but bore his mark away
Of honour; all the Year was *Cromwell's* day:
But this, of all the most auspicious found,
Twice had in open field him Victor crown'd:
When up the armed Mountains of *Dunbar*   145
He march'd and through deep *Severn* ending war.
What day should him *eternize* but the same
That had before *immortaliz'd* his *Name?*
That so who ere would at his Death have joy'd,
In their own Griefs might find themselves imploy'd;   150
But those that sadly his departure griev'd,
Yet joy'd remembring what he once atchiev'd.
And the last minute his victorious *Ghost*
Gave chase to *Ligny* on the *Belgick Coast*.
Here ended all his mortal toyles: He lay'd   155
And slept in Peace under the *Lawrel shade*.
   O Cromwell, Heavens Favorite! To none
Have such high honours from above been shown:
For whom the Elements we Mourners see,
And *Heav'n* it self would the great *Herald* be;   160
Which with more Care set forth his Obsequies
Then those of *Moses* hid from humane Eyes;
As jealous only here lest all be less,
That we could to his Memory express.
   Then let us to our course of Mourning keep: 165
Where *Heaven* leads, 'tis *Piety* to weep.
Stand back ye Seas, and shrunk beneath the vail
Of your Abysse, with cover'd Head bewail
Your *Monarch*: We demand not your supplies
To compass in our *Isle;* our Tears suffice;   170
Since him away the dismal Tempest rent,
Who once more Joyn'd us to the Continent;
Who planted *England* on the *Flandrick shoar*,
And stretch'd *our frontire* to the *Indian Ore;*
Whose greater *Truths* obscure the *Fables* old,   175
Whether of *Brittish Saints or Worthy's* told;

And in a valour less'ning *Arthur's* deeds,
For Holyness the *Confessor* exceeds.
   He first put Armes into *Religions* hand,
And tim'rous *Conscience* unto *Courage* man'd:
The Souldier taught that inward Mail to wear,
And *fearing God* how they should *nothing fear*.
Those Strokes he said will pierce through all below
Where those that strike from Heaven fetch their Blow.
Astonish'd armyes did their flight prepare,
And cityes strong were stormed by his prayer;
Of that for ever Preston's field shall tell
The story, and impregnable Clonmell.
And where the sandy mountain Fenwick scal'd,
The sea between, yet hence his pray'r prevail'd.
What man was ever so in Heav'n obey'd
Since the commanded sun o're Gibeon stay'd?
In all his warrs needs must he triumph, when
He conquer'd God, still ere he fought with men:
Hence, though in battle none so brave or fierce,
Yet him the adverse steel could never pierce.
Pity it seem'd to hurt him more that felt
Each wound himself which he to others delt;
Danger itself refusing to offend
So loose an enemy, so fast a friend.
Friendship, that sacred virtue, long does claime
The first foundation of his house and name:
But within one its narrow limits fall,
His tendernesse extended unto all.
And that deep soule through every channell flows,
Where kindly nature loves itself to lose.
More strong affections never reason serv'd,
Yet still affected most what best deserv'd.
If he Eliza lov'd to that degree,
(Though who more worthy to be lov'd than she?)
If so indulgent to his own, how deare
To him the children of the Highest were?
For her he once did nature's tribute pay:
For these his life adventur'd every day:
And 'twould be found, could we his thoughts have cast,

Their griefs struck deepest, if Eliza's last.
What prudence more than humane did he need
To keepe so deare, so diff'ring minds agreed?
The worser sort, so conscious of their ill,
Lye weak and easy to the ruler's will;
But to the good (too many or too few)
All law is uselesse, all reward is due.
Oh! ill advis'd, if not for love, for shame,
Spare yet your own, if you neglect his fame;
Least others dare to think your zeale a maske,
And you to govern only Heaven's taske.
Valour, religion, friendship, prudence dy'd
At once with him, and all that's good beside;
And we death's refuse nature's dregs confin'd
To loathsome life, alas! are left behind.
Where we (so once we us'd) shall now no more,
To fetch day, presse about his chamber-door;
From which he issu'd with that awfull state,
It seem'd Mars broke through Janus' double gate;
Yet always temper'd with an aire so mild,
No April sunns that e'er so gently smil'd;
No more shall heare that powerful language charm,
Whose force oft spar'd the labour of his arm:
No more shall follow where he spent the dayes
In warre, in counsell, or in pray'r, and praise;
Whose meanest acts he would himself advance,
As ungirt David to the arke did dance.
All, all is gone of ours or his delight
In horses fierce, wild deer, or armour bright;
Francisca faire can nothing now but weep,
Nor with soft notes shall sing his cares asleep.

   I saw him dead, a leaden slumber lyes,
And mortal sleep over those wakefull eyes:
Those gentle rays under the lids were fled,
Which through his looks that piercing sweetnesse shed;
That port which so majestique was and strong,
Loose and depriv'd of vigour, stretch'd along:
All wither'd, all discolour'd, pale and wan,

How much another thing, no more that man?
Oh! humane glory, vaine, oh! death, oh! wings,   255
Oh! worthlesse world! oh transitory things!
Yet dwelt that greatnesse in his shape decay'd,
That still though dead, greater than death he lay'd;
And in his alter'd face you something faigne
That threatens death, he yet will live again.   260
Not much unlike the sacred oak, which shoots
To Heav'n its branches, and through earth its roots:
Whose spacious boughs are hung with trophies round,
And honour'd wreaths have oft the victour crown'd.
When angry Jove darts lightning through the aire,   265
At mortalls sins, nor his own plant will spare;
(It groanes, and bruises all below that stood
So many yeares the shelter of the wood.)
The tree ere while foreshortned to our view,
When fall'n shews taller yet than as it grew: 270
So shall his praise to after times encrease,
When truth shall be allow'd, and faction cease,
And his own shadows with him fall; the eye
Detracts from objects than itself more high:
But when death takes them from that envy'd state,   275
Seeing how little we confess, how greate,
Thee, many ages hence, in martial verse
Shall th'English souldier, ere he charge, rehearse;
Singing of thee, inflame themselves to fight,
And with the name of Cromwell, armyes fright.   280
As long as rivers to the seas shall runne,
As long as Cynthia shall relieve the sunne,
While staggs shall fly unto the forests thick,
While sheep delight the grassy downs to pick,
As long as future time succeeds the past,   285
Always thy honour, praise and name, shall last.

   Thou in a pitch how farre beyond the sphere
Of humane glory tow'rst, and raigning there
Despoyl'd of mortall robes, in seas of blisse,
Plunging dost bathe and tread the bright abysse: 290
There thy great soule yet once a world does see,

Spacious enough, and pure enough for thee.
How soon thou Moses hast, and Joshua found,
And David, for the sword and harpe renown'd;
How streight canst to each happy mansion goe? 295
(Farr better known above than here below;)
And in those joyes dost spend the endlesse day,
Which in expressing, we ourselves betray.

    For we, since thou art gone, with heavy doome,
Wander like ghosts about thy loved tombe; 300
And lost in tears, have neither sight nor mind
To guide us upward through this region blinde.
Since thou art gone, who best that way could'st teach,
Onely our sighs, perhaps, may thither reach.

    And Richard yet, where his great parent led, 305
Beats on the rugged track: he, vertue dead,
Revives; and by his milder beams assures;
And yet how much of them his griefe obscures.
He, as his father, long was kept from sight
In private, to be view'd by better light; 310
But open'd once, what splendour does he throw?
A Cromwell in an houre a prince will grow.
How he becomes that seat, how strongly streigns,
How gently winds at once the ruling reins?
Heav'n to this choice prepar'd a diadem, 315
Richer than any eastern silk, or gemme;
A pearly rainbow, where the sun inchas'd
His brows, like an imperiall jewell grac'd.

    We find already what those omens mean,
Earth ne'er more glad, nor Heaven more serene. 320
Cease now our griefs, calme peace succeeds a war,
Rainbows to storms, Richard to Oliver.
Tempt not his clemency to try his pow'r,
He threats no deluge, yet foretells a showre.

To his Noble Friend Mr. Richard Lovelace, upon his Poems.

Sir,
    Our times are much degenerate from those
Which your sweet Muse which your fair Fortune chose,
And as complexions alter with the Climes,
Our wits have drawne th'infection of our times.
That candid Age no other way could tell   5
To be ingenious, but by speaking well.
Who best could prayse, had then the greatest prayse,
Twas more esteemed to give, then weare the Bayes:
Modest ambition studi'd only then,
To honour not her selfe, but worthy men.   10
These vertues now are banisht out of Towne,
Our Civill Wars have lost the Civicke crowne.
He highest builds, who with most Art destroys,
And against others Fame his owne employs.
I see the envious Caterpillar sit   15
On the faire blossome of each growing wit.
    The Ayre's already tainted with the swarms
Of Insects which against you rise in arms.
Word-peckers, Paper-rats, Book-scorpions,
Of wit corrupted, the unfashion'd Sons.   20
The barbed Censurers begin to looke
Like the grim consistory on thy Booke;
And on each line cast a reforming eye,
Severer then the young Presbytery.
Till when in vaine they have thee all perus'd,   25
You shall for being faultlesse be accus'd.
    Some reading your *Lucasta*, will alledge
You wrong'd in her the Houses Priviledge.
Some that you under sequestration are,

To ... Lovelace, upon his Poems.   12 *Civicke crowne*: a garland of oak leaves and acorns, bestowed upon a soldier who had saved the life of a citizen in battle.
  21–22 The Printing Ordinance of June, 1643, against unlicensed books, which prompted Milton's *Areopagitica* of November, 1644, was in force (Mac.).
  28 *wrong'd*: abused (Mar.); *Houses Priviledge*: that of free speech (Mar.).

Because you write when going to the Warre, 30
And one the Book prohibits, because *Kent*
Their first Petition by the Authour sent.
   But when the beauteous Ladies came to know
That their deare *Lovelace* was endanger'd so:
Lovelace that thaw'd the most congealed brest, 35
He who lov'd best and them defended best.
Whose hand so rudely grasps the steely brand,
Whose hand so gently melts the Ladies hand.
They all in mutiny though yet undrest
Sally'd and would in his defence contest. 40
And one the loveliest that was yet e're seen,
Thinking that I too of the rout had been,
Mine eyes invaded with a female spight
(She knew what pain 'twould be to lose that sight.)
O no, mistake not, I reply'd, for I 45
In your defence, or in his cause would dy.
But he secure of glory and of time
Above their envy, or mine aid doth clime.
Him, valianst men, and fairest Nymphs approve,
His Booke in them finds Judgement, with you Love. 50
                        Andr. Marvell

Upon the Death of the Lord Hastings

Go, intercept some Fountain in the Vain,
Whose Virgin-source yet never steept the Plain.
Hastings is dead, and we must finde a store
Of Tears untoucht, and never wept before.
Go, stand betwixt the *Morning* and the *Flowers*; 5

---

30 Reference to Lovelace's famous song "To Lucasta, Going to the Wars."
33 Lovelace, who presented the Kentish petition in support of the king to the House on 30 April 1642, was imprisoned (Mar.).
Upon the Death of the Lord Hastings. One of several verses commemorating the young nobleman's death on 24 June 1649, of smallpox. The eldest son of Ferdinando, sixth Earl of Huntington, he was to have married on the following day the daughter of Sir Theodore Turquet de Mayerne, physician to the king (Mar.).

And, ere they fall, arrest the early *Showers*.
Hastings is dead; and we, disconsolate,
With early *Tears* must morn his early *Fate*.
    Alas, his *Vertues* did his *Death* presage:
Needs must he die, that doth out-run his *Age*.   10
The Phlegmatick and Slowe prolongs his day,
And on Times Wheel sticks like a *Remora*.
What man is he, that hath not *Heaven* beguil'd,
And is not thence mistaken for a *Child?*
While those of growth more sudden, and more bold,   15
Are hurried hence, as if already old.
For, there above, They number not as here,
But weigh to Man the *Geometrick* yeer.
    Had he but at this Measure still increast,
And on *the Tree of Life* once made a Feast,   20
As that of *Knowledge*; what Loves had he given
To Earth, and then what Jealousies to Heaven!
But 'tis a *Maxime* of that State, That none,
Therefore the *Democratick* Stars did rise,
And all that Worth from hence did *Ostracize*.   25
    Yet as some *Prince*, that, for State Jealousie,
Secures his neerest and most lov'd *Ally*;
His Thought with richest Triumphs entertains,
And in the choicest Pleasures charms his Pains:
So he, not banisht hence, but there confin'd,   30
There better recreates his active Minde.
    Before the *Chrystal Palace* where he dwells,
The armed *Angels* hold their Carouzels;
And underneath, he views the *Turnaments*
Of all these Sublunary *Elements*.   35
But most he doth th'*Eternal Book* behold,
On which the *happy Names* do stand enroll'd;
And gladly there can all his Kindred claim,
But most rejoyces at his *Mothers* name.

---

12 *Remora*: a fish which adheres to other large fishes and to vessels by means of a suctorial disk. The ancients believed it capable of checking or stopping vessels.

18 *Geometrick yeer*: heavenly justice is weighed in geometric proportion (Mac.).

  The gods themselves cannot their Joy conceal,   40
But draw their veils, and their pure Beams reveal:
Onely they drooping *Hymeneus* note,
Who for sad *Purple*, tears his *Saffron*-coat;
And trails his Torches th'row the Starry Hall
Reversed, at his *Darlings* Funeral.   45
  And *Æsculapius*, who, asham'd and stern,
Himself at once condemneth, and *Mayern*;
Like some sad *Chymist*, who, prepar'd to reap
The *Golden Harvest*, sees his Glasses leap.
For, how Immortal must their race have stood,   50
Had *Mayern* once been mixt with *Hastings* blood!
How sweet and Verdant would these *Lawrels* be,
Had they been planted on that *Balsam*-tree!
  But what could he, a good man, although he bruis'd
All Herbs, and them a thousand ways infus'd?   55
All he had try'd, but all in vain, he saw,
And wept, as we, without Redress or Law.
For *Man* (alas) is but the *Heavens* sport;
And *Art* indeed is Long, but *Life* is Short.
        Andrew Marvel   60

An Elegy upon the Death of my Lord Francis Villiers

Tis true that he is dead: but yet to chuse,
Methinkes thou Fame should not have brought the news
Thou canst discourse at will and speak at large:
But wast not in the fight nor durst thou charge.
While he transported all with valiant rage   5
His Name eternizd, but cut short his age;
On the safe battlements of Richmonds bowers
Thou was espyd, and from the guilded Towers

An Elegy upon...Villiers. Born on 2 April 1629, Lord Francis Villiers, the posthumous son of the first Duke of Buckingham, met his death on the field of battle on 7 July 1648.

Thy silver Trumpets sounded a Retreat,
Farre from the dust and battails sulphry heat.   *10*
Yet what couldst thou have done? 'tis alwayes late
To struggle with inevitable fate.
Much rather thou I know expectst to tell
How heavy *Cromwell* gnasht the earth and fell.
Or how slow Death farre from the sight of day   *15*
The long-deceived *Fairfax* bore away.
But untill then, let us young *Francis* praise:
And plant upon his hearse the bloody bayes,
Which we will water with our welling eyes.
Teares spring not still from spungy Cowardize.   *20*
The purer fountains from the Rocks more steep
Destill and stony valour best doth weep.
Besides Revenge, if often quencht in teares,
Hardens like Steele and daily keener weares.
    Great *Buckingham*, whose death doth freshly strike   *25*
Our memoryes, because to this so like;
Ere that in the Eternal Court he shone,
And here a Favorite there found a throne;
The fatall night before he hence did bleed,
Left to his *Princess* this immortal seed.   *30*
As the wise *Chinese* in the fertile wombe
Of Earth doth a more precious clay entombe,
Which dying by his will he leaves consignd:
Till by mature delay of time refind
The christall metall fit to be releast   *35*
Is taken forth to crowne each royal feast:
Such was the fate by which this Postume breathd
Who scarcely seems begotten but bequeathd.
    Never was any humane plant that grew
More faire then this and acceptably new.   *40*
'Tis truth that beauty doth most men dispraise:
Prudence and valour their esteeme do raise.
But he that hath already these in store,
Can not be poorer sure for having more.
And his unimitable handsomenesse   *45*
Made him indeed be more then man, not lesse.
We do but faintly Gods resemblance beare

And like rough coyns of carelesse mints appeare:
But he of purpose made, did represent
In a rich Medall every lineament.   50
    Lovely and admirable as he was,
Yet was his Sword or Armour all his Glasse.
Nor in his Mistris eyes that joy he tooke,
As in an Enemies himselfe to looke.
I know how well he did, with what delight   55
Those serious imitations of fight.
Still in the trialls of strong exercise
His was the first, and his the second prize.
    Bright Lady, thou that rulest from above
The last and greatest Monarchy of Love: 60
Faire *Richmond* hold thy Brother or he goes.
Try if the Jasmin of thy hand or Rose
Of thy red Lip can keep him alwayes here.
For he loves danger and doth never feare.
Or may thy tears prevaile with him to stay?   65
But he resolv'd breaks carelesly away.
Onely one argument could now prolong
His stay and that most faire and so most strong:
The matchlesse *Chlora* whose pure fires did warm
His soule and only could his passions charme.   70
    You might with much more reason go reprove
The amorous Magnet which the North doth love.
Or preach divorce and say it is amisse
That with tall Elms the twining Vines should kisse:
Then chide two such so fit, so equall faire   75
That in the world they have no other paire.
Whom it might seeme that Heaven did create
To restore man unto his first estate.
Yet she for honours tyrannous respect
Her own desires did and his neglect.   80
And like the Modest Plant at every touch
Shrunk in her leaves and feard it was too much.

  61 Mary Villiers became the wife of James Stuart, fourth Duke of Lennox and first Duke of Richmond (Mar.).

But who can paint the torments and that pain
Which he profest and now she could not faigne?
He like the Sun but overcast and pale: 85
Shee like a Rainbow, that ere long must faile,
Whose rosiall cheek where Heaven it selfe did view
Begins to separate and dissolve to dew.
   At last he leave obtaines though sad and slow,
First of her and then of himselfe to goe. 90
How comely and how terrible he sits
At once and Warre as well as Love befits!
Ride where thou wilt and bold adventures find:
But all the Ladies are got up behind.
Guard them, though not thy selfe: for in thy death 95
Th'Eleven thousand Virgins lose their breath.
   So *Hector* issuing from the Trojan wall
The sad *Iliades* to the Gods did call
With hands displayed and with dishevell'd haire
That they the Empire in his life would spare. 100
While he secure through all the field doth spy
Achilles for *Achilles* only cry.
Ah ignorant that yet e're night he must
Be drawn by him inglorious through the dust.
   Such fell young *Villiers* in the chearfull heat 105
Of youth: his locks intangled all with sweat
And those eyes which the Sentinell did keep
Of love closed up in an eternall sleep.
While *Venus* of *Adonis* thinks no more
Slaine by the harsh tuske of the Savage Boare. 110
Hither she runns and hath him hurried farre
Out of the noise and blood, and killing warre:
Where in her Gardens of Sweet myrtle laid,
She kisses him in the immortall shade.
   Yet dyed he not revengelesse: Much he did 115
Ere he could suffer. A whole Pyramid
Of Vulgar bodies he erected high:
Scorning without a Sepulcher to dye.
And with his steele which did whole troops divide
He cut his Epitaph on either Side 120

Till finding nothing to his courage fit
He rid up last to death and conquer'd it.
   Such are the Obsequies to *Francis* own:
He best the pompe of his owne death hath showne.
And we hereafter to his honour will   125
Not write so many, but so many kill.
Till the whole Army by just vengeance come
To be at once his Trophee and his Tombe.

Appendix

Music Settings

Nicholas Lanier (reproduced by permission)

The selection of music settings of songs and lyrics transcribed in the following pages has been determined largely by a desire for representativeness—of poets, of composers, of types of setting—and for music contemporaneous with the verse to insure that a like aesthetic has guided both composer and poet. Throughout the centuries the makers of song have demonstrated through their creations that sometimes musical values have been of primary importance, and that sometimes, conversely, poetical considerations have played the dominant role. In only a very few periods of English song have the two arts been joined together in a relationship which displays the nicest balance—and the late sixteenth and early seventeenth centuries provide the best examples. Hearing the settings makes clear the significance of this joint relationship; examining them further leads to the consideration of ways of deepening an appreciation of them.

One approach to the study of music and poetry is to uncover some artistic principle which, more likely subconsciously than consciously, seems to have motivated both composer and poet in the process of creation. For example, Vincent Duckles, in "John Jenkins's Settings of Lyrics by George Herbert" (*The Musical Quarterly*, xlviii, 1962), has shown how both engage in "a kind of willful distortion of meaning that comes from forcing the familiar into strange contexts," and that in the music "tension comes from the wide-ranging melodic lines, from the abrupt speech rhythms, and from the rather loose-knit imitation." Since the composer's work virtually always follows the poet's and is a kind of commentary upon it (at least in a sophisticated tradition), Calvin S. Brown proceeds, in the central chapters of *Music and Literature: A Comparison of the Arts* (Athens, Georgia, 1948), to distinguish between a literal setting of a text and a dramatic setting of a text. The former he treats as one which "seizes on all words which are capable of musical imitation and exploits their possibilities," and the latter as one which "pays little attention to single words or ideas" but which "considers them in context and aims at suggesting or reinforcing the dramatic elements of the total situation." Obviously, since the work of song-writers is seldom mated with that of poets in such extreme polarities, much of the pleasure and profit of utilizing this approach in analysis lies in observing the varying mixtures of the two. More specifically literary in its ends, since it aims to show how existing music, or a music tradition, may condition verse, is that portion of Bertrand H. Bronson's essay on literature and music in *Relations of Literary Study: Essays on Interdisciplinary Contributions* (edited by James Thorpe for the Modern Language Association of America, New York, 1967) which deals perceptively with Herrick's stanzaic forms. Finding the poet "a tireless and delicate experimenter" with the straight ballad meter, he conjectures that "Herrick, for all his fastidious classicism, was in familiar touch with the popular singing tradition."

A more traditional approach, since its emphasis is historical, is to link English developments in music with continental movements, and in keeping with this concern, Nigel Fortune, in his chapter on the renaissance solo song included in *The New Oxford History of Music* (volume iv, London, 1968), shows the precise way in which a figure like Ferrabosco, in setting a Donne lyric, assimilates features of the new Caccinian *arioso* style. One can also trace genres of song, as Ian Spink has done, in centering his attention on one type of song in "English Seventeenth-Century Dialogues" (*Music & Letters*, xxxviii, 1957), to demonstrate how its development inevitably led to and sustained a dramatic kind of recitative writing. Or one can focus on the artistic achievements of a single composer, as McDonald Emslie has done in "Nicholas Lanier's Innovations in English Song" (*Music & Letters*, xli, 1960). In this article he traces the contributions of a figure of no little eminence in the evolution of the English declamatory song, a type quite different from the lutenist ayre of Jacobean times, whose "voice-line, like that of a recitative but to a less degree, models itself on the time-movement, and to a certain extent the pitch-movement that the words would have if given spoken declamation."

Less historical and more analytical in nature is Eric Ford Hart's procedure in "Introduction to Henry Lawes" (*Music & Letters*, xxxii, 1952). Hart shows how the composer made use of the principal song forms of midcentury, the declamatory song (either strophic or "through-composed"), the "ballad," the glee, the catch, and the dialogue; and then having noted Lawes's predilection for the first of these, he demonstrates how he exploited to the full "the emotional effects of major and minor tonality, of modulation, of musical form (e.g., in alternating recitative and air movements), and of powerful diatonic or chromatic harmony." Emphasizing the rhetorical nature of his declamation, Hart shows further how the composer used rests dramatically, stressed words by setting them to long or high notes (and sometimes both), and constantly concerned himself with making syntactic relationships of the text comprehensible. He points out that Lawes's capacity for capturing speech-rhythms in his music is clearly indicated in his revisions of his songs; viewed first in manuscript and then in their printed texts, they show again and again his meticulousness in his second thoughts on stress and its problems.

Since it often is valuable to see ditties in the aggregate in order to analyze the precise nature of the verses which possess settings (as opposed to those merely intended for settings), three anthologies of words alone, with informative introductions and annotations, are indispensable: E. H. Fellowes's *Madrigal Verse, 1588–1632,* first published in 1920, but revised and amplified in a third edition by F. W. Sternfeld with David Greer (London, 1967, and New York, 1968); J. P. Cutts's *Seventeenth Century Songs and Lyrics* (Columbia, Missouri, 1959); and Edward Doughtie's *Lyrics from English Airs, 1596–1622* (Cambridge, Massachusetts, 1970). It is similarly useful to view music settings of the same class in song anthologies. For the sophisticated tradition the collection entitled *Poèmes de Donne, Herbert et Crashaw mis en musique par leurs contemporains* (Paris, 1961) is especially valuable for showing how its editors, André Souris and Jean Jacquot, have met the problems of presenting fully realized accompaniments in a suitable style for songs which survive only in *cantus* and *bassus* parts. For the popular tradition Claude M. Simpson's *British Broadside Ballad and its Music* (New Brunswick, N.J., 1966) provides a compendium of tunes of the period to which ditties could be framed, for on some occasions a traditional tune or a well-known meter was in the poet's mind as he wrote his verse.

For readers interested in a still more comprehensive treatment of the secular art-song, with both historical depth and geographical breadth, a full and compact survey is available in *A History of Song* (London, 1960); Denis Stevens, editing the contributions of several specialists, supplies the chapter on the renaissance. A recent issue of *Comparative Literature* devoted to the interdependence of literature and music (xxii, No. 2, 1970) includes a summary article by C. S. Brown which resurveys the field and leads an ample gathering of articles exploring various aspects of the two arts.

The lyrics as transcribed in the following pages have no independent authority to justify their frequent departures from the received text as printed without the music. Their variant readings are largely to be interpreted either as composers' modifications for their own musical purposes or as scribal idiosyncrasies. The old spelling is preserved in the lyrics accompanying the music, but the punctuation, virtually nonexistent in those items transcribed from manuscript, is silently supplied by the editor.

1. Send home my long strayde eies*

John Donne   [Giovanni] Coprario
                                         [c. 1575-1626]

Send home my long strayde eies to mee, which O, which O, to[o] longe have dwelt on thee, and if they

*Tenbury MS 1019, f.1ᵛ.   Full text: page 50.

1214

theare have learnt such ill, such false fash-ions and forst pas-sions that they bee made by thee fitt for no good

1215

sight, keepe them still.

2. Goe and catch a fallinge star*

John Donne   Anon.

Goe and catch a fall-inge star, gett with child a

[Lute]

Man-drake Roote, tell me where all past tymes are,

*Brit. Mus. Egerton MS 2013, f. 58ᵛ.   Full text: page 22.

1216

or who clefte the Divells foote, teach me to heare Mer-maydes sing-inge or to keepe off En-vyes sting-inge, And find what winde serves to ad-

1217

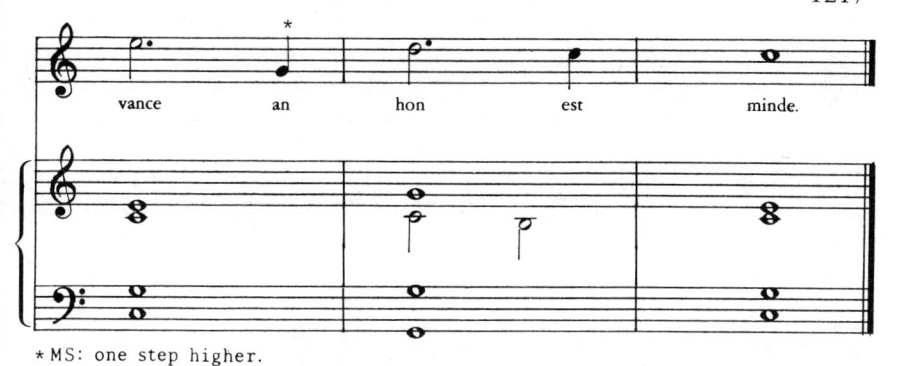

vance an honest minde.

* MS: one step higher.

3. Deerest love, I doe not goe*

John Donne   Anon.

Deer-est love, I doe not goe, for wear-i-nes of thee, or that all the world can show a fit-ter love for mee;

*Tenbury MS 1018.   Full text: pages 30–31.

1218

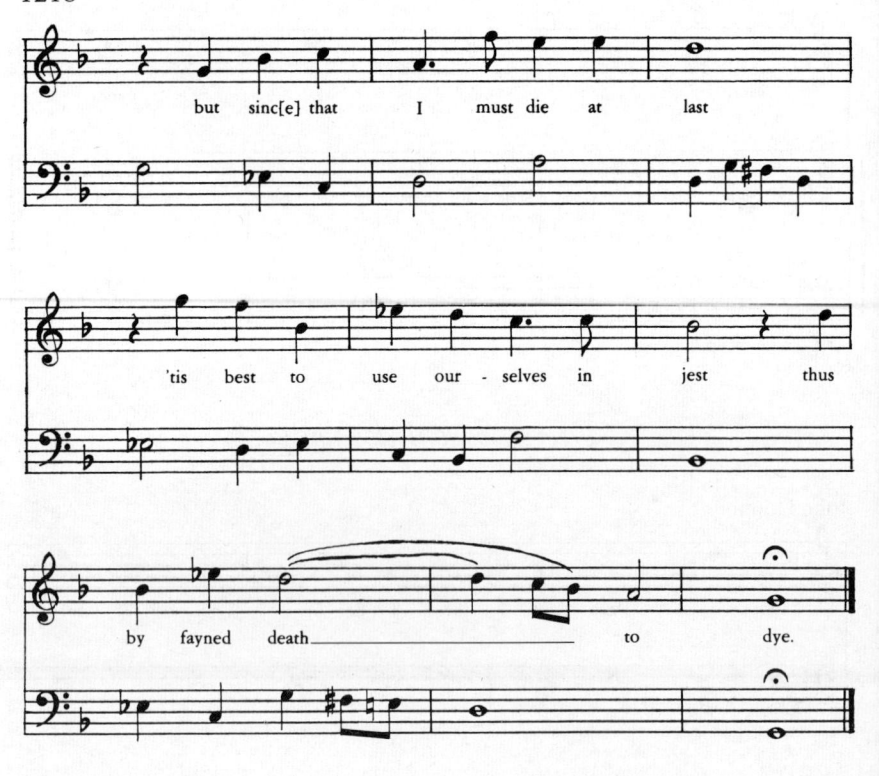

but sinc[e] that I must die at last

'tis best to use our-selves in jest thus

by fayned death to dye.

4. *So, so, leave off* *

John Donne Anon.

So, so, leave off this last la-ment-ing

[Lute]

*Oxford, Bod. MS Mus. Sch. f.575, f.8ᵛ.   Full text: page 71.

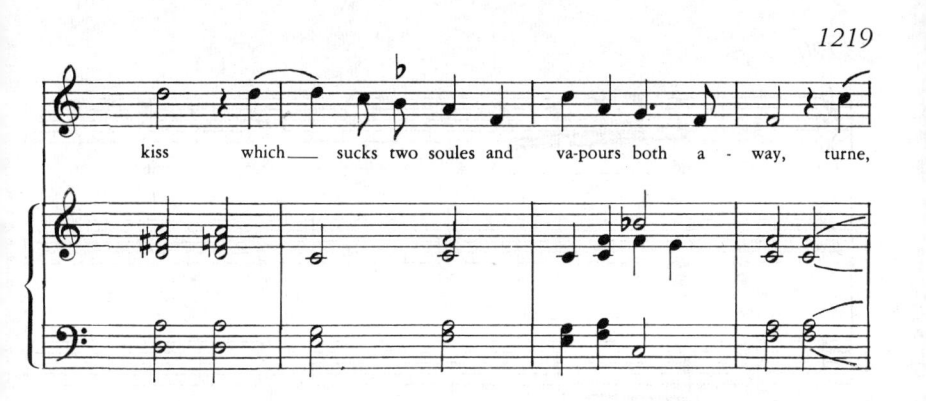

kiss which sucks two soules and va-pours both a - way, turne, thou ghost, that way and let mee turne this and let our- selves be-night our hap - py day. Wee ask no leave to

1220

love nor will wee owe any so cheap a death as saying goe.

5. Wilt thou forgive the sinne*

John Donne
John Hilton
[c. 1599–1657]

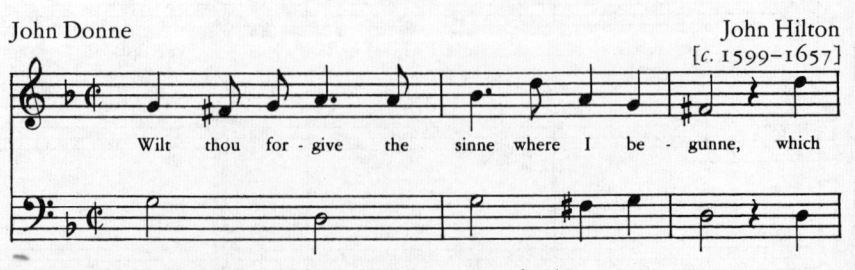

Wilt thou for-give the sinne where I be-gunne, which

*Brit. Mus. Egerton MS 2013, f.13ʳ.   Full text: pages 168–69.

is my sinne though it were done be-fore?

Wilt thou for-give those sinnes through which I runne, And doe them still, though still I doe de-plore?

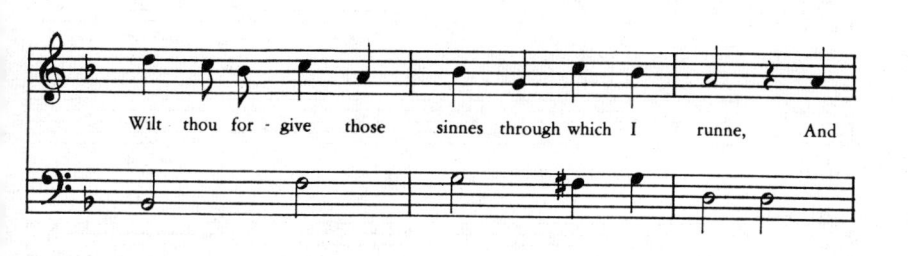

When thou hast done, thou hast not done, for I have more.

6. Lord, when the sense of thie sweet grace*

Richard Crashaw
Anon.

Lord, when the sense of thie sweet grace sends up my soul to see thie face, thy bless-ed eyes breed such de-sire, I dy in Loves de-li-cious fire. O Love, I am thy sac-ri-fice; be still tri-um-phant, bless-ed Eyes:

*Oxford, Bod. MS Doncaster C57, p. 68. Full text: pages 720–21.

still shine on me, faire Suns, that I may still be-hold though still I dy. Though still I dye I live a-gaine; still long-ing to be still so slayne, so gain-full is such losse of breath, I dye evn in de-sire of death. O wel-come high and

1224

Heaven-ly art of life and death in one poore heart, for while thou sweet-ly slay'st me dead to my-self, I live in thee.

7. Bright spark*

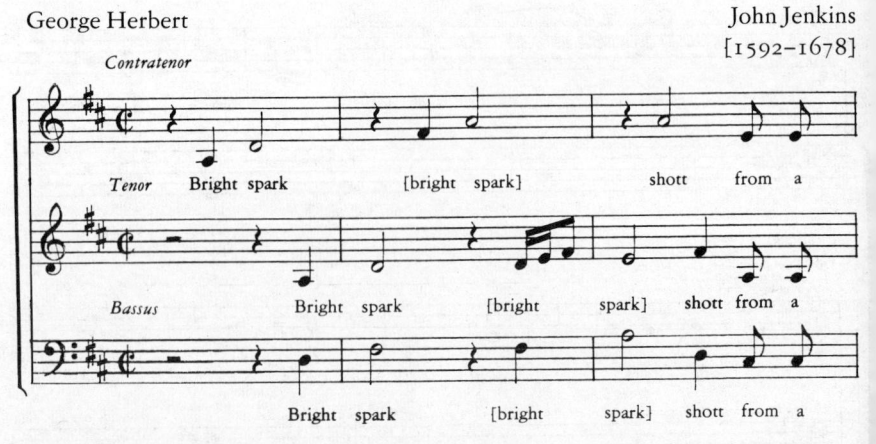

George Herbert   John Jenkins
                                [1592–1678]

Contratenor

Tenor Bright spark [bright spark] shott from a

Bassus Bright spark [bright spark] shott from a

Bright spark [bright spark] shott from a

*Oxford, Christ Church MSS 736–38, No. 18. Full text: pages 254–55.

1225

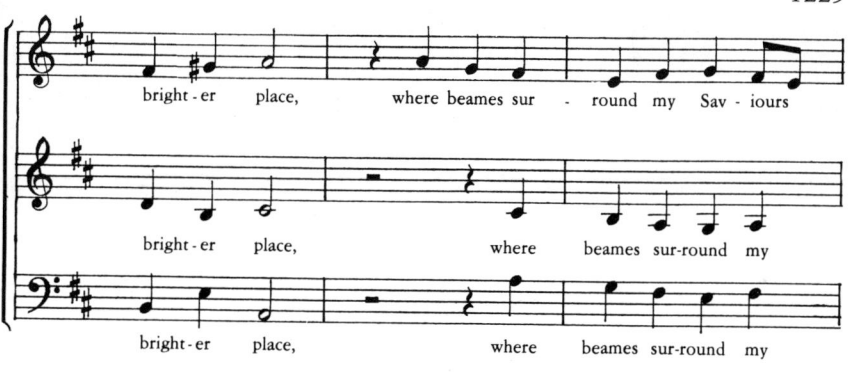

brighter place, where beames surround my Saviours face; Canst thou be any where so well as there; so well as there? yet if thou wilt from

1226

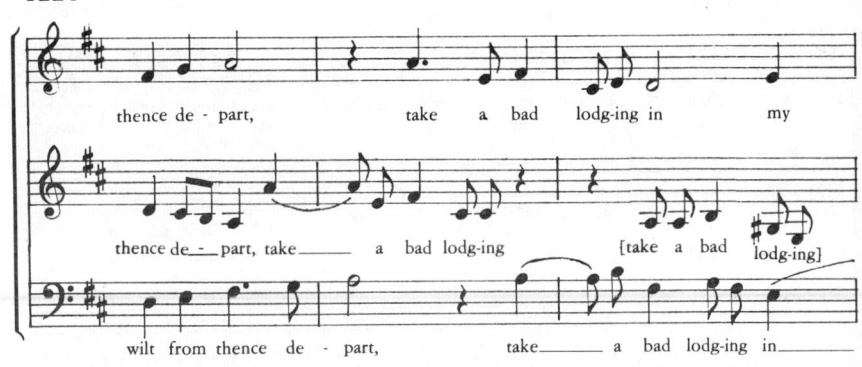

1227

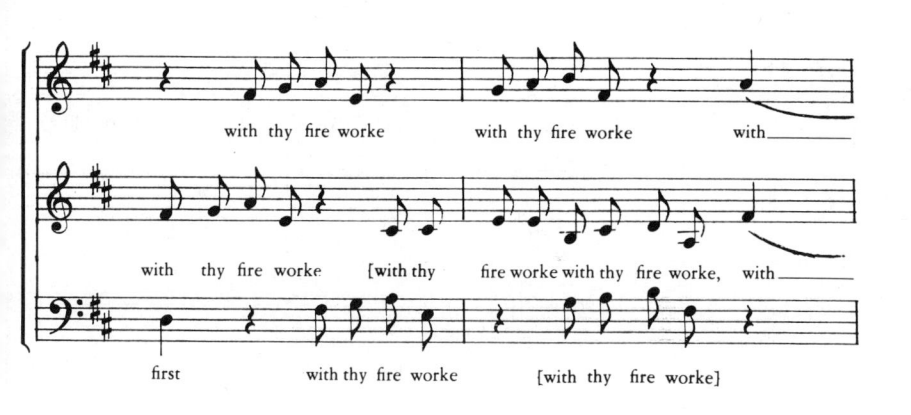

1228

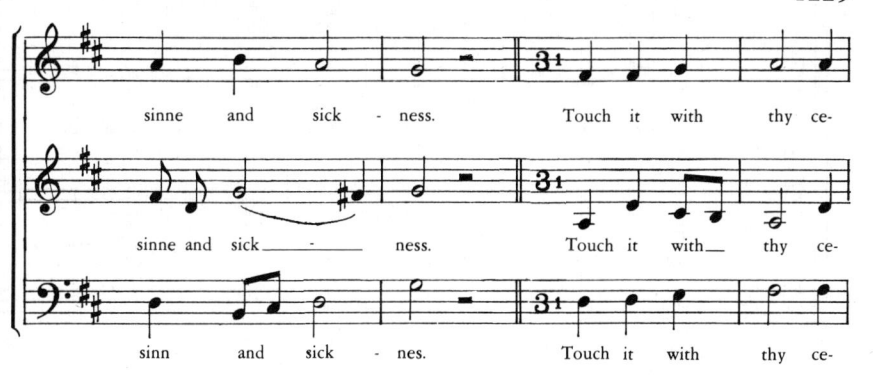

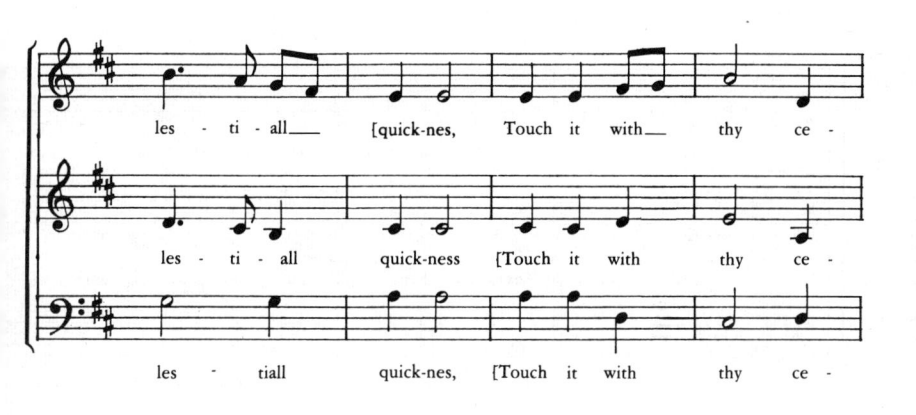

sinne and sick-ness. Touch it with thy ce-
sinne and sick — ness. Touch it with thy ce-
sinn and sick — nes. Touch it with thy ce-

les - ti - all [quick-nes, Touch it with thy ce-
les - ti - all quick-ness [Touch it with thy ce-
les - tiall quick-nes, [Touch it with thy ce-

les - tiall quick-nes] that it may hang and move
les - tiall quick-nes] that it may
les - tiall quick-nes] that it may hang and

1230

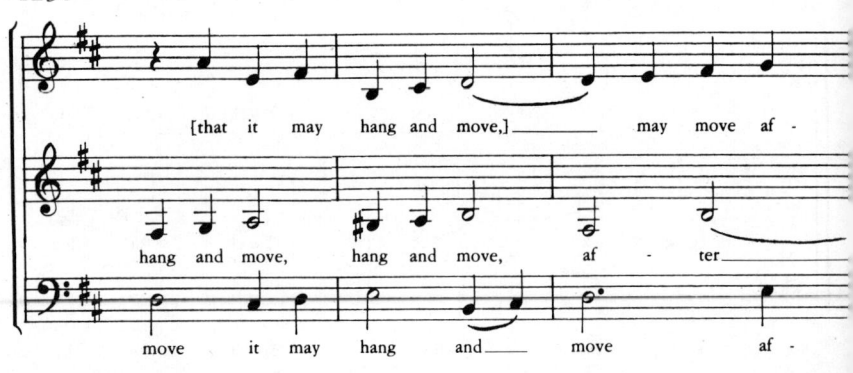

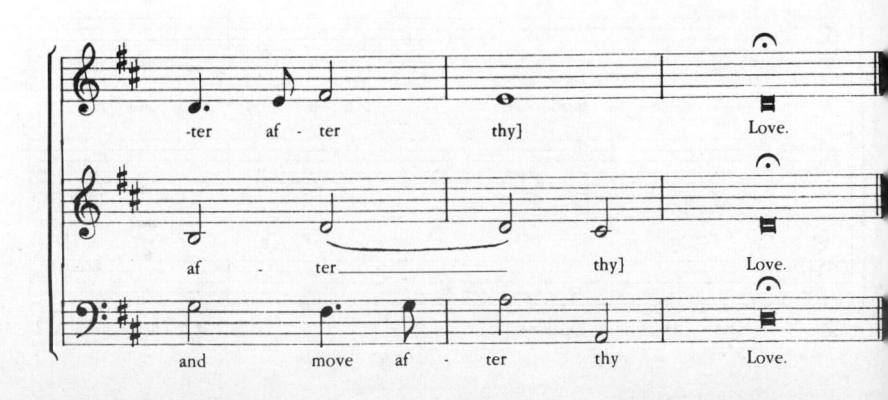

8. See, O see, who is heere come a Maying*

Ben Jonson

Martin Peerson
[c. 1572–1657]

*Martin Peerson, *Private Musick...fit for Voyces and Viols* (1620), No. XXIII. Full text: page 898.

1232

see, who is heere, who [is heere] come a May-ing, And

see, who is here, come a May-ing, The Master of the Ocean,

see, who is heere come a May-ing,

see

see,

1233

1234

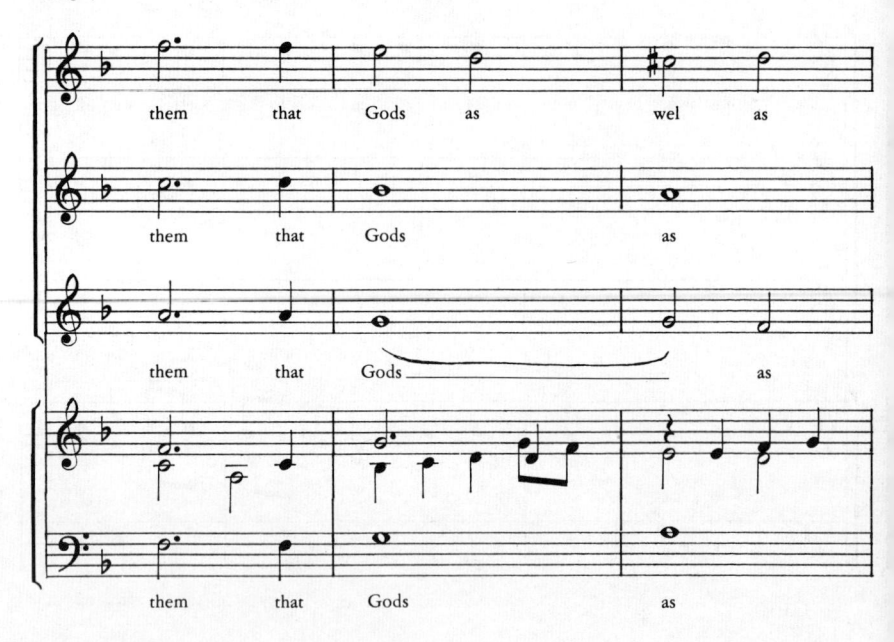

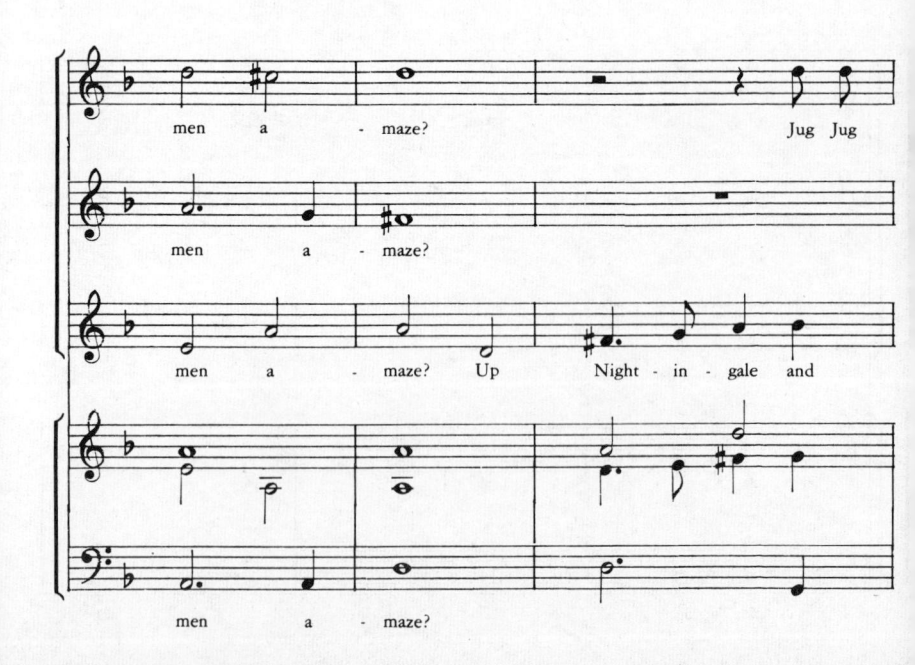

Jug, Jug Jug Jug, Jug Jug Jug,

Jug, Jug, Jug, Jug, Jug, Jug,

sing, Jug, Jug, Jug, Jug, Jug, Jug,

Jug Jug, Jug Jug,

Lark, raise thy note, _____ thy note _____ and

Thy note _____ and

1236

1237

1238

like were nev-er seen for good and faire

like were nev-er seene for good and faire, nor

like was nev-er seene for good and faire,

like was nev-er seene for good and faire,

Nor can be though fresh

can be, nor can be though fresh

Nor can be though fresh

though fresh

May should ev - ery day, should ev - ery day,
May should ev - ery day, should ev - ery day
May should ev - ery day, should ev - ery day in-
May should ev - ery day, should ev - ery day
in - vite a sev-erall payre, a sev - erall
in - vite a sev - erall payre, in - vite a sev- erall
-vite a sev - erall paire, in - vite a sev-erall, sev - erall

1240

9. O the Joyes that soone should wast*

Ben Jonson
[Nathaniel Giles]
[c. 1558–1633]

*Oxford, Christ Church MS 439, pp. 38–9. Full text: pages 889–90.

1242

tast
[weare I to tast]
such an - oth - er
[such an - oth - er
such an - oth - er]
it would be my
wissh-inge
that I might dye
that [I might
dye]
kiss-inge.

10. Yf I freely may discover*

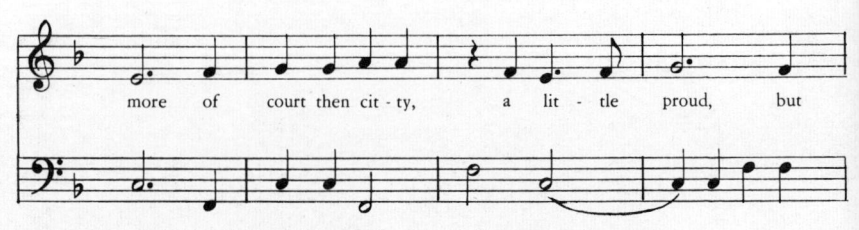

Ben Jonson   Anon.

Yf I free-ly may dis-cov-er what would please_ mee in my lov-er: I would have her faire and wit-ty, sav-ouring more of court then cit-ty, a lit-tle proud, but

*Brit. Mus. Additional MS 24665, pp. 62, 60.   Full text: page 893.

full of pit-ty, light and am-o-rous in her toy-ing, oft build-ing hopes, and soone dis-troy-ing, long but sweet in her en-joy-ing nei-ther too eas-y, nor too hard, but all ex-

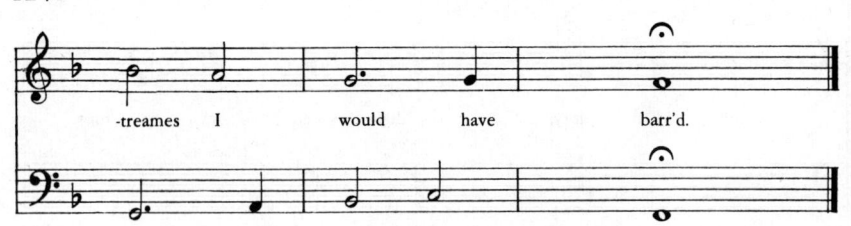

1246

-treames I would have barr'd.

11. *What softer sounds are these salute the Eare**

Ben Jonson *A Dialogue* William Lawes [1602–1645]

Joy: What soft-er sounds are these sa-lute the Eare, from the large Cir-cle of the Hem-i-spheare, as if the Cen-ter of all sweetes melt heere?

Delight: It is the breath and soule of Ev-erie thing, putt forth by Earth, by Na-ture and the spring to speake the

*Brit. Mus. Additional MS 31432. Full text: pages 899–900.

1247

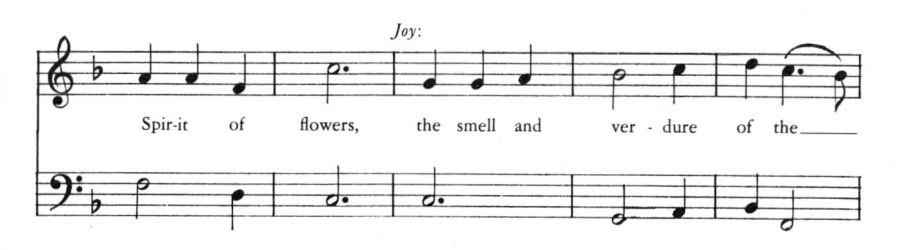

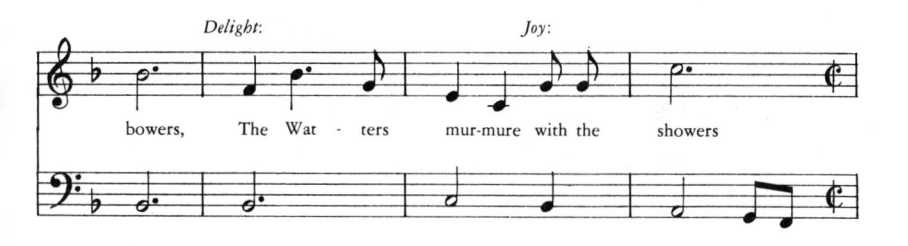

Joy: welcome, the Welcome of the King: *Delight:* The Joy of plants, the Spirit of flowers, *Joy:* the smell and verdure of the bowers, *Delight:* The Waters *Joy:* murmure with the showers Both: [Joy] Distilling on the new fresh howers, The whistling [Delight] Distilling on the new fresh howers,

1248

winds and birds that sing wel-come, wel-come

The whist-ling winds, and birds that sing wel-come, wel-come:

Wel-come, wel-come to our Roy-all King:

Wel-come, [wel-come to our Roy-all King.]

1249

Chorus.
[Treble I and II]

Wel - come O wel - come is the gen-er-all Voyce wher-

[Tenor and bass]

in ___ all Crea-tures prac - tice to re - joyce.

12. Heare me, O God*

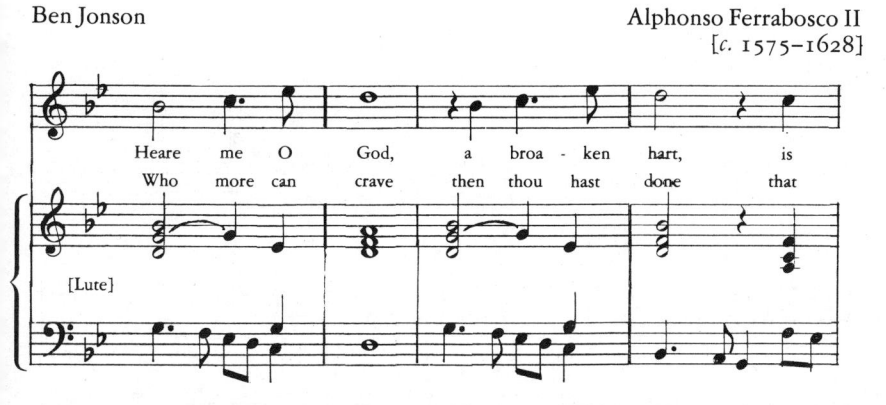

Ben Jonson Alphonso Ferrabosco II
[c. 1575–1628]

Heare me O God, a broa-ken hart, is
Who more can crave then thou hast done that

[Lute]

*Brit. Mus. Egerton MS 2013, 57ᵛ–58ʳ. Full text: pages 818–19.

1250

my best parte, use still thy rodd, that I may
gav'st thy Sonne to be a slave first made of

prove, therein thy love; Yf thou hadst
nought which all sinne bought. Sin, death, and

not bin sterne to me, but left me
hell his glorious name quite over-

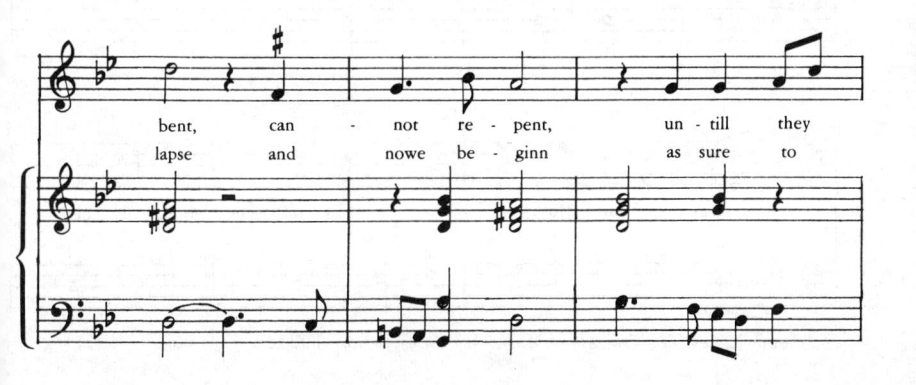

free, I had forgott myselfe and
came yet I rebell and plight the

thee; For sinn's soe sweete, as minds ill
same; But Ile come in before my

bent, cannot repent, untill they
lapse and nowe beginn as sure to

meete their pun-ish-ment.
winne be-neath the crosse.

13. White though you be*

Robert Herrick

Nicholas Lanier
[c. 1588–1666]

White though you be, yet *Lil-lies* know from the first ye were not so: But Ile tell you what be-fell ye; Cu-pid and his Moth-er lay in a Cloud while both did play:

*Henry Lawes, *The Treasury of Musick* II (1669), p. 58.   Full text: page 963.

He with his pre-ty fin-ger prest the Ru-by Nip-ple of her Breast; out of the which the Cream of Light like to a dew fell down on you, and made you White.

14. *Goe, goe, perjur'd man**

Robert Herrick

Robert Ramsey
[*fl.* 1628–1644]

Goe, goe, perjur'd man, and if thou ere re-

*Oxford, Bodleian MS Doncaster C. 57, f.11ʳ. Full text: pages 958–59.

1254

-turne to view the small remainder in my urne, when thou wilt laugh att my religious dust and aske wher's now the colour, forme, or trust of womens beauty or perhaps with rude hands scatter the flowers which the virgins strewd, know

1255

...I have pray'd to pitty that some winde may blow my ashes up and strike thee blinde.

15. When as Leander (yong) was Drown'd*

Robert Herrick
Henry Lawes
[1596–1662]

When as Leander (yong) was Drown'd, no heart by Love receiv'd a wound, but on a Rock him-selfe sat by,

*John Playford, *The Second Book of Ayres and Dialogues* (1655), p. 12.   Full text: page 955.

1256

there weeping superabundantly. His head upon [his] hand he layd, and sighing (deeply) thus he sayd: Ah cruell Fate! and looking on't wept as hee'd drown the Hellespont. And sure his tongue had more exprest, had not his tears, had not his tears for-bad the rest.

16. *Gather your rose buds while you may**

Robert Herrick William Lawes
à 3 voc.

Cantus
Gath-er your rose buds while you may, old

Tenor

Bassus

time is still a-fly-ing, And that same

flower that smiles to-day, to-mor-row will be dy-ing.

*John Playford, *Select Musicall Ayres and Dialogues* (1652), Pt. II, p. 25.   Full text: page 964.

17. Let me sleepe this night away*

Robert Herrick William Webb
[ob. 1653–1660]

a. 4 *A Canon in the Unison*

Let me sleepe this night a way till the dawn-ing of the day, till the dawn-ing of the day; then at the o-pening of mine eyes, at the o-pening of mine eyes, I and all the world shall rise, I and all the world shall rise.

*John Playford, *Catch that Catch Can* (1652), p. 109.

18. When death shall snatch us*
A Dialogue

Andrew Marvell William Lawes

Dorinda: When death shall snatch us from these Kidds, and shutt up our devided Lidds, Thirsis, O tell me, prith-y doe, whith-er thou and I shall go.

Thirsis: To E-lu-zium,

Dorinda: but wher ist?

Thirsis: A chast soule can nev-er mis't.

Dorinda: I know noe way but to my home, is our cell E-lu-zium?

*Brit. Mus. Additional MS 31432, ff.12ᵛ–14ʳ. Full text: pages 1165–66.

[Thirsis:]
Cast thy face to yon - der sky, there the milk-y
Both:
Tis a straight and eas-ie way, that leads to
path doth lye. Tis a straight [and eas-ie way] that
Dorinda:
ev - er - last-ing day. There birds may pearch,
leads to [ev-er- last - ing day.]
but how can I, that have nor wings and can-not fly?
Thirsis:
O doe not

sigh, deare Nimph, for fyre that hath noe wings, still doth a-spire, Un-till it knock a-gainst the Pole. Heaven is the Cen-ter of the soule.

Dorinda: But in E-lu-zium how doe they passe Et-ter-ni-ty a-way?

Thirsis: They know not what it is to feare, free from the Wolfe and ho-rid Beare;

1262

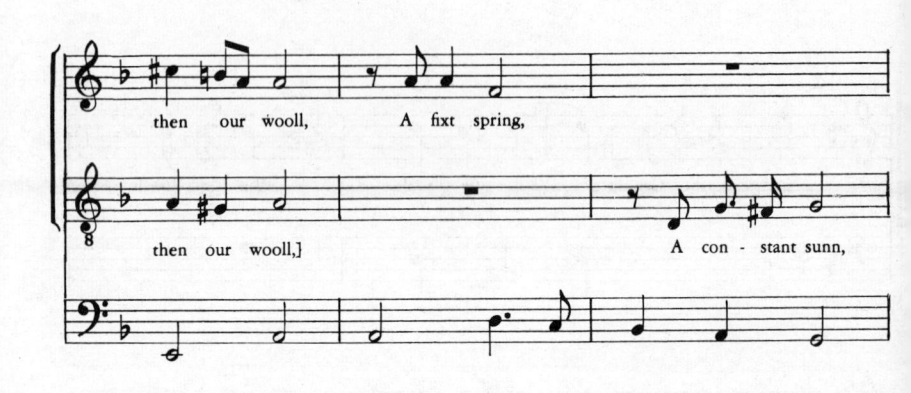

pipes like gold that play A never [ceasing roun - de-
gold that play A never ceasing roun - de-
lay,] A never ceasing Roun - delay.
-lay, A never ceas-[ing Roun - de-lay.]

Flow-ers
Perpetuall Rivers ther doe flow,

1264

1265

Why then should we heere make de-lay
Why then should [we heere make de-lay]

since we may bee as free as they?
since we [may bee as free as they?]

Notes

John Donne

POEMS

SONGS AND SONETS

The good-morrow
  2 lov'd? Dob., 1639] lov'd, 1633-35.
  5 'Twas] T'was 1633.
  7 'twas] t'was 1633.
Song
  9 to'advance] to advance 1633.
The undertaking Title from 1635] omitted 1633.
  2 *Worthies* 1639] worthies 1633.
  7-8 art... it, Dob., D., 1669] art,... it 1633.
The Sunne Rising
  8 offices; Dob., 1639] offices, 1633.
  23 us; 1669] us, 1633.
  24 alchimie. D.] alchimie; 1633.
Loves Usury
  12 Lady'of] Lady of 1633.
  13 sport: Dob.] sport 1633-35.
  20 covet, most D.] covet most, 1633.
The Canonization
  4 improve, 1650] improve 1633.
  15 more Dob., 1639] more, 1633.
  19 wee'are] wee are 1633.

  22 Dove, Dob., D., 1639] dove, 1633.
  30 legend D.] legends 1633.
  36 Love: 1639] Love. 1633.
  37 us: Dob.] us; 1633.
  44 from] frow 1633.
  45 your Dob., D.] our 1633.
The triple Foole
  17 Love] Love, 1633.
  18 read;] read, 1633.
  19 songs, D.] songs: 1633.
  20 published;] published, 1633.
Lovers Infinitenesse
  2 all; Dob., D.] all, 1633-35.
  3 move, D.] move; 1633.
  4 fall, D.] fall. 1633.
  8 ment. Dob.] ment, 1633-35.
  20 it Dob., D.] is 1633.
  21 mine;] mine, 1633.
  27 heart;] heart, 1633.
Song
  4 mee; 1650] mee, 1633.
  20 recall; D.] recall? 1633.
  36 fulfill; Dob.] fulfill, 1633.
The Legacie
  13 none. Dob.] none, 1633-35.
  14 me,'and] me, and 1633.
  15 mee'againe,] mee againe, 1633.
  24 'twas] twas 1633.
A Feaver
  5 know; Gr.] know, 1633.
  10 'tis] tis 1633.
  25 'twas] t'was 1633.

1269

Aire and Angels
  18 overfraught. D.] overfraught, 1633.
  22 scatt'ring] scattring 1633.

Breake of day
  1 day; 1639] day, 1633–35.

The Anniversarie
  2 glory'of] glory of 1633.
  12 divorce: Dob.] divorce, 1633–35.
  17 love, Dob.] love; 1633–35.
  22 wee Dob., D.] now 1633.
  28 nobly,'and] nobly, and 1633.
  30 threescore; Dob.] threescore, 1633–35.

A Valediction: of . . .] *A Valediction of . . .* 1633–35.
  1 herein Dob., O'F., N.] herein, 1633.
  4 was. D.] was, 1633–35, Dob.
  11 undoe; D.] undoe, 1633.
  29 Sinew,'and] Sinew, and 1633–35.
  32 scatter'd] scattered 1633.
  34 flow 1639, Dob.] flow, 1633–35.
  43 thy'inconsiderate] thy inconsiderate 1633.
  56 To'an] To an 1633.

Twicknam garden
  4 thing: 1639] thing, 1633–35.
  18 line is not indented in 1633.
  24 womans D.] womens 1633.

A Valediction: of the booke Title: Dob.] *Valediction to his booke* 1633–35.
  18 Records: N.] Records. 1633–35, Dob.
  22 instruments; D.] instruments, 1633–35.
  25 and Goths inundate D.] and the Goths invade 1633.
  32 amuze Dob., D.] amuze, 1633–35.

  36 Beauty'a] Beauty a 1633.
  38 titles Dob.] titles, 1633.
  47 grounds;] grounds, Dob., 1633–35.
  53 their nothing 1635, Dob., N., O'F., D.] there something 1633.

Communitie
  Title 1635] omitted 1633.
  3 there 1635] these 1633., Cy.
  7 had Dob.] had, 1633–35.
  15 betrayes: 1650] betrayes, 1633–35.
  21 well: Dob.] well, 1633–35.

Loves growth
  6–7 spaced in 1633–35.
  20 awaken'd] awakened 1633–35.

Loves exchange
  6 Onely'I] Onely I 1633.
  28 Love O'F.] love 1633.
  30 th'Idolatrie O'F.] the Idolatrie 1633.
  36 For this, Love O'F.] for, this love 1633.

Confined Love
  Title 1635] omitted 1633.

A Valediction: of weeping] *A Valediction of weeping* 1633–35.
  6 thee; Dob.] thee, 1633–35.
  22 soone. D.] soone, 1633.
  25 purposeth; Dob.] purposeth, 1633.

The Flea
  The poem is placed here in the sequence of the 1633 edition. In 1635–69 editions, it is placed at the beginning of *Songs and Sonets*.
  6 shame, 1635] shame 1633.

The Curse
  3 only,'and] only, and 1633.
    only'his] only his 1633.

8 torne. D.] torne; 1633.
27 Mynes Dob., O'F.] Myne 1633-35.
28 ill Dob., 1669] ill, 1633.
30 Be'annex'd] Be annex'd 1633.

The Message
Title 1635] omitted 1633.
14 crosse Dob., D., Cy.] breake 1633-35.

A nocturnall...
1 'Tis] Tis 1633.
7 Whither] Whither, 1633-35.
20 have;] have, 1633-35.
31 know; 1639] know, 1633.
34 love; Gr.] love, 1633-35. invest. 1639] invest, 1633-35.
36 shadow,'a] shadow, a 1633.
41 all; Gr.] all, 1633.

Witchcraft by a picture
2 eye: Dob.] eye, 1633.
4 espie. O'F.] espie, 1633-35, Dob.
6 kill, Dob.] Kill? 1633-35.
8 I'have] I have 1633.

The Baite
Title 1635] omitted 1633.
3 brookes,] brookes: 1633.
18 with 1635] which 1633.
23 sleavesilke 1635] sleavesicke 1633.
26 bait;] bait, 1633-35.

The Apparition
5 thee,... vestall,] thee... vestall 1633.
15 thee;'and] thee'; and 1633.

The broken heart
12 some; Dob.] some, 1633-35.
23 alas, O'F.] alas 1633, Dob.

A Valediction: forbidding...]
A Valediction forbidding... 1633-35.

1 mildly'away] mildly away 1633.
4 no: Dob.] no. 1633.
7 'Twere] T'were 1633.
17 by'a] by a 1633.
20 and 1669] omitted 1633.
35 drawes D.] makes 1633.

The Extasie
8 string. D.] string, 1633.
18 lay; Gr.] lay, 1633.
25 knew 1635, Dob.] knowes 1633.
31 sexe,] sexe 1633.
42 Interinanimates Dob.] Interanimates 1633.
51 They'are... we, N.] They are ours, though not wee, 1633.
52 The'intelligences] The intelligences 1633.
spheare. N., D.] spheares 1633-35.
55 forces, sense, to us Dob.] senses force 1633-35.
59 Soe Dob.] For 1633-35.

Loves Deitie
20 To'ungod] To ungod 1633.

Loves diet
12 mee. Dob.] mee; 1633.
25 reclaim'd 1635, Dob., D.] redeem'd 1633.
27 sport 1635] sports 1633.

The Will
10 give;] give, 1633-35, Dob.
16 by'appointing] by appointing 1633.
34 Love,] love, 1633.

The Funerall
6 then to Dob., D., Cy.] unto 1633-35.
12 These Dob., D.] Those 1633-35.
16 condemn'd] condem'nd 1633.

17 with 1635] by 1633.
22 To'afford] To afford 1633.

The Blossome
10 labourest 1635-69, Dob.] labours 1633.
23 tongue, Dob., D.] tast, 1633-35.
24 you'a Dob., D.] your 1633.
38 would Dob., D.] will 1633-35.

The Primrose ... situate
Title: 1635] *The Primrose* 1633.
17 study'her,] study her, 1633.
her, not 1635-39] her, and not 1633.
25 number; D.] number, 1633.
26 Belonge Dob., D.] Belongs 1633-35.

The Relique
9 hop'd D.] thought 1633.
a D.] some 1633.
17 be'a] be a 1633.
26 doe; Dob.] doe, 1633-35.
27 wee Dob.] wee, 1633-35.
29 seales Dob.] seales, 1633-35.
30 free. Dob.] free, 1633-35.

The Dampe
20 professe. O'F.] professe, 1633-35.

The Prohibition
5 thee Cy.] mee 1633.
what to me Cy.] that which 1633.
20 love'is] love is 1633.
22 Stage, 1635, Cy.] stay, 1633.

The Expiration
2 away: Dob.] away, 1633.
4 day; Dob.] day, 1633.

The Computation
6 doe, Gr.] doe. 1633.

The Paradox
Title: 1635] omitted 1633.

6 yesterday? Gr.] yesterday. 1633.
15 which Gr.] which, 1633.
17 lov'd N., O'F.] love 1633-35.
20 lye O'F.] dye. 1633.

Farewell to love
First printed in 1635 edition. Copy text: 1635.
2 love, 1650] love 1635.
10 sise, O'F.] sise 1635.
12 highnesse] hignesse 1635.
26 This,] This; 1635.
29 be,] be 1635.
30 Eagers desire Gr.] Eager, desires 1635.

A Lecture ... Shadow
First printed in 1635 edition, where it concludes the *Songs and Sonets*. Copy text: 1635. Title from 1650, 1669] *Song*. 1635, 1654.
4 here, two Dob., O'F., N.] here; Two 1635.
26 first A18 and O'F.] short 1635.

Sonnet. The Token
First printed in the 1649 edition. Copy text: 1649.
1 Token] token O'F., Cy.: Tokens, 1649.
4 passion O'F.] passions 1649.
11 with O'F.] in 1649.
14 desir'd, because best ... best; O'F.] desired 'cause 'tis like the best; 1649.
17 store, O'F.] score, 1649.

[*Self Love.*]
Untitled; first printed in the 1650 edition, where it concludes the *Songs and Sonets*. Copy text: 1650. Indentations follow O'F. Stanza

divisions are editorial. Title: Gr.
4 'gaynst O'F.] against 1650.
6 can all O'F.] cannot 1650.
15 others,... Dots signify omission in 1650 and O'F.
16 He'can] He can 1650. want nor crave; O'F.: omitted 1650.
17 payes O'F.] prays, 1650.
19 payes not, O'F.] payes, not, 1650.

ELEGIES, SATIRES, VERSE LETTERS

Elegie II
  Title: *Elegie II* 1633] Elegy: *The Anagram*. 1635.
  51 shee'accuse] she accuse 1633.
  52 confesse,] confesse. 1633.
  53–54 From Dob., Cy., and N.] omitted 1633.

Elegie V. His Picture
  Title: 1635] *Elegie V.* 1633.
  1 Picture;] Picture, 1633. farewell, D.] farewell; 1633.
  20 to'disus'd] to disus'd 1633.

Elegie IX. The Autumnall
  Title: 1635] *Elegie. The Autumnall.* 1633.
  2 face;] face, 1633.
  5 'twere] t'were 1633.
  6 Affection... takes Dob., D.] Affections... take 1633.
  8 shee's Dob., D.] they'are 1633.
  15 Love O'F.] love 1633.
  28 past. O'F.] past; 1633.
  40 made; Dob.] made 1633.
  41 to'a] to a 1633.
  44 be. D.] be; 1633.
  47 natural lation A18, D.] motion natural 1633.

Elegie [XI]. The Bracelet
  First printed in the 1635 edition. Copy text: 1635. Title from 1635; Gr. supplies number.
  6 are ty'd Dob., O'F., N.] were knit 1635.
  22 ty'd Dob., O'F.] tyed 1635.
  24 them... rott O'F.] these, their Countries naturall rot 1635.
  26 So leane, so pale, so lame O'F., Dob.] So pale, so lame, so lean 1635.
  35 which Dob., O'F., N.] that 1635.
  52 lustyhead] lusty head 1635.
  55 Oh Dob., O'F., Cy.] And 1635.
  58 they] he 1635.
  60 scheames Dob., O'F., Cy.] scenes 1635. fulfills O'F., Cy.] fils full 1635.
  85 a one Dob., O'F., Cy.] an one 1635.
  87 which Dob., N.] that 1635.
  90 few fellowes] few-fellowes 1635.
  92 So much that N.] So, that 1635.
  I'almost] I almost 1635.
  98 Countrey,'and] Countrey, and 1635.
  that and thy pay N.] it and thy pay 1635.
  103 thee; 'and] thee; and 1635.
  105 hurt which ever Gold hath Dob., Cy.] evils that Gold ever 1635.
  106 mischiefes Dob., Cy.] mischiefe 1635.
  which] that 1635.

108 love; and Dob., N.] *and* omitted 1635.
111 thee, Dob.] thee 1635.
113 if with it Dob.] if from it 1635.
114 'twere] twere 1635.

Elegie XVI. On his Mistris
First printed in the 1635 edition, where it is titled "Elegie on his Mistris."
1 interview, D.] interview 1635.
18 From... t'ward Dob., D.] my soule from other lands to thee 1635.
28 mindes; D.] minde, 1635.
39 Page, D.] Page 1635.
46 greate D.] greatest 1635.

Elegie XVIII. Loves Progresse
Title ed.] *An Elegy on Loves Progresse.* 1669. Copy text: 1669.
5 strange O'F., Cy., N.] strong 1669.
25 Beauty's not] beauty is not O'F., Cy., N.: Beauties no 1669.
30 abound;] abound, 1669.
32 in D.] on 1669.
40 face!] face? 1669.
42 springes] springs 1669.
47 first O'F., Cy., N.] sweet 1669.
53 Her... to which O'F., Cy., N.] Unto her swelling lips when 1669.
57 There O'F.] Then 1669.
60 Ore past, and the strayt O'F., Cy., N.] Being past the straits 1669.
63 that O'F., Cy., N.] yet 1669.
64 scatter'd] scattered 1669.
65 Sailing] Sailng 1669.
67 thence] there 1669.
thy] the 1669.
68 wouldst] should'st 1669.
73 Art; O'F.] Art, 1669.
83 the'imperial] the imperial 1669.
90 elements MSS.] enemies 1669.

Elegie XIX. To his Mistris...
First printed in 1669 edition. Title from 1669.
10 is your Dob., O'F.] it is 1669.
16 which'on] which on 1669.
17 safely Dob., O'F.] softly 1669.
20 Receiv'd by Dob.] Reveal'd to 1669.
21 Paradice; Dob.] Paradice, 1669.
22 white, Dob.] white; 1669.
26 Behind,... below; Dob., Cy.] Before, behind, between, above, below, 1669.
27 new-found-land! Dob.] new-found-land, 1669.
28 Kingdom, safeliest when Dob.] Kingdom's safest, when 1669. man'd!] man'd 1669.
30 blest am I Dob.] am I blest 1669.
thee! Gr.] thee? 1669.
32 be: Dob.] be, 1669.
36 balls, Dob.] ball: 1669.
38 covett theirs Dob.] court that, 1669.
41 are mystick... which only we Dob.] are only mystick..., which we, 1669.
43 reveal'd] revealed. 1669.
know, Dob.] know; 1669.
44 to a Dob.] to thy 1669.
45 hence;] hence 1669.
47 first Dob.] first, 1669.
48 man?] Man. 1669.

Satyre I
1 fondling 1633] changeling 1635-69.
5 conduits, grave Divines: 1649-69] conduits; grave Divines, 1633-39.
6 Philosopher: 1649-69] Philosopher. 1633-39.
7 jolly 1633] wily 1635-69.
13 love, here, in 1635-69] love in 1633.
40 or 1633, 1669] omitted 1635-54.
46 hee'was] hee was 1633.
47 weare,] weare 1633.
52 goe. 1635-69] goe, 1633.
58 infant 1633-54] Infantry 1669: Infanta Gr.
to'an] to an 1633.
60 Scheme 1635-69] Sceanes 1633.
61 fashion'd 1635-69] fashioned 1633.
62 subtile-witted] subtile wittied 1633.
63 canst] can 1633.
66 conscience? 1635-69] conscience, 1633.
69 imprison'd] imprisoned 1633.
70 high 1633] his 1635-69.
73 them 1635] then 1633.
78 stoops 1635] stoopt 1633.
81-82 Or... to you, 1635] omitted 1633.
83 me,'and] me and 1633 Do'you] Do you 1633.
84 favour'd] favoured 1633.
89 us: 1635] us, 1633.
92 colour'd] coloured 1633.
95 s'all 1633] all 1635-69.
97 plight 1633] pleite 1635-39.
101 travail'd. Long? No,] travailed long? no, 1633.

103 reply'd] replyed, 1633.
104 answer'd] answered 1633.
108 lechery. 1635-39] liberty; 1633.

Satyre III
16 is. Gr.] is; 1633.
22 discoveries? Gr.] discoveries, 1633.
23 Salamanders, Gr.] Salamanders? 1633.
28 words?] words, 1633.
33 foe:] foes W.: foe, 1633. Devill W.] devill h'is 1633.
34 please,] please: 1633.
40 it selfes death Gr., 1635, most mss.] it selfe death 1633.
42 loath. Gr.] loath; 1633.
44 here Gr.] her 1633.
46 agoe;] agoe, 1633.
47 her Gr., most mss.] the 1633.
54 drudges.] drudges: 1633.
57 bid Gr., MSS] bids 1633.
84 night. Gr., 1635] night, 1633.
85 doe: Gr.] doe. 1635, D., W.: doe 1633.
86 too Gr., some mss.] to 1633.
99 strong? cannot Gr.] strong cannot 1633.
101 chang'd; Gr.] chang'd 1633.
103 is; Gr.] is, 1633.

To the Countesse...
7 to'encrease] to encrease 1633.
13 all Dob.] all, 1633.
14 reach: Dob.] reach, 1633.
16 voice Dob., D., 1635] faith 1633
teach: Dob.] teach; 1633.
17 good, Dob.] good: 1633.
18 it; Dob.] it: 1633.

36 This 1635, Dob., Cy.] Thy 1633.
To Sir Edward Herbert ...
Title: At] at 1633.
10 minde! Gr.] minde? 1633.
35 show; Gr.] show, 1633.

THE ANNIVERSARY POEMS

A Funerall Elegie
106 well the 1633] well, the 1611.
The First Anniversary 1612 title] omitted 1611. Marginalia from 1612.
129 trie 1633] trie; 1611–25.
153 close-weaving 1633] close-weaning 1611–25.
195 Angels, 1612] Angels. 1611.
217 there 1612 errata] then 1611.
259 there 1612 errata] then 1611.
262 Townes 1612 errata] Towres 1611.
474 fame 1612 errata, 1633] same 1611–25.
The Second Anniversarie
1 confesse 1633] confesse. 1612–25.
10 Though 1612 errata] Through 1612–25.
16 meet 1621, 1633] meet. 1612.
17 soule; 1621, 1633] soule, 1612.
46 safe-sealing Gr.] safe-fealing 1612.
47 till thou 1612 errata] till, thou 1612.
48 'Tis 1612 errata] T'o 1612.
Hydropique 1612 errata] Hydroptique 1612.
50 be, Man.] be 1612.
67 was 1612 errata] twas 1612.
69 all shee Gr.] all, shee 1612.
82 is 1633] is. 1612.
116 goe, Man.] goe. 1612.
119 rite 1612 errata] right 1612.
137 wonne 1612 errata] worne 1612.
153 a long] along 1612.
197 retards 1612 errata] recards 1612.
198 bee; 1633] bee, 1612.
232 there 1612 errata] then 1612.
246 thought,)] thought, 1612.
268 'tis Gr.] ty's 1612.
lay. 1621] lay 1612.
281 recant, 1633] recant. 1612.
292 taught 1612 errata] thought 1612.
308 aye] aie 1612.
314 print 1612 errata] point 1612.
338 will 1612 errata] wise 1612.
353 thought 1612 errata] thoughts 1612.
359 herselfe a state, 1633] herselfe, a state 1612.
378 ill,) 1635] ill, 1612.
380 whither 1612 errata] whether 1612.
398 vow 1612 errata] row 1612.
417 t'erect 1612 errata] to'rect 1612.
423 world 1633] worlds 1612–25.
435 up 1633] upon 1612.
449 joye, 1633] joye. 1612.

476 Man. 1633] Man, 1612.
477 Redresse 1612 errata] Reders 1612.
522 doe, 1612 errata] doe 1612.

DIVINE POEMS

To the Lady . . . .
    4 know, Walton, 1675] know Walton, 1670.

HOLY SONNETS
[LA CORONA]

La Corona
    14 nigh.] nigh, 1633.
Nativitie
    8 effect Gd., most mss.] effects 1633. doome.] doome; 1633.
Temple
    4 those Gd., most mss.] the 1633.
    11 'tis] 'Tis 1633.
Crucifying
    8 to'a span, Gr., Gd., many mss.] to span 1633.
    9 inch. Loe Gr.] inch, loe 1633.
Resurrection
    1 soule 1635] soule, 1633.
    12 deaths Gr., Gd., some mss.] death 1633.
Ascention.
    10 lambe, Gr., Gd.] lambe 1633.

A LITANIE

    Title: Gd., MSS] *The Litanie* 1633.
    30 serpents, Gr., Gd.] serpents 1633.
    34 instinct, Gd., some mss.] instinct 1633.
    56 Grandfathers] Grandfathers, 1633.
    61 satisfied Gd., Gr., most mss.] sanctified 1633.
    100 Thy Gd., most mss.] The 1633.
    109 Academe Gd., some mss.] Academie 1633.
    122 too, Gr., Gd.] too 1633.
    153 fame Gr., Gd., MSS] flame 1633.
    163 through Gr., Gd., MSS] though 1633.
    173 spoile, Gd.] spoile; 1633.
    178 soule they . . . expresse, Gr., Gd.] soule, they . . . expresse 1633.
    191 that MSS] which 1633.
    214 offices; Gr., Gd] offices, 1633.
    231 well 1633, most mss.] will some uncorrected copies of 1633.
    239 doe, Gr., Gd.] doe 1633.
    245 againe, Gr., Gd.] againe 1633.

HOLY SONNETS

1
    9 in Gd., many mss.] on 1633.
3
    4 last point Gd., most mss.] latest point 1633, Gr.
    6 soule Gr., Gd., most mss.] my soule 1633.
    14 flesh,] flesh the 1633.
4
    6 dearth Gr., Gd., W.] death 1633, most mss.
    8 woe.] woe, 1633.
5
    12 memorie; Gr.] memorie, 1633.
    14 forget.] forget, 1633.

6
    8 deliverie.] deliverie 1633.
    10 dost Gr., Gd., MSS] doth 1633.
    14 more, Death Gd., MSS] more, death 1633.

7
    8 glorified. Gr., Gd] glorified; 1633.
    12 intent: Gr., Gd.] intent 1633.

8
    10 timorous. Gr.] timorous, 1633.

9
    4 that Gr., Gd., most mss.] his 1633.
    6 fell, Gd.,] fell 1633.
    14 assures Gr., Gd., MSS] assumes 1633.

10
    9 loved Gr., MSS] lov'd 1633.

12
    9 those Gd., some mss.] these 1633] thy Gr., some mss.
    11 all-healing Gr., Gd., most mss.] thy all-healing 1633.
    12 kill.] kill 1633.
    14 that Gd., most mss.] 1633.

13
    1 decay?] decay, 1635.
    7 feebled Gd., MSS] feeble 1635, Gr.

15
    6 lands Gr., Gd., some mss.] land 1635.
    11 have burnt Gr., Gd., some mss.] burnt 1635.
    12 fouler; W.] fouler, 1635.

16
    10 vile Gr., Gd., some mss.] stile 1635.
    14 Thy true griefe... in W.] Thy greife... into 1635.

17
    12 Angels,... divine,] Angels... divine W.

18
    2 What,] What W.

OCCASIONAL POEMS AND HYMNS

The Crosse
    13 affliction, Gr., Gd.] affliction 1633.
    14 none. Gr., Gd.] none; 1633.
    26 And Gd., some mss.] But 1633.
    33 make, 1635] make: 1633.
    37 oft Alchimists] oft, Alchimists 1633.
    50 others Gd., MSS] other 1633.
    52 Points Gr., some mss.] Pants 1633.
    61 fruitfully Gr., Gd., MSS] faithfully 1633.
    63 That Gr., Gd., MSS] The 1633.

Upon the Annuntiation...
    Title: Gd., MSS] *The Annunciation and Passion,* 1633.
    33 these MSS] those 1633.

Goodfriday...
    4 motions Gr., Gd., MSS] motion 1633.
    27 Made 1633, Gr., some mss.] Make Gd., many mss.

A Hymne to Christ...
    12 sea Gr., Gd., MSS] seas 1633.

A Hymne to God the Father
    1633] variant version in MSS titled *To Christ,* or, *Christo Salvatori.* Gr. prints both texts.
    7 which I have wonne 1633] by which I wonne some mss., Gd.

Hymne to God my God...
  5 now Gd., MSS] here 1635, Gr.

12 theire Gr., Gd.] those 1635.
19 but streights, Gr., Gd.] but streights 1633.

George Herbert

THE TEMPLE

THE CHURCH-PORCH
  24 feet and 1633] feet, B.
  36 worldly 1633] wordly B.
  57 Lust and 1633] Lust, and B.
  75 those that 1633] those, that B.
  144 Lock and] Lock and 1633: Lock, and B.
  148 up and 1633] up, and B.
  162 with all] withall B.
  213 servant that 1633] servant, that B.
  298 cards.) Steale] Cards) steale B.] cards) steal 1633.
  308 truth a discourtesy B.] truth discourtesie 1633.
  345 see 1633] See, B.
  360 they. 1633] they B.
  361 thine corr. to thy B.
  393 food, 1633] food. B.
  433 blessing which 1633] blessing, which B.
  449 wee, folly. punctuation from 1633] wee folly. B.

Superliminare
  5 Avoyd, Punctuation from P., H.] Avoyd Profanenes come not heere, B.] Avoid profanenesse; come not here: 1633.

THE CHURCH

The Sacrifice
  7 bread: 1633] bread B.
  58 meeke] meek 1633: meeke, B.
  83 command: 1633] command B.
  105 eares, 1633] eares B.
  119 All understanding, more then 1633] all understanding more, then B.
  129 him... him B., W.] me... me 1633.
  130 his B., W.] my 1633.
  131 he B., W.] I 1633.
  mist.] mist B.
  137 they 1633] thy B.
  141 mee; they punctuation from 1633] mee they B.
  157 array; punctuation from 1633] array. B.
  208 Such sorrow as, if H., P.] Such sorrow, as if B., W., 1633.

The Thankes-giving
  48 Victorie! 1633] Victorie. B.

The Reprisall
  In quatrains in W., 1633.
  3 behind; punctuation from 1633] behind B.

The Agony
  5 behove: 1633] behove B.
  18 feels as 1633] feels, as B.

The Sinner
    13 grone, 1633] grone. B.
Redemption
    14 Your 1633] *your* B.
Sepulcher
    13 braine thee, punctuation from 1633] braine thee. B.
Easter
    14 long: 1633] long B.
    17 part, 1633] part B.
Easter wings
    In B., W., lines are horizontal on the page, as here, but all early editions present them vertically. The two stanzas in B. are side by side, on facing pages.
H. Baptisme
    [*I*] added, ed.
    5 vent B.] rent 1633.
H. Baptisme
    [*II*] added, ed.
Sinne
    [*I*] added, ed.
    10 eares B.] eares: 1633.
    11 Without, our shame, within our consciences, B.] Without, our shame; within, our consciences; 1633.
Affliction
    [*I*] added, ed.
    25 paine, punctuation from 1633] paine B.
Faith
    2 sinne as, when H.] sinne, as when B., W., 1633.
Prayer
    [*I*] added, ed.
    2 man returning 1633] Man, returning B.
The H. Communion
    ll. 25–40 appear alone in W., with title, *Prayer*, and are set off from the rest of the poem in B. But the Eucharistic imagery of ll. 37–40 (absent in W.) signifies the intent to incorporate it with the proceeding portion.
    3 for mee B.] from me 1633.
    39 please, 1633] please B.
Antiphon
    [*I*] added, ed.
Love II
    1 Heat 1633] heat B.
The Temper
    [*I*] added, ed.
    15 wretch? 1633] wretch B.
The Temper
    [*II*] added, ed.
Jordan
    [*I*] added, ed.
    7 lines? 1633] lines B.
    11 sing: 1633] sing B.
    12 Prime: 1633] prime B.
Imployment
    [*I*] added, ed.
The H. Scriptures I
    5 all health, health thriving till W.] all health health, thriving till B.] all health, health thriving, till 1633.
    13 handsell: heaven punctuation from 1633] no punctuation, B.
The H. Scriptures II
    3 onely how 1633] onely; how B.
    13 misse: 1633] misse B.
Whitsunday
    25 same,] Same. B.
    26 light: 1633] light B.
Praise
    [*I*] added, ed.
    6 fly; punctuation from 1633] fly B.
    15 poore, 1633] poore B.
Affliction
    [*II*] added, ed.

13-15 one, ed. Elsewhere, B.'s punctuation] All my delight, so all my smart:/Thy crosse took up in one,/By way of imprest, 1633.
Sinne
[*II*] added, ed.
Even-song
In quatrains in 1633.
13 diet, care, and 1633] diet care and B.
32 more then 1633] more, then B.
Church-monuments
6-line stanzas in 1633.
Anagram
In 1633, between "Avarice" and "To all Angels and Saints."
Church-lock and key
11 too, yet 1633] too yet B.
Content
31 digestion, 1633] digestion B.
Humility
29 bandying 1633] banding B.
Frailty
17 lest if what 1633] least if, what B.
21 Love: punctuation from 1633] Love B.
Constancy
25 Sunne 1633] Sonne B.
27 those whom 1633] those, whom B.
33 share, 1633] thare B. ill. 1633] ill B.
Affliction
[*III*] added, ed.
The Starre
17 light, 1633] light B.
Sunday
9 art, 1633] art B.
33 ope; 1633] ope B.
Imployment
[*II*] added, ed.

Christmas
18 deeds. 1633] deeds B.
Ungratefulnes
22 allure 1633] allures B.
23 Bone B.] box 1633, H.: Boxe W.
Sighes and Grones
4 mee: punctuation from 1633] mee. B.
16 light: 1633] light B.
20 vial] viall 1633: viol B.
The World
6 Pleasure] pleasure B.
15 Grace] grace B.
16 Death] death B.
Coloss: 3. 3.
Italics supplied from 1633 to set forth the acrostic more clearly.
Vanity
[*I*] added, ed.
14 Her 1633] Her changed to His B.
20 drest] drest. B.
22 sought 1633] wrought B.
Lent
31 forti'th 1633] fortith B.
Vertue
3 to 1633] too B.
7 his B.] its 1633.
The Pearle
Math. 13.45. 45 added, ed.
1 Learning; punctuation from 1633] Learning. B.
4 huswife, 1633] huswife B.
11 Honour, punctuation from 1633] Honour. B.
21 Pleasure, punctuation from 1633] Pleasure. B.
26 unbundled B.] unbridled 1633.
Affliction
[*IV*] added, ed.
12 pink B.] pinke W.: prick 1633.

16 life.] life B.: life: 1633.

Man
    8 no fruit B., 1633] more fruit W.
    53 World serve B.] world serves 1633.

Antiphon
    [*II*] added, ed.
    16 since 1633] since, B.

Life
    8 part 1633] part. B.
    14 liv'd, 1633] liv'd B.

Justice
    [*I*] added, ed.

Affliction
    [*V*] added, ed.

Mortification
    18 houre W.] house B., 1633. *Houre* is probably right, as the bell customarily tolled at the time the person was passing out of life. Cf. l. 30.

Decay
    18 retreat, 1633] retreat B.

Misery
    33 shame, 1633] shame B.
    46 all night B.] all night: 1633.
    48 shute B.] shoot 1633.
    60 flow: 1633] flow B.
    75 a B.] the 1633.

Jordan
    [*II*] added, ed.

Prayer
    [*II*] added, ed.
    4 easines, ed.] full stop B., 1633.

Conscience
    8 sphere; 1633] sphere B.

Sion
    6 seeers B.] seers 1633.
    23 mount like larks, they B.] mount, like larks they 1633.

Home
    33 away, 1633] away B.
    52 thee. 1633] thee B.

The British Church
    In 3-line verses 1633.
    3 Both 1633] both B.
    4 the B.] her 1633.

Vanity.
    [*II*] added, ed.

The Dawning
    9 doe B.] dost 1633.

Jesu
    5 was *I*, ed.] was, *I*, B.] was *J* 1633] the vowel I and the consonantal J are identical in B.
    6 where *ES* 1633] Where, *Es* B. where *U* was 1633] where, *U*, was B.

Busines
    9 work: 1633] work. B.
    29 spare B.] space 1633.
    32 Tells to all he meets, 1633] Tells to all, he meets B.

Dialogue
    31 smart— 1633] smart. B.
    32 more: 1633] more. B.

Dulnes
    9 light, 1633] light B.
    14 show, 1633] show. B.
    17–18 Question marks added from 1633. B. has, "Where are my lines then, my approaches, veiws/ Where are my window-songs."
    23 could 1633] cold B.

Love-joy
    7 *Joy* 1633] *joy* B.

Providence
    13 preist: punctuation from 1633] preist. B.
    21 teach, 1633] teach B.
    23 hand you stretch, 1633] hand, you stretch, B.
    34 all: 1633] all. B.

37 both; 1633] both. B.
39 all: ed.] all, B.] all. If 1633.
42 can neither 1633] can, neither B.
79 warres 1633] warres. B.
82 perill: 1633] perill. B.
98 that which 1633] that, which B.
127 can, punctuation from 1633] can B.
129 dry. 1633] dry B.
135–36 Punctuation from 1633] Frogs marry, Fish and flesh, Bats, Bird and Beast, Sponges, Non-sense and Sense. Mines, th'earth and plants. B.
138 ours, H.] ours; B., 1633.
139 under-chaw B.] under-jaw 1633.
140 B. evidently takes *elephant* as plural, the species.] leans or stands 1633.

Hope
1 Hope 1633.] hope B.
5 viall 1633] violl B.

Gratefulnes
7 given heretofore B.] giv'n him heretofore 1633.

Peace
4, 9, 20 Caps. supplied from 1633.
21 demand, H.] demand; B., 1633.

Confession
28 day, 1633] day. B.

The Bunch of Grapes
4 vaine, Punctuation from 1633] vaine B.
7 Red 1633] red B.
15 too 1633] to B.
18 not last. 1633] not at last. B.
22 wine 1633] vine B. (cf. 1. 24).

Love-unknowne
10 Better 1633] Better, B.
18, 37, 56 Ital. supplied from 1633, to emphasize friend's part in the dialogue.
35 pan,] pan B.] pan; 1633.
38 it's B.] 'tis 1633.
61–70 Ital. from 1633.
65 too 1633] to B.

Mans medly
4 measure, 1633] measure B.
6 is. 1633] is B.
18 trimming, not 1633] trimming not B.
22 he must B.] must he 1633.

The Storme
6 Amuse B.] Amaze 1633.
17 stormes: ... best; punctuation from 1633] stormes. ... best B.

Paradise
11 *Pare* 1633] pare B.
13 *Frend* 1633] frend B.

The Method
22 done, 1633] done. B.
26 those 1633] those, B.

Divinity
6 sky: punctuation from 1633] sky. B.
19 day! 1633] day B.
24 all that 1633] all, that B.

4 Ephes: 30
6 dead. B.] dead? 1633.
10 part, 1633] part B.
12 expresse; 1633] expresse, B.
30 crystall, punctuation from 1633] crystall. B.

The family
3 puling B.] pulling 1633.
10 Order 1633] order B.; cf. ll. 9, 13.

The Size
12 spices, is't H.] spices. Is't B.

16 Exact B.] Enact 1633, H.
38 all. 1633] all B.
39 The stanzaic pattern demands an extra line of two feet here, but it is mising.
44 dreame, punctuation from 1633] dreame B.
47 Ital. from 1633.

Artillery
9 spheres 1633] sferes B.

Churchrents or schismes
Title in 1633, H.: *Church-rents and schismes.*
1 chair 1633] place B. *Place* does not rhyme; *chair* was evidently inferred by the editor of 1633 from context, rhyme, and use in l. 10.
7 perceive it, blew thee B.] perceive, it blew them 1633.
9 glories. Onely 1633] glories onely B.
10 bitten, in 1633] sitten in B.
18 vaded B.] faded 1633.

Justice
[*II*] added, ed.

The Pilgrimage
14 would,] would B.: wold; 1633.

The holdfast
10 nought. 1633] nought B.

Complaining
5 calls. 1633] calls B.
17 houre, 1633] houre B.
20 releife. Punctuation from 1633] releife B.

The Discharge
3 licorous eye 1633] licorous eye? B.
30 grow. 1633] grow B.
48 to morrow 1633] too morrow B.

54 distrust: 1633] distrust B.

Praise
[*II*] added, ed.

An Offering
2 fooles? Punctuation from 1633] fooles B.

Longing
5 sighs, my 1633] sighs my B.
19 heare! 1633] heare B.
42 Sayes 1633] sayes B.
83 which 1633] with B.

The Bagge
30 cry'd, 1633] cry'd. B.

The Jewes
2 cyens 1633] sinnes B. As H. notes, *cyens*, a spelling of *scions*, (slips for grafting) continues the metaphor of *sap, juice*, and gives the disyllable required by the meter; *sinnes* may be a copyist's alteration of an unfamiliar word.

The Collar
3 What? shall 1633] what shall B.
4 road, punctuation from 1633] road B.
34 word, 1633] word; B.

The Glimpse
5 to my B.] for my 1633.

Assurance
40 throat: 1633] throat B.

Praise
[*III*] added, ed.
25 one 1633] on B.

Josephs coat
3 note: such 1633] note. such B.

The Pulley
6 way,] way; 1633: way B.

The Preisthood
17 those 1633] those, B.

18 shows. 1633] shows B.
38 skill: 1633] skill B.
The Search
   51 say, 1633] say B.
The Crosse
   16 harmony): H.'s punctuation]
     no punctuation B., 1633.
   26 bow, 1633] bow B.
The Flowre
   32 zone] zone, B., 1633
   43 *Love,* punctuation from
     1633] *Love* B.
The Sonne
   6 sunnes 1633] sonnes B.
A true Hymne
   17 Although the verse 1633]
     Although verse B.
A Dialogue Antheme
   4 *King.* 1633] *King* B.
   8 worst. 1633] worst B.
Selfe-condemnation
   4 owne state B.] own estate
     1633.
   10 is; 1633] is B.
   22 taken B.] ta'ne 1633.
Bitter-sweet
   2 strike,] strike B.
The Glance
   14 Soule, punctuation from
     1633] Soule B.
The 23^d Psalme
   18 mine B.] my 1633.
   24 thy B.] my 1633.
Mary Magdalene
   6 tred,] tred. B.: tread: 1633.
The Odour. 2 Cor. 2.15.
   15 added, ed.
   12 *My servant* 1633] *My servant* B.
   23 meet] meet, B., 1633.
The Fore-runners
   6, 10, 32 *Thou art . . . God.* Ital
     from 1633. B. encloses

phrase in parentheses at ll.
10, 32.
19 cane, 1633] cane B.
25 dong, punctuation from
   1633] dong B.
26 shame: 1633] shame B.
31 not; 1633] not. B.
32 all 1633] all, B.
Discipline
   28 Needs must 1633] Needs,
     must B.
The Invitation
   36 All should 1633] All, should
     B.
The Banquet
   40 short, 1633] short B.
   49 his pitty B.] this pitie 1633.
   53 breath; 1633] breath. B.
The Elixir
   16 cleane. punctuation from
     1633] cleane B.
   18 divine: 1633] divine B.
   20 fine. 1633] fine B.
   22 gold: 1633] gold B.
Death
   15 grace, 1633] grace B.
Doomes day
   6 Brother? punctuation from
     1633] Brother. B.
   13 away, 1633] away. B.
Heaven
   9 wholly. 1633] wholly? B.
Love
   [*III*] added, ed.
   17 meat: 1633] meat B.
The Church Militant
   27 shone, 1633] shone B.
   70 slaine. punctuation from
     1633] slaine B.
   72 yeare. 1633] yeare B.
   115 *God,* punctuation from
     1633] *God;* B.
   126 ev'ry 1633] evry B.

1286 · Notes

133 came with B.] came both with 1633] came in with. W.
161 *Sinne*] Sinne B.
209 *O* 1633] o B.
220 *Sinnes*] sinnes B.
223 *Sin*] sin B.
252 povertie. 1633] povertie B.
256 her ancient B.] our ancient 1633.
266 *Sin*] sin B.
267 their round B.] the round, 1633.
269 round.] the round B.: them round 1633.
272 *Sin...Darknes*] sin...darknes B.

Henry Vaughan

SILEX SCINTILLANS
PART I
Authoris...
    4 praemonuit.] praemonuit 1650.
    10 Lapis.] Lapis 1650.
To my...
    1 God! 1655] God, 1650.
    2 thee; 1655] thee. 1650.
    3 life 1655] life, 1650.
    6 heart; 1655] heart, 1650 those 1655] these 1650.
    9 Indeed 1655] Indeed, 1650.
    12 thee 1650] the 1655 love; 1655] Love, 1650.
    13 But 1655] But, 1650 bent, 1655] bent 1650.
    14 Beg, 1655] Begge 1650.
Regeneration
    63 desir'd,] desir'd 1655.
Death
    [*I*] added, ed.
    18 contempt;] contempt, 1655.
Resurrection and Immortality
    18 dust?] dust. 1655.
The Search
    84 pray'r 1655] Pray'r, 1650.
    89 Dust 1655] Dust; 1650.
Isaacs Marriage
    3 date, 1650] date. 1655.
    4 renew't 1655] renew't, 1650.
    9 multipli'd 1655] multiply'd, 1650.
    11-12 1655] But being for a bride, sure, prayer was/Very strange stuffe wherewith to court thy lasse, 1650.
    14 odde dull 1655] odde, corse 1650.
    18 dayes 1650] daye 1655.
    19 1655] When sinne, by sinning oft, had not lost sence, 1650.
    23 Retinue; 1650] Retinue 1655.
    25 wind 1655] wind, 1650.
    35-36 1655] But in a frighted, virgin-blush approach'd/Fresh as the morning, when 'tis newly Coach'd; 1650.
    38 lock, 1650] lock. 1655.
    43 knewest 1655] knewst 1650.
    49 restor'd 1650] resto'd 1655. flye 1650] flee 1655.

51 ayer] ayre 1650] ayer. 1655.
52 pray'r. 1650] pray'r 1655.
53 Well 1655] Well, 1650.
55 her Ch.] his 1650, 1655, M., F.
58 thirstie 1650] thirst 1655.
62 sacrifice. 1650] sacrifice 1655
66 Infancie. 1655] Infancie, 1650.
67 to't 1655] to't, 1650.

The Brittish Church
3 head 1650] head. 1655.

Mount of Olives
[*I*] added, ed.

The Call
1 head!] head 1655.
11 How] how 1655.
19 are] ate 1655.

[*Silence, and stealth . . .*]
19 snuff] snuft 1655.
21 known] known, 1650, 1655.

The Resolve
25 wits] *Wits Recreation*, 1650] wits, 1655.

The Match
36 thee!] thee? 1650, 1655.

Rules and Lessons
76 stifle] stiffle 1655.
82 at Ch., M.] all 1655.

Corruption
9 till,] till 1655.
20 those!] those 1655.

Disorder and frailty
23 tast,] tast 1655.

Repentance
6 power,] power; 1655.

The World
11 sour M.] so our 1655.

The Shepheards
1 lives 1655] livers M.'s emendation.

12 'Twas M.] 'Iwas 1655.

Misery
58 Cel, M.] Cel 1655.

Mount of Olives
[*II*] added, ed.

Begging
[*I*] added, ed.

PART II

Ascension-day
20 wears!] wears? 1655.
21 yields] yields, 1655.
23 with the 1655] with Thee Ch.

The Proffer
11 husband 1655] husbands Ch., M.

The Garland
1 below,] below. 1655.
21 bowres,] bowres 1655.

The Timber
42 story)] story 1655.

Begging
[*II*] added, ed.
1 I, 1655] O 1654, in *Flores Solitudinis*.
9 slow 1655] hard 1654.

Jesus weeping
[*I*] added, ed.
1 City!] City? 1655.

Jesus weeping
[*II*] added, ed.

The Ornament
19 one M.] once 1655.

St. Mary Magdalen
6 an] and 1655.
40 Blood] Blood, 1655.

The Rain-bow
26 weather.] weather 1655.

[*As time one day . . .*]
22 shine] shine; 1655.
36 blood.] blood 1655.

The Ass
  48 prize,] prize 1655.
Childe-hood
  15 *men!)*] *men!* 1655.
The Night.
  John 3.2 ed.] 2.3 1655.
  2 noon,] noon 1655.
Abels blood
  33 I,] I 1655.
  40 *things*] *things.* 1655.
Righteousness
  6 Heav'ns] Heavns 1655.

  30 pains Ch., M.] prayers 1655.
The day of Judgement
  [*II*] added, ed.
Death
  [*II*] added, ed.
The Feast
  19 I,] I 1655
The Water-fall
  16 before,] before. 1655.
  26 goes!] goes? 1655.

Richard Crashaw

From STEPS TO THE TEMPLE [1646]

DIVINE EPIGRAMS

Easter day
  3 thee, 1648] thee 1646.
  6 Nest. 1648] Nest, 1646.
  12 lids, punctuation from 1648] lids 1646.

From THE DELIGHTS OF THE MUSES

Musicks Duell
  10 Syren, harmlesse 1648] Syren. harmlesse 1646.
  43 wrangles. 1648] wrangles; 1646.
  69 whence M., MSS] when 1646, 1648.
  72 laboureth 1648] laboureth. 1646.
  73 soyle. It. M., some mss.] soyle it 1646, 1648.
  74 lyre,] lyre. 1646, 1648.
  78 men, 1648] men. 1646.
  84 noyse, 1648] noyse. 1646.
  99 graver 1648] grave 1646.
  104 *Enthusiast.*] *Enthusiast* 1646.
  118 higher.] higher 1646, 1648.
Wishes
  36 owes. 1648] owes 1646.
  85 send 1648] send, 1646.
  90 flowers. 1648] flowers, 1646.
  92 sunnes, 1648] sunnes; 1646.
  104 worth 1648] worth, 1646.
On Marriage
  In 1646, in *Steps to the Temple*, but more appropriately placed with the secular verses, *Delights of the Muses*, in 1648.

CARMEN DEO NOSTRO

To the Noblest . . .
  10 parenthesis added, ed.
  16 deny'd. 1653] deny'd, 1652.
  40 IRRESOLUTE,] IRRESOLUTE 1652.

58 delay; ed.] delay 1652.
To the Name...
   17 see 1648] see. 1652.
   45 sing. 1648] sing 1652.
   54 you,] you 1652.
   68 ne'er] nére 1652.
   74 your 1648] yours 1652.
   75 e're 1648] ére 1652.
   101 Delights] Dilights 1652.
   120 Guest] guest 1648: Guest. 1652.
   186 spices 1648] species 1652.
   188 thence. 1648] thence 1652.
   210 therein 1648] them in 1652. ends. 1648] ends 1652.
   223 o'reflowd] 'oreflowd 1652.
   239 thee. 1648] thee 1652.
In the Holy Nativity...
   15 been, 1646] been 1652.
   16 Thrysis 1648] Thysis 1652, cf. l. 24 th'hast 1648] th-hast 1652.
   23 Comma, etc. added here and sqq. to indicate repetition of entire chorus.
   28 eyes'] eyes's 1652, cf. l. 30.
   37 I) ed.] I.) 1652.
   41 ye 1648] the 1652.
   43 ye 1648] the 1652.
   48 morn, punctuation from 1648] morn. 1652.
   54 bed: punctuation from 1648] bed 1652.
   56 cold. 1648] cold 1652.
   60 wings 1648] wing. 1652.
   85 silk, punctuation from 1648] silk. 1652.
   91 flyes 1648] flyes. 1652.
   105 bring, 1646] bring 1652.
New Year's Day
   12 rose. 1648] rose 1652.

In the Glorious Epiphanie...
   14 Eyes. 1648] Eyes 1652.
   41 sphear] spheare 1648] spear 1652.
   48 (1.) 1648] (2.) 1652.
   94 worn 1648] worn. 1652.
   132 us. 1648] us 1652.
   133 (1) 1648] (2.) 1652
   136 love-sick 1648] love-sick, 1652.
   163 (1.) 1648] (2.) 1652.
   167 Punctuation from 1648] LIGHT 1652.
   182 learn] learni 1648: learn, 1652
   183 (1.) 1648 (2.) 1652.
   188 it 1648] in 1652.
   195 descant 1648] dscant 1652.
   196 what 1648] that 1652.
   197 his 1648] this 1652.
   204 you.] you: 1648: you 1652.
   222 for 1648] for, 1652.
   244 (1.) His GOLD... 1648] (3.) His GOLD... 1652.
To the Queen's Majesty
   1 race, 1648] race. 1652.
   4 Day] day. 1648: Day. 1652.
   5 face, 1648] face. 1652.
   17 whole 1648] whose 1652.

THE HOWRES

For the Hour of Matines
   14 FATHER'S] FATHER' 1652] Fathers 1648.
For the Hour of Prime
   3 open.: These petitions here and subsequently should be read as in Responsor for Mattens.
   13 lyes, 1648] lyes. 1652.
   16 fires, the] fires the 1652.
   29 losse.] losse 1652.

30 O Lord JESU-CHRIST...:
Prayer as in *Mattens* repeated
here and at the end of each
Hour.

The Third
14 than] then 1648] them 1652.
20 side 1648] side. 1652.

The Sixt
7 be.] be 1652.
8 in.] in 1652.
31 CROSSE] CROSSE. 1652.

The Ninth
15 no more; 1648] no more 1652.
25 world's] word's 1652.

Evensong
38 CROSSE] CROSSE. 1652.

Compline
7 be.] be 1652.
8 in.] in 1652.
15 touch 1648] touch. 1652.
19 punctuation from 1648] HEART. 1652.
31 Prayer omitted here, but added in MS AI (M.).

The Recommendation
8 BREATH. 1648] BREATH 1652.

Vexilla Regis...
17 move 1648] move. 1652.

Charitas Nimia
7 merchandise 1648] merchandise. 1652.
33 thou 1648] you 1652.
53 need, 1648] need? 1652.

Sancta Maria Dolorum
10 owne 1648] one 1652.
28 smart,] smart 1652.
30 again.] againe. 1648: again 1652.
87 If 1648] is 1652.

Upon the Bleeding Crucifix
10 good, 1648] good. 1652.
36 drown'd. 1648] drown'd 1652.

Upon the Crowne...
2 yet 1648] yet. 1652.
4 find 1646] find; 1652.
7 Thornes 1648] Thrones 1652.

The Hymn of Sainte Thomas...
33 Lord, my Faith, my Hope 1648] lord, my Hope 1652.

Lauda Sion Salvatorem
19 LORD] LORD. 1652.
25 bid 1648] bid. 1652.
29 no punctuation 1648] wine. 1652.
34 place, 1648] place 1652.
35 good 1648] good. 1652.
38 beleive.] beleive 1652.
39 names] Names 1648: name 1652.
63 WINE,] *Wine*, 1648: WINE. 1652.

Dies Irae Dies Illa
1 what 1648] with 1652.
16 call. 1648] call 1652.
20 fly.] flye. 1648: fly 1652.
38 me: 1648] me 1652.
48 word,] word 1652.
60 ital. from 1648.

The Himn O Gloriosa Domina
2 SON, 1648] SON 1652.
6 son.] son 1652.
10 things 1648] thing 1652 thee] the 1652.
35 from 1648] line omitted 1652.

In the Glorious Assumption...
1 come. 1648] come 1652.
18 here. 1648] here 1652.
29 tree] three. 1652: Tree, 1648.

46 be 1648] be. 1652.
The Weeper
   47 Punctuation from 1648] Tear. 1652.
   58 they 1648] they, 1652.
   Stanza XVI: number omitted in 1652.
   91 woes 1648] woes. 1652.
   98 thee!] thee? 1648: you! 1652. Cf. l. 100.
   104 Vine 1648] wine 1652.
   132 opportunity. 1648] opportunity 1652.
   141 praier 1648] paire 1652.
   144 drop.] drop, 1652.
   147 waits,] waites, 1648] waits. 1652.
   155 yeares] years 1648] yeares. 1652.
   159 fire.] fire 1648] fires 1652.
   163 ye 1648] the 1652.
   172 your 1648] their 1652.
A Hymn to the Name ...
   2 word, 1648] word. 1652.
   11 fill: 1648] fill, 1652
   14 child. 1648] child 1652.
   40 weake 1648] what 1652.
   61 line from 1648] omitted 1652.
   68 punctuation from 1648] MARTYRDOM 1652.
   74 so. 1648] so 1652.
   92 Thee,] thee. 1646, 1648: Thee. 1652.
   109 with. Thus 1648] with thus 1652.
   121 ever. There, 1648] ever there, 1646: ever there 1652.
   122 thou shalt first 1648] you first 1652.
   147 line from 1648] omitted 1652.

155 writt, 1648] writt. 1652.
167 punctuation from 1646] crown. Sons 1652.
169 punctuation from 1648] soul, goe 1652.
175 keeps 1646] keep 1652.
An Apologie
   19 heav'n,] Heav'n, 1648] heav'n 1652.
   26 hatch'd 1648] word omitted 1652.
   29 enow 1648] now 1652.
The Flaming Heart ...
   8 mistake. 1648] mistake 1652.
   18 see. 1648] see 1652.
   22 Her. 1648] Her 1652.
   48 THEE.] THEE 1652.
   58 kindly takes 1648] gives 1652.
   65 things, 1648] things. 1652.
   74 heart. 1648] heart 1652.
   76 darts, punctuation from 1648] darts. 1652.
   104 SERAPHIM!)] SERAPHIM! 1652.
A Song
   11 breath, punctuation from 1648] breath 1652.
Prayer
   7 thy 1648] the 1652.
   17 your 1648] their 1652.
   19 the ghostly foes] the Ghostly foe 1648] their ghostly foes 1652. your part 1648] their part 1652.
   20, 33 your 1648] their 1652.
   54 ith' 1648] th' 1652.
To the Same Party ...
   4 may 1648] my 1652.
Alexias ...
   Title. Complaint] Complaint. 1652.

The First Elegie
   17 way, 1648] word omitted, 1652.
   25 graves 1648] graves. 1652.
   29 Here t'was 1648] Here' was 1652.

The Second Elegie
   10 the beauteous skyes] the beauteous Skies 1648: the skycs 1652.

The Third Elegie
   14 wife. 1648] wife 1652.
   33 approach: 1648] approach 1652.
   54 thousands 1648] thousand 1652.

Description...
   18 spheare] *Spheare* 1648] spear 1652.
   19–20 Paines... themselves; from 1648] omitted 1652.
   23 dying 1648] ding 1652.
   33 and make M.] make 1652] and keep 1648]

An Epitaph...
   19 And] 'And 1652.
      light,] Light, 1648: light. 1652.

Death's Lecture...
   Title: at 1648] and 1652.

   7 YOUTH,] YOUTH 1652.
   8 ye 1648] the 1652.
   12 here: 1648] here 1652.
   15 wide 1648] Wild 1652.

Temperance.
   Title: *Or the*] *Of the* 1652.
   5 physick. Doat] physick Doat 1652.
   27 face; *Hyg.,* M.] face 1652.
   31 way *Hyg.,* M.] way, 1648: way. 1652.

Hope
   16 bed. 1646] bed 1652.
   18 Thee,] Thee 1652] thee. 1648.
   25 th'eye] the eye 1648] th-ey 1652.

M. Crashaws Answer...
   10 morn.] morne. 1646, 1648: morn 1652.
   21 Heav'n!] Heaven! 1646, 1648: heav'n 1652.
   22 eternity. punctuation from 1646] eternity 1652.
   35–36 lines from 1648] omitted 1652.
   37 fair fallacy! by punctuation from 1646] fair fallacy by 1652.

Ben Jonson

From EPIGRAMMES

III
   4 have, F2] have F.
XIV
   2 Know,] Know. Ff.
XV
   4 't will] t'will Ff.

XXIII
   6 no' F2] no F.
LXXXVIII
   12 him,] him Ff.
XCII
   14 twelve] twelves. Ff.
   17 lock'd F2] look'd F.

CVIII
  8 pen. F2] pen F.
CXXXIII
  30 the F2] thee F.
  48 Sans] Sans' Ff.
  119 voyc't,] voyc t Ff.

THE FORREST

III
  25 friends,] friends; Ff.
  46 lent H & S following MSS] lend Ff.
VI
  20 they] they, some copies F.
XI
  57 bowers, F2] bowers F.
  69 Peace,] Peace Ff.
XII
  93–100: on what... sonne. *om* Ff. B. M. Harleian MS. 4064, ff. 243ᵇ–245ᵇ]. Another early draft is in Bod. MS. Rawlinson poetry 31. In the following notes these are A and B respectively. A is the copy text.
  94 lost, B] lost A.
  95 regard, B] regard A.
  96 prepard B] prepard, A.
  98 yeare, B] yeare A.
  99 run, B] Run A.
XIII
  123 finde; F2] finde? F.
XIV
  2 dance, F2] dance. F.
  8 by,] by. Ff.

From UNDER-WOOD

To the Reader. same leave,] same, leave F.
  Ancients] Ancients, F.

Under-Wood] Under-woods F2.
[I.*1*] *To the Holy Trinitie*
  2 Unitie,] Unitie. F2.
  9 sacrifice,] sacrifice. F2.
  32 Of] of F2.
  41 Sanctifier,] Sanctifier. F2.
[I.*2*] *A Hymne*
  12 sweet,] sweet. F2.
  22 With all] withall F2.

[II] *A CELEBRATION OF CHARIS*...

1 20 young,] young. F2.
  22 decay,] decay. F2.
2
  19 looke.] looke, F2.
3
  6 me:] me F2.
  9 Love] love F2.
  12 shaft.] shaft F2.
4
  3 Dove,] Dove F2.
  4 guideth.] guideth F2.
  25 o' the] of F2.
5
  23 in;] in? F2.
  45 thou,] thou F2.
  50 spi'd.] spi'd F2.
6
  1 Charis,] Charis F2.
  4 faire,] faire. F2.
7
  7 gone.] gone F2.
  12 long;] long, F2.
9
  37 him;] him F2.
10
  6 understood.] understood F2.
[III] *The Musicall strife*...
  14 wake.] wake, F2.
[VIII] *The Houre-glasse*
  7 Mistress] Mrs. F2.

[IX] *My Picture* . . .
  15 yeares,] yeares. F2
[X] *Against Jealousie*
  6 fire:] fire, F2.
  11 were.] were, F2.
  13 forth.] forth F2.
  15 please;] please, F2.
[XI] *The Dreame*
  12 againe,] againe; F2
[XIX] *An Elegie*
  6 wings;] wings. F2.
[XXIII] *An Ode* . . .
  32 reproofe,] reproofe. F2.
[XXVII] *An Ode*
  16 voice?] voice. F2.
  27 Muse] Muse, F2.
  32 sing?] sing, F2.
[XXVIII] *A Sonnet*
  5 it] it. F2.
[XXIX] *A Fit* . . .
  1 Rime,] Rime F2.
  3 Conceipt,] Conceipt F2.
  15 Art] are F2.
  32 protection,] protection! F2.
  39 restore] restore, F2.
  55 Sense, . . . meet] Sense . . . meet, F2.
[XXXVI] *A Song*
  2 love] love; F2.
  9 worlds] world F2.
  13 stil'd,] still'd some copies of F2.
[XXXVIII] *An Elegie*
  7 it:] it, F2.
  30 before.] before, F2.
  32 can;] can, F2.
  35 now;] now, F2.
  50 unjust.] unjust, F2.
  60 have!] have? F2.
  74 skie,] skie; F2.
  92 die,] die F2.
  94 apply;] apply F2.
  105 Mistresse] Masters F2.
  111 Fibres] Fivers F2.
    doe] doth F2.
  115 away;] away F2.
  117 heart.] heart F2.
  121 have;] have, F2.
[XXXIX] *An Elegie.*
  Attrib. to Donne first in the *Poems* of 1663 as "Elegie." Copy text: Jonson F2.
  2 you?] you. F2.
  8 perjuries?] perjuries; F2.
  24 thee;] thee F2.
  29 back,] back F2.
  30 streames:] streames F2.
  37 he,] he F2.
  41 pittie;] pittie F2.
  44 infamie;] infamie F2.
  45 he] be F2.
  47 dyes,] dyes F2.
  53 revive; Donne] receive; F2.
  58 make.] make F2.
  62 wayes;] wayes F2.
[XL] *An Elegie*
  9 me, Mistress,] me M^{rs} F2.
  19 light,] light F2.
  20 rarified] retified F2.
    spright;] spright F2.
  25 Mistress] Masters F2.
  38 belie] belie. F2.
  48 not] nor F2.
[XLI] *An Elegie*
  2 Heare,] Heare F2.
    Mistress,] Masters, F2.
  19 it.] it, F2.
[XLII] *An Elegie*
  1 cold;] cold F2.
  8 horse?] horse F2.
  21 not,] not F2.
  44 force,] force. F2.
  47 Chaires] Chaires; F2.
  52 That] that F2.
  53 An] And in some copies of F2.

66 see,] see F2.
74 none,] none F2.
[XLIII] *An Execration* . . .
  5 attempted, *Vulcan*.] attempted *Vulcan* F2.
  12 Bride,] Bride. F2.
  16 blasphemie,] blasphemie? F2.
  20 scurrile] surrile F2.
  33 fiftie] fittie F2.
  52 Geese,] Geese. F2.
  63 in;] in F2.
  76 lungs;] lungs F2.
  78 catch;] catch, F2.
  79 *Pamphlets*] *Pamplets* F2.
  80 Alley;] Alley. F2.
  91 made] mad F2.
  92 not] omitted F2.
    doe,] doe. F.
  105 ruines,] ruines F2.
  112 none:] none F2.
  123 Wise-men] Wise-man F2.
  140 Stewes;] Stewes. F2.
  144 the H. & S. following most mss] in F2.
  148 sigh'd a Sister,] sigh'd, ah Sister F2.
  187 Lanthorne,] Lanthorne F2.
  196 Losse] Losse, F2.
  198 fill;] fill. F2.
  213 thee,] thee F2.
  215 *Bess Broughtons* 1640 Q ed. of poem and H. & S. following all MSS] B. Bs. F2.
[XLVII] *An Epistle* . . .
  4 gold;] gold, F2.
  7 eyes,] eyes; F2.
  8 compromise.] comprimise. F2.
  17 dead;] dead F2.
  22 received] receiv'd F2.
  58 crack'd,] crack'd F2.
  59 will,] will; F2.
  60 can,] can F2.

  62 thence] then F2.
[LII] *My Answer*
  17 handling] handling, F2.
  19 But,] Put F2.
  22 face,] face F2.
[LVII] *To* . . . *Burges*
  10 refuses] refuses, F2.
[LXVI] *An Epigram to the Queene* . . .
  8 wrought] wrought. F2.
  9 Isle] Isle! F2.
[LXVII] *An Ode* . . .
  26 Daughter] Daughtrr F2.
  51 divine,] divine! F2.
  54 *Caroline!*] *Caroline*. F2.
[LXX] *To the immortall memorie* . . .
  44 fall'st,] fall'st F2.
  68 bald] bold F2.
  84 *Ben,*] Ben F2.
  91 long] Long F2.
  100 indentur'd] indenture F2.
[LXXIX] [Untitled]
  5 warpe,] warpe. F2.
A New-yeares-Gift . . .
  12 Shep. in F2 at 14.
  16 Nym. in F2 at 18.
  20 Shep. in F2 at 22.
  23 Chor. in F2 at 22.
  24 Nymp. in F2 at 25.
  27 Chor. in F2 at 25.
    Valleys,] Valleys F2.

[LXXXIV] *EUPHEME;*
OR, THE FAIRE FAME

  Title. Fame] Fame. F2.
The Dedication . . .
  19 Boyes,] Boyes F2.
The Mind
  1 Painter,] Painter F2.
[Prose pass.]
  2 Mother] Mother, F2.
  8 it.] it F2.

Elegie on my Muse
   F repeats title before 1 prefaced
      by *An* ....
   48 doome;] doome. F2.
   77 actions] actions, F2.
   123 the] tee F2.
   149 elect,] elect F2.

MISCELLANY

To the memory ...
   29 didst] didstst F.
   40 Sent] sent F.
   60 Such] such F.

The Songs in
CYNTHIAS REVELLS

[*Echo's*] *Song*
   4 sings."Q 1601] sings. F.
   7 ours":Q] ours: F.
[*Prosaites'*] *Song*
   4 Hey day; hey day, Q]
      Hey ... day, &c. F.
   5-33 Beare-wards ... day
      Q] omitted F.
   23 commaunders] commaunders. Q.
   24 Turn'd] turnd Q.
Song [*Mercury and Crites*]
   5 You F 1616] We Q 1601.

The Songs in POETASTER

Song
   6 toying, Q] toying F1.
[*Crispinus'*] *Song*
   2 scant one] scant-/one F1.

From BARTHOLOMEW FAYRE

Nightingale's Song
   3 beare,] beare. 1631 edition of
      Bartholomew Fayre.
   9 warning for and] warning,
      for and, 1631.
   32-33 youth [thou ... purse.]
      ed.] better, &c. 1631.
   39 At] at 1631.
   43-44 better [bin ... purse.]
      ed.] youth, &c. 1631.
   48 Advance] Adnauce 1631.
   51 say).] say 1631.

From A PRIVATE ENTERTAINMENT

Song
   8 Jug, ... jug; Line from Martin
      Pearson's *Private Musick*
      (1620)] Jug, jug, jug, jug, &c,
      F1.
   13 King] King; F1.

Song from THE KING'S ENTERTAINMENT ....

   7 plants, the] plants. The F2.
   22 'tis] 't is F2.

Songs from LOVE FREED ...
   20 streames.] streames, F1.
   23 away;] away F1.
   39 lines] lives Ff.
An Expostulacion ...
   49 taske.] taske MS.
   74 shop-philosophy.] shop-philosophy MS.

Robert Herrick

From HESPERIDES

A Lyrick...
  13 Gotiere] corr. Errata, 1648.
A Nuptiall Song...
  158 that Two Emended after Gen. XXV.23.] that, That most copies of 1648 ed.
Oberons Feast
  1 *the*] omitted 1648.
To... Pembroke
  2 *of*] *or* 1648.
To his Nephew...
  3 *Coxie*] *Coxn* 1648.
The mad Maids Song...
  9 woe is me, woe, woe is me] corr. Errata in 1648.
A Pastorall...
  3 fails.] fail. 1648.

32 *Sil.*] *Scil.* 1648.
41 *Sil.*] *Scil.* 1648.
Oberons Palace
  40 great-ey'd kine,] great-ey'd-kine, 1648.
The parting Verse...
  8 let] yet corr. Errata in 1648.
Upon her feet
  Started] played some copies of 1648.
An Ode...
  10 having] corr. Errata in 1648.
The Hag
  18 working.] working, 1648.
Charon...
  15 That] that 1648.
  19 Can] can 1648.
  21 *Ph.*] *Ch.* 1648.

Andrew Marvell

MISCELLANEOUS POEMS

A Dialogue...
  Title.] Dialogue, F.
  51 soft, Mar.] cost F.: All that's costly, fair, sweet, Cooke.
To his Coy Mistress
  29 dust;] durst; F.: Dust; Cooke.
  34 lew, Mar.] glew, F.

Tom May's Death
  21 Emathian Cooke] Emilthian F.
  26 translated, Cooke] transflated, F.
  34 command,] command F.
  55 thee] the F.
  68 World's Cooke] World F.
Musicks Empire
  6 tuned Cooke] tun'd F.
  21 VI.] VII F.

The Garden
  23 your Cooke] you F.
Fleckno ...
  104 By Cooke] But F.
To his worthy Friend ...
  Text from F., but some variant readings adopted from James Primrose, *Popular Errors* (1651), transl. from Latin by Robert Witties.
  4 off 1651] of F.
  30 Cawdles, 1651] Cawdies F.
  32 fall.] fall, F.
  33 hastning F.] hasting 1651.
On Mr. Milton's Paradise Lost
  Text from F., but some variant readings adopted from version in John Milton, *Paradise Lost* (1674), 2nd edition.
  33 treatst 1674] treats F.
  45 mightst 1674] might F.
Upon the Hill ...
  12 fright.] frght. F.: fright, Cooke.
  27 further Cooke] furthe F.
  34 Plume Cooke] Plum F.
Upon Appleton House ...
  22 Mote] Mose F.: Mole Cooke.
  139 Man Cooke] Mant F.
  323 *Paradise* Cooke] *Puradise* F.
  328 Thee] The F.
  389 *Israalites*] *Israaliies* F.: *Israelites* Cooke.
  454 Beast. Cooke] Breast. F.
  464 *Constellations* Cooke] *Constellatious* F.
  472 astonish'd Cooke] astonish F.
  556 *Sin,*] *Sin.* F.
  562 *Birds* Cooke] *Btrds* F.
  755 *Aranjuez*] *Aranjeuz* F.: *Aranjeuz* Cooke.
On the Victory ...
  Text from F., but some variant readings adopted from edition in John Bulteel, *New Songs and Poems* (1674).
  9 Intrails 1674] Intails F.
  66 unsung.] unsung. F.
  80 as] as as F.
  97 strength, 1674] strength. F.
  104 oblig'd] obilg'd F.
  125 brought] brought. F.
  129 aspire, 1674] a Spire F.
  139 neither] netheir F. fly;] fly, F.: flie; 1674.
  152 Ill.] Ill F.
  160 lost.] lost, F.
A Dialogue ...
  Text from F. A version with music appears in John Gamble's *Ayres and Dialogues* (1659), 66 ff. This is A in the following notes. An earlier version, corrupt through truncation and paraphrase, appears in William Lawes's autograph MS song book, Brit. Mus. Add. Ms. 31432, ff. 12^v–14^r. See Contents for this version herein reproduced with music.
  1 Death] death A: Death, F. part A] snatch F.
  2 Lids, F.] Lids; A.
  4 shall A] must F.
  5 Elizium: F.] Elizium. A. (*Dorinda.*)] (*Dorinda*) F., oh F.] Oh! A.
  is't] i'st F.
  6 Soul A] Soul, F.
  7 way A] way, F. home: A] home F.
  8 Cell A] omitted F.

9 Cast F.] Turn A.
10 lye; F.] lye, A.
13 There ... nest, F.] There ... nest. A. Assigned to Thyrsis in A.
but F.] But A.
shall A] can F.
14 fly? A] fly. F.
15 sigh (fair Nimph) F.] sigh, fair Nimph, A.
fire F.] Fire, A.
16 wings, yet F.] wings but A.
aspire F.] aspire; A.
17 hit A] hit, F.
18 Heaven's F.] Heavens, A.
19 Elizium F.] Elizium, A.
20 away? A] away. F.
21 Oh! A] Ho, F.
ther's] there is A.
22 Ther's F.] there is A.
no Fox, no] nor Fox, nor A.
Bear; A] Bear. F.
24 away; F.] away: A.
25 No Oatepipes needful, there thy Eares A] And there most sweetly thine Ear F.
26 feast F.] sleep A.
Spheares A] Sphear. F.
27 *Dorinda*. Appears as catch word of F., but omitted as prefix.
Oh Sweet! A] omitted F.
state, A] state F.
Antidate: F.] antidate A.
29 spend A] spend, F.
to A] omitted F.
come A] come, F.
31 on: F.] on: A
There A] There, F.
32 sweetest A] softest F.
33 There A] There, F.
Consort, A] Consorts, F.

34 Cool A] Cold F.
flow. F.] flow: A.
35 There A] There, F.
is] is, F.
36 ever A] ever, F.
begun. F.] begun; A.
37 there A] there, F.
38 Nimph's a F.] Nymph a A.
39 F. prints as two lines. (*Thyrsis*.) ed.] *Thyrsis*. F. Ah me!] Ah me, ah me. F: Ah! me. A.
40 dye: F.] die; A.
41 Convince A] Convinc't F.
now A] now, F.
true, A] true; F.
42 bidding, F.] bidding A.
mee, F.] me A.
adieu. A] adieu F.
43 *Thyrsis*. A] omitted F.
live A] live, F.
thee, I; A] thee, I F.
44 I'le A] Will F.
45 Corilla A] Corellia F.
46 poppies, A] poppies F.
47 weep: A] weep, F.
48 smoothly F.] omitted A.
in sleep. F.] in a sleep. A.

The Character of Holland. Text from F., but some variant readings adopted from 1665 and 1672 editions, when the poem was published separately as a pamphlet. Both 1665 and 1672 present a different conclusion in the last eight lines.
43 see the *rising Sun* F.] sees the rising Sun, 1665: sees the Rising Sun 1672.
45 leak, 1665, 1672] leak F.
48 Shov'l and be a Magistrate.

1300 · Notes

F.] Shovel and be a Magistrate 1665, 1672.
59 Besides 1672, F.] Beside 1665.
61 for their *God* F.] to be God 1665, 1672.
65 *Marg'ret* F.] *Marg'et* 1665, 1672.
88 a 1665] omitted F.
90 But... *End*: F.] (But... End:) 1665, 1672.
101–52 in F. only. The following eight lines end the poem in 1665 and 1672:

Vainly did this Slap Dragon fury hope,
With sober English valour ere to cope:
Not though the Primed their barbarous mornings-draught
With Powder, and with Pipes of Brandy fraught:
Yet Rupert, Sandwich, and of all, the Duke,
The Duke has made their Sea-sick courage puke.
Like the three Comets, sent from heaven down
With Fiery Flailes to swinge th'ingratefull Clown.

An Horatian Ode...
Title. Horatian Th.] Horation F.
31 highest] hightest F.
85 *Commons* Th.] *Common* F.

The First Anniversary.
Text from F., but some variant readings adopted from 1655 Quarto.
41 an 1655] and F.
60 joyning 1655] joyng F.
105 won, 1655] won. F.
286 wouldst 1655] would F.

Two Songs...
Title. Lady] Ludy F.

A Poem upon... O.C.
48 his growing Th.] her growing F.
108 celebrates Th.] celebrate F.
121 lead] dead F.
185–324 not in F. Supplied from Th.
201 does claime Grosart] desclaime Th.
229 refuse] refuge Th.
272 cease,] cease; Th.
273 fall; Grosart] full Th.

To His Noble Friend... Text from Richard Lovelace, *Lucasta* (London, 1649).

Upon the Death...
Text from *Lachrymae Musarum*, collected and set forth by R. B[rome], London, 1649 and 1650. The text of the 1650 edition is reprinted here.

An Elegy...
Text from the anonymous and apparently unique printed version in the library of Worcester College, Oxford. It carries a handwritten attribution to Marvell.

Index to Titles and First Lines

All titles are set in italics, first lines in roman type. Titles which begin with English articles are alphabetized by the second word; first lines are alphabetized to the very first word.

Aaron, 363
A bachelour I will, 937
Abels blood, 581
About the sweet bag of a Bee, 947
A broken Altar, Lord, thy servant reares, 205
A crowne, a crowne, for Loves bright head, 906
Admission, 486
Affliction (Peace, Peace; It is not so. Thou doest miscall), 494
Affliction, I (When first thou didst entice to thee my heart), 225
Affliction, II (Kill mee not ev'ry day), 241
Affliction, III (My heart did heave, and there came forth, O God!), 254
Affliction, IV (Broken in pieces, all asunder), 271
Affliction, V (My God, I red this day), 278
After many scornes like these, 821
After the Feast (my Shapcot) see, 991
After the rare Arch-Poet Johnson dy'd, 986
Againe, 943
Against Jealousie, 832
Against Love, 953
The Agony, 217
The Agreement, 588
Ah Ben!/Say how, or when, 1017
Ah! he is fled!, 430
Ah my deere angry Lord, 360
Ah! what time wilt thou come? when shall that crie, 485
Aire and Angels, 33
Alas, how pleasant are their dayes, 1092
Alas I can't, for tell me how, 1022
Alas, poore Death, where is thy glory?, 358
Alexias, 727
All after pleasures as I ridd one day, 261
All Kings, and all their favorites, 35
All men are wormes: But this no man. In silke, 765
Almighty Judge, how shall poore wretches brooke, 377
Almighty Lord, who from thy glorious throne, 380
The Altar, 205
The Amber Bead, 1013
Ametas and Thestylis making Hay-Ropes, 1117
Among thy Fancies, tell me this, 980
Amorphus' Song, 890
Anagram, 246
The Anagram (Elegie II), 77
An Anatomy of the World, 105
An Apologie, 715
And art thou greived, sweet and sacred Dove, 321
And do they so? have they a Sense, 460
And must I sing? what subject shall I chuse, 802

And now th'art set wide ope, The Speare's sad Art, 624
And why to me this, thou lame Lord of fire, 849
Anguish, 585
The Anniversarie, 35
The Anniversary Poems, 101
Annunciation, 137
Another (Art thou not destin'd? then, with hast, go on), 1046
Another (Thou had'st the wreath before, now take the Tree), 987
Another, I (In the morning when ye rise), 1022
Another, II (If ye feare to be affrighted), 1022
Another Ladyes exception present at the hearing, 829
The Answere, 357
Anthea bade me tye her shooe, 938
Antiphon, I, 232
Antiphon, II, 274
The Apparition, 54
The Apparition of his Mistresse calling him to Elizium, 1003
A Prayer, that is said alone, 1045
The Argument of his Book, 931
Artillery, 325
Art thou not destin'd? then, with hast, go on, 1046
Ascention, 139
Ascension-day, 523
Ascension-Hymn, 525
As due by many titles I resigne, 151
As he, that sees a dark and shady grove, 223
As I one evening sat before my cell, 325
As Men, for feare the starres should sleepe and nod, 319
As on a window late I cast mine eye, 299
As one put drunk into the Packet-boat, 1106
The Ass, 574

As shews the Aire, when with a Rain-bow grac'd, 954
Assurance, 342
As time one day by me did pass, 566
As travellours when the twilight's come, 501
As virtuous men passe mildly' away, 56
A sweet disorder in the dresse, 946
At the round earths imagin'd corners, blow, 152
Authoris (de se) Emblema, 407
The Autumnall (Elegie IX), 79
Avarice, 257
Awake, glad heart! get up, and Sing, 472
Awake, sad heart, whom sorrow ever drownes, 294
A Ward, and still in bonds, one day, 412
Away despaire! my Gracious Lord doth heare, 338
Away thou fondling motley humorist, 91
Away with silks, away with Lawn, 988
A wreathed Garland of deserved praise, 375

A Bachanalian Verse, 1018
Bad are the times..., 989
The Bagge, 338
The Bag of the Bee, 947
The Baite, 53
The Banquet, 370
Bartholomew Fayre, 896
Batter my heart, three person'd God; for, you, 155
Be dumb course measures, jar no more; to me, 537
Before I sigh my last gaspe, let me breath, 62
Begging, I, 522
Begging, II, 550

Index to Titles and First Lines · 1303

Begging another, on colour of mending the former, 826
Beginne with Jove; then is the worke halfe done, 980
Bermudas, 1082
Be still black Parasites, 531
Bid me to live, and I will live, 971
The Bird, 544
Bitter-sweet, 360
Blasted with sighs, and surrounded with teares, 38
Blessed, unhappy City! dearly lov'd, 553
Blest be the God of Harmony, and Love!, 452
Blest be the God of Love, 243
Blest Infant Bud, whose Blossome-life, 483
Blest Order, which in powre dost so excell, 348
The Blossome, 64
Blush, folly, blush: here's none that feares, 895
Boast not these Titles of your Ancestors, 877
The Book, 603
The Bracelet (Elegie XI), 81
Brave Infant of Saguntum, cleare, 864
Brave Rose, alas where art thou? in the chair, 326
Breake of day, 34
Bright, and blest beame! whose strong projection, 483
Bright Babe! Whose awfull beautyes make, 656
Bright Queen of Heaven! Gods Virgin Spouse!, 558
Bright shadows of true Rest! some shoots of blisse, 479
Bright sparke shott from a brighter place, 254
The British Church, 291
The Brittish Church, 430
The broken heart, 55
Broken in peices, all asunder, 271
The Bunch of Grapes, 312

Buriall, 453
The Burial Of an Infant, 483
Busie old foole, unruly Sunne, 24
Busines, 295
Busy inquiring heart, what wouldst thou know?, 330
But cause thou hearst the mighty king of Spaine, 912
But that thou art my Wisedome, Lord, 276
Buz, quoth the blue Flie, 900
By miracles exceeding power of man, 138
By our first strange and fatall interview, 84
By those bright Eyes, at whose immortall fires, 833

The Call (Come my heart! come my head!), 438
The Call (Come my Way, my Truth, my Life), 344
Camden, most reverend head, to whom I owe, 764
The Canonization, 27
Canst be idle? canst thou play?, 295
The Carkanet, 938
Carmen Deo Nostro, 639
A Celebration of Charis in ten Lyrick Peeces, 820
Ceremonies for Candlemasse Eve, 1015
The Character of Holland, 1167
Charis, guesse, and doe not misse, 825
Charis one day in discourse, 826
Charitas Nimia, 678
Charmes, 1021
Charmes and Knots, 277
Charm me asleep, and melt me so, 966
Charon and Phylomel, 1011
Charon! O Gentle Charon! let me wooe thee, 1011
The Cheap Physitian Upon the Translation of Lessius, 735

Chearfulness, 455
The Check, 474
Childe-hood, 577
Christmas, 261
A Christmas Caroll, sung to the King in the Presence at White-Hall, 1039
Christs Nativity, 472
The Church, 205
The Church-floore, 246
Church-lock and key, 246
The Church Militant, 380
Church-monuments, 244
Church-Musique, 245
The Church-Porch, 185
Churchrents or schismes, 326
Church-Service, 452
Clasping of hands, 344
Clayming a second kisse by Desert, 825
Cleere are her eyes, 1001
Climb at Court for me that will, 1129
Clora come view my Soul, and tell, 1094
Clorinda and Damon, 1083
Clothes do but cheat and cousen us, 988
Cock-crowing, 533
The Collar, 340
Coloss: 3. 3. Our life is hid with Christ in God, 265
Come away,/Make no delay, 376
Come! bring thy gift. If blessings were as slow, 333
Come bring your sampler, and with Art, 935
Come, come, what doe I here?, 444
Come down, and dance ye in the toyle, 934
Come, drop your branches, strow the way, 551
Come follow me, my wagges, and say as I say, 888
Come, let us here enjoy the shade, 838
Come little Infant, Love me now, 1089
Come live with mee, and bee my love, 53
Come Lord, My head doth burne, my heart is sick, 289
Come, Madam, come, all rest my powers defie, 89
Come my Celia, let us prove, 798
Come my heart! come my head!, 438
Come my Way, my Truth, my Life, 344
Come sapless Blossom, creep not stil on Earth, 515
Come, skilfull Lupo, now, and take, 952
Come then, and like two Doves with silv'rie wings, 1003
Come thou, who art the Wine, and wit, 997
Come we shepheards whose blest Sight, 650
Come with our Voyces, let us warre, 829
Come ye hither All, whose tast, 369
Communitie, 41
Complaining, 330
Compline, 673
The Computation, 72
Confession, 310
Confined Love, 44
Connubii Flores, or the well-wishes at Weddings, 1007
Conscience, 287
Constancy, 252
The Constellation, 508
Content (Peace muttring thoughts, and doe not grudge to keep), 248
Content (Peace, peace! I know 'twas brave), 446
Content thee, greedy hart, 323
Corinna's going a Maying, 960
The Coronet, 1078
Corruption, 470

Index to Titles and First Lines • 1305

A Country life: To his Brother, M. Tho: Herrick, 948
Courage my Soul, now learn to wield, 1073
Crispinus' Song, 894
The Crosse (Since Christ embrac'd the Crosse it selfe, dare I), 162
The Crosse (What is this strange and uncouth thing!), 352
Crucifying, 138
The Curse (Who ever guesses, thinks, or dreames he knowes), 49
The Curse (Goe perjur'd man; and if thou ere return), 958
Cynthias Revells, 888

Damon come drive thy flocks this way, 1083
Damon the Mower, 1112
The Dampe, 68
Daphnis and Chloe, 1099
Daphnis must from Chloe part, 1099
The Daugher of Herodias, 554
The Dawning (Ah! what time wilt thou come? when shall that crie), 485
The Dawning (Awake, sad heart, whom sorrow ever drownes), 294
Day of Judgement, I, 421
The day of Judgement, II, 591
Dean-Bourn, farewell; I never look to see, 947
Dear, beauteous Saint! more white then day, 560
Deare Freind sitt downe. The tale is long and sad, 313
Deare friend sit down, and bear awhile this shade, 536
Deare love, for nothing lesse then thee, 45
Dear friend! whose holy, ever-living lines, 463
Dear, heavn-designed Soul!, 724

Dear hope! earth's dowry, and heavn's debt!, 738
Dear Lord, 'tis finished! and now he, 410
Dear Reliques of a dislodg'd Soul, whose lack, 734
Death (Death thou wast once an uncouth hideous thing), 375
Death, I ('Tis a sad Land, that in one day), 416
Death, II (Though since thy first sad entrance by), 594
Death, and darkness get you packing, 491
Death be not proud, though some have called thee, 153
Death's Lecture at the Funeral of a Young Gentleman, 734
Death thou wast once an uncouth hideous thing, 375
Decay, 280
Dedication [Silex Scintillans], 409
The Dedication [The Temple], 185
The Dedication of her Cradle, 872
Dear God,/If thy smart Rod, 1038
The Definition of Love, 1103
Deigne at my hands this crown of prayer and praise, 136
Delight in Disorder, 946
The Delights of the Muses, 628
Deniall, 260
Description of a Religious House and Condition of Life, 731
Dialogue, 297
A Dialogue... (What gentle formes are these that move), 907
A Dialogue Antheme, 358
A Dialogue between the Resolved Soul, and Created Pleasure, 1073
A Dialogue between the Soul and Body, 1084
A Dialogue between Thyrsis and Dorinda, 1165
Dies Irae Dies Illa, 694
The Difference Betwixt Kings and Subjects, 936

The Dirge of Jephthahs Daughter, 1036
The Discharge, 330
Discipline, 368
Discontents in Devon, 941
Disorder and frailty, 476
Display thy breasts, my Julia, there let me, 968
The Dissolution, 69
Distraction, 434
Divine Epigrams, 623
Divine Meditations, 151
Divine Poems, 135
Divinity, 319
Doe but consider this small dust, 831
Doe not beguile my heart, 330
Doe what you come for, Captayne, with your newes, 779
Donne, the delight of Phœbus, and each Muse, 766
Doomes day, 376
Dotage, 355
Down with the Rosemary and Bayes, 1015
The Dream (Me thought, [last night] love in an anger came), 939
The Dreame (Deare love, for nothing lesse then thee), 45
The Dreame (Or Scorne, or pittie on me take), 832
Dressing, 489
Drinke to me, onely, with thine eyes, 802
Drinke up/Your Cup, 1018
Droop, droop no more, or hang the head, 933
Dulnes, 298
Dust and clay/Mans antient wear! 525
The dwelling-place, 571

Each blest drop, on each blest limme, 623
Easter, 221
Easter day (Rise, Heir of fresh Eternity), 626
Easter-day (Thou, whose sad heart, and weeping head lyes low), 491
Easter Hymn, 491
Easter wings, 223
Echo's Song, 888
An Elegie (By those bright Eyes, at whose immortall fires), 833
An Elegie (Let me be what I am, as Virgil cold), 847
An Elegie (Since you must goe, and I must bid farewell), 846
An Elegie (That Love's a bitter sweet, I ne're conceive), 845
An Elegie ('Tis true, I'm broke! Vowes, Oathes, and all I had), 839
An Elegie (To make the Doubt cleare that no Woman's true), 843
Elegie II. The Anagram, 77
Elegie V. His Picture, 79
Elegie IX. The Autumnall, 79
Elegie XI. The Bracelet, 81
Elegie XVI. On his Mistris, 84
Elegie XVIII. Loves Progresse, 86
Elegie XIX. To his Mistris going to Bed, 89
Elegie on my Muse, 878
An Elegy upon the Death of my Lord Francis Villiers, 1202
The Elixir, 374
The end of his worke, 1023
Enough: and leave the rest to Fame, 1129
Ephes. 4:30. Greive not the holy spirit, &c., 321
Epigrammes, 761
An Epigram to K. Charles, 861
An Epigram to the Queene, then lying in, 861
An Epistle answering to one that asked to be Sealed of the Tribe of Ben, 856
Epistle. To Elizabeth Countesse of Rutland, 807

Epistle. To Katherine, Lady Aubigny, 810
Epitaph on Elizabeth, L. H., 782
Epitaph on S. P. a child of Q. El. Chappel, 781
An Epitaph upon⸺, 1129
An Epitaph Upon a Young Married Couple, 733
Epode, 803
Ere cherries ripe, and straw-berries be gone, 774
Eternal God! maker of all, 603
Eternitie, 1033
Eupheme; or, The Faire Fame, 871
The Evening-watch, 451
Evensong (Beginne with Jove; then is the worke halfe done), 980
Even-song (Blest be the God of Love), 243
Evensong (Lord, by thy sweet and saving Sign), 672
An Execration upon Vulcan, 849
The Expiration, 71
An Expostulacion with Inigo Jones, 909
The Extasie, 57
The Eye, 958
Eyes and Tears, 1079

Fair and yong light! my guide to holy, 567
Faire Daffadills, we weep to see, 979
Faire Fame, who art ordain'd to crowne, 872
Fair, order'd lights (whose motion without noise, 508
The Fair Singer, 1096
Fair, solitary path! Whose blessed shades, 582
Faith (Bright, and blest beame! whose strong projection), 483
Faith (Lord, how couldst thou so much appease), 229
False glozing Pleasures, casks of happines, 355
False life! a foil and no more, when, 601
False world, good-night: since thou hast brought, 796
Fames pillar here, at last, we set, 1024
The family, 322
Farewell! I goe to sleep; but when, 451
Farewell, thou child of my right hand, and joy, 769
Farewell thou Thing, time-past so knowne, so deare, 956
Farewell to love, 73
Farewell you Everlasting hills! I'm Cast, 432
Father John Burges, 860
Father of Heaven, and him, by whom, 140
Father of lights! what Sunnie seed, 533
Father, part of his double interest, 156
The Favour, 538
The Feast, 595
A Feaver, 32
Fight thou with shafts of silver, and o'rcome, 942
Fine Madame Would-bee, wherefore should you feare, 771
The First Anniversary, 105
The First Anniversary of the Government under O.C., 1174
First, April, she with mellow showrs, 943
The First Elegie (I late the roman youth's lov'd prayse and pride), 727
First, for Effusions due unto the dead, 944
First [Song] (The Astrologers own Eyes are set), 1185
First was the World as one great Cymbal made, 1118
A Fit of Rime against Rime, 837
The Flaming Heart, 717
The Flea, 48

Fleckno, an English Priest at Rome, 1121
The Flowre, 354
The foile, 365
Follow a shaddow, it still flies you, 800
The Fore-runners, 365
For every houre that thou wilt spare mee now, 26
For Godsake hold your tongue, and let me love, 27
For his Mind, I doe not care, 829
For Loves-sake, kisse me once againe, 826
The Forrest, 790
For the first twenty yeares, since yesterday, 72
For the Hour of Matines, 665
For the Hour of Prime, 667
For Those my unbaptized Rhimes, 1026
4 Ephes: 30. Greive not the holy spirit, &c., 321
Frailty, 251
From spanish shrugs, french faces, smirks, irps, and all affected humours, 891
From the dull confines of the drooping West, 1011
From the Temple to your home, 1007
The Frozen Heart, 934
The frozen Zone: or, Julia disdainfull, 954
Full of Rebellion, I would die, 224
The Funerall, 63
A Funerall Elegie, 101

The Gallery, 1094
The Garden, 1119
The Garland, 539
Gather ye Rose-buds while ye may, 964
Gentle knights,/Know some measure of your nights, 905
Get up, get up for shame, the Blooming Morne, 960
Giddines, 311
Give me that man, that dares bestride, 947
The Glance, 360
Glide gentle streams, and beare, 955
The Glimpse, 341
Glorie, 1006
Goddesse of Youth, and Lady of the Spring, 969
God hath two wings, which He doth ever move, 1027
God is above the sphere of our esteem, 1027
God is all-sufferance here; here He doth show, 1034
God is not onely said to be, 1027
God makes not good men wantons, but doth bring, 1043
God not to be comprehended, 1028
Gods Anger without Affection, 1027
God when He's angry here with any one, 1027
God will have all, or none; serve Him, or fall, 1033
Goe, and catche a falling starre, 22
Goe happy Rose, and enterwove, 968
Goe now; and with some daring drugg, 735
Goe perjur'd man; and if thou ere return, 958
Goe smiling soules, your new built Cages breake, 623
Goe thou forth my booke, though late, 1023
Go, go, queint folies, sugred sin, 478
Go hence, and with this parting kisse, 995
Go, intercept some Fountain in the Vain, 1200
Good, and great God, can I not thinke of thee, 815
Good day, Mirtillo..., 965
Good Friday, 219
Good Friday: Rex Tragicus, 1047

Index to Titles and First Lines · 1309

Goodfriday, 1613. Riding Westward, 165
Good men afflicted most, 1043
The good-morrow, 21
Good morrow to the Day so fair, 988
Good wee must love, and must hate ill, 41
Go prettie child, and beare this Flower, 1033
Grace, 240
Gratefulnes, 307
Great Charles, among the holy gifts of grace, 861
Greife, 352

Had we but World enough, and Time, 1090
The Hag, 1009
Haile Mary, full of grace, it once was said, 861
Hail, most high, most humble one!, 697
Hail, sister springs!, 702
Happy those early dayes! when I, 442
Hark. *See also* Hearke.
Harke, how the Birds doe sing, 315
Hark! she is call'd, the parting houre is come, 699
Have ye beheld (with much delight), 991
Having bin Tenant long to a Rich Lord, 220
H. Baptisme, I, 223
H. Baptisme, II, 224
The H. Communion, 231
Heare mee, O God!/A broken heart, 818
Heare ye Virgins, and Ile teach, 978
Heark how the Mower Damon Sung, 1112
Hears't thou, my soul, what serious things, 694
Heaven, 378

Hedon's Song, 889
He is starke mad, who ever sayes, 55
Hellen, did Homer never see, 835
Helpe me! helpe me! now I call, 935
Hence they have born my Lord: Behold! the Stone, 1050
Here lyes Johnson with the rest, 1017
Here lyes to each her parents ruth, 766
Here take my Picture; though I bid farewell, 79
Here we securely live, and eate, 1001
Here where our Lord once lay'd his Head, 675
Her Eyes the Glow-worme lend thee, 1005
Her man described by her owne Dictamen, 827
Her of your name, whose fair inheritance, 135
Her pretty feet, 1001
Her Triumph, 822
Hesperides, 929
He that cannot chuse but love, 75
He that feares death, or mournes it, in the just, 767
He, that is weary, let him sitt, 259
The hidden Treasure, 576
The Himn O Gloriosa Domina, 697
His Answer to a Question, 936
His Cavalier, 947
His coming to the Sepulcher, 1050
His Confession, 1026
His Creed, 1035
His discourse with Cupid, 823
His Excuse for loving, 820
His fare-well to Sack, 956
His last request to Julia, 1023
His Letanie, to the Holy Spirit, 1029
His Noble Numbers, 1025
His Prayer for Absolution, 1026
His Picture (Elegie V), 79
His Prayer to Ben. Johnson, 1005

His request to Julia, 942
His returne to London, 1011
His teares to Thamasis, 1019
His Winding-sheet, 997
Hither thou com'st: the busie wind all night, 544
The holdfast, 329
Holines on the Head, 363
Holland, that scarce deserves the name of Land, 1167
H. Baptisme, I, 223
H. Baptisme, II, 224
The H. Communion (Not in rich furniture, or fine array), 231
The Holy Communion (Welcome sweet, and sacred feast; welcome life!), 492
H. Scriptures (Welcome dear book, souls Joy, and food! The feast), 471
The H. Scriptures, I (Oh Booke! infinite sweetnes! Let my heart), 238
The H. Scriptures, II (Oh that I knew how all thy lights combine), 238
Holy Sonnet 1 (As due by many titles I resigne), 151
Holy Sonnet 2 (Oh my blacke Soule! now thou art summoned), 151
Holy Sonnet 3 (This is my playes last scene, here heavens appoint), 152
Holy Sonnet 4 (At the round earths imagin'd corners, blow), 152
Holy Sonnet 5 (If poysonous mineralls, and if that tree), 153
Holy Sonnet 6 (Death be not proud, though some have called thee), 153
Holy Sonnet 7 (Spit in my face you Jewes, and pierce my side), 154
Holy Sonnet 8 (Why are wee by all creatures waited on?), 154
Holy Sonnet 9 (What if this present were the worlds last night?), 155
Holy Sonnet 10 (Batter my heart, three person'd God; for, you), 155
Holy Sonnet 11 (Wilt thou love God, as he thee! then digest), 156
Holy Sonnet 12 (Father, part of his double interest), 156
Holy Sonnet 13 (Thou hast made me, And shall thy worke decay?), 157
Holy Sonnet 14 (O might those sighes and teares returne againe), 158
Holy Sonnet 15 (I am a little world made cunningly), 158
Holy Sonnet 16 (If faithfull soules be alike glorifi'd), 159
Holy Sonnet 17 (Since she whome I lovd, hath payd her last debt), 159
Holy Sonnet 18 (Show me deare Christ, thy spouse, so bright and cleare), 160
Holy Sonnet 19 (Oh, to vex me, contraryes meete in one), 161
Holy Sonnets, 136
Holy Sonnets, 1633, 150
Holy Sonnets, 1635, 157
Holy Sonnets, Westmoreland MS, 159
Home, 289
Hope (Hope whose weak beeing ruin'd is), 737
Hope (I gave to Hope a watch of mine: but hee), 305
Hope whose weak beeing ruin'd is, 737
Horace's Ode, 894
An Horatian Ode upon Cromwel's Return from Ireland, 1171
The Houre-glasse, 831
How, best of Kings, do'st thou a scepter beare!, 763
How blest art thou, canst love the

countrey, Wroth, 793
How dull and dead are books, that cannot show, 981
How fresh, ô Lord, how sweet and cleane, 354
How he saw her, 820
How I doe love thee Beaumont, and thy Muse, 770
How is man parcell'd out? how ev'ry hour, 496
How Life and Death in Thee, 625, 678
How Lillies came white, 963
How Love came in, I do not know, 944
How rich, O Lord! how fresh thy visits are! 472
How should I praise thee, Lord? how should my rimes, 234
How shril are silent tears? when sin got head, 486
How soone doth Man decay!, 279
How sweetly doth My Master sound! My Master, 364
How vainly men themselves amaze, 1119
How well her Name an Army doth present, 246
How wisely Nature did decree, 1079
The H. Scriptures, I (Oh Booke! infinite sweetnes! Let my heart), 238
The H. Scriptures, II (Oh that I knew how all thy lights combine), 238
H. Scriptures (Welcome dear book, souls Joy, and food! The feast), 471
Humility, 250
Hymn. *See also* Himn.
The Hymne (Queene, and Huntresse, chaste, and faire), 890
A Hymne on the Nativitie of my Saviour, 819
A Hymne to Christ, at the Authors last going into Germany, 167

Hymne to God my God, in my sicknesse, 169
A Hymne to God the Father (Heare mee, O God!), 818
A Hymne to God the Father (Wilt thou forgive that sinne where I begunne), 168
The Hymn of Sainte Thomas in Adoration of the Blessed Sacrament (Adoro Te), 688
A Hymn to the Name and Honor of the Admirable Sainte Teresa, 709

I am a little world made cunningly, 158
I am the Doore, 624
I am two fooles, I know, 28
I beheld her, on a Day, 820
I blesse thee, Lord, because I Growe, 317
I bring ye love:..., 1019
I can love both faire and browne, 25
I cannot ope mine eies, 242
I cannot reach it; and my striving eye, 577
I cannot skill of these thy waies, 277
I cannot thinke there's that antipathy, 772
Idle Verse, 478
I do believe, that die I must, 1035
I do not go! thou know'st, I'le dye!, 550
I dream'd this mortal part of mine, 939
I dreamt the Roses one time went, 934
If any have an ear, 572
If as a flowre doth sprid and dy, 237
If as the winds and waters here below, 317
If faithfull soules be alike glorifi'd, 159
If I freely may discover, 893

I fixe mine eye on thine, and there, 52
If poysonous minerals, and if that tree, 153
I freeze, I freeze, and nothing dwels, 934
If Rome so great, and in her wisest age, 773
If this worlds friends might see but once, 564
If to admire were to commend, my praise, 784
If wee Could see below, 365
If when these Lyricks (Cesar) You shall heare, 969
If ye feare to be affrighted, 1022
If yet I have not all thy love, 29
I gave to Hope a watch of mine: but hee, 305
I have been wanton, and too bold I feare, 1023
I have considerd it, and find, 217
I have consider'd it, and find, 462
I have done one braver thing, 23
I have it now, 569
I have lost, and lately, these, 938
I joy, Deare Mother, when I veiw, 291
I know it is my sinne which locks thine eares, 246
I know the waies of Learning; both the head, 269
I late the roman youth's lov'd prayse and pride, 727
Ile come to thee in all those shapes, 960
Il'e write no more of Love; but now repent, 1023
I'll tell thee now (deare Love) what thou shalt doe, 39
I long to talke with some old lovers ghost, 60
I made a posy, while the day ranne by, 276
I make no haste to have my Numbers read, 1006

Immensitie cloysterd in thy deare wombe, 137
Immortall clothing I put on, 1013
Immortal Heat, o Let thy greater flame, 234
Immortal Love, Author of this great frame, 233
Imployment, I, 237
Imployment, II, 259
Impossibilities to his friend, 963
The Incarnation, and Passion, 437
The Indifferent, 25
I never stoop'd so low, as they, 70
I now thinke, Love is rather deafe, then blind, 831
In shade of death's sad Tree, 681
In sober mornings, doe not thou reherse, 933
Instead of Orient Pearls of Jet, 938
In the Glorious Assumption of Our Blessed Lady, 699
In the Glorious Epiphanie of Our Lord God, 656
In the Holy Nativity of Our Lord God, 650
In the houre of my distresse, 1029
In the morning when ye rise, 1022
In this world (the Isle of Dreames), 1044
The Invitation, 369
Inviting a friend to supper, 776
In what torne ship soever I embarke, 167
Isaacs Marriage, 428
I saw a Flie within a Beade, 1013
I Saw Eternity the other night, 504
I saw the Vertues sitting hand in hand, 250
I scarce beleeve my love to be so pure, 42
I see the Temple in thy Pillar rear'd, 586
I see the use: and know my bloud, 448

I send, I send here my supremest kiss, 1019
I sing of Brooks, of Blossomes, Birds, and Bowers, 931
I sing the birth, was borne to night, 819
I sing the brave adventure of two wights, 785
I sing the just, and uncontrol'd Descent, 873
I sing the Name which None can say, 643
Is this a Fast, to keep, 1046
I struck the board, and cryd, No more, 340
It cannot be. Where is that mighty joy, 235
I that have been a lover, and could shew it, 836
I threatned to observe the strict decree, 329
I travaild on seeing the hill, where lay, 328
It will be look'd for, booke, when some but see, 762
I walkt the other day (to spend my hour,), 519
I who have favour'd many, come to be, 982
I wonder by my troth, what thou, and I, 21
I Would be married, but I'de have no Wife, 637
I wrote it down. But one that saw, 588

Jacobs Pillow, and Pillar, 586
A Jeat Ring sent, 69
Jesu, 295
Jesu is in my heart, his sacred name, 295
Jesu, no more! It is full tide, 685
Jesus, my life! how shall I truly love thee?, 540
Jesus weeping, I, 553
Jesus weeping, II, 555

The Jewes (Poore nation, whose sweet sappe and juice), 339
The Jews (When the fair year), 548
Jordan, I, 236
Jordan, II, 284
Josephs coat, 346
Joy, 537
Joy, I did locke thee up. But some bad man, 312
Joy of my life! while left me here, 447
Judgement, 377
Julia, if I chance to die, 942
Julia was carelesse, and withall, 937
Julia when thy Herrick dies, 997
Justice, I, 277
Justice, II, 327

Kill mee not ev'ry day, 241
Kinde pitty chokes my spleene; brave scorn forbids, 94
King of Comforts! King of life!, 487
King of Glory, King of Peace,/I will love thee, 332
King of Glory, King of Peace,/With the one make warre to cease, 389
King of Mercy, King of Love, 522
The Kings Entertainment at Welbeck, 899
The Kisse (Among thy Fancies, tell me this), 980
A Kisse (What is a Kisse? Why this, as some approve), 1006
Kisse me, sweet: The warie lover, 799
The Knot, 558
Know'st thou This, Souldier? 'Tis a much-, 687
Know you faire, on what you looke, 626

La Corona, 136
Laid out for dead, let thy last kindnesse be, 941

The Lampe, 431
Lauda Sion Salvatorem, 690
The Law, and the Gospel, 502
Leanders Obsequies, 955
A Lecture upon the Shadow, 74
The Legacie, 31
Lent, 267
L'Envoy (King of Glory, King of Peace), 389
L'Envoy (O the new worlds new, quickning Sun!), 605
Let all the world in ev'ry corner sing, 233
Let forraine Nations of their Language boast, 356
Let it not your wonder move, 820
Let mans Soule be a Spheare, and then, in this, 165
Let me be what I am, as Virgil cold, 847
Let me powre forth, 46
Let witts contest, 372
Life, 276
Life of my life, take not so soone thy flight, 962
Like the vain Curlings of the Watry maze, 1174
Listen sweet Dove unto my song, 239
A Litanie, 140
Little think'st thou, poore flower, 64
Live, live with me, and thou shalt see, 999
Loe, what my countrey should have done (have rais'd, 771
Loe where a Wounded Heart with Bleeding Eyes conspire, 701
Lo here a little volume, but great Book!, 721
Longing, 335
Look how our foule Dayes do exceed our faire, 1026
Look up, languishing Soul! Lo where the fair, 676
Lord, bind me up, and let me lye, 512

Lord, by thy Sweet and Saving Sign, 665
Lord how can Man preach thy eternal word?, 247
Lord, how couldst thou so much appease, 229
Lord, how I am all Ague, when I seeke, 218
Lord, how is Gam'ster chang'd! his haire close cut! 766
Lord I am like to Misletoe, 1044
Lord I confesse my sinne is great, 228
Lord in my silence, how doe I despise, 251
Lord I will meane and speake thy praise, 345
Lord Jesus! with what sweetness and delights, 523
Lord, let the Angels praise thy name, 281
Lord make mee coy and tender to offend, 275
Lord, my first Fruits present themselves to thee, 185
Lord, since thou didst in this vile Clay, 480
Lord, thou art mine, and I am thine, 344
Lord, Thou hast given me a cell, 1031
Lord! what a busie, restles thing, 435
Lord, what is man? why should he coste thee, 678
Lord, when the sense of thy sweet grace, 720
Lord, when thou didst on Sinai pitch, 502
Lord! when thou didst thy selfe undresse, 437
Lord, who createdst Man in wealth and store, 223
Lord who hast form'd mee out of mudd, 248
Lord with what bounty and rare Clemency, 262

Lord, with what care hast thou begirt us round?, 225
Lord, with what courage, and delight, 455
Lord, with what glory wast thou serv'd of old, 288
Love, I, 233
Love, II, 234
Love, III, 379
Love, and Discipline, 500
Love and my selfe (beleeve me) on a day, 940
Love, any devill else but you, 43
Love bad mee welcome. Yet my soule drew back, 379
Love brought me to a silent Grove, 1015
Love built a stately house, where Fortune came, 265
Love Freed from Ignorance and Folly, 906
Love is blinde, and a wanton, 894
Love-joy, 299
Lovers infinitenesse, 29
Loves Alchymie, 47
Loves Deitie, 60
Loves diet, 61
Loves exchange, 43
Loves growth, 42
Love-sick, 540
Love's play at Push-pin, 940
Loves Progresse (Elegie XVIII), 86
Loves Usury, 26
Love, thou art Absolute sole lord, 709
Love-unknowne, 313
Lucy, you brightnesse of our spheare, who are, 775
Luke 11. Blessed be the paps which Thou hast sucked, 625
Luxurious Man, to bring his Vice in use, 1111
A Lyrick to Mirth, 953

Madame, had all antiquitie beene lost, 778
Madame, I told you late how I repented, 772
The mad Maids song, 988
Make, make me Thine, my gracious God, 1032
Make me a heaven; and make me there, 958
Man (My God, I heard this day), 272
Man (Weighing the stedfastness and state), 518
Man is a lumpe, where all beasts kneaded bee, 99
Mans fall, and Recovery, 432
Mans medly, 315
Marble, weepe, for thou dost cover, 768
Marke but this flea, and marke in this, 48
Mark you the floore? that square and speckel'd stone, 246
Marry, and love thy Flavia, for, shee, 77
Martial, thou gav'st farre nobler Epigrammes, 767
Mary Magdalene, 362
Master Surveyor, you that first begann, 909
The Match (Dear friend! whose holy, ever-living lines), 463
The Match (Nature had long a Treasure made), 1109
Mattens, 242
Mattens, or morning Prayer, 980
Matthew 8. I am not worthy that thou should'st come under my roofe, 624
Matthew. 27. And he answered them nothing, 624
May his pretty Duke-ship grow, 970
May none, whose scatter'd names honor my booke, 764
May others feare, flie, and traduce thy name, 765
M. Crashaws Answer for Hope, 738
Meeting with Time, slack thing, sayd I, 306

The mellow touch of musick most doth wound, 936
Melt earth to sea, sea flow to ayre, 902
The Men of War, 572
Men that are safe, and sure, in all they doe, 856
Mercy and Love, 1027
The Message, 50
The Method, 318
Me thought, (last night) love in an anger came, 939
Midnight, 445
The Mind, 875
Misery (Lord, bind me up, and let me lye), 512
Misery (Lord, let the Angels praise thy Name), 281
M. Crashaws Answer for Hope, 738
Money gets the masterie, 942
'Mongst those long rowes of crownes that guild your race, 664
Mony, thou Bane of blisse, and sourse of woe, 257
More discontents I never had, 941
The Morning-watch, 449
Mortification, 279
Mount of Olives, I, 436
Mount of Olives, II, 517
Mourning, 1097
The Mower against Gardens, 1111
The Mower's Song, 1116
The Mower to the Glo-Worms, 1115
Moyst with one drop of thy blood, my dry soule, 139
The Musicall strife, 829
Musicks Duell, 628
Musicks Empire, 1118
The Mutinie, 506
My Answer: The Poet to the Painter, 859
My comforts droppe, and melt away like snow, 357
My dear, Almighty Lord! why dost thou weep?, 555

My faithful friend, if you can see, 963
My God and King! to thee, 585
My God, a Verse is not a Crowne, 250
My God, how gracious art thou! I had slipt, 461
My God, if writings may, 285
My God, I heard this day, 272
My God, I'm wounded by my sin, 1028
My God, I red this day, 278
My God! thou that didst dye for me, 409
My God, when I walke in those groves, 422
My heart did heave, and there came forth, O God!, 254
My joy, my life, my crowne!, 357
My Love is of a birth as rare, 1103
My masters and friends, and good people draw neere, 896
My Mind was once the true survey, 1116
My name engrav'd herein, 36
My Picture left in Scotland, 831
My Soul, there is a Countrie, 457
My stock lyes dead, and no encrease, 240
My wearied Barke, O Let it now be Crown'd! 1024
My words and thoughts doe both expresse this notion, 265

Nativitie, 137
Nature, 224
Nature had long a Treasure made, 1109
Nay, nay,/You must not stay, 904
Negative love, 70
Neutrality loathsome, 1033
Never my Book's perfection did appeare, 969
Never was Day so over-sick with showres, 959
The new Crie, 774

Index to Titles and First Lines · 1317

New yeares, expect new gifts: Sister, your Harpe, 868
A New-yeares-Gift sung to King Charles, 1635, 869
New Year's Day, 654
The New-yeeres Gift, or Circumcisions Song, sung to the King in the Presence at White-Hall, 1040
The Night, 579
Night hath no wings, to him that cannot sleep, 1035
Nightingale's Song, 896
The Night-piece, to Julia, 1005
The Ninth [Hour], 671
Noblest Charis, you that are, 823
No cause, nor client fat, will Chev'rill leese, 768
A nocturnall upon S. Lucies day, 51
No despight to the dead, 1006
No Lover saith, I love, nor any other, 72
No more let Greece her bolder fables tell, 784
Non Vi, 640
Nor art thou lesse esteem'd, that I have plac'd, 1012
No roofes of gold o're riotous tables shining, 731
Nor yet, nor yet, O you in this night blest, 904
No Shipwrack of Vertue, 943
No Spouse but a Sister, 937
No Spring, nor Summer Beauty hath such grace, 79
Not he that flies the court for want of clothes, 781
Nothing could make mee sooner to confesse, 119
Not in rich furniture, or fine array, 231
Not that in colour it was like thy haire, 81
Not to know vice at all, and keepe true state, 803
Now does Spains Fleet her spatious wings unfold, 1160

Now each one drie his weeping eyes, 892
Now, my cunning lady, Moone, 901
Now, now the mirth comes, 1020
Now that the harth is crown'd with smiling fire, 813
Now thou hast lov'd me one whole day, 23
Now Westward Sol had spent the richest Beames, 628
A Nuptiall Song, or Epithalamie, on Sir Clipseby Crew and his Lady, 972
The Nymph complaining for the death of her Faun, 1085

Obedience, 285
Oberons Feast, 977
Oberons Palace, 991
Oberon, the Faery Prince, 900
Oblig'd by frequent visits of this man, 1121
O Book! lifes guide! how shall we part, 604
The Obsequies, 598
Occasional Poems and Hymns, 162
O come away,/Make no delay, 595
O day of life, of light, of love!, 591
An Ode (Hellen, did Homer never see), 835
Ode (Swell me a bowle with lustie wine), 894
An Ode for him, 1017
An Ode, or Psalme, to God, 1038
An Ode, or Song, by all the Muses, 862
An Ode. To himselfe, 834
An Ode to Sir Clipsebie Crew, 1001
Ode: To Sir William Sydney, on his Birth-day, 813
O doe not use mee, 263
The Odour. 2 Cor: 2.15, 364
O dreadfull Justice, what a fright and terrour, 327

Of Death, 767
An Offering, 333
The Office of the Holy Crosse, 665
Of Love, 944
Oft have I seen, when that renewing breath, 418
Of what an easy quick accesse, 284
Of your Trouble, Ben, to ease me, 827
Oh All ye, who passe by, whose eies and mind, 206
Oh Blessed body, whither art thou throwne, 220
Oh Booke! infinite sweetnes! Let my heart, 238
Oh Day most calme, most bright, 255
Oh doe not die, for I shall hate, 32
Oh doe not wanton with those eyes, 830
Oh glorious spirits, who after all your bands, 258
Oh King of greif (a title strange, yet true, 215
Oh my blacke Soule! now thou art summoned, 151
Oh my Cheif Good, 219
O holy, blessed, glorious three, 541
O holy, blessed, glorious Trinitie, 816
Oh, to vex me, contraryes meete in one, 161
O Joyes! Infinite sweetnes! with what flowres, 449
O knit me, that am crumbled dust! the heape, 434
O might those sighes and teares returne againe, 158
O Mighty Nothing! unto thee, 624
O my chief good!, 458
On a Drop of Dew, 1077
On, as thou hast begunne, brave youth, and get, 987
On Chev'rill the Lawyer, 768
On Court-worme, 765

On English Mounsieur, 773
On Giles and Jone, 769
On Himselfe (Il'e write no more of Love; but now repent), 1023
On Himselfe (The worke is done: young men, and maidens set), 1024
On his Mistris (Elegie XVI), 84
On Lippe, the Teacher, 772
On Lucy Countesse of Bedford, 772
On Margaret Ratcliffe, 768
On Marriage, 637
On Mr. G. Herberts booke intituled the Temple of Sacred Poems, 626
On Mr. Milton's Paradise lost, 1127
On my first Daughter, 766
On my first Sonne, 769
On reformed Gam'ster, 766
On Sir Voluptuous Beast, 767
On Spies, 770
On the famous Voyage, 784
On the same Beast, 767
On the Victory obtained by Blake over the Spaniards, in the Bay of Sanctacruze, 1160
On the water of our Lords Baptisme, 623
Or lookt I back unto the Times hence flown, 1010
The Ornament, 559
Or Scorne, or pittie on me take, 832
O sacred Providence, who from end to end, 299
O spitefull bitter thought, 342
O tell me whence that joy doth spring, 602
O that I could a sinne once see, 243
O, that joy so soone should waste!, 889
O the new worlds new, quickning Sun!, 605
O thou that lovest a pure, and whitend soul!, 489
O thou! the first fruits of the dead, 453

O Thou, the wonder of all dayes!, 1036
O thy bright looks! thy glance of love, 538
Our times are much degenerate from those, 1199
O what a cunning guest, 310
Oh what a thing is man! how farre from powre, 311
O when my God, my glory brings, 585
O who shall, from this Dungeon, raise, 1084
O who will give me teares? Come all ye springs, 352
O who will show me those delights on high?, 378
O Yeares! and Age! Farewell, 1033
O yet, how early, and before her time, 905

Painter, yo'are come, but may be gone, 875
Palinode (From spanish shrugs, french faces, smirks, irps, and all affected humours), 891
Palm-Sunday, 551
The Palm-tree, 536
A Panegerick to Sir Lewis Pemberton, 982
Paradise, 317
The Paradox, 72
The Parasceve, or Preparation, 1034
The Parcæ, or, Three dainty Destinies, 940
The Parliament of Roses to Julia, 934
A parody, 373
The parting Verse, or charge to his supposed Wife when he travelled, 995
Part of the worke remaines; one part is past, 1023
The Passion, 458
A Pastorall sung to the King: Montano, Silvio, and Mirtillo, Shepheards, 989
A Pastorall upon the birth of Prince Charles, Presented to the King, 965
Peace (My Soul, there is a Countrie), 457
Peace (Sweet Peace, where dost thou dwell, I humbly crave), 308
Peace muttring thoughts, and doe not grudge to keep, 248
Peace, peace! I blush to hear thee; when thou art, 474
Peace, peace! I know 'twas brave, 446
Peace, Peace; It is not so. Thou doest miscall, 494
Peace Pratler, doe not lowre, 287
The Pearle, 269
Perirrhanterium, 185
Phillis, Tomalin, away, 1188
Philosophers have measur'd mountains, 217
Phosphorus, 905
The Picture of little T.C. in a Prospect of Flowers, 1105
The Picture of the Body, 874
The Pilgrimage (As travellours when the twilight's come), 501
The Pilgrimage (I travail'd on seeing the hill, where lay), 328
The pillar of Fame, 1024
Play I co'd once; but (gentle friend) you see, 964
Play-wright me reades, and still my verses damnes, 770
A Poëme sent me by Sir William Burlase, 858
Poems of Devotion, 816
A Poem upon the Death of O. C., 1190
Poetaster, 893
Poets, 1006
The Poets good wishes for the most hopefull and handsome Prince, the Duke of Yorke, 970

The Pomander Bracelet, 938
Poore hart lament, 318
Poore Nation, whose sweet sappe and juice, 339
Poore silly Soule, whose hope and head lyes low, 293
The Posy, 372
Praeludium, 802
Praise (King of Comforts! King of Life!), 487
Praise, I (To write a verse or two is all the praise), 241
Praise, II (King of Glory, King of Peace), 332
Praise, III (Lord I will meane and speake thy praise), 345
Prayer (A Prayer, that is said alone), 1045
Prayer, I (Prayer the Churches banquet, Angels age), 231
Prayer, II (Of what an easy quick accesse), 284
Prayer: An Ode, Which was Præfixed to a little Prayer-book, 721
Prayer the Churches banquet, Angels age, 231
Praying! and to be married? It was rare, 428
Praysed be the God of Love, 274
Pray thee take care, that tak'st my booke in hand, 762
Predestination, 1045
Predestination is the Cause alone, 1045
The Preisthood, 348
Prepare for Songs; He's come, He's come, 1040
Presse me not to take more pleasure, 366
The Primrose, 66
A Private Entertainment at High-Gate, 898
The Proffer, 531
The Prohibition, 70
Prosaites' Song, 888
Providence (O sacred Providence, who from end to end), 299

Providence (Sacred and secret hand!), 557
Psalm 65, 592
Psalme 104, 541
Psalm 121, 494
The Pulley, 347
The Pursuite, 435
Put off Thy Robe of Purple, then go on, 1047

Queene, and Huntresse, chaste, and faire, 890
The Queer, 602
Quickness, 601
The Quiddity, 250
The Quipp, 292
Quite spent with thoughts I left my Cell, and lay, 441

The Rain-bow, 562
Rare are thy cheeks Susanna, which do show, 1001
The Recommendation, 675
Redemption, 220
Regeneration, 412
The Relapse, 461
Religion, 422
The Relique, 67
Repentance (Lord I confesse my sinne is great), 228
Repentance (Lord, since thou didst in this vile Clay), 480
The Reprisall, 217
Reproach we may the living; not the dead, 1006
The Resolve, 462
Resurrection, 139
Resurrection and Immortality, 418
Retirement, 498
The Retreate, 442
Rich, churlish Land! that hid'st so long in thee, 729
Righteousness, 582
Rime, the rack of finest wits, 837
Rise heart; thy Lord is Risen. Sing his praise, 221
Rise, Heire of fresh Eternity, 626

Rise, Royall Sion! rise and sing, 690
Rise, thou best and brightest morning!, 654
The Rose, 366
Rules and Lessons, 465

Sacred and secret hand!, 557
The Sacrifice, 206
Sad, purple well! whose bubling eye, 581
Sainte Mary Magdalene, 701
St. Mary Magdalen, 560
Salute the last and everlasting day, 139
Salvation to all that will is nigh, 137
Sancta Maria Dolorum, 681
The Sap, 515
Satyre I (Away thou fondling motley humorist), 91
Satyre III (Kinde pitty chokes my spleene; brave scorn forbids), 94
Satyrs' Song, 901
The Scar-fire, 942
The Search ('Tis now cleare day: I see a Rose), 425
The Search (Whither, ô, whither art thou fled), 349
The Second Anniversarie. Of The Progres of the Soule, 119
The Seconde Elegie (Though All the joyes I had fleed hence with Thee), 728
Second Song (Phillis, Tomalin, away), 1188
The Seed growing secretly, 564
See how the arched Earth does here, 1130
See how the Orient Dew, 1077
Seeke you majestie, to strike?, 903
See, see, ô see, who here is come a Maying!, 898
See Sir, how as the Suns hot Masculine flame, 150
See the Chariot at hand here of Love, 822
See with what simplicity, 1105
Selfe-condemnation, 359
Self Love, 75
Send home my long strayd eyes to mee, 50
Send me some Token that my hope may live, 75
Senec. Traged. ex Thyeste Chor. 2, 1129
Sepulcher, 220
Shapcot! To thee the Fairy State, 977
Shark, when he goes to any publick feast, 976
Shee'is dead; And all which die, 69
The Shepheards, 510
Shew me thy feet; shew me thy legs, thy thighes, 988
Sho'd I not put on Blacks, when each one here, 1016
The shooe tying, 938
Show me deare Christ, thy spouse, so bright and cleare, 160
The Showre, 434
Sighes and Grones, 263
Silence, and stealth of dayes! 'tis now, 451
Silex Scintillans, 407
Since Christ embrac'd the Crosse it selfe, dare I, 162
Since dying for me, thou didst crave no more, 598
Since I am comming to that Holy roome, 169
Since I in storms us'd most to be, 602
Since in a land not barren stil, 500
Since Lord to thee, 224
Since she whome I lovd, hath payd her last debt, 159
Since you must goe, and I must bid farewell, 846
Sinne, I, 225
Sinne, II, 243
The Sinner, 218

The Sinners Sacrifice, 816
Sinnes round, 305
Sion, 288
Sions true, glorious God! on thee, 592
Sir Inigo doeth fear it as I heare, 913
Sit further, and make room for thine own fame, 1126
Sitting, and ready to be drawne, 874
The Sixt [Hour], 669
The Size, 323
Slow, slow, fresh fount, keepe time with my salt teares, 888
Soft Musick, 936
So long you did not sing, or touch your Lute, 967
Some act of Love's bound to reherse, 790
Some man unworthy to be possessor, 44
Some that have deeper digg'd loves Myne then I, 47
Some would know, 936
Son-dayes, 479
Song (A crowne, a crowne, for Loves bright head), 906
Song (Blush, folly, blush: here's none that feares), 895
Song (Come follow me, my wagges, and say as I say), 888
A Song (Come, let us here enjoy the shade), 838
Song (Gentle knights,/Know some measure of your nights), 905
Song (Goe, and catche a falling starre), 22
A Song (Goe perjur'd man; and if thou ere return), 958
Song (If I freely may discover), 893
A Song (Lord, when the sense of thy sweet grace), 720
Song (Love is blind, and a wanton), 894

Song (Melt earth to sea, sea flow to ayre), 902
Song (Nay, Nay,/You must not stay), 904
Song (Nor yet, nor yet, O you in this night blest), 904
Song (Now each one drie his weeping eyes), 892
Song (Now, my cunning lady, Moone), 901
A Song (Oh doe not wanton with those eyes), 830
Song (O, that joy so soone should waste!), 889
Song (O yet, how early, and before her time), 905
Song (See, see, ô see, who here is come a Maying!), 898
Song (Slow, slow, fresh fount, keepe time with my salt teares), 888
Song (Sweetest love, I do not goe), 30
Song (Then, in a free and lofty straine), 895
Song (The solemne rites are well begunne), 903
Song (Thou more then most sweet glove), 890
Song (Wake, our mirth begins to die), 894
The Song, by two Faies, 903
The Song of her Descent, 873
Song: That Women are but Mens shaddowes, 800
Song: To Celia, I, 798
Song: To Celia, II, 802
A Song to the Maskers, 934
The Sonne, 356
Sonnet. The Token, 75
Sonnet To the noble Lady, the Lady Mary Worth, 836
Sorry I am my God, sorry I am, 305
So smooth, so sweet, so silv'ry is thy voice, 942

Index to Titles and First Lines · 1323

So, so, breake off this last lamenting kisse, 71
Soules joy, when thou art gone, 373
Spies, you are lights in state, but of base stuffe, 770
Spit in my face you Jewes, and pierce my side, 154
Stand still, and I will read to thee, 74
The Starre (Bright sparke shott from a brighter place), 254
The Starre (What ever 'tis, whose beauty here below), 535
The Star-Song: A Caroll to the King, 1042
Stay, the cheerefull Chanticleere, 902
Steps to the Temple, 623
Still yong and fine! but what is still in view, 562
The Stone, 569
The Storm, 448
The Storme, 317
Strength of my Countrey, whilst I bring to view, 780
Submission, 276
The succession of the foure sweet months, 943
Sunday, 255
The Sunne Rising, 24
Superliminare, 204
Suppose he had been Tabled at thy Teates, 625
Sure, It was so. Man in those early days, 470
Sure, there's a tye of Bodyes! and as they, 456
Sure thou didst flourish once! and many Springs, 546
Sweet Day so coole, so calme, so bright, 269
Sweete, sacred hill! on whose fair brow, 436
Sweetest love, I do not goe, 30
Sweetest of sweets I thanke you.
When displeasure, 245
Sweetest Saviour, if my soule, 297
Sweet, harmles lives! (on whose holy leisure, 510
Sweet Peace, where dost thou dwell, I humbly crave, 308
Sweet were the daies, when thou didst lodge with Lot, 280
Swell me a bowle with lustie wine, 894

Take heed of loving mee, 70
Tamely fraile body'abstaine to day; to day, 164
Teach mee, my God and King, 374
The Teare sent to her from Stanes, 955
Tears, 585
Tell us, thou cleere and heavenly Tongue, 1042
The Temper, I, 234
The Temper, II, 235
Temperance, 735
The Tempest, 496
The Temple, 185
Temple (With his kinde mother who partakes thy woe), 138
Tempora cinxisset Foliorum densior umbra, 930
Tentâsti, fateor, sine vulnere sœpius, & me, 407
The Thankes-giving, 215
A Thanksgiving to God, for his House, 1031
Th'Astrologers own Eyes are set, 1185
That for seven Lusters I did never come, 945
That Love's a bitter sweet, I ne're conceive, 845
That Providence which had so long the care, 1190
That Women are but mens shaddowes, 800

The fleet Astronomer can bore, 266
The forward Youth that would appear, 1171
The God of Love my Shepheard is, 361
The Hag is astride, 1009
The Harbingers are come. See, see their mark, 365
The lucky world shewd me one day, 559
The merry world did on a day, 292
Then his chast wife, though Beast now know no more, 767
Then, in a free and lofty straine, 895
These Houres, and that which hover's o're my End, 675
The solemne rites are well begunne, 903
The wanton Troopers riding by, 1085
The worke is done: young men, and maidens set, 1024
They are all gone into the world of light! 527
They'have left thee naked, Lord, O that they had!, 687
Think'st Thou that this Love can stand, 1117
The Third Elegie (Rich, churlish Land! that hid'st so long in thee), 729
The Third [Hour], 668
This Crosse-Tree here, 1049
This Day is Yours Great Charles! and in this War, 1014
This Ile tell ye by the way, 1021
This is my playes last scene, here heavens appoint, 152
This morning, timely rapt with holy fire, 772
Thou art not, Penshurst, built to envious show, 790
Thou art not so black, as my heart, 69
Though All the joyes I had fleed hence with Thee, 728
Though since thy first sad entrance by, 594
Thou had'st the wreath before, now take the Tree, 987
Thou hast made me, And shall thy worke decay?, 157
Thou more then most sweet glove, 890
Thou sail'st with others, in this Argus here, 943
Thou, that hast given so much to mee, 307
Thou that know'st for whom I mourne, 439
Thou, that mak'st gaine thy end, and wisely well, 763
Thou who condemnest Jewish hate, 359
Thou! who didst place me in this busie street, 574
Thou who dost dwell and linger heere below, 358
Thou, who dost flow and flourish here below, 539
Thou, whom the former precepts have, 204
Thou, whose sad heart, and weeping head lyes low, 491
Thou, whose sweet youth, and early hopes inhance, 185
Three lovely Sisters working were, 940
Thrice, and above, blest (my soules halfe) art thou, 948
The Throne, 594
Through that pure Virgin-shrine, 579
Throw away thy rod, 368
Thus have I back again to thy bright name, 715
Thy God was making hast into thy roofe, 624
Till I shall come again, let this suffice, 982
The Timber, 546
Time, 306

Time was upon, 1028
'Tis a sad Land, that in one day, 416
'Tis dead night round about: Horrour doth creepe, 431
'Tis growne almost a danger to speake true, 810
'Tis hard to finde God, but to comprehend, 1028
Tis lost, to trust a Tombe with such a ghest, 101
'Tis not the work of force but skill, 640
'Tis now cleare day: I see a Rose, 425
'Tis the yeares midnight, and it is the dayes, 51
'Tis true, I'm broke! Vowes, Oathes, and all I had, 839
Tis true that he is dead: but yet to chuse, 1202
'Tis true, 'tis day; what though it be?, 34
To a Freind an Epigram of him, 913
To all Angels and Saints, 258
To all, to whom I write, 764
To a Love-Feast we both invited are, 1034
To Alphonso Ferrabosco, on his booke, 783
To Anthea, who may command him any thing, 971
To a weake Gamster in Poetry, 780
To Captayne Hungry, 779
To Celia, I, 798
To Celia, II, 802
To Crowne it, 1024
To Daffadills, 979
To day old Janus opens the new yeare, 869
To Dean-Bourn, a rude River in Devon, 947
To Dianeme, 988
To Doctor Alablaster, 1012
To draw no envy (Shakespeare) on thy name, 885
To Edward Allen, 773

To Electra, 960
To Elizabeth Countesse of Rutland, 807
To E. of D. with six holy Sonnets, 150
To finde God, 1026
To Fine Lady Would-bee, 771
To Francis Beaumont, 770
To God, I, 1032
To God, II, 1034
To God, III, 1043
To God, IV, 1044
To God: an Anthem, sung in the Chappell at White-Hall, before the King, 1028
To God, on his sicknesse, 1038
To Heaven, 815
To his Booke (While thou didst keep thy Candor undefil'd), 932
To his Booke (Goe thou forth my booke, though late), 1023
To his Coy Mistress, 1090
To his dying Brother, Master William Herrick, 962
To his Friend, on the untuneable Times, 964
To his Girles who would have him sportfull, 1022
To his Mistris going to Bed (Elegie XIX), 89
To his Mistresses, 935
To his Muse, 931
To his Nephew, to be prosperous in his art of Painting, 987
To his Noble Friend Mr. Richard Lovelace, 1199
To his Saviour, a Child; a Present, by a child, 1033
To his sweet Saviour, 1035
To his worthy Friend Doctor Witty upon his Translation of the Popular Errors, 1126
To Inigo Marquess Would be A Corollary, 912
To John Donne, 776
To Julia, 997
To Katherine, Lady Aubigny, 810

To keep a true Lent, 1046
To Kenelme, John, George, 877
To King James, 763
To Lucy Countesse of Bedford, 772
To Lucy, Countesse of Bedford, with Mr. Donnes Satyres, 775
To make a final conquest of all me, 1096
To make the Doubt cleare that no Woman's true, 843
To Mary Lady Wroth, 778
To Master John Burges, 860
Tom May's Death, 1106
To M. Denham, on his Prospective Poem, 1010
To me my Julia lately sent, 938
To M. Henry Lawes, the excellent Composer of his Lyricks, 1014
To Mr. Josuah Sylvester, 784
To Musique, to becalme his Fever, 966
To my Booke, 762
To my Booke-seller, 763
To my meere English Censurer, 765
To my most merciful, my most loving, and dearly loved Redeemer, 409
To night, grave sir, both my poore house, and I, 776
To Our B. Lord, 678
To paint thy Worth, if rightly I did know it, 858
To Penshurst, 790
To Phillis to love, and live with him, 999
To Play-Wright, 770
To rest, to rest; The Herald of the day, 905
To Robin Red-brest, 941
To see both blended in one flood, 625
To Sicknesse, 800
To Sir Edward Herbert. At Julyers, 99
To Sir Raph Shelton, 781
To Sir Robert Wroth, 793
To Sir William Sydney, on his Birth-day, 813

To the Countesse of Bedford, 97
To thee, my way in Epigrammes seemes new, 765
To the Ghost of Martial, 767
To the High and Noble Prince, George, Duke, Marquesse, and Earle of Buckingham, 969
To the Holy Bible, 604
To the Holy Trinitie, 816
To the immortall memorie, and friendship of that noble paire, Sir Lucius Cary, and Sir H. Morison, 864
To the Infant Martyrs, 623
To the King (If when these Lyricks [Cesar] You shall heare), 969
To the King and Queene, upon their unhappy distances, 945
To the King: Upon his comming with his Army into the West, 944
To the King, Upon his taking of Leicester, 1014
To the King, Upon his welcome to Hampton-Court, 1018
To the Lady Magdalen Herbert, of St. Mary Magdalen, 135
To the learned Critick, 765
To the memory of my beloved, The Author Mr. William Shakespeare, 885
To the Most Illustrious, and Most Hopefull Prince, Charles, Prince of Wales, 930
To the most learned, wise, and Arch-Antiquary, M. John Selden, 982
To the Name Above Every Name, the Name of Jesus, 643
To the Noblest and best of Ladyes, the Countesse of Denbigh, 640
To the Painter, to draw him a Picture, 952
To the Queene, 969
To the Queen's Majesty, 664
To the Reader, 762
To the reverend shade of his religious Father, 945
To the right honourable, Philip,

Index to Titles and First Lines · 1327

Earle of Pembroke, and Montgomerie, 981
To the Rose, 968
To the same (Kisse me, sweet: The warie lover), 799
To the Same Party Councel Concerning Her Choise, 724
To these whom Death again did wed, 733
To the Virgins, to make much of Time, 964
To the World, 796
To true Souldiers, 780
Touch but thy Lire (my Harrie) and I heare, 1014
To urge, my lov'd Alphonso, that bold fame, 783
To Virgins, 978
To what a combersome unwieldinesse, 61
To William Camden, 764
To William Lord Mounteagle, 771
To write a verse or two is all the praise, 241
The Transfiguration, 1013
Trinity-Sunday (Lord who hast form'd mee out of mudd), 248
Trinity-Sunday (O holy, blessed, glorious three), 541
The triple Foole, 28
A true Hymne, 357
Truth and falsehood, 1022
Truth by her own simplicity is known, 1022
'Twas so, I saw thy birth: That drowsie Lake, 434
Twelfe night, or King and Queene, 1020
The 23d Psalme, 361
'Twere time that I dy'd too, now shee is dead, 878
Twice or thrice had I loved thee, 33
Twicknam garden, 38
Twixt Kings and Subjects ther's this mighty odds, 936
Two Songs at the Marriage of the Lord Fauconberg and the Lady Mary Cromwell, 1185

The undertaking, 23
Under-wood, 816
The unfortunate Lover, 1092
Ungratefulnes, 262
Unkindnes, 275
Unprofitablenes, 472
Up, O my soul, and blesse the Lord. O God, 541
Upon a Gentlewoman with a sweet Voice, 967
Upon Appleton House, to my Lord Fairfax, 1133
Upon Ben. Johnson, 1017
Upon God, 1027
Upon her Eyes, 1001
Upon her feet, 1001
Upon his Sister-in-Law, Mistresse Elizab: Herrick, 944
Upon Julia's breasts, 968
Upon Julia's Clothes, 1013
Upon Julia's Fall, 937
Upon Julia's Recovery, 933
Upon Julia's Riband, 954
Upon Julia's Voice, 942
Upon Love, 1015
Upon Love: by way of question and answer, 1019
Upon M. Ben. Johnson, 986
Upon Mistresse Susanna Southwell, 1001
Upon M. William Lawes, the rare Musitian, 1016
Upon our Saviours Tombe wherein never man was laid, 625
Upon Shark, 976
Upon the Annunciation and Passion falling upon one day, *1608*, 164
Upon the Bishop of Lincolne's Imprisonment, 959
Upon the Bleeding Crucifix, 685
Upon the Body of Our Bl. Lord, Naked and Bloody, 687
Upon the Crowne of Thorns, 687

Upon the Death of the Lord Hastings, 1200
Upon the Hill and Grove at Bill-borow, 1130
Upon the H. Sepulcher, 675
Upon the Infant Martyrs, 625
Upon the losse of his Mistresses, 938
Upon the Nipples of Julia's Breast, 991
Upon this Primrose hill, 66
Upon Time, 1028
Up publike joy, remember, 862
Up to those bright, and gladsome hils, 494
Urging her of a promise, 826

Vain, sinful Art! who first did fit, 554
Vain Wits and eyes, 411
A Valediction: forbidding mourning, 56
A Valediction: of my name, in the window, 36
A Valediction: of the booke, 39
A Valediction: of weeping, 46
Vanity, I, 266
Vanity, II, 293
Vanity of Spirit, 441
Vertue, 269
Vexilla Regis, the Hymn of the Holy Crosse, 676
The Vine, 939

Wake, our mirth begins to die, 894
Wantons we are; and though our words be such, 1006
The Water-course, 358
The Water-fall, 599
Water, water I desire, 942
Weary of this same Clay, and straw, I laid, 506
The Weeper, 701, 702
Weepe with me all you that read, 781
Weighing the stedfastness and state, 518
Weigh me the Fire; or, canst thou find, 1026
Welcome dear book, souls Joy, and food! The feast, 471
Welcome deare Feast of Lent: who loves not thee, 267
Welcome, Great Cesar, welcome now you are, 1018
Welcome, most welcome to our Vowes and us, 944
Welcome sweet and sacred Cheere, 370
Welcome sweet, and sacred feast; welcome life!, 492
Wellcome white day! a thousand Suns, 528
Well may my Book come forth like Publique Day, 930
Well meaning readers! you that come as freinds, 717
What can the man do that succeeds the King?, 576
What doth this noise of thoughts within my hart, 322
What ever 'tis, whose beauty here below, 535
What gentle formes are these that move, 907
What God is, 1027
What happy, secret fountain, 571
What heav'n-intreated Heart is This?, 641
What hee suffered, 821
What if this present were the worlds last night?, 155
What is a Kisse? Why this, as some approve, 1006
What is this strange and uncouth thing?, 352
What softer sounds are these salute the Eare, 899
What's that we see from far? the spring of Day, 972
What sweeter musick can we bring, 1039
What though my Harp, and Violl be, 1038

When as in silks my Julia goes, 1013
When as Leander young was drown'd, 955
When Blessed Mary wip'd her Saviours feet, 362
When by thy scorne, O murdresse, I am dead, 54
When Death shall part us from these Kids, 1165
When ere my heart, Love's warmth, but entertaines, 953
When first I saw true beauty, and thy Joys, 517
When first my lines of heavenly joyes made mention, 284
When first thou didst entice to thee my heart, 226
When first thou didst even from the grave, 476
When first thy Eies unveil, give thy Soul leave, 465
When first thy sweet and gracious eye, 360
When for the Thorns with which I long, too long, 1078
When God at first made man, 347
When he would have his verses read, 933
When I am dead, and Doctors know not why, 68
When I a Verse shall make, 1005
When I beheld the Poet blind, yet bold, 1127
When I dyed last, and, Deare, I dye, 31
When I thy singing next shall heare, 943
When my Devotions could not peirce, 260
When my grave is broke up againe, 67
When that rich soule which to her Heaven is gone, 105
When the fair year, 548
When through the North a fire shall rush, 421

When to my Eyes, 445
When with these eyes clos'd now by thee, 594
When with the Virgin morning thou do'st rise, 980
Where do'st thou carelesse lie, 834
Where, like a pillow on a bed, 57
Where the remote Bermudas ride, 1082
While Beast instructs his faire, and innocent wife, 767
While that my soule repaires to her devotion, 244
While the milder Fates consent, 953
While thou didst keep thy Candor undefil'd, 932
Whil'st that, for which, all vertue now is sold, 807
Whilst yet to prove, 73
The white Island, 1044
White Sunday, 528
White though ye be; yet, Lillies, know, 963
Whither away delight?, 341
Whither Mad maiden wilt thou roame?, 931
Whither, ô, whither art thou fled, 349
Whither? Say, whither shall I fly, 954
Whitsunday, 239
Who ere shee bee, 633
Who ever comes to shroud me, do not harme, 63
Who ever guesses, thinks, or dreames he knowes, 49
Who ever loves, if he do not propose, 86
Who is the honest Man?, 252
Who on yon throne of Azure sits, 498
Who read a Chapter, when they rise, 277
Who sayes that fictions onely and false haire, 236

Who sayes that Giles and Jone at discord be?, 769
Who shall doubt, Donne, where I a Poet bee, 776
Why are wee by all creatures waited on?, 154
Why, Disease, dost thou molest, 800
Why doe I languish thus drooping and dull, 298
Why I write not of Love, 790
Why? though I seeme of a prodigious wast, 859
The Will, 62
Wilt thou forgive that sinne where I begunne, 168
Wilt thou love God, as he thee! then digest, 156
The Windowes, 247
Wishes: To his (supposed) Mistresse, 633
Witchcraft by a picture, 52
With all the powres my poor Heart hath, 688
With golden Censers, and with Incense, here, 1043
With his kinde mother who partakes thy woe, 138
Within this sober Frame expect, 1133
With sick and famisht eyes, 335
With thy small stocke, why art thou ventring still, 780
With what deep murmurs through times silent stealth, 599
Woe, woe to them, who (by a ball of strife), 945
Womans constancy, 23
The World (I Saw Eternity the other night), 504
The World (Love built a stately house, where Fortune came), 265
Would'st thou heare, what man can say, 782
Would you beleeve, when you this Mounsieur see, 773
The Wounded Heart, 935
Wounded I sing, tormented I endite, 346
A Wreath (A wreathed Garland of deserved praise), 375
The Wreath (Since I in storms us'd most to be), 602
Wretched and foolish Jealousie, 832

Ye living Lamps, by whose dear light, 1115
You, that decipher out the Fate, 1097
Young Love, 1089